UNITED STATES ARMY IN WORLD WAR II

Special Studies

THE EMPLOYMENT OF NEGRO TROOPS

by

Ulysses Lee

D1523470

CENTER OF MILITARY HISTORY

UNITED STATES ARMY

WASHINGTON, D.C., 1994

Library of Congress Catalog Card Number: 66–60003

First Printed 1963—CMH Pub 11–4–1

For sale by the U.S. Government Printing Office
Superintendent of Documents, Mail Stop: SSOP, Washington, DC 20402-9328
ISBN 0-16-042951-X

UNITED STATES ARMY IN WORLD WAR II
Stetson Conn, General Editor

. . . to Those Who Served

Foreword
To the First Paperback Edition

As in the case of some other titles in the United States Army in World War II series, Ulysses Lee's *The Employment of Negro Troops* has been long and widely recognized as a standard work on its subject. Although revised and consolidated before publication, the study was written largely between 1947 and 1951. If the now much-cited title has an echo of an earlier period, that very echo testifies to the book's rather remarkable twofold achievement: that Lee wrote it when he did, well before the Civil Rights movement of the 1960s, and that its reputation—for authority and objectivity—has endured so well.

The U.S. Army Center of Military History thus takes pleasure in publishing this first paperback edition of a landmark study in military and social history. As a key source for understanding the integration of the Army, Dr. Lee's work eminently deserves a continuing readership.

Washington, D.C.   HAROLD W. NELSON
14 April 1994   Brigadier General, USA
                                                    Chief of Military History

The Author

Ulysses Lee, now Professor of English at Morgan State College, Baltimore, was a member of the Office of the Chief of Military History from 1946 to 1952, concluding a decade of active Army officer service in ranks from first lieutenant to major. In World War II he served as an Education Officer and Editorial Analyst in the field and in the headquarters of Army Service Forces; for seven years thereafter he was the military history specialist on Negroes in the Army and prepared this volume.

A graduate of Howard University, Dr. Lee taught at Lincoln University, Pennsylvania, and attended the University of Chicago as a Rosenwald Fellow between 1936 and his entry into military service in 1942. He received his doctorate in the history of culture from the University of Chicago in 1953, and from then until going to Morgan in 1956 he taught at Lincoln University, Missouri. Co-editor of *The Negro Caravan,* an anthology of writings by American Negroes published in 1941, he was author-editor of the Army Service Forces manual, *Leadership and the Negro Soldier,* published in 1944, and has been the author of many reviews and articles published before and since. Dr. Lee has also been associate editor of *The Midwest Journal* of the College Language Association and a member of the editorial board of *The Journal of Negro History.*

Preface

Recognizing that the story of Negro participation in military service during World War II was of national interest as well as of great value for future military planning, the Assistant Secretary of War in February 1944 recommended preparation of a book on this subject. The opportunity to undertake it came two years later with the assignment to the Army's Historical Division of the author, then a captain and a man highly qualified by training and experience to write such a work. After careful examination of the sources and reflection Captain Lee concluded that it would be impracticable to write a comprehensive and balanced history about Negro soldiers in a single volume. His plan, formally approved in August 1946, was to focus his own work on the development of Army policies in the use of Negroes in military service and on the problems associated with the execution of these policies at home and abroad, leaving to the authors of other volumes in the Army's World War II series, then taking shape, the responsibility for covering activities of Negroes in particular topical areas.

This definition of the author's objective is needed in order to understand why he has described his work "in no sense a history of Negro troops in World War II." Writing some years ago, he explained: "The purpose of the present volume is to bring together the significant experience of the Army in dealing with an important national question: the full use of the human resources represented by that 10 percent of national population that is Negro. It does not attempt to follow, in narrative form, the participation of Negro troops in the many branches, commands, and units of the Army. . . . A fully descriptive title for the present volume, in the nineteenth century manner, would read: 'The U.S. Army and Its Use of Negro Troops in World War II: Problems in the Development and Application of Policy with Some Attention to the Results, Public and Military.'" Thus, in accordance with his objective, the author gives considerably more attention to the employment of Negroes as combat soldiers than to their use as service troops overseas. Even though a large majority of the Negroes sent overseas saw duty in service rather than in combat units, their employment in service forces did not present the same number or degree of problems.

The volume opens with background chapters recalling the experience of Negroes in the Army in World War I, the position of Negroes in the Army between wars, and Army planning for their use in another great war, as well as the clash of public and private views over employment of Negroes as soldiers. It continues with chapters on the particular problems associated with absorbing large numbers of Negroes into the Army—the provision of separate facilities for them, their leadership and training difficulties, their physical fitness for service, morale factors influencing their eagerness to serve, and the disorders that attracted so much attention to the problems of their service. The concluding eight chapters are concerned principally with the employment of Negro soldiers overseas, in ground and air combat units and in service units.

The author wrote most of this volume between 1947 and 1951, and the University of Chicago accepted its opening chapters as a doctoral dissertation. After Dr. Lee left the Army to return to teaching, he revised his work in the light of comments and criticisms received from the many reviewers of his original draft. As revised by Dr. Lee, the work was still too long for publication as a single volume; and in my capacity of General Editor I have reduced the revised manuscript considerably in length and reorganized and consolidated certain of the original chapters. The changes made by me were along lines agreed to in conferences with Dr. Lee and in consonance with his expressed wishes, or at least with my interpretation of them.

Certain other volumes of this series, as planned in 1946, gave particular attention to the Army's use of Negroes, notably *The Procurement and Training of Ground Combat Troops,* by Robert R. Palmer, Bell I. Wiley, and William R. Keast; *The Women's Army Corps,* by Mattie E. Treadwell; and *The Army and Industrial Manpower,* by Byron Fairchild and Jonathan Grossman. Bell I. Wiley's Army Ground Forces Study No. 36, "The Training of Negro Troops," offers an interesting comparative treatment of that topic. Dennis D. Nelson's study, "The Integration of the Negro into the United States Navy, 1776–1947," deals mostly with the Navy's policies and practices during World War II, and the monograph by Jean Byers, "A Study of the Negro in Military Service," describes policies and practices in both services during the war. The volume by Charles E. Francis, *Tuskegee Airmen: The Story of the Negro in the U.S. Air Force* (Boston, 1956), and the one by Lee Nichols, *Breakthrough on the Color Front* (New York, 1954), offer useful insight into the military service of Negroes during and after the war. The reader is also referred, for more detailed maps of the many theaters of war in which Negroes served, to the theater volumes of the Army's World War II series.

In its planning, this work owes much to the Army's first Chief Historian, Dr. Walter L. Wright, Jr. The original draft, less the two concluding chapters, was carefully reviewed and criticized by a panel under the chairmanship of his successor, Dr. Kent Roberts Greenfield, which met on 4 January 1952. Panel critics in addition to Dr. Greenfield were Dr. John Hope Franklin, then Professor of History at Howard University; General

Wade H. Haislip (USA Ret.), then Chief of the General Staff's Personnel Division; Lt. Gen. Arthur G. Trudeau (USA Ret.), then Commandant of the Army War College; Dr. William T. Hutchinson, Professor of History at the University of Chicago; Col. (now Brig. Gen.) George C. O'Connor, then Chief, Histories Division, OCMH; and Dr. Donald R. Young of the Russell Sage Foundation. Paralleling this panel review all or parts of the author's work went to a large number of knowledgeable critics, many of them the leaders of Negro troops during the war, and the work as revised for publication has also been reviewed by several individuals qualified to do so. To all of these, named and unnamed, who have read and criticized this work, the author and the Office of the Chief of Military History owe a debt of gratitude.

Acknowledgment is due also to those who have contributed materially in preparing this work for publication: Mrs. Loretto C. Stevens, assistant editor; Miss Barbara J. Harris, editorial clerk; Mrs. Norma B. Sherris, photographic editor; and Billy C. Mossman, map compiler. Mrs. Dorothy Neill McCabe prepared the index.

Prefaces usually conclude not only with acknowledgments of assistance but also with a statement of the author's sole responsibility for any errors of fact or flaws of interpretation. Since Dr. Lee has not been able to participate fully in the final revision and editing of his work, it would be improper to hold him responsible for the contents of the work as printed. I accept this responsibility.

Washington, D.C.   STETSON CONN
18 June 1965   Chief Historian and
                                             General Editor

The U.S. Army Center of Military History

The Center of Military History prepares and publishes histories as required by the U.S. Army. It coordinates Army historical matters, including historical properties, and supervises the Army museum system. It also maintains liaison with public and private agencies and individuals to stimulate interest and study in the field of military history. The Center is located at 1099 14th Street, N.W., Washington, D.C. 20005–3402.

Contents

Tables

Maps

Illustrations

All illustrations are from Department of Defense files, with the exception of the portrait on page 79 by Fabian Bachrach, courtesy of Judge William H. Hastie, and the photograph on page 534, courtesy of Col. Julian G. Hearne, Jr.

THE EMPLOYMENT OF NEGRO TROOPS

CHAPTER I

After World War I

For a decade or more after World War I the American public as a whole was little concerned with the peacetime Army. It was considerably less concerned with the Army's plans for the current or future use of national manpower. For a time in the middle and late twenties, war memoirs, fiction, and drama enjoyed a vogue, but the general interest in contemporary military matters was aroused mainly by war revelations, public controversies such as that surrounding Brig. Gen. William Mitchell's advocacy of an autonomous air force, and changes in the high command of the services. Demobilization, disarmament, international agreements for peace, and economy in public expenditures were successively central to the thinking of the times. They deflected public interest from serious concern with the internal problems and needs of the armed forces. There was a general idea abroad that in the event of a national emergency the Army, backed by the civilian population, should be prepared. But the likelihood of a national emergency seemed remote indeed in an era devoted to arms reduction and treaties of peace and friendship.

American Negroes shared the general public attitude. In the period immediately following World War I, they had current and pressing domestic problems of their own to claim their attention.

Northern manufacturing areas, where heavy migrations of Negro labor from the South introduced a set of problems generally unknown before the war, were in the throes of postwar readjustment. Full-scale race riots had broken out during the war and in the years immediately thereafter in East St. Louis, Houston, Chester, Washington, Chicago, and Tulsa. Racial troubles on a smaller scale flared elsewhere. The Negro press, churches, and social work organizations —the directing forces of Negro public opinion—had their hands full dealing with these new postwar problems.

The Military Orientation of the Negro Public

Concern with the pressing problems of the postwar period did not cause the Negro public wholly to lose sight of its relations with the armed forces. The Army and military life had long occupied a position of relatively greater concern and importance to the Negro public than to Americans in general. Soldiering had been an honored career for the few Negroes who were able to enter upon it. In the restricted range of economic opportunities open to them, the military life ranked high. Thus the Army and its policies remained a significant center of interest to Negro organizations, to the press, and to the public as a whole. It was one of the few national endeavors in which Negroes had had a relatively secure position and which, at least in time of war, could lead to national recognition of their worth as citizens and their potential as partners in a common undertaking.

Since the Civil War, the Army had maintained four Regular Army Negro regiments, the 9th and 10th Cavalry and the 24th and 25th Infantry. The men of these regiments were the legatees of the Civil War troops out of which the units had been organized and of the Indian fighters and plains soldiers who filled their ranks until the turn of the century. Until World War II there were few Negro communities that did not have several honored men of the Grand Army of the Republic who could be pointed to with pride. Retired infantry and cavalry sergeants from the Regular Army were often leading spirits in Negro community life. Some of the oldest and best known of the Negro schools—Howard, Hampton, Fisk—were founded by Union generals. One of the schools, Lincoln Institute, later Lincoln University, in Missouri, was established with funds given by the enlisted men of regiments of the United States Colored Troops after the Civil War. Wilberforce, in Ohio, was proud of its pre-Spanish-American War status as the only Negro college with a department of military training to which Army instructors were detailed.

Orators and ministers, educators and politicians, had extolled the Negro soldier as an example of courage and loyalty and skill to such a degree that the names of Old and New World military heroes of the colored races—Toussaint L'Ouverture, David Dumas, Chaka,

Antonio Maceo, Peter Salem—were familiar enough to be freely used on any patriotic occasion. Battles and regiments were widely and fully commemorated in books and pamphlets.[1] Lithographs of Negro troops in action and of military heroes were common in Negro homes. The participation of Negroes in past wars was one of the richest veins of material that could be worked by the supporters of Negro rights and opportunities.

Negroes, generally, were convinced of the unbroken record of loyalty and courage of their soldiers. They were certain of the benefits which participation in each of America's wars had brought them. In 1918, when William E. B. DuBois, editor of *The Crisis,* official organ of the National Association for the Advancement of Colored People (NAACP), sought to defend the thesis that winning the war must take precedence over fighting for the Negro's rights, he wrote:

The Crisis says, *first* your Country, *then* your Rights! . . . Certain honest thinkers among us hesitate at that last sentence. They say it is all well to be idealistic, but is it not true that while we have fought our country's battles for one hundred fifty years, we have *not* gained our rights? No, we have gained them rapidly and effectively by our loyalty in time of trial.

Five thousand Negroes fought in the Revolution; the result was the emancipation of slaves in the North and abolition of the African slave trade. At least three

---

[1] George W. Williams, *A History of the Negro Troops in the War of the Rebellion 1861–1865* (New York: Harper and Brothers, 1888); Theophilus G. Steward, *The Colored Regulars in the U.S. Army* (Philadelphia: A.M.E., 1904). In addition, many of the regiments of the United States Colored Troops and state regiments of the Civil War had their own histories.

thousand Negro soldiers and sailors fought in the War of 1812; the result was the enfranchisement of the Negro in many Northern States and the beginning of a strong movement for general emancipation. Two hundred thousand Negroes enlisted in the Civil War, and the result was the emancipation of four million slaves, and the enfranchisement of the black man. Some ten thousand Negroes fought in the Spanish-American War, and in the twenty years ensuing since that war, despite many set backs, we have doubled or quadrupled our accumulated wealth.[2]

There was little doubt among Negroes during World War I that the record of the loyalty and courage of their soldiers would be preserved in France and that the peace would be followed by gains in status and opportunity similar to those listed by DuBois for wars past. War gave them a renewed opportunity to demonstrate their loyalty and patriotism. Their full support would bring its own reward.

In World War I the bulk of the 404,-348 Negro troops (including 1,353 commissioned officers, 9 field clerks, and 15 Army nurses) were in the Services of Supply—in quartermaster, stevedore, and pioneer infantry units. Two infantry divisions, the 92d and 93d, were formed and sent to France. The four Regular regiments were assigned to defensive positions in the continental United States and its island territories.

The 93d Division was not a true division but four separate infantry regiments without trains or artillery. These regiments, three of them National Guard, were assigned to the French, reorganized according to French tables, and used as integral parts of French divisions on the Western Front. They operated in Champagne, the Vosges, and in the Oise-Aisne offensive from the early summer of 1918 to the end of the war. The 92d Division, largely made up of draftees, spent fifty-one days in a "quiet" and two days in an active sector in France. One of its regiments, the 368th Infantry, was used for liaison between the French and American armies at the beginning of the Argonne offensive while the remainder of the division was in reserve. After five days the regiment, having experienced considerable disorder and confusion, was withdrawn from the line. On 10 and 11 November, the whole 92d Division was sent into action with the other three front-line divisions of the U.S. Second Army to attack the second Hindenburg Line.

Both the 92d and 93d Divisions had Negro officers in junior grades but were otherwise generally commanded by white officers. The 93d's National Guard regiments also had Negro field grade officers, but with the exception of one regiment totally staffed with Negroes (except for its commander in the last months of the war) few remained assigned throughout the war. Both divisions experienced considerable shifting of Negro and white officers among their various units, with many Negro officers being eliminated.

In assessments of Negro participation in World War I, the two infantry divisions got the bulk of public and official

[2] Editorials, "Our Special Grievances" and "The Reward," *The Crisis*, XVI (September, 1918), 217. The first line here quoted is the last line of "Our Special Grievances"; the remainder is the opening section of "The Reward." The two editorials were printed in sequence as answers to criticisms of a previous editorial, "Close Ranks," in which the magazine had urged its readers to "forget our special grievances and close our ranks" in the fight for democracy.

attention both during and after the war.
Their employment and conduct produced a fog of reports, rumors, and
legends which grew and changed with
the passage of time. The Negroes' view
of their participation was considerably
at variance with that of the Army's
senior commanders and of white officers
of Negro units. Both views influenced
heavily the developing attitudes of the
public and the Army toward the participation of Negro troops in future emergencies. Both views had continuing
importance, for many of the Army's
senior commanders of World War II
were the younger generals and field
grade officers of World War I and many
of the leading Negro protagonists and
spokesmen of World War II were the
Negro officers and enlisted men of World
War I. Both had memories coming
from direct experience or from the accounts of their contemporaries. The
two wars were not separated by so long
a span of years that one did not directly
influence the other.

Praise in the Press

During World War I itself, few weeks
passed without a detailed reporting of
the bravery of American Negro soldiers
in the nation's press. Nationally circulated magazines carried feature articles
on Negro fighters abroad and the Negro
journals quoted from the great metropolitan papers with approval. The
United Press reported:

American Negro troops proved their
value as fighters in the line east of Verdun
on June 12. . . . The Germans attempted
a raid in that sector but were completely
repulsed by the Negroes. The Boches began a terrific bombardment at one minute

after midnight (throwing over between
3,000 and 4,000 shells from guns ranging
in size from 67 to 340 millimeters). The
bombardment was concentrated on small
areas. Many of the shells made holes from
ten to fifteen feet across.

In the midst of this inferno the Negroes
coolly stuck to their posts, operating machine guns and automatic rifles and keeping up such a steady barrage that the
German infantry failed to penetrate the
American lines. The Americans miraculously sustained only two wounded.[3]

Confirmation of the skill and courage
of Negro soldiers was reported in other
ways. The news of Pvts. Henry Johnson and Needham Roberts, of the
369th Infantry (New York National
Guard), who together put to flight a German raiding party, killing or wounding
twenty or more of the enemy, was carried in newspapers all over the country
and became a subject for commendatory
editorials. The Boston *Post,* under the
heading No Color Line There, commented: "In the service of democracy
there is no such distinction. General
Pershing's late report places on the roll
of honor the names of two soldiers of
one of our colored regiments, Privates
Johnson and Roberts. . . . This is the
true ideal of service. No matter what
the color of the skin, we all recognize
it." And the Pittsburgh *Chronicle Telegram* said, quoting General Grant's Civil
War comment: " 'The Colored troops
fought nobly.' That was more than half
a century ago. They 'fought nobly' in
the plains, in the islands of the Pacific
and the Atlantic, wherever they have
been called upon to fight. . . . And

[3] Quoted in *The Crisis,* XVI (September, 1918),
238. The regiment referred to was the 371st Infantry,
93d Division, assigned to the French 157th Division
but operating with the French 68th Division.

now in France they are living up to the reputation they have won on other, far distant fields." [4] When their unit returned, Johnson and Roberts were the subjects of laudatory newspaper and wire service interviews read all over the country.

Interest in the Negro units continued high. A correspondent of the New York *Times* wrote of one Negro unit:

The regiment's inspiration to great deeds on the front was explained by a Negro lieutenant.

"One of my men came to me several days ago," he said, "and asked me why I had joined the army. He reminded me that I was above draft age and he wanted me to tell him what I was fighting for. I told him I was fighting for what the flag meant to the Negroes in the United States. I told him I was fighting because I wanted other oppressed people to know the meaning of democracy and enjoy it. I told him that millions of Americans fought for four years for us Negroes to get it and now it was only right that we should fight for all we were worth to help other people get the same thing. . . .

"I told him that now is our opportunity to prove what we can do. If we can't fight and die in this war just as bravely as white men, then we don't deserve an equality with white men, and after the war we better go back home and forget about it all. . . ." [5]

When the French Government awarded the Croix de Guerre to three of the regiments of the 93d Division, to a company of the fourth regiment, and to the 1st Battalion of the 367th Infantry, 92d Division, each award was chronicled in the press. *The Literary Digest* summed up opinion on the award to the 369th Infantry:

Exceptional tho the award of the coveted French War Cross may be, the deeds of valor by which this negro regiment won it are less exceptional than typical of the way in which all our colored troops measured up to the demands of the war. This is the verdict of newspaper correspondents and of soldiers invalided home from the Western Front. Survivors of the fighting now arriving in New York have "nothing but praise for the colored troops," writes a reporter in the New York *Evening Sun*. "They proved their valor on countless occasions, and it was one of the common stories that Jerry feared the 'Smoked Yankees' more than any other troops he met." [6]

As the troops continued to return home, articles assessing the role of Negro troops in the war began to appear. "Like the Senegalese forces of the French Army," *Current History* reported, "the black American troops held their own on European battlefields and stood the test of courage, endurance and aggressiveness in moments of the greatest stress. They fought valiantly at Château-Thierry, Soissons, on the Vesle, in Champagne, in the Argonne, and in the final attacks in the Metz region." [7] On the return of the 369th Infantry, first of the Negro regiments to parade

---

[4] Quoted in *The Crisis*, XVI (July, 1918), 130–31, along with excerpts from the Buffalo *Evening News*, Brooklyn *Times*, Boston *Evening Transcript*, New York *Times*, and the New York *Tribune*. See also *The Literary Digest*, LVIII (September 7, 1918), 48, 50; Arthur W. Little, *From Harlem to the Rhine* (New York: Covici, Friede, 1936), 192–201.

[5] "The Looking Glass: Over There," *The Crisis*, XVI (August, 1918), 179.

[6] "Croix de Guerre and Rare Praise for American Negro Troops," *The Literary Digest*, LX (January 18, 1919), 55–56. The account continues with narratives of individual soldiers. For other accounts and comments see "The Looking Glass: Lost Echoes," *The Crisis*, XVII (January, 1919), 133.

[7] "The Negro in the War: How French and American Black Troops Performed Deeds of Valor on Many Battlefields," *Current History*, XI (December, 1919), 540.

up Fifth Avenue in massed formation, the New York *Times* wrote: "New York's Negro soldiers, bringing with them from France one of the bravest records achieved by any organization in the war, marched amid waving flags . . . ," and Nicholas Murray Butler, President of Columbia University, offered a resolution reading, "No American soldiers saw harder or more constant fighting and none gave a better account of themselves. . . . When fighting was to be done, this regiment was there."[8] Even the regimental band, "the band that introduced jazz to France," came in for high praise. It was considered one of the four best in the world, ranking with the British Grenadiers, the Garde Républicaine, and the Royal Italian Bands, one journal declared.[9]

There was praise, too, for the Negro service troops in France, especially for the stevedores, and for the high motivation of Negro draftees. A reporter writing a series on the National Army camps told of a unit of 1,600 men at Camp Lee:

Ten days after they arrived in camp with the first quota last fall, the call came for them to go immediately to France for special service. The call was sudden and unexpected. General Cronkhite [Maj. Gen. Adelbert Cronkhite] knew that the men had not expected to leave this country for several months. He thought that some of 1,600 might have good reasons for not wanting to leave at once, so he called for volunteers from the 5,000 other colored troops who were in camp to fill whatever vacancies there might be in the oversea unit. Every one of the 5,000 volunteered for immediate oversea service. Then the unit was marched to a hall. The general

said that there were volunteers to take the place of any who wished to remain behind. Only 20 per cent of the 1,600 availed themselves of the opportunity to stay at home.[10]

Under the Surface

While statements of praise presented a highly flattering picture of Negro troops in World War I, the public was not unaware that beneath the surface other rumors were running thick and fast. The 369th Infantry, "characterized by some as 'possessing black skins, white souls and red blood,' " *The Outlook* commented, "ought to silence for all time the slanderous charge that Negroes are cowards and will not fight; and the service which these representatives of their race have rendered in the war to make the world safe for democracy ought to make forever secure for that race in this their native land their right for life, liberty, and the pursuit of happiness."[11]

Cowardice was not the only charge that worried Negroes at home. During the war other disturbing reports had spread through the larger cities: Negro troops were being abused by their white officers; systematic attempts were being made to "break" and demote Negro officers; American white officers were attempting to import the worst features of color prejudice into France; Negro troops were being employed as "shock troops" in the most dangerous battle zones and as labor troops where the work was hardest. Other rumors of

[8] New York *Times*, February 18, 1919.
[9] *The Independent and Harpers' Weekly*, XCVII (March 1, 1919), 286.

[10] William S. McNutt, "Making Soldiers in Dixie," *Collier's Weekly*, LXI (April 27, 1918), 7. See also David L. Ferguson, "With This Black Man's Army," *The Independent and Harpers' Weekly*, XCVII (March 15, 1919), 368, 385.
[11] "Honor to Whom Honor Is Due," *The Outlook*, CXXI (February 26, 1919), 329.

wholesale arrests of Negro officers and enlisted men made the rounds. Many of these allegations were dismissed as German propaganda, and all of them were formally denied by General John J. Pershing.[12] But the Houston riot of 1917, involving troops of the 24th Infantry, was no rumor. Committees were still working in 1919 to reverse the death sentence of the soldiers involved.

As reports came back from Negro soldiers themselves, many of these rumors, especially those dealing with discriminatory treatment of Negro officers and men, revived. During the course of the war, Negroes had expressed two major grievances. One centered on retirement in June 1917 of Col. Charles Young, highest ranking Negro Regular Army officer, on the eve of what many Negroes had expected and hoped would be his appointment to a field command.[13] The other had to do with the formation and staffing of the 92d Division.

It was widely believed that the 92d Division was established by Secretary of War Newton D. Baker and approved by President Woodrow Wilson over the objections of the Army's General Staff. Before it left the country for France, there were rumors that the division had not been given properly selected men and that there were deficiencies in the technical training of both officers and enlisted men. Deficiencies in literate

COLONEL YOUNG AS A CAPTAIN

and skilled men might have been remedied by transfers of men from other regiments, but, *The Crisis* informed its readers, permission to make these transfers had been denied. "Unless this decision is reversed," the magazine predicted, "the Ninety-second Division is bound to be a failure as a unit organization. Is it possible that persons in the War Department wish this division to be a failure?" the magazine asked.[14] After the war, Negroes linked the retirement of Young and the staffing of the 92d as part of the same official strategy. The Army General Staff "knew what Young could have made of

[12] Emmett J. Scott, *Scott's Official History of the American Negro in the World War* (Chicago: Homewood Press, 1919), pp. 344–53.

[13] *Ibid.*, pp. 64–65; "Army's Only Colored Colonel, 'Hero of Race,' Laid at Rest," Washington *Evening Star*, June 1, 1923, quoted in Abraham Chew, *A Biography of Col. Charles Young* (Washington: R. L. Pendleton, 1923), pp. 7, 11–12.

[14] Editorial, "The Negro and the War Department," *The Crisis*, XVI (May, 1918), 7–8.

the 92d Division," *The Crisis* said after his death.[15]

Young's retirement dashed the high expectations of Negroes, and the colonel soon became a symbol of their disillusion. They pointed out that he was one of the few field grade officers with Pershing in Mexico whom the general had recommended to command militia in the federal service.[16] Others subsequently supported the claim that Young was retired "because the army did not want a black general" by quoting white officers who had said as much in public addresses.[17]

Colonel Young, over the years, attained the stature of a martyred hero. The Negro public became convinced that if Young, with his rank and West Point background, could be treated so, the lot of other Negro officers must have been difficult. Stories of wholesale inefficiency on the part of Negro officers reached the press, but Negroes were frankly skeptical of their accuracy. As early as the spring of 1919, DuBois, who had gone to France immediately after the armistice in search of material for a projected history of the war, concluded: "So the word to acknowledge the Negro stevedore and the fighting black private has gone forth, but the American army is going to return to America determined to disparage the black officer and

eliminate him from the army despite his record." [18]

The Negroes' version of their part in World War I was that the root of all trouble in the Negro units lay in animosities that developed between American white and Negro troops, and especially in those originating with white American officers. American Army attitudes, as contrasted with French public attitudes, were blamed for developing racial frictions. The American high command refused, according to this view, to regard Negro troops as full-fledged American soldiers, whereas the French, unexposed previously to large numbers of Americans, insisted upon treating Negroes as a part of the 1918 Army of Liberation to be accepted in the same manner as any other American troops. Negroes remembered the 92d Division's Bulletin 35, issued at Camp Funston, Kansas, in March 1918. This bulletin urged the men of the division to avoid raising the color question, "No MATTER HOW LEGALLY CORRECT," and advised them that "the success of the Division with all that success implies is dependent upon the good will of the public. That public is nine-tenths white. White men made the Division, and they can break it just as easily if it becomes a trouble maker." The bulletin was interpreted as symbolic of the Army's approach to racial matters. Mass meetings were called to demand the resignation of the division's commander. "At no time during his incumbency as the head of the Division was General Ballou [Maj. Gen. Charles C. Ballou] able to regain the confidence

---

[15] *The Crisis*, XXVI (July, 1923), 106. See also William E. B. DuBois, *The Gift of Black Folk* (Boston: Stratford Co., 1924), p. 131.

[16] Ltr, CG Punitive Expedition, U.S. Army, Colonia Dublan, Mexico, to TAG, 21 Aug 16, sub: Recommendation of Officers To Command Militia in Federal Service, quoted in *The Crisis*, XV (March, 1918), 218.

[17] Addie W. Hunton and Kathryn M. Johnson, *Two Colored Women with the American Expeditionary Forces* (Brooklyn: Brooklyn *Eagle* Press, 1920), p. 43.

[18] William E. B. DuBois, "The Black Man in the Revolution of 1914–1918," *The Crisis*, XVII (March, 1919), 223.

of the colored masses, with whom he had been immensely popular prior to this episode," wrote Emmett J. Scott, assistant to Secretary of War Baker.[19]

In May 1919, DuBois published a series of war documents, including letters requesting the removal of Negro officers before they had been tested in battle, orders giving evidence of discriminatory treatment, and a copy of a letter written by the 92d Division's chief of staff to a United States senator proposing that never again should a division with Negro officers be organized.[20] The publication of these documents renewed again the fears of the Negro public. After the Post Office Department banned from the mails the issue of *The Crisis* in which the documents were printed, Negroes were certain that they were genuine and that the full facts of the war, as seen by Army officers, were destined to be hidden from the public. They were certain that if the facts were revealed they would show that: (1) Negro soldiers and officers performed well when given a chance to do so; (2) if they did not perform well it was because of faulty white leaders too preoccupied with their own prejudices to perform their military jobs well; and (3) Negro soldiers and officers, especially the latter, performed jobs better than they were credited with doing. Credit had to be withheld, for otherwise there could be no justification for denying full rights and privileges as citizens to Negroes who had won their position as Americans and as capable leaders on the field of battle.

Shortly before DuBois' publication of the war documents, a service magazine expressed its opinion that perhaps mulattoes might make capable officers, able to lead Negro troops, but that it was not satisfied that pure-blooded Negroes had developed sufficient capacity for education and mental discipline for leadership.[21] Colonel Young, in response, asked if this "surprising generalization of lack of leadership and the capacity of the Negro officer was derived by consultation of the records of the War Department, the press, both white and Negro, and the reports of *impartial* officers. The black officer feels," he continued, "that there was a prejudgment against him at the outset, and that nearly every move that has been made was for the purpose of bolstering up this prejudgment and discrediting him in the eyes of the world and the men whom he was to lead and will lead in the future." Young proceeded to list French and American decorations won by Negro officers in World War I and to cite examples of pure-blooded Negro officers of the past, such as the Civil War's Maj. Martin Delany and Haiti's Toussaint L'Ouverture.[22]

Testimonials to the efficiency and good conduct of Negro troops were collected from other American and French officers and from the mayors of French towns. Court-martial figures were cited to disprove charges of misconduct to-

---

[19] Scott, *History of the American Negro in the World War*, p. 97.

[20] "Documents of the War," collected by William E. B. DuBois, *The Crisis*, XVIII (May, 1919); Scott, *History of the American Negro in the World War*, p. 438.

[21] Editorial, "The Negro Officer," *National Service With the International Military Digest*, V (March, 1919), 134.

[22] Quoted from the New York *Post* in "The Looking Glass: Negro Officers," *The Crisis*, XVIII (June, 1919), 96.

LIEUTENANT ALEXANDER AND FELLOW OFFICERS OF THE 9TH CAVALRY. *(Lieutenant Alexander is second from the left, top row.)*

ward the French civilian population.[23] The loyalty of Negro troops in the face of German propaganda focused upon the racial disadvantages of the Negro in America was described with approval.[24] Counterexplanations of the performance of the 92d Division were advanced by

Negro junior officers of the division. "The Ninety-Second Division was a tragic failure," two officers wrote. "It was a failure in organization. It was a failure in morale. It was a failure in accomplishment. . . . the Negro division was the object of special victimization, superimposed upon its sacrifice," they bitterly continued.

The evidence advanced by the two officers for their interpretation of the division's "special victimization" was voluminous. The division trained in sections and was never assembled in one place until the last days of the war. It was given "the most ignorant and physically disqualified Negroes in the United States . . . ," with 40 percent of its men

[23] Cf., "Rap," *The Crisis*, XVIII (May, 1919), 12–13; Charles H. Williams, *Sidelights on Negro Soldiers* (Boston: Brimmer, 1923), pp. 74–76; Robert R. Moton, *Finding A Way Out, An Autobiography* (New York: Doubleday, Page, 1920), pp. 251–65.
[24] Scott, *History of the American Negro in the World War*, pp. 417–25; *Second Report of the Provost Marshal General to the Secretary of War on the Operations of the Selective Service System to December 20, 1918* (Washington, 1919), pp. 195–96; Monroe Mason and Arthur Furr, *The American Negro Soldier with the Red Hand of France* (Boston: Cornhill, 1920), pp. 115–17.

illiterate. Its white officers were unsympathetic to the Negro men and hostile to the Negro officers. They were all Southern "in accordance with tradition," some even introducing themselves to Negro troops with the announcement that they "had once suckled black mammies' breasts." The model officer held up to the Negroes by the commanding general was 2d Lt. John H. Alexander, who "knew how to stay in his place." [25] The Houston riot of 1917 and the implied threats thereafter demoralized the officer trainees at Des Moines, Iowa. The white instructors at Des Moines, from the Regular units, expected the officer trainees to conduct themselves like the old Regular enlisted men. Commissions were not awarded on the basis of merit, but "they went to those regulars who had given satisfaction as privates and 'noncoms.' Very few of those men had even a fair education. . . . They did their best as they saw it. But the unalloyed truth is that commissions were often awarded to those who were more likely to fail than succeed. [One man] won a commission by singing plantation songs." Officers were assigned without regard to training; infantry officers were "indiscriminately" assigned to artillery, machine gun, and other units for which they had no special training. A graduate of the Sheffield Scientific School was sent to the infantry while a senator's butler, "commissioned by graft," went to the heavy artillery.

Training difficulties, the officers' account went on, were slight when compared with the lowering of the division's morale in France. Among other things, it was charged that the men were kept out of schools; leaves were prohibited; rather than training, the men spent their time at police duties; staff officers were changed constantly; white officers were transferred into the division and out again as soon as they had obtained desired promotions; Negro officers were "terrorized" by wholesale arrests and transfers; officers, untrained in the duties of those arms, were assigned to artillery and the engineers, then blamed for having failed; the division went into its sectors without the proper equipment and into the short Argonne engagement without proper briefing, artillery support, rifle grenades, wire cutters, or horses. The enthusiasm of the whole division was dampened by the restrictions placed upon the contacts of the men with French civilians. "The sole charge of the division staff was to make the life of the Negro soldier unendurable." The old Regular Army enlisted men, now officers, assisted in breaking the morale of the division in an effort to "curry favor." There were a few officers whom the men respected; as for the rest, "the division had no trust in them."

The two officers concluded that while the division was distinctly a failure as an organization it could not be considered a combat failure, for it "never had its mettle tried. It cannot be said that it either failed or succeeded in battle. The 368th Infantry was sent 'over the top' for the avowed purpose of demonstrating a failure. For their failure General Ballou should be court-martialed." The division was "crippled" in training; no corps command wanted

---

[25] The World War I Camp Alexander at Hampton Roads was named for Lieutenant Alexander, second Negro graduate of West Point.

it. Yet it cost the United States four million dollars a month, they observed.[26]

Most writings on World War I by Negro authors had a more moderate approach. That the Negro troops were not given proper equipment or clear orders, that a failure of command and the inexperience of troops were responsible for their showing, that even so the Negro officers and men performed well enough to receive numerous medals and awards—these constituted the standard Negro version of World War I. That there was general, though varying, discrimination and unfairness toward Negro troops was an accompanying theme.[27]

During the twenties and thirties Negroes became more and more convinced that, if left alone, the Army would contrive in any future war to limit the use of Negroes to labor units and to avoid, if possible, the use of Negro

officers altogether. Some believed that many of their most promising young men in World War I had been assigned to pioneer infantry and stevedore regiments rather than to combat units. They felt that with a little more care and watchfulness the Army might have seen to it that combat units received a larger share of these men, with profit both to the men and to the units. They feared that in another war, instead of demonstrating progress over World War I, the employment of Negro troops might be on a more restricted basis than what they considered it to have been in World War I. They therefore placed more than ordinary emphasis on the importance of combat service and of service under their own officers. In this view they were aided by the normal and natural tendency to consider warfare as the clash of armed divisions on the field of honor rather than as a gigantic economic and logistical struggle in which combat units are but a small part of the total war endeavor. Without heroes in the combat arms, without leaders of their own race, war from the Negro point of view would remain but an extension of the everyday chores which they were accustomed to perform anyway.

The Negro public could not know the extent and nature of reports on Negro officers and troops contained in War Department files, but as memoirs of military leaders appeared after the war this public became convinced that more than a little had gone wrong in the use of Negro troops in World War I. With the accounts of senior officers added to, if not exactly agreeing with, those of their own troops, the picture of Negro participation in World War I became a clouded one.

---

[26] All quotations in this paragraph and the preceding three are from letters, William N. Colson and A. B. Nutt, "The Failure of the Ninety Second Division," *The Messenger*, II (September, 1919), 22–25. For later accounts by other participants see Howard H. Long, "The Negro Soldier in the Army of the United States," *Journal of Negro Education*, XII (1943), 307–15; and Charles H. Houston, "Saving the World for Democracy," Pittsburgh *Courier*, July 20–October 12, 1940.

[27] Scott, *History of the American Negro in the World War*, pp. 433, 439; William E. B. DuBois, "The Black Man in the Revolution of 1914–1918," *The Crisis*, XVII (March, 1919), 223; William E. B. DuBois, "An Essay Toward a History of the Black Man in the Great War," *The Crisis*, XVIII (June, 1919), 80–83; Colson and Nutt, article cited n. 26, above, p. 24; Hunton and Johnson, *Two Colored Women with the AEF*, p. 48; Long, article cited n. 26, above, *passim*; Williams, *Sidelights on Negro Soldiers*, pp. 163–66; Carter G. Woodson, *The Negro in Our History* (Washington: The Associated Publishers, 1922), p. 520 (1931 edition); Sgt. William O. Ross and Cpl. Duke L. Slaughter, *With the 351st in France* (Baltimore: Afro-American Co., 1919); Mason and Furr, *The American Soldier with the Red Hand of France*, *passim*.

In 1925, when Maj. Gen. Robert L. Bullard, commander of the American Second Army, published his memoirs, the controversy about Negro participation in the war reopened once again.[28] From his wartime diary, General Bullard quoted: "Poor Negroes! They are hopelessly inferior. I've been talking with them individually about their division's success. That success is not troubling them. With everyone feeling and saying that they are worthless as soldiers, they are going on quite unconcernedly." And, of the final attack: "The poor 92d Negroes [Diary, November 11th] wasted time and dawdled where they did attack, and at some places where they should have attacked, never budged at all."[29] As fighting troops, General Bullard concluded, Negroes were simply failures. He declared: "If you need combat soldiers, and especially if you need them in a hurry, don't put your time upon Negroes. The task of making soldiers of them and fighting with them, if there are any white people near, will be swamped in the race question. If racial uplift or racial equality is your purpose, that is another matter."[30]

As successive memoirs appeared in later years, uncertainty and recriminatory doubts about the entire career of Negro soldiers in World War I gained ascendancy over the optimistic reception of the first news from the front.[31]

Negroes believed that an impartial account would reverse these reports. They suspected that all the unfavorable narratives about Negro participation in World War I were the result of a planned attack aimed at discrediting their courage. This idea took root in the Negro mind and flowered there. Negroes had volunteered their best college-trained youths for officer training. They refused to believe that the generation to whom they looked for the future could have been responsible for the problems of Negro combat units. Hostile forces within the Army were to blame. "Nothing would have been more fatal to their plans than a successful Negro regiment officered by Negroes," DuBois wrote in 1925. "The Negro haters entrenched in the Army at Washington began, therefore, a concerted campaign [of slander]. Bullard voices the re-vamped lie which was plotted in 1918."[32] This notion, firmly believed in many Negro circles, conditioned the attitudes of young Negroes toward the Army for a full generation, for it was not allowed to die by Negroes nor was it killed off by any word of revision from the Army.

An Army Postwar View

The Army's judgment on the future of Negroes as a part of America's man-

[28] Maj. Gen. Robert L. Bullard, *Personalities and Reminiscences of the War* (New York: Doubleday Page, 1925), especially Chapter XXX.

[29] *Ibid.*, pp. 295–96. Brackets are in the original.

[30] *Ibid.*, p. 298.

[31] Representative later accounts are: General John J. Pershing, *My Experiences in the World War* (New York: F. A. Stokes Co., 1931), 2 vols.; Maj. Gen. Robert Alexander, *Memories of the*

World War, 1917–1918 (New York: Macmillan, 1931); William A. Percy, *Lanterns on the Levee* (New York: A. A. Knopf, 1940). Accounts by officers of Negro units are: Capt. Chester D. Heywood, *Negro Combat Troops in the World War: The Story of the 371st Infantry* (Worcester, Mass.: Commonwealth Press, 1928); Little, *From Harlem to the Rhine.*

[32] "Opinion of W. E. B. DuBois: Bullard," *The Crisis*, XXX (September, 1925), 218–29.

power available for military use in time of war proceeded from quite different premises. Soon after World War I, Army organization and personnel agencies determined that a definite policy on the employment of Negroes was needed if the best use was to be made of all available manpower in time of war. Such a policy was nonexistent in 1917. With little access to the more technical products of social research, Army planners generally relied upon the testimony of World War I commanders and traditional public attitudes in judging the capabilities of Negroes and in determining possibilities for the use of Negro manpower in time of war. Of the sources available to the Army, World War I testimony was perhaps the most important, though traditional attitudes played their part.

Most of the testimony from World War I was contained in personal documents submitted to the War Department and the Army War College by commanders of the 92d Division and, to a lesser extent, by commanders of the separate regiments of the 93d Division. These documents, remaining in typescript, were seldom available to more than a few officers. Through frequent repetition in successive studies and conferences, however, specific excerpts became relatively familiar. Other types of testimony appeared in commercially published memoirs and reminiscences. A third class, of increasing importance through the years, was the oral account —the personal reminiscence or anecdote —passed on in officers' clubs, schools, and at social gatherings. Only the first group is pertinent here, since it was upon this testimony, gathered within a short time after the close of the war, that both

initial and subsequent attitudes affecting planning were primarily based.

Most of the testimony came from regimental and higher commanders of units of the 92d Division, the only full-sized Negro combat division with the American Expeditionary Forces. This testimony was almost uniformly condemnatory so far as the performance of Negro combat troops, and particularly of Negro officers, was concerned. Infantry commanders were especially convinced that the training and performance of their troops had been a failure. Commanders of supporting units, such as engineers and field artillery, reported relatively greater success, but they too felt that combat duties, especially under Negro officers, should not be assigned to Negro troops. Commanders of regiments of the 93d Division, whose experience was with combat troops organized in separate regiments fighting with French divisions, made similar comments on the inadvisability of employing Negroes as combat troops, especially under Negro officers, although their reports showed that their own organizations were relatively more successful than those of the 92d Division. No formal comments were received from the officers of the four Regular Negro regiments, for these units were not sent to France. The testimony was therefore confined to units of volunteers, draftees, and National Guardsmen.[33]

The commanding officer of the 368th Infantry, 92d Division, for example, felt that Negro soldiers were "absolutely dependent" upon the leadership of white officers. Since, he said, combat units may expect heavy officer casualties, "I

[33] Letters and reports in AWC 127-3-24 (1920).

onsider the Negro should not be used as combat soldier." The commanders of he 371st and 372d Infantry, 93d Division,[34] agreed, saying that in a future var Negroes should be used principally n labor organizations. The 372d's commander added that if they had to be sed in combat organizations, "then ombatant officers should be all white— lso the non-commissioned officers." he commander of the 365th Infantry, 2d Division, along with others, added further provision, "a period of training at least twice as long as is necessary n the training of white troops—otherwise they should be used as pioneer or abor troops." Frequently, comments ncluded a statement such as that of the ommander of the 367th Infantry, 92d Division: "As fighting troops, the negro nust be rated as second class material, his due primarily to his inferior intelligence and lack of mental and moral ualities." Others, like the commanding general of the 92d Division, recommended that no Negro units larger than regiment be formed in the future,[35] nd some, including the division's chief f staff, felt that a separate extra Negro egiment might be added to every division, "actually making it a service regiment."

The emphasis on the necessity for vhite leadership arose from the conviction, almost universally held, that, with

few exceptions, the Negro officer was a failure in World War I. The commanding general of the 92d Division's 183d Brigade, for one, said, "Negro officers did not take proper care of their men. They not only lacked initiative but lacked standing with their own men." In the judgment of the commander of the 184th Brigade, "The Negro as an officer is a failure, and this applies to all classes of Negro officers, whether from the Regular Army or from the Officers' Training Camp." The division's chief of staff did not remember "in thirteen months service a single report coming from a Negro officer that ever gave sufficient information to base any plan thereon and practically every report had to be checked up by some white officer."

The reported experience of those units which replaced their Negro officers with white officers apparently proved the point fully. "After the negro lieutenants of the regiment were replaced by white the improvement was such that its efficiency was but little less than that of the average white engineer regiment," the commander of the 317th Engineers, 92d Division, reported. The commander of the 372d concluded that: "The replacement of the combatant colored officers of the 372d Infantry by white officers had, for its effect, a better state of morale and discipline throughout the regiment; better instruction and better tactical control. . . . Its work in sector warfare there under white officers was far more satisfactory than it had been two months previous under colored officers." Commanders of other regiments in which white officers replaced Negroes expressed similar opinions.

---

[34] The 371st was a Southern draft regiment with l white officers; the 372d was a National Guard giment from New England, Ohio, Maryland, and ic District of Columbia in which white officers placed most of the Negro officers.
[35] This recommendation was bulwarked by a mparison of the performance of the separate giments of the 93d with those of the 92d Division.

It was clear that most commanders of
Negro combat troops in World War I
had little to recommend for the employment of Negro troops in a future war
except labor duties under white supervision. Yet many admitted mitigating
circumstances in judging the performance of the combat units and some
indicated that the bare recorded facts of
combat did not tell the whole story.
General Ballou, the commander of the
92d Division, wrote:

The Secretary of War gave personal attention to the selection of the white officers
of the higher grades, and evidently intended to give the Division the advantage
of good white officers. This policy was not
continued by the War Department . . . the
92d . . . was made the dumping ground for
discards, both white and black. Some of
the latter were officers who had been eliminated as inefficient, from the so-called 93d
Division. . . .
   In the last battle of the war the Division
did some very aggressive work, so far as
the companies were concerned, and the
same could have been done in the Argonne
had there not been too much eagerness to
get the negroes out while their credit was
bad, as many preferred it should remain.
   The Colonel of one regiment came to
me, at the request of his officers, to beg me
to send them to the front, and pledging
me to a man that they would go to the
rear only by my order, or on a stretcher.
Those men would have been dangerous at
that time, and ought not to have been
humiliated by being sent to the rear.

. . . .

To officer a Division in which the best
possible leadership was required, only one-
half as many students were summoned to
the training camp as were summoned from
which to select the officers of a white Division. [College degrees were required for
admission to the white camp but] only
high school educations were required for
. . . the colored . . . and in many cases
these high school educations would have

been a disgrace to any grammar school.
   For the parts of a machine requiring the
finest steel, pot metal was provided.[36]

Field grade officers commented on training and personnel problems:

   It was my experience at Camp Meade
that there was a tendency to use the negro
for special fatigue in road building or other
improvements. Where a single negro unit
is placed in a white divisional camp these
things have to be guarded against. . . .
While I was promoted out of the 92d Division a few days after its arrival in France,
it was my opinion that its being scattered
in different camps in the U.S. had materially effected the training and formation
of the Divisional Staff. The division could
not expect to have the same team play as
one which had trained together at one
camp.[37]

. . . .

   . . . in my opinion the negro race did not
take advantage of the opportunity offered
them and send their leaders into the war
as officers. Many of the negro officers had
been barbers, waiters and had earned a
living in similar capacities before the war.
There were negroes with whom I came into
contact, civilians, who were men of ability
but the occasions were rare.[38]

No matter what mitigating circumstances were advanced, the general conclusion was that Negro troops could not
be employed satisfactorily in combat
units unless such careful selection, intensified training, and superior leadership
as had not been forthcoming in World
War I could be provided. Since such
selection and such leadership, whether
white or Negro, would be limited, the

[36] Excerpts from Ltr, Col Charles C. Ballou to
Asst Comdt Gen Staff College, 14 Mar 20, AWC
127–19.
   [37] Ltr, Col William P. Jackson, IGD, to Asst
Comdt Gen Staff College, 28 Mar 20, AWC 127–16.
   [38] Ltr, Maj Walter E. Prosser (CO 350th FA) to
Asst Comdt Gen Staff College, 14 Apr 20, AWC
127–10.

bulk of Negro troops should be used in service units. Of combat units, those of supporting types could best use Negroes, though a proportion would have to be placed in front-line organizations. These should be confined to small units if a satisfactory method of employing them in conjunction with larger white units could be achieved.

The full testimony and experiences of World War I commanders nevertheless left considerable room for doubt as to the complete validity of any but the most general conclusions, for even those commanders who reported least success indicated that in any given unit careful planning and execution of a different order from what had been common in World War I might have produced different results. Reports from the more successful units suggested that the picture was not universally bleak. Officers of certain of the infantry units, while recommending changes in organization and employment, did not always agree with the general conclusion that there were inherent difficulties barring the way to the formation of successful Negro combat units. The white commander of the only one of the eight Negro infantry regiments in France to continue with all Negro officers, except himself, wrote, "I found the men of the 370th Infantry generally amenable to discipline, exceedingly uncomplaining under hardship, and the majority willing and ready to follow an officer anywhere and at any time. . . . Of course there was a large amount of illiteracy, which complicated the non-commissioned officer problem." Some of the Negro officers, he reported, were good, but the majority showed a "lack of sense of responsibility and of initiative." That the regiment func-

tioned as well as it did, he added, was "largely due to the influence of a few good men, [officers who] were loyal, hardworking and reliable men. . . ." [39]

He felt that a large error had been made in training Negro officers in separate classes:

. . . men of the two races should be compared and if the Negro suffers from the comparison, he should not be commissioned. As I understand the question, what the progressive Negro desires today is the removal of discrimination against him; that this can be accomplished in a military sense I believe to be largely possible, but not if men of the two races are segregated.

In saying the foregoing, I appreciate the tremendous force of the prejudice against association between negroes and whites, but my experience has made me believe that the better element among the negroes desires the removal of the restriction rather than the association itself. [40]

The commanding officer of the 371st Infantry, the only all-draft Negro regiment staffed completely with white officers from the beginning, felt that with white leadership "a small number" of Negro infantry divisions could be adequately trained and used by the army "as shock divisions . . . to equalize the losses among the races." He would not deny commissions to Negroes, for he believed that incentives to enlisted men were essential, but he would confine the use of Negro officers to noncombat units and would insist on "absolute equality of requirements between negroes and white candidates for promotion." Initiative, he declared, while rarer among Negroes than among whites, was "not wholly lacking," and he then cited ex-

---

[39] Ltr, Maj Thomas A. Roberts to Asst Comdt Gen Staff College, 5 Apr 20, AWC 127–17.
[40] Ibid.

amples from his regiment to prove his point. The examples included a company clerk who went forward to the battlefield from the rear echelon when he learned that his company had lost all its officers, and a linesman who, after being seriously wounded, worked several more hours to keep the telephone lines open, until he dropped from exertion and loss of blood.[41]

The conviction that the Army, instead of limiting the use of Negro combat troops, should attempt to increase their efficiency was strongly expressed in some of the reports. To heighten their self-identification as a vital part of the Army team some observers recommended that smaller Negro units be attached to or integrated into larger white units. One commander wrote:

Personally I think it is a waste of time to consider whether we shall have colored troops and colored officers. It is quite possible that in the future as in the past circumstances will arise to compel us to have both.

I think our past policy of massing them by themselves has not been wise. I believe under conditions as they are this policy should be modified by doing away with the colored regiments and putting a colored unit in every regiment, said unit not to be smaller than a company and not larger than a battalion. I believe in having colored officers for these colored units to the extent that suitable colored personnel is available under the conditions for qualifying for the position of an Army officer.[42]

Although other commentators had similar reactions, the adverse testimony of most officers of the 92d and 93d Divisions was so preponderant that it was difficult for Army General Staff officers to come to any conclusion other than the one widely held among them in the period between wars: Negro combat troops in World War I failed to come up to Army standards. If such a failure was to be prevented in a future war, plans that took into account the testimony of World War I commanders and avoided the organizational errors of World War I had to be laid to determine the best and most efficient means of employing Negro troops in a time of national emergency.

_____

[41] Ltr, Col Perry L. Miles to Asst Comdt Gen Staff College, undated but received 13 May 21, AWC 127–22.

[42] Ltr, Col Vernon A. Caldwell to Asst Comdt Gen Staff College, 14 Mar 20, AWC 127–15. Colonel Caldwell had commanded a Negro company in Cuba and in the Philippines in the War with Spain. For a time, he commanded the 365th Infantry in France.

CHAPTER II

Peacetime Practices and Plans

During the years of peace, the War Department and its General Staff proceeded, as was their duty, to develop plans for the mobilization of manpower in the event of war. Plans for the use of Negroes explored various organizational possibilities. Some of these were derived from the recommendations of World War I commanders. Others came from the study of historical and sociological treatises. Still others were the products of a priori reasoning. At times, the plans were ahead of the contemporary thinking of comparable civilian institutions. Religious denominations, public school systems, and industrial plants, like the Army, had to deal with problems of racial adjustment on a broad scale. Many of these, again like the Army, had developed separate methods and subinstitutions for their relations with Negroes. At other times, Army plans fell behind developing contemporary practices. But they always included social and political considerations along with purely military problems.

The major problem, generally recognized in planning for the mobilization of Negro troops, was how best to build efficient military units from a portion of the population which, in general, had had little experience in the skills and responsibilities that go with efficient military administration and leadership and which, under existing peacetime conditions, had little opportunity to develop them. Neither in civilian economic and political life nor in military pursuits had Negroes generally attained positions of the type that required the development of technical, managerial, and leadership skills. While the lack of opportunities for the development of demonstrable native capabilities was certainly a factor in the low status of Negroes in the general American society, the lack of development itself, no matter what the cause, could not be overlooked if the Army was seriously to attempt to create efficient Negro military units on a large scale.

Presumably, it could build such units from the available material by removing the burden of military responsibilities and leadership from the Negroes themselves and passing it on to white officers and possibly to white noncommissioned officers. This method had been widely used in the organization of the United States Colored Troops in the Civil War and in Negro units in World War I. A second method would be so to reduce the numbers of Negroes called for military service that the importance of the question would diminish to a near-vanishing point. A third method would be to abandon altogether the attempt to build Negro units and place Negroes in units along with white soldiers.

The first procedure would be ideal from the point of view of providing units with more experienced leadership, but almost every commentator was quick to see that, aside from the possibility that through the subtle two-way interplay of racial prejudices Negro units with all-white leaders might be no more efficient than in the past, this plan would be attacked at once because of its implicit denial of opportunities and incentives to all Negroes, whether qualified or not. Both of the other approaches, it was felt, would be political and social dynamite. As for reducing the number of Negroes to such a point that the problem of how to employ them would become a small one, this might work in peacetime, but in time of war, political and social pressures could be counted upon to create demands from both Negroes and whites for increased rather than diminished use of Negroes in the military services. If planned units for Negroes did not exist, attempts to place them in existing white units might be made. The majority of Army officers and War Department officials charged with determining policy on the employment of Negro troops did not believe that, within the existing social structure, there was any possibility of creating units racially mixed on an individual basis. It might be customary for Negroes and whites to work together in most parts of the country, but it was not customary for them to live and play together. Nor was the working relationship generally comparable to that which is required of men operating in a military team.

Where Negroes and whites worked together in civilian life, Negroes were generally in subordinate positions or in types of jobs traditionally reserved for them. They were the unskilled workers and helpers where whites were the skilled workers and foremen; they were the porters and janitors and watchmen in office buildings where whites were the accountants and salesmen and managers; they were the domestics and heavy laborers for white employers. The skilled and professional workers, the tradesmen and craftsmen among them, though engaged in a broader variety of pursuits than was generally realized, were few in comparison with the vast majority of unskilled workers who held neither responsible nor leadership positions in civilian life. Working relations between Negroes and whites in the same plant were seldom characterized by the upward and downward flow of both authority and confidence so essential to *esprit* in a military unit. Army planners took note that the United States Navy no longer employed Negroes in peacetime at all, except as mess boys, because of the problem of "mixing the races" aboard ship. Even the Navy's traditional Negro mess boys were giving way to Filipinos, Chamorros, and Japanese. Abandoning the separate Negro units was not seriously considered by the Army at all.

The Army recognized that large numbers of Negro troops would have to be employed in another war. They would probably have to be employed in separate Negro units which would fall heir to all the difficulties experienced in World War I, where separate Negro units with racially mixed leadership, especially in combat units, were the rule. The question was how to minimize these difficulties while still maintaining separate Negro organizations.

"There Is Not Enough Army to Go Around"

In its planning for the future the Army, as already noted, had a core of Negro Regulars to consider. Their presence affected both military plans and the reaction of the Negro public to the Army as an institution.

The four Negro regiments, the 9th and 10th Cavalry and the 24th and 25th Infantry, were established by legislation enacted in 1866 and 1869. The first of these acts, under which the Army was reorganized, increased the Regular Army to ten cavalry regiments and forty-five infantry regiments. Of the four new cavalry regiments two were to have Negro enlisted personnel, and of the thirty-five new infantry regiments four were to be Negro. The act of 1869 ordered the reduction of the infantry regiments to twenty-five as rapidly as a consolidation of the existing regiments could be made. Under the terms of this act, two of the Negro regiments, the 38th and 41st, were consolidated as the 24th Infantry and the other two, the 39th and 40th, became the 25th Infantry.[1] The Revised Statutes of 1878, Sections 1104 and 1108, provided that the enlisted men of two cavalry regiments and two infantry regiments should be Negroes. There was no express repeal of these sections of the Revised Statutes in any later legislation concerning the Regular Army.

Therefore, although the National Defense Act of 1920, under which the peacetime Army was organized, did not require the continued existence of any of the Regular regiments—it spoke of units and not of regiments—it was generally considered within the Army and by the Negro public that the Negro regiments were required by law. During the period of successive reductions of the size of the Army after World War I, the Judge Advocate General advised that since repeals by implication were not favored and that since earlier opinions had held that to alter the composition of an arm or service by increasing or diminishing the number of Negro organizations would be an exercise of legislative power by the Executive, Negro units would have to be retained.[2]

The question was of importance in 1922 for two reasons. In the reduction of the size of the Army many white regiments had been placed in an inactive status. With prospects of further reductions in the total Army strength, other regiments might be made inactive. "It seems to me an absurdity," the Deputy Chief of Staff wrote to the Judge Advocate General, "that with the reduction of the Army the War Department should be obliged to maintain these four regiments of colored soldiers. Carried to the logical extreme, if the Army were reduced to four regiments, it would necessarily have to be an exclusively colored army."[3] The second reason was that by law the 9th Cavalry, then in the Philippines, was due to return 400 men to the United States. There had to be an

[1] WDGO 17, 15 March 1869. The original 24th Infantry became a part of the 11th Infantry; the original 25th became a part of the 18th Infantry.

[2] In October 1904 and again in April 1907, the question of the enlistment of Negroes in the Coast Artillery had been raised and the Judge Advocate General had ruled that this question could only be determined by legislative and not by administrative action. Memo, JAG for DCofS, 15 Mar 22, AG 322.97 (3–1–22) (1).

[3] Memo, DCofS for JAG, 1 Mar 22, AG 322.97 (3–1–22).

organization on the mainland which could receive these men. The prospect for the 10th Cavalry was that it would become a recruit depot for the shifting of men to and from the overseas regiment. The need to retain these two regiments if their current assignments were continued seemed strong. At the same time, further reduction of the Army appeared to make it possible that the 2d Division might have to be broken up, making two of its regiments inactive, and that the 24th and 25th Infantry might have to be included in the 2d Division. This would be "contrary to the policy heretofore held of not brigading the two colors together." [4]

While the Judge Advocate General did not believe that any of the four Negro regiments could be inactivated except by legislative action, he did suggest two practical solutions: portions of them might be made inactive, as had been done in 1890 when two companies of each infantry regiment and two troops of each cavalry regiment, white and Negro, were skeletonized to effect an over-all strength reduction; [5] or the incorporation of existing Negro nonregimental detachments into the infantry and cavalry regiments might achieve an over-all

reduction of Negro strength though the regiments remained. [6]

Further reduction of the Negro cavalry regiments was not going to be an easy matter. Under a general reorganization and reduction of the cavalry in 1921, six troops of the 9th and seven of the 10th Cavalry had already been ordered demobilized. [7] Enlistments of Negroes, other than those who had been in the Army before April 1917, had ceased in 1919. [8] A further general reduction of the Army was ordered by an act of 30 June 1922. The 24th Infantry's authorized strength was thus reduced, and the regiment had to absorb the Colored Detachment at Fort Benning, Georgia, acquiring a surplus of Negro infantrymen that could not be absorbed elsewhere. The surplus was prorated among all infantry regiments, with each white regiment's actual strength reduced by a proportionate share of the 24th's surplus. This reduction in actual strength amounted to thirty men per regiment. Each full-strength white regiment was to cease recruiting until its strength reached its authorized strength less thirty. [9] A temporary cessation of new enlistments in the Negro regiments was ordered. [10]

The Negro regiments were filled to capacity—and remained so. Re-enlistments on the day following discharge,

---

[4] Memo, DCofS for JAG, 4 Mar 22, AG 329.97 (3-4-22). In 1919 it had been announced that the 184th Brigade, to contain the 24th and 25th Infantry, would be attached to the 7th Division, with the 9th Cavalry also assigned to this division and the 10th Cavalry assigned to the 36th Division. This was an interim organization, when twenty infantry divisions, each with one cavalry regiment assigned, and one cavalry division, were planned. *Army and Navy Journal,* (April 5, 1919); *National Service with the International Military Digest* (September, 1919), pp. 186–88.
[5] WDGO 72, 21 July 1890; WDGO 79, 25 July 1890.

[6] Memo, JAG for DCofS, 15 Mar 22, AG 322.97 (3-1-22) (1).
[7] Ltr, TAG to CG's All Corps Areas, 20 Aug 21, AG 320.2 (8-11-21).
[8] WD Cir 271, 1919; WD Cir 355, 1919; WD Cir 365, 1919; WD Cir 392, 1919.
[9] Ltr, Actg TAG to CG's All Corps Areas, 6 Jul 22, AG 322.212 (7-1-22) Enlisted RA. The act of 30 June 1922 reduced the Army to 125,000 enlisted men. Of these, 49,107 were allotted to the infantry.
[10] Ltr, Actg TAG to CG's All Corps Areas, 3 Jul 22, AG 342.1 (6-30-22) RA Rtg No. 21.

or within twenty days for noncommissioned officers, were regularly high. The Negro units lost few men through normal discharges. Even before World War I these regiments had had a high percentage of career soldiers; during the period of reductions nearly all men of these regiments were professional soldiers. Vacancies and promotions became rarities in most Negro units.

In 1931 the Army found it necessary to reduce further the strength of the Negro units. An expansion of Air Corps units had been authorized by Congress in 1926. This expansion was to take place in five yearly increments. The men for the Air Corps units were to come from allotments to units of other branches. Negro ground units were not required to contribute to the first four increments, but in the fifth, or 1931 increment, they took their share of the reductions all at once.[11] The reductions were coupled with the absorption of scattered detachments by the regiments and with changes in locations which split the 10th Cavalry and the 25th Infantry among several stations.

The increase of Air Corps units out of the Negro allotments meant more than the shift of men from one arm to another. It meant a general reduction in the strength of Negroes in the Army. Unlike the white units the Negro units had no new compensatory vacancies available in the Air Corps, since the Air Corps did not accept Negro enlistments.[12] The Negro units once more found themselves overstrength both in numbers and in ratings. The War Department had to order a temporary cessation of enlistments, re-enlistments, and promotions for Negroes. Because excess men could be absorbed only by transfer among the few Negro units, the cessation of enlistments and promotions, planned to last not more than six to twelve months, persisted until 1934 in an acute form.[13] Further, the strength of the Army was reduced at a time when, because of economic depression, the demand by Negroes for enlistment was higher than usual. Of the five years available for the Air Corps' increase, none, so far as relations with the Negro public went, was worse than 1931.

Although the original War Department letter of instructions plainly indicated that the orders suspending recruiting for Negro units were "*Not* for Press Release," [14] it was difficult to keep the news quiet. Before the month was out, the NAACP had received copies of the orders from "two sources" and had written President Herbert C. Hoover to inquire about their authenticity. "If we interpret these facts correctly," the NAACP said, "it appears . . . that it is the intention of the War Department to abolish the so-called colored regiments." [15]

---

[11] Personal Ltr, Maj Gen Douglas MacArthur, CofS, to Maj Gen Edwin B. Winans, CG Eighth Corps Area, 17 Aug 31; Ltr, Frederick H. Payne, Actg SW, to Walter White, Secy NAACP, 11 Aug 31. Both in AG 320.2 (6–17–31) (1) sec. 1. See also letters in AG 620 (4–23–41) (1) sec. 2.

[12] The 65th Infantry (Puerto Rican) was similarly affected.

[13] Ltr, TAG to CG's, 2 Jul 31, AG 320.2 (6–17–31) Enlisted, based on Memo, G–3 for TAG, 17 Jun 31, AG 320.2 (6–17–31); Ltr, TAG to CG's Corps Areas, 25 Jun 34, AG 320.2 (6–25–34) Enlisted.

[14] Marginal note, signed C.C., on Ltr, TAG to CG's, 2 Jul 31, cited in note 13, above.

[15] Ltr, Walter White to President Hoover, 29 Jul 31, AG 320.2 (6–17–31) (1) sec. 1.

The fact that the directive was to receive no publicity added a note of deep and dark mystery. Within a few weeks the Negro press was carrying articles suggesting that the Negro regiments were being gradually disbanded. American Legion posts and civic groups were writing their congressmen to obtain definite reports on what the future of Negro troops was to be.[16] The War Department answered certain of the inquiries, including those from the White House, by saying:

The War Department does not distinguish between its soldiers and treats white and black absolutely alike. Apparent effort is now being made to establish the principle that the negro soldier shall receive preferential treatment over the white soldier. The War Department wishes emphatically again to go on record that it believes it would be most harmful to establish any differential treatment between soldiers of the American Army because of difference of race or color.[17]

This justification, based on the equity of reductions in Negro units similar to previous ones in white units and on the fact that over 40 percent of the white units were split among several stations, enabled the NAACP to prepare a rejoinder in which it agreed fully with the principle as stated. "It is our most earnest desire," Walter F. White, the NAACP secretary, wrote, "that Negro and white soldiers receive the same treatment and the same consideration, with no preference for either white or black units." On the surface, he said, the present plan seemed fair and impartial, but in actual operation it created the very preferential treatment which the War Department had disavowed:

It is the conception of this Association that non-preferential treatment for white and colored soldiers, if adhered to by the War Department, would result in the Tenth Cavalry being kept together at one post; in Negroes being enlisted in the Air Corps and every other service of the Army; in full armament equipment being distributed to Negro combat units, that is, trench mortars, howitzers, machine guns, etc; in full staffs of colored noncommissioned officers in existing colored units; in free and unobstructed admission of Negro cadets to the United States Military Academy at West Point; and eventually in colored officers being promoted and assigned to commands on the basis of their ability and not their color.

The letter was not answered, but Maj. Gen. George Van Horn Moseley, Deputy Chief of Staff, noted: "This is a very good letter. General MacArthur will probably be interested in reading it when he returns." [18]

The dissatisfaction of Negroes continued. President Robert R. Moton, successor to Booker T. Washington at Tuskegee Institute, made impassioned pleas to President Hoover for the preservation of the units, pointing out that, from his own observations at nearby Fort Benning, the fate of the 24th Infantry had been a slow withering away. Moton wrote:

The original declaration was that these Negro troops from the 24th Infantry were transferred to Fort Benning as a *special training unit*. Whatever the original intention, this program has been entirely

[16] AG 320.2 (6–17–31) (1) sec. 1, Protests; AG 620 (4–23–31) (1) sec. 2.

[17] Ltr, Gen MacArthur to Walter H. Newton, Secy to President, 3 Sep 31; Ltr, Actg SW Payne to Newton, 18 Sep 31. Both in AG 620 (4–23–31) sec. 2.

[18] Ltr, Walter White to Gen MacArthur, 10 Sep 31, AG 620 (4–23–31) (1) sec. 2, and attached note.

abandoned. Negro troops at Fort Benning are without arms or equipment of any sort that could be used in training for combat service. They are called out twice a week for what are virtually the rudiments of drill, the only elements of training which they get.

Continuing, Moton urged the President:

I would respectfully ask you to consider the long and honorable career of Negro troops in the service of the United States. It is the universal testimony that they are excellent soldiers and possessed with eager willingness in the performance of their duties under all conditions of service. It is more than unfortunate, it is an injustice, that regiments that have distinguished themselves in the way the 10th Cavalry and the 25th Infantry have done, should be reduced from combat service to be menials to white regiments, without chance for training or promotion and be excluded from other branches of the services. It is merely a pretense that Negroes are accorded the same treatment in the United States army as are given to white troops. It has never been the case and is not so now. This applies both to the rank and file, as witness the presence of the highest ranking Negro officer in the United States army at Tuskegee Institute at the present time, who, by reason of his color is denied service according to his rank and with his own regiment.[19]

Republican clubs and workers suggested that it would help considerably in the coming campaign if the matter could be adjusted.[20] The President, having writ-

ten one personal note to the Secretary of War for information, now wrote another, saying: "We do not seem to be able to get the thing quiet. I am wondering if there is anything you can do in the matter."[21]

"The matter" was not helped when *The Cavalry Journal,* which, in the opinion of laymen, ought to have known what it was talking about, carried an epitaph for the 10th Cavalry. Its text confirmed all the convictions of Negroes that the War Department had so completely denied:

The passing of the 10th Cavalry as a combat regiment is an event of note and will come as a shock to many distinguished officers and soldiers who have served with it. The 10th Cavalry *returns saber* with a proud consciousness of duty well done. The past will preserve for it a record second to none.

For the future we can confidently predict that it will carry on in its new role with the same loyalty and high spirit that has given its motto a living meaning, "Ready and Forward."[22]

A photograph of 10th Cavalry master and first sergeants accompanying the article bore the legend: "Vale: The 10th Cavalry 'Key Men' Returning Saber for the Last Time."

Nor was the War Department's public position on the necessity for splitting the 10th Cavalry improved when similar orders for the 25th Infantry were revoked following vigorous protests, mass meetings, and petitions from white residents in the vicinity of Fort Omaha, Nebraska,

---

[19] Ltr, Moton to Hoover, 18 Sep 31, forwarded to WD 22 Sep 31, AG 620 (4–23–31) (1) sec. 2B; see also Ltrs, Moton to Hoover, 31 Aug 31 and 27 Oct 31, same file. The officer referred to was Col. Benjamin O. Davis.
[20] Ltr, Newton to Actg SW, 15 Sep 31; Resolution, Third Ward Regular Republican Organization, Chicago, to the President, 5 Oct 31; Telg, New Jersey State Republican League, 28 Oct 31; Ltr, Comdr Tacitus E. Gaillard Post, Veterans of Foreign Wars, Kansas City, Mo., to the President, 15 Jan 32. All in AG 620 (4–23–31) (1) sec. 2B.

[21] Ltr, Hoover to SW, 30 Oct 31, AG 620 (4–23–31) (1) sec. 2B.
[22] "Organization Activities," *The Cavalry Journal,* XL (September–October, 1931), 59. The source of this article was the 10th Cavalry itself. It revealed the expectation of the regiment upon receipt of orders.

where two companies of the 25th were to have been sent. The War Department declared that there was no connection between the two events, but the Negro citizens of Omaha, who had been as vigorously pressing for the location of the 25th's companies in their city, could not be convinced that the Army had not given in to white protests on the 25th while refusing to heed Negro protests on the 10th Cavalry. In order to assure their city's receipt of part of the 25th Infantry, they disavowed the NAACP's campaign to have both Negro units kept together and urged the War Department to change no orders at all.[23]

No matter what was done about the splitting of the regiments among several posts, the strength problem would have to be met. "In the adjustment of our military program," General Moseley wrote to Claude A. Barnett, director of the Associated Negro Press, "the fact is there is not enough Army to go around. This makes the problem often very difficult. As you probably know, we are abandoning a number of posts and this has brought down upon us violent protests from our white brethren. Thus far we have been able to withstand these attacks."[24]

Even after the resumption of enlistments in 1934, the tight vacancy situation in Negro units allowed for little recruiting. Because enlistments could be accepted for vacancies only, a Negro who wished to join the Regular Army

could not present himself at a recruiting station, make application, be examined, and be accepted or rejected. During the earlier years of the depression, the same situation with regard to an excess of applicants over vacancies existed for white units. White recruiting, however, never came to a complete halt, and in the middle and late thirties recruiting stations were nearly always able to accept well-qualified white applicants. But a Negro seeking to join the Army had to find out what posts had elements of a Negro unit, discover where vacancies existed, apply to the commanding officer of the post or unit where service was desired, and present himself at the post at his own expense once enlistment was authorized. The Army explained that it had no funds for transporting recruits over the great distances outside their own corps areas which many Negroes had to travel to reach posts where vacancies existed.[25] Often a trip from the east coast to Arizona, where the 25th Infantry was stationed, was involved. As a result, few prospective enlistees got beyond the stage of making inquiries at a recruiting station. But the popularity of prospective military service was such that requests for enlistments in the old regiments sometimes came from great distances—even from as far away as the Philippines.

The restrictions on size, number, and types of Negro units, added to the high proportion of re-enlistments and the consequent inability to take many recruits, made it difficult for the Negro units to prepare themselves for the job

[23] Ltrs, various dates, AG 620 (4–23–31) (1) sec. 2A; Ltr, Omaha NAACP to SW, 5 Oct 31; Ltr, Actg CofS to Omaha NAACP, 9 Oct 31; Telg, John A. Singleton, President Omaha NAACP, to SW, 1 Nov 31. Last three documents in AG 620 (4–23–31) (1) sec. 2B.
[24] Ltr, DCofS to Barnett, 15 Oct 31, AG 620 (4–23–31) (1) sec. 2B.

[25] Ltr, TAG to Senator Elmer Thomas, Okla., 13 Apr 39, AG 291.21 (4–10–39).

of providing a nucleus of young, trained Negro men who might be valuable in an expanded wartime Army. Because all elements of the regiments were seldom assembled and stationed at the same posts, and because so many of the elements and detachments were used for housekeeping duties, training beyond the level of the disciplined life of the garrison soldier was difficult. The regiments, or those portions available, did participate in field exercises with other units of the Army from time to time, but for the most part they had little save ceremonial and rudimentary training duties to perform. The Negro press and public, in their long campaign for increased enlistment opportunities, did not overlook the ready opportunity to cite the disadvantages of a situation in which recruiting posters and stations were in evidence in the business sections of most cities while potential Negro trainees lacked vacancies in which they could be placed. The young Negro who successfully found his way into the Regular Army as an enlisted man was looked upon as an extremely fortunate young man.

The opportunity for the young Negro to become a Regular Army officer was even more limited. Between 1920 and 1940 only one Negro was graduated from the Military Academy at West Point, though others were appointed.[26] In 1940 two other cadets, in the classes of 1941 and 1943, were enrolled at the academy. The total number of Negro

Regular Army officers was five, of whom three were chaplains.

The Civilian Components

During the period between world wars several large cities had National Guard units allotted to Negroes; most of the units had existed before World War I and some before the War with Spain. Only one of these, the 369th Infantry (New York) was maintained with all of its elements. The 8th Illinois Infantry was maintained minus one battalion. The 372d Infantry, with two battalions and one company of a third, was split among Massachusetts, Ohio, and the District of Columbia, with a New Jersey unit added just before mobilization in 1940. Maryland had a separate company, which became the Service Company of the 372d in 1940. The regiment's headquarters, band, and medical detachment were unallotted; agreement among the states concerned was necessary before a commanding officer and other field officers could be appointed. Split as it was, among four states in four corps areas, supervision of this regiment for peacetime training as a unit was practically impossible.

Senior infantry units of the Reserve Officers' Training Corps (ROTC) were established at Howard University in Washington and at Wilberforce University in Ohio. Although Negro students at other Northern universities were permitted to take ROTC training in mixed units provided that they could qualify, Negroes in ROTC units outside of Howard and Wilberforce were rare. Charges were made in peacetime that at certain schools "qualifications" included being white. Despite investigations,

---

[26] Up to 1940 a total of four Negroes had been graduated from West Point: Henry O. Flipper, Cavalry, 1877; John H. Alexander, Cavalry, 1887; Charles Young, Cavalry, 1889; Benjamin O. Davis, Jr., Infantry, 1936.

such charges were difficult to prove, for the decision on academic qualifications rested with the school authorities.[27]

Negro Reserve officers, numbering 353 eligible reservists in 1940,[28] were assigned to regiments of the Organized Reserves and were given summer camp training when they requested it. The only Negro Reserve regiment which was even nearly staffed was the 428th Infantry (District of Columbia). Correspondence and lecture courses were open to Negro reservists and, where their numbers were large enough, separate lectures were organized for them. Junior ROTC's, "55c" units, and high school cadet corps were available to Negroes in certain schools, such as Hampton Institute in Virginia, Tuskegee Institute in Alabama, North Carolina Agricultural and Technical College, and Prairie View College in Texas, and in certain public high schools, notably in Washington, D.C.,[29] Chicago, and Gary.

Citizens' Military Training Camps were organized and located on the basis of applications received. There were periodic criticisms of the Army for not operating camps to which Negro youths could be assigned in each corps area.[30] At various times, these camps were operated in the Third, Seventh, Eighth, and Ninth Corps Areas. In the late thirties the Third Corps Area camp was staffed by Negro officers.

Relatively few Negroes were directly affected by the opportunities in the civilian components for military experience. The Reserve elements and the National Guard units were so distributed geographically that the vast bulk of the Negro public hardly knew of their existence and had no means available for taking advantage of them. After being guaranteed retention of their National Guard units and after the establishment of ROTC units, most Negroes paid little attention to the training activities of the civilian components, although there were sporadic signs of concern over limited ROTC and Citizens' Military Training Camp opportunities. Like the rest of the population between wars Negroes were disposed to think of the Army primarily in connection with parades, veterans' organizations, and new and sensational weapons discussed in Sunday magazine supplements.

The Planning Problem

The Army in the meantime was developing its plans for employing Negro manpower in the event of war. The central theme of this planning was that types of units must be found in which Negroes could serve with greatest profit to the country, the Army, and themselves. Since cultural considerations— the Army's estimate of the state of domestic race relations, an estimate strongly supported by most social and political institutions in the twenties— made separate Negro units an undisputed reality, maintaining a workable balance between white and Negro units

---

[27] Ltr, Walter D. McClure, Jr. (Roxbury, Mass.), to SW, 13 Apr 41, and answer, TAG to McClure, 18 Apr 41, AG 291.21 (4-13-41) (1); Rpt, Lt Col Willis J. Tack, PMS&T, University of Akron, re Allegations . . . [of] Samuel R. Shepard [concerning racial discrimination in ROTC], 3 Dec 41, AG 291.21 (11-17-41) (3).

[28] Tab C to Memo, G-1 for CofS, 28 Sep 40, AG 210.31 ORC (9-28-40).

[29] The Negro units of the Washington High School Cadet Corps evidenced their esteem for the Regular Army Negro units by designating their regiments the 24th and 25th, composing the 9th Brigade of Washington High School Cadets.

[30] See *The Crisis*, XXVII (February, 1924), 151.

was of prime importance to the development of a citizen army capable of defending the country without unduly offending either Negroes or whites. To this assumption several others were corollaries. It was generally assumed that Negro troops would respond to the training techniques that were effective with white troops, although it was frequently stated that their training period might have to be longer. Because of their civilian backgrounds and the reports from World War I, it was generally considered that they would be more useful as service than as combat troops. It was expected that they would respond to the same types of motivation and methods of leadership which were effective with white troops, although much emphasis was placed on the use of white officers if the best was to be obtained from Negro units. Any marked departure from the normal training standard for purposes of increasing the efficiency of Negro troops, it was felt, would be considered discriminatory.

Since most of the reports from World War I did not emphasize training or leadership deficiencies, except in relation to the use of Negro officers, the problems of leadership and training did not loom large in comparison with those of the formal organization of Negro troops for effective military service. It was assumed that no matter how Negro units were organized, they would have to be used as integral parts of corps and armies and not as units grouped separately into corps or armies of their own.[31] How Negro units could best be

organized for use with white units as part of a unified military team was an important issue but it was lost sight of in the attempt to find the answer to the primary question: How could the Negro portion of the nation's manpower best be employed in time of war? And then: How could Negro manpower be used with the least stress on military effectiveness and on social customs?

Units and numbers became the important considerations, while training, leadership, and utilization techniques became secondary. The provision of Negro units in "proper" proportions would satisfy the major requirements. No serious attempt was made to use the existing peacetime Negro units as laboratories for experience in methods of training or leading Negro troops, nor was a serious attempt made to insure the development of adequate leadership or of improved training methods through the use of the Reserve components available to the Army. It was assumed that these problems would be no greater than in the past.

Most of the proposals outlined in plans made for the utilization of Negro troops were put into effect in one way or another during the course of World War II. Many of the administrative and organizational problems of the employment of Negro troops therefore may be better understood in light of both the World War I testimony and the developing plans of the War Department General Staff. In the unfolding story of the employment of Negroes in World War II, many details of plans made after

---

[31] Only once in the history of the United States Army was a Negro unit of corps size organized; this organization, the XXV Corps, was formed toward the end of the Civil War. Like all Civil War corps it was a great deal smaller than a World War II corps.

World War I and then virtually forgotten may be discerned. From the evolving policy it is also possible to see reasons for certain developments, such as the initial choice of particular types of units for Negroes, the imbalance existing between Negro and white inductions in the early period of mobilization, and the uncertainty which attended such questions as the provision and assignment of Negro officers and the commitment of Negro units to overseas duty.

The 1922 Plan

The basic features of the policy on the use of Negro manpower in time of war were formulated in 1922. The plan distributed at the end of that year remained essentially the same until it was rescinded in 1938. No expansion of the four Regular Army regiments, except to war strength, was provided. The formation of Negro National Guard units was left entirely to the states. Any Negro units requested by the states were to be separate organizations in addition to the eighteen National Guard divisions which had been authorized. The establishment of Reserve units for Negroes was left entirely to each corps area commander. Only two corps areas, the Fourth and Fifth, had provided any Reserve units for Negroes and none had made provision for Reserve combat units. The 1922 plan, therefore, had to provide an entirely new outline of what was needed if mobilization plans were to be representative of manpower as it existed in the population of the country.

The 1922 staff study on which the plan was based made several primary assumptions which eventually became

part of Army doctrine on the subject of the employment of Negro troops.[32] Among these were:

1. The use to be made of Negroes of military age in the event of complete mobilization is a basic problem in mobilization planning.

2. If mobilization plans do not include "a comprehensive policy in this regard that will be sound and fair and will appeal to intelligent judgment," political pressures will ensue that will force the War Department to shoulder the responsibility alone. "The possibility of arriving at a satisfactory solution under such circumstances is slight."

3. For the general social and economic good of the country, Negroes must be utilized in combat as well as in service units. "To follow the policy of exempting the negro population of this country from combat service means that the white population, upon which the future of the country depends, would suffer the brunt of loss, the negro population, none; the rising white generation 34 percent, and the rising negro population, nothing."[33]

4. Military realities and not "social, ethnological and psychological" theories must be the deciding factors in determining the use to be made of Negro manpower. "Briefly, these [military realities] are: that the negro is a citizen of the United States, entitled to all of the rights of citizenship and subject to all of the obligations of citizenship; that the negro constitutes an appreciable part of

---

[32] Memo, G–3 for CofS, 28 Nov 22, AG 322.97 (11–28–22) (1).

[33] The 34 percent loss figure was based on the percentage of casualties in the mobilized force of Great Britain during World War I, a figure which was considered comparable to the losses which the United States might expect in event of all-out war.

our military manhood; that while not the best military material, he is by no means the worst; that no plan of mobilization for the maximum effort can afford to ignore such a fraction of the manhood, especially in these times when war makes demands upon the physical defectives and the women; and finally, that in a democracy such as ours political and economic conditions must be considered, and that decision must rest upon these two considerations alone."

The study offered solutions for the three major controversial questions raised by World War I: the use of Negroes as combat troops; the size and nature of Negro units; and the race of officers for Negro units.

On the question of the employment of Negroes as combat troops, the study concluded that, from World War I examination records, at least half of the Negro effectives were eligible for combat service and should be so assigned. Psychological test data from World War I showed that Negroes ranked lower than whites. But there were "some Negroes in all intelligence grades." The 1922 study concluded that: "As a matter of fact, we have to sift our white population for suitable combat material. The fact that the sifting would result in relatively fewer Negroes for combat duty is not an excuse for not sifting the Negro population at all."

As far as the size of Negro combat units was concerned, the paper agreed that smaller units led by white officers and operating "either separately or in conjunction with other white troops" had achieved a greater measure of success in the past than large Negro units. The study therefore recommended: ". . . to play safe . . . Negro units should not be grouped exclusively in organizations as large as a division, but smaller units should be grouped with white units. We know that white regiments and negro regiments have operated successfully side by side, and, this being the case, there appears no good reason why they should not be brigaded together." Since there was no past experience in grouping Negro and white battalions in the same regiment, this type of organization was not recommended.

The use of Negro officers was the third controversial question which the study attempted to answer. The lack of success of Negro divisional troops in World War I may have been due to the "preponderance of Negro officers," but, the study pointed out, "the record of Negro regiments which operated with the French is not discreditable, even though in the case of at least two regiments, the Negro officers greatly predominated." [34] While the successful performance of Negro troops was dependent upon "proper leadership" by "white officers or by white officers in command of principal units," the study warned that

"it is not reasonable to expect that the negro will be willing to serve in the ranks with no hope of a commission. Moreover, it cannot be fairly stated that no negro possesses the necessary qualities of leadership to make him an efficient officer. . . . Not all our white officers are selected from the ranks of the most intelligent. As a matter of fact, we commission many white officers of only average intelligence. It follows that there must be some negroes of intelligence equal to some of the whites

---

[34] This point was not pursued to a discussion of any further differences which may have existed between the employment of these regiments by the French and by the AEF.

whom we commission. The trouble in the past has been that we have not demanded from the negro the same standard of intelligence, grade for grade, as from the white.

Even in separate training camps giving identical courses "there was no means of comparing results." The only solution, the study concluded, was "to establish a rigid standard and to require whites and negroes alike to measure up to it."

Since the composition of National Guard units was under state control—and the study argued that it should so remain—and since the four Regular regiments already provided for representation in the Regular Army, the 1922 plan confined its attention to the provision of units in the Organized Reserves, the only remaining component of the Army. Reserve units, thought of as "moulds into which the draft should be poured," were allotted to corps areas, whose commanders were to organize these units with a full complement of Reserve officers and a cadre of noncommissioned officers and specialists.

A major feature of the 1922 plan was the recommendation that corps area commanders, after "a careful study of the distribution of the Negro population," should block out regimental and battalion areas, properly subdivided into subordinate unit areas. From the units allotted to the corps areas, commanders would provide units for Negro troops. These units were not to be developed "for the present" except where properly qualified Negro officers were available to command them. Where no officers existed, units would remain unorganized until officers were developed.

The 1922 plan was approved by the Secretary of War, John W. Weeks, on

23 December and its provisions were communicated confidentially to corps area commanders on 27 December, with instructions that each corps area should make plans and recommendations for the use in initial mobilization of about 50 percent of the Negro effectives available in its area, half of these to be placed in combat organizations and the remainder in noncombatant organizations.[35] Negro units were to be taken from unit allotments already made to the corps areas, except that extra infantry units might be formed if needed. All were to be nondivisional units. The instructions included sample suggestions for individual corps areas. For example, it was suggested that the First Corps Area (New England) might form an infantry or field artillery battalion, or several batteries of coast artillery for harbor defense. The Third Corps Area (Pennsylvania, Maryland, District of Columbia, Virginia) might form from its 24,000 Negroes available for combat duty one infantry regiment in the vicinity of Philadelphia and another in Washington. Nondivisional combat units could absorb the remaining 17,000 men. The Fourth Corps Area (southeastern states), which contained the greatest number of Negroes, might provide ten or twelve extra infantry regiments, while the Ninth Corps Area (west coast and mountain states), with a small number of effectives, might provide a regiment of artillery or companies of harbor defense troops. All units were to have Negro officers, except that where they could not be obtained white officers might fill vacancies, provided that no

[35] Ltr, TAG to CG's Corps Areas, Depts, Chiefs Branches and Bureaus, CG District of Washington, 27 Dec 22, AG 322.97 (11–28–22) (Misc Div).

Negro officer should command a white officer.

Corps area commanders submitted their own plans for the use of the Negro manpower in their areas as requested. The only objections to the general plan came from two corps area commanders who felt that the Negro units should be in addition to their current allotments in order to prevent disruption of units already set up for white personnel. Extra cavalry units recommended by corps area commanders were not approved, but units of other arms and services were included in the authorized lists of units for Negroes. To prevent an unduly large number of extra infantry units, commanders were authorized to clear allotted artillery units of white personnel "if, in their opinion, it can be done without injury to morale" and then set these units aside for Negroes. The plans submitted by the commanders and the policy itself were approved and confirmed on 12 July 1923.[36]

The only large question concerning the use of Negro troops in service units of the Organized Reserves was raised by the Engineers. The Chief of Engineers, in 1921, and again in 1923, opposed the allocation of Negroes to general service units, pointing out that these units required officers and men with considerable technical skill and that their duties "compel these troops to be exposed to the same conditions of fire and all the severe circumstances of front line fighting . . . without the opportunity to relieve the nerve strain by returning the fire of the enemy." He recommended that the War Department adopt and "promulgate" the policy that all engineer units, except auxiliary (separate) battalions, be white or, "if troops of other colors, that the personnel be specially selected. . . ." The War Department answered that it did not plan to restrict the use of Negroes to "any particular types of organizations in any branch of the service" so far as corps area assignment to the Organized Reserves was concerned. The Engineer objection was nevertheless filed for consideration in future revisions of mobilization plans. Though general service units were not entirely removed, the majority of them were replaced by auxiliary and, later, by separate battalions.[37]

Modifications and Developments 1923–33

Later mobilization plans did not generally follow the 1922 policy so far as the ratios of combat to noncombat units was concerned; nor did they provide for the employment of Negro manpower in proportion to the general effective population available for military service. In addition to Reserve units, moreover, provision was made for Negro inactive Regular Army units which could be organized at specified periods after the beginning of mobilization. A 1928 plan, for example, provided for Regular Army inactive field artillery units among the combat arms; the bulk of Negroes were allotted to Regular Army inactive am-

---

[36] Ltr, TAG to CG's Corps Areas, 12 Jul 23, AG 322.97 (6–30–23) (Misc) M–C.

[37] Ltr, CofE to TAG, 24 Dec 21, and 1st Ind, TAG to CofE, 27 Jan 22, AG 320 Orgd Res (12–24–21); Ltr, OCE to TAG, 20 Jul 23; Ltr, TAG to CofE, 30 Jul 23. Last two in AG 322.97 (11–28–22) (1).

munition trains, engineer auxiliary battalions, and quartermaster units.[38]

During the 1920's the subject of the
future employment of Negro troops came
to be considered so sensitive that it was
felt that it was not in the best interest
of the service to disseminate information
concerning it too widely. The policy of
cloaking plans for the use and designation of Negro units in secrecy went so far
in the late twenties that Negro units, as
such, virtually disappeared from all except the War Department's own plans.
After 1928, corps area commanders were
not permitted to show on their mobilization plans those units which were to
receive Negro troops. These instructions
were not rescinded until 1938, when
corps area commanders and chiefs of
arms and services were directed to indicate "appropriately" the Negro units in
their plans.[39] As a consequence, it was
widely assumed both outside and inside
the Army that no comprehensive plan
for the employment of Negro troops in
time of war existed.

The basic assumptions of the 1922
plan nevertheless remained in operation. Four introductory points of a
summary of existing plans prepared in
1931 by the War Department Personnel
Division (G–1) for the Deputy Chief of
Staff are representative of those elements of peacetime planning for the
utilization of Negro manpower which
remained constant:

1. The negro being a citizen of the
United States must, in a major emergency,
bear his proportionate share of the war
burden.

2. The negro manpower is 10.73% of
the whole.

3. Lack of policy regarding the use of
the negro manpower caused the War Department to adopt during the World War,
a course in regard to its use that was dictated more by political and racial conditions than sound military policy.

4. Unless our mobilization plans provide
for the use of the negro manpower in
combat units the War Department will be
forced to do so after the emergency arises.
This may be a cause of great embarrassment.[40]

Fractional percentages for Negro
strength shifted during the period, as
new census figures and estimates became available. But the available proportionate Negro manpower remained
slightly above or below 10 percent of the
population throughout the two decades
between wars, and this percentage was
used in policy papers. Providing for the
full use of this proportionate share of
population was a central theme in manpower studies and plans of the peacetime period.

In 1931 a new study of the Negro
manpower problem provided a plan
which emphasized the desirability of de-
ferring the organization of Negro units
until after an emergency was well under
way. No units larger than a battalion
were to be organized in the first year of
mobilization. The advantages to be obtained by this procedure were: fewer
officers would be required for Negro
units at a time when capable officers
would be in great demand elsewhere;
more rapid mobilization would be
achieved by minimizing the problem of

---

[38] Memo, G–3 for TAG, 28 Jul 28. AG 322.97
(5–16–31).

[39] Ltr, TAG to All CG's Corps Areas and All
Chiefs Arms and Svs, 28 Jul 28, AG 381 (7–28–28)
(Misc) ; Ltr, TAG to All CG's Corps Areas and All
Chiefs Arms and Svs, 1 Jan 38, AG 381 (1–11–38)
(Misc) A–M.

[40] Memo, G–1 for DCofS, 25 May 31, AG 322.97
(5–16–31). The summary itself was prepared from
G–3 files.

where to locate and house large Negro units; greater latitude in employment would be obtained through attachment of small Negro units to larger white or Negro organizations; [41] and the importance of the failure of a large Negro unit in combat would be minimized. The battalions would be inactive Regular Army units,[42] making them available for staffing by Regular Army officers and obviating any legal or ethical necessity of assigning Negro officers to them. Thirty-six battalions of infantry, six squadrons of cavalry, and twenty-four battalions of field artillery were to be provided. They were allotted to the corps areas and remained so allotted until 1940, although they had disappeared from mobilization plans by 1938. They were not to be organized until an emergency had arisen. To organize them earlier, it was felt, would present problems of administration and invite political pressures which would be less likely after M-day, the date of the beginning of mobilization for war.

For the first twelve months of war, these units were to operate with white regiments, "arousing friendly rivalry and increasing racial pride." At the end of the first year of a war, they were to be supplemented by the mobilization of the Negro regiments of the Organized Reserves. Negro officers would be eligible for assignment to these Reserve regiments. Any larger units to be formed of

Negro enlisted men could be grouped from the existing smaller units in the theater of operations once the smaller units had proved their combat efficiency.[43]

For initial mobilization, a plan of 1933 showed four infantry regiments (including two National Guard regiments), the separate combat battalions, two companies of infantry, two regiments of cavalry, nine engineer separate battalions, and two quartermaster service regiments. This provided for far less than a proportionate share of the manpower in the initial mobilization. Out of a total of 1,526,380 men in the initial mobilization, only 31,245 or 2.05 percent would be Negro, while current estimates of the available manpower showed that 9.45 percent would be Negro.

The 1937 Plan

The War Department Personnel Division, again studying the manpower problem in 1937, pointed out that failure to provide larger percentages of Negroes in initial mobilization would result in the repetition of mistakes made in World War I. The study described certain of the errors which it hoped to avoid. In the first registration of manpower between 21 and 30 years of age in 1917, 9,562,518 (89.87 percent) were white while 1,078,333 (10.13 percent) were Negro. Of these, 3,110,659 (32.53 percent) of the whites and 556,917 (51.-65 percent) of the Negroes were placed in Class I (unlimited service). During the period of the first registration (5 June to 11 September 1917), enlist-

---

[41] Attachment of not more than one Negro infantry battalion, field artillery battalion, or cavalry squadron of the Regular Army to white infantry, field artillery, or cavalry regiments had been approved in 1927. G-3/6541-Gen-151, 26 Mar 27.

[42] Inactive units, in theory, exist but they have no enlisted men. Officers may be carried on assignment to inactive units, and enlisted men may be provided at any time.

[43] Memo, G-1 for DCofS, 25 May 31, and Incl, AG 322.97 (5-16-31).

ments in this age group were approximately 650,000 whites and 4,000 Negroes. This disproportion was the result of an almost total prohibition on the voluntary enlistment of Negroes because of the failure to provide units to which Negroes could be sent. Therefore, when selective service calls began in September, the percentage of Negroes called was necessarily higher than that for whites (36.23 percent as compared with 24.75 percent up to 15 December 1917). The result of this situation was that at first white citizens objected to the removal of large percentages of whites from regions in which Negroes, though heavily represented in the population, were not being enlisted at all and Negroes objected because they were being refused enlistment by the Army. After the operation of selective service began, the complaints were reversed: Negroes objected to their higher draft rates and whites objected to the removal of disproportionate numbers of Negro agricultural workers as well as to heavy concentrations of Negro soldiers in Southern camps. The system produced an unbalanced force within the Army, with Negroes, who could be expected to require a longer time for training, entering the Army later than men who were presumed to require less.[44]

To avoid the development of a racially unbalanced army in time of war, the G–1 plan of 1937 proposed that, from M-day on, Negroes and whites should be mobilized in proportion to population. In order to do this, mobilization plans should be required to provide enough Negro units for the initial period of expansion to guarantee a ra-

cially proportionate Army. To achieve this result, Negroes would have to be enlisted in the early stages of mobilization at a rate in excess of their proportion in the population, for in the existing Regular Army and National Guard they were below proportionate strength. Unless their initial disproportion were compensated for at the beginning of mobilization by a higher rate of enlistment and induction, they would remain below proportionate strength. Not only must additional units for Negroes be provided in mobilization plans, but also a greater opportunity for Negro citizens to volunteer during the enlistment period must be provided if a racially proportionate Army were to be achieved from M-day on. A greater number of units than those shown in current mobilization plans would have to be earmarked for the receipt of Negro volunteers and drafted men if the errors of 1917 were not to be repeated. In 1937 the strength of the Regular Army and the National Guard stood at approximately 360,000. Of this number 6,500 or approximately 1.8 percent were Negroes. To mobilize a million men, an additional 552,000 whites (86.25 percent) and 88,000 Negroes (13.75 percent) would have to be called if a proportion of 90.55 to 9.45 was to be attained. Thereafter, mobilization could proceed in an approximate ratio of 90.-55 to 9.45 in all future stages of expansion.[45]

The 1937 G–1 study resulted in changes in basic War Department policy on the mobilization of Negro manpower. Not the least of these was the approval of the recommendation that all policies concerning Negro manpower, with one

---

[44] Memo, G–1 for CofS, 26 Apr 37, G–1/14615.

[45] Ibid.

exception, be removed from the "Secret" classification and the resulting air of mystery which had surrounded the question for more than a decade. The exception was the recommendation that Negro combat units have 50 percent more company officers attached than called for in tables of organization. This recommendation arose from the conviction that Negro troops, in addition to requiring more intensive training, would also require closer supervision in operations—supervision which their noncommissioned officers would be unable to insure unless far larger numbers of highly qualified noncommissioned officers were available than was the case in World War I. While the 50 percent officer overstrength policy was to be followed, it was not to be published.[46]

Policies on the utilization of Negro manpower were to be announced in the same way that all other policies were announced, so that everyone concerned would understand what the full attitude of the War Department was before the beginning of an emergency. The 1937 plan implied that full publication in sources to which the public would have access was desirable. But, in addition to reservations which War Department agencies had about the full and free publication of any of the general plans for an emergency, there were special and continuing misgivings about publicizing basic policies on the use of Negro manpower. The Army War College commandant gave a representative summary of objections:

I doubt the wisdom of the War Department announcing this policy at large. Its early announcement will give time for its

careful study by those seeking political capital, for points on which the War Department may be attacked, or embarrassed.

For example, to announce that there will be no discrimination against the negro race in the question of opportunity to bear its proper share of combat and non-combatant duties; to announce that the negro population of the United States is approximately 9%; and then say . . . that "Existing units of the Regular Army and National Guard contain approximately 1.8% negroes," might serve as the basis for a drive for additional colored regiments in the Regular Army, or for the replacement of white regiments by colored, to make the proportion correct.[47]

Though the 1937 policies were removed from the "Secret" classification they did not become readily available to either the public or to the Army.

The New Mobilization Regulations

The approved recommendations of the 1937 plan were incorporated into Mobilization Regulations then being rewritten.[48] While this method of publication removed the plans for Negro participation from their former "Secret" classification, Mobilization Regulations had a restricted circulation. They were distributed in limited numbers to the highest headquarters only: to the chiefs of arms, services, and bureaus, and to the commanders of corps areas, armies, and departments; and to general and special service schools. Neither the general public nor the majority of the Army had ready access to them. No one was given authority to publicize or discuss

---

[46] Memo, OCS for G–1, 17 Feb 38, OCS/15384–5.

[47] Memo, Comdt AWC for G–1, 17 Apr 37 (Second Draft), G–1/14615 (4–26–36).

[48] They were published in MR 1–1, Personnel: Basic Instructions; MR 1–2, Personnel Requirements; MR 1–3, Officers; and MR 1–4, Officer Candidates, along with other pertinent regulations.

any part of their contents with individuals either in or out of the Army who were not directly concerned with mobilization planning. Moreover, from six to twenty-four months were needed to process, edit, and publish these regulations. As portions of the regulations were prepared, mimeographed copies were distributed to the higher headquarters of the Army for use and comment. This procedure created a time lag between the approval of the major features of the 1937 plan and their promulgation to even the restricted audience that they finally reached in their printed form. Thus, despite the decision to publish the Negro policy in detail in Mobilization Regulations—an advance over previous procedures in which only the most general statements were made—the Army's specific plans for the use of Negro troops remained an esoteric subject so far as the general public and most of the Army were concerned. By 1940 when the regulations were all completed and in print, the Army had already begun to move into its initial period of expansion, and mobilization had moved out of the realm of theory and into the realm of practice. References to the use of Negro troops in the new regulations represented a generally unabsorbed and unfamiliar policy.

The approved features of the 1937 War Department G–1 plan, as published in the Mobilization Regulations as they made their successive appearances, included the following provisions:

1. Negro manpower was to be indicated in mobilization plans, "when applicable," at a percentage of the total mobilized strength approximately equal to the ratio between the Negro manpower of military age and the total manpower of military age.[49]

2. Each corps area was to furnish manpower approximately in the ratio of the total manpower mobilized, period by period, which the area's male population of military age bore to the total population of military age. "In the application of this provision whites and negroes will be computed separately." [50] Each corps area would therefore provide Negroes in a ratio equal to the ratio of its Negro manpower of military age to the total Negro manpower of military age.

3. "Unless conditions require modification in the interests of national defense, the ratio of Negroes mobilized in the arms as compared with those mobilized in the services will be the same as for white troops." [51]

4. "Where desirable for training or other purposes, the War Department will provide for the early mobilization of negro units at war strength." [52]

5. Negroes, except when assigned to pools, were to be placed in Negro organizations.[53] All warrant officers and en-

---

[49] MR 1–2, 1 Sep 38, par. 2. Modified in the 1 May 1939 revision by the proviso "Where the situation will permit and warrant such action." Dates given in these notes on the regulations will be those of initial publication, usually in mimeographed copies distributed for comment. Where significant changes occurred in later versions they will be so noted.

[50] MR 1–2 (1938), par. 2.

[51] Ibid.

[52] Ibid., par. 11b. In the 1 May 1939 revision, par. 2a, the limitation was added: ". . . will, so far as practicable, provide in its plans." Both 1939 versions added that the War Department's plans would include appropriate instructions where the foregoing procedures were inapplicable. MR 1–2 (1939), par. 2b.

[53] MR 1–1, 23 Aug 38, par. 9a (5) (c). Later refined to include Negro units or subdivisions of installations, MR 1–1, 10 Feb 39.

listed men of Negro organizations were to be Negroes.[54] "Negro personnel requirements for units are provided for and established by the negro units scheduled for mobilization by the War Department."[55] Warrant officer and enlisted personnel of another arm or service attached to Negro units were, except as otherwise prescribed by the War Department, to be Negroes.[56]

6. Reserve officers for Negro units of the Organized Reserves, officers for Negro organizations in installations, and chaplains for Negro Regular Army units might be Negro.[57] For National Guard units, Negro officers were to be restricted to those positions in Negro units authorized for Negro officers. Whether such authorized positions were to be filled by Negro officers would depend upon the availability of qualified personnel.[58]

7. The number of Negro officer candidates would not exceed the number required to provide officers for organizations authorized to have Negro officers, account being taken of the necessary loss replacements and of the number of Negro officers already available on initiation of mobilization. "The actual number procured, trained, and commissioned will depend, as for all other eligibles, upon the number who qualify under the prescribed standards."[59] "The prescribed standards will be rigidly applied on the basis of individual merit, without exception as to such factors as race, religion, financial status, or social position."[60]

8. Negroes were to be assigned to service command and War Department overhead installations in a percentage "not less than" the percentage of Negroes in the total male population of military age within the corps area in which these installations were located. In overhead installations controlled by the chiefs of arms and services, Negroes were to be employed in a percentage "at least equal to the percentage of Negroes in the total male population of military age." Rare exceptions might be made by the War Department on the basis of the merits of each case.[61]

9. So far as practicable, Negroes assigned to zone of interior installations such as reception centers, replacement centers, and unit training centers for processing, training, or permanent duty during mobilization, were to be assigned to installations in the general areas where they were procured.[62]

Percentages and Types

In a letter supplementing the issuance of the new Mobilization Regulations, the percentage ratio of Negroes to whites for the United States at large and for the installations under the control of chiefs of arms and services was fixed at approximately 9 percent. For the several corps areas and installations of the War Department not under the control of chiefs of arms and services located therein the percentages were fixed as follows: First Corps Area, 1.26 per-

[54] MR 1–2, 15 Jul 39, par. 19b (5).
[55] MR 1–2 (1938), par. 11b; 15 Jul 39, par. 19b.
[56] MR 1–2 (1938), par. 5b (4).
[57] MR 1–2, 1 May 39, par. 11b; par. 11c (4). The 15 July 1939 version changed "may" to "will" for these officer requirements. (Par. 10e.)
[58] MR 1–2, 15 Jul 39, par. 10e.
[59] MR 1–2 (1938 and May 39 versions), par. 11d, and 15 Jul 39 version, par. 13b.
[60] MR 1–4, 17 Oct 38, par. 1b.
[61] MR 1–2 (1938), par. 11e; 15 Jul 39, par. 19c.
[62] MR 1–1 (1938), par. 9a (5) (c).

cent; Second Corps Area, 4.26 percent; Third Corps Area, 11.25 percent; Fourth Corps Area, 33.37 percent; Fifth Corps Area, 6.45 percent; Sixth Corps Area, 4.25 percent; Seventh Corps Area, 5.58 percent; Eighth Corps Area, 10.52 percent; Ninth Corps Area, 1.03 percent.[63] These percentages were approximately the ratios of Negro to white manpower in each corps area. They provided a forecast of the distribution of Negro enlisted men by geographical area.

The 1937 plan provided that Negroes should be organized into the following types of units:

Infantry regiments, GHQ Reserve
Cavalry regiments, GHQ Reserve
Artillery regiments, heavy, long-range calibers, GHQ Reserve
Harbor defense troops
Corps and army ammunition trains
Engineer general service regiments, separate battalions, and dump truck companies
Quartermaster service, remount, and truck regiments; service and port battalions; railhead and salvage companies; and pack trains
Ordnance companies (ammunition)
Corps area service command units
War Department overhead

Significantly, the list omitted the separate battalions of the combat arms which had been authorized in 1927 and which had appeared in the 1933 mobilization plans,[64] thereby effectively re-

scinding the provision for separate battalions of Negro troops which could be attached to larger white units.[65]

The 1937 plan and policy, as outlined above, was the one in effect in 1940, the first year of active preparation for defense through a general peacetime expansion of the Army. But policy and practice, again, were not identical.

From the listing of Negro units in the Protective Mobilization Plan (PMP) of 1940, as shown in Table 1, it is obvious that, even within the limits of planning, in which inactive units could be shifted as necessary, the published mobilization planning policy as it affected Negroes was not being adhered to. The 1937 policy required that Negro manpower be maintained at a ratio approximately in proportion to the total manpower available, that is, from 9 to 10 percent. The units provided in the 1940 PMP contained 5.81 percent Negroes in the total of enlisted men.[66] The policy required further that the ratio of Negro combat troops to service troops be the same as that of white troops. Of the 5.81 percent Negro personnel in the PMP, by far the largest proportions were assigned to the Infantry, the Engineers, and the Quartermaster Corps. Other arms had no Negro units or disproportionately small numbers of Negro units. None of the revisions of the PMP since 1938 had complied with the provision on the ratio of combat to service troops. In those

[63] Appendix D, Percentages of Negro Manpower, to Ltr, TAG to Chiefs Arms, Svs, and Bureaus; Army, Corps Area Comdrs; CG GHQ AF; Superintendent USMA; Comdts Gen Sv Schools; CG's PofE's; CG's Gen Depots, 3 May 39, AG 381 (3-3-39) (Misc) A-M.
[64] G-3/6541-Gen-151, 26 Mar 27, approved 16 Apr 27.

[65] Additional Memo, G-1 for CofS, 8 Feb 38, G-1/14615.
[66] War Department overhead and corps area service commands were maintaining 9 percent Negro personnel in plans submitted to G-1 for action. Memo, G-3 for CofS, 3 Jun 40, G-3/6541-Gen-527. Replacement centers on M plus 90 were to have 4.4 percent Negroes. An. 2, WD PMP 1940.

TABLE 1—NEGRO UNITS IN PROTECTIVE MOBILIZATION PLAN, 1940
(CONTINENTAL UNITED STATES)[a]

Unit	Corps Area	Status[b]	Enlisted War Strength
Total...	....	....	44,537
24th Inf Regt.......................................	IV	RA–PA	2,660
25th Inf Regt.......................................	VIII	RA–PA	2,660
369th Inf Regt......................................	II	NG–A	2,660
8th Illinois Inf Regt (less 1 Bn)...................	VI	NG–A	1,910
372d Inf Regt			
2d Inf Bn.......................................	V	NG–A	750
3d Inf Bn.......................................	I	NG–A	750
Rifle Co A......................................	III	NG–A	188
1st Sep Inf Rifle Co................................	III	NG–A	188
9th Cav Regt.......................................	VII	RA–PA	1,272
10th Cav Regt......................................		RA–PA	1,244
94th Field Arty Regt (8-in. How)...................	IV	RA–I	1,968
44th Coast Arty Regt (155-mm. Gun TD)...............	III	RA–I	1,865
41st Engr Regt (Gen Service)........................	IV	RA–I	1,176
59th Engr Bn (Sep).................................	IV	RA–I	1,079
66th Engr Bn (Sep).................................	IV	RA–I	1,079
65th Engr Bn (Sep).................................	V	RA–I	1,079
99th Engr Bn (Sep).................................	IV	RA–I	1,079
62d Engr Bn (Sep).................................	III	RA–I	1,079
63d Engr Bn (Sep).................................	IV	RA–I	1,079
67th Engr Bn (Sep).................................	IV	RA–I	1,079
69th Engr Bn (Sep).................................	V	RA–I	1,079
70th Engr Bn (Sep).................................	VI	RA–I	1,079
98th Engr Bn (Sep).................................	VI	RA–I	1,079
16th Engr Co (Dump Truck)..........................	II	RA–I	150
17th Engr Co (Dump Truck)..........................	V	RA–I	150
21st Engr Co (Dump Truck)..........................	VII	RA–I	150
47th QM Regt (Truck)...............................	VIII and IX	RA–PA	1,300
48th QM Regt (Truck)...............................	IV and V	RA–PA	1,300
354th QM Regt (Service)............................	IV	RA–I	2,518
255th QM Regt (Service)............................	IV	RA–I	2,518
201st QM Bn (Gas Supply)..........................	II	RA–I	388
202d QM Bn (Gas Supply)..........................	VI	RA–I	388
203d QM Bn (Gas Supply)..........................	V	RA–I	388
204th QM Bn (Gas Supply)..........................	V	RA–I	388
205th QM Bn (Gas Supply)..........................	IV	RA–I	388
206th QM Bn (Gas Supply)..........................	IV	RA–I	388
207th QM Bn (Gas Supply)..........................	VII	RA–I	388
208th QM Bn (Gas Supply)..........................	VII	RA–I	388
209th QM Bn (Gas Supply)..........................	III	RA–I	388
210th QM Bn (Gas Supply)..........................	III	RA–I	388

See footnotes at end of table.

TABLE 1—NEGRO UNITS IN PROTECTIVE MOBILIZATION PLAN, 1940
(CONTINENTAL UNITED STATES)[a]—Continued

Unit	Corps Area	Status[b]	Enlisted War Strength
211th QM Bn (Gas Supply)	VI	RA–I	388
212th QM Bn (Gas Supply)	VI	RA–I	388
391st QM Bn (Port)	II	RA–I	807
394th QM Bn (Port)	IX	RA–I	807
86th QM Co (Railhead)	II	RA–I	100
88th QM Co (Railhead)	IV	RA–I	100
92d QM Co (Railhead)	VII	RA–I	100

[a] Total in units (white and Negro), PMP, 1940, continental U.S., 769,666; percentage of Negro personnel in units, PMP, 1940, 5.81 percent.
[b] RA, Regular Army; A, active; PA, partially active (some elements inactive); I, inactive.

Source: Tab B, Memo, G–3 for CofS, 3 Jun 40, G–3/6541-Gen-527.

branches which contained both combat and noncombat types of units, Negro troops were placed principally in the noncombat types, such as engineer separate battalions. Aside from the active units of infantry and cavalry in the Regular Army and the National Guard, the number of combat units in the PMP was limited to one field artillery and one coast artillery regiment.

This condition was brought about largely by objections on the part of chiefs of arms and services who opposed the assignment of Negro personnel to their branches.[67] Many of the objections of the branches may be traced to the legacy of World War I. To these must be added two other considerations influencing decisions: first, a large residue of popular beliefs and stereotypes concerning Negroes, many of which appeared in "documented" tracts and pseudoscientific studies of the first dec-

ades of this century, and second, imperfectly understood theories of intelligence and adaptability.

Student officers, many of whom later occupied policy making positions in their respective branches, absorbed the materials of successive school studies, adding to them whatever new materials might be readily available, producing by agglutination new school studies to be used in like manner by later classes. Out of these studies and accompanying discussions came a semiofficial credo matching in many ways beliefs widely held among the general public. Some of the more elaborate school studies were occasionally borrowed for use by staff divisions; their more important influence, however, was in molding the attitudes of the students who produced and used them. In the absence of other materials, their use was frequent.

One of the most complete of the brief summaries appearing in such a study, one produced at the Army War College by a committee of field grade students,

[67] Memo, G–3 for CofS, 3 Jun 40, G–3/6541-Gen-527.

most of whom were to play important parts in World War II, provides a representative summary example of the personality problem which commanders expected to meet in the employment of Negro troops:

As an individual the negro is docile, tractable, lighthearted, care free and good natured. If unjustly treated he is likely to become surly and stubborn, though this is usually a temporary phase. He is careless, shiftless, irresponsible and secretive. He resents censure and is best handled with praise and by ridicule. He is unmoral, untruthful and his sense of right doing is relatively inferior. Crimes and convictions involving moral turpitude are nearly five to one as compared to convictions of whites on similar charges.

On the other hand the negro is cheerful, loyal and usually uncomplaining if reasonably well fed. He has a musical nature and a marked sense of rhythm. His art is primitive. He is religious. With proper direction in mass, negroes are industrious. They are emotional and can be stirred to a high state of enthusiasm. Their emotions are unstable and their reactions uncertain. Bad leadership in particular is easily communicated to them.[68]

"Intelligence" as a factor in the employability of Negroes was especially stressed by branches which considered their duties to require relatively high skills and considerable specialized training. By World War I "intelligence" test scores, nearly 80 percent of all Negroes were grouped in the two lowest

classes. The conclusion was reached, in certain studies, that here was proof of the innate lower intelligence of Negroes.[69] But within the range of information afforded by these tests, doubts that general racial conclusions of this sort could be drawn soon arose. Later studies pointed out that the test scores of Negroes varied within and among groups from different sections of the country. The example of Negroes from Northern industrial states, where both economic and educational opportunities were highly developed, who scored higher than whites from Southern agricultural states, where similar opportunities were less well developed, was often cited to show that opportunity and environment evidently had much to do with the

[68] Memo for Chairman of Com 3, 12 Nov 36, prepared by Subcom 2, in Rpt of Com 3, Course at AWC, 1936-37, Preparation for War Period, Part I, G-1 Subcourse, AWC 1-1937-3. This statement expresses in summary form most of the attitudes and assumptions of earlier War College and other school studies. For fullness, compare with Guy B. Johnson, "The Stereotype of the American Negro," Characteristics of the American Negro, Otto Klineberg, ed. (New York: Harper and Brothers, 1944), pp. 3-4.

[69] Of the World War I intelligence tests, no competent, full-scale critical analysis on the basis of later developments in testing has been made. One of the earliest critical statements was made in 1927:

"It is necessary to avoid the confusion likely to result from the familiar quibble over terms. By intelligence we may understand the ability to perform problems that reflect an understanding of a familiar environment. But this is not the sort of thing the Army examiners undertook to measure. The Army Memoir defined intelligence as the thing measured by the tests. . . . 'by "intelligence" we mean the ability that manifests itself quantitatively in a set of consistent scores in all the types of examination upon which our data are based.' Defined in this manner, the tests, or any other conceivable tests that anyone may wish to set up, are an irrefragable, indisputable, and perfect measure of intelligence."

Edward B. Reuter, The American Race Problem (New York: Thomas Y. Crowell, 1927), p. 89n. The confusion of terms continued throughout the discussion of World War I tests and persisted through World War II, where the general classification test was almost universally considered an intelligence test. See Otto Klineberg, "Racial Psychology," in Ralph Linton, ed., The Science of Man in the World Crisis (New York: Columbia University Press, 1945).

scores made on World War I tests.[70] The
more advanced Army studies took these
factors into consideration. Some predicted that, as opportunities improved,
so would test achievements, but most
reached the conclusion that the reasons
for the differentials in test scores did not
alter the fact that Negroes, rated by the
same standards on the same tests, generally scored lower than whites.

Therefore, it was reasoned, the
chances of producing efficient military
units with Negroes were considerably
lower than with whites. As a result, even
though the General Staff might approve
an equitable representation of Negroes
in all branches, the chiefs of branches
who had immediate responsibilities for
the production of trained units were reluctant to designate units in mobilization plans, or later, in troop bases, for
their reception. Long and detailed
justifications for their inability to do so
were a commonplace. The continuing
reluctance of all arms and most services
to provide units for Negroes was a major
deterrent to the application of War Department policies on the utilization of
Negro troops throughout the first half of
World War II.

The Revisions of 1940

In the summer of 1940, the War Department Organization and Training
Division (G–3) sought to correct flaws
in the application of the 1937 policy to
the Protective Mobilization Plan. Certain of the provisions such as the authorization of Negro personnel for corps and
army ammunition trains were out-
moded, since these units had been elim-

inated from the Army. The problem of
the lack of balance between Negro combat and service troops remained. To
solve it, G–3 recommended that the list
of units authorized Negro personnel be
expanded and that all arms and services,
except Air Corps and Signal Corps, be
required to accept for assignment in appropriate units a "reasonable proportion" of Negroes. Restrictions on Negro
separate battalions, G–3 pointed out,
should be relaxed, since in the future
separate battalions might prove desirable in certain arms, such as coast artillery harbor defense and antiaircraft
units. Moreover, separate battalions
would lessen the problem of the absorption of Negro officers should it be decided
to replace them with white officers after
the beginning of mobilization. G–3
recommended that the new policy provision read: "The largest unit of any
arm or service to be organized of Negro
personnel is the regiment." This would
allow for the organization of separate
battalions or smaller units and, at the
same time, block any efforts of Negro
civilian organizations to effect a brigade
grouping of infantry regiments in the
National Guard. "Otherwise," G–3 felt,
"difficulty may be experienced during
mobilization in absorbing negro general
officers." [71]

Both the Personnel Division and the
War Plans Division disagreed with G–3
on that part of its proposal which would
exempt the Air and Signal Corps from
providing units for Negro troops. War
Plans indicated that, in its opinion,

. . . it is neither desirable nor practicable
in a major mobilization to exclude Negro

[70] Klineberg, "Racial Psychology."

[71] Memo, G–3 for CofS, 3 Jun 40, G–3/6541–
Gen–527.

manpower per se from any Arm or Service. Furthermore, it is the opinion of this Division that Negro manpower can be as successfully employed in some capacities in both the Air Corps and the Signal Corps as it is in the other Arms and Services. . . . Any limitation in the use of Negroes in the Arms and Services must be predicated upon the actual availability of personnel with required qualifications rather than upon any arbitrary elimination of the Negro as a whole on the grounds of lack of technical capacity. Our greatest difficulty with the Negro troops in the World War came not primarily from a lack of technical capacity, but from psychological factors and from faulty leadership.

The only limitation to be placed on the organization of Negro units should be that accomplished by a "strict maintenance of equality between the qualifications" required for Negroes and whites in similar units.[72] The Personnel Division withheld its concurrence on different grounds. G–1 felt that under the action recommended by G–3, proper racial proportions could not be maintained. G–1 believed that each arm and service should take as its share of Negroes approximately 9 percent of its total strength and that a proper proportion of this percentage should be placed in front-line units so that "the negro manpower of the country may bear its proportionate losses in the event of war." This could be accomplished, G–1 believed, only by the assignment of "some Negro regiments of infantry and field artillery to our infantry divisions." It recommended that this be done, since the assignment of Negro units to the GHQ Reserve would fail to meet the desired requirements in the peacetime Regular Army or under the mobilization plan.[73]

In support of its proposals G–3 cited the stands taken by the chiefs of the Air and Signal Corps. The Chief of the Air Corps had indicated that no air units, combat or service, could employ Negroes. The Chief of the Air Corps went on to say that when the Air Corps expansion bill was before Congress, the matter was studied intensively. The bill was so worded that the Civil Aeronautics Authority (CAA) was allotted responsibility for the training of Negro pilots, and the Secretary of War had adopted a policy that Negro pilots would not be trained by the Air Corps but by the CAA at one of the schools used by the Air Corps. Negro pilots, the Chief of the Air Corps continued, could not be used by "our present Air Corps units" since this would result in the "impossible social problem" of having Negro officers serving over white enlisted men; and to organize an all-Negro air corps unit would take several years in order to train the necessary enlisted men as competent mechanics.[74]

The Signal Corps believed that "it would be difficult to obtain properly qualified personnel, or personnel who could be properly trained for duty with and function efficiently in units such as Signal Battalions, Signal Companies, Signal Troops and Signal Service Companies." The Signal Corps was willing to consider an exception in the event that "a Negro Division is ever organized." Even then, it felt, it would be difficult to obtain properly qualified men

---

[72] Memo, WPD for G–3, 29 Jun 40, Tab H to G–3/6541–527.

[73] Memo, G–1 for G–3, 20 Jun 40, G–1/146515.
[74] Memo, CofAC for G–3, 31 May 40, Tab E to G–3/6541–Gen–527.

such as radio electricians, telephone technicians, and radio operators.[75]

G–3 felt that further explanation was unnecessary. It did not concur with G–1's proposal that Negro regiments of infantry and artillery be assigned to white divisions because that would mean the replacement of corresponding white units in each active division of the Regular Army and the National Guard. If new divisions were organized with a portion of their infantry and artillery composed of Negroes, G–3 said, "Not only would the training time of a mixed division be much longer but the relative combat efficiency of white and negro units might vary to such an extent as to affect adversely tactical operations." Moreover, G–3 continued, there was nothing to prevent a theater of operations commander from attaching separate Negro regiments to divisions for combat operations if he should so desire; this would be quite different from requiring him to accept a mixed division with "doubtful combat efficiency." Only the authorization of all-Negro divisions, G–3 concluded, would assure the Negro's sharing of proportionate battle casualties. Such an authorization G–3 did not advocate.

On the Threshold of Mobilization

The plans of 1937 and 1940 indicate not only the tenor but also the range of thinking within the War Department on the subject of the employment of Negro troops in a national emergency. Despite the 1937 provision that information on Negro troops should be disseminated

[75] Memo, OCSigO for G–3, 28 May 40, OCSigO–320.2–Gen.

in the same manner as information on other Army policies, little general knowledge of the Army's plans spread beyond the confines of the Mobilization Regulations to either the military as a whole or to the public at all. This was unfortunate, for up to the beginning of World War II the impression was widely held that the Army probably had no concrete plans for the use of Negro troops other than a grudging admission that in time of war they would be useful primarily as laborers and that they must be kept completely segregated from white troops. That any thinking had been done on such questions as the types and sizes of units, methods of employment of Negro troops, or the provision of opportunities for Negroes as specialists and in positions of leadership was generally unknown.

Much of the public agitation and questioning of the Army's purposes in regard to the use of Negro troops might have been avoided by full and frank discussion of the question in the years before the emergency had built itself to the high point of the summer of 1940. Because so little of what the Army was planning was known, racial and political pressure groups were unable to make concrete proposals which might have benefited their own interests as well as those of the Army and the nation. Of the Army's plans the public knew nothing except what it could infer from small bits of information and a few examples of official action. These, when added together, appeared to Negroes less than encouraging so far as full and equitable use of Negro manpower was concerned. The fulfillment of predictions concerning the effects of political and racial pressure, concerning the difficulties inherent in any plan which did not provide for a racially balanced Army from the beginning of expansion, and concerning the relative difficulties of maintaining a fair and workable balance among types of Negro units might also have been avoided had the Army's own personnel been aware of the thinking and reasoning behind the policy on Negro troop utilization. Instead, the Army's officers, as a whole, were relatively unfamiliar with much of the reasoning behind the policies. Many were unfamiliar with the policies as a whole or in significant part. Proposals from individual commanders and staff agencies, many of which had already been considered and discarded, made their appearance periodically during the early period of preparations for national defense. Many of the existing policies were misinterpreted, ignored, or sidetracked, usually because of lack of familiarity with the whole fabric of which specific directives formed only individual threads. Only if the general trends of high level thinking had been known could this have been avoided.

It should be kept in view also that the Army, in its employment of Negro troops, did not consider itself a free agent, psychologically, politically, or in any other sense. Aside from influences of personal feelings, neither all agencies of the War Department nor all field commands were at any one time fully agreed on the merits of current policies on the use of Negro manpower. Though there were many inside and outside the Army and the War Department who felt that there was much that could be done within the Army to provide for a fuller use of Negro manpower, the War Department itself took the position that it was operating within a social framework which it did not create and which it did not have the power to alter in any significant manner. As G–1 expressed it in 1939, and as other agencies echoed it throughout the war:

The War Department has given serious thought to questions involving the induction of Negroes into the military service. However, the War Department is not an agency which can solve national questions relating to the social or economic position of the various racial groups composing our Nation. The War Department administers the laws affecting the military establishment; it cannot act outside the law, nor contrary to the will of the majority of the citizens of the Nation.[76]

In general, the position of the War Department on the subject of the utilization of Negro troops in the summer of 1940—on the eve of the beginning of the greatest expansion which the Army of the United States had known—may be summarized briefly as follows:

1. Negroes would be mobilized in proportions equal to their representation in the nation's manpower of military age. Preferably, they should be mobilized early, both to allow numbers to be built up to and maintained at a percentage level approximating 9 plus percent, and to provide earlier training, since adequate training might take a longer period than normal.

2. Negroes would be utilized in both arms and services and in all types of units for which they could qualify. Combat arms assignments for Negroes should be in the same ratio as for whites. Full agreement on their use in all arms and services had not been reached among staff agencies or by the chiefs of all

[76] Memo, G–1 for Public Relations Bureau G–2, 11 Oct 39, G–1/15640–11.

arms and services, but a strong stand on their proportionate use in all branches had been taken by the Personnel Division.

3. Negroes would be utilized in units with all-Negro enlisted personnel, but these units did not need to be employed separately. A strong group believed that Negro units should be kept small and used in attachment or assignment to larger white units. A less widely held view was that only as parts of otherwise white divisions could Negro combat units operate successfully and in a manner which would guarantee their sharing proportionately in battle losses and in battle credits.

4. Officers for Negro units might be Negro or white. They were to be assigned in 50 percent greater numbers than to similar types of white units. Negro officers were to be chosen and trained according to the same standards as white officers and, preferably, trained in the same schools. Negro officers were to serve only with Negro units and in overhead installations, and should command Negro troops only. Specific units for which Negro officers were authorized would be designated. Initially, these would include only the Reserve and National Guard units and such service units as might be so designated. For that reason, most Negro units in the Protection Mobilization Plan were designated "Regular Army—Inactive."

5. In their utilization, Negro troops were to be trained, officered, quartered, clothed, and provided with all facilities in the same manner as white troops.

In the working out of these plans, many apparently minor points arose which grew into major ones. Though the plans were well-laid, much intervened between planning and execution. Some of the causes and results of the difficulties and the successes encountered in the attempt to transfer plans to action will be discussed in succeeding chapters. Vestigial remains of many of the alternate plans reviewed here will be seen in many of the proposals and changes made during the course of World War II.

CHAPTER III

The Negro Position Defined

As the conflict which was to become World War II approached, Negroes asked with increasing frequency for the opportunity that they believed to be rightfully theirs in the first place: the opportunity to participate in the defense of their country in the same manner and on the same basis and in the same services as other Americans. Not all Negroes were agreed on the details of this participation. Some refused to compromise on anything short of complete integration into the armed forces without segregation of any sort. Others were willing to accept varying measures of segregation in the hope of achieving compensatory advances in the form of additional opportunities for service, promotion, and status within a segregated system. All were agreed that at least some of the restrictions existing in the peacetime Army of 1939 should be relaxed.

They had seen how the Navy, in the years between wars, had been able to eliminate almost all Negroes. They believed that the Army had quietly ceased the combat training of the old Negro regiments. They entered the period of expanding national defense with the conviction that, left to its own devices, the Army, citing the Navy as precedent and using World War I as justification, might very well refuse to expand its Negro strength any more than it had to. Knowing little or nothing about existing War Department plans for an emergency, Negroes were resolved to prevent the increase of restrictions and, through the use of every available means, to remove all limitations which operated to prevent the full employment of Negro manpower within the Army.

By the late 1930's a steadily rising flow of queries on the subject of Negro employment in the Army came into the War Department from the National Association for the Advancement of Colored People, newspapers and press associations, National Guard unit officers, groups of World War I veterans, men wishing to enlist, and members of Congress inquiring on behalf of their constituents. Queries and protests about the use of Negro troops were normally answered by the War Department until 1940 in a routine and noncommittal manner, according to "precedent letters" similar to those employed for answering general correspondence on many other subjects. Such letters, usually prepared by staff agencies and approved by the Office of the Secretary of War or by the Office of the Chief of Staff, were deposited with The Adjutant General, who could then use them as a basis for answering similar letters on the same subject. In the area of Negro queries, the answers summarize the Army's position on several basic questions, but usually they did not give detailed or specific answers to direct questions.

If the correspondent questioned the

restrictions placed on Negro enlistments by virtue of the small number of Negro units maintained or by reason of the organization of Army units by race, the reply was likely to read:

In time of peace the Army must be so organized as to assure a balanced force, containing, in the proper proportions, elements of all arms and services, and capable of rapid and orderly expansion in time of war without major changes in the basic peacetime organization. Consequently, it is necessary to set up specific units to which colored personnel may be assigned, and these organizations must have a definite and proper place in the balanced force organizations of the Army as a whole. These organizations now include units of the infantry, cavalry, quartermaster corps, and medical corps. They meet our peacetime requirements, and provide the necessary nucleus for war-time expansion.[1]

If the correspondent became insistent and requested further information or presented an argument for a change in policy, his letter was simply acknowledged, or he might be told:

Your remarks and the contents of the accompanying paper have been carefully noted. However, under a long established rule the War Department refrains from participation in controversial discussions arising from time to time in connection with articles appearing in the press, or statements made by public speakers or debaters, when the activities of the Army or its personnel are subjected to criticism.[2]

By 1940, correspondence on the policy toward the use of Negro manpower had become so heavy that The Adjutant General provided duplicated form letters for replies. Addresses and, when required, additional pertinent materials might be typed on these.

Congressmen, newspapers, organizations, and individuals receiving the War Department's form letter replies often concluded that no actual plans existed for the use of Negro troops other than those dictated by expediency. The precedent letters helped to convince correspondents that there was scant hope of promoting the cause of the Negro by appealing to the War Department directly. The natural alternative was public agitation that would stir the President and Congress into action. Thus a succession of public campaigns on the question of the employment of Negro troops gained in momentum and support as the need for national defense projects became more widely accepted.

Beginning Campaigns

In 1938, the Pittsburgh *Courier*, then the largest and one of the most influential Negro papers of national circulation, opened a campaign for the extension of opportunities for Negroes in the military services. The paper published an open letter to President Roosevelt, organized a Committee for Negro Participation in the National Defense, and encouraged its readers to send letters, telegrams, and delegations to congressmen and other national political leaders asking for an opinion on the wisdom of forming an all-Negro division in the peacetime Army. Many of these letters, especially those to congressmen, were forwarded to the War Department for information. As the campaign spread to other papers and

---

[1] Ltr, TAG to Charles E. Russell, Chairman Inter-Racial Committee of the District of Columbia (NAACP), 30 Oct 39, AG 291.21 (10–19–39).

[2] Ltr, TAG to Charles E. Russell, 28 Jul 40, AG 291.21 (6–7–40). See also Ltrs, TAG to Handsel G. Bell, various dates, AG 291.21 (4–18–39); TAG to Levi Pierce, various dates, AG 291.21 (10–10–39); TAG to various persons and organizations, AG 322.97 (2–23–38) (1).

to local organizations, similar letters arrived from other sources.[3] This campaign was well organized and well publicized. Quantities of correspondence poured into the War Department. When the department did not commit itself the Negro press, having obtained no positive information, became even more cynical and critical.

In the late thirties various other agencies and organizations interested in Negro affairs became aware of the problem of the Negro in the armed forces. A 1939 conference of the National Youth Administration (NYA) on the problems of the Negro and Negro youth, in addition to requesting the further extension of educational and vocational opportunities which had been stressed throughout the thirties, made a number of other recommendations to the War Department: Funds for military training in land grant colleges should be allocated equitably to Negro and white youths. Educational facilities provided by the Civilian Conservation Corps (CCC) should be increased so that Negroes might be trained "to take their places in the leadership of the Camps." Federally supported service schools such as West Point and Annapolis should be maintained without discrimination in the admission of students. Restrictions on enlistments in the armed services should be eliminated. Negroes should be included in the expansion of the air arm. Negro combat units should be used for other than custodial and personal services. And the President should appoint a commission charged with recommending methods of "integration [of Negroes] into all the armed forces without segregation." [4]

Older organizations, such as the Federal Council of Churches of Christ in America and the Southern Interracial Commission, joined with newer groups like the Council for Democracy and Fight for Freedom in expressing concern about the Negro in the armed forces. Most of the newer organizations were interested in solidifying public opinion on the side of the Western Powers. They could not proceed with their public appeals in the name of the preservation of democracy, many of these organizations felt, while Negroes constantly reminded them of inequities existing at home. Fight for Freedom, whose board of sponsors included Senator Carter Glass, Mrs. Calvin Coolidge, and James H. Hubert, secretary of the New York Urban League, issued a statement reading in part: "During the past war we made brave promises of interracial justice—after the war would be over. The promises were forgotten. Today we must prove as we march towards war that we mean to advance freedom for ALL men here in America." The Council for Democracy, whose board included Ernest Angell, Fred Bartlett, Abraham Flexner, Robert Littell, and Leon M. Birkhead, published a pamphlet, *The Negro and Defense: A Test of Democracy,* which contained similar ideas. The interest of these and other civilian groups was not limited to the War Department but extended to three other federal agencies that had loose ties with the Military Establishment.

[3] AG 322.99 (2–23–38) (1); Pittsburgh *Courier,* February 19, 1938 to September 28, 1940.

[4] Forwarded by Administrator of NYA to SW, 2 Mar 39, AG 291.2 (3–2–39).

The Civilian Conservation Corps, a depression-born agency originally planned as a relief measure for unemployed youths, developed into a major youth training program in the late thirties. It did not provide military training, but its campers were supervised and served by military personnel of the Officers' Reserve Corps. Between April 1933 and June 1940 approximately 300,000 Negro youths went through CCC camps.[5] While Negroes were underrepresented in the CCC on the basis of relative needs, after 1936 the 9 to 10 percent of Negroes in the total enrollment of the camps represented approximately their percentage in the single male population in the 15–24-year age group.[6]

In the summer of 1937, the War Department noted that, out of a total of 1,849 CCC companies, 167 were Negro. Two of these, at Gettysburg, Pa., and Elmira, N.Y., were officered in line and staff by Negro Reserve officers. Thirty-three medical officers and eight chaplains in the CCC at that time were Negroes.[7] Negro educational advisers were employed in the all-Negro camps. In June 1940 approximately 30,000 Negroes were in the 151 all-Negro and the 71 mixed camps, most of the latter being in New England and the Middle West.[8]

While the CCC was administered in a manner that carefully avoided giving the impression that these camps had any direct relation to military service, the educational, vocational, health, and group-living training of the youths concerned, and especially of the Negro youths, was considered by many to be of tremendous value to the nation as a whole. Criticism of the CCC for not giving greater opportunities for the development of Negro administrative leadership began to appear in the pre-Pearl Harbor years. By 1939, as indicated in the recommendation of the NYA conference mentioned above, the relation of these camps to the development of latent leadership qualities was widely recognized.[9]

The National Youth Administration helped train mechanics and technical specialists both for use in defense industries and for possible use in the armed forces. NYA training was superimposed upon courses which had been developed during the Great Depression. There was little complaint about these courses, for they generally provided opportunities for Negro students in most fields of training. The major complaint was that the courses alone were not enough.[10]

The third of the agencies whose activities were looked upon as vital to the interests of Negro participation in national defense was the Civil Aeronautics Authority (CAA), which in 1939 began to give pilot training to students in cooperation with colleges and a few private airfields. This program was begun as part of an effort to increase the airmindedness as well as the practical aviation training of American youth.

---

[5] Edgar G. Brown, *What the Civilian Conservation Corps Is Doing for Colored Youth* (Washington: Federal Security Agency, Civilian Conservation Corps, June, 1940), p. 1.

[6] Richard Sterner and others, *The Negro's Share: A Study of Income, Consumption, Housing and Public Assistance* (New York: Harper & Brothers, 1943), pp. 256–58.

[7] Memo, G–3 for SGS, 14 Jul 37, AG 322.97 (7–7–37) (1).

[8] Brown, *op. cit.*, p. 1.

[9] Cf., *The Crisis*, XLVII (November, 1940), 343.

[10] Cf., James L. H. Peck, "When Do We Fly?" *The Crisis*, LXVII (December, 1940).

Initially, no provision was made for the specific inclusion of Negro trainees. Since no courses were given in co-operation with Negro schools or colleges and few Negroes were enrolled in schools that had courses, there was no significant Negro participation. This situation brought about the first of a series of legislative enactments designed to clarify and increase the military training opportunities for Negroes.

The Air Corps and Public Law 18

In March 1939, while debating a bill to expand the nation's defense program, the Congress incorporated into the bill an amendment proposed by Senator Harry H. Schwartz of Wyoming. This amendment provided that, from among the civilian aviation schools to which the Secretary of War was authorized to lend equipment for aviation training, one or more should be designated by the Civil Aeronautics Authority for the training of Negro pilots. An earlier amendment had been presented to the Clerk of the Senate by Senator Styles Bridges of New Hampshire. When the Schwartz amendment was presented from the floor, Senator Bridges offered his own amendment as a substitute. It provided "That the Secretary of War is specifically authorized to establish at appropriate Negro colleges identical equipment, instruction, and facilities for training Negro air pilots, mechanics, and others for service in the United States Regular Army as is now available in the Air Corps Training Center." [11] This additional amendment failed to pass, but

it is illustrative of the type of legislation which had support in many quarters. By some members of Congress, it was discussed and voted upon as though it would accomplish the same ends as the Schwartz amendment which was adopted. Both amendments were direct outgrowths of a campaign for admission of Negroes to the Air Corps. This campaign was the most widespread, persistent, and widely publicized of all the prewar public pressure campaigns affecting the Negro and the Army.

Negroes had been attempting to gain entrance to the Air Corps since World War I. In 1917, when they tried to enlist in the Air Service of the Signal Corps, they received the answer that no colored aero squadrons were being formed "at the present time." Applications for that branch therefore could not be received; but, if, "later on," it was decided to form colored squadrons, recruiting officers would be notified to that effect.[12] Requests for service as air observers also were made during World War I. A plan was broached in the Office of the Director of Military Aeronautics for the use of Negroes for fatigue and police duty at airfields to relieve regular men, but this was not looked upon with favor.[13] A few Negroes were in construction companies of the Air Service, but none engaged in any form of flying or of aircraft maintenance.[14]

Early postwar requests for the establishment of Negro air units of the Or-

---

[11] *Congressional Record*, March 7, 1939, pp. 2367–70.

[12] Ltr, OCSigO to Charles S. Darden, Los Angeles, Calif., 17 Aug 17, AAF 322.9 (Negro Det).

[13] Memo, Chief Pers for Exec Office OCSigO, 7 Aug 18, AAF 291.2A.

[14] Ltr, OCAS to H. T. Douglas, Bridgeport, Conn., 13 Nov 20, AAF 291.2; Ltr, CAS to AGO, 1st Ind to Ltr, Secy Maryland War Records Commission, 15 Dec 22, AAF 322.3 Units A-1.

ganized Reserves were considered "impossible" to grant on the ground that no Negro officers had previously held commissions in the Air Service and that, since no Negro air units existed, there was no justification for the appointment of Negroes as flying cadets.[15] In 1931, when existing Negro ground units were reduced to provide for the fifth increment of the Air Corps expansion, critics pointed out that the only way to prevent the reduction from working an injustice would be to open the Air Corps to Negroes so that they might at least retain the over-all strength originally allotted to them.[16] To suggestions in this vein the War Department replied that from the beginning, the Air Corps "gathered in men of technical and mechanical experience and ability. As a rule, the colored man has not been attracted to this field in the same way or to the same extent as the white man. Particularly is this so of aerial engineering." So many applications from college trained men were being received, the War Department added, that "many white applicants are being denied places." [17] To this the secretary of the NAACP answered:

It is obvious that colored men cannot be attracted to the field of aviation "in the same way or to the same extent as the white man" when the door to that field is slammed in the colored man's face. . . . There are thousands of excellent colored mechanics in the country and if the War Department did not prejudice the case by definitely excluding them, we feel sure that there would be no difficulty in finding and developing men with all the qualifications required of pilots, mechanics, and all the other functions included in the air service.[18]

Eight years later Senator Schwartz summed up the point of view of those who felt that legislation was the only guarantee of full Negro participation in the military defense of the nation when he remarked:

Somebody may say, "There is no provision in the bill now which would prevent a Negro receiving such training," but, Mr. President, I can only judge the future by the past. I believe the situation is such that unless we give this specific and affirmative recognition, possibly our qualified Negro citizens will not have an opportunity to become air pilots.[19]

This argument for the inclusion of specific references to Negroes in national defense bills was to arise frequently in succeeding months. It was to culminate in the provisions concerning race written into the Selective Training and Service Act of 1940.

The Schwartz amendment was enacted as a part of Public Law 18, effective 3 April 1939.[20] Its subsequent

---

[15] 1st Ind, CAS to AGO, on Ltr, C. E. Mertin, Oakland, Calif., 29 Dec 22, AAF 326.6 ROTC.

[16] Ltr, Walter White, Secy NAACP, to Actg SW, 1 Sep 31; Ltr, Robert R. Moton, Tuskegee Institute, to President Hoover, 18 Sep 31, and other papers in AG 620 (4–23–31) sec. 2B; Ltr, Walter White to CofS, 15 Sep 31, AG 320.2 (6–17–31) (1) sec. 1.

[17] Ltr, Actg CofS to Walter White, 21 Sep 31, AG 620 (4–23–31) sec. 2B.

[18] Ltr, Walter White to Actg CofS, 25 Sep 31, AG 620 (4–23–31) (1) sec. 2B.

[19] Congressional Record, March 7, 1939, p. 2367. According to Bureau of Census figures read into the Congressional Record, there were 123 licensed Negro commercial and student pilots in the country in 1937. Many of the licenses were not kept in force.

[20] It was incorporated into Section 4 of H.R. 3791 and, as approved, read: "The Secretary of War is authorized, in his discretion and under the rules, regulations, and limitations to be prescribed by him, to lend to accredited civilian aviation schools, one or more of which shall be designated by the Civil Aeronautics Authority for

history illustrates some of the many difficulties involved in legislation of this type. It also illustrates the influence which such legislation had on Army planning.

When it became clear that the bill, including the Schwartz amendment, was likely to be approved by both Houses and signed by the President, there was some inclination within the Air Corps to believe that the amendment might make it necessary for the Air Corps to train Negro pilots and to form at least one Negro air unit. At the request of Brig. Gen. Barton K. Yount, chief of the Training Group of the Office of the Air Corps, the Air Plans Section prepared a plan for the training of Negro pilots and a Negro unit based on the assumption that it *"will"* be necessary for the Air Corps to proceed with such training. "However, further study of the act by several different individuals on the General Staff and in the C. A. A. has developed the belief that such steps will not be necessary," the chief of the Plans Section reported.[21]

As interpreted by the Air Plans Section, the bill merely authorized the Secretary of War to lend equipment to accredited civilian aviation schools at which personnel of the Military Estab-

lishment were pursuing a course under competent War Department orders. One or more of these schools would be designated by the CAA for the training of any Negro pilot. The CAA would name one of the schools which the Air Corps was to use for primary training. This school would offer Air Corps training, and also civilian training. "The letter of the law would certainly be fulfilled, and it is believed that the spirit would also be fulfilled 100%. There is absolutely nothing that directs us to enlist negro flying cadets. The original intent was to use the C.A.A. and the matter crept into this bill thru misunderstanding. By being left in, it assures the Negro of training at a school of such high standards that 'personnel of the Military Establishment are pursuing a course' there." [22]

General Yount agreed that all that was necessary under the law was for the Air Corps to request the CAA to designate "one of *our* approved schools (Chicago, for example) where negroes may be trained under *Civil Aeronautics Authority regulations* and by the *Civil Aeronautics Authority.*" Still, he felt, the War Department, under its interpretation of the law, might rule that Negro pilots must be enlisted as flying cadets and that they must be trained in the same manner as white pilots under the expansion program. In that case, CAA would probably have to designate one of "our approved schools" for Negro training. After completing training at a civilian school, Negro cadets could be sent to Randolph Field and later to Kelly Field. "It is possible that this would

the training of any Negro air pilot, at which personnel of the Military Establishment are pursuing a course of education and training pursuant to detail thereto under competent orders of the War Department, out of aircraft, aircraft parts, aeronautical equipment and accessories for the Air Corps, on hand and belonging to the Government, such articles as may appear to be required for instruction, training, and maintenance purposes."
[21] R&R, Chief Plans Sec to CofAC, 8 Apr 39, AAF 353.9-4–A. Italics in original. This plan is described on page 64, below.

[22] R&R cited n. 21, above.

create a difficult situation although it could be taken care of," General Yount thought.[23]

But, once begun, the process of training would not end here. The Air Corps' Reserve Division had already pointed out that, if a Negro flying cadet successfully completed training at the Air Corps Training Center, he "must reasonably be considered as being qualified" for a Reserve commission. While commissioning such a trainee was not mandatory under the law, "it would, at the same time, prove difficult, if not impossible," to refuse such a commission.[24] Once a Negro cadet was commissioned, General Yount felt, a demand, "backed by politics," would be made for the continuation of his training.[25]

Continued training would be possible by assignment of Negro reservists to white units. In Yount's view this would be "ruinous to morale." One or more Negro Reserve or Regular Army units in which Negro Reserve officers could continue their training might be established. Neither funds nor estimates existed for either type of unit. Either type, because of the time needed to train enlisted men, would have to have white senior officers, noncommissioned officers, and mechanical personnel. "This is not considered practicable," General Yount concluded. Reserve units, moreover, could be expected to multiply as Negroes in different parts of the country requested them. Therefore, General Yount recommended, the Air Corps should confine its action to a request for authorization to plan training in "one of our approved schools and under the jurisdiction of the Civil Aeronautics Authority." [26] His recommendation was approved by General Arnold, who then requested War Department approval.[27]

The Judge Advocate General, when asked for his opinion, more than agreed with the Air Corps. He further construed the act to contain a directive to the CAA only, with absolutely "no duty . . . imposed by such language on the War Department." The War Department nevertheless decided that, "in the present instance and notwithstanding such interpretation," it would be advisable to co-operate with the CAA in carrying out "what appears to be" the intent of Congress. The Air Corps was therefore directed to confer with the CAA to obtain its designation of an accredited civilian flying school and to agree upon the aircraft and equipment required.[28]

The Air Corps proceeded to follow the line of action approved by the War Department. General Yount conferred informally with Robert Hinckley, chairman of the Civil Aeronautics Authority, who agreed to designate a school and train a number of Negro pilots under the CAA program. "Inasmuch as this may be discussed in the press and may cause some political repercussions . . . ," the Chief of the Air Corps wrote, "it is recommended that the entire subject be discussed with the Secretary of War in order that he may be thoroughly informed as to the War Department pro-

[23] R&R, OCofAC to Gen Arnold, 14 Apr 39 AAF 353.9–4–A. Italics in original.
[24] R&R, Chief Reserve Div OCofAC to Chief Tng Gp, 3 Apr 39, AAF 353.9–4–A Training of Negro Pilots.
[25] R&R, OCofAC to Gen Arnold, 14 Apr 39, AAF 353.9–4–A.

[26] Ibid.
[27] Memo, CofAC for CofS, 18 Apr 39, AG 011 (8–18–39), AAF 353.9–4–A.
[28] 2d Ind to Memo, CofAC for CofS, 18 Apr 39, JACO to TAG, 27 Apr 39, and 3d Ind, TAG to CofAC, 4 May 39. Both in AAF 353.9–4–A.

cedure in this case, i.e., 'The Civil Aeronautics Authority will train the negro pilots in accordance with the provisions of H.R. 3791.' " [29]

Despite the cautious analysis of and approach to Public Law 18, the decision as reached was to cause continued misunderstanding and dissatisfaction. Negroes and many of the congressmen supporting the amendment had considered that it ended once and for all the discussion of whether or not the Air Corps would train Negro pilots.[30] The Air Corps, seeking to explain its interpretation of the law, had prepared a letter to Senator Morris Sheppard, chairman of the Senate Military Affairs Committee. But before it was sent the Office of the Chief of Staff informed the Air Corps not only that "for the time being" the War Department would take no action in connection with the training of Negro pilots but also that "no more publicity will be given this matter than is absolutely essential." [31] In light of

these directions, the prepared letter was not sent.[32]

Informing the Senate committee was nevertheless necessary, General Arnold thought. Senator Schwartz had visited him and General Yount with urgent demands that training for Negro pilots be initiated. Representatives of Negro organizations had "called and expressed an opinion that they will continue to agitate in Congress for the passage of additional legislation if something definite is not done for pilot training for their race in the very near future." Informing Senator Sheppard of the proposed plan "may do much to allay this agitation," General Arnold felt.[33] On 25 May he took the matter up personally.[34] As a result, a suggested letter went to Secretary Woodring for his signature. But this letter was lost or mislaid and a substitute was not sent forward until 10 June.[35] The letter was dispatched to Senator Sheppard on 12 June, too late to accomplish its original purpose, for in the meantime the hearings on H.R. 6791, the Supplemental Military Appropriation Bill for 1940 providing funds for the Air Corps expansion program, had produced testimony that further convinced congressmen and the public that the Air Corps, under Public Law 18, was going to train Negro pilots.

Senator Schwartz, on 26 May, had told the committee of his conviction that

[29] Memo, CofAC for CofS, 9 May 39, AAF 353.9-4-A.

[30] Statement, Edgar G. Brown, *Hearings, Senate Subcommittee on Appropriations, Military Establishment Bill for 1940 (H.R. 4630)*, pp. 152–53; Statements, Edgar G. Brown, J. Finley Wilson, and Senator Harry H. Schwartz, *Hearings, House Subcommittee on Appropriations, Supplemental Military Appropriation Bill, 1940 (H.R. 6791)*, pp. 339–44; Senator Styles Bridges in debate on H.R. 7805, 25 Jan 40, *Congressional Record*, 86, p. 671; Debate, *Military Establishment Bill for 1941 (H.R. 9209), Congressional Record*, 86, pp. 4017–19; Statement, Rayford Logan, 14 May 40, *Hearings, Senate Subcommittee on Appropriations, Military Establishment Appropriation Bill for 1941 (H.R. 9209)*, pp. 365–76; Senator Styles Bridges, discussion and questions, 14 May 40, *Hearings*, above, p. 368.

[31] Memo, SGS for CofAC, 16 May 39, AAF 353.9-4-A.

[32] R&R, Chief Tng and Opns Div for CofAC, 22 May 39, AAF 353.9-4-A.

[33] Memo, CofAC for CofS, 24 May, 39, AAF 353.9-4-A; Statement, Senator Schwartz, *Hearings, House Subcommittee, Supplemental Military Appropriation Bill, 1940*, 26 May 1939, pp. 342–43.

[34] Penciled note on R&R, AAF 353.9-4-A.

[35] Memo, CofAC for CofS, 10 Jun 39, AAF 353.9-4-A.

the appropriation bill required an amendment providing a specific amount for training Negro pilots. Both General Yount and General Arnold had told the Senator that they were encountering difficulties in carrying out the provisions of the existing act. "Of course," the Senator said, "you understand the same as I do, whether we want to admit it or not, that back under this is a feeling in the Army and in the Navy that bringing these Negro pilots and giving them this opportunity will result in some embarrassment one way or another on account of social or economic conditions." He indicated that General Arnold had told him that the Air Corps, "without trouble," could give Negro pilots training for ninety days at a civilian school, ninety days at Randolph Field, and ninety days at Kelly Field, with the Randolph Field phase probably added to a civilian school. The Kelly Field phase, where "they are flying in squadrons," would be more difficult, but the War Department could handle this. "I hope the committee will amend the bill because I do think the War Department needs a little urging," Senator Schwartz continued.[36] Similar proposals for specific sums to be earmarked for the training of Negro pilots were made by Negro witnesses.[37]

Representative D. Lane Powers of New Jersey sought to determine the need for legislation earmarking special funds for this purpose. On 5 June he asked Secretary of War Harry H. Woodring if, under Public Law 18, one or more schools would be designated for Negro pilot training. Secretary Wood-

ring, who had not yet received the draft letter to Senator Sheppard, replied that the matter was being considered. "We are trying to work this out in fairness to those colored people who are rightfully entitled to this training. We are going to try to work this out honestly in the interests of every citizen of the United States," the Secretary said.[38] "You are definitely going to train some Negro pilots, are you not?" Powers asked. Woodring replied, "We are planning to do so." [39]

To further questions the Secretary continued to answer in the affirmative. Though he did not say specifically that the War Department itself was going to train or use Negro pilots, the impression was left that the Secretary had committed the Army to a program of training and using Negro pilots, trained in the primary phase at a civilian school, from which they would go into military training. This impression had been heightened by the general understanding that, although CAA was to train primarily civilian pilots, these men would constitute a military reservoir from which the Travelling Flying Cadet Board could pick the best for further training.[40]

When the appropriations bill came to the floor of the House, Representative Louis Ludlow of Indiana proposed a new amendment providing that one million dollars of the eight million planned for expanding the training of military pilots be set aside for training Negro pilots. This would be "sheer justice," Ludlow said, for, if war comes,

---

[36] Hearings, House, Supplemental Military Appropriation Bill, 1940, (H.R. 6791), pp. 312–44.
[37] Ibid., pp. 339–42.

[38] Ibid., p. 281.
[39] Ibid., p. 282.
[40] Hearings, House and Senate, Training of Civil Aircraft Pilots, H.R. 5073, S. 2119, Senate Hearings, pp. 16–17, 86–87, House Hearings, pp. 14–15.

Negroes will be conscripted on a wide-spread scale, and it is just as certain as anything in the future can be that a considerable proportion of Negroes with aviation training will be sent into air combat detachments. It would be positively cruel and inhumane to assign Negroes to the combat air service without giving them the means to protect themselves. The protection to which they are entitled is a thorough course in combat air training, the same course that is given to white air pilots. . . . Now is the time to begin that training.[41]

The Ludlow amendment passed the House but it did not remain in the bill.

Nothing in the meantime happened in the training of Negro military pilots. In the fall of 1939 the CAA did establish, under its own authority, Civilian Pilot Training (CPT) units at several Negro colleges, including Tuskegee, Howard, Hampton, West Virginia State, North Carolina Agricultural and Technical, and Delaware State. A few Negroes also enrolled in CPT courses at other colleges and universities in the North. During the first year of the CPT program, 100 Negro college students were given training; of these 91 qualified for civil licenses—a record as good as that of white students, a national magazine remarked.[42] The CAA also announced the designation of the North Suburban Flying School at Glenview, Ill., as the school required by Public Law 18, but no Negroes were sent to this school, though new barracks had been built there and white flying cadet classes

were being sent there. To the continuing requests for information on training Negroes for duties with the Air Corps, the War Department had a standard answer—a variation on what had become a familiar theme to the more persistent inquirers:

It has long been a policy of the War Department not to mix colored and white enlisted men in the same tactical organization and, since no provision has been made for any colored Air Corps units in the Army, colored persons are not eligible for enlistment in the Air Corps.[43]

The general public impression that there was a connection between the CAA program and the opening of the Air Corps to Negro flying cadets and enlisted men meanwhile continued. The actual participation of Negroes in the CPT program did not allay agitation for full participation in Air Corps training; rather, it increased the range of such agitation. The refusal of cadet boards to consider the applications of Negroes who were successful participants in the college program gave further leverage to the campaign.

Nor was the legal interpretation of Public Law 18 clearly understood. In January 1940, during the debate on the supplemental appropriations bill,[44] Senator Bridges sought to discover the status of flying training for Negroes. Reading from a letter in which the War Department returned a Negro's application for flying cadet training because "there are no units composed of colored men,"

---

[41] Congressional Record, June 21, 1939, p. 7667. This amendment, according to Representative Ludlow, was sponsored by, among others, the following Negro organizations: United Government Employees, National Alliance of Postal Employees, National Airmen's Association, and the Elks Civil Liberties League.

[42] Time, October 28, 1940, p. 19.

[43] Ltr, TAG to Representative William H. Larrabee (Indiana), 21 Dec 39, AG 291.21 (12–12–39).

[44] H.R. 7805, Supplemental Appropriation for the Military and Naval Establishments, Coast Guard, and Federal Bureau of Investigation for the Year Ending June 30, 1940.

Senator Bridges declared, referring to Public Law 18:

I find that that provision of the law was not carried out. . . . I think that is a rather serious thing. I am in sympathy with these appropriations and the general purpose of this bill for the national defense; but I should like to have it a matter of official record that the law was passed. It was passed, I assume, by Congress in good faith to provide training for the colored men of this country who desire to participate and secure training as aviators in he United States Army; and apparently the law today has been ignored.

Turning to Senator Elbert Thomas, Senator Bridges asked ". . . has the Senator any suggestion as to just how Congress should go about seeing that the law is carried out?"

Similar questions about Public Law 18 arose from time to time in committees and on the floors of both Houses. Most of the answers given left the impression that the CAA program was initiating training which would be continued by the Army once enough pilots and mechanics had obtained rudimentary training. In March the Chief of the Air Corps, Maj. Gen. Henry H. Arnold, informed the House committee on appropriations that he felt that the Chicago school would take care of the matter of training Negro pilots.[45] The Chief of Staff, General George C. Marshall, on at least two occasions left a similar impression with committee members. On one of these, after explaining that "there is no such thing as colored aviation at the present time" but that the CAA was the proper place to begin it, the general was asked by Representative Ludlow, "So you expect to give reasonable consideration to the Negro in that respect?" Marshall replied, "We are doing that right now."[46] It was implied by the White House and so interpreted to the Negro public that the War Department would accelerate and expand CAA training and that, when enough specialists and pilots were available, Air Corps units composed of Negroes would be organized.[47] Delays at Glenview were explained by the difficulty of obtaining the twenty qualified students needed to begin instruction.[48]

The completion of CPT courses by the first Negroes naturally raised the question of what the next step in their training and use would be. The Air Corps and the Army were developing their own internal approach to the question. Despite the general statements of the impossibility of forming Negro air units, within the General Staff there was strong minority opinion that all branches, including the Air and Signal Corps, should be required to absorb their proportionate share of Negro enlisted men in time of war. The question was: how could this be done in the Air Corps while maintaining racial separation?

In the Air Corps, traditional officer-enlisted men relationships had been up-

---

[45] Hearings, House Subcommittee on Appropriations, Military Establishment Appropriation Bill for 1941, 76th Cong., 3d sess., March 7, 1940, p. 549.

[46] Hearings, House Committee on Appropriations, 2d Supplementary National Defense Bill for 1941, July 21, 1940, p. 133; see also Hearings, Senate Committee on Appropriations, 2d Supplementary National Defense Bill for 1941 (H.R. 10263), August 5, 1940, pp. 17–18.

[47] Time, October 28, 1940, p. 19; Ltr, Col Edwin M. Watson, Secy to President, to Walter White, Secy NAACP, The Crisis, LXVII (December, 1940), pp. 376–77.

[48] Memo, CofAC for CofS, 25 May 40, AAF 353.9–4–A.

set by the appearance of the pilot-officer who had to work with enlisted men who might not be under his command at all. A pilot's plane might be serviced by enlisted men who were members of a base squadron on an airfield several hundred miles from his home station. He might have to work with men of a strange weather unit or operations section. Visions of wholesale breaches of the codes of interracial etiquette arose whenever it was considered that a Negro pilot might be forced to land at a strange airfield for an overnight stay.

As great a quandary was created by the question of making use of existing facilities to train Negro pilots and enlisted men for whom neither units nor a body of experience capable of forming initial units and ground crews was available. Recognition of the cost and unwieldiness of duplicating training facilities in a service in which complete separation of the races was unlikely led to the suggestion that the Air Corps might make a departure from Army practices and train Negro and white airmen together. "The training of white and negro pilots in the same unit is out of the question," G–3 answered. "The idea of mixed units does not prevail among the educated negroes, who were members of a committee which met with C. A. A. and Army members to make arrangements for the course of instruction at the Chicago School of Aeronautics, as they favor the idea of colored units." [49] On the other hand, in face of the Air Corps' opposition, the provision of separate units for Negroes seemed unlikely. "There are no type units, combat or service, for which it is recom-

mended that negro personnel be used . . . ," the Air Corps had informed G–3.[50] Arguments against training Negro pilots included the scarcity of experienced Negroes in commercial aviation, the "lack of interest" of Negroes in aviation as evidenced by the number of private licenses which they had allowed to lapse, the absence of Negro units in the air forces of other countries, and the time ("several years") which would be needed to train enlisted men to become competent mechanics for use in ground crews of separate Negro units. Another potent argument was based on the fact that Negro pilots would make necessary a large increase in the number of Negro officers. Extracts from the testimony of World War I were cited to demonstrate that their superiors, their subordinates, and Negro officers themselves lacked confidence in their abilities. It was concluded that "the hazards of flying either in peace or war are such that the lack of confidence in any pilot of a combat unit not only creates timidity in the other pilots of the formation, but creates a mental hazard which in reality becomes a material hazard. Thus any such unit whether it is composed of white or negro pilots is useless as a combat unit either in peace or war." [51]

This reasoning was not known to the Negro public in detail. Negroes summed up the Air Corps' position by simply asserting that the Air Corps had no intention of admitting that Negroes could fly and that it had less intention of being found in error by giving them the chance to prove that they could. Lack of op-

---

[49] Memo, G–3 for CofS, 5 Jun 40, AG 291.21 (5–14–40) (1).

[50] Memo, CofAC for G–3, 31 May 40, Tab E, G–3/6541–Gen–527.
[51] Memo, G–3 for CofS, 5 Jun 40, AG 291.21 (5–14–40) (1).

portunities for Negroes to find employment in defense industries, especially in
aircraft factories, was tied in with the
protests. *The Crisis* used as the cover
of its July 1940 issue a photograph of
planes on an assembly line across which
was printed: FOR WHITES ONLY. The
caption read: "War-planes—Negro Americans may not build them, repair them,
or fly them, but they must help pay for
them." Varying the same theme, the
magazine's December 1940 cover showed
a training ship over a beautifully laid
out field. This time the caption read:
"FOR WHITES ONLY—a U.S. Army Air
Corps training plane over the 'West
Point of the Air'—Randolph Field,
Texas. Negroes are not being accepted
and trained by the Army Air Corps at
any field in the Nation, despite all the
talk of national unity and of the urgency
of every group serving in national defense." On the same cover the magazine headlined two protest articles,
"When Do *We* Fly?" by James L. H.
Peck and "Jim Crow in the Army
Camps," by "A Negro Soldier." [52]

Negro critics did not know that out of
Public Law 18 had come, in 1939, a plan
for the training of a Negro air unit.
The plan forecast that, since there was
no reservoir of Negro pilots and mechanics, it would take "several years"
before a Negro unit could be realized.
Holding that "the training of pilots
should present no special problem," the
authors of the plan explained:

It is believed that it would be fairly easy
to obtain a small number of qualified
candidates for as many classes as desired.
It might be necessary and desirable to
establish a special section or class at the
Training Center for those who survived
the primary course. Specially qualified
graduates could be sent to the Technical
School for courses in engineering, armament, photography, and communications,
if desired. The training of negro pilots
should be so timed that a negro unit would
be available for their active duty. Likewise, the training of negro enlisted men
should present no great problem, as separate classes could be held at the Technical
Schools. The greatest difficulty would probably be in getting the quality of enlisted
men necessary for this technical training.
A high school education would be desirable.[53]

According to this plan any type of
unit could be organized, but from the
point of view of complexity in maintenance and operation difficulties a single-
engine unit was deemed best. This
narrowed the choice to pursuit or observation squadrons. A single pursuit
squadron would have to fit into a group,
but an observation squadron could be a
comparatively independent unit. Therefore the latter was the recommended
"initial unit." The process of forming
the Negro unit would be gradual, with

[52] A third article, a laudatory "Salute" to Brig.
Gen. Benjamin O. Davis with a biographical sketch
of the first Negro general, appeared in the same
issue. Similarly, the July issue had contained an
account of a Negro youth in Chicago who, having
applied for Air Corps training, had "not been
turned down by mail" and an aeronautical engineer who had become a probationary employee
at Douglas Aircraft in Los Angeles. "It is not
known," the magazine commented, "what will become of the two men, but at least their initial
efforts have not been rebuffed as in the past.
However, there is as yet no indication that the
vast national defense program of the United States
will include the Negro as employees in factories,
mechanics and helpers in the huge ground crews
for airplanes, or by enlistment in all the branches
of the armed forces." These articles illustrate the
protest journals' anxiety to report achievement and
progress as well as problems to their leaders. *The
Crisis,* LXVII (July, 1940), 199.

[53] Memo, Chief AC Plans Sec for CofAC, 7 Apr
39, AAF 353.9-4-A.

initial key supervisory and technical enlisted personnel white. White officer personnel would be necessary to start with, except for "plain piloting and observing." As Negroes became proficient, they would move into responsible positions. It was nevertheless believed that at least three white officers should be left with the unit permanently. The unit should be Regular Army, for though the initial cost would then be higher, continuing costs would be less. If a Reserve or National Guard organization was formed, "the probability of political demands for additional units would probably run the resulting cost to a much higher figure than shown for a single Regular Army unit." A practical problem was posed by the lack of an allotted unit which could be used. There were but two new observation squadrons planned for the expansion, one for Hawaii and one for Panama. Conversion of an existing unit was considered inadvisable "as the services of the unit would be practically lost during the conversion period." The alternative was to request funds and authorization for an additional unit, which, if an observation squadron, would cost nearly four and a half million dollars. A new station, probably near Chicago, was considered desirable.[54]

This plan, while not used in 1939, was essentially the same as that which was put into operation in 1941. If the legislation of 1939 provided nothing else, it produced the first few Negro civilian pilot trainees and a plan which the Air Corps could employ later to initiate training of Negroes as military pilots.

Subversives and Patriots

By 1940 concern arose that, unless some assurances were given Negroes that they would have an opportunity to participate in the defense of the nation, subversive influences would find a fertile field for fifth column activities among a disaffected Negro population. A concrete basis for this apprehension appeared to be demonstrated by the circulation of such articles as "Negro Yanks Ain't Coming Either—Remember 1917" which appeared in a New York communist publication aimed primarily at a Negro audience; [55] by the use of the Negro issue in the isolationist press's attacks on the proposed selective service bill; by open criticism of such Negro leaders as A. Phillip Randolph, Walter White, and their organizations for being too conservative and ineffective; and by the development of exotic Negro cults which held that the bearing of arms was against the tenets of their new-found faiths.[56]

Certain newspapers did not hesitate to use the Negro issue in their campaigns against American entrance into the war. The New York *Daily News*, for example, carried full-page pictures of the Ku Klux Klan and of Southern sharecroppers. The captions read, "Should We Fight to Save the World . . . While These Things Continue at Home?" and "Negroes have No Freedom of Speech, No Freedom From Terror in the South." "Tell your president, senators, and congressmen," the paper suggested to its readers, "that you want democracy to work properly at home before you fight

---

[54] *Ibid.*

[55] *The Review*, February 1, 1940.

[56] Institute for Propaganda Analysis, "Negroes Ask about Democracy," *Propaganda Analysis*, IV (August 26, 1941).

for it abroad." [57]   In similar vein, isolationist magazines carried articles such
as "Should Negroes Save Democracy?" [58]

In April 1940, at its annual meeting in
Washington, the National Negro Congress, a loose federation of Negro groups
organized in 1936, passed a resolution
that if America ever went to war with
the Soviet Union they would refuse to
fight.   "This is treason," Representative
Robert G. Allen of Pennsylvania informed the House.[59]   A. Phillip Randolph, head of the Brotherhood of Sleeping Car Porters and twice president of
the congress, refused re-election to a
third term and then resigned from the
organization, explaining that the congress, having accepted financial support
from the Communist Party, had lost its
independence and would lose all possibility of mass support from Negroes.
"It seems to be beyond the realm of
debate," he said, "that the Negro people
cannot afford to add to the handicap of
being black, the handicap of being
'red.' " [60]   After this, Representative
Hamilton Fish of New York, a former
officer of World War I's Negro 369th
Infantry, declared that "99½ percent of
American Negroes are loyal American
citizens." [61]

During 1940 and 1941, street corner
and park speakers harangued crowds
about the necessity of unity among the
world's darker peoples, of whom the
Japanese, as the most powerful, were
the natural leaders.   They played upon
the latent anti-Semitism of Negro areas
to show that Nazi Germany had reason
and logic behind its racial policies.
The British record of colonialism in Africa and the West Indies came in for its
share of opprobrium.   The old Universal Negro Improvement Association
(remnant of the Garvey Back-to-Africa
Movement of the twenties), the Ethiopian Pacific Movement, the World Wide
Friends of Africa, the Peace Movement
of Ethiopia, the Brotherhood of Liberty
for the Black People of America, the
Development of Our Own, and various
cult groups of "Moorish" and "Arabic"
Negroes, some dating back thirty years
with escapist members who denied their
kinship to American Negroes and gave
their allegiance to none but the crescent
flag of Islam, all came under suspicion
as foci of subversive infection.   "You
have no stake in the war," many of these
cults' street speakers confided to their
Negro audiences.   "You will not be allowed to fight the Germans anyway—
they're white; if you are sent to fight
anyone it will be the Japanese, your
colored darker brothers." [62]

---

[57] New York *Daily News*, June 4, 1941.
[58] E. E. Johnson, "Should Negroes Save Democracy?" *Scribner's Commentator*, XI (November,
1941), 57-62. For analyses see: Horace M. Bond,
"Should the Negro Care Who Wins the War?"
*The Annals of the American Academy of Political
and Social Science*, CCXXIII (September, 1942),
81-84; Adam C. Powell, Jr., "Is This a 'White
Man's War?' " *Common Sense*, XI (April, 1942),
111-13.
[59] *Congressional Record*, April 30, 1940, p. 5253.
[60] A. Phillip Randolph, "Why I Would Not
Stand for Reelection for President of the National
Negro Congress," quoted in Extract of Remarks,
Representative Arthur W. Mitchell (Ill.), *Congressional Record*, April 30, 1940, app. 2945.

[61] *Congressional Record*, April 30, 1940, p. 5254.
[62] Cf. Powell, *op. cit.*; Roi Ottley, "A White
Folks' War?" *Common Ground*, II (Spring, 1942),
29; Lunabelle Wedlock, *The Reaction of Negro
Publications and Organizations to German Anti-
Semitism* (Washington: Howard University Studies
in the Social Sciences) III, No. 2 (1942), 116-93;
Alfred M. Lee, "Subversive Individuals of Minority
Status," *The Annals of the American Academy of*

Although these organizations had few members, their activities were taken as signs that the traditional loyalty of Negroes might be weakening. Stafford King, Civilian Aide to the Secretary of War for the State of Minnesota, who had previously written to the War Department several times on the problems of CMTC and CAA training for Negroes in his state, now wrote:

We are, if we can believe one-tenth of what we hear and read, facing the definite possibility of revolution from within or invasion from without, or both. A united people is the one and only defense against either of these contingencies. No subdivision of government should by arbitrary rule bar a whole class of citizens from volunteer service. There is no physical, moral or patriotic reason why the colored man, after passing the regular tests, should be denied enrollment in the regular army, the National Guard, the ROTC or the CMTC.

I have no hesitation in suggesting to you, Sir, that if and when the colored men are so denied the volunteer service which is given to their white, yellow and brown brothers, they become easy prey to the smooth tongue of him who reminds them of their inequalities and promises that under some new type of government, Communist, Fascist, or Nazi, such inequalities will be erased.[63]

Newspaper columnists and Army officers sounded the same warning. The commanding general of the Fifth Corps Area reported to the War Department that, of several hundreds of Negroes applying to recruiting stations in his area, most had to be turned away. "Their disappointment and dissatisfaction after having met with failure in their efforts to get into the Army, makes them fertile ground for the activities of subversive agents, in the opinion of some of our Recruiting Officers," he wrote.[64]

Replying to such inquiries and comments with what were essentially form letters began to seem inappropriate to Maj. Gen. Emory S. Adams, The Adjutant General. To one of the earlier letters of Stafford King, he prepared a form answer and delivered it to the Secretary of War with a memorandum attached:

1. The attached reply to Mr. Stafford King on his letter regarding the status of Negroes in the Regular Army has been prepared in accordance with past policies and precedents, but fails to reach the crux of the situation in my opinion because the policies and precedents are not in accord with the state of affairs in the United States.

2. The colored race is entitled to greater and better representation in our Army for obvious reasons, many of which are set forth in Mr. King's letter, and this whole subject should have careful and immediate study to determine the future policy of the War Department in the premises.

3. It is recommended that this study be initiated without delay.[65]

To this recommendation, G–1 replied that it was collaborating with G–3 on just such a study.[66]

Political and Social Science, CCXXIII (September, 1942), 167–68; Louis Martin, "Fifth Column Among Negroes," Opportunity, XX (December, 1942), 358–60; Roi Ottley, "New World A-Coming": Inside Black America (Boston: Houghton, Mifflin, 1943), pp. 322–42.

[63] Ltr, Stafford King, State Auditor of Minnesota and Civ Aide to SW, to SW, 8 Jul 40, AG 291.21 (7–8–40) (I). Mr. King had informed the War Department earlier that a Negro classmate of his son, standing high in the CAA classes at the University of Minnesota, had been refused further pilot training "for no reason except that he is colored."

[64] Ltr, CG Fifth Corps Area to TAG, 5 Aug 40, AG 291.21 (8–5–40) 9 (2).

[65] Memo, TAG for SW, 18 May 40, AG 291.21 (5–3–40) (1).

[66] Memo, G–1 for CofS, 20 May 40, AG 291.21 (5–3–40).

The preparation of studies in itself did little to solve the dilemma of the use of Negro troops. Negroes and their partisans, knowing nothing of the contents of these studies or of the importance attached to them, continued to carry their case to the public and the Congress. Comparisons with World War I were used skillfully by Negro spokesmen, with a constant overtone of "We want no repetition of the tragic errors of that war." They made speeches, they wrote articles, they consulted with men in high places, they appeared at Congressional hearings, they utilized the services and sought the aid of the better-known members of the boards of their organizations. They hoped that, by working before the declaration of war, before the beginning of large-scale expansion of the Army, they might escape the necessity of deciding which was to come first once war was declared: a struggle to obtain additional rights and privileges or a quiescent acceptance, once war began, of a *status quo* which they were convinced had long since been proved impractical. Their aim was full integration of Negroes into the armed services as Americans and not as a special class of citizens. "We will be American soldiers. We will be American ditchdiggers. We will be American laborers. We will be anything that any other American should be in this whole program of national defense. But we won't be black auxiliaries," Dean William H. Hastie of the Howard University Law School declared.[67] Under known Army policies,

it seemed doubtful to many Negroes that they would be anything other than grudgingly accepted auxiliaries.

New Bills and Units

In the summer of 1940, two new Congressional bills to increase the size of the Army, incidentally affecting the employment of Negro troops, engaged the attention of the War Department. One would have given the President authority to assign officers and enlisted men during fiscal year 1941 to the various branches of the Army in "such numbers as he considers necessary. . . . Provided, that no person shall be excluded from any branch of the military establishment on account of race, creed, or color." The G–3 Division felt that passage of legislation containing this provision would "disrupt completely plans for the organization of an effective military force."[68] G–1 predicted that such a provision would make it impossible to limit Negro enlistments to a number proportionate to the Negro population. Conceivably, the bulk of the Regular Army might become Negro. Because of the uncertainty of the number of Negro enlistments, no "balanced force" could be maintained if Negro and white units were to be kept separate. The legislative proposal might force the Army to organize Negro units in every arm and service.[69] After getting the General Staff divisions' views, Secretary Woodring summarized the department's objections to the provision, linking them to the Japanese threat and to the possibility

---

[67] Quoted in Walter White, "It's Our Country, Too: The Negro Demands the Right to Fight For It," Reprinted with permission from *The Saturday Evening Post*, CCXIII, 63. Copyright 1940 The Curtis Publishing Company.

[68] Memo, G–3 for CofS, 12 Jun 40, AG 011 (6–12–40) (1).
[69] *Ibid.*; Memo, G–1 for CofS, 13 Jun 40, AG 011 (6–12–40) (1).

that passage might endanger the maintenance of segregated units:

It is impossible to forecast definitely what its effect might be. Its retention in the bill might result in the enlistment of Negroes or Japanese in numbers out of all proportion to the colored population of the country. Such a result would demoralize and weaken the effect of military units by mixing colored and white soldiers in closely related units, or even in the same units. It might also have a dangerously adverse effect upon discipline should it be necessary to have colored and white troops in the same units or closely related units. I have no objection whatever to negro troops but must not be required to take them in such numbers as to prevent the proper organization of the army. I strongly urge the conferees to strike this provision from the bill.[70]

The joint conferees of the House and Senate substituted a provision which read, as passed: "Provided, That no Negro, because of race, shall be excluded from enlistment in the Army for service with colored military units now organized or to be organized for such service." [71] This substitution left the manner of the enlistment and employment of Negroes exactly where it had been before.

But the net effect of the original proposal was to increase the allotment of Negro combat units in the Army for the first time in twenty years and to provide types of units in which Negroes had not previously been employed. For, although the provision, as originally worded, was stricken from the bill, the War Department could not be certain that it would not reappear and become a part of final legislation. In an effort to "forestall the reinclusion of this provision," the Chief of Staff authorized Maj. Wilton B. Persons, Office of the Secretary of War, to inform "appropriate conferees" that the War Department was making definite plans to organize "a considerable number" of additional Negro units of the ground forces under the provisions of a second bill, authorizing an increase of the Regular Army by another 95,000 men. Major Persons reported that the matter was "handled with satisfactory results." [72]

The new Negro units added under this compromise were: one 155-mm. gun field artillery regiment; two coast artillery antiaircraft gun regiments; one general service engineer regiment; twelve quartermaster truck companies; and one chemical decontamination company. Each of these units, except the second coast artillery regiment and the chemical company, was within the Negro allotment contained in the current Protective Mobilization Plan, although not all of those activated were units designated specifically in the PMP as Negro. The total strength of the new Negro units was to be 4,595, or 8.4 percent of the 55,000 increase authorized for ground troops. The Negro strength of the Army was to be more than doubled by the addition of the new units.

Providing this augmentation illustrated some of the difficulties and administrative annoyances inherent in expanding the Army's Negro strength. They foreshadowed many of the later

---

[70] Ltr, SW to Senator Morris Sheppard, Chairman Senate Mil Affairs Com, 13 Jun 40, AG 011 (6–12–40) (1).

[71] Public Law 703, 76th Cong., approved 2 Jul 40; published to the Army in WD Bull 17, 2 Aug 40.

[72] Memo, OCS (initialed G.C.M.) for Maj Persons, 20 Jun 40, OCS 20602–2, and penciled note thereon, AG 011 (6–20–40); Memo, OCS for G–1, G–2, G–3, G–4, and WPD, 19 Jun 40, OCS 20602–61.

problems which the Army was to face. In the first place, since the PMP represented a balanced force, the addition of Negro units could not be accomplished simply by constituting new Negro units to be added to the PMP. Several of the new Negro units had to be provided from among organizations that already existed but that were designated for whites. The 349th Field Artillery (155-mm.), for example, was withdrawn from the Organized Reserves, reallotted to the Regular Army, changed to a motorized regiment, and designated Negro.[73] The 502d and 503d Coast Artillery (AA) regiments, white Reserve units, were redesignated 76th Coast Artillery (AA) and 77th Coast Artillery (AA) and made Negro Regular Army units. The 1st Chemical Decontamination Company, which was white in the PMP, was made a Negro unit. Of the new units, only the 41st Engineer Regiment and the 48th Quartermaster Regiment had been Negro all along.[74]

In the augmentation plans and activation orders, companies of the 48th Quartermaster Regiment were designated for activation with Negro personnel, but the 48th, although so indicated in the PMP, was not designated "Negro" in the War Department's orders. The Third Corps Area, to which the unit was allotted, therefore had to ask the War Department whether its intention was to activate the companies of this regiment with Negro enlisted men. The query was natural, since the 47th Quartermaster Regiment, now designated Negro, had

been white in the 1939 PMP and since the mid-1940 augmentation had originally included eight companies of the 47th which were now deleted. The War Department replied that its intention was to activate the 48th Regiment with Negroes.[75]

The new white units in the expansion of the Army were opened for enlistment on 1 August, but enlistments in Negro units were delayed until 15 August. Certain of the Negro units could not be housed at their assigned stations until the construction of "Negro housing" was completed. They were to be activated at temporary stations and moved later. Providing cadres for the new types of units was a difficult problem. Time was needed to prepare the Negro cadremen, who had to be obtained from existing units of the traditional branches, for their task of establishing and training units in new branches.

The organization of new Negro units in the Regular Army raised questions within the Army. Would these units become permanent parts of the Regular Army? Would the branches have difficulty in inactivating them once the emergency was over? Would their establishment mean that other arms and services besides the Infantry and Cavalry would now have a peacetime "Negro problem?"[76]

Certain of the arms and services still did not believe that they should be given the task of organizing Negro units at all. Specific objection came from the General Headquarters (GHQ) Air Force,

[73] This regiment had been an element of the World War I 92d Division.
[74] Memo, G-3 for TAG, 10 Jul 40, AG 320.2 (7-10-40) (2); Ltr, TAG to CG's, Chiefs, and CO's of Exempted Stations, 20 Jul 40, AG 320.2 (7-10-40) M (Ret) M-C.

[75] Msg, CG Third Corps Area to WD, 23 Jul 40 and Rad, WD to CG Third Corps Area, 26 Jul 40, WD G-3/41389 and AG 320.2 (7-23-40).
[76] Cf., Memo, G-3 for G-1, 7 Oct 40, AG 210.31-ORC (9-28-40).

which asked that the 1st Chemical De-contamination Company be exchanged for a white unit. Such a company in air operations, the GHQ Air Force said, must be broken down into small detachments for use at various bases and distributing points. The detachments must live and mess with other Air Corps units. Since all other units of the GHQ Air Force were white, the decontamination company should also be white.[77] The Chief of the Air Corps asked for favorable consideration of the request. G–3 pointed out that the method of utilization described by the GHQ Air Force was but one of many and that during peacetime such a unit need not be used in this manner at all, unless it could be so employed with minimum difficulties. The request was not approved and the unit was activated with Negroes.[78]

Opening enlistments for Negroes in new Regular Army combat units was distinctly news in the civilian press. In Detroit, for example, Army recruiting made an all-time record for the city on 15 August, the day when recruiting of Negroes began. "Those enlisted today included 29 Negroes, the first Negroes to be enlisted for combat units here since 1920," the Detroit News reported. Chicago recruiting offices broke the national record by enrolling over 100 men in a day.[79]

The pattern set in the establishment of these new units was in several ways typical of later Army experience. The redesignation of white units to receive Negroes, the semiconfusion of the racial identity of units, delays in assembling units caused by lack of housing and trained cadres, objections to the receipt of Negro units by branches of services, and the readiness of Negroes to enter new units were to be repeated many times during mobilization and during the course of World War II.

The legislative compromise out of which the new units came had additional significance. It was the first of a series which, by adding a few units here, and subtracting a few there, caused a relatively haphazard development in the expansion of Negro strength. The expansion was often based more on expediency than on either military necessity or sound planning. Existing plans were often altered by factors, frequently non-military, which interfered with the orderly procedures visualized for the expansion of Negro strength.

The Selective Training and Service Act

The legislation of 1940 primarily affecting the employment of Negro troops by the Army was the Selective Training and Service Act. When first proposed, this legislation contained a preamble which read in part: "The Congress further declares that in a free society the obligations and privileges of military training and service should be shared generally in accordance with a fair and just system of selective compulsory military training and service." Nevertheless, Negroes and supporters of their efforts to obtain full military training, remembering that Public Law 18 of April 1939 had produced no pilots,

---

[77] Ltr, CG GHQ AF to TAG, 13 Jul 40, AG 320.2 (7–13–40) (1).

[78] Memo, G–3 for TAG, 25 Jul 40, AG 320.2 (7–13–40) (1).

[79] Detroit News, August 15, 1940, read into the Congressional Record by Senator Arthur Vandenburg (August 19, 1940), p. 10472; Chicago Defender, September 7, 1940.

pressed for additional safeguards.

Rayford W. Logan of Howard University, chairman of the civilian Committee on Participation of Negroes in the National Defense Program, testified before the House Committee on Military Affairs that amendments to the Selective Service bill which stated specifically the intent of Congress should be inserted. He asked that a new subsection be added: "No provision of this act shall be construed or administered so as to discriminate against any person on account of race, creed, or color," or, as an alternative, "In the selection and training of men as well as in the interpretation and execution of the provisions of this act there shall be no discrimination against any person on account of race, creed or color." [80] Other spokesmen, Charles H. Houston, NAACP civil rights lawyer, and Owen D. Young, representing the American Youth Commission, urged the adoption of amendments similar to those proposed by Logan. Proposals that Negroes be given safeguards leading to fuller service made a favorable impression on the committee, for much of the testimony before it had been from pacifist and other groups opposed to the bill. Representative Paul J. Kilday of Texas asked Professor Logan, "You are not asking for the exemption of your race, but you are asking that they be put into it?" Logan replied, "Yes, and it seems to me extraordinary that they are not." "I think your stand is in marked contrast to some of those who have been here," Kilday commented.

Antidiscrimination amendments were introduced in both the House and Senate, despite the fact that the bill, as reported out by the committees, contained sections forbidding discrimination against volunteers and requiring selection "in an impartial manner." Representative Hamilton Fish of New York introduced an amendment in the House which was essentially Logan's alternative amendment. It applied to selectees only. Senator Robert F. Wagner, also of New York, sought to include specific mention of aviation units as well as to make it mandatory that men be selected "without regard to race, creed or color." Both proponents urged that Negroes be guaranteed the right to serve in any branch without restrictions because of color.

There was little direct Congressional opposition to the amendments as such, but the debate on the subject of Negroes in the proposed Army training program illustrated not only the effect of political pressures on the Congress but also the political results of public interest in the subject. The debates covered the range of public reaction to the question of legislative guarantees of Negro participation in the preparedness program. Some congressmen asserted that the amendments were not aimed at the prevention of discrimination against Negroes at all but at the breakdown of segregation within the Army. Senator Allen J. Ellender of Louisiana objected that the amendment would lead to racially mixed units and his colleague, Senator John H. Overton, arguing on the distinction between discrimination and segregation, said:

I understand from members of the general staff that there is no discrimination whatever against the colored race. They are, however, placed in separate units,

---

[80] *Selective Compulsory Military Training and Service, Hearings . . . on H.R. 10132,* 76th Cong., 3d sess., p. 587.

while the desire on the part of a certain class of our population is that there should be mixed units. If we should undertake to establish mixed units in the Army, it would be subversive to discipline, subversive to morale, and would not be of benefit either to the colored or to the white race. . . . I think I am justified in making the observation that if they are excluded from the air forces it is because the Army is not ready yet to have separate units. I think that would be the only reason.[81]

Senator Tom Connally of Texas, recalling the Civil War, and the Houston riot of World War I, said of the Wagner proposal:

I think the Senator from New York does not properly interpret the spirit of the colored race. He may interpret the spirit of one or two of them who are on salaries around here to agitate the colored people; he may speak for one or two colored lobbyists; but he does not speak for the great mass of the American colored people. Most of them are hard working, most of them mean well; most of them want to do right; most of them want to serve their country —if their country needs them. A few of them want continually to agitate, disturb, stir up discussion, and raise the devil about what they speak of as their political and social rights.[82]

Senator W. Warren Barbour of New Jersey, on the other hand, contended that anything less than equitable distribution of Negroes among the arms and services would constitute discrimination. In World War I, he said, many Negroes were

. . . wholly and only in labor battalions. They were given only this sort of work which, while important in itself, was discriminatory. The fact that so much of that really non-military duty was confined to that one race proved that it was discriminatory; and this is not fair, it is not right, it is not American.[83]

Senator Schwartz recalled that, a year before, the Congress had passed a bill (Public Law 18) which authorized the Army to train colored pilots. The Army, he continued, had not been able to "work out that provision" because of the social implications involved. He reminded the Senate that recruiting notices reading "white only" had disturbing effects among the Negro population. Negroes with whom he had talked, he pointed out, believed that "a very large number of colored men were not with colored regiments, but they were with a white artillery regiment and with other regiments, taking care of horses—polo ponies, probably." Though the War Department had not created "what they call the social situation in the South and in the Army," he continued, "they are trying to meet the situation for they must and will work with it and produce a plan where Negroes, such as pilots, would not have to be working with white pilots." [84]

When the Selective Service Act was finally passed, it contained two specific provisions against discrimination because of race or color. The first, in section 3 (a), provided: "That within the limits of the quota determined under section 4 (b) for the subdivision in which he resides, any person, regardless of race or color, between the ages of eighteen and thirty-six, shall be afforded an opportunity to volunteer for induction into the land or naval forces of the United States for the training and service prescribed. . . ." The second, in sec-

---

[81] Congressional Record, 86, p. 10890.
[82] Ibid., p. 10894.

[83] Ibid., p. 10890.
[84] Ibid., p. 10891.

tion 4 (a), read: "That in the selection and training of men under this act, and in the interpretation and execution of the provisions of this act, there shall be no discrimination against any person on account of race or color." [85]   The inclusion of these provisions did not of itself satisfy those opponents of discrimination who visualized a draft Army which, with segregation as a pattern, would spread discriminatory practices over the entire United States.

Although the Army had stated several times that, if the Selective Service bill passed and became law, Negroes would be inducted in proportion to their strength in the manpower covered by the law, there was an additional provision in the law which caused Negro leaders some concern. Section 3 continued:

Provided further, That no man shall be inducted for training and service under this act unless and until he is acceptable to the land or naval forces for such training and service and his physical and mental fitness for such training and service has been satisfactorily determined: Provided further, That no men shall be inducted for such training and service until adequate provision shall have been made for such shelter, sanitary facilities, water supplies, heating and lighting arrangements, medical care, and hospital accommodations, for such men, as may be determined by the Secretary of War or the Secretary of the Navy, as the case may be, to be essential to public and personal health.

The questions raised by this section were: Would Negroes be "acceptable to the land or naval forces?"   Would the force of "unless and until" provide a means of limiting service "unless and until" the armed forces had a need for

the individual Negro?   Could lack of shelter or hospital accommodations for Negroes be made a limiting factor in their induction? [86]

Announcements and Appointments

To obtain answers to these and other questions, leaders of Negro organizations prepared a memorandum setting forth what they considered minimum requests. The text of this memorandum was presented to President Roosevelt, Secretary of the Navy Frank Knox, and Assistant Secretary of War Robert P. Patterson at a White House conference on 27 September 1940.[87] The portion of the program applying to the armed services read:

The following are important phases of the integration of the Negro into military aspects of the national defense program.

1. The use of presently available Negro reserve officers in training recruits and other forms of active service. At the same time, a policy of training additional Negro officers in all branches of the services should be announced. Present facilities and those to be provided in the future should be made available for such training.

2. Immediate designation of centers where Negroes may be trained for work in all branches of the aviation corps. It is not enough to train pilots alone, but in addition navigators, bombers, gunners,

---

[85] Public Law 783, 76th Cong., 16 Sep 40.

[86] Cf., Walter White, "It's Our Country, Too: The Negro Demands the Right to Fight," *Saturday Evening Post*, CCXIII (December 14, 1940), 27, 61–68.

[87] The Negroes presenting this program were Walter White, T. Arnold Hill, formerly industrial secretary of the Urban League and at that time adviser on Negro Affairs in the National Youth Administration, and A. Phillip Randolph. Cf., Walter F. White, *A Man Called White* (New York: Viking, 1948), pp. 186–89; Pittsburgh *Courier*, October 19, 1940.

radiomen, and mechanics must be trained in order to facilitate full Negro participation in the air service.

3. Existing units of the army and units to be established should be required to accept and select officers and enlisted personnel without regard to race.

4. Specialized personnel such as Negro physicians, dentists, pharmacists and officers of chemical warfare, camouflage service and the like should be integrated into the services.

5. The appointment of Negroes as responsible members in the various national and local agencies engaged in the administration of the Selective Service Training Act of 1940.

6. The development of effective techniques for insuring the extension of the policy of integration in the Navy other than the menial services to which Negroes are now restricted.

7. The adoption of policies and the development of techniques to assure the participation of trained Negro women as Army and Navy nurses as well as in the Red Cross.[88]

The White House had already directed the War Department, on 5 September, to prepare and hold a statement to the effect that "colored men will have equal opportunity with white men in all departments of the Army."[89] General Marshall informed his Personnel Division that, at a cabinet meeting on 13 September, the President had stated that "he had been troubled by representations of the Negroes that their race under the draft was limited to labor battalions." The Army informed the President that it planned to give Negroes "proportionate shares in all branches of the Army, in the proper ratio to their population—approximately 10 percent." The President then sug-

gested that the War Department, "in conjunction with the Navy," publicize this fact. "The Secretary of War wishes an exact statement of the facts in the case, and as to how far we can go in the matter," the Chief of Staff wrote.[90]

On 16 September 1940, the day the Selective Service Act was approved, the War Department issued a press release headed "Expansion of Colored Organizations Planned." When the Selective Service System began to operate, the release reported, 36,000 of the first 400,000 men called would be Negroes. The release listed all Negro units, including the new August units, and mentioned the CAA program, adding that "the creation of additional colored combat organizations is now under consideration." It implied, but did not state, that these would include Air Corps units.

On 8 October 1940, Assistant Secretary Patterson, "as the result of a conference in your office on September 27," submitted to President Roosevelt a full statement of policy, already approved informally by the Secretary of War and the Chief of Staff. The President penciled his "O.K." and initials on this memorandum, thereby giving his approval to a policy which remained in effect throughout the war. On the morning of 9 October it was released to the press by the White House.[91] This first comprehensive statement on the subject read:

It is the policy of the War Department that the services of Negroes will be utilized on a fair and equitable basis. In line with

[88] *The Crisis*, LXVII (November, 1940).

[89] Memo, OCS for G-1 and G-3, 5 Sep 40, OCS 20602-78.

[90] Memo, CofS (initialed G.C.M.) for G-1, 14 Sep 40, OCS 20602-79.

[91] Memo, ASW for President, 8 Oct 40; Ltr, Secy to President (Stephen Early) to ASW, 9 Oct 40, AG 291.21 (10-9-40) (1).

this policy provision will be made as follows:

1. The strength of the Negro personnel of the Army of the United States will be maintained on the general basis of the proportion of the Negro population of the country.

2. Negro organizations will be established in each major branch of the service, combatant as well as noncombatant.

3. Negro reserve officers eligible for active duty will be assigned to Negro units officered by colored personnel.

4. When officer candidate schools are established, opportunity will be given to Negroes to qualify for reserve commissions.

5. Negroes are being given aviation training as pilots, mechanics and technical specialists. This training will be accelerated.

6. At arsenals and army posts Negro civilians are accorded equal opportunity for employment at work for which they are qualified by ability, education, and experience.

7. The policy of the War Department is not to intermingle colored and white enlisted personnel in the same regimental organizations. This policy has been proven satisfactory over a long period of years, and to make changes now would produce situations destructive to morale and detrimental to the preparation for national defense. For similar reasons the department does not contemplate assigning colored reserve officers other than those of the Medical Corps and chaplains to existing Negro combat units of the Regular Army. These regular units are going concerns, accustomed through many years to the present system. Their morale is splendid, their rate of reenlistment is exceptionally high, and their field training is well advanced. It is the opinion of the War Department that no experiments should be tried with the organizational set-up of these units at this critical time.[92]

The White House, in releasing the statement, implied that it was the result of the 27 September conference with Negro leaders. The measure of the protests which went up from Negroes was the measure of the distance between the White House announcement and their proposed program. The men who had attended the White House conference were especially annoyed by the implication that they had endorsed the announced policy.[93] They were specifically disturbed about points five and seven. The announcement embodied the main points of a policy adopted (although not announced) by the War Department in 1937, in its planning for mobilization; and the final paragraph repeated, in almost identical phrases, the statements made in the many Adjutant General letters which had gone out to individuals all over the country. Nevertheless, this statement, which contained the basic Army policy in force throughout the war, was afterward referred to within the War Department as the Presidential directive on the use of Negro troops and as a Presidential sanction for policies derived therefrom.[94]

Had the policy announcement been made earlier, as had been intended in the 1937 recommendations, reaction to it might have been slight, for the details of the announcement went beyond what the Negro press and public had expected or requested as late as the beginning of 1940. Coming as it did, after the Selec-

---

[92] Incl to Memo, ASW for President, 8 Oct 40, distributed to Army 16 Oct 40 by Ltr, AG 291.21 (10–9–40) (1).

[93] Pittsburgh *Courier*, October 19, 1940; *Time*, October 28, 1940; White, *A Man Called White*, pp. 186–89.

[94] Examples: (1) "This procedure [training Negroes at Tuskegee] would be necessary to follow out the President's policy of segregation of the races." R&R, OCofAC, Pers to Gen Arnold, 30 Jan 40 [41], AAF 353.9–4–A; (2) Min of Gen Council, 16 Jun 42, p. 3.

tive Service Act, which had already legalized proportionate representation of Negroes through the operation of a random choice lottery, the question of manner of service was the only one left which was of primary concern. The statement on air training had less than the ring of conviction about it, since no training of the sort was being given by the Army. The reference to Regular Army units, over half of which were less than two months old, helped clinch the belief, held by most Negroes, that there was a wide gap between the words and the intentions of the War Department. "Of all the shabby dealings of America with a tenth of her citizens," *The Crisis* commented in its issue following the announcement, "none is more shameful or more indefensible than the refusal to give Negroes a fair chance in the armed forces." The editorial continued:

The citizens' army that is to be trained under the Selective Service Act will find shortly that the Army and the Navy are being run very much like country clubs. Americans discovered that in 1917, but there was a war to be fought at once then and there was not much they could do about it. Now it should be different and the peacetime army and its civilian relatives, given a space to think and act before actual warfare interferes, may force some changes.[95]

Thereafter, and throughout the war, *The Crisis*, and most of the Negro press, while praising the signs of change within the Army which meant greater opportunities for Negroes, continued to attack the Army's segregation policy, even in connection with such installations as the Tuskegee Army Flying School, which trained the Negro pilots for which the

press had worked so long, and in connection with the activation of Negro divisions. A Negro journalist commented shortly after Pearl Harbor that no Negro leader in 1942 could write a "Close Ranks" editorial of the 1918 model if he expected to maintain his influence. "For in the last war," he argued, "in spite of the acknowledged bravery of Negro troops, they suffered all forms of Jim Crow, humiliation, discrimination, and indeed slander—a pattern being followed today." [96] One of the NAACP's most prominent officers, William Pickens, for example, was discharged by the organization as an apologist for segregation after he had commended the Army's work at Tuskegee and at Fort Huachuca.

By no means all comments on the announcement of Army policy, by or on behalf of Negroes, were adverse.[97] It was often pointed out that, under the new policy, Negroes would have broader opportunities than they had had in the past. Some Negroes wrote to the War Department to say that they thought it a "fine thing" to give the Negro a place in the armed services in proportion to population. Others, including Negro college officers and presidents, offered their services as advisers to the Secretary of War and in capacities in which they would be able to stress the need of national unity to Negro audiences.[98] But

[95] *The Crisis,* LXVII (December, 1940), 375.

[96] Roi Ottley, "A White Folks' War?" *Common Ground,* II (Spring, 1942), 28–29.
[97] See *Nation,* CLI (October 26, 1940), 378–79; Father John LaFarge, "Our Jim Crow Army," *America* (October, 1940).
[98] Ltrs in AG 291.21, Oct–Nov 40. See especially Ltr, Brig Gen Spencer C. Dickinson (Illinois N. G., Ret.) to Gen Marshall, 10 Oct 40, AG 291.21 (10–10-40), praising the Army for its new policy. In an accompanying memorandum, General Marshall wrote to G–1, "The writer of the attached letter is a colored man, who commanded the 8th Illinois

GENERAL DAVIS

the majority of the comments and correspondence criticized one or another of the announced policy decisions.

In the wake of criticisms, other commitments were made. Bishop Richard R. Wright, chairman of the Colored Division of the National Democratic Headquarters, asked Stephen Early, Press Secretary to the President, if anything had been done by the Republicans since the Spanish-American War to make permanent additions of Negro Regulars to the Army and if it was "a fact that under the present administration the Negro has gotten more recognition in

the Army than ever before, and what is the record?" G–1 made no attempt to answer the first of these questions, but in response to the second it compiled a list of the new Negro units recently approved and of those planned for the near future.[99] On the basis of this information Assistant Secretary Patterson informed the White House that, in addition to the new units already provided, three infantry regiments, one engineer regiment, eight engineer battalions, "and the necessary ordnance and quartermaster troops" would be formed in the spring from Selective Service men.[100] "Also from Selective Service personnel, 2,250 men will be trained in Air Corps units," Patterson's memorandum concluded.[101] The next day a supplementary memorandum, delivered to the White House by Maj. Walter Bedell Smith, indicated that the 4th Cavalry Brigade was being formed and that it would be one of two, the other brigade to be white, forming the 2d Cavalry Division.[102] Thus, in answer to the demands of the 1940 political campaign, the War Department committed itself to action in terms of specific units, filling out the announcement of 9 October that though Negroes would remain in separate units they would be represented in

Infantry. He is a medical graduate of the University of Heidelberg, I believe. It is just as well to have this man in mind in case of attacks of our not having given enough to the negro pressure." Memo, CofS for G–1 and Maj [W. B.] Smith, signed GCM, CofS, 14 Oct 40, AG 291.21 (10–10–40).

[99] Memo, G–1 for CofS, 21 Oct 40, AG 322.97 (10–21–40).
[100] Memo, ASW for William D. Hassett, The White House, 21 Oct 40, AG 322.97 (10–21–40). G–1 had also listed an artillery brigade headquarters and headquarters battery, one signal contruction company, an additional chemical company, a cavalry brigade weapons troop, two ponton companies, and the numbers of Negroes to be trained in the replacement centers of each arm and service. These details were not forwarded to the White House.
[101] Memo cited n. 100.
[102] Memo, Gen Marshall for William D. Hassett, 22 Oct 40, AG 322.97 (10–21–40).

all arms and services. These units were all to be provided, but the manner and nature of their provision was yet to be worked out. The question of the manner and nature of their employment was still further in the future.

Two more steps were taken within this same pre-election week. On 25 October Col. Benjamin O. Davis, senior Negro officer in the Army, was nominated for promotion to brigadier general.[103] On the same day Secretary Stimson appointed William Hastie, Dean of the Howard University Law School, as his Civilian Aide on Negro Affairs.[104]

The first of these appointments received widespread attention in the na-

JUDGE HASTIE

---

[103] The Senate received the nomination along with others on 7 November. (*Congressional Record* 86, 13610, 13827.) General Davis, born in Washington on 1 July 1877, had had a long Army career. He had been a 1st lieutenant in the 8th U.S. Volunteer Infantry in the Spanish-American War; in 1899 he enlisted in the 9th Cavalry. He was appointed 2d lieutenant, Cavalry, in 1901; by 1930 he had been promoted to colonel. He had served with the 10th Cavalry during the Philippine insurrection, with the Mexican Border patrol, and with the American legation in Liberia. The remainder of his career had been spent as a National Guard and ROTC instructor and in other special duties. Negro newspapers had been hinting for some time that "rumor" had it that, like Col. Charles Young, he would be retired rather than promoted. Retired originally on 31 July 1941, General Davis returned to active duty the next day, 1 August 1941. After 50 years in the Army, General Davis went on inactive duty in July 1948.

[104] Dean Hastie had had a distinguished public career. Negro press comments on his appointment indicated that the Negro public had high respect for his abilities. Hastie had been assistant solicitor for the Department of the Interior, Federal District Judge of the Virgin Islands (the first Negro to be appointed to the federal bench), chairman of the National Legal Committee of the NAACP, and a prominent member of civic improvement groups in the city of Washington. Various Negro organizations, including the press, had been asking for the appointment of such an adviser.

tional press, for this was the first time that a Negro had achieved general officer's rank in the United States Army. The second appointment was widely noted as a sign that the Army intended to expand its Negro strength with a minimum of difficulties. The political significance of the appointments was not overlooked. Some viewed the Davis promotion as a Roosevelt administration attempt to counteract Negro opposition to the October policy announcement. In promoting General Davis, *Time* commented, the administration was already violating its announced policy, since he would leave his all-Negro command, the 369th New York National Guard Regiment, for the new 4th Cavalry Brigade, containing the 9th and 10th Cavalry Regiments, both of which, as Regular

Army outfits, had all white officers. The white officers could be replaced by Negro Reserve officers, but even then the policy would be violated, since Negro Reserve officers were not to be used in Regular Army units. The easiest way out, the magazine continued, would be to retire General Davis on his sixty-fourth birthday due the next July, for "By then the election will be over." [105] The Negro press, in general, greeted the promotion with approval, though indicating that it alone was not enough.

For the Hastie appointment, the Secretary of War had a World War I precedent. In 1917, Newton D. Baker had made Emmett J. Scott, secretary to Booker T. Washington at Tuskegee, his Special Assistant with approximately the same purpose in mind—the provision of some means of liaison and some source of interpretation between the Negro public and the War Department. Moreover, the appointment of special advisers on questions affecting the Negro public had been an increasing tendency among federal agencies during the preceding eight years.

Judge Hastie undertook his duties on 1 November 1940. In his letter of appointment, Secretary Stimson described these duties to be "to assist in the formulation, development and administration of policies looking to the fair and effective utilization of Negroes in all branches of the military service." [106] The Secretary's letter continued:

I hope that you will be able to assist us in the development of and improvements in the War Department's plans for the organization of Negro units in each major branch of the service, and for the utilization of Negro reserve officers, candidates for commissions, and aviation cadets. I also hope that you will be of assistance to us in connection with policies involving the employment of Negroes on civilian status at army establishments and by army contractors.

It will be part of your duties to investigate complaints concerning the treatment of Negroes in the military service or in civilian employment in the War Department. In this connection, I hope it will be possible for you to spend time visiting camps, posts and stations for the purpose of observing and reporting to me upon matters of Negro participation in the national defense.

It is my expectation that you will cooperate with the Negro representatives on the Selective Service Committee and in the Labor Section of the Advisory Commission to the Council of National Defense, where appropriate.

Such recommendations as you may from time to time wish to make should be submitted to me through the Assistant Secretary of War.

You may be assured that the officers and establishments of the War Department will cooperate with you in carrying out the tasks which I have outlined. Instructions are being issued that you be consulted on matters affecting Negroes in the army, and that all information necessary to the effective execution of your duties be made available to you.

---

[105] *Time,* November 4, 1940, p. 20. See also Pittsburgh *Courier,* November 2, 1940; Walter White, "It's Our Country, Too," *loc. cit.;* Editorial, "Negro Self-Respect and Politics," *The Christian Century,* LVII (November 13, 1940) , 1403; Ollie Stewart, "The Negro—American Nationalist," *Scribner's Commentator,* IX (March, 1941) , 68; Walter White, "Brown Americans," *Coronet,* XVII (November, 1944) , 86.

---

[106] Ltr, SW to Dean William H. Hastie, 25 Oct 40, OASW Personnel #301, and Memo, ASW to Maj Gen James H. Burns, 25 Oct 40, same file. Technically, Hastie was carried on the rolls as Head Attorney under Executive Order 8044.

Judge Hastie considered these manifold duties to be the "general task of facilitating the equitable integration of the Negro into so much of the National Defense Program as falls within the jurisdiction of the War Department." [107] His office, consisting of himself, one assistant, and a secretary, proceeded to gather information from General Staff divisions and from the chiefs of arms and services in an attempt to determine and appraise the existing plans and developments in the Army's use of Negro troops. Hastie, acting upon the information available to him, initiated recommendations, generally through the Secretary of the General Staff, occasionally through one or another of the assistant chiefs of staff, and at times directly to the Assistant Secretary (later, Under Secretary) of War, Judge Patterson. Most of the policy proposals specifically affecting Negroes were referred to the Civilian Aide for comment, although Judge Hastie complained early that too frequently such matters did not come to his attention until the proposals had been completely formulated and presented for final approval. As a result of the publication of a directive concerning the construction of welfare and recreational facilities for Negro troops on which Judge Hastie had not been consulted, the chiefs of arms and services and the General Staff divisions were instructed that "Matters of policy which pertain to Negroes, or important questions arising thereunder, will be referred to Judge William H. Hastie, civilian aide to the Secretary of

War, for comment or concurrence before final action." [108]

Individual complaints from soldiers and civilian employees of the Army, proposals and complaints from Negro organizations, and problems ranging from the employment of Negro hostesses and librarians in service clubs to the constitution of Negro combat units were referred to the Civilian Aide's office for comment and consultation. Routine requests for information and "daily visits and inquiries by persons seeking employment" consumed a large part of the time of the office and prevented the Civilian Aide from giving his full attention to the larger aspects of his duties.[109] Nevertheless, through personal contacts with the chiefs of War Department agencies and through informal inquiries, Judge Hastie, in the first few months of mobilization, considered a variety of questions of major importance, including: the proportionate distribution of Negroes in the arms and services; the use and training of Negro officers, chaplains, and nurses; recreational and welfare facilities for Negro troops; the use of Negro civilian personnel in Army installations; Negroes in Civilian Conservation Corps camps; Negroes in National Youth Administration projects on Army posts and stations; and the relations of the War Department with the Negro press.

At the outset Hastie was furnished a complete list of existing units and of those planned through June 1941. He

---

[108] Ltr, TAG to Chiefs Arms and Svs and Divs of WD Gen Staff, 18 Dec 40, AG 291.21 (12–17–40) M–OCS–M, based on Memo, ASW for TAG, 15 Dec 40, and Memo, SGS for TAG, 17 Dec 40, AG 291.21 (12–17–40) (1).

[109] Memo, Civ Aide for USW, 7 Feb 41, AG 322.97 (3–18–41) (1).

---

[107] Memo, Civ Aide for USW, 7 Feb 41, AG 322.97 (3–18–41) (1).

was assured that Negroes would be excluded from no arm or service, though it was explained that the Armored Force was not an arm but a combination of arms and services. "There are no negro units in the armored corps," G–1 said, "but there are mechanized units in the 9th and 10th Cavalries." [110] Negro aviation units, about which Hastie had inquired specifically, would follow when the National Youth Administration and Civil Aeronautics Authority programs had trained enough civilian pilots and mechanics. "If this program is to be safe," G–1 said, "it must progress carefully, step by step. Plans are now being developed for training of negro military pilots, when this program has progressed sufficiently to provide the requisite ground personnel." Negro officers, dentists, and doctors would be used in the three existing National Guard regiments and in the one new regiment to be formed in February. Nurses would be procured for "hospitals which are used exclusively for negro patients" and qualified pharmacists were free to compete for Reserve commissions. "With representative units in all arms and services the problem of utilization of skilled negroes is in general no different from that of the skilled whites," G–1 noted. "The utilization of the exceptionally skilled white is limited, and it will be the same in the case of the negro." In the classification and reception of Negroes at reception centers or in the admission of men to specialist schools, no discrimination would be permitted. Selection for schools would depend entirely upon the "particular suitability of the selectee for the duties for which he is to be trained." [111]

The Lines Form

General interest in the question of the employment of Negro troops widened during the year 1940. A number of year-end articles on the subject appeared in nationally distributed publications. Walter White, secretary of the NAACP, summed up his views in the opening words of an article:

From the man-power angle, the largest defense headache ahead of the United States Government is likely to be the status of that 10 per cent of our population which is Negro. The Negro insists upon doing his part, and the Army and Navy want none of him.[112]

To a large extent, despite the War Department's announced expansion of its employment of Negroes, White's brief picture was correct. The use and status of Negro manpower did become one of the major "headaches" of the war. What White did not state was that a profound difference in interpretation of the Negro's "part" existed. There were those who insisted that there was no possible meeting ground between the two opposing points of view.

Many Negroes saw no way in which

---

[110] Memo, G–1 for Judge Hastie, 20 Nov 40, G–1/15640–57.

[111] *Ibid.*

[112] Walter White, "It's Our Country, Too," *loc. cit.* Among other articles appearing at about the same time were: "Role of the Negro in National Defense," *School and Society*, LII (December 7, 1940), 580; Mrs. F. D. Roosevelt, "Defense and the Minority Group," *Opportunity*, XVIII (December, 1940), 356–58; Paul E. Bowen, "The Historical Background of the Negro as Soldier," *Virginia Teachers Bulletin*, XVII (November, 1940), 29–31; Lawrence Sullivan, "Negro Vote," *Atlantic Monthly*, CLXVI (October, 1940), 477–94; Metz Lochard, "Negroes and Defense," *Nation*, CLII (January 4, 1941), 14–16.

any denial of the individual's right to serve in any capacity for which he was fitted, without reference to race, could be reconciled with the professed ideals for which the war was being fought. With appeals to democracy and continued obeisance to the ideal of the dignity of the individual highly in evidence as justifications for the struggle in which the world was locked, Negroes continued to point out discrepancies in the active expression of the "democratic faith" so frequently propounded by the heads of the government. "A lily-white navy cannot fight for a free world. A jim crow army cannot fight for a free world. Jim crow strategy, no matter on how grand a scale, cannot build a free world," *The Crisis* said immediately after Pearl Harbor.[113]

The Army, on the other hand, insisted that its job was not to alter American social customs but to create a fighting machine with a maximum economy of time and effort. The War Department made it clear that it saw no point in debating "at every point" policy decisions already made, for though it would answer specific inquiries, it felt that Negroes, and especially the NAACP, were simply trying to keep alive a controversy which served no valid military purpose in time of national crisis.[114] The War Department felt, moreover, that it had offered Negroes the opportunity to serve in all capacities and that that itself was a major removal of discriminatory barriers and a major concession. From the Army's viewpoint, the promise of proportional use of Negroes in all types of units provided more opportunities for service than Negroes were able to take advantage of. Separate units continued segregation, but the Army felt that segregation was a practice which it had found in the civilian community and which it had no right to alter until the civilian community itself had changed its own methods or had given the Army, through the Congress, a clear mandate to do so.

The Selective Service Act had ordered that inductees be selected and trained without discrimination and, the War Department reiterated, it did not itself discriminate against any of its soldiers. Here was one of the major points of disagreement, for, as shown in the Congressional debates on the inclusion of nondiscriminatory clauses in the Selective Service Act, the distinction between discrimination and segregation in normal usage was not always clear. The meaning of these terms then and later depended in large measure upon the view of the user. Segregation, implying only separation, was often considered nondiscriminatory by those who believed that equal facilities and opportunities could be provided to both races. To others, including most Negroes, the concept of enforced segregation was itself discriminatory. The fact of separation not only prevented freedom of movement and action on the part of the segregated minority (and was therefore considered an abridgment of basic personal liberties) but also produced inequalities of facilities and opportunities for the minority. The minority, being numerically smaller and weaker, had no means of enforcing guarantees of equal facilities and opportunities.

[113] Editorial, "Now Is the Time Not to Be Silent," *The Crisis*, XLIX (January, 1942), 7.
[114] Ltr, TAG to Dr. Amanda V. G. Hillyer, Chairman Program Committee, D.C. Branch, NAACP, 12 Apr 41, AG 291.21 (2–28–41) (1).

Moreover, the argument ran, the very act of formal segregation implied inescapable differences among men which made common action impossible and which, by denying the common aims and similar objectives of men was, per se, discriminatory. On the other hand the courts, through World War II, held that segregation, as such, was not discriminatory where equal facilities were provided. Field commanders therefore saw nothing anomalous in announcing that their racial policy was "segregation without discrimination" or that no discrimination could exist in a command or camp which had Negro enlisted men only.

To those for whom the aspirations of Negroes were a cause, no amount of special consideration in the way of separate units of diverse types was compensation for the continuing conviction that the root of all difficulties in the Army's use of Negro manpower lay in the restriction of Negroes to these particular segregated units. The crowning irony to many Negroes was that the Army, while insisting upon separate units, did not go all the way in its segregated pattern and insist that these units be commanded wholly by Negro, and not by white, officers. "We deplore segregation in any form," said Professor Rayford Logan, representing ten Negro organizations and speaking for seven co-witnesses in 1940, "especially when it is practiced by the Federal Government. But in accepting these separate units which are forced upon us, we do so only because of the hope that these units will be commanded by Negro officers." [115]

Negroes therefore used their political pressures in two directions: the first toward the elimination of segregation and discrimination in the extension of the use of Negro manpower, and the second in an attempt to exploit to the fullest the possibilities for the use of Negroes within a segregated system.

The conflict between the self-defined interests of the Army and of Negroes continued throughout the war. Appeals to political power were made by both sides, but no clear legislative decision was reached. Segregation as a concept remained the root question affecting the cleavage between the Negro public and the Army; it was basic to Negro soldiers' attitudes toward the Army and the war; it was useful for political campaign purposes; and it provided a convenient basket to catch most of the problems arising in the employment of Negro troops. Yet it was seldom mentioned in a direct way by either Negroes or the Army during the war, for it was easier to place greater stress upon the many other facets of difficulty which the employment of Negro troops provided. Negroes emphasized clearly discriminatory practices growing out of segregation, such as the lack of opportunities for advancement, differentials in facilities, and limitations upon employment. The Army emphasized the low classification scores, the lack of vocational skills, and other real or apparent deficiencies of Negroes which, though admittedly they might be the result of deprivations in civilian life, obviously, in the Army's view, prevented Negroes from carrying their full share of the military load. These alone, not to speak of civilian patterns in the sections of the country from which most Negroes

[115] *Hearings, Senate, Military Establishment Appropriation Bill for 1941 (H.R. 9209),* 14 May 40, p. 365.

came, were sufficient argument, from the Army's point of view, to oppose the end of separate units.

But there was other support for their maintenance. In an opinion survey conducted in March 1943, the Office of War Information found that nine out of ten whites in five key cities felt that white and Negro troops should be kept separate, while eight out of ten Negroes in the same cities were opposed to segregation.[116] It was obvious that both whites and Negroes could not be satisfied on this point if public opinion was to decide the question.

It could be expected that the Army would attempt to avoid as much as possible the difficulties arising out of providing units for Negroes. The simplest method would have been to reduce the number of Negroes entering the Army to a minimum, though under the Selective Service Act this could not be done legally. But there might be other ways. There were the protective clauses in Section 3 which provided that no man should be inducted "unless and until he is acceptable to the land or naval forces" and until "adequate provision shall have been made for such shelter, sanitary facilities, water supplies, heating and lighting arrangements, medical care, and hospital accommodations. . . ." There were always actual shortages of housing, equipment, and units for Negroes. Educational and literary qualifications might be placed at a point where large numbers of Negroes could be excluded.

But the Negro public and its sympathizers, remembering World War I and now more potent politically than twenty years before, watched carefully for any evidence of failure to adhere fully to the terms of stated policy. Moreover, white citizens in areas with sizable Negro populations did not take kindly to the deferment of large numbers of Negroes while white men were being drafted. A stream of letters continued to come into the White House and the War Department; congressmen were kept busy with inquiries from their constituents; delegations and lobbyists arrived in Washington with great regularity; new and different points of attack were discovered as soon as older ones were cleared up or answered. All of these added up to continuous public pressure, backed by the possibility of further political pressures.

For Negroes as a whole, throughout the war, felt that "Our boys in camps [are] being treated so bad"; "They're not being given a fair chance"; and "They're putting up their lives for nothing to fight for."[117] Relatively few felt that their sons' chances were good in any of the armed services; only three out of ten felt that their chances for advancement in the Army included a chance for a commission. Few felt that their troops would actually be used in battle. Nearly all reported less than full confidence in the Army's desire to use Negro manpower to the fullest possible extent.[118] In voicing their disapproval of the assignment of the majority of Negro troops to noncombatant duties, most Negroes simply said, "This is supposed

---

[116] OWI, The Negroes' Role in the War: A Study of White and Colored Opinions (Memorandum 59, Surveys Division, Bureau of Special Services), 8 Jul 43. This survey was conducted in five cities: Birmingham, Raleigh, Oklahoma City, Chicago, and Detroit.

[117] OWI, The Negroes' Role in the War.
[118] Ibid.

to be a colored man's country, too," or "We should all fight side by side." A few added "They [the whites] will say we did not fight and were behind the lines, so that they can keep us behind after it's over."[119] Their leaders summed up their position in the slogan that Negroes had to fight for the right to fight.[120]

Interest in the progress of plans for defense continued high among Negroes. When interest slackened the Negro press awakened it. The biggest single bloc of news to become available in years was that dealing with opportunities for Negroes in defense preparations, civilian as well as military. Despite the expansion of defense industries, as 1940 closed the unemployment rate among Negroes had been cut only slightly over that of the darkest depression years. The possibility of enlistment in the armed forces had so much greater appeal and promise for impoverished but ambitious youth than the CCC or the NYA that papers needed to do little to awaken the interest of their readers.

As a source of news about Negro troops, the Negro press was unchallenged, for few general circulation dailies carried the normal press releases about the activities of Negro troops. The importance of these papers in molding attitudes and affecting the morale of the youths who would become the Negro troops of World War II was very great. Long before entering the Army many Negroes had formed definite opinions of their chances in the armed forces from their reading of the Negro press and

from the inevitable family and barbershop discussions which followed. Few felt that their chances for advancement or fair treatment were good, but most knew that new opportunities were possible daily. The importance of news of the armed forces to the Negro press, evident though it was in the first months of mobilization when the front pages of Negro papers were filled with news of the armed services, was not fully realized within the War Department until later in the war. Only then was a serious effort made to supply the missing details and add to the variety and veracity of the many armed forces stories carried by the Negro papers, thereby reducing, though not completely removing, the aura of mutual distrust surrounding relations between the Army and the Negro press.

At the end of 1940 it was not possible to answer all the questions raised by the newly announced policies on the employment of Negro troops. Some were not yet asked. A certain tally was, however, possible. The Congress had passed a Selective Service Act with nondiscriminatory clauses. The War Department, urged by pressures generated by the political temper of an election year, had announced a basic policy calling for a proportionate use and distribution of Negro troops. The Army had begun the expansion of its Negro units and it had acquired its first Negro general officer. The Secretary of War had acquired an adviser on Negro affairs.

Future actions of the War Department and the Army were critically awaited by the Negro public. Negro selective service men had not yet begun to be called into the new Army. How the new policy on proportionate Negro

---

[119] Ibid.
[120] Cf. Walter White, "It's Our Country, Too," loc. cit.; The Journal of Negro Education, XII (Summer, 1943).

representation in Army strength would work out, how the Army would provide units in all its major branches, was still anyone's guess. Actually, neither Negroes nor the Army had high hopes for the immediate rapid expansion of Negro strength. No one in 1940 foresaw the huge size to which the Army would ultimately grow or, by virtue of the proportionate representation policy, the unprecedented numbers of Negroes which the Army was committed to take and use. Too many details, ranging from such homely matters as providing training facilities for the new draftees to more world-shaking questions of international strategy had yet to be worked out. At the end of the year the major questions affecting the employment of Negro troops were distinctly of the homelier, though by no means unimportant, variety. Upon these homely questions and upon the pressures which they generated, rather than upon the broad outlines of policy as laid down in mobilization plans or as dictated by the changing military situation, depended the decisions around which the employment of Negro manpower in World War II developed.

CHAPTER IV

Expanding Negro Strength

From the beginning of World War II in Europe to Pearl Harbor the active Negro enlisted strength of the Army increased more than twenty-five-fold, from 3,640 men on 31 August 1939 to 97,725 on 30 November 1941.[1] By the end of December 1942, Negro enlisted strength had risen to 467,883.[2] As already noted this expansion, like the expansion of the whole Army, was far greater than prewar plans had contemplated. In achieving its Negro strength the Army faced and overcame many administrative problems. Others it was unable to solve. Many of these problems revolved about the question of maintaining a proportional balance between Negroes and whites, a question that was ever-present between 1941 and 1943. It affected most of the normal processes incident to the expansion of over-all Army strength.

The Army's difficulty in making room for additional Negroes meant much more than a simple adjustment to large numbers of Negro inductees. The expansion of the Army to its maximum authorized strength was theoretically limited only by the nation's manpower, by appropriations, and by the Army's ability to provide training facilities.

Training facilities involved not only the need for new housing and equipment but also plans for new units, cadres, training and replacement centers, and officers to supervise training and tactical units. All too frequently one or more of these elements were unready or unavailable in carrying out the expansion as planned. These uncertainties affected white trainees too, but not to the same extent as Negro trainees, for white units existed in all branches and in most types. Existing units could provide for the relatively orderly reception and training of white recruits, but the few Regular Negro units were unable to form the needed base for the twenty-five-fold increase in Negro strength before December 1941. In the fall of 1940, Negro recruits destined for most arms and services were assured neither units, billets, nor training cadres.

Initial Expansion

The plan of 1937 for the utilization of Negro manpower in the event of mobilization had provided for an initial rate of increase of Negro strength which would be higher than that for whites in order to bring the proportion of Negroes in the Army up to their proportion in the available manpower of military age. Thereafter, the rate of increase was to continue at the level of the population

---

[1] Misc Div AGO, Returns Sec, 9 Oct 39, 30 Nov 41.

[2] Tab B, Memo, G-3 for CG's AGF and SOS, 25 Jan 43, WDGCT 320.2 Gen (1-25-43).

ratio. Since separate Negro units were to be continued, all calculations had to be based on a close accounting of men by race. The development of the necessary administrative machinery for determining and controlling racial quotas presented immediate difficulties. Furthermore, since the census of 1940 had not been completed by the time the Selective Service Act went into effect, the exact proportions and the geographical distribution of Negroes in the manpower of military age were not available until Selective Service registration figures could be compiled. The dual method of receiving men by ordinary volunteer enlistments and through inductions, the latter including volunteers who entered the Army through Selective Service, complicated the matter of fixing quotas by race. Quota calls, fixed by the Army, had also to be adjusted to the availability of housing and units as well as to the rate of acceptance of volunteers.

To make matters even more complex, in the first year of mobilization a little more than 13 percent of those classified I–A (available for immediate induction) were Negroes instead of the 9 or 10 percent expected. The 3 or 4 percent variation from the estimate may not appear to have been very far off, but when this percentage was applied to large numbers of men it made a considerable difference, in this case, forty to fifty thousand additional men. As time went on, the proportion of Negroes in Class I–A showed every likelihood of increasing instead of diminishing. Relatively few Negroes had industrial, technical, and professional jobs that carried a deferred classification. Proportionately more Negroes than whites were

therefore available for Class I–A. Neither the Navy nor the Marine Corps used Selective Service in the first years of the draft and neither accepted Negroes, except that the Navy used them as messmen and in a few other classifications. White volunteers for the naval services were likely to reduce further the proportion of whites as compared to Negroes in the Selective Service Class I–A category.

If "the balance of Negro and white manpower" was to be maintained, quota calls had to be divided not only among the nine corps areas and subsequently into state and local board quotas but also into racial quotas within those areas according to local racial distributions. To add to the administrative complexities of the situation, the Army, basing its theory on World War I test scores and actual distribution of skills among Negroes, desired proportionately more Northern than Southern Negroes for technical and combat units. As if these complications were not enough, no final decisions on locations, types of units, or housing facilities for Negro selectees had been made by the fall and winter of 1940–41. Several branches—notably the Signal Corps and the Air Corps—were still attempting to avoid accepting any Negroes, and others were attempting to keep their number as small as possible. All of these factors helped to delay the mobilization of the Negro portion of the Army considerably, and as a result the expansion of the Army began without obtaining anything like the officially desired initial proportionate balancing of white and Negro troops.

Since calls for Negro troops, according to the Selective Service Act and according to the laws of chance by which the

draft lottery was operated, should have
occurred on the whole at the same rate
as for white troops, Selective Service
proceeded to classify Negroes as their
names appeared on local board listings.
When their numbers were reached, Selective Service, lacking sufficient Army
requisitions for the numbers of Negroes
available, sent them "notices of selection." These notices indicated that the
recipients had been selected for induction and that they would be ordered to
report at a later date—how far off Selective Service could not say. Many Negroes quit or lost their jobs because of
these notices. Some, not actually inducted for months, complained bitterly
about the delay and about their resulting
unemployment, for employers were reluctant to hire a man who already had a
notice of selection. Of course delayed
inductions affected white as well as
Negro inductees, but in a much lower
proportion of instances.

With the low and uncertain economic
position of Negroes as the dominant factor and with the "passed over" policy
as an added incentive, many Negroes
volunteered through Selective Service.
As of 30 September 1941, the number
of Negro volunteers was 38,538, or 16.1
percent of the total number of volunteers entering the Army through Selective Service and more than a third of all
the Negroes in the Army. Of the volunteers awaiting induction on this date,
25.3 percent were Negroes.[3] The vol-
unteer-through-Selective-Service figures
were made higher because of an additional factor: it was still almost impossible for Negroes to volunteer through

regular recruiting stations. All volunteers moved to the top of local Selective
Service board lists without regard to
race. In some cases, the rate of Negro
volunteering was so high that local
boards did not have to call on selectees
at all to fill their quotas.

Calls for Negroes up through January
1941 were deferred. The February call
was for but a small part of the Negroes
originally allotted for that month. In
New York, for example, 900 Negroes
were selected in January 1941 and notified to expect induction in February.
Because of construction delays at Fort
Devens, Mass., where they were to have
been sent, approximately 500 of these
men were not inducted in February but
were carried over to March. Those
originally scheduled for the February
and March calls were consequently delayed. In the District of Columbia,
1,100 white men and no Negroes at all
were called for March.[4]

Time did not improve the situation.
By September 1941, the total number
of Negroes passed over and awaiting
induction was 27,986, with the possibility that 17,399 of these would remain
uncalled on 1 January 1942. To these,
the Negroes who were reached in October, November, and December and were
not to be inducted in those months had
to be added.[5] For February 1942, the
voluntary enlistment of Negroes
through recruiting stations was reduced
to fifty a week—five from each corps area.
The March selectees were reduced to a
minimum in an attempt to avoid the
threatened congestion of available housing in reception centers, units, and in-

[3] *Selective Service in Peacetime: First Report of
the Director of Selective Service, 1940–41* (Washington, 1942), p. 256.

[4] *Ibid.*, pp. 254–56.
[5] Incl to Ltr, Dir Selective Sv to SW, 4 Oct 41,
AG 324.71 (10–4–41).

stallations.[6] By early 1943, the War Manpower Commission estimated that approximately 300,000 Negroes had been passed over to fill white calls.[7]

Some local boards protested vigorously. "We do hereby record our belief and opinion," an Ohio local board wrote, "that the February call for nine *white* men is unfair, unjust, and discriminatory against both the white and colored races. This arbitrary method of induction of men by color rather than by order number we believe is a flagrant and totalitarian violation of both the letter and spirit of the law." [8] South Carolina boards likewise objected that too few Negro selectees were being called.[9] The Director of Selective Service warned:

This general situation permits both Negroes who have volunteered for induction and white men who have higher order numbers, but who are inducted before the Negroes with lower order numbers, to claim, whether justified or not, that there is discrimination contrary to the provisions of the law.[10]

He recommended that "unusual efforts" be made to bring requisitions for each state into line with the racial distribution of the population of the state.

This situation did not grow up over-night, nor was the War Department unaware of the possibility of its development. From the time of the debates on the Selective Service Act, the General Staff divisions had warned of the necessity for prompt action to prevent such a racial imbalance in the expanding forces. But the staff divisions could not agree on how, short of strict induction by order number, such a situation could be prevented. Induction by order number, the staff divisions feared, might produce what was considered an even more undesirable imbalance: a tremendous disproportion of Negroes in comparison with whites which would, at the end of the first year's training, be followed by a reverse imbalance.

In October 1940, G–1 urged that the War Department make provision to bring the Army's proportion of Negroes up to 10 percent, since new census estimates indicated that, instead of the expected 9 percent provided for in the 1940 PMP, 10.07 percent of the population affected by the draft would be Negroes. "The longer the delay in setting up such requirements," the Personnel Division warned, "the greater will be the number of Negroes which will ultimately have to be taken to meet the requirements of the law and satisfy public demand." [11] Though G–3 objected that disruption of construction of housing and hospitalization facilities or an increase in the number of Negroes in overhead would result, the War Department, in December 1940, directed that the troop basis for the distribution of trainees be refigured so that by July 1941 10 percent of the

[6] Memo, G–1 for TAG, and Memo for Record, 31 Jan 42, G–1/15640–135; Rad, TAG to CG's Corps Areas, 4 Feb 42, AG 342 (1–31–42) E–R–A.
[7] Ltr, Paul V. McNutt, Chairman War Manpower Commission, to SW, 17 Feb 43, AG 324.71 (2–17–43).
[8] "Resolution—Protest," Selective Sv Local Bd 13, Cuyahoga County, Ohio, 3 Feb 41, Incl to Ltr, Dir Selective Sv System to SW, 14 Feb 41, AG 324.71 (9–19–40), sec. 1. Italics in original.
[9] Memo, G–3 for TAG, 26 Feb 42, and attached Memo for Record, G–3 6547–399.
[10] Ltr, C. A. Dykstra, Dir Selective Sv System, to SW, 14 Feb 41, AG 324.71 (9–19–40) sec. 1.

[11] Memo, G–1 for CofS, 21 Oct 40, AG 381 (8–31–39) (1) sec. 1.

men in training under the Selective Service Act would be Negroes.[12]

Answering Selective Service's objections to the disproportionately low acceptances of Negro selectees, the War Department explained that it had been impossible to take a "proper percentage of negroes because of lack of shelter and cadres." The department promised Selective Service that it would "make every effort" to keep the proportions of white and Negro selectees balanced if Selective Service would keep a check on the states to prevent them from placing "an undue proportion" of Negroes in Class I–A.[13]

In March 1941, G–3 estimated that because of their higher rate of volunteering, their lower economic status, and their consequent lower percentage of draft deferment, the proportion of Negroes entering the Army might go as high as 14 percent. Replacement center allocations should therefore be increased to provide for a 13 to 14 percent proportion of Negro selectees and existing Negro units should be brought up to full strength. An infantry replacement center for Negroes should be established at Fort Huachuca, Arizona, and a 10 percent overstrength should be authorized for Negro units and overhead troops. To provide for additional Negro troops, new construction and the substitution of Negroes for white troops to the extent necessary were recommended. G–3 observed as well that, unless the War Department made reasonably prompt provisions for the induction of Negroes, legal action might compel it to do so.[14]

The Supply Division pointed out that it would be more economical to convert white units in the PMP to Negro and use existing or planned housing rather than construct additional housing especially for Negroes. G–4 estimated that $13,-554,400 would be needed to build a replacement center at Fort Huachuca and to provide the additional construction needed elsewhere for the accommodation of Negro selectees.[15] Maj. Gen. William Bryden, Deputy Chief of Staff, agreed that this expenditure was not justified. Housing vacated by National Guard units departing at the end of their year's training might be used by Negroes. Moreover, General Bryden felt, if the Army refused to induct illiterates the number of Negro selectees would be reduced.[16] The G–3 recommendations were approved by the Chief of Staff with the stipulation that no additional construction was to be authorized. Temporary overstrength was to be housed in tents, and if necessary excess personnel was to be sent direct to units instead of to replacement centers.[17]

When the first requisitions for inductees were submitted to the states by corps area commanders in November 1940, it was impossible to determine by race the number that would appear. Some states had not broken their regis-

---

[12] Memo, OCS for G–1, 26 Nov 40, AG 381 (8–31–39) sec. 1; Ltr, TAG to CG's, Corps Area Comdrs, etc., 11 Dec 40, AG 381 (10–21–40) M–A–M.

[13] Memo, G–1 for CofS, 20 Feb 41, G–1/15640–79; Ltr, Actg SW to Dr. C. A. Dykstra, Dir Selective Sv System, 24 Feb 41, AG 324.71 (2–14–41) M.

[14] Memo, G–3 for CofS, and attached papers, 10 Mar 41, G–3/6541–Gen–527.

[15] Memo, G–4 for CofS, 11 Apr 41, G–4/31981. Earlier, G–4 had suggested unit conversions as an economy measure. Cf., Memo, G–4 for G–1, 13 Nov 40, AG 381 (8–31–39) sec. 1.

[16] Memo, DCofS for CofS, 26 Apr 41, OCS 20602-161.

[17] Memo, OCofS for G–3, 5 May 41, OCS/20602-161.

trants down by color. Only the Fourth Corps Area [18] submitted requisitions to the states by color, and the Fourth was able to do so only because delays in construction caused a corresponding delay in the submission of the corps area's requisitions. This delay gave the commanding general time to request permission of the War Department to submit, on his first call, separate requests for whites and Negroes.[19] An excess of men over available space was likely in any event, for the National Guard units already inducted had brought more men than anticipated. The allotted strength of Guard units had been increased for the fiscal year 1941 and many of these units had recruited to full peacetime strength. A number of inactive Guardsmen had also been called to duty. Moreover, Regular Army enlistments under the authorized increase from 242,000 to 375,000 enlisted men had exceeded expectations. As a result of shelter shortages, instructions were sent to all corps area commanders directing them to specify the numbers of men desired by color in all future periods.[20] Since no information on the total number of Negroes and whites who would be inducted would be available until the first induction period closed on 28 November, all corps area commanders were authorized to use reception centers for temporary assign-

ments to take care of any excess in either race.

This did not settle the matter. The First Corps Area (New England) discovered that Connecticut boards were not inducting by color. The First's requisitions had to be increased to cover this contingency. It was instructed to hold at Fort Devens Reception Center any excess Negroes who might appear. They could be used in the 336th Infantry, scheduled for activation in February 1941.[21]

Corps areas were not mutually exclusive organizations in the disposition of selectees. The Fourth Corps Area, by its own request, was given authority to submit requisitions to the states for 5,500 white and 1,000 Negro men. But the Second Corps Area (New York, New Jersey, and Delaware) was authorized to ship 500 Negroes to Fort Benning, Georgia, in the Fourth Corps Area for the 24th Infantry and 290 to Fort Huachuca, Arizona, in the Eighth Corps Area (southwestern states) for the 25th Infantry. The commanding general of the Fourth Corps Area radioed the War Department that shelter was not available at Benning for the 24th's new men. The Second Corps Area was then instructed to ship no men to Benning but to send the entire 790 to the 25th Infantry.[22]

The result was that for several months Negro inductees were assigned to units neither by occupational specialities, by educational background, by tested aptitudes, nor by any other classification method. They were assigned accord-

---

[18] Of corps areas, the Fourth (the southeastern states, excluding Virginia and Kentucky) contained by far the largest number and percentages of Negroes.

[19] Memo, G–1 for the CofS, 8 Nov 40, AG 324.71 (11-8-40).

[20] WD Ltr, AG 324.71 (10–15–40), dated 17 Oct 40, had already provided for requisitions by color, but this provision had been canceled.

[21] Memo, G–1 for TAG, 23 Dec 40, AG 324.71 (12–23–40) (1).

[22] Memo, G–1 for TAG, 20 Nov 40, AG 324.71 (11–18–40).

ing to the numbers of men received and according to the availability of space in units. A unit which required 250 men in order to reach its authorized strength would not receive them if its station had no additional housing for Negro troops, while a unit which needed no additional men but whose post had available housing might be swamped with successive increments of men. Normally, reception centers assigned men on the basis of occupational skills, n accordance with tables which had been worked out for each branch of service, and, later, for each type of unit. These tables showed the approximate proportion of each occupational speciality which a given type of unit would require. But so long as replacement centers were not receiving Negroes and so long as the number of Negro units was small, Negro selectees had to be assigned primarily on the basis of the numbers and not the types of men required. The new Negro units, from the beginning of the expansion of Negro strength, therefore received large numbers of men who did not fit the needs of the unit. This was frequently true for white units as well, but seldom for the same reasons and seldom with so little probability of correction.

The 41st Engineer General Service Regiment, one of the new units activated in August 1940, discovered by the end of December 1940 that most of its selectees did not have "the qualities of intelligence, education and initiative highly enough developed to qualify them for duty in a general service regiment." [23] Engineer general service regiments were supposed to be able to do all types

of engineer work in army areas, including construction of roads and bridges and operation of utilities. The unskilled labor unit with which these units were often confused was the engineer separate battalion. It was not widely realized that general service regiments required a high percentage of skilled labor and a relatively high average of ability on the part of the individual men. The Chief of Engineers recommended that reception centers send only men of average or better classification to these units. The War Department in denying his request stated that it was impossible, at the time, to assign Negroes on any other than a numerical basis. It suggested that whenever new Negro engineer units with lower requirements, such as separate battalions, became available, the 41st could transfer its unsuitable men to these units. [24]

The 7th Aviation Squadron illustrated the opposite effect of assignment by availability. Aviation squadrons were, primarily, labor units assigned to air bases. Of the 7th Squadron's 220 men, most of whom had come from the Middle Atlantic States, approximately half had high school and college training at a time when new combat units were bemoaning the lack of adequately schooled selectees. The occupational qualifications of the men in this unit, as compared with their educational qualifications, illustrated another major difficulty in organizing new Negro units. Despite the relatively high educational qualifications of the men of this unit, few skilled occupations were represented. Aside from teachers and students, the better-trained men, on the

[23] Ltr, OCofE to TAG, 24 Jan 41, AG 324.71 (1–24–41) (1) sec. 12.

[24] Memo, G–1 for TAG, 1 Feb 41, and 1st Ind, 5 Feb 41, both in AG 324.71 (1–24–41) (1) sec. 12.

average, had no higher occupational skills than the less well trained men. Most of those with a year or more of college training had been working as porters, shipping clerks, sales clerks, maintenance men, bartenders, chauffeurs, kitchen helpers, and miners. What secondary skills these men might have had could not be determined from their occupational histories. The more highly skilled men, such as auto mechanics, sheet metal workers, power pressmen, factory foremen, carpenters, and photographers were seldom high school graduates. The relationship of jobs to education was directly related to the prewar economic status of Negroes. Young graduates of high schools and colleges had had to take whatever jobs were available; skilled jobs were scarce. Nevertheless Judge Hastie felt that these men, despite the misuse of their training in civilian life, would have been more useful in technical and combat units than in the squadron to which they were assigned.[25]

In an attempt to rectify the situation produced by numerical assignment without specific relation to qualifications, a series of shifts in procurement requisitions took place in the spring of 1941. Fifty semiliterate selectees, to be employed as aircraft hands, painters, mess attendants, and guards, were ordered transferred from the 34th Coast Artillery Brigade (AA) to the Air Corps at Chanute Field, Illinois. These men were to be replaced by fifty relatively skilled men—receiving and shipping clerks, electricians, automobile mechan-

ics, metal workers, radio operators, and draftsmen—from the Second Corps Area. The shift was explained as necessary in order to give the 34th Brigade a better distribution of intelligence and skills. The Second Corps Area, it was thought, could best provide the skilled men desired by the 34th and at the same time provide the skilled men needed to complete the Chanute Field requirement, while the 34th Brigade could provide the unskilled men needed at Chanute from its own overabundant supply of untrained men.[26]

Similarly, a requisition on the Sixth Corps Area (Michigan, Wisconsin, and Illinois) for 596 selectees for shipment to the Ordnance Replacement Center at Aberdeen Proving Ground, Maryland, was canceled. The 34th Brigade was directed to send 300 low scoring selectees to Aberdeen. The Second Corps Area would send 596 selectees to the 34th Brigade with qualifications determined by antiaircraft regimental tables of organization, and 296 men to the Ordnance Replacement Center. The reasoning was the same: some 300 men of the Fourth Corps' 34th Brigade were in low classification grades or illiterate; ordnance ammunition companies "need approximately 50 percent skill and intelligence; 50 percent should be 'strong backed' labor." It was assumed that the Second Corps Area could provide the skill and intelligence needed by both types of units, while the Fourth Corps Area could provide the "strong backed" labor from men already misassigned to the 34th Coast Artillery Brigade.[27]

[25] Memos, Civ Aide to SW for TAG, 5 Sep 41 and 21 Oct 41, both in AG 327.31 (9-19-41) (1) sec. 12; Memo, G-1 for TAG, 29 Oct 41, G-1/8645-762.

[26] Memo, G-1 for TAG, 20 Mar 41, AG 327.31 (9-19-40) (1) sec. 12.
[27] Memo, G-1 for TAG, 27 Mar 41, AG 327.31 (9-19-40) (1) sec. 12.

Similar shifting of procurement quotas continued through the spring of 1941. New Fourth Corps Area allotments for the 99th and 100th Coast Artillery (AA) (SM) to be activated at Camp Davis, North Carolina, were canceled and reallotments were made to include Northern and Middle Western areas in order to give these regiments "required occupational skills and intelligence not available in colored selectees from the Fourth Corps Area." [28]

Shifts of personnel, though calculated to relieve the maldistribution of skills and training in certain units, could also relieve the pressures created by large numbers of passed-over Negro selectees in politically sensitive areas. For one shift, G–1 noted that "postponing induction of 1608 colored selectees from June to July in the Fourth Corps Area will have no repercussions in that corps area," while for another shift it was explained that passed-over Negro selectees in Illinois could be taken care of by a reallotment of corps area quotas. [29]

Actually, the shifts for purposes of improving the distribution of skills had little good effect. Despite the fact that Northern corps areas had a greater percentage of skilled Negroes than Southern, the availability of the desired types of men at a given time in a given reception center was limited. So long as assignment by numerical availability and not by careful classification methods was employed, Negro units in which the shifts occurred were not much better off after the shifts than before. Many other units in which maldistribution resulting from numerical block assignment occurred had no opportunity to benefit from subsequent transfers of men.

Other annoyances arose out of the necessity of balancing white and Negro manpower by units. Occasionally a unit appearing as Negro in the War Department mobilization plan or, later, in the troop unit basis was carried as white by the corps area or command to which it was allotted. Radiograms directing reallotments of whites and Negroes then bounced back and forth between the War Department and the corps area and camp commanders concerned. At times, such difficulties were corrected before shipment was made. [30] In a few instances Negro troops appeared when whites were expected and sometimes the reverse occurred.

The situation arose, in part, from the decision to remove the term "colored" as an inseparable part of a unit's designation. Older Negro units had carried the identification as a part of the unit name, for example, 47th Quartermaster Truck Regiment (Cld). In 1940, as a result of protests over the similar designation of certain National Guard units and as part of the decision that all Army units were to be trained, equipped, and employed alike, regardless of race, the identifying term was dropped. [31] Des-

---

[28] Memo, G–1 for TAG, 9 May 41, G–1/15640–85, AG 327.31 (9–19–40) (1) sec. 12.

[29] Memo, G–1 for TAG and attached Memo for Record, 27 Mar 41; Memo, G–1 for TAG and Memo for Record, 6 Jun 41. Both in AG 327.31 (9–19–40) (1) sec. 12.

[30] Memo, G–1 for TAG, 28 Apr 41, AG 327.31 (9–19–40) (1) sec. 12.

[31] Tel, NAACP to SW, 13 Jun 40, Ltr, NAACP to the President, 13 Jun 40, and Inds, TAG and CofNGB, 17–18 Jun 40, all in AG 080 (NAACP) (6–13–40) (1); Ltr, TAG to Chiefs, CG's, CO's Exempted Stations, 18 Jul 40, AG 320.2 (6–15–40); AR 220–5, par. 7, 18 Sep 42; WD Cir 351, 21 Oct 42.

ignations such as "this is a colored unit" or "a colored unit" were permitted, if needed. Obviously, such designations were cumbersome and might easily be overlooked. To avoid repeating these awkward phrases, the custom of using an asterisk and an accompanying footnote indicating race soon came to be the accepted means of identifying Negro units in station lists, orders, or in any list of units.[32] Since asterisks could easily be transposed to the wrong unit or omitted entirely, station and troop lists became notoriously unreliable in this respect. To prevent such errors, agencies shipping men were ultimately required to notify the receiving agency that the shipment contained Negroes. If the men were accompanied by officers, their race was to be indicated as well. The receiving agency was, by this means, enabled to prepare billets and other facilities on a separate basis in advance of the arrival of troops, thus avoiding all-around "embarrassment." [33] Troop lists, despite all precautions, remained unreliable in their identification of Negro units. Occasional mix-ups occurred throughout the war.

Housing

The amount of construction needed to house the new Army was tremendous. Vast acreages had to be purchased or leased, and graded and laid out, before construction could begin. Contracts had to be let, construction gangs had to be recruited, transported, and housed, and emergency changes in construction plans had to be made. Priorities for projects had to be established.[34] Despite initial allotments of a portion of the new construction to Negroes, the provision of housing for Negro troops was relatively slow and uncertain.

In the spring of 1941, G–4 conducted a survey of all camps and exempted stations to determine where housing, without additional construction, was already available. Most exempted stations replied that they had no housing available for Negro troops, and, in some cases, that they had no housing available at all.[35] Corps areas reported few camps with facilities for more than a small number of additional Negroes: 50 at Fort Eustis, 343 at Fort Belvoir, 5 at Fort Myer, 132 at Fort Knox, 640 at Fort Riley, 40 at Jefferson Barracks, 92 at Fort Ord, 202 at Camp Luis Obispo, and 32 at Camp Edwards were typical of the reports. The entire Fourth Corps Area had facilities, without additional construction, for only 4,851 more Negroes, 2,646 of whom could be placed in station complements at fourteen posts.[36]

Much of the difficulty arose from the physical layouts of posts and from the varying definitions of what constituted available housing for Negroes. Not every area of currently unused housing was available for Negro troops. An area constructed to house divisional troops

---

[32] The footnote asterisk became official with the publication of AR 220–5, 18 September 1942.

[33] Memo, AGF DCofS for AGF Opns Div, 2 Jun 42, and M/S, AGF Opns Div to AGF DCofS, 4 Jun 42, both in AGF 322.999/70 (Cld Trps); Ltr, TAG to CG's, 7 Jul 42, AG 291.21 (7–24–42).

[34] Leonore Fine and Jesse A. Remington, Construction in the United States, MS in preparation for a volume in UNITED STATES ARMY IN WORLD WAR II, ch. VI.

[35] Exempted stations included depots, arsenals, and similar installations, many of which had no troops authorized and therefore had no housing. Other exempted stations, such as ports, were still in the planning and construction stage.

[36] Ltrs and Msgs in AG 600.12 (5–24–41) (1).

would normally be held for divisional use. A division required a continuous block of housing and the attendant motor parks, shops, and recreational and mess facilities which were necessary to its efficient training as a unit. Because the maximum size of a Negro unit in the first years of expansion was set at the brigade level, divisional areas were not available for Negro troops at all. Negro units had to be put in the barracks and tent areas that remained after divisions and their attached units had been housed.

Theoretically, new housing was allocated to Negro units on a proportionate basis, but many posts had not expected to receive a proportionate number of Negroes. Moreover, the number of Negroes on a given post was expected to be small enough to allay the fears of surrounding communities—small enough, that is, to be certain that the white troops present could control any racial disorders that might arise. This meant that not too many Negroes— though the numbers often exceeded 10 percent—could be assigned to a given post.

Again, housing for Negroes had to be located so as to carry out the principle of segregation by units. This required an extension of segregation into the allotment of housing. The main portion of a camp, often constructed in a huge arc with parade grounds and headquarters near the center and hospital wards and warehouses at either end, was allotted to divisional and attached units or to other large units assigned to the camp. Off at a tangent from the main sweep of camp buildings, a regimental or smaller area was constructed for Negro troops. All Negro units assigned to

the post had to be fitted into this or similar blocks of housing. Initially these areas, as at Fort Dix, New Jersey, and Fort Devens, Massachusetts, were at a considerable distance from the main camp area. Later construction filled in the intervening spaces, usually with warehouses, stockades, and motor parks rather than with barracks. Usually the Negro areas remained distinct and separate, though in some of the newer camps, such as Camp Breckinridge, Kentucky, and Camp Ellis, Illinois, they were merely separated from identical white quarters by a parade ground or a fire break. The Negro area came to be known as such; often it was so shown on camp layouts. It was, essentially, a separate camp adjoining the major portion of the post. It was usually provided with its own branch exchange, its own recreation hall, and, later, its own motion picture house, its own chapel, and, if the area were large enough, its own service club and guest house.[37]

In most cases, the result was that available housing for Negroes was not measured by available vacancies but by vacancies in the Negro area. Conversely, available housing for whites was limited to housing outside the Negro area, unless all Negroes could be removed from the section of the post involved. An objection from Fort Leonard Wood explained a type of housing-strength problem arising from this procedure:

The schedule attached to the basic letter includes 1,760 white trainees for the week of December 7–13, which number is apparently based on the assumption that one battalion of white trainees could be

_____
[37] The provision of recreational facilities is treated in Chapter XI, below.

substituted for one of colored trainees in order to fill this center to its limit of capacity, inasmuch as the schedule provides for a total of 8 battalions of white trainees and two of colored trainees. Such a substitution is not practicable. There are barracks at this station for 7 battalions of white trainees in one area, and for 3 battalions (one battalion less one company) of colored trainees in another area well separated from the area for white trainees. Further, the enlisted cadres of 3 battalions (one battalion less one company) are colored troops.[38]

Housing by race meant that if Negro increments did not arrive in training centers according to schedule the whole training process for Negro troops was delayed. Delays in filling a training unit meant delays not only for that unit but for the next unit to follow. The influx of Negro trainees into the Camp Wheeler (Georgia) Infantry Replacement Training Center was so slow in the summer of 1941 that the 16th Training Battalion, consisting of Negro trainees, was not able to start training three of its five rifle companies until September, though all companies had been scheduled to start training in August. Housing for the October load therefore was not available until November when the delayed companies had completed their training. Eight hundred and eighty trainees had to be deferred until housing became available for them.[39] Similarly, at the Fort Bragg (North Carolina) Field Artillery Replacement Training Center, the arrival of Negroes in small groups produced an excess of trainees over housing capacity. Small groups for specialist training had to wait until their numbers were built up to a point where classes were of sufficient size to make training feasible. The waiting men took up space which grew cumulatively more valuable as successive increments arrived. "The shipment of colored trainees in small groups results in unsatisfactory specialist training," the center reported.[40]

The housing shortage slowed up or postponed the training of many of the new Negro units. The 41st Engineer General Service Regiment, activated in August 1940, could not expect housing accommodations for its full complement of 1,176 men until 15 January 1941. In October 1940 the unit requested 800 additional men as soon as possible since by 15 February 1941 it was scheduled to furnish cadres totaling 562 men. The unit was told that housing difficulties precluded expansion beyond a total of 835 men and that space had been allotted for only 140 new men. Abandonment of unit training to the extent necessary to provide for cadre training was authorized. By December the unit had 697 men, with 425 new selectees due from the Fourth Corps Area in January. When the unit asked for permission to enlist locally a maximum of 375 men to make up its deficiency, the request was denied since the Third Corps Area (Pennsylvania, Maryland, District of Columbia, and Virginia) had 375 passed-over selectees whom it could and would send to the unit as soon as housing was available.[41] The 54th Coast

---

[38] 1st Ind, Hq ERTC Ft. Leonard Wood, Mo., to TAG, 8 Sep 41, AG 327.71 (7–3–41).

[39] Ltr, CG Cp Wheeler, Ga., to TAG, 4 Sep 41, AG 324.71 (9–4–41).

[40] 1st Ind to Ltr, TAG to CG FARTC, Ft. Bragg, N.C., 10 Sep 41, AG 324.71 C (9–31–41).

[41] Ltrs, AG 221 (10–19–40), AG 221 (10–31–40); Memo, G–1 for TAG, 13 Nov 40, G–1/15640–52; Rad, CG Fourth Corps Area to TAG, 19 Dec 40, and Memo, G–1 for TAG, 21 Dec 40, both in AG 341 (7–10–39) sec. 2A, pt. 3.

Artillery, originally scheduled for activation at Barrancas, Florida, was moved from that station at the request of the Navy Department. Its activation was subsequently delayed by slow construction of Camp Wallace, Texas, its new station. The arrival of both the regiment's cadre and its selectees was held up until construction could be completed. Lack of housing was also the bottleneck holding up The Surgeon General's entire program for the use of Negroes, for Negro Medical Department personnel could not begin training until separate shelter and housekeeping facilities were constructed.[42]

A minor byproduct of the housing shortage in 1941 was the effect upon training and discipline in units already activated. Often, Negro units awaiting fillers, who were, in turn, awaiting space in replacement training centers and reception centers, shared vacant housing with other units. Later, the fact that the sharing unit failed to receive adequate space of its own left the host unit with crowded quarters. The 41st Engineer General Service Regiment complained that "on a basis of neighborly obligation" it had shared its infirmary and officers' quarters with the 96th Engineers. This arrangement created friction through division of responsibility, intermingling of soldiers, and crowding of quarters. The 41st requested quarters for "our sister organization" so that each unit could control all activities in its own area. The 758th Tank Battalion and the 371st Infantry made similar requests for housing for units which

had to share their areas' supply, mess, and infirmary facilities.[43]

Camp Locations

In addition to the availability of housing at stations designated for the receipt of Negro troops, the physical location of camps to which Negroes were to be sent was itself a determining factor in procurement and assignment. Finding suitable camps for training Negro troops was to vex the War Department—and Negro soldiers—throughout the war. The answer was not simply one of locating suitable barracks space and training facilities within areas under Army jurisdiction. Purely military considerations played but a small part in determining the location of Negro troops in the early period of mobilization. The main considerations were: availability of housing and facilities on the post concerned; proportions of white and Negro troops at the post; proximity to civilian centers of Negro population with good recreational facilities that could absorb sizable numbers of Negroes on pass; and the attitude of the nearby civilian community to the presence of Negro troops.

Many communities objected to the presence of any Negro troops at all. Others objected to the presence of certain categories: military policemen, combat troops, officers, Northern troops. Community attitudes also fluctuated from time to time. It had long been one of the canons of War Department

[42] Memo, SGO, Maj Arthur B. Welsh, to Gen Love, 27 Dec 40, SGO 291.21–1940.

[43] Ltr, Hq 41st Engr Gen Sv Regt, Ft. Bragg, N.C., to CG Ft. Bragg, 23 Dec 41, approved, 9th Ind, AGF to CofE, 18 Apr 42, AG 600.13/476; Ltr, Hq 758th Tk Bn (L) GHQ Reserve, to CO Cp Claiborne, La., 5 Mar 42, AGF 600.12/539; Ltr, Hq CT 371, Cp Robinson, Ark., to CG Cp Robinson, 10 Nov 42, and 7 Inds, AGF 620/234.

policy, based on a past history of riots and disturbances there, that no Negro units should be mobilized in Texas.[44] Although the order on which this policy was based was rescinded in 1937,[45] the prohibition still operated in fact. The policy did not prevent citizens of less prosperous areas in Texas from requesting camps near their towns. The postmaster of Calvert, Texas, pointed out that there was a large Negro population in his town, that the two races got along well together, and that plenty of wood, good soil, and natural gas were available. "Our cotton crop on our upland East of Calvert was a failure, we haven't had a C. C. Camp in our county, our town, also our county population certainly needs something to stimulate business and employment," he added.[46] On the other hand Arizona citizens, who had requested Negro troops in 1940, were ready by 1943 to petition that Negro troops be withdrawn and that no more be sent to the state.[47]

A great many communities could not be convinced that the exigencies of the situation demanded the stationing of Negro troops in their vicinities. They often made their views known through their congressmen. An early and typi-cal protest came from Representative Patrick H. Drewry of Virginia on behalf of the citizens of Petersburg. In September 1940, before the opening of Camp Lee and before the large expansion of Negro manpower, Representative Drewry visited General Marshall and the chief of the War Plans Division to ask that, in view of racial difficulties in Petersburg during World War I, no Negro troops other than a small number of labor troops be stationed at Camp Lee.[48] One of the first "correctives" to the fear of potential race riots was formulated in connection with this request. As a supplement to plans already made to establish quartermaster and medical replacement centers at Lee with a peak load of 19,000 trainees, 3,500 of whom would be Negroes, G–3 proposed that a rifle company of the 12th Infantry be made available if necessary to help prevent race riots. The Chief of Staff approved the G–3 proposal and Negro troops were assigned to Camp Lee.[49] The 12th Infantry's rifle company was never needed.

Another type of protest, based on the inability of a camp town to provide recreational facilities for Negroes on pass, came from Wyoming. Early in 1941, Senator Schwartz asked that the number of Negroes stationed at Fort Warren be reduced because of the small Negro population in Cheyenne. In April 1941, the June quota of 500 Negroes for Fort Warren was accordingly changed to 500 for Camp Lee.[50] This

---

[44] Memo, OCS for G–3, 17 Jun 29, OCS 13984–127; Memo, G–3 for CofS, 22 Jun 29, G–3/6541–Gen–272; Ltr, TAG to CG Eighth Corps Area, 25 Jun 29, AG 381 (6–17–29) (1).

[45] Ltr, TAG to CG Eighth Corps Area, 3 Dec 37, AG 391 (11–24–37) (Misc) A.

[46] Ltr, A. K. Tyson to Representative Luther A. Johnson, 28 Oct 40, and Ltr, Representative Johnson to SW, 4 Nov 40, both in AG 680.1 (11–4–40) (7).

[47] Ltr, Santa Cruz Chamber of Commerce, Nogales, to NAACP, 24 Oct 40, AG 291.21 (10–28–40) (1); AGF DF, 22 Jul 42, AGF 291.2 (7–17–42); Memo, TIG for DCofS, 2 Mar 43, IG 333/1–93d Inf Div (Sp); Memo, G–3 for CG's, 1 May 43, AGF 322.999/7 (Cld Trps).

[48] Memos, WPD for CofS, 26 Sep 40 and 10 Oct 40, AG 324.71 (9–26–40) (1).

[49] Memo, G–3 for WPD, 5 Oct 40, and D/S, OCofS to G–3 and WPD, 16 Oct 40, AG 324.71 (9–26–40) (1).

[50] Memo, G–3 for TAG, 21 Apr 41, AG 324.71 (4–21–41).

reduction produced a local housing snag at Fort Warren. The Seventh Corps Area declared that the reduction of Negroes and the substitution of white men could not be accomplished if strict segregation was to be held to:

Substitution can be made but segregation can not repeat can not be accomplished stop no housing available for any increased quota of white selectees except in barracks adjacent to colored selectees stop strongly recommend that white and colored selectees be segregated stop consider vacant space in area for colored troops Ft Warren replacement center advisable rather than quartering white and colored together repeat strongly recommend no substitution . . . of white for colored selectees be made at QMRC end.[51]

In the meantime the city provided local recreational facilities for Negroes and Cheyenne protests were modified.[52]

In 1942, protests about the location of Negro troops continued to pour into the War Department from all over the country. The state of Mississippi and Camp Wheeler, Georgia, wanted no Negro officers.[53] The citizens of Rapid City, South Dakota, were afraid that their town could not offer the proper entertainment facilities for Negro troops. A "thunder of complaints" went up from all over the state when a Negro cavalry regiment was ordered to Fort Clark, Texas.[54] Albuquerque, New Mexico, and Spokane, Washington, citizens ob-

jected to stationing Negro Air Forces units at nearby fields, for they felt that their own Negro populations were too small to provide social contacts for Negro men. Las Vegas, Nevada, and Battle Creek, Michigan, objected to military police and field artillery units respectively. When the citizens of Morehead City, North Carolina, heard that a white coast artillery station at nearby Fort Mason was going overseas and would be replaced by a Negro unit, they asked their senators and congressmen to intervene.[55]

In November 1941 General Marshall directed his staff to resurvey the allocation of Negro units, "with the idea of planning a proper proportion of Negro personnel at locations adjacent to communities with a large colored population." [56] The staff consulted army and corps area commanders, and post, camp, and station commanders reported their observations and recommendations through the corps area commanders. These reports indicated that, aside from small station complement detachments of service troops, few post or higher commanders felt that additional Negro troops could be accommodated without causing protests or resentment from nearby civilian communities. Negro troops, according to the post commanders, would be resented at five out of six Northern posts, over half of the Southern posts,

---

[51] Rad, Seventh Corps Area to TAG, 26 Apr 41, AG 324.71 (4–25–41). See also Ltr, CG Ft. Warren QMRC to CG Seventh Corps Area, 18 Jun 41, AG 324.71 (6–18–41).

[52] Ltr, Senator Schwartz to Gen Marshall, 29 Apr 41, AG 324.71 (3–22–41) (1).

[53] Memo, AGF G–1 for G–3, 5 May 42, AGF 210.31/102.

[54] Ltr, CG AGF to Representative Charles L. South, 24 Jun 42, AG 322.17/1 (9th Cav); Min Gen Council, 30 Jun 42.

[55] Memo, AG for TAG, 13 Mar 42, AGF 322.999/8 (Cld Trps); Ltr, Spokane Chamber of Commerce to SW, 17 Dec 42, AG 291.21 (12–4–42) (8); Ltr, Senator Mon C. Wallgren to SW, 10 Dec 42, AG 291.21 (12–10–42) (12–4–42) (2); Ltrs, AG 333.9 (10–12–42) (1); Memo, OUSW for CofS AGF, 6 Aug 42, and CofS AGF to Special Asst USW, 6 Aug 42, AGF 322.999/132.

[56] Memo, SGS for G–1, G–3, and CofAS, 25 Nov 41, AG 322.97 (11–25–41) (1).

and practically all of the southwestern and western posts. Nearly all commanders of Southern posts indicated that Northern Negro troops would produce greater resentment than Southern Negro troops. Post commanders felt that large numbers of Negroes should not be stationed at any one post and that in no case should more Negro than white troops be placed on a given post, except that the commanding general of the Eighth Corps Area recommended that an all-Negro post of 20,000 capacity be located in eastern Texas near Italy, a town which was reasonably close to several centers of Negro population. Some commanders felt that the attempt to place Negroes near large centers of Negro population could produce new problems. The commanding general of the Second Army felt that large towns should be avoided because of the possible interaction of the presence of Negro troops and large groups of Negro civilians. The commanding general of the Second Corps Area felt that Negroes should not be placed near big cities such as New York and Philadelphia.[57]

In January 1942 G–3, indicating that no military purpose would be served by further shifts of Negro troops and that most permanent stations were "as suitable as is practicable at this time," specifically recommended that:

1. No changes be made in the permanent stations of Negro troops, except for military reasons.
2. The size of nearby Negro civilian communities be a determining factor in selecting stations of newly activated or transferred units.
3. Insofar as practicable, Negroes in-

ducted in the North be stationed in the North.
4. No Negro unit larger than a brigade be stationed at any post within the continental limits of the United States, except that one infantry division may be stationed at Fort Huachuca, Arizona.[58]

While these proposals were not remedies for the conditions which made finding acceptable locations for Negro troops so difficult, the first provision strengthened the position of assigning agencies in their insistence that military needs take precedence over local attitudes, the second would be likely to reduce the strain on local community attitudes in areas where large numbers of Negroes, in or out of uniform, were an unfamiliar sight, and the fourth lessened the possibility of the establishment of a group of all-Negro posts, isolated from the rest of the Army if not from civilians.

Only the third provision was completely ineffective and unworkable. Yet this proposal, that Northern Negro troops be kept in the North, was made frequently in recommendations to the War Department, and was echoed in the Southern press. The Dallas *Morning News*, for example, editorialized:

The federal government apparently has never learned that it cannot without unfortunate consequences billet northern-trained Negro troops in the south. Until it does learn that axiomatic fact, there will continue to be trouble.[59]

Mobilization Regulations had provided that Negroes in the zone of the interior should be assigned to stations in the general areas where they were pro-

[57] Memo, G–3 for CofS, 18 Jan 42, AG 322.97 (11–25–41) (1–18–42).

[58] Memo, G–3 for CofS, 18 Jan 42, AG 322.97 (11–25–41) (1–18–42).
[59] Dallas *Morning News*, November 4, 1941.

cured.[60] Within the War Department, the Morale Branch agreed that Northern Negroes should not be sent to Southern camps.[61] A meeting of Southern governors assembled at Hot Springs, Arkansas, in the spring of 1942 made two requests: that no Negro military police be used around Southern airports or anywhere else that might make it necessary for them to direct or control white soldiers and civilians and that Southern Negroes be kept South and Northern Negroes, North. This last request, although communicated to the Army in May 1942, was not practical.[62] All major replacement training centers and many camps were in the South. Further, since Negro skills and educational qualifications were not evenly distributed geographically, it would add to the difficulties of building potentially useful Negro units. It would complicate the problem of locating Negro units at posts that were suitable both from the training and the social point of view. It would mean Northern duplication of such facilities as the Army Flying School at Tuskegee, Alabama, and it would interfere with maneuvers, for maneuver areas were primarily in the South.[63]

Once the War Department determined that military needs must take precedence over local attitudes, it billeted Negro troops at most camps, stations, and airfields in the United States. After the reorganization of the Army in March 1942 each major command controlled the location of troops under its jurisdiction. The commands soon determined that shifting troops not only interfered with the continuity of training but that it did little more than transfer objections from one community to another. For example, Army Ground Forces pointed out that Little Rock had a sizable Negro population and that the choice of Camp Robinson was therefore logical, and emphasized that if Negroes were not stationed at Robinson they would have to go elsewhere "where they will be resented as much, if not more, than in Arkansas." Continuing, the Ground Forces stated: "We have 3,000 set up for Camp Swift, Texas, where the Mayor asked his Congressman to inform the President that he would personally shoot the first one who came into town." [64]

The headquarters of the major commands became convinced that the problem of locations was one which could be settled best by strong and wise local commanders whose knowledge of their troops and of the nearby communities must be relied upon to reduce areas of tension between white and Negro troops on posts and between troops and civilians in nearby towns. Lt. Gen. Lesley J. McNair, the commander of Army Ground Forces, summed up what came to be a general War Department attitude when he held that the only solution to the problem of locations for Negro

---

[60] MR 1–1, Personnel, par. 17d (3).

[61] Memo, OCofMB for G–3, 2 Dec 41, AG 322.97 (11–25–41) (1).

[62] Ltr, AGF to G–3, 24 Apr 42, AGF 291.2/17 and reply, G–3 to AGF, WDGCT 291.21 (4–24–42).

[63] When he was informed that Lt. Gen. Ben Lear, after his experiences with racial friction in the Arkansas maneuvers of 1941, had recommended that no Negro troops be sent South for maneuvers in the future, Secretary Stimson noted marginally on the recommendation: "No. Get the Southerners used to them!" Memo, WPD for CofS, 25 Mar 42, AGF 322.999/2.

[64] Memo, TIG for DCofS, 2 May 42, AGF 333.1/18; Ltr, TAG to CG AGF, 22 May 42, AG 291.21 (5–8–42); M/S, AGF Opns Div to CofS AGF, 9 Apr 42, AGF 322.999/3.

troops lay in competent commanders "who can forestall racial difficulties by firm discipline, just treatment, strenuous training, and wholesome recreation." [65] He later expanded this to include advice against shifting Negro troops as a result of community pressures:

It is inadvisable to yield to pressure to move colored troops elsewhere, since such action shows weakness of command and fosters complaints from the civil population. Colored troops are unavoidable under the law, their assignment to station is made after careful consideration of the many factors involved, and a community receiving such troops must accept the situation created and handle it as they handle other social problems. On the other hand, a civil community has every right to expect colored units to be commanded effectively, and prevented from committing outrages such as occur all too frequently.[66]

To lessen the chance of racial difficulties, the War Department recommended that an advance check be made by the assigning agency to determine the adequacy of recreational facilities at both the station and in nearby communities, for "proper recreational facilities and opportunities for association in nearby communities will assist to a great extent in lessening the possibility of racial difficulties." Sufficient notice of the arrival of Negroes was to be given commanders of the new station so that adequate preparations for their reception and accommodation might be made.[67]

Though the principle that pressure to move Negro troops would be resisted and that Negro troops could be distributed generally throughout the Army's posts where similar types of units were trained was held to, no definite directives on the question of retaining Negro troops at posts in the face of public opposition were issued. Cases were dealt with as they arose. In most cases, the Army urged protesting communities to consider the necessity of training Negro troops where facilities existed, that is, in nearly every camp in the country. Appeals were made to high community patriotism and to community leaders of both races. After communities understood that they were sharing the distribution of Negro troops with other areas all over the country, most protests were withdrawn. Uncertainty, fear, and sometimes open animosity reflected in troop-town relations continued to exist in some towns. In others, local church, school, welfare, and recreation groups, with the help of national bodies, especially the United Service Organizations (USO) and the American Red Cross, combined to provide troops with community services that reduced and relieved tensions which could otherwise have been counted upon to produce friction and open disturbances of one sort or another if allowed to continue unchecked. Nevertheless, a few cases of shifting units for other than military reasons occurred throughout the war. While particular units were thus shifted, clearing a camp of all Negro units for other than military reasons became a rarity. Sometimes these shifts were to the advantage of the units themselves when they involved movement from an area relatively unprepared for their pres-

---

[65] Memo, AGF for TAG, 14 Jun 42, AGF 322.999/78.

[66] Memo, Gen McNair for CG Second Army, 1 Sep 42, AGF 319.1/112 (8–24–42).

[67] Ltr, TAG to CG's, 7 Jul 42, AG 291.21 (7–24–42); Ltr, Hq AGF to CG's Armies, VI, VII, IX Corps, 12 Jul 42, AGF 370.5/410 (7–7–42), in AGF 291.2/5.

ence to one which could provide better facilities.

No particular advantage, other than a clearing of the administrative air, was gained by the decision itself, for by the time it was decided that the location of Negro troops was primarily a matter of military necessity that could be justified as such, the possibility of further major shifts of Negro troops was definitely limited by the available space. By 1942, most camps which were to house Negro troops in sizable numbers throughout the war were already doing so.[68] Most ports of embarkation and their subsidiary posts housed Negro troops. To illustrate further the geographical range of camps with permanent concentrations of Negro troops, once the Air Forces began to employ large numbers of Negro units virtually every air station had at least one aviation squadron and at least one quartermaster platoon (aviation) composed of Negro troops.

The larger the unit, the more difficult was the choice of a location. This situation lasted throughout the war. It encouraged the organization of small Negro units and discouraged the activation of large units. The first of the all-Negro divisions, the 93d Division, was located in the spring of 1942 at Fort Huachuca, Arizona, a post which had housed Negro troops traditionally and which was far enough away from civilian communities to minimize local protests over sending so large a unit there. Even so, the commanding general of the post's service command had not recommended it as a division camp for Negro troops.[69] When the second Negro infantry division, the 92d, was to be activated in the fall of 1942, no single post could be found for it. The division was therefore activated at four widely separated posts in Alabama, Arkansas, Kentucky, and Indiana. This division could not be assembled until the 93d left Fort Huachuca. Several attempts were made to find other divisional camps for Negroes, with Fort Meade, Maryland, Fort Dix, New Jersey, and Camp Butner, North Carolina, favorably mentioned because of their location near Negro centers of population.[70] When the 2d Cavalry Division was about to become all Negro, no single camp was available, though Fort Clark, Texas, could have been adapted to the whole division if it had not been Negro. The division was therefore divided between Fort Clark and Camp Lockett, California, both of which had then to be expanded with

---

[68] These installations included: Camps Stewart and Gordon and Fort Benning, Georgia; Camps Livingston, Polk, Beauregard, and Claiborne, Louisiana; Fort Riley, Kansas; Camps Haan, Cooke, and Stoneman and Fort Ord, California; Fort Dix and Raritan Arsenal, New Jersey; Fort Custer, Michigan; Fort Lewis and Vancouver Barracks, Washington; Fort Leonard Wood and Camp Crowder, Missouri; Forts Sam Houston and Bliss and Camps Hulen, Wolters, Bowie, and Swift, Texas; Fort Knox, Kentucky; Camp Forrest, Tennessee; Edgewood Arsenal, Aberdeen Proving Ground, and Fort Meade, Maryland; Fort Jackson and Camp Croft, South Carolina; Fort Bragg and Camp Davis, North Carolina; Camps Van Dorn, Shelby, and McCain, Mississippi; Forts Eustis and Belvoir and Camp Lee, Virginia; Fort Devens and Camp Edwards, Massachusetts; Fort Huachuca, Arizona; and Fort Sill, Oklahoma.

[69] M/S, AGF Opns Div to Constr Div, 2 Apr 42, AGF 320.2 (3-8-42) Opn/00910.

[70] Fort Meade became an AGF depot. The Fourth Corps Area questioned the wisdom of adding a division to its Negro strength, though it suggested Grenada, Rucker, Sutton, Gordon, and five others in addition to Camp Butner. 1st Ind, Fourth Corps Area to Ltr, TAG to CG Fourth Corps Area, 8 Mar 42, AG 320.2 (3-8-42) MJC-C.

housing and stables to take care of this last of the horse cavalry divisions.[71]

Cadres for Units

The vast and rapid increase in the strength of the Army posed another problem that was much more serious for new Negro units than for corresponding white units. New units are built around cadres supplied by older "parent" units of the same or similar types. Cadres are supposed to be made up of experienced, trained men, properly balanced in numbers, skills, and leadership abilities according to the needs of the new unit being activated. New units then receive fillers from reception or replacement centers to bring themselves to full strength. Among Negro units there were neither enough older units nor enough units of similar types to supply the cadre needs of new units. Only the four Regular regiments and a few other detachments had existed long enough before mobilization to be trained at all. From the beginning, therefore, Negro units were hard put to furnish cadres in sufficient numbers and of sufficient quality to provide for the proper organization and training of new units of varying types in all arms and services. Many a unit complained bitterly that cadres for younger units were stripping it of all noncommissioned officer and specialist material before the unit itself had got its own training well under way. The new units, in turn, after receiving the best that the parent units had to offer, often complained that their cadres could not meet their needs.

The problem of cadres was one whose ultimate effect was far-reaching, for original units trained with less than adequate cadres produced in turn new cadres for younger units that were likely to be even more inadequate. The lifeblood of cadres was well-trained, well-disciplined, well-informed personnel with high leadership abilities. As activations of new units continued to increase, the quality of the cadres deteriorated rapidly and the lifeblood sapped from the older units grew so thin that many of the newer units began their careers with cadres poor enough to constitute a handicap from which some of them never recovered.

The older Negro units, composed primarily of career cavalrymen and infantrymen, could not, all at once, provide the required cadres for new artillery, chemical warfare, and engineer units. But because there was no other source they had to provide cadres for most of the earlier units, with the result that they themselves were weakened. It is questionable whether the traditional Regular units were ever able to provide adequate cadres for new units of even their own arms. Despite their reputation of containing large numbers of well-disciplined and responsible career soldiers, the older units had long been in need of additional training and men. They were brought to full strength relatively slowly and their heavy losses through the production of cadres and through other necessary transfers kept them from acquiring the finished training which they were too often assumed to have had. The regiments had been at reduced strength for several years before the beginning of mobilization and, "although classed as combat regiments,

---

[71] Memo, Hq AGF for CG SOS, 22 Sep 42, and attached Memo for Record, AGF 20/3.

[the cavalry regiments] actually were used as service troops at Forts Myer, Leavenworth and Riley and at the United States Military Academy." [72] In May 1941, Brig. Gen. Terry Allen explained that the Negro regiments of the 2d Cavalry Division were "several months behind the Third Cavalry Brigade, owing to delay in organization and because they had only a small nucleus of trained men to start with." [73] During the period 1940–42, nevertheless, these units and their infantry counterparts, which were no better prepared for their tasks, were continuously furnishing cadres to new Negro units in all arms and services.

Because of the lack of adequate Negro cadres, the early coast artillery regiments were activated with sufficient white noncommissioned officers assigned to assist in training these units to carry on "work connected with their specialities." The white NCO's remained assigned to these regiments until July 1941, when they were transferred to white units. They actually remained on detached service with the Negro regiments for some time thereafter, or until Negroes became available for promotion to the first three grades and until accommodations for Negro enlisted men were made available at the Coast Artillery School. [74] Negro coast and antiaircraft artillery regiments were unable to furnish all the cadres

needed for the Coast Artillery Replacement Training Center at Fort Eustis, Virginia, and, despite the objections of the center, white cadremen were used as instructors until Negroes could replace them.

As early as January 1941, The Quartermaster General reported that all Negro quartermaster units in all corps areas were depleted by cadre calls to such an extent that they could supply no further cadres to units. He suggested that commanders requiring cadres for new Negro quartermaster detachments for station use should organize, supervise, and train their detachments with whatever personnel was available. If none was available, key personnel should be enlisted locally. [75] Fort Knox reported in December 1940 that Company K, 48th Quartermaster Regiment, stationed there, had already trained two cadres and was to furnish another in January. It therefore could not take care of more selectees due to arrive at Knox in January 1941. The post needed twenty-two enlisted men from another source at once to provide a cadre for the new quartermaster service company into which the January selectees were to be put. Fort Knox was informed that, if necessary, white personnel might be utilized temporarily to organize the Negro company. [76]

Medical units faced similar difficulties in attempting to provide cadres from an insufficiency of properly trained men.

---

[72] Tab B, Cavalry Units in PMP, 1939, to Memo, G–3 for CofS, 5 Aug 40, AG 320.2 (8–5–40) (3).

[73] Ltr, Gen Allen, CG 2d Cav Div, to Gen Marshall, 13 May 41, AG 320.2 (5–13–41) (3).

[74] Memo, G–3 for TAG, 15 Nov 40, AG 320.2 (11–15–40); Memo, OCofCA for TAG, 10 Jun 41, AG 320.2 (6–10–41); Ltr, TAG to CG First Army, 16 Jun 41, AG 320.2 (6–10–41) EA. Regiments involved in this procedure included the 54th Coast Artillery and the 76th, 99th, and 100th Coast Artillery (AA).

[75] Memo, OQMG for G–1, 10 Jan 41, AG 220.31 (5–22–40) (1) sec. 6.

[76] Ltr, Hq Ft. Knox, Ky., to CG Fifth Corps Area, 21 Dec 40; Ltr, TAG to CG Ft. Knox, 18 Dec 40, both in AG 220.31 (5–22–40) (1) sec. 6; Memo, G–1 for TAG, 11 Jan 41, and Rad, TAG to CG Fifth Corps Area, 11 Jan 41, both in AG 220.3 (12–21–40) (5–22–40) (1) sec. 6.

Cadres for the medical detachments of Negro regiments and battalions, including the Regular Army units, were furnished by the Colored Medical Detachment at West Point and by medical personnel at Fort Huachuca.[77] These sources could furnish "necessarily small" cadres only. As a result, the fourteen-man cadre sent to Fort Bragg in March 1941 had to be shared by medical detachments of three regiments, and the eleven-man cadre sent to Camp Livingston was shared by the detachments of three regiments and one separate battalion. Within a month these new detachments were being called upon to furnish cadres for other units.[78]

The cadre problem persisted, sometimes taking other forms. As late as the summer of 1942, staff officers at Headquarters, Army Ground Forces, were still pondering the wisdom of requiring one type of unit to furnish a cadre for a different type of unit, though this measure had been resorted to many times before. They pointed to the example of a truck company which, although it had no such technicians, was called upon to furnish a cadre, including shop foremen, for a light maintenance company. Ground Forces G–3 explained that the sole Negro light maintenance companies then active had only their original cadres. Neither of the Quartermaster Replacement Training Centers could furnish further technicians from their limited instructor and overhead personnel without seriously affecting training at the centers. The only

Negro units left with a certain amount of mechanical training were the truck companies. Ground Forces G–4 suggested the use of graduates of the Hampton Quartermaster School, but these men lacked the military and leadership training necessary for good cadremen.[79] In another case, half of the men sent to two new signal construction companies by an antiaircraft regiment were rated so poor in ability by the receiving unit that it felt that it would be impossible to train and use them as cadremen. No investigation was ordered because, after fifteen indorsements and several weeks of effort, Army Ground Forces had been unable to fix the responsibility for the equally poor quality of the cadre previously sent out by the same regiment.[80]

Cadre problems in Negro units lasted up to the end of the war. In the late fall of 1944, for example, the Engineer Training Center at Fort Lewis, Washington, was using white cadres to train Negro troops. As fast as Negroes completed training and qualified for occupational specialities, they replaced the white cadremen. Nevertheless, in May of the following year, some cadres there were still all white, some were mixed, and only one was all Negro. While the white cadremen could be employed in the training center, and while the use of mixed cadres was proceeding without difficulty, the white cadremen could not be assigned to the organized units themselves. It was therefore necessary to devise all possible means to develop

---

[77] Ltr, TAG to All Army and Corps Area Comdrs and Superintendent USMA, 29 Feb 41, AG 320.2 (1–24–41) E–C.

[78] Ltr, First Army to TAG, and 2 Inds, 2 Apr 41, AG 320.2 (4–2–41).

[79] M/S, AGF G–4 Trans to AGF G–3 Opns, 10 Jul 42; Opns to Trans, 16 Jul 42; G–4 Trans to G–3 Opns, 20 Jul 42. All in AGF 320.2/1 (Cadre).

[80] Ltr, Hq AGF to CG AAC, 24 Jul 42, and attached DF, AGF 320.2/120 (AA Comd).

Negroes to replace white cadremen when units left the center.[81]

The initial problems in the expansion of Negro strength, with the exception of cadre difficulties, were relatively minor when compared with later questions involving the use of Negro troops and when compared with the larger questions of full-scale mobilization involving the Army as a whole. They affected the administrative processes of the Army more than they affected the troops themselves. They did serve to delay and at times to confuse the orderly process of establishing and training Negro units.

They had as well a nuisance value that affected the views of higher headquarters on the entire question of the employment of Negro troops. The larger questions affecting directly the planned employment of Negro troops and the training, morale, and efficiency of these troops were yet to come. These were primarily internal Army problems which could not be settled by adjusted quotas, expanded construction, or by appeals to civilian communities urging them to remember their higher obligations to the nation in time of war. They could be solved only by a rigorous examination of Army organization, practice, and policy as they affected the employment of Negro manpower.

---

[81] Ltrs, Maj Charles H. Flournoy to CofE, 5 Dec 44 and 26 May 45, both in OCE 291.2.

CHAPTER V

Units: The Quota Phase

According to the policy of the War Department announced in October 1940, Negro units were to be provided in all arms and services of the Army. According to mobilization regulations, assignments of Negroes to the combat arms were to be in the same ratio as those of whites. In reality, during the early months of mobilization certain branches remained exempt from using any considerable portion of Negro troops. Other branches found themselves absorbing Negroes greatly in excess of their proportion of the draft. This development had been clearly foreseen by the planners of the late thirties, but attempts to distribute Negroes in equal proportion to all branches were resisted by the chiefs of those arms and services which had not traditionally contained Negro units. Though the War Department G-1 and G-3 Divisions continued to warn that these branches must make provision for receiving increased numbers of Negroes and although most of these branches began to make plans for the eventual increase of their Negro units, the actual provision of units, outside of the Corps of Engineers, the Quartermaster Corps, and the Chemical Warfare Service, advanced slowly.

The Distribution Problem

At the end of 1941, the bulk of the nearly 100,000 Negroes then in the Army were in the branches to which they had been allotted in mobilization plans. Three-fifths of the entire number were almost equally divided among infantry, engineer, and quartermaster units. Another fourth were in field and coast artillery units. The small number remaining were scattered among all other branches. Despite the large percentage of all Negroes who were in the infantry, including Regular and National Guard units, only 5 percent of all infantry enlisted men were Negroes. In the Air Corps, Medical Department, and Signal Corps less than 2 percent of all enlisted men were Negroes. But approximately every fourth man in the Corps of Engineers and every sixth man in the Quartermaster Corps was a Negro. Every seventh man (14.6 percent) in the Chemical Warfare Service was a Negro. Of all men who were unassigned or who were in miscellaneous detachments, 27 percent were Negroes.

In the next seven months, during which the number of Negro enlisted men in the Army reached 200,000, their distribution tended to become even more unbalanced. The proportions of Negroes in the Quartermaster and Engineer Corps increased to the point where it appeared possible that every nontechnical unit in those branches would soon be Negro. Proportions in the Medical Department increased slightly. On the other hand, in the Air and Signal Corps

Negro representation declined to less than 1 percent of total enlisted strength. Since the Air Corps and the Arms and Services with Army Air Forces (ASWAAF) were increasing in strength at a faster rate than any of the ground arms and services, what had long been apparent now became even more obvious: the distribution of Negroes among the arms and services had to be made more nearly equitable, and the Air Corps, especially, had to increase its percentage of Negro enlisted men. The overrepresentation of Negroes in engineer and quartermaster units and their underrepresentation in the units of other branches also led to reconsideration of their employment in types of units, including divisions, other than those originally provided.

Selective Service pressure on the Army to accept increasingly large numbers of Negroes as they became available through the draft accentuated the need for new units. Selective Service and the War Department discussed "this extremely troublesome problem" frequently, with Selective Service, on occasion, threatening to abandon the procedure of delivering white and Negro selectees on the basis of separate calls as requested by the Army in favor of selection by order number without regard to color quotas.[1] The disproportionate numbers of Negroes passed over in filling Army color quotas was proving embarrassing to Selective Service in its public relations. The legality of the whole procedure of separate calls by color was being questioned.

War Department agencies suggested

several replies to Selective Service's proposal to abandon calls by separate color quotas: Troop units had been planned on the basis of population ratios and could not be altered without a complete reorganization; Negroes in excess of 10.6 percent who happened to be in Class I–A could not be inducted without raising the question of Negroes carrying more than their fair share of the military obligation of the country; new units, especially for the Air Forces, were being planned; and, since the Selective Service Act did not limit the obligation for training Negroes to the Army, the Navy, too, should be requested to assume its share of the responsibility. The War Department formally answered Selective Service in a "non-committal" fashion stating that it was not unmindful of the problem and that Selective Service would be kept informed of studies of reallocation and reorganization then under way.[2]

In the summer of 1942, the first critical shortage of men needed to fill units activated in excess of original plans occurred. For July the Army sent a supplemental call for 65,000 white and 10,000 Negro men to Selective Service. The Director of Selective Service, Maj. Gen. Lewis B. Hershey, refused to honor the call until its racial proportions were readjusted. He accepted a revised call for 50,000 whites and 20,000 Negroes with the understanding that the August call would contain an even heavier proportion of Negroes. "Otherwise, we feel," G–1 explained, "that popular demands will cause the question to be placed before the War Manpower Board. This should be avoided at all costs as it

---

[1] Ltr, Dir Selective Sv to SW, 18 Sep 41, AG 324.71 (9–18–41).

[2] Ltr, and Memo for Record attached, TAG to Dir Selective Sv, 11 Oct 41, AG 324.71 (9–18–41).

would probably result in the Army being forced to accept [men] from the Selective Service System in accordance with their order numbers without regard to color." [3]

While successive communications from Selective Service and the interested public were coming in, various plans for the placement and utilization of Negro inductees were proposed and a few of these were tried. But the only plan which would serve to keep the backlog of selectees low enough to satisfy Selective Service would be one that provided enough units for Negroes. Accordingly, the arms and services were told again and again that each must make available a proportionate share of its units for Negro enlisted men. Under the pressure of providing sufficient units for Negroes, the organization of units for the sake of guaranteeing vacancies became a major goal. In some cases, careful examination of the usefulness of the types of units provided was subordinated to the need to create units which could receive Negroes. As a result, several types of units with limited military value were formed in some branches for the specific purpose of absorbing otherwise unwanted Negroes. Conversely, certain types of units with legitimate and important military functions were filled with Negroes who could not function efficiently in the tasks to which they were assigned.

Ground Units for the Air Forces

The branch singled out for much of the public, political, and internal military pressure to expand its use of Ne-

groes was the Air Corps. Public pressures, as explained previously, were the result of long-term campaigns which succeeded in achieving political and press support. Military pressures came from other arms and services and from the general staff divisions. As the lack of balance in proportionate distribution became greater among the arms and services, the War Department and the ground arms and services became convinced that at least part of the answer to the problem lay with the Air Corps. If the Air Corps, rapidly becoming the largest of the Army's branches, absorbed more Negroes, pressure on the ground arms and services to provide more and more Negro units would be lessened. This thinking was later applied as well to the Air Forces as a whole, for if the Arms and Services with the Army Air Forces accepted more Negro units, they could absorb part of the Negro personnel which the ground arms and services would otherwise have to accept.

Because of its high enlistment appeal the Air Corps, in the earlier period of expansion, was able to obtain a majority of its men through regular enlistment channels. Since only selectees were affected by the Selective Service Act's racial clauses, only that portion of the Air Corps personnel which came through the draft was affected by rulings on proportionate Negro strength.

In the fall of 1940, the Air Corps was informed that it would receive 25,000 selectees as its 1941 spring quota. Of these, 9 percent, or 2,250 would be Negro. The Air Corps proposed, initially, that these Negro enlisted men be placed in "air base detachments." These units were to be trained and employed as parts of air base groups. De-

[3] Memo, G–1 for CofS, 5 Jun 42, WDCSA 291.21 (6–5–42).

tachments would be authorized when Negro selectees were sent to a given air base. Although they were to be carried in the tables of organization of air base groups, the base "detachment" was intended to prevent mixing Negroes and whites in the same unit. In a "corrected version" suggested by G–3, the Air Corps substituted 250-man "training squadrons (separate)" to be over and above the regular Air Corps allotment of selectees and to be completely separate from air base groups. This arrangement, by which the Air Corps allotment of selectees rose from 25,000 to 27,250 men, would prevent interference with the planned use of the original 25,000 white selectees on whom the Air Corps had counted for its combat group expansion program.[4]

Before activation of the first nine aviation training squadrons in June 1941, it was explained that they were being organized "solely to take care of the colored selectees allotted to the Air Corps...."[5] They were later described as activated "to aid in the many duties which must be performed to keep in order the stations of the AAF within the continental limits of the United States." They were intentionally left with their duties vaguely defined so that local commanders might have discretion in the uses to which they were put.[6]

Aviation squadrons, as these units were later called, were established at every major air base. The troop basis of the Army Air Forces, by 30 June 1942, provided for 184 such squadrons. A total of 266 were eventually activated.[7] A few of these squadrons operated under specific tables of organization, but the vast majority came under the bulk allotment system, under which personnel was allotted to particular commands and headquarters which, in turn, allotted personnel to particular units as required by the using installation. Their strengths therefore fluctuated according to the determined needs of the station to which they were assigned. Aviation squadrons were thereby enabled to absorb, within reasonable limits, as many or as few selectees at a given time as were necessary to maintain the desired distribution of Negroes within the Air Corps.

Another type of Negro unit widely employed by the Air Forces was the aviation quartermaster truck company or air base transportation platoon. These were technically units of the arms and services with the Air Corps and not Air Corps units. They served to absorb the initial proportion of Negroes allotted to the services with the Air Corps. In December 1940, the Air Corps learned that it was being allotted 3,627 Negro enlisted men for duty with its arms and services. "If this is correct," the chief of the Air Corps Plans Division observed,

[4] Ltr, OCofAC to TAG, 3 Oct 40; Memo, G–3 for TAG, 12 Oct 40; Ltr, OCofAC to TAG, 10 Oct 40; Memo, OCofAC for G–3, 10 Oct 40. All in AG 320.2 Air Corps (10–3–40) (1).
[5] Memo, G–3 for G–1, 4 Mar 41, AG 580.7 (1–27–41).
[6] Memo, DCofAS for Asst CofAS, Tng, 9 Oct 42; Memo, CofAS for DCofS, 14 Oct 42; Ltr, Air AG to CG AFCC, CG TTC, 6 Mar 42. All in AAF 291.2B.

[7] Most of these, permanently assigned to airfields, were inactivated in 1944, their personnel being absorbed in one or another of the sections of the new AAF base units. While these sections were technically parts of the same base unit, the fact that each had its own commander and morning report made each a separate unit in conformity with the 16 October 1940 policy requiring separate Negro units.

"it appears that every Quartermaster Truck Company assigned to duty at Air Corps stations will be colored. There may be additional colored personnel of some other service at a few stations." [8] Preparations were made to receive these units, which averaged 70 enlisted men each. It was suggested that future barracks construction at each station provide one or two barracks units separated from others so that "necessary segregation" would be possible if and when the allotment of Negro troops to the Air Corps was increased further by the War Department. The truck companies, but not the transportation platoons, were generally assigned to service groups. Companies were organized either under definite tables or by allotment. Platoons were generally allotment units.

By the end of 1941 the authorized squadrons and service units with the Air Forces could no longer absorb all of the men which the Air Forces had to take if it was to come close to its proportionate share of Negro strength. As long as the Air Forces did not absorb its share of the increase of Negroes, G–3 insisted, ground branches could expect to continue to be "overloaded with colored due in part to the fact that in the past they have absorbed a considerable number of the colored personnel resulting from expansion of the Army Air Forces." [9] During 1942 the Army was to expand to 3,600,000 men. Of these, 337,750 were to be Negroes. The Air Forces, which was to expand to 997,687 —more than a quarter of the entire Army—was allotted 53,299 Negroes in 1942, or 10.6 percent of its total increase

of 502,822 men. This number, added to the 24,293 Negroes previously allotted (most of whom had not yet been accepted), would give the Air Forces a total of 77,592 Negroes.[10]

The Air Forces contended that the maximum number of Negroes which it could use was 20,739 in the Air Corps and 23,468 in its services, a total of 44,207.[11] If the Air Forces allotment were reduced, ground units would then have to absorb the excess 33,385 Negroes in addition to the 260,158 already allotted them. Ground forces could do so only if two white divisions in the troop basis were converted to Negro or if two white divisions plus several nondivisional units were deleted and unneeded Negro separate rifle battalions were substituted. To prevent this, G–3 recommended that the Air Forces be required to accept its 53,299 Negroes out of the 1942 increase in the Army. The Chief of Staff approved, adding the stipulation that air base defense units "for the number of air bases found necessary" be organized and that Negro personnel be used for this purpose as required.[12]

Initially 23,000 Negroes were allotted to airdrome defense units, as the air base security battalions were originally called. While all of the original units were Negro, the Chief of Staff's decision required that provision be made for the future use of similar white units. Nevertheless, except for a few white units formed for almost immediate overseas use in specific areas, most units activated were Negro.

---

[8] Memo, CofAC Plans Div to Chief Buildings and Grounds, 9 Dec 40, AAF 291.2A.

[9] Memo, G–3 for CofS, 6 Jan 42, OCS 20602–249.

[10] *Ibid.*

[11] Memo, AAF A–1 to WD G–3, 29 Jan 42, AAF 291.2B.

[12] Memo, DCofS for G–3, 12 Feb 42, OCS 20602–249.

The air base security battalions were designed to protect air bases against riots, parachute attacks, and air raids. They were to be equipped with rifles, machine guns, and 37-mm. (and possibly 75-mm.) guns.[13] Though there was some confusion in the minds of commanders and civilian officials on the point, these battalions were in addition to and not substitutes for military police, guard squadrons, and aviation squadrons. Army Ground Forces was given jurisdiction over the activation and training of these units. Upon completion of training, the battalions were to pass to Army Air Forces control. From the beginning the personnel allotted to the units counted toward the Air Forces quota of Negro troops.[14]

The air base security battalions were the last of the special units employed to help absorb the Air Forces quota of Negro enlisted men. The original 1942 program called for a total of 67 air base security battalions, 57 of them to be Negro. The program was later expanded to a total of 103 units. Through 1943, 296 were planned, 261 of which were to be Negro. Not all of these were activated. Future Air Forces expansion into new types of units for Negroes took place in the Arms and Services with the Air Forces and in the combat and related units of the Air Corps.

Flying Units

The question of Air Corps flying units for Negroes was an old one.[15] In the fall of 1940, after a public announcement in September that Negro troops were being developed for "the aviation service," the Chief of Staff called upon G–3 to consider and make recommendations for the training of Negro aviation mechanics with the ultimate objective of establishing a Negro combat unit.[16] For weeks, Air Corps agencies found flaws in all suggestions made for beginning this training. The Chicago School of Aeronautics, suggested by G–3, gave flying training but not mechanic training and therefore could not be used. The Aeronautical University of Chicago gave mechanic training, but its students were housed in a Y.M.C.A., "which makes it manifestly impossible to assign colored students under the existing arrangement." [17] Civilian schools could be made to take Negro students but, because of locations, housing, messing arrangements, and concurrent civilian and military classes, "such assignment would be unjustified without their consent." The Air Training and Operations Division felt, therefore, that Negro mechanic trainees should be assigned to the Air Corps Technical School at Chanute Field where they and the facilities they were to use would be completely under military control. The Air Plans Division on the other hand was certain that if this assignment was made "disturbances and possibly riots will probably ensue both at Chanute Field and the nearby communities." As an alternative it proposed Tuskegee Institute in Alabama as the place to initiate such a

---

[13] Ltr, Hq AAF to CofAC, CG AF, CG ACTFC, 25 Feb 42, AAF 291.2.
[14] WD Cir 59, 1942; Memo, G–3 for CG AGF, 14 Mar 42, WDGCT 320 (3–14–42).
[15] See above, pp. 55–65.

[16] Memo, SGS for G–3, 17 Sep 40, OCS 20602–80; Memo, SGS for G–3, 20 Sep 40, OCS 20602–83; Memo, G–3 for CofAC, 25 Sep 40, AAF 353.9–4–A.
[17] Memo, prepared by T&O Div OCofAC for G–3, 3 Oct 40, AAF 353.9–4–A.

course. "If colored units are to be formed," the Air Plans Division stated, "colored schools should be provided for their training [and] separate schools for colored pilot training likewise should be organized." [18] The Training and Operations Division, in view of the small number of Negroes expected and in view of the lack of qualified instructors, supervisors, and equipment, held out for Chanute Field as "the best expedient." [19]

At this point of threatened impasse General Arnold, Chief of the Air Corps, asked, in a marginal note, "Gen. Johnson How should we go about training the colored mechanics for *1 squadron* with the least trouble and effort?" [20] Within a week, the Air Corps prepared a plan. It recommended to G–3 that, "if it is imperative that negro tactical units be formed," instruction should be undertaken to provide men for one Corps and Division Observation Squadron, with training concentrated at "a recognized colored school, such as Tuskegee" in order to eliminate the possibility of racial difficulties which might occur elsewhere. "Although a definite decision may have been reached at this time to organize colored units in the Air Corps," the memorandum continued, "no country in the world has been able to organize a satisfactory air unit with colored personnel." Three years, the Air Corps remonstrated, would be necessary to train a crew chief, two more years for a hangar chief, and a total of

ten years for a line chief.[21] That a Negro combat unit could be formed in time to be of value to the national defense at all was doubted. The day after it received this memorandum G–3 called for the submission of a plan to train a Negro single engine pursuit unit.[22]

In December 1940, the Air Corps submitted its full plan, calling for the employment of 429 enlisted men and 47 officers in a pursuit squadron, a base group detachment, weather and communications detachments, and services. White noncommissioned officers were to be used as inspectors, supervisors, and instructors for an indefinite period of time. Initial training of technical and administrative officers and enlisted men was to be given at Chanute Field. Negro officers, when qualified, would replace white officers in the squadron and in administrative positions on the squadron's base. Training was to proceed by stages through the basic, advanced, and unit phases. The elementary phase of flying training was to be omitted initially by utilization of Negro graduates of the CAA's civilian pilot training courses.[23]

For a time, the Air Corps sought to acquire a field in the vicinity of Chicago for the training and eventual station of this unit.[24] But the high cost of land, the presence of heavily traveled air lanes, and the location of available sites in areas subject to bad weather and fre-

[18] Memo, Chief of Air Plans Div for Chief of T&O Div OCofAC, 5 Oct 40, AAF 353.9–4–A.
[19] Memo, T&O Div for ExO, 15 Oct 40, AAF 353.9–4–A.
[20] *Ibid.*, marginal note, signed HHA. Italics in original.

[21] Memo, OCofAC for G–3, 22 Oct 40, AAF 353.9–4–A.
[22] RS, G–3 for CofAC, 24 Oct 40, Tng of Pers for Cld Avn Units, G–3/42914; Memo, OCofAC for TAG, 18 Dec 40, AG 580.7 (12–18–40) (2).
[23] Memo, OCofAC for TAG, 18 Dec 40, AG 580.7 (12–18–40) (2).
[24] Ltr, OCofAC to CofAC, 18 Nov 40, AAF 353.9–4–A.

quent flooding caused the Air Corps to look elsewhere. An area in the vicinity of Tuskegee, where Tuskegee Institute had been carrying on a CAA college student flying training program and where the institute's president, Frederick D. Patterson, had been urging the location of additional training facilities, was finally settled upon as an airfield location for flight training. This plan was supplemented in the spring of 1941 by the authorization of a civil contract school for elementary flying training of Negro cadets. The school, operated under contract by Tuskegee Institute, was located near the town of Tuskegee.[25]

Under Secretary Patterson presented the Air Corps plan to Judge Hastie for comment. Hastie had already conferred with General Arnold about the possibility of finding Negroes with training and experience in aircraft maintenance with a view to filling Air Corps needs in connection with the planned project.[26] Now he could see no reason, "apart from a desire for racial separation," which justified the establishment of a separate station for the training of a Negro squadron. He saw many valid reasons in favor of training Negroes in existing Air Corps installations. They included maintenance of training standards, economical use of instructional personnel, and inculcation of morale. Hastie observed:

A squadron in the Air Corps does not function in such a way that it can be separated from other units, as can such an organization as a coast artillery regiment. . . . Acquaintance, understanding and

mutual respect established between blacks and whites at the three regular Air Corps Training centers can be the most important factor in bringing about harmonious racial attitudes essential to high morale. Indeed, I can think of no other way of accomplishing this objective. It cannot be overemphasized that the contacts which the Air Corps seem to fear cannot be avoided. Such contacts should be established normally in the training centers.[27]

Hastie predicted that "whatever the attitude of Tuskegee may be, there would unquestionably be very great public protest if the proposed plans should be adopted."

Such protests did come from the Negro press and public. They were to be typified in the epithet "Lonely Eagles," applied to the Tuskegee cadets. Chicago Negroes and their press were especially critical of the plan. General Arnold, somewhat baffled by this turn of events, remarked later that "these people are willing to take a chance on losing the whole Tuskegee opportunity in order to gamble on obtaining training on different circumstances which they claim will give them a more even break. . . . It looks as if it is a case of the whole or nothing that this group of people are waiting for." [28]

In support of its plan, the Air Corps pointed out that Randolph, Maxwell, and Moffett Fields were already congested and that the Tuskegee site would provide a minimum of delay in getting the training of Negroes under way. The school would be under the direct supervision of the commanding general

[25] Memo, OCofAC for TAG, 11 Mar 41, AG 580.7 (3–11–41).

[26] Memo, Civ Aide to SW for DCofS, 18 Jan 41, AAF 291.2A.

[27] Memo, Civ Aide to SW for USW, 31 Dec 40, AG 580.7 (12–18–40) (2).

[28] Memo, DCofS for CofS, 20 May 41, AG 580.7 (5–20–41).

of Maxwell Field, Alabama.[29] Judge Hastie, while not concurring in the plan, withdrew his formal opposition on 8 January 1941. The plan was approved by Under Secretary Patterson the same day.[30]

While the approval of this plan to extend the combat employment of Negroes to the Air Corps, at least on an experimental basis, did not materially increase Air Corps absorption of Negro selectees—the Negro units planned for Tuskegee were primarily made up of three-year enlistees—it did serve to increase the variety of types of units provided for Negroes.[31] The 99th Pursuit Squadron was activated on 22 March 1941; it was followed by the 100th Squadron, activated on 19 February 1942. Three school squadrons, two air service squadrons, two fighter control squadrons, additional fighter and training squadrons, two group headquarters, and communications, weather, and service detachments necessary for these units and for the new airfield were all provided in 1942. Many of these units were not filled for months after activation. They did not, therefore, immediately affect the relative standing of the Air Corps in the employment of its share of Negro troops.

The decision to use only Negro attached units with the new squadrons made it necessary to constitute and activate several types of units of the ground arms and services not previously planned. These included chemical, ordnance, and medical detachments for the Tuskegee station, two signal aircraft warning companies originally intended for task force and fighter group assignment, and signal, quartermaster, medical, and ordnance units for the original squadrons and for the service group. The activation of these Air Forces types of ground units gave force to the Army's announced policy of establishing Negro units in all branches of the service.

At a press conference announcing the decision to form a Negro pursuit squadron, Under Secretary Patterson stated that it was of course part of the policy of the Army to have Negro units in each branch of the service. A newsman followed with the question, "That means a Negro tank corps?" Judge Patterson answered, "Everything." When pressed for plans on the "tank corps," the Under Secretary admitted that he did not know that the War Department had "gone down into that," but an aide reminded the press that although there were no plans for tank units, Negroes were already in the infantry.[32] This could have been taken to mean that since the Infantry was one of the arms contributing units to the Armored Force, the question of the distribution of Negroes to that service was settled, but the statement was taken to mean that if the Air Corps had taken Negroes, the Armored Force would not be far behind.

Nondivisional Ground Combat Units

As a matter of fact, the Armored Force had already been instructed to make a provision for Negro units. The

[29] Memo, CofAC for ASW, 6 Jan 41, AG 580.7 (12–18–40) (2).

[30] Memo, CofAC for SGS, 8 Jan 41; RS, G–3 to TAG, 23 Dec 40, approved 8 Jan 41. Both in AG 580.7 (12–18–40).

[31] Memos, G–1 for TAG, 28 Feb 41; CofS, 11 Mar 41. Both in AG 580.7 (1–27–41) (12–18–40) (2).

[32] Memo for SW, 17 Jan 41, Press Conf of Patterson, USW, 16 Jan 41, 3:00 p.m.–3:35 p.m., in Gen Council Room, copy in AAF 291.2A.

MAJ. GEN. WALTER R. WEAVER DELIVERS THE INAUGURAL ADDRESS *opening the new Air Corps School for training Negro aviators at Tuskegee.*

Armored Force, like the Air Corps, had contended that, except for experimental purposes, it could not afford during an emergency to take a proportionate share of Negroes. It was too busy with the problems of welding a unified force out of what was essentially a combination of arms to have time for the activation and training of Negro armored units. The Armored Force suggested that its representation be provided by using Negroes in lieu of white soldiers in service detachments at the Armored Force School and Replacement Center. These detachments, to include 574 and 403 men, respectively, would be used to provide chauffeurs, janitors, firemen, cooks, basics, and bandsmen.[33]

G–3 concluded that service detachments alone would not satisfy requirements. Though the Armored Force could argue that it was not, technically, a separate branch of the service but a combination of arms and services which were already taking proportions of Negroes, G–3 pointed out that the Armored Force functioned as a separate branch of the service and was accepted by the public as such. It therefore recommended that the Armored Force, in addition to the two service detachments, activate the 78th Light Tank Battalion at Camp Claiborne, Louisiana, with Negro per-

---

[33] Memo, Hq Armd Force to Ln Off Armd

Force, 5 Dec 40, AG 320.2 (6–5–40) (3) sec. 3–D. A "basic" was an enlisted man with the minimum essentials of military training assigned to tasks requiring little experience and no specialized training.

THE LONELY EAGLES.   *Air Corps cadets standing in review on the field at Tuskegee.*

sonnel.[34] This battalion was to be activated on 1 June 1941, with 32 white enlisted instructors attached to compensate for the lack of a trained Negro cadre.[35] Despite strong objections from the Armored Force,[36] two additional tank battalions were scheduled. The 761st was activated on 1 April 1942 and the 784th Tank Battalion a year later on 1 April 1943. The three battalions, with the 78th redesignated as the 758th, formed the 5th Armored Group, activated on 23 May 1942.

In the artillery, the expansion of the number of Negro units proceeded in an orderly fashion, in accordance with theories developed during peacetime. On the basis of World War I reports, it was believed that Negroes could be employed profitably in supporting artillery units, especially in the heavier types where direct contact with the enemy would be least likely. Two antiaircraft artillery regiments and one field artillery regiment were provided in the August 1940 expansion.[37] Two National Guard infantry regiments were subsequently converted and inducted into the federal service as artillery units, one as field

---

[34] Memo, G–3 for CofS, 15 Feb 41, approved 25 Feb 41, G–3/6541–Gen–527; Ltr, TAG to Chief Armd Force, 4 Mar 41, AG 320.2 (2-25-41) M (Ret) M–C.

[35] Ltr, Hq Armd Force to TAG, 6 Mar 41 and 1st Ind, TAG to Chief Armd Force, 31 Mar 41, AG 320.2 (3-6-41).

[36] Memo, CofS for USW, 14 Apr 41, USW 291.2 Race, Negro.

---

[37] The 76th and 77th Coast Artillery (AA) and 349th Field Artillery. Headquarters and additional battalions of these units were not provided and filled until 1941.

artillery and the other as antiaircraft artillery.[38] One coast artillery, two more antiaircraft artillery, and three more field artillery regiments, and a field artillery brigade headquarters were activated in 1941.[39] By the end of 1942 eight Negro antiaircraft artillery regiments, four barrage balloon battalions, six separate antiaircraft battalions, and two separate searchlight batteries had been activated.[40] Two more searchlight batteries, which were never filled, were also constituted and partially activated. At the same time, in addition to the one field artillery brigade headquarters and division artillery, a total of seven field artillery regiments, with fourteen battalions (two 75-mm. gun, two 155-mm. gun, eight 155-mm. howitzer, and two 8-inch howitzer) had been activated.

When antitank battalions were redesignated tank destroyer battalions in December 1941, thus creating what was in all major respects a new combat arm, two Negro battalions for the new service were activated with cadres from two of the older field artillery regiments.[41] In

1942, five more Negro tank destroyer battalions were activated, with six more scheduled for 1943. Of these latter six, four only were activated.

The Traditional Arms: Divisions

Although infantry and cavalry regiments were the traditional types of Negro combat units, expansion in these arms did not proceed smoothly. The general plans for expansion called for few separate infantry and cavalry regiments, and at the beginning of mobilization all-Negro divisions were looked upon with disfavor from almost every Army quarter.

As a unit for Negroes the separate regiment had a number of advantages over the division. The regiment was a self-contained unit, able to operate alone. It did not require organic supporting elements demanding personnel with knowledge, training, and abilities which might not be easily obtained in sufficient numbers from among available Negro enlisted men. Moreover, it did not require the extensive pyramiding of leadership and administrative abilities which divisions needed if they were to function efficiently. In the zone of interior, regiments could be used as defense or school troops. Separate Negro regiments might be attached or assigned to other units for operational purposes. After demonstrating the quality of their fighting ability, separate regiments might be combined into divisions if a theater commander felt that such a move was either desirable or advantageous. Separate Negro regiments might be employed as organic elements of divisions in which other regiments and units were white.

[38] The 8th Illinois Infantry, inducted 10 February 1941 as the 184th Field Artillery; 369th Infantry (N.Y.), inducted 13 January 1941 as the 369th Coast Artillery (AA).

[39] The 54th Coast Artillery; 99th and 100th Coast Artillery (AA); 46th Field Artillery Brigade; 350th, 351st, and 353d Field Artillery.

[40] The additional regiments were the 90th, 612th, and 613th Coast Artillery (AA). A tenth, the 84th Coast Artillery (AA), was constituted but two batteries only were activated in September 1942. This unit had been intended to receive excess continental Negroes remaining from a reorganization of the 99th Regiment, then in Trinidad, and Puerto Rican Negroes. The unit later became the 84th Antiaircraft Artillery Gun Battalion, a wholly Puerto Rican outfit.

[41] These were the 846th Tank Destroyer Battalion, activated on 15 December out of the 349th Field Artillery, and the 795th Tank Destroyer Battalion, activated the next day from the 184th Field Artillery.

This last possibility went beyond the theory stage. The two Negro Regular cavalry regiments were assigned from time to time after World War I to the new cavalry divisions along with white regiments. The 9th and 10th Cavalry had so operated with white regiments in the past, both in Indian warfare and in Cuba, where during the Spanish-American War the 9th Cavalry had been brigaded with the 3d and 6th Cavalry to form the 1st Cavalry Brigade and the 10th Cavalry had been brigaded with the 1st Cavalry and the 1st U.S. Volunteer Cavalry (Roosevelt's Rough Riders) to form the 2d Cavalry Brigade. Upon organization of the 1st Cavalry Division in 1921 the 10th Cavalry was assigned to its 1st Cavalry Brigade and remained so assigned for a little more than a year.[42] In 1927 the 10th Cavalry, along with the 11th Cavalry, was assigned to the 5th Cavalry Brigade of the inactive 3d Cavalry Division.[43] Under the Four Army Organization in 1933, the 9th Cavalry was similarly assigned to the 3d Cavalry Division, replacing the 11th Cavalry in the 5th Brigade, and the 24th Infantry was assigned to the 7th Brigade of the 4th Division along with the 29th Infantry.[44] Although, except for occasional maneuvers such as those of the 1st Cavalry Division in Texas in the fall of 1929 in which the 10th Cavalry participated, the Negro regiments were not in close contact with the white regiments, their assignment to divisions with white troops was not without precedent.

In August 1940, when the cavalry requirements of the Protective Mobilization Plan were revised, the 9th and 10th Cavalry were designated for GHQ Reserve. The number of horse cavalry divisions was reduced from six to two. The 1st Cavalry Division was to be complete, while the 2d Cavalry Division was to have its horse cavalry regiments "and such other elements as available personnel and equipment permit." [45] Consideration was given at this time to including the two Negro regiments in the Regular Army cavalry divisions.[46] At the beginning of mobilization, the 2d, 3d, 11th, and 14th Cavalry were assigned to the 2d Cavalry Division. Of these, the 3d and 11th Cavalry were not available because of their designations for other missions. Approved plans for the placement of selective service men called for the concentration of the 2d, 14th, 9th, and 10th Cavalry at Fort Riley, Kansas, by January 1941. "Although the Tabs showing the utilization of selective service trainees do not definitely assign any particular regiments to the 2d Cavalry Division the only conclusion from them," G–3 stated in October, "is that the 2d, 14th, 9th and 10th are so assigned." [47]

The Chief of Cavalry objected strenuously to this organization. "I submit,"

<hr/>

[42] Ltr, TAG to CG's All Corps Areas, 20 Aug 21, AG 320.2 (Misc Div); Ltr, TAG to CG's, 11 Sep 22, AG 370.5 Mex Border (7-20-22).

[43] Ltr, TAG to CG's All Corps Areas, AG 320.2 (7-5-27).

[44] Ltr, OCofInf to TAG, 8 Mar 33, AG 320.2 (8-6-32) sec. 1-A; Annex 1, Changes to Conform to the Four Army Organization, 1933, Incl 1 to Directive for Four Army Organization, AG 320.2 (8-16-33) (Misc) M-E.

[45] Ltr, TAG to CG GHQ, Army, Corps Area and Dept Comdrs, Chiefs Arms and Svs, 14 Aug 40, AG 381 (8-31-40) M-C-M.

[46] Tab C, Differences Between WPD Reqmts (Tab A) and PMP Allotments (Tab B), to Memo, G–3 for CofS, 5 Aug 40, AG 320.2 (8-5-40) (3).

[47] Memo for Record attached to Memo, G–3 for TAG, 8 Oct 40, AG 320.2 (10-8-40) (2).

CAVALRYMEN OF THE 4TH CAVALRY BRIGADE *leaving West Riding Hall at Fort Riley in March 1941.*

he wrote to the Chief of Staff on 20 September 1940, "that no consideration of convenience or expediency should govern the formation of the fighting division . . . ." More specifically, he stated:

It appears to me to be obvious that such a unit nonhomogeneous—half white and half black, cannot be as effective as a homogeneous or all black or all white unit. There is not only a difference in color but there is a difference in emotional reactions. The concentration of a large body of troops in one place, approximately half white and half black, involves the risk of bitter rivalries and racial clashes. I consider this to be an unwise improvisation.

The Chief of Cavalry opposed not only the composition of the new division but also its proposed location. He felt that an all-white 2d Cavalry Division should be located on the southern border, at Fort Huachuca, Arizona, at Deming, New Mexico, or at Fort Bliss, Texas, leaving the Negro regiments at Fort Riley, Kansas; otherwise, the division should stay at Fort Riley, with the Negro regiments going to Fort Huachuca or to Fort Meade, South Dakota. Nevertheless, his chief objection was to the mixed division. "In making a decision on this matter," he concluded, "fighting efficiency should be considered the controlling factor." [48]

Despite the objections of the Chief of Cavalry, the 2d Cavalry Division was announced for organization "early in 1941" at Fort Riley. Its 3d Cavalry Brigade was to contain the white 2d and 14th Cavalry and its 4th Cavalry Brigade the Negro 9th and 10th Cavalry.[49] According to plan, the activation of other division elements was deferred. Brigade headquarters troops and weapons troops were provided in February 1941, but the division headquarters and headquarters troop was not activated until 1 April 1941.[50] The early organization and training of the division were therefore considerably hampered. Not until November 1941 were all its remaining inactive units authorized.[51] All of its organic units, except the Negro brigade and the truck unit of the quartermaster squadron, were activated with white troops. Aside from its Negro brigade, which made it, in the language of the Chief of Staff, "unique" among the divisions,[52] the 2d Cavalry Division as constituted in 1941 played no special part in the provision of units for the placement of Negro troops, for it was able to absorb only those selectees necessary to fill the 9th and 10th Cavalry.

In the spring of 1942, when the War Department decided to increase the numbers of armored and motorized divisions, Army Ground Forces recommended that one of the new divisions be provided by conversion of the 2d Cavalry Division, less its Negro 4th Cavalry Brigade, to an armored division. This recommendation was approved, with the exception that the 2d Cavalry Division was retained as a cavalry division with only its 4th Cavalry Brigade remaining active while its white elements were relieved and reassigned to the new 9th Armored Division.[53]

Retention of the 2d Cavalry Division provided for the future absorption of larger numbers of Negro selectees. Moreover, there was always the possibility that need might arise for a trained horse cavalry division. "Contrary to general opinion," Brig. Gen. Terry Allen, then commander of the 2d Cavalry Division, had written to General Marshall, "I feel that the cavalry still has a distinct role in modern warfare, when given proper missions and when properly trained and led." [54] It was not considered politically expedient to reduce the cavalry arm to one division only, nor was it considered good public relations to eliminate the two Regular Negro regiments. This combination of factors provided a new, all-Negro 2d Cavalry Division, ready to receive excess Negro

---

[48] Action Memo, CofCav for CofS, 20 Sep 40, AG 320.2 Cav (9-20-40).

[49] Ltr, TAG to CG's et al., 10 Oct 40, AG 320.2 (10-8-40) M (Ret) M-C.

[50] Ltr, TAG to CG's Seventh Corps Area and Second Army, 12 Feb 41, AG 320.2 (1-31-41) M (Ret) M-C; Ltr, TAG to CG's Second Army and Seventh Corps Area, Chiefs Arms and Svs concerned, 26 Mar 41, AG 320.2 (3-12-41) M (Ret) M-C.

[51] Ltr, TAG to CG 2d Cav Div, 24 Oct 41, AG 320.2 (7-17-41) MR-M-C.

[52] Ltr, Gen Marshall to Brig Gen Terry Allen, 23 May 41, AG 320.2 (5-13-41) (3). Certain other units were assigned both Negro and white elements, for example, the 18th Field Artillery Brigade and the 34th Coast Artillery Brigade (AA). Such brigades, however, were by no means comparable to a division in the nature of their tactical employment.

[53] Memo, Hq AGF for G-3, 12 May 42; Memo, G-3 for CG AGF, 14 May 42. Both in AGF 320.2/ 165 GNGPS (5-11-42).

[54] Ltr, Allen to Marshall, 13 May 41, AG 320.2 (5-13-41) (3).

selectees should it be needed for this purpose.[55] In November the War Department directed that new units constituted for refilling the division be ready for activation on 25 February 1943.[56] On this date, the 2d Cavalry Division, the first division in World War II to have Negro components, became the third with all Negro enlisted men, for in the meantime two Negro infantry divisions had been organized.

While the 2d Cavalry Division was the only unit of its size actually activated with Negro and white regiments, consideration had also been given to the formation of an infantry division with a combination of Negro and white troops. The Chief of Staff, in the fall of 1940, had "in mind, in case we are forced to organize a colored division," taking the two infantry regiments scheduled for location at Fort Huachuca, and adding a third Negro infantry regiment, the Negro medium artillery regiment (349th Field Artillery), and white light artillery to form a division.[57] The G–3 Division, asked for comment, replied that it did not "look with favor on the mixing of colored and white troops in a unit (white light artillery units in the colored Infantry Division) if there is any way of avoiding it, especially where the preponderance of troops in the unit are colored." [58] There is no evidence that subsequent experience with the 2d Cavalry Division served to alter either point of view.

Shortly before activation of the first Negro infantry division, the 93d, in the spring of 1942, the Chief of Staff's office noted an increasing volume of mail asking for the organization of a volunteer mixed Negro and white division.[59] Among those urging the formation of a mixed division were a number of widely known civilians, including Dorothy Canfield Fisher, the novelist; Samuel McCrea Cavert, General Secretary of the Federal Council of the Churches of Christ in America; Msgr. John A. Ryan, Director of the National Catholic Welfare Association's Department of Social Action; and Mary E. Woolley, former president of Mt. Holyoke College.[60] Letters from organizations such as the NAACP and The Council Against Intolerance, from their members, and from college professors and students also came into the War Department in large numbers. Many of the letters spoke of the symbolic importance that such a unit would have on both the national and the international scene as an earnest of national faith in democracy and as an answer to Japanese propaganda that the war was a color-based conflict.

In answering these letters, the War Department pointed out that the volunteer system was "an ineffective and dangerous" method of raising combat units and that the use of the volunteer system

[55] Ltr, TAG to CG's AGF, AAF, SOS, 21 Jul 42, AG 320.2 (7–17–42) MS–C–M; Ltr, TAG to CG's AGF, AAF, SOS, 28 Aug 42, AG 320.2 (8–27–42) MS–C–M.

[56] Ltr, TAG to CG Third Army, 23 Nov 42, AG 320.2 (11–21–42) OB–I–GN–M.

[57] Memo, SGS for G–3, 7 Nov 40, AG 320.2 (11–27–40) (2).

[58] Memo, G–3 for CofS, 27 Nov 40, AG 320.2 (11–27–40) (2).

[59] The suggestion for the formation of this division appears to have originated at a conference of Negro editors, held on 8 December 1941, the day after Pearl Harbor. The NAACP and Negro newspapers supported the suggestions. See below, pp. 143–44.

[60] DF, G–3 for CofS, 10 Feb 42, AG 291.21 (2–6–42) MB; Ltrs in AG 291.21 (12–22–41) (1); Ltrs in AG 291.2, Jan–Feb 42.

would interfere with the "scientific and orderly selective processes" used by the Army. "Although, as you point out," Mrs. Fisher was told, "it would be an encouraging gesture towards certain minorities, the urgency of the present military situation necessitates our using tested and proved methods of procedure, and using them with all haste. It prohibits our initiating experiments except where they will lead to the fulfillment of pressing military needs." [61]

Despite the volume of requests for a volunteer mixed division—and such requests continued to reach the War Department periodically until near the end of the war—when Negro divisions were finally decided upon, the motivating influence for their formation was more the need for additional organizations to take care of the increasing number of Negroes available to the Army than either the military or the public pressures involved. After Pearl Harbor, when it was obvious that the Army would increase its total size ever more rapidly—bringing with it more and more Negroes—the advantages of forming all-Negro divisions gained in attractiveness and support. Divisions could absorb 15,000 and more men each. With their elements and supporting units, furthermore, they afforded representation in almost every arm and service. They provided, as well, an answer to requests for a "division" without committing the Army on the volunteer mixed unit question or on any of the possible combinations of white and Negro units which had been suggested during the period of planning.

By the end of 1941, as the 1942 Troop Basis took shape, it appeared that the

Army of 3,600,000 men scheduled for 1942 would have a total of 71 divisions, 32 of them new infantry divisions and 4 of them new armored divisions. The Army would have to take 177,000 new Negroes during the year as a proportionate share of its increased strength. Even if the Air Forces and the ground arms and services took the maximum number of Negroes in the nondivisional units provided, a considerable excess would still remain. If all types of units were to have Negro representation, it was argued, divisions should be included. Infantry divisions, it was pointed out, would not have to be built up from scratch, for separate Negro infantry regiments already existed. They could be used to give divisions a leaven of experience. The peacetime 24th and 25th Infantry Regiments, the new 366th, 367th, and 368th Regular regiments, and the 372d National Guard Regiment were available for this purpose. The 366th Infantry, activated on 10 February 1941; the 372d, inducted 10 March 1941; the 368th, activated 1 March 1941; and the 367th, activated on 25 March 1941, all had had considerable training by the end of 1941.

During the period of discussion of the Troop Basis for 1942, estimates of the total number of divisions needed if the Army should be called upon for offensive operations reached 200.[62] That four of these (plus half a cavalry division) should be Negro did not at the time appear to be excessive since, on a proportionate basis, twenty divisions would have been Negro. The first of the Negro divisions, the 93d, was planned for activation in the spring of 1942. It

[61] Ltr, CofS to Mrs. Dorothy Canfield Fisher, 16 Feb 42, OCS 20602–254.

[62] Ltr, CofS GHQ to G–3, 6 Dec 41, GHQ 320.2/58.

would utilize two of the existing infantry regiments, the 25th and the 368th, as a nucleus and expand to full size. If the Army Air Forces took its full quota and all services and separate units of the arms took the maximum practicable number of Negroes, "three additional colored divisions are the minimum essential to provide for the disposition of approximately 177,000 additional Negroes that will enter the Army . . . ," G–3 determined. The Troop Basis for 1942 therefore scheduled four Negro infantry divisions.[63]

But snags developed in this program. G–1 pointed out that if too many Negroes entered the Army in the early months of 1942 they would have to be placed in camps where recreational facilities were not available. G–4 could make no commitment on the dates when suitable stations would be available for large numbers of Negroes. Although divisions were large units which, with overstrength, could absorb large numbers of Negroes, the problem of locations and housing, not to mention training, was vastly more complicated for them than for nondivisional units. The activation dates of the three additional divisions could be placed near the end of the calendar year, but since they were to furnish cadres to each other in turn it would be next to impossible to activate them all at nearly the same time. It was decided to limit the activations of Negro divisions in 1942 to two and carry the additional two divisions into 1943. Thus, the 93d Division could provide the cadre for the 92d Division in October 1942; the 92d could cadre another division in April 1943 and this new division

could provide a cadre for the fourth Negro infantry division in August 1943.[64] The 93d and 92d Divisions were activated as scheduled, but the deferment of the other two of the 1942 Negro divisions left 29,000 Negroes to be placed in smaller units during the calendar year.

The decision to retain the 2d Cavalry Division, whose inactive elements were to be provided by early 1943, helped alleviate the pressure for the maintenance of a balance among combat units. Although it was clear that they would be activated only as a last resort, the additional Negro infantry divisions remained in the projected troop basis for 1943 for the same reason as well as to absorb projected increases of Ground Forces Negro strength should they be needed for this purpose.

Service Units

The demand for service units became an ever increasing one in the expanding Army. The provision of service units for Negroes, especially in the Corps of Engineers and Quartermaster Corps, was originally accompanied by little debate, for it was generally agreed that Negro troops could be employed to advantage in such units. By April 1942, 42 percent of all engineer and 34 percent of all quartermaster units were Negro. Unlike those of some other arms and services these engineer and quartermaster units, even when created to absorb men made available by other branches' canceled allotments, were usually activated to fill specific military needs.

Although only one Negro engineer

[63] Memo, G–3 for CofS, 9 Jan 42, AG 381 (Mob and Tng Plan 1942) (12–12–41).

[64] Incl 1 to Ltr, Hq AGF to CG's All Newly Activated Inf Divs, 23 Apr 42, AGF 320.2/9 (Inf).

general service regiment was provided in the 1940 PMP, from the formation of the 41st Regiment in August 1940 to the end of 1942 twenty-seven engineer general service regiments were activated with Negro enlisted men. An equal number was to be added in later years. One engineer aviation regiment and nineteen battalions were activated by the end of 1942, with a larger number following in succeeding years. Separate engineer battalions, engineer water supply battalions and companies, and dump truck and aviation engineer companies accounted for the majority of the remaining engineer units activated with Negroes in the period 1940–42.

Quartermaster truck and service units were always in demand in the expanding Army. Later, as more and more troops were shipped to overseas theaters, requests for these units were generally greater than the number and the shipping space available. The many types of Negro quartermaster units activated between 1940 and the end of 1942 included truck, service, car, railhead, bakery, salvage repair, salvage collecting, laundry, fumigation and bath, gas supply, sterilization, and pack units, ranging in size from regiments to detachments. Before the war was over, there were more than 1,600 Negro quartermaster companies, plus headquarters, bakery, laundry, and driver detachments, separate platoons, and provisional units of various types and sizes. During the same period, the Quartermaster Corps, before the establishment of a separate Transportation Corps, organized Negro port battalions and companies. Subsequently, the Transportation Corps itself organized a considerable number of port and amphibian truck companies for employment at home and overseas.

In the rapid expansion of its Negro units, the Quartermaster Corps could not avoid problems common to other branches of the Army. As early as August 1941 the personnel requirements of Negro quartermaster units began to exceed the current supply of trainees graduating from quartermaster replacement training centers. To fill high priority quartermaster units scheduled for the autumn of 1941, certain quartermaster units were furnished men from the engineer, field artillery, coast artillery, infantry, and cavalry replacement training centers. Each of these centers had a surplus of Negro trainees who, as overstrength—lacking units for assignment—would otherwise present housing and assignment difficulties for their branches. Filling high priority quartermaster units with this surplus helped solve the problem of placing these men.[65]

A third branch, the Chemical Warfare Service, continued to provide units for more than its proportionate share of Negro troops from the activation of the 1st Chemical Decontamination Company onward. It was generally felt that Negroes could serve well in chemical units. Additional decontamination companies were provided. Negroes were also placed in smoke generator companies; chemical maintenance companies, aviation; chemical depot companies, aviation; and chemical platoons, airdrome. One chemical service, one chemical motorized, and one chemical processing company were activated in 1942. The

[65] Memo, G–3 for TAG, and attached Memo for Record, G–3/46578, 7 Aug 41, AG 324.71 (8–7–41) (15); Ltr, TAG to CofAAF, 26 Aug 41, AG 324.71 (8–7–41) E–C.

majority of the new chemical units for Negroes were smoke generator companies, many of them added to the troop basis during 1942 to fill expected needs of offensive operations being planned in that year. A number of these units were to be activated, trained, and initially used by defense commands.[66]

The Medical Department, as already noted, experienced considerable difficulty in providing units for its share of Negro selectees. The whole question of medical units, as distinct from medical detachments with units of other arms and services, was inextricably interwoven with that of the utilization of Negro physicians, dentists, and nurses, which in turn was part of the larger question of the use of Negro officers in general. Initially, Negro selectees designated for the Medical Department could be placed in the medical detachments of Negro regiments and battalions. As long as these were understrength, the question of the Medical Department's increasing its proportion of Negro selectees was primarily an academic one. But this situation, in which vacancies exceeded the available number of men, did not last long.

In the late summer and fall of 1940, the Medical Department made over-all plans for the employment of its share of Negro troops. These plans included provisions for both officers and enlisted men. The major feature affecting the provision of units for Negro troops was the proposal for a separate Negro unit which became the medical sanitary company of World War II. Originally called "medical companies, separate, colored," by The Surgeon General's Office, these companies were later termed sanitary companies, in conformance with the policy that no units were to be designated by race and that no special tables of organization were to be made for Negro troops which did not apply to white troops as well.[67]

The sanitary companies were originally intended to provide ward and professional services for hospitals having one hundred or more Negro patients, cared for in separate wards. After it was determined that such services would be administratively uneconomical, the units were thought of as hospital service units, containing men who could replace the approximately 180 white enlisted men normally used as chauffeurs, cooks, cooks' helpers, orderlies, and basics in a general hospital. The units would be assigned or attached to general hospitals. They would be housed, messed, and administered separately, under the command of Negro officers. Where Negro professional personnel were assigned to a hospital, these companies would provide messing and other facilities for them.

As they actually developed, the medical sanitary companies became primarily labor units employed in addition to the general hospital personnel.[68] They became general service units which might be used for any duty considered appropriate by the commander of the unit or

---

[66] Memo, OPD for CG's AGF and SOS, 6 May 42, AGF 320.2/14 (CWS); Ltr, WD to CG's Central and Western Defense Comds and Edgewood Arsenal, Md., 16 May 42, AG 320.2 (5-15-42) MR–M–GN.

[67] Memo, G-3 for G-1, 5 Nov 40, G-3/42108; Memo, G-1 for TAG, 13 Nov 40, and 1st Ind, TAG to SGO, 15 Nov 40, 2d Ind SGO to TAG, 20 Nov 40. Last three in AG 320.2 (8-2-40) sec. 6.
[68] Memo, G-1 for CofS, 15 Jan 41, AG 320.2 (10-25-40) (8-2-40) (4), sec. 6.

station to which they were assigned. While the companies were to be assigned to all hospitals having 1,000 or more beds, lack of funds for the construction of the necessary additional housing delayed the activation of the sanitary companies until the need for new Negro units to absorb the Medical Department's quota became more pressing.[69]

Only two medical sanitary companies were activated in 1941. These two were activated "because of pressure on G–1 to put colored medical personnel on duty" and not, as in the case of certain other units, primarily for the purpose of absorbing surplus Negro selectees.[70] Fifty-four were added during 1942. A larger number was planned for 1943, but not all of the units scheduled were activated. The 1943 companies were available for activation whenever monthly Army Service Forces Negro quotas could not be absorbed elsewhere.[71] Thirty companies were eventually activated in 1943 and one in 1944. Many of the 1943 companies were inactivated or disbanded in the fall of 1943 or in 1944 when more vitally needed service units were being filled for immediate overseas use.

Aside from station hospitals at Tuskegee and at Fort Huachuca, four field hospitals, and scattered veterinary, ambulance, and administrative units, medical sanitary companies remained the major medical units provided for Negroes.

Negro military police units were not provided until after local experiments with Negro military police detachments showed that their use in areas with large Negro troop populations paid dividends in better order, better relations between troops and the military police, and better relations with civilians in those communities which had learned to look upon Negro military policemen as something less than a threat to local customs. Most of these units were small detachments of men detailed to military police duty from station complements. Among them there was little uniformity in procedure, organization, or training. Some posts used Negro military police on special duty assignments; others used them on a full-time basis. Until the establishment of the Corps of Military Police on 26 September 1941, these units were generally under the direct control of post and service commanders.

The directive establishing the new Corps of Military Police required responsible commanders to report the designation, station, and strength, by race, of existing units.[72] There were twenty-two of these detachments of Negro military police on 30 June 1942, ranging in size from two men at Fort Sam Houston, Texas, to sixty-five at Camp San Luis Obispo, California.[73] Ten Negro military police battalions (zone of interior) and three companies were activated in August 1942. Two more battalions were scheduled, but the War Department decided not to activate any more Negro units of this type and they therefore received white personnel. Two Negro prisoner of war escort com-

[69] Memo, G–4 for G–1, 21 Jan 41, G–4/32470; Memo, SGO for TAG, 4 Mar 41, AG 320.2 (3–4–41) (8–2–40) (4) sec. 6.
[70] Memo for Record, attached to Memo, G–3 for TAG, 27 Feb 41, AG 320.2 (2–27–41).
[71] Cf. Min of Gen Council, 8 Feb 43.

[72] Ltr, TAG to PMG et al., 26 Sep 41, AG 320.2 (9–26–41) MR–M–A.
[73] Tab A to Memo, Chief MP Div OPMG for Dir Mil Pers SOS, 23 Oct 42, AG 210.31 (2–14–42) (3).

MILITARY POLICE UNIT AT COLUMBUS, GEORGIA, APRIL 1942

panies were included in the 1942 Troop Basis but, on the request of the Provost Marshal General, they too were activated with white personnel, with G–3 stipulating that future plans provide for the use of Negroes in this duty.[74]

The Ordnance Department provided ammunition companies and almost no others for the receipt of Negroes. Aviation ordnance depot and aviation ordnance supply and maintenance companies were provided in the Army Air Forces; several medium automotive maintenance companies in the Army Ground Forces were activated with Negro enlisted men.

Signal Corps units for the receipt of an increased proportion of Negro enlisted men were confined to construction and to Air Forces types of signal units. One construction company was activated in May 1941 and saw early duty in Panama. Except for three construction companies, and three construction battalions, all other Negro signal units activated in 1942 were Air Forces units. These included eleven construction battalions, two aircraft warning companies, and one service group signal company. The Signal Corps remained below its

[74] Memo, G–3 for PMG, 11 Feb 42, G–3/42107; Memo, SOS for G–3, 10 Aug 42; Memo, G–3 for CG SOS, 12 Aug 42, and Inds. Last three in WDGCT 320.2 Actv (8–10–42).

proportionate share of Negro troops throughout the war.

Miscellaneous Units and Minor Problems

A number of miscellaneous units were provided for Negro troops in 1940–42. Chief among these were bands, replacement companies, postal units, service command units (SCU's) at posts and at civilian educational institutions, and a special service company. Various provisional units, training units, school detachments, and overhead supply detachments were also utilized for the placement of Negro troops. Many of these units, such as bands and replacement companies, were needed to service Negro trainees.

Occasionally, specific requests for the activation of Negro units were made by commanders who needed additional troops for tasks connected with the operation of their posts. Such a request came from Fort Knox in 1942. An engineer separate battalion was needed there to construct roads, training facilities, and firing aids in an expanded range and training area. The Chief of Engineers, believing that all units should be trained for future theater of operations use, objected to the activation of units for full-time employment on local tasks. This unit was therefore activated with the stipulation that it be trained in its usual duties by rotating its companies between training and necessary work and that it "not be used solely for labor while at Fort Knox." [75]

The commander at Fort Belvoir, Virginia, similarly asked for authority to advance the activation date for a medical sanitary company, ostensibly because a First Army medical inspector had indicated that it was desirable to start training this type of unit as soon as possible. When First Army asked for further reasons for advancing the activation date for the unit, it developed that the post commander expected that the organization could be used to good advantage in mosquito control and general camp sanitation without interfering with its training. [76]

Truck regiments, provisional and permanent, for use at service schools, and school detachments to replace civilians, such as janitors and table waiters for instructors' and student officers' living quarters and messes, accounted for a number of units provided for Negro troops. The Field Artillery School at Fort Sill, Oklahoma, explained its need for additional Negro enlisted men in its school detachment:

Until recently, civilian colored kitchen police and table waiters were available in sufficient numbers to maintain officer and instructor messes without difficulty. Lately, we have not been able to employ the required number, since a large percentage of this labor has been drafted. Other eligible men who would be desirable in the messes are now employed elsewhere at more attractive wages and better working hours. The problem of securing adequate kitchen police and table waiters is becoming more acute. [77]

The Parachute School at Fort Benning wanted a Negro service company to

---

[75] Ltr, Hq Armd Force to TAG, 23 Feb 42, and Incls, AG 320.2 (2–23–42) (11–15–40) (1) sec. 11; Ltr, TAG to CG's, 12 Mar 42, AG 320.2 (2–23–42) MR–M–C.

[76] Ltr, Hq Ft. Belvoir to CG Third Corps Area, 25 Feb 42, AG 320.2 (11–15–40) (1) sec. 11.
[77] Ltr, FA School to CG R&SC, 2 Oct 42, AGF 352/402 (FA School).

TABLE 2—RACIAL DISTRIBUTION BY TYPES OF SERVICE (ENLISTED ONLY)
31 DECEMBER 1942

Type of Service	White	Negro	Percentage of All Negroes in Each Type of Service	Percentage of All Men in Army	
				Whites	Negroes
Army total	4,532,117	467,883	10.3	100.0	100.0
Combat units	1,815,094	92,772	4.8	40.0	19.7
Service units	616,851	161,707	20.7	13.6	34.5
AAF and ASWAAF	1,190,363	109,637	8.4	26.4	23.5
Overhead a	363,820	65,880	15.3	8.0	14.1
RTC's	238,500	27,500	10.3	5.3	5.9
OCS	72,200	800	1.1	1.5	0.2
Unassigned	235,289	9,587	3.9	5.2	2.1

a Includes replacement depots and hospitals.

Source: Extended from Tab B, Memo, G–3 for CG's AGF and SOS, 25 Jan 43, WDGCT 320.2 Gen (1-25-43).

relieve its own students of such duties as kitchen police, guarding installations, and policing training areas, hangars, and administrative buildings.[78] Other units were formed for demonstration purposes at certain schools. Occasionally, needed units were activated overseas from experienced units already in the theater, fillers being provided from the mainland.[79]

The provision of certain types of units for Negroes sometimes ran counter to local civilian customs and attitudes toward the types of tasks for which Negroes should be trained and employed. The

Alabama State Firemen's Association objected to the employment of Negro soldiers in the fire department at Fort McClellan. The association wanted these traditionally "white" jobs kept for white men.[80] California longshoremen's unions objected to the formation of Negro port battalions and stated: "This move can only be interpreted by us as being directed against union labor." [81] Many areas objected to the use of Negro guard and air base security battalions, on the ground that they violated local mores. The War Depart-

[78] Ltr, Prcht School to CG AGF, 27 Jul 42, AGF 322.999/2 (Cld Trps) (7-27-42).

[79] Examples are aviation engineer battalions, requested by the South Pacific Base Command in 1942, to be activated in the theater with cadres from the 810th and 811th Engineer Battalions (Avn), which "will furnish the new units with a higher level of experience than can be obtained from any existing unit in the United States." DF, Hq AAF to Hq AGF, 4 Aug 42, AGF 320.2/347.

[80] Ltrs, Senator J. H. Bankhead and others, various dates, April–June 1941, AG 291.21 (5-3-41) (1).

[81] Telg, International Longshoremen's and Warehousemen's Union to President Roosevelt, 9 Apr 41, AG 080 Los Angeles, Calif. (4-10-41) (1) and Ltrs in AG 080 International Longshoremen's and Warehousemen's Union (8-26-41) and AG 080 San Francisco, Calif. (8-27-41) (1). These include letters from United Hotel Employees, CIO, supporting the IL&WU.

ment's assurance that these units were being formed for military needs only and that their primary use, after the completion of training, would be outside of the United States, brought an end to this type of protest.

By the end of 1942, despite difficulties in carrying out the plan, the War Department had made tremendous progress toward achieving the goal of proportionate distribution. At that time every arm and service had Negro units with the exception of the Finance Department, and even Finance had Negroes on individual assignment with other units. But the basic distribution problem had not been solved, for the proportions of Negroes assigned to the arms as compared with those assigned to the services did not match the ratios of white troops so assigned. *(Table 2)*

Proportionate distribution, which on paper and at first glance appeared to be an eminently fair procedure for the provision of Negro units, both from the points of view of the branches and of Negroes, had revealed serious disadvantages by the end of 1942. Block assignment of Negroes according to the numbers which the Army had to take in monthly induction quotas; allowing some of the branches to immobilize large numbers of men who required housing, supplies, and officers although their ultimate usefulness was doubtful; distributing men on the basis of proportionate quotas rather than according to the needs of the service and the abilities of the men —the wisdom of continuing these policies among others came into question. The War Department finally came to realize that the continued provision of units on the basis of numerical proportions involved more and more minor problems which showed every sign of growing into major ones.

CHAPTER VI

Proposals and Counterproposals

During 1941 and 1942 many papers and studies directed toward a solution of the question of the proper and equitable employment of Negro troops were prepared in War Department agencies. They arrived, with few exceptions, at no new conclusions, except to recommend again that the necessary additional units to absorb Negroes be provided and that each arm and service continue to accept its proportionate share.

The few exceptions in this continuing round of studies appeared at widely separated intervals and under quite different circumstances. In September 1941 the Civilian Aide to the Secretary of War, William H. Hastie, after ten months of "observation, discussion, and action in the War Department and in the field," produced an "overall description of what is happening to the Negro in the Army" and suggested corrective measures. In March 1942 the War Plans Division produced a study calling for a complete reassessment of the basis for the use of Negro manpower. Out of G–3 in October of the same year came a third study suggesting changes in the entire approach to the problem.

Though only a few of the suggestions made in the studies were acted upon, these three studies indicate the range of corrective suggestions made before the pattern of Army racial organization in wartime had set too firmly for significant changes to be made. They, and the reactions to them, are indexes to the extent of recognition of the problems involved and to the resistance that ideas and new proposals can meet.

The Hastie Survey

Judge Hastie's survey and recommendations, written while the Army was still undergoing its peacetime expansion and training, considered nearly every large question involved in the employment of Negro troops, but it was his recommendation on the organization of units that created most concern within the staff divisions of the War Department.[1]

The basic contentions of Judge Hastie's survey were that the Army could utilize many more Negroes in many more varieties of service than it was currently doing and that Negro troops could be organized more effectively for military service. In an introductory section, headed "The Fundamental Error of Philosophy and Approach," Hastie opened his report:

---

[1] Survey and Recommendations Concerning the Integration of the Negro Soldier into the Army, Submitted to the Secretary of War by the Civilian Aide to the Secretary of War, in Memo, Civ Aide to SW for SW through USW, 22 Sep 41, G–1/15640–120. (Referred to hereafter as Hastie Survey.)

The traditional mores of the South have been widely accepted and adopted by the Army as the basis of policy and practice affecting the Negro soldier. . . . In tactical organization, in physical location, in human contacts, the Negro soldier is separated from the white soldier as completely as possible. . . . The isolation of Negro combat troops, the failure to make many of them parts of large combat teams, the refusal to mingle Negro officers—most of whom have had little opportunity to command and train soldiers —in units with experienced officers of the Regular Army, all are retarding the training of Negro soldiers.

Hastie's major premise, thus stated, predisposed certain agencies to react unfavorably to his recommendations out of fear that the results would involve the Army in social as well as military problems.

Hastie's survey of the current status of the Negro soldier in the Army indicated a marked contrast between practice and announced policies. On 30 June 1941, the Army had 74,309 Negro enlisted men out of a total strength of 1,448,500. They represented only 5 percent of the whole. Plans current at that time set a goal of only 6 percent, for though about 10 percent of Selective Service inductees were Negroes, only 3 percent of three-year Regular enlistees and less than 2 percent of National Guard enlisted men were Negroes. Moreover, Hastie added, "The newly enlisted Negro soldiers have been disproportionately concentrated in the Corps of Engineers, the Quartermaster Corps, and Overhead installations." Hastie felt that the imbalance had come about because these were the branches which could use Negroes "most easily in detached units, rather than as an integral part of larger combat teams." The "most glaring disproportion," he continued, was in the overhead installations, which G–3 was considering increasing to 20 percent of all Negroes. The intention was to confine Negroes to small service detachments "performing nonmilitary duties of unskilled and menial character" that should be performed by civilian employees not available for military service. "Where there are both colored and white service detachments in the Overhead of a particular station, the most undesirable duties are assigned to the colored detachment," he continued.

The suggestion that the high proportion of Negroes assigned to labor functions was justified by the proportionately large numbers of Negro selectees in Class V, the lowest class of the Army General Classification Test (AGCT), "must be discounted," Hastie argued, for illiterates were no longer to be accepted, selective service volunteers had higher basic abilities, and college students deferred for the first year of mobilization were rapidly being called to duty. "Finally," Hastie reported, "the evidence of field commanders indicates that a high percentage of the men with little education or acquired skill at the time of their induction, can be used effectively in combat units. Many such men have basic intelligence and are eager to learn for the very reason that opportunity has been denied them in civilian life. And even for men of small intelligence there are many important jobs in Combat organizations." As an illustration, he cited the 77th Coast Artillery, "composed in large measure of Negro Selective Service trainees of low classification," whose training record showed that it had "progressed faster than a white artillery regiment which is a component of the same brigade." [2]

The growing Selective Service backlogs, failure to use more Negroes in newer types of organizations, poor classification and assignment methods, the location of three-fourths of Negro trainees in the South where they had to accommodate themselves "to humiliation and insult imposed by those who insist upon traditional Southern practices designed to keep the Negro humble and subordinate, when the Army should, on the other hand, insist that every man in uniform be treated as a man and a soldier," and lack of opportunities for the development of capable Negro officers were among the other major matters treated by Hastie in his survey.

The chief difficulties which the Army was experiencing and which, he predicted, would increase, Hastie attributed to the pattern of rigid separation by units within the Army:

Many of the underlying problems of morale and administration discussed in this report are inherent in the fundamental scheme of separate units for colored soldiers. Difficulties begin in Selective Service calls where the requirement of separate units has led to separate calls for white and colored soldiers in violation of the spirit of the Selective Service lottery. It will be remembered that in at least one state local officials refused for a period to honor such racial calls. The danger of such rebellion is again imminent. Many of the problems of placing Negro soldiers according to training and ability result from the necessity for finding a separate Negro unit and a vacancy in such a unit before the soldier can be assigned to duty. . . .

All of this will not be changed over night. The disturbing thing, however, is that there is no apparent disposition to make a beginning or a trial of any different plan. The beginning of the training of Negro pilots for the Army Air Corps offered such an opportunity for a fresh start along sound lines. For example, a substantial portion of the Armored Force is being trained at Pine Camp, New York, in an area where racial tensions are not serious. Integration of highly competent Negroes, selectees and volunteers for 3-year enlistments, into such an organization would be an important first step in the desirable direction. It is strongly recommended that some such beginning be made in the Air Corps, in the Armored Force, or in any organization which in its nature requires carefully selected men of superior intelligence and special competence.

I believe the Military authorities do not comprehend the amount of resentment among soldiers and civilians, white as well as black, over the rigid pattern of racial separation imposed by the Army. Today, soldiers and civilians are more critical than they were 25 years ago in their examination of our professed ideals. Insistence upon an inflexible policy of separating white and black soldiers is probably the most dramatic evidence of hypocrisy in our profession that we are girding ourselves for the preservation of democracy.[3]

In his specific recommendations for the organization of Negro troops, Judge Hastie proposed four points "in order that the progressive integration of Negro soldiers into the Army shall proceed in such manner as to achieve the greatest possible Military advantage." These recommendations were:

1. New organizations must be provided as speedily as possible to accommodate the anticipated excess of Negro selectees.

2. Negro combat regiments should be made components of higher units; isolated single companies and detachments should be eliminated.

---

[2] Hastie Survey, p. 5.

[3] *Ibid.*, pp. 18–19.

3. Isolated small units which are the only Negro troops at their stations should be transferred to other stations (in order to obviate the need of providing expensive separate recreational facilities for them).

4. At some place in the armed services a beginning should be made in the employment of soldiers without racial separation.

Judge Hastie's recommendations were submitted to Under Secretary Patterson. Judge Patterson, in sending the paper to General Marshall, asked: "Will you please give this your careful consideration and let me have your views on it? It will probably be best to have an oral discussion of these issues." [4] Full replies to the memorandum, with changes, alterations, and comments, were prepared over a period of weeks by the assistant chiefs of staff and by interested agencies to whom the report was sent. In mid-November 1941, Judge Patterson reminded General Marshall that he had not yet heard from him and that he still wanted to discuss "at an early date Judge Hastie's memorandum of suggestions on Negro troops in the Army, which I sent to you with my memorandum of October 6th." [5] General Bryden, Deputy Chief of Staff, discussed the matter with Under Secretary Patterson on 5 December 1941, two and one-half months after the recommendations had been made and two days before Pearl Harbor, an event which effectively altered the course of discussion of the Hastie recommendations.

No one quarreled seriously with the first three recommendations of Judge Hastie. New Negro units, as described above, were activated as rapidly as possible. The possible organization of all-Negro divisions, although Hastie had not urged it, was expected to answer the question of making smaller combat units parts of larger units. The organization of the 2d Cavalry Division, although Hastie was not so told, was considered proof that "the Department is not opposed in principle to the inclusion of negro regiments in higher units." The GHQ tank battalion (the 78th, later 758th) and the 99th Pursuit Squadron were cited as evidence of willingness to activate units in "new type" organizations. More would be activated as qualified men became available, but comparative AGCT scores seemed to indicate that such an event was unlikely.[6]

Judge Hastie's proposal for a beginning in desegregation and his belief that with carefully selected men of high qualifications such a beginning might safely be made on a small scale, overshadowed his other recommendations in the eyes of most commenting agencies. Hastie himself had assumed that such a beginning should be made in peacetime since in his view, with the country at war, any alteration of existing relationships might be considered as a dangerous experiment for a time of national emergency. He had also assumed that from both the

---

[4] Memo, USW for CofS, 6 Oct 41, G-1/15640-120.

[5] Memo, USW for Gen Marshall, 19 Nov 41, OCS/20602-226.

[6] Measures Which Have Been Taken or Which Are Being Taken in Connection With Some of the Recommendations Made by Judge W. H. Hastie in Memorandum Dated September 22, 1941, prepared by G-1 in collaboration with G-3 as Incl to Memo prepared for CofS for submission to SW, 1 Dec 41, OCS/20602-219, Incl not used and returned to G-1; D/S, 2 Dec 41, G-1/15640-120. See Chapter IX, below, for a discussion of AGCT scores and their significance.

point of view of economy in the use of manpower and in military efficiency such a beginning would be desirable. Most of all, he felt that such a step, taken concurrently with his other recommendations, would have tremendous symbolic value:

I sincerely believe that much of the difficulty being experienced in arousing the nation today is traceable to the fact that we have lost that passion for national ideals which a people must have if it is to work and sacrifice for its own survival. We have lost that motivative drive because we have let our own behavior become inconsistent with our wordy professions. Whatever we may think of the ideals of Germany or Russia, fascism on the one hand and communism on the other had to become a national obsession, a driving force revealed in domestic behavior, before these nations could be keyed to a great war effort for the preservation and extension of their ideologies.
Until the men in our Army and civilians at home believe in and work for democracy with similar fervor and determination, we will not be an effective nation in the face of a foreign foe. So long as we condone and appease un-American attitudes and practices within our own military and civilian life, we can never arouse ourselves to the exertion which the present emergency requires.[7]

The General Staff took the point of view that Hastie wished the Army to carry out a complete social revolution against the will of the nation. An unused memorandum proposed by G–1 with the concurrence of G–3 clearly stated the case for the staff divisions:

It is the opinion of these Divisions that, under no circumstances should the War Department concur in those recommendations which are based largely upon racial and social issues. The immediate task of

the Army is the efficient completion of our Defense Program. Nothing should be permitted to divert us from this task. Contrary to the bulk of the recommendations, every effort should be made by the War Department to maintain in the Army the social and racial conditions which exist in civil life in order that the normal customs of the white and colored personnel now in the army may not be suddenly disrupted. The Army can, under no circumstances, adopt a policy which is contrary to the dictates of a majority of the people. To do so would alienate the people from the Army and lower their morale at a time when their support of the Army and high morale are vital to our National needs.[8]

In the formal memorandum of the Chief of Staff to the Secretary of War on the subject, dated 1 December 1941, General Marshall wrote:

A solution of many of the issues presented by Judge Hastie in his memorandum to you on "The Integration of the Negro Soldier into the Army," dated September 22, would be tantamount to solving a social problem which has perplexed the American people throughout the history of this nation. The Army cannot accomplish such a solution, and should not be charged with the undertaking. The settlement of vexing racial problems cannot be permitted to complicate the tremendous task of the War Department and thereby jeopardize discipline and morale.

. . . .

The problems presented with reference to utilizing negro personnel in the Army should be faced squarely. In doing so, the following facts must be recognized; first, that the War Department cannot ignore the social relationships between negroes and whites which has been established by the American people through custom and habit; second, that either through lack of educational opportunities or other causes the level of intelligence and occupational skill of the negro population is considerably

[7] Hastie Survey, p. 24.

[8] Memo, G–1 for CofS, 6 Nov 41, G–1/15640–120.

below that of the white; third, that the Army will attain its maximum strength only if its personnel is properly placed in accordance with the capabilities of individuals; and fourth, that experiments within the Army in the solution of social problems are fraught with danger to efficiency, discipline, and morale.[9]

To all practical intents and purposes, Hastie and the Army's high command had reached an impasse on this particular question before the formal entry of the United States into war.

The Editors' Conference and Its Aftermath

Just at the time that the Chief of Staff's formal reply to the Hastie recommendations was sent to the Secretary, the Bureau of Public Relations and Judge Hastie were arranging a conference of Negro editors and publishers.[10] They had scheduled their meeting for 8 December 1941, a date whose significance was to be known only after the Sunday, 7 December, attack on Pearl Harbor. This type of conference, planned to provide the Negro press with factual information concerning the functions of the various War Department agencies and to endeavor to create better relations between the Army and the Negro public, had been used successfully in World War I.[11] At round table discussions, the editors were to hear representatives of The Adjutant General's Department, the Bureau of Public Relations, the Morale Branch,

The Inspector General's Department, the Provost Marshal General's Office, the Judge Advocate General's Office, and the Civilian Personnel Division. A tour of the Bureau of Public Relations, an exhibition of films, and a demonstration of modern warfare at Fort Belvoir, Virginia, would follow. The conference was to open with remarks by General Marshall.

For General Marshall's address, the G–3 Division prepared two reports. The first contained current statistics on the employment of Negro personnel. It listed the achievement of the Army in activating the 99th Pursuit Squadron and the 758th Tank Battalion, in planning the activation of tank destroyer units, in distributing Negroes "in all our arms and services," in the use of Negro officers, and in general advances in training. The second, "furnished for background purposes, only," contained statements that might be useful in "refuting charges that discrimination is being practiced against negroes." It contained statistics comparing white and Negro AGCT score distributions (at that time, 13.34 percent of the white and .64 percent of the Negro soldiers were in the highest class; 5.51 percent of the whites and 45.05 percent of the Negroes were in the lowest class); comparisons of AGCT scores of white and Negro high school graduates and then of college graduates; racial comparisons of occurrence rates of occupational specialists (44.2 percent white to 5.3 Negro clerks per 1,000; 99.5 white to 118.8 Negro truck drivers; .586 white airplane mechanics to .045 Negro; 8.9 white to 31.5 Negro cooks; .346 white to .011 Negro telegraph operators per 1,000); and selected comments of World War I com-

---

[9] Memo, CofS for SW, 1 Dec 41, OCS 20602–219.

[10] Memo, Bureau of Public Relations for TAG, 1 Dec 41, AG 291.21 (12–1–41) (1).

[11] Emmett J. Scott, "The Participation of Negroes in World War I: An Introductory Statement," *Journal of Negro Education*, Yearbook No. XII (1943), p. 293.

manders on the combat efficiency of Negro troops as compiled by the Army War College.[12]

In his talk General Marshall pointed out the progress that had been made and that was in the offing. Here he made the first public announcement that a Negro division was being considered. He made clear his recognition of the problem faced by the War Department and said that the department was not satisfied with the progress it had made. In an aside General Marshall added, "And I am not personally satisfied with it either." Coming as they did in the emotionally charged atmosphere of the morning after Pearl Harbor and just before the Congress of the United States assembled to hear the President's request for a declaration that the nation was in a state of war with Japan, General Marshall's remarks, especially the added comment on his personal feeling in the matter, made a profound impression on the Negro editors. But, an hour later, Col. Eugene R. Householder, of The Adjutant General's Department, read from a prepared paper:

The Army did not create the problem. The Army is made up of individual citizens of the United States who have pronounced views with respect to the Negro just as they have individual ideas with respect to other matters in their daily walk of life. Military orders, fiat, or dicta, will not change their viewpoints. The Army then cannot be made the means of engendering conflict among the mass of people because of a stand with respect to Negroes which is not compatible with the position attained by the Negro in civilian life. This principle must necessarily govern the Army not only with this subject of contention but with

respect to other dogma be it religious, political, or economic. The Army is not a sociological laboratory; to be effective it must be organized and trained according to the principles which will insure success. Experiments, to meet the wishes and demands of the champions of every race and creed for the solution of their problems are a danger to efficiency, discipline and morale and would result in ultimate defeat.[13]

The editors, comparing this presentation with General Marshall's, were appalled. They attacked the position outlined. In their discussions they pointed out that whether it wished to or not, an army carried within itself certain social forces. They took the phrase "The Army is not a sociological laboratory" and used it as a cynical summation of Army policy. They contended that current practices extended segregation and prejudices to sections of the country where such patterns had not formerly existed. They took Colonel Householder's statement to mean that the Army had no intention of modifying its racial practices. They took General Marshall's statement to mean that, on the contrary, change within the Army was not only possible but desirable. General Marshall's, as the more hopeful and more responsible attitude, was the one they chose to accept, though they could not ignore the implication that it might not be shared by all of his subordinates.

The announcement of the new division for Negroes was headlined by most of the Negro papers as the biggest news coming out of the meeting. But the assembled editors interpreted the con-

---

[12] Memo, G–3 for CofS, 3 Dec 41; Memo, G–3 for Col W. B. Smith, SGS, 4 Dec 41. Both in AG 322.97 (12–3–41) (1).

[13] Speech, The Adjutant General's Department, AG 291.21 (12–1–41) (1).

ference's main significance to be that more serious consideration of the Negro's position in the Army by its responsible chiefs would bring "steady but slow improvement," as an editor of the Pittsburgh *Courier* expressed it. He explained:

This does not mean that all desires of the Negro citizen are to be favorably acted upon immediately. It does not mean that segregation in the Army is going to vanish overnight [nor does it mean that the Army has been persuaded that] now is the time to begin planning to abolish segregation. . . . [General Marshall's statement] means, of course, that the directing head of the War Department and the United States Army knows about our problem, is personally interested in it and personally desires that restrictions against the advancement of the Negro soldier be lifted.
I think General Marshall was honest when he made the statement. I think that his present attitude, in the light of the past, represents an improvement due to greater knowledge of our problem and greater understanding. I think that General Marshall's attitude, so far as we're concerned, is growing better and better.[14]

Or, as the Norfolk *Journal and Guide* put it:

It was the general consensus of those attending the conference that a surprisingly new outlook was vouchsafed by key men in the War Department setup, that they seem more open-minded to a new deal in relation to the Colored American in the armed forces, and have actually initiated some fundamental changes without a lot of fanfare.[15]

Not all papers reacted so favorably. The Chicago *Defender* stated editorially that:

Mr. Hastie, though a very capable gentleman, has no appreciable authority and scarcely any influence with the big wigs of the War Department. He can make no commitments, and he cannot explain away the segregative and discriminatory practices to which the high officials of his own department are clinging. What then is the purpose of this conference? It is an obvious attempt to appease belligerent Negro editors who have taken a critical view of the whole panorama of national defense.[16]

The conference may "properly be placed in a compartment and marked 'File and Forget,'" the Newark, New Jersey, *Herald-News* commented, for ". . . it convinced no one, not already convinced, that racial segregation or color proscriptions have any place in the official policy of a nation dedicated to the defense of democracy and democratic institutions." [17]

During the discussions of the assembled editors, Claude A. Barnett, director of the Associated Negro Press, suggested that if the process of integrating Negroes into units as individuals was hampered by personal objections and prejudices of white and Negro soldiers, the Army might open one or more units on a volunteer basis to those Negroes and whites who would prefer service in a nonsegregated unit. A few weeks after the conference, Walter White of the National Association for the Advancement of Colored People, "emboldened . . . by your statement [of] your personal dissatisfaction with the progress made to date with respect to integration of Negroes into the United States Army," took this suggestion and offered the aid of his organization to General Marshall for the formation of a volunteer divi-

---

[14] P. L. Prattis, "The Horizon: Conference of Negro Editors Was Challenge to War Department Officials," Pittsburgh *Courier*, December 18, 1941.
[15] Norfolk *Journal and Guide*, December 18, 1941.

[16] Chicago *Defender*, December 18, 1941.
[17] Newark *Herald-News*, December 20, 1941.

sion "open to all irrespective of race, creed, color or national origin." Citing correspondence received by his organization and others "from all parts of the United States including the South," White stated that authorization for such a unit would "serve as a tremendous lift to the morale of the Negro which at present is at a dangerously low ebb. We are convinced that it also would have tremendous psychological effect upon white Americans and it would give the lie to the attacks made by Nazi Germany and other Axis powers to the effect that the United States talks about democracy but practices racial discrimination and segregation." [18]

White's letter was referred in a routine manner to The Adjutant General by an assistant secretary of the General Staff. In the meantime, White wrote a second letter to General Marshall, correcting an erroneous reference to a regiment in his first letter when he had intended to write "division" and suggesting that since he was to be in Washington in January perhaps a conference to discuss his proposal could be arranged.[19] The Adjutant General answered in what was essentially a form letter:

The Chief of Staff has requested that I acknowledge receipt of your letter of January 2, 1942, relative to the organization of a volunteer division of the Army open to all without respect to race or color, and requesting a conference with regards to the matter.

The War Department does not contemplate the organization of a division such as suggested, and consequently a conference on the subject is not deemed necessary.[20]

This reply caused Walter White and the Negro editors to believe that the program presented at the 8 December conference had been another case of the War Department's using a public approach different from the private path it intended to pursue, a path which would not lead to any real change in the status of Negro participation in the war. The Assistant Secretary of War, John J. McCloy, informed of the unfavorable reaction, suggested in a note to Maj. Gen. Emory S. Adams, The Adjutant General:

There have been some repercussions resulting from what has been considered to be the undue curtness of the reply of January 8 to Walter White, Secretary of the National Association for the Advancement of Colored People. I have not the slightest doubt of the unwisdom of having any such unit as was proposed in White's letter to Marshall, but I am inclined to think that in the future it may be advisable to handle these matters by an interview. Of course, it isn't necessary that General Marshall should take part in any such interview but some officer might well do so.

I am told that the very good effect which General Marshall's appearance before the negro editors made has been somewhat dissipated by this letter and some failure to act on several other much less objectionable requests put forward by Judge Hastie.

I am sending this down to you merely because your name was on the letter. I have no doubt that it was drafted elsewhere and merely sent out by you as a routine matter, but I thought you might be able to trace it.[21]

[18] Ltr, Walter White, Secy NAACP, to Gen Marshall, 22 Dec 41, AG 291.21 (12-22-41) (1).

[19] Ltr, Walter White to Gen Marshall, 2 Jan 42, AG 291.21 (1-2-42) (12-22-41) (1).

[20] Ltr, TAG to Walter White, 8 Jan 42, AG 291.21 (1-2-42) MB (12-22-41) (1).

[21] Memo, ASW for TAG, 13 Jan 42, AG 291.21 (1-13-42) (12-22-41) (1). General Adams penciled on the memo, "I drafted the reply personally after ascertaining from A.C.S. G-3 that no such division was contemplated by the W.D. E.S.A."

General Adams sent a copy of the McCloy note to Lt. Col. James W. Boyer, Jr., of the Miscellaneous Division, Adjutant General's Office. Colonel Boyer had been in frequent consultation with the Hastie office and with members of the Negro press. He had helped draft many letters to White. In a memorandum for General Adams, Boyer detailed a complex of reactions to the situation representative of the position of many of those administrative officers who had to deal daily with the matter of the employment of Negroes in the Army:

2. I yield to no one in the War Department in the matter of tolerance for the Negro. I have dealt on a most pleasant basis with Judge Hastie, not only on the basis of the relationship of his position in the War Department, but on the basis that he himself is a fine and intelligent person. Incidentally, I know of no failure to act on requests put forward by Judge Hastie. All of his requests have had expedited service so far as I know.

3. The War Department is confronted, however, with a condition that bids fair to be insidious, even cancerous. Judge Hastie makes no bones about it that "the time for minorities to make their gains is the time of national emergency." With utmost frankness, then, it is the purpose of Judge Hastie and his backers to advance the colored people as a race at the expense of the Army. Not satisfied with any gain, and there have been many, he intends to go from one disputed point to another. When the War Department recedes from an announced position he is prepared to submit some other equally debatable issue. While many of these issues are small in themselves, the cumulative effect is being felt throughout the War Department among those who deal with Negro problems. Incident after incident could be recounted wherein he has demonstrated willful persistence in breaking down the Department's long considered policies.

4. Of course, Judge Hastie considers himself a representative of the National Association for the Advancement of Colored People first, and a representative of the War Department second. I do not believe that he has helped solve any problem of significance but has created them. I believe that the Secretary of War should know that this is true.

5. With respect to Mr. White, the letters addressed to him may have been curt. His letters to the War Department have been increasingly insolent on subjects which are of no concern to the National Association for the Advancement of Colored People. Should Mr. White be justified in his action, so also could be the Jewish Welfare Board or an association of the Japanese-American, or any other group, social or otherwise, set up to be special pleaders for minority causes. It is inconceivable that any other minority would be treated with such tolerance. Should the National Commander of the American Legion address the Department as White has done, he would receive scant consideration.

6. I can see no useful purpose in any officer dissipating his time to discuss with Mr. White or anyone else the creation of a volunteer division composed of whites and Negroes. There may be some super-tolerant people that would join a Negro outfit but their numbers would be few. Other whites that would join a Negro outfit would be of the same class of whites that would live in a Negro community. This Judge Hastie knows and admits and he does nothing to cut down useless and persistent correspondence on the subject.[22]

The ideas here expressed were not held by one officer alone. They were a fair reflection of the resentment to Hastie which had grown within the War Department. It had affected many of the objections to attempts to achieve changes in the employment of Negro troops. As early as the spring of

[22] Informal Memo, J.W.B. for Gen Adams, n.d., AG 291.21 (1–13–42) (12–22–41) (1). Omitted matter in Paragraph 1 is introductory only.

1941, G–1 observed that Judge Hastie, through his personal contacts with War Department officers and through his desire to "extend his activities to corps areas and troop units," [23] had succeeded in securing numerous concessions. "If this action is continued the whole program may get out of hand," the Personnel Division feared.[24]

Gradually, during 1941, Hastie began to be left out of consultation on issues affecting Negroes which arose within the department. He was not told, for example, of the decision to establish a separate school for Negro quartermaster trainees at Hampton Institute. When he discovered that this school had been authorized, Hastie objected to it and, finding that he was too late, urged that it as well as all other schools be opened to both Negroes and whites. Nor was he consulted on the removal of the 54th Coast Artillery from Camp Wallace, near Galveston, upon the request of white and over the objections of Negro citizens. Galveston, he observed, was as good a town as any for Negro troops. "I wish again to emphasize the fact," he reminded Under Secretary Patterson, "that the principal usefulness of this office is destroyed if we are not consulted with reference to such matters." [25]

At times notations with the force of "Not to be shown to Judge Hastie" were attached to papers dealing with phases of Negro troop utilization. A draft letter prepared by several officers of The Adjutant General's Office and of the G–1 Division in September 1941, for example, carried an appended note: "G–1 in passing upon this proposed letter, urged that it not be coordinated with the Office of the Civilian Aide, Judge Hastie. . . ." [26] The draft was in reply to an Office of Civilian Defense request for information on the question of Negro civilian morale as reflected by conditions in the Army, a matter which President Roosevelt wished to discuss with Mayor Fiorello H. La Guardia, then Director of Civilian Defense. This request was forwarded to the Civilian Aide by the Morale Branch. In the absence of Judge Hastie, Truman K. Gibson, Hastie's assistant, referred it to The Adjutant General's Office, which urged that "no such requests should be complied with unless they are channeled to this office through the Office of the Administrative Assistant." The reply, as drafted, developed a rationale of Negro-Army relations based on the idea that subversive activities against the Army were central to the current pressure tactics of Negroes:

It is well known, of course, that the Negro population has been a focal point of subversive agitation. It has appeared that this agitation has crystallized in several instances against War Department policies respecting the non-mingling of Negroes with other troops. Additionally, there has been agitation against sending Negro soldiers to southern camps where undoubtedly there exists a traditional dislike of "black Yankees". . . .

As you are of course aware, the handling of the Negro in the Army will be, at all times, a problem. There are now in service nearly 80,000 Negroes, many of whom cannot be profitably employed in the

[23] In his letter of appointment, Secretary Stimson had authorized Hastie to visit the field.

[24] Memo, G–1 for CofS, 18 Mar 41, G–1/15640–83. See also Walter White–Brig Gen Frederick Osborn Corresp, 1–6 Apr 42, SSB 291.21 (9–27–41) (1).

[25] Memo, Civ Aide for USW, 15 Jul 41, USW 291.2 Judge Hastie's Office.

[26] Remarks and Memo, ExO G–1 for Col Boyer, 3 Sep 41, AG 291.21 (9–4–41) (1).

service excepting as labor troops. This is due to the low average mentality. However, in response to urgings upon the War Department, they are now represented in every major branch of the Army, including the Air Corps. No effort has been spared to provide equal opportunity and accommodations, for the Negro soldier.

It is doubtful that there will be any simple solution. Many leaders of the Negro race agitate for more and more consideration, far beyond the capabilities of their people. Cleverly, they seek to create problems rather than obviate them, "Why should Negroes be segregated from whites?" "Why should Negro regiments have any white officers?" "Why should the War Department permit enforcement of state laws relative to segregation in southern states?" As one question is disposed of, another takes its place inspired by inflammatory reasoning.

While the events which have so far transpired have been scattered, there appears to be underlying all such events a pattern of centralized stimulation. The fact that to date there has been comparative lack of conflict among the large bulk of 80,000 Negroes in service is because, perhaps, that there has been good common sense used by the Negroes themselves. Commanders of cantonments in the field, it is felt, are zealously endeavoring to meet the situation. . . .

It should be understood that the Negro is not the only problem confronting the War Department, because there are a variety of other special pleaders who set up specious claims that they too are being discriminated against as a class. Among the latter are those in specialized professions such as chiropracters, osteopaths, naturopaths, pharmacists, male nurses, barbers, etc., who have organized their efforts much after the pattern of the Negro agitators to claim special recognition. . . .

Those Negro leaders who seek to prove discrimination because of color employ special pleading for a race which as a class, has not as yet the attained mental equipment to be employed in military functions other than those where brawn is prerequisite.

The opportunities for this group have reached a point of saturation.[27]

The points of view of Judge Hastie and his supporters were clearly at variance with those of many of the officers in the War Department who had to deal with policy decisions on the employment of Negro troops. What to Hastie appeared to be a minimal approach to symbolic democracy, became to many of those with whom he was attempting to work a plot to change the existing American social structure and a threat to the Army's system of military discipline. What to officers in the War Department appeared to be a logical and rational solution to a difficult problem, based on civilian precedent backed by years of experience, appeared to Hastie to be a perversion and extension by the Military Establishment of the least desirable features of Negro-white civilian relations and a willful disregard of the more advanced and workable solutions to racial problems being practiced in civilian life.

In the resulting stalemate, the basic organization of Negro troops remained unchanged and untouched, while the questions raised concerning the efficiency of this organization continued to vex the War Department.

Action on the Hastie Proposals

Discussion of the proposals made in the Hastie Survey did not cease with

---

[27] Draft Ltr, TAG to Brig Gen L. D. Gasser, WD Representative OCD, 2 Sep 41, in Memo, G–1 for Col Boyer (AGO), 3 Sep 41, AG 291.21 (9–4–41) (1). The letter actually sent, dated 4 September 1941, deleted most of the material quoted here. The draft, according to penciled notes attached, had been worked on and approved by several officers.

the December letter from the Chief of Staff or with the December conference between the Under Secretary of War and the Deputy Chief of Staff. In subsequent conferences, Judge Patterson and Judge Hastie continued to explore the possibilities of action on those phases of the proposals which had not been acted upon and upon which agreement might be reached. Among the proposals for further employment of Negroes adopted by January 1942 were the use of Negro military police in areas where there were Negro troops and the constitution of a Negro division, considered a feasible partial solution to the problem of scattered small units. Once the activation of the initial division was confirmed, Hastie favored the formation of additional large units. It was understood that small units would be shifted to posts where more Negro troops and, therefore, better physical and recreational facilities were located. The main questions affecting organization which remained unanswered were those of the continued increase of Negro strength and the employment of Negroes in the Air Forces. "Although the Air Force is advertising for men, Negroes are not taken except for special Negro units which were filled long ago," Judge Patterson wrote to General Bryden. "Perhaps an additional Negro Air squadron should be formed," he suggested.[28]

On 13 January, Judge Hastie, Judge Patterson, and Secretary Stimson conferred once more. Again the questions of consolidating small detached Negro units, the constitution of additional Air units, and the provision of an increased number of units generally to absorb Selective Service's excess Negroes were discussed. Stimson mentioned the suitability of Negro soldiers for operations in the tropics. Patterson and Hastie urged the announcement of the formation of an additional division or of several regiments. Hastie linked the scarcity of Negro officer candidates, a matter then under discussion by the Negro press and public, to the existence of small detached units which did not regularly receive quotas for officer candidate training. Without getting support from the Secretaries, he again urged the beginning of integration of Negroes and whites, even in the smallest way.[29]

Action on the matters discussed and agreed upon was slow. Hastie, in the meantime, produced a critical examination of the 1942 Troop Basis. "I have now been permitted," he informed the Under Secretary on 5 February, "to examine so much of the troop unit basis for 1942 as embraces Combat Divisions, Army Troops, Corps Troops, GHQ Reserve Troops, Harbor Defense Units, Military Police Units, and Tank Destroyer Battalions. . . . The Secretary of War, has announced that about 175,000 more [Negroes] will be added to the Army in 1942. . . . A study by G–3 contemplates the addition of some 240,000 Negro soldiers, as contrasted with the number of 175,000 mentioned by The Secretary. But there is no organizational structure yet approved for the 175,000 new men." [30]

To Hastie, the "one element of ad-

---

[28] Memo, USW for DCofS, 10 Jan 42, ASW 291.2 Race, Negro (Misc).

[29] Memo, USW for SW, 16 Jan 42, ASW 291.2 Race, Negro (Misc).

[30] Memo, Civ Aide to SW for USW, 5 Feb 42, attached to Memo, DCofS for USW, 16 Feb 42. Both in ASW 291.2 Race, Negro (Army Misc).

vancement" in the 1942 Troop Basis was the inclusion of Negroes in divisions. He considered this "the most effective method for modifying the present pattern of placing Negroes in scattered, small units." He criticized the continued increase of Negroes in the Quartermaster Corps "in which dispersion of small units is most extreme"; the provision of 11 percent Negroes in the Medical Corps, "practically all of them in Sanitary Companies" with "no white Sanitary Companies whatever"; and the concentration of Negroes in engineer general service regiments and in "scattered" ammunition companies. "Certainly," he wrote, "the Negro soldier should do his full share of manual, unskilled labor, but the cited examples represent an unreasonable preponderance, in some places the exclusive assignment of Negroes to functions of this type." Finally, pointing out that the Selective Service backlog of uninducted Negroes who remained at the top of the selectee lists "invites court action by any white selectee chosen for induction ahead of eligible Negroes whose name precedes his," he urged that provision be made for a larger absorption of Negroes by the Army, by the Navy, or by both services.[31]

A week later Deputy Chief of Staff Bryden informed Under Secretary Patterson that it was deemed impracticable to assemble small Negro units because of the nature of the functions they performed. "To assemble them would result in an excess of these elements at the places where assembled and would require replacement by similar white service elements," he indicated. A

letter to the field on the equal treatment of soldiers, regardless of race; instructions insuring an opportunity for every soldier to apply for officer candidate training; assurance that Negroes equaling the population percentages would be taken into the Army; and assurance that new combat units would be activated were included in General Bryden's report of plans.[32]

To Hastie's criticisms of the current troop basis, General Bryden later replied that the distribution of Negroes to ground units, to air and air service units, and to miscellaneous categories compared favorably with the white distribution. Of 338,000 Negroes provided for, 177,000 (53 percent) were allocated to ground units; 78,000 (23 percent) to the Army Air Forces and services; 82,000 (24 percent) to miscellaneous categories. These percentages compared favorably with white percentages of 48, 27, and 24. Bryden pointed out that the War Department had endeavored to employ Negro manpower in types of units proved suitable for Negroes and also in other types where they might be expected to develop to desired standards. He added:

In spite of the fact that American battle experience has indicated a battle efficiency of Negro divisions below that required—as well as below that demonstrated by white divisions—the current troop basis includes two complete Negro divisions. . . . It has, however, been found necessary to assign Negroes in considerable numbers to small units in which specialist and intelligence requirements are not exacting. Those small units, generally carried in GHQ Reserve, are necessary for the proper support of divisions in combat. The term "reserve"

[31] Ibid.

[32] Memo, DCofS for USW, 13 Feb 42, ASW 291.2 Race, Negro (Misc).

does not mean that they will not be employed in active combat. . . .[33]

The difficulties of finding locations for large Negro units and the possibility that they might not be useful overseas, the failure of Selective Service deferments to equalize the eligible white and Negro selectees on the basis of population percentages, the failure of the Navy to take its share of Negroes, and the desirability of having the troop basis reflect actual needs were all cited as factors contributing to the department's problem. General Bryden stressed, moreover, that "with the advent of actual War the primary responsibility of the War Department is to conclude the building of an Army which can operate when and where needed at maximum effectiveness. It is obvious, in times as critical as these, the needs of the Nation must transcend the favored consideration of any particular group." [34]

The explanations and detailed justifications for War Department policies in the employment of Negro troops, delivered almost *ad seriatium* and in almost identical terms, were not convincing evidence to Hastie that the Army had done all that it could. He renewed his recommendations from time to time, citing new evidence in support of his resubmissions. Many of Hastie's strictures on current organizational policies as they affected the over-all efficiency of Negro troops came to have obvious foundation in fact as the year wore on. As more and more Negroes entered the Army and as more and more of them appeared destined for units of limited apparent value, discussions of the "Negro problem" became more frequent. No one had as yet made an official statement on the matter, but the attempt to distribute Negroes proportionately was proving considerably more difficult than had been apparent in paper plans; moreover the simple physical problem of the intake of proportionate numbers of Negroes without regard to their proportionate distribution was proving to be an onerous administrative burden.

A War Plans Approach

Seeking a method of employing not only a proportionate but any number of Negroes that might become available, the War Plans Division in March 1942 prepared a study which showed that using Negroes exclusively in certain types of noncombatant units could have increased by 26.2 percent the number of Negroes employed in ground units in the 1942 Troop Basis. Although this study was not sent to the Chief of Staff as originally intended, it presented several arguments for consideration in future planning which were pertinent to what the War Plans Division felt to be "the most effective use of colored manpower above and beyond population percentage." These suggestions were formulated with two ends in view:

1. Release of white manpower from noncombatant units to make available the greatest possible percentage of reliable troops for combat units.

2. To permit the deferment of the maximum number of skilled defense workers consistent with the balanced requirements of an army of any given figure.[35]

---

[33] Memo, DCofS for USW, 16 Feb 42, ASW 291.2 Race, Negro (Misc).

[34] *Ibid.*

[35] Memo, WPD for CofS (not used), Mar 42, OPD 291.21/3, 3-25-42.

These considerations were to figure heavily in later discussions and in action taken. But the chief innovation suggested was the proposal to abandon the 10 percent quota in favor of a maximum use of Negroes in the Army by concentrating the employment of Negro troops in the services.

The study, recognizing "the necessity for a certain number of colored tactical units (due to unavoidable reasons)," proceeded on the assumption that holding Negro combat units to the percentages already set up for 1942 would allow additional Negroes to be usefully employed in service units to an extent greater than their percentage in the population. The best men, of whom larger numbers would be expected in this increased number of Negroes drafted, could then be placed in the combat units, releasing submarginal personnel for the service units. In its emphasis upon highly selected men for combat units the plan had overtones of older "elite unit" suggestions and of later "selective screening" proposals.

The plan envisioned the use of Negroes exclusively in all quartermaster port, bakery, laundry, sterilization and bath, mobile shoe and textile, refrigeration, salvage collecting, service, railhead, gasoline supply, and car units; in all engineer depot, general service, separate, water supply, and air base units; in all medical sanitation units; and in all chemical decontamination, depot, and impregnating companies.[36]

In addition to advocating the use of these units for Negro personnel, the plan proposed the creation of two new types of units to absorb Negroes: station maintenance companies, to be used for "policing areas now the responsibility of tactical units, for fighting range fires, for landscaping and grading, and for such other duties as would vitiate the tactical training or specialized functions of other units"; and metropolitan service companies, to be used to "move office furnishings, fixtures and supplies around cities and large headquarters, and generally to make Army installations lacking sufficient organic service troops independent of unskilled civilian labor without diverting the time and energies of skilled headquarters personnel."[37]

Had the plan been submitted and approved, it would have accomplished more than the stated release of white manpower for combat units and the further deferment of skilled workers. It would have made possible the employment of a larger number of Negroes, estimated at 861,000 by the end of 1943. This number would have been 171,600 over the flat 10 percent figure. It would have provided a partial guarantee of the continuity of the Negro combat units. Under this plan, it would not only have been possible to supply the combat units with higher caliber men from the increased draft but it might also have been unnecessary to strip the combat units for personnel for critically needed service units in 1943, since a large reserve of men available for use in orthodox service units could have been obtained from the proposed "station" and

---

[36] *Ibid.,* and attached list, White Units Due for Activation Between March 1 and December 31, 1942 and Suitable for Activation by Colored Troops.

[37] *Ibid.*

"metropolitan" service units. Moreover, the plan would have lessened later difficulties encountered in the deployment of Negro troops overseas, for theater commanders requisitioning needed service units would have had no choice except to take Negro organizations if they were the only ones of their types available in the Army.

The plan had several major drawbacks. It ignored the War Department's public position, still being reiterated, that Negroes would be used more extensively in all arms and services and the corollary policy that no type of unit would be exclusively white or Negro. It violated the principle that the number of Negroes employed by the Army would be proportionate to their numbers in the registered population, a maximum beyond which few in the Army were willing to go and one which the Army was experiencing considerable difficulty in reaching. It assumed that the provision of types of units into which men of relatively lower vocational and educational experience ought to fit would be successful, regardless of the leadership, officer and noncommissioned, that was supplied. But since the plan did not get beyond the War Plans Division, it had no formal effect upon the major department-wide discussions of the employment of Negro troops in 1942. It can nevertheless be considered a straw in the wind for the renewal, in 1943, of proposals that the majority of Negro troops be placed in the services of supply, and for the growing conviction that Negro troops should be employed in ways that would release white troops for combat and technical duties.

The Chamberlain Plan

The third set of suggestions involving major changes in policy—greater than any that Judge Hastie or the War Plans Division had suggested—came in the fall of 1942 when the 1943 Troop Basis was taking final form. The chief of the Organization-Mobilization Group of G–3, Col. Edwin W. Chamberlain, proposed an end to the further activation of Negro units.

Accepting the point of view that Negroes in the mass, as shown by classification test scores, were less able and less useful to the Army than whites in the mass, and that the Army in 1943, especially in the face of the refusal of the naval services to take their full share, would be forced to take an even larger proportion of Negroes, Colonel Chamberlain argued that separate units resulted in a considerable waste of manpower, funds, and equipment. Negro selectees, with their poor backgrounds, could not continue to attempt to man needed units effectively. Friction between white and Negro troops, Chamberlain believed, was "aggravated if not caused in its entirety by segregation practices both within and without the Army." The War Department policy of creating units in order to provide assignments for Negro personnel, coupled with the limitations which lower qualifications placed on the number and variety of Negro units, would produce "insurmountable" difficulties in 1943. Then, if the policy was continued and if the Army was required to induct its full proportion of Negroes while the Navy continued to take few, 21 percent of the planned augmentation would be Negro.

To continue to place these men in special units not vital to the prosecution of the war or in normal units which could not be expected to come up to the highest standards was a waste of manpower. Both the friction and the waste could be avoided if Negroes were placed in otherwise white units in the ratio of one Negro to nine whites. Colonel Chamberlain admitted that his proposal would be "abhorrent to those who view the situation only superficially since it bears the earmarks of the integration of Negroes with whites—a thing to which WD policy has long been opposed," but he felt that closer study would convince "reasonable men" that the solution was "no more integration of the white and colored races than is the employment of Negroes as servants in a white household." [38]

If current registration proportions continued, 89 of the average 100 men received from Selective Service in 1943 would be white and 11 would be Negro. On the basis of current AGCT performances, Chamberlain determined the 100 would divide as follows:

Group	White	Negro
Superior (Grade I)	7	0
Above Average (Grade II)	26	1
Average (Grade III)	29	2
Below Average (Grade IV) . . .	19	3
Inferior (Grade V)	8	5
	89	11

The whole number of Negroes below Grade III in the average 100 would be considerably fewer than the whole number of whites. Negro selectees would be assigned to units by normal reception center classification. The eight out of

eleven in below average classifications could be used as the cooks, orderlies, chauffeurs, truck drivers, kitchen police, and basics who made up from 10 to 20 percent of the strength of the average unit. "It should be borne in mind," Chamberlain continued, "that the assignment of the Negro to these lesser tasks comes about wholly through the natural selection—based on his capabilities—incident to the organization of a new unit from 100 men delivered more or less at random from reception centers." [39] The remaining Negroes with demonstrated average and better qualifications could be transferred to existing Negro units. Their abilities could be used to provide a gradual improvement in these units, increasing their employability and, at the same time, providing an outlet for the ambitions and capabilities of the better qualified men.

Negroes who complained of discrimination, Chamberlain felt, could not object to a solution that assigned a soldier wholly on the basis of his capabilities as determined by universally administered tests and that, at the same time, increased the possibility of Negro participation in the war effort. While he conceded that the plan was "radical" and that it would be "difficult to sell both in the WD and to the country at large," Colonel Chamberlain concluded that "either a solution such as the one proposed must be adopted or we must reconcile ourselves to the fact that we face a loss in equivalent manpower in the order of three quarters of a million men." [40]

This proposal was sent by Brig. Gen.

---

38 Draft Memo (initialed E.W.C.) for Gen Edwards, G–3 Negro File, 1942–44.

39 *Ibid.*
40 *Ibid.*

Idwal H. Edwards, the Assistant Chief of Staff, G–3, to several of the officers and agencies immediately concerned, including the Deputy Chief of Staff, the Operations Division, the new Advisory Committee on Negro Troop Policies, and the commanding generals of the Air, Ground, and Service Forces. Army Ground Forces was vitally concerned about the matter, since its combat units, seriously under their proportions of Negroes, would be directly affected. Its reactions were therefore a notable gauge both of the range of dissatisfaction with existing troop organization as it affected Negro soldiers and of the force of objections to proposals for the individual integration of Negroes into the Army. These reactions illustrated, as well, the recognition within the Army that there were more desirable methods of organization than the one being pursued.

Aside from the general reaction that cooks, chauffeurs, and truck drivers could not necessarily be provided from low scoring men ("the jobs either require schooling or the passing of an aptitude test, neither of which grade 5 men are capable of doing," Ground G–4 wrote [41]), reactions in the Ground staff ranged from flat refusal to consider the proposals seriously to careful studies of portions of the plan considered useful. Ground G–3 wrote:

There is no more reason why the two races can live closely together in the Army than in the Navy. If white and colored can live together in a company they can live together on a battle ship. The proposal involves a great deal more integration "than does the employment of negroes as servants in a white household." . . . I be-

lieve we should state that the proposal is inadvisable due to the certainty that internal strife, dissension, and lowered morale would result.[42]

Ground G–4 commented further that the time had come to return to the plan of attaching Negro regiments to white divisions: "This will accomplish the same result as is indicated in the basic memo without the integration and will assure a proportionate share of battle casualties." [43] The Ground Plans Division argued that the integration of individuals into white companies would be no more successful than it had been in the Civilian Conservation Corps and that if a new plan were adopted it should be such that it could be used throughout the Army. The Plans Division proposed a scheme based on General Rommel's method for mixing Italian units with German troops. According to this proposal, the following units in each division would have Negro enlisted men and white officers: quartermaster battalions, service companies, and service batteries; one rifle company in each infantry battalion; one firing battery in each artillery battalion; one company in each engineer battalion; one company in each tank battalion of armored divisions. Of nondivisional combat units, 90 percent could be mixed in the same manner, using all white officers; 10 percent of the separate combat battalions could be all Negro except for officers. Thirty percent of the nontechnical service units, such as service battalions and truck regiments, could be Negro with Negro officers; all officer candidates for

[41] AGF M/S 4, G–4 to Plans, 2 Nov 42, AGF 322.999/1.

[42] AGF M/S 3, G–3 to G–1, 1 Nov 42, AGF 322.999/1.
[43] AGF M/S 4, G–4 to Plans, 2 Nov 42, AGF 322.999/1.

these units would be chosen from among noncommissioned officers of the first four grades who had demonstrated their leadership abilities for a period of six months.[44]

General McNair, in the final answer of Army Ground Forces, limited his acceptance to the idea which he had espoused before: that separate Negro battalions for attachment to other units of similar types should be the solution. In presenting his reaction to the proposal, General McNair restated the major objections to proposals for integration as thoroughly as the War Department staff had done a year before:

2. I agree with you [General Edwards, War Department G–3] that we must treat the problem of utilizing the negro from the purely military viewpoint.

3. I am unalterably opposed to the incorporation of negroes in small units with white soldiers. Inevitably, such action would weaken the unit, since it would introduce men of comparatively low intelligence. We have a sufficiency of such men among white soldiers. A commander in the field disposes his forces principally according to, (1) the task ahead and (2) the capabilities of the units in connection with such tasks. Decisive operations usually call for specialized units at critical points. Weaker units can be disposed where their weakness will cause no serious ill effects. The introduction of negroes throughout our fighting units would tend to leave a commander with no outstanding units.

4. In this war, shipping is the bottleneck of our military effort. It is entirely likely that we shall not be able to exert our maximum effort on account of shipping. It follows that we must see to it that every shipload of troops has the maximum of fighting power. Shipping should not be wasted on mediocrity.

5. It is appreciated that the negro

problem must be solved, since it can not be disregarded. We already are placing negroes in service and auxiliary units to the maximum, and this practice, of course, should be continued. As to combat units, we are forming two infantry divisions wholly of negroes—the 92d and 93d divisions. The basic memorandum proposes a solution diametrically opposed to these two divisions. I agree that a colored division is too great a concentration of negroes to be effective, and feel that an intermediate solution would be better than either of these two extremes.

6. The proposal to eliminate the regimental echelon for all units except the infantry is believed sound. In fact, there is much to recommend the battalion as the fighting unit of infantry; the British Army employs such an organization. If the size of negro combat units were limited to separate battalions they would be fully suitable for battle employment, yet the organization would permit the maximum of flexibility in such employment. They could be put in here and there where the situation was such that they could be useful and effective. It is believed that a policy along this line would solve satisfactorily the social problems involved and minimize the military difficulties.

7. I favor:

a. The maximum workable proportion of colored troops in service and auxiliary units.

b. Colored combat units not larger than a battalion, organized so as to be self-administered.[45]

A variant in the Chamberlain plan was proposed by G–3 in the spring of 1943.[46] This proposal was primarily an attempt to spread Negro laboring personnel over a wider area of usefulness and to overcome the problem of obtaining adequate technical and supervisory

---

[44] AGF M/S, Plans to DCofS, 4 Nov 42, AGF 322.999/1.

[45] Memo, Gen McNair for G–3, 11 Nov 42, AGF 322.999/1 (Cld Trps). Paragraph 1 (omitted) introductory only.

[46] Memo, G–3 for CG ASF, 23 Mar 43, WDGCT 291.21 (3–23–43).

leadership for Negro service units. White and Negro enlisted men would be combined in units whose battalion headquarters and headquarters companies contained white technical and supervisory personnel—specialists and noncommissioned officers—while the remaining companies used Negro supervisory and laboring personnel. All specialists for these units were to be white; Negro supervisory leadership was to come from men no longer needed in the technical positions in battalion headquarters. General hospitals with Negro sanitary companies and port battalions with white operating companies and Negro stevedore companies were suggested examples of how this plan would work.

Army Ground Forces G–1, in considering this proposal, added another possibility: Negro service companies or battalions could be attached to white units such as engineer general service regiments or quartermaster salvage and repair depots, thus relieving white "laboring" strength for use elsewhere. Other Ground Forces staff divisions, including the Ground G–3, Medical, Ordnance, Signal, Chemical, and Quartermaster sections, did not concur. "The result, if started in Ground Force units, would be amalgamation of the Negro enlisted personnel," Army Gound Forces explained.[47]

Army Service Forces branches were no happier over the new G–3 proposal. The Corps of Engineers observed that such an experiment might work in its separate battalions but nowhere else. Engineer functions, the corps pointed out, did not require "hand labor" except in those cases where the proper associated services had not furnished enough manpower, thereby causing engineer units to be taken away from construction projects while their equipment stood idle. If anything, the engineer separate battalions, "a relic of 1917," should be reorganized to include more equipment and specialists or abolished outright. Where separate battalions were converted to general service regiments, the change had had "a marked effect on the efficiency of the colored units concerned even though a large percentage of the men are in grades IV and V in intelligence rating. It has been possible to select and train machinery operators and other specialists satisfactorily when given the necessary time," the Engineers reported. In no event would the Engineers recommend the assignment of white noncommissioned officers to Negro units. "To do so will make it almost impossible to develop organizational esprit among the colored men since they would have no opportunities for advancement. The matter of discrimination also enters," the corps added.[48] The Transportation Corps considered the proposal workable "altho it would destroy the morale of almost any unit if working sections were denied [a] chance for grades and rates in Headquarters." On the other hand, by careful selection, training, and supervision, and by the addition of heavy lift experts from the headquarters and headquarters com-

---

[47] Memo, AGF for G–3, 16 Apr 43, AGF 322.999/359.

[48] 1st Ind, CofE to CG SOS, 18 Feb 43, to Memo, Hq ASF for Chiefs Svs, Surg Gen, QMC, PMG, and Dir SSD, 6 Feb 43, SPOPU 381.2 (2–6–43).

pany and from mobile port headquarters, Negro battalions as presently organized would operate as well as white battalions, the Transportation Corps believed.[49] With both service and ground combat branches opposed, the proposal was abandoned.

The Advisory Committee

Most subsequent proposals for changes in the organization of Negro troops or other matters of Army-wide policy affecting Negroes were channeled through a new medium, the Advisory Committee on Negro Troop Policies, formed on 27 August 1942 with the Assistant Secretary of War, John J. McCloy, as chairman.[50] The appointment of this committee came as a surprise to Judge Hastie and to Under Secretary Patterson. Not only was Hastie not appointed to the committee, but nearly a month had passed when he informed Judge Patterson that he had heard indirectly that it had been organized. "This was news to me," Patterson told McCloy, "although I have been charged with discussion of matters concerning

negroes with Judge Hastie. The creation of this board, without notice to him or participation by him, has-caused him a good deal of uneasiness, and it is one of the factors that has led him to question his usefulness as Special Aide to the Secretary of War on Negro Affairs. As you know, he has indicated before that he would like to resign and he has again told me that he does not believe he is accomplishing anything of a useful nature."[51] To the War Council, Patterson reported that Hastie had been constructive and helpful and that his resignation would be most unfortunate.[52] After discussing the matter with Hastie, Patterson reported to Stimson similarly, saying: "I had not heard of the establishment of the committee until I received Hastie's letter, and I was not in a position to tell him what the purpose of the committee was. I can understand his feeling that his usefulness has been impaired."[53]

Of the exact purpose of the committee, Secretary McCloy did not profess to be certain. It was indicated that, since it was made up primarily of military men, including two assistant chiefs of staff, the group would concern itself "strictly with military problems in the use of negro troops and that the broader social problems were only incidentally involved."[54] The committee had been formed as a result of a recommendation made by G–1 in July, approved by the Chief of Staff on 30 July, and by the

[49] M/S, ACofTC for Opns to Col Hodson, 7 Apr 43; Memo, Col Hodson for CofTC Tng Div, 7 Apr 43. Both in TC 353 Tng Negro Units (Gen Files, 2d Sec).
[50] Ltr, TAG to ASW, 27 Aug 42, AG 334.8 (7-18-42) OF-A. In addition to Mr. McCloy, the committee members were Brig. Gen. Benjamin O. Davis, Inspector General's Office; Brig. Gen. Idwal H. Edwards, WD G-3; Brig. Gen. Donald Wilson, WD G-1; Brig. Gen. Joseph H. Dalton, SOS; Col. Edward Barber, AGF; Col. John H. McCormick, AAF. While the personnel of the committee changed from time to time, the same staff agencies and major commands were permanently represented. This committee was known variously as the Negro Troop Committee, the Special Troop Policies Committee, and the McCloy Committee. For convenience, it is referred to hereafter as the Advisory Committee.

[51] Memo, USW Robert P. Patterson for ASW McCloy, 23 Sep 42, ASW 291.2 NTC.
[52] War Council Notes, 23 Sep 42, WDCSA files.
[53] Memo, USW for SW, 24 Sep 42, USW 291.2 Race, Negro, Army.
[54] Memo, Lt J. M. Hall, OASW, for Mr. McCloy, 28 Sep 42, ASW 291.2 NTC.

Secretary of War on 25 August 1942.[55] The recommendation grew out of the reports of Col. Elliot D. Cooke of The Inspector General's Department, who, in the spring of 1942, made an extensive tour of posts, camps, and bases having Negro troops. Colonel Cooke found varying practices and policies with respect to the command of Negro troops at the many places visited.[56] As a result, G–1 proposed the appointment of a permanent War Department committee of officers "who, informed by experience, can evaluate racial incidents, proposed social reforms, and questions involving the training and use of negroes, male and female, in terms of an intimate understanding of War Department policies." [57]

The suggested committee was to consist of a representative of each division of the General Staff, the Army Ground Forces, the Army Air Forces, the Services of Supply, the Chief of Engineers, The Quartermaster General, The Surgeon General, and the Women's Army Auxiliary Corps. G–1 proposed further that a white man "who is an outstanding leader in the mechanical and industrial education of young negro men, for example, the President of Hampton Institute" be appointed as adviser to this special committee. The committee as proposed was considered too large; the recommendation as approved by the Chief of Staff carried the provision that

the committee "be kept small and headed by Mr. McCloy." [58]

The chairman of the new committee, reflecting opinion that had grown within the War Department during the past few months, had already expressed his view of the nature of the Army's racial problem. Earlier in the summer, after a discussion of the attitude of the Negro press and organizations toward the war and the Army, Hastie informed Secretary McCloy that he was disturbed "that you seem to have been persuaded (1) that Negroes should not agitate for the elimination of undemocratic practices at home during these critical times; and (2) that the continuation of such agitation would do more harm than good." When these matters were discussed from time to time, Hastie continued, he hoped that the Assistant Secretary would point out "the basic issues of this war and the impossibility of foreclosing those issues at home while we stir people up to fight for them all over the world." [59]   To this McCloy replied:

I think I probably ought to state in writing what my attitude is. Of course, there is no group in the country that should not agitate for the elimination of undemocratic practices. Like sin, everyone is against undemocratic practices. What I urge upon the Negro press is to lessen their emphasis upon discriminatory acts and Color incidents irrespective of whether the White or the Colored man is responsible for starting them. Frankly, I do not think that the basic issues of this war are involved in the question of whether Colored troops

[55] Memo, G–1 for CofS, 18 Jul 42, AG 334 Advisory Com on Negro Trp Policies (11 Jul 42) (1). (1); D/F, G–1 to TAG, 11 Aug 42, AG 334 Advisory Com on Negro Trp Policies (11 Jul 42) (1).

[56] Ltr, OTIG (Col Elliot D. Cooke) to TIG, 25 Jun 42, and 1st Ind, TIG to CofS, 29 Jul 42, WDCSA 333 (6–29–42).

[57] Memo, G–1 for CofS, 18 Jul 42, AG 334 Advisory Com on Negro Trp Policies (1).

[58] Penciled note dated 30 Jul 42, signed D. W., [Gen Wilson] on Info Memo OCS signed J. T. M. [Gen McNarney] for CofS, 27 Jul 42, in AG 334 Advisory Com on Negro Trp Policies (18 Jul 42) (1).

[59] Memo, Civ Aide for ASW, 30 Jun 42, ASW 291.2 NT 1942.

serve in segregated units or in mixed units and I doubt whether you can convince the people of the United States that the basic issues of freedom are involved in such a question. In its policy of playing up the incidents of which I speak, I believe that papers like the Pittsburgh Courier and, perhaps, some others, serve to take the mind of the Negro soldier and the Negroes generally off what you term the basic issue of the war. If the United States does not win this war, the lot of the Negro is going to be far, far worse than it is today. Yet, there is, it seems to me, an alarmingly large percentage of Negroes in and out of the Army who do not seem to be vitally concerned about winning the war. This, to my mind, indicates that some forces are at work misleading the Negroes. I bespeak greater emphasis on the necessity for greater out and out support of the war, particularly by the Negro press, and I feel certain that the objects for which you aim will come closer to achievement if the existing emphasis is shifted than if it is not.[60]

After the establishment of the Advisory Committee Judge Hastie continued to work on some matters through Judge Patterson's office; he presented other suggestions through Assistant Secretary McCloy's office for consideration of the Advisory Committee. The committee made recommendations of its own from time to time. It considered the broad plans originating in the staff divisions, attempted to keep abreast of the developing racial situation in the country, and proposed measures which it hoped would have a beneficial effect upon racial matters within the Army. G–1 and G–3 prepared summaries of existing policies for discussion and, at the second meeting of the committee on 24 October, the Chamberlain plan was presented by G–3, Brig. Gen. Idwal

H. Edwards. Reaction to the plan, and especially to the proposal to experiment with mixed personnel on a small scale, was favorable, "but there was a marked reluctance to recommend such a radical step all at once," one member reported.[61]

At the same meeting a proposal came from Brig. Gen. Frederick H. Osborn's Special Service Division that segregation in Army motion picture houses be abandoned. This proposal grew out of a conference on segregation in theaters on Massachusetts posts between Hastie; his assistant, Truman K. Gibson, Jr.; Dr. Donald Young of the Joint Army-Navy Committee on Welfare and Recreation and the Special Service Division; and Matthew Bullock. It was agreed that Young would urge the Special Service Division and the Joint Army-Navy Committee to recommend issuance of a policy statement that "colored personnel be neither excluded from nor segregated in any theater located within a military reservation," with the added provision that a local commander could submit to the Commanding General, SOS, recommendations for exceptions to avoid serious trouble. The conferees thought that complete elimination would encounter no serious trouble but that the addition of a modifying provision would increase the chances for success.[62] The proposal was discussed at length. It had been approved by Under Secretary Patterson, but Assistant Secretary McCloy had secured a reversal. The Advisory

---

[60] Memo, ASW for Judge Hastie, 2 Jul 42, ASW 291.2 NT 1942.

[61] M/S, Col Edward Barber for CofS AGF, 24 Oct 42, AGF G–1/380.

[62] Memo, Donald Young for Francis Keppel, Secy JANCWR, and Gen Osborn, 10 Sep 42, SSB 291.2 (9–27–41) (1); Memo, Howard C. Peterson, Special Asst to USW, for Mr. McCloy, 14 Oct 42, ASW 291.2 Gen 1942.

Committee agreed to seek more information and, if possible, avoid public announcement of policy on the subject. It would deal with each situation as it came up.[63]

In November, Hastie suggested several matters which the Advisory Committee might wish to consider. These included a renewal of his criticisms of the Troop Basis for 1942, which, he believed, applied to the 1943 Troop Basis as well. He made new recommendations for increasing opportunities for the technical training of Negro enlisted men and officers and he reminded the committee of the need for a definite War Department policy against racial discrimination in Army theaters, post exchanges, and similar facilities.[64]

Brig. Gen. Benjamin O. Davis, in the meantime, worked out a proposal for the operation of the Advisory Committee.[65] Davis proposed that the committee recommend "the breaking down of the so-called 'Jim Crow' practices within the War Department and on the military reservations, and the securing of the cooperation of the communities near the reservations to that end." He proposed, as Hastie had done earlier, the issuance of a directive "announcing that military necessity required a closer unity and comradeship among all races constituting our citizenry." In addition, he proposed orientation courses, emphasizing the contribution of Negroes to America and attempting to make white soldiers realize the "great respon-

sibility" resting upon them in achieving unity of aims within the Army. General Davis included a recommendation that the term "colored" instead of "Negro" be used to designate race in official Army materials. Like many other Negroes, Davis believed that many of the internal racial difficulties of the Army and the civilian community at large, sprang from the ill-considered use of epithets such as "nigger." In connection with the original Hastie Survey, a staff discussion of the wisdom of issuing a directive outlawing the use of this and similar terms extended over a period of several months. General Davis, while agreeing that it was desirable to reduce this source of racial friction, felt that general orientation in Army race relations was preferable to a directive outlawing the term.[66] Neither set of recommendations submitted by General Davis was dealt with immediately, though features of both proposals were later adopted under other circumstances.

In December, the Advisory Committee, after surveying the field through reports from staff agencies, recommended the use of Negroes in harbor defense units in order to reduce their employment in antiaircraft units; the activation of a Negro parachute battalion "for purposes of enhancing the morale and esprit de corps of the negro people"; the assignment of Negroes to combat engineer units to avoid "what may prove to be a perfectly justifiable charge of discrimination against the negro through his assignment almost exclusively to general service engineer regiments"; and the

---

[63] M/S, Col Barber for CofS AGF, 24 Oct 42, AGF G–1/380.

[64] Memo, Civ Aide for ASW, 4 Nov 42, ASW 291.2 NTC.

[65] Memo, Davis for Committee [Fall of 1942], ASW 291.2 NTC.

[66] Memo, TIG for CofS, 13 Nov 41; Memo, Civ Aide for USW, 30 Dec 41; Memo, USW for DCofS, 10 Jan 42. All in G–1 15640–15646.

use of Negroes in ambulance battalions in lieu of white troops, thus reducing the numbers who otherwise would have been placed in medical sanitary units. On these recommendations General Marshall noted marginally, "Seems O.K." for harbor defense units, "Start a company" for the parachute battalion recommendation, and "excellent" for each of the other two recommendations.[67]

Because of the difficulty of locating harbor defense units so that they would not cause objections from the towns which they were supposed to protect, and because the need for such units rapidly diminished as the danger of attacks on the American coast lessened, no Negro harbor defense units, as such, were formed. The 555th Parachute Company was constituted on the inactive list in February 1943, activated at the end of the year, and raised to a battalion in November 1944.[68] Twelve motor ambulance companies were activated in 1943 and two others were added later. Though the Chief of Engineers and Army Ground Forces continued to object to the activation of combat engineer units other than those necessary to divisions, combat engineer battalions were eventually activated from personnel of converted units of the arms in 1943, 1944, and 1945. Most of these later became construction and general service units.

Throughout its career the Advisory

PARATROOPER TRAINEES *in column formation about to board an Army transport at Fort Benning.*

Committee, acting in part as a clearing house for staff ideas on the employment of Negro troops and in part as a channel and consultation board for civilian ideas on the use of Negro troops, continued to exercise a lively interest in and, at times, partial control over the provision and use of Negro units. Its activities gradually extended into an interest in the entire racial pattern within the Army as well as into a concern with Army-civilian relations where racial matters were involved. But, before the end of 1942, the committee had taken no positive action upon either Judge Hastie's or General Davis's recommendations on the improvement of race relations within the Army. Hastie's resignation at the beginning of the New Year helped

---

[67] Memo, Advisory Com on Negro Trp Policies (Col John H. McCormick, A.C., recorder) for CofS, 24 Dec 42, WDSA 291.21 (12–24–42).

[68] AG 320.2 (2–1–43) OB–I–GNGCT, 25 Feb 43; AG 322 (7 Dec 43) OB–I–GNGCT, 8 Dec 43; AGF 322/129 (Inf) GNGCT, 19 Dec 43. The company was activated 30 Dec 43; the battalion, 25 Nov 44.

galvanize the committee into action on certain of these proposals.

Air Forces Proposals and Hastie's Resignation

Since the establishment of the Air Corps flying school at Tuskegee, Judge Hastie had watched developments in the Air Forces with particular concern. The Tuskegee school had been vigorously opposed by the NAACP and by most of the more influential members of the Negro press. In the first months of its existence, the school was studiously ignored by the larger newspapers. Negro public figures, when referring to the pilots in training there, began to term them "Lonely Eagles," men destined to fly and fight separately from the rest of the Air Forces if at all.

In the summer of 1942, as successive classes of pilots were being graduated, interest in the school rose, and the Negro press covered Tuskegee closely. No longer was the seriousness of the Air Forces training program doubted. Negroes were now concerned about the seriousness of the intentions of the Air Forces to use the units being formed at Tuskegee, about the restriction of Negroes to single-engine pilot training, and about the long lists of eligible applicants awaiting entry to the flying school. Critics of the program pointed out that the percentage of single-engine pilots needed by the Air Corps was limited,[69] and therefore that Negroes who did not qualify for single-engine training were automatically deprived of an opportun-

ity to pursue any other type of flying training. The physical size limitations on single-engine trainees—maximum height and weight limitations of five feet, nine inches, and 160 pounds—cut further the number of Negroes eligible for this one type of training.[70]

The limitation of Negro nonpilot officer training to the few aerial observers and weather, armament, and engineering officers required by units then in being was further questioned and criticized. The Air Forces' refusal to accept applicants for appointment as service pilots and its requirement that Negro medical officers take courses in aviation medicine by correspondence and in local branch schools were cited as evidence that the Air arm had not kept up with the rest of the Army in providing full opportunities for qualified Negroes. The Air Forces denied that it was pursuing restrictive practices. It was filling authorized vacancies and training men according to existing War Department policies and within the limits of available resources.[71] The major difficulty seen by the Army Air Forces in carrying out its Negro training program was one of maintaining this training without undue enlargement. "We are pressed on every side," General Arnold declared, "by negro sympathizers to increase the program beyond any bounds of its usefulness. The increase cannot be made until an opportunity has been afforded the 99th Pursuit Squadron to

---

[69] Estimated at 36 percent of the cadet training program in the spring of 1942. 3d Ind, AAF Div of Individual Tng to CG AAFFTC, 19 Apr 42, AAF 353.9 Tng of Negroes.

[70] Ltr, AAFFTC to Air Surgeon, 28 May 42, AAFFTC 291.2 (5–28–42). These limitations did not apply to the first Tuskegee classes.

[71] See CofAS for Col St. Clair Streett, 31 Oct 41, 13 attachments and subsequent correspondence in ASWA 291.2. See also AAF 291.2 Cld Trps and AAF 353.9 Cld Tng.

prove its worth in actual combat operations."[72]

It was on the question of how training for units then in being was to be carried out as well as on developments at Tuskegee that Judge Hastie finally resolved to resign. One of the reasons for his original position in 1940, of neither approving nor yet of actively opposing the establishment of the Tuskegee school, was that the immediate gain in Negro utilization outweighed the advantages of continued opposition to the separate training station.[73] Flying training would begin at a station where Negro cadets could learn to fly and Negro officers would ultimately have the opportunity of command not only in the projected flying unit but also in the post's staff positions. Hastie was not disposed to support either a diminution of the expected gains or an extension of the separate Tuskegee pattern to other Air Forces—and, by possible precedent, to other Army—training activities.

Having established a logic for the Tuskegee installation, the Air Forces faced the necessity of extending that logic to all training connected with the units at the Tuskegee station. This was at first attempted by trying to confine most of that training to Tuskegee itself, a development involving attendant changes in plans for the control of activities there. When Tuskegee grew too crowded to accommodate further training projects, the extension of the same pattern elsewhere was proposed. The result was the war's most extended and most detailed attempt to define and to apply theories of the benefits of separate training for Negroes.

In the meantime, Hastie became concerned about the intentions of the Air Forces to meet commitments already made. In July 1942, he inquired about the Air Forces progress in training Negroes to replace white administrative officers at Tuskegee.[74] General Arnold replied that, since the school actually opened in October 1941, the year required to train replacements was not yet up. "There has been no change in our original plans of the procedure to be followed," he assured Hastie.[75]

The following fall, Hastie inquired again about plans to replace white officers with Negroes. The question by this time had assumed greater importance, for several Negro officers assigned to Tuskegee, including finance, chemical warfare, medical, and athletic officers, some of them of considerable standing in the Negro peacetime community, had been given subordinate and, in some cases, no actual assignments at all. This time the inquiry was referred to the Southeast Army Air Force Training Command (SEAAFTC) at Maxwell Field, under whose jurisdiction Tuskegee came. The command indicated that it considered it unwise to use Negro officers in post administrative positions at the field. SEAAFTC reminded AAF that the plan which Hastie referred to was a prewar plan. No subsequent direc-

---

[72] Memo, CG AAF to CofS, 2 Jul 42, AAF 353.9 Tng of Negroes.
[73] See chs. III and V, above.

[74] The following were white officers at this time: Commanding Officer, Director of Training, Executive, Adjutant, Administrative Inspector, Senior Surgeon, Utilities Officer, Signal Officer, Intelligence Officer, Public Relations Officer, Post Quartermaster, and twelve flying instructors.
[75] Memo, CG AAF for Hastie, 10 Aug 42, AAF 353.9 Tng of Negroes.

tive requiring the substitution of Negro for white officers had been issued. In any event the original plan, calling for 11 white officers, 15 white noncommissioned officers, and a full garrison of only 47 officers and 429 enlisted men, was no longer applicable, since Tuskegee now had 217 officers and 3,000 enlisted men. SEAAFTC argued that considerable effort to locate and develop reliable Negro officers had been made, but that none had been forthcoming. Anyway, the command pointed out, every commanding officer has the prerogative of selecting his own staff officers. "In general, colored officers do not possess the necessary technical background to qualify them to occupy supervisory positions now filled by white officers," SEAAFTC said. "They are definitely lacking in the qualifications essential for leadership and the urgency of the war situation does not justify experimentation." Furthermore, the best qualified Negro officers available to it, the command continued, were assigned to Task Force units at Tuskegee. The remainder would be needed for new fighter and service groups, which, at the time, had almost no personnel. The responsibilities of the Tuskegee commander and of his staff were multiple and the replacement of white by Negro officers would "not only reduce the present efficiency of the station but in all probability tend to defeat the purpose of this effort." The command considered Hastie's interest in the matter "more racial than military. The purpose and function of this command is military training and it has no interest in the racial question. . . . Unless instructed to the contrary, military efficiency and military expediency will continue to be the determining factors

in the selection of training personnel at Tuskegee as is the policy at all other stations under the jurisdiction of this headquarters." [76] The possibility that Tuskegee would become an all-Negro post, as originally planned and as consistent with the objective of complete segregation, was not bright.

But, consistent with the goal of training the Negro squadrons with the least difficulty, the Air Forces continued to add training facilities at Tuskegee, thereby relieving itself of the necessity of training Negro specialists and technicians at its established schools, many of which were in the South. To the addition of technical schools to the Tuskegee program Hastie objected in June 1942. "Thus the Army Air Forces carry one step further a plan of confining as much of the training of Negroes as possible to the Tuskegee project. It must be expensive and uneconomical utilization of personnel and materials thus to duplicate training facilities for relatively small numbers of men," he observed to Robert A. Lovett, the Assistant Secretary of War for Air. Pointing out that technicians and mechanics for the two squadrons already activated had been trained at Chanute Field, Illinois, and that in the rest of the Army Negroes were being trained in existing schools, he predicted that the new plan would develop the same defects as pilot training: it would be slow, expensive, and circumscribed. He hoped that the plan would be re-examined. Secretary Lovett penciled a note to his executive officer: "Col Coiner

[76] 2d Wrapper Ind, Hq SEAAFTC to CG AAFFTC, Ft. Worth, Tex., 19 Nov 42, AAF 291.2 Negro Misc. See also, 1st Ind, AAF for Civ Aide, 29 Oct 42, AAF 353.9 Cld Tng.

—pls investigate; why was Chanute dropped?" [77]

"It appears to me that Judge Hastie and his assistant are interested only in having their people trained at the well-known Chanute school—not in the training or the facility thereof," Colonel Coiner observed as he began to investigate the reasons for abandoning Negro training at Chanute.[78] After conferring with Col. Luther S. Smith, the Air Forces Director of Individual Training, who as director of Training at the Southeast Air Corps Training Center in 1941 had been responsible for organizing the training program at Tuskegee, Colonel Coiner informed Secretary Lovett that training at Chanute had been dropped because it was only reasonable to expand training for Negroes at the place where their units were located. An additional construction program for Tuskegee to provide facilities for technical training had been authorized some months before and the program was now "either completed or so far along as to be classed completed." [79]

Plans for technical training at Tuskegee were nevertheless being changed. The 99th Pursuit Squadron was scheduled to be committed to action by 1 October 1942. Pilots and mechanics for the 100th Pursuit Squadron, which was to be the senior squadron in a planned fighter group, were in training. The full group was to be completed during the fiscal year 1943. Since the group was to be activated and trained at Tus-

kegee at the same time that the station was carrying on other flying training activities, the Air Forces was considering the establishment of a separate technical school for Negroes at another site to relieve Tuskegee of the responsibility for conducting the two distinctly different types of training at the same time.[80] In August the Air Forces informed its Technical Training Command (AAFTTC) that facilities tentatively provided at Tuskegee for technical training would not be used for this purpose. "If deemed advisable by you, you will be authorized to establish a detachment at Tuskegee for the training of negro officer candidates," AAFTTC was told. Contract facilities at a Negro university or similar institution might be obtained for other technical training.[81]

By autumn the situation had changed further. The Army Air Forces was now expecting to take over the basic training of all its personnel of the arms and services (ASWAAF), including 6,000 Negroes a month for the remainder of 1942 and 9,000 per month for 1943.[82] With flying training expanding at Tuskegee, the need for technically trained enlisted and officer personnel was increasing rapidly. The Technical Training Command considered acquiring Prairie View College in Texas for this purpose, and the Third Air Force, seeking a location for the tactical training of units that would be removed from the crowded Tuskegee station, looked over a site at Fort Davis, Alabama, southeast of the

---

[77] Memo, Civ Aide for ASWA, 30 Jun 42, and attached note, ASWA 291.2.
[78] Memo, Lt Col Richard T. Coiner (ExO ASWA) for Lovett, 4 Jul 42, ASWA 291.2.
[79] Note for Lovett, dated 21 Jul 42, signed RTC, ASWA 291.2.

[80] Memo, CG AAF for CofS, 2 Jul 42, AAF 353.9 Tng of Negroes.
[81] Ltr, Hq AAF to CG AAFTTC, Knollwood Fld, N.C., 5 Aug 42, AAF 353–A Negro Tng.
[82] Draft Ltr attached to R&RS, AFRIT–3 (Individual Tng) for CofAS, 26 Oct 42, AAF 353–A Negro Tng.

Tuskegee school on the other side of the town of Tuskegee. This site, previously considered for the flying school location, was abandoned, partly because of protests from the white citizens of Tuskegee who felt that with Tuskegee Institute, a Veterans' Administration Hospital, and one Army and one contract flying installation already existing to the north, east, and west of the town, an additional installation for Negroes to the south would encircle the town completely.[83] As yet, there was no over-all plan for the training of Negroes who could not be accommodated at Tuskegee.

On 25 October, the Technical Training Command submitted a plan which called not only for the establishment of a separate technical school for Negroes but also for separate officer training, officer candidate, and clerical schools plus a basic training center, all to be concentrated at Jefferson Barracks, in St. Louis. Thus, all Negro training for the Air Forces would be on a completely segregated basis, concentrated at Tuskegee and at Jefferson Barracks.[84]

Independent of the remainder of the plan and of geographical considerations, the concentration of all Negro replacement training for the Air Forces at one post had certain advantages, the Air Forces believed. The Air Forces had experienced some difficulty in extracting the desired number of technical trainees from its aviation squadrons. Among their other duties, these squadrons gave

basic training to Negro selectees assigned directly from reception centers. On 19 August 1942, the Air Forces sent a circular letter asking aviation squadrons to report qualified enlisted men for technical school training. By 5 October only 44 out of 85,000 men had been reported available. "The results so far obtained from the above referred to letter are of no value whatever," Army Air Forces informed its field commanders. Pointing out its desire to start a large-scale program, the Air Forces again instructed its commands to report qualified enlisted men by number and course, but most reports continued to be negative.[85] Concentration of replacement trainees at one post would permit proper classification and assignment of potential technical trainees before units found other jobs for them to do.

There was not complete certainty within the Air Staff of the wisdom of the proposal to concentrate all training for Negroes at separate posts. A policy letter on the subject, addressed to the Technical Training Command, was prepared by the Director of Individual Training on 26 October for the signature of the Chief of the Air Staff. This letter began: "Confirming past verbal directives, the training of negroes will be accomplished through segregation." It directed the commanding general of the Technical Training Command to select "a suitable site or sites" for the basic training of enlisted Negroes of the Air Forces and of the Arms and Services with the Air Forces, for technical training of

[83] Record of Corresp received, 27 Sep 42, No. 601-Tex., in ASWA 291.21; Ltr, Hq AAFSETC, Maxwell Fld, Ala., to CG AAF, 20 Nov 42, AAF 666 Ft. Davis, Ala.; Memo, A–4 for Gen Arnold, 21 Nov 42, AAF 676.3 Installations–H.
[84] Ltr, AAFTC, Knollwood Fld, N.C., to CG AAF, 25 Oct 42, AAF 353.01 Est.

[85] Ltr, Hq AAF to CG's Tng Sv Comds and Numbered AF's, 19 Aug 42, AAF 220.9; Ltr, Dir Pers AAF (Col J. M. Bevans) to same, 5 Oct 42, AAF 353.9 Tng of Negroes; Rpts in AAF 353.9 Tng of Negroes.

enlisted men and officers, for the administrative training of officers, and for such individual training as the Services of Supply could not provide for Negro ASWAAF personnel. The draft of this letter was submitted to the Air Training Division for approval before submission to the Chief of the Air Staff. Though pointing out that "former training policies regarding negro troops have not favored segregation, however recent developments indicate that it is desirable to accomplish this type of training thru segregation," the Training Division concurred. The office of the Chief of the Air Staff then routed the proposal to the Director of Program Planning (AFDPU) for concurrence. AFDPU did concur but recommended that the directive be given "a very limited distribution and any reference thereto be definitely confined to a limited number of people." The Chief of Air Staff, Maj. Gen. George E. Stratemeyer, then directed that the Assistant Chief of Air Staff, A–1, indicate concurrence or nonconcurrence "by his own signature." A–1 concurred.[86] But, after a personal conference with Maj. Gen. Walter R. Weaver of the Army Air Forces Technical Training Command, General Stratemeyer recommended that the letter be withdrawn. There was no need for it, since the proposal covered was already projected for Jefferson Barracks. The policy appeared to be settled. All Air Forces training for Negroes would be given at racially separate schools and posts.[87]

Action was being taken to comply with the Technical Training Command's plan[88] when news of the change at Jefferson Barracks reached St. Louis. Irate white citizens and organizations protested vigorously. "All Hell broke loose out there and the Mayor called me and talked to me for about a half hour last night," General Weaver informed Brig. Gen. Thomas J. Hanley, the Deputy Chief of the Air Staff. "The city of St. Louis is up in arms about this thing, and I thought I'd better tip you fellows off up there," he continued.[89] Washington had already heard of the St. Louis reaction. Missouri congressmen had been querying the War Department about the proposal. The Air Forces was advised to discuss the matter with the Advisory Committee, and decision on the full proposal was postponed.

In the meantime, the Individual Training Section of the Air Staff had prepared a justification for providing the Technical Training Command with a policy for carrying out its proposals. This staff section argued that the central, north-south border location of Jefferson Barracks near a metropolitan area with a large Negro civilian population would "absolutely minimize the tremendous problem arising from racial prejudice."

Smith noted on the R&RS (handwritten): "File without further action—Cleared verbally with Lt Col Libby. LSS" and "Barbey: This constitutes a policy for further action—LSS 11/6."

[88] R&RS's, 4 Nov 42 and 6 Nov 42; R&RS, AFRIT for AFCAS, 11 Nov 42; Memo, AAF (DCofAS) for CofS, attention G–3, 13 Nov 42, all in AAF 353.9 Cld Tng (dispatched 17 Nov 42); Ltr, TAG to CG's Major Comds, Sv Comds, RTC's, 7 Nov 42, AG 324.71 (11–7–42) OC–S–M.

[89] Tel Conv, Maj Gen Walter Weaver, Knollwood Fld, N.C., and Brig Gen T. J. Hanley, Washington, 11 Nov 42, AAF 291.2 Negroes. See also AAF 291.2 (Races) binder 1.

---

[86] R&RS's, AFRIT–3 to AFCAS, AFCAS to AFDPU, AFDPU to AFCAS, AFCAS to AFFAP, AFAAP to AFCAS, 26 Oct to 2 Nov 42, AAF 353A Negro Tng.

[87] R&RS, AFCAS (Lt Col Millard A. Libby) for AFRIT, 2 Nov 42, AAF 353A Negro Tng. General

Jefferson Barracks would reduce the hazards to training arising from racial discrimination. Segregation of Negro troops there was regarded as a safeguard against discrimination:

The problem must be faced candidly and impartially, for the following reasons:
(1) A poorly selected location geographically will irritate and amplify racial prejudices, which seriously hamper individual training. We cannot allow such a consideration to in turn hamper our individual training efforts, which are designed for the sole purpose of producing efficient fighting-fit troops.
(2) We cannot allow racial prejudices to interfere with our administration of present policy, as well as human justice, which dictate that the Army Air Forces will provide training opportunities for colored troops which are equal to those given to white troops.

. . . .

e. Segregation must be followed, particularly for phases of individual training, as a safeguard against charges of racial discrimination, and to permit of proper inspections in this phase.
f. Jefferson Barracks is one of the best posts of the Army Air Forces, for any types of troops. It is rich in traditions and honorable history, being one of the oldest posts in our Army's history. . . . It is believed that Jefferson Barracks will lend itself admirably to being publicized as the "Colored Miami Beach Schools," in the same manner as we have publicized the flying school at Tuskegee as the "Colored West Point of the Air." [90]

Neither Air Personnel nor Air Training concurred in this presentation of the proposal,[91] but the Deputy Chief of Air

Staff, General Hanley, did concur and the next day initiated action for the preparation of a formal proposal based on Individual Training's reasoning for presentation to the Chief of Staff and the Advisory Committee. "General Arnold, the Chief of Air Staff and the Deputy Chief of Air Staff concur in the idea that the segregation of negroes, as outlined in this paper, is the best way to train them in the Army Air Forces," Hanley indicated to Col. Aubry L. Moore, of Program Planning, when directing preparation of the necessary papers. There should be no publicity or action toward carrying out the policy until the plans clear through the Advisory Committee, the Deputy Chief of Air Staff added.[92] The formal request, dated 13 November, was forwarded to G–3 on 17 November but was returned without action, for in the interval still other changes in the program had occurred.[93]

The Technical Training Command on 16 November had renewed its request for approval of the concentration of all Negro training at Jefferson Barracks, adding that pending approval or the issuance of other directives the flow of Negro recruits to the command should be stopped. This proposal was returned to the Technical Training Command as not favorably considered,[94]

scattered throughout the country." Both comments dated 11 Nov 42. R&RS cited n. 90.
[92] R&RS, DCofAS for AFDPU (Col Moore) 12 Nov 42, AAF 353–A Negro Tng.
[93] Memo, AAF (DCofAS) for CofS (Attention G–3), 13 Nov 42, prepared in AFDPU, draft fwd to DCofAS 14 Nov, dispatched 17 Nov 42, AAF 352.01 Est, AAF 353–A Negro Tng.
[94] Immediate Action Ltr, AAF Hq Tech Tng Comd, Knollwood Fld, N.C., to CG AAF, 16 Nov 42, and 1st Ind, Hq AAF to CG AAF TTC, 19 Nov 42, AAF 353 Cld Tng.

[90] R&RS, Dir Individual Tng for AFAAP, AFACT, AFCAS, in turn, 11 Nov 42, AAF 353–A Negro Tng.
[91] AFAAP (Col F. Trubee Davison) simply wrote "Non-concur" (penciled); AFACT ("R. W. H.[arper]," also penciled) explained: "Non-concur in conversion of Jeff Bks to all-colored. Segregation better done by small number of colored units

for by the time the request arrived, a new draft, first circulated on 18 November, calling for concentration of most Negro training at Chanute Field, Illinois, was in process of preparation by the Air Staff's Directorate of Individual Training.[95]

On 30 November the Technical Training Command forwarded a substitute proposal, calling for the use of Jefferson Barracks for officer candidate and cooks and bakers training only, with other training conducted at other schools. The proposal, while its written form was in the mails, was given by phone to Headquarters AAF, coinciding with the completion of the 18 November (Chanute Field) draft. Its features were incorporated into the 18 November draft letter. The new proposal authorized the training of (1) officer candidates at Jefferson Barracks; (2) enlisted specialists at Chanute Field; and (3) the continuation of basic training in aviation squadrons. Permanent party ASWAAF personnel were to be distributed to the various units of their arms and services and the unassigned personnel to "your various basic training centers in exactly the same manner as white personnel of this category."[96] This plan, too, had to be discarded, for Chanute could not handle all specialties. The new formal proposal of the Technical Training Command as originally written was substituted and approved by the Director of Individual Training on 9

December.[97] It provided for training sites as follows:

Officer Training

Jefferson Barracks	OCS
Grand Rapids	Weather
Yale	Engineer, armament, communications
Boca Raton	Radar (V–1)
Harvard	Statistical

Enlisted Training

Boca Raton	Radar mechanics
Chanute Field	Machinist, metal work, parachute, welding, link trainer, teletype repair, electrical, propeller, and instrument specialists
Scott Field	Radio
Jefferson Barracks	Cooks and bakers
Fort Logan	Clerks
Lincoln	Airplane mechanics
Buckley Field	Armorers
Lowry Field	Bombsight specialists; photographers

One of the problems involved in Negro officer training, unstated formally in the planning for the separate OCS at Jefferson Barracks, was that ground officer candidate training for the Air Forces was located in luxury hotels at Miami Beach, Florida. At the time, this city normally permitted no Negroes to remain overnight in its precincts; on its behalf, numerous inquiries and protests on the possibility of locating Negro troops in its hotels came in to the War Department. Air Forces agencies had given assurances that no Negro troop or officer candidate training was planned

---

[95] Draft Ltr, Dir Individual Tng for CG AAFTTC, 18 Nov 42, and attached drafts and comments, AAF 353–A Negro Tng.

[96] Ltr, Dir Individual Tng for CG AAFTTC and Incl, Outline of Plan, 1 Dec 42, AAF 353–A Negro Tng.

[97] Ltr, Hq TTC to CG AAF, 30 Nov 42, and 1st Ind, Hq AAF (Brig Gen L. S. Smith) to CGTTC, 9 Dec 42, AG 353, AAF 353 Cld Tng.

for the Miami Beach schools.[98]   Though the remainder of the Army was training Negro officer candidates in established schools, the AAFTTC, out of all its original plan, retained only the separate Negro OCS.   With its enlisted trainees scheduled for regular schools, this persistence in establishing a separate OCS, when coupled with the AAF's insistence upon concentrating all of its Negro flying training at Tuskegee, gave to the Air Forces an appearance of willful adherence to its own plans to keep officer training on a separate basis despite the policies of all other branches of the Army.

It appeared to Judge Hastie toward the end of 1942 that the Air Forces was formulating its own policies without reference to his office or to general Army policies.   During the planning for Jefferson Barracks, Hastie was neither consulted about nor advised of the discussions.   Throughout this planning he was in continuous communication with the Air Forces on the training of Negroes.   He had inquired about statistical errors made in the Air Staff on success rates in pilot training at Tuskegee —errors which, when called to the attention of the Air Staff, were then compounded instead of corrected.   He had asked about training flight surgeons by correspondence, to which the Air Forces at first replied that with the great bulk of aviation medicine trainees, both Negro and white students were using extension courses and branch schools.   When Hastie asked specifically if Negroes were excluded from Randolph Field's medical courses, the answer came back: "It is

not the policy of the Air Corps to exclude Negro officers from training at the School of Aviation Medicine."   He had asked about placing washed-out cadets in other types of training and about cadet training for qualified Negroes in meteorology, armament, and engineering.[99]   But plans for expanding this training, including the difficult problem of concentrated and separate training versus training in established schools, had not been mentioned to him in the Air Forces communications on these subjects.

Late in November, Judge Hastie learned from St. Louis newspapers that the Air Forces had planned to turn Jefferson Barracks into an all-Negro training center.   After hearing about questions put to Secretary Stimson at a press conference, he asked Secretary Lovett toward the end of November if there was any truth in the rumors about Jefferson Barracks.[100]   Three weeks later, the reply came that "present Air Forces plans do not provide for the conversion of Jefferson Barracks into an all-Negro post" and that "the training program in general contemplates assignment of Negro personnel for training to installations in areas from which procured."   Complaints from St. Louis, the communication continued, indicated that "it would be wiser not to effect the reported conversion." [101]   The reply was technically correct though no specific mention was made of the latest plan to establish an officer candidate school and a cooks and bakers school at Jefferson Barracks nor

---

[98] Ltr, Representative Pat Cannon to ASW McCloy, 16 Jun 42, and subsequent corresp, ASWA 291.21.

[99] See papers in ASWA 291.2, Oct–Nov 42.
[100] Memo, Civ Aide for ASWA, 26 Nov 42, ASWA 291.2.
[101] Memo, ASWA for Civ Aide, 17 Dec 42, ASWA 291.2.

of the decision to utilize established technical schools for specialist training.

On 1 January Jefferson Barracks issued a press release informing the public that a new officer candidate school for Negroes would open there on 15 January. On 5 January Hastie informed Secretary Stimson and Under Secretary Patterson that in the Air Forces "further retrogression is now so apparent and recent occurrences are so objectionable and inexcusable that I have no alternative but to resign in protest and to give public expression to my views." [102] Despite the "several substantial gains of the past two years in the handling of racial issues and particular problems of Negro military and civilian personnel" and despite the two secretaries' expressed confidence that he could do more within the War Department than out, Hastie began, he did not think that his presence was longer useful:

I have believed that there remain areas in which changes of racial policy should be made but will not be made in response to advocacy within the Department but only as a result of strong and manifest public opinion. I have believed that some of these changes involve questions of the sincerity and depth of our devotion to the basic issues of this war and thus have an important bearing, both on the fighting spirit of our own people and upon our ability as a nation to maintain leadership in the struggle for a free world." [103]

So long as he remained in the War Department he could not express himself freely and publicly on these matters. Therefore, he was submitting a formal resignation separately to take effect on 31 January.[104]

Except for a statment to the press issued on 16 January in which, to quiet growing rumors, he announced that he had submitted his resignation and that he had asked his two assistants, Louis Lautier and Truman K. Gibson, Jr., to stay at their posts, Hastie refrained from any public statement during the remainder of the month. He had, however, outlined in detail his objections to the course of Air Forces policy in his memorandum to the secretaries. He included a sharp denunciation of misleading information given him by the Air Forces as well as criticisms of its policies:

In establishing a separate Officer Candidate School for Negroes at Jefferson Barracks the Air Forces are deliberately rejecting the general practice of unsegregated Officer Candidate Schools which has proved so eminently successful throughout the Army and which has been so hopeful an augury. I did not know that such a school was contemplated until the matter appeared a few days ago in an Army press release. Worse, still, I was given misleading information by the Air Forces at a time when the plan must have been well advanced. . . . In such circumstances the failure of the Air Forces, after written request, to advise this office candidly and fully of a plan so soon to be publicly announced cannot be considered an excusable inadvertence.[105]

This latest development had to be placed in its proper setting, Hastie continued. He recalled that "the policy of using Negro personnel in the Air Forces at all was imposed upon a Command, reluctant from the outset. Resistance, bred of that reluctance has been

---

[102] Memo, Civ Aide for SW through USW, 5 Jan 43, ASW 291.2 NT–Civ Aide.
[103] Ibid.

[104] Memo, Civ Aide for SW through USW, 6 Jan 43, ASW 291.2 NT–Civ Aide.
[105] Memo, Civ Aide for SW through USW, 5 Jan 43, ASW 291.2 NT–Civ Aide.

encountered repeatedly." He went on to cite the Air Forces' establishment of aviation squadrons; its establishment of a separate clerical school; its refusal to train and use qualified service pilots, weather officer applicants, and other officer specialists which, in national recruiting campaigns, it had said it needed badly; the inadequacy of its training for Negro flight surgeons; its refusal to use Negroes in positions of responsibility at Tuskegee; and its refusal to continue technical training in its established schools in the pattern begun at Chanute Field where "the results were excellent." Moreover, Hastie asserted, the Air Forces was failing to produce results with its methods. While efforts were being made to set up segregated technical training at Tuskegee or elsewhere, "successive classes of pilots were being trained, but no supporting technical schooling of ground crew members was in progress. Thus even the segregated system has gotten badly out of balance in the effort to accomplish its extension. The prospect is that in 1943 Negro pilots will be ready before and faster than adequate members of trained ground crews are available." The situation at Tuskegee, where separate messes, quarters, and washrooms were maintained, Hastie concluded, had reached the point where it might "jeopardize the entire future of the Negro in combat aviation. Men cannot be humiliated over a long period of time without a shattering of morale and a destroying of combat efficiency. . . . If the group of white officers at Tuskegee insist upon this—and I have no evidence that they do—they are psychologically unsuited to train Negroes for combat. If they do not so insist, the racial attitude of the local commander

or of higher authority is all the more apparent." [106]

Hastie's memorandum was forwarded to the Air Staff, where inquiries began.[107] General Stratemeyer called a halt to the preparations for the new school, telling a representative of Individual Training:

I don't want any colored school any place to be conducted as a segregated school. With reference to colored Officer Candidates at Miami Beach, I want them treated just like white Officer Candidates. They will go to the same classes, to the same drills, and eat in mess halls the same as the whites. If there are any questions, tell General Smith to call me.[108]

General Stratemeyer then had the Hastie paper analyzed for Assistant Secretary McCloy. Judge Hastie was correct about aviation squadrons, the Air Staff said, but he had overlooked the fact that the majority of Negroes with low general classification scores had to be employed somewhere. On everything else, the Staff declared, Hastie was in substantial error. His information about the establishment of a segregated officer candidate school at Jefferson Barracks "had no basis in fact." A plan had been prepared "in an operating division of Headquarters, Army Air Forces but it had neither been referred to nor approved by the Chief of the Air Staff. Negroes with sufficiently high general classification and mechanical aptitude

[106] Ibid.
[107] R&RS, Dir Pers to Dir Individual Tng, 5 Jan 43, and Comment 2, Dir Individual Tng to Dir Pers, attention Mil Pers Div, 9 Jan 43. Both in AAF 353-A Negro Tng.
[108] Immediate Action Ltr, Hq AAF (Brig Gen L. S. Smith, Dir Individual Tng) to CG TTC, Knollwood Field, N.C., 10 Jan 43, AAF 353–A Negro Tng. Quotation marks are in the original, a transcript of General Stratemeyer's telephone conversation forwarded to Knollwood.

scores were being used as noncommissioned officers or were being sent to officer candidate schools and to training courses "throughout the school system of the Technical Training Command." The separate clerical school at Atlanta University was being conducted by the Services of Supply. As for Tuskegee, the location of the school there had been urged by the officials of the Tuskegee Institute and instead of training being harmed there, both Brig. Gen Benjamin O. Davis and the Commanding General, Third Air Force, had found the fighter squadron there to be in a "superior state of training." It was "now ready to be committed to combat." Moreover, the Air Staff's analysis continued, directives would be issued to insure compliance with War Department policies on racial discrimination in the matter of separate messing and toilet facilities for Negro and white officers, though the commanding officer at Tuskegee would be within regulations if he established a regimental mess for the new 332d Fighter Group "providing no racial restrictions were placed on officer messing facilities established for other officer personnel." The policy of placing Negro officers in posts of responsibility at Tuskegee had not changed though "implementation . . . will depend upon the best judgment of the responsible commander." Sufficient weather, armament, communication, engineering, and administrative officers to care for Negro units were being trained, but "excessive numbers of Negro specialists would be wasteful and inadvisable," the Air Forces added, remarking that War Department assignment policies of Negro officers which would limit the usefulness of additional specialists were still in force.

Service pilots would be employed as needed within the limits of War Department policies on the assignment of Negro officers, and directives insuring the training of flight surgeons in resident student status had been issued.[109]

Hastie observed that perhaps General Stratemeyer was correct about the new school—"I hope, of course, that no such project has been or is going to be inaugurated," he said—but, in addition to the press release, "this office checked informally with the Air Forces Technical Training Command and received verbal confirmation from that office." Moreover, General Stratemeyer's statement did not clearly say whether "the Air Forces are not going to have a segregated Officer Candidate School or merely that the Chief of Air Staff had not approved the proposal at the time my memorandum was written." Hastie declared that he doubted that the four or five thousand Negroes who, according to General Stratemeyer's figures on test scores, had the required aptitude for technical training, were receiving it, that badly needed weather officers could not work anywhere "except at the Tuskegee Base or with a Negro unit in the field," and that the judgment of the Air Staff on what was happening at Tuskegee could be reconciled with conclusions "based on my own observations and on the views of persons living and working there every day." To him, this analysis was only one more example of the Air Forces' lack of candor in facing the issue of its use of Negro troops.[110]

[109] Memo, CofAS for ASW, 12 Jan 43, ASW 291.2 NT–Civ Aide. Draft prepared by Col John H. McCormick, then assistant A–1 and Air Forces representative on the Advisory Committee.
[110] Memo, Civ Aide for ASW, 19 Jan 43, ASW 291.2 NT–Civ Aide.

Secretary Stimson accepted Hastie's resignation on 29 January.[111] As one of his last official acts in the War Department, Hastie forwarded to Assistant Secretary McCloy the next day a memorandum on two additional issues "which seem to be of immediate importance": the placement and promotion of Negro officers, including provisions for the removal of excess officers from the all-Negro units since "field and company officers tend to deteriorate when they seem to be in a blind alley"; and the overseas use of Negro combat organizations, especially those which had been in training for long periods of time.[112] Both of these problems were to engage the attention of the War Department for many months to come.

Gibson and the Aide's Office

A search for a successor to Hastie was already under way. The names of Negro college presidents, federal and state government officials, and, occasionally, of unknown but favored former students of distinguished law professors—sometimes solicited by Assistant Secretary McCloy and sometimes offered by interested persons outside the Department—were suggested during January 1943.[113] The Negro press, lauding Hastie for his stand, indulged in its own predictions. The Associated Negro Press reported that "the consensus of opinion as expressed freely and frankly is that he did the right thing in stepping out of a posi-

tion that was becoming untenable." [114] Typical of editorial opinion was the New Orleans *Louisiana Weekly*'s assertion that Hastie's resignation was

. . . a tribute to the new type of leadership that is coming to the forefront for the Negro masses. . . . He performed admirably under the difficulties. . . . He must indeed have been a patient man to have been pushed around and given the "brush off" by the Army "swivel chair corps" who apparently care little for the Negro in the Army other than as a laborer. However, there is a limit to every man's patience, even Judge Hastie's. We think by his action he rises in stature and becomes one of our living heroes and leaders whom Pearl Buck says we so desperately need.[115]

In the meantime, the work of the Civilian Aide's office continued with Hastie's assistant, Truman K. Gibson, Jr., designated Acting Civilian Aide on 5 February,[116] pending appointment of a successor to Hastie.

Hastie, in his resignation statement, had indicated that, instead of a consistent policy leading to the useful employment of Negro troops, un-co-ordinated and often divergent patterns within the Army were leading to supportable charges of a lack of direction in the utilization of Negroes and a potential waste of manpower. Here was a concrete matter

---

[111] Ltr, SW to Hastie, 29 Jan 43, ASW 291.2 NT–Civ Aide.

[112] Memo, Civ Aide for ASW, 30 Jan 43, ASW 291.2 NT–Civ Aide.

[113] See ASW 291.2 Files, 1943.

[114] ANP dispatch, headed "War Department Wasted Talents," Atlanta *Daily World*, 29 Jan 43.

[115] Editorial, "Judge Hastie's Resignation," *Louisiana Weekly*, January 30, 1943.

[116] Memo, ExO to ASW for Gen Surles (BPR), 4 Feb 43; Memo, SW for Truman K. Gibson, 5 Feb 43. Both in ASW 291.2 NT–Civ Aide. The directive that matters of policy pertaining to Negroes be referred to the Civilian Aide's office for comment or concurrence was reissued with Gibson's name substituted for Hastie's. WD Memo, W600–13–43, 13 Feb 43, Policies Pertaining to Negroes, AG 291.21 (2–13–43) OB–C–MB–FH.

upon which action could be taken on its practical merits rather than on the ethical grounds from which many of the Hastie proposals, despite their practical aspects, had proceeded. The Advisory Committee, which had previously held few meetings, now came to vigorous life. As already noted, this committee had been set up to "evaluate racial incidents, proposed social reforms, and questions involving the training and use of negroes." [117]   How closely the three went together was now clearer than before. The Advisory Committee now realized more fully that its was a continuing problem of evaluation and consideration of multitudinous problems going beyond the technicalities of the distribution of Negroes in the troop basis. Truman Gibson, in discussions with Secretary McCloy, impressed upon him that, with the serial presentation of Hastie's objections in the press [118] and with the steady worsening of Negro troop problems, immediate steps to solve the major questions which Hastie had called to the secretaries' attention should be taken and the public should be so informed.[119]

Hastie's resignation itself had been followed by certain immediate changes, especially in the Air Forces, which quietly dropped its Jefferson Barracks plan, promoted the commander at Tuskegee and replaced him, made plans to remove the new tactical group from Tuskegee, and ordered flight surgeon trainees to

school at Randolph Field.   Just before Hastie's resignation took effect, the Air Forces announced publicly that it was expanding its training program for combat fliers and supporting services and that Negroes were being trained "throughout virtually the entire Technical Training Command of the Air Forces as well as at the Air Forces Officers' Training School at Miami." [120] After the first of February, when Hastie announced publicly that Air Forces policies had been the chief cause of his resignation, the Air Forces indicated that it had no intention of making a further reply, since it believed that it had complied fully with the Secretary of War's instructions on Negro troop policies.[121]

In the weeks following Hastie's departure, Gibson presented serially, in conferences and memoranda, separate analyses of many of the problems remaining unsolved.   The Civilian Aide's main channel of action now shifted definitely from Under Secretary Patterson's office to Assistant Secretary McCloy's, with Gibson working closely with Charles Poletti, ex-lieutenant governor of New York and, at the time, a special assistant to the Secretary, and, later, with Col. William P. Scobey and Lt. Col. Harrison A. Gerhardt, executives to the Assistant Secretary.   While he pursued the same objectives as Hastie, Gibson generally approached his problems singly, presenting alternatives for action phrased in terms of their probable effect upon the Army, the public (white and

[117] Memo, G–1 for CofS, 18 Jul 42, AG 334 Advisory Com on Negro Trp Policies (18 Jul 42) (1).
[118] Hastie's statements to the press were later developed into a pamphlet, *On Clipped Wings: The Story of Jim Crow in the Army Air Corps* (New York: NAACP, 1943), 26 pp.
[119] Memo, Gibson for ASW, 3 Feb 43, ASW 291.2 NTC.

[120] Press Release, Bureau of Public Relations, 28 Jan 43, "Army to Expand Its Program for Training Negro Fliers."
[121] Rpt of AAF Representative, (Gen Hanley), Min Gen Council, 1 Feb 43.

Negro), and the developing military situation.[122]

To McCloy and to Poletti, Gibson again outlined the problems of both his office and of its relations with the Advisory Committee, enclosing for Poletti a copy of the Hastie Survey containing marginal notes on what had been done and what remained to be accomplished in the Hastie program.[123] To the new secretary of the committee, Col. Joseph S. Leonard, formerly commander of the 366th Infantry at Fort Devens, he offered the files of his office so that the committee might become more familiar with the main problems with which the Civilian Aide had been faced. Both Gibson and the Advisory Committee began to give closer attention to the help that they might get from Brig. Gen. Frederick H. Osborn and his Special Service Division in the area of the morale of Negro troops. To General Osborn, Gibson outlined the Air Forces problem for use in a conference to be held with Judge Patterson.[124]

This conference was an outgrowth of one of the many inquiries coming into the War Department after Hastie's resignation. After one of these, involving a meeting of Under Secretary Patterson, Assistant Secretary Lovett, and General Stratemeyer with Wilbur LaRoe and a delegation from the Washington Federation of Churches, Judge Patterson, Assistant Secretary Lovett, Howard Petersen, and General Osborn met to consider developments within the Air Forces. One result was an agreement that Air Forces—Negro relations should be handled by the Advisory Committee and that Patterson would thereafter refer questions on these relations to the committee.[125] This agreement ended the Under Secretary's formal concern with Negro troop problems. Another result was that, as a consequence of Patterson's expression of dissatisfaction with the progress and numbers of Negro personnel which the Air Forces was training, Secretary Lovett and General Stratemeyer discussed the entire situation, suggesting that the Air Forces investigate and take action to:

1. Make certain that some Negroes were assigned to the college training program in northern colleges where CPT training was being given, even at the expense of filling quotas set for Tuskegee.

2. Investigate and increase the activities in which Negro pilots might participate, paying particular attention to securing all possible candidates for service pilot ratings, assigning them to liaison units which could work with Negro ground units.

3. Make an attempt to train pilots and navigators as transport crews which could be assigned to Roberts Field in Liberia "for the purpose of flying cargo or ferrying

---

[122] Examples: Memos, Gibson for Poletti and Gibson for ASW, 20 Feb 43, on command in the 366th Infantry; Memo, Gibson for ASW, 4 Mar 43, on ambiguous policy on assignment and promotion of Negro officers; Memo, Gibson for Poletti, 5 Mar 43, on use of Negroes in military government plans; Memo, Gibson for Poletti, 16 Mar 43, on Liberia Task Force problems; Memo, Gibson for Poletti, 18 Mar 43, on adequacy of investigation of problems in 76th CA; Memo, Gibson for Poletti, 22 Mar 43, on Air Forces training program; Memo, Gibson for Poletti, 23 Mar 43, on revised policy on promotion of Negro officers. All in ASW 291.2 NT and ASW 291.2 NT–Gen, 1943. During much of this period, Assistant Secretary McCloy was out of the country; this, in part, accounted for the high proportion of items presented to Poletti rather than directly to the Assistant Secretary.

[123] Memo, Gibson for ASW, 3 Feb 43, and Memos (2), Gibson for Poletti, 9 Feb 43. All in ASW 291.2 NTC.

[124] Memo, Gibson for Osborn, 11 Mar 43, SPSP 291.21.

[125] Memo, Osborn for Gen Joe N. Dalton, 11 Mar 43, SSB 291.21 (9–27–41) (1).

airplanes forward to combat theaters from that installation. It is understood that there is a colored U.S. citizen in Canada who has piloted bombers across the North Atlantic four or five times and who is available for, and who has requested assignment to the Army Air Forces. Investigate this through A–1, and see if his services cannot be secured for the purpose of either bringing his entire crew with him to operate for the Air Transport Command in Liberia or to train a colored crew which can be used by the Air Transport Command from Roberts Field."

4. Investigate and prepare plans to start the training of additional colored ground personnel and have them on hand to work with and assist in the training of a medium or light bombardment group "which we must necessarily activate and organize if and when our present experiment with the fighter group is successful." [126]

While most of these proposals were not carried out, planning for the increased use of Negroes did begin within the Air Forces and a medium bombardment group did materialize. Moreover, co-operation between the Air Forces headquarters and the Civilian Aide's office gradually improved. After a visit to Tuskegee in April, Gibson informed Secretary Lovett that he had been greatly impressed by "the very able and conscientious manner in which Lieutenant Colonel Noel Parrish, the Commanding Officer, has attacked the many difficult problems with which he has been confronted. There has been a decided upswing in the morale of the Negro officers and men stationed there." Though many of the criticisms of Tuskegee were justifiable, he continued, "the training program has been conducted in a fair and impartial manner. For this, the

Air Forces is deserving of credit and has received favorable comment even from some of the most vocal critics of the whole program." He regretted that previous disagreements of his office with various Air Forces policies had resulted in "the development of an attitude that a feeling of hostility exists" preventing "the free discussion of possible solutions for what is admittedly a troublesome and difficult problem" and preventing "adequate discussions on the adoption of some continuing plan for the use of Negroes in the Army Air Forces." He pointed out the dangers of adherence to unchanging formulas and offered the facilities of his office for planning beyond the needs of the fighter units then under way.[127] Secretary Lovett noted on the memorandum: "Copy given to Col. McCormick, Personnel. He is to see Gibson & get his cooperation on matters wherever possible before any step is taken."

While Gibson's attempts to obtain a closer working relationship between his office, the Advisory Committee, and the offices of the two assistant secretaries did not always meet with unalloyed success, events and a greater concern on the part of participants to deal adequately with them produced a better machinery for action than had been. Gibson, though he was never given membership on the committee, gained early an advantage closed to Hastie: after March, upon Secretary McCloy's recommendation, he attended Advisory Committee meetings regularly.[128] Although the committee had no staff other than its secretary and

[126] R&RS, Stratemeyer to ACofAS G–3, copy to Arnold, Lovett, Dir Individual Tng, A–1, 11 Mar 43, copy in ASWA 291.21, action proposals and recommendations in AAF 353–A, Negro Tng.

[127] Memo, Gibson for ASWA, 1 May 43, ASWA 291.2.
[128] Min of Mtg of Advisory Com, Col J. S. Leonard, 22 Mar 43, ASW 291.2 NTC.

no other full-time member, its meetings provided a forum and clearing house where the chiefs of policy-making branches and the representatives of the major commands of the Army could compare notes and gain perspective on questions affecting the employment of Negro troops. The Civilian Aide was therefore able to present his views on questions as they arose. Though the committee often temporized and deferred action, when a major proposal was agreed upon its movement through the staff divisions was expedited by familiarity with the proposal gained in committee meetings. With the Advisory Committee and the Civilian Aide working more closely than formerly, the War Department began to acquire a more generally agreed upon approach to Negro troop policies, though it still lacked a central co-ordinating body for the collection, evaluation, and dissemination of information upon and decisions made about proposals and counterproposals affecting these policies.

Gibson held his position as acting aide until 21 September 1943, when he was made permanent Civilian Aide.[129] Between February and September many of the problems brought to the attention of the War Department by Hastie came to a head. A number of modifications in policy and practice occurred, for many of the difficulties foreseen by Hastie and the staff sections in 1941 and 1942 came to full growth by the spring of 1943. With these, Gibson, McCloy, and the Advisory Committee had to deal. But the pattern of the organization and employment of Negro troops had so set by 1943 that many situations could only be modified and not appreciably altered. In the meantime, the course of policies and problems in the field, met at their high points by reactions and new policies in the War Department, continued to develop.

---

[129] Memo, ASW for Admin Asst (John W. Martyn), 21 Sep 43, ASW 291.2 NT–Civ Aide.

CHAPTER VII

Officers for Negro Troops

The War Department from the beginning of mobilization recognized that the effectiveness of troops and troop units depended in large measure on the quality of their leadership. Negro units, in the quest for competent leadership, had to compete with a general need for officers that grew with great rapidity in the expanding Army. As the size of the Army increased, the ratio of officers to men increased even more rapidly. New and larger headquarters and units, new administrative, technical, and supervisory positions, and new planning and control functions generally absorbed larger proportions of officers than enlisted men. At the same time the pool of available officer material shrank with greater rapidity than the pool of available manpower. Too often the men in demand for administrative, control, and technical duties were likely to be the type of men so urgently needed for troop leadership in units. In any event, winnowing out the potential leaders from millions of anonymous men was not an easy task.

The War Department had also recognized in its prewar planning that Negro units needed more officers than corresponding white units. The plan of 1937 had visualized the provision of 50 percent more officers for Negro units than tables of organization (T/O's) called for. The extra officers were expected to provide the needed counterbalance to the lack of military background and civilian educational and vocational experience which handicapped so many Negro soldiers. Extra officers would make possible closer supervision and greater individual attention, thereby shortening the time needed to prepare a unit for combat. The Army discovered, not long after it began to grow, that the 50 percent overstrength policy, however useful it might be, was not going to work. There simply were not enough officers to go around. Negro units, like all other units, were going to be lucky if they received even their proper table of organization allotments. In the summer of 1942, when there was a serious general shortage of officers, some Negro units had one officer only and in some cases one officer was commanding two or more units.[1] In the general shortage, no matter what policies were laid down on the desirability of excellent officers with, as the Deputy Chief of Staff, Lt. Gen. Joseph T. McNarney phrased it, "common sense and appreciation of the racial questions which confront the Army," [2] Negro units received too few officers for the

---

[1] For examples, see Memo, G-1 for CG SOS, 11 Jun 42, AG 210.31 (2-14-42) (3); Memo, G-1 for CG AGF, AGF 320.2; and Ltr, Hq IV Army Corps OTIG, Cp Beauregard, La., to TIG, 15 Jun 42. All in AGF 333.1/31 IV Army Corps.
[2] Remarks of General McNarney in the General Council, 18 Aug 42.

best results and too few officers who met the desired requirements for service with them. This last was especially true since it was difficult to describe with exactness the kind of officer best fitted for service with Negro troops in terms which did not coincide with the definition of a good officer for any situation.

Initial Procurement Policies

When mobilization began in 1940 the Army had certain definite, if vaguely expressed, notions of what it wanted in the way of leadership for Negro troops. World War I and earlier testimony had indicated that white officers were preferable to Negro officers. The white officers chosen should have some acquaintance with Negroes; therefore it was often assumed that, since few individuals from other parts of the country had come into frequent contact with Negroes, they should be Southerners. It was assumed, too, that Negro officers would have to be used, but that their numbers should be kept to a minimum. Since most commentators believed that few Negroes possessed potential combat leadership abilities, they held that Negro officers should be assigned primarily to overhead and service units. Further refinements of qualifications were not prescribed for either Negro or for white officers with Negro troops. The subtler forms of cultural and psychological qualifications, often speculated upon by writers and students of the question, were not officially endorsed by the War Department. The provision of officers for Negro units therefore revolved, from the beginning, about two conflicting ideas: that the best officers for Negro units should be white and that sufficient Negro officers must

be supplied to satisfy the Negro public and enlisted men that race was not a barrier to advancement of Negro men in a wartime army.

A considered statement of the problem from the point of view of a World War I commander was that of Col. Malvern-Hill Barnum, a brigade commander of the 92d Division. Colonel Barnum thought that while most Negroes, because of educational deficiencies, would have to be employed in line of communications work, combatant units should be organized in the infantry, cavalry, and artillery and these units should be officered by Negroes to the extent to which competent men could be found. He wrote:

The colored race in our Country is making great advances in education and in commercial and professional channels. It would not be in accordance with the policy of our Country to close to the colored man the door of opportunity to become officers, and to rise as high as their merit will permit. . . .
The greatest difficulty to be overcome [in World War I officer training] was the natural lack of aggressiveness on the part of the colored man. It could not for a moment be expected that a race which had for two hundred years, or more, been kept in a subordinate position would suddenly manifest aggressiveness such as was required in the desperate fighting which occurred during the last year or two of this war.
Some may say that colored men are not competent to become officers of the Army. This statement is entirely too sweeping, for there is no doubt but that we had many colored officers who were thoroughly competent, the fact that we had a good many incompetent ones should not be allowed to give rise to the feeling that all were incompetent.[3]

---

[3] Ltr, Col Malvern-Hill Barnum to Col Allen J. Greer, 19 Apr 19, AWC–127–21.

The point of view taken by Colonel Barnum was approximately the one that governed the provision of officers to Negro units in World War II, although the experience of World War I, supported by extracts of testimony, was generally summed up in statements like "It is generally conceded that Negro officers serving in the American Expeditionary Force during the World War were failures as combat officers." [4]

The War Department under policies in effect in the summer of 1940 planned initially to provide white officers for all units which were not Reserve or National Guard. Additional units to which Negro officers could be assigned were to be designated from time to time as Negro officers became available from the officer candidate schools. Negro chaplains could be used with any Negro unit and medical officers could be assigned to designated units. Warrant officers in Negro units were to be Negroes. Negroes were to command other Negroes only.

None of these original policy rulings was strictly held to. General Davis, for example, was assigned in 1941 to command the 4th Cavalry Brigade, which contained the two Negro cavalry regiments. Both regiments, because they were Regular Army units, had an all-white complement of officers. The 25th Infantry, early in 1942, was assigned to the 93d Division. The assignment of Negro junior officers to this Regular regiment was authorized to keep the unit parallel in composition to the other regiments of the division.[5] Variant policies, as in the case of warrant officers, developed out of the original ones as the supply of available officers and the numbers and types of Negro units changed. Despite the announced policy on warrant officers, repeated requests for clarification were made. Could Negro warrant officers be appointed to units with all white officers? All Negro officers? White and Negro officers? [6] The War Department sought to clarify the matter by reminding assignment agencies that all warrant officers authorized for Negro units should be Negroes.[7] Alternative requests continued to come in, one of them from a tank battalion that wanted white warrant officers for its existing vacancies and an authorization for nine additional white warrant officers.[8] Ground Forces refused to consider the request because other Negro tank battalions would want the same arrangement; besides, it violated current War Department policy that requirements for Negro and white units should be exactly alike.[9] "If we ever placed a note on a T/O differentiating in any way between white and colored," wrote an officer well indoctrinated in War Department policies, "we should all go to Hell." [10] Nevertheless, a compromise was arranged which allowed second lieutenants to be assigned to warrant officer vacancies "where it is definitely determined that negro warrant officers of

[4] Memo, G-3 for CofS, 5 Jun 40, AG 291.21 (5-14-40).

[5] Memo, G-3 for CofS, 4 Feb 42, approved by SW, 11 Feb 42, G-3 645-444.

[6] Memo, TAG for Dir Mil Tng SOS, 14 Jul 42, AG 200.3/92 (WO).

[7] WD Memo W610-1-42, 17 Aug 42, AG 220.2 WO (7-26-42) (OB-A-PS).

[8] Ltr, CO 758th Tk Bn to CG TDC, 28 Jan 43, app. CGTDC in 3d Ind, 210 GNTDA, dated 30 Jun 43, and forwarded by CG Armd Comd without comment, AGF 210/28 WO.

[9] Ibid., 5th Ind, Hq AGF.

[10] AGF M/S, RQT to Ground G-1, 11 Jul 43, AGF 210/28 WO.

appropriate qualifications" are not available. In this event, white second lieutenants were to be assigned to units having all white officers and Negro second lieutenants to units with Negro junior officers.[11] Many Negro units already had and continued to retain white warrant officers despite the official ruling in the matter.

White Officers and Their Leadership Dilemma

From the beginning the majority of all officers with Negro units were white. This situation was not only in accordance with the long established Army belief that white officers possessed better leadership qualifications than Negroes and that they were preferred by Negro troops but was also a result of the initial shortage of Negro officers. In the absence of available Negro officers, even in the units for which they were authorized, white officers had to be used. Initially, providing officer leadership for Negro troops was primarily a problem of selecting white officers who were both qualified for and compatible with their assignments.

The presence of white officers was accepted as natural by a great many Negro troops. Such acceptance did not prevent the development of strained relationships having their roots in racial attitudes. The fine line between good and poor officer-enlisted men relations, a line drawn finer in a rapidly expanding wartime Army by the presence of mili-

tarily inexperienced officers as well as untrained enlisted men accustomed to the relatively unrestricted civilian mode of living, buckled dangerously when soldiers could attribute any and every unpleasant task or disappointment to a possible racially-based antipathy on the part of their commanders. For, while many Negro enlisted men accepted the presence of white officers as natural and inevitable, they were not at all certain, in the face of the many signs to the contrary, that their white officers accepted the presence of Negro enlisted men in the Army as either natural, inevitable, or even desirable.

Many commanders recognized that the major problem of white officers serving with Negro troops was one of attitude as much as positive professional qualifications. "Negro troops are not a problem," one battalion commander told an assembly of officers. "The minute you make them a Problem you take away their self-respect and self-confidence. They must be handled with the right attitude of mind and with a spirit of fair play. They have a rich heritage and a historic background and have the right to expect treatment as human beings and comrades in the cause for which we are fighting."[12] The hurdles to be overcome by the white officer in gaining the confidence of his Negro enlisted men were many. He had to watch his language as well as his actions to avoid the wholesale—and, sometimes, apparently sudden—alienation of an entire command. "The use of profane language shows ill-breeding, conduct unbecoming

[11] 1st Ind, Hq AGF to CG Second Army, 8 May 43, AGF 210 CWO; Ltr, TAG to CG's Major Comds, Armies, Corps, Defense Comds, Sv Comds, R&SC, Overseas Theaters, and Base Comds, 6 Sep 43, AG 210.31 WO (10 Aug 43) PO–A–A.

[12] Remarks of Lt Col John R. Harris, QMC, CO 243d QM Bn, to All Offs Assigned to Negro Trps in the Ft. Lewis Area, 16 Sep 42, AGF 322.999/299½.

an officer and a gentleman," the same commander cautioned his audience. "The word 'Nigger' or any abusive language or any reference tending to lower the standards of a soldier is Out." [13]

At the conclusion of a letter describing his techniques of leadership, the commander of an antiaircraft regiment already overseas summarized his findings with a sense of discovery:

It is funny. I have been thinking over what is in this letter and it applies, all of it, to white troops as well as colored. I guess it is merely the details that count. Nevertheless, I am sincere in my admiration for these troops and I say that with full knowledge, that if I get a chance to take them into battle my own life and all that I have to live for will depend on them. I am supremely confident of their ability. There is not one iota of doubt in my mind that you people in Washington are building a mountain out of a molehill when you speak of "The Negro Problem in the Army." My God, these men are human and only waiting to be led. They are actually eager to do what is right. That sounds as though I am a negrophile whereas I am not. I am only a realist wanting to see the army make full use of this vast reservoir of man power. It must be used.[14]

Men who in all their lives had never considered it necessary, in their relation with Negroes, to practice the ordinary courtesies in human relations which make the civilized life of complex societies tolerable to its individual members were not always able to reach suddenly the conclusion that "these men are human" and only waiting, like other men, to be led. That the Army had a genu-

ine need of the manpower which Negroes represented posed a difficult problem in re-evaluation for many officers.

A great deal depended upon the wisdom and approach of commanders. The officers of a given unit usually reflected the approach taken by the commander of that unit, and, sometimes, by the commander of the post on which the unit was located or of the higher unit to which the organization was assigned or attached. Of three Negro engineer regiments activated at the same time on the same post from soldiers of the same military experience—all of them drawn from six converted battalions—one was markedly different from the other two. "Quite by accident we had commanding officers who placed their best officers where they would be most effective," a white junior officer of this regiment explained. "A more liberal attitude on the part of the command in the regiment resulted in our being generally accepted as the best of the three units." [15] Since the men, training, and external environment were the same in the three cases, it was a fair assumption that the differences among the units reflected differences in the qualities of leadership.

Of two similar antiaircraft gun battalions arriving at Camp Beauregard, Louisiana, from Camp Davis, North Carolina, in 1944 a parallel observation was made. One battalion was commanded by a young, "vigorous, hard-driving, enthusiastic" officer, "interested in his career and determined to do his best."

---

[13] Ibid.

[14] Personal Ltr, CO 99th CA (AA) Regt, to "an officer of WD," 2 Feb 43, circulated in hectograph form by Lt Col Marshall S. Carter in Memo, OPD, 8 Feb 43, OPD 322.97.

[15] E. T. Hall, Jr., "Race Prejudice and Negro-White Relations in the Army," The American Journal of Sociology, LII (March, 1947), 402. The author, an anthropologist, used as standards of judgment the venereal rates, number of courts-martial, number of men absent without leave, and performance in the field of each unit.

The officers under him, white and Negro, were well qualified technically and were good troop leaders, with the Negro officers comparing favorably with the white in knowledge of technique; they were "interested, working hard, gentlemanly . . . racially sensitive but apparently philosophical and following example set by Battalion Commander." The sister battalion was commanded by an older officer "with practically no interest or enthusiasm in his job." The white officers under him were "average, nothing brilliant, not well selected, and reflecting Battalion Commander's lack of enthusiasm in their work . . . [the] Negro officers not bad, not good, just run of the mine." Eight months later, when the first battalion was seen on Saipan by the same observer it had deteriorated somewhat, though it was still a "passably effective" unit. "Its current deficiencies may be summed up very quickly by saying that it has lost its vigorous battalion commander who furnished the spark and driving energy," the observer reported.[16]

The War Department discovered that a balance had to be maintained between the professional and the personal qualifications of the leader of Negro troops if only because the officer found himself in what was essentially—for him—an artificial situation. Balanced leadership required that the officer give no hint at any time that he had allowed a personal conception of racial differences to affect his own judgment in any given situation.

A notable example of the effect of the belief that actions of commanders stemmed from racial notions occurred in 1943 in one of the Negro divisions then in training within the continental limits of the United States. A rumor, fostered if not founded in the distrust which the men of the division felt toward their commander, grew up and persisted for several months. It built itself into a fantastic structure, involving the FBI and the White House, culminating in the assertion that the soldiers of the division were planning to assassinate their commanding general. In June 1943, Mrs. Roosevelt forwarded to the War Department a letter sent to her that quoted the commanding general as having said, on 20 May, in a meeting of the division mess sergeants and supply officers, that " 'Nigger' soldiers will not eat spinach and if given a Chicken Salad with Celery as part of its ingredients the 'Nigger' soldiers will eat the chicken and leave the celery. I have thousands of 'Nigger' soldiers in my division who will not eat this and will not eat that. I once had a Nigger Mess Sergeant who explained to me why the men would not eat celery." [17] The version of the general's remarks sometimes differed, with carrots substituted for spinach, but the story spread widely. A second story, emanating from the same division, ran: A jeep turned over and injured a Negro soldier. The commanding general was reported to have inquired, "Did it hurt my truck?" By the fall of 1943, an Indianapolis beauty parlor operator who had visited the post concerned was reporting that there was a plot among the Negro soldiers to kill their general and that he had already been shot at a num-

---

[16] Narrative of Incident of Disorder, Negro and White Soldiers at Camp Beauregard, La., September, 1944, Incl to Ltr, Brig Gen Edward Barber to Col Leonard, Secy Advisory Com on Special Trp Policies, 24 Jul 45, ASW 291.2.

[17] M/R, Tel Conv, Asst G–3 AGF to CofS Third Army, 21 Jun 43, AGF 322/2.

ber of times. The motivation? The general's contempt for his men as symbolized in the language and content of these rumored remarks.[18] The fact that these rumors, however untruthful, could spread so widely, endure several months, and receive credence among many persons indicated the severity of the strain existing between white officers and their Negro soldiers in many situations.

The white officer assigned to all but the best located and commanded Negro units had many forms of annoyance which he would not have had if he had been assigned to duty with a white unit. His satisfaction in his assignment was not increased by this knowledge. Extra duties and extra tensions increased his resentment toward his Negro unit and its men. One officer reported that in Texas "Prejudice was even applied to white officers serving with Negro troops, as though they had become tainted. One of the very first questions asked by a civilian on meeting an Army officer was, 'What type of troops do you have?' "[19] The officer with Negro troops was often made to feel that his was a secondary role and that, as an officer, he was not contributing as fully and seriously to the conduct of the war as those men who were assigned to white units. At times, officers assigned to Negro troops felt that they were being penalized or that they were not considered fully competent. A commander, attempting to determine the attitudes of his officers, most of them recent graduates of OCS serving in their initial assignments, reported that "the consensus was that each of them had been disap-

pointed on learning of his assignment to a Negro unit. Several of them stated that they had failed to measure up and thought that they were assigned to inferior service."[20]

Sometimes, special additional duties were allotted to officers with Negro troops. Even when these duties were normal ones which might have been required from time to time of officers in any unit, the reaction was that they were especially connected with duty with Negro troops. In one post,

most of the colored units were along one street; and for reasons known only to those in command, every unit had to assign an officer and three enlisted men to patrol this street between the hours of 6:00 P.M. and 11:00 P.M. This meant that as many as six jeeps and command cars could be seen roving up and down about three-quarters of a mile of road, sometimes within a hundred feet of each other. The officers felt the duty ridiculous and unnecessary; the men quite naturally knew that it was for no other reason than that someone was afraid of an outbreak.[21]

In this same post, two officers were assigned each night to ride buses to town forty miles away; others were assigned to stand at the door of the USO club in a nearby town. In another unit, the officers were required to make block purchases of railroad tickets at the nearby town for men going on pass to discourage queues of Negro soldiers in the railroad station. Having purchased the tickets, the officers then stood at the door of the post buses on pass days, handing each man his proper ticket as he boarded the

[18] Rpt, ASF, Hq Fifth Sv Comd, 17 Nov 43, and other papers in AGF 322/5.

[19] Hall, *op. cit.*, p. 401f.

[20] Rpt, Investigation 828th TD Bn, Cp Hood, Tex., 24–27 Aug 42, p. 5; and exhibit D, p. 90, IG 333.9-828th TD Bn 8-12-42.

[21] Hall, *op. cit.*, p. 402.

bus.[22]   Any officer, regardless of his personal view, finding himself in a situation where extramilitary duties of an onerous nature consumed much of his time, would prefer to be assigned to a unit where such duties were not required. Aside from these additional annoyances, the greater physical and mental labor required for duty with Negro troops, large numbers of whom were deficient in general as well as in specific educational background and in technical skills, frequently produced a situation in which the chances of maintaining proper leadership relations between officers and men were reduced to near zero.   Many officers showed their resentment to their assignment to Negro units openly, in ways unmistakable to the men serving under them.   In these instances the gulf between them and their men was greatly deepened.

Commanders of large units attempted to select and weed out officers unsuited for duty with Negro troops.   During the course of its existence, many white officers, from lieutenants to lieutenant colonels, of the 92d Division were relieved at the request of the division for "unsuitability for duty with colored troops." [23]   Beginning while its officer cadre was in training at Fort Benning, the 93d Division attempted to weed out officers exhibiting "evidence of carelessness and irresponsibility" and lack of tact which would make them unsuitable for duty with the Negro division.[24]   One corps commander, whose practice was to send for commanders of Negro units coming into his corps to interview them personally, had found it necessary, in a number of instances, to change the officers of the units in an attempt to improve leadership.[25]   In sixteen months, one nondivisional regimental commander had 254 changes in officer personnel, most of them for "inability to cope with existing conditions." [26]   Investigations of complaints of racial discrimination within units and of unit disorders often resulted in recommendations that one or more officers be relieved or transferred.[27]

Since the "unsuitability" of officers might become apparent, or develop, weeks or months after assignment, it was not always possible to ward off in advance officer sources of friction.[28]   Nor was it always possible to tell when an officer, by deliberately demonstrating "unsuitability" for an onerous duty, might be using a simple means to acquire a transfer to a unit which he would prefer.   An officer of one of the Negro divisions, writing to a friend asking if he could get him transferred from the division, complained that things had "taken a change for the worse, very much worse!"   There would be no more cadres, no more schools, no more transfers, "which means we are all stuck here in the division.   It was bad enough train-

---

[22] Personal observation of the author.

[23] 92d Div Files, 210.3 x 220.3.

[24] Rad, Hq AGF to CG Third Army, 4 Apr 42, and Telg, Hq AGF to Brig Gen E. M. Almond, Inf School, Ft. Benning, Ga., AGF Classified Radiograms (AGF-Out) Mar–Aug 42, AGF 210.35/78; 93d Div 210.31 Files, passim.

[25] Ltr, CG VIII Corps to CG AGF, 20 Aug 42, AGF 322.999/23 (Cld Trps).

[26] 1st Ind, Hq 364th Inf, APO 980, to TAG, 25 Apr 44, to Ltr, Officer Hq Co 2d Bn 364th Inf, 4 Apr 44, OPD 322.97/40.

[27] For examples see Ltr, Asst IG Hq DTC to CG DTC, 11 Aug 42, and Inds, AG 291.21 (7–17–42) (1); Investigation . . . 457th Avn Sq, AAF Files Bulky, 333.5 457th Avn Sq; Memo, TIG for CG ASF, 23 Nov 44, IG 250–Camp Ellis and Incls.

[28] Cf., ASF Conf of CG's Sv Comds, Dallas, Tex., 17–19 Feb 44, p. 141.

ing these colored, but no one had the idea we'd go overseas with them. That would be sheer suicide. These troops are not ready and never will be ready for or capable of combat. They are for the most part afraid and the few smart ones have no desire to fight. . . . I have to get out of this outfit, but can't unless someone asks for me. . . . Every white officer here is writing, phoning, and sending wires to everyone he knows. We are all trying to get out." [29] The division, when queried, had categorical explanations for the desire of white officers for transfers. The isolation of the post at which the division was stationed; the prospect of six months more training before going overseas which faced officers who were anxious to get into combat; the difficulty and slowness of training enlisted men, 86 percent of whom were in AGCT Classes IV and V; and the "natural preference" of white officers for service with white troops were cited as reasons for dissatisfaction. Yet, the division said, there were relatively few requests for relief on the basis of inability to accept Negro troops.[30] But when requests were made on the basis of objections to service with Negro troops, they were often completely explicit. An officer requesting relief from the 92d Division gave as his reasons:

Incompatibility with colored people to which the colored soldier has proven no exception. Having been raised in Montana which is remote from areas of race prejudice I had accepted my association with the colored personnel with an open mind. In fact, upon a previous association incident to a four year residence in Tennessee an initial sympathy changed to a feeling of disgust towards practically all colored individuals, because of their practically universal worthlessness and ineffectiveness. I can still feel a strong admiration for those who demonstrate real competence; a feeling even accentuated by contrast to relative achievement. Furthermore, to those who deserve recognition for sustained meritorious performance I have no feeling of aversion. Although I can still find such interest in a few specific individuals, for the rank and file I can feel only disgust for their inherent slovenliness, and their extreme indolence, indifference and frequent subtle insolence. From personal observation I have concluded that they are so completely indolent and indifferent as to fail to take simple measures and safeguards in the interest of self preservation, even under pressures applied by their white officers. I am likewise convinced that with few exceptions colored officers with whom I have come into contact are thoroughly incompetent, and for the most part are to be viewed in a light little different from the enlisted men.

The officer continued, saying that he had asked not to be assigned to the division and that, after being so assigned, he found that he could not sleep at night and that he was lying awake with worrying and with headaches. He asked to be transferred to a replacement depot.[31] The request was approved by both the regimental commander and the division, the division adjutant adding defensively that "the prejudice outlined was not stated until Major ——— was informed that his assignment was for duty with troops and not staff duty." [32]

Commanders of Negro troops had long since discovered that no value lay in the retention of an officer with these attitudes, for troops would sense them almost immediately. The commander

[29] Papers in AGF 322/4.
[30] Ibid.

[31] Ltr, Major ———, Hq Bn 370th Inf, 31 Jan 45, to CG 92d Div, 92d Div Files, 210.3 x 220.3/23.
[32] Ibid., 2d Ind, 92d Div to Fifth Army.

of one training center with a large proportion of Negro troops explained ". . .
we all get discouraged, and get a rather
defeatist attitude ourselves [when trying
to develop NCO's from men of AGCT
IV and V ratings]. The negroes are
extremely sensitive almost to the point
of clairvoyance in sensing such an attitude on the part of their superiors." [33]

White Officers: The Search
for Standards

In 1942, after the recognition of a
serious morale problem among Negro
troops, a special inspector reported to
the War Department that there was a
tendency to assign white officers of mediocre caliber to Negro units and that
leadership in many units was therefore
deficient. In many instances commanders "failed completely to appreciate the problems which their units presented in that particular locality, and
had taken no steps to solve them," the
Deputy Chief of Staff said when directing a critical examination of unit practices. He emphasized that officers of
high professional qualities, "particularly
[of] judgment and common sense, tact,
initiative, and leadership" were desired
in Negro units. Officers who are "better
trained in a military way," but "without
the knack" of serving with Negroes "not
only fail to accomplish the task but create the conditions which breed trouble." [34]

The commands had little to go on in

surveying their unit officers other than
age and efficiency reports. Army
Ground Forces examined the records of
all Regular Army officers assigned to
Negro units. Without exception these
officers were rated superior or excellent.
In many cases their ratings were higher
than those of officers in new white divisions. But their ratings did not reflect
their ability to command Negro troops,
for, as Army Ground Forces pointed out,
the number of officers in the Army with
experience in "handling colored troops"
was practically negligible.[35] Special inspections of Negro units to determine
the fitness of their officers were ordered
in some commands. Most of the officers
in the Negro units surveyed were young,
inexperienced graduates of officer candidate schools—as were most of the junior officers which the Army was using.[36]
It was difficult to say whether or not they
would develop into satisfactory company
officers. This uncertainty militated
against their wholesale removal.

The Deputy Chief of Staff's letter on
professional qualifications did have an
important secondary effect. It fixed the
notion in the minds of commanders and
staff agencies that the War Department
desired special consideration for Negro
units in the assignment of competent
officers. But where were they to come
from? Commanders were unwilling to
give up their best officers to supply the
needs of Negro units. Sometimes orders transferring white officers to Negro
units, disregarding the effect that such
phrasing might have on the officers' approach to their new permanent assign-

---

[33] Leadership, Address by Brig Gen Horace L.
Whittaker, Notes, ASF Fifth Tng Conf, ASFTC, Cp
Barkeley, Tex., 24 Oct 44.
[34] Ltr, DCofS to CG's Major Comds, Defense
Comds, and Armies, 10 Aug 42, WDCSA 291.21
(10-19-42).

[35] Ltr, Hq AGF to DCofS, 20 Aug 42, AGF
322.999/23 (Cld Trps).
[36] M/S, Hq AGF, Ground G-1 to CofS AGF,
11 Oct 42, AGF 322.999/25.

ment, indicated that the transfer was pursuant to the letter "Professional Qualifications of Officers Assigned to Negro Troops." [37] Some major commands resorted to the arbitrary ruling that no officer with a rating of less than "excellent" was to be assigned to a Negro unit.[38] The War Department followed, later, with a similar blanket ruling for all Negro units undergoing training in the United States.[39] Reports were rendered on certain officers with Negro units who fell below the desired standards, but many headquarters reported that most of these officers could be brought up to standard in a short time.

Some observers felt that an all-round high efficiency rating was not nearly so desirable as excellence in the leadership column of the efficiency report.[40] Others felt that at least a measure of improvement would be obtained if all white officers assigned to Negro units had at least served an apprenticeship in white units. Adding the errors of green troop leaders to the difficulties of Negro units could then be avoided. In any event, it became obvious that the formal efficiency rating, especially if earned with white troops, was no guarantee of good leadership for Negro units. Army Service Forces suggested to the Chief of Staff that since the information available from the officer's Qualification Card was

"entirely inadequate" for the purposes of assignment to Negro units, personal interviews and letters from present commanders be substituted to determine whether or not officers for assignment had:

a. A primary requirement of demonstrated leadership ability in a command assignment.

b. Mature judgment and common sense.

c. Even disposition and patience.

d. Demonstrated stability under pressure and ability to handle emergency situations.

e. Ability to organize and foster athletic and recreational programs.[41]

These criteria were approved by the War Department on 18 October 1944 and the requirement of an excellent efficiency rating was rescinded.[42] ASF had also recommended that officers who did not meet these requirements be relieved, but the War Department did not include this recommendation in its directive. In instructions to its own commanders, ASF recommended that officers having these qualities be considered for promotion, that all officers be retained long enough to demonstrate these qualities, and that the turnover of suitable officers be held to a minimum.[43]

The quest for standards in judging the improvement of leadership in Negro units continued to the end of the war. It is doubtful that any of the formulas

---

[37] Cf., Ltr Order, Hq 35th Inf Div to 4 Named Officers, 12 Sep 42, AG 210.31 (2–14–42) (3).

[38] Ltr, Hq AGF to CG's, 10 Aug 42, AGF 322.999/23.

[39] Memo, G–1 for TAG, 21 Mar 44, WDGAP 210.31; Ltrs, TAG to CG's Major Comds, 24 Mar 44, AG 210.31 (21 Mar 44); Ltr, Hq ASF to CG's and MDW, Chiefs Svs, TQMG, TSG, CSigO, 1 Apr 44, SPX 210.31 (24 Mar 44); AAF Ltr 35–8, 18 May 44.

[40] Notes, Fifth ASF Tng Conf, 24 Oct 44, Cp Barkeley, Tex., p. 102.

[41] S/S, Hq ASF for CofS, 13 Oct 44, WDCSA 210.31 (13 Oct 44), AG 210.31 (21 Mar 44) (2).

[42] Ibid.; Ltr, TAG to CG's Major Comds, 1 Nov 44, AG 210.31 (13 Oct 44), AGPO–A–SPGAM.

[43] Ltr, Hq ASF to CG's Sv Comds, Chiefs Svs, TQMG, TSG, and CSigO, 1 Nov 44, SPXPO–A–SPGAM–210.31 (13 Oct 44); Ltr, Hq ASF to CG's, DCofS for Sv Comds, et al., 15 Nov 44, SPXPO–A 210.31 (7 Nov 44).

had any broad-scale effect other than to keep the attention of higher headquarters focused upon the seriousness of the problem and to reinforce the feeling in many headquarters that the supervision of Negro units was much more trouble than it was worth. For while various higher headquarters continued to blame weak commanders for conditions such as those which resulted in the Camp Claiborne riots of 1944,[44] agencies responsible for recommending officer assignments had little means of knowing much about the personal characteristics of officers assigned to Negro units. When units were reported as having unsatisfactory complements of officers, the best that could be done, in most cases, was to replace the unit commanders and hope that their subordinates would mend their ways either by precept or by following the example set by the new commander.[45] Interviewing on a large scale was impossible and formal tests for judging officers for Negro troops did not exist. Though higher headquarters might prescribe careful checks of officers' records and, sometimes, individual interviews before assignment to Negro units, time and the lack of experience in lower echelon assigning agencies often conspired to defeat these efforts. The process, as it operated within one command which required both a check of officer records and multiple interviews before assignment to a Negro unit, was described by the personnel officer in charge as "a case of try and try again. You never can tell what kind of officer is suitable for assignment to colored troops."[46] His subordinate officer in charge of working out assignment details elaborated on the technique as it operated:

You see, my instructions were to get officers in there regardless of qualification. . . . What we had to do was take any officers and assign them to the organization. These were the only ones made available to me for transfer. . . . The whole history is, I mean just cold facts, we will call up Daniel Field and say we have got to have an officer for a colored aviation squadron. They will check and say OK, I will give you S———. He is made available and we transfer him to Herbert Smart. That's just the way these things actually come up.[47]

In the meantime, pronouncements on the qualities desired in a commander of Negro troops continued to be made.

These pronouncements had one thing in common: the traits described were desirable in equal measure in officers assigned to any troops. Occasionally an officer sought to apply age-old leadership formulas with a shift in emphasis to explain differences between the command of Negro and white troops. Brig. Gen. Horace L. Whittaker, commanding

[44] Memo, Col Leonard for ASW, 3 Oct 44, sub: Summary Rpt of Recent Visit of Observation at Southern Cps Relative to Racial Matters, Incl 1, Rpt on Racial Conditions at Cp Claiborne, SPTR 291.2 (3 Oct 44).

[45] 1st Ind, OCS to CG ASF, 10 Jan 44, to Memo, CG ASF for CofE, 31 Dec 43, SPTRU 333.3 (IG) (Eng) (23 Dec 43); Ltr, CG VIII Corps to CG AGF, 20 Aug 42, AGF 322.999/23 (Cld Trps); Ltr, OASW to Mrs. Roosevelt, 12 Aug 43, based on WDGAO/322.99 (1 Jun 43) dated 9 Aug 43, ASW 291.21 Alpha; ASC Survey of Negro Organizations, 1944, AAF 333.5 Bulky.

[46] Statement, Maj Axel G. Cask, Chief Pers and Tng Div, Hq Warner Robins ASC, Robins Fld, Ga., 28 Jun 44; Ltr, Hq ASC OAI to CG ASC, Patterson Fld, Ohio, 11 Jul 44, Rpt of Investigation re Alleged Conditions in the 456th and 457th Avn Sqs . . . , ASC IG–5–EWS, AAF 333.5, Bulky.

[47] Capt James B. Lucy, Chief Officers' Br Mil Pers Sec, Hq WRASC, 28 Jun 44, ASC IG–5–EWS, AAF 333.5, Bulky.

the Fort Warren AFSTC, told a training conference:

With colored troops the three fundamentals of leadership are still present and, I must emphasize, even more important than with white troops. The only difference is in the importance of each. With white troops, I would say that the importance of knowing your work is the most important of the three. With colored troops it is the least important. The reaction of colored troops makes it more important that their officers convince them that they are getting a fair and square deal. It is next to most important that they be convinced that the officer is interested in them.[48]

Essentially, all formulas failed because the Army could not find enough officers who both understood them and were able to carry them out. General Whittaker declared that in his experience at a training center he had seen no more than twenty-five company commanders who were efficient enough to exercise the required leadership and at the same time bring their units up to technical standards.[49] At no time did the Army have enough officers with both the characteristics and the experience which together produced excellent balanced leadership, and no one knew where to get them in sufficient numbers in the limited time available. Officers with the desired Solomonic "maturity" enabling them to approach the manifold problems of Negro units with confidence were especially elusive. Reports of the mediocre caliber of officers assigned to Negro units therefore continued to flow into higher headquarters.[50]

Plans for Mobilizing Negro Officers

Negro officers were not immune themselves to many of the problems of adjustment to service with Negroes which affected adversely the leadership abilities of so many white officers serving in Negro units. Though their problems were of a different order, Negro officers and officer candidates had enough of their own to keep them from providing an adequate answer to the leadership needs of Negro units. Moreover, Negro officers never existed in numbers sufficient to supply all Negro units, nor is it likely that enough qualified officer candidates could have been drawn from the Negroes in the Army to do so.

When mobilization began in 1940 the War Department anticipated that, in accordance with existing policy, the small number of Negro officers available would be absorbed entirely in the few units authorized all Negro officers. As noted earlier, there were then only five Negro officers in the Regular Army, three of whom were chaplains.[51] The three National Guard regiments were staffed with Negro officers who were expected to remain with these units when they were called into federal service. The bulk of Negro officers available for assignment in the early period of mobilization were in the Reserve Corps.

[48] Leadership, Address by Gen Whittaker to ASF Fifth Tng Conf, 24 Oct 44, ASFTC Cp Barkeley, Tex., Notes, pp. 101, 103.

[49] *Ibid.*, p. 103.

[50] Memo for Files, Gen Edward S. Greenbaum, 8 Mar 43, AGF 322/1 (93d Div); Ltr, Hq AGF

to R&SC, 25 Nov 43, AGF 353.92/262; Ltr, CG Cp Wheeler, Ga., to CG AGF, 7 Dec 43, AGF 322.999/381; 2d Ind, Hq Ft. Huachuca to CG 9th Sv Comd, 23 Mar 45, on Hq ASF to CG's Sv Comds, etc., 30 Jan 45, SPX 291.2 (26 Jan 45) OB–S–SPDCCC), Ft. Huachuca 291.2, 9th Sv Comd 291.2. See also: Lt. Col. Herbert S. Ripley, M.C., O.R.C., and Maj. Stewart Wolf, M.C., O.R.C., "Mental Illness Among Negro Troops Overseas," *American Journal of Psychiatry,* CIII (January, 1947), 510.

[51] See above, p. 29.

TABLE 3—NEGRO NATIONAL GUARD OFFICERS
24 SEPTEMBER 1940

Unit	Infantry	Medical	Dental	Chaplains	Total
Total...............................	136	11	2	1	150[a]
372d Infantry					
D.C..................................	3	1	0	0	4
Maryland............................	3	1	0	0	4
Massachusetts.......................	15	1	0	0	16
Ohio.................................	14	1	0	0	15
184th Field Artillery................	44	3	1	0	48
369th Coast Artillery................	57	4	1	1	63

[a] Does not include enlisted men holding NGUS commissions.

Source: Tab B, Memo, G–1 for CofS, 28 Sep 40, AG 210.31 ORC (9-28-40).

The War Department had not determined in advance of mobilization such questions as the service of Negro officers in units with white officers, the relative rank and promotion policy for Negro officers, or the types of units and overhead positions to which they were to be assigned. These questions were settled as they arose and when they could no longer be ignored. As with Negro units, the policy on the provision and use of Negro officers was developed bit by bit, to fit current needs. In the process, the provision of leadership, as it related to the provision of Negro officers, became a distinctly secondary consideration.

In September 1940 the G–1 Division proposed five possible plans for using Negro Reserve officers: [52]

Plan One would maintain the three National Guard regiments overstrength in officers. All Negro Reserve officers would be assigned to these units. This

[52] Memo, G–1 for CofS, 28 Sep 40, AG 210.31-ORC (9-28-40).

plan had two disadvantages: it provided a large surplus of officers in the three regiments and, G–1 thought, would be unsatisfactory to organizations "now advocating Negro representation throughout the Army."

Plan Two, a modification of Plan One, provided revised requirements for the Guard regiments. Under this plan only 79 Reserve officers would be used in these regiments initially. The remainder would be used to fill any shortages developing among the 150 eligible Negro Guard officers.

Plan Three provided for the addition of a fourth Negro tactical regiment to be staffed entirely with Negro Reserve officers. This Regular Army infantry unit, to be organized at Fort Devens, Massachusetts, would absorb 122 Negro officers, including medical and dental officers and chaplains. The remainder would fill out the National Guard units. This plan had the virtue, G–1 felt, of providing representation in the Regular Army as well as in the Guard and

TABLE 4—NEGRO RESERVE OFFICERS ELIGIBLE FOR ACTIVE DUTY
30 JUNE 1940

Branch	Colonels	Lieutenant Colonels	Majors	Captains	1st Lieutenants	2d Lieutenants	Total
Total...................	1	3	9	42	145	153	353
Infantry.................	1	2	4	30	73	152	262
Quartermaster............	0	0	1	1	1	1	4
Medical..................	0	1	3	4	52	0	60
Dental...................	0	0	0	2	6	0	8
Chaplains................	0	0	1	4	9	0	14
Chemical Warfare.........	0	0	0	0	1	0	1
Veterinary...............	0	0	0	0	3	0	3
Military Intelligence.......	0	0	0	1	0	0	1

Source: Tab C, Memo, G–1 for CofS, 28 Sep 40, AG 210.31 ORC (9-28-40).

placing "all negro officers on their own, where they must produce results or fail in their responsibilities." It, along with the other two plans, had the disadvantage of placing all Negro officers with tactical units, opening the War Department to the possible charge of "placing them all in positions of greatest danger." In addition, Plan Three provided for an excess proportion of Negro Reserve officers, based on the number of Negro Reservists as compared with the total strength of the Officers' Reserve Corps. All three of these plans, G–1 felt, had the positive merit of avoiding the mixing of white and Negro officers either in units or in replacement centers and other installations.

Plan Four was the same as Plan Three, except that several units in corps area service commands were substituted for the single Negro Regular Army regiment. These units were to be Quartermaster service and truck companies, headquarters detachments, and similar organizations. This plan would enable

the Army to absorb all Negro Reserve officers remaining after filling the Guard regiments, it would guarantee a proportionate representation of Negro Reservists, and it would provide a flexible means of maintaining Negro Reserve officers on duty at all times. Its disadvantages were that if the National Guard finally furnished a full complement of officers to the three regiments, all Negro Reserve officers would be "thrown into" corps area service commands. A second objection which G–1 saw was that Negro Reserve officers would be placed on duty in stations with white officers.

Plan Five contemplated the completion of the National Guard complement of Negro officers with Negro Reserve officers and the assignment of the remainder to the four traditional Regular Army Negro regiments or to new Regular Army units, limiting the Negroes to company grades. This plan, though it would provide a wider distribution of Negro officers, would, at the same time, violate the "policy of mixing white and colored officers in the same organization," G–1 pointed out. G–1 doubted further that Negro Reserve officers would be of value in "Regular Army organizations of Negro enlisted men of long service under white officers." Nor would this plan provide position vacancies for the seven Negro infantry field grade officers.

G–1 recommended that Plan Three be approved and that the number of reservists ordered to active duty be divided proportionately among the arms and services based on the numbers commissioned in each branch. Because the only arm in which Negro reservists were commissioned was the infantry, G–1 recommended that Negro infantry Reserve officers also be considered eligible for assignments to the artillery branches, since two of the three National Guard regiments were to be changed from infantry to the two artillery arms. In addition, G–1 recommended that "the policy which seeks to avoid mixing white and negro officers in the same tactical unit should be continued." [53]

The Operations and Training Division, G–3, objected to Plan Three. It would do no more than solve the immediate problem, provide "an all negro unit in the Regular Army from now on," and bring an unnecessarily large number of Negro Reserve officers into the Army.[54] The War Plans Division wanted extra Negro officers placed in engineer separate battalions and ordnance ammunition companies rather than in a new infantry regiment, explaining: "The separate battalions and ammunition companies, being labor units, will suffer least from being officered by negroes. With three negro combat units (National Guard) officered by negroes on active duty, it is entirely reasonable to provide some service units also officered by Negroes. Unless all of these units are completely isolated, they would, regardless of type, be located at stations where there are also white or negro units with white officers. . . ." Moreover, the War Plans Division added, when "the present emergency" was over, the Army would be reduced. "The first units to be demobilized should be those least needed, purely labor units such as separate battalions. This will afford an opportunity of eliminating, with their units, the negro reserve officers on duty with Regular Army units." [55]

Only The Adjutant General and the Executive for Reserve Affairs concurred in G–1's recommendations. G–1, reiterating its objections to the use of Negro officers in small units, admitted that the use of Negro reservists in service as well as combat units was "reasonable," but it again pointed out that this would mean employing small groups of Negro officers on posts with large numbers of white officers. Plan Three, G–1, stated, "at least groups them in organizations of sufficient size that they may provide their own organizations for entertainment and recreation." Since two of the National Guard regiments were to be converted from infantry to artillery, it would be reasonable to supply infantry Reserve officers to these units, but none of the infantry officers were "suitable for assignment to Engineer or Ord-

---

[53] *Ibid.*

[54] Memo, G–3 for G–1, 7 Oct 40, AG 210.31 ORC (9–28–40).

[55] Memo, WPD for G–1, 15 Oct 40, AG 210.31 ORC (9–28–40).

nance units. However, a new Infantry
regiment would be no more permanent
than new service units, all of which are
Regular Army inactive units." [56] Despite G–1's advocacy of its Plan Three,
assigning all reservists to the three
Guard regiments and to a new Regular
infantry regiment, the Chief of Staff's
office, in approving the proposals on 22
October substituted Plan Four, providing for the use of Negro officers in corps
area service commands in lieu of the
fourth regiment.[57]

This decision did not stand long.
President Roosevelt, disturbed by representations of Negroes that their Reserve officers were apparently not going
to be used widely, penciled a note to the
Assistant Secretary of War:

Patterson
Colored Reserve Officers must be
called just as White Reserves.
Assign to new units & not just
to Nat Gd. units.
F.D.R.[58]

Thereupon General Marshall instructed G–1 that Negro reservists were
to be assigned to new Regular units.
"You will have to check up on our plans
and see how best to do this considering
the qualifications of the officers," he
wrote.[59] On 28 October General Marshall gave oral approval for a subsequent
change back to Plan Three, which G–1
had advocated all along, with a modification providing for proportional use of
Negro reservists.[60] On 9 November 1940

the approved plan was communicated to
the Army, in the following terms:

The number of Negro Reserve Officers to
be called to extended active duty will be in
the same proportion to the total number of
eligible negro Reserve officers as the number of white Reserve officers. They will be
assigned to the three colored National
Guard regiments (372d Infantry, 184th
Field Artillery, and 369th Coast Artillery),
as required, to complete the officer complements of those regiments. In addition, one
new colored regiment of Infantry, to be organized later, will be officered by negro
Reserve officers, so far as they are available.[61]

The Policy in Operation

Before Negro Reserve officers could be
assigned to National Guard units, the
number of Guard officers who would
pass their physical examinations and be
inducted had to be determined. This
number was estimated at 150 officers.
For the three Guard regiments and one
new Regular regiment, an estimated
368 officers would be required. More
than half of these would therefore have
to come from the Reserve.[62]

Eligible Negro Reserve officers were
not uniformly distributed through the
nine corps areas. Therefore, authority
to order Negro officers to active duty was
retained by The Adjutant General
rather than decentralized to the corps
areas as in the case of white officers.[63]
The available Reserve pool fluctuated
somewhat as new officers were added

[56] Additional Memo, G–1 for CofS, 16 Oct 40,
AG 210.31 ORC (9–28–40).
[57] Memo, G–1 for CofS, 28 Sep 40, OCS 20602–103.
[58] Note, President Roosevelt to ASW Robert Patterson, attached to Memo, Gen Marshall for G–1,
25 Oct 40, AG 210.31 ORC (9–28–40).
[59] *Ibid.*
[60] Memo, G–1 for CofS, 29 Oct 40, AG 210.31
ORC (9–28–40).

[61] Ltr, TAG to CofS GHQ, CG's Armies, Corps
Areas, and Chiefs of Arms and Svs, 9 Nov 40, AG
210.31 ORC (11–6–40) M–A–M, based on Memo,
G–1 for TAG, 5 Nov 40, AG 210.31 ORC (9–28–40).
[62] Memo, G–1 for TAG, 29 Nov 40, AG 210.31
ORC (11–29–40).
[63] *Ibid.;* Ltr, TAG to CG's, 24 Oct 40, AG 210.31
NGUS (10–3–40) M M–A.

from schools, as inactive officers regained their eligibility for active duty, as active officers were discovered to be over-age for troop duty, and as new officers were added from unexpected sources. The unexpected sources included officers in the Philippines, Hawaii, and Puerto Rico, whose race at times was not clearly or indisputably indicated in their records. The pool, even before the staffing of the approved units began, was called upon for officers for other uses, thus reducing the number of officers available for assignment to units. The Second Corps Area, for example, asked for eight Negro junior officers for duty at its reception centers. Four of these officers were furnished with the understanding that they would be sent to the new infantry regiment, now designated the 366th, in February 1941. Selective Service requested first one, and, later, a second Reserve officer for its national headquarters. When plans for the new Negro pursuit squadron and its air base detachment matured, Negro officers were required for nonflying duties. A proportion of these came from the Reserve.[64] A few reservists were assigned to the new military police battalions. A few others, with technical training or needed specialities, went to new Signal units, into the Specialists Corps, or later, when that branch was organized, into Special Services. Those eligibles of troop age remaining uncalled went from temporary duty at the Infantry School to the 369th Infantry, the 93d Division's

new selectee regiment.[65] But the general interpretation of the directive governing the assignment of Negro Reserve officers was that the Negro reservists would be employed only in the four designated tactical units.

This limitation aroused apprehension among Negro specialists, especially in the medical profession, both within and without the Officers' Reserve Corps. The four tactical units could absorb only twelve medical and five dental officers.[66] There were a number of Negro doctors and dentists, primarily graduates of Howard University, who held infantry Reserve commissions dating from the completion of their college training. Many of these men had been attempting to secure transfers to the Medical Department Reserve, only to be told by the corps areas that there were no vacancies or that the procurement objectives had been reached.[67] Moreover, applications from Negro civilian dentists and physicians for appointments in the Reserve were being returned by corps areas despite the drive to obtain additional Reserve officers from these professions.[68] Negroes were fearful that these physicians and dentists would be called to active duty as infantry officers, as some actually were, or as selectees and that their professional training would be a loss to them and to the Army.

---

[64] Immediate Action Ltr, TAG to CG's Corps Areas et al., 10 May 41, AG 320.2 (4-15-41) MT-C-M; Ltr, Hq SEATC, Maxwell Field, Ala., to TAG, 18 Jul 41, AG 320.2 (7-18-41). At least 66 Negro Reserve officers applied for the four branch immaterial positions which were originally announced.

[65] Rad, TAG to CG Fourth Corps Area, 9 Mar 42, Fourth Corps Area 353 ORC (EAD), item 480-F.

[66] Memo, G-1 for CofS, 29 Nov 40, AG 210.31 ORC (10-22-40).

[67] Ltr, A. N. Vaughn, M.D., President National Medical Association, to SW, 16 Mar 41, Incl to Memo, Col E. R. Householder, AGD, for ExO AGD, 20 Mar 41, AG 210.1 Med (2-19-41) M.

[68] Memo, G-1 for TAG, 12 Feb 41, and attached Memo for Record, AG 210.1 Med Reserve (2-12-41).

The War Department belatedly reminded corps areas and departments
that directives covering applications for
Reserve appointments applied to Negroes as well as to whites.[69] It then
developed that further adjustments
were required.

The approved peacetime procurement objective for Negro Reserve officers of the corps area assignment group
provided for 120 medical and 44 dental
officers. In 1940, 55 medical and 34
dental officers were required to complete
this objective. Many corps areas, it was
then discovered, had filled their complete allotments of medical officers and
all had filled their dental allotments
while ignoring the existence of a Negro
objective included within the larger
allotments. There was, by November
1940, an overage of 513 officers commissioned in the Dental Reserve.[70]
One of the questions was where the allotments to complete the Negro objective were to come from. The other
was where the Negro medical and dental
reservists, aside from the few needed in
the four tactical units set aside for Negro Reserve officers, would be assigned
should the procurement objective be
completed.

The Surgeon General's Office, expecting the Medical Department to be assigned about 4,000 Negro enlisted men
and several hundred officers as its proportionate share of the Negroes to be
received during the 1940–41 military
program, had been studying this question since August 1940. The Surgeon

General proposed in October 1940 that
Negro Medical Department officers be
used "in all units officered by Negroes,
but that medical officers in units with
white officers remain white as heretofore," that officers and nurses be employed in "colored wards" of all station
and general hospitals with an average
of 100 Negro patients, and that hospitals
used for Negroes exclusively be staffed
with Negro medical personnel, including
nurses. The colored professional personnel in hospitals was to be cared for
by the medical sanitary companies proposed in the same paper.[71] This plan,
in its general aspects, was approved on
11 December 1940, with the additional
provision that the National Medical Association, the Negro counterpart of the
American Medical Association, be requested to suggest the names of Negro
physicians who might be used by the
Army and that both Negro and white
medical officers be used in units with all
white line officers.[72] Negro wards,
eight at each post, with all Negro profes-
sionals, were authorized for Fort Bragg,
North Carolina, and for Camp Livingston, Louisiana, the two stations with
the largest Negro populations.[73] Additional Negro wards were to be designated to absorb Negro medical officers as
additional commissions were granted.

These Medical Department plans,
like the other War Department plans
for mobilizing Negro officers, had grown
out of recognition that some Negro officers would have to be employed if the
War Department was to avoid charges of

---

[69] Ltr, TAG to Corps Areas, Depts, and TSG, 15 Feb 41, AG 210.1 Med Reserve (2–13–41) R–A.
[70] Ltr, TAG to Corps Areas, 10 Jul 39, AG 381 (6–8–39) Misc M–A; Memo, G–1 for CofS, 29 Nov 40, AG 210.31 ORC (10–22–40).

[71] Ltr, OSG to TAG, 25 Oct 40, AG 320.2 (10–25–40) (8–2–40) (4) sec. 6.
[72] Memo, G–1 for CofS, 15 Jan 41, AG 320.2 (10–25–40).
[73] Ibid. These wards required 17 doctors, 2 den-tists, and 28 nurses at each hospital.

discrimination. These plans were in accordance with the provisions of the publicly announced policy of October 1940. Though the War Department had insisted in all policy statements upon the maintenance of single standards in the appointment of both white and Negro officers, it had paid little attention to other effects of these plans. It had given little attention to the provision of the best possible leadership for the units concerned. The primary motivation of the planners was to satisfy a demand for the use of Negro officers in a way that would intrude them in the least direct manner upon the Army as a whole and, as the War Plans Division expressed it, to place them in units which would "suffer least" from them. The debate over the virtues of additional tactical units and service units for the assignment of Negro officers did not revolve about the capacity of the officers to execute efficiently duties involved in either type of unit nor about the potential usefulness of the units themselves; rather, it revolved about the desirability of containing Negro officers in self-sufficient units where they could provide their own entertainment and where housing and messing contacts between Negro and white officers could be held to a minimum. Concern about the numbers of Negro officers and the possibility of reducing their numbers once the emergency was over exceeded concern about regulating numbers in terms of their qualifications and their usefulness to the training and leadership of the units to which they were to be assigned. In any event, no measurement of the leadership abilities of the existing officers in the civilian components was available. Without a fair trial, certain

agencies urged, no judgment on the abilities of the Negro officers could be given. Disquieting suspicions, coming from World War I, might be held, but since the object during the period of peacetime mobilization was to train both officers and men as rapidly as possible and with the least friction, the provision of position vacancies for Negro officers and not the provision of leadership for Negro troops became the criterion for policy decisions.

Command Problems in the Negro Regiments

In the two infantry Guard regiments being converted to artillery before induction into the federal service, all officers as well as enlisted men would have to be retained in their new branches. These were the 369th Infantry, converted to the 369th Coast Artillery (AA), and the 8th Illinois Infantry, converted to the 184th Field Artillery. Both regiments lost their commanders before being called into federal service. The third unconverted regiment, the 372d Infantry, had not been a cohesive unit between wars since it was split among several states and corps areas. It had no commander and no true headquarters. The infantry Reserve officers, in the first two cases, would be no more unfamiliar with the arm and mission of the regiments than their permanent Guard officers were. In the third case they, like most of the Guard officers, would be entering upon acquaintance with the regiment as a whole with no appreciably greater disadvantages than the Guard officers.

The command of these regiments and of the new Regular regiment, the

366th Infantry, almost immediately became a question of vexing importance. While many white Guard units lost officers and commanders through physical examinations and reclassification procedures, few were in positions comparable to the Negro units. Regular officers could be supplied to the white units but the Negro units, if they were to remain all-Negro in command, had to rely wholly upon the few Guard and Reserve officers who were available. There were no Negro Regular officers who could replace officers from the civilian components. After Colonel Davis, commander of the 369th, was promoted to general, he was no longer available for regimental assignment; his son, Capt. Benjamin O. Davis, Jr., the only other Negro line officer in 1940, went, after brief duty at Fort Riley, into training in the Air Corps, and was thereby lost to the ground regiments.

In some instances the regiments, so far as their top command positions were concerned, became enmeshed in complications from which they never recovered. The 8th Illinois Infantry lost its original commander, who as a member of the Illinois state legislature could not hold both positions under the statutes of the state. He therefore resigned and retired. The senior lieutenant colonel was found physically disqualified and he, too, was scheduled for retirement. Chicago Negroes became alarmed, fearing that upon induction the regiment would find itself, as had happened midway of World War I, with a white commander. An Illinois congressman suggested that the second-in-command be re-examined.[74] In the

meantime, the governor of the state appointed a new commander, who was found to be physically qualified. The regiment was inducted (as the 184th Field Artillery) on 6 January 1941 with its new commander in charge.[75] The re-examination of the disqualified commander remained pending and the permanent command of the regiment was in doubt. In the next few months, it developed that the governor's appointee was not, in actuality, the next senior lieutenant colonel in the regiment. When, upon re-examination, the former commander was found permanently disqualified, Lt. Gen. Ben Lear, Second Army Commander, recommended the alternate lieutenant colonel—the true senior officer—for promotion, making the governor's appointee second-in-command. The four months of entangled internal command problems were no boon to the development of good leadership in this regiment.[76]

The 366th Infantry was to be staffed entirely from eligible Reserve officers. Unlike Guard regiments, Regular regiments had no provision for the attachment of instructors. One white colonel and four lieutenant colonels, Regular Army, were therefore assigned to temporary duty during the period of organization of the 366th, the colonel to command and all five to remain "for such time as the Commanding General, First Army, considers necessary." [77]

[74] Memo, OCS (Col Orlando Ward, SGS) for G-1, 7 Jan 41, OCS 20602-132.

[75] Memo, G-1 for Ward, 7 Jan 41, AG 210.72 184th FA (1-7-41) (1); Memo, G-1 for TAG, 11 Feb 41, AG 291.21 (1-13-41).

[76] Ltr, SGS to Rep Raymond S. McKeough, 6 Mar 41, and other exchanges in OCS 20602-132.

[77] Memo, G-1 for CofS, 8 Nov 40, AG 210.31 ORC (11-8-40) (3); Ltr, TAG to CofInf, 22 Nov 40, and Ltr, TAG to CG Third Corps Area. Both in AG 210.31 ORC (11-8-40) M-A.

The organizational period of the regiment, because of the delays in housing and other facilities incident to filling most Negro units, lasted longer than had been expected. In July, when asked if the white officers could be dispensed with, the regiment had "just organized" its last battalion, was still short in essential equipment, and had had no unit training.[78] Because the white Regular officers were assigned rather than attached, they had displaced the Negro officers in the command of the regiment and of its battalions. G–1, while believing that the Regular officers should remain until the regiment became a "going concern," was reluctant to allow this condition to continue indefinitely. It recommended that organization of the unit be expedited to allow the Negro field grade officers, whose existence and rank had been one of the arguments for staffing the regiment with Negroes in the first place, "an opportunity to actually exercise command" during their year of active duty.[79] Throughout the year, however, First Army continued to recommend retention of the white officers, saying "the Reserve Field Officers are not yet qualified to assume complete command at this time." [80]

A year after the activation of the regiment, it had four full colonels, three white and one Negro, and a fifth full colonel, white, under orders and due to

report, plus two additional white lieutenant colonels assigned. Its Negro officers continued to be "understudy" commanders. A new complication arose when the original white colonel of the regiment was relieved about 4 March 1942, leaving the Negro colonel, now over age for troop duty, in command with four white officers, including two colonels, under him. This violated the policy on the assignment of Negro officers. A new white commander was due to report and the Negro colonel was recommended to be "immediately relieved from the regiment because of over age and be assigned to duty elsewhere, preferably at another station." If a Negro commander were desired, VI Corps recommended, the next senior Negro officer, a lieutenant colonel, should be promoted, the white colonels should be relieved, with one remaining attached to assist and guide the new commander and to train one of the four Negro majors for duty as executive.[81] Another year passed before this regiment, intended to be staffed entirely by Negro officers from the beginning, was so staffed.

The 372d Infantry, after its first seven months of training, was reported as making little progress. Command of the regiment was again the central problem. The regimental commander, a 62-year-old Negro colonel who, it was reported, "is deficient in basic education, has displayed a decided lack of administrative ability, and appears to be ignorant of modern methods of training" was considered a liability. Moreover, the officers lacked confidence in the regi-

[78] 2d Ind, VI Army Corps to CG First Army, 9 Jul 41, to Ltr, TAG to CG First Army, 18 Jun 41, AG 210.31 ORC (6–16–41) OE–A, based on Memo, G–1 for TAG, 16 Jun 41, G–1/8165–490.

[79] Memo, G–1 for CofS, 17 Jul 41, AG 210.31 ORC.

[80] Ltr, VI Army Corps to CG First Army, 15 Sep 41, and 4 Inds, AG 210.31 ORC (9–15–41) (11–8–40) (3) ; Ltr, TAG to CG First Army, 10 Feb 42, and subsequent exchanges in AG 210.31 ORC (2–7–42).

[81] Inds to Ltr, Hq ETO and First Army, 16 Feb 42, AG 210.31 ORC (11–8–40) (3).

ment's three white National Guard instructors. With the exception of the senior instructor, they were not qualified, the officers felt, and the senior instructor was useless to the regiment because he was not being used efficiently by the regimental commander.[82] The colonel of the regiment was persuaded to request relief from active duty because of age, the executive officer was recommended for reassignment, certain other officers were reclassified, and a new Negro commander, fresh from courses at Fort Benning, was brought into the regiment.[83]

Of the four original all-Negro regiments, only the 369th Coast Artillery avoided serious top command difficulties within the first year. In the case of the 184th Field Artillery, later internal difficulties in command may be traced in large measure to the initial command situation and the political implications involved. The long-confused command picture in the 366th Infantry, when the command responsibilities of the Negro "understudy" field officers were questioned by subordinate officers and enlisted men and where the future of command responsibility in the "all-Negro" regiment was in doubt, helped undermine command discipline and stunt the growth of initiative and responsibility within the regiment. Command and unified leadership in the 372d Infantry were further vitiated, even after

the relief of the original commander, by the assignment of the regiment to its first mission: the defense of New York City and various points in its environs, a mission lasting for over two years and effectively splitting the regiment into small units.[84] To add to the command difficulties in these regiments, officer shortages continued for months and, in some cases, for over a year after the initial induction of the units. The 372d Infantry, with a strength of approximately 3,000, over half of whom were totally untrained selectees, had a shortage of thirty officers, not including authorized overages, in September 1941.[85] The 369th Coast Artillery, though receiving all the Negro graduates of the Antiaircraft Officers' Candidate School, was still short twenty-seven second lieutenants in May 1942. This regiment went overseas with a shortage of officers.[86] Nevertheless, on 30 September 1941, 250 eligible Negro Reserve officers, of whom 150 were officers of the combat arms, remained uncalled to active duty. The 222 then on active duty represented less than half the available Negro Reserve officers.[87] "The familiar reluctance of National Guard Commanders to requisition Reserve officers operates in this case as it does generally," Judge Hastie commented.[88]

---

[82] Memo, OTIG for CofS, 17 Oct 41, G-1/15640-118.

[83] Papers in OCS 21177-297 and G-1/15640-118. A white colonel from a Regular Negro regiment was later ordered to the regiment as "instructor," then as commander, but his orders were revoked. He was then assigned to Headquarters, Second Corps Area, with inspection duties for the 372d Infantry. G-1/15640-54, 25-30 Mar 42.

[84] Ltr, TAG to CG Second Corps Area, 13 Dec 41, AG 370.5 (12-11-41) MC-C-M; Ltr, TAG to CG Second Corps Area, 26 Apr 42, AG 370.5 (4-22-42) MC-E-M.

[85] Msg, First Army to TAG, 8 Sep 41, AG 210.31 ORC (9-8-41).

[86] Comd Pers Repl Req, 369th CA (AA) to TAG, 10 May 41, 3d Wrapper Ind, Hq AAC to TAG, 3 Jun 42, 341/B-99 (5-10-42), AG 210.31 (5-20-42); Ltr, Hq AAC to TAG, 12 Sep 42, AG 210.31 (2-14-42) (3).

[87] TAGO Machine Rec Sec, 3 and 4 Nov 41, Tabs G and H in G-1/15640-120.

[88] Hastie Survey, p. 12, G-1/15640-120.

Officer Candidates

The National Guard units had felt that they could supply officers from their own ranks and requested that they be allowed to do so.[89] The 369th Coast Artillery was granted permission to continue its own officers' training school and to continue to have men commissioned during the period between federalization and the opening of officer candidate schools.[90] The regiments, though taking some Reserve officers, expected to fill further vacancies from officer candidate school graduates, preferably chosen from among their own men.

In the first months of the schools' operations Negro candidates were few. Between July 1941, when the schools opened, and mid-September 1941, only 17 out of the 1,997 students enrolled in candidate schools were Negroes. Ten of these were candidates at the Infantry School, 1 each at the Field Artillery and Cavalry Schools, and 5 were at the Quartermaster School.[91] In the next two months, only six more Negro candidates entered officers' schools. Two of these were in the Quartermaster School. The Infantry, Field Artillery, Ordnance, and Finance Schools each received one candidate.[92]

Judge Hastie, realizing that the disproportionately small number of Negro candidates, constituting less than 1 percent of the whole, would produce unfavorable reactions among the Negro public, urged a general revision of policy on the use of Negro officers. He considered the small number of units in which Negro officers could be used and the limitation of Negro officers to units in which the entire staff was Negro to be major deterrents to both the appointment of candidates and to the efficiency of leadership in units. He believed that mixing white and Negro officers in the same units was both inevitable and desirable. Competent Negro officers would not become available until Negro junior officers had been developed "in regular course" by being assigned to regiments then commanded entirely by white officers. "Moreover," he wrote, "in the general replacement of National Guard and Reserve Officers, who have not rendered satisfactory service, it is probable that numbers of field officers, colored as well as white, will be relieved of command. Experienced and qualified successors for numbers of these colored officers will necessarily be procured from available white personnel. The immediate effect of these procedures would be the intermingling of white and colored junior officers in units now commanded by white officers exclusively, and in a few cases, white and colored field officers in regiments now commanded by an entire Negro personnel. Such a course seems necessary and desirable." [93]

Hastie felt that no increase in Negro officer candidates could be expected

[89] 4th Ind, Hq 369th CA (AA) NYNG to CofNGB, 18 Nov 40, to Ltr, NGB to AG of New York, 30 Oct 40, NGB 325.4 (CA) N.Y.–52; 6th Ind, Hq 184th FA to CG Sixth Corps Area, 22 Jan 41, to Ltr, NGB to AG of Illinois, 13 Dec 40, AG 210.31 ORC (12–31–40) M.
[90] Memo, CofS for CofCA, 10 Apr 40, OCS 19308–4; Ltr, Acting DCofS to Maj Gen W. N. Haskell, 11 Apr 40; Ltr, NGB to AG of New York, 30 Oct 40; Memo, OCNGB for Col Wharton, 28 Nov 40. All in NGB 325.4 (CA) N.Y.–52.
[91] Memo, TAG for Admin Asst OSW, 16 Sep 41, AG 291.21 (9–12–41) M.
[92] Memo, TAG for Civ Aide to SW, 18 Nov 41, AG 291.21 (10–30–41) RB.

[93] Hastie Survey, G–1/15640–120. See also Memo, G–1 for TAG, 1 Jan 42, and attached Memo for Record, Incls, OCS 20602–239.

through the normal operation of quotas, especially since most Negroes were in small units. "The realities of the situation are that many Commanders in the field approach the selection of Officer Candidates with bias against the Negro as an officer in the United States Army," he declared. Since no plan existed for the use of Negro officers in certain branches, such as the Quartermaster Corps, Corps of Engineers, and Cavalry, in which large numbers of Negroes were being trained, commanders were prone to overlook potential Negro officer candidates. "It is believed that nothing less than a directive or confidential memorandum to commanders charged with the selection of Officer candidates, indicating that certain minimum percentages of Negro candidates are to be selected, will be effective," Hastie concluded.[94]

In the meantime, prompted by the slowness of the development of Negro officer candidate training, Edgar Brown, one of the prominent Negro legislative lobbyists of 1939–41, suggested to the President and to the Secretary of War that nothing "would be more salutary for the morale and patriotism of 15,000-000 Negro citizens and soldiers," than a separate school for Negro officer trainees modeled on the Des Moines school of World War I.[95] A radio commentator picked up Brown's suggestion and broadcast to the nation that "a large group of the most responsible Negro leaders in the country" were opposed to the President's policy of training Negro officers with white trainees and had asked for separate schools.[96] The reaction of Negroes was immediate. The NAACP called upon the White House and the War Department to reveal who the "so-called responsible leaders" were, adding, "We respectfully submit that no leader considered responsible by intelligent Negro or white Americans would make such a request."[97] A second telegram from the NAACP, signed by 47 Negro editors, college presidents, judges, bishops and ministers, businessmen, and heads of professional and fraternal organizations, and accompanied by the promise of the names of as many more Negroes in opposition to the suggestion, indicated that the proposal had little backing among Negro leaders.[98]

To subsequent inquiries on the possibility that separate officer candidate schools might be established, the War Department replied that separate schools would be uneconomical and inefficient. "Our objection is based primarily on the fact that negro officer candidates are eligible from every branch of the Army, including the Armored Force and Tank destroyer battalions, and it would be decidedly uneconomical to attempt to gather in one school the materiel and instructor personnel necessary to give training in all these branches," a senator was told. School troops, quarters, and staffs would have to be duplicated if two separate sets of schools were organized. The War Department seldom failed to point out, in

[94] Sources cited n. 93.

[95] Ltr, Edgar G. Brown, President United Government Employees, Inc., to President Roosevelt and to SW, 15 Oct 41, AG 291.21 (10–15–41) (1).

[96] Fulton Lewis, MBS, 20 Oct 41, Daily Radio Digest, 21 Oct 41, AG 291.2 (10–21–42) (9).

[97] Telg, Walter White, NAACP, to Secy Stimson and President Roosevelt, 23 Oct 41, AG 291.21 (10–23–41) (3).

[98] Telg, Walter White to Secy Stimson, 29 Oct 41, AG 291.21 (10–29–41) (1).

explaining the small numbers of Negro candidates, that, in general competition with white candidates, Negroes were at a disadvantage since only 5 percent, in comparison with 45 percent of the whites, had the General Classification Test qualifications for admission to officer candidate schools. "It is more efficient to send these candidates to the regular schools of their respective branches where they take the same training as white officer candidates," the department declared. "Further, to make such a segregation of negro candidates on a fixed percentage basis rather than on ability would be a discrimination against white candidates," another inquirer was told.[99]

The meager production of new Negro officers before December 1941 had other explanations. The numbers of Negroes entering the Army had not yet reached the proportionate levels aimed for and the pools of reservists had not yet been exhausted. No revision of the Negro officer assignment policy had been made, and the relationship of the new officers, trained to be platoon leaders, to the old policy was vague. Nor had the relationship of Negro candidates to the problem of leadership for Negro troops in the new Army—in units which were now being spread through all arms and services —been explored. For the use of Negro officers in general had not been looked upon as a potential answer to leadership problems. Rather, it was a use born of necessity and from which not too much was expected in the way of strong, firm, and effective leadership.

---

[99] Ltr, SGS to Senator Carl Hayden (Arizona) 12 Dec 41, AG 352 (12–12–41) M; Ltr, G–3 to Representative James N. Fitzpatrick, 12 Dec 41, AG 352 (12–12–41) MT.

CHAPTER VIII

The Quest for Leadership Continues

After Pearl Harbor the provision of Negro officers to fill needed leadership positions in Negro units received more serious consideration within the War Department. Throughout most of 1941 the guiding principle in this effort was the requirement that Negroes be represented in commissioned ranks in accordance with the policy statement of October 1940. The officers so provided were to be given training for a year. They would then return to inactive duty or reserve status. The declaration of war altered these conditions completely. Negro units, steadily increasing in number as a result of the operation of the Selective Service Act, now had to be viewed as a part of a fighting force in preparation for use in an actual war. Mounting shortages of white officers in all units increased the real need for Negroes to fill officer vacancies in Negro units.

Plans After Pearl Harbor

In early 1942 the War Department, acting in part upon Judge Hastie's recommendations,[1] began to take steps to increase the numbers of Negro officers available for duty with troops. A complete revision of the policy of assignment necessarily resulted. For, if Negro officers were to be used in increasing numbers in existing and planned units, places and methods for their use had to be found. The policy of assigning Negro officers to a limited number of units in a few branches and in units staffed exclusively with Negroes had to be modified.

In late January G–3 called a conference of representatives of the arms and services to discuss their Negro officer requirements. Most arms and services had barely considered the matter, for, under persuasive pressures emanating from the General Staff, they were only beginning to visualize the use that they might make of their proportionate quotas of Negro enlisted men. What use each branch would make of Negro officers had to be determined before the War Department could embark on a program to increase the number of Negro officer candidates. For, under Mobilization Regulations, the number of Negro officer candidates was governed by the officer requirements of the units to which Negro officers were to be assigned.[2] The War Department's plan therefore contemplated the prior desig-

---

[1] Memo, USW for SW, 16 Jan 42, ASW 291.2 (Race, Negro); Memo, USW for Judge Hastie, 17 Feb 42, ASW 291.2 (Race, Negro, Misc); Memo, DCofS for USW, 13 Feb 42, WDCSA 322.97 (11–21–42).

[2] MR 1–2, par. 13 b, 15 Jul 39, reaffirmed in 1943 in Memo, Hq AGF for G–1, 7 Apr 43, AGF 352/72 and D/F, G–1, 8 Apr 43, WDGAP 322.99.

nation of units in which Negro officers could be placed.

Most branches, under the impetus of designating units for the use of Negro officers, shifted their focus from officer requirements to a consideration of the number of Negro officers which they thought they could absorb, duplicating, to some extent, the procedure which they were following in the provision of Negro units. The Quartermaster Corps reported that it had enough truck companies to absorb all Negro lieutenants made available by its school.[3] The Corps of Engineers said that it could take its share of Negro officers in aviation battalions, separate battalions, replacement training center battalions, and divisional combat battalions, provided that the officers were all in the grade of lieutenant.[4] The infantry could use enough to fill the two infantry regiments and enough in company grades to fill the infantry companies of the not yet activated 93d Division. Divisional officers would be promoted to higher grades and positions as they became "capable through training." The 92d Division would be filled in the same manner. All together, 1,098 Negro officers, constituting 4.19 percent of all infantry officers on duty with troops and 2.58 percent of all infantry officers, could be used by the infantry in 1942.[5]

The Field Artillery, similarly, could use Negro officers to complete the staffs of the 184th Field Artillery, the newly activated 795th Tank Destroyer Battalion, and the gun batteries of the two divisions planned for 1942.[6] The coast artillery was prepared to fill the batteries of two 155-mm gun regiments with Negro officers, which, with the 369th Infantry, would make a total of 201 officers for 1942.[7] The Medical Department brought out its existing plan, adding that the 93d Division at Fort Huachuca would have a complete Negro medical service and that for the post's hospital "The Surgeon General is willing in the interests of nondiscrimination to promote colored doctors, dentists, etc. to grades comparable in a like hospital set up for white patients providing of course that colored Medical officers are qualified to perform the duties. . . ." Therefore, no grades for Negro officers were specified by The Surgeon General, but he did point out that in regiments with white commanders the regimental surgeon should be white so that the white officers could have a physician of their own race. Medical administrative officers could be assigned to sanitary companies and as mess and supply officers or detachment commanders at hospitals with Negro services. The Surgeon General believed that his plan would provide vacancies, including higher grades for "all competent colored officers that will be available to the Army."[8] The Air Forces had already planned to use Negro flying and administrative officers at Tuskegee and in the service units necessary for the operation of that base.

Other arms and services had less well

[3] Memo, OQMG for G-3, 3 Feb 42, QM 352 P-MT (OCS).

[4] Memo, OCofE for G-3, 29 Jan 42, CE 320-2-TO.

[5] Memo, OCofInf for G-3, 28 Jan 42, CI 210.31/9879.

[6] Memo, OCofFA for G-3, 27 Jan 42, FA 210.31 A-137.

[7] Memo, OCofCA for G-3, 27 Jan 42, AG 210.31 (2-14-42) (3).

[8] Memo, SG for G-3, 30 Jan 42, Incl to Memo, G-3 for TAG, 18 Mar 42, AG 210.31 (2-14-42) (3).

formulated plans. Some were willing to activate units specifically for the purpose of absorbing Negro officers. The Ordnance Department reported that it had but one Negro officer, a second lieutenant recently graduated from Aberdeen and, at the time, assigned to Raritan Arsenal. He would be held at the arsenal until other Negro officers were available, whereupon all would be assigned to companies. If enough officers were available, they would be assigned in full complements to ordnance companies, a group at a time; otherwise they would be assigned to companies in pairs as available. Initially, three ammunition companies would be activated for the purpose of absorbing Negro officers. Additional assignments to ten other companies would be made as soon as locations were found where other units with Negro officers were available to provide messing and housing facilities for the few officers carried by each ordnance company.[9] What the Ordnance Department proposed as a means of assigning Negro officers to units—simultaneously by groups or blocks, by providing units for them when none existed, and by locations considered expedient—contained the basic elements of later War Department practices.

The Signal Corps was of the opinion that "relatively few, if any" Negroes could meet its standards for assignment to tactical Signal Corps units. It recommended that all tactical units be officered exclusively by white officers and "that any colored officer who must be absorbed" be assigned to Corps Area and War Department overhead, in depots, repair shops, or administrative offices.[10] The Cavalry indicated that it would have no large use for Negro officers, since they could be used only at the cavalry replacement training center and in the reconnaissance troops of the Negro divisions in ranks not above lieutenant.[11] The Regular cavalry regiments, like the Regular infantry regiments, already had all white officers under policies then current.

The Provost Marshal General decided that in his four types of military police units, uses for Negro officers would be rare. Since there were to be no Negro armies or corps, Negro tactical military police units would be limited to divisions; those divisions which were colored "throughout" could have Negro military police and Negro officers. The Provost Marshal would "not object" to Negro officers in the zone of the interior units set up in the Second and Ninth Corps Areas. Since no colored prisoner of war escort units had been organized, the question of officers for them had not arisen, but if such units were organized the Provost Marshal would recommend against Negro officers since there were but two officers to a unit. Officers in these units normally messed with post administrative officers at prisoner of war camps and there were no Negro administrative officers in these camps. In corps area service command units, Negro officers could be employed in military police detachments, but the decision should be left with detachment commanders, depending upon local conditions.[12]

---

[9] Memo, OCofOrd for G-3, 27 Jan 42, CofOrd 210.3/275.

[10] Memo, OCSigO for G-3, 27 Jan 42, OCSigO 210.31 Gen.

[11] Memo, OCofC for G-3, 27 Jan 42, Incl to Memo, G-3 for TAG, 18 Mar 42, AG 210.31 (2-14-42) (3).

[12] Memo, PMG for G-3, 2 Feb 42, PMG 210.31.

The Negro Officer Troop Basis

G–3, from the information that it had gathered, proceeded to determine a procurement basis and to construct a troop basis for the assignment of Negro officers for 1942. This document provided for the assignment and grades of Negro officers in units of the arms and services, in training units at replacement training centers, and in station hospitals. All assignments were to be in the grades of first and second lieutenant, except that possibilities for promotion up to the rank of colonel were provided in the Coast Artillery, Field Artillery, and Infantry, and in the Medical Department, and that chaplains, to be Negro in all Negro units, could be promoted to whatever rank tables of organization authorized. Units in the Negro Officer Troop Basis would retain white officers until Negro officers became available.[13]

To assure an increase in the number of Negro officer candidates, commanders were directed to suballot proportionate quotas to Negro units and installations within their commands and to make every effort to secure qualified Negro candidates.[14] There was some expectation that in the process of expansion the number of Negro officer candidates would grow to become proportionate to the strength of Negroes in the Army.[15]

After the beginning of the Volunteer Officer Candidate (VOC) program, under which potential officers not yet called by Selective Service could volunteer for

officer training and remain free to return to their homes if not successful, the War Department discovered that few Negro applicants were being accepted and inducted. It reminded corps area commanders of the "acute shortage of Negro officers, especially in such technical branches as Field Artillery, Antiaircraft Artillery, Engineers, Chemical Warfare Service, Signal Corps, and Ordnance Department" and urged that they exploit the VOC program as a source of suitable Negro officer material for the branches in which the shortages would be most acute. Examining boards and draft boards were instructed to examine carefully the educational and vocational backgrounds of all Negro applicants so that none with qualifications for officer training should be overlooked in the VOC program.[16] The Air Forces, which had on file several applications from Negro civilians who appeared to be highly qualified officer material but who could not be used by the Air Forces, was requested to forward their names to the Officers Procurement Section of the Reserve Division for possible use by other branches.[17]

The complex and detailed Negro Officer Troop Basis, listing the permitted grades in every unit to which Negro officers might be assigned, did not remain fixed, not even during 1942. Changes were provided for in the original plan. G–3, in consultation with G–1, G–4, and the chief of the branch concerned, was authorized to substitute "like units" for those shown at any time prior to the actual assignment of Negro

Memo, G–3 for CofS, 14 Feb 42, approved 7 Mar 42, AG 210.31 (2–14–42) (3) (5).
[14] Ltrs, TAG to CG's, Chiefs Supply and Admin Svs, 24 Feb 42, 19 Apr 42, AG 350 (2–21–42), AG 352 (4–13–42).
[15] Ltr, SW to Archibald MacLeish, Office of Facts and Figures, 27 Apr 42, WDCSA 291.21 (4–3–42).

[16] Ltr, TAG SOS to CG's Corps Areas, 2 Jun 42, SPX 352 (5–21–42) OB–SPGA.
[17] Memo, G–1 for CG AAF, 22 Jun 42, WDGAP 322.99, G–1 291.2 (Alpha).

officers.[18] After the reorganization of the War Department in March 1942, the authority to make changes was decentralized to the major commands, in consultation with each other where appropriate.[19] New units were added to the list to absorb excess graduates of some schools and to replace other units which had moved overseas, were alerted, or in which, for any other reason, a major change of officers was not considered feasible or desirable. Quartermaster truck companies, aviation, numbered 821 to 845 inclusive, were added, for example, because all graduates of the 15 July 1942 class of the Quartermaster OCS were allotted to the Army Air Forces and to units previously authorized to be filled; these Air units were needed to absorb the Negro members of that class.[20] Similarly, the Ordnance Department required additional units for its troop basis to take care of additional OCS graduates.[21] By July 1942, the Antiaircraft Artillery Command had filled all of its units authorized Negro officers except the 369th Coast Artillery (AA). The 369th had already gone overseas understrength, but it had fifty candidates in training. These officers were to be used to fill the 369th and then to fill additional units to be added to the approved list.[22] The Corps of Engineers suggested adding 31 units, all general service regiments, separate battalions, or aviation engineers. Not all could be added, for some had been deleted or altered in the full troop basis, but 18 new units, exclusive of air types, were authorized Negro officers.[23] As a temporary expedient to absorb excess officers in field artillery, infantry, and cavalry, Army Ground Forces proposed that air base security battalions be authorized Negro officers in all grades and positions except commander and executive.[24] When the 795th, the one tank destroyer battalion with Negro officers, was filled, including overstrength, AGF nominated four other tank destroyer battalions to receive Negro lieutenants.[25] Sometimes the Negro Officer Troop Basis had to be altered because of an omission or other error, as when the 245th Quartermaster Battalion (Service), a Puerto Rican unit that already had all-Negro officers, was added to the list in April.[26]

The list of units to which Negro officers could be assigned grew and fluctuated as more and more units and a more liberal supply of officers became available. Priorities among authorized units

---

[18] G-3/6457-444 file.

[19] Memo, G-3 for CofS, 9 Mar 42, approved 12 Mar 42, AG 210.31 (2-14-42).

[20] Ltr, TAG to CG's AAF and SOS and TQMG, 27 Jul 42, AG 210.31 (7-21-42) MS-SPGA.

[21] D/F, MPD SOS to G-1, 6 Oct 42, SPGA O/210.3 Ord (10-2-42)-14, AG 210.31 (10-2-42) (2-14-42) (3).

[22] Ltr, Hq AAC to CG AGF, 23 Jul 42, AG 210.31 (7-23-42) (2-14-42) (3).

[23] Ltr, OCofE to CG SOS (Dir MPD), 3 Aug 42, CE SPEAM 210.3 (Engrs, Corps of), AGF 210.31 (8-3-42), AG 210.31 (8-3-42) (2-14-42) (3); Ltr, TAG to CG's, CO's PofE's, Chief Armd Force, Chiefs Supply Svs SOS, 8 Sep 42, sub: Assgmt of Negro Offs to Engr Units, AG 210.31 (8-3-42) MO-SPGAO-M.

[24] Memo, Hq AGF for CofS, 12 Sep 42, AGF 322.999/16 (Cld Trps); 1st Ind, Hq AGF to CG R&SC, 17 Sep 42, AGF 210.31 GN GAP-A (9-10-42).

[25] Ltr, Hq AGF to G-1, 29 Oct 42, AGF 210.31/392; Ltr, TAG to CG AGF, 2 Nov 42, AG 210.31 (10-29-42) OB-S-A.

[26] Ltr, Hq Puerto Rican Dept to TAG, 25 Apr 42, 210.31-Gen, AG 210.31 (4-25-42) (2-14-42) (3). The race of this unit was administratively determined, as men and officers were never clearly differentiated in Puerto Rican units by continental racial standards.

for the assignment of Negro officers were worked out in some branches and commands. For example, Army Ground Forces established the following unit priorities for the assignment of Negro officers:

Infantry
 1. 93d Infantry Division
 2. 92d Infantry Division
 3. 758th Tank Battalion
 4. 24th Infantry
 5. 366th Infantry
 6. 367th Infantry
 7. 372d Infantry
Field Artillery
 1. 184th Field Artillery
 2. 795th Tank Destroyer Battalion
 3. 93d Infantry Division
 4. 92d Infantry Division
 5. Field Artillery Replacement Training Center
Cavalry
 1. 93d Reconnaissance Troop
 2. 92d Reconnaissance Troop
 3. 795th Tank Destroyer Battalion
 4. Cavalry Replacement Training Center
Coast Artillery
 1. 369th CA (AA)
 2. 99th and 100th CA (AA), elements at Camp Davis, N.C.
 3. Tng Bns at Fort Eustis, Va.
 4. 99th and 100th CA (AA), elements which have left Camp Davis, N.C.

Within the 93d Division, the Chief of Infantry had already requested the following priorities: 369th, 368th, and 25th Infantry, with the 369th at the top because it was the one new regiment in the division, therefore permitting the least displacement of officers already assigned.[27]

Nevertheless, the 1942 Negro Officer Troop Basis was not considered satisfactory. It was too restrictive, and be-

cause of its relative inflexibility it was subject to too frequent amendment. In year's end conferences the policy of 1942 was revised. The new policy continued to authorize the assignment of Negro officers to previously designated units, but it attempted to clarify the methods and conditions for their assignment. Under the 1942 policy, methods of introducing new Negro officers into units already activated with white officers were not clearly defined, nor were sources of requisitions for them or jurisdiction over assignments always clear. Additional categories of units, covering practically all types, were agreed upon by the conferees, but the determination of specific units within those types was to be left to the command having jurisdiction over the units. The designating authority would then report the units selected to the War Department. Overhead activities to which Negro officers could be assigned, while limited to those that had considerable numbers of Negro troops, were to be specifically listed. Assignments of Negro officers were to be made "in block" and not by individuals. Thus all attached officers, such as chaplains and medical officers, were to be assigned in groups in all authorized grades. When all Negro lieutenants were authorized a unit, they were to be assigned in company or battalion groups depending on the size of the unit. Opportunities for the promotion of Negroes to higher grades than those initially authorized were to be provided by the accumulation of qualified officers of the arm or service concerned. When sufficient officers to staff a battalion or smaller unit became available they would be promoted in a block and assigned to a new unit in the grades which the unit required. These

---

[27] Ltrs, Hq AGF to CG R&SC, 29 Apr 42, and to CG AAC, 29 Apr 42, both in AGF 210.31/88; Memo, OCofInf for G-3, 28 Jan 42, CI 210.31/9879.

officers could be held in pools while awaiting reassignment.[28]

This policy, instead of simplifying the operation of the Negro officer assignment policy over the existing rules as had been hoped, not only complicated the paper work involved but also made it more difficult to provide good leadership for Negro units. Neither of these considerations was paramount in the formulation of the new policy of assignment in groups by grades. The major aim was to provide Negro officers to units while inviting the least possible friction from combining Negro and white officers in the same units. The published policy included again a prohibition against the assignment of Negro senior officers, except chaplains and medical officers, to units having white officers in a junior grade.[29] The new policy intensified the assignment problem by making it more difficult to place Negro officers in units. It guaranteed, by its promotion provisions, low morale for officers once they were assigned. For now individual assignments, reassignments, and promotions were predicated upon the availability of enough other officers qualified to fill a given unit in the grades required and not on the merit of the officers involved.

The Negro Officer Candidate Supply

Soon after the number of Negro students in officer candidate schools was increased in 1942, it became apparent that Negroes would not be able to fill all officer vacancies in Negro units in any event. The OCS requirement of a 110 score on the Army General Classification Test removed automatically the great bulk of Negroes from consideration as potential officer candidates. Formal educational requirements removed others. In some quarters it was expected that so few Negroes would qualify as officer candidates that the Army would have no real problem in employing the small numbers of Negroes who would finally graduate and be commissioned.

Of the Army's 3,500,000 men in August 1942, 244,000 or 7 percent were officers, of whom 41,400 or 1.2 percent were OCS graduates. Of the 228,715 Negroes then in the Army, only 817, or 0.35 percent, were officers, of whom 655 or 0.28 percent were graduates of OCS. "The foregoing figures," a Ground Forces staff officer asserted, "confirm our conclusion reached previously, i.e., the colored race cannot produce enough military leadership to officer the colored units. A good estimate would be that enough can be produced to meet 10% of the total requirements for colored units." [30]

While the conclusion that Negroes would be unable, in the time available, to supply officers for all Negro units was correct, figures alone could not fully reveal the facts in the case. Negro officer candidates, chosen on the basis of unit

---

[28] Memo, Chief of Off Br for Brig Gen White (ACofS G–1), 31 Dec 42, Tab A to Memo, G–1 for TAG, 4 Jan 43, AG 210.31 (1–4–43) (1).

[29] Ltr, TAG to All CG's, CinC SWPA, CinC Armd Force, CO's Base Comds, 10 Jan 43, AG 210.31 (1–4–43) B–S–A.M.

[30] M/S, AGF G–1 to CG AGF, 12 Oct 42, in papers attached to Memo, Hq AGF for G–1, 20 Oct 42, AGF 322.999/26. At peak officer strength, in August 1945, there were 7,768 Negro male officers, nurses, dieticians, physical therapists, warrant officers, flight officers, and WAC officers in the Army and 687,496 Negro enlisted men and women. Of these, 6,140 were male commissioned officers. Strength of the Army, 1 Jan 46, STM–30. See Table 12.

quotas, were rather more unevenly distributed as to quality than appeared on the surface. Numbers and quotas and not potential leadership ability became the criterion for the acceptance of Negro candidates. Some units, because of assignment by numerical availability practiced in many reception centers, were more than able to fill their candidate quotas with men who not only had the required paper qualifications but who also possessed outstanding leadership abilities. Other units were unable to fill quotas with either type of man. Still others, struggling along with few men of the caliber required for their noncommissioned officer ranks, were reluctant to encourage their best men to apply for OCS. In certain cases, the best men themselves, knowing that a sergeancy carried with it little of the assignment and adjustment difficulties and risks of a second lieutenancy—which many soldiers considered the permanent rank of Negro officers—were reluctant to give up the known certainties and privileges of their noncommissioned rating for the uncertainties of the officers' rank.

Many Negroes felt that antipathy for Negro officers held by Southern civilians, by white enlisted men, and by white officers, was greater than antipathy for Negro soldiers in general. Stories, many of them apocryphal but others with a basis in fact, were legion, especially in connection with difficulties encountered with military courtesy, with obtaining transportation facilities while traveling on government transportation orders, with obtaining assignments to units once on post, and with housing, messing, and even laundry facilities for Negro officers. Many of these stories were in bad taste and, like most jokes,

exaggerated for effect, but they are indicative of the Negro enlisted man's—and officer's—reaction to the status of the Negro officer. These reactions served to undermine attitudes basic to good discipline.

Despite the fact that the AGCT requirement alone was sufficient to cut the potential number of Negro officer candidates far below the proportion that the number of Negro enlisted men could have been expected to produce mathematically, by the end of 1942 the number of available Negro officers was beginning to exceed the number of available assignments. For, as the over-all supply of officers began to increase, a concurrent reluctance to assign Negro officers to units—bolstered by reports of difficulties in units already so staffed—grew as well.

Assignment Difficulties

Aside from the limited number of units authorized them, other barriers to the assignment of Negro officers developed. Of major importance were those arising out of the social matrix imposed by American racial attitudes. The Fourth Service Command, for example, reported that it had positions for Negro over-age officers, but that suitable housing, messing, and recreational facilities were not available generally, for, in fact, "only makeshift arrangements have been made to accommodate colored chaplains in colored enlisted areas." [31] The Northwest Service Command indicated

[31] Ltr, Hq Fourth Sv Comd to TAG, 6 May 42, 4th SC 210.31–Gen (DF) (5–6–42) (3). When Judge Hastie complained earlier that these "makeshift arrangements" were all too prevalent, the Chief of Chaplains and The Inspector General were of the opinion that conditions could not be too bad, since only one chaplain had complained. Since assignment to quarters and the provision of

that it had potential vacancies for Negro officers in units along the Alcan Highway, but observed that it had no separate facilities and that no towns with Negro populations existed along the highway to provide social outlets. Each of the Negro battalions had a Negro chaplain, but the command wanted no additional officers.[32] The 733d Military Police Battalion, in which all white officers were to be replaced by Negroes, found itself moved from the northern part of the Ninth Service Command to the Southern Land Frontier Sector. The sector felt that the Negro officers could hardly be used as provost marshals in Phoenix or Tucson, or in Nogales, Calexico, and other border towns where action in cooperation with commanders and provost marshals of exempted stations, civil authorities, and a potentially anti-Negro civilian population was necessary. "I am closely in touch with the sentiment of the people in this Sector," Brig. Gen. Thoburn K. Brown wrote to Lt. Gen. John L. DeWitt, "and while they are beginning to be tolerant in their attitude toward colored troops, it is only because they have the greatest confidence in the officers commanding these colored troops. This confidence, I am sure, would not extend to colored officers." [33]

No additional Negro officers were sent to this unit. The sixteen Negro officers already assigned were gradually transferred to military police detachments and to other units.[34] Decisions that Negro officers would not be welcome were not in all cases the product of local commanders' impressions. Representations often came from communities themselves. The entire Mississippi Congressional delegation, for example, sent a joint petition to the War Department requesting that no Negro officers be stationed in Mississippi at all, and Georgia congressmen objected to stationing regiments with Negro officers at Camp Stewart.[35]

Low Proficiency and other Limitations

A second barrier to the full and free employment of Negro officers was a continuing disbelief in their abilities. This disbelief was typified and re-enforced by the progressive troubles of certain of the older, all-Negro staffed units, coupled with the firm conviction that Negro troops preferred service under white officers, or at least served better under them.[36] The attitude itself was responsible, in the long run, for so limiting opportunities to develop leadership

---

messing facilities was a responsibility of local commanding officers and since Negro chaplains themselves had not complained, both officers recommended that the War Department make no inquiries and take no action. Memo, Civ Aide to SW for TAG, 6 Sep 41, and 6 Inds, AG 291.21 (9–6–41) (2).

[32] Ltr, NWSC to TAG, 11 Jan 43, AG 210.31 (1–11–43) (1 Jan 43) (1).

[33] Ltr, Hq SLFS WDC to CG WDC and Fourth Army, 20 Sep 42, and Inds, 210.31, AG 210.31 (2–14–42) (3). General Brown was also commanding general of the 4th Cavalry Brigade; most of his ground units in the Southern Frontier Land Sector contained Negro enlisted personnel.

[34] Memo, OPMG for MPD SOS, 23 Oct 42, SPAA 370.093; Ltr, TAG to TPMG, 18 Nov 42, AG 210.31 (9–20–42) PO–A, AG 210.31 (2–14–42) (3).

[35] Rpt of G–3, Min Gen Council, 4 May 42, p. 6; D/F, G–3 for Hq AGF, and Memo, Hq AGF for G–3, 5 May 42, both in AGF 210.31/102; Memo for Record, 19 Mar 43, and M/S, Hq AGF, 19–20 Mar 43, both in AGF 322.999/354 (Cld Trps).

[36] Memo, SGO Plng Sub-Div for Gen Love, 2 May 41, SGO 291.2 (Negro Pers) 1941; Ltr, Maj Gen Fred W. Miller to Gen McNair, 8 Apr 43, AGF 322/1 (93d Div).

potentialities that it tended to become a self-proving proposition.

No matter what other obstacles confronted the older tactical units in their development, the most evident thing about them was that they were all—or nearly all—Negro-staffed. When successive inspection reports showed rapid fluctuations in the status of the units— now a commendation for one training task done well and a few months later a condemnation for the same or other tasks done poorly—the Negro officers were considered incapable of controlling their units to the point of maintaining them at a high level of efficiency in all departments at once. So many adverse reports on one unit came into Washington that staff officers in G–3 and in AGF considered that it would always be "a source of trouble" so long as it continued intact in the same location and with the same officers. "Washout" the headquarters and "Shanghai the Colonel and the Chaplain to some remote part away from their political stamping grounds," Army Ground Forces Plans recommended.[37] Of the commander of this unit, Lt. Gen. Ben Lear, commanding the Second Army, remarked later that "he has demonstrated his loyalty, a willingness to cooperate and interest and that he possesses professional training and ability to the extent reasonably to be expected from a nonprofessional negro officer of his grade and experience." To this, Lt. Gen. Lesley J. McNair, commanding Army Ground Forces, commented: "In my view . . . report[s] on the regiment indicate rather clearly that the regimental commander is incapable of building a satisfactory regiment. The fact

that he is loyal and willing does not make him competent." [38] But AGF demurred when General Lear, arguing that no Negro replacements were available, sought to remove the Negro commander and executive of another unit through reclassification proceedings in order to replace them with white officers. The War Department had established the unit as all-Negro and desired that opportunities for promotion of Negroes be kept open. "The problem of finding places to assign Negro officers of grades higher than lieutenant is becoming increasingly difficult," AGF said. "It is expected that additional units will have to be designated to have all Negro officers at an early date." To clinch the point, AGF offered as a replacement for the reclassified commander or his executive a Negro officer of field grade recommended for promotion by the Commanding General, Third Army.[39] No more was heard of this particular reclassification proceeding.

Continued dissatisfaction with the progress of Negro units later led General Lear, placing the blame squarely on Negro officers, to request that no further Negro units be staffed with Negro officers in the grade of major or higher. "Reluctantly I have come to the conclusion," he said, "that [Negro units'] unsatisfactory progress is largely due to deficiencies in leadership as demonstrated by many negro officers. . . . Their progress has been in direct proportion to the percentage of white offi-

---

[37] M/S, Hq AGF Plans to DCofS, 30 Aug 42, AGF 319.1/112.

[38] 1st Ind, Hq Second Army, to CG AGF, 9 Dec 42; M/S, CG AGF to AGF G–3, 29 Dec 42. Both in AGF 333.1/51.
[39] Rad, Hq Second Army to CG AGF, 15 Feb 43, AGF Radio File–IN 396; Ltr, Hq AGF to CG Second Army, 17 Feb 43, AG 210.31/2 (TD).

cers assigned to the units. Those with all white officers have made reasonable progress; those with all negro officers are definitely substandard." The request was approved "in principle" by AGF and by the War Department.[40]

A request that came from the Antiaircraft Command reinforced General Lear's recommendation. The 538th Antiaircraft Artillery (AW) Battalion, formerly the 2d Battalion of the 100th Coast Artillery (AA), had come under the jurisdiction of the Antiaircraft Command in a low state of morale, training, and general efficiency. For six months previously it had had Negro lieutenants, who were transferred out to fill other units. Though authorized Negro officers, it had been assigned white officers temporarily since no Negro officers were available to the Antiaircraft Command at the time. Now the unit had improved considerably under its white officers and the command did not wish to return to Negro officers.[41] Ground G–1 again remarked that it was becoming increasingly difficult to assign Negro officers.[42]

Developing doubts of their technical as apart from their administrative and leadership proficiency played their part in the reluctance to accept Negro officers in certain units. Sometimes intermediate headquarters through which assignments had to go interposed objections to the placement of Negro officers even though they had received the required training. The chief of the Chemical Warfare Service was prepared to assign Negro officers to two smoke generating companies at Fort Brady, Michigan, but the Central Defense Command objected on the ground that only officers with excellent meteorological backgrounds and a high degree of technical training could be used in these units. The Chemical Warfare Service then asked SOS if the Central Defense Command could object, since the units were on the War Department's approved list. G–1, when queried, replied that the Central Defense Command would have to accept the officers, give them a trial, and, if it then found them unsatisfactory, use the normal procedures for removal prescribed in Army Regulations.[43] The fear that requisitions, arriving when no Negro officers were available from pools, would be filled by substandard officers transferred from overstrength units also operated to reduce assignment possibilities.[44]

Technically trained Negro officers, once initial vacancies were filled, were difficult to place. After the disbandment of the junior of the two signal aircraft warning companies activated at Tuskegee in 1942, over two dozen Negro second lieutenants of the Signal Corps were left without assignments. Despite attempts to place them in other commands, suitable position vacancies were never found for all of them.[45] "There are only six units to which these officers could be assigned," AGF informed AAF, "and all of them are now 200% over-

[40] Ltr, CG Second Army to CG AGF, 13 Apr 43, and MR attached, AGF 210.31/500.
[41] Ltr, Hq AAA Comd to CG AGF, 4 Jun 43, AGF 210.31/521.
[42] M/S, Off Div G–1 to G–3, 8 Jun 43, AGF 210.31/521.
[43] Ltr, OCofCWS to CG CDC, 4 Feb 43, and 3 Inds; D/F, G–1 to TAG, 23 Feb 43. All in AG 210.31 (1–4–43) (1).
[44] Ltr, Hq 828th TD Bn to CG TDC, Cp Hood, 13 Sep 43, AGF 210.31/571.
[45] Ltr, Hq Tuskegee Army Air Fld to CG AAFSETC, Maxwell Fld, Ala., 27 May 43, and 2 Inds, AAF 210.31 Signal Corps.

strength." [46]   While a few were later assigned to signal construction battalions and to miscellaneous Air Forces units, the others were employed about the Tuskegee station in various base capacities, ranging from assistants in base communications through assistants in special services to officers in charge of specific barracks of the base unit. A few remained in these and similar jobs until the end of the war, unable to obtain suitable assignments, unable to put their training into practice, and hoping that a vacancy would occur in one of the units which could use them.

Where overhead and staff positions were involved, new applications for specialists were added. To the initial request by Judge Hastie that consideration be given to the use of Negro officers in Judge Advocate General's Department functions, the stumbling block was their use in Negro divisions, which seemed to the Judge Advocate General to be a natural place for the use of officers who were lawyers. But the Ground Forces had an informal policy that "as long as the Division Commander is a white officer the heads of general and special staff sections of his headquarters should be white officers." AGF, while considering the advisability of using Negroes as assistant division judge advocates on a special allotment basis, advised that Negro officers for the judge advocates on a special allotment be employed elsewhere than in divisions. [47]   After numerous protests on the

lack of Negro officers in the Judge Advocate General's Department, G–1, late in the war, directed the Judge Advocate General to arrange to use Negro lawyers as officers. The Judge Advocate General's Office determined that six officers would be the most that it could place. The Military Personnel Division, Army Service Forces, then directed the Judge Advocate General to procure four officers for assignment to the Third, Fourth, Eighth, and Ninth Service Commands, since they had the largest numbers of Negro troops. But the service commands contended that these assignments would be "impracticable." Two officers were thereupon assigned to posts, one at Camp Claiborne and one at Fort Huachuca. The Army Air Forces was already using one Negro officer as post judge advocate at Tuskegee. The other two field assignments were never made, though a third officer was used when one of the first two was assigned overseas. [48]

Mechanics of Assignment

The policy of block assignments made the assignment of Negro officers no easier. It had been designed to facilitate assignment and to minimize friction between white and Negro officers which was expected to arise if Negro junior officers were sent individually to units which still had white officers in the same or lower grades. As practiced, it produced more serious leadership crises than the inadequate assignment system that it supplemented. The simultaneous removal of all white lieutenants from a unit and the substitution of Ne-

[46] Ltr, Hq AGF to CG AAF, 20 Jan 43; 1st Ind, Hq AAF to CG AGF, 9 Jul 43; 2d Ind, Hq AGF to CG AAF, 16 Jul 43. All in AGF 210.31/449.

[47] Ltr, Civ Aide SW to G–1, 15 Aug 42; D/F, G–1 for CG AGF, 17 Aug 42; M/S, AGF G–1 to CofS, 19 Aug 42; 1st Ind, AGF to G–1, 23 Aug 42. All in AGF 322.999/144.

[48] Ltr, MPD SOS to JAG, 25 Jun 45, SPGAO 322.9 (Gen–25 Jun 45)–41; MS, Distribution of Military Personnel, I, p. 147, in OCMH.

gro officers, most of whom were getting their first experience in command and some of whom might have been waiting for weeks in a pool while the group was being built to a large enough size for block assignment, not only suddenly destroyed on a unit-wide basis the leadership relations between officers and men, but often interrupted training, setting the unit back by several weeks in extreme cases; destroyed whatever *esprit* had been built up among the officers and men of the unit; and forced each element of the organization to alter its entire mode of operation.[49] The resulting letdown in operating efficiency, discipline, and morale was often attributed to deficiencies in the new Negro officers when the method of substituting new—and in these cases quite different—officers for the old, familiar troop leaders, schooled in their knowledge of the men of the unit, and the peculiarities of life for the unit under its particular headquarters and on its particular post, was as often at fault.

To lessen the effect of mass transfers of white officers out and Negro officers into a unit, commanders of armies, corps, and other field units having assignment jurisdiction over units were authorized, in 1943, to direct attachment rather than relief of white officers for a period of from three to six months. The retained white officers were to train the new Negro personnel and help make the transition from one group of officers to the other a smoother and more gradual process.[50] In units, the greatest care and

watchfulness had to be maintained lest the Negro officers become mere assistants to the older white officers, learning little and dissipating what sense of responsibility and initiative as well as military knowledge and self-respect they had brought with them upon assignment to the units. The units, in the meantime, had an excess of officers engaged in duplicate duties. The division of control often affected these units adversely from top to bottom.

As the numbers of Negro officers available began to exceed the numbers of vacancies allotted, and as the numbers of service units authorized Negro officers increased, the 25 percent overage of officers authorized the all-Negro units was extended to include all units with any Negro officers. In Quartermaster truck companies, authorized three lieutenants, the 25 percent overstrength was construed as permitting an additional officer.[51] In some units, the overages went far above 25 percent. Even with this provision, sizable numbers of Negro officers collected in pools. The policy of assigning Negro officers in groups rather than as individual replacements accounted for the presence of the larger number of unassigned Negro officers in organized pools, for assignment directly from schools to units had to be delayed until enough officers were gathered together to fill an entire unit's allotted grades. Pools were expected to hold officers and at the same time enable them

---

[49] Min Gen Council, 12 Jul 43; Ltr, CG Second Army to CG AGF, 19 Feb 43, AGF 210.31/464.

[50] Ltr, CG Second Army to CG AGF, 19 Feb 43, AGF 210.31/464; Ltr, Hq AGF to CG's Armies, IX, XIII, XV Corps, II Armd Corps, AB Comd, Amph TC, AA Comd, DTC, MTC, R&SC, TDC, Chief Armd Force, 24 Feb 43, AGF 210.31/467.

[51] Ltr, OQMG to CG SOS, 13 Aug 42, and Memo, Dir Mil Pers SOS for CG AGF, 19 Aug 42, both in SPGAO/210.3 (8–13–42); D/S, G–1, 21 Aug 42, WDGAP 322.99; D/S, G–3, n.d., WDGCT 291.21 (8–13–42); 1st Ind, TAG to TQMG, 5 Sep 42, AG 210.31 (8–13–42) OA.

to continue their technical training. Special, separate pools for Negro officers were provided at Fort Huachuca and sometimes at the service schools.[52] At other times, Negro officers were simply retained at the schools, awaiting assignment. To await disposition, they were occasionally dispatched to a post, such as Tuskegee, where housing existed and where considerable numbers of other Negro officers were assigned. The pools, gathering and retaining large numbers of newly commissioned, inexperienced officers for whom no assignments existed, became a source not only of low officer morale but also of many of the leadership difficulties experienced later by and with Negro junior officers. Often there were more officers gathered at a given post or center than could be absorbed by available housing or by available training assignments. "This is a situation which tends to breed discontent and to induce a state of mind where minor incidents are exaggerated, and a tendency toward carping criticism developed among officers who are not sufficiently busy to occupy their minds," one training center commander observed of his Negro pool officers.[53]

As a result of the scarcity of authorized position vacancies, plus the tendency to assign and retain white junior officers in Negro units, certain Negro organizations suffered from an excess of officers while others, at the same time, had a shortage.

As early as August 1942, when many other Negro units were reporting officer shortages, the 93d Division was being swamped by the daily arrival of new lieutenants. Housing and messing facilities available to the division at Fort Huachuca could accommodate 636 officers of all grades, but the 93d had 644 lieutenants alone. "Many lieutenants are sleeping two and three in a room in some organizations. . . . The problem of training the increasing number of new arrivals is difficult," the division reported in a request that no more lieutenants be assigned.[54] A year later, when many Negro air base security battalions were disbanded, their 330 white and 238 Negro officers had to be given new assignments. The white officers were divided among RTC units and Second Army field units. The Negro officers, with the exception of 27 men, were divided equally between the 92d and 93d Divisions, with the result that the 93d Division again had a large officer surplus.[55]

Occasionally, schools had no requisitions at all for Negro graduates and authority to assign them had to await War Department decisions.[56] Negro overage and limited service officers, for whom few assignment vacancies in overhead and staff duties existed, contributed numbers of officers to pools.[57] Some of these men were disposed of by assignments to USO liaison, ROTC, and

[52] Ltr, Hq AGF to Hq FA RTC, Ft. Sill, Okla., 24 Feb 43, AGF 210.31 GNRSP; Ltr, OTSG SOS to Dir Tng SOS, 10 Mar 43, AG 210.31 (4 Jan 43) (1); Ltr, R&SC to Hq AGF, 17 Nov 43, AGF 210.31/449.
[53] Ltr, Hq ERTC, Ft. Leonard Wood, Mo., 13 Jul 43, and 1st Ind, Hq Seventh Sv Comd to CofE, 27 Jul 43, OCofE 291.2. See also Ltr, Hq FA RTC, Ft. Sill, Okla., to CG AGF, 15 Jun 43, AGF 210.31/529.

[54] Ltr, CG 93d Inf Div to CG AGF, 11 Aug 42, and 2 Inds, AGF 210.31/1 (93d Inf Div). Some of these officers were intended to serve as cadre for the 92d Division.
[55] M/S, AGF Inf Br G–1 Sec to Off Div AGF, 28 Sep 43, AGF 210.31/576 (1943).
[56] Ltr, OQMG to CG SOS, 26 Jun 42, SPQPO 210.31.
[57] Ltr, TIG to CG R&SC, 22 Jul 43, and 14 Inds, dated to 5 Dec 43, AGF 210.31/545.

special service duties, for which not all so assigned were fitted either by temperament or training. "Made jobs," such as assistant directors of schools, town "liaison" officers, advisers to various staffs or headquarters, roving inspectors, and "special" officers of various types, were sometimes devised for over-age and limited service officers of higher ranks.

The difficulty of assigning them to T/O jobs was obvious to many Negro officers, for often on the same posts where certain Negro units had enough officers to fill nearly every vacancy twice over, there were other units which had either too few officers or which had white officers only. Nearly every supernumerary Negro officer knew or thought he knew of a unit or a job where he could have been used to greater advantage than in the "extra" position in which he found himself. The policy of unloading excess officers into particular units while retaining white officers or allowing T/O vacancies to remain in other units was a major contributing factor in the low morale of Negro junior officers.

Negro Officers' Leadership Dilemma

Restrictions on their activities, even when Negro officers were assigned to positions where their services were needed, were central factors operating to reduce their efficiency and usefulness. The grade, assignment, and promotion policy had been instituted as a means of providing greater opportunities for Negroes to serve as commissioned officers. But the policy by which Negro officers could serve in designated units and grades only, and by which no Negro officer was supposed to outrank or command any white officer in the same units limited these same opportunities. Negro officers considered the entire policy "discriminatory and unjust," General Davis reported. The policy confirmed "a different status for colored officers, [who feel] that, since they are called upon to make the same preparation and sacrifices, the promotion and assignment policy should be the same for all officers." [58] It gave an overt sanction to theories that no Negro, no matter how competent, could perform assigned duties better than any white man, no matter how incompetent. It confirmed in the minds of enlisted men the belief that their Negro commissioned leaders were not full-fledged officers in the first place, thus further confounding leadership problems. It created invidious and ineradicable distinctions between officers in the same units.

At the outset grade restrictions, coupled with the large numbers of over-strength and non-T/O vacancy officers in the same units, effectively blocked promotions. Later, authority to transfer eligible Negro officers to other units where they could fill higher grades was granted. This policy, interpreted as barring promotion unless officers transferred from their units, was "a body blow to their morale and efficiency, as well as to organizational *esprit*," a commanding general of the 93d Division observed. "It also caused a loss of confidence in leadership which was not confined to leadership in the 93d Division. They felt that the War Department had broken faith with them." [59] It gave sanction for the feeling among Negro

[58] Memo, Gen Davis for TIG, 7 Aug 43, AGF 210.31/449, AG 210.31 (4 Jan 43) (1).
[59] Ltr, Maj Gen F. W. Miller to Lt Gen L. J. McNair, 8 Apr 43, AGF 322/1 (93d Div).

officers that development of ingenuity and assumption of responsibility in their units were useless.

The policy, coupled with the social pressures and sanctions of which it was born, was responsible for additional practices which damaged officer morale and the development of good leadership. At Camp Shelby, in 1944, 11 Negro officers were assigned to overhead duties as personnel consultants, 9 with a special training unit, 1 as an assistant special service officer, and 1 as commander of the post's Negro casual detachment. The last two, by approved classification standards, were misassigned from the beginning. The nine had no direct contact with the white enlisted cadre which operated the units. All suggestions and recommendations which they made had to be passed on to the white cadre by a white officer "who is chief personnel consultant despite the fact that in one battalion he is unqualified for the work and in all battalions [he] is junior to the other officers who are his assistants." [60] The Negro officers, when they should have been at their primary duties, had two additional duties to perform: athletic supervision and orientation presentations. No other officers and no cadre men assisted in those duties. The further training and efficiency of these officers were limited by post restrictions. They were not allowed to attend the post-operated school on courts-martial; their quarters, mess, and recreational facilities compared unfavorably with those of white officers of similar rank; their contact with other officers and consequently the possibility

of their learning by example from other officers was sharply curtailed by the oral appointment of one of their number—an officer junior to all but two of the group—as "spokesman." The spokesman was responsible for making all contacts with the headquarters to which these officers were assigned. One battalion commander, when questioned about the propriety of ignoring seniority in these cases, replied that "this was Mississippi and he was not concerned over the seniority of Negro officers." [61] It would hardly be expected that these officers could develop into able leaders.

Mixed Staffs and Their Problems

A major barrier to the development of leadership in Negro units lay in the use of white and Negro officers in the same units under conditions which emphasized differences in officers' origins rather than similarities in their goals and responsibilities. These conditions were reinforced and made official by shifting policies which, having prescribed a differential for the assignment and promotion of Negro officers, proceeded to expand the boundaries of the limitations imposed by providing for the eventual though not guaranteed replacement and transfer of white officers. Therefore neither white nor Negro officers were secure with respect to continued duty, responsibility, or advancement within a given unit. Nor were they secure in their relations with each other. In these units, the leadership of men became secondary to the preservation of personal interests and status.

---

[60] Memo, Tng Inspector for Dir Mil Tng ASF, n.d., but inspection of 4–8 Jun 44, ASW 291.2 Cp Shelby.

[61] *Ibid.*

Mixed staffs had certain advantages. They provided a leaven of experience and some instruction, if by no other means than by example, for newly commissioned officers. They increased the possibility of filling staffs in many units that otherwise would have limped along with officer shortages. Through their commanders, they facilitated co-operation between white and Negro units of similar types which might not have existed otherwise. In those instances where the commanders and higher staff members looked upon the leadership of the unit as a profitable military and not a revolutionary social venture, they afforded the possibility of sufficient contact between white and Negro officers to enable both the unit and the officers to gain benefits from the greater experience, training, and confident stability of the one group as well as from the greater knowledge and understanding of racial problems and practices of the other. The two officer groups in these cases worked together to the mutual benefit of each other and of the unit.

But mixed staffs could have equally marked disadvantages. There were times when the functioning of many mixed staffs appeared to be about to break down completely. While many commanders, through the force of their own personalities and their own high standards of leadership, were able to weld excellent working teams from units with mixed officers, there were others who found themselves caught up in a maelstrom of personal animosities born of and fostered by racial taboos and tensions. At times the split in staff relations, resulting from long standing social customs reinforced by the physical separation of housing, messing, and club facilities and from policies that assigned all white officers to headquarters staff and unit command positions and all Negroes to platoon leader positions, was almost inevitable. At other times, it was clearly preventable. But in either event, the difficulties of these units, rather than the successes of other, and generally smaller, units came to the attention of higher headquarters and caused grave doubts about the wisdom of mixed staffs.

The feeling of white officers that service with Negro troops involved additional and onerous duties was accentuated in many units with mixed staffs. Psychological tensions often appeared on both sides. Neither Negro nor white officers, as a group, either by training or by prior civilian experiences, had learned to work normally and naturally together. The conscientious white officer found the necessity of being constantly on his guard, constantly aware of the new and restricted world of racial discriminations and sensitivities which he had unwittingly, and often unwillingly, entered, an additional burden which he often came to consider hardly worth the bearing. Extra duties, in addition to more intensive and longer training schedules, sometimes fell to the lot of white officers assigned to units with mixed staffs simply because of the presence of Negro officers. At some posts, white officers only could be assigned to such duties as officer of the day, town patrol officer, officer of the guard, post exchange inventory, finance certification officer, or to other routine, rotating duties. Some headquarters, requesting labor or other special details from Negro units, stipulated that the men be in charge of a white officer. The services of white officers on these hardly to be sought for but nevertheless necessary tasks came more frequently, therefore, if they were assigned to a unit whose Negro officers were exempted from duties in which they might encounter "delicate situations." [62] Negro officers, by the same token, felt that they were being ignored or overlooked in the full performance of the duties of an officer. Often they were certain that preferred duties were being denied them. At times they attributed to racial prejudice the distribution of unpleasant duties and extra details within the unit.

One commander, after pointing out that certain duties could not very well be allotted Negro officers, protested that "It has been my policy in the sixteen months I have had this regiment that there shall be no discrimination based on race, color or creed. All officers of the regiment use the same messes, sleeping accommodations, and bath houses. . . . I believe [the] one cause for friction is the mixing of junior white and colored officers." But sensitive duties involving the civilian population and other units were not given to his Negro officers.[63] Other units solved this portion of their problem by requiring both white and Negro officers to perform the same "unpleasant duties without reference to color," applying the same standards to both, and by removing "those who failed to measure up to army standards, regardless of color." [64] When the responsibilities and duties of officers were allotted and shared by Negroes and whites as officers rather than as two varieties of officers, little difficulty arose from this source of friction and better leadership developed.

Housing and messing problems plagued many units without regard to the unit commanders' desire in the matter. In general, the initial Army pattern was to house and mess Negro and white officers separately, though in later years of the war in many units and installations this tended to modify itself to housing and messing by rank, by senior choice, or by priority of arrival. Requests, such as Fort Bragg's for $14,221.70 in April 1942, to provide an additional barracks for Negro officers to "afford equal and separate accommodations for white and colored officers" were not unusual.[65] Providing separate facilities if officers were to be segregated militated against the assignment of Negro officers to units so located that separate housing was not available. Complaints that Negro officers arrived without forewarning at certain posts were often based on the necessity for providing separate facilities in advance.[66] In some instances, one or two Negro officers occupied an entire standard barracks in spacious solitude. In others, the

[62] Hall, "Race Prejudice and Negro-White Relations in the Army," *The American Journal of Sociology*, LII (March, 1947); Memo, Tng Inspector for Dir Mil Tng ASF, n.d., but inspection Jun 44, ASW 291.2 Negro Troops; Ltr, CO Station Hospital, Cp Livingston, La., to TAG, 9 Jun 41, Tab D to Memo, G–1 for CofS, 4 Aug 41, G–1/15640–54; 2d Ind, CO Station Hospital, Cp Livingston, La., 13 May 41, to TAG Ltr, 1 May 41, AG 210.31 ORC (4–29–41) R–A.
[63] 1st Ind, Hq 364th Inf to TAG, 25 Apr 44, OPD 322.97/40.

[64] Hist 100th Ord Bn (Ammo), 4 May 1942–9 May 1945.
[65] Ltr, Hq Ft. Bragg, N.C., to CG Fourth Corps Area, 4 Apr 42, app. 4th Ind, Hq AGF, 22 Apr 42, AGF 600.12/470.
[66] Ltr, Second Army to Hq AGF, 6 Jan 43, and Memo, Hq AGF to Dir Mil Pers SOS, 8 Jan 43, both in AGF 210.31 GNGAP–B (1–6–43).

two or three Negro officers who happened to be assigned permanently to a post's overhead, to a station complement, to a band, or to a quartermaster service or a medical sanitary company, were given a small house, usually removed from the main housing areas of the post, to use as quarters. In still other cases, Negro officers were housed and messed with Negro enlisted men.[67] Chaplains, often the lone Negro officers in a unit or on a post, had especial difficulties with billeting and messing.[68] Payment of membership fees in clubs and messes was at times required by posts which did not expect Negro officers to use these facilities, but practices in various localities varied from the free use of all facilities through the use of designated or agreed upon tables and areas to the use of enlisted men's messes and quarters or none at all. To an early inquiry from Judge Hastie on the Army's position on the use of facilities by Negro officers, G–1 replied:

The Army has always regarded the officers' quarters and the officers' mess as the home and the private dining room of the officers who reside and eat there. They are an entity within a military reservation which has always enjoyed a minimum of regulation and the largest possible measure of self-government. The War Department considers this to be a fundamentally correct conception. Both from the standpoint of practice of long standing and from the standpoint of propriety, the War Department should be most reluctant to impose hard and fast rules for every human

relationship involved in the operation of officers' messes and officers' quarters. For a variety of reasons, problems arising in the officers' home cannot be solved by fiat.[69]

One result was that, in many units, especially the larger ones, little contact, "even for discussion of, and conversation pertaining to, professional subjects" existed among white and Negro officers.[70] In other cases, where rigid lines of demarcation between officers were maintained, the Negro officers became allied with their enlisted men against the white officers, a situation leaving white senior officers with lessened control over their units. At other times white officers were supported by Negro enlisted men against the Negro officers, especially in those cases where Negro officers, assigned in blocks, attempted to assert control in organizations whose higher ranking noncommissioned officers had formerly had carte blanche in the operation and regulation of the "domestic" life of the unit. In neither case could a high state of discipline or of effective training be achieved.[71] As for leadership: under such circumstances, it could hardly exist at all.

The separation of officers by race in the use of facilities remained a stumbling block in the development of officer *esprit* and unified leadership, but the War Department continued its reluctance to invade what it considered to be the sphere of local and unit com-

---

[67] Ltr, Hq Sec I, 2138 AAF Base Unit (8 Negro officers) to TIG, 30 May 44, AAF 250.1 Morals and Conduct, #3; Ltr, Off, Hq 2d Bn 364th Inf, 4 Apr 44, OPD 322.97/140.

[68] Memo, Civ Aide to SW for TAG, 6 Sep 41, and 6 Inds, AG 291.21 (9–6–41) (2); Memo, TIG for Chief of Special Inspection Div OTIG, AG 291.2 (8 Mar 43) (1).

[69] Memo, G–1 for Judge Hastie, 15 Sep 41, AG 291.21 (9–15–41) (1).

[70] Memo, Gen Davis for TIG, 7 Aug 43, AGF 210.31/449.

[71] Hist 100th Ord Bn (Ammo) 4 May 42–9 May 45; AGF M/S, Ground G–1 to Sec, 31 Jul 43, AGF 322/2 (92d Inf Div); 1st Ind, Hq 364th Inf to TAG, 25 Apr 44, to Ltr from Off, Hq Co 2d Bn 364th Inf, APO 980, 4 Apr 44, and statement of —— to CO 364th Inf, 21 Apr 44, OPD 322.97/40.

manders' responsibility. At Fort Huachuca, where colored and white officers of the 93d Division were reported in 1942 to "eat in the same mess, live in the same barracks, serve in the same companies and apparently are striving to the end of making an efficient fighting division," the construction of separate clubs for white and Negro officers was an initial source of friction. General Davis reported to The Inspector General that while the garrison at Huachuca may have been large enough to require two clubs, commanders "could have met the problem without these clubs having been designated as clubs for either white or colored officers." [72] General Davis recommended, with Maj. Gen. Virgil L. Peterson concurring and General Marshall approving, that in large camps where the garrison was predominantly Negro the War Department provide no facilities for the exclusive use of white or Negro personnel "but that the disposition and use of these facilities be left to the decision of the local commanders who are most familiar with the racial problems involved." [73]

While this policy decision removed War Department sanction from the practice of designating facilities by race in the few instances where large camps had predominantly Negro troops, it brought no change in general practices. It merely made it all the more essential that commanders of Negro units be men of more than ordinary wisdom. Some units were able to solve the problems of housing, messing, and club facilities to the complete satisfaction of their staffs; others were in constant turmoil over one or another phase of these purely social matters which, though nonmilitary in a strict sense, affected profoundly the military training and performance of units. They symbolized the lack of trust, faith, and belief in the equality of men which existed within many of these units. There were units which developed their own small messes into clubs for the use of the officers of the unit only. There were others in which unskilled leadership practices in the purely social areas ruined, to a large extent, the efficiency of units long before they reached a port of embarkation. At least one large combat unit spent nearly two years in a wrangle over the status of Negro and white officers culminating in the arrest of over one hundred and the trial of three Negro officers. Thereby, almost without reference to other factors, the unit remained uncommitted to combat at the close of the war. [74]

Despite an obvious desire on the part of higher headquarters not to interfere in these problems, their effect upon units and upon unit leadership rather than questions of efficiency in training or leadership ability in the abstract, were at the core of the difficulties of many Negro units. The result in some areas was that some commanders recommended that the Army return to its

---

[72] Memo, TIG for CofS, 6 Aug 42, AG 333.1 Ft. Huachuca (8–6–42) (1). See below, ch. XII.
[73] Memo cited n. 72.

[74] "Ad Equum Rescribere" ["The Training of Negro Combat Units by the First Air Force"], Hq Air Defense Comd, Mitchel Field, N.Y., History of the First Air Force, Monograph III, May 46, Air Hist Gp, 420.04; Hist 477th Bombardment Gp (Med), all installments and versions, AF Archives; Papers in ASW 291.2 NTC and ASW 291.2 Alpha.

policy of using all white or all Negro officers only in a given unit.[75]

That this was no solution was clear to those who had a larger view of the provision of leadership for Negro troops. In the first place, there were units with mixed officer staffs which were not subjected to internal rancor. Most of the tank, tank destroyer, engineer, and smaller service units had little trouble of this sort. In the second place there were units with all white and all Negro staffs whose problems of leadership were as great as or greater than those with mixed staffs. Moreover, with the bulk of Negro officers newly commissioned and with the general shortage of officers, the use of mixed staffs was the only logical policy to follow. The success of one or another practice in the provision of officers depended primarily upon the officers concerned and, most of all, upon the commanders under whom they served. Those commanders who themselves were willing to make an attempt to erase the causes of internal discord within the units with mixed staffs and who sincerely believed that those causes could be eliminated achieved greater success with mixed staffs. Not enough commanders of this sort were available to guarantee the smooth functioning of most units. Under the circumstances, it was easy to conclude that the mixed staff was an undesirable emergency measure which should have been avoided at all costs.

Men of the Spirit

There was one Negro member of mixed staffs who had traditionally been welcomed as an officer leader of Negro troops. This was the chaplain. To many commanders, the presence of chaplains, required by Mobilization Regulations to be Negro in Negro units, promised an assuaging answer to the more difficult problems of leadership facing them. When officers and men became entangled in the many problems of a racial nature which could affect command in Negro units, the first person to whom the problem was likely to be given was the chaplain. As guardians of the spiritual and moral life of the soldier, with a firm and solid tradition of leadership in Negro community life, chaplains were expected to possess special techniques for developing positive relationships between men and command, and for providing the needed links of understanding upon which sound leadership could be built. They were expected to provide aid in combating the internal stresses often present. Often they did, in the realm of religion and the spirit. But the problems of leadership in Negro units were not always answerable in these terms.

From the earliest period of mobilization, Negro chaplains "of the right sort" had been in demand. "A good chaplain who commands the respect and confidence of the men is invaluable," one commander with experience with Negro troops reported.[76] Said another, in a unit which had no chaplain, "The services of such an officer have long been

[75] 3d Ind, 28 Apr 44, to Ltr, Hq Co 2d Bn 364th Inf, APO 980, Lt Gen S. B. Buckner, Jr., to TAG, OPD 322.97/40. See also 3d Ind, Hq 25th Inf (Col E. M. Yon) to CG 93d Div, 22 Jul 44, on basic Ltr, Hq 28th Rpl Bn and Assignment Sec to CG 93d Div, 12 Jun 44, 93d Div Files 210.1 Reclassification and 210.31 Assignments.

[76] Lt Col James L. Lewis, 93d Engr, Notes on Service with the 93d Engineer Regiment (GS) in Extreme Cold and Wet Climates, Engr School 8715.

needed and can accomplish immeasurable good, if an intelligent, sympathetic and energetic one can be secured." [77] An inspector supported his recommendation that there was an "urgent need" for a Negro chaplain at a special troop headquarters with the statement that "The morale of the enlisted men in the 40th Signal Construction Battalion and the 562d Quartermaster Service Battalion, the units with colored personnel at this station, is very low." [78]

The expectation of many commanders was that Negro chaplains, as many were, would be a helpful link between the command and the troops, interpreting each to the other and smoothing the rougher stretches in the path of leadership. Often the chaplain was the only Negro officer in the unit or in the area. At times he was the only person available with previous experience in interracial matters. Often he was, like the average chaplain of the peacetime Army, not only a spiritual adviser but also a guardian of all morale, with recreation, athletic, and orientation duties to perform.[79] Until late 1941 the chaplain of a Negro regiment was specifically charged with the instruction of soldiers in "the common English branches of education." [80] Usually he was expected to, and often he was

directed to, explain to Negro troops the more difficult problems which arose. One officer, during the course of an investigation, commented: "I don't know whether the men took this matter up with the Chaplain or not but if they did I feel rather disappointed because I feel that the Chaplain could have straightened the matter out." [81]

To enlisted men, the chaplain's relation to leadership was a plain one. Where the chaplain was held in esteem —and this esteem could arise from many approaches to the problems facing him —his influence for good was felt widely. Otherwise, the chaplain had a small congregation, few consultants, and little influence. No instance of serious friction or disorder in a unit whose chaplain had both the ear of command and of enlisted men has been found. Alert and confident chaplains could, and did, prevent physical disturbances at times. Twice on the weekend of 12 July 1942, Chaplain Lorenzo Q. Brown, by promising the full support of the commanding officer, dispersed a potential mob of over five hundred soldiers bent on "rescuing" men of their battalion from the hands of civilian police who had, according to rumor, killed some of them.[82] But, in many units, chaplains were a disappointment to their commanders and, in some cases, to their enlisted men.

---

[77] Ltr, Hq 758th Tk Bn, Cp Hood, Tex., to CG AGF, 30 Mar 43, AGF 210.31/84 (Chaps).

[78] Ltr, Hq 16th Detachment Special Trps, Second Army, Cp Tyson to CG Second Army, 19 Nov 43, AGF 210.31/84 (Chaps).

[79] In the 20 February 1941 AR 60–5 the chaplain was specifically exempted from detail to these duties. Post exchange duties, courts-martial, defense counsel duties, and the proscriptions of the Geneva conventions only had been listed as outside the chaplain's duties in the 1937 version of this regulation.

[80] Dropped from the November 1941 revision of AR 60–5.

[81] Rpt of Investigation of Conditions at Ft. Clark, Texas, conducted by Lt Col Lamar Tooze, IGD, Asst IG Hq Third Army, 23–28 Jul 43, 2d Cav Div 333, filed with 9th Armd Div Files.

[82] On Monday, the missing "dead" men were presented to the assembled battalion by the chaplain and battalion commander. Cleveland *Call and Post,* August 1, 1942; Ltr, CofCh to Dean William Stuart Nelson, Howard University, 18 Jan 44, SPCHI 211 NC.

Sometimes, chaplains became as enmeshed in unit quandaries as other Negro officers and men. As one chaplain, neither a Negro nor working with Negro troops and therefore meeting the dilemma faced by many Negro chaplains in a less extreme form, expressed it: "The army measured a chaplain's success in terms of the degree to which he expedited army discipline; but the men judged him on his ability to unbend that discipline." [83] The Negro chaplain often found that, in the process of laying the groundwork for better discipline and morale, he had already alienated either his men or his superiors, with the result that he could effectively influence neither.

Despite vigorous efforts pursued throughout the duration of the war, the Army never obtained a large enough number of Negro chaplains to be able to determine what their fullest effect might have been had enough been readily available. In addition to the three Negro chaplains in the Regular Army in 1940, there were seventeen in the Reserve Corps, of whom three were on active duty with the Civilian Conservation Corps. [84] The normal distribution of chaplains was one to every 1,200 officers and enlisted men (1944 standard), with chaplains divided between units and bases or higher headquarters. Chaplains were authorized, denominationally, from among the major church bodies in proportion to their representation in the census of religious bodies. [85]

Negro denominations were given their population-based quotas along with all other denominations that represented considerable portions of the nation's church membership. Negro ministers of predominantly white denominations were represented proportionately to their numbers and availability within their denominations. Many of the Negro units of battalion size were just under the strength of 900 required for a unit chaplain and were therefore authorized none. Some services attempted to acquire special authorizations for chaplains for such units. [86] But the Office of the Chief of Chaplains was making valiant attempts to supply the ministers needed under current authorizations. Few chaplains from among those available could be spared to provide for special requests.

In December 1940 teachers of religion and directors of religious life in 25 Negro colleges and in 8 Negro and 11 primarily white theological seminaries were requested to submit the names of promising Negro candidates for the Army chaplaincy. [87] Thereafter, speakers at assemblies of clergymen continued to emphasize the need for chaplains and to urge qualified Negro ministers to apply for Army commissions. In the main, however, even when the constant upward readjustment of the quotas for chaplains as the size of the Army grew is taken into account, the supply of available Negro chaplains always fell considerably short of the goal. There were corresponding shortages of white chap-

[83] Morris N. Kertzer, *With an H on My Dog Tag* (New York: Behrman House, 1947) , p. 11.

[84] Ltr, OCofCh to Inez M. Cavert, Federal Council of the Churches of Christ in America, 10 Jun 40, CofCh 211 Negro Chaps.

[85] The 1916 census was used. The 1936 census, published in 1939, was substituted in May 1945.

[86] Ltr, Hq AA Comd to CG AGF, 26 Jun 43, and 1st Ind, Hq AGF to CG AA Comd, 12 Aug 43, AGF 210.31/1 (Chaps).

[87] Ltr, OCofCh to Schools and Colleges, 30 Dec 40, OCofCh 211 Negro Chaps.

lains in many denominations, but among Negro chaplains the shortage was general in all denominations.

For 1943, the existing Negro units were expected to require 455 chaplains. Of these, 445 were allotted to the Negro denominations and to the Methodist Church. It was hoped that Negro ministers of other denominations would supplement these quotas. With the 1943 estimate before them, the Negro churches had the following goals in mid-January: [88]

Denomination	1943 Quota	On Duty	Shortage
National Baptist (U.S.A. 159; America, 18)	177	48	129
African Methodist Episcopal	93	32	61
Methodist (Central Jurisdiction)	69	25	44
African Methodist Episcopal Zion	55	6	49
Colored Methodist Episcopal	51	5	46
	445	116	329

The shortage of chaplains was seriously felt in some units. None of the divisions could obtain, initially, their full quotas of chaplains. Training units at replacement centers were sometimes entirely without them. Units often lost their chaplains to higher priority units preparing for shipment overseas. The shortage was such that, sometimes, white chaplains were assigned to Negro units as a temporary expedient, though a few were assigned

because the Office of the Chief of Chaplains had not been informed that the unit was Negro.[89] On posts with units too small to be authorized Negro chaplains and on posts where the bulk population of Negroes was too small to require the services of a station chaplain, Negro troops were usually ministered to by white chaplains. At times, white chaplains disappointedly reported that they had had little success in attracting Negro troops to chapel services. One chaplain, believing that the fault lay with the available choice of music in the *Army-Navy Hymnal,* suggested that Negro troops be supplied with a special hymnal of spirituals.[90] Sometimes Negro civilian pastors from nearby towns offered their services, but the practice of using these volunteers was not favored by most commanders.

One result of the shortage of chaplains was the acceptance of a number of individuals who had less than superior qualifications. Of the chaplains sent to the Chaplain School, few failed to graduate. But those who did fail were sent to the field anyway; they were already commissioned and chaplains were scarce. Many of those failing in the school were Negroes; many, but not all, of the disappointing performances in the field came from men who had failed their courses at the school for chaplains.[91] A number were marginal

---

[88] Ltrs, CofCh to Bishop R. R. Wright, Jr., and others, 23 Jan 43, SPCHP 210.1 (1–23–43). The Central Jurisdiction embraced most of the Negro membership of the predominantly white united Methodist Church. The other church bodies with specific quotas were independent Negro denominations.

[89] Ltr, Pers Off CofCh to Port Chaplain, Hampton Roads PofE, 14 Dec 42, and Ltr, OCofCh to Chaplain Edgar F. Siegfriedt, Cp Claiborne, La., 10 Mar 43, both in OCofCh 211 Negro Chaps; Ltr, Pers Off CofCh (Chaplain John F. Monahan) for Corps Chaplain XVIII Corps, 15 Feb 44, SPCHP 210.4 XVIII Corps (10 Feb 44).

[90] See corresp in OCofCh 080 SPCHS Cong-Christian, 21 Sep 42, 28 Sep 42, 3 Oct 42.

[91] MS, OCofCh, Hist of Mil Tng, Supplement, pp. 7–8, in OCMH.

ministers from the beginning. Some of these helped to undermine the reputation of Negro chaplains, and, by extension, of Negro officers and leadership as a whole both among commanders and among enlisted men. In one army camp in the space of three months one of the two Negro chaplains misused funds entrusted to his keeping by enlisted men while on maneuvers; the other became notorious among the troops after persuading the wife of an enlisted man to remain behind after the departure of her husband's unit. Bad check charges and marital difficulties plagued some. Another resigned for the good of the service as a chronic alcoholic. Cases such as these were not common, nor were they confined to Negro chaplains. But they occurred frequently enough among Negro chaplains to lessen the influence of all Negro chaplains in some areas and to make the jobs of sounder chaplains more difficult both with soldiers and with their commanders.

Negro chaplains divided sharply over the issue of the precedence of their responsibilities to their men as soldiers and Negroes and to their calling as ministers and as officers. Their general influence upon enlisted men, barring unusual circumstances, was unquestioned. As the only available Negro officers in many commands, demands upon them by their men and by the Negroes of neighboring units and communities were often beyond those normally made upon men of their calling. As chaplains they were the recipients of grievances and complaints without limit. Many of these were rooted in the beliefs and fears of soldiers as Negroes. Chaplains skilled in human and interracial relations were able to

deal judiciously with problems of this sort that came to their attention; many were able to alter and influence patterns of racially based behavior for the better. Others were unable to steer a clear path between the importunings of their men and the official duties which they had undertaken. Some withdrew from active concern in the problems of men and commands. Still other chaplains, seeing a sufficiency of injustices about them, undertook the unflinching defense of all men in all cases, the guilty with the innocent. One such case, rather widely circulated among War Department staff agencies as part of an interview with a provost marshal returning from overseas, was that of a chaplain in Australia who "worked hard to defend 'a pore colored boy' who had killed two white officers in cold blood." [92] While many had a stabilizing effect on units, others did not. In many commands, chaplains therefore became suspect as bearers of discord, contributing to, rather than alleviating, leadership problems.[93]

Even when these chaplains were morally right, their lack of tact in the difficult area in which they had to operate created additional morale strains within the units whose men they had hoped to help. By late 1943, a number of chaplains, sometimes to the accompaniment of considerable publicity in

---

[92] ASF Interim Rpt to ASF Staff Divs and ASW, 26 Aug 44, SPINT R–575.
[93] See, for example: Memo, G–3 for G–1, 10 Sep 41, G–3/42659, and G–1 Memo for Record, 22 Sep 41, G–1/15640–114; Tel Conv, R&SC with OCofCh, 26 Jul 43, OCofCh 211 NC, I; Statement for Record and Memo, both 29 Dec 42, Chaplains Rpts, and 333 Investigation, 93d Div Files; Memo, TIG for Chief Special Inspection Div OTIG, AG 291.21 (8 Mar 43) (1).

the Negro press, had resigned by request, been reclassified, or tried by courts-martial and dismissed from the service. A few of these sought—and those who sought it received—a sympathetic reception among the Negro public, for they were viewed as the vigorous champions of the downtrodden carrying forward the great traditions of their churches. But they left in their wake commanders and supervising chaplains who viewed their successors with suspicion as potential sources of disruptions; they left behind them enlisted men whose faith in the Army and their officer leaders was further weakened.

Publicity resulting from the release of certain of these chaplains, added to general press comments on racial relations within the Army, further hampered the recruiting program of the Chief of Chaplains. After a conference with representatives of the National Baptist Convention, U.S.A., the largest Negro church body and the church with the fourth largest chaplains' quota and with the smallest portion of its quota filled, the Chief of Chaplains decided that, until the urgent need for Negro chaplains was met, consideration would be given to applicants with two or more years of college or seminary work and three years of pastoral experience in lieu of the ordinarily required bachelor's degree, provided that other requirements were met.[94] This was the only case where different standards were pre-scribed for Negro commissioned personnel.

One answer to this proposal was quickly forthcoming. At their convention in Kansas City in September 1943, the National Baptists, contrary to the expectations of the conferees, were presented with a resolution that the convention would "refrain from further endorsement of members of our Denomination to serve as Chaplains in the United States Army" so long as bias in the treatment of chaplains resulting in "the public humiliation of outstanding members of the Baptist Clergy [through] tacit agreement of the Chief of Chaplains, the Chaplain's office, and the War Department" continued.[95] While all chaplains were volunteers, no chaplain could be accepted by the Army without denominational endorsement.

The developing attitude among Negro clergymen represented by this resolution was reinforced the next year when the Fraternal Council of Negro Churches in America issued a manifesto which placed revisions in the armed forces' racial policy at the top of its list of desired reforms.[96] The inability of a number of Negro ministers to meet even the lowered standards, plus many clergymen's disbelief that they could give full service in the armed forces, permitted the shortage of chaplains to grow larger. In mid-July 1943, just before standards were lowered, the total number of Negro chaplains on duty was 246.[97] Their number hovered around

---

[94] Ltrs, CofCh to Representatives, National Baptist Convention USA, 30 Jul 43, SPCHC 080 Nat Bapt USA (23 Jul 43) ; Ltr, OCofCh to Chaplain Albert Percy Smith, 97th Engr Bn, 17 Sep 43, OCofCh 211 Negro Chaps; Ltr, OCofCh to Reverend Willard M. Wickizer, Ex-Secy Com on War Svs, Indianapolis, Ind., 21 Jul 43, SPCHP 080 Disciples of Christ (21 Jul 43) .

[95] CofCh 080, National Baptist USA, vol. I.

[96] The manifesto was reprinted in full in *Congressional Record*, September 14, 1944, p. A 4255.

[97] Ltrs, CofCh to Representatives National Baptist Convention USA, 30 Jul 43, SPCHC 080 National Baptist USA (23 Jul 43) .

this figure for the rest of the war. On 31 August 1944 there were slightly fewer, 238, while on 31 July 1945 the total number of Negro chaplains on duty was 259.[98] Quotas, in the meantime, rose as total Army strength rose. At the end of the war, the Negro denominations were still far below their quotas. As of 19 October 1945, when the Chaplain's Corps was at approximately its conclusion of hostilities strength, the Negro denominations had the following quotas and chaplains on duty: [99]

Church	Quota	Chaplains on Duty
National Baptist (U.S.A. and America)	612	79
African Methodist Episcopal	77	69
African Methodist Episcopal Zion	62	18
Colored Methodist Episcopal	39	8
	790	174

Even if they had all been able to affect positively the problems of leadership and morale, Negro chaplains remained to the end of the war too few in number to exert to the fullest the influence expected of them.

"Weeding Out": Rotation and Reclassification

Gradually, a general malaise, destructive to morale and therefore to leadership potentialities, settled upon a great many officers serving with Negro troops. Many white officers felt that they were "figuratively sitting on kegs of powder." Though they would try to carry out the desires of the War Department they felt that they were "sunk" in their assignments. Many Negro officers became convinced that they were the victims of discriminatory practices which prevented the fullest development of their capabilities.[100] That few white officers would choose to serve with Negro troops became a generally accepted belief. That few Negro officers were capable and efficient was as widely believed.[101]

To help dispel the belief that service with Negro troops was a blind alley, The Inspector General recommended in 1943 that rotation of white officers on duty with Negro troops be considered.[102] Rotation was not to be mandatory, for though it was obvious that the majority preferred service with white troops, some officers had stated that they preferred duty with Negro troops. The commanding general of the 93d Division agreed that such a plan would be helpful in his division.[103] "While assignments in War cannot be based on individual preferences," Headquarters,

---

[98] Strength of the Army, 6 Oct 44, 6 Sep 45, STM-30.

[99] The quota for all chaplains was 8,500; 7,584 were on duty on this date. In this tabulation Negro chaplains of the Central Jurisdiction of the Methodist Church as well as Negro chaplains of other primarily white denominations were included in the figures for their parent churches. On 31 October 1945 the total number of Negro chaplains, including those of primarily white denominations, was 201. Statistics compiled from MS history, CofCh, Military History of the Second World War:

The Corps of Chaplains, pp. 21–22, in OCMH and Strength of the Army, 14 Dec 45, STM-30.

[100] Memo, WD for TIG, 13 Oct 43, AGF 210.31/592.

[101] Memo, Col Leonard for ASW, 3 Oct 44, ASW 291.2; McNair-Miller Corresp, extracts in AGF 322/1 (93d Div); papers in AG 291.2 (23 May 42), Participation of Negro Trps in Post-War Mil Establishment.

[102] Memo, WD for TIG, 13 Oct 43, AGF 210.31/592.

[103] Memo, Hq 93d Inf Div for CG CAMA, n.d., Incl to Ltr, CG IV Corps to G-1 AGF, AGF 210.31/592.

Army Ground Forces, wrote to its field commanders, "it is believed reasonable that, so far as practicable, service with colored troops should be rotated." [104]

The procedure worked out by the Ground Forces was that commanders of Negro divisions and separate units would report to the appropriate higher commander not to exceed 5 percent of the total number of white officers, distributed approximately by grades, who had had eighteen months of continuous service with colored troops, did not desire further service with them, and had an efficiency rating of very satisfactory or better. Higher commanders would then reassign these officers to white units, provided that replacements for them were available. General officers and regimental commanders were to be rotated by Headquarters, Army Ground Forces. The rotation policy was to be published to higher commanders only.[105]

The belief that rotation of officers was a solution to the problem of dissatisfaction among white officers assigned to Negro units persisted throughout the war. That rotation ran directly counter to the provision that successful commanders be kept with Negro units; that it would contribute further to the rapid turnover of officers in Negro units about which so many inspectors had complained; and that, without a backlog of excellent leaders to draw on for replacements, rotation was impractical as a device for guaranteeing effective leadership did not dim its chimerical appeal. Though it did not work in practice, as evidenced by the number of negative

reports submitted by commanders, it was nevertheless accepted by officers in high and low ranks as the next best thing to no service with Negro troops at all.[106]

No similar hope of relief was available to those Negro officers who felt that they had served long enough against odds in specific units. Requests for transfer sometimes came from Negro officers in batches, but since there were few opportunities for transfer, most of these could not be honored. Requests for transfer were often a prelude to reclassification for both Negro and white officers, especially in the larger units, for they called attention to the dissatisfaction and to the resulting unsatisfactory work of officers. Even when units sought to alleviate pressures on officers in an attempt to help their adjustment and improve their leadership abilities reclassification sometimes proved the only possible answer.

One white junior officer, after progressively demonstrating his inability to adjust to service with Negro troops, was removed from duty with troops and given special headquarters duties, but there he spent most of his time looking up regulations and circulars and writing letters trying to arrange a transfer. Eventually he informed his regimental commander that he would have to get away from serving with Negro troops even if he brought court-martial charges against himself. He was finally sent before a reclassification board. There he appeared with affidavits from other officers which declared that most of them

---

[104]Ltr, Hq AGF to CG's Armies, Corps, Comds, CAMA, TDC, 31 Dec 43, AGF 210.31/592 (31 Dec 43) GNGAP.
[105] Ibid.

[106] AG and SF Redistribution "Sound-Off" Reports Files, TID (I&E) Div; Ltr, CG USAFIL to TAG, 18 Oct 43, OPD 320.2 Liberia, sec. 1; Ltrs in 92d Div 210.3 Transfer of Officers.

felt the same way that he did. But who would operate the unit if every officer were transferred? the board wanted to know. This particular officer, the board decided had gone so far in placing his personal dislikes above the demands of duty that he was recommended for discharge from the service.[107]

Successive transfers in some instances caused a discontinuity in command which had its effects upon unit training and discipline. One company of divisional special troops had seven commanders and nearly as many first sergeants in two years, while the division itself had five divisional staff officers in the same technical service during the same period. When the latest company commander requested relief because "an attempt was made on my life by a shot being fired thru my tent and into my bunk, thru my mosquito bar a bare few inches from my pillow" with the result that he could "never again have any faith in the company as a Company Commander should have because of a constant fear of some unknown person possibly waiting to try again," the request was disapproved. "If every time an officer gets in a tough spot and asks to transfer," the division's chief of staff observed, "we won't get far. I can understand how he feels, I can understand that there may be for a time a degree of lack of interest and lack of confidence on his part. However, if he is any good, and I know he is, and will apply himself to his task, he will make good."

---

[107] Unless otherwise indicated, the information and specific examples in this and succeeding paragraphs of this section were derived from unit files which are unidentified in order to preserve the anonymity of the individuals concerned.

Three successive special staff officers occupying the same position were reclassified in the same division. The first was recommended for relief "as being unsuited for duty with a colored unit." His successor was reclassified a year later upon his determination that he could no longer handle a situation which showed no sign of improving:

When I first came to this Division I was not prejudiced against the colored race and had high hopes of accomplishing a great deal. I have worked hard and faithfully and felt that I had succeeded to some extent. However, in the past few months, incidents have occurred which indicate that the feeling was an illusion. Not only have I been unable to eradicate race prejudice as a basis for the many difficulties encountered but I have found it most difficult to work with this command. I have twice been called disloyal by the Chief of Staff and once by the Commanding General because I have had the courage to express my views concerning morale in this Division.

The recent episode with the ——— Company, in which a definite planned attempt to discredit the Battalion Commander and to cause him to be relieved, has destroyed all hope I ever had to accomplish anything here. I was told that we, the whites, are all plotting to discredit the negroes, that they do not trust any white officer. They feel that their Battalion should have all Negro officers as another white officer would merely be a repetition of the previous ones. I so lost control of myself that I told several negro officers in the ——— Company that, where I had not been prejudiced before, I was now definitely prejudiced.

I find that I am definitely turning into a Psychoneurotic. I have been unable to sleep, complain of various aches and pains which have no organic basis. This morning while in conference with the Commanding General . . ., concerning the ——— Battalion situation, I broke down with hysterical weeping for over an hour. This is an indication of my mental state, which does not differ from that of a number of other officers on the staff. I know that I am not psychiatric material and a change of environment will clear these symptoms up. I feel that I have a lot of excellent service left in my system but if I am forced to remain with this Division I shall end up a liability to the government. I believe someone else, with a fresh point of view, could handle the job with greater efficiency.

This officer, according to his commanding general, had performed in an excellent manner; therefore, the division recommended his transfer to any except another Negro unit. But, lacking a proper vacancy for him, higher headquarters recommended reclassification. By this time, his successor was already being reclassified because he did not have "the knack or ability to handle negroes."

Sometimes, desired transfers and reclassifications were not achieved. Two regimental commanders in one division in training were listed for relief or transfer, although one had been previously recommended for promotion to general officer rank. One was recommended for transfer because of age and the other because of lack of "the mental and physical energy" needed to command effectively. At the same time, special troop commanders and special staff officers were recommended for removal from the division. But the approach of maneuvers caused a reconsideration since "any change if made at this late time would probably be more detrimental than helpful." One of the two regimental commanders remained with the division until the end of the war.

In a separate battalion, reclassification of several officers was recommended. The commander was "totally out of sympathy with Negro troops and grossly ignorant of what was required of a Battalion Commander." The executive officer was considered "a type who is unfit to command, one whose idea of efficiency is to have an inspection of polished shoes at midnight and for identification tags at 3 o'clock in the morning and to give mass company punishment by requiring soldiers to march from midnight to 8 A.M." A lieutenant was judged unfit to command troops because of his use of improper language and because of a "generally abusive attitude," though, it was added, he appeared to have had considerable provocation. A fourth officer had kicked and stoned a soldier who had been "most disobedient and discourteous to him, which actions however, could not excuse the officer's action." [108] But in this case, by the time recommendations had reached headquarters and then been reopened by direction of the assistant to the Deputy Chief of Staff, the unit was overseas. With the determination that it would be "impracticable" to return the officers to the states, reprimands only were sent them.[109]

Reclassification procedures for Negro officers in the divisions usually began with assignment to divisional officers' schools. Upon reports of progress in the schools depended the disposition made of the officer student. These schools, originally designed to improve leadership and technical qualifications, soon came to be looked upon as a means of weeding out unwanted officers, especially since usually only Negro officers

---

[108] R&RS, The Air Inspector to Secy Air Staff, 1 Nov 43, AAF 250.1, binder 3.
[109] R&RS and drafts of reprimands, AAF 250.1 Misc.

were assigned to them. Some were frank in stating their opinions of the schools. Said one officer: "On being assigned to the Division Officers School I was called in by the Regimental Commander, who made it clear that I was being sent to school not because of inefficiency, but because of my attitude toward the policies of the Regiment as to Negro officers." Said another: "Completely ignoring my several ratings of 'excellent' and no ratings of unsatisfactory, I was ordered to the Division school to prove my efficiency, causing me greater humiliation."

The reclassification of Negro officers was usually supported by statements of their lack of ability, aggressiveness, or interest, supplemented by statements of their race consciousness and sensitivity. A number of officers disputed these charges, declaring that they were being reclassified, subjected to psychiatric examination, or punished for showing resentment to discriminatory practices. When men already slated for reclassification replied with charges of discrimination, their accusations usually reinforced the original charges of lack of co-operation and development of prejudices against superior white officers. But, at times, officers who had previously been considered exemplary leaders surprised commanders by submitting requests for relief or resignation phrased in similar terms. One, from an officer whose commander disapproved the request "in view of the excellent record of this officer in his organization, and the spirit and thoroughness by which his duties are performed," began:

By my own admission, I can no longer willingly and cooperatively discharge the duties of an officer as I have done faithfully and cheerfully during more than two years of service in a commissioned status. A proper regard for the opinions of all concerned demands that with clarity and forthrightness I set forth the causes which do now propel this course of action.

a. I am unable to adjust myself to the handicap of being a Negro Officer in the United States Army. Realizing that minorities are always at odds for consideration commensurate with the privileges enjoyed by the greater number, I have tried earnestly to find this expected lack of equality, and nothing more, in the relationships and situations around me here. Prolonged observation reveals that inconsistencies over and above a reasonable amount are rampant. Sins of omission, sins of commission, humiliations, insults—injustices, all, are mounted one upon another until one's zest is chilled and spirit broken.

b. In my opinion there is mutual distrust between the two groups of officers. As a result of this, it is my belief, nowhere is there wholehearted cooperation or unity of purpose. Prejudice has bred a counterprejudice so that now neither faction can nor will see without distortion. In garrison the situation is grave; in the field where one's life and success of mission are dependent upon that cooperation and unity, disastrous.

c. Being exposed to this atmosphere for so long a time, I have not remained unchanged; to deny this would be dishonest. For so long have I endured the frustration and mental torture of being ostracized from, discriminated against, discredited, that my resentment has become an insurmountable barrier against my sense of duty. Whereas I was once fired with ambition and zeal to do a necessary job willingly, I now find myself with the willingness no longer. Enthusiasm has given way to apathy; ambition, to a sense of futility. . . . Feeling as I do, a sense of fairness to myself, to those who command me, and most important, to those who must serve under me directs that I can but offer my resignation.

When this officer learned that his request had aroused indignation at battalion and regimental headquarters and that reclassification proceedings would be instituted instead, he tried to withdraw his resignation. The regimental commander, though admitting that he had previously thought him an excellent officer, proceeded to certify him a "failure" because of "1. Prejudice against white officers" and "2. Inability to adjust himself willingly and conscientiously cooperate with those in authority." Supporting statements, including those of the regimental and battalion commanders, indicated that though he was a willing officer performing in an excellent manner, it had been noticed that he had developed "a shiftiness" in his eyes and a tendency to "wincing" which indicated insolence, untrustworthiness, deceit, and distrust. Only the company commander continued to hold that this was an excellent officer, though he added that since the officer had admitted that he could no longer discharge his duties well, his services to the company would be unsatisfactory.

Most cases of reclassification were clear-cut. The officers concerned had deteriorated week by week and most knew that reclassification was being considered. Headquarters often reported that they were engaged in weeding out unsatisfactory officers. With white officers, recommendations might be made for retention in the service for duty anywhere except with Negro troops, but with Negro officers the recommendation was usually for separation from the service. Even then, while papers were forwarded and returned, officers awaiting reclassification remained in their units where others, to

their own discomfiture and concern, soon learned of the scheduled event. White officers, in many instances, could be placed on detached or special duty in headquarters during this waiting period, with the result that Negro officers in some units felt that they alone bore the brunt of reclassifications.

The attempt to improve leadership by transferring and reclassifying unsatisfactory officers therefore became enmeshed in the same racial problem that ensnared officer leaders in other areas, particularly in promotions and assignments. The commander of a regiment with 150 officers, one hundred of them Negroes and fifty white, explained:

. . . The officer being reclassified, either white or colored, thinks he is getting a raw deal. This sentiment is largely shared by his friends and acquaintances. When four cases are pending at one time, as there are at present in this regiment, the reaction in morale amongst officers of the unit is particularly noticeable. Once the officers being reclassified depart the atmosphere will gradually clear and officer morale will get back on even keel.

. . . Where white and colored officers are mixed, particularly in companies, two psychological complexes are present, both equally false. Almost every white officer, no matter how mediocre he is in ability, feels that he is superior to the colored officer. In this connection it must be borne in mind that officers of company grade are young, and have not attained the tolerance and fair judgment towards other races which may be found in older and more experienced officers. The colored officer, no matter how capable, is quick to interpret any criticism, correction or punishment given by white officers as racial discrimination. The same is true when the colored officer does not obtain a promotion or assignment he desired. These two complexes create an abnormal situation peculiar not only to this regiment but to the division as a whole. Almost without exception every assignment or promotion in company grades and sometimes field grades is believed by one or the other group to have an ulterior motive connected therewith.

The company commander, in particular, has a most difficult task to live in harmony with and maintain unity and efficiency amongst his officers, particularly if he has the courage to weed out the unfit. In some instances, rather than rate a junior officer "unsatisfactory" on his 66–1, commanders have given a "satisfactory" purely to avoid the charge of discrimination that invariably accompanies such an action. When questioned, the company commander admits that the officer has not been performing satisfactorily but he has hopes that the officer will improve. The undersigned has ordered reclassification proceedings to be initiated in many cases and has informed the officer in question that his reclassification was being directed, —all this to avoid criticism and charges of discrimination being directed at the battalion or company commander concerned.

Little was, or perhaps could, be done about these developing strains on leadership until matters had gone too far for correction by any other means. On the surface, intra-unit relations often appeared to be smooth, but the "undercurrent of racial antipathies, mistrusts and preconceived prejudices" in some units made an unhealthy situation from the beginning.[110] Administrative and troop leadership talents of both Negro and white officers were often expended in the defense of real and imagined personal prerogatives which had little to do with leadership and nothing to do with a concerted military effort. Despite the efforts of higher commanders, the

development of leadership for troops who could use the very best available often bogged down in areas where it had no business pausing for the briefest halt.

Unending Quest

Leadership for Negro troops was thus lost in a welter by the physical necessity of assigning all white, all Negro, or both white and Negro officers to Negro units and by the policies governing these assignments. That all officers for Negro units would have to come into frequent contact with other officers, Negro and white, from nearby units under the same command or headquarters and that all officers assigned to Negro units would have to adjust to service with Negro enlisted men was axiomatic. But that all officers assigned to Negro units, as a first step in the development of their leadership potentialities when on duty with Negro troops, had to be able to accept with equanimity any and all of the problems and petty frictions which might arise out of these necessities was barely understood. When it was, obtaining the required paragons of interracial dexterity was difficult.

Leadership of the type normally associated with well-functioning units, though it did exist, was rarer among Negro units than elsewhere in the Army. With the rapid turnover of officers, the temperamental clashes between officers and troops, the friction between Negro and white officers, the frequent regular and special inspections from higher and adjacent headquarters, the constant striving for results apparently not to be forthcoming, and the lack of firm, positive leadership on the points at issue, this could hardly have been otherwise.

---

[110] Pers Ltr, Lt Col Marcus H. Ray, 600th FA Bn, APO 92, to Truman K. Gibson, 14 May 45, copy in OPD 322.97 III.

Leadership principles in many units were forgotten while officers pondered their own fates. Many white officers were filled with a feeling of defeat and discouragement over their own inglorious assignments to troops in whom they had no confidence and about whom their white associates, when they did not completely ignore their existence, were frankly sceptical. Many Negro officers were filled with resentment toward the social matrix in which they were caught and which confined them to subordinate positions where they felt that they were neither fully officers nor enlisted men but uniformed symbols, doomed to receive at best a grudging acceptance as officers from their superiors and only a token recognition as leaders from their subordinates. Neither group, as a whole, concentrated upon its major problem: the leadership of men.

The provision of leadership in Negro units became, therefore, as difficult a problem as any that the War Department faced in the employment of Negro troops. Men who had in sufficient measure General McNarney's prescribed "common sense" simply could not be found in quantities large enough to supply Negro units with the leaders whom they so desperately needed.

CHAPTER IX

Units: Men and Training

Housing, camp sites, units, and officers were all prior necessities to the main task in the mobilization of Negro manpower: the induction and training of soldiers for employment in war. Private soldiers and noncommissioned officers were the final key to that employment. Upon their capabilities, qualifications, and adaptability depended, in the last analysis, the performance of the units, the effectiveness of the leadership of their commissioned and noncommissioned officers, and the effectiveness of the training facilities provided by the Army.

Army planners had counted on advances between wars in the civilian training and experience of Negroes to make feasible the provision of a greater number of types of Negro units than those activated in the first months of mobilization. But differences in Selective Service rejection rates, in Army test scores, and in the training progress of Negroes as a whole when compared with whites as a whole soon revealed a general lag between Negro registrants of draft age and the rest of the country. To construct and employ, on the same master plan, separate but parallel units in all arms and services with one of the two parallel groups of units recruited entirely from a relatively unprepared portion of the population barely susceptible to the selection and classification procedures applied to the rest of the Army was a difficult task at best. This task was made more difficult not only by the selection and employment policies of the Army, but also by widespread variations and deficiencies within the Negro population. These variations and deficiencies began to show up early. They created problems in the employment of Negro manpower both early and late.

Standards and Inductions

In World War II, Negroes were accepted for military service at a consistently and continuously lower rate than whites. As of 30 September 1941, when the number of Negroes classified in the immediately available class (I–A) by Selective Service was 13.1 percent of the total in that class, and therefore higher than the approximately 10.7 percent proportion of Negroes among those registered, the number of Negroes in Class IV–F (rejected by Selective Service) showed an even greater disproportion. Of men rejected as a result of physical examination, 12 percent were Negroes; of men rejected for obvious physical or mental disabilities without physical examination, 15.8 percent were Negroes; and of men rejected because of any other reason without physical examination, including failure to meet minimum educational requirements, 35.6 percent were Negroes.[1] Of the registrants classified between 15 May and 15 September 1941, 1.1 percent of the whites, or 60,001 were deferred for educational deficiency, while 12.3 percent of the Negroes, or 83,466 were so deferred.[2] By the end of 1943, of all white men examined at induction stations, 30.3 percent had been rejected, but of all Negro men examined 46 percent had been rejected. During 1943, over half of the Negroes examined at induction stations (432,086 out of 814,-604) were rejected as compared with 33.2 percent of the whites examined.[3] The number of Negroes classified for limited service only was also excessive in comparison with the number of whites so classified.[4] The higher proportion of Negroes available in I–A in the earlier months of mobilization reflected the smaller numbers of men deferred in essential categories rather than a higher percentage of physically and mentally fit men.

Of the Negroes rejected, the largest numbers fell into two classes: venereal disease cases and the educationally deficient.[5] Of the two, educational deficiency was by far the more important manpower problem, since facilities for relatively rapid treatment of venereal diseases were known. Once cured, the venereals ceased to be a problem, except in cases of reinfection after induction where duty time was lost. Moreover, after March 1943, when facilities for rapid cures became generally available, most venereals became eligible for induction. But the cure for educational deficiency, while also known, was a long, slow, corrective process whose end result could not be predicted. The best that could be expected in a short period of time was to raise men to a "functionally literate" level. This, of course, was "education" in a highly limited sense.

The Army itself was not directly concerned with rejected Negroes. Since they were not subject to Army training, they became part of the problem of over-all use of national manpower as surveyed and controlled by the War Manpower Commission. But the state of affairs symbolized by the high rejection rates of Negroes was, nevertheless, of the greatest significance to the military use of Negro manpower. It meant that, in manpower calculations, the number of Negroes in the age group eligible for service who could meet initial Army standards fell short of expectations. Therefore the ability of the Negro population to share fully in the defense of the nation was limited from the beginning by disadvantages to which Negroes were subject in their civilian lives.[6] It meant, further, that of those Negroes inducted into the Army, a large proportion would be men who barely crossed the line of acceptability by Army standards. For the same circumstances which caused so large a number of rejections left a large group of men who barely met the minimum in-

[1] Selective Service in Peacetime, First Report of the Director of Selective Service, 1940–1941 (Washington, 1942), pp. 254–55.

[2] Ibid., app. 29, p. 401.

[3] Selective Service as the Tide of War Turns: Third Report of the Director of Selective Service, 1943–1944 (Washington, 1945), pp. 559, 615, 627.

[4] Ibid., p. 206.

[5] Ibid., pp. 207, 629. For whites, the largest number was rejected for mental disease.

[6] Martin D. Jenkins et al., The Black and White of Rejections for Military Service (Montgomery, Ala.: American Teachers Association, 1944).

duction requirements. This heavy weighting of Negro personnel toward the lower end of the acceptable scale became apparent in the first year of mobilization. As induction standards changed, the problem posed by the qualifications of Negro inductees was intensified. Each change in standards meant subsequent administrative changes for the reception and absorption of Negro soldiers.

During the first few months of mobilization, no definite mental or educational standards for induction were prescribed. Mobilization Regulations merely required that no registrant who had previously been discharged from the Regular Army, Navy, or Marine Corps because of inaptness or who could not "understand simple orders given in the English language" would be inducted.[7]

In the spring of 1941 the Personnel Division urged that standards be raised to reduce the numbers who could not readily absorb instruction so that more of the nation's men of higher abilities could receive the benefits of a year's training. G–1 was aware that the largest reduction of low grade men resulting from any upward revision of standards would come in the Fourth and Eighth—the Southern—Corps Areas and that a new standard would serve to reduce the numbers of Negroes eligible for the Army. Such a reduction was not considered too serious, since as yet neither housing nor units in sufficient numbers were available for Negroes. Nevertheless, a "hostile public reaction" might come from the South. G–1

therefore suggested that any test applied be a simple one which local boards could give. Accordingly, beginning 15 May 1941, the ability to read, write, and compute "as commonly prescribed in the fourth grade in grammar school" became the standard for induction. Those men who had not completed the fourth grade were eligible for induction only upon passing the Minimum Literacy Test prescribed by the War Department.[8] This standard remained in effect until 1 August 1942, when the Army began to accept illiterates in numbers not to exceed 10 percent of all white and 10 percent of all Negro registrants accepted in any one day.[9]

Classification Tests

Once inducted, the selectee received additional tests and classification interviews at reception centers. The chief test on which classification was based was the Army General Classification Test (AGCT). This test, given generally from March 1941 on, had been devised to help the Army sort soldiers according to their ability to learn. It was designed to separate the fast learners from the slow.[10]

---

[7] MR 1–7, Reception of Selective Service Men, Change 2, 3 Nov 40. In effect from November 1940 to 15 May 1941.

[8] Memo, G–1 for CofS, 31 Mar 41, AG 381 (11–3–37) (1) sec. 1–7–a; MR 1–7, Reception of Selective Service Men, Change 9, 18 Apr 41; Roy K. Davenport and Felix Kampschroer, Personnel Utilization: Classification and Assignment of Military Personnel in the Army of the United States During World War II, pp. 81–82, MS OCMH.

[9] WD Cir 169, sec. IV, 1 Jun 42.

[10] Walter V. Bingham, "The Army Personnel Classification System," The Annals of the American Academy of Political and Social Science, CCXX (March, 1942), 21; Walter V. Bingham, in Ambrose Caliver, ed., Post War Education of Negroes; Educational Implications of Army Data and Experiences of Negro Veterans and War Workers (Washington: Federal Security Agency, U.S. Office of Education, 1945), p. 25.

The AGC test contained three kinds of tasks: first, "verbal items of increasing difficulty, sampling the person's grasp of the meaning of words and their differences; second, items involving solution of arithmetical problems and mathematical computations; third, items requiring ability to visualize and think about relationships of things in space." [11] It attempted to measure the effects of at least four elements influencing the rate of learning: (1) native capacity, (2) schooling and educational opportunities, (3) socioeconomic status, and (4) cultural background.[12] That it measured native intelligence alone or completely, Dr. Walter V. Bingham, Chief Psychologist of the Classification and Replacement Branch of The Adjutant General's Office, denied:

It does not measure merely inherent mental capacity. Performance in such a test reflects very definitely the educational opportunities the individual has had and the way in which these opportunities have been grasped and utilized. Educational opportunities do not mean schools merely. Learning goes on about the home, on the playground, at work, when one reads a newspaper, listens to a radio, or sees a movie. There is nothing in the title of the Army test that says anything about native intelligence. It is a classification test. Its purpose is to classify soldiers into categories according to how ready they are to pick up soldiering—how likely they are to learn easily the facts, skills, and techniques necessary for carrying out Army duties.[13]

In three of the elements whose effects

were measured, Negroes as a whole entered the Army with grave deficiencies. School facilities for Negro inductees had been measured and found to be inadequate by general standards.[14] The effect of playgrounds, newspapers, radios, and motion pictures as a part of their learning process could only be estimated, but it was known that in many communities with large Negro populations one or more of these influences upon learning was missing from the backgrounds of most Negro inductees. The socioeconomic status of Negroes the country over was generally lower than that of the rest of the population, and the general cultural background of Negroes was lower still. Native capacity, unexercised and untried, had also faced many impediments to development in civilian life.

The Army was not primarily interested in native capacity or in cultural background but in the working ability that the inductee had attained and in the promise of future development in a short time which that level of ability indicated. On the AGCT, the most rapid learners—those making scores of 130 or above—were ranked at the top in Grade I and the slowest learners—those making scores of 69 or below—were placed in Grade V. With 100 as the average, the AGCT was designed to obtain scores that would reflect a normal distribution curve, as follows: Grade I, 7 percent; Grade II, 24 percent; Grade III, 38 percent; Grade IV, 24 percent; and Grade V, 7 percent.

These grades had broad and general usefulness to classification and assignment. Grades I, II, and III were ex-

---

[11] Bingham, in *Post War Education of Negroes*, p. 25.

[12] Roy K. Davenport, "Implications of Military Selection and Classification in Relation to Universal Military Training," *Journal of Negro Education*, XV (Fall, 1946), 590.

[13] Bingham, in *Post War Education of Negroes*, p. 25.

[14] See files, *Journal of Negro Education, passim;* Jenkins *et al., op. cit.*

pected to produce leadership for the Army, with officer candidates coming wholly from Grades I and II—from men with scores of 110 and over. Grades I, II, and III were also expected to furnish the Army's enlisted specialists and technicians. The lower grades could be expected to produce only semiskilled soldiers and laborers.

Seldom did a given unit's distribution work out in the expected ratios. But the average unit and the Army as a whole were not too far from the predicted figures. On the other hand Negro inductees, out of whom units of all types were to be constructed, fell almost wholly in the two lowest classes. From the beginning, therefore, the tests had special significance in the organization and training of Negro units.

While Negroes generally ranked lower on the AGCT than whites, Negroes and whites of comparable backgrounds made comparable scores. High scorers among Negroes learned as rapidly as·high scorers among whites, provided that motivation, surroundings, and instruction were of the same quality. That there were fewer Negroes with average backgrounds measured in terms of educational and vocational experiences was not the fault of the tests. That there would be fewer high scorers among Negroes per hundred than among whites was expected. How great a disparity existed was fully demonstrated after the first months of testing. (*Table 5*)

In addition to the General Classification Test the Army also gave newly inducted men a Mechanical Aptitude Test. While both Negroes and whites, in general, scored lower on the Mechanical Aptitude Test than on the AGCT, here the racial disparities between the highest and lowest classes were, as would be expected from an examination of the vocational opportunities and experiences of Negroes, even more marked. (*Table 6*)

Scores and Units

While the percentages of illiterate and low-scoring Negroes were much higher on both tests than among whites, their numbers were no greater. The problem created centered therefore not around the numbers of low-scoring men to be absorbed by the Army (for the total percentage in each grade, as shown in the totals columns of Tables 5 and 6, was not markedly affected by the inclusion of Negroes) but around the high percentages to be absorbed in specific, separate units. Because of the biracial organization of the Army, this problem became immeasurably greater among Negro than among white units. The 351,951 (8.5 percent) white AGCT Grade V men inducted between March 1941 and December 1942 could be distributed among the total of 4,129,259 white men received, while the 216,664 (49.2 percent) Negro men received in the same period—135,000 men fewer—could be distributed only among the total of 440,162 Negro men received. Low-scoring white men could be distributed as fillers to existing white units and installations containing men who had already had varying amounts of training. The further progress of these units and installations was not seriously hampered by the addition of relatively small numbers of slow learners. The cushion of trained Negro men already in units in early 1941 was small. The few Negro units were therefore much less able to absorb slow learners. The mechanical

TABLE 5—DISTRIBUTION OF ARMY GENERAL CLASSIFICATION TEST SCORES
MARCH 1941–DECEMBER 1942

AGCT Grade	White		Negro		Total	
	No.	Percent	No.	Percent	No.	Percent
Total.............	4,129,259	100.0	440,162	100.0	4,569,421	100.0
I...........................	273,626	6.6	1,580	0.4	275,206	6.0
II..........................	1,154,700	28.0	14,891	3.4	1,169,591	25.6
III.........................	1,327,164	32.1	54,302	12.3	1,381,466	30.2
IV..........................	1,021,818	24.8	152,725	34.7	1,174,543	25.7
V...........................	351,951	8.5	216,664	49.2	568,615	12.5
Percentage.................	....	90.4	....	9.6	....	100.0

Source: Tab A, Memo, G–3 for CofS, 10 Apr 43, AG 201.6 (19 Mar 43) (1).

aptitude problem was an even greater one within units. For example, the mechanical aptitude distribution of 2,136 Negro soldiers arriving at Camp Gordon Johnston for training in the fall of 1943 as amphibian truck drivers was:

MAT Grade	Percentage
I	0.4
II	1.5
III	10.2
IV	31.1
V	56.8

The skills of these men were comparably underdeveloped:[15]

Job	Required	Available	Shortage
Mechanic, auto....	156	39	117
Repairman, auto body.......	72	4	68
Welder, combination.....	36	9	27
Amphibian truck driver.....	1,188	365	823

[15] Mil Tng Div OCofTC, Transportation Corps History—Training of Units, Feb 45, p. 48, MS OCMH.

Although illiterate and unskilled men were an Army-wide problem, the average white unit could expect to receive, in the normal course of events, a few illiterate and low-scoring men, while the average Negro unit could be equally certain of receiving up to half of its men in the unskilled, illiterate, and Grade V classifications.

With or without classification tests as verifying evidence of the poorer civilian backgrounds of Negro inductees, the training of units formed primarily from men from the lower economic and cultural strata of American life would have presented difficulties. But the tests and test scores had a negative as well as a positive aspect in the classification and training of Negro enlisted men. Since the bulk of Negroes fell in the two lowest classes, their scores served as a psychological barrier to effective training. Officers and training headquarters, expecting a normal spread of classification and aptitude grades, tended to assume that any other distribution was fatal to success in training. To officers and

TABLE 6—MECHANICAL APTITUDE TEST SCORE DISTRIBUTIONS FOR MEN PROCESSED AT RECEPTION CENTERS, SEPTEMBER–DECEMBER 1942

Grade	White		Negro		Total	
	No.	Percent	No.	Percent	No.	Percent
Total...............	1,800,413	100.0	180,863	100.0	1,981,276	100.0
I......................	72,224	4.0	223	0.1	72,447	3.7
II.....................	343,178	19.1	2,682	1.5	345,860	17.5
III....................	623,968	34.6	14,579	8.1	638,547	32.2
IV....................	494,305	27.5	44,836	24.8	339,141	27.2
V.....................	266,738	14.8	118,543	65.5	385,281	19.4

Source: Tab A, Memo, G–3 for CofS, 10 Apr 43, AG 201.6 (19 Mar 43) (1).

training supervisors, the low cross-sectional scores of Negro units became portents of inevitable training failure about which little could be done. Furthermore, although the psychologists who developed the tests insisted that their results should not be equated with a measurement of absolute intelligence, the nonpsychologists who made up the bulk of the Army users of the tests early and consistently referred to AGCT scores as indexes of intelligence. If the tests measured the ease with which a civilian could learn to be a soldier, why wasn't it a test of intelligence? If white soldiers consistently rated higher than Negro soldiers in their AGCT scores why was not the conclusion that Negro soldiers were of inferior intelligence justified? Granted that a background of poor educational and cultural opportunities produced low scores, was this not evidence that poor background stunted mental growth and thereby produced poor intelligence? The tests themselves, with their results coldly recorded in finite figures, therefore became a hazard to effective training.

The Army's psychologists, while warning against the use of AGCT scores as "intelligence" indexes, neglected to add a warning against comparing scores of men from two different groups whose backgrounds and prior experiences were not parallel. For tests to show comparable aptitudes, both groups should have had relatively the same familiarity with the language and concepts used; formal schooling should have been comparable, not only in grades available and completed but also in the content and quality of the courses; motivation and rapport with testers should have been about the same.[16] In most of these respects, Negro and white troops taking the same AGC test differed. Even if the tests had been designed to take into consideration the cultural and economic backgrounds of the two groups of soldiers, methods of administering the tests would probably have prevented obtaining truly comparable scores. And if the administrative circumstances could have been kept identical, the two groups

[16] Otto Klineberg, *Race Differences* (New York: Harper and Brothers, 1935), pp. 152–77.

tested still could not be compared absolutely on the basis of the original tests, for they had been standardized with the mid-point of the scale at "the central tendency of the distribution of scores made by the adult white male population of military age." [17]

Unfavorable AGCT distributions prevalent among Negro troops were used in some arms and services to justify restrictive practices in the employment of Negro manpower.[18] They provided a ready explanation in resisting public pressures for the wider use of Negro troops.[19] Preoccupation with AGCT scores reached such a point in some units and training centers that attempts at

effective classification and training were virtually abandoned.

Unit after unit complained formally of the poor "intelligence" distribution of the men it was receiving. Many of the complaints, in the light of expected distributions, seemed justified, especially when combined with the numbers of illiterates received in some units.[20] Several of the larger Negro units, formed before the initial restrictions on the induction of illiterates were made in May 1941, judged themselves to be severely handicapped in terms of the new standards. The 367th Infantry, the new Negro Regular Army regiment activated in March 1941, requested permission to discharge 815 illiterates whom it would not have received under the new standards. The Third Army, in forwarding this request to the War Department, observed that its 46th Field Artillery Brigade and 93d Engineer Battalion were no better off, and recommended that the illiterates from these Negro units be transferred to service organizations. The War Department approved the transfers "when and if new Colored units of a labor type" became available.[21]

But, since Negro units of all types were being made available at a rate barely able to absorb incoming selectees, units which began with an overload of substandard men were generally unable

<hr>

[17] Walter V. Bingham, "Personnel Classification Testing in the Army," *Science,* C (September 29, 1944), 276. In later standardizations, Negro samples were included.

[18] In arguing against the use of medical sanitary company personnel in general hospitals as originally planned, the Medical Department, for example, wrote:

It cannot be expected that individuals with such degrees of intelligence as manifested in the Army General Classification Tests . . . can be entrusted with the care of the sick or trained to perform the more technical functions incident thereto. This is in keeping with the study submitted by G–3 which states that at the present time it has been found necessary to recommend the demobilization of certain colored units because of low intelligence. . . . It is not expected that such people should be used in the care of the sick, except for those very few who may be employed in the care of the sick of their own race at those places where colored medical service has been established.

Memo, OSG (Brig Gen Albert G. Love) for Col James Wharton (G–1), 5 May 41, SGO 291.2 (Negro Pers).

[19] Memo, Maj Claude B. Ferenbaugh for Maj Gen [Wade H.] Haislip, 29 Apr 41, and covering note, Maj Bowman for ASWA Lovett, ASWA 291.21 (4–29–41); Memo, G–3 for CofS, 3 Dec 41, and Memo, G–3 for Col [W. B.] Smith, SGS, 4 Dec 41, G–3/6541–Gen; Ltr, William H. Hastie, Civ Aide to SW, n.d., OCS/20602–219; Memo, DCofS for USW, 16 Feb 42, ASW 291.2 Race.

[20] The term "illiterate" was used by units to refer to low-literates as well as to completely illiterate men. At times it included all Grade V scorers as well. "Illiterate," as used by units to describe their men, was therefore a flexible term, meaning generally men who could not read with facility or understanding, as well as the completely unlettered men.

[21] Ltr, Hq 367th Inf Regt, Cp Claiborne, La., 2 May 41, to CG Third Army, and 3 Inds, AG 350.5 (5–23–41) (1).

TABLE 7—ARMY GENERAL CLASSIFICATION TEST SCORES OF ENLISTED PERSONNEL,
46TH FIELD ARTILLERY BRIGADE, CAMP LIVINGSTON, ALABAMA
30 APRIL 1942

Unit	Grade I		Grade II		Grade III		Grade IV		Grade V		Total
	No.	Percent	No.	Percent	No.	Percent	No.	Percent	No.	Percent	
	2	.023	117	2.6	495	13.8	1,053	25.6	3,615	57.8	5,282
Hq Btry 46th FA Brigade.........	0	0	10	8.0	36	29	37	30	42	33	125
350th FA Band....	0	0	0	0.0	5	20	11	44	9	36	25
350th FA..........	0	0	32	2.3	125	9	296	22	933	68	1,386
351st FA..........	0	0	32	2.0	148	10	278	20	1,034	69	1,492
353d FA..........	2	.14	26	2.0	118	8	256	18	996	71	1,398
846th TD Bn......	0	0	17	2.0	63	7	175	20	601	70	856

Source: Incl 1, Ltr, Hq IV Army Corps, OTIG, Cp Beauregard, La., to CG IV Army Corps, 15 Jun 42, AGF 333.1/13 (IV Army Corps). [Tables corrected.]

to exchange them with other units. The 46th Field Artillery Brigade, cited by the Third Army, still had an unfavorable distribution of Army General Classification Test scores at the end of April a year later. (*Table 7*) The Inspector General now recommended that a portion of the Grade V men in this unit be replaced by men in higher grades. The IV Army Corps thought that at least a thousand of the unit's 3,651 Grade V men should be transferred from the brigade. But the brigade was authorized to transfer 250 men only. They were to go to two new ordnance ammunition companies. The ordnance companies were to supply the brigade with replacements from among the best men whom they received as fillers.[22]

Problems of score and skills distribu-

tions plagued Negro units continuously. The Armored Force, having received excessive numbers of low-scoring Negro fillers, asked in 1942 that reception centers be required to send physically qualified Negroes with scores not lower than Grade IV to Negro tank battalions.[23] The 1st Airbase Security Training Group reported in 1943 that in a four-month period it had received 4,600 "unculled" fillers for ten battalions. Of these, 91 percent were in Grades IV and V with over 50 percent in Grade V. The 9 percent remaining were not enough to provide the necessary noncommissioned officers and specialists for ten battalions.[24] One antiaircraft battalion protested in 1942 that the unsatisfactory state of its records disclosed by an

[22] 3d and 4th Inds to Ltr, Hq IV Army Corps to CG IV Army Corps, 15 Jun 42, AGF 333.1/13 (IV Army Corps).

[23] Ltr, Hq Armd Force to CG AGF, 20 Aug 42, AGF 322.999/125.

[24] Ltr, CO 1st Air Base Security Tng Gp, Cp Rucker, Ala., to CG Second Army, 20 Mar 43, AGF 327.3/459.

inspection was caused by the lack of adequate clerks. Of the ten battery clerks and assistants, three were in AGCT Grade III, six in Grade IV, and one in Grade V. They were incompetent and showed little interest in improving their efficiency. "These clerks are fully aware of the improbability of disration [reduction in rank], owing to a dearth of suitable intelligent replacements," an inspector reported. The situation in this unit was soon to be aggravated by the loss of a battalion cadre and of men entering officer candidate schools.[25]

Complaints about the receipt of excessive numbers of low-scoring and unskilled men were usually answered with a reference to the generally poor AGCT and experiential distribution among Negro selectees. Preferential standards, the War Department explained, could not be established while most other Negro units had equally unfavorable distributions. In some instances, as in the case of the antiaircraft battalion mentioned above, the total percentages of Negroes in Grades I, II, and III in the units and training centers of the requesting branch were higher than similar percentages for the Army as a whole. In these cases commands were told to search their service units for men qualified for more technical jobs.[26]

Screening Proposals

Various types of screening programs to provide men having higher scores for selected units were suggested from time to time but these presented practical difficulties which generally prevented their use.[27] In the first place, all units required a measure of higher-scoring men to provide a necessary minimum of capable noncommissioned officers. The suggestion had been made that such service units as port battalions might solve this problem by using white noncommissioned officers and Negro laborers, thus releasing qualified Negro administrative and leadership personnel to tactical units. The morale problem created by any proposal which denied the possibility of advancement within their own units to Negro enlisted men was considered well-nigh insurmountable.[28] Nevertheless, this proposal for the use of white noncommissioned officers, especially as it related to service units, continued to crop up from time to time.[29]

Nowhere was the poor distribution of high-scoring men felt so keenly as in the Negro divisions. The distribution in each division was always heaviest in the lowest AGCT grades. Despite several attempts to correct the divisional situation, no workable means of doing so was discovered. Despite the fact that large numbers of inapt men had been cleared from the 93d Division during its training period, regiments of the division arrived

---

[25] Ltr, TIG Cp Stewart, Ga., to CG AAATC Cp Stewart, Ga., 5 Dec 42, and 3d Ind, Hq AA Comd, AG 220.31 (12–5–42) OC–T (1–16–43).

[26] 6th Ind, TAG to AGF (Hq AA Comd), 16 Jan 43, to Ltr, TIG Cp Stewart, Ga., to CG AAATC Cp Stewart, 5 Dec 42, AG 220.31 (12–5–42) OC–T (1–16–43).

[27] 1st Ind, Office of Civ Aide to SW, 2 Jul 42, to G–3, on Memo, G–3 for Judge Hastie, 29 Jun 42, WDGCT 220.3 (5–9–42).

[28] Citing this reason, Brig. Gen. John C. H. Lee, then commanding the new San Francisco Port of Embarkation, requested that if port units assigned there were to be Negro, noncommissioned officers should also be Negro. Memo for Colonel [Orlando] Ward, 13 May 41, sub: Tel Call from General Lee, PofE, San Francisco, AG 320.2 (5–13–41) (1).

[29] Memo, G–3 for CG's ASF, AGF, AAF, 23 Mar 43, WDGCT 291.21 (3–23–43).

overseas with AGCT distributions which normally would have been considered prohibitive of effectiveness.[30]

Before its formal activation, the 92d Division attempted to obtain a more favorable distribution of skills and ability than would be expected from a random shipment of fillers. The division argued that its units at Fort McClellan, Alabama, could expect to receive a large percentage of their fillers from the Fourth Service Command. These fillers would not meet the requirements of a division. It requested a special schedule instead, with reception centers supplying men according to requirement rates for each type of unit. The War Department approved a special schedule, based not on the likelihood of obtaining high-scoring men but on the basis of past proportions of Negroes furnished by each service command.[31] While the headquarters and special troops units received a disproportionately high percentage of men from the Second and Fifth Service Commands— over three-fourths of all the men received by the division came from these

Northern areas—the division's regimental combat teams were left to absorb an equally disproportionate number of men from the Southern Fourth and Eighth Service Commands. If the purpose had been to provide the division with a true cross-section of the nation's Negro manpower, such a schedule would have been adequate; if it was to guarantee a higher percentage of high-scoring and skilled men such a schedule could not have been successful. For, as with Negro troops as a whole, the fillers for the 92d came in largest numbers from the areas that had previously furnished not only the largest percentages of men but also the largest proportions of low-scoring men.

In the spring of 1943, G-3 proposed that all of the 7,000 Grade V men then in the 92d Division in excess of 10 percent be screened out and replaced by higher-scoring men. The Grade V soldiers could be used in new quartermaster service battalions and similar units, under noncommissioned officers especially selected for the purpose. Men from replacement training centers could provide enlisted leadership for the division's new personnel. On further study it developed that, in order to obtain 7,000 replacements with higher scores, it would be necessary to induct and screen 12,500 men, of whom 5,500, based on past induction experiences, would be Grade V's. These low-scoring men added to the original 7,000 taken from the division would comprise 12,500 men —almost enough for another division— to be placed in other units. There were not enough unactivated units in the troop basis to absorb this many Grade V men at once, nor was there a source from which their "selected" non-

---

[30] The AGCT distribution of the 369th Infantry, the one all-new non-Regular regiment in the division, on 1 September 1944 was, for example:

Grade	Number of Men	Percentage
Total.................	3,010	100.00
I..................	4	0.13
II.................	80	2.62
III................	319	10.60
IV................	1,290	42.85
V.................	1,317	43.80

Hist Rpt, 369th Inf Regt, Supplementary Papers, AGO 393-70.4 (21783).

[31] Memo, AGF G-1 for AGO Classification and Replacement Branch, 11 Aug 42, AGF 322.999/1 (Cld Trps) (R).

commissioned officers, who would have to be obtained over and above the 12,500 figure, could be obtained. Moreover, the replacement center men whom the Ground Forces had originally hoped to use as selected noncommissioned officers for the 92d Division were, during the period of discussion, already dispersed to other units. To embark on another projected induction and training plan to obtain sufficient high scorers to provide noncoms for 12,500 Grade V's, increased by the number of additional low scorers it would be necessary to induct in order to obtain the required high-scoring noncoms for the original 12,500, looked like mounting a permanent treadmill. Moreover, Army Service Forces protested the proposal because of the effect which it would have on future service units. Army Ground Forces therefore recommended that the plan be dropped.[32]

Screening proposals for units of less than divisional size might fail for reasons other than that of the sheer numbers involved. The time needed to arrive at a decision and the then current location of the unit might affect plans adversely. The 76th Coast Artillery (AA), one of the pair of antiaircraft regiments activated in August 1940 and therefore one of the oldest of the new Negro units in the Army, had, in March 1941, the following AGCT distribution among its new selectees: AGCT Grade I, none; II, 2; III, 28; IV, 124; V, 385; illiterate, 351; unclassified, 7; total, 897. According to basic classification theory, this group of selectees should have been able

to produce only thirty noncommissioned officers at best. Of these, only two would have been eligible for OCS consideration. This unit, like others, complained of the poor material sent it but, receiving no other, proceeded to do the best that it could. In May 1942, when the regiment had completed the major part of its training and was tactically disposed in the Eastern Defense Command, a representative of the Second Corps Area Engineer answered the unit's call to check its malfunctioning searchlights. He reported:

The condition of their lights is directly traceable to a lack of preventive maintenance and maladjustment of the equipment through ignorance and inaptitude of the operating personnel. The non-commissioned officers, as well as the men of lower grades are, in general, lacking in the qualifications necessary for the successful operation of a Searchlight Battery. They do not have sufficient capacity for understanding and mechanical instinct is lacking. Inspection of equipment indicated that even the simplest adjustments and operations were not being correctly performed, even though the men had been told repeatedly how to do them. The non-commissioned officers cannot be trusted to do any of the second echelon work without continuous officer supervision, which is impossible with the myriad of other duties officers must perform in the course of a normal day.

Men of the caliber of those in this regiment, the Engineer concluded, should not have been assigned to operate such "delicate and expensive" equipment.[33] This single paragraph contains the basic elements of most complaints about the quality of Negro enlisted men and its effect on units.

---

[32] Memo, G–3 for CG AGF, 5 Mar 43, WDGCT 291.21 (1–14–43); G–3 Rpt, Min Advisory Com on Negro Trp Policies, 22 Mar 43, ASW 291.2–Com; Min Gen Council, 15 Mar 43.

[33] Ltr, Engr Hq Second Corps Area to CofE, 9 May 42, in AGF 353/1 (CAC Tng).

The report on the 76th Coast Artillery received serious attention from several agencies but none thought that much could be done about the unit so long as it continued with its existing low-scoring personnel. Like the analysis, suggested methods for improvement contained the basic elements of most correctives advanced to meet such complaints. The antiaircraft command concluded that the unit's main problem was that "colored soldiers lack the mechanical interest and capacity for understanding searchlight operation and maintenance," since few had had mechanical or technical experience in civilian life. It predicted that other Negro antiaircraft regiments awaiting activation would be no better off, and suggested that it was a mistake to man such units with Negro personnel in the first place.[34] Army Ground Forces thought that similar conditions prevailed in other Negro units of this type, but envisioning no hope of stopping the activation of additional Negro antiaircraft regiments, proposed extending their training time.[35] Judge Hastie felt that these were dangerous generalizations and assumptions based on incomplete data; such generalizations were often cited and acted upon long after surrounding circumstances were forgotten. He suggested that evaluations of the 369th Antiaircraft, which had a higher caliber of enlisted men and noncommissioned officers, and of the 99th and 100th Regiments, might produce different conclusions about the suitability of Negroes for antiaircraft employment. Judge Hastie agreed that the

men of the unit under study were not of the best quality, but the blame lay, he felt, with faulty classification and assignment procedures. He had seen the regiment's first contingent of men shortly after they arrived. They "were mostly young men from the rural south, many of them illiterates at loose ends in the community, who had volunteered or had been called for induction at the top of the Selective Service list." Reception centers, Hastie continued, had made no effort to select men particularly fitted for antiaircraft work. As a result, the 76th's men were below the average of Negro soldiers, including those in service organizations. Hastie recommended mass transfers of higher-scoring men from service organizations to combat units where they would be of more value. The large induction centers near industrial and urban areas should be authorized to send to the 76th Coast Artillery 50 or 100 men with high AGCT scores.[36]

These remedies—elimination of unit types, extending training periods, transferring substandard men, and preferential selection for combat units—were to be suggested frequently in 1942 and 1943. At times these suggestions had overtones of the post-World War I suggestions that Negro troops be divided into a few elite combat and a mass of service units. In most cases, as in this case, nothing happened. By the time discussion of the 76th Coast Artillery was concluded, the summer was half over. The unit had left the Eastern Defense Command and was already over-

[34] 2d Ind, Hq AAC to Hq AGF, 4 Jun 42, 470.3/K, to Ltr cited n. 33.
[35] 3d Ind, Hq AGF to TAG, AGF 322.17/2 (76th CA) GNOPN, to Ltr cited n. 33.
[36] 1st Ind, OCA to SW, 2 Jul 42, to G-3 on Memo, G-3 for Judge Hastie, 29 Jun 42, WDGCT 220.3 (5-9-42).

seas.[37] G–3 hoped that in the future units under the defense commands could be given refresher training that would obviate difficulties such as those affecting the 76th Coast Artillery. Significantly, this was the only indication by a commenting agency or echelon that a part of the remedy might be found outside the area of the unit's AGCT distribution. Later, after the urgency of coastal defense had passed, the problem of retraining or converting other units, white and Negro, assigned to defense commands, became an important one.

Only in the Air Forces were screening techniques for Negro technical and combat units both possible and effective. The Air Forces, having stated at the outset that it doubted the possibility of finding enough Negroes to fill the required skilled positions in air combat and technical units, proceeded on the assumption that initial screening was even more vital to its Negro than to its white units. It was better able to follow through on its screening processes than either the ground or the service forces. It had fewer combat and technical units in proportion to the numbers of Negroes in the command. Highly qualified men could be transferred or diverted from its large proportion of service units, most of which, like the aviation squadrons, required few specialists. The greater attractiveness of the Air Corps as a branch of service and the opportunities to volunteer for service with this branch caused a larger number of more highly qualified Negroes to attempt to get into the Air Forces either through the aviation cadet boards or

through volunteering for specific units. As a result of the limited flying training program for Negroes, the Air Forces had a reserve supply of highly qualified aviation cadets rejected in single-engine flying training who, until 1943 when some became available for transfer to the Field Artillery for liaison pilot training, were ineligible for any other type of flying training and who, therefore, could be assigned to the combat or technical units activated at Tuskegee as needed enlisted men. Tuskegee itself was a miniature replacement depot, able to transfer men to units where they could be more readily utilized. Moreover, the Air Forces had virtually complete control over the internal distribution of selectees to its units.

Plans for the original Negro air units called for men with particular skills and ratings. The original 97 Negro selectees for the Air Corps, for example, were drawn from a much larger number of men already in units. They fitted required specification serial numbers.[38] The 276 recruits for the first Air Corps unit—the men who, with the 97 selectees, were later to be assigned to the 99th Fighter Squadron—were drawn from volunteer 3-year enlistment applicants coming from all over the country. Besides meeting general Air Corps enlistment standards, they had to pass the examination for the Air Corps Technical School prior to being enlisted. At the time, approximately 50 percent of all white Air Corps enlistees failed to qualify for further training in technical schools. The examination requirement not only assured the new Negro unit a higher quality of enlisted cadre from the

---

[37] Memo, G–3 for Judge Hastie, 8 Aug 42, WDGCT 220.3 (5–9–42).

[38] Ltr, OCofAC to TAG, 18 Mar 41, AG 324.71 (3–12–41).

99TH FIGHTER SQUADRON TRAINEES *sending and receiving code at Tuskegee.   The instructor was formerly in the 39th Coast Artillery Antiaircraft Brigade.*

beginning, but it also enabled the Air Corps to avoid enlisting 550 or more Negro 3-year volunteers to obtain 276 qualified men.[39]

For other technical units the Air Forces followed similar initial screening methods.   For its 689th Signal Reporting Company, Aircraft Warning, Frontier, scheduled for task force use by 1 September 1942, the Air Forces had only

[39] Memo, G–1 for TAG, 4 Mar 41, G–1/15640–75.

one officer and three enlisted men on 15 May 1942.   The Signal Corps, at the time, was producing neither Negro officers at its OCS nor enlisted men at its RTC's.   The Air Forces therefore arranged with The Adjutant General's Office that out of the first week's quota of Negro selectees received in June 1942, 96 men, all high school graduates or better and all in the top three AGCT grades, would be earmarked for the

689th. It was willing to take five Negro officers with "some" radio or communications experience wherever it could find them.[40] From this group it proceeded to build a unit which was highly regarded throughout its career.

As a result, Air Forces Negro technical and combat units were generally, in AGCT scores and technically qualified men, closer to normal than other Negro units.[41] Where proficient specialists were not available for these units, men of higher potentialities learned the duties of forecaster, armorer, or mechanic about as rapidly as white men of equivalent scores, among whom there were also many with little experience in the newer fields in which there was a huge national shortage of trained men. The Air Forces also used reverse screening at times, with training centers requesting low-scoring men, white or Negro, in exchange for potential specialists.[42]

Contributing to the failure of plans to guarantee higher-scoring men to specific Negro units was the disbelief of certain staff and command agencies in the importance of AGCT scores. They insisted that, with good leadership, effective units could be formed despite disproportionately low AGCT scores. They felt that, with few exceptions, men with low scores would make good soldiers if not good leaders. This reasoning applied to both white and Negro units. Before the 92d Division's request for a more normal distribution than prevailing reception center assignment methods could insure, the 5th Armored Division had asked that corrections be made in the score distributions of its fillers. The Services of Supply refused to consider the request, declaring that it believed that 67 percent of Grade V men were capable of becoming acceptable soldiers, 29 percent could be used to advantage in limited service, and only 4 percent were of no use to the Army and therefore should be discharged. A score of 70, the dividing line between AGCT Grades IV and V, SOS said, was the equivalent of a seventh or eighth grade education. Since the median educational level for men in the 1940 census was 8.3 school years, larger percentages in the two lower classes than previously predicted could be expected. Moreover, SOS continued, AGCT scores were variable, not fixed, and therefore might be raised through study and training, as Aberdeen Proving Ground had done with fifteen Grade V men, fourteen of whom had moved into Grade IV after receiving special training in reading.[43] A Ground Forces staff officer commented on a similar request from the 81st Infantry Division:

G–1 sees no cause for alarm as an analysis shows that approximately 96% of the men who made Grade V on the AGC Test have had some schooling and of these over 30% have completed grade school or better. Most men classified in Grade V can be made into first class soldiers. The principal difference being that we cannot expect

---

[40] Ltr, Hq AAF to SOS, 15 May 42, and attached M/R, AAF 210.31 Assignment of Offs.

[41] The range for the 477th Bombardment Group, for example, was lower in the two end classes, but higher in the upper-middle range: Grade I, 1.4 percent; II, 23 percent; III, 41 percent; IV, 30 percent; and V, 4.6 percent. Hist, 477th Bombardment Gp, 15 Jan–15 Jul 44, Air Force Hist Div.

[42] 5th Ind, Hq AAF Gulf Coast Tng Center to CG AAF, 24 Jul 43, on Ltr, Hq Tech School, AAF TTC, Truax Fld, Wisc., 21 Jun 43, to CG 2d Dist AAF TTC, St. Louis, Mo., and Inds, AAF 220.31 #20.

[43] Memo, Dir Mil Pers Div SOS for CG AGF, 21 May 42, SPGA/8645–514.

to draw on this class for any proportion of leadership.[44]

Nor were all units and commanders in the field convinced that AGCT scores alone were deterrents to adequate training. The Infantry Replacement Training Center at Fort McClellan, for example, objected to a suggested mandatory increase in training periods for units with more than 45 percent of their personnel in Grades IV and V, warning that the measure would produce "apparent or real race discrimination," since all white troops could be so distributed that no white training unit would have an excessive number of low-scoring men. "In respect to colored troops," the center reported, "the percentage of the present five battalions is 84% of grades 4 and 5. It is not believed, however, that the achievement of the colored troops as a group in the mechanical elements of training subjects such as weapons firing, marches, etc., is much below that of white battalions. As a matter of fact, the colored are equal in many elements and superior in some." [45]

That the AGCT score was "not a reliable index of the worth of a man" became accepted doctrine in many quarters. "There are many other qualities which must be taken into consideration such as perseverance, honesty, physical stamina and loyalty and loyalty is not the least of these," one commander of Negro troops told a training conference.[46] A commander of a Negro antiaircraft artillery regiment, describing an educational program for his troops, said ". . . I have come to the fixed opinion that the AGCT is not worth a damn with colored troops. I have a 1st Sergeant in Group V that I will stack up against any Noncom in any army as a leader of men. And I know and am convinced that despite the ratings, I have one of the best groups of soldiers in the Army right here in this Regiment." [47]

Nevertheless, reports from the bulk of units and inspectors continued to emphasize the importance of AGCT scores. The number and insistence of such reports became so great that to ignore them was impossible. Low AGCT scores meant low intelligence and poor performance to most parts of the Army which had to deal directly with the training of units, largely Negro, with below average scores. Unfavorable AGCT score distributions were not confined to fillers for Negro units. Two divisions with low-score problems have been mentioned above. Nondivisional white units had similar problems.[48]

---

[44] M/S, AGF G–1 to DCofS, 29 Jul 42, AGF 327.3/246 (Drafted Men).

[45] Memo, Hq IRTC Ft. McClellan, Ala., to CG R&SC, 24 Sep 43, AGF 353.01/68.

[46] Unit Training, Address by Col Lawrence B. Wyant, Mil Tng Div Hq ASF, to Fourth ASF Tng Conf, Ft. Monmouth, N. J., 15–17 Mar 44, Files Fourth Conf, pp. 4–5.

[47] Remarks, CO 99th CA (AA) Regt, to VD Symposium, 30 Jul 43, G–3 291.21. See also, 1st Ind, Hq SOS USF China, APO 627, to CG U.S. Forces China Theater, APO 290, AG 291.2 (23 May 45) (2).

[48] One corps reported that several of its white units were having AGCT score difficulties. Its 650th Engineer Topographical Battalion, a more highly specialized unit than most Negro units, had complained that of 103 fillers received, 70 percent were in Grades IV and V and 95 percent had less than a grade school education. The 50th Engineer Combat Battalion, a type of unit rarely used for Negroes, had 51 percent in Grades IV and V, while the 74th Ordnance Maintenance Battalion, a unit of another type seldom used to absorb Negroes, received 544 fillers in October 1942, 71 percent of whom were in Grades IV and V or illiterate. Ltr, CG IX Corps to Lt Gen Lesley J. McNair, CG AGF, 30 Nov 42, AGF 324.71/212 (Drafted Men).

Despite a tendency to misinterpret and overemphasize their importance, AGCT scores, or, rather, the poor academic, vocational, and cultural backgrounds which they charted, were of singular significance to the careers of Negro enlisted men and their units. They were the one measure of potentialities upon which new units were built in most arms and services. They, coupled with occupational histories, were the visible evidence of the fitness of masses of otherwise anonymous men for assignment to different types of units and training centers. They were a basic criterion for the selection of men for leadership positions, officer or enlisted, regardless of other qualities which might be desired. Many Negro soldiers, on the basis of their scores alone, were restricted in their ability to take fullest advantage of the Army's huge and complex training program. Many units, as a result of low scores, found it impossible to obtain the necessary specialist training for sufficient numbers of their men, for many specialists' programs prescribed minimum AGCT scores before an application could be accepted. But the continuing, all-embracing problem raised by the low AGCT grades prevalent in Negro units was their relationship to training units for effective use within the standard time periods allotted by training programs.

Despite the widespread discussion of the problem among commanders and staff agencies, it was impossible to say what the direct relationship was between AGCT score distributions and unit training progress. It was logical to conclude that training difficulties in units made up of large numbers of illiterate or near-literate men unable to make full use of the masses of training literature and printed training aids supplied by the Army would be greater than in units whose men came from environments where all educational processes—those of the home and the community as well as the school—combined to contribute to their general intellectual growth. To raise the level of Negro men entering the Army, preferably to the point where it would parallel, class by class, the AGCT groupings of white enlisted men, was one solution proposed in the spring of 1943. It would have been possible to take the existing AGCT percentages of white enlisted men and so control Negro inductions that percentages in each AGCT grade would be approximately the same as those of white soldiers. Though this method, arrived at through limiting selectees to men with an eighth grade education (twice the fourth grade limitations for continentals), was later used with success for the induction of Puerto Rican troops,[49] it had several disadvantages for use among continental Negro troops. In the first place, Army nondiscriminatory policies required that all rules and regulations be applied to Negroes and whites alike. Such a procedure would have been immediately open to the charge of being discriminatory, since screening standards would be based on the scores of white troops with the implication that only units built in the AGCT image of existing white troops could be used by the Army. In the second place it would have reduced the intake of Negro inductees to too low a point to satisfy either the terms of the

[49] The Puerto Rican Induction Program and The Use of Puerto Rican Troops, sec. VI, Antilles Department Historical Studies, ch. IV, MS OCMH.

Selective Service Act or the public pressures for the fuller use of Negroes. A third reason was that too drastic curbs on the induction of low-scoring manpower might work disadvantageously to the Army should larger numbers of Negroes or whites be needed as unskilled labor at any future date. Therefore, the problem of raising the qualifications of Negro inductees had to be discussed and applied within a framework of general requirements for all manpower and at the same time be so constructed that it would affect primarily the large numbers of substandard Negro men eligible for military service. Plans and proposals necessarily had to approach the problem through efforts to raise the standards of border-line cases while insuring that the over-all numbers and the racial proportions of men received by the Army would not be affected.

Special Training Plans

Army and Mobilization Regulations had provided that commanders should establish special training schools or units for men of poor educational backgrounds when their numbers made such units advisable. The number of such local, unit-conducted schools for illiterates and low-literates increased rapidly in 1942 and in early 1943. Since they were not centrally controlled or reporting units, their exact numbers and enrollment cannot be determined, but, in May 1943, just before centrally controlled special training units went into effect, 384 units and stations, Negro and white, were receiving directly The Adjutant General's "Our War" and "The Newsmap Supplement," publications intended for use in literacy classes. Many more units

were receiving these materials through local distribution agencies.[50]

The operation of unit and post controlled special training units provided an extra burden for commands which already had their hands filled with their normal training duties. Many commanders were interpreting regulations to mean that the establishment of these units was mandatory.[51] Some means of giving illiterates elementary courses in reading and writing before formally assigning them to units had to be devised, for illiterates were a handicap to the receiving units. Though illiterates might be well received and quite useful, units had neither the time, the instructors, nor the teaching aids to make them quickly available for regular training.[52]

The Services of Supply proposed by mid-1942 that centrally controlled "development" units, patterned after World War I development battalions, be established. Illiterates coming into the Army, SOS argued, were increasing and, because of the rule to take effect on 1 August 1942,[53] they would continue to increase in numbers. Portable Civilian Conservation Corps buildings, and CCC instructors who were experienced in training illiterates, could be used to house and train these men.[54] While AAF and G–1 concurred in the proposal,

[50] Among the units receiving materials directly were twenty-five divisions, including the 2d Cavalry and 92d Infantry Divisions. Ltr, TAG to CO's Units and Posts, 28 May 43, AG 353 (5–28–43) OT–C.

[51] Memo, AGF for G–1, 27 Nov 42, AGF 353/2025 GNGAP–I.

[52] Lt Col James L. Lewis, Notes on Service with the 93d Engineer Regt (GS) in Extreme Cold and Wet Cold Climates, Engr School 8715.

[53] See above, p. 241.

[54] Memos, CG SOS for CofS, 6 Jun 42 and 20 Jul 42, SPGAE/8645–731.

AGF and G-3 did not. The additional administrative and overhead load added by these units and the relatively small numbers of men to be trained militated against ready acceptance of the proposal.

By the spring of 1943 G-3 was ready to propose its own plan. The new plan went considerably farther and was intended to do more than simply prepare illiterates and low-literates for regular training. It was designed to raise the general quality of Army enlisted men in three ways: (1) to screen all personnel at induction stations so as to eliminate all but the upper 10 percent of Grade V's,[55] (2) to discharge from the Army all men who had demonstrated their inability to absorb military training, and (3) to establish combination labor-development battalions to rehabilitate the remaining backward men.[56] The current percentage of Grade V's in Negro units was so high "as to present an almost insurmountable obstacle in the attempt to organize effective Negro units," G-3 said. With the Army then scheduled to reach a maximum strength of 8,208,000 officers and enlisted men and women, the necessary 783,000 Negroes, "the majority of which must be assigned to tactical units," should be as high a quality as possible. With shipping a bottleneck, G-3 continued, the War Department could send Negro units overseas only if they were not inferior to white units. Otherwise, in 1944, "Negro units will be piled up in the United States to an unwarranted degree and the Negro race will be denied its fair share of battle honors as well as battle losses." To mo-

bilize and train units which could not be used overseas was "a flagrant waste of manpower and time," G-3 argued. "The Army is open to severe and just criticism for this wasted Negro manpower which, if left in civil life, would contribute materially to an important phase of the war effort," [57] G-3 continued. Most Negroes in the lowest AGCT classes were from the rural South, where they could best contribute to the war effort, G-3 felt, by remaining on the farms. Men in the higher classifications were from the North, where few were deferred for essential activities. The proposed solution could be instituted "without serious repercussion. The gain in the effectiveness of white units would not be so pronounced as in Negro units, but, "to avoid discrimination," the plan must be applied to both white and Negro personnel.

The plan itself was expected to work in this manner:

1. After 1 May 1943, the Army would reject all selectees in Grade V in excess of 10 percent. A special "intelligence" test, combined with an interview at induction stations, would be designed to screen out men lacking the capacity to be soldiers while retaining men who lacked sufficient education to pass the general classification test. The men screened out would comprise approximately the lower three-fifths of those currently classified in AGCT Grade V. As a result, approximately 1 percent of the whites and 20 percent of the Negroes then being accepted would be rejected. Since the Army had to accept 10.6 percent Negroes, Selective Service would have to increase its calls to insure the

---

[55] The percentage shifted as various proposals were considered during discussions of the plan.

[56] Memo, G-3 for CofS, 10 Apr 43, AG 201.6 (19 Mar 43) (1).

[57] Ibid.

Army's receipt of its required quota of Negroes.

2. Within the Army, streamlined machinery would be established to permit the speedy discharge, without stigma, of men found "as a result of actual lack of performance" and not as the result of test performances to be incapable of becoming effective soldiers.

3. Other men in the Army, classified in Grade V, would be transferred to units whose function was chiefly labor and which could use men with lower qualifications to best advantage.

4. Backward men, not inapt enough to warrant discharge, were to be transferred to rehabilitation or development battalions to be located at the larger posts in the continental United States. "These battalions would be combination labor and training battalions operating on a schedule in which days of labor on the post where stationed and days of training or instruction would be alternated." As soon as a man was sufficiently trained to be advanced to a unit, he would be transferred out of these battalions.[58]

Objections to the proposal—many of which were accepted by G–3 before the final plan was presented for approval—were several. G–3 hoped that the combination labor-training provision for the battalions would soften basic objections to the plan's implied recognition of the Army's need to embark on a large-scale educational program. Army Ground Forces objected to the establishment of development battalions in any form; Army Air Forces wanted safeguards against potential malingering that it thought the plan involved; G–2 though

also believing that the danger of malingering was a great one, was noncommittal. The Services of Supply had had grave doubts about the plan as originally proposed because of its provision for the rejection and discharge of large numbers of men, the larger percentage of whom would be Negroes. The plan "has been studied with the viewpoint that the Army only must be considered and that any sociological problems arising as a result thereof must be disregarded," SOS observed. "However, it is considered pertinent to point out that the plea of the southern states particularly those in the Southeast is 'when is the Army going to take more colored.' Any increased rejection of colored and increased return of colored now in the Army to civilian life will bring repercussions both economic and political," SOS feared.[59]

Neither the Services of Supply nor Truman Gibson, Acting Civilian Aide to the Secretary of War, agreed that an arbitrary line between men who could and who could not be used by the Army was possible as a result of existing tests. Gibson proposed that the original statement that units with an excess of Grade V men above 8 percent could not function be re-examined. "Most Negro units have more than 8% Grade V men," he pointed out. "Certainly some of these have performed in competent and creditable manners. . . . I know of no study in the War Department conducted in a large number of individual units for the purpose of ascertaining even an approximate percentage of Grade V men the different organizations

---

[58] *Ibid.*

[59] Memo, Mil Pers Div SOS for G–3, 19 Mar 43, AG 201.6 (16 Mar 43) (1).

could effectively absorb." Standard AGC tests are not claimed to be measurements of intelligence, he continued. The ABC nonverbal test, when given, produced higher grades for many men in Grade V. In the ABC, "more than 30% of the Negroes retested who have been placed in Grade V initially, in the AGCT, enter a higher classification, in some places going even to Grade I," Gibson contended. Test scores were by no means the only factors involved in the training of Negro units; the manner of making assignments was just as important, he concluded.[60]

SOS also reminded G-3 that its arbitrary statement of the Army's ability to use men rated as inferior according to a series of tests was subject to question. What was the essential difference between a Grade IV and a Grade V man anyway? SOS wanted to know. All might be utilized if training schedules for slow learners were made more realistic and if development battalions, as suggested earlier by SOS, were put into use. The command hoped that limitations would be placed on their use: (1) intelligence rather than literacy should be stressed; (2) only the lower part of Group V rather than an arbitrary 90 to 94 percent should be screened out; (3) each major component should continue to be required to accept Negroes in proportion to its size; (4) no transfers should be made from one command to another on the basis of test scores; (5) no mass discharges or transfers to development battalions of men who had had basic training should be made; (6) mobilization training of units should be geared to their capacity to learn—in many cases, for Negro units, at least 50 percent slower than for white units; and (7), Negro units should be sent overseas in definite proportions "in order that colored troops may receive their percentage of casualties." [61]

General Davis, as a member of the Advisory Committee on Negro Troop Policies, approved the plan, but warned that the Grade V limitations might prove too stringent. "In this connection," he observed, "I would state that during my tour of duty in the United Kingdom, I observed a number of colored units composed of a large number of Grade V men. These units were highly commended for the services being rendered. The port battalions were commended by the British officials from whom they had received instruction." [62] Goldthwaite H. Dorr, Special Assistant to the Secretary of War, thought that, instead of being discharged, inapt and low-scoring men should be put on inactive duty in the same manner as men in the 38- to 45-year age group recently released by the Army.[63]

The revised draft, taking into consideration many of the proposals of other divisions, was presented to the Advisory Committee by General Edwards on 2 April. The committee unanimously approved it and recommended immediate adoption.[64] Subject to the inclusion of Dorr's suggestion, Secretary Stimson approved the G-3 plan for Grade V personnel.

---

[60] Memo, Actg Civ Aide to SW for G-3, 1 Apr 43, AG 201.6 (19 Mar 43) (1).

[61] Memo, Dir of Mil Pers Div SOS for G-3, 19 Mar 43, AG 201.6 (19 Mar 43) (1).

[62] Memo, OTIG for G-3, 25 Mar 43, AG 201.6 (19 Mar 43) (1).

[63] Memo, Dorr to SW (initialed G.H.D. and H.L.S.), 17 Apr 43, in AG 201.6 (19 Mar 43) (1).

[64] Min Advisory Com, 2 Apr 43, ASW 291.2 NTC.

The Plan in Operation

The chief feature of the special training plan in operation was not the elimination of large numbers of Grade V men, as proposed in the original plan, but the institution of a new induction screening process and the establishment of new special training units for the more effective use of that portion of Grade V registrants which ranked highest in potentialities. At induction stations, a preliminary interview established whether or not graduates of standard English-speaking schools were mentally qualified. Transcripts, certificates, and other proofs of schooling were accepted at this stage. Large numbers of men were thereby excused from further phases of the new induction process and were declared eligible for induction. Mental qualification tests for induction were given to all men who could not present documentary proof of schooling. These tests were designed to screen out registrants who would make AGCT scores above the lower three-fifths of Grade V. For illiterates and non-English-speaking men, a nonlanguage group test for the same purpose was available. For men failing the Mental Qualification Test, individual tests were given. All men failing the individual test were then interviewed again to prevent error and malingering.[65]

The new plan went into effect at induction stations in June 1943. At intervals, The Adjutant General reported that the plan was working satisfactorily, and that the lower three-fifths of Grade V men already inducted were being eliminated while the 10.6 percentage of Negroes was being retained, the difference being made up by the induction of larger numbers of illiterates who gave promise of higher potential abilities. Of the 40,446 men—35,872 (88.7 percent) white and 4,574 Negroes (11.3 percent)—processed between 1 and 5 June at induction centers and between 13 and 19 June at reception centers, 963 (2.4 percent) Grade V's (420 of them white and 543 colored) and 1,159 (2.9 percent) illiterates (484 white and 675 colored) were inducted. Of the total number of men inducted, 1.3 percent of the whites and 14.8 percent of the Negroes were illiterate. Though the mental qualification for illiterates had been raised, the percentage of illiterates inducted had risen from 1.7 to 2.9 percent. At the same time, the percentage of Grade V men inducted was being reduced, for many inducted illiterates made higher scores on their nonverbal tests. Between January and April 1943, 7.2 percent of all men inducted were in Grade V. With the elimination of the lower three-fifths of Grade V's, 2.8 percent would now be desired. During the period 13–19 June 1943, 2.4 percent of the men inducted were in Grade V, constituting a reduction of 3 percent for white and 24.3 percent for Negroes. Of the total number of men processed between 13 and 19 June, 11.3, slightly more than the required 10.6 percent, were Negroes.[66]

In many areas there was, nevertheless, objection to the new procedure. It rejected too many men, especially Negroes,

[65] Memo, Classification and Repl Br AGD for Dir Mil Pers ASF, 27 Apr 43, AG 201.6 (19 Mar 43).

[66] Memo and Incl, Classification and Repl Br AGD for Dir MPD ASF, 25 Jun 43, AG 201.6 (19 Mar 43) (1).

from a given group called. The Qualification Test, which had been purposely
kept simple, was a primary target.
From the Fort Jackson, South Carolina,
induction station came objections which
embodied those of many other observers.
At the station, 4,916 white men and
4,756 Negroes were examined in June
1943. Of these, 4,427 whites or 90.05
percent and 2,360 Negroes or 49.62 percent were accepted. The disproportionate results, Fort Jackson argued,
indicated that the tests had been standardized for whites and that they were
not applicable to Negroes:

The Qualification Test No. 1 consists of
seventeen questions, and the first type of
questions are comparatively simple. For
example: "write the smallest of the following numbers in the blank space; 142 175
180 191 125," which, of course, is 125. This
item is of elementary level and it does have
general application, and we find that the
white and negro respond with almost equal
success on this item. The next four questions deal with analysis. As for example:
an arrow pointing between north and west,
and the four points of the compass are
given, the question is asked; "in which
direction is the arrow pointing"? It is
found that the negro misses this type of
question in greater numbers than the white,
because this demands a detection of the
correct bearing of the direction and in interpreting this the relationships have a
scheme. The negro, in the majority of
cases interviewed, is seeing this for the first
time, while the white has had many experiences in this type of thinking. It is felt
that if the negro was given this question in
the field he would have little trouble in
answering it correctly. Hence, it is not felt
that because the negro misses this question,
that he does not have the intelligence to be
able to answer the same question if given to
him under regular conditions to which he
is used to. . . . Item twelve, it is required
to know the number of pounds in a ton.
Since the adult negro has been out of

school for sometime, and it is doubtful
[whether] there are many negroes who have
bought coal by the ton, it is felt that he has
completely forgotten, or what is likely,
never knew how many pounds in a ton. In
items thirteen and fourteen, a disadvantage
lies in the set-up of the objective answer
required, which the negro is unaccustomed
to, since it has not been introduced on any
wide scale into their school training. In
most cases of our southern negroes, the new
type of testing has not been introduced into
the schools in anywhere near the same proportion as it has into the white schools.
Hence this type of question is entirely
foreign to them. Also, it is felt that the
average negro under the conditions which
he is subjected to in his testing, is more at
a disadvantage than the white, and is
slower at thinking, or especially objective
thinking than the white person. This involves an adjustment that fails in the insight upon the first experience without
instructions, hence a different method
should replace this type of response where
the negro is concerned.[67]

While Fort Jackson's Post Inspector
found no evidence of malingering, the
commanding general believed that men
"could easily be trained in how to fail
to pass this test." The Director of Selective Service for South Carolina was
"quite upset" by the high rejection rates
of Negroes, the commanding general reported. Letters and his own observation had convinced him that "a large
number of gentlewomen with children
and without children are being left in
communities and also in the communities are large numbers of negro laborers." Many of the Negro rejects could
be used, perhaps in "farm battalions."
The state would otherwise be unfairly
burdened with furnishing a "very high

[67] Ltr, Office of the Post Inspector, Hq Ft. Jackson, to CG Ft. Jackson, 13 Jul 43, AG 201.6 (19
Mar 43) (1).

percentage" of white men.[68] The Fourth Service Command, approving the South Carolina recommendations, observed that the South Carolina situation was duplicated in all states of the command.[69]

The arguments concerning the validity of the test for Negroes were ignored by the War Department, for the Negro rejection rate was almost exactly what the Army had hoped it would be. The Fourth Service Command was informed, however, that induction proportions in the South were being preserved. The 1940 census showed 31 percent of the population of the command to be Negro while the induction rate of Negroes for the period 14 June–14 August was 33 percent.[70] The War Department was satisfied that the Negro induction rate was being preserved by the new system.

Service Command Special Training Units

Special training units "to relieve organizations, unit training centers and replacement training centers from expending regular training effort" on the expected increase in illiterates and low-literates were authorized for each service command.[71] The units were set up with the expectation that nearly twice as many Negroes as whites would receive this special training and that the heaviest loads would be in the two southern commands. Actually, there were always more white than Negro trainees in these units, with nearly 70 percent of the men at any one time being white.[72] Instead of the predicted 1 percent of the whites and 20 percent of the Negroes processed at reception centers, 9 percent of all whites and 49 percent of all Negroes inducted after June 1943 went to special training units. This number represented about 11.5 percent of all men received through reception centers. Eighty percent of the trainees were illiterate or non-English-speaking; the remainder were AGCT Grade V men. From June 1943 through May 1945, over 260,000 men went through these units, of whom over 220,000—about 85 percent of the white and 86 percent of the Negroes—were forwarded to regular basic military training.[73]

Men assigned to special training units received three hours of academic and five hours of military training daily instead of alternating between training and labor as originally planned. With a maximum three months of training authorized, 79 percent of the men in training during the fiscal year 1945 completed training in sixty days or less and 44 percent required less than thirty days. Negroes completed special training in approximately the same average time as whites. With the exception of a few stations, the training given was of a high order.

Although the special training units in their two years of operation, proved the value of accelerated, elementary literacy training for men of limited educa-

[68] 3d Ind to Ltr cited n. 67, Hq Ft. Jackson to CG Fourth Sv Comd, 19 Jul 43, AG 201.6 (19 Mar 43) (1).

[69] 4th Ind to Ltr cited n. 67, Hq Fourth Sv Comd to TAG, 23 Jul 43, AG 201.6 (19 Mar 43) (1).

[70] 5th Ind to Ltr cited n. 67.

[71] Par. 15, AR 615–28, 28 May 42.

[72] Army Service Forces Annual Report for the Fiscal Year 1945, p. 142.

[73] Ibid., pp. 142–43.

tional, mental, and language abilities, the units were not an unqualified success in correcting the situation which the plan they evolved from was designed to combat. They did make available to the Army larger numbers of white and Negro men—the equivalent of more than a dozen divisions—who would otherwise have been rejected as illiterate and they did provide elementary training for these men. Though marginal soldiers no longer delayed the training of regular units, training centers complained that special training unit men, especially when placed in units where they had little need to practice their newly learned literacy skills, quickly deteriorated. Many of the men, a few months after being certified as "functionally literate," were still signing payrolls with X's. This deterioration was not the responsibility of the special training units; nevertheless, commanders of Negro T/O units, many of whom received practically all of their fillers from special training units, tended to complain that the units had not done their jobs well. There was some evidence that in certain of the units AGC tests were given repeatedly to men until they raised their scores to Grade IV. These men were then classified "literate" and released to regular training. This practice, contrary to the purpose of the units, was ordered stopped, with the warning that "the ability to read and write is not in itself a requirement for successful military training, however, that ability materially accelerates the rate of progress." [74]

There were suggestions that the problem of slow learners and backward men could not be solved by the limited training available in the special training units. The Neuropsychiatry Division of the Surgeon General's Office, seeking a method for the utilization of physically qualified men discharged from these units as inapt, recommended the organization of slow learners into supporting and construction companies modeled on the American pioneer units of World War I and the British Pioneer Corps of World War II. The British had included in their units even those men who were so backward that they could not be trusted with lethal weapons. "With good officers and non-commissioned officers these men are magnificent," British reports ran.

In the last six months of 1943, 90,172 educationally deficient men were inducted. Of these 66,258 went to regular training after a stay in special training units. The question of what to do with the other 24,000 physically fit men remained. The average slow learner could not keep pace with the quick learner. "Such competition forces him to find an escape consciously (AWOL) or unconsciously (psychoneurosis), and the process holds back the possible speed of training for the normal," Lt. Col. William C. Menninger, director of the Neuropsychiatry Division, explained. Many, with more time, could be adequately trained, though a few would be unable to finish basic training no matter how much time was given them. If men who scored less than 70 on the AGCT were placed in special units, operating as construction crews, maintenance units, stevedores, and on manual

[74] Ltr, Hq TD RTC to CG R&SC, 23 Aug 43, AG 353 (5-1-43) and 31 Incls; Ltr, TAG to CG's Sv Comds, 11 Oct 43, AG 353 (23 Aug 43) OC-LT.

jobs, the amount of maladjustment in the Army would be reduced.[75]

ASF and G–1, in rejecting this proposal, took the position that the number of men discharged from special training units as unteachable or unadaptable to military training was too small to be administered effectively without special supervisory personnel. Since these men, if retained in special units, would have to be counted in the Troop Basis, other organizations would have to be removed in order to keep the Army within its manpower ceiling. The men discharged from special training units were not thought of as a loss of trained manpower, for the Army actually gained by replacing them with better qualified men from the nation's manpower pool.[76]

Neither the old literacy training efforts conducted by T/O units nor the newer reception center special training units did more than guarantee Negro units fewer totally illiterate and low Grade V men. By their very nature, they were unable to affect markedly the upper AGCT grades so thinly distributed in Negro units. Of Negro men released from special training units in the first six months for assignment to regular training, 99.2 percent were in Grades IV and V, but the number in Grade IV was considerably larger than that in Grade V. While these men were man-

ifestly better able to enter regular training than the unsorted and untrained daily 10 percent of illiterates and random percentage of Grade V's previously received, they relieved rather than solved Negro units' difficult problem of absorbing too many men of poor backgrounds. While special training units could not solve completely the problems of units which continued to receive disproportionately large numbers of low-scoring men, they did succeed in their main purpose: to relieve regular units of the burden of special training and to make available for regular training larger numbers of illiterate and low-literate men of higher potentialities.

Instructional Problems

Since lower scores generally meant slower learning, it was assumed that extending training periods would go far to correct deficiencies in the progress of Negro units. In 1943, shortly after the establishment of the new special training units, G–3, on the recommendation of the Commanding General, Fourth Service Command, and of the Army Service Forces, authorized extended training programs for units which, because of a preponderance of low-grade personnel, "unusual mental attitude," or other reasons were not progressing satisfactorily. Extended military training programs, to be identified by the letter A (as in MTP 10–1A) and requiring up to six months' training, were to be prepared. Units were to be designated formally as substandard to prevent their being committed to an overseas theater before receiving sufficient training. Disciplinary training was to be intensified. Officers

---

[75] Memo, Neuropsychiatry Div (Lt Col William C. Menninger, Dir), on Organization of "Armed" and "Unarmed" Pioneers, 20 Mar 44, Incl to Ltr, Col Menninger to Col Arthur G. Trudeau, Mil Tng Div ASF, SPTR 220.3.

[76] Memo Mil Tng Div ASF for TSG (Dir Neuropsychiatry Div), 25 Mar 44, SPTR 220.3 (21 Mar 44); Memo, MPD ASF for G–1, 31 Mar 44, SPGAC/221 Gen (25 Mar 44)–122; Memo for Record attached, 19 Mar 44, SPTR 220.3 (21 Mar 44).

for these units were to be especially chosen.[77]

Extended military training programs were slow in preparation. After they were ready, training headquarters were sometimes reluctant to designate units substandard. A unit which was in demand was needed within a minimum time while a unit which was not in demand would have an automatic extension of its training period. What training commands and centers wanted was better men from reception and replacement training centers rather than substandard program authorizations. When sixteen Transportation Corps amphibian truck companies at Camp Gordon Johnston, Florida, were declared substandard and placed on a 26-week substandard training program in October 1943, the Transportation Corps protested that if better personnel had been sent to it, this training delay would not have occurred. As matters stood, at least five of these units would have to be committed in their current status of training when about halfway through the extended program.[78]

Extended training periods, without corresponding adjustments in instructional techniques and leadership approaches to the problems of Negro units, were in no case enough to guarantee an effectively trained unit. For though there had been general agreement as far back as the post-World War I planning period that it would take longer to train Negro units, there was no indication that units with extended periods were better fitted to carry out their missions than many others which had a normal training period or than many of those which were shipped overseas without completing training.

The difficulties of carrying out effective instruction in units with large numbers of low-scoring men were, however, generally recognized. In those everyday, taken for granted practices in living, thinking, and working common to most Americans, the low-scoring Negroes of many units had basic deficiencies for which no corrective existed in Army instructional doctrines. Few commanders of small units had either the time or the inclination to peer behind every shortcoming of their troops to determine both the origin and remedy for these basic deficiencies. That directions framed in such terms as "discipline," "sentinel," "compensation," "maintain," "observation," "barrage," "counter-clockwise," or even "exterior" might be meaningless,[79] no matter how patiently or repeatedly given, occurred to few instructors charged with training Negro units. To reduce what was ordinarily accepted as understandable language to an even lower level was not easy to do without subconsciously berating one's listeners for that lack of "intelligence" which required annoying additional effort on the part of the instructor.

Proper instructional methods for slow

---

[77] Memo, G–3 for CG's ASF, AGF, AAF, 9 Aug 43; Memo for Record on G–3 Div M/S, 22 Aug 43; Memo, G–3 for CG's AAF, AGF, ASF, 24 Aug 43. All in WDGCT 291.21 (12 Jul 43).

[78] Ltr, Dir Mil Tng TC for Mob Div ASF, 28 Oct 43, SPTR 220.3.

[79] These words are taken from a list of 500 words occurring with high frequency in *The Soldier's Handbook, The Soldier's Reader, Army Life,* general orders, and bulletin board notices, over half of which were not known to Grade V men, white and Negro, tested at a replacement training center. Less than 50 percent of the men tested understood the words listed here. See WD Pamphlet 20–6, Command of Negro Troops, 29 Feb 44.

learners of poor experiential backgrounds were hardly stressed in a functional manner as a necessary adjunct to good leadership techniques as they affected the training of Negro troops.[80] While American troops in general required instruction in the reasons for mobilization and, later, in the reasons for America's entry into the war,[81] Negro troops often had to be instructed as well in the bare rudiments of existence in a machine age and, at that, in terms to which most available teaching personnel, Negro as well as white, were unaccustomed. Supervision of their training sometimes required more personnel than usual. The training of a maximum of 170 officers and 3,600 enlisted men at Camp Gordon Johnston required a Headquarters and Headquarters Company of fifty officers and 265 enlisted men.[82]

The range of subjects in which even a nontechnical unit was expected to gain proficiency was far wider than the limited horizons of many low-scoring men had ever before included. The twenty-six week training program of a quartermaster railhead company, as an example, included the following in addition to the basic military training subjects: storage and issue (warehousing, space utilization, prerequisites for issue) ; vehicle loading; daily telegrams and the computation of supplies on the basis of information furnished therein; railhead arrangement; use of road nets and sidings; receiving, sorting, and checking supplies; accounting for supplies; inspection of subsistence stores; salvage operations; selection of sites for railheads, including plans for defense, camouflage, and protection from air attacks; practical operation of railheads; map reading; security (including reconnaissance, defense against guerrilla, chemical, air, and paratroop attacks, concealment, dispersal, and camouflage) ; decontamination apparatus and its use; demolitions; safety measures; night operations. In addition, the unit was to conduct specialist training of chauffeurs and clerks in event these men could not be supplied by the specialist schools.[83]

Moreover, in a unit of this sort, as in many other small units which might have to operate independently with reduced personnel, the training of all enlisted men was supposed to emphasize the importance of individual responsibility when direct supervision was not available. In this area alone, because of their immediate past, many Negroes required a complete reorientation and retraining in their daily living habits. Individuals were to be trained to perform different tasks, such as supervision of loading details, guiding traffic, and all phases of railhead operation so that a single man might function effectively in many positions to allow for inter-

---

[80] For later attempts to stress instructional methods, see WD Pamphlet 20–6, Command of Negro Troops, 29 February 1944, and ASF Manual M–5, Leadership and the Negro Soldier, October 1944, both of which are discussed below, Chapter XIII. These publications came too late in the war to affect the vital training periods of the bulk of the units.

[81] See Shirley A. Star, "The Orientation of Soldiers Toward the War," in Samuel A. Stouffer *et al., The American Soldier: Adjustment to Army Life* (Princeton: Princeton University Press, 1949) ; Capt Ulysses G. Lee, Army Orientation, Hist of Mil Tng ASF, (1945), MS OCMH.

[82] Mil Tng Div OCofTC, Transportation Corps History—Training of Units, Feb 45, p. 50, MS OCMH.

[83] TM 10–379, Handbook for the Quartermaster Railhead Company, AG 300.7 (4 Nov 43), pp. 15–19.

changeable team and labor pool use of men in varying situations. The range of subjects to be covered in twenty-six weeks was greater than many of the men assigned had encountered in all the preceding years of their lives. Large numbers of slow learners of poor backgrounds were an obvious handicap to the efficient training progress of such a unit.

In addition to the general difficulties of training low-scoring men in a variety of tasks in a short time, there were a number of specific areas of difficulty which units and their men faced because of the preponderance of slow learners. In order to complete their training and become available for operational use, all units, including the less technical types, had to have available the specialists required for unit functions. Specialists required by port companies, in addition to cargo-handling personnel, included, for example: mechanic foreman, mess sergeant, stevedore foreman, supply sergeant, hatch foreman, company clerk, blacksmith, cargo checker, carpenter, clerk-typist, cook, cooper, crane operator, hatch tender, longshoreman, general mechanic, tractor mechanic, rigger, tractor operator, truck driver, combination welder, and winch operator. Obtaining key specialists for service units was sometimes baffling to training directors. One reported to a training conference:

For example, the problem of training negroes to successfully fill key and technical positions of an Engineer General Service Regiment or an Engineer Construction Battalion is almost, if not entirely, unsurmountable. Such key positions as Construction Supervisor (059), Electrician, General (078), Surveyor, General (227), Designer, Electrical (078), Designer, Road Construction (382), Designer, Structural

(074), Foreman, Machine Shop (086), Draftsman, Mechanical (071), Draftsman, Structural (074) and Foreman, Bridge (541) and many others of this nature require considerable civilian background and experience. The key and technical positions for Engineer units mentioned above should be filled with men who have had a civilian background commensurate with the job to be done so that within a reasonably short course of military instruction, inductees could fill the required positions. Wide search will fail to reveal negroes whose background reflects experience in such required key positions. . . . Since personnel must be trained for the above key positions in 20 weeks, it can be readily seen that upon activation, two strikes are already called on a technical unit allotted negro personnel. The specialists required may be named, may be rated, and may draw the pay of specialists, but the real specialist is not there. Who does the technical work of these so-called specialists? It is probable that the white officer does, if it is accomplished, thus being forced to neglect his own work.[84]

Officers themselves were not always able to give much aid. At the Third Engineer Aviation Unit Training Center, MacDill Field, Florida, where nearly all Negro aviation engineer units were trained in the last half of the war, inspectors found training officers who were not able to identify tools and who could not identify component parts of engineer sets and chests.[85]

---

[84] Address, Col William H. Craig, Fourth Sv Comd, Problems of a Service Command Training Division, Notes, ASF Fifth Training Conf, 24 Oct 44, ASFTC Camp Barkeley, Tex., p. 163. Numbers in parentheses are Military Occupational Specialty (MOS) numbers. See also, Unit Training in the Corps of Engineers, 1 July 1939–30 June 1944, pp. 17–18, MS OCMH.
[85] Ltr, Hq EAUTC, Office Dir and Maint, MacDill Field, to Dir of Supply and Maintenance, 316th AAFBU (EAUTC), MacDill, Fla., 16 Jan 45, copy in EAUTC MacDill Fld Hist Rpt, Installment VIII, AAF 2158–4.

Schools were set up to transform the thousands of young men with little civilian experience into the specialists required, as well as into the pilots, gunners, and cannoneers for which there were no civilian counterparts.[86] But standards for entrance to many specialist schools were higher than the available enlisted men of most Negro units could meet.[87]

Certain units requested that requirements for specialists' courses be lowered. They argued that their lower-rated men could do the required classroom work and that, in any event, they were the only ones who could be spared. For Engineer courses, units suggested broadening the base to include men from the upper fifth of the command. This request was approved.[88] Army Air Forces, pointing out the immediate need for signal construction companies, urged the lowering of minimum scores and the substitution of equivalent experience for specialist training in Signal Corps schools. In this case the approval was conditioned by the attachment of a white signal construction unit to help intensify training in the Negro units.[89]

Other units gave retests of the AGCT in an attempt to qualify men for specialist and officer candidate schools. Some of these were genuine retests, in which adequate explanations of the tests and adequate time, both often lacking in reception centers, resulted in a marked improvement in scores. How much of this improvement may be traced to newly acquired knowledge and experience cannot be gauged. At other times, men were retested several times, until their scores were raised. This latter procedure, frowned upon by the Classification and Replacement Branch, had little validity in a determination of the actual scores of the men concerned. That units took the time to administer these retests indicates how serious the shortage of AGCT qualified men was.[90]

Many units were genuinely hard put to fill quotas allotted them for officer as well as specialist training. Since the requirement of a score of 110 (Grade II) or better for appointment to officer candidate schools left a relatively small number of Negro eligibles, the problem of filling allotted quotas became a desperate one in some units.

---

[86] For comprehensive accounts of methods of training used by the armed services, see series *Publications of the Commission on Implications of Armed Services Educational Programs*, American Council on Education (Washington, 1947) (12 monographs).

[87] Requirements for most courses were not excessively high, but in a random choice among units few Negroes with both the necessary scores and the required background could be found to meet requirements such as the following: Water Purification: proficiency in elementary arithmetic and use of formulas, aptitude for or experience in electrical and mechanical work and elementary chemistry; Mechanical Equipment: elementary arithmetic and use of formulas with aptitude for or experience in electrical and mechanical work; Drafting: proficiency in arithmetic with an aptitude for drafting, some knowledge of algebra, plane geometry, and trigonometry desirable. Ltr, OCE to TAG, 3 Jul 41, AG 220.63 Engr Sch (7-3-41) (1).

[88] Ltr, 1st Hq and Hq Detachment Special Trps, Armd Force, Ft. Knox, Ky., to CG Armd Force, 15 Jan 43, AGF 352/127 (Engr Sch).

[89] Ltr, Hq AAF to CSigO, 1 Mar 43, AAF 353 Cld Tng.

[90] Materials on the numbers of retests given in specific units and their results are lacking, for obvious reasons. That retests were given, sometimes legitimately and sometimes with such frequency as to negate the purpose of the AGCT, cannot be doubted. See Ltr, Hq Btry 93d Div Arty to CG 93d Div, 15 Aug 42, Misc Corresp Hq 93d Inf Div Arty; Ltr, T/5 L. A. P——— to Btry CO, 7 Aug 42. Both in same file.

In 1942, inspecting officers, one of whose responsibilities was to determine whether or not unit commanders were exploiting fully the opportunity to send Negro candidates to OCS, found that in many units there were practically no opportunities to exploit. While in the average white unit 30 percent or more of the men fell within the two top grades eligible for appointment, in the average Negro unit less than 5 percent of the men were eligible on the basis of scores without regard to other qualifying criteria.[91] Reductions for other disqualifying reasons left many Negro units without possible candidates. School retests of candidates left more than the suspicion that many Negro units were not too careful in certifying AGCT scores for men sent to OCS. Candidates, once they were sent to the schools, were usually allowed to remain. Some of the borderline cases successfully completed their courses, but many others were rapid failures. The predominance of low-scoring men hampered even high-scoring men in their attempts to take full advantage of Army training opportunities, for sending men to officer candidate schools often removed most of the enlisted leadership material from the unit.

For admission to the Army Specialized Training Program (ASTP) at civilian colleges, Negro enlisted men were at an even greater disadvantage, for the requirement here was a score of 115 or better. Since only about 2.5 percent of all Negroes in the Army had scores of 115 or better, Negroes eligible for ASTP constituted less than one-fourth of 1 per-cent of all men in the Army. In December 1943, at the program's peak, 105,265 students were enrolled. Of these, only 789 were Negroes. They represented three-fourths of 1 percent of the total.[92]

Barriers to Advanced Training

Despite the difficulty of securing enough men with the required qualifications for specialist and advanced training, there existed additional barriers to the selection of well-qualified men for training. The percentage of Negro eligibles was so small that their distribution to varying units of the arms and services made it difficult to locate men who might have made excellent candidates for specific types of advanced training. Judge Hastie suspected that there were many Negro men "lost" within the Army in units which had no need of their qualifications while other units suffered shortages in the same field. Sufficient evidence, in the form of requests for assignment and occasional inspectors' comments, existed to support this view. G-3, realizing that numbers of Negro men were in units such as aviation squadrons and medical sanitary companies which had no true specialists' requirements, requested a sampling survey of these units to determine if enough men of high caliber were available there to fill some of the requirements of more critically needed units. The results of the survey were discouraging; there was

---

[91] Memo, Hq Third Army for Col Newcomer, 4 Jun 42, CofE 352 (Engr OCS) pt. 3.

[92] Of these students, 569 were in the 5 units located at Negro schools; 220 were in 36 units located at mixed schools in the north and west. Memo, Chief Standards Sec ASTP for Chief Curricula and Standards Br ASTP, 29 Jan 45, SPTR 291.2 (29 Jan 45).

no excess of highly qualified men reported from these units.[93]

Later, in a blanket attempt to salvage men of higher capabilities from units which required proportionately fewer men of this type, the War Department directed that certain types of units be cleared of men of greater potentialities. "Specifically," the directive read, "excess of men with high intelligence in units such as aviation squadrons, sanitary companies, and service units of the Quartermaster Corps and Engineer labor units will be reassigned to units where their skills and intelligence can be utilized more effectively." [94] But the one word, "excess," defeated the purpose of this directive. The common shortage of men qualified as noncommissioned officers forced many of these units to report that they had no "excess" among high-scoring men.

There were other units in which little attempt was made to screen out possible applicants for advanced training. Often, officers of these units and the enlisted men themselves, having received no specific instructions in the matter, were equally uncertain of what applications, if any, could be made with a chance of acceptance by the men of a Negro unit. Even units and commands with definite training requirements were uncertain of either the procedure or the possibility of sending Negro soldiers to certain schools. Inquiries on

specific training policies as they affected Negroes were frequent. Will there be a separate school for tire maintenance? the Civilian Aide's office asked. Can Negro enlisted men be trained as guard patrolmen at Miami Beach? First Air Force wanted to know. May they be sent to the corps area horseshoeing school? Fourth Corps Area was asked. Are Negroes eligible for the General Mechanics Course at Motor Transport Schools? the Replacement and School Command and the Antiaircraft Command inquired. Can Negroes be given observation aviation training? Scott Field asked. Where can we send Negro medical enlisted men for training? Second Army and the Flying Training Command inquired.[95] Occasionally an officer, observing that no applications for specialists' or advanced training had ever come from the enlisted men of the unit, made specific inquiries. Up to July 1943, the 61st Aviation Squadron, with 300 men, had not processed a single application for aviation cadet training. "And being uncertain as to the course we should pursue," Moore Field's Aviation Cadet Examining Board wrote, "we have not made a direct appeal to them as part of our current recruiting campaign." From their records, however, the board had

[93] Memo, Actg Civ Aide to SW for G–3, 19 Mar 43, and Memo, G–3 for G–1, 26 Mar 43, WDGCT 291.21 (3–19–43); Memo, TAG ASF for G–1, 10 May 43, AG 201.6 (5–10–43) DC–A; Memo, G–1 for G–3, 12 May 43, WDGAP 322.99; Info Action Sheet, C&R Br AGO to G–1, 14 May 43, AG 201.6 (5–14–43) OC–A.
[94] Ltr, TAG to CG's, etc., 17 Jun 43, AG 353 (10 Jun 43) B–D–A.
[95] Memo, Truman Gibson, Asst to Civ Aide to SW, for Lt Col Walter B. Smith, OD CofS, 27 Jun 41, AG 353.9 (6–27–41) (1); Ltr, Hq AFEDC and First AF to CG AAF, 8 Jun 43, and 1st Ind, Hq AAF, 15 Jun 43, AAF 353 Cld Trps; Msg, Hq Fourth Corps Area to Comdr Inf Sch, Ft. Benning, Ga., 9 Apr 42, Fourth Corps Area CA 220.632–Inf Sch 92–E–2; Msg, CG R&SC to CG AGF, 18 Jul 42, AGF 352/37 (MTS); Ltr, Hq AAC to CG AGF, 23 Sep 42, AGF 352/42 (Ord Sch); Ltr, Asst Adj Scott Fld, Ill. to CG 2d Dist, AAFTTC, St. Louis, Mo., AAF 353 Cld Trps; Rad, Second Army to Hq AGF, 17 Aug 42, Rad, Hq AGF to Second Army, 17 Aug 42, AGF 322.999/168.

concluded that several of the squadron's men seemed well qualified "and would probably welcome the opportunity to file applications if they were specifically invited to do so." [96]

Units might well have pondered the wisdom of advising their men of all training openings announced by the Army, for at times training agencies reported that they had no facilities for training Negroes and at other times Negro trainees reporting to training stations were summarily transferred elsewhere. Certain training facilities were considered "inadequate" for Negroes and assigning agencies were directed to use other facilities. School policies, moreover, shifted from time to time. The Air Forces, desiring the Signal Corps to train Negro enlisted men for the 1000th Signal Company, 96th Service Group, learned that Signal Corps was training no Negroes in the required specialties. The Air Forces proceeded to make a search to obtain men from civilian life who already had the required training and experience.[97] Some six weeks later, it learned that Signal Corps was now training Negro soldiers in these specialties.[98] Negro enlisted men arriving at the Parachute School in 1942 were immediately transferred on the grounds that the school had no facilities for training them and the Army had no units to which they could be assigned.[99] Ordnance trainees

were ordered to Aberdeen or other Army installations rather than to affiliated schools because trainees in civilian plant and other private schools were billeted in YMCA's and hotels where only "unsuitable" facilities were available for Negroes. This restriction applied to all affiliated ordnance schools except Hampton Institute.[100] The existence of special separate schools like the Hampton automotive training school, established by the Quartermaster Corps in April 1941 as a stopgap program for training the increasing Negro personnel of the Army, and the course for Negro physical therapists at Fort Huachuca established by the Medical Department for civilians and, later, for Wacs, in 1943, further confused the issue of the eligibility of Negroes for any and all Army schools.

The location of training facilities in schools and colleges operating under state segregation laws, most of whose contracts with the Army contained the usual federal nondiscriminatory clauses, posed a further problem at times. Generally, where these schools objected to Negro students and where duplicate facilities existed elsewhere, Negro trainees were sent to schools in other areas, but in some instances, as at the School for Personnel Services at Washington and Lee University, Negro trainees were accepted in regular courses. No general policy on this matter was formulated.

While these additional barriers to full participation in the Army's facilities for training did exist, the main deterrent to the full and adequate training of Negro

[96] Ltr, Avn Cadet Examining Bd, Moore Fld, Tex., to Hq AAF, 6 Jul 43, and 1st Ind, 14 Jul 43, Hq AAF to Avn Cadet Examining Bd, Moore Fld, AAF 353 Cld Tng.

[97] R&RS, AAF Dir of Communications to AAF Dir of Base Svs, 6 Feb 43, AAF 353 Cld Tng.

[98] R&RS, AAF MPD to AAF Dir of Communications, 29 Mar 43, AAF 353 Cld Tng.

[99] M/R, AGF G-1 Enl Div, 16 Dec 42, AGF 220.3/1152.

[100] Ltr, Hq AGF to CG's Armies, Corps, Commands, DTC, Chief Armd Force, 12 Oct 42, AGF 322.999/4.

specialists continued to lie in the inability of a large enough number of men to meet the formal requirements for advanced training. Most Army schools were open to Negroes and most Negro units received the regularly allotted quotas for school training along with all other units of their types. The units' chief problem was to find men who were suitable candidates for training in courses which varied from horseshoeing at Fort Riley to airplane mechanics at Lincoln Air Base, from bakers and cooks at stations like Fort Benning to clerks at schools like Washington and Jefferson College. To add to the difficulty, many units lacked sufficient men qualified by temperament or certified ability to fill all existing needs for the noncommissioned officers so essential to unit training and to unit operations. The result was that most units blamed their lack of training progress on a variety of factors, most of which they traced back to the lack of knowledge and preparation of their enlisted men as exemplified, visibly, in the AGCT scores inscribed on each man's Form 20 card. AGCT scores, illiteracy, and "low intelligence" became the major villains besetting Negro units. Special training units were a help, and locally operated "leadership" and specialist schools filled many a gap in unit training opportunities, but most units felt that if they could just receive fillers with more nearly normal AGCT scores most of their problems would be solved.

Often the existence of low AGCT scores in a Negro unit became a bulwark against adverse criticisms of training progress and discipline. Unit officers learned very early that the maldis-tribution of AGCT scores in Negro units as measured against white unit norms was generally an acceptable explanation for nearly all difficulties which a Negro unit might be undergoing. If noncommissioned officers were poor, it was because too few men were in the leadership producing Grades, I, II, and III. If training progress was slow, it was because too many men were in the slow learning Grades, IV and V. If venereal disease rates were high, if morale was low, if discipline was poor, if AWOL rates were high, if mess halls and barracks failed to pass sanitary inspections, if vehicles and equipment were improperly maintained, low AGCT scores—low "intelligence"—were to blame. In many units the AGCT score became the refrain for a continuous jeremiad used as a fraternal greeting for inspectors. "When the Inspector General inspects a Negro unit," one officer experienced in the training of Negro soldiers explained, "the Unit Commander frequently calls his attention to the big percentage of men below Class II. The inspector thinks, 'Good Heavens, a unit like that can't be much good' and he starts looking for trouble. Sometimes he will say in his report, 'Unit will not be ready for movement overseas until a higher percentage of men in Class I, II, and III is assigned.' . . . Now the fact is that some very serviceable units can be made of personnel of this type. It would be a little silly to assume that all German soldiers are of Class III or better in spite of their claims of superiority. The Russians might lose some of their confidence if they knew the dreadful truth about their mental gradations. . . . Many of our officers are giving the results of these tests more weight than was ever intended." [101]

Something of what could be done when the situation demanded it and when full use of resources was made was illustrated by training centers such as the 3d Engineer Aviation Unit Training Center at MacDill Field, Florida, where eighty-eight enlisted instructors were used in the last half of the war. Most of these men were young, with a median age of 24. Most were from the South by birth and most had had limited civilian experience before induction into the Army. Their education ranged from the second year of elementary school through completion of college; exactly half had had four years of high school or some college training. All had been in the Army from twelve to eighteen months. Exactly half were in the first three grades, half were in IV and V. Nearly half had been manual laborers, with the remainder spread through a varied list of skilled and semiskilled civilian occupations, few of which had direct connection with the engineering trades. Of these soldiers and their backgrounds the training center reported:

The list of specific occupations will suggest the civilian experience on which Army specialist training could be grounded. Perhaps one-third of the list, including the bartender and the asylum attendant, are difficult to connect with the task of building runways for advancing air power. Even so, native human capacities under the spur of need and the stress of opportunity often do respond in unsuspected ways.[102]

While the AGCT scores and the poor backgrounds of Negro enlisted men which they measured were certainly central to the slow progress of many units, they alone could not be held responsible for all training difficulties which Negro soldiers and their units faced. While low scores were characteristic of most Negro units, not all units faced the same varieties of training problems, nor were all units equally affected by comparably low scores. Those unit commanders who discounted the paramount value of scores in judging the potentialities of units found there were other factors of equal importance involved in the successful training of Negro units. With an examination of these factors in the life and training of Negro units, the role of AGCT scores loses lustre as the touchstone for understanding the major problems of Negro units and their training.

[101] Unit Training, Address by Col Lawrence B. Wyant, GSC Mil Tng Div ASF, to Fourth ASF Tng Conf, Ft. Monmouth, N.J., 15–17 Mar 44, Files Fourth Conf, pp. 4–5.

[102] EAUTC Hist Rpt, Ex No. 43, Fldr 1 (18 Mar 43–1 May 44), pp. 126–27, AF Hist Div Archives.

CHAPTER X

Physical Fitness

The physical fitness of the Negro population of military age was less decisive than Army General Classification Test scores in its effect upon the employment of Negro troops, but it was nevertheless a matter of major importance to the Army. As with mental and educational standards, changing physical standards for induction and employment often caused administrative and training complications in the absorption and assignment of Negro men. Physical fitness problems affecting Negro inductions, employment, and discharges were closely connected with the same factors which made educational deficiencies so important to Negro units.

Health and Inductions

Studies of the civilian health of Negroes conducted before the war had shown that Negro life expectancy was shorter than that of white Americans. Death rates were higher among Negroes than among whites. Illness rates were also higher.[1] Poor health facilities in many of the areas from which Negroes came, poor economic circumstances which prevented many families from taking advantage of the medical and dental facilities that did exist, poor housing and inadequate diets which contributed to physical deficiencies, and cultural standards which failed to produce precautions and sanctions against social diseases were factors contributing both to higher death and illness rates for civilians and to those physical disabilities which resulted in high rejection rates for Negro registrants for military service.

All men inducted into the Army during the first half of the war were very largely free of serious physical defects. Sixty percent of the Negroes and 57 percent of the whites available for general service between November 1940 and December 1943 had no discoverable defects at all. Defects in the remainder were minor. Among limited service personnel, available for induction after June 1942, the major defects among white men were those of the eyes and teeth, while among Negroes they were the venereal diseases.

Negro men inducted for limited service (Selective Service Class I–B) constituted no large problem for the Army, for relatively few Negroes were accepted for limited service as such. The original experimental call in June 1942, designed to determine how well physically

---

[1] For comprehensive discussions of the findings of health studies, see Samuel J. Holmes, *The Negro's Struggle for Survival: A Study in Human Ecology* (Berkeley: University of California Press, 1937); Julian H. Lewis, *The Biology of the Negro* (Chicago: The University of Chicago Press, 1942); and E. Franklin Frazier *The Negro in the United States* (New York: Macmillan, 1949), pp. 567–92.

substandard men could be absorbed by the Army for use on nonstrenuous duty, contained 800 whites and 200 Negroes. The next call, in August 1942, required 2,500 whites only. Thereafter, Class I–B was discontinued, physical standards were lowered, and limited service men were progressively reclassified I–A (immediately available) if they had no major disqualifying defects. At first 10 percent and, later, 5 percent of the men of each race accepted each day at each induction station could be limited service men. These color percentage quotas were dependent upon regular induction calls and acceptances by race. They therefore fluctuated considerably. At various times white limited service men up to 20 percent of the men accepted and no Negroes were called, with the result that, in 1943, 99,846 white as compared with 4,184 Negro limited service men and, in 1944, 34,352 white as compared with 1,747 Negro limited service men were inducted. After May 1944, acceptance of limited service men ceased.[2]

Excepting the venereal diseases, all principal disorders among Negroes examined by local boards and induction stations occurred proportionately about the same number of times as among whites, with somewhat lower percentages of defects of eyes, ears, teeth, lungs, and the musculoskeletal system among Negroes accepted and rejected than among whites. Figures on rejections could not always be compared with accuracy, nor could they be taken as a complete cross-sectional picture of the

nation's health. The data on defects were based on 10 to 20 percent samples of available reports. They did not include examinations of volunteers, Regular Army men, National Guardsmen, and others entering the Army outside of the Selective Service System. Nor did they report the health of deferred men. Physical standards and reporting systems varied, at times, from board to board and station to station. Complete listings of all disqualifying defects were not always reported by examining stations. Selective Service found that the tendency to record or summarize only the most serious defects of Negro registrants was especially marked. Therefore, the immediately disqualifying defects might be listed while less important disorders were ignored. While they might not give a complete picture of the state of selectees' health, first examination reports did give a reliable accounting of the availability of manpower for immediate service. Since nearly all Negroes entered the Army through the Selective Service System, the Negro figures when taken alone had a higher validity as a gauge of Negroes' availability; but since proportionately fewer whites entered through Selective Service, comparative figures were a less valid index to comparative racial health.[3]

The Venereal Disease Problem

The first two million serologic reports of selectees re-emphasized the importance of the venereal diseases as deter-

---

[2] Mil Pers Div ASF, The Procurement of Military Personnel, II, 326–29, MS OCMH; *Quotas, Calls, and Inductions* (Selective Service System Special Monograph 12, Washington, 1947), I, 97–99.

[3] Cf. *Physical Examination of Selective Service Registrants* (Selective Service System Special Monograph 15, Washington, 1947), I, 149–80, and Tables in III, 46, 50.

rents to the full use of American manpower. Unless some method could be found to reclaim and use venereals, many of whom were otherwise free of physical defects, a great body of potentially valuable manpower would be lost to the military services. The venereal diseases became, therefore, a major target for medical attack in preparation for and in prosecution of the war. The venereal diseases, though they were by no means the only physical factor involved, became the principal physical disability markedly limiting the military employment of Negro as compared with white manpower. Combined with educational deficiencies, they sharply reduced the proportions of Negro registrants initially available for general service. Primarily because of these two disproportionately frequent defects, over half of the Negro registrants examined, as compared with less than two fifths of the white registrants, were not eligible for general service on their first examinations.[4]

The problem posed for the Army by the high rates of venereal disease among Negroes was threefold. Venereal diseases complicated and slowed up, through deferments and rejections, the selection and induction of Negro registrants during the first years of the war. They caused a disproportionate loss of administrative, training, and duty time once Negroes were inducted. They placed a further strain on morale in the training and supervision of Negro units. The presence of venereal diseases bulwarked personal prejudices in the training and use of Negro troops. No

amount of instruction in the nature of transmission of these diseases could overcome completely the aversion of most noninfected men to venereals. Nor did the circulation and posting of reports detailing the high rates of infection occurring in many Negro units aid in dispelling the notion, often alluded to in officers' letters requesting transfers, that Negro troops were personally careless and dirty.

At the beginning of mobilization, registrants with venereal diseases were rejected completely, although some cases of men with gonorrhea, the venereal disease most common and at the same time most difficult to detect by routine examination methods, did get into the Army.[5] After March 1942, registrants with adequately treated syphilis could be inducted, but the criteria of adequate treatment were such that few registrants with a history of syphilis could meet them. Registrants with uncomplicated gonorrhea became available for limited service at the same time. In October 1942, men with uncomplicated gonorrhea up to 2 percent of each race at each induction station (later raised to 4 percent) could be inducted for general service. In December 1942, regulations were again relaxed, with the number of venereals accepted geared to the number of beds and rapid treatment facilities actually available in reception centers. It was March 1943 before enough treatment facilities became available to allow the Army to accept very many venereals and to treat them

---

[4] *Ibid.*, I, 160.

[5] Maj. Ernest B. Howard, MC, "Gonorrhea from the Standpoint of the Army," *American Journal of Syphilis, Gonorrhea, and Venereal Diseases*, CXXVII (1943), 607–15.

before their assignment to regular training.[6]

The higher incidence of syphilis among Negroes was such that maintaining equal ratios of venereal inductions by race in the first months of 1943 did not allow a sufficiently rapid absorption of previously rejected Negro men. In August 1943, therefore, induction stations were authorized to accept Negroes with syphilis up to one third of the total Negro call. Nevertheless, on 1 April 1945, when all inductions were slowing down, it was estimated that 265,100 or 5.7 percent of all the 4,629,000 registrants aged 18-37 then in the rejected classes were syphilitics. An additional 18,400 or 0.4 percent were so classified for other venereal diseases. Of these, over half in each category were Negroes.[7]

Those venereals who were inducted under the relaxed Army standards of 1943 were treated and cured of their diseases before entering regular training through the use of new rapid treatment methods employing sulfa drugs and, later, penicillin. Within Army units, therefore, the problem of venereal disease was very largely one of the prevention and control of new infections. While chaplains were free and in most commands were urged to stress moral principles and control through conti-

nence, the Army approached its prevention and control program from a practical medical point of view closely related to manpower economics.

Although Army control methods succeeded in keeping Negro military rates below those of the Negro civilian population, Negro units in a given area or command continued to account for disproportionate numbers and percentages of venereal infections. Until the treatment of uncomplicated cases on duty status became possible, Negro soldiers lost a large number of days from duty. During the first four months of 1942, when Negroes constituted 7 percent of the strength of the Southeast Air Force Training Center, they accounted for 42 percent of the center's cases. In the First Air Force for October and November 1942, when Negroes amounted to 11 percent of the command, they represented 40 percent of the cases. In September 1942 the 93d Infantry Division, with 107 cases (a rate of 99 per 1000 per annum), lost 2,226 man days from duty, two and a half times as many days as any other division then under Ground Forces control.[8] In light of the training difficulties of Negro units, excessive losses of duty time from venereal diseases augured no good if allowed to proceed unchecked.

The Antivenereal Disease Campaign

The United States Public Health Service's campaign against venereal diseases, underway during the last half of the

[6] Major regulations governing the induction of venereals were contained in MR 1-9, 31 Aug 40; MR 1-9, 15 Mar 42; State Dir Adv No. 77, 26 Sep 42; MR 1-9, 15 Oct 42; State Dir Adv 126, 17 Dec 42; Ltr, AG 372.02 PR-I, 25 May 43; Local Bd Memo 178, amended 6 Jan 44; MR 1-9, 19 Apr 44.
[7] Data from National Headquarters Selective Service System Report, Venereal Disease in Selective Service Registrants. On the incidence of syphilis in the civilian population, see Thomas Parran, "The Role of the United States Public Health Service in Venereal Disease Control," Federal Probation, VII (April-June 1943), 5.
[8] Rpt, Capt Robert Dyar, MC, to the Air Surgeon, 6 Jun 42, AAF 726.1; 2d Ind, Hq AAF EDC and FAF to CG EDC and First Army, 31 Dec 42, on Ltr, Hq AAF to CG FAF, 11 Dec 42, AAF 726.1; AGF Statistical Bull 30, 25 Nov 42.

thirties, had barely begun to affect the country's Negro population by 1940. Despite concerted efforts at education in the danger, prevention, and cure of venereal diseases, many Negro communities, lacking good health and medical attention generally, had not come to a realization of either the importance of or the possible treatments of venereal diseases. General sanitary facilities were often such that minimum venereal disease control at best was all that was possible. The names of the common venereal diseases themselves were often unknown. Unless the problem was discussed with soldiers in the more familiar slang terms, lectures on the dangers of syphilis and gonorrhea often made little impression. The sufferer from "bad blood" did not always connect his disorder with that which the lecturer was discussing. Often lecturers, with their charts and technical terms, failed to make their main points clearly, especially to slow learners. One officer found a soldier who admitted that he had had trouble using the chemical prophylaxis kit provided because he found it very difficult to swallow its white tube.[9] Others confirmed the existence of cultural barriers to the full efficacy of the control program offered by the Army. Superstitions about the nature of venereal diseases were widespread. Among both white and Negro troops they acted as deterrents to educational programs, but Negro troops were the more likely to have learned that it is impossible to contract venereal diseases during the full of the moon or that drinking lemon juice was a sure cure for

gonorrhea.[10] Resistance to prophylaxis was high, furthermore, because of widespread beliefs that prophylactic measures and devices reduced virility. Reluctance to visit prophylactic stations was increased in many situations—where stations were located in or near police stations, where there was any question of their free use by Negroes, where they were located away from the Negro sections, or where they were so far from bus or train stations that the risk of missing transportation back to camp was sufficient to make a soldier go directly to the station rather than out of his way for prophylaxis. Moreover, the leading citizenry, Negro as well as white, in many towns either had little interest in or were reluctant to participate in venereal disease control measures. In some towns, it was difficult to find a location for a prophylactic station which was not objected to by the citizenry.[11]

Even in areas where the May Act had been invoked, Negro rates continued high. The May Act permitted federal intervention in the control of prostitution in areas around Army camps when local authorities were unable to act.[12] Organized prostitution, against which the May Act was primarily aimed, was rare among Negroes in most areas, but available and willing women were not. The control measures of the May Act were difficult to enforce where the free lance prostitute, the bar girl, and the woman described only as "friend" were

[9] Capt Marcellus H. Goff, MC, 366th Inf, VD Among Colored Trps, Incl to Ltr, Hq First Sv Comd to CG ASF, 20 Aug 43, SPOCS 726.1.

[10] Memo, Capt James W. Fisher for Chief Experimental Sec, Research Br ASF, 2 Jan 45, AAF TI&E Div Files.

[11] Ibid.; Hist Tuskegee Army Air Fld From Conception to 6 Dec 41, AF Hist Div; Ltr, Hq Greenville AAB to CG Third AF, Tampa, 29 Oct 42, AAF 726.1 Genito-Urinary, etc., Diseases, binder 1.

[12] U.S. Code, Title 18, sec. 51a.

the major sources of infection. Even with well-planned precautionary methods, rates might remain high.

Despite its efforts at control, one engineer separate battalion located in a May Act area had twenty-four cases in five weeks out of an average strength of 1,185 men, giving the battalion a rate of 211 per thousand per annum. The twenty-four cases accounted for 277 man days lost from duty and training. This unit scheduled lectures by the battalion surgeon or exhibitions of venereal disease prevention training films twice a month. Company commanders lectured on sex hygiene once a month. Platoon sergeants also lectured once a month. For purposes of dispelling fear of prophylaxis treatment, demonstration prophylaxis was given in every squad of the organization. Mechanical prophylaxis kits were supplied to every man going on pass. Individual kits were given to each man going on overnight pass or furlough. Each man returning from pass was required to report to the dispensary and state whether or not he needed prophylactic treatment. The location of prophylactic stations was posted in every barrack. Posters advertising the value of prophylaxis were widely displayed. Passes were restricted as much as possible consistent with maintaining morale. And efforts were being made to provide sufficient recreation on the post to keep men away from the camp towns. Yet a number of factors limited the full success of this program. Following preventive instructions was not easy for the men of this battalion. In the largest of the nearby towns the prophylactic facilities were hardly adequate. The colored

station, approximately one mile from the center of the Negro district, while accessible in the summer, was less so in the winter. The white station, more conveniently located in the center of town, had refused admittance to several men of the organization who had applied for prophylaxis, thus reducing sharply the number of potential applicants. After remonstrances, the white station began to take Negro soldiers "provided they are not obnoxious to local civilians." Despite the fact that the rate in the Negro organizations on the post was several times that of the white, the Control Board concluded, the preventive facilities, including recreational diversions, available for Negro soldiers were generally inferior to, and therefore less effective, than those for whites.[13]

Surveys elsewhere uncovered similar problems. Standard remedies in addition to venereal disease education programs became, first, cleaning up surrounding camp towns, and second, furnishing increased on-post activities in order to reduce the number of exposures.

With or without facilities that provided "wholesome" recreation for soldiers away from camps, most camp towns had enough of a tenderloin district to cause unit officers to despair of reducing their venereal rates. An officer of one Negro unit reported that conditions in the nearby camp town were "inimical to the efficiency, health, and welfare of soldiers." Prostitution was rampant in cafes in the Negro section; the restaurants themselves were "especially unclean." The officer reported:

[13] Ltr, IG Second Army to CG Second Army, 17 Nov 42, and 3 Inds, AGF 333.1/53 Second Army.

As things go now a man going on pass has little to improve his morale. Buses are crowded. Hours may be spent to catch a bus. Our Negro troops are segregated in mixed buses. Little recreation is possible. Almost no good place to eat. At least one popular place is unsanitary. Vice is tempting. This puts the soldier in a complaining frame of mind. The latter is especially in evidence in relations with our soldiers and the Military Police. . . . [There is an] apparent lack of interest in the Negro section by the [town] administrative officers.[14]

In another town, most of the Negro houses of prostitution were located around the USO. The house across the street from the USO contained eleven girls, ten of them infected. Six of these had two diseases.[15]

In many towns, the Negro district was served by neither running water nor by a sewage system. This condition made simple sanitation difficult. It made the use of soap-impregnated prophylactic materials provided in Army kits almost impossible and certainly discouraging. In a few cases no hot water was provided in prophylactic stations, either in town or on post, with the result that soldiers would not use the stations.[16] Under these circumstances, preventive instructions had little effect except among that portion of a command which heeded the

advice to remain continent. Where recreational facilities were as limited as they were in many towns and on many posts, and where troops felt that release from frustrations and pent-up emotions was necessary at any cost, such advice was not often heeded for long.

The Fry Problem

A special problem was that which existed at Fort Huachuca, Arizona, training home of the two Negro infantry divisions and, before that, of the old Negro cavalry and infantry regiments. Located in the Huachuca Mountains of southeastern Arizona, Fort Huachuca had been a post since 1877. It had no camp town at all. The nearest towns were Bisbee, 35 miles away and 10 miles from the border; Douglas and Agua Prieta, 60 miles away on and across the Mexican border; Nogales, 65 miles away on both sides of the border; and Tucson, 100 miles away. Each of these towns, with the exception of Bisbee, was visited frequently by as large a number of troops as could get away on pass.[17] Prostitution was rife in most of them, though Tucson and Douglas had relatively few Negro prostitutes and only a small resident Negro population. The Mexican towns, with their tourist attractions and their bordellos, usually lying just outside of the city limits, and therefore subject to little municipal control, were patronized generously by soldiers from Fort Huachuca. The welcome there was warmer than in the Arizona towns. In Nogales,

---

[14] Incl 4, S–2 333d FA to CO 333d FA, Cp Gruber, Okla., 10 Feb 43; 1st Ind, 8th Hq Sp Trps Third Army to Ltr, Hq AGF to Third Army, 29 Jan 43, AGF 726.1/74 (VD).

[15] Ltr, Maj George McDonald to Hq AAF, 21 Jan 43, AAF 726.1 binder 2. The commander of the nearby post did not believe conditions were so bad as this and made McDonald specify locations and describe them in detail.

[16] Ltr cited n. 15; 1st Ind, 384th Engr Bn (Sep) to Ltr, IG Second Army, 17 Nov 42, AGF 333.1/58 (Second Army); Memo, Hq ASF for Chief Experimental Sec, Research Br I&E Div ASF, 2 Jan 45, in AAF TI&E Div Files.

---

[17] Bisbee, a mining town, had few facilities for visiting soldiers, though it was nominally the post town. At its own request, it was placed off-limits to nonresident Fort Huachuca personnel.

Sonora, for example, all but two dance halls and restaurants were open to Negro soldiers; they were "welcome to all the cantinas (bars) and cheap restaurants and particularly to the red-light district for which they represent its principal source of income."[18] Local fears, growing vice conditions, and mounting racial tensions gradually caused most of the Arizona towns, or major portions of them, to be closed at times to Fort Huachuca personnel. But the Mexican towns and the nearby unincorporated settlement of Fry, lying just outside the gates of the post, remained open. Fry offered, in exaggeration, all the allure, if none of the exotic glamor, of the Mexican towns.

Because it was surrounded by a desert with no nearby communities and because it was located in a part of the country with practically no Negro population, Fort Huachuca, since the days when it was a frontier post garrisoned with Negro soldiers of the old regiments, had considered Fry a quasi-necessary adjunct. White Arizonians, thinking of Fry as a safety valve, tended to agree. In Fry lived women. Some of them were employees of the post and some were members of soldiers' and civilians' families, but most of them—and sometimes the former were included in this number—were prostitutes and camp followers. As the post commander described it in 1942:

The small town of Fry is dirty, unsanitary and squalid. It has been so for many years. It was made worse in these respects during the construction of the cantonment when two or three thousand white laborers were employed here. During this period, when a much lesser number of soldiers was stationed here, the expulsion of prostitutes from Fry was directed by the Commanding General, Eighth Corps Area. A considerable number of prostitutes left, most of whom are believed to have drifted back in a short period of time. When the drive was on, soldiers, including N. C. O.'s, married a considerable number of prostitutes rather than see them leave. Some of this latter group are known to have continued to ply their trade. Following this action there was noticeable a restless and disgruntled attitude on the part of the soldiers which showed itself in various ways. White women in Fry became so alarmed with reference to their security that the unions at work on the cantonment threatened to have their laborers leave the job as they said they would not work where their families were not secure. I personally addressed mass meetings of these unions, guaranteed their families security and persuaded them to remain at work.[19]

As the numbers of laborers in Fry decreased, the number of soldiers on the post increased, leading the post commander to observe that the number of prostitutes in Fry had probably increased, too, "as a natural reaction to the law of supply and demand."[20] Many of them were transients arriving for a few days, renting or sharing a shanty, then leaving to return at a later date.

Venereal disease control was at best a difficult problem, but with a Fry and its Blue Moon area, made up of tin shanties, lean-to's, and tents inhabited by an undetermined number of camp followers, the problem of control at Fort Huachuca, especially after the arrival of large units,

---

[18] Dispatch, L. S. Armstrong, American Consul, Nogales, Sonora, to Secy of State, 16 Jul 42, No. 375, in 93d Div Files 291.

[19] 1st Ind, Hq Ft. Huachuca to CG Ninth Sv Comd, 4 Aug 42, to Ltr, Ninth Sv Comd to CO Ft. Huachuca, 28 Jul 42, copy in 93d Div Files.
[20] Ibid.

became more difficult. Fry became widely known and discussed both at Fort Huachuca and elsewhere. The post commander admitted that, after considering several possibilities, his sympathies lay with retaining Fry in an improved and regulated form. He believed that repression of prostitution in Fry would be a danger to surrounding communities and to morale on the post. Moreover, scattering prostitutes in an area where there were no communities that wished to receive them would be most difficult. To the post commander there were but three solutions to prostitution in Fry:

a. What is in my opinion the best solution, is prohibited by War Department policy. That solution is: Definitely segregated areas which the Federal, State and County health authorities can control and outside of which no prostitution would be permitted. With such a system, infected women could be put out of circulation and treated and the military authorities could arrange for every man entering such a segregated area taking prophylaxis treatments.

b. The second solution is to let the prostitution situation drift along as I have found it and endeavor, with the cooperation of the Federal, State and County authorities, to arrange for the treatment of infected women and at the same time take every possible precaution by means of education, persuasion, and thoroughness in operations, to insure the greatest number of prophylactic treatments to men who become exposed.

c. The third solution, is to entirely eradicate prostitution in the town of Fry and other towns visited by soldiers and to prohibit soldiers from entering Mexico. It is believed that little good would be accomplished by prohibiting prostitution in Fry and permitting it to exist in other towns in the vicinity, including Mexico. Probably more harm than good would be done as we can control more definitely,

prophylaxis treatments at Fry than we can in other towns. . . .[21]

With the first solution not approved by the War Department policy and the third one not feasible, Fry was left with the military authorities taking "every possible precaution," though a version of the first solution was briefly tried. Toward the end of 1942, since neither county nor state officials had moved to repress prostitution in the area, post authorities, with the co-operation of local civilian authorities, moved the more notorious and easily detected prostitutes into a wire enclosure, carrying their shanties and tents bodily with them. This area, one of whose boundaries was provided by the post's fencing, became known as "The Hook." On the Fry side of the post all roads and paths from the bus station, the Gate theater, the USO clubs, and the Green Top, led directly to The Hook, whose gates, guarded by a military police checking station and a prophylactic station, the latter supplemented by another inside, saw hundreds of soldiers come and go daily.[22]

Meetings with residents of Fry were held in early 1943 at which it was explained that both the laws of Arizona and the May Act gave sufficient authority to close every place in town. At one meeting, where over a hundred residents were present, the post commander announced that the discussion was "not for those living a virtuous life with their family." Nobody left.[23] He then ex-

[21] 1st Ind, Hq Ft. Huachuca to CG Ninth Sv Comd, 4 Aug 42, papers in CSOIG 333.9 Ft. Huachuca, Ariz. (18).
[22] Hq 92d Div to Unit CO's, 2 Jul 43, 726.1 92d Div Files.
[23] Memo, Office Judge Advocate 93d Div for CG 93d Inf Div, 13 Jan 42, 93d Div Files 250.

plained rules for the registry, photographic identification, and weekly examination of every woman in The Hook. Nobody objected.

Fry and The Hook, with their new regulatory measures, came to the attention of other federal agencies and of civilian social hygiene associations. The regional Venereal Disease Control Committee, made up of representatives of the Army, Navy, U.S. Public Health Service, and the Federal Security Agency was less than satisfied with the Huachuca solution. At a meeting in Houston at the end of January 1943, representatives of the American Social Hygiene Association and the Federal Security Agency complained that so long as all officials of the Mexican border cities knew that Fort Huachuca was "conducting a stockade" the Pan American Sanitary Commission could hardly hope to establish effective border control of venereal disease.[24] Protests to the War Department that the post was violating Army directives brought action against the Huachuca solution. The Ninth Service Command, on orders from Army Services Forces, directed that Fort Huachuca stop using military personnel to control and examine prostitutes in Fry.[25]

The fences around The Hook were removed and repressive measures were again attempted. After the departure of the 93d Division in April 1943, many of the women residents left the area. Those remaining were ousted by the county sheriff in May. When, as part of the pressure against prostitution, one

of the landowners in the area was persuaded not to renew his leases and rental contracts, thus forcing the users of the land to move, another landowner leased or sold new land to the camp followers, who picked up their tents and shanties and started a new settlement a short distance from the old. Others moved to nearby towns. The local USO and, later, the newly constructed Fry Amusement Center (the Green Top) helped matters, but Fry and vestiges of The Hook, still going under the same name, remained. To the new full-time post venereal disease control officer Fry seemed "the strangest situation in the American Army." No camp in America, he continued, had "vice and corruption at its front door" like Fort Huachuca. Venereal disease might become a secondary matter in Fry, he concluded. "Soldiers entering the huts in that area may well bring into this camp the most dreaded diseases of modern times. From a public health point of view, typhus, the plague and cholera loom a serious menace and an actual possibility."[26]

After trying a number of other expedients, including the medical examination of all men entering or leaving it, Army authorities declared "the famous Hook area" and neighboring places off-limits to Fort Huachuca soldiers at "12 o'clock noon," Sunday, 22 August 1943.[27] That afternoon the venereal disease control officer saw "unaccustomed thousands" of men in the stands

[24] Ltr, Surg (VDCO) AAF Gulf Coast TC to Maj Robert Dyar, Hq AAF, 29 Jan 43, AAF 726.1 binder 2.
[25] Rad, Ninth Sv Comd to CO Ft. Huachuca, 13 Feb 43, Ft. Huachuca 726.1.

[26] Office VDC Ft. Huachuca to Post Surgeon, 10 May 43, Ft. Huachuca 726.1 (VD Control).
[27] Office VDC Ft. Huachuca, Venereal Disease Bulletin, 20 Aug 43; Ltr, 92d Inf Div Surgeon to CG VIII Corps, Brownwood, Tex., 28 Aug 43. Both in Ft. Huachuca 726.1 (VD Control).

at the ball game and "countless hundreds" lined up in front of theaters. Fry was "all but a deserted village. Infected prostitutes in The Hook, whose pockets in the past have bulged, were fleeing the area by the scores."[28] Thereafter many of the women moved back to Fry, some returning to one or another house, others becoming transient, using local taverns and the Green Top as soliciting points.[29] Some became mobile purveyors of their wares, cruising the surrounding area in automobiles, often with their mattresses tied to the tops of their cars.[30]

Nevertheless Fort Huachuca, relying on its compulsory prophylaxis system, with men ordered to check in and out of prophylaxis stations when leaving or entering post or Mexican border areas, supplemented by an intensive educational program and an extensive use of the off-limits power as main measures of control, did reduce its problem. The post's weekly Venereal Disease Bulletin, written with exceptional vigor and directness, was ordered read to all enlisted men at a formation before being posted on unit bulletin boards. The bulletin listed all new danger spots—local, on the border, and sometimes as far away as Memphis, Tennessee. Appeals made in the bulletin ranged from straight educational doctrine and the publication of comparative unit rates with honor rolls and black lists, through appeals to race pride, family honor, the future, religious considerations, and mere self interest, to sardonic attacks on the foolishness of the victim who, having been warned, continued to take

his chances. Intensive and unremitting campaigns for the last six months of 1943 reduced the post's rate from ten times the Army standard to twice the standard at the end of the year.[31] The service command's venereal disease control officer was able to write in November, "everyone up here is most pleased with the way things are going."[32]

Fry was not alone among the towns which allowed relatively uncontrolled vice to concentrate, for much the same reasons, in their Negro districts. While the problem was not so large elsewhere, both because the number of troops was smaller and the isolation less, the absence of community, and at times of command, support for cleaning up camp towns was a frequent obstacle to control measures. Civilian Negro communities in general were reluctant to become involved in antivenereal or other programs which had connection, actual or implied, with local police and municipal authorities. "The answer," one Negro observer declared, "is racial fear and skepticism, which makes them want to be left alone and attend to their own business. In most things for community good they will tell you 'I don't want to interfere' or 'I don't want to be mixed up in it.' They want to stay hidden in the background and live a quiet life for themselves and family."[33] The resistance of Negro citizens to participation in venereal disease control

---

[28] Ft. Huachuca, VD Bull, 27 Aug 43.
[29] Ibid., subsequent issues.
[30] Ibid., 24 Dec 43.

[31] Ibid., 9, 16, 30 Jul, 31 Dec 43.
[32] Ltr, Maj Wayne W. C. Sims, MC, Ninth Sv Comd VDCO to Col E. B. Maynard, MC, Surg Ft. Huachuca, 12 Nov 43, Ft. Huachuca 726.1.
[33] Address, Maj. George McDonald, Negro Prostitution and Methods of Control, delivered before the Alabama State Conf on VD, State Capitol, 9 Jul 43, Montgomery, copy in AAF 726.1 Genito-Urinary, binder 4.

programs was overcome in a few communities, notably those with good general public health programs where the co-operation of white citizens and communities was available. Various devices to reduce the exposure risk among soldiers were tried. Appeals to race pride were common. One post bulletin, announcing a venereal disease campaign slogan contest for Negro troops chided, ". . . the Negro has excelled in every phase of warfare except the control of V.D." [34] The First Air Force issued a pamphlet, "Who, Me?" especially for Negro soldiers. At some posts the unit with the best record got a trophy for excellence; on at least one post, the unit with the worst got a booby prize—a handsomely mounted eight ball.[35] Still others tried various systems of identifying nonprostitutes, with some areas of heavy incidence resorting to the use of "health cards," obtained from local physicians or clinics. At MacDill Field, Florida, all women visitors to the "Colored Area" of the field were required to have "V-ette" cards, obtained without charge at the Negro USO in Tampa. These cards, similar to those used for white visitors to the base, served as substitutes for passes issued by organizations. They were available after the local USO had checked several references and had ascertained that the applicant was in good health.[36]

The Tuskegee Program

None of these varied plans and improvisations worked so well as a program begun at Tuskegee Army Air Field, later prescribed for the Air Forces at large and, still later, in slightly altered form, for the Army as a whole. This program was essentially a combination of measures already in effect at other places plus some innovations which were to spell the difference between the success of the Tuskegee program and the failure of so many others.

Tuskegee, essentially a flying school with roughly 1,300 men in addition to cadets, found its venereal rate climbing steadily through the first half of 1942. The post was located in a high civilian incidence area near several other airfields and camps. As the military installations in the area expanded, infected women flocked to nearby towns where honky-tonks and dance halls offered easy pickings for the soldiers of Gunter, Maxwell, and Craig Fields, near Montgomery; Camp Rucker and Napier Field to the south; Fort Benning at Columbus; Fort McClellan, near Birmingham; and Tuskegee, halfway between Montgomery and Columbus and not too far from Birmingham and Atlanta.

---

[34] VD Bull 1, Keesler Field, Miss., July 1943. Also, Lecture on VD for Narration of a Proposed Film, Incl to 4th Ind, McDonald to Surgeon Tuskegee AAF, 17 Sep 43, on basic VDC Br Air Surgeon's Office to CG AAFTC Ft. Worth, 25 Aug 43, AAF 726.1 Genito-Urinary Diseases, binder 4; Ft. Huachuca, VD Bull, 6 Jul 44 (vol. 2, No. 9), Ft. Huachuca 726.1.

[35] Ltr, Selfridge Fld Station Hosp to Air Surgeon, 14 Oct 43, AAF 726.1, binder 4.

[36] Ltr, Hq Cp Area MacDill Fld, Fla., to CO's All Cld Orgs, MacDill Fld, 26 Aug 43, no file No.; Ex L, Hist Rpt EAUTC MacDill Fld, 18 Mar 43–1 May 44, folder 2, exhibits A–S, AF Hist Archives. In some towns, "health cards" were sources of numerous incidents of racial friction as women with soldier escorts were stopped and asked to show them. Cf. Memo, TIG for CofS, 4 Jun 43, AG 291.21/22; Frank Yerby, "Health Card," Harper's Magazine, CLXXXVIII (May, 1944), 548–53.

Tuskegee's new venereal disease control officer, Maj. George McDonald, who had operated a successful municipal control program in Baltimore before entering the Army, found early that the simplest control measures—getting rid of infected women or of the places in which they were to be found--were not simple where Negro troops were concerned. "Some might argue," he told the Alabama governor's conference on venereal diseases, "that if we could get rid of the honky-tonks we would get rid of the chief meeting places of a large group of prostitutes. The answer to that was forcefully brought out to me during the beginning of our VDC Program. We found that fully 70 percent of all our venereal disease cases were contracted in Montgomery. We went to the Commanding Officer and seriously begged him to put Montgomery off-limits for our station. His answer was a question—'Where else or what else have you got to offer in its place?' I must admit, I was stumped." [37]

The Tuskegee program emphasized a system of "subvenereal disease control officers" in addition to the usual program of films, lectures, and command discipline. The subvenereal disease control officers were enlisted men, mainly noncommissioned officers, thoroughly trained in venereal disease control theories and practice. Each unit contained one or more such officers, supplementing the normal program. As enlisted men, these workers were able to uncover considerably more information concerning contacts in surrounding communities than the average commissioned officer could locate. Their lectures and discussions with groups of soldiers, plus pamphlets especially prepared for the men of the field, had greater effect than those of medical officers alone. Impetus to a reduction of rates was given by a periodic publication of the rates for each unit at the station, including comparisons with rates of other units and stations in the training center, thus enlisting both local competition and racial pride on the side of VD control. Communications from the post commander to unit commanders stressed their responsibilities for control as part of their over-all efficiency as commanders. Better planned and more frequent surprise physical inspections were instituted. Prophylactic kits were made readily available and demonstrations of their proper use were given frequently.[38] Within a comparatively few months the Tuskegee program had reduced the station's rate from one of the highest in the area to one of the lowest—from 300 to 400 per thousand per annum in the summer of 1942 to 20 and 28 in October and November, with the rate at the Primary Field falling to a flat zero in those months.[39]

After his success at Tuskegee, Major McDonald was requested by the Army Air Forces to make a tour of airfields,

[37] Address, Maj. George McDonald, Negro Prostitution and Methods of Control, 9 Jul 43, copy in AAF 726.1 Genito-Urinary, binder 4.

[38] See A VDC Program for Colored Troops, AAF 726.1. This mimeographed description of the program, with station unnamed, was distributed to service and training command headquarters, which, in some cases, reproduced it for fields, camps, and stations. See, for example, Ltr and Incl, Hq Ninth Sv Comd to CO's Posts, Camps, and Stations, 26 Jul 43, 726.1 SPKIM.

[39] Off Def Health and Welfare Svs, Social Protection Sec, Conf Bull II, 5 (8 Mar 43); Memo, Brig Gen Benjamin O. Davis for TIG, 6 Jun 44, AAF 333.1 Misc, Tuskegee.

where he gave talks and demonstrations to Negro troops. At the same time, he made supplementary reports on the venereal disease situation as it existed in the areas surrounding the fields visited.[40] But, as he informed Army Air Forces headquarters when future lecturing trips were proposed for him, the amount of good coming from short term intensive work was purely temporary. To be of lasting value, a program had to be in operation day in and day out.[41]

In May 1943, a special school for the instruction of noncommissioned officers in venereal disease control as developed at the field was authorized at Tuskegee. Men were sent to the successive courses of this school from all over the Air Forces and many of the fields with smaller units began to obtain more effective results.[42] Both the 92d Division and the post at Fort Huachuca instituted the subvenereal control system in mid-1943, helping reduce the rates at Fort Huachuca for the rest of the year.[43]

After the courses at Tuskegee became generally available, upon application for quotas, to all Air Forces stations—

and to other posts that requested attendance for their men—failure to make use of the Tuskegee method was regarded within the Air Forces as an indication of laxity in venereal disease control measures. Temporary schools, modeled on the Tuskegee curriculum, were set up both for white and for Negro students at other posts.

The Tuskegee plan was officially extended to the rest of the Army in expanded form after a conference on Venereal Disease Problems among Colored Troops, held by The Surgeon General on 13 October 1943. The new system of control, directed in February 1944,[44] went further when it authorized a Negro venereal disease control officer for military installations with a Negro strength of 5,000 or more. This officer was to serve as an assistant to the station venereal disease control officer.[45] His duties were: directing venereal disease education for colored personnel; securing contact information from infected colored soldiers; supervising prophylactic facilities for Negro personnel; and maintaining close liaison with the post special service officer in providing recreation for Negro troops.

Continuing and better educational aids were provided. Original educational materials had paid little attention to the Negro phase of the problem as such. New filmstrips included Negro materials as aids to recognition and awareness on the part of Negro troops; an

[40] Ltrs, AAF 726.1, binder 2 (1942–43).

[41] Ltr, Maj McDonald to Maj Julius R. Scholtz, Hq AAF, 2 Aug 43, AAF 726.1 Genito-Urinary, binder 4.

[42] Ltr, ACofAS Pers Hq AAF to CG's AF's and AF Comds, 11 May 43, AAF 726.1; Ltr, Hq AAF to CO Tuskegee AAF, 17 Sep 43, AAF 726.1 Genito-Urinary, binder 4; Rpt, Maj Robert Dyar, CofAAF VDC Br, to the Air Surgeon, no date, but Incl to Ltr, CofAS to CG's AAF SEATC, AAFTTC, 20 Jun 43, AAF 726.1 Misc; Rpt of Insp Trip to Third AF, 31 Mar–2 Apr, 8 Apr 43, Incl to Ltr, Actg Air Surgeon to CG Third AF, 19 Apr 43, AAF 726.1 Misc.

[43] Ltr, Office Dir Med Div Ft. Huachuca to CO Ft. Huachuca, 25 Jun 43, 726.1; Ltr, Hq 92d Div to CO's All Units, 23 Jun 43, 726.1 GNMAM, Div Files.

[44] WD Cir 88, 28 Feb 44, Venereal Disease Control Among Negro Troops.

[45] During the last half of 1943, twenty stations, all Ground and Service Forces training centers, had 5,000 or more Negro troops, with the bulk of Negroes at stations with smaller numbers of troops. Incl 2 to Memo, SGO for TAG, 18 Dec 43, AG 726.1 (18 Dec 43) (3).

antivenereal disease film with Negro characters was produced. Pamphlet and poster material aimed at Negro troops, using Negro figures, were produced locally and by central distribution agencies.

Compliance with the directive to furnish Negro venereal disease control officers at the larger camps proceeded slowly, with many of the officers coming directly from the Medical Administrative Corps' officer candidate schools. The stations successful in lowering their venereal disease rates were those which developed continuing intensive programs. Specific responsibility for the Negro program vested in one individual as a full-time job brought best results. Differences observed between two camps some months after the publication of the new system illustrated the need for comprehensive, continuous programs. Both stations were located in similar environments. Although neither was currently operating at the 5,000 strength required for the appointment of a Negro venereal disease control officer, the more successful station had had a regularly detailed Negro technical sergeant—called locally the Health Educator—performing the duties of such an officer for approximately two years. The sergeant conducted intensive courses in venereal disease control for noncommissioned officers of new units, utilizing lectures, projects, and practical problems as teaching methods. Efforts of the post were aided by the existence of a good venereal disease control program as a part of the larger public health program of the county in which the post and largest camp town were located. Two organizations, both known as "The Health Crusaders,"

were an important link between the county health agency and the community. The local white Young Men's Business Club adopted venereal disease control as its main community program for the coming year. The town's Negro ministers were either co-operative or at least not opposed to the program. All hostesses and junior hostesses at the USO received instructions concerning the program. The local prophylactic station was an unusually well-run one, with Negro medical technicians on duty twenty-four hours a day. The only difficulties experienced at this post were an inability to obtain 100 percent use of the town dispensary by the men and an inability to obtain complete co-operation from some company commanders who, despite the offer of post assistance, remained lukewarm toward the program.[46]

The program at the second camp in the same general area was much more spotty and therefore less successful. At this post there was no continuing day in and day out stimulation by a specialist. Attitudes and efforts, unit by unit, ranged from "spirited execution to neglect and lack of cooperation on the part of company officers." One company officer, when asked about his unit's consistently high rate, told the visiting medical officer that he had never found himself unable to "write a satisfactory indorsement." The second camp, moreover, had less co-operative surrounding communities and less advantageously located prophylactic facilities. All three of the dispensaries maintained in the three nearby towns were used by

---

[46] Memo, Capt James W. Fisher for Chief Experimental Sec, Res Br ASF, 2 Jan 45, AAF TI&E Files.

white and Negro soldiers, two of them with separate waiting rooms and none of them located near the Negro sections of the towns. A fourth area visited by the men of the post was the nearest large town, with two dispensaries, one for whites and one for Negroes. Both were unattractive, with dirt floors and inadequate space. Both were poorly located, with the Negro dispensary on the ground floor of the Negro USO building and the white station under a staircase in the rear of a police station. Both locations discouraged use. Attendants' hours at the Negro station were irregular, with the result that Negro soldiers complained of being refused by the white dispensary when their station was closed. The saving factor of the second camp's program was that the towns frequented by its soldiers had fewer venereal disease contacts than the town frequented by the soldiers of the camp with the better program. Consequently, the lower rates at the first camp indicated that providing "direct and active assistance to units on the company level [was] the most important deterrent to contraction of venereal disease and the resulting high rates." [47]

The relatively more intensive measures of control needed for Negro troops were constant and additional burdens for commanders. Instruction and control was a continuing problem, both in training and overseas. Some commanders connected high venereal diseases rates with increased pay rates coupled with the low AGCT scores of Negro troops; some found in them confirmation of the inability of Negro troops to conform to standard mores and con-

trols; and some viewed them as yet another example of innate differences between Negro and white troops. At times, therefore, the venereal situation among Negro troops helped bulwark initial resistance to the use and command of Negro troops, and especially to the use of Negro officers.

Specific instances reinforced this latter resistance in some units. Within a month of activation, one combat team of a division was faced with the problem of what to do about three Negro officers hospitalized for venereal diseases. The fact that one case was a "recurrence" of an old infection of eight years standing did not help matters. Aside from the necessary paper work and discussion of the proper procedures to be followed under new regulations and policies for dealing with venereal cases, the symbolic dangers of the situation to the division were clear.[48] Their regimental commander later requested that the officers be transferred, as "the fact of [their] treatment is generally known among the officers of the regiment and in all probability among the enlisted men also. . . . It is believed the future usefulness of these officers in this regiment has been seriously impaired." [49] No matter what action was taken the damage to the division, especially in terms of relations between white and Negro officers and in terms of the respect of enlisted men for their Negro officers, had been done.

---

[47] Ibid.

[48] Interoffice Ref Sheet, 92d Inf Div Surgeon to CofS, 12 Nov 42, 92d Div Files, sheet 2, No. 44.
[49] Ltr, CO 370th Combat Team to CG AGF, 23 Nov 42, 92d Div Files, sheet 2, No. 44. Two of the officers were court-martialed; sufficient evidence in the third case was not available for charges to be brought.

General Fitness for Full Duty

While venereal diseases, as recorded by race on statistical charts in reports, were dramatically evident problems among Negro troops, they were not the sole concern of unit commanders in the area of health. Though the Negro venereal rates remained high, the common complaint of commanders was not so much that excessive numbers of their men contracted venereal diseases, for the number of patients in a given unit at any one time was likely to be low despite the high rates indicated by the thousand men per annum count. The average unit was more likely to complain that the general physical fitness and stamina of its men was low.

If it is assumed that Army physical standards were adhered to at induction stations for both Negroes and whites,[50] it is difficult to explain the apparently rapid physical deterioration of many Negro enlisted men after induction into the Army. A variety of factors— better dietary and sanitary surroundings than large numbers of Negro soldiers were accustomed to in civilian life, regulated physical exercise and development, adequate medical and dental

care [51]—should have, and undoubtedly did, raise the physical standards of many Negro soldiers. Yet the average Negro unit reported generally lower physical stamina among its enlisted men than the average white unit reported.

Occasionally suggestions were made that Negro soldiers, especially those from the Deep South, had lower resistance that might be attributed to chronic deficiency diseases. In the 4th Cavalry Brigade of the 2d Cavalry Division during freezing and subzero weather in the winter of 1942, there were over 200 cases of frostbite, ranging from minor freezing of ears, fingers, and feet to more serious cases. Eighteen serious cases, mostly of frozen feet, occurred in a single truck convoy of the 10th Cavalry en route from Omaha, Nebraska, to Fort Riley, Kansas. On the same occasion none of the thirty white truck drivers in the same convoy suffered frostbite. Moreover, during the same period in the remainder of the division, whose other components were white, there were only eight minor cases. Most of the Negro victims were from Arkansas, Louisiana, and Texas. Ignorance and faulty guidance on the part of troop leaders, ignorance or failure to obey orders on the part of enlisted men, or inability of troop commanders to obtain replacements of worn-out or lost items of clothing may have played their part, but the fact remained that

---

[50] Suggestions were made from time to time to the effect that the initial examinations of Negro registrants at some induction stations may not have been so carefully conducted as those for white inductees. If this was true, of course a higher percentage of men with undetected or unrecorded defects would have become available for induction. See Robert Wormser, "Race and Draft," *The Nation*, CLVI (May 29, 1943), 790; Notes, ASF 5th Tng Conf, Cp Barkeley, Tex., 24–26 Oct 44, p. 171, ASF Control Div Files; Lt. Col. Herbert S. Ripley, MC, and Maj. Stewart Wolf, MC, "Mental Illness Among Negro Troops Overseas," *The American Journal of Psychiatry*, CIII (January, 1947), 507.

---

[51] There were investigations of sporadic charges that the medical and dental care of Negro men were being neglected. These charges, usually made in letters of enlisted men, their relatives, or their friends to the White House or the War Department, were seldom sustained. See, for examples: Ltr, AGO to CG AAF, 17 Feb 44, AG 291.2 (9 Feb 44) (1); Ltr, Hq AAF WCTC to CG AAF WCTC, 31 Jul 43, AAF 201.601 Disability.

many more Negro than white soldiers in the same command suffered from frostbite under the same conditions.[52]

Troops were generally less physically fit in the later years of the war when many men previously rejected were inducted into the Army. Progressively lower physical standards affected white units as well, but with a greater number of units in a given training command and a larger number of overhead installation position vacancies to which men rejected during preparation for overseas movement (POM) could be sent, the problem was less concentrated than among Negro units.

Moreover, in many Negro units large numbers of physically substandard men appeared long before the last phases of the war. As of March 1943, less than a year after activation, the 93d Division had discharged 3,790 men—a full quarter of a division's authorized strength—for physical disabilities. Of these, 414 were discharged with certificates of disability, 155 through Section VIII procedures,[53] and 3,221 through clearing field forces procedures for the physically unfit.[54] Many other units complained of physically unfit men who either could not or would not pass the required physical tests. Many of these men were cast-offs shifted from unit to unit on successive transfers, becoming, as one training inspector expressed it, "one of a rotating pool, a border line

case subject to conflicting medical opinion, [who] bounces around like a pellet in a pin-ball machine, because he represents a type that will do productive work only under constant supervision to say nothing of his contribution to the delinquency records." [55] A company commander described the situation in his unit:

There are some men in this Company who should not be in the Army, from the way they walk. Whether it is done on purpose or not I do not know but some of them walk on the side of their heels. We have one man who says he has to be wet all the time, that he cannot stand the heat, and gets excited quickly. Some of them are being written up now by the Medical Officer for discharge.[56]

Of fifty filler replacements received at one post for use in committed units, twenty-five were physically unfit for overseas duty. One was blind in one eye with defective vision in the other; others had heart disease, high blood pressure, venereal diseases, or drug addictions. Granting that sending stations tended to adjudge men more highly qualified than receiving stations did, this was a case requiring explanation. The surgeon of the sending station declared that these men were examined at his station and at general hospitals; they were believed to be eligible for full duty. Physically perfect men were becoming scarce, he remarked, and added: "It must be remembered that the type and class of

---

[52] Ltr, IGD (Lt Col McFarland Cockrill) to CG 2d Cav Div, Cp Funston, Kans., 12 Jan 42, 2d Cav Div File 333, filed with 9th Armd Div Files.

[53] Section VIII, AR 615–300, provided for the discharge of constitutionally inapt and undesirable men.

[54] Memo, Maj Gen Fred W. Miller, CG 93d Inf Div, for Lt Gen Courtney H. Hodges, CG Third Army, 27 Mar 43, AGF 322/1 (93d Inf Div).

[55] Memo, Hq ASF for Dir Mil Tng ASF, 20 Jan 44, SPTRU 333.1 (Engr).

[56] Statement, Lt Everett Paris, CO Co B, 378th Engr Bn, Freda, Calif., exhibit B, p. 7, Incl to Ltr, Asst IG Hq Desert Tng Center to CG DTC, 11 Aug 42, AG 291.21 (7-17-42) (1).

colored soldiers now being inducted is not what one would desire." [57]

A case might be made that some of the men in units, casual pools, and detachments who were considered physically unfit did suffer from disabilities aggravated by military training and service or that, as physical standards were changed, men with limiting disabilities were brought into the Army too freely. During mid-1943, when reclassifications out of Class IV–F (physically or mentally disqualified) were at a peak, proportionately more Negroes than whites were shifted from IV–F to classes eligible for induction. Twenty-three percent of the men placed in Class IV–F during this period were Negroes, but 36 percent of those leaving IV–F for induction were Negroes. Many of these men had previously been rejected under higher physical standards; others had been administratively rejected as being in excess of permitted quotas of limited service men, syphilitics, and illiterates which the Army could accept.[58] One officer, observing large numbers of them, commented: "These men, having been told they were unfit several times before, believe they are still unfit for military service and spend much of their time attempting to convert the Army to their point of view." [59]

Willfully or otherwise, the mental attitudes of these men played a large

part in their low physical state. By the end of 1942 nearly a third of the patients on medical wards at Fort Huachuca were already exhibiting signs of combined mental and physical illnesses, heightened, one observer felt, by contacts with other patients which produced a monotonous repetition of similar "simple patterns of psychogenic symptoms." The report specified:

About 30 percent of the patients occupying beds assigned to the medical service had psychogenic symptoms produced by the desire to get out of the Army. These symptoms were seldom referrable to the emotional or intellectual sphere and thus complicated psychoneuroses were rare. A few patients had neurocirculatory asthenia. The majority complained of sticking pains at the left nipple, pain in the chest, shortness of breath on exertion and pains in the legs. A few complained of nervousness and would begin to shake for the examiner's benefit. The remainder complained of back pain, pains in the extremities, or of pains in old surgical wounds or in scars of injuries or in old injuries all of which had been dormant for years before induction. Thus the heart, the back and the extremities, or old scars and injuries were the loci to which the primitive minds projected the symptoms born of a desire to escape.[60]

Few of these patients, even when they had only minor difficulties that were not sufficient to make further combat training unprofitable, showed any desire to keep up with training.

Though medical officers could seldom find cogent reasons for the poor physical condition of many of the complaining men, they were equally unsuccessful in any significant number of cases in proving willful shirking of tasks requir-

[57] Ltr, CO Cp Rucker, Ala., to CG Fourth Sv Comd, 24 Jan 44; Ltr, Surgeon Cp Gordon Johnston to CG ASFTC, Cp Gordon Johnston, Fla., 9 Feb 44, and Inds and Incls to both Ltrs, Hq Cp Rucker, Ala., 333.1.
[58] Physical Examination of Selective Service Registrants (Selective Service System Special Monograph 15, 1947), I, 158f.
[59] Memo, Capt William B. Bryant for Chief Fld Sv Br, I&E Div ASF, 7 Mar 45, Wyo., A–AF TI&E Files.
[60] Ltr, Asst to Dir Mil Pers Div Ninth Sv Comd to CG NSC (The Surgeon), 28 Dec 42, copy in Ft. Huachuca 333.1 Insps-Post Camps Stations.

ing physical endurance. Many unit officers and some medical officers were nevertheless convinced that malingering, and not physical disorders, was the answer to the complaints of many of the soldiers. In the absence of proof of malingering or of medical reasons for transfer or discharge, the "sick men" became liabilities to their units. "Malingering is about to run me crazy," one infantry battalion commander commented. "There are entirely too many 'cripples'—men complaining of . . . 'hurting' in de grine and . . . misery in de back.' You take them over to the medics. The medics may say they're all right, but they'll continue their limping. You don't know what to do with them." [61] One of this officer's company commanders declared:

You may watch most any company coming off the field and you'll see a line of from five to twenty-five stragglers or 'cripples.' They will fall out on the march, go over and sit under a mesquite bush, laugh and talk, and yell at other men to come and fall out with them. They are by no means whipped; they have stamina left. But they have not the pride in themselves as men and soldiers to go ahead and finish the march.[62]

Other commanders were similarly convinced that many complaints of physical disabilities were willful evasions of duty or were faked to avoid passing inspections for overseas readiness—a certain indication of low unit and individual morale where it occurred.

One service commander observed of the men in a battalion which had already been twice rejected for overseas service:

Recently, one of my inspecting officers, who had so far not appeared at that particular unit, was mistaken by my colored friends for one of General Peterson's inspectors. About five or six of them promptly told him reasons why they were not fit for overseas duty. Five of them claimed they had physical defects. A couple more of them had never fired their weapons. They, of course, were promptly checked. The five had never appeared on sick call. They were re-examined and found to be excellent physical specimens. The other two men had certainly fired their rifles, and had done very well, incidentally.[63]

Some camps separated the chronic complainers into special casual or "ZI" units in order to minimize their effect on other soldiers. Some of these special units grew large toward the end of the war; others, aided by a supervised change in mental outlook, had a remarkably high percentage of restorations to physical fitness. A training center commander reported his experience with the latter:

I had a lot of trouble with the people that were basically malingerers. The thing I was most concerned with was that they were like bad apples in the barrel. Every time one of them went along chinning himself on the ground, he got the other fellows feeling bad, and they got to going around the same way. . . . Every time I saw a malingerer, I grabbed him up. I set up a rest camp or special training camp for them at a mountain about 35 miles west. It is up at an elevation of 8300 feet, 35 miles from the nearest road or railroad. We told them there were a lot of bears in the mountains, too.

---

[61] Maj Ralph L. Todd, CO 1st Bn 365th Inf Regt, 92d Div, to AGF Hist Off (Maj Bell I. Wiley), 20 Jun 44, quoted in Wiley, The Training of Negro Troops, AGF Hist Study No. 36.

[62] Ltr, CO Co D 1st Bn 365th Inf Regt, formerly of the 25th Inf, 92d Div, to AGF Hist Off, 19 Jun 44, AGF Hist Study No. 36.

[63] Maj Gen Sherman Miles, CO First Sv Comd, 18 Feb 44, in Rpt, ASF Conf of CG's Sv Comds, Dallas, Tex., pp. 141–42, ASF Control Div Files.

I obtained a medical officer, a psychiatrist, a dietitian, and a physical trainer that Colonel McDonald [station hospital] hired for me, and sent them all up there for perfect service. If a man had a bad arm, he got exercises all day long, especially prescribed to develop the arm. Most of the fellows were very bad off. If it was a bad leg, they got leg exercises; if it was their backs, they got back exercises; all prescribed by a professional physical trainer. If they had too many pains, that probably were caused by acid in the system—too much meat—they got a special diet—and they did not get pork chops.

We put the lights out at nine P.M., so they had plenty of sleep. They needed their rest, so they got it. I made quite a few cures. We have run about 900 men through there so far, and the system has proved fairly fruitful. It worked out well.

The people I have down in the main camp now are doing all right. I get very few of these sick ones any more, and Saturday before I came down here, I was able to close the rest camp. . . .[64]

But not all commands were so successful in dealing with the physically unfit. The 92d Division in July 1944, after the departure of its 370th Combat Team for Italy, and on the eve of its own movement to a port of embarkation, still had 1,700 men who were not physically qualified for combat, many of them POM rejects of the 2d Cavalry Division, the 364th Infantry, the 366th Infantry, and half a hundred other miscellaneous units.[65] How these men got into the division was not always clear. Some of them had come on orders issued by neither Fourth Army nor by

Army Ground Forces. But that they were men culled from other units was abundantly clear. Many, upon arrival, had already been classified as physically unfit for full service. As the division prepared for overseas movement, the number of such men showed signs of growing larger. By August it had reached 2,000. A covey of colonels, white and Negro, including a medical officer, some from Fourth Army and others detailed by Army Ground Forces from Washington and from other field units, descended upon Fort Huachuca to investigate, assess the situation, and make recommendations.

They found that the division had received, in the preceding twelve months, 6,242 enlisted men from 61 other organizations. In the same period it had sent out to other organizations 2,243 enlisted men as replacements. The division had sent out better men than it had received. Its casual detachment, despite discharges and the arbitrary return of 10 percent of the men to each organization, was filled with unfit men. Most of them had been tried in as many as three position vacancies within the division. Upon discovery, on marches or maneuvers, that they could or would not keep up, these men were given medical examinations. The casuals were of two general types: Class C and D men, medically certified to be in the poorest physical condition and therefore eligible for clearance from tactical organizations; and "Q-minus" men, medically qualified personnel who nevertheless failed to pass physical tests. Of the 2,272 men reported to be in this camp by the Fourth Army, about 950 were rated Class "Q-minus."

The casual camp, separate and at some

[64] Statement of Brig Gen Horace L. Whittaker, in Notes, ASF Fifth Tng Conf, Cp Barkeley, Tex, 24–26 Oct 44, p. 107, ASF Control Div Files.

[65] Ltr, Hq 92d Inf Div to CG Fourth Army, 21 Jul 44, 92d Div Files, 220.31–D; Memo, Enl Div, G–1 Sec, Hq AGF, for CofS AGF, 16 Aug 44, AGF 333.1/1 (92d Div.)

distance from the division area, was self-supporting as to messing, housing, and administration, though the men were still carried on their organizations' rolls. No training was given them, but they did furnish their own and some division details. They required additional officer and noncommissioned officer supervisors, but nevertheless until the first week of August there was insufficient leadership personnel to exercise full discipline and control. "Generally these men moved slowly to their assigned tasks, dragging or limping as their illness, feigned or real, dictated," one of the investigating colonels reported, "If 'allergic' to wearing helmet liner, shoes, leggings, belts, they were required to carry them along wherever they went."[66] One result of this policy was described by a group of observers:

The men were observed to form ranks slowly. Some of them carried their helmets instead of wearing them, others carried their shoes instead of having them on their feet, wearing low cut shoes instead, and some were carrying chairs, suit-cases, and other impedimenta. Many of the shoes were cut open over the toes or were unlaced. Some of the men wore no socks. The men did not march in cadence. Many of them limped and some were stooped or bent at the waist.[67]

Placing the potentially reclaimable with the actually unfit aggravated the problem to such an extent that it was doubted that any of these men were by then of future value to the Army. Observed one of the inspecting colonels:

The retreat formations where these men are allowed to move at will to the parade ground, instructed to sit down in formation if they can not stand and to move back to their areas at will . . . is a spectacle that is not only devastating to morale, but is giving aid and comfort to these men in their beliefs of being physically unfit, and from which, it will be most difficult for them to recover.[68]

Said another:

When the men present marched off the field, *all* took up a peculiar, shuffling gait of a nature which the undersigned has never before seen. It was beyond the possibility of any coincidence that all men in ranks should be so afflicted as to be unable to march off the field at a gait faster than about one-half mile per hour.[69]

Officers, medical and line, white and Negro, were often convinced that many of these men were physically fit and that they should not be discharged but made to work at noncombat assignments, preferably overseas, for the good of the morale of the rest of the 92d Division. "This Casual Detachment now constitutes a menace to the morale of the Division," one medical officer declared:

Right now we are having trouble in preventing men with hitherto good records from going over to join it. I believe it would be a mistake to discharge this large

---

[66] Memo, Col Edward O. Gourdin [CO 372d Inf Regt] to CG AGF, 17 Aug 44, AGF 333.1/1 (92d Div).

[67] Memo, Maj John S. Tarr, IGD Fourth Army (Lt Col Thomas A. O'Neil, Actg G–1, Lt Col William E. Wilkinson, MC, and Capt Jones B. Huskey, Inf, all of Hq Fourth Army concurring), for CofS Fourth Army, 10 Aug 44, AGF 333.1/1 (92d Div). For accounts of men bent at the waist see P. G. Hamlin, "Camptocormia: The Hysterical Bent Back of Soldiers," *Military Surgeon*, XCII (March, 1943), 295–300; Lt Col S. A. Sandler "Camptocormia: A Functional Condition of the Back in Neurotic Soldiers," *War Medicine*, VIII (1945), 36–45. Thirteen of the 19 soldiers studied

by Sandler were Negroes. Most recovered when told they were to be discharged.

[68] Memo, Col Anderson F. Pitts [IGD Second Army] for CG AGF, 16 Aug 44, AGF 333.1/1 (92d Div).

[69] Memo, Col N. P. Morrow [Hq AGF] for CG AGF, 14 Aug 42, AGF 333.1/1 (92d Div).

number of men as undesirables; neither should they be assigned to soft jobs. It is true there are some borderline physical cases, which can and should be sorted out, by more careful examination. The great majority of these men are malingerers; they should be forced to do duty involving some hazard and hard work. . . . It is too bad the division did not proceed direct overseas at the end of maneuvers.[70]

Unproved but persistent rumors that these men, when on pass or when visiting nearby Fry where they were no longer under the surveillance of officers, were quite able to move with an alacrity and ease markedly absent during duty hours lent further support to these views. There was no suggestion that general medical care at Fort Huachuca was not of the best; reports on this camp throughout the war commented on the excellence of the medical equipment and staff at its two hospitals.[71]

While there were differences of opinion on the number of men who were true malingerers, all observers agreed that physical and mental ills were combined in the cases of many of these men and that grouping them together had made their ills, real or fancied, a fixed part of their behavior. All had taken on the liabilities of the others, magnifying their own disabilities in the shadow of the continuing complaints of their neighbors. The investigating officers' conclusions ranged from a belief that the physical disability of these men would be difficult to determine to esti-

mates that from 10 to 85 percent of the men were consciously malingering.

Since so large a proportion of the men in this casual camp had had one or more venereal diseases, it occurred to some that residual infections might be at the root of the problem. "I was definitely assured by the Division Surgeon," an observer reported, "that this was not the case. He pointed out that the type[s] of cases to which I referred were in all cases proper cause for discharge from the service, so that this source of disease could be eliminated from our consideration in regard to this personnel." [72]

That many of the men chronically complaining of their physical inability to perform normal duties were suffering from more than the elementary physical disorders of which they complained was undoubtedly true. One Army psychiatrist, writing on the general problems of maladjusted soldiers, both white and Negro, indicated that "It is remarkable that the clinical picture in maladjusted soldiers is almost stereotyped. The pattern may be compared with schizoid reaction types. His behavior is marked by a more or less manifest hostility to the Army, a feeling of ill health, and an inability to perform duties or get along with fellow soldiers." Among the case histories which he cited were the following:

A 25 year old Negro recently inducted complained of pains and stiffness in his back following a spinal tap at induction. In addition, he had difficulty in breathing with his gas mask on. He had feared entry into the Army because he had heard that he would be mistreated and probably shot if he came to a Southern Camp. After

---

[70] Capt James K. Batts, MC, 365th Inf, quoted in Memo cited n. 69.

[71] For examples, see Rpt, Surgeon Consultant Ninth Sv Comd for TSG, 5 Jul 44; Rpt of Orthopedic Consultant for TSG, 22 Aug 44; Ltr, Consultant in Surgery Ninth Sv Comd Surgeon for TSG, 8 May 45. All in SPRSM 333.1 Ft. Huachuca.

[72] Memo, Enl Div G-1 Sec, AGF, for CofS, 16 Aug 44, AGF 333.1/1 (92d Div) (Incl).

being in the Army for 3 months and finding everyone friendly he felt better, and had less pains in his back. He was transferred to the Special Development Unit but after two weeks he was complaining of weakness of his bladder which he blamed on cold weather.

. . . .

A 33 year old colored soldier [had] complaints of pains in the chest. . . . He had innumerable conflicts because of a prejudice concerning his own race. He felt that he was quite a bit better than most other negroes. At the same time, discrimination bothered him. He was not able to get along well on his Post with other soldiers since he felt superior to them and it bothered him that he had to live with them or was treated in the same way. At the time of his examination he was assigned to work on a salvage truck. This work evidently did not satisfy him. This was in contrast to the real situation, since in civilian life he never had much of a job.[73]

Few units were equipped to deal properly with men whose physical ills had a psychological basis. But that all men who had been transferred to casual detachments as physically unable to keep up with their units' training should have been so disposed of was also questionable. Some organization commanders had used the existence of casual detachments as a means of getting rid of men who, with better training, might have

been able to come up to performance standards. Once the men were shunted to casual detachments progressive deterioration set in.[74]

The disposition of the physically unfit devolved upon the service commands as units moving overseas transferred their substandard men. With few overhead installation vacancies and with increasing complaints from training centers that the Negro soldiers being received from ground unit transfers were usable neither in technical units nor in those performing heavy labor, the service commands were at a loss to absorb these men. While discharge provisions had been liberalized, there were no provisions for the discharge of men classified physically fit for general service. Moreover, there were not enough zone of interior assignments to absorb the genuine limited assignment Negro personnel gathering in service command installations.

The Army eventually disposed of most of these men through a new procedure which authorized the discharge of all enlisted men below the minimum physical standards for induction for whom no suitable assignment was available.[75] When added to the prevailing means of discharge for physical or mental disability, inaptness, undesirable habits or traits of character, conviction by a civil court, and convenience to the government, the route for discharge of most surplus men, including the excess of physically unfit Negroes, was open. During the war years, discharges as physically and mentally unfit accounted

[73] Capt. Morris H. Alder, "The Management of the Maladjusted Soldier at the Basic Training Center," *Journal of Clinical Psychopathology*, VII (April, 1946), 713–29. See also Maj. Isidor Weiss, "Psychoses in Military Prisoners," *Journal of Clinical Psychopathology*, VIII (April, 1947), 689–705; William C. Menninger, *Psychiatry in a Troubled World* (New York: Macmillan, 1948) 214–21; Lt. Col. Herbert S. Ripley, M.C., O.R.C. and Maj. Stewart Wolf, M.C., O.RC, "Mental Illness Among Negro Troops Overseas," *American Journal of Psychiatry*, CIII (January, 1947), 510; Capt. Rutherford B. Stevens, M.D., "Racial Aspects of Emotional Problems of Negro Soldiers," *loc. cit.*, pp. 493–98; Memo, Col Edward O. Gourdin for CG AGF, 17 Aug 44, AGF 333.1/1 (92d Div).

[74] Memos, Col Anderson Pitts for CG AGF, 16 Aug 44, and Col Edward O. Gourdin for CG AGF, 17 Aug 44, AGF 333.1/1 (92d Div).
[75] WD Cir 370, 1944.

TABLE 8—SEPARATIONS OF NEGRO ENLISTED MEN BY SELECTED CAUSES
DECEMBER 1941–MAY 1945

Year	Honorable		Other Than Honorable[c]	Transfers To Inactive Status "Less Over 28"	Total Separations[d]
	Physical and Mental Disqualification[a]	Misc. (Honorable) Over 28; Overage; Retired[b]			
Total....................	131,221	15,639	13,222	8,202	168,284
(Percent).....................	(77.9)	(9.3)	(7.9)	(4.9)	(100.0)
1941 (December)................	276	24	18	50	368
1942..........................	5,497	169	427	127	6,220
1943..........................	51,807	13,062	2,889	7,049	74,807
1944..........................	58,824	1,530	7,546	845	68,745
1945 (Through May)............	14,817	854	2,342	131	18,144

[a] Includes certificate of disability and inaptness or neurosis.

[b] Includes non-Army commissions, to enter USMA, USNA, and USCGA, minority, dependency, importance to national health, safety or interest, and others.

[c] Includes undesirable habits, misconduct, and concealment of desertion, or discharge other than honorable. Dropped from the rolls, resulting from AWOL, not included in separations.

[d] All figures exclude battle and nonbattle deaths, missing, prisoners of war, interned, declared dead, separated to accept Army commissions, and demobilization discharges.

Source: Strength of the Army, 1 Jul 45, STM-30.

for more than three fourths of all Negro separations, excluding casualties, demobilization separations, and discharges to accept commissions.[76] (Table 8)

Nevertheless, in the summer of 1945 the problem of the disposition of "left-over" personnel medically declared fit for service still remained. From Fort Huachuca alone, between five and six hundred men, described as individuals "who would not work and who would not let anyone else work" had been organized as a provisional ordnance company and sent to Umatilla Ordnance Plant, Oregon, where they were found to be "entirely unsatisfactory." They were returned to Fort Huachuca by the Ninth Service Command for disposition. Some 185 more were due in from a California station. Four disposition

teams were busily engaged at the station hospital examining these men.[77]

The problem of physical fitness, with the venereal diseases as its constant component and with physical and psychological deterioration an increasingly widespread phenomenon in units, was clearly a major one in the employment of Negro troops in World War II. It played a continuous and distinctive role, both in the selection and in the later use of Negro manpower by the Army. It slowed up training. It impeded the preparation of Negro units for overseas movement. It consumed disproportionate time on the part of commanders and of medical and personnel officers. And throughout the war it affected another and even more difficult problem to assess—the general morale and motivation of Negro troops and units.

[76] The percentage of all men separated from the Army as physically and mentally unfit during the same period was 42 percent. (Strength of the Army, 1 Jun–1 Jul 45.)

[77] Ltr, Deputy Chief for Hospitals and Domestic Opns to TSG (through CO Ft. Huachuca, CG NSC), 8 Jun 45, Ft. Huachuca 333.1 Insp—Post, Camp, Stations, Hospitals.

CHAPTER XI

Morale

Concern with the importance of high morale to training and utilization of troops was more widespread in World War II than in previous wars.[1] Increasingly the War Department realized that success in training and employing Negro troops depended as much upon measures to improve morale as upon attempts to improve leadership and methods of training *per se*. Efforts to improve the conditions and terms of service of Negro troops, with the hope that their morale and motivation would thereby be improved, were assiduously made after the middle of 1942. These efforts constitute a distinct phase in the story of Negro troop employment in World War II.

The sources of low morale among Negro troops were many. Some were similar to those affecting all troops; others were unique. For Negroes, conditions changed on given posts as successive post and unit commanders arrived and departed. The fact that rules and practices applying to Negro troops, to their relations with white troops, and to their use of camp facilities varied so widely from post to post and from time to time on the same post was itself a major contribution to low morale.

On a new and unfamiliar post, the

first few days could be filled with disturbing questions for the Negro soldier who wished to avoid embarrassment and possibly serious entanglements with local rules and customs. Would he be served if he tried to make a purchase at the main post exchange, or was there a special branch exchange for Negro units? Which theater, which bus stop, which barber shop could he use? Where could he place a long distance call? Which prophylactic station could he use? Was he free to enter the main Red Cross office? The gym? The bowling alley? Would the station cleaning and pressing concessionaire accept his soiled clothing? How would he be received in the nearby camp town? To many Negro soldiers the uncertainty of their status was as damaging to morale as the knowledge of definite restrictions. Rumors and attitudes fostering low morale and disaffection throve under the circumstances. With the racial customs of the average post not clearly defined, new men and units took their cues from older men and units. From the mouths of these oracles came much misinformation about local conditions. From the need for basic facts about post life came much of the predisposition to accept as fact the rumor and gossip that more rationally oriented men, under different circumstances, might have rejected.

Negro soldiers, finding a maze of

---

[1] See History of the Special Services Division, ASF, and History of the Information and Education Division, ASF, MSS in OCMH.

Watching a Boxing Match at Camp Claiborne, La., 1942

shaded meanings in the racial rules of conduct as applied from camp to camp and as viewed against the stated war aims of lecturers who described the reasons for America's participation in the war, found it difficult to assign to themselves acceptable roles in the military and social conflict of which they were a part. The larger effects of the situations in which they found themselves were not, however, nearly so obvious either to Negro troops or to the War Department and its agencies as the physical factors in which these effects were partially rooted. The number of physical disadvantages that Negro soldiers could name to support their convictions as to their relatively unfair status in the Army was legion. But a few—recreational facilities, camp-town and soldier-civilian relationships, and transportation —were constant in their bid for primary attention as deterrents to high morale. Since they impinged upon so many areas of related concern, physical facilities and arrangements received considerably more attention than all other obstacles to high morale combined. They were the visible, traditional symbols of close attention to the morale and welfare of enlisted men that the men themselves and their commands, as well as individual civilians and public organizations, brought most frequently to the attention of the War Department and its agencies. The continuing attempts of the War Department and of individual commanders to ameliorate or remove conditions productive of low morale and its concomitants were therefore most frequently directed toward the pragmatic solution of the problem of facilities for soldier recreation and entertainment.

Recreational Facilities

Early in the period of mobilization Judge Hastie inquired about provisions for the welfare and morale of Negro soldiers. He was especially concerned about small units and detachments on posts relatively isolated from large centers of Negro population.[2] The Adjutant General, in whose office the Morale Division was then located, replied that his Morale Division was responsible only for supplying facilities. Responsibility for morale remained "distinctly a matter of command from which it cannot be separated." The Morale Division planned to secure funds from Congress to purchase athletic equipment, books, magazines, newspapers, and other recreational equipment for furnishing service clubs, and to pay the salaries of librarians and hostesses. Facilities and funds for welfare and recreational purposes were to be based on organization and strength. Within the limits of their strengths, facilities would be allotted to Negro units on the same basis as they were to all other units:

. . . welfare and recreational facilities for colored troops which are a part of a composite garrison will be provided on the same basis as if the colored contingent formed the garrison of a separate camp. At stations where the total strength of the negro complement is comparable to that of

a company, facilities will be provided which would normally be provided for a company organization, i.e., company day rooms, etc. As the strength of the colored complement increases to that comparable to a battalion, additional facilities will be provided such as E–2 type Exchange, RB–1 type Recreational Building, and separate chapels will be provided on the basis of one (1) for each 2,000 enlisted personnel or major fraction thereof. As stated in paragraph 6 twenty (20) modified guest houses are approved for small colored groups and each camp situation will have to be decided on its individual merits. Small detachments of colored troops are being given facilities not available to White Garrisons of a corresponding size because of the particular situation, but at the present time it cannot be foreseen to what extent this can be carried.[3]

Adequate and satisfactory physical facilities were not a guarantee of high morale, but they were expected to help commanders build morale. In view of their availability to some units, their absence in others could be a ready contribution to a decline in morale. Among Negro troops, even their presence as substitute facilities gauged to the size of the Negro portion of a command often highlighted differentials between Negro and white troops on the same post. These differentials were many. Though not all of them obtained at every post, enough were a part of the military experiences of Negro soldiers at most posts to affect markedly their morale and their approach to the terms of their service.

The housing policy had often assigned Negro soldiers the less choice sites on posts, removed them from the center of post activities, and left them far from

[2] Memo, Civ Aide to SW for Chief of Morale Div AGO, 17 Dec 40, AG 353.8 (12–17–40) (1).

[3] Memo, TAG for Civ Aide to SW, 28 Jan 41, AG 353.8 (12–17–40) (1); see also WD Memo 210–18–42, 1 Dec 42, par. 5.

well-stocked exchanges, field houses, post transportation lines, and welfare agencies. On every large post some troops, white and Negro, would normally be at a disadvantage in this respect, but Negro troops sometimes concluded that their removal from proximity to main post areas was a general and approved Army policy, designed to prevent their use of main post facilities and prevent direct contact between them and white troops.

Because recreational facilities were provided on the basis of the number of men who would use them, Negro service clubs and recreation halls were often too small to provide for more than a few activities at a time.[4] The smaller Negro units, often crowded into areas not planned for such use, frequently lacked normal day room space. The guest house might be identical with the one or more provided for white troops, but nevertheless it might be inadequate for the accommodation of visiting parents, wives, and sweethearts for whom it was provided. For even when camps were located near towns with sizable Negro populations, available private lodgings of a quality approaching that of a camp's guest house were usually limited. Most boarding facilities in nearby towns were already occupied by the resident families of enlisted men, since as late comers in a time of general shortages, few Negroes were able to obtain family quarters on the average post. The guest houses, therefore, were often crowded beyond capacity. The service club hostess, of-

ten serving as social director, librarian, and cafeteria manager of the club—in many instances, the club had not been expected to serve enough troops to require more than one or two professional workers—had the additional problem of fitting excess numbers of visitors into the limited space available in the guest house.

As the Negro strength of certain posts grew, the provision of planned facilities could not keep pace with the growth of commands. After June 1942, when restrictions were placed on construction not considered necessary to the health and training of a command, it became increasingly difficult to provide additional facilities. Motion picture theaters, recreation halls, and guest houses were the chief sufferers. At Fort Sill, Oklahoma, for example, only six rooms were available for the use of guests of a garrison of 2,500 Negro soldiers. At Camp Wolters, Texas, the guest house was also inadequate. In both instances, The Inspector General recommended additional facilities as morale factors, but neither recommendation could be approved because of the new construction policy.[5]

From the beginning of the program for the construction of recreational facilities, murmers of protest against the specific designation of facilities by race began to filter into the War Department. The protests came most frequently from residents of those states that had antidiscrimination laws and customs. On 15

[4] Originally, only two service clubs for Negro troops—at Fort Bragg, N.C., and at Camp Livingston, La., where 5,000 Negroes were expected—were planned.

[5] Ltr, Brig Gen Benjamin O. Davis to TIG, 24 Jun 42, IG 333.1–Spec Insp (Cld Trps) Ft. Sill (1942), AGF 333.1/12 (Ft. Sill) and 3 Inds; 3d Ind, Hq AGF and Memo for Record to CofS, AGF 333.1/2 (Cp Wolters).

August 1942, the commanding generals of service commands and the Chief of Engineers were directed to cease providing recreational facilities at posts, camps, and stations "where the garrison is preponderantly colored, and both white and colored officers are on duty with the same units," with instructions "explicit or implied" that the facilities were for the exclusive use of either race.[6] This directive affected very few stations, primarily Fort Huachuca and Tuskegee Army Flying School, and at those stations affected the local commanders, as distinct from service commanders and the Engineers, could still designate facilities by race at their discretion. The scarcity of facilities for Negroes therefore continued in most camps where specific provisions for Negro troops had not been planned.

Separate facilities by race, though not a part of the announced Army policy, were an extension of the announced policy of separate units by race. The Special Service Division, which was charged with the provision and, later, with training and furnishing officers and civilians for the operation of recreational facilities, concluded from surveys made in May and September 1942 that most white soldiers favored some form of segregation policy.[7] On the basis of a separate survey in May 1942 of Air Forces enlisted men, members of a service which at that time had barely begun to use Negro manpower in any form, the Special Service Division reported that while only one in ten Air Forces soldiers opposed the idea of training Negroes as pilots, bombardiers, and navigators, "Northerners and Southerners tend to *agree* that the Negro should be *segregated as a matter of Army policy.*" However, the division pointed out, "They tend to *disagree on willingness to work personally alongside the Negro.* Two-thirds from the North *are* willing, two-thirds from the South are *not* willing." [8]

For the purposes of support of existing policy, the results of these surveys appeared to be convincing evidence of the need for continuing separate facilities and units. At a meeting in December 1942, of the commanding generals of service commands, with whom control of most posts rested, Brig. Gen. Frederick H. Osborn, director of the Special Service Division, observed:

I think that the results of this study are sufficient evidence of the wisdom of the policy of the Army in segregating Negro and white troops. It is perfectly evident—this and the following page make it perfectly evident—that if you dropped the general policy of segregation and forced white and Negro troops together in the same units, you would build up friction which you couldn't handle. That would seem to be the meaning of these reports. At the same time, as you see, there is a considerable and very fine recognition of the right of Negroes to be trained in even the highest and most skilled services, such as pilots.[9]

---

[6] Ltr, Hq SOS to CG's All Sv Comds and CofE, 15 Aug 42, SPX 353.8 (8–14–42) MS–SPOP–M.

[7] The results were published in What the Soldier Thinks, 8 December 1942, issued at the time as a confidential document for the use of commanders only.

[8] What the Soldier Thinks, pp. 30–31. Italics in original.

[9] Address, Brig Gen Frederick H. Osborn, Proceedings of the Conference of Commanding Generals, Service Commands, Third Session, 18 December 1942, New Orleans, La., pp. 38–39. The pages referred to by General Osborn were those of What the Soldier Thinks, copies of which were distributed at the meetings.

A second survey, covering both Negro and white soldier attitudes, was completed in March 1943. This time, 13,-000 Negro and white men from 92 organizations were asked differently phrased questions.[10] "Do you think it is a good idea or a poor idea for Negro and white soldiers to have separate service clubs in Army camps?" the soldiers were asked. Forty-eight percent of the Negro soldiers and 85 percent of the white soldiers replied that it was a good idea; 13 percent of the Negroes and 6 percent of the whites were undecided; and 39 percent of the Negroes and 9 percent of the whites thought it a poor idea. To the question, "Do you think it is a good idea or a poor idea for white and Negro soldiers to have separate PX's in Army camps?" 40 percent of the Negro and 81 percent of the white soldiers thought it a good idea; 12 percent of the Negroes and 9 percent of the whites were undecided; and 48 percent of the Negro soldiers and 10 percent of the whites thought it a poor idea. To the question, "do you think white and Negro soldiers should be in separate outfits or should they be together in the same outfits?" 38 percent of the Negro and 88 percent of the white soldiers thought that they should be in separate outfits; 26 percent of the Negro and 9 percent of the white soldiers said that it made no difference or they were undecided; while 36 percent of the Negro and 3 percent of the whites checked a preference for the same outfits.

As the Special Service Division phrased it, " a minority of Negro soldiers —but a substantial minority, from thirty-eight to forty-eight percent—say they consider some form of separation a good idea." But this time the division added in its published report: *"Many of the Negroes and some of the whites who favor separation in the Army indicate by their comments that they are opposed to segregation in principle. They favor separation in the Army to avoid trouble or unpleasantness arising from race prejudice. This point is most often made in connection with service clubs, where social relations are most important. Negroes who oppose segregation in the Army indicate most frequently that their reasons are related to the idea that we are fighting for democracy and equality."* The report added that the longer a Negro served in the Army, the less likely he was to favor separation of the races, and that Southern Negroes with the least

---

[10] This was one of a series of studies made by the Research Branch, Special Service Division, on the attitudes of both Negro and white soldiers. The total sample questioned was selected by lot from Army organizations carefully chosen to give proper weight to all types of installations in all regions. As on all surveys, in order to insure frank answers, men were questioned in an atmosphere of anonymity. Local or unit officers were not present and Negro enlisted men only were present in the cases of Negro groups answering questionnaires. The questionnaires in the March survey were based on repeated pretests of over 2,400 soldiers. The first pretest showed that Negro enlisted men did not reveal their personal opinions to white interviewers or in the presence of white enlisted questionnaire administrators. Opinions expressed to white interviewers differed greatly from those given to Negro interviewers. When the men filled out their own questionnaires in groups where anonymity was assured, their written answers were about the same as those given orally to Negro interviewers, but markedly different from those given white interviewers. Negro enlisted men were therefore used as group leaders and interviewers of Negro soldiers on this and on all subsequent surveys in order to insure frank answers from Negro troops. Research Branch, Special Service Division, Attitudes of the Negro Soldier, 28 July 1943.

education were most likely to favor racial separation in the Army.[11]

While the full significance of these last two statements as a guide to future planning for the employment of Negro troops may have been lost, the validity of the statements was amply demonstrated before the close of the war. To the surprise of some inspectors, Southern Negroes of relatively long service often turned out to be the chief complainants in investigations of charges of discrimination conducted during the last half of the war. Northern Negroes of considerable education were early and continuously credited with being the chief sources of dissatisfaction in many Negro units. Judge Patterson's remark in the War Council that in his opinion the illiterate Negro would probably make a better soldier than the educated Negro [12] was a direct reflection of the feeling, gaining ground as the dissatisfaction of Negro soldiers increased, that better educated Negroes were less likely to adjust well to Army life and that they caused more trouble than their numbers in the nation's manpower warranted.

In many instances the desires of Negro troops were not for the more elaborate forms of recreational facilities, though their provision for neighboring white troops and not for Negroes continued to be a source of resentment. Sometimes, lacking any facilities at all, Negro troops simply wished for a place to gather. The noncommissioned officers attending the first classes of the Air Forces' Venereal Disease Control School at Tuskegee Army Flying School in June 1943 expressed an interest in two problems related to but not specifically a part of their course of instruction:

One was the undesirable conditions of vice prevailing in many negro civilian communities, and the other was the inadequacy or even complete lack of recreational facilities for negro troops at many Army Air Forces bases. It is of interest to note that these criticisms of recreational facilities stemmed from practically every command represented (Second Air Force, Third Air Force, Air Service Command, Proving Ground Command, School of Applied Tactics, Gulf Coast Training Center and West Coast Training Center) except the Southeast Training Center, which is reported to have a colored recreation center (combined chapel, recreation room and theater, RBC-A-T-, one story, 37' x 108') on nearly all its installations. Their desires were not for swimming pools and bowling alleys, but for some building, some center, that might serve as a nucleus of recreational activities. The opinions of this group of intelligent colored men regarding the recreational needs of negro soldiers cannot be overlooked in the consideration of the possible adjuncts to medical measures for venereal disease control.[13]

Less obvious discriminatory items also drew comments from Negro troops. The

[11] What the Soldier Thinks, Number 2, August 1943, pp. 58–59. Italics in original. For a detailed postwar analysis of this survey, see Shirley A. Star, Robin M. Williams, Jr., and Samuel A. Stouffer, "Negro Soldiers," in Stouffer et al., The American Soldier: Adjustment During Army Life, "Studies in Social Psychology in World War II," vol. 1, (Princeton: Princeton University Press, 1949), pp. 566–80.
[12] Notes on War Council Meeting, WDCSA, 25 May 42.

[13] Report, Maj Robert Dyar, Chief AAF Venereal Disease Control Branch, to the Air Surgeon, no date but Incl in Ltr, CofAS to CG's AAF SEATC, AAFTC, 20 Jun 43, AAF 726.1 Misc. The Southeast AAF Training Center also had the lowest venereal disease rates for most reporting periods, despite its location in a high incidence area.

condition and time for the issuance of equipment, the paving or graveling of roads and walks in the Negro areas ("We improve an area and then they move us farther out and we improve that one" was a common complaint of Negro troops in the new camps in the first years of mobilization), and the apportionment of post duties were all additional grounds for complaint at various times and in various places.

Negro units with athletic teams or posts with all Negro teams—and organized athletics were encouraged on many posts to reduce the pull of the camp town as well as for physical conditioning and recreation—sometimes found their morale lowered rather than rasied by virtue of having teams. Free time in gymnasiums or on athletic fields that were not used simultaneously by Negro and white soldiers was often at a premium. On posts where sanction for matches between Negro and white teams was not freely given, it was hard to find a team to oppose. Many a Negro athletic team found its opponents among state reform school and penitentiary Negro teams or in distant as well as nearby Negro high school, college, or other Army post teams. The post championship football team might not have played a Negro team at all. As the war went on, this situation changed gradually. Athletic competitions became one of the chief contributions to morale. Posts such as Fort Lewis, Washington, Fort Dix, New Jersey, and Camp Lee, Virginia, organized postwide leagues and used Negro players on post football, baseball, boxing, and basketball teams. The Army-wide exhibition tour of Joe Louis in 1943 and 1944, in which the heavyweight champion, then a sergeant,

boxed not only with members of his own traveling troupe but also with various local and unit champions, white and Negro, helped broaden the base of athletic competition on many posts.

In religion and in the arts as well, contrasts unfavorable to Negro troops were sources of irritation. On large, otherwise well-equipped stations, chapel, motion picture house, gymnasium, and recreation hall might be in one building in the Negro section of a camp, complicating the scheduling of activities. Traveling shows from the United Services Organization (Camp Shows, Inc.), visiting sports celebrities, lecturers, and concert artists might perform for Negroes in mess halls or buildings converted for the purpose while the main body of the post enjoyed them in the central post theater, field house, or chapel. "Special arrangements," usually consisting of a block of reserved seats, were sometimes made for Negro troops in the main post theater on the occasion of performances scheduled by particularly outstanding Negro and sometimes white celebrities, but it is difficult to say whether these arrangements helped or hindered the morale of Negro soldiers. Sometimes word of these special arrangements did not reach Negro troops in time for them to take advantage of them; at other times, troops made no attempt to do so. One Negro celebrity, the singer Lena Horne, concluded a tour of Army posts in anger because arrangements were such at one post that she was scheduled to perform for Negro troops at a noon mess where German prisoners of war, she felt, had better opportunities to hear her than the Negro soldiers, while her scheduled performance at the main post theater had

had few white and no Negro soldiers present.[14]

An obvious means of insuring more adequate facilities for Negro troops on posts was to broaden the use of existing facilities. It was hoped that such a procedure would lessen the need for Negro soldiers to frequent neighboring and often unfriendly towns for recreational purposes and thereby reduce opportunities for interratial friction off post. Since much of the morale problem was occasioned by recreational facilities designated "Colored" or "White," one of the difficulties could be solved by directing the removal of such designations and arranging for other methods of use.

Accordingly, the 15 August 1942 directive, which had forbidden the construction of racially designated facilities on any post with a majority of Negro soldiers and both white and Negro officers, was rescinded. A new directive, forbidding the designation of any recreational facilities "including theaters and post exchanges" by race, was issued on 10 March 1943. "Where necessary, recreational facilities may be allocated to organizations in whole or in part, permanently or on a rotation basis, provided care is taken that all units and personnel are afforded equal opportunity to enjoy such facilities," the directive read.[15]

This directive required the removal of remaining "White" and "Colored" signs in the designation of facilities and required, if but one recreational facility of its type existed on a post, that arrangements be made for its use by troops of all units, and therefore of both races. It did not, however, abrogate the policy of providing facilities for Negroes as though they constituted a separate post,[16] nor did it alter the policy of separate use of existing facilities.

Use of facilities by designated units and areas now took the place of use by designated races. What had been the Colored Service Club now became Service Club No. 2, or whatever other number was assigned it; what had been the Colored Area Exchange now received a branch number or a named area designation. In some cases, the Negro club or theater was designated Number 1 to avoid the implication of its being a second-class establishment. In others, the theater serving the Negro area received and showed motion picures first for the same reason, as well as to avoid attendance at the main post theater on the ground that the current movie had not yet been scheduled in the Negro area. On many posts, however, the directive requiring the removal of racial designations from facilities was not honored; for many months inspectors reported unfavorably on the continued use of racial designations for facilities. Moreover, the directive did not succeed in producing sufficient changes in the use of facilities to alter appreciably either the recreational situation or its morale consequences among Negro soldiers. The letter had been phrased in such general

---

[14] Later investigation showed that general arrangements at the post and between the post and Camp Shows, Inc., were poor. Miss Horne, after leaving the post, made an appearance before a large group of soldiers at the nearby town's Negro USO. Ltr, Post IC to CO Cp Robinson, Ark., 28 Dec 44, CofS Files 291.2 Misc.

[15] Ltr, TAG to CG's, All Sv Comds, CofE, 10 Mar 43, AG 353.8 (3–5–43) B–S–A–M and Memo for Record attached to Memo, G–1 for TAG, 5 Mar 43, WDGAP/353.8.

---

[16] Memo, Hq SOS for CofE, 26 Apr 43, and Memo for Record attached, AG 353.8 (14 Aug 42) (1).

terms that only the commander who wanted official backing for local changes was influenced by it. But the directive did establish the principle that Negro troops were to be given the opportunity to use all existing facilities provided for the welfare and recreation of soldiers.

Camp Towns

No such principle could be established by War Department directive in camp towns, where recreational facilities for Negro troops were often far less adequate and more segregated than on posts. Since most Army camps were located in the South and Southwest, most Negro troops were stationed in camps whose neighboring civilian communities had definite laws and customs regulating relations between Negroes and the white civilian population. Except when near the largest towns, most camps of the North and Northwest were in areas that had practically no Negro population. Nearby Negro communities, sometimes small and often economically depressed whether North or South, usually offered little to soldiers in the way of wholesome recreation. Civilians and local law enforcement agencies seldom welcomed Negro soldiers either with open arms or with disinterested forbearance. But the pull of the towns, even when conditions in them were unfavorable, was strong. Not only did the towns mean release from camp discipline and duties, but if they had any Negro population at all, they also meant associations on a social level usually nonexistent in the camps.

Except for the well-meaning but often ineffective efforts of church groups, most camp towns made few plans for Negro soldiers before circumstances produced undesirable results. It was often debatable whether what most towns offered was not more detrimental than advantageous to soldiers. Most camp towns, if they had a Negro business or recreational district, had so restricted it that it was either one with or contiguous to the local vice district. Often the Negro USO club, placed in the only available building, was some distance from the Negro business and recreational areas or was otherwise inconveniently located away from main transportation lines. The one or two restaurants and movie houses serving Negroes in the entire town were very likely to be in the heart of a prostitution district. Bars, when they existed legally, were often centers of vice and criminality. In one town, of the five Negro restaurants available, all were judged "Absolutely filthy and insanitary in every respect." [17] In another, practically every place—the Chat & Chew Cafe, Pete's Place, the Life Saver's Cafe, Squeeze Inn, Jean's Tavern, Angamama Restaurant, the Blue Bonnet Hotel, and the Dunbar Hotel—turned up constantly as a point of procurement leading to venereal contacts.

The difference between facilities in large and small towns was not great in quality, but the small towns had the additional disadvantage of being even more bleak and uninviting than the larger ones. While the large towns had poor facilities, the small ones had virtually none. The only nearby community available to Negro troops stationed

---

[17] Report of Inspection Trip, 13–14 Oct 43, Incl to Ltr, AAFCFTC to CG AAF, 16 Oct 43, AAF 726.1, binder 4. Of the thirteen white restaurants inspected in the same town, all showed varying degrees of cleanliness, but none was so bad as the Negro places.

at one post was described by an inspecting officer:

The colored section of the city of Pampa, "The Flats," is approximately five short blocks by two, the population is about 400; this in addition to the 15,000 white persons in the city. The majority of those living in "The Flats" are married. It appears that they would just as soon not have too many of the colored enlisted men "hanging around," especially when the male members of such homes are absent. There is a colored U.S.O. in "The Flats," one room approximately 30 feet by 100 feet. The colored soldiers who take pride in their appearance would hesitate before going through several inches of mud to the U.S.O. in inclement weather. There are very few colored girls with whom the colored soldiers may associate. In some instances, the Commanding Officer of Pampa Army Air Field arranged for bus transportation with appropriate chaperons to bring girls from Amarillo and other surrounding towns, in order to attend dances at the colored service club. There is one colored taxicab company, "The Brooks" taxicab company, which is run by the proprietor of the colored hotel (The Brooks). The rate from Pampa, Texas, to Pampa Army Air Field, a distance of 14 miles, is $2.50, one way. There are no motion picture shows in the City of Pampa, for colored persons. In "The Flats" there is one grocery store, and one Cafe, the "Busy Bee." [18]

To the enlisted men at the field, the town and post recreation situations were part of a continuous pattern. One soldier characterized the spare time activities of the men of the post located near the town described above:

The only form of amusement we have on the Field is to go to the theatre. We do have our own service club here on the Field. The club is quite adequate to meet any needs we might have but we have no drawing card. I wouldn't advocate dances because of the fact that being where we are there is nobody to invite. We do not have movies in the service club. We have no cafeteria but on two occasions we have had hot cocoa and doughnuts. On these two occasions we didn't have post support but I understand that all of the equipment is provided by the Post Welfare Fund. The facilities are adequate but in Pampa it is just that we have nobody to invite to the service club. The colored section is small and you don't find the type that would be suitable.

The post theatre is about our only form of amusement but attending the movies is good recreation. I think the section that is set aside for our organization is adequate but it is jammed every night because of the way our boys work. Most of our men are assigned to the mess halls. They are off one day and on one day. There are never more than half of our men off at one time. The men get to see all the movies because they usually show two days. . . .

We have a separate U.S.O. in town. The building itself is very nice. Very few go there because it is not properly managed. Two civilians from town are in charge. They are colored. They tell the boys to come over and write letters. Why spend thirty-five cents to write a letter? There is no attraction.[19]

Most towns, large and small, had no adequate recreational facilities for Negroes, as they often pointed out in requests to the War Department that Negro soldiers be moved elsewhere.[20] Nor were most towns convinced that it was a practical expenditure on their part to help provide such facilities. Often, service groups found it difficult to rent

---

[18] Memo, Hq AAF (AFTAJ) (Col. Lewis A. Dayton) for CG AAF, 14 Feb 44, AAF 333.5. The inspector concluded that the situation here was similar to that encountered by Negroes at other airfields, especially in the South where the majority of fields were located.

[19] Statement, Actg 1st Sgt George L. Chambers, 328th Avn Sq, Pampa AAF, Tex., 13 Dec 43, to Col Lewis A. Dayton, AAF 333.5.

[20] See above, Chapter IV.

acceptable buildings for use as a club for Negro troops. "Civic groups will frequently bestir themselves with 'drives' to provide a Cadet Club, but are not receptive to suggestions for a similar facility for colored troops," the Air Forces found from experience. "Often the only available gathering places for Negro troops in the community adjacent to the bases are juke-joints and taverns, strictly at the 'dive' level. [Illustrating] the acuteness of this situation is the comment of a Negro soldier at one station, when the possibility was suggested of placing two such places in the nearby community off-limits. He remarked that 'Then we just wouldn't have *no* place to go.' " [21]

The one advantage of the larger towns with a sizable Negro population was that such towns might be better organized to provide for the needs of Negro soldiers. In any event, the Negro population might, through its local leaders, seek to protect soldiers from the abuses that were relatively more common in many of the small towns. The larger towns were more likely to have a sense of the civic need of avoiding racial difficulties growing out of relations between town police and other officials and soldiers on pass; municipal administrations were more likely to attempt correctives when requested by civilian or military agencies. In exceptional instances, the Negro population of the larger towns cooperated to obtain more wholesome recreation for Negro soldiers than the town normally provided. The USO

and the Special Services Division, ASF, in co-operation with the Federal Security Agency and the Office of Defense Health and Welfare Services, sought to help such communities in planning activities for Negro troops.

While the relations of Negro troops and surrounding communities varied with the size of the towns to which the soldiers had access, a more important factor was the attitude of the towns to the presence of Negroes in uniform. Troops located near cities such as Boston or Tacoma, Washington, without a considerable Negro population, but with a modicum of recreational facilities available and with local authorities and commercial interests that were not particularly inhospitable to Negroes, had few complaints. Troops near cities such as Berkeley and Oakland, California, where the city administration and police were co-operative with the command, had fewer venereal and disciplinary problems. Troops located near cities such as Little Rock, Arkansas, or Savannah, Georgia, with sizable Negro populations but few facilities and strained relations in any of the many areas of civilian or military racial tension, might abandon many of their complaints upon improvement in facilities or in race relations. But troops located near towns like Spokane, Denver, Battle Creek, or small New England towns in which there were few Negroes and small accommodation to the presence of Negro soldiers, might suffer both from the lack of recreational outlets and from the absence of a congenial Negro population. In these cases morale and discipline might decline as readily as in areas where overt segregation and discrimination were a part of the accustomed pat-

---

[21] A Venereal Disease Control Program for Colored Troops, Incl to Ltr, Hq AAF to CG's (Attn: Surgeon), 3 Jun 44, AAF 726.1 Misc. Italics in original.

tern. The primary rules laid down as a guide to the location of Negro troops—that they be near centers of Negro population and near towns which already had facilities available to them—were therefore generally adequate, and the absence of one or the other might not be too important, The absence of both usually portended morale difficulties.

The All-Negro Posts

At times these yardsticks, when applied to what seemed to be nearly ideal situations, were less than accurate. The Site Board for the location of a flying school for Negroes thought it had solved the difficult location problem for an all-Negro post [22] when it recommended a site fifteen miles from Tuskegee, Alabama. Under the heading, "General Suitability for Air Corps Station," it wrote:

The close proximity of Tuskegee Institute makes this site ideal for the training of Negroes, since that Institute furnishes many precepts and examples in conduct and attitude. It is a center of Negro learning and culture, and it has temporary accommodations for Negro personnel. Further it is an Institute whose leaders exert great influence in the affairs of the Negro race.

The County of Macon in which Tuskegee Institute is situated is predominantly Negro, and a Negro flying field is welcomed by the community.

Tuskegee is predominantly white, while the Tuskegee Institute is naturally entirely a Negro community. This condition would assist largely in handling the problem of segregation.

But, as the white officer historian of the Tuskegee station observed, these beliefs "may be considered the beginning of the lack of understanding relative to this station." [23]

While it guaranteed to the infant field the close administrative co-operation of nearby Tuskegee Institute, whose officials had urged the acceptance of a site in the school's vicinity, the location did not come close to producing the ideal environment that the Site Board had envisioned. The very fact that Macon County was predominantly Negro and the site of the institute as well as of a Veterans' Administration hospital militated against the full welcome of yet another Negro installation by the population of Tuskegee and the surrounding countryside. Negro members of the school's staff and residents of the institute area were disturbed by the threatened disruption of their accustomed manner of living. White citizens feared the sudden influx of Negroes—Northern Negroes to be trained in the use of arms at that. Townspeople, Negro and white, resented the spending ability of soldiers crowding into the few shops and restaurants available. Institute authorities soon let it be known that they did not favor enlisted men showing attentions to female students, thus closing off, or at least making more difficult, one of the major expected advantages of the location—the provision of a social outlet for the soldiers of the field. The male students at the institute resented the appearance of the field's soldiers on their campus. Messing on contractual ar-

---

[22] All-Negro posts had Negro units only, but not all-Negro personnel in units or overhead.

[23] History of Tuskegee Army Air Field from Conception to 6 Dec 41 (Maj Edward C. Ambler), 14 Oct 43, rev. 5 Mar 44, AF Hist GP 289.28–1, vol. 1, Hist Tuskegee Army Air Field, p. 10.

rangements with the institute caused further strained relations. The mess hall often closed early, little food was left for the last men, and the food served was poor by Army standards. The expected living accommodations turned out to be twelve apartments, nine houses, and one hotel of forty-three rooms for whites. For Negroes there were nine houses for rent and Dorothy Hall, the school's dormitory for visitors. The rapidly increasing profiteering on rental quarters, indulged in by landlords, mainly Negro, some of whom were no less rapacious than the more widely publicized landlords of urban Negro slum districts and of other unfavorably located Army towns, did not help relations between town and post.

Nor was the complete segregation between white and Negro communities of particular aid to the field. The presence of the institute, coupled with the soldiers' knowledge of the part it had played in securing the location of the field in its vicinity, served to alienate further those men at the Flying School, most of them from the North and most of them of better than average education, who saw in the institute a living symbol of entrenched advantage gained from segregation and a subtle supporter of segregation on the airfield itself. The presence of the institute in its relation to segregation and discrimination did not lessen racial friction either on the field or in the town.

In some ways, the proximity of the institute heightened racial tensions both among soldiers and among white civilians. The long experience of institute area residents in the latent racial frictions and animosities of the region,

when communicated to the soldiers, heightened the apprehensions of men whose contacts with the area were new. Viewing the collaboration of the institute and the air base with alarm arising from the belief that the institute might have found a valuable ally in the soldiers of the airfield, local whites had old fears renewed. The early racial disturbance at Tuskegee was an outgrowth of this interplay of fears and friction.

But if the location of the Air Forces' all-Negro post at Tuskegee did not meet all the suitability standards expected, the location of the Ground Forces' all-Negro post at Fort Huachuca, Arizona, was even less inspired from the point of view of camp-town relations. Soldiers from Tuskegee Army Air Field, when they found little in the town of Tuskegee, could go to Montgomery, forty miles away, or to Atlanta, about a hundred miles farther away. Citizens of nearby Tuskegee and of Montgomery, and the staffs of the Negro schools located in the two towns attempted, through USO, social, athletic, and other activities, to ease the difficult recreation problem in the area. Negro colleges and community organizations as far away as Atlanta helped the field solve its recreational problems. But there was no town near Fort Huachuca to care for a garrison that was much larger than Tuskegee's. Distances in Arizona were greater than in the east, and after they were covered soldiers often had arrived at no better a destination than if they had not gone so far. The larger Arizona communities within reach of the post—Tucson, Phoenix, Bisbee—soon tired of the visits of Fort Huachuca soldiers. One by one they became increasingly inhospitable, with some of them eventually banned to all Negro soldiers save those whose relatives resided in the towns.[24]   Fort Huachuca was, moreover, heir to Fry which, as previously described, had little to offer troops aside from prostitution and a large USO club.

With the help of Truman Gibson, Jr., assistant to the Civilian Aide to the Secretary of War, Col. Edwin N. Hardy, the post commander, encouraged private Negro capital from Chicago to invest in the improvement of Fry.   Thus Colonel Hardy hoped to establish "a large amusement hall which will provide for dancing, drinking (nothing stronger than beer), skating, shooting galleries, restaurants, music, etc.   Girls would be available to serve soldiers, dance with them, and put on floor shows." [25]   Eventually, he hoped, private capital would construct a residential district with housing for the fluctuating Negro population, both military and civilian.   Fry did acquire its amusement casino, known locally as the Green Top, but it was never "brought up to proper standards of sanitation and genteel conditions in other respects" as the colonel had hoped.

The existence of Fry and the absence of a Negro population in surrounding towns were not the only differences between Fort Huachuca and other posts at which Negro troops were located, nor

between it and Tuskegee.   Tuskegee was a new station where the discomforts inherent in the establishment of a new camp were shared by all personnel stationed there, officers and enlisted men, Negroes and whites alike.   Fort Huachuca, on the other hand, was an old, established post for which a new training cantonment alone had to be constructed. Tuskegee was a post constructed primarily for the training of Negroes, while Huachuca, though used for that purpose entirely, could have been transferred at any time to the training of any units other than the two Negro divisions successively located there.   At Tuskegee all facilities were constructed and geared to the needs of a small post whose population was, from the beginning, scheduled to become, eventually, almost entirely Negro.   Fort Huachuca had no such intimations.   At Tuskegee, therefore, there was but one station hospital, one post exchange, one set of officers' quarters, one system of messes, one set of barracks and quarters for civilian employees, one movie, one service club. Though there was some dissatisfaction on the part of Negro personnel that the post exchange restaurant at Tuskegee was divided racially during most of the war and though signs bearing racial designations at one time made their appearance, Negroes at Tuskegee had few immediate reminders of segregation policies.   It was clear that whatever was on the post was primarily for their use. The disadvantages of segregation, as it related to the provision of facilities, were almost entirely on the side of the white officer and enlisted personnel at Tuskegee, as that station's intelligence officer continuously pointed out in suc-

---

[24] The situation was complicated in Phoenix by successive disturbances involving troops stationed there, a situation affecting Fort Huachuca's troop population adversely although it had not been involved. See ch. XII, below.

[25] 1st Ind, Hq Ft. Huachuca to CG Ninth SC, 4 Aug 42, to Ltr, Ninth SC to CO Ft. Huachuca, 28 Jul 42, 250.1 SPKIM.

cessive installments of his historical reports.[26]

At Fort Huachuca, on the other hand, duplicate facilities were the rule: two complete station hospitals, one with a full white and the other with a full Negro staff; two sets of civilian quarters; a pair of officers' clubs; and so forth. While white officers and enlisted men at Tuskegee complained of having to travel to Auburn over bad roads in order to find acceptable living quarters, Negro officers and enlisted men had similar complaints at Fort Huachuca about towns as far away as Tucson and Phoenix.

Both of the all-Negro posts recognized many of the problems of their isolation, greater in the case of the one than the other but felt in both, and of their relationships with the surrounding civilian communities. Both tried, therefore, to exploit to the fullest the advantages of on-post recreation in order to reduce the pull of the towns. Tuskegee, the first of the wartime flying schools to obtain authorization for a service club, maintained a prodigious schedule of on-post activities, a schedule which often won commendation from inspectors for the post's special service and athletic personnel. Both posts received close attention from the prominent Negro performers of the USO's and Camp Shows' circuits. Often performers and bands

playing in nearby cities would make special, unscheduled trips to these posts, both to perform for and to visit with the soldiers there. Fort Huachuca, in addition to a full complement of recreational facilities, had the only full-time Theater (theatrical production) and Education officers assigned to an individual post in the Army.[27] If recreation had been the key to morale in relation to training, the Negro soldiers of Fort Huachuca and Tuskegee, who received greater attention in this area than the Negro troops at most other stations, should have had the highest morale in the Army. Actually Negro soldiers at both posts shared more of the problems of other Negro soldiers than they missed by being stationed at their all-Negro posts.

Transportation

One of these problems, transportation, was administratively more difficult than most for the Army to handle. It involved different modes of travel, varying state and local laws and customs, and, above all, negotiations with commercial firms whose facilities were, at best, heavily taxed by wartime travel and whose patience was equally taxed by local and federal restrictions on the use of equipment and on the extent of services. Here, both on posts and in towns, Negro soldiers came into frequent contact with law enforcement agencies and men who, as bus drivers and train conductors, carried the weight of law enforcement of-

[26] These installments of the History of Tuskegee Air Field, Air Force Hist Gp 289.28-1, all save the last written by Maj Edward C. Ambler, the post's white intelligence officer and historian, devote considerable space to the living and entertainment problems of white personnel. Their complaints paralleled, both in substance and in quantity, almost exactly those of Negro personnel at many other stations, lacking, of course, references to discrimination against them on the post or in nearby towns.

[27] Theater and Education officers, originally members of the Army Specialists Corps and later of Special Services, were usually assigned only to service command or overseas area staffs as field directors of amateur and professional theatricals and of off-duty educational programs.

ficials in the observance of local laws and customs and in the control of the discipline of their passengers while on trips. At loading points conflict between soldiers and civilians was frequent. In addition, the presence of military and civilian policemen on the trains and buses sometimes led to clashes, serious and trivial, verbal and physical, which made transportation a key point of racial tension. Because transportation was a problem of varying proportions, depending largely upon local laws and ordinances, neither its full dimensions nor it solution was readily apparent to the War Department.

In rail transportation, there were fewer chances for difficulties than in bus travel, for individual soldiers used trains less frequently than they used the buses that connected posts with nearby towns and cities. Rail transportation was important, however, not only for individual furloughs home but also for the official shipment of troops and individuals transferring from post to post. Its general problems came to the attention of the Army as soon as considerable numbers of troops began to move back and forth across the country on new duty assignments. It became, therefore, in the earlier months of mobilization, one of the more vexing War Department administrative as well as command problems arising out of the increased use of Negro troops.

The problem divided itself into two phases: the adequacy of coach facilities and the use of pullman facilities. Dining cars and arrangements for meals en route shared in the latter problem. All were affected by the laws of states through which the trains passed. Administrative decisions therefore de-

pended in large part upon the state of and interpretation of laws affecting the subject of rail travel by Negroes.

Rail transportation south of the Missouri-Ohio-Potomac line had long been a major source of complaint from Negroes who had to travel considerable distances. All that the words segregation and discrimination implied was conjured up by the term "Jim Crow car." The Jim Crow cars were not infrequently the least well-kept of a given train's coaches; often a half coach only, occupying part of a baggage or smoking car, was designated for Negro passengers. Since all Negroes riding a given train were expected to use it, the "colored coach" was sometimes crowded while cars immediately behind were less than full. To the Negro soldier one of the more tangible evidences of entrance into the South was the direction to change at Washington to the colored coach at the front of southbound trains.[28] One Negro soldier remarked: "I hate Washington even if it is the capital of the country; there you have to change to Jim Crow cars and then you know what kind of country you've got." [29] Negroes generally argued that the Jim Crow car was always "separate" but never "equal."

Negro passengers seeking to ride first class were so few before the war that no separate pullman accommodations were made available to them except in cases of group travel when cars might be chartered; to the passenger

---

[28] Similar directions were less frequently encountered on the north-south lines of the Mississippi Valley. Trains leaving Chicago for the South usually, until after World War II, departed with their Negro passengers already seated in separate coaches.
[29] Statement, Sergeant of the 477th Bombardment Group, Atterbury AAB, to the author, Sep 44.

who insisted on purchasing a first class ticket in those larger cities where they were sold to Negroes, the standard practice of the railroads was to assign a room or compartment for the price of a berth.[30] With the beginning of mobilization and the tremendous increase of rail traffic, rooms as well as all other space began to acquire premium value at the same time that Negro and white civilian and military requests for first class space on trains rose sharply.

Early in the period of mobilization the War Department began to receive requests for directions on the shipment of groups of soldiers by rail. Shipments too small to require the use of troop trains were usually sent on government transportation requests as individuals or as a group under the control of a commissioned or noncommissioned officer. Many post transportation officers were uncertain whether or not to issue to Negroes transportation requests calling for first class travel, despite the fact that Army Regulations provided that noncommissioned officers traveling individually or in parties of nine or less be furnished lower berths at public expense.[31] In April 1941, Sgt. Floyd N. Alexander, traveling from Fort Huachuca, Arizona, to Fort Meade, Maryland, under orders as the noncommissioned assistant to the officer in charge of a group of selectees who had been transferred from Meade to Huachuca, was refused pullman accommodations on the way back through

Texas. At Seneca, Missouri, Sergeant Alexander was awakened and given a pullman berth. The 1302d Service Unit, the headquarters unit of which Sergeant Alexander was a member, asked for guidance for future situations of a similar nature.[32]

A few days before Sergeant Alexander departed from Fort Huachuca, the Supreme Court had handed down its decision in the Mitchell case in which the circumstances were similar.[33] In this case, involving Congressman Arthur Mitchell of Illinois, the court held that Negroes purchasing first class tickets must be furnished equal comfort and convenience. This decision, plus the Army Regulations concerning official travel of noncommissioned officers of the first three grades, caused the Judge Advocate General's Office to rule that "the refusal of the railroad concerned to honor the Government's transportation request for such accommodations in Sergeant Alexander's case constitutes a clear violation of the law as announced in the Mitchell case" and that as long as regulations remained unchanged noncommissioned officers "are entitled to the prescribed accommodations without discrimination and the railroads are bound to furnish such accommodations, when available, without discrimination." [34] The Quartermaster General, whose office was responsible for military travel, then requested the American Association of Railroads to take meas-

[30] Ltr, Vice President, Association of American Railroads, to Manager, Military Transportation Section, Association of American Railroads, Washington, D.C., 3 Nov 41, in AG 291.21 (5–2–41) (2). See also Charles S. Johnson, *Patterns of Negro Segregation* (New York: Harper & Brothers, 1943), pp. 45–48, 167–68.

[31] AR 30–925, 8 Oct 35, 2a.

[32] Ltr, 1302d Sv Unit to Third Corps Area, 2 May 41, sub: Rpt of Trans Furnished, AG 291.21 (5–2–41) (2).

[33] Mitchell v. U.S. *et al.*, 61 Supreme Court 873, 23 Apr 41.

[34] 8th Ind, JAGO (Col Fred W. Llewellyn) to TAG, 3 Jul 41, Mil Affairs JAG 291.2.

ures to prevent "further unlawful discriminations." [35]

The matter of railroad transportation of Negro military personnel was not, however, so easily concluded. Before The Quartermaster General's request could be forwarded, Arthur H. Gass, Manager of the Association of American Railroads, Military Transportation Section, received a request from the General Superintendent of the Richmond, Fredericksburg, and Potomac Railroad Company that another situation be "handled." On 8 July 1941 four Negro second lieutenants, on their way from Fort Ontario, New York, to Fort Eustis, Virginia, for temporary training duty, had been directed to move to the Negro coach at Washington. When the conductor returned to their coach, he found them still seated there. Despite arguments from the conductor and a railroad agent, they continued into Richmond without moving. "We feel these men should comply with the State Law, in moving in regular passenger trains and we would thank you to give it such handling as you deem proper," the railroad's superintendent stated.[36] Gass felt that the officers, since they would be returning from Fort Eustis at the completion of their training, should be instructed to comply with the state law. The Office of the Quartermaster General referred the request to The Adjutant General for action and for reference to Judge Hastie.[37] The Adjutant General sent the case to the Judge Advocate General's Office for an opinion.

This case, the Judge Advocate General's Office decided, differed from the Alexander case. "Upon the assumption that the accommodations provided for these colored passengers were in fact equal to those furnished white persons, the situation presented in this case is one of segregation rather than one of discrimination," the Judge Advocate wrote. "As to discrimination, the law is clear that there is a duty of the carrier to provide equality of transportation facilities," the opinion continued, citing the Mitchell case. There was no federal statute in conflict with the laws of Virginia pertaining to segregation, and the railroad was acting within its rights, the Judge Advocate concluded. He recommended that the officers be informed of their "obligations in this regard" and concurred in the recommendation that the matter be referred to Judge Hastie "as the issue here considered may have been misunderstood in view of recent decisions." [38]

Hastie did not agree with the Judge Advocate's opinion. "The Virginia State Segregation Law," he wrote, "has no valid application to the officers in question because they were traveling in interstate commerce." The principal cases cited by the Judge Advocate in support of the constitutionality of the state laws were, he continued, "explicit in limiting their application to travel in

[35] Ltr, OQMG to Arthur H. Gass, Manager, Military Transportation Section, Association of American Railroads, Washington, D.C., 17 Jul 41, QM 201 T–CT (Alexander, Floyd N., Sgt).

[36] Ltr, W. A. Aiken, General Superintendent RF&P RR, Richmond, Va., to A. H. Gass, 12 Jul 41, Incl to Ltr, A. H. Gass to TQMG, 18 Jul 41, AG 291.21 (7–18–41).

[37] 1st Ind, OQMG to TAG, 22 Jul 41, on Ltr, Gass to TQMQ, 18 Jul 41.

[38] 3d Ind, JAG (Col E. C. McNeil) to TAG, 12 Aug 41, on Ltr, Gass to TQMG, 18 Jul 41, JAG 291.2.

intrastate commerce." [39] In a further comment, the Judge Advocate agreed that there was some judicial authority on both sides of the question of the constitutionality of state segregation laws in interstate commerce, but added that "all are agreed that the carrier may, if it furnishes equal accommodations and does not discriminate therein, establish rules requiring segregation of white and colored passengers." The Judge Advocate concluded that: "Although the validity of the Virginia State segregation law as applied to passengers in interstate commerce may not be free from doubt, nevertheless, until the law is declared by a court of competent jurisdiction to be inoperative when directed to such passengers, officers of the Army traveling without troops should comply with its provisions, and in any event, should comply with such regulations to the same effect as have been adopted by the carrier for the conduct of its passengers." [40]

Hastie again disagreed. Since there was a "considerable body of authority to the effect that passengers in interstate commerce are not subject to state segregation laws," he wrote, "it is believed that this Department should not acquiesce in the application of such laws to Army personnel travelling in interstate commerce but rather should obtain the opinion of the Attorney General on the issue in question." The Attorney General should also be asked to comment on the circumstances under which military personnel in interstate commerce were subject to the segregation regulations of

carriers.[41] The Judge Advocate General had also requested that an expression of opinion be obtained from the Attorney General. Accordingly, The Adjutant General wrote a letter of inquiry to the Attorney General for Secretary Stimson's signature.[42]

In the meantime the railroads in the ten states having rail segregation laws had instructed their operating forces, by individual action following the Mitchell decision, that requests for pullman accommodations from a Negro passenger, either civilian or military, on an interstate journey would be filled if space was available. "In other words," the Association of American Railraods informed its Military Transportation Section, "you may assure the Quartermaster General that there is no intent on the part of the American Railroads to discriminate against members of the Military Forces." [43] Hastie then suggested that, in view of past difficulties and the consequent hesitancy of some stations to authorize pullman travel for Negro soldiers, the situation would be helped if all appropriate officers were informed of the association's action. The Quartermaster General concurring, a circular was prepared for the field on the matter.[44]

On the other question, that of inter-

[39] Memo, Civ Aide to SW for Adm Asst to SW, 18 Aug 41, AG 291.21 (7-18-41).
[40] Memo, JAG for TAG, 15 Oct 41, JAG 291.2 (Mil Affairs).

[41] Memo, Civ Aide to SW for Adm Asst to SW, 20 Oct 41, AG 291.21 (5-2-41) (2).
[42] Ltr, SW to Attorney General, 14 Nov 41, AG 291.21 (10-15-41) MB.
[43] Ltr, Vice President Association American Railroads to Gass, 3 Nov 41, Incl to Ltr, Gass to TQMG, 10 Nov 41, AG 291.21 (5-2-41) (2).
[44] 2d Ind, Civ Aide to TAG, 28 Nov 41, and 4th Ind, OQMG to TAG, 10 Dec 41, to Ltr, Gass to TQMG, 10 Nov 41, AG 291.21 (5-2-41) (2); Transportation Accommodations for Negro Members of the Army, prepared 18 Dec 41, issued as sec. II, WD Cir 269, 26 Dec 41.

state rail segregation in coaches, the Attorney General replied on 19 December 1941, stating that since the Supreme Court had not settled the question and that since there was division of opinion among lower courts, the policy of acceptance of local laws and customs outlined by the Judge Advocate General would be satisfactory to the Department of Justice "pending final determination of the question by the Supreme Court." [45] Consequently, the official Army interpretation of the responsibilities of troops traveling individually by rail in the Southern states henceforth during the war was that they should abide by local laws and by carriers' regulations.

Train travel under crowded wartime conditions was filled with incidents damaging to morale. When jammed trains pulled into stations, many a Negro soldier bound for home on furlough found himself unable to board the coach or coaches reserved for Negroes. At rail stations such as the one at Chehaw, Alabama, the station for the Tuskegee Army Air Field, Negro soldiers often overflowed from the coaches into the baggage car where they rode the forty miles into Montgomery on boxes and trunks while seats were available in the remaining coaches of the train. Even if the white coaches were equally crowded, the reaction was that a greater choice of coaches would have increased the

chances of boarding a given train. The new pullman policy was no great aid to the traveling soldier; even if he had the funds to spare for first class travel, it was virtually impossible to obtain space on short notice except in the larger cities.

Irritable, overworked, and often bitter bus and train personnel accounted for a number of clashes, most of which, fortunately, did not develop into full-scale racial disorder. On a train from New Orleans to Hattiesburg, Mississippi, in November 1942, for example, a conductor attempted to hurry a Negro soldier who had difficulty finding his ticket. The soldier eventually found his ticket, saying "Here it is, Buddy." The conductor, angered by the soldier's use of the word "Buddy," called the train's military police. The police, after learning what the incident was about, refused to arrest the soldier, whereupon the conductor went to the baggage car and got a pistol. The soldier moved to a smoking car where a first sergeant and several other noncommissioned officers of his regiment were seated. He told them of the incident, indicating that he would point the conductor out when he next came through the train. As the conductor returned from the baggage car, he was identified by the soldier in a low voice, but the conductor nevertheless overheard. As he reached the doorway between the smoking compartment and the coach, he stopped, pulled his pistol out of his pocket, pointed it at the soldiers, and shouted, "If any one of you black sons-of-bitches make another chirp, I will kill every damn one of you." Whatever the psychological effects of the incident, the soldiers did not react as they might have and no physically

[45] Ltr, Attorney General to SW, 19 Dec 41, AG file cited n. 44. "It is not altogether unlikely," the Attorney General wrote, "that when the question of the validity of both the State statutes and the regulations of carriers is fully presented to the Supreme Court, it will hold them to be unconstitutional, but until the question is finally determined by that Court any opinion which I might render would not be controlling."

tragic results occurred. Third Army, in reporting the incident to the railroad, observed that such misconduct on the part of the conductor "could have resulted in a tragedy, his own death, or even a race riot. The misconduct of the conductor, directed against these colored soldiers, who are in the state of Mississippi by reason of Military necessity, shows not only an overbearing and cowardly disposition, but an utter disregard of patriotism, and lack of consideration for those in the Military Service, who are patrons of the Southern Railway System." [46]

At times the tension of travel was increased by the misconduct of soldiers.[47] Drinking, resulting in intractable conduct, was a frequent complaint of carriers against both white and Negro soldiers before restrictions on the sale of intoxicants and before the gradual disappearance of club cars brought about by the conversion of those cars to "paying space" reduced the availability of liquor on trains.[48] But in cases of Negro soldiers, the problem was complicated by the growing antagonism between Negro soldiers and white military police [49]

and the continuing antagonism between Negroes and train officials as representative of a restricting Jim Crow railway system. Reports of misconduct on trains were not so frequent, however, as reports of the more usual types of individual difficulties growing out of the nature of rail travel for Negroes.[50] Nor did rail transportation, despite the extent of negotiations concerning it in the earlier months of mobilization, approach bus transportation in its effect upon individual and group morale. Neither was it so important for local and post administration and discipline, since the bulk of military travel from post to town or from post to major rail points of departure was by bus and not by train.

"I think to straighten out the trouble on the bus stop in town would be the cure for a lot of the trouble here," one Negro sergeant told an inspector. Many another Negro soldier and eventually many of those charged with the amelioration of Negro morale difficulties agreed with him.[51]

---

[46] Ltr, Hq Third Army, Office of the CG Ft. Sam Houston, Texas, 9 Feb 43, to Ernest E. Norris, President, Southern Railway System, Washington, D.C., AGF 333.1/64 (Third Army).

[47] Cf. Inland Transportation of Individuals for the Army During World War II, Monograph 20, Historical Unit, OCofTrans, ASF, pp. 148–50, 162–63, in OCMH; Ltrs, TAG to CG's, 12 Apr 42, AG 250.1 (3–24–42) MB–M, and 21 Jul 42, AG 250.1 (7–14–42) MB–SPAA–PS–M.

[48] Memo, CofS for Gen Gullion (TPMG), 4 Nov 42, WDCSA 250.11 (11–4–42); Memo, same, 17 Nov 42, WDCSA 250.11 (11–17–42); Memo, PMG for CofS, 23 Nov 42, SPMG 250.1 Gen; WD Instructions for Mil Pol on Railroad Trains (Not Troop Trains) and in Railroad Terminals and Stations, 1943.

[49] In general, Negro MP's were not assigned to train duty, though service commanders were free

to do so should they deem it advisable. It was thought that Negro military policemen would require duplicate teams on trains, one of white MP's and one of Negro MP's, with the latter's duties restricted and complicated by the segregation laws of Southern states and by the necessity of their dealing with strange and perhaps unsympathetic military and civilian officials. Memo, PMG for DCofS for SC's ASF, 29 Nov 44, ASF CofS for SC's File 291.2 Misc, and attached Tabs A and B.

[50] Ltr, West Point Route to CO Maxwell Fld, Ala., 4 Feb 42, Incl to Ltr, Hq Fourth Corps Area to Hq AGF, n.d., 370.5–T–Misconduct on Trains, AGF 250.1/18; Rpt of Inv, Hq 2 Cav Div. 3 May 43, 333, 9th Armd Div (2d Cav Div), AGO Records.

[51] Testimony, SSgt George L. Chambers, 328th Avn Sq, Pampa AAF, Tex., 13 Dec 43, in Incl to Memo, Hq AAF (AFTAI) for CG AAF, 14 Feb 44, AAF 333.5; Memo, Col Leonard for ASW, 3 Oct 44, ASW 291.2; Rpts, ASF Insp Team, Rel Racial Matters, various dates 1944–45, in ASF DCofS Files 291.2.

Negro troops, in heavy proportions, traveled back and forth from camps to nearby towns, usually by buses run into the camps on a scheduled commercial or chartered service. In states with segregation laws the practice of restricting Negroes to seats at the rear of buses was usually the rule. Where the local laws left the proportioning of space to the numbers of passengers involved in a given trip, Negroes were seated from the back and whites from the front. At the same time, white passengers were usually loaded first. Wherever buses were crowded or wherever passengers failed to change their seats to accommodate altered racial proportions, arguments over seating and loading, often with disastrous results, were possible.

When a bus left a terminal at the center of a post and picked up Negro troops along its route through the post on the way to town, all seats and most standing room were likely to be taken by the time Negro soldiers were reached. Negro troops then waited for the next bus, or crowded into the already filled bus, giving rise to numerous altercations and disturbances.

Some posts authorized military policemen to load a particular number of Negro soldiers first—eight or twelve or whatever number could be expected to fill a fair proportion of the seats normally allotted them—in order to eliminate friction arising from the necessity of their pushing through from front to back or from finding their allotted seats already occupied by white passengers. Others arranged separate buses and schedules for Negro soldiers.

Neither practice, though both guaranteed a specific number of seats, was satisfactory. The first at times was so construed that the number of Negro soldiers riding a given bus was limited to the number of seats allotted and not to the number of passengers available. In these cases, buses might leave several Negro soldiers behind though some seats were empty. Sometimes instructions to military police about the number of seats to be reserved for Negroes were vague; sometimes they did not include provision for white soldiers standing while Negroes sat; nor did they always include instructions covering cases where white soldiers, in contravention of local laws insisted that "it was all right" for Negro soldiers to share seats with them.[52] Any or all of these possibilities could be and were productive of arguments, arrests, and, occasionally, violence.

When separate buses were provided, they usually ran on less frequent schedules, for there were usually fewer Negro soldiers to be accommodated on a given post. But because they were on a less frequent sechedule, the separate buses were often as crowded as the main line buses had been. Negro soldiers awaiting the arrival of the "Colored" bus watched with envious and resentful eyes whenever the more frequently scheduled "white" buses passed, especially if they contained empty seats or standing room.

Transportation jams at terminals and camp gates were often tremendous, with long lines of men waiting to be loaded on buses. These waiting, irritable crowds often provided fertile ground for racial incidents. A few posts used divided waiting rooms for Negro and white troops. At least one post, seeking to ease the bottleneck at its main gate,

---

[52] Ltr, Office Camp Inspector, Cp Rucker, Ala., to CG Cp Rucker, 18 Mar 43, Cp Rucker 333.1, AGO Records.

near which the Negro area was located, cut special entrances for Negro troops going on pass and built a new waiting station at the bus stop.[53]

In towns, the bus problem for the soldier attempting to get back to camp was the same, except that the direction of travel was reversed and the pressure of loading was increased. Often the Negro AWOL's excuse that "the bus left me" or that "the bus was too crowded to get on" was perfectly accurate. In some commands the problem was alleviated by the use of government vehicles, usually trucks, but with vehicle and gas shortages and with restrictions on the use of vehicles this was seldom possible as a continuing practice. Many Negro soldiers found the difficulty of getting to and from town too great to be worth the effort, especially in light of the deficient facilities in many camp towns.

By 1944, the prominent role that bus transportation difficulties played in racial friction and low morale among Negro soldiers was generally recognized. Inspector after inspector alluded to the problem. Cases of racial friction involving buses had appeared frequently enough in the civilian press to make it a major symbol of racial difficulties in Army camps. But one camp solved its problem and, through a newspaper account inserted in the *Congressional Record* by Representative Herman P. Eberharter of Pennsylvania, helped to solve the problem elsewhere. The article, "How One General Solved Bus Problem for Negroes by Deal with Company," [54]

was reproduced by Army Service Forces and sent "for your information" to all post, camp, and station commanders in Virginia and in the Fourth and Eighth Service Commands.[55]

The article itself was a reporter's survey of bus transportation problems of Negro soldiers in a number of southern camps. He found two camps, Camp Shelby, Mississippi, and Camp Lee, Virginia, in which "direct, intelligent effort" to solve the bus problem had been made. Of the two, the solution reached at Camp Lee was the one that had done most for morale. "Now things are different," he wrote. "Any Negro soldier who is in town can always get a bus back —with no Jim Crowism and no more than ordinary delay, such as happens on buses everywhere." He outlined what he considered to be the reasons that "Negro soldiers at Camp Lee were high in morale, proud and snappy":

The "revolution" was accomplished by white-haired Brig. Gen. George Horkan, a West Pointer, a Georgian and a man whose name will be treasured in the hearts of many northern Negroes all their lives.

.   .   .   .

General Horkan, within a few days after he took command, learned about the intolerable bus service—that Negro soldiers were jammed into inadequate Jim Crow seats, or passed up altogether and forced to walk to and from camp. There had been a few minor fracases on busses, the general told me . . . the kind of thing that leads to deep resentment, if not to race riots.

"I knew something had to be done," the general said, "also, I knew I couldn't do anything about the State (Jim Crow) law." So, he simply made an agreement with

---

[53] Historical Report, Engineer Aviation Unit Training Center, MacDill Field, Fla. (18 Mar 43–1 Aug 44), Folder 1, AF Archive 3767–179.

[54] By Orrin C. Evans, Philadelphia *Record*, inserted in *Congressional Record*, 22 May 1944, pp. A2679–A2680.

[55] Ltr, Hq ASF to CG's Third, Fourth, and Eighth Sv Comd's, 29 May 44, SPX 291.2 (23 May 44).

the Petersburg-Camp Lee bus company under which an adequate number of vehicles were operated between town and camp exclusively for soldiers. He established a depot in the Petersburg business section, equally convenient for white and Negro soldiers.

There is no segregation on the buses. The rule is first come, first served—and there has been no trouble.[56]

A few weeks after this account had been circulated to post commanders, a new general letter on facilities for Negroes was published by the Army. General Horkan's solution to the bus problem, arrived at independently, was directed for all government owned or operated motor transportation:

4. *Transportation.*—Buses, trucks, or other transportation owned and operated either by the Government or by a governmental instrumentality will be available to all military personnel regardless of race. Restricting personnel to certain sections of such transportation because of race will not be permitted either on or off post, camp, or station, regardless of local civilian custom.[57]

Those camps affected by this directive saw a marked decrease in racial friction on buses. No serious case of such friction was reported from any bus line operated in this manner during the remainder of the war.

The Impact of Intangibles

Physical facilities provided, from the beginning, visible, tangible items whose contribution to the low state of morale

among Negro soldiers could be observed and evaluated with relative ease; but they were only the more obvious deterrents to high morale and motivation. More significant blocks to high morale in Negro units often occurred on different, less easily apprehended levels. It was on the level of belief in the importance of the job assigned to the individual soldier and to his unit that morale foundered in many Negro units. It was on the level of belief in the Army's and in their commanders' good faith and good intentions that Negro soldiers' morale often met important tests. It was on the level of belief in the ultimate significance of their roles in the Army's and in the country's eyes that motivation for superior efforts and performance fell short in many units. Where these blocks to high morale were demolished, units flourished despite deficiencies in physical facilities. Where they continued to exist, units and individuals felt the full force of their destructive power.

Early in the period of expansion, both Judge Hastie and General Davis wished the War Department to take a firm stand on one of the critical immediate causes of friction and disillusionment among Negro troops—the use of offensive epithets applied to Negroes.[58] After much discussion of the value of direct orders barring the use of epithets such as "nigger," G–3 prepared a letter for commanders which reminded them of the provisions of Army Regulations on the matter:

1. Organization commanders of Negro troops have found that emphasis on the

[56] *Ibid.*

[57] Ltr, TAG to CG's AAF, All Sv Comd's, MDW, 8 Jul 44, AG 353.8 (5 Jul 44) OB–S–A–N, based on DF WD G–1 for TAG, 5 Jul 44, WDGAP 291.2 (29 Jun 44).

[58] Hastie Survey, 22 Sep 41, G–1/15640–120 and papers attached.

substance of the following provisions of paragraph 3, Army Regulations, 600–10, is especially applicable in sustaining and improving morale:

"Superiors are forbidden to injure those under their authority by tyrannical or capricious conduct or by abusive language. While maintaining discipline and the thorough and prompt performance of military duty, all officers, in dealing with enlisted men, will bear in mind the absolute necessity of so treating them as to preserve their self-respect. A grave duty rests on all officers and particularly upon organization commanders in this respect."

2. In this connection the use of any epithet deemed insulting to a racial group should be carefully avoided. Similarly, commanders should avoid all practices tending to give the colored soldier cause to feel that the Army makes any differentiation between him and any other soldier.

3. As the Army expands and new and relatively inexperienced officers assume and share functions of command, it will be increasingly important that all officers have a full realization of the significance of such factors as are discussed herein for the maintenance of discipline and high morale.[59]

All commanders of subordinate units and exempted stations were to be informed of this War Department view.[60]

Some subordinate commands issued their own directives. These, as in the following example, were often general warrants of good intentions:

I. NEGRO TROOPS
1. The following directives on the above subject apply to all personnel of this Training Center:

a. The treatment of colored personnel will be in all respects fair and impartial; it will be characterized by a kindly, sympathetic attitude, and by a sincere de-

sire to assist them in every way possible toward a high morale and toward a full and effective part in our war effort.

b. Station commanders are responsible that officers assigned to duty with colored units are qualified by character, temperament and training to achieve the objectives stated, or implied, in paragraph a above.

c. The use, in speaking to or referring to colored units or individuals, of any degrading or insulting term is forbidden.

d. As soon as possible, separate and adequate Post Exchange, recreational and welfare facilities will be provided for colored personnel at each station. Station commanders will immediately report to this Headquarters deficiencies in this respect which cannot be met locally.

e. The establishment by proper agencies of suitable recreational facilities and activities in nearby communities will be encouraged and assisted.

f. On all inspections of stations of this command, Inspectors General assigned to this Headquarters will examine into and report upon the fulfillment of the above directives.[61]

Other commands were at times more direct and blunt in their admonitions. The commanding general of the 28th Infantry Division, when stationed at Camp Livingston, Louisiana, directed his men that:

1. There is sufficient possibility of difficulties between white and colored soldiers in this area that every effort must be made by white soldiers to avoid provocation of trouble.

2. The word "nigger" is a provocative word when used in speaking to or about colored soldiers.

3. This word will not be used in this Division at any time; all officers will be emphatically so instructed and they will

[59] Memo, G–3 for TAG, 11 Feb 42, G–3/6451–399.
[60] Ltr, TAG to CG's Corps Areas, Def Comds, Hawaiian Dept, CofAAF, CO's Bases, 14 Feb 42, AG 322.97 (2–11–42) MSC–C–M.

[61] Extract of Circular 158, Hq Gulf Coast Air Corps Training Center, Randolph Field, Texas, 1 Oct 42.

use every effort, in a quiet and discreet manner, to see that the word is not used.[62]

Admonitory directives such as these did not necessarily improve morale in Negro units. "Kindly, sympathetic" attitudes were no substitutes for a sense of military usefulness, lacking in many an aviation squadron or sanitary company from the beginning. "Separate and adequate" facilities provided constant jolts to attempts to develop self-esteem in Negro troops. They did little to assure the Negro soldier that the Army made no "differentiation between him and any other soldier." Directives alone could not erase the conviction of Negro troops that they were not wanted by the Army to the same extent and degree as white soldiers.

Military usages with reference to them were critical to Negro soldiers. They, like the Negro public at large, naturally expected fairness and impartiality from the federal government and its agencies toward all citizens. Civilian customs and practices in areas surrounding training camps could be galling and morale damaging, but most Negro soldiers, anticipating no rapid changes in civilian attitudes toward them, looked to military authorities for at least nominal protection against the more flagrant abuses possible in camp towns. They considered the military reservation, ideally, to be an island refuge from local legal and custom-supported discriminations. Their morale was bound to suffer with the adoption and extension of civilian practices in military installations where Negro soldiers expected that, even within the framework of separate mili-

tary units, equal treatment for men in training for a common effort would prevail. In many instances, the realization that the post offered little more than the town—and in some areas of the country, particularly the Northeast and Northwest, it offered less—contributed heavily to the morale difficulties of Negro units.

Matters of race and problems connected with race often came to outweigh most other problems in the minds of many Negro soldiers. To inspectors and investigators this development came to be described as "racial sensitivity." When, in an Army-wide survey conducted in the spring of 1943, soldiers were invited to answer the question, "If you could talk with the President of the United States, what are the three most important questions you would want to ask him about the war and your part in it?" half of the Negro soldiers asked questions relating to racial discrimination.[63] Fewer than 0.5 percent of white troops thought the matter of racial discrimination worth asking the President about. The four items of most concern to white soldiers were questions and complaints about Army life (31 percent), conditions in the postwar United States (29 percent), the length of the war (24 percent), and questions and criticisms about the conduct of the war (23 percent).[64] No single category, except racial discrimination, even approached these in importance for the Negro soldier. Only 17 percent of Negro soldiers asked about the length of the war, and a goodly number of the 13 percent who

---

[62] Memo, Hq 28th Inf Div, Camp Livingston, for R, SB, and Sv Comd Co's, 8 Jun 42, in AGF 322.999/5 (Cld Trps).

[63] Attitudes of Negro Soldier, 28 July 1943, Research Branch, Special Service Division.

[64] Percentages on questions added up to more than 100 percent since each soldier was asked to list three questions.

had questions and complaints about the Army asked them in racial terms.

That many of the conditions which produced deep concern among Negro soldiers lay outside the purely military sphere was indicated in their questions. Over a quarter of Negro soldiers (29 percent) asked questions about the racial pattern after the war: "Will I as a Negro share this so-called democracy after the war?" "Will it [the war] make things better for the Negro?" "Will colored people be continued [sic] subjected to the humiliating law of Jim Crow and segregation as before the war?" Fifteen percent protested against current and past discrimination and civil violence: "Why are Negroes barred from certain defense jobs they are capable of doing?" "Why don't he stop so much lynching?" "Our life is worth as much to us as the White's life is to them." "Why don't they make the people in the South treat the Negro right and *then* try to make the people in other countries do right?"

When Negro soldiers' questions revolved about conditions within the Army they were extensions, a fortiori, of their civilian experiences phrased in terms of their Army experiences: "Why aren't Negro troops allowed to fight in combat as well as white troops?" "If white and colored soldiers are fighting and dying for the same thing, why can't they train together?" "Why is there discrimination even in the Army?" "Why can't Negroes have fine things like the white boys in the Army?" Army practices, though generally less stringent than civilian practices which most Negro soldiers had experienced, acquired added meaning simply because they were Army

practices, carried out in the midst of wartime hortatives on teamwork and national unity for a common goal. They therefore assumed greater significance as Negro soldiers compared them with what they conceived to be ideal practices consonant with the nation's stated war aims.

Though Negro soldiers, as a whole, never abandoned the hope that their status, military and civilian, would improve—many of them agreed fully with the statement attributed to Joe Louis: "There may be a whole lot wrong with America, but there's nothing that Hitler can fix" [65] —the continued presence of questions such as these, voiced and unvoiced, for which the Army had no answers acceptable to the questioners, affected adversely the development of high motivation and morale. The construction put upon events and situations, all subject to variable interpretations, depended largely upon the full setting in which they occurred. With a civilian born and nourished predisposition to expect the worst in any situation involving a competition of racial interests, the morale of Negro troops could be ruptured and destroyed while officers were reading the latest directive on morale and discipline.

Evidence of their officers' good faith and good intentions was a critical item in morale. "The greatest thing I have noted to improve efficiency and morale in Negro troops," one commander who had been training Negro troops since the

---

[65] Attributed to Joe Louis by a public speaker; quoted in Sterling A. Brown, "Out of Their Mouths," *Survey Graphic*, XXXI (November, 1942), 483.

beginning of mobilization said near the end of the war, "is to sell them in the beginning and keep on selling them on how interested you and your officers are in them and their welfare, and to convince them someway or somehow by any means available that you and your officers are the biggest hearted and fairest minded men in the United States." [66] In many cases, however, officers were too far removed from their troops to be able to judge with accuracy what the temper of their morale was. In many cases, officers who thought that morale was good, that minor differences had been ironed out, discovered suddenly and with surprise that morale had been badly undermined or destroyed, sometimes unwittingly, by the actions of the officers themselves. Others found that they had wholly misinterpreted both their abilities as "salesmen" and the meaning placed on events by their men.

There were many types of distance and symbol-based difficulties between command and men which blocked easy recognition of morale problems. These included:

(1) *Lack of Belief in Officers' Personal Integrity.* In one unit whose men accused their officers of discriminatory treatment, including an attempt to bring "the segregation and prejudice from Mississippi to a place [the desert] that knows no segregation," one officer explained, "They said they thought they should be allowed to go where they wanted as they were up north but I got the Chaplain to come up and explain

the situation and they are all right now." The men of the unit, on the other hand, insisted that things were not "all right now." Though they had been told to stay away from all but a few places by their officers, they discovered that they were welcomed by townsfolk in other shops and business houses. "When we first came here," one soldier stated, "we had places set aside where we could go. We were told we could go to other places to make purchases but had to leave the store as soon as we made our purchase and that we could not hang around in the white section occupied by the white people. The colored places out here are dirty and most of us have gone to the other places and been treated swell. The people seemed glad to have us come in." Another said: "We have been told to go north of the tracks for our entertainment but a S/Sgt. and myself on our own hook went over south of the tracks; they received us very pleasantly, they seemed glad to have the colored soldiers." The soldiers therefore concluded that their officers had deliberately and unnecessarily sought to keep them away from town establishments and that they could not be trusted further as custodians of the unit's welfare. [67]

(2) *Ignorance of Effects of Language and Action.* Not only were the officers of this same unit unaware of how the experience described above had undermined morale and faith in their integrity, but they were also unaware of the general effects which other aspects of their behavior toward their men had produced. One officer, charged by the

---

[66] Brig Gen Horace L. Whittaker, ASFTC, Fort Francis E. Warren, Wyo., 20 Feb 45, in Questionnaire for Camp and Troop Commanders, ASF 291.2.

[67] Ltr, Asst IG DTC Hq, to CG DTC, 11 Aug 42, and Incls, AG 291.21 (7–21–42) (1).

men with having ordered noncommissioned officers to strike soldiers and with
having cursed and nagged his men, replied that though he knew it was improper, he had ordered beatings but
that he had done no more. "As far as
I know," he told the investigating officer,
"I have not cussed or nagged any of the
soldiers. You know how Niggers are,
if you don't keep after them they simply
lie down on the job. If I cussed any of
them at any time it was done unconsciously, however I do not believe I
ever did." In the record of this case
there is no indication that either the
officer or the inspector was aware that
both the officer's actions and his language were sufficient to alienate his
troops and that both offenses were
contrary to regulations and to customs
of the service. The inspector recommended the officer's transfer, observing
laconically, "Once this race turns against
one it is seldom that they will work for
one afterwards." [68]

(3) *Inability to Gauge Depth
of Morale Problems.* When asked
whether or not he knew anything beforehand about a petition of grievances
presented to him by the noncommissioned officers of his battalion, a unit
commander professed that "Prior to
the receipt of the petitioning letter I had
no knowledge or no suspicion that anything was amiss with the morale of the
battalion. Of course, I was generally
aware of conditions governing the normal routine of negroes, both civilian
and soldier, in the vicinity of Louisville
and Fort Knox, Kentucky. That did
not occur to me to be of any importance

or to have any connection with the petitioning letter, because I had been
aware of those conditions all my life and
subconsciously assumed that the members of the colored race were aware of
it as an existing fact over which neither
they nor I had any control." [69]

(4) *Ignorance of Temper of Command Based on Insulation from Enlisted
Men.* When at morning roll call, nearly
all enlisted men present in an aviation
squadron shouted in unison "We want a
new CO!" the action came "like a bolt
out of the blue" to the squadron commander. Two first lieutenants in the
unit had been aware of brewing troubles
but had not informed the commander.
The commander asked two of the enlisted men for reasons, which they gave.
After agreeing to meet with his top noncommissioned officers, the commander,
instead, dismissed the squadron and
preferred charges of creating and failing
to suppress a mutiny against those who
spoke up. He later admitted that he
"did not understand the colored race,
did not know how to handle them, and
that that was, in all probability, the
reason for his failure to click as a Commanding Officer." Investigation revealed, however, that in addition to
using language offensive to his men, the
commander had failed to secure for his
unit privileges and equipment equal to
that of neighboring units and was considered by his noncommissioned officers
to have placed too little reliance upon
them, with the result that co-operation
between the commander, his junior

[68] *Ibid.*, and attached comments of Civ Aide to SW, AG 291.21 (7-21-42) (1).

[69] CO 828th TD Bn, Cp Hood, Texas, to Investigating Officer, 26 Aug 42, in IG 333.9-828th
TD Bn (3-13-42).

officers, and his noncommissioned officers was lacking.[70]

(5) *Excessive Faith in Effectiveness of Hortatives.* Faced with disorder and threatened disturbances in a Negro unit on his base, a colonel on the post commander's staff, who afterward said that he himself would have "ordered that outfit up with packs, and I would have hiked them until they had a little bit of that out of their system, and then I would have found some place to bivouac for a while and they would do a little more hiking," was certain that he had straightened out all difficulties when, "as one soldier to another," he addressed the assembled men of the unit:

I told them that there were certain things that weren't available for them on the base, and due to certain conditions in the South, they were just to bear with us until we could get these things built. I asked their 1st sergeant, and the 1st sergeant of the 456th—I started off with an orientation talk. Some of my activities overseas, and then asked for questions from the group, and at that time one of the men had appeared with a clipping out of a Northern negro newspaper in which the Secretary of War was supposed to have said that he didn't want colored men to salute the flag. And there was some talk about that. And we thought the best thing to do was to get them to the theater and straighten them out on the right angles right away. I told them about having served joint guard duty with the 9th cavalry, and where I served in France where we had a colored labor

battalion and that many times they helped to get my trucks out of the mud, and that I had seen negro troops overseas, and that I sat on the Awards and Decorations Committee of the 8th Overseas Air Force Service Command and that I helped recommend many colored boys for bravery, and about the soldiers who went into a fire and unloaded 1,000 pound bombs. I gathered at that time that they had the impression that because they were an aviation squadron, that they were just a highly advertised labor battalion. I told them that when we went into Africa in the invasion, that all the different branches were unloading material on the docks, regardless of whether you had been trained to operate a telegraph key, a typewriter, or whatnot, everybody worked. It didn't make any difference whether you were white, yellow, black or whether you were a Jew, Protestant, Catholic or what. It had nothing to do with the theater of operations. I asked for questions, and this was brought up about the[ir] saluting the flag, and something was said about officers not saluting, or returning a salute, and I said any time I didn't return a salute of theirs, I wanted it brought to my attention through my commanding officer. I told them I was the oldest soldier on the field and I didn't see any difference between a colored soldier and a white soldier; we were all in this thing for the same thing, and what was good for one was good for the other. I got a big hand from them—and the next day they had their sit-down strike.[71]

In these cases, little by way of improved morale could be expected so long as the major questions posed went

[70] Reorganizations in this squadron—including removal of the officers and the first sergeant and reduction of seven noncoms—cleared the air; within the month the unit received commendation from the Air Freight Forwarding Squadron at Biak and from its wing headquarters for the "faithful and diligent manner in which it has performed its duties." Hist Rpt, 54th Troop Carrier Wing JA (Capt Paul Boucher, JAGD, Wing JA), in Hist, 54th Troop Carrier Wing, Sep 44 (on 345th Avn Sq), Biak, Air Archive WG–54–HI Sep 44.

[71] Statement, 27 Jun 44, to IGD Inv O, in Rpt of Inv of Irregularities surrounding Training and Conduct of 457th Aviation Squadron conducted at Warner Robins Air Service Command and Herbert Smart Airport. . . . 26 June–3 July 1944, AAF Files Bulky, 333.5 14 Oct 44. In this case the soldiers involved were not asking primarily for improved physical facilities nor for assurances of their usefulness in the Army, but for a more effective squadron commander and more efficient training.

unanswered. Command and men were operating upon assumptions that had no common meeting ground—the distance between them was too great for easy bridging. In what may not have been a majority, but in what was certainly all too many cases, the realization of command that all was not as it appeared on the surface came too late for effective corrective measures to be taken.

Symbols and Apprehensions

Events in areas which might not directly touch them physically sometimes heightened the belief of troops that training for military duties was not to be taken too seriously by Negro units. Thus, when plans to use particular units to help harvest cotton in Arizona were discussed in 1943 and when, in the same year, Negro troops were used to clean snow from the streets of cities such as Richmond, Virginia, and Seattle, Washington, where snow seldom falls and where, as a result, the cities lacked equipment to keep open main highways over which essential war transportation moved, no logical explanation could obviate the conclusion of units hundreds of miles away as well as those involved that here was direct evidence that Negro troops were esteemed as laborers only.[72]

Wheat or potatoes would have been bad enough, but to pick cotton, with all that this traditional plantation crop symbolized in the lives of Negroes, or to shovel snow, when Negroes felt their outfits were scheduled to become "pick and shovel" units sooner or later anyway, were considered crowning indignities.

Similarly, the Red Cross blood bank controversy, in which Negro blood for dried plasma was at first refused and later accepted, but segregated despite the scientific fact that all human blood, for transfusion purposes, is alike, was an additional reminder to Negro troops of the reasoning which sometimes governed their status even in those areas where objective scientific approaches might have been expected to prevail.[73] The Negro press, in the meantime, continued to editorialize on the contrast between the acceptance of serums and

---

[72] The proposal that troops be used to help harvest the Arizona cotton crop involved both white and Negro troops, including a small body of Air Forces troops. But the main body of troops involved would have been elements of the 93d Division at Fort Huachuca and the 364th Infantry at Phoenix. After the War Manpower Commission advised on 24 February that the request was not justified by the Arizona labor situation, arrangements to move troops to cotton fields were halted. News of this planned use of troops had, however, been printed in the public press. Minutes of the General Council, 22 Feb 43, p. 5; *Ibid.*, 1 Mar 43,

p. 2; Ltr, Walter White to SW, OSW 291.2; Editorial, *The Crisis*, L. (March, 1943), p. 72.

[73] Negro plasma was labeled "AA" (Afro-American). The Surgeon General's Office, after a time, began to explain the Blood Bank policy to persistent inquirers with:

This action was taken in the interest of removing any possible objection to this form of therapy on the part of a patient who holds a prejudice against the injection of Negro whole blood or plasma processed therefrom, notwithstanding the assurance of competent authorities [that] there is no biological difference between any human serum.

With the two types of dried plasma at hand a white or colored patient may have his choice of serum which removes a possible alibi for refusing a form of treatment that is not universally popular. Ltr, Asst to TSG to Laurence Foster, Pennsylvania State Temporary Commission on the Condition of the Urban Colored Population, 8 Apr 43, SGO 291.2 1943. See also Memo, Civ Aide to SW for TAG, 26 Dec 41, AG 707 (12–26–41) (6–18–41) (1); American Red Cross National Headquarters, Statement of Policy Regarding Negro Blood Donors, 21 Jan 42; Ltr, Adm Asst to SW to Sen Arthur H. Vandenberg, 23 Jan 42, AG 291.21 (12–27–41) (1); Ltr, Edward H. Cavin, Asst Adm Gen Services, Red Cross, to Truman K. Gibson, 6 Nov 43, ASW 291.2 Alpha.

antitoxins developed from horses and cows with the refusal of Negro blood for plasma use. The irony of the situation was further heightened by the widely publicized fact that a pioneer researcher in blood preservation, medical supervisor of the emergency Blood Plasma for Britain project in 1940, and director of the first American Red Cross Blood Plasma Bank, a pilot unit for the armed services established in 1941, was Dr. Charles R. Drew of the Howard University School of Medicine.[74]

News of this sort of action, once it got to troops, lowered general morale. Realizing this—and blaming the Negro press for inciting dissatisfaction among Negro troops by carrying such news items, as well as accounts of racial friction in camps—many posts, despite lack of approval from higher headquarters, banned Negro papers, or particular issues, from libraries and from sale in exchanges. While lack of news from the Negro world or from the home towns of Negro troops, added to the knowledge that a particular paper was no longer readily available, might act as an additional deterrent to morale, some banned papers usually arrived through the mails to those men who were subscribers. The news which they contained, now doubly valued, made the rounds of the Negro portion of a post anyway. The bans did little more than convince troops of the insecurity of their commands and heighten their belief that the banned news must be all the more important.[75]

Incidents such as these were easily interpreted as real affronts. They reinforced the growing opinion among Negro troops that they were the objects of special treatment designed not to increase their preparation for participation in war but to neutralize the effect that their military service might have upon their status as soldiers and citizens. They increased the mixed feelings of Negro soldiers toward the Army's intention of treating them as responsible members of and equal partners in the Military Establishment. They increased the feeling that Negro troops had no important or carefully considered part to play in the unfolding war.

Esprit

The development of *esprit de corps,* or pride in organization, was more difficult to achieve in Negro units than in most white units, both because of the generally lower morale of Negro troops and because of other factors described in preceding chapters. Certain small units of Negro troops did achieve a sense of unity, especially after entering operational areas, but the large units remained, for the most part, organizations whose parts, in their relations with the whole, were never firmly cemented either through emotion or logic. In none of the Negro divisions, for example, was high individual personal or unit identification with the division as a whole achieved.

The size and the remoteness of the divisions as a physical entity was partly at fault. The concept of a division was itself difficult for men with the limited horizons of many Negro enlisted men. Its actual size, its potential abilities, and

---

[74] "Prologue to Blood Plasma," *What's New* (Abbott Laboratories), Dec 44, pp. 8, 27.

[75] Memo, Bureau of Public Relations for CofS, 10 Nov 43, AG 461 (10 Nov 43) (1), and attached papers.

its function as a great foundation block for modern corps and armies had little specific meaning for the Negro division's individual soldiers. To many a member of a subordinate divisional unit, "Division" simply meant that headquarters from which unpleasant orders and directives emanated. The division commander, insulated by his full staff, all white, might as well have dwelled "in a moated castle in a far countree." Few men had affection or high regard either for him or for the division; many men never knew their current division commander's name.

Initially, in the case of the 92d Division, the headquarters and special troops were physically several hundreds of miles distant from each of the regiments and artillery battalions, for the division was activated with its headquarters and special troops at Fort McClellan, Alabama, while the combat teams of the division were located at Camp Joseph T. Robinson in Arkansas, at Camp Breckinridge in Kentucky, and at Camp Atterbury in Indiana. Despite the rapidity of modern transportation and communication, the elements of this command were sufficiently far removed from each other to hamper division-wide development of *esprit* in the formative period of the organization. Different procedures and different atmospheres, all affecting morale, developed in each of the four enclaves of the division, all affected by the personalities of the four commanders and the racial climate of the four geographical regions. Despite attempts of the commanding general and the combat team commanders to maintain equivalent standards of discipline and morale

throughout the division, the assembly period at Fort Huachuca in the late spring of 1943, which might have been followed by an upward swing in division-wide morale, saw instead a slackening, as members of the four groups compared and criticized differences and similarities among them.

The consolidation of the division reinforced and brought into sharper focus dormant antipathies which, when the division was divided, did not appear to be significant at any one post but which, when all the division could be observed together, appeared to Negro officers and enlisted men to have sinister significance. On both sides of the racial fence notes could be compared, attitudes could solidify, and mutually antagonistic positions could be bulwarked. It was not long before successive events, interpreted by Negro soldiers to mean that the newly assembled division had adopted the least instead of the most desirable features of each of its parts, began to be felt. These included an increase in segregation in officers' messes and barracks, with one Negro assistant mess officer removed because he refused to participate in setting up separate tables; an increase in objectionable individual acts including the use of epithets toward Negro officers and enlisted men; the "obvious transfer of Negro officers to preclude command"; the recognition that only Negro officers were assigned to a School of Application and Proficiency, thought of as a prelude to reclassification, when "it did not seem reasonable to them that there could only be inefficient Negro officers in the Division"; and an increase in chaplains' dissatisfaction with and interference in command matters.[76] Correctives, usually made promptly in accordance with division policies which condoned none of these actions, did not alter the belief that these and similar irritants and not officially stated policies were the true gauge of the command's attitude toward its Negro personnel.

General Davis, after a visit to the 92d Division in the summer of 1943, noted the effect on morale which these and other occurrences had had. He contrasted the situation before and after assembly:

During the period 21 January to 19 March, 1943, the three combat teams and divisional units were inspected by the inspector general. During these inspections the morale of the Division was found to be superior. There appeared to be the best of feeling existing between the colored and white officers. There were no complaints or reports of racial discriminations. At the Division Headquarters mess there was no segregation of colored officers. The inspector general noted that colored officers were seated with their white comrades at several tables in the Headquarters mess, and the best of comradeship was displayed. At a reception held at Fort McClellan colored and white officers were present. General Almond was held in the highest respect by all officers. The colored officers were especially profuse in their praise of him for his fairness and deep concern for their advancement and welfare. He had on all occasions shown a personal interest even in their comforts and entertainment.

Now, there seems to be an opinion among the colored officers and men that General Almond has been unduly influenced by some officers in the Division and that his attitude has changed since his arrival at

Fort Huachuca. In justice to General Almond the record shows that in all cases where white officers deviated from his policy of fairness, action has been taken. Such officers were transferred, court-martialed, or disciplined under AW 104. In some cases, the disciplinary action was delayed, incident to the necessary investigations, etc., and the action taken was therefore not always associated by the colored officers and enlisted men with the offenses. . . .

General Almond has, in the opinion of the inspector general, overlooked the human element in the training of this Division. Great stress has been placed upon the mechanical perfection in the execution of training missions. Apparently not enough consideration has been given to the maintenance of a racial understanding between white and colored officers and men. The execution of ceremonies with smartness and precision, and the perfunctory performance of military duties is taken as an indication of high morale. This is not true with the colored soldier. He can be driven to perform without necessarily having a high morale. . . . However, General Almond appears to be an able officer, and it is believed that now—since he is well aware of the situation and because of the fact that in all cases of unfairness or misconduct involving racial issues he has taken remedial action—action will be taken to remove the causes of unrest. . . .[77]

Evidences of the decline in morale and the growth of dissatisfaction and resentment within the division were at times spectacular in shape and proportion. A car in which white officers were riding through Fry was stoned by enlisted men. A white lieutenant, asleep in his tent during a field exercise, was severely injured by a blow on the head with a shovel. Twelve Negro lieutenants had been recommended for trial by general court-martial. Four second

[76] Ltr, Div IG to CG 92d Div, 28 Jun 43; Interoffice R/S, CofS 92d Div to Div IG, 10 Jul 43; Interoffice R/S, Div IG to CofS 92d Div, 12 Jul 43. All in Corresp Regarding Pers and Sundry Papers, item 19, Div Files.

[77] Memo, Davis for TIG, 7 Aug 43, copy in AGF 210.31/449.

lieutenants were in confinement awaiting trial. Two captains, three first lieutenants, and nineteen second lieutenants had been recommended for disciplinary action.[78] While Army Ground Forces had recognized that the dispersion of the division at four posts would retard training,[79] the possible effect of assembly at Fort Huachuca upon *esprit* and general morale was apparently not considered too fully.

The 93d Division was formed from two separate Regular regiments—one an old peacetime unit and the other a new unit activated for a little more than a year—and a new selectee regiment.[80] The Regular regiments, during their independent existence, had evolved a kind of solidarity of their own which might have been developed, under skillful

handling, into a division-wide *esprit*. While the 93d did not suffer all the divisive experiences of its younger sister division, there is no evidence that it ever achieved division-wide *esprit* under any of the five commanders assigned to it.

The 2d Cavalry Division, after going through its original reorganization, remained in an anomolous position, for alone among divisions activated in World War II it continued to occupy separate posts, Camp Lockett in California and Fort Clark in Texas. Since some of its units, preparatory to the conversion of the division to service functions, did not move overseas with the rest of the division, the 2d Cavalry Division was never assembled as a whole in any one place. *Esprit* here remained on the subordinate unit level until after conversion, after which a nostalgic *esprit* for the disbanded division developed among some of its former members.

In none of the Negro divisions, moreover, was it possible to use constructively the device of unit tradition to achieve *esprit de corps*. The 93d Division, having fought in World War I as separate regiments, had no past tradition as a division to draw upon, nor did it have any of its regiments of World War I to utilize as separate foci of unit pride.[81]

---

[78] *Ibid.* General Almond took strong exception to General Davis' report of the situation at Fort Huachuca, terming it unfair to him and to the division, but he did not make a formal official rejoinder. He informed General Peterson that General Davis' report was based on the view of the division taken by imaginative, race-conscious personnel of the post complement, especially the medical officers of Station Hospital No. 1. In his view the division had high morale and the incidents cited by General Davis had less than their indicated significance. Some were not accurately or fully reported: the two captains awaiting disciplinary action were white; the car stoner did not belong to a unit of the division and was drunk; messing problems had been solved and neither they nor the shovel attack had been followed by any resentment except as fostered by agitators and post complement personnel; policy in the division had not changed, only the attitudes of officers resenting reclassification proceedings had altered. Personal Ltr, Gen Almond to Gen Peterson, 14 Sep 43, with Incl, Analysis of Memo for TIG, dated 7 Aug 43, Correspondence Regarding Personnel and Sundry Papers, No. 21, Div Files. Also Personal Ltr, Almond to Davis, 8 Sep 43, same file.

[79] Memo, AGF for Logistics Group OPD, 25 Jan 43, AGF 353/167 (Readiness Rpt).

[80] Respectively, the 25th, 368th, and 369th Infantry regiments.

---

[81] The 93d did have as a component the 25th Infantry with the El Caney blockhouse in its coat of arms, but its 369th Infantry was not the legitimate descendant of the famed 369th of World War I. This latter unit had become the 369th Antiaircraft Artillery Regiment, taking its World War I battle honors with it. The division's 368th Infantry had been a component of the 92d Division in World War I; it had become a Regular Army regiment at the beginning of mobilization but, out of its World War I history little could be gleaned for troop morale, for it was the regiment most frequently cited to show the ineptitude of the 92d Division in that war.

The only legitimate World War I traditional element left to the division was its shoulder sleeve insignia, a blue French helmet.

This insignia was considered unspectacular and a negative morale factor by the 93d.[82] Believing that it had Army Ground Forces' approval for a change, the division opened a competition for a design for a new insignia. From a host of deserts, mountains, tropical palms, and yellow panthers, wildcats, and tigers—the latter all rejected because the color yellow signified cowardice—the division finally selected a black panther head, so that it could be called the "Panther Division." But even here, its attempts to build up morale were unexpectedly frustrated. Ground Forces, citing the historical significance of the blue helmet, the cost of the change, and the desire of the War Department to retain all possible World War I insignia as reasons, withdrew its approval for the change.[83]

The 92d Division, on the other hand, had as its insignia a black buffalo dating its symbolism back to the Negro regiments of Indian warfare days.[84] During World War I "The Buffaloes" had been the 367th Infantry,[85] then a member of the 92d Division, which in World War II had become a separate unit. Besides obtaining a buffalo calf mascot, christened Buffalo Bill, and besides using the "Buffalo" designation freely, the division did little to capitalize on the tradition behind its shoulder sleeve insignia. Each of its regiments had its own World War I traditions and honors, two of them having been decorated either in whole or in part.[86] But little successful indoctrination of new selectees in the meaning and continuity of regimental traditions was achieved.

In contrast to the divisions, certain of the separate Negro organizations developed considerable unit pride. In most cases these were smaller units, with a highly developed sense of mission. They usually continued with few top command changes during their careers. The air combat units were of this type, as were the three tank battalions. Of his 99th Fighter Squadron, Lt. Col. Benjamin O. Davis, Jr., explained in a press conference held in the War Department upon his return from the Mediterranean:

. . . It is a very significant fact, I believe, that all members of this organization were impressed at all times with the knowledge that the future of the colored man in the Air Corps probably would be dependent largely upon the manner in which they carried out their mission.

Hence, the importance of the work done by this squadron, the responsibility carried

---

[82] The original patch, a red hand, desired by two of the division's regiments as former members of the French 157th (Red Hand) Division, had been denied the division at the close of World War I.

[83] Ltr, Hq AGF to CG 93d Div, 28 Oct 42, AGF 421.7/298 and 10 Inds; Ltr, Hq 93d Div to TQMG, 17 Dec 42, and 1st Ind, Hq AGF, 30 Dec 42, 93d Div Files 421.7.

[84] Negro soldiers of the Regular regiments, especially the cavalry regiments, were known as "Buffalo Soldiers" by the Indians. See Fairfax Downey, *Indian Fighting Army* (New York: Scribner's Sons, 1941).

[85] See Lt. O. E. McKaine, "The Buffaloes," *Outlook*, CXIX (May 22, 1918), 144–47.

[86] The 371st Infantry as a whole and Company C, 370th Infantry, both units of the 93d Division in World War I, received the Croix de Guerre with palm, unit decorations which were rarer in World War I than in World War II. The third regiment, the 365th, had received divisional commendation for meritorious conduct in the Bois Frehaut in the last days of the war; however, the direct descendant of the old 365th, like the 93d's 369th, was not the infantry regiment but the 184th Field Artillery.

by every man, be he ground crewman or pilot, meant that very little pleasure was to be had by anyone until the experiment was deemed an unqualified success.[87]

In this case, delays in assignment, attacks in the public press, restrictions and annoyances, plus the positive sense of the individual responsibility of each man consolidated that group loyalty and pride upon which *esprit* is founded. Colonel Davis continued:

In the meantime, the squadron received the attention of the press. When was the unit going to the combat zone? Why the delay? Much attention was directed toward the segregated aspects of the Tuskegee Airfield. This publicity had a profound effect upon the individual member of the Ninety-ninth. The eyes of the Nation were upon this organization.

It was true that he felt hurt to find that his training station at Tuskegee Army Airfield was being regarded by some outside the Military Establishment as being a discriminatory set-up.

However, he had had the good sense to realize that the best means he had to defeat the end of supporters and philosophers who relegated him to a subsidiary role in the life of the United States was to do the job in such a way that the world would know that he was capable of performing a highly specialized and technical piece of the work in a creditable manner.

. . . .

Every man in the Ninety-ninth will go through any ordeal concocted by combat or garrison existence to assure the successful completion of the experiment. At all times every man realizes that the pleasures and relaxations that are available to men in other organizations are not available to him because his task is far greater, his responsibility is much heavier, and his reward is the advancement of his people.[88]

Like the air combat units, the tank battalions, training as the 5th Tank Group though often located at different posts, had a high sense of mission. Though higher headquarters had frequent doubts as to the wisdom of continuing these units, these doubts were not communicated to the men of the battalions. Rather, through their group and higher commanders, the units learned to think of themselves not only as units from which important results were expected but also as units which could expect to produce important results. Their men were no better in AGCT's or in civilian psychological preparation than those of many other units; but the visible progress of their training and of their potential usefulness, stimulated by their growing familiarity with their tanks and the gradual appearance of Negro officers who moved up to command some of the units' companies, gave these units a sense of movement toward a visible goal. From maneuvers and exercises, with both white and Negro regiments and divisions, they gained confidence in each other, in their officers, and in their units, as they should have done, but as many Negro units did not do. More important, higher commanders not only visited them, but what they reported to commanders in the way of commendation was communicated to the men; what they said in addresses was well enough said to be remembered and acted upon. Hortatives to which many white units became accustomed struck home to units unaccustomed to being

[87] Statement, Lt Col Benjamin O. Davis, at Press Conference, 10 September 1943, reprinted from Washington *Afro-American*, 18 Sep 43, in *Married Men Exemption, Hearings . . . U.S. Senate . . . on S. 763* [*Drafting of Fathers*], 1943, pp. 437–42.

[88] *Ibid.*

taken as valuable members of a team. The commander of one of the training centers, Brig. Gen. Ernest J. Dawley, addressed the men of one of the units, the 761st Tank Battalion, on three occasions. Once, in speaking to the men of the various things that might or might not happen during wartime for which there would be no obvious explanation but which must be laid to the "fog of war," he concluded: "When you get in there, put in an extra round of ammunition, and fire it for General Dawley!" This speech made a lasting impression on the men. When the 761st entered combat, one of its tanks was named "The Fog of War." "And to top it off, several extra rounds of ammunition were put in, and fired 'for General Dawley,'" the unit's historian recorded.[89] Men of this battalion, when hospitalized and subsequently transferred, tried to return; the reputation of the unit spread into the rear areas and requests for transfers into it, not all of which came through the proper channels, became common enough for the unit to provide forms for transfer requests.[90] Even after V–E Day, when the unit expected to be redeployed to another theater, either direct or through the United States, requests for transfer in or return to the unit continued, some of them coming from men of other combat units already inactivated or scheduled for inactivation and others from service unit soldiers, including former members.[91]

For service units which saw little military value in their daily activities, developing unit pride was more difficult. Inspectors were likely to recommend, especially for those with observable difficulties, a considerable morale building program, often beyond the abilities of company officers to carry out.[92] A typical recommended corrective program included: a more forceful unit commander, more drill and purely military training, an instructional and educational program stressing loyalty and military subjects, more educational films and explanations pointing out joint responsibility for national defense, musicals and plays on Army and patriotic themes produced by the units, good speakers on Americanism and the progress of the Negro race, an educational program to increase the literacy level of soldiers, lectures to instill confidence in leaders, explanations of the dangers of spreading rumors, complaint periods scheduled by and with the post commander, and transfers of agitators to other units.[93]

The average small unit had neither the personnel, the physical equipment, nor, if training and duties were to be accomplished, the time to engage in so extensive a program. Yet, where any significant part of such a program was

---

[89] Pvt Trezzvant W. Anderson, "Come Out Fighting" [761st Tank Battalion, 1942–45], p. 15.

[90] 761st Tank Bn Corresp Files, Sep 44–Oct 45, Org Rec Br, AGO.

[91] Ltrs in 761st Tank Bn Corresp Files, AGO Records.

[92] The less technical units, often in greater need of such programs, usually had fewer officers, thus reducing the amount of attention to such corrective programs that the unit could give. Quartermaster fumigation and bath or troop transport companies, with an average of 85 and 110 men, for example, had three, five, or more officers; aviation squadrons, with 250 or more men, usually had three and sometimes fewer officers assigned.

[93] For examples, see Memo, Hq AAF AFTAE for CG AAF, 14 Feb 44, AAF 333.5; Memo, TIG for CofS, 4 Jun 43, AGF 291.2/22; Ltr, TIG to DCofS, 8 Jun 43, AG 291.2/25.

put into operation, beneficial results were obtained. One quartermaster service company, described as the "worst" unit in its service command, "which set fire to the previous Company Commander's Quarters, trying to burn him while he was asleep," and in which an enlisted man, a candidate for discharge under Section VIII procedures, had struck a company officer in the face with his fist, was hardly a promising candidate for such a program. High absence without leave and venereal disease rates, accompanied by high courts-martial rates, were the rule of this company. The situation was made worse, if not originally precipitated, by the undefined functions of the unit. Activated in January, it had been used more or less as a casual company up to the end of June 1944. Its seventeen-week training program did not begin until then. It had had a large turnover of personnel, including the disciplinary cast-offs of "all the other Quartermaster Companies" at its training center. After the appointment of a new company commander and the transfer of new noncommissioned officers to the company, matters improved. The downward trend in morale and discipline, constant since activation, was stemmed without resource to great emphasis on physical facilities for recreation and entertainment. Simply through attention to the purposes of training, the company improved remarkably. By the time of its technical training period, consisting of on the job operations at the Lincoln Ordnance Depot in Springfield, Illinois, the commander of the Quartermaster Training Section at Camp Ellis, its training station, reported that the unit could and would function successfully. Upon departure from its three weeks of training at Lincoln Depot, it received a letter of commendation from the depot commander which spoke highly of "the splendid performance of work and the excellent discipline" of this formerly troubled unit.[94]

Mission and Morale

Lack of belief in the seriousness and importance of their training became a critical problem in many another unit. In some cases, this disbelief was shared and even fostered by unit officers. "In conversation with a number of senior officers," General Davis reported of the 371st Regimental Combat Team of the 92d Division in March 1943, early in the division's training period, "it was learned that there is a widespread belief within the Division, based upon rumors, that these two divisions [92d and 93d] are not to be committed to combat. This belief is having a disturbing effect." [95] Of the 93d Division another observer reported in the same month: "Among the white officers the outstanding question [is] as to whether the division will ever be able to perform combat service. The feeling is that it will not and that nobody on the staff would dream of sending it to combat duty. The result of this feeling is that the officers and men who do not want to fight are just marking time in a spiritless

[94] Memo, TIG for CG ASF, 23 Nov 44, 250–Camp Ellis, Ill., and Incls; Ltr, CO 3143 QM Service Co, Camp Ellis, to TIG, 15 Nov 44; and Memo, Hq QM Gp, ASFUTC Camp Ellis, for Col William H. Browne, IGD. All in SPTR 291.2.
[95] Ltr, IG to TIG, 24 Mar 43, IG 333.1–Cp Jos. T. Robinson, AGF 333.1/1 (92d Div).

way and those who do want to fight feel that they are in a blind alley." [96]

No one was more surprised when the 93d Division was committed to an active theater than men of the division. The quarterly report of one of the division's elements, written after arrival in the Pacific, described the reaction of the unit to the knowledge that the division would move overseas:

The 93d Infantry Division Artillery has come a long way since the beginning of the year. Even the most skeptical of us no longer deny the fact that the Division will see action. It is up to each officer and enlisted man to acquit himself creditably when the time comes for him to put into use the knowledge that he has acquired during training. . . .

The Division was alerted for oversea duty the first of the year and the morale of the men was something to be proud of. There were those of us who held tenaciously to the belief that we would never see action or go overseas; however that fallacy has been dispelled. Time took care of that. When all of the men finally awoke to the fact that we were definitely going over, they, as the slang goes, "straightened up and flew right." [97]

The effect of the awakening was marked by an upswing in morale and discipline. When the division's troop trains left for the staging area, the unit historian continued, morale was excellent and "according to the authorities, our unit was one of the most perfectly conducted units that has ever gone through Stoneman . . . ." [98] The unit behaved on

the transport from San Francisco like a "picnicking outfit." [99]

Disbelief in the importance and ultimate purpose of units, coupled with its deleterious effect on morale and training, was not confined to the larger combat organizations. Many of the smaller, more nearly anonymous units had similar qualms. The "most serious handicap" of medical sanitary companies was lack of knowledge of what their ultimate mission would be in the field. Garbage and trash collection and disposal, duties given to some of the units, were, according to Army Regulations, functions of the Corps of Engineers and not of the Medical Department. Some companies had difficulty finding even so "meaningful tasks" for their men to perform. [100] The aviation squadrons, into which most of the Air Forces' Negroes went, often asked searching questions about their roles in the war. Investigation revealed that, though it might be but part of the problem, the undefined character of these units and the nature of their work often lay at the root of their low morale.

Many of the men in these and in other service units had had no formal basic military training and had no clear idea of the relation of their units to the winning of the war. "Negro outfits, if trained in the same manner as ours, cannot be fit for modern warfare or any other group task," members of one aviation squadron complained in a letter to the War Department. The list of

---

[96] Memo for Files (Col Edward S. Greenbaum, Asst to USW), 8 Mar 43, copy in AGF 322/1 (93d Div).

[97] History, Hq and Hq Btry, 93d Inf Div Arty, Quarterly Report, 1 Jan–31 Mar 44, AGO Hist Rec Br, 493–11.4 (6367).

[98] Camp Stoneman, Calif., a part of the staging area of the San Francisco Port of Embarkation.

[99] History cited n. 97.

[100] Memo, SGO for G–3, 26 Feb 42, SGO 320.2 (2–26–42), AG 320.2 (11–15–40) (1) sec. 11; Unit Hist, 715th Medical Sanitation Co, AGO Hist Rec Br, 98–45–1 (15258).

grievances included an assertion that upon activation the unit had begun training but, sixty days later, "individual understanding of duty is as low as upon activation, with squadron discipline disrupted beyond recovery by Non-Coms and our present Commanding Officer." The communication made no reference to discrimination, though subsequent investigations directed by higher headquarters revealed grounds for complaint here which the communicants had ignored. Before the original letter could be investigated, the squadron had demonstrated against its commanding officer, upon removal of its first sergeant, by refusing to respond to the duty sergeant's call for morning formation. Four investigations were made, three of the squadron and one of two of the inspectors, one of whom, in a brief survey, had found the squadron mutinous, the other of whom, in a more thorough investigation, had decided that at most the conduct of the squadron could be described as prejudicial to good order, since testimony was given that the squadron formed quickly upon appearance of an officer and marched smartly to a hurriedly called squadron meeting.[101] Another communication, from two similar units, read:

You must please, please understand that we do not resent serving our country (we are proud to serve) but we would like and want very much to serve it in a more important capacity than we are at this time. We can and would fight [for] it if trained to do so, but as yet we hardly know what a

gun, tank, combat plane, hand grenade, machine gun look like.

We haven't had any drilling to speak of that could be classed as drilling. We had three (3) weeks of Basic Training. It takes that long to learn to do the Manual of Arms (arms are something we haven't seen, except a 45 on the M. P.'s side, ready to blow your brains out if you resent being treated like a dog and being called a Nigger or a Black Son of a B——) much less call it Basic Training.[102]

Such complaints, resulting in incipient disorder in the first case, were the end products of disbelief in the importance of the missions of certain service units. They matched in their significance for morale the conviction in many combat units that their titular missions would never see fulfillment.

The damage done by these convictions was considerable. It continued throughout the training periods of units so affected. A few weeks before the departure of the 92d Division for overseas assignment, an inspector reported:

It is apparent that a general impression prevailed in the 92d Division that the unit would never be committed to overseas combat service. Platoon leaders have testified that in trying to bring out realism in the training problems they explained how certain exercises would be used in overseas services, but that they detected knowing glances among the non-commissioned personnel implying that this was only training talk. It was further reported that before going to maneuvers, General Almond called an officers' meeting and pointed out that the rumors that the 92d Division was never going overseas were unfounded. It is fur-

[101] Ltr, signed Members 457th Aviation Squadron, Herbert Smart Airport, Ga., to Secretary Stimson, Gen Arnold, CO Patterson Field, Ohio, CO Herbert Smart Airport, 2 May 44, and other papers in AAF Files, Bulky, 333.5 457th Avn Sq.

[102] Ltr, 328th Avn Sq and 908th QM Co to Secretary Stimson, 22 Nov 43, AAF 333.5. This letter was written by one or possibly two men with the stated concurrence of certain other men in the units. It was taken home by one of the men on furlough and mailed from there.

ther reported that he often tried to eliminate the spirit of defeatism in the division and tried to insert realism and purpose in their training problems.[103]

Complicating the problem of lack of understanding and motivation in many units was the additional uncertainty caused by frequent transfers and the long periods in unassigned and casual status experienced by many soldiers. At times whole units remained relatively idle, without apparent training or work progress. Inactivity of this type, seemingly pointless, militated against good training habits and tended to destroy discipline, morale, and the effectiveness of whatever training had been accomplished. This was true of all units and individuals in pools or in uncertain status. But with white soldiers, Army red tape or perhaps an individual error somewhere along Army channels could be blamed. In Negro units, sitting and waiting could be interpreted as anything from a normal delay in their planned use to a complete confirmation that nobody ever intended to use them anyway.

Units so highly motivated by their individual significance and training successes as the tactical units at Tuskegee found their morale slipping when, after being alerted for movement overseas in the Liberia Task Force in August 1942, they found that 1943 had arrived without a sign of actual movement to a port. During the months that they had been in various stages of alert they had seen certain units of the original task force disbanded; they could not be certain that the same thing would not happen to

the remaining units. The men of the 99th Fighter Squadron, 83d Fighter Control Squadron, and 689th Signal Air Warning Company had finished their training; though refresher training was carried on constantly "the newness had worn off." No furloughs were possible and often pass privileges were withdrawn when successive immediate movement communications, which did not result in movement orders, were received.

Mental strain in these units was increased by the sense of urgency and significance of their role, a role not shared by less critical units. Tension mounted as the fear that "something" might happen to prevent their use in combat grew. Every accident, minor or major, was viewed as a threat to the program of which they were a part. Lt. Mac Ross, the first Negro pilot to survive the loss of a military plane in flight, thought, while bailing out, "I've wrecked a ship worth thousands of dollars. Maybe they'll start saying Negroes can't fly." [104] The distinction of being the first Negro member of the Caterpillar Club did not dim this concern. Further accidents during the more than six months alert period caused similar qualms to develop among the men of all the station's units.[105] That the squadron might dry rot before ever getting overseas, and that, as a result, its members might be charged with demonstrating the inability of Negroes to fly in combat was a major concern of many of its men dur-

---

[103] Memo, Enlisted Div G–1 Sec Hq AGF for CofS AGF, 16 Aug 44, AGF 333.1/1 (92d Div).

[104] Quoted by Lt. Charles H. DeBow, "I Got Wings" (as told to William A. H. Birnie), *American Magazine*, CXXXIV (August, 1942), 29.
[105] History of Tuskegee Army Air Field (Maj Edward C. Ambler), 1 Jan 43, pp. 44–47; 29 Feb 44, pp. 94–95; AF Hist Gp 289.28–3, vol. I.

ing these months of waiting. Concern about their commitment, frequently expressed in the Negro press, which began to recount the speed of shipment of white units and pilots with less training time, did not decrease the pressure upon the morale of these units.

In units with a less critical view of their significance, greater deleterious effects resulted from long periods of inactivity. "Colored troops at this station," an ASF inspecting committee reported a post commander as saying in 1944, "have been in training nearly a year and a half, most of it at this station. They are bored, over-trained, domesticated, and subject to any bad influence upon their emotions. It is recommended that every effort be made to move these troops to some other locality, preferably in the direction of their ultimate destination. The mere activity of moving would satisfy them for a reasonable length of time, and strange surroundings would quiet their restlessness." [106] But many units remained undisturbed at their posts, continuing routine training and, on occasion, performing miscellaneous duties of barely visible importance.

A number of observers shared the opinion that moving Negro troops to new locations would divert them enough to check falling morale and allay unrest before it became serious. In some cases, general improvement noted in units was attributed to the receipt of movement orders.[107] But the first sergeant who had felt that most of the troubles of his unit could be solved if

the bus situation could be improved, went on to remark:

I don't know any cure for the rest of it. Just not content. It all goes back to the mess halls. It is unfortunate that anyone has to be in a place he doesn't like but this is war and these men don't realize they must suffer discomfort for their country. I think what they would rather have than be near home is to be out on the [flying] line. They don't want to mess around pots and pans. They want to learn something in the Army. They want to gain something. Some men by being here are becoming stagnant.[108]

Most of the men in this squadron were assigned to cadet, officers', and consolidated messes, many of them as kitchen police. The squadron had some counterindications of high morale: first unit on the post to reach 100 percent in war bond allotments; best venereal record on the field, with no new case in the preceding 76 days; and a good disciplinary record both on and off the post. When his men had tried to obtain transfers, the squadron commander had therefore thought that "They merely want to leave Texas." [109]

A more striking instance of the relationship between awareness of usefulness and both morale and efficiency was provided at Seymour Johnson Field, North Carolina. There, since the summer of 1943, serious malassignments had existed in the field's aviation squadron. A number of the men, for example, had been trained in Signal Corps radio schools and in colleges as members of the Enlisted Reserve Corps.

[106] Leonard Committee Report to ASF Mil Tng Div, 3 Oct 44.

[107] Memo, OTIG Sixth Sv Comd for CG Sixth Sv Comd, 28 Jan 44, Cp Ellis 333.1, AGO Records.

[108] Chambers testimony cited n. 51. See above, page 321, Sergeant Chambers' statement on buses.

[109] Capt Nathan M. Shaw, Jr., AC, 19 Dec 43, in Incl to Memo, Hq AAF (AFTAI) for CG AAF, 14 Feb 44, AAF 333.5.

When they were called to active duty and sent to basic training centers, they were classified for further specialist training. Instead, however, they were assigned to Seymour Johnson Field and placed on squadron duty, where they performed menial labor with no prospect of further training.

This condition was not unusual, but Seymour Johnson Field, through the Technical Training Command, managed to have many of the men transferred to other fields where, it was hoped, they could be more efficiently used. Others of these better qualified men were left on the field. Some of them were used in administrative positions taking advantage of their intelligence and general education if not of their specialized training; others were placed in the station hospital, as medical corpsmen and as medical and dental laboratory technicians. With the reduction of station and hospital strength that came in 1944, these men were no longer needed; some of them, now trained as medical technicians, were transferred from the field.

The field began to find itself short of qualified maintenance personnel as white soldiers were withdrawn for assignments to units preparing for overseas duty. The field's Classification Section checked the Form 20 record cards of all Negro men. Only two Negroes with AGCT scores of 100 or better were being used in basic specialties, one man as automotive equipment operator and one as head waiter in the Officers' Club. Those whose backgrounds, AGCT scores, or mechanical aptitude scores warranted, were then assigned to the flight line. Beginning in May 1944 un-

trained white and Negro men selected to bolster the fast crumbling supply of maintenance men were trained locally:

All men assigned to the flight line with the prospect of receiving technical training were assigned to Production Line Maintenance and put to work on the plane-washing rack. If they showed promise and proper interest and attitude, they were sent to the P–47 school conducted by the Ground Training Department. Most of these men were classified as laborers and attended the school which was conducted for both white and colored soldiers who attended the same classes. Personnel in charge of the P–47 school were enthusiastic, in general, concerning the response of the Negro soldiers. . . . It was impossible to comment too favorably on two aspects of the situation—morale and the aid to the manpower problem.

No segregation whatever was practiced—in on-the-job training, in the P–47 school, or on the flight line. The colored soldiers working on the line were quite naturally most outspoken in their praise of the policy and in their opinion that it was definitely a pioneering step. None of them, either from personal experience at other bases or from the experiences of friends with whom they corresponded knew of any other field where such a policy had been adopted. One of the colored soldiers, a radio man in FLM Communications and a college graduate, commented that he had been malassigned until the First Air Force took over the Base. In spite of experience in radio and signal work, he had been detailed to duty as a carpenter in the squadron area, realizing all the while that he could have been of more use elsewhere. Very strong in his admiration for the overall handling of the racial question at Seymour Johnson Field, he emphasized that no (t) enough praise could be given the amicable relationship that existed between the colored and white soldiers on the line.

The officer in charge of FLM Communications stressed the fact that two of his section chiefs, white men from Southern states, were as satisfied with the work of the colored men under them as with the white men assigned to them. One of the section chiefs protested strongly when the officer in charge suggested the transfer of one of the Negro soldiers to another crew.

It was generally agreed that practically all the mechanically inclined men in C Squadron had applied for assignment to the flight line and most of those qualified had been given the opportunity. Although a great deal of skepticism had existed among the colored soldiers, when the plan first went into effect, the favorable reports from the first men to work on the line counteracted that feeling.

The pride and satisfaction of the Negro soldiers was plainly shown by their preference for work on the flight lines as privates, often on the night shift, than to work at the Officers' Club with a chance to earn extra duty pay. A factor which had much to do with the excellent morale was the promotional policy under which the Negro soldiers had—theoretically and actually—the same chance for advancement as white soldiers working on the same jobs.[110]

Not only did the morale of the squadron rise as a result of this policy, but also administrative and disciplinary problems were greatly reduced, though Negro soldiers still presented more than their share of disciplinary problems, mainly in town situations.

The post commander, some months after the beginning of maintenance training for Negro soldiers, commented:

Although, frankly, the program was undertaken with some trepidation and the feeling that some of the more advanced technical work would be beyond the limitations of the Negro soldiers, the result has been most gratifying. They are now working efficiently and reliably in the refueling system and at the various stations in PLM,

including hydraulics, and in radio repair. It has been found that they perform the duties which are commensurate with their AGCT score.

It is satisfying to note the great improvement in the morale of the Negro soldiers since the plan started and also to note how amiably they work alongside white soldiers with no friction or ill-will whatever.[111]

On airfields, where planes and shops were available to give even the least technical units a sense of mission, it may have been easier to stem falling morale through job assignments that had immediate, visible usefulness in terms of the conduct of the war. But in the less glamorous branches the sense of usefulness could also be enhanced with a corresponding response in morale and efficiency. At Indiantown Gap's Army Service Forces Training Center, in Pennsylvania, where large numbers of port companies—many of them made up of personnel formerly in medical, sanitary, antiaircraft, and other now inactivated units—were trained, a special orientation program for Negro troops emphasizing their relation to past and present wars was developed in 1944 under the direction of a Negro officer[112] and a staff of enlisted men of good academic backgrounds. Without elaborate physical facilities—the makeshift service club, the exchanges, and restaurants available at this post were, if anything, below average—but with intensive attention to both instructional and command staff on the part of the

[110] The History of Seymour Johnson Field, 1 Jan 45–31 Mar 45 (Installment 3), AAF 288.57, vol. I. See also The History of Seymour Johnson Field, 6 Jul 44–1 Oct 44 and 1 Oct 44–31 Dec 44, AF 288.57–5, 6.

[111] Interv, SSgt Donald R. Sutherland with Col Dudley B. Howard, AC, Comdr Seymour Johnson Army Air Field, 31 Mar 45, app. 1 to History of Seymour Johnson Army Air Field, 1 Jan–31 Mar 45, AF Hist Gp 298.57 vol. II.

[112] Lt. Everett C. Morrow, a former member of the staff of NAACP.

centers' commander, Col. Forrest Ambrose, an officer once assigned to the 24th Infantry, this post succeeded in convincing the majority of the men trained at the center that ships, docks, and the necessary port companies were an important part in the wartime team and that the Army was doing its best in utilizing their services. By the last year of the war Indiantown Gap had become a major example of what could be done by a command to lessen the debilitating effects of a decline in motivation and morale among Negro troops. Because of its location, near the big eastern cities, it was available as a prime exhibit of what the Army could do for morale. In January 1945 Truman Gibson, after visiting this and other posts, determined that the main ingredients of success at this training center were the high caliber of the officers and their leadership plus their willingness to attempt answers to the puzzled queries of enlisted men, both in words and in actions. He observed to Assistant Secretary McCloy:

At Indiantown Gap, I inspected the physical facilities and talked at length with many of the officers and enlisted men of the ASFTC which Colonel Ambrose commands. In talking with the enlisted men, I was impressed with their high morale. Never in the four years that I have visited Army installations have I seen more trust and confidence placed in officers by enlisted men. This was made all the more unusual by reason of the fact that the stevedore training which the men receive is very arduous. Particularly effective was the Orientation Program in which intelligent answers are given the many difficult questions that the enlisted men raise. The white and colored officers seemed to get along well during their duty and off-duty hours. A Negro officer is the coach of the basketball team which I saw play and on which there are only two Negro players. Together both races use the Officers' Club freely and without strain in the Training Center.[113]

Roy Wilkins, acting secretary of NAACP, who had accompanied Gibson, remarked of the commanding officer, "It is a great pity that the Army does not have a couple of hundred more men like him." [114]

A quartermaster service battalion training in the California-Arizona maneuver area also showed the benefits of careful instruction on the purposes and value of their organization to the prosecution of the war. An inspector reported:

The battalion had just commenced basic training at the start of the maneuvers and the utilization of this battalion was absolutely necessary in support of the troops in the combat zone. Investigation discloses that the work of this battalion was outstanding and interrogation of negro soldiers from private to master sergeant reveals a surprisingly high morale and pride in their work. Large numbers stated openly and freely that they knew the type of work being accomplished by them was absolutely necessary and just as important as actual fighting. . . . One Sergeant, a welder by trade, when asked if he would like to go to school and continue in that type of work stated that he preferred to remain a sergeant in his present unit. . . .[115]

Not all posts and units were able or willing to alter the outlook of Negro soldiers by exerting the effort to convince them that what they were doing had ultimate value to the war effort. But where men and units felt that theirs

[113] Memo, Civ Aide to SW for ASW, 13 Jan 45, ASW 291.2 NT.
[114] Ltr, Roy Wilkins to John J. McCloy, 11 Jan 45, ASW 291.2 NT.
[115] OTIG, Hq DTC to CG DTC, 20 Mar 43, AG 291.2 (3–5–43) (1).

was a position of responsibility and import in the conduct of the war, where they were made to feel that an honest attempt had been made to use their services, and where they were convinced that their superiors were both cognizant of their problems and judicious in their decisions concerning them, high morale could be achieved. In most units a sincere attempt in any one of these directions was sufficient to hold the morale line. Where none of these courses was adopted, morale and motivation crumbled to the point that neither the routine of training and employment, the expansion of physical facilities, nor the hortatives of the well meaning had significant effect.

CHAPTER XII

Harvest of Disorder

When adequate corrective measures for the low morale of Negro troops were not taken, when adequate leadership was not available, when post–community co-operation could not be secured, and when "incidents" without a positive indication of concern on the part of commanders and higher headquarters continued to occur, the chances for open disturbances involving troops remained many and varied. Despite the large number of racial clashes involving soldiers that did occur, when the opportunities for disturbances are considered the actual rate of serious, generalized outbreaks of racial violence involving Negro troops in World War II was small. Nevertheless, cases of physical racial friction, ranging from minor brawls to serious disturbances, ran into the hundreds. They were a continuing cause for concern within the War Department and in the Army's higher commands. They continued to be a threat to discipline, to relations between Negro and white troops, to relations between the Army and civilians, and to unity in the war effort on the home front. As fodder for propaganda against the Army and, in the hands of the enemy, against the nation, they were unsurpassed.

The concern of the War Department in the area of racial disturbances was constant. Local patterns of violence which strengthened and confirmed its anxiety were set early. The pattern of reactions of troops, commands, and the public was set equally early. Racial friction of one sort or another continued through the war, with the early summer of 1943 marking the high point both of incidents of violence and of official concern. Relatively few disturbances involved mass violence between white and Negro troops, although a number had their root causes in individual incidents between officers and men of the two races. Sometimes erupting disorder had city, state, or military law enforcement agents as its main protagonists; sometimes it involved civilians; sometimes there was no violence at all, but mass demonstrations and "acts to the prejudice of order and discipline," some of them approaching mutiny. Sometimes the "violence" was only that common to the semi-underworld and tenderloin districts of all big cities, the street brawls or Saturday night party fights given additional significance because one and sometimes all participants were in uniform.

No matter what the nature of the disturbance the reaction was much the same. To higher headquarters, in receipt of numerous reports, complaints, and warnings from the distant field, the fact that Negro troops were located on a given post was enough to indicate the possibility of racial disorder there or in nearby communities. To security agencies each disturbance stressed again the need for constant vigilance, both to head off possible repercussions in the civilian society and to stem subversive influences, either of which might interfere seriously with the war effort. To Negro troops, the threat of disorder that might involve them was omnipresent; at times it was thought of as just one more of the inevitables of military service, or, at the least, of passes into certain nearby towns. Early in the war, the Negro public was convinced that the life of the Negro soldier was one of constant fear and danger while his unit was still in training. The white public, especially in the towns near heavy troop concentrations, was often certain that the threat of town or post race riots was constant. Enough "incidents" occurred during the war years to lend support to each of these views and to each of their infinite variants.

The major significance of disturbances was seldom in the events themselves but in their potentialities. Overt racial friction, military or civilian, affected, in turn, units and stations elsewhere. The more serious disturbances were carried by the news services into the columns of the nation's press. There they affected civilian attitudes, white and Negro, toward the Army and the prosecution of the war. The cumulative effect of racial disturbances on the War Department was to add another item to the growing list of matters to be considered in planning for the employment of increasing numbers of Negro troops, both in training at home and in deployment overseas. It was generally considered a most important addition to this list.[1]

The March of Violence

In April 1941, shortly after the first Negro selectees began to enter the Army, the first major symbolic event in the long chain of racial violence occurred. In a wooded section of Fort Benning, Georgia, the body of a Negro soldier, Pvt. Felix Hall, his hands tied behind him, was found hanging from a tree. How he got there was uncertain. Negroes concluded that he had been lynched. Post authorities suggested that it might have been suicide, but surrounding circumstances were against this solution. The ensuing investigation did not solve the mystery of Hall's death. Speculation continued, but in the absence of proof of foul play, no considerable agitation took place. A queasy uneasiness among Negro troops and the public lingered.[2]

Later in the same month another kind of incident occurred. On Sunday afternoon, 20 April 1941, white Civilian Conservation Corps (CCC) enrollees and Negro troops of the 48th Quartermaster Regiment became involved in an altercation over the use of a diving platform at the YMCA Lake area at Fort Jackson, South Carolina. Already, in the nearby city of Columbia, ill feeling among troops, Negro civilians, and mili-

---

[1] Min Gen Council, 21 Jun 43, 2 Aug 43; Ltr, Gen Marshall to CG's, 13 Jul 43, WD 291.2 (13 Jul 43); Proceedings ASF Conf of CG's Sv Comds, 23 Jul 43, Chicago, pp. 17–18, 103; Hq ASF, Classified Checklist of Current Problems, SPTR 291.2 (28 Jan 44).

[2] See Ltrs, Petitions, Rpts, and Resolutions in AG 291.21 (4–14–41) (2) and in AG 291.21 (4–26–41) (10) dated 14 Apr through 3 Jun 41.

tary police had developed. Between afternoon and evening, stories of the clash spread through Fort Jackson. That night, considerable tension was present in the area of the 48th Quartermaster Regiment. At about 9:30 P.M., the Fort Jackson Military Police Company learned that a disturbance was underway. White soldiers from the 30th Division, some in civilian clothes and some in uniform, were assembling in groups, planning to rush the Negro area. There shots were fired as "unknown individual members" incited the men with "greatly exaggerated versions of incidents occurring during the afternoon." Officers of the post, the field officer of the day, the 8th Division officer of the day, members of the main guard of the 30th Division, and the provost marshal halted the movement and dispersed the groups.[3]

Thereafter, difficulties between Fort Jackson's military police and Negro soldiers and civilians in Columbia continued until well into 1942. Beginning in June 1941, fracases involving military policemen, city policemen, soldiers, and civilians occurred frequently in the Negro business area of the city. The Colored Citizens' Committee of Columbia protested in letters, petitions, and visits to post authorities. "Something must be done," the Citizens' Committee declared in January 1942, "as our Colored Citizens are growing restless, suspicious, and what occurred in Alexandria, La., and Fayetteville, N.C., thus far has been averted, because of our vigilance, and talking to our people, but we cannot always hope to hold them down with

so much disregard to 'Citizenship rights.' "[4]

The Alexandria and Fayetteville affairs mentioned by Columbia's committee were two of the major similar disturbances that occurred during 1941–42. These were basically conflicts between troops and military police, involving as well town police, Negro and white citizens, and, at times, all five groups. Arguments, rough handling, fights, and near riots were common in these disturbances. A street brawl in Tampa, Florida, on 15 July 1941, was typical of these fracases. At about 11:20 p.m., a Negro soldier, after an argument with a white military policeman in the presence of other Negro soldiers and civilians, was arrested and sent to the military police headquarters in Tampa. The military policeman and a second MP remained in the area. A second Negro soldier, a sergeant who later admitted that he had been drinking, approached the military policeman who had made the arrest and engaged him in conversation. The sergeant, ostensibly trimming his fingernails with a knife, whispered, according to the MP, that he would cut the policeman's throat. The policeman struck the Negro sergeant with his club and drew his pistol; the sergeant knocked the pistol from his hand and threw the policeman to the ground. The second military policeman and a nearby city policeman came to the aid of the MP; the city policeman shot the Negro sergeant while he was on the ground. A third Negro

[3] Rpt of Proceedings of Bd of Offs at Ft. Jackson, S.C., 25 Apr 41, Incl 5 to Incl 3, AG 291.21 (10–2–41) (3).

[4] Ltr, James M. Hinton, Secy, The Colored Citizens' Committee, Columbia, S.C., to TIG, 30 Jan 42, AG 291.21 (1–30–42); Rpt, Acts of Mil Police at Ft. Jackson, S.C., in Connection With Negro Civilians of Columbia, AG 291.21 (3–25–41) (1).

soldier was shot while attempting to disarm the city policeman. Though the setting was there for a full-scale free-for-all with potentially fatal results, no further violence followed.[5] But trouble between Negro soldiers and military policemen on the streets of Tampa went on through the summer.

The pattern of disturbances, all potentially productive of serious riots, continued to develop. The Fayetteville disturbance, on the night of 5–6 August 1941, was the first of a series of serious bus incidents involving military police and Negro soldiers. A large group of Negro soldiers, following pay-day passes, gathered at a bus stop to await transportation back to Fort Bragg. A number had been drinking. As the waiting crowd grew larger, disorder at the bus stop increased. When a bus arrived, disorderly soldiers threatened unarmed Negro military policemen, whose duty it was to ride the buses, and prevented them from coming aboard. The driver refused to move without police protection. This delay in departure increased the confusion and disorder, while the crowd outside awaiting the next bus continued to grow. A detachment of white military police reinforcements, attempting to quiet the passengers, boarded the halted bus. They succeeded in stirring up further disorder among the jostling, cursing, busload of men. Attempting to arrest the chief troublemakers, military policemen began to use their night sticks. One soldier on the crowded bus grabbed

a military policeman's service revolver from its holster. He discharged its full six shots in the direction of the disarmed MP. Another military policeman shot toward the soldier, and other shots from outside the bus followed. When the confusion subsided, one white military policeman and one Negro soldier were dead, two other white military policemen and three Negro soldiers were wounded. The gun fight in Fayetteville was bad enough, but the aftermath at Fort Bragg, especially as reported in the nation's press, was a serious portent of future difficulties. The post's provost marshal ordered all Negro soldiers, except those already in barracks, collected and brought to the stockade adjacent to the guardhouse, where they were held until morning. Men arriving on later buses were searched and threatened by military policemen. No explanation of what had happened or of the purpose of this roundup was given to the men herded into the stockade. Military policemen, angry and resentful over the death of their comrade, and Negro soldiers, equally resentful of the death of the Negro soldier and the methods used to round them up, created a new tension on the post. For days accounts of the brutality used in the forced checking of men who could not have been involved in the bus disturbance reached the public through the press and through soldiers' letters. The revolvers and ammunition of the military police who had been at the scene were not collected on the spot, confounding the possibility of a definite determination of responsibility for the shooting on the bus and thus lending color to the rumors current that military police activities at the post

---

[5] Ltr, Hq MacDill Fld, Fla., to TAG, 30 Jul 41, and other papers in AG 333.9 MacDill Fld (7-30-41).

were based not on good police work, but on elemental anger.[6]

The outbreaks of violence during the summer of 1941 reached a climax during the Second Army maneuvers. These maneuvers were marked by incidents between townsfolk and white as well as Negro troops, and were occasioned both by the lack of military discipline and the resentful attitudes of citizens dwelling within maneuver areas toward the presence of large bodies of troops. Before the maneuvers, Lt. Gen. Ben Lear, commanding the Second Army, cautioned the commanders of both the 5th Division, to which the 94th Engineer Battalion was attached, and of the 2d Cavalry Division, to conduct conditioning lectures for their Negro troops before departing for maneuvers.[7] At Murfreesboro, Tennessee, and at Gurdon, Arkansas, Negro troops on maneuvers ran into armed resistance from citizens and state police. The second incident was the more spectacular, and, in the shadow of Fayetteville, came to national attention through the wire services.

Troops of the 94th Engineer Battalion from Fort Custer, Michigan, became embroiled in a series of incidents in the vicinity of Gurdon. Some of the soldiers felt that their difficulties began at Little Rock, Arkansas, where individuals of the unit and white city police engaged in an altercation in a night club. Others, pointing out that neigh-

boring Negro troops from Camp Shelby, Mississippi, had not been molested, felt that the trouble arose because they were Northern troops with Northern white officers. Only in their persistence and intensity were the incidents at Gurdon different from those occurring in many another Southern small town area.[8]

On 11 August 1941, some two or three hundred soldiers of the Negro engineer battalion visited the town of Gurdon in search of recreation. The town had neither recreation to offer nor the desire to offer it. The appearance of so large a body of Negro soldiers from the Chicago-Detroit area excited adverse comments from the white residents of the small town, but nothing untoward happened except that the soldiers congregated in small groups while white military police attempted to keep them moving. In the meantime a rumor, later proved false, spread among the soldiers that one of their number had been arrested and severely beaten by military police. Excitement and resentment mounted when military police instructions were circulated that the town was to be cleared by 10 o'clock. With no transportation available, the soldiers gathered in groups and, in a crude and noisy formation liberally spiced with profanity and uncompli-

[6] Papers in AG 333.9 Ft. Bragg (8-7-41) (1); Memo, G-3 for DCofS, 19 Sep 41, G-3/46778, AG 322.97 (8-24-41) (1); Memo, TIG for CofS, 5 Sep 41, IG 370.093-Mil Police. The post provost marshal at Fort Bragg was replaced after this affair.

[7] Maj Bell I. Wiley and Capt Thomas P. Govan, History of the Second Army, AGF Hist Sec Study 16, 1946, pp. 59-62.

[8] This paragraph and the two following are based on: Ltr, Inds, and Incls, CG Second Army to TIG, 24 Aug 41, with three investigations inclosed, Second Army AG 250.1-5 (FE'41) (A) AG 322.97 (8-24-41) (1); Ltr, Fiorello H. LaGuardia, Dir of Civ Defense, to SW, 28 Aug 41, inclosing nine letters and affidavits, three clippings, etc., on Gurdon troubles, AG 322.97 and Bulky Package; Ltr and Inds, CG Second Army to TIG, 9 Sep 41, Second Army AG 250.1-5 (FE'41) (B), AG 322.97 (9-9-41); Memo, Civ Aide to SW for USW, 16 Oct 41, and Memo, DCofS for USW, 28 Oct 41. Last two in WD 322.97 (10-17-41), AG 322.97 (8-24-41).

mentary remarks about the South, proceeded along the main street of the town toward their bivouac area. Many, apparently fearing interference, had armed themselves with clubs and missiles. Though no difficulties between them and civilian authorities of the town of Gurdon occurred that evening, the noisy movement of the group of apparently unorganized soldiers through the town, coupled with seeming insubordination toward the few of their officers who were attempting to control the situation during the four-mile trek from the town to their bivouac, intensified the fears of local citizens. Town authorities and the town marshal, who freely declared his intention to use force of arms in the event of trouble, proceeded to swear in new deputies to augment the town police force. Through the night sensational rumors spread, both among members of the battalion and among citizens of the town. The Commanding General, Seventh Corps Area, declared the town of Gurdon off limits and directed that the battalion move its bivouac several miles distant. These decisions were communicated to town and police authorities on 12 August during the working day.

Nevertheless, on the evening of the 12th at about 10 p.m., Arkansas state police with drawn firearms approached the 94th's bivouac area and ordered the camp guard—armed with rifles but without ammunition—off the highway at the entrance to the camp, striking several of the sentries in the process. Troops visiting Prescott, another nearby town, were harassed by state police who followed their trucks into town, threatening the men upon arrival. On

14 August elements of the battalion, its men demoralized and its officers uncertain, began to move to their new bivouac area. State police, through misrepresentation, excitement, or misunderstanding, notified the provost marshal of the Second Army that a group of unsupervised and disorderly Negro soldiers was proceeding down the highway. The provost marshal, accepting the report as fact, requested the state authorities to take charge until military police arrived. Fully armed state police and deputies started for the reported scene of disorder. In the meantime, the provost marshal, with an assistant, proceeded to the scene and, upon observing the troops moving along in good order, assumed that the area of difficulty must be farther along the road toward Gurdon. He dropped his assistant and set out toward the town. Following his departure, a sergeant of state police arrived with state troopers and a deputized force. State troopers, using insulting epithets to both the troops and their officers, ordered the marching unit off the road and into a ditch lately filled with rain and into nearby woods, while armed deputies, in civilian clothes and therefore civilians as far as the troops could see, stood by. When one of the officers protested the police actions and epithets, a state policeman removed his glasses and struck the "Yankee nigger lover" in the face. Military police had by now arrived at the scene but, until the white lieutenant was struck, their commander, the provost marshal's assistant left at the scene earlier, made no move to interfere. Some of the Negro soldiers, observing that neither they nor their white officers apparently had police protection in

Arkansas, left their battalion and, hitch-hiking or by public transportation, made their way back to Fort Custer. At least one soldier, without money and feeling that moving north or east through the Gurdon area was too dangerous, went southwest through Texas into California. He picked cotton in Arizona and picked figs and cut grapes in Fresno for money for food; he then hopped trains to Fort Warren, Wyoming, where he intended to give himself up, hoping for transportation back to Fort Custer. On learning through rumor that "fugitives" from Arkansas were to be returned there, he left on a wine tank car for Omaha, rode other trains into Michigan, and eventually reached Detroit on 5 September.

The bewilderment and fear of the troops in the face of the Gurdon incident and its implications for morale and discipline among Negro troops in general were probably of greater import than the incident itself. A soldier's letter on the affair reveals to some extent the disorganization and demoralization it caused:

We are scared almost to death. Yesterday we went on a 10 mile hike alongside of the highway off the concrete. All of a sudden six truck loads of mobsters came sizzling down the highway in the other direction. They jumped out with guns and sub-machine guns and [revolvers] drawn, cursing, slapping and saying unheard of things. Sis it was awful. They took us off the highway into the woods. Daring anyone to say a word, they hit two of our white officers who try to say something back. But the bad part of it all, the military police were among them and against us. The State police passed out ammunition to the civilians. We are now about five miles down in the woods hoping that they don't come down here. No one has pitched a

single tent today, nor yesterday, we are afraid to, half of our company has left for Michigan already, hoboing. Few have train fare, others went deeper into the woods.

We had a detail down here in a little town called Guidon [sic] working at the depot, when some of the officers went down there they had been stopped by a mob, threatened their lives if they did not leave town in five minutes—yet they could not go down the highway, the only way they know to go. Our officers are nearly all as afraid as we are. They call them "Yankee Nigger lovers," us black "Yankees."

We have guards, guarding a place and the State police deliberately came off the highway, took his gun (rifle) which was empty and beat Yankee Doodle on his head. These people are crazy, stone crazy. Or I am. Yesterday one of our trucks went to get some eats and they wouldn't let us get any. The officers asked that we all be sent back to Fort Custer. None of us can show our faces except in these woods, we can't be seen on or even near the highway. We are undecided now, we all want to know what we are going to do? [9]

Many troops became certain that there was no protection available for them in the South and little understanding from the Army, especially after six of their number were tried by courts-martial and several of their officers whom the men considered to have aided them were relieved.[10] Despite Hastie's recommendation that, to dispel the notion that the Army had viewed the disturbance with complacency, the War Department should issue a statement summarizing the facts in the case, announce the punitive steps taken toward

[9] Excerpt, Ltr of a soldier to his family (unnamed), Incl to Ltr, Civ Aide to SW to TAG, 20 Aug 41, AG 291.21 (8-20-41). See also New York *Times* and Chicago *Tribune* for 15-20 Aug 41; Bulky Pkg, AG 322.97 (8-2-41) Cabinet 8175.
[10] Memo, SGS for G-3, 6 Oct 41, OCS 20602-193; Memo, Hastie for USW, 16 Oct 41, WD 322.97 (10-17-41).

the military police officers as well as toward members of the battalion, and announce the referral of the record to the Department of Justice for such action as might be proper under federal statutes, it was decided that no useful purpose "so far as the best interests of the Army are concerned" would be served by so doing.[11] Both informal and, later, formal requests for the opinion of the Attorney General in the matter resulted in the decision that, since state troopers interceded at the request of military police, there was no suitable basis for federal action.[12]

Months later the battalion had not regained normal morale and discipline, as evidenced by excessively high rates of company punishment, confinements, and arrests; excessive hospital, sick in quarters, and venereal rates; lax military courtesy; and general deficiencies in appearance and posture.[13]

Other incidents, all indicative of a more or less serious state of affairs, continued to occur during that last peacetime summer: in Galveston, a disturbance between Negro troops from Camp Wallace and Negro city policemen, at Camp Livingston, Louisiana, a disturbance following newspaper publication of photographs of a staff sergeant

beaten during an arrest; rumors and reports of murders at Camp Claiborne, Louisiana, and Camp Shelby, Mississippi; brawls between soldiers and military police at Camp Davis, North Carolina; and reports of unrest and a "difficult situation" at Camp Stewart, Georgia.[14]

Through all of these ran the common thread of friction between Negro soldiers and both city and military policemen. Where Negro military policemen were used, generally on a temporary basis in the Negro sections of towns, they were usually unarmed, increasing their difficulties in the control of troops. Most of the disturbances were followed by newspaper publicity, not always accurate—the papers could not always get facts from local or other public relations officers and took what they could find to support what became, in the Negro press, a campaign for armed Negro military police and, at times, in the local white press, a campaign for the removal of Negro military police embracing, in some instances, the removal of all Negro soldiers. Widely publicized incidents were followed by what amounted to avalanches of letters and petitions of protest or suggestions to the War Department, most of them coming from sincere persons and organizations but some of them from antipreparedness, isolationist, far left, anti-Negro, and anti-Army sources.[15]

[11] Memos, DCofS for USW, 15 Oct 41, Hastie for USW, 16 Oct 41, and DCofS for USW, 28 Oct 41, all in AG 322.97 (8-24-41) (1). The military police officer was relieved as was the battalion commander, but these changes were announced only through special orders.

[12] Memo, DCofS for USW, 28 Oct 41; Memo DCofS for USW, 2 Jan 42; Ltr, USW to Francis Biddle, Attorney Gen of the U.S., 8 Jan 42; Ltr, Dept of Justice to Robert P. Patterson, USW, 12 Feb 42. All in AG 322.97 (8-24-41) (1).

[13] Ltr, TIG Second Army to CG Second Army, ——Jun 42, Ft. Custer, Mich., AGF 333.1/26 Second Army.

[14] Binder AG 291.21 (6-11-41) (1); Rad, CG Eighth Corps Area to TAG, 25 Aug 41, AG 333.9 Galveston, Tex. (8-21-42); Memo, Lt Col J. W. Boyer for OinC Misc Div AGO, 11 Aug 41, AG 291.21 (8-11-41) (4); Ltr "From a Negro Soldier" to President, 11 Jul 41, AG 333.9 (6-11-41) (1); Ltr, Hq 2d Cav Div to CG 2d Cav Div, 19 Sep 41, Div Files, 333.5, AGO Record.

[15] Letters and petitions in AG 291.2 and 333.9 files for June of 1941 through the following summer.

The War Department dispatched investigators to the scenes of most of these disturbances, while local authorities made their own inquiries. Investigations and resulting recommendations, running into the hundreds, sometimes took months and seldom applied to more than the specific case at hand. They had general corrective application only insofar as they served as precedents for later cases. Nevertheless, it was obvious by 1942 that the relations between Negro soldiers and both military and civilian police had reached so unhealthy a point in many parts of the country that future disorders could be expected unless steps were taken to prevent them.[16]

As yet no major disturbances in which Negro troops were the mass aggressors had occurred. But the events of early 1942 left doubts that Negro troops, with access to ammunition and with increasing tensions growing out of their relations with town and military police, would long remain quiescent. The first of a new series of disturbances occurred on 10 January 1942 in Alexandria, Louisiana, the crowded camp town for Camps Polk, Livingston, Beauregard, and Claiborne and for three airfields: Alexandria, Pollock, and Esler. Alexandria, sometimes used by as many as 30,000 soldiers at the height of the war, was the scene of numerous tension-born incidents. The 1942 trouble reached riot proportions, involving hundreds of soldiers and civilians, after the clubbing of a Negro soldier by a military policeman in front of a theater in

the heart of the Negro district. In March, large crowds gathered in Little Rock while military police attempted to arrest a Negro soldier. The soldier was finally shot by a civilian policeman. "I would not be surprised if this is not the Alexandria situation repeated, reason and methods both," the editor of the Kansas City *Call* wired to Judge Hastie.[17] On 1 April, at Tuskegee, Alabama, friction between armed Negro military police from the nearby airfield and townsfolk, brewing since January, came to a head. A Negro military policeman took a soldier from the custody of a white city policeman at gunpoint. City police, reinforced by a deputy sheriff, two Alabama state policemen, and about fifteen white civilians armed with shotguns, took the soldier back from military police in a scuffle, during which a military policeman who had drawn his pistol was beaten and the remainder of the military patrol disarmed. A large group of soldiers and civilians gathered. White officers from the post residing in the town rounded up most of the soldiers and returned them to camp, but not before soldiers on the post had become alarmed at the prospect that armed townsfolk might attack the airfield. At Fort Dix, New Jersey, on 2 April, a gun battle between white military police and Negro soldiers, developing out of an argument over the use of a telephone booth, resulted in the deaths of one white MP and two Negro soldiers. In May, a fight between two Negro soldiers from Mitchel Field developed into a free-for-all between civilian

---

[16] Memo, TIG for CofS, 5 Sep 41, AG 320.26 (8–7–41) (3) (1); Memo, Civ Aide to SW for PMG, 16 Feb 42, PMG 291.2.

[17] Incl 8 to Memo, TIG for TAG, 30 Mar 42, IG 333.0–Foster, Thomas D.

police and colored civilians in Hemp-stead, New York.[18] Moreover, inspectors and observers were reporting that smoldering resentments lay just under the surface in many other places, ready to burst forth on provocation.

First Correctives

After the disturbances of the summer of 1941, the first steps toward needed correctives were taken. Following the Fort Jackson incident, directions to adhere more closely to regulations on the protection of ammunition were issued.[19] After Fort Bragg, closer attention to the selection and training of military policemen and provost marshals was recommended. The organization of temporary detachments of untrained military policemen, the failure to use Negro military policemen in camps and towns with large numbers of Negro soldiers, and the close liaison between civilian and military police in many towns, a condition tending to indoctrinate soldier police with the methods and points of view of local civilians, were all severely criticized. The improper training and conduct of military police as revealed during the summer of 1941 and the lack of a central agency to establish

doctrine, provide training, and supervise organization and procurement of personnel for military police units were remedied by the establishment of the Corps of Military Police under the Provost Marshal General on 26 September 1941. With the urging of Judge Hastie and upon the recommendation of Maj. Gen. Allen W. Gullion, the new Provost Marshal General, the use of Negro military policemen by camps with sizable bodies of Negro troops was directed.[20] Some local commanders and the Provost Marshal General resisted certain of the recommendations, especially those which directed that, for psychological reasons, town military police headquarters be divorced from city police stations.[21] Townsfolk sometimes resisted the use of Negro military police, especially in cities where local Negroes had been exerting pressures for appointment of Negro civilian police.[22] The seriousness of the situation was impressed upon local commanders not only by communications from the War Department and service commands but also by recurring incidents of friction.

A continuing problem was the quality of military policemen available for duty. Although personnel officers and the Corps of Military Police tried to obtain

---

[18] Memo, TIG for DCofS, 22 Jan 42, and other papers in SPMG 291.2 Gen; Ltr, Hq Cp Beauregard, La., to CG Fourth Corps Area, 16 Jan 42, and Inds, AG 320.2 (8–7–42) (3) sec. 5 Mil Police Corps; Memo, TIG for TAG, 30 Mar 42, IG 333.9; Proceedings before Grand Jury for Eastern District of Arkansas, Western Div, 10 Jun 42, Little Rock, to 13 Jun . . . , AG 291.2 (3–30–42) (1) Bulky; Hist TAAF, 7 Dec 41–31 Dec 42, AAF Hist Gp 289.28 vol. I, 39–41; Memo, G–2 for G–3, 17 Jun 42, WDGCT 291.21 (6–17–42); Memo, ExO G–1 Sec Hq AGF for TIG, 4 Sep 42, AGF 291.2/15; New York *Times*, April, 3 and 4, 1942.
[19] Rpt of Proceedings of Bd of Offs at Ft. Jackson, S.C., 25 Apr 41, AG 291.21 (10–2–41) (3).

[20] Memo, G–3 for CofS, 7 Aug 41, G–3/43414; 1st Ind, TPMG, 16 Sep 41, on Memo, G–3 for G–1, 11 Sep 41, AG 320.2 (8–7–41) (3) sec. 1; Memo TIG for CofS, 5 Sep 41, IG 370.093–Mil Police; Memo, G–3 for CofS, 27 Oct 41, AG 320.2 (8–7–41) (3) sec. 1; Memo, PMG for G–3, 11 Oct 41, G–3/44246; Memo, TPMG for TAG, 11 Oct 41, AG 320.2 (10–11–41) (1); WD Cir 224, Sec III, Establishment of Mil Police Detachments (Cld), 22 Oct 41.
[21] Inds 5 to 14, 22 Sep 41 to 7 Nov 41, to Ltr, Hq MacDill Fld, Fla., to TAG, 30 Jul 41, AG 333.9 MacDill Fld (7–30–41) (1).
[22] Memo, OPMG for TAG, 25 Feb 42, and other papers in AG 322.999 MP Corps (2–16–42).

high caliber men, the number of poorly qualified men gravitating to it remained large. "I am fully conscious of the importance of the primary war effort and the need for first-class fighting troops and I am willing that the military police units shall have their share of those who are morally and physically crippled," General Gullion protested in March 1942, "but I think I ought not to be required to take them all." [23]

Between station complement and tactical units on the same post tense feelings were often common. With military police detachments a part of station complements this feeling was often heightened when tactical units were Negro. It was sometimes necessary for commanders to make strong remonstrances about the treatment of Negro soldiers by police under post control. In one instance, where a post reported that, since "the force employed by the Military Policeman was not excessive or unwarranted" no disciplinary action for beating a soldier need be taken, the division commander of the soldier involved sharply replied:

1. I do not concur with the conclusions reached by your investigating officer. The use of unwarranted force by members of your Military Police Detachment is becoming altogether too prevalent and I feel that some of your Military Police are going out of their way to look for instances.

2. In this particular case it seems to me that the Military Policeman went out of his way to find fault with a soldier who was complying with his orders. He was told to return to the Post and upon turning away to comply with the order he located the tie and put it on. It appears to me that the Military Policeman was beyond his rights

in following the soldier and accusing him of lying.

3. I do not understand why it is necessary for two Military Policemen to use their clubs to subdue one man. The use of clubs should be rare indeed, and I feel that too many instances are being reported to this headquarters which are entirely unwarranted and which reveal a tendency on the part of your people to assume a bullying attitude unnecessarily. [24]

Ill feeling between troops and military police, founded on experiences of this type, was not uncommon nor was it confined to Negro troops and white police. At Fort Huachuca, where Negro police were used, it existed to some extent; a Thanksgiving Day 1942 disturbance in Phoenix, Arizona, was between members of a Negro infantry unit and Negro military police. [25] But where both troops and police were of different colors, where both brought their civilian attitudes into the Army with them—the one a distrust of police conditioned by long experience and the other a disregard for Negroes conditioned by an equally long apprenticeship—special care in training, discipline, and supervision was necessary to prevent recurring irritations of old, still unhealed wounds.

In the average command, action designed to prevent physical friction consisted of more or less elaborate precautionary directives on the handling and use of ammunition in Negro units. To officers, the receipt of such precautionary directives often produced a new

[23] Memo and five Incls, TPMG for Chief Admin Svs SOS, 26 Mar 42, SPPMG 220.31.

[24] 3d Ind, Hq Ft. Clark, Tex., to CG 2d Cav Div, Ft. Clark, 11 Sep 43; 4th Ind, Hq 2d Cav Div to CO Ft. Clark, 13 Sep 43, 2d Cav Div 333, filed with 9th Armd Div, AGO Records.
[25] Interoffice Memo, OPMG, 23 Jun 44, SPMG 291.2 Gen; Memo, G-1 for CG SOS, 3 Feb 44, WDGAP 291.2.

burden to be added to the many others already required in duty with Negro units. One commander found his headquarters' precautionary orders somewhat baffling:

Colonel H—— stated that these secret orders grew out of the great concern of the higher command over the possibility of a negro riot or outbreak. He mentioned an incident with which I was unfamiliar purported to have taken place in 1940 in Brownsville, Texas. He mentioned a 1917 episode at Houston, Texas, and also a quite recent incident near Beaumont, Texas, where a negro soldier was shot by a civilian police officer. This action indicating concern of the higher command was somewhat surprising to me because my observation of my own battalion gave me no indication of the faintest possibility of such an occurrence. In fact those familiar with the newness of this organization and the inexperience of the personnel of this organization have complimented the battalion numerous times on the many different phases of its administration and training.[26]

Thereafter this battalion commander was visited by the executive officer of his training group and the incoming post commander, who personally repeated the instructions. Yet no indications of a tendency on the part of his men, either openly or surreptitiously, to collect ammunition had been noted. The commander explained the excessive caution of his check methods to his men by pointing out the necessity of saving their short supply of ammunition and by the necessity of guaranteeing individual safety.[27]

In many another unit no satisfactory explanation was possible. The detailed

searches of barracks areas conducted on some posts, including the use of mine detectors to aid in the location of ammunition presumably buried under barracks, increased the apprehension of soldiers and bulwarked their distrust of headquarters' attitudes toward them. In some areas the unrelieved tenseness of units itself was responsible for incidents which might not have occurred otherwise. Normal precautions in the safeguarding of weapons, where followed in all units, could be productive of good results, but abnormal methods, especially when obviously centered on Negro units, often heightened rather than lessened the possibility of disturbances.

Reactions and Resolutions

Judge Hastie, attempting to find a positive solution to racial friction such as that at Fort Bragg, suggested to the Morale Branch of The Adjutant General's Office shortly after that disturbance that informal discussion groups among representative Negro and white soldiers on the same post might cause them to arrive at a "better understanding and more wholesome relationships. It is apparent, I believe," Hastie continued, "that we do not solve such problems by trying to keep colored and white soldiers away from each other." Brig. Gen. James A. Ulio, then chief of the Morale Branch, replied that any discussion of such a proposal would have to await the result of the investigation in progress at Fort Bragg.[28] Hastie, citing the experience of the Sixth Corps Area

---

[26] Testimony of Witnesses, Exhibit D of Investigation . . . 828th TD Bn, Cp Hood, Tex., 24–27 Aug 42, p. 91, IG 333.9–828th TD Bn 8/13/42.
[27] Ibid., p. 92.

[28] Memo, Civ Aide for SW for Chief Morale Br, 18 Aug 41, and Ltr, Chief of Morale Br for Civ Aide for SW, 21 Aug 41, both in MB 353.8 Ft. Bragg (8–19–41).

at its Savanna, Illinois, ordnance depot, had already suggested that camps with large Negro populations could make good use of Negro morale officers. At the same time that his soldier discussion proposal was returned, he was reminded that the assignment of morale officers, like morale itself, was a function of command and that the War Department would endeavor to supply morale officers only upon indication that they were not available within commands.[29]

The establishment in late 1941 of an autonomous War Department Special Service Branch, with General Osborn as director, provided a new vehicle for considering the general problem of military and civilian disorders and tensions affecting Negro-white relations. When inviting Dr. Donald Young, University of Pennsylvania and Social Science Research Council authority on minority problems, to attend a meeting of morale officers on 26-27 January 1942, General Osborn expressed himself "increasingly concerned" about the influence of the Negro press and intelligentsia on the Negro soldier. He was thinking, he wrote Young, of obtaining a Negro for his Planning Division.[30] No War Department headquarters planning office, at this time, had a Negro, civilian or military, on its staff, and General Osborn wanted advice on this as well as on broader problems.

In February, Young and the chief of General Osborn's Planning Division discussed the contributions which the new branch and related agencies might make toward reducing tensions arising out of the increased use of Negro troops. Young suggested that two or three Negro officers be assigned to the Special Service Branch for general duties and to act as sources of information and liaison with the press, civilian groups, and individuals. Civilian consultants, as for example Negro physicians, might be used on special projects. The Negro press, Young cautioned, had limited circulation and an overestimated influence; if special information was sent to Negro papers, their approach might change. Neither the press nor Negroes in general expected major changes in policy, Young believed, but their news stories had to follow racial interests. To make Negro civilians feel that their interests were not being ignored, as was currently the case, unfavorable incidents could be countered by accounts of positive action taken on related matters. Both the Bureau of Public Relations and the Special Service Branch should provide more publicity—posters, movies, and news about Negro soldiers. Moreover, Young counseled, Negro troops should be used in a routine, matter-of-fact way wherever possible, at home and abroad, and news about them should be handled accordingly.[31] No similar set of positive ameliorative recommendations was to reach the War Department during the war. Though each recommendation was eventually adopted in some form, in the winter of 1941-42 no one was ready to take action on any one of these measures. General Osborn inclined to the belief that too much discussion and

[29] Memo, Civ Aide for SW for Chief Morale Br, 13 Jun 41, and Memo, Chief of Morale Br for Hastie, 20 Aug 41, both in MB 353.8.

[30] Ltr, Chief Sp Sv Br to Dr. Young, 15 Jan 42, SSB 291.21 (9-27-41) (1).

[31] Memo, Chief Planning Div SSB for Chief SSB, 26 Feb 42, SPSP 291.21 (10-31-42).

emotional emphasis on the problem had already proved harmful.[32]

In the meantime, Hastie continued his efforts to lessen growing tensions between white and Negro troops. After a visit to Fort Dix in the spring of 1942, he suggested two more ameliorative steps, the first of which, in different forms, was to be suggested many times from many sources before it was adopted: that the Bureau of Public Relations and the Special Service Branch co-operate on an educational program designed to influence the racial attitudes of both white and colored soldiers,[33] and that the General Staff be urged to adopt a policy of assigning Negro special service officers to units whose tables of organization called for such an officer. The Negro officer, Hastie felt, would generally be more aware of the educational needs of Negro soldiers and would find such soldiers more responsive to him than to a white officer.[34] Later in the month, the NAACP suggested to General Osborn that a series of lectures be prepared for troops by a committee consisting of persons like Mark Ethridge, Frank P.

Graham, Hastie, Herbert Agar, and Charles Houston. General Osborn thought this proposal a good one.[35] Under Secretary Patterson and his assistant, Howard C. Petersen, agreed that the Hastie proposals had "real merit."[36] Special Service was willing to undertake the job, but, it reminded the Under Secretary, assigning officers to field units was outside its powers. Nevertheless, it would encourage the selection of Negro officers for special service duties.[37] In its educational film program, Special Service had already taken the first steps toward the preparation of a film on Negro soldiers "including a history of colored soldiers since Attucks of the Revolutionary War fame."[38] But neither this, the larger educational program, nor the program on the use of Negro morale officers in the field was to come to fruition for more than a year.

Surveying the situation in June 1942, the War Department's Intelligence Division emphasized the possibility of German and Japanese plus Communist and Negro press agitation as sources of disturbances. But, at the same time, the division reported that, after surveying investigations of previous disorders, no known subversive influences among Negro troops could be connected with dis-

[32] Ltr, Ralph Barton Perry to Gen Osborn, 24 Nov 41 and Ltr, Osborn to Perry, 9 Dec 41, MB 353.8 Cambridge, Mass. (11-24-41); Ltr, Walter White, Secy NAACP, to Osborn, 1 Apr 42; Ltr, Osborn to White, 3 Apr 42, and Ltr, White to Osborn, 6 Apr 42, last three in SSB 291.21 (9-27-41) (1).

[33] The first orientation program on the nature and progress of the war, mainly handled through materials prepared in the Bureau of Public Relations and through lectures by professional speakers, had already begun at this time. See Capt Ulysses Lee, History of Military Training, ASF, Army Orientation, (Sep 45), MS in OCMH.

[34] Memo, Civ Aide to SW for Howard C. Petersen, Sp Asst to USW, 18 May 42, SSB 291.21 (9-27-41) (1). At this time, special service officers were charged with both educational and recreational activities on posts and in units.

[35] Memo, Osborn for Petersen, 30 May 42, SPSP 291.21 (5-21-42).

[36] Memo, USW for Osborn, 22 Jun 42, SPSP 291.21 (6-25-42).

[37] Memo, Osborn for USW, 25 Jun 42, SPSP 291.21 (6-25-42).

[38] Ltr, Maj Frank Capra to Lillian Hellman, 18 Apr 42, SS 413.56 (4-6-42) sec. IIA. In May 1942, a team, consisting of two Negroes, Maj Alston W. Burleigh formerly with the 366th Infantry and Carlton Moss, and Marc Connelly, white author of Green Pastures, began a tour of posts and camps to survey motion picture possibilities. Schedules and letters in SPSP 413.56 May-Jun 42.

orders that had occurred. "The investigators have been aware of the several types of subversive groups at work among the Negro population," G–2 reported, "but have been unable to discover evidence of action by these groups in the Armed forces, by actual agents." G–2 concluded that the location of troops, the lack of discipline, police—especially military police—methods, and lack of recreational facilities were all factors leading to disturbances among Negro troops. The division recommended that military police be more highly trained and more thoroughly supervised in localities with Negro troops; that more attention be paid to disciplinary training among Negro troops; that movement and stationing of Negro troops in areas differing from their home environments be kept at a minimum; that racial tolerance and respect for the uniform "irrespective of the race, color, or previous condition of servitude of the wearer" be increasingly emphasized in the initial training of all inductees and that it be insisted upon throughout the services; and that "all possible steps should be taken to reduce and control the publication of inflammatory and vituperative articles in the colored press." [39]

While the G–2 paper was a comprehensive summary of the situation as it existed and of the types of correctives frequently proposed up to then, the other staff divisions and the major command headquarters to which it was circulated for comment were not too strongly impressed. G–3 informed G–2 that it was sending the study to other offices and "also that the recommendations were already covered by War Department policy." [40] "It appears to contribute nothing very tangible," General McNair of Army Ground Forces noted when his G–3 suggested that the report be distributed to army and corps commanders. [41] General Peterson, The Inspector General, who received the same survey later, [42] replied by citing the findings and recommendations made by Col. Elliot D. Cooke on his special mission for the Chief of Staff completed in the late spring of 1942. [43] Colonel Cooke had concluded that "Bi-racial incidents in the Army are not premeditated and most of them could have been avoided through proper education, leadership and discipline"; that "the colored soldier is loyal, but an increasing amount of propaganda is being promulgated by outside agencies in an effort to foster demands for post-war privileges in payment for present military services"; and that "racial prejudice exists to some extent in the Army itself. Many officers and men find it difficult to alter hereditary feelings and emotions." He had felt that his mission had focused the attention of commanders on the necessity of furnishing "all troops with equal facilities, of treating them justly, and enforcing like discipline." The Inspec-

---

[39] Memo, G–2 for G–3, 17 Jun 42, WDGCT 291.21 (6–17–42).

[40] Memo for Rec on G–3 DF to CG's Major Commands, 2 Jul 42, WDGCT 291.21 (6–17–42). Actually, not all of the G–2 recommendations were covered by current policy, *i.e.*, indoctrination of trainees in racial tolerance with insistence upon respect for the uniform irrespective of the race of the wearer; nor were all formally adopted policies being carried out, *i.e.*, stationing of Negro troops in areas similar to their home environment.

[41] M/S, Hq AGF, Comment 5, CG for CofS, AGF 291.2/14.

[42] DF, G–3 to TIG, 18 Aug 42, WDGCT 291.21 (6–17–42).

[43] Memo, TIG for G–3, 11 Sep 42, IG 291.2–Misc.

tor General agreed then and later with these observations. But he felt in September 1942 that too little time had passed to permit a general judgment on progress achieved in adjusting racial relations. Reports of inspection, "particularly those of The Inspector General and Brigadier General B. O. Davis," showed satisfactory progress in the matter, General Peterson observed.[44]

Though there were no further large disturbances in the summer of 1942, signs of possible outbreaks continued. Developing "signs of growing tension and deliberate stimulation of racial antagonisms in the South," were worthy of closer attention, Judge Hastie informed Under Secretary Patterson in August. The situation was serious enough, Hastie suggested, for the President to mention in a radio speech the importance of race relations at home and abroad as they affected global conflict. Secretary Stimson, he continued, might issue a statement concerning the seriousness of the military situation, pointing out that "Military authorities must and do rely upon public officials and private citizens to cooperate in the maintenance of amicable relationships between the military and civilian communities." Citing the experience of Houston, Texas, where military and civilian leaders had established a successful interracial citizens' committee to work on local tensions, Hastie suggested that local commanders and public relations officers "be enjoined to increase their efforts" to win local civilian co-operation in handling local problems. Military intelligence might be asked to channel information about organized efforts to stir up violence

against Negro soldiers and defense workers so that the Department of Justice might co-operate where advisable. Hastie again recommended that soldiers be indoctrinated with the necessity for inter racial co-operation:

> Such a campaign might effectively be launched by a special order to be read simultaneously throughout the armed forces (as was done recently in tribute to our Chinese allies) pointing out the important role and essential service of Negro, Filipino, American Indian, foreign born, and other minorities in our Army, and calling for close cooperation based upon the mutual respect of men whose lives are dedicated to victory in a common cause. Of course, much of the effectiveness of such a proclamation would depend upon the follow-up of local commanders within their respective units.[45]

Under Secretary Patterson, after a discussion with Maj. Gen. Alexander D. Surles of the Bureau of Public Relations and Judge Hastie on the matter, suggested in the War Council that the problem had grown too large to be handled by the War Department alone and that perhaps Secretary Stimson should take it to the President or send "some discreet officer to talk with mayors and chiefs of police in the Southern States in the hope of obtaining cooperation." [46]

Public Approaches

The War Department, answering most citizens' inquiries and complaints about racial violence involving soldiers, at first relied on precedent letters similar in tone to those of 1939–40, while continuing to deny that much was wrong.

---

[44] *Ibid.*

[45] Memo, Civ Aide to SW for USW, 12 Aug 42, USW 291.2 Race, Negro (Judge Hastie's Office).
[46] Notes on War Council, 17 Aug 42.

The Negro press and organizations were indirectly accused of helping foment disturbances and of using them as leverage for greater demands. "It appears to the War Department," Under Secretary Patterson wrote to Fiorello La Guardia, the Director of Civilian Defense, "that, with respect to the isolated cases referred to, certain organizations and certain sections of the press are utilizing them to promote, in the Army, social gains which have not been attained in the country as a whole and [are] using the Army as a means of promoting such gains among the civilian population. I believe that you will agree with the War Department that such activities are most unfortunate, because they materially impede the War Department in its present desire to build promptly and efficiently an Army capable of defending the nation in the existing crisis and organized so that it will fit into the accepted social order of this country." He emphasized further that the vast majority of Negro men and units had been involved in no difficulties and that the press had ignored those "commendable conditions and the excellent relationship between a large part of our negro units and our white units and between negro soldiers and civilians." [47]

Magazines and newspapers of varying points of view began to show concern over disorders as they grew more widespread. After the Alexandria riot, the magazine *Common Sense*, which had shown an interest in the military handling of racial matters before, suggested that the Army's difficulties were a part of a larger whole:

The incident, regardless of who was in the right, is a symptom. The leaders of the most responsible Negro organizations have said that the 13,000,000 Negroes in America are not "wholeheartedly and unreservedly" behind this war. It is not Hitler's fault that they are not. It is our fault. Negroes are discriminated against in our armed forces. They are discriminated against in defense industries. They are even discriminated against by many unions. . . .[48]

Commenting on the same disturbances, the Catholic journal, *The Commonweal*, observed that "The natural reaction of the colored population is to wonder just how much it is worth their while to join in a fight which is generally advertised as a fight for 'democracy' when their own share of democracy is at present so small and gives no promise of being much greater in the future." [49] After Fort Dix, Douglas Southall Freeman's Richmond *News Leader* editorialized:

If Negro soldiers are to be drafted into the army or are to be accepted as volunteers, they must be treated as fellow-soldiers and not as vassals or as racial inferiors. Those white Americans who prefer to put racial discrimination above national defense must justify their creed by their conduct. If they insist on having Negroes in the Army, they must themselves do more. As the decision has been to employ Negro troops of every type, those troops must not be the victim of any sort of discrimination. They are entitled to the same uniform, the same food, the same facilities that other soldiers enjoy. As the South well knows upon longer and closer experience than the North has had, this does not mean that either whites or Negroes are at their best in the same com-

---

[47] Ltr, USW for Dir Civ Def, 24 Sep 41, WD 333.9 (9–3–41) MB, based on Memo, G–1 for TAG, 13 Sep 41, G–1 1/15640–115. See also Ltr, Gen Osborn, Sp Sv Div, to Ralph Barton Perry, American Defense, Harvard Group, 9 Dec 41, MB 353.8 Cambridge.

[48] Editorial, *Common Sense*, XI (February 1942), 57.

[49] "The Racial Front," *The Commonweal*, XXXV (January 23, 1942), 332–33.

pany, the same branch, the same mess. They are not . . . [but] boys can be brought to see that they must fight—together and not against each other.[50]

The New York Negro paper, the *Amsterdam Star-News*, like most other Negro journals, took a more trenchant view of matters:

They [Negro soldiers] cherish a deep resentment against the vicious race persecution which they and their forbears have long endured. They feel that they are soon to go overseas to fight for freedom over there. When their comparative new-found freedom is challenged by Southern military police and prejudiced superiors, they fight for freedom over here.[51]

Emergency agencies of the government, especially those whose job it was to deal with aspects of civilian morale and mobilization for the full wartime use of national human resources, began to show their own interest in the Army's racial problems. Archibald MacLeish's Office of Facts and Figures had found that from among the many grievances standing between full psychological support of the war by the Negro public in the first months after Pearl Harbor, the "fact of discrimination in the armed services of the United States is perhaps the most bitter."[52] Fiorello La Guardia's Office of Civilian Defense was finding similar barriers to its work with civilian groups.[53] From the point of view of

their civilian interests, both offices wished to know what, in addition to its already announced policies, the War Department was planning to do to reduce existing tensions.

In the late summer of 1942, the Office of War Information, successor agency to the Office of Facts and Figures, and the Research Branch of Special Service began to plan joint surveys of camps and communities. The military agency was to study camps and quasi-military institutions, such as USO clubs, while the civilian agency worked with civilian communities on civilian attitudes, contents of local newspapers, and civilian institutions such as stores and dance halls. Their aim was to develop "a procedure which would enable us to deploy representatives of our branch and the Office of War Information to any tension area on a few days' notice, such that we can come back in a couple of weeks or less with a quick and reliable report."[54] While such quickly deployable teams were not developed, both agencies subsequently directed general surveys with similar aims.

From civilian communities, renewed agitation for the immediate removal of Negro troops from certain locations and qualms about placing them in others followed in the wake of concern over disturbances. The reiterated order to keep northern Negroes North and southern Negroes South, found primarily impractical, was a product of this period.[55] The difficulty in finding a camp location for the 92d Division was partially the result of this concern. When the "ex-

[50] Editorial, " 'Together' Not 'Against'," Richmond *News Leader*, April 3, 1942.
[51] Editorial, "The Fort Dix Straw," New York *Amsterdam Star-News*, March 28, 1942.
[52] Excerpts from Survey of Intel Materials, 16 Mar 42, Bureau of Intel OFF, Incl to Ltr, Archibald MacLeish to SW, 7 Apr 42, AG 291.21 (4-7-42) (4).
[53] Ltr, TAG to Brig Gen Lorenzo D. Gasser, OCD, 4 Sep 41, and Remarks attached to Incl to Memo, G-1 for AGO, 3 Sep 41, AG 291.21.

[54] Memo, Samuel A. Stouffer, Research Br, for Gen Osborn, CofSS, 1 Sep 42, SPSP 353.8 (8-24-41) (2) sec. II.
[55] Ltrs in AG 291.21 (6-11-41) (1).

plosive" situation at Little Rock was advanced as a reason for not placing a combat team there, Army Ground Forces, citing Secretary Stimson's strictures against the exclusion of Negroes from maneuvers scheduled for Arkansas, and stating that disturbances had occurred in a number of other places, resignedly observed that "It is believed that racial difficulties will occur in almost all sections of the United States, and that some means of dealing with the problem, other than removing Negro troops from otherwise desirable stations will have to be found." [56]

Renewal and Reassessment

In the spring of 1943 serious disorders began again. In the preceding months, though isolated skirmishes and incidents occurred at individual posts, becoming a common occurrence at some, no significant event which could be considered a general outbreak of racial friction had transpired. During these months the slow process of building toward an open flare-up had been aided by a steady downward drop of morale in many Negro units. By early summer, the harvest of racial antagonism was beginning to assume bumper proportions. Serious disorders occurred at Camp Van Dorn, Mississippi; Camp Stewart, Georgia; Lake Charles, Louisiana; March Field and Camp San Luis Obispo, California; Fort Bliss, Texas; Camp Phillips, Kansas; Camp Breckinridge, Kentucky; and Camp Shenango, Pennsylvania. Other camps had lesser disorders and rumors of unrest.

The disorders of 1943 differed from those of preceding years. They involved, for the most part, a larger number of troops. They occurred more frequently in the camps themselves where the possibility of mass conflict between men of Negro and white units was greater. Negro troops were as likely to be the immediate aggressors as white troops and civilians. Two of the disorders, those at Camps Van Dorn and Stewart, were especially serious, both for their potentialities and for their effects on the revision of plans for the general employment of Negro troops. Both incidents involved combat troops of particular units, rather than anonymous groups of soldiers from several units, aided and abetted or provoked by civilians and police in the crowded centers of towns on pay nights. Often disorders symbolized the breaking point both of the patience of the troops involved and of the tolerance of the War Department and its higher commands.

Trouble at Camp Van Dorn in May, involving the 364th Infantry, had its beginnings months before. It was intimately entwined with the previous career of the regiment. The 364th had been activated as the 367th Infantry, one of the new Regular Army units, on 25 March 1941. Much of its training took place at Fort Jackson, South Carolina, during the period of the Columbia friction. Despite the usual low range of AGCT scores and lack of wide civilian experience among its men, it became, in its first year, a relatively well-trained unit. The 367th, less its first battalion, was selected to furnish the 24th Infantry with personnel qualified for foreign service when that regiment became the first Negro infantry unit to move overseas in

[56] Memo, CofS AGF for DCofS, 7 May 42, GNOPN AGF 333.1/19.

April 1942. Its 1st Battalion was alerted for duty with the Liberia Task Force in March 1942, separating from the regiment and proceeding to the Charleston port the following month. Not until January 1943 did it sail from New York. In the meantime, the remainder of the regiment, not knowing that its 1st Battalion had been redesignated the 367th Infantry Battalion (Separate), waited either to refill or to rejoin its 1st Battalion. Necessarily, because of the secrecy of wartime movements, it could not be informed of the destination of its 1st Battalion nor of its future relations with it. Requests on the part of the regiment to be allowed to refill its 1st Battalion could not be met, for there was no provision in the troop basis for an additional battalion in a regiment all of whose battalions were already active. Because the 1st Battalion had been shipped, with all equipment marked as belonging to the 367th Infantry, the regiment, minus its 1st Battalion, was finally redesignated the 364th Infantry. A new 1st Battalion was formed, for by now it was clear that the remainder of the regiment would not join the detached battalion.[57] The regiment, by now refilled with a considerable proportion of new men and faced with retraining, was assigned to the Western Defense Command's Southern Land Frontier Sector for protective guard duty.

While stationed in Phoenix, Arizona, the regiment became involved in two serious disturbances. In the first of these about 500 men of the unit refused to disperse when ordered to do so by the regimental commander. In the second,

occurring on Thanksgiving night of 1942, approximately 100 men of the regiment engaged in a shooting affray with a detachment of Negro military police in Phoenix, with the result that one officer, one enlisted man, and one civilian were killed and twelve enlisted men were seriously wounded. As a result of this disturbance, sixteen members of the regiment were tried by general court-martial, each receiving a sentence of fifty years. The regiment received a new commander and executive officer. These officers tried to eliminate individuals who might be a source of future difficulties. About fifty men were transferred from the regiment during this process. To overcome some of the basic causes of friction within the regiment, a new camp with improved recreational facilities was provided. The new commander was certain that the regiment had returned to a normal state of discipline. The men of the unit, according to intelligence operatives, were equally certain that they had profited from the changes following the clashes.

The Western Defense Command now began to recommend that the regiment be put to other use, and, specifically, that it be considered for employment overseas since "its long retention at this station is likely to produce a deterioration in its present efficiency."[58] In May 1943 the regiment was ordered to Camp Van Dorn, Mississippi, for retraining by Army Ground Forces, a procedure generally followed for units from the defense commands before shipment overseas.

Camp Van Dorn was not only in Mississippi, a fact which members of the

---

[57] Ltr, Hq AGF to CG Third Army, 9 Jun 42, AGF 320.2/8 Inf; Ltr, TAG to CG's, 10 Jun 42, AG 320.2 (6-8-42) MR-M-GN.

[58] Memo, G-3 for CG AGF, 16 Apr 43, WDGCT 291.21 (4-8-43).

regiment, arriving from Phoenix, viewed as a change distinctly for the worse; it was also one of the more isolated of the larger camps located in that state. The nearest town, Centreville, had a normal population of less than 1,200. The nearest sizable towns, McComb, Baton Rouge, and Natchez, were from forty to fifty miles away. Centreville had little to offer any troops in the way of recreation or entertainment, and the prevailing segregation laws and absence of compensating facilities on the post made the men of the 364th especially resentful. Some viewed the change in location as punishment for their continuing difficulties in Phoenix, which had grown distinctly cooler toward their presence as the months passed.[59]

The 364th arrived at Van Dorn in two groups, the first on 26 May and the second on 28 May. The first group, bragging that they were going to "take over" the camp, the town of Centreville, and, if necessary, the state of Mississippi, began to show their resentment to the area to which they had been transferred the day after their arrival. A number of 364th men, visiting the Negro area service club, refused to obey the rules of the club. They arrived in various states of partial uniform, refused to doff caps, used indecent language to the hostesses, and brought beer into the club from a post exchange in violation of camp rules. An hour after the regular closing time, the hostess and the noncommissioned officers in charge were still attempting to clear men of the unit from the building. The following night, after the ar-

rival of the second contingent of the regiment, an exchange manager closed his building because of the threatening conduct of men who insisted that exchange employees had been rude and uncivil to them. Later, several hundred men, most of them from the 364th, broke into the exchange, rifling the stock and damaging equipment. On the next night, a Saturday, a group of about 75 men from the unit visited Centreville and roamed about the town, reportedly using indecent and profane language. The group was accosted by the town chief of police and a number of deputized townsfolk armed with shotguns. Upon arrival of a military police officer, the group dispersed and returned to camp.

On Sunday evening, 30 May, the incident occurred which, considering the rising temper of the regiment, the town, and the remainder of the camp, could have caused a general outbreak. A private from the regiment was accosted outside the reservation by a military policeman and questioned about his improper uniform and lack of a pass. During a fight which followed, the county sheriff arrived. The soldier, attempting to flee, was shot and killed by the sheriff. The commanding officer of the regiment, informed of his soldier's death, dispatched all officers to their respective units and proceeded, with the regimental staff, to the barracks area of the company to which the soldier belonged. There he found the entire company milling around in an uproar, threatening to break into the supply room for rifles and ammunition. He ordered firing pins removed from all rifles and placed an officer guard over the supply room. While this company was being quieted, men of another company

---

[59] Memo, TIG for DCofS, 8 Jun 43, and Ltr, OTIG to TIG, 21 Sep 43, both in AGF 291.2/25.

stormed their supply room and obtained a number of rifles. Shortly thereafter a crowd of several hundred soldiers gathered near the regimental exchange. A riot squad, made up of Negro military policemen, fired into the crowd when it attempted to rush them. One soldier was wounded by this volley. The regimental commander and his chaplain arrived at this point. After talking and pleading with the men, the commander quieted the group, assembled his battalions, and marched the regiment to its barracks area where the entire unit was confined. It took several days of constant searching, which itself served to keep tension high, to locate and recover all missing rifles. Citizens of the nearby town and county began to arm themselves and to call for an immediate transfer of the regiment.

When apprised of the situation the commander of Army Ground Forces, General McNair, whose command in the past had been faced frequently with demands for the removal of Negro troops from specific communities, determined that to transfer the 364th Infantry to another station would be the worst possible solution, since it was not only what the local citizens wanted but also a possible motive for the unit's actions. He proposed that the regiment be confined to its own area until it disclosed "its real troublemakers" and that it be deprived of all its privileges until it "demonstrated its worthiness." He proposed further that the citizens of Centreville and other nearby communities be assured that no member of the unit would be permitted to enter these towns until the citizens themselves asked that the ban be lifted. In the meantime, using extra officers if necessary, a training pro-

gram would be provided which would keep the regiment too busy to allow time for any further demonstrations.[60]

The Inspector General agreed that the proposed action, though "drastic and yet untried," might be valuable under the circumstances. Citizens of the area would probably protest the retention of the regiment at its station, and Negroes would probably protest the disciplinary action taken, but, nevertheless, except for giving the local citizenry control of the future policy of permitting troops to visit surrounding towns—military authorities should be left to determine, on the basis of future developments, when the regiment should return to a normal status—General Peterson recommended that the action proposed be tried. The War Department approved.[61]

Though restrictive disciplinary measures, plus command efforts, brought an outward calm to the regiment, the resentment and disturbed morale of the unit did not alter significantly. Men of the regiment were now aware that they were to be retained at Camp Van Dorn and that over their unit lay the stigma of unusual punishment. A month after the initial Van Dorn disturbances, the unit became embroiled again in an on-post demonstration of near-riot proportions. On the evening of 3 July 1943, a large number of girls had been brought in from neighboring towns for a dance. To help pay their transportation costs, tickets to the dance were sold to soldiers at fifty cents each. Before the dance could start, soldiers, most of them from

---

[60] Ltr, TIG for DCofS, 8 Jun 43, AG 291.2/25.
[61] Memo, OCofS for CG AGF, 9 Jun 43, and 1st Ind, AGF to Third Army, 14 Jun 43, AGF 291.2/25.

the 364th Infantry,[62] began pouring into the service club where the dance was to be held. Coming through side doors and windows as well as through the main entrance, they overran the club. The club assistants, with the help of a number of first sergeants of the regiment, tried to get the building cleared, but the crowd refused to leave. As fast as a few departed through doors, others poured in through windows. The regimental guard and a detachment of Negro military police were called. The field officer of the day, a lieutenant colonel, arrived and, using the public address system set up for the dance, explained the rules for the dance and directed all soldiers to leave the building. The crowd remained. The officer of the day then called for assistance from an alerted white unit, a battalion of the 99th Infantry Division. This battalion arrived, cleared the hall, and dispersed the crowd, now grown to about 2,000.[63]

With the approach of the departure date of the alerted 99th Division, the retention of the 364th Infantry at Van Dorn as the largest single infantry unit on the post took on new significance. Although no ammunition had been issued the unit and the bolts of all rifles had been removed, The Inspector General felt that, "due to the attitude of civilians in this locality relative to racial matters and to the presence of large numbers of northern Negroes, there exists considerable danger of racial dis-

turbances in the general vicinity of this camp." The inspecting officer recommended that the unit be transferred overseas.[64]

The Third Army, however, was now convinced that the unit would not be ready until 1 March 1944.[65] No active theater required a separate infantry regiment. The Operations Division, requested to prevent further deferment of the regiment beyond 1 March, finally arranged for it to replace a white separate regiment in the Aleutians. There it performed garrison duties for the rest of the war.

Decision on the 364th Infantry was complicated by events of the few days following its initial difficulties at Camp Van Dorn. At Camp Stewart, Georgia, near Savannah, in the first week of June, another and larger disturbance involving units of the Antiaircraft Training Command occurred.

The disturbance at Camp Stewart had been brewing for some time. Adverse conditions on this post and in Savannah had been brought to the attention of the War Department as early as 1941.[66] Savannah was a war-crowded town. In addition to its normal population of about 95,000, there were two shipyards close to the city employing about 15,000 people. Camp Stewart had a normal strength of between forty and fifty thousand men. The Savannah Army Air Base at Hunter Field had approximately 9,000 men. In addition, Marine Corps men from Parris Island and Navy and Coast Guard men on liberty used Savan-

---

[62] Aside from small headquarters detachments, other Negro troops on the post included two quartermaster truck regiments, one service battalion, one medical ambulance battalion, and a quartermaster laundry company, totaling about 6,500 troops.

[63] Ltr, OTIG for TIG, 21 Sep 43, AGF 291.2/25.

[64] Ibid.

[65] M/S, Hq AGF, Ground G–3 to Ground CofS, 1 Oct 43, AGF 291.21/25.

[66] Memo, Lt Col J. W. Boyer for OinC Misc Div AGO, 11 Aug 41, AG 291.21 (8–11–41) (4).

nah for recreation. On Saturday nights, shipyard workers, marines, sailors, airmen, and soldiers all came to town. Camp Stewart sent weekly into the city a convoy of about 100 trucks, carrying between 1,200 and 1,500 men, sometimes 75 percent of them Negroes. Neither city nor military police, neither civilians nor volunteer organizations were able to do a great deal to provide adequately for such an influx.[67] Negro troops had been complaining for months about the treatment they received from white civilians and military personnel in Savannah and at Camp Stewart. In the spring of 1943 the situation grew rapidly worse.

At this time there were fourteen Negro antiaircraft units at Camp Stewart.[68] Some of these were old battalions, recently reorganized from regiments being re-formed as groups; others were newly organized battalions, three of them formed with cadres from the 369th AAA Regiment returned from Hawaii. Another of the units was the 100th AAA Gun Battalion, which had been tactically deployed at Fort Brady, Michigan, as part of the defenses of the Sault Ste. Marie area. Just before the outbreak at Camp Stewart, General Davis and Lt. Col. Davis G. Arnold had completed an investigation arising out of the receipt in the War Department of anonymous letters, petitions from civilian organizations, and others concerning conditions at the camp.[69]

General Davis found that dissatisfaction in the 100th Battalion and in the cadre from the 369th was general. These men, mainly from the North, many of them well educated, and fresh from service in areas where civilian customs were more favorable to them, were joined by other units in objections to the designation of latrines and other facilities by race in violation of War Department orders. They reported the usual difficulties with white military police in entering and leaving camp on pass, dissatisfaction with recreational facilities on post, with bus transportation, with treatment by military and civilian police, and with the lack of overnight lodging and meals at reasonable prices in Savannah in comparison with those available for white soldiers. The enlisted cadremen were considered quite capable—the commanding officer at the training center said, "They have the snappiest gun crews that I have ever seen in this whole place, and I go out everyday." But, in presenting their grievances to General Davis, including complaints that their officers, whom they unabashedly referred to as ninety-day wonders, did not have sufficient experience and training, they spoke so rebelliously and so recklessly that General Davis had to caution them on the demeanor expected from disciplined soldiers.

On the basis of the Davis-Arnold report, General Peterson recommended that attempts be made to improve the recreational situation in Savannah, that pass privileges be staggered to prevent overcrowding of both buses and the available facilities, that more Negro military police be employed at entrucking points, and that closer co-ordination be

---

[67] Ltr, Air Provost Marshal, Hunter Fld, Ga., to DCofS for Sv Comds ASF, 7 Jun 43, AAF 726.1, Binder 3.

[68] These were the 100th, 207th, 208th, 458th, 477th, 538th, 484th, 492d, 493d, 503d, 741st, 790th, 818th, and 846th AAA Battalions.

[69] Memo, TIG for CofS, 4 Jun 43, AGF 291.2/22.

developed among the proper staff and command agencies to prevent serious consequences from the existing unrest.[70]

Before General Peterson's recommendations could start on their way, violence flared at Camp Stewart. The central unit involved was neither the 100th Battalion nor any of the units with returnee cadres, but a unit which, approaching the end of its training, was alerted for overseas movement.

On the evening of 9 June the rumor spread through the Negro area at Camp Stewart—four of the battalion areas were empty, save for guards, because their units were on a field exercise—that a Negro woman had been raped and murdered by white soldiers after they had killed her husband. One version included military policemen among the murderers. The rumor, which was later determined to have been false, was heightened in effect by actual occurrences of the preceding few days: military policemen in vehicles with machine guns had been used to disperse a crowd gathered outside a service club during a dance, and a Negro soldier, asking for a drink of water at an ice plant in nearby Hinesville, had received a blow on the head with ice tongs instead. At about 8:30 nearly a hundred soldiers, some armed with rifles, gathered in the Negro area. Officers sought to halt the growing mob. A wild shot was fired. Military police and vehicles were ordered to the area. The first crowd moved back and broke up but a second mob, tense with excitement and anger, formed later. Gun racks and supply rooms of several Negro battalions were broken into and ammunition, rifles, and submachine guns

were removed. Some troops, bent on revenge, joined the mob; some went into the nearby woods in fear; others remained to "fight it out" and to defend their areas. To add to the confusion of the evening, gas alarms rang out in nearly every battalion area.

At about ten o'clock an approaching military police vehicle was fired on from the area of the 458th Battalion. General firing then started from this and several other battalion areas, continuing for the next two hours. Four military policemen were wounded, one seriously; a civilian bus driver, fired on as he approached the area, was slightly wounded. Shortly before midnight, a military police detail crossing a small parade ground on foot was fired on; one military policeman was killed. At 12:30 members of two white battalions moved into the area in half-tracks. The firing ceased shortly thereafter.

In the aftermath of the riot, which had not involved actual fighting between Negro and white troops, a board of officers appointed at Camp Stewart to investigate determined that the disturbance was essentially an outgrowth of long pent-up emotions and resentments. The majority of the Negro soldiers were convinced that justice and fair treatment were not to be had by them in neighboring communities and that the influence of these communities was strongly reflected in the racial policies of the command at Camp Stewart. Many Negro troops feared for their personal safety. Others, gripped by a feeling of desperation, had determined to fight back against existing abuses without regard to consequences. While frequent rumors circulated rapidly throughout the Negro units, no evidence of an organized cam-

[70] Ibid.

paign fostering discontent was uncovered. The arrival of the men and officers from the 100th Battalion and 369th Regiment may have aroused "latent resentment" existing in the minds of soldiers already stationed at the camp, but the board found no evidence that the men of these units were responsible for the dissatisfaction leading to the disturbances. The one unit with all Negro officers, commanded by Lt. Col. DeMaurice Moses, was called into formation by its commander and his staff after the start of the disturbance and remained calm throughout the period. The board, despite its own findings, nevertheless fell back on older formulas, ascribing the difficulties to the stationing of Northern Negroes in the South and to the "average negro soldier's meager education, superstition, imagination and excitability" which, coupled with regimentation, made him "easily misled" and developed a "mass state of mind." It therefore recommended that charges be placed against any individuals involved against whom concrete evidence of criminal activities existed; that better machinery for getting rid of "deliberate agitators" be supplied; that special training for military police in "handling Negro soldiers" be devised; that an educational program be planned for Negro troops to "teach dangers of rumor mongering, acceptance of rumors as truth, avoidance of 'chip on shoulders' attitude," and attempting to take the law into their own hands; and that the 458th Battalion be disbanded, with its enlisted men distributed to other organizations.[71]

These recommendations did not reach to the heart of the board's own findings. The commanding general of the Antiaircraft Command therefore did not concur with the recommendation that the chief offending unit be disbanded. Any guilty noncommissioned officers could be reduced and punished in due course; new men could be transferred into the unit. Army Ground Forces agreed with the command, saying that "This unit appears to have had an excellent record of accomplishment prior to the riot" and the time, money, and effort invested in it could still be utilized.[72] All necessary disciplinary action was already provided for in Army Regulations; the matter of indoctrinating troops was a local problem that required no sanction from higher headquarters.

In the early summer of 1943 events of a similar nature continued to come to the attention of higher headquarters. Before Camp Stewart, there were disturbances at the Fort Bliss, Texas, Antiaircraft Training Center, followed by another later in June on the local celebration of Texas' Emancipation Day (19 June, "Juneteenth"), both of which were accompanied by "isolated incidents of beating of negro troops, rock throwing, and chasing of negroes (by white troops)."[73] At Lake Charles, Louisiana, in May a pre-embarkation disturbance arose from "last fling" activities of soldiers on pass, the arrest of a Negro soldier by a white military policeman despite the local ground rule that only Negro MP's would arrest Negro soldiers,

---

[71] Ltr, Brig Gen Samuel L. McCrosky, President of Bd, to CG AAATC, Cp Stewart, AGF 322.999/6.

[72] M/S, AGF G-1 to AGF G-3, G-2, CofS, and 3d Ind, Hq AGF to CG AAATC Cp Stewart, 8 Jul 43, both in AGF 322.999/6.
[73] Ltr, AAATC Ft. Bliss, Texas, to CG AAATC, 2 Jun 43, AGF 250; Ltr, Hq AGF to CG AAC, 24 Jul 43, AGF 322.999/370.

and a failure of other military police, including officers, to function properly.[74] Angered by rough treatment of their fellows in Starkville on the Fourth of July, about fifteen Negro soldiers from Camp McCain, Mississippi, set out with arms and ammunition on the next night, heading for Starkville, seventy miles away. At nearby Duck Hill, along the Illinois Central tracks, they stopped and fired into the nearer town in retaliation. At Camp Claiborne, Louisiana, where there were approximately 8,500 Negro and 40,000 white troops, a chain of disturbances indicating low morale and poor discipline occurred during the late spring and summer, including mass raids on exchanges, involving loss of merchandise and damage to equipment; attempts by soldiers to overturn buses; and a near riot in a service club when an angry crowd, protesting the mistreatment of a soldier by a white officer, dispersed only after a tear gas candle was used.[75] At the Shenango (Pennsylvania) Replacement Depot, on the evening of 14 July 1943, an altercation between Negro and white soldiers in a post exchange expanded until it involved large numbers of troops in the exchange area. This first disturbance, brought under control by white and Negro military police, was followed by another when two new prisoners, picked up for a pass violation, spread news of the ear-

lier fracas to men in the guardhouse. Negro prisoners broke out of the guardhouse and, joined by other soldiers, seized firearms and ammunition from supply rooms. Military police, again white and Negro, killed one and wounded five other soldiers in quelling the second disturbance.[76]

Individual Violence

Not all of the violence and disorder in which Negro troops became involved resulted from racial friction or mass grievances. Much of it was of a purely indigenous nature, sometimes growing out of cultural traits and patterns of behavior brought into the Army from civilian life and sometimes growing out of contacts between soldiers and civilians whose lives were enmeshed in the semi-underworld of the honky-tonk sections of many camp towns. Throughout the war these provided backdrop and counterpoint to racial violence sometimes difficult to distinguish from the main action and theme. In the prevailing atmosphere of alertness and sensitivity to potential racial disorders, many a street squabble or local fight, normal in war-crowded towns and camps, received attention out of proportion to its importance, for none could draw the line between a minor disorder and one that might portend a major outbreak of violence.

Sometimes civilian crowds, opposed to law enforcement in any form or conditioned to suspect that Negro soldiers

---

[74] 1st and subsequent Inds, TAG to CG Third AF, 17 May 43, AG 291.2 (5-13-43) (1).

[75] Memo for TIG, 16 Jul 43, IG 312.1-Misc. The situation at Camp Claiborne continued to deteriorate until riots, including attacks on unit officers barricaded in orderly rooms, occurred in August and September 1944, as a result of which a number of soldiers were tried and convicted of mutiny and of inciting to riot.

---

[76] Memo, TIG for CG ASF, 26 Jul 43, 333.1–Shenango Pers Repl Depot (5); Ltr, ASW McCloy to Walter White, Secy NAACP, 4 Sep 43, WD 291.2 (14 Jul 43) OB–C.

would receive less than fair treatment from police officers, came close to precipitating mass violence. In Louisville, Kentucky, in June 1943, street crowds became disorderly when white and Negro military police arrested Negro soldiers. The crowd, seeing soldiers bleeding—they had been fighting among themselves—and concluding that they had been beaten by arresting police, heaped imprecations upon the military police, calling the Negro MP's "mouthpieces for the white people." [77] When an arrested soldier refused to enter a police car in Tampa, Florida, a crowd of civilians gathered, urging other soldiers to take him away from military police. Not until an armored car arrived did the crowd disperse. Persons in the upper stories of houses continued to hurl bottles, flowerpots, and other objects into the street and upon the armored car below.[78] In another type of disorder not involving racial friction, a feud between two units over the success of one soldier in dating "a much-sought-after colored girl," erupted into disorder in the Quartermaster service area at Camp Rucker, Alabama, following a beer party in one of the units.[79] General disorder at a USO dance at Fort Dix, New Jersey, resulted in the death of one soldier, the wounding of two others, and

the beating of one military policeman after Negro military police were called.[80]

In some units, where a high state of discipline had never been achieved, acts of violence were a commonplace. Soldiers of one battalion, while on a recreation trip to Las Vegas, Nevada, became involved in an altercation with civilian and military police, colored and white, in a bar just a short distance from the truck park where their accompanying officers were asleep. One soldier was killed and three others were injured in the ensuing fight. Within the organization itself, during the training period, several men were shot accidentally or by guards while "kidding around." Shortly before the unit moved to a port of embarkation one of its mess sergeants was hacked to death in his kitchen with a cleaver by a technician fifth grade and two accomplices bent on robbing him.[81] In 1944, after three years of dispersed duty in and around New York City, the 372d Infantry was removed to Camp Breckinridge, Kentucky, for retraining. There, in process of reorganization and swollen to nearly twice its normal size by new men—"infantry volunteers" who were often culls from other units—it became the victim of rapidly deteriorating discipline accompanied by continuing breeches of decorum and by acts of violence. The camp commander, as support for a request for additional military police, listed one general and twenty-five specific examples of disorder and breeches of discipline occurring on the post between 24

[77] Ltr, Betty Bailey, Louisville, 7 Jun 43, and investigation, especially 3d Ind, 8 Jul 43, Hq Ft. Knox, Ky., to CG Fifth Sv Comd, Fifth Sv Comd 291.2, AGO Records.

[78] Ltr, Office of Provost Marshal Tampa Area to Provost Marshal Third AF, Tampa, 20 Feb 44, AAF 250.1 Misc.

[79] Rpt, Hq Cp Rucker to CO Cp Rucker, 28 Jan 44, Cp Rucker 333.1 Gen 17, AGO Records. The beer party was held to have been merely incidental to the bitter feeling existing between the units.

[80] Memo, Dir Sec and Int Div Second Sv Comd for CofS Second Sv Comd, 13 Jan 45, Second Sv Comd 291.2, AGO Records.

[81] Decimal files, 827th TD Bn, AGO Records.

May and 16 August 1944. Most of these he attributed to this unit.[82] These were purely disciplinary cases, to be handled as other violations of law and order. But the line between them and racially based violence was often vague, especially in the minds of those involved as participants or as immediately responsible commanders.

Civilian Disorders

Complementing and complicating the tenseness and disorder within the military establishment were civilian racial disorders. During the summer of 1943 serious disturbances occurred in Los Angeles, Detroit, Beaumont, and New York. Rumors of riots in the offing appeared in other cities: In Houston for "Juneteenth," in Charleston for the last week in June, in Richmond over the Fourth of July weekend, in Washington on the evening chosen for a mass meeting of Negroes protesting the refusal of the local street car company to employ Negro operators, in Pittsburgh over the weekend of 10 July when 300 Negroes stormed a police station to protest the arrest of two men who refused to "move on" when ordered to do so by the police.[83] That civilian and military disorders had connecting links could not be overlooked. Soldiers and sailors were involved in the Detroit and Los Angeles riots. In the Harlem riot of 1943, the precipitating event involved a Negro soldier and a white city policeman, with the policeman accusing the soldier of attempting to interfere with the arrest of a disorderly Negro woman. The rumor spread quickly that the soldier had been killed by the policeman. Rioting, most of it against property rather than against whites themselves, followed, resulting in at least five deaths and several hundred injured.[84] The possibility of further repercussions from these disturbances within the Army was viewed as a real danger.[85] In Harlem, Negro and white soldiers sent into the area to clear the streets and restore order were greeted with cheers. In Detroit, however, the action of the service command in using 2,000 white soldiers only for riot duty brought immediate repercussions in Negro units. Eighty Negro soldiers at nearby Oscoda Army Air Base, mainly members of the 332d Fighter Group and the 96th Service Group, protested to the President that they, too, should have been called for this duty, charging that white soldiers helped white rioters against Negroes and saying that the

---

[82] The list included: attempted and completed rapes of colored Wacs and wives of colored and white soldiers; robberies of service clubs, exchanges, and taxi drivers; attacks on guards; arrests and complaints of prowlers in civilian and WAC areas; and disregard of camp rules (nonracial) about the use of recreation areas, resulting in disorder and friction. Memo and Incl, CG ASF for G-3, 22 Aug 44, Cp Breckinridge, SPINT 291.2; Memo, G-3 for CG AGF, 22 Aug 44, WDGCT 291.21 (22 Aug 44); Ltr and Incls, Col Russ Throckmorton, CO Cp Breckinridge, to Col Frederick L. Hayden, CofS Fifth Sv Comd, 20 Sep 44, Fifth Sv Comd 291.2, AGO Records.

[83] Monthly Summary of Events and Trends in Race Relations, I (August 1943), 8; Joseph E. Weckler and Theo E. Hall, *The Police and Minority Groups* (Chicago: International City Managers' Association, 1944), pp. 1–5.

[84] William Cecil Headrick, "Race Riots—Segregated Slums," *Current History*, V (September 1943), 30–34; T. T. Brumbaugh, "The Fault Dear Brutus," *The Christian Century*, LXI (May 24, 1944), 634–44; S. Edward Young, "Black Restlessness," *The Christian Century*, LXI (November 1, 1944), 1252–53.

[85] Min of Gen Council, 21 Jun 43, 2 Aug 43.

handling of the riot brought out in bold relief the helpless physical position of Negro soldiers and civilians.[86] The greater fear arising from these continuing disturbances in both the civilian and military spheres was that, with all their interacting potentialities, they would interfere seriously not only with training but also with war production, handing at the same time free copy to enemy propagandists. With the political campaigns of 1944 approaching, attempts to make political capital of the increasingly serious problem were on the horizon. It would therefore behoove the Army, its legislative experts felt, to "keep its skirts clean in the matter" and avoid involvement in the coming campaign.[87]

Army Service Forces, which had primary responsibility for service commands and, through them, for posts, acquired after the middle of 1943 direct responsibility for increasing percentages of Negro troops. ASF began to place prevention of racial friction high on its list of problems toward the end of 1943. There was still a tendency to place the major blame for disturbances upon inadequate recreational facilities, inadequate command, and outside agitation.

A representative of The Inspector General, addressing a conference of commanding generals of service commands in midsummer 1943, summed up the situation and the War Department's view of both its origin and its importance:

In my opinion the toughest problem confronting service commanders today is the one of preventing disturbances involving colored troops, since it involves some matters which are not under your control. The number of such disturbances has materially increased in the last few months. High officials of the War Department are not so much concerned as to how commanders functioned in quelling the disturbances, but rather what had they done to learn that a riot or disturbance was probable and what action had they taken to prevent it.

General Peterson's information indicates that in too many instances commanding officers are too far removed from their colored troops; they are not sufficiently interested in their day-to-day welfare in providing them with reasonable recreational facilities within the post and in seeing that reasonable transportation is provided to and from recreational areas off the post; they are not enough concerned about the discrimination that may be practiced against Negroes in the surrounding country and in the lack of recreational facilities therein; they permit on their own posts discriminations which are contrary to the War Department policies and instructions; they fail to maintain appropriate standards of discipline in Negro units; they grudgingly accept Negro officers assigned to their commands and thereafter spend a good deal of time griping about the unfitness of a Negro to be an officer, rather than requiring him to meet officer standards.

. . . .

In stations where conditions exist as I have just described, there grows up the feeling of unrest and resentment, which is flamed by troublemakers within the organization until it gets to the point that only a spark, which is ordinarily a false rumor,

[86] Oscoda was a subbase of Selfridge Field, at which most of these troops were stationed when, a few weeks before, on 5 May, the post commander, having ordered his car to base headquarters in the early morning hours, shot the Negro driver assigned to it on sight and without provocation. The protest itself was not unprecedented. In the Springfield Riots of 1908, units of the 8th Illinois, prepared to answer the governor's call for riot duty, protested that the use of white National Guardsmen only worked a specific hardship on the Negro citizens of Springfield which could have been avoided by the use of the Negro units as well. History of the First Air Force Army Air Base at Selfridge Field, Mich., 1 January–31 December 1943, pp. 141, 152, MS in AAF Hist Gp 288.52–3 I; Pittsburgh *Courier*, July 31, 1943.
[87] Rpt, L&L Div, Gen Council Meeting, 12 Jul 43.

converts an organization into a riotous mob. Some officials in Washington believe that some of the disturbances that have occurred could have been prevented had the commanders concerned functioned appropriately. I do not want to give the impression that disturbances are the fault of the commanders, but by failing to act appropriately, they facilitate the work of groups or individuals who are attempting to create unrest and later riots among Negro troops.[88]

As more and more Negro troops came under its direct control, Army Service Forces and its agencies explored ways and means of improving the control of racial tensions within camps and stations. Early in 1944, the continuing examination of policy concerning Negro troops was placed at the top of Army Service Forces' Classified Checklist of Current Policies, with the director of its Military Personnel Division made responsible for close observation of matters arising under these policies.[89] The Inspector General, from mid-summer 1943 to the end of the year, made a series of comprehensive surveys of conditions in several camps and groups of camps. Nine specific recommendations were forwarded by him for War Department consideration. Many of these had been covered before, but from the findings of inspectors they were considered to be in need of further attention. Moreover, The Inspector General, from past reports and observations, viewed the situation as a complex of many strands which, singly or in combination, led to unrest and eventual disorder. The corrective

recommendations included: (1) directives "by appropriate authority" to commanders concerned for the purpose of stressing, in the training programs of Negro troops, the necessity of "their accepting and striving to attain the proper standards of military discipline"; (2) utilization of additional Negro military police to provide more adequate and centralized control; (3) the establishment of an "active, attractive, interesting and fully coordinated recreational and entertainment program, including additional facilities therefor;" (4) the necessity of affording Negro officers "the same privileges and opportunities for advancement as those granted white officers" with the requirement that they "be held to the same high degree of leadership, efficiency, performance of duty and discipline"; (5) a clear statement of War Department policy to correct "an unwillingness of commanding officers to bring offenders to trial when the seriousness of the offense manifestly indicated the need therefor"; (6) attainment of closer co-operation of federal and state authorities toward control of venereal diseases; (7) directives to local public relations officers requiring them to gather information on Negro personnel at posts, camps, and stations, to furnish releases to Negro papers and encouragement to the papers to use such releases "with a view to elimination from their publications of erroneous, distorted or inflammatory articles," failing which, "drastic steps" should be taken by appropriate government authorities "in cases of publication of articles which adversely affect the War effort;" (8) recommendations to commanding officers that "when there is reason to believe or suspect that there is racial unrest or that

---

[88] Address, Col Pierre V. Kieffer, IGD, Annual Inspection of Service Commands, Proceedings, ASF Conference of Commanding Generals, Service Commands, July 22, 1943 to July 24, 1943, Chicago, Illinois, pp. 17–18.

[89] Classified Checklist of Current Problems, SPTR 291.2 (28 Jan 44).

racial disturbance is imminent within their commands, they should exercise, in such situations as may warrant it, the military censorship of postal matter authorized by the provisions of paragraph 3d, War Department Training Circular 15, dated 16 February 1943, using the utmost care and secrecy in so doing;" and (9) bringing to the attention of appropriate agencies, with a view to correction "where practicable," the lack of established eating and lodging facilities for Negro personnel traveling in the South.[90]

All of the matters in this portmanteau recommendation had previously come to the attention of one or another of the agencies concerned. Many of them had reminiscent overtones of the recommendations made by Judge Hastie in his pre-Pearl Harbor survey.[91] Much had been done to carry out certain of them. That they were still unfinished business midway of the war was an indication of the difficulty which the War Department had had with them. The degree of relationship which the areas of recommended action bore to the problem of violence and discipline differed considerably; that all were contributing to the general problem of the employment of Negro troops could not be denied.

[90] Memo, OTIG for ASW, 24 Jul 43, ASW 291.2 NT.

[91] See above, ch. VI.

CHAPTER XIII

Toward an Objective

The explanations, recommendations, and remedies advanced to deal with recurring signs of unsatisfactory progress in the training of Negro troops were many. Few observers failed to describe the situation as a complex one. Certain of the threads which went to make up a tangled skein were common to most observations and recommendations. The influence of real and imagined neglect of and discrimination against Negro soldiers; the educational and experiential backgrounds of the soldiers themselves; the lack of proper leadership and discipline in their units; the influence of the press, especially of the Negro press; the influence of local conditions, especially in the South; the orientation of white troops and police, especially military police, toward Negro troops; the failure to move Negro units overseas in large numbers; and the imperfect dissemination of War Department policies to officers in the field were the chief points at issue.

That these matters were all linked together, with interacting implications, began to be recognized more widely by mid-1943. While there was still a tendency to blame outside forces—the press and agitators in particular—for the major difficulties experienced, there was also a growing recognition that the root of the matter was both deeper and broader than these. Eighty-five percent of the Army, as one member of the Advisory Committee on Negro Troop Policies observed somewhat later, had ideas about Negroes that could not be changed quickly.[1] But that did not prevent Assistant Secretary McCloy and the Advisory Committee from devoting considerable time and effort to improving the general situation.

McCloy was convinced that a fair appraisal would show that the Army, by mid-1943, was ahead of the rest of the country in recognizing and attempting to do something about its racial problems. He pointed out again and again that rumors and press concern over discriminatory practices obscured the attempts of the War Department to eliminate both racial friction and the major deterrents to effective training. Writing to Eleanor Roosevelt, the President's wife, he explained:

There has arisen a tendency in the Negro soldier to believe any wild story of discrimination or abuse. The story will spread like wildfire and the Negro soldier has been so sensitized by references to his abused position that he is prepared to believe anything and does. The Negro press has been quite careless in reporting and playing up accounts of alleged mistreatment. By no means all the blame can be traced to the Negro or the Negro press and . . . there is room for great improvement

---

[1] Maj Gen Miller G. White, during discussion, Meeting of Advisory Com on Negro Troop Policies, 4 Jan 44, ASW 291.2 NTC.

in our handling of the Negro in the Army. General Marshall has recently issued a strong directive to the Army commanders which should initiate a much closer attention to the handling of those matters by the responsible officers.

The problem is a national one but the War Department is making every endeavor to see that the general condition of Negro troops in the Army is improved and that causes of friction between them and the white troops are removed. Unfortunately, the steps which one side feels would remove the trouble, almost invariably stimulates trouble from the other side and a solution in one part of the country in a particular situation can rarely be applied generally.[2]

Proceeding from the general point of view that racial conditions in the Army were considerably better than painted to the public and yet not good enough for the best utilization of all manpower, Secretary McCloy and the Advisory Committee set about examining the situation with the intention of improving it so that Negro troops might be more of an asset and less of a problem in the training and deployment of an Army at war.

Advice to Commanders

General Marshall's "directive," referred to by Secretary McCloy in his note to Mrs. Roosevelt, was the result of discussions and urgings in the Advisory Committee.[3] A subcommittee, consisting of General Davis of The Inspector General's Office, Brig. Gen. Miller G. White, representing G–1, and Lt. Col.

Willard S. Renshaw, representing Army Ground Forces, had drawn up a report on the general problem, which became the basis for General Marshall's letter to the field. The subcommittee's account of the provenance of disorders, taken from Inspector General reports, became the standard War Department view of the problem. It was essentially the same account that McCloy gave to Mrs. Roosevelt, but here the central emphasis was on command and control difficulties.

Most of the disturbances, the committee reported and General Marshall so described to the field,[4] began with real or fancied incidents of discrimination or segregation against Negro troops. No positive action was taken by commanders to overcome the causes of irritation and unrest. Gossip and rumor circulated. A minor incident occurring thereafter often brought on a general disturbance. There was a widespread failure of commanders of some echelons to appreciate the seriousness of the matters involved and their responsibility for dealing with them. Few commanders took preventive measures to forestall impending general disorder. In many cases commands made allowances for the improper conduct of white or Negro soldiers, among themselves or toward each other, until discipline was generally undermined. General Marshall in his

---

[2] Ltr, ASW to Mrs. Roosevelt, 26 Jul 43, ASW 291.2 NT.

[3] Memo, Civ Aide to SW for ASW, 14 May 43, Memo, Secy Advisory Com for ASW, 25 May 43, and Memo, ASW for Gen White, 29 May 43, all in ASW 291.2 NT–Gen; Min, Advisory Com, 28 Jun, 2 Jul 43, ASW 291.2 NT–Com.

[4] The report was presented to the Advisory Committee on 2 July 1943, sent by the committee to the Chief of Staff on 3 July (Memo, Advisory Com for CofS, 3 Jul 43, ASW 291.2 NT), and sent to the major commands in altered (excerpted) form over the signature of General Marshall (Memo, CofS for CG's Major Comds, 3 Jul 43, WDCSA 291.21). The major commands, by indorsement, sent it to the field. See, for example, 1st Ind, ASF AG, 13 Jul 43, to CG's, Sv Comds, etc., SPX 291.2 (13 Jul 43).

letter reminded commanders that the maintenance of discipline and good order between soldiers and the civilian population was a "definite command responsibility," and that those guilty of derelictions must be punished by prompt and effective disciplinary measures. "Failure on the part of any commander to concern himself personally and vigorously with this problem will be considered as evidence of lack of capacity and cause for reclassification and removal from assignment," he concluded.

The Advisory Committee, in its recommendations to the Chief of Staff, urged that the troop commander not only be impressed with the importance and difficulty of the problem but also that he be required:

(1) To maintain close personal contact with the situation.

(2) To follow implicitly the War Department policies and instructions, in letter and spirit, with respect to discrimination and the provision of equal facilities.

(3) To take positive action to insure early determination of the existence of unrest and disaffection among troops and to remove the causes therefor, whether they result from conditions under his jurisdiction or from unsatisfactory relationships with the civilian population.

(4) To develop definite programs within his own jurisdiction for the elimination of causes of friction on military reservations.

(5) To maintain close relations with the civil authorities and secure co-operative action by them to remove or correct causes of friction between soldiers and the civil population.

(6) To discover and suppress inflammatory gossip, rumors, or propaganda among the troops themselves, preferably by countermeasures to offset same. When unrest and the causes therefor are known to exist, he must see that the troops themselves are aware that he is so informed and are them-

selves informed as to the measures the commander is taking to remove the causes.

(7) When conditions so warrant and when it is apparent that the means under his jurisdiction are ineffectual to obtain corrective or remedial action, to immediately report all facts of the circumstances to his superior.[5]

The committee recommended as well that the commanding generals of the Air, Ground, and Service Forces be directed to submit specific recommendations for changes in policies on the treatment of Negro personnel, the use of camp facilities, the organization of Negro soldiers into units, and the employment of those units. Negro combat troops, the committee urged, should be dispatched to active theaters at an early date: "In the opinion of the Committee, such action would be the most effective means of reducing tension among Negro troops." [6] The three principal commands, moreover, should be directed to report to the Chief of Staff the action they had taken to carry out these recommendations.

Though much of the action suggested by the committee was implied in the letter of the Chief of Staff, the specific recommendations were not forwarded to the major commands. The committee knew that standing War Department policies and instructions were not being carried out fully in all commands, and that in some instances they were not even fully known; it knew that commanders were not paying sufficient attention to the seriousness of what was, after all, but one of many problems with which they were faced. It believed that training

---

[5] Memo, Advisory Com for CofS, 3 Jul 43, ASW 291.2 NT. Punctuation in original changed by author.

[6] Ibid.

problems and disturbances were linked with the over-all question of Negro troop utilization and that War Department policies themselves were in need of revision.   But there was still a reluctance to interfere with command responsibilities by pointing out more than that these responsibilities existed.   Ameliorative efforts therefore proceeded in other directions.

The Bureau of Public Relations and the Press

On the question of the relationship of the press to morale, the Bureau of Public Relations, which was centrally concerned with public and press reactions, was especially disturbed not only by Army relations with the Negro press but also by recurring suggestions from G–2 and from field commanders that portions of the Negro press be censored or otherwise controlled.[7]   In the summer of 1942 when such suggestions had been frequently made as a result of the Negro press coverage of the racial disturbances of that year, the bureau replied that it was attempting to help, rather than hinder, the Negro press in obtaining and printing accounts of Negroes in the Army.   "The policy of this Bureau," it told G–3, "has been to work for a higher degree of factual accuracy in published reports of the activities of Negro troops, to emphasize the many favorable aspects of Army practices and policy in racial matters, and to encourage the reconsid-

eration of articles or editorials of a critical or controversial nature."[8]   The bureau gradually became a center for the regular visits of Negro reporters and it in turn sent its representatives for visits to the Negro publishers and to their annual conferences.   A weekly illustrated mat service especially planned for Negro papers and the encouragement of public relations officers in the field to stimulate the reporting of news of Negro activities brought an increase of information on Negro soldiers in both the Negro and the metropolitan white press.   A Special Interest Section to serve the needs of the Negro press was organized within the bureau in the summer of 1942 and Negro officers were brought in to operate it in 1943.   Visits to maneuver areas were arranged for Negro reporters so that the progress and seriousness of the training of Negro troops could be observed at firsthand.

The bureau maintained a weekly analysis service of trends in the Negro press which sorted stories according to their favorable or unfavorable presentation of news concerning the Army.   These analyses, plus those of Elmer Davis' Office of War Information, showed early that the Negro press was hungry for news of Negro soldiers and that it would use almost every item which the bureau could supply.   In the summer of 1942, when so many unfavorable reports of the treatment of Negro soldiers in the Army appeared in the Negro press, a bureau analysis of the contents of one issue of the Pittsburgh *Courier* showed twenty-six articles attacking racial discrimination in general, eight attacking racial

---

[7] Memos, G–2 for G–3, 29 May 42 and 17 Jun 42, both in G–3 291.21; Memo, Maj Gen Alexander D. Surles for ASW, 13 Apr 43, ASW 291.2 NT–Gen; Ltr, CG Cp Lee, Va., to Dir BPR, 6 Jan 43, and Incls, ASW 291.2 NT–Com; Censorship Rpt (AGO Form 912a) Hq USAFISPA, 24 Sep 43, on the Chicago *Defender*, 24 Jul 43, ASW 291.2 NT.

[8] Memo, BPR for G–3, 31 Aug 42, G–3 291.21 vol I.

discrimination in the Army, and one attacking discrimination in the Navy. Of general news concerning Negroes in the Army, there were twenty-three articles, all favorable, and two on the Navy, both favorable. The ratio of critical Army to critical general articles (8 to 26) was considered by the bureau an improvement. The preponderant effect, the bureau concluded, was not produced by editorials but by headlines and pictures. It proposed to keep a steady supply of news items and pictures flowing to the Negro papers.[9] This it did, with the flow increasing as more war news became available. Most of the bureau news releases found wide use.

Despite these efforts, the reporting of events in a manner critical of the Army continued. In the opinions of field commanders, such articles were damaging to the morale of troops. In addition to making suggestions that all or particular Negro papers be placed under surveillance for possible subversive activities, a number of posts and stations from time to time banned one or another paper from sale in exchanges or libraries.[10] Few posts went so far as the Antiaircraft Training Center at Fort Bliss, Texas. There, after the 1943 disturbances, Negro newspapers which, in the opinion of the commanding general, contained material of "such an agitational nature as to be prejudicial to military discipline within the training center" were banned from the post entirely. All mail received at the Fort Bliss post office for Negro battalions was delivered to the camp's postal officer, who extracted "objectionable newspapers." The remaining mail was then delivered, with the training center commander directing the final disposition of newspapers. While the legality of this procedure was endorsed by the Eighth Service Command's Director of Military Intelligence and by the Censorship Officer, El Paso Branch, Office of Postal Censorship, the Antiaircraft Command, when informed of the practice, sought further advice from the War Department.

Army Ground Forces, upon receipt of the Antiaircraft Command's report, telephoned the commanding general of the Antiaircraft Command to have the commanding general of the Fort Bliss training center discontinue his practices immediately. As an emergency measure, Ground Forces G–2 thought, a commander might properly stop a particular paper or an issue, but to do so permanently "would only serve to supply ammunition for agitation to colored papers." [11]

Evidence of the unauthorized prohibition of Negro newspapers in libraries, reading rooms, service clubs, and post exchanges continued to reach the Bureau of Public Relations. Inquiries of service commands had revealed no formal bans, for actions of this type had not been taken through regular channels. But in some cases post intelligence officers, without an order from the post commander, had proceeded to ban papers. In at least one case a unit intelligence officer did so after receiving

---

[9] *Ibid.*

[10] TM 21–205, The Special Services Officer, 12 May 1942, gave commanding officers authority to destroy reading material considered "subversive, obscene, or otherwise improper." See Ltr, TAG, 24 Jun 41, AG 461 (6–20–41) MC–M; Ltr, TAG, 18 Jun 42, AG 461 (5–28–42) MS–B–M.

[11] Ltr, Hq AA Comd to CG AGF, 19 Aug 43, AGF 000.73/3.

from his service command the information that though the service command had no approved or disapproved list of papers, on certain posts specific papers, which were named, had been banned. The bureau felt that if it had not pursued its investigations below the level of camp commanders, it "might have been placed in the position of stating that there was no truth in the report . . . ." It took the position endorsed by Army Ground Forces earlier that so long as newspapers and magazines enjoyed post office privileges local commanders should not ban them from installations without War Department approval. The bureau was certain that, through its liaison officers, it would be able to remedy public relations situations considered damaging to morale. The bureau's position was approved by the War Department and commanders were so informed.[12]

Both Negro and white editors and publishers became concerned with the influence which their papers had upon tense racial situations. How irresponsible editing had helped foment the Harlem riot of 1943 and how rumor clinics and careful handling of news had helped avert threatened racial difficulties in Indianapolis and Washington were discussed in the official organ of the American Society of Newspaper Editors. Certain Southern dailies, such as the Mobile, Alabama, *Register* and the Shelby, North Carolina, *Star* made determined efforts to describe regularly in their columns the activities of Negro men and women in the war, giving Negro readers "the feeling that their work in defense of democracy is appreciated," and giving to the general public some picture of Negro participation in the war.[13] Negro editors and publishers, when defending their own editorial practices, often arrogated to themselves much credit for initiating changes in Army policy,[14] but they also began to check more frequently with the Bureau of Public Relations and the Office of the Civilian Aide before printing accounts of disturbances and discriminatory practices.[15] They could and did point out that they had refrained from using many of the stories which came to their attention.[16] But enough stories remained on their front pages to make Negro papers easy targets as sources of disaffection during most of the war.

The Bureau of Public Relations learned early that the manner of presen-

---

[12] Memo, BPR for CofS, 10 Nov 43, approved by DCofS, 25 Nov 43, and circulated to the field as Ltr, TAG, 29 Nov 43, AG 461 (10 Nov 43) OB–S–BPR–M.

[13] The quotation is from Virginius Dabney, "The Press and the Interracial Crisis," *The Bulletin of the American Society of Newspaper Editors,* September 1, 1943, pp. 1–2. See also, in the same issue, Ben McKelway, "Rumor Clinic Technic Allayed Race Riot Fears in Washington," p. 3; Walter Leckrone, "Leckrone Tells How Indianapolis Averted Threat of Race Rioting," *The Bulletin* . . . , October 1, 1943, pp. 5, 8.

[14] See Ernest E. Johnson, "The Washington News Beat," *Phylon,* VII (1946), 126–31; P. L. Prattis, "The Role of the Negro Press in Race Relations," *Phylon,* VII (1946), 273–83.

[15] See correspondence files (unindexed) of Office of the Civilian Aide, AGO Records.

[16] Ltr, P. L. Prattis to T. S. Matthews, in *Time,* July 7, 1944 (copy forwarded to Truman K. Gibson, Jr.), ASW 291.2 NT–Civ Aide; See also Ltr, Deton J. Brooks, Jr., Asst Editor, Chicago *Defender,* to Gibson, 12 Aug 43, ASW 291.2 NT–Puerto Rico, Alpha; Binder, Alleged Attack upon a Negro Soldier at Scooba, Miss., AG 291.21 (2–2243) (1); Ltr, unnamed correspondent, to Cleveland *Call and Post,* Incl to Memo, Gibson for Lt Col Harrison A. Gerhardt, 7 Mar 44, ASW 291.2 NT–Combat; Memo, Gibson for ASW, 22 Nov 44, on tel conv with William G. Nunn, Managing Editor, Pittsburgh *Courier,* ASW 291.2 NT–Combat.

ANP CORRESPONDENT AND MEN OF A SIGNAL CONSTRUCTION BATTALION *somewhere in France, 13 July 1944.*

tation and phrasing of news releases about minorities was as critical in the development of favorable attitudes as the news facts themselves. "Being cognizant of [the] adverse effect of publicizing most Negro troops serving overseas in World War I, as 'labor battalions,'" the bureau had the War Department inform overseas commands in June 1942 that "the War Department announced the recent arrival of Negro troops in Northern Ireland without reference to composition." But the move

was "nullified" by theater statements that these troops were intended for the Services of Supply only. These statements, the bureau cautioned, were interpreted as an attempt to label all Negro troops overseas as noncombatant. While both the War Department and overseas commanders were to "see that overseas arrival of Negro troops is well publicized at each opportunity," the arrival of noncombatant Negro troops was to be discussed in each instance as "Negro troops" without reference to their composition, the communication directed.[17] News and pictures of Negro soldiers which reinforced the traditional beliefs that the Army had little intention of employing Negroes as combat soldiers, the bureau realized, were almost as damaging as none at all.

News of Negro soldiers was not only useful in public relations but it was also a morale factor among soldiers themselves. Negro troops were quick to notice the absence of news about them or about their units in newspapers, magazines, and newsreels. The men of the 93d Engineer General Service Regiment constructing the Alcan Highway from the Alaska end, for example, felt that their work received no public recognition in comparison with that of other units on the highway. "They want their friends to read about their regiment and feel that they understand their outfit is making an important contribution to the war effort," an officer of the regiment reported. The failure of correspondents to visit their portions of the road or to mention them in their articles "had a bad effect on morale and esprit de corps of the individual soldier and his regiment."[18]

As larger numbers of Negro units were deployed overseas, the Bureau of Public Relations co-operated with Negro newspapers in getting their war correspondents into the theaters. In 1943, the Bureau of Public Relations and the Civilian Aide encouraged thirteen papers to organize a pool of correspondents so that better coverage might be available to all from among the limited number of correspondents available.[19] By the end of the war, every major theater had been visited by at least one Negro war correspondent.

Films

Aiding the Bureau of Public Relations in its attempt to improve public and soldier attitudes through the news was the film, *The Negro Soldier*,[20] completed in the fall of 1943 and distributed in early 1944. This film was begun within the Special Service Division as one of a series of educational films designed to supplement the *Why We Fight* orientation films. As a pioneer venture in Army and film history, it received careful attention from a number of people. When Frank Capra sent the first complete script to General Osborn it had already had the benefit of a full memorandum on "Things to Do and Not to Do" by the division's consultant, Dr. Donald Young, and the skills of some of the best film and drama technicians.[21] The finished script, done by Jo Swirling and Ben Hecht, was, Capra felt, "far superior to anything we have had. Done with taste and repression, this may not only be an information picture, but may also serve as an emotional glorification of the Negro war effort."[22] It was just this emotional quality of the script that worried the Washington headquarters. "It is

[17] Ltr, TAG to CG's Major Comds, Theaters, Def Comds, Bases, 23 Jun 42, AG 291.21 (6–20–42) MB–BPR–M.

[18] Lt Col James L. Lewis, Notes on Service with the 93d Engineer Regiment (GS) in Extreme Cold and Wet Cold Climates, Engr School 8715.

[19] Memo, BPR for ASW, 25 Oct 43, and Memo, Civ Aide for ASW, 23 Oct 43, both in ASW 291.2 NT–Publicity.

[20] Film No. RF–51.

[21] Memo, Maj Capra, Chief Motion Picture Sec SSB, for Chief SSB, 30 Mar 42, and Ltr, Maj Samuel Griskin to Maj John B. Stanley, 16 Oct 42, both in SS 413.56 (7–12–41) (1) sec. II.

[22] Ltr, Col Capra (Los Angeles Br Office SSB) to Gen Osborn, 26 Aug 42, SPSP 413.56 (8–26–42).

undoubtedly a powerful script but the fact that it is, as you say in your letter, an emotional glorification of the Negro war effort," General Osborn replied to Capra, "puts it in a different class from the one we had intended and makes us very doubtful about showing it to troops without changes that would mean practically recasting the script." [23]

Dr. Young and Capt. Charles Dollard, analyzing the script from an audience reception angle, felt that it had been improved over an earlier version by the addition of a minister and mother as narrators. But, they pointed out, the new characters must be handled carefully:

The woman should not be a "mammy." Her race should be determinable only by her color; not by her dress or manner. The preacher might well be a relatively young man, typical of the new clergy of the cities. The emotional element in the situation should not be overstressed either in the language of the script or in the diction of the characters.

Much of the sermon and the soldier's letter was "just plain corny"; too often Negroes were reminded of the more bitter experiences of their past. The authors inadvertently "probe[d] at least one old wound on every page." Young and Dollard recommended that since the film was to be shown as "produced by the War Department" it was doubly important that the script adhere rigidly to fact, and that it avoid all reference, direct or indirect, calculated to remind Negroes of old grievances. [24]

After much discussion, the film went into production in January 1943. [25] Within the framework of a Negro church service, enabling the use of a choir with the minister's sermon as the connecting narrative thread, the film unfolded a chronicle of the Negro soldiers' participation in past American wars. Then, through the medium of a letter read by a proud mother in the congregation, it detailed the story of a Negro recruit, his training, and his rise to a second lieutenancy. The film was produced with a restraint and dignity previously rare in films on Negro subjects. Eventually, it was ordered shown to all troops "without special emphasis or introduction to the audience." [26]

Before the film was ordered shown to all personnel, it was previewed by two groups of soldiers, one white and one Negro, both so chosen as to be representative of the Negro and white Army populations. The film was well received by both Negro and white soldiers, with nine-tenths of the Negroes and two-thirds of the whites saying they "liked it very much." There was less than 10 percent difference between Northern and Southern white soldiers in the percentage liking the film. Most soldiers felt that the film gave an accurate picture of the Negro soldier, with less than three

---

[23] Ltr, Osborn to Capra, 2 Sep 42, SPSP 413.56 (8–26–42).

[24] Memo, Young and Dollard for Osborn, 1 Sep 42, SPSP 413.56 (8–26–42).

[25] Msg, Col Edward L. Munson, Jr., for Gen Osborn, 29 Aug 42; Msg, Gen Osborn to Col Munson, 2 Sep 42; Msg, Capra to Munson, 10 Sep 42; Ltr, Dep Dir SSB to Col Capra, Fox-Western Studio Br Office SSD, Los Angeles, 10 Sep 42, all in SPSPX 413.56 (9–10–42); Memo, ASW for Dir SSD SOS, 23 Jan 43, ASW 291.2 NT.

[26] WD Cir 208, 25 May 44, Sec III. The film produced unexpected queries when initially shown at Fort Huachuca; unwise introductions and discussions elsewhere were avoided after this admonition.

percent of the Negroes and five percent of the whites thinking the film mostly one-sided or untrue.[27] A short version of the film was made available in June 1944 for civilian exhibition.

Appearances of Negro soldiers in Army-produced films, except in glimpses, were rare until after the production of *The Negro Soldier*. Subsequent films, such as *Westward Is Bataan*,[28] paid greater attention to the role of Negro soldiers, especially service troops. The orientation film for Americans in Britain, *Welcome to Britain*,[29] contained a brief treatment of the difference between the British and American points of view about race. The Air Forces produced for the third anniversary of the Tuskegee Army Air Field a film, *Wings for This Man*,[30] recounting the achievements of that training school and its graduates. At the request of the theater, a producing team went to Europe in 1944 for a film on the Negro's part in the European offensive, released as *Teamwork*.[31] While not all of these ventures were unqualified successes, they were useful as morale and informational material for Negro and white soldiers and for the general public.

Instruction in Leadership

Taking advantage of materials newly collected by the Research Branch of the Special Service Division, the Advisory Committee sponsored in 1943 the publication of an unprecedented pamphlet intended to inspire improved leadership in Negro units and to inform officers in the field of the official War Department position on the employment of Negro troops. Such a statement had been urged from time to time in the Advisory Committee, whose members had felt that much of the difficulty experienced in Negro units was traceable to a lack of knowledge and to misinterpretation of War Department policies and points of view. The need for definitive information was pointed up by continuing requests from unit commanders and by the use, on certain posts, of unauthorized instructional materials culled from sources of varying reliability. The War Department pamphlet, issued as Command of Negro Troops,[32] was prepared in the Special Service Division and in the Joint Army-Navy Committee on Welfare and Recreation as one of a series on command policies.[33] The Special Service Division, in its manual for orientation officers, the Guide to the Use of Information Materials, in use since October 1942 as an office memorandum and distributed generally in December 1942,[34] had already set the tone for this publication

---

[27] "Reactions of Soldiers to the Film, *The Negro Soldier*," What the Soldier Thinks, No. 5, 25 Apr 44. But in some places, as at Hondo Field, Texas, it was felt that the film "did more harm than good. It was resented by many men. A less obvious, a less 'frontal' approach seems wiser. Such a judgment may be dismissed as 'pussy-footing' but it is not necessarily 'pussy-footing' to question the wisdom of irritating a prejudice by making a direct attack upon it." Hist Hondo AAF, 1 Sep–1 Nov 44, AF Archive 284.46–6.

[28] Film No. OF–27.

[29] Film No. GI–33.

[30] Film No. SFP–151.

[31] Film No. OF–14.

[32] WD Pamphlet 20–6, 29 Feb 44.

[33] Dr. Young and Major Dollard were primarily responsible for the preparation of this pamphlet. It served as a basis for the later Navy pamphlet, Guide to Command of Negro Naval Personnel, NAVPERS–15092, 12 Feb 45, prepared primarily by Dr. Young.

[34] A later revision was issued as WD Pamphlet 20–3, 10 Dec 43.

by declaring: "Problems of race are a proper concern of the Army only so far as they affect the efficiency of the Army, no more, no less," and "To contribute by act or word toward the increase of misunderstanding, suspicion, and tension between peoples of different racial or national origin in this country or among our Allies is to help the enemy." Though limitations to its concern were set, that the Army had a concern with "race" was freely admitted in a way which would have been impossible in 1940. The division's "Pocket Guides" and "Language Guides" for American troops in foreign countries were contributions to an understanding between soldiers and alien but friendly populations.

The pamphlet on the command of Negro troops recognized an equal or greater problem of understanding between soldiers of different races within the American Army and attempted to deal with it within the framework of military necessity. Though the preparation of the pamphlet on command was begun early in 1943, and though its first appearance was on 27 September of that year, it represented such a major departure from previous Army practice that its actual distribution to the field, after successive readings and many suggestions by members of the Advisory Committee and by other interested agencies, was delayed until early 1944. It was then distributed to all Army units containing Negroes and to their higher headquarters.

The pamphlet, divided into sections on Negro manpower and on problems of command, was intended "to help officers to command their troops more effectively by giving them information which will increase their understanding

of their men." [35] It stressed the fact that "Colored Americans, like all other Americans, have the right and duty to serve their country to the very best of their individual abilities" and that "the Army has the right and duty to see to it that its personnel of all races do so serve." [36] It examined the problem of Negro adjustment to the Army, comparing it with the adjustment problems of "a white soldier from California" as they differed from "a white soldier from Maine or Florida." While showing that the Negro population, on the average, had had inferior schooling, less skilled work experiences, and that "its role in the life of the Nation has been limited," it went on to counter stereotyped notions of Negroes by pointing out that "No statement beginning 'All Negroes' is true, just as no statement beginning 'All Frenchmen,' 'All Chinese,' or 'All Americans' is true." [37] Comparing the status of Negroes in World War I with progress made in World War II, it sought to reassure troop leaders of the potential value of their units.

The problems of low AGCT scores, classification and assignment, illiteracy, resentment on the part of Negro troops, and other sources of difficulty for Negroes and their commanders were discussed briefly and in simple language under such headings as "Know Your Men," "Good Soldiers Are Made, Not Born," "Little Expected, Little Gained," and "Negro Soldiers Are Americans." The pamphlet went specifically into the dangers of loose and offensive language, going farther than

---

[35] Command of Negro Troops, p. 1.
[36] *Ibid.*
[37] *Ibid.*, p. 2.

either General Davis or Judge Hastie had originally requested.   It advised:

Many people who do not mean to be insulting use terms, tell jokes, and do things which are traditionally interpreted by Negroes as derogatory.   Such words as "boy," "Negress," "darky," "uncle," "mammy," "aunty," and "nigger," are generally disliked by Negroes.   There is also dislike of the pronunciation of the word "Negro" as though it were spelled "Nigra," because it seems to be a sort of general compromise between the hated word "nigger" and the preferred term "Negro." Colored and Negro are the only words which should be used to distinguish colored soldiers from white. . . . It is difficult, if not impossible, to characterize all behavior which is resented by Negroes, but perhaps the simplest, if too general, way to express it is to say that troop morale will suffer if the words or acts of officers imply either racial hostility or a patronizing, condescending attitude.[38]

The burden of the text was that the commander of Negro troops was faced with no new problems but only with the task of extending "to a specific situation the teachings of everyday experience in the handling of men." [39]   To this end, a catechetical check list of fifteen points for commanders was appended to the pamphlet and included as well on an inserted, pocket sized card which the commander could remove and consult at any time.   This check list, suggested by Colonel Leonard, the Secretary of the McCloy committee, posed the following questions for the commander:

1. Have I made due allowances for any lack of educational opportunity in my men?
2. Have I made proper effort to teach my men skills they have not previously had opportunity to acquire?

3. Have I provided literary classes for those needing them?
4. Have I used words and phrases that my men cannot fully comprehend?
5. Have I taken great pains with AGCT IV's and V's to explain to them the consequences of AWOL and venereal diseases?
6. Have I provided the most intelligent and responsible soldiers with a good chance to earn promotion and to use their best abilities, even at the expense of having them transferred from my command?
7. Have I done or said things that might wound the sensibilities of my men?
8. Have I protected the rights of my men in their relations with the public?
9. Have I required of my troops soldierly discipline, appearance, and conduct in their relations with the public?
10. Have I provided my public relations officer with as many items as possible relating to commendable performances by my outfit and individual soldiers in it?
11. Have I exacted the highest degree of discipline, care of equipment, care of grounds and buildings, etc., while making allowances for limitations on ability to perform where lack of education and mechanical skills may be a handicap?
12. Have I given my organization the opportunity to acquire pride and confidence in itself by giving it missions for which my men show superior qualifications?
13. Have I excused my own shortcomings as a commander by attributing inadequate training to lack of ability on the part of my command instead of to my own failure to correct shortcomings?
14. Have I constantly kept before my men the reasons why we fight?
15. Have I subordinated all else to my duties as a commander, and have my men been brought to realize the paramount place of the war effort?

The most elaborate of the intracultural educational media designed to aid training and diminish disciplinary and attitude problems was Leadership and the Negro Soldier, begun at the end of 1943 and issued as ASF Manual M–5 in

[38] *Ibid.*, p. 11.
[39] *Ibid.*, p. 10.

October 1944. This document was prepared at the request of Army Service Forces' Military Training Division for use as a course text in ASF officer candidate and officers' schools. It was especially desired by the Transportation Corps, which was then receiving large numbers of officers by transfer from overstaffed branches like antiaircraft artillery for whom retraining materials preparatory to their duty with Negro troops were needed. The manual came equipped with tests and questionnaires for classroom use. For a ten-hour course, each of its eight chapters was to provide "the main substance" of a one-hour lecture; another hour was to be devoted to a showing of the film, *The Negro Soldier*, and another to a discussion of the pamphlet, Command of Negro Troops. A digest of state and federal laws of importance to Negro troop commanders and a list of readily available reading materials were appended. Officers and civilians within the Army and in other agencies whose primary work was concerned with minority relations in the military or in the general cultural life of the nation were requested to prepare drafts of chapters dealing with aspects of the Negro soldier which they were especially fitted to discuss.[40]

The manual, essentially a more detailed extension of Command of Negro Troops, was intended to give a general description of Negro life in America as it affected military service and command. In addition to its use in ASF schools, the manual was distributed to each company of Negro troops in ASF, to all orientation officers, and to any requesting agency or unit of the other major commands. "The issue is not whether the Negro will be used in the War," the foreword to the manual pointed out, "it is how effectively he will be used. This question cannot be evaded. Furthermore, it cannot be met successfully by uninformed judgments on the basis of civilian associations and personal views on the subject. The problems involved are as technical as any other problem of personnel, and can be solved only with the benefit of special study, full information, and a serious interest in their resolution."

These instruments of deeper understanding and of a more serious application of principles of command to special problems in which too few of the Army's officers were well-grounded were warrants of the Army's determination to assure the maximum and most effective use of all manpower. That they came so late in the war was regrettable, but unavoidable. There was still a residual fear that the Army's efforts in this direction might be misinterpreted and that they might create new problems by focusing attention upon old ones. "It is essential that there be a clear understanding" Manual M–5 therefore warned, "that the Army has no authority or intention to participate in social reform as such but does view the problem as a matter of efficient troop utilization."

Concern over the possible misinterpretation of the purpose of this and similar materials was real. A clear statement of purpose disavowing any other intent that might have been implied was necessary to avoid public controversy of the

---

[40] The planning and execution of this document was also under the direction of Dr. Young, again with the assistance of members of the Research Branch, Morale Service Division, and of his associates in the JANCWR.

sort which, during the period of distribution of command of Negro Troops and preparation of Manual M–5, centered about the proposed use of another pamphlet by the Army. In January 1944, the Orientation Branch, Morale Services Division, ASF, ordered 55,000 copies of *The Races of Mankind,* prepared for the Public Affairs Committee, a private educational organization, by Professor Ruth Benedict and Dr. Gene Weltfish of the Department of Anthropology of Columbia University, The pamphlet was intended for distribution in kits supplied to information and education officers and to orientation centers. It was selected, the branch explained, for "adequacy of content and simplicity of statement of the essential facts regarding races." It was to be used as an aid in refuting Nazi "master race" theories.

Before the pamphlet could be delivered to and distributed by the Army, it had become a subject of public controversy involving two civilian service organizations. United Service Organizations barred the pamphlet from its service centers as promoting special interests, whereupon the Congress of Industrial Organizations' War Relief Committee, calling it "one of the best answers to Hitler's Aryan creed," announced that it would mail the pamphlet to all servicemen on its lists. Argument for and against the pamphlet became entangled in the domestic race issue, especially in relation to the quotation of World War I Alpha test scores of Northern Negroes and Southern whites cited to show the influence of environment and education upon mental test results. When the Army's purchase of the pamphlet became known, press comments upon the purchase, both pro

and con, were widespread, despite the fact that the Orientation Branch, by 29 February, had decided not to use the pamphlet. The House of Representatives Committee on Military Affairs became interested. On 26 April its special subcommittee investigating the distribution of publications to Army personnel released a report concluding that "The committee is convinced that wartime is no time to engage in the publication and distribution of pamphlets presenting controversial issues or promoting propaganda for or against any subdivision of the American people." [41] The sponsors of Army materials giving a background in racial and minority matters wished to precipitate no similar controversy over their instructional material.

Two other attempts to improve leadership through providing instructional materials, both of them in the same area and both of them illustrative of the possibilities for misunderstanding inherent in all save the most carefully prepared materials, were made at the War Department and branch levels. One misfired and the other never went off.

Disturbed by the mixed effect of chaplains on leadership and morale in Negro units as reported both by senior chap-

---

[41] Memo for Ch, Fiscal Br, MSD, 24 Jan 44, SPMSO 352.11 (24 Jan 44); Memo, MSD for Sp Asst to SW, 12 Feb 44, SPMSO 353.11 (Feb 44); Washington *Evening Star,* March 5, 1944; Memo, Programs Sec, Orientation Br, for Br Ch, 29 Feb 44, TI&E files; Washington *Post,* March 5, March 8, April 28, 1944; St. Louis *Post-Dispatch,* March 7, 1944; N.Y. *Times,* March 8, 1944; Washington *Daily News,* April 27, 1944; *The Detroit News,* April 28, 1944; Memo, Actg Dir MSD for O–in–C, Orientation Br, 10 Mar 44, SPMSO 352.11 (10 Mar 44); Inv of the National War Efforts, Rpt, Com on Mil Affs, 78th Cong., 2d Sess, pursuant to HR 30, April 26, 1944.

lains and by field commanders, the Chief of Chaplains, "in the hope that a careful reading will help toward a more harmonious relationship," reproduced and circulated to all Negro chaplains, their commanders, and to the Chaplain School copies of a letter on leadership sent by a Negro chaplain to Chaplain Arnold. The letter had been received during the discussions of reducing the standards for Negro chaplains to help overcome the shortage of applicants for the chaplaincy.[42] It had been proposed for publication to Negro chaplains at the time, but it did not appear until just after the National Baptists had discussed in bitter terms the problems of Negro chaplains. The letter read in part:

> . . . It is with extreme regret that I contemplate the recent difficulties experienced by some Negro Chaplains, resulting in Court Martial. Much material is available from which a Chaplain may glean information and instruction, but there is little or nothing designed to counsel the new Negro Chaplain in his unique task. Many habits of thought and speech, customary to the newly commissioned colored minister, must be re-thought and adjusted to Army Service. Success in the parish ministry is not a guarantee of success in the Chaplaincy. This is especially true of the successful Negro ministry. For instance, the 'rabble-rousing' success of most successful colored ministers will always be disastrous, when used, in military service. This technique, while effective in the parish, is at basis undisciplined and therein we find its inefficacy for a useful Chaplain. I say "useful" Chaplain because utility is the objective of the successful Chaplain; Utility for the good of the service. Religion in the Army is designed I believe to make its contribution towards the creation and maintaining of a victorious Christian Army. There is a time and place for the Chaplain to make his

contribution toward the controversial aspects of Labor, Politics and even Race, but that time and place is not the time of war; not in the service. Unless the new Chaplain is acquainted early in his career, with these truisms, he will sooner or later run afoul Army regulations.

. . . .

> The Race Problem and Race Leadership are naturally a part of the Negro minister's responsibility. In many communities he is the focal point for adjustment and intercourse. Unless he is apprised differently early in his career, the colored Chaplain is apt to imagine himself the Protector of his troops from the expected injustice of their white officers. This attitude is probably at the root of the difficulties, recently experienced by some Negro Chaplains. It is an attitude guaranteed fatal to the success of the Negro Chaplain's work. With it, he can never be a good Chaplain in terms of usefulness to both officers and enlisted men. He thereby alienates the officers, some of whom need and would request his counsel and ministry. Again, he lays himself open to the charge of Complaint-monger, and will find himself with little time to devote to the soldier-consultant who has a perfect record but who still needs the religious advice and counsel of his Chaplain.

. . . .

> Very often when dealing with colored troops, a white officer's disciplinary rulings may be construed as prejudicial. The Negro Chaplain may immediately conclude that Racial prejudice is being practiced. This may be the case, but unless it is undeniably true, admittedly true or can be explained in no other way it should not be so charged. In other words, "for the good of the Service" Race prejudice is never present unless without the shadow of a doubt. If a Chaplain will only consider the matter objectively he will realize that it is very difficult in all cases, and impossible in most, to distinguish between racial prejudice and the many other types of prejudice with which ordinary human relations abound. Again, if the Chaplain is not careful he will sometime find himself ap-

---

[42] See above, p. 230.

pealing for Race prejudice, when an un-prejudiced judgment would harm some man he is trying to aid. At any rate the technique of deferred judgment as concerns racial prejudice will not only react to the advantage of the enlisted men involved but it will give the officer concerned the benefit of the doubt to which he is entitled. Loose talking and thinking in these matters is detrimental to the morale of the unit and will eventually weaken the Chaplain with officers and thoughtful enlisted men alike. Lousy and indifferent soldiers, of which every unit has its fair share, will charge all their misfortunes to Race prejudice; the Chaplain will be tempted to do the same. One day he will find himself a questionable champion of his Race, but an unquestion-able failure as a chaplain. . . .[43]

Reactions from chaplains ranged from "I am in hearty accord with spirit of the letter. . ." to "Careful reading of this letter many times to be certain of avoid-ing misunderstanding causes me to re-gret deeply that any man of God, Negro or otherwise, should feel justified in making some of the statements and ob-servations therein." Some chaplains felt that they would have benefitted had such a statement been available earlier in their careers. Some disliked the im-plication that many successful civilian ministers were "rabble-rousers." Some thought there was overemphasis on fail-ures which might form the basis for "dubious and widespread generaliza-tion."[44] Most respondents were trou-bled by the implications of the letter's comments on chaplains and racial fric-tion. "I can not close my eyes to what I feel to be a truth upon the assumption that 'race prejudice is never present un-less without a shadow of a doubt,' " one chaplain wrote.[45] And another felt that: "The writer of that letter is certainly an impractical or an inexperienced chap-lain. The chaplain who fails to combat these [discriminatory] practices is not worthy to carry the CROSS."[46]

In reply to the more troubled chap-lains, the Office of the Chief of Chap-lains expressed sentiments such as: "No two men agree fully on any subject, especially the race question. Anyway, the problem exists and it behooves each negro and white chaplain to recognize its breadth and depth and act in the Christian spirit to alleviate as much of the tension as possible . . . ."[47] To a chaplain who objected to the indorse-ment of the letter by the Chief of Chaplain's Office, the reply went: "You are advised that this office did not in-dorse all the statements and terms used in the letter sent to all Negro chaplains and their commanding officers. It was believed that the letter contained sound counsel and would be suggestive reading for all concerned. The response from Negro chaplains has proven the wisdom of this judgment."[48]

The Advisory Group of Church Rep-resentatives of the Joint Army and Navy Committee on Welfare and Recreation, headed by Charles P. Taft, determined after this episode to give its attention to the problem of the chaplaincy and its relation to the Army's racial problems.

---

[43] Ltr, Chap (Capt) A. L. Smith, 97th Engr Gen Sv Regt, to Brig Gen William H. Arnold, CofChaps, 31 Jul 43; Incl to Ltr, CofChaps to all Negro Chaps, CO's, Units to which Negro Chaps are assigned, Negro Chap Students, Chaplain School, 24 Sep 43, SPCHT 211 Chaps Negro (16 Sep 43).
[44] Ltrs and extracts from letters of Negro chap-lains, in CofChaps 211 Negro Chaps (2, 6 Oct and 29 Dec 43) .

[45] Ibid., 16 Nov 43.
[46] Ibid., 17 Nov 43.
[47] Ltr, Chap Frederick W. Hagan to Chaplain——, 17 Nov 43.
[48] Ltr, Hagan to Chaplain——, 26 Nov 43.

In the winter and spring of 1944 a subcommittee of this group[49] prepared a manuscript, The Chaplain and the Negro in the Armed Services. It was primarily a reworking of the material in the War Department pamphlet, Command of Negro Troops, with the addition of materials on the religious background of Negro soldiers and specific suggestions on the aid which both white and Negro chaplains might give to commands and to soldiers in problems of racial relationships. After committee discussions with members of the Chief of Chaplain's staff, who were at first disposed to co-operate in its preparation,[50] the manuscript was presented to the Advisory Group of Church Representatives in July. The Advisory Group voted unanimously to transmit it to the Chiefs of Chaplains of both Army and Navy after suggested changes were incorporated. Chaplain Arnold suggested at this meeting that copies be sent by his office to senior chaplains for comments before presentation to the War Department. The manuscript was transmitted to the Chief of Chaplains on 4 September,[51] the same day that Maj. Gen. Stephen G. Henry, the new G–1, urged in the General Council that all staff divisions handling matters of racial

relationships co-ordinate their efforts with all other interested agencies.[52] Acting upon an extracted reminder from the Director of Personnel, ASF,[53] the Chief of Chaplains thereupon forwarded the manuscript asking if the proposed review procedure was in harmony with this policy.[54]

The Director of Personnel, ASF, then forwarded the manuscript to G–1, concurring in the proposal that it be circulated among experienced white and Negro chaplains for review and that its revision be submitted by the Chief of Chaplains through G–1 to the Advisory Committee on Negro Troop Policies for final approval.[55] But G–1 determined that "The general tone of the proposed publication is one bordering upon effecting social readjustment," and believed that "publication of this manuscript would be subject to misinterpretation by agitators on both sides of our national racial problem. The War Department has consistently held that it is not a medium to effect social reforms." With the concurrence of Chaplain Arnold, it recommended both against publication and against circulation to Negro and white chaplains for review and comment.[56] Despite Truman Gibson's objections that the reading in G–1 must have been superficial to merit such a conclusion—he pointed out as an example that the manuscript's statement that "the Negro is just another man" bore the penciled marginal query "social

---

[49] Dean William Stuart Nelson, Howard University School of Religion, chairman; Roswell P. Barnes, Federal Council of Churches of Christ in America; Bishop Richard R. Wright, Jr., Wilberforce University; Rev. Harold M. Kingsley, Good Shepherd Congregational Church, Chicago; Rev. John LaFarge, editor of America; with Truman K. Gibson and Donald Young as ex officio members. The committee was divided between Negroes and whites with most major branches of the church represented.
[50] Cf., Ltr, CofChaps to Dean Nelson, 18 Jan 44, SPCHI 211 N.C.
[51] Ltr, Charles P. Taft, JANCWR, to Gen Arnold, 4 Sep 44, ASW 291.2 NTC (Separate Envelope).

[52] Min of Gen Council, 4 Sep 44.
[53] Memo, Dir Pers ASF, 5 Sep 44, SPAP 291.2.
[54] Ltr, CofChaps to Dir Pers ASF, 9 Sep 44, SPCHG 291.2 Negro (5 Sep 44).
[55] 1st Ind to Ltr cited n. 54, Dir Pers ASF to G–1, 11 Sep 44, SPAP 291.2 (9 Sep 44).
[56] DF, G–1 to Adv Com (thru OCS), 18 Sep 44, WDGAP/291.2.

equality?" and that an examination of the underscored sections indicated that the reader of the manuscript believed that "the matter of race in the Army should not be discussed at all"—the pamphlet was held in the Advisory Committee where action upon it was deferred.[57] Partly because the Advisory Committee held few meetings for the remainder of 1944 and partly because the using service was by now no more enthusiastic about it than G–1, the manuscript was filed without action and without further revisions. Other than the letter on their responsibilities—a letter which the Chief of Chaplain's Office denied endorsing fully—and materials prepared for line officers, chaplains received no specific instructions on the role they should play in the leadership of Negro troops.

New Instructions on Facilities

Most members of the Advisory Committee thought that the directive of 10 March 1943 had clearly defined policy on the use of post facilities by all troops. This directive forbade the designation of facilities by race but it permitted their allocation to units provided that all personnel and all units were given equal opportunity to use them. Reports from inspectors and from commanders in the next few months indicated that there was still a lack of information on how the War Department intended this policy to operate with regard to specific facilities, such as post exchanges.[58] Dur-

ing a discussion of the problem, Secretary McCloy asked the members of his committee if another order should be issued, whereupon Maj. Gen. Miller G. White, the G–1, suggested that existing instructions be rewritten instead. No exchange could refuse to serve any soldier but the instructions had not made this clear. McCloy therefore asked that a clarification of the 1943 directive be prepared by General White and that, if necessary, a new one be written and distributed. The Inspector General was requested to add a report on discrimination in the use of facilities to his routine inspections. Truman Gibson later requested that special emphasis be placed on the use of exchanges, transportation, and Army motion picture theaters, for it was around these facilities that most reported difficulties had arisen.

The new letter, supplementary to that of March 1943, outlined specific requirements:

3. *Exchanges.*—While exchanges and branch exchanges may be allocated to serve specific areas or units, no exchange will be designated for the exclusive use of any particular race. Where such branch exchanges are established, personnel will not be restricted to the use of their area or unit exchanges but will be permitted to use any other exchange on the post, camp, or station.

4. *Transportation.*—Buses, trucks or other transportation owned and operated either by the Government or by a governmental instrumentality will be available to all military personnel regardless of race. Restricting personnel to certain sections of such transportation because of race will not be permitted either on or off post, camp, or station, regardless of local civilian custom.

5. *Army Motion Picture Theaters.*—Army motion picture theaters may be allocated to serve certain areas or units but no theater or performance in any theater will be de-

---

[57] Memo, ASW for Col Leonard, 29 Sep 44, ASW 291.2 NTC (Separate Envelope).

[58] Discussion, Advisory Com, 4 Jan 44, ASW 291.2 NTC; Memo and Incls, Civ Aide to ASW, 24 Jan 44, no sub, ASW 291.2 NT–Pub. See ch. XI, above.

nied to any group or individual because of race.

6. Effective compliance with War Department policies enunciated herein will be obtained through inspection by responsible commanders and inspectors general. Each inspector general will be directed that if, during a periodic inspection [of] a post, camp, or station, he discovers evidence of racial discrimination or indirect violation of War Department policies on this subject, he will inform the commanding officer of the installation that such discrimination is contrary to War Department policy. If subsequent inspection of the installation indicates that proper remedial measures have not been taken, the commanding general of the service command will initiate action to insure full compliance with the announced policy.[59]

This directive did not immediately affect all of the enumerated services at all posts but, as subsequent inspections by service commands and Army Service Forces headquarters showed, it gradually dispelled tensions on posts where restrictions of movement had been a constant threat to good order. The directive was generally distributed to the lowest echelons by late summer. It was not generally reproduced for troops on posts, although some posts published it in daily bulletins. But the press, and particularly the Negro press, had long since announced the fact of its issuance, and, eventually, printed copies of the order itself. "Extra! U.S. Army Bans Jim Crow in PX's, Buses and Theaters," one paper headlined its story.[60] Another captioned an editorial: "Four Years Late." Subsequently it published the full text of the directive itself, under the first page headline, "Here It is!" [61] With the directive readily available in the more widely circulated Negro papers, it was not long before most Negro soldiers knew of its existence.

Some commanders and some governors and congressmen of Southern states were disturbed over the intent and effect of the directive. Replies to inquiries clarified War Department policy as much as the new letter. Replying to a protest of Governor Chauncey Sparks of Alabama that the new directive would break down segregation in the South, Acting Secretary Robert P. Patterson restated the War Department's views:

There has been no change in the War Department's practice concerning segregation of races. The most recent publication is a letter of July 8th which reiterates a previously announced policy and enjoins compliance therewith. I presume that the notice mentioned in your telegram stating that the War Department has ordered the termination of race segregation refers to this letter.

The War Department has maintained throughout the emergency and present war that it is not an appropriate medium for effecting social readjustments but has insisted that all soldiers, regardless of race, be afforded equal opportunity to enjoy the recreational facilities which are provided at posts, camps and stations. The thought has been that men who are fulfilling the same obligations, suffering the same dislocation of their private lives, and wearing the identical uniform should, within the confines of the military establishment, have the same privileges for rest and relaxation.

I appreciate greatly your interest in this problem but I am sure you will understand the War Department's viewpoints in reference to it.[62]

---

[59] Ltr, TAG to CG's AAF, All Sv Comds, MDW, 8 Jul 44, AG 353.8 (5 Jul 44) OB–S–A–M, based on DF, G–1 for TAG, 5 Jul 44, WDGAP/291.2 (29 Jun 44).

[60] Baltimore Afro-American, August 5, 1944.

[61] Editorial, Pittsburgh Courier, August 19, 1944; article, September 2, 1944.

[62] Ltr, Actg SW to Sparks, 1 Sep 44, WDCSA 291.2 (26 Aug 44).

While the point of view that within the military reservation standard treatment of all soldiers was to prevail was not included in any official War Department statements to the field, the new interpretation that racial separation applied to units only and not to other activities became standard within the higher levels of the War Department. Subsequent answers to similar inquiries on the same directive were based on this letter.[63] General Marshall's redrafted version added another slant: "Occasionally it is necessary to reiterate former announcements, as was done in this instance, in order to admonish those who may not be diligently complying with a prior order." Continuing, he observed: "It is unfortunate that this directive has been publicized as setting forth a new War Department racial policy, and I see no justification for such publicity. The intent of the War Department was to insure continued fair treatment of all military personnel in the use of recreational facilities at military reservations and in the use of government transportation." [64] Secretary Stimson, in answering the reply of one of the protesting congressmen who had already received the War Department's interpretation, reiterated this viewpoint and distinguished between interference with local customs and the conduct of affairs within the Military Establish-

men.[65] Thus the new letter, through these interpretations, provided for the first time a clear distinction between Army racial policies to be applied on federal military reservations and local civilian laws and customs to be observed by members of the Military Establishment when off-post.

Most posts gradually adapted themselves to the specific instructions of the letter on facilities. Post facilities could still be designated for specific units or areas, but no facility could now be designated exclusively for specific units or areas. For the most part the new clarification of the use of facilities was adopted in whole or in significant part, although examples of evasion and indirect discouragement continued to be found by inspectors. A few months after the issuance of the directive, Colonel Leonard, the secretary of the Advisory Committee, observed that:

It was significant that the recent War Department letter on this subject was interpreted by both white and colored personnel as a radical change in policy. Commanding officers believed it necessary that conferences be held for the organizations of the command to explain the meaning of this letter, and many colored soldiers believed that all local instructions on these subjects were rescinded.

Bus transportation in general has been improved, due in part to the reduction of personnel at many camps. However, at some camps, as at Camp Claiborne, bus transportation is still considered unsatisfactory by colored personnel. Continuous study of this subject is necessary by camp authorities to insure fair treatment to all.

The principal difficulties at Post Exchanges had to do with restaurant service,

---

[63] See, for examples, Ltr, SW to Congressman A. Leonard Allen, 7 Sep 44, WDCSA 291.2 Negroes (1 Sep 44); Ltr, SW to Hon. Thomas L. Bailey, Governor of Miss., 8 Sep 44, WDCSA 291.2 Negroes (30 Aug 44); Ltr, SW to Congressman John Newsome, WDCSA 291.2 Negroes (26 Aug 44); also many similar letters in same file.

[64] Ltr, Marshall to Governor Spessard L. Holland of Florida, 9 Sep 44, WDCSA 291.2 Negroes (2 Sep 44).

[65] Ltr, SW to Representative A. Leonard Allen of Louisiana, 20 Sep 44, WDCSA 291.2 Negroes (13 Sep 44).

particularly for civilian patrons, and also white attendants objected to serving Negro personnel. These difficulties have been satisfactorily arranged.

At several camps, there was objection to any separation at theaters, particularly by the Air Force personnel at Fort Knox and at Walterboro Air Base. At Fort Knox the Commanding Officer believes it for the best interest to all to separate theater audiences into four groups as follows: officers, both white and colored; soldiers accompanied by women; unaccompanied white soldiers; and unaccompanied colored soldiers. At Walterboro Air Base colored personnel refused to attend theaters until the orders requiring separation were withdrawn.

Camps have become adjusted to the above-mentioned letter and no further trouble is anticipated.[66]

The fact that anyone could use any facility was enough to turn the tide of Negro soldiers' morale upward on many posts. Men often continued to use the exchanges and theaters in their own areas—they were closest—but they now had less reason to resent the existence of facilities which were no longer forbidden territory. On some posts, facilities were so arranged that it was less convenient for Negroes to use any others than those which had formerly been specifically designated for them. At Fort Bragg, North Carolina, by late 1944 it was reported:

No racial discrimination is practiced although there is a general tendency for the units made up of Negro soldiers to use the facilities most convenient to them. This, however, is due to personal desire and convenience: All soldiers are permitted to use any post theater, exchange, or other facilities. . . . No discrimination or segregation is practiced. Negroes may ride on any bus and occupy any seat on the intra-camp of

[or] Fort Bragg-Fayetteville service. However, to expedite service specified buses are assigned runs to designated areas and of the twenty-three (23) buses regularly assigned seven (7) operate direct to the colored area. Of the thirty-two (32) regularly assigned schedules, five (5) are scheduled to the colored area. . . .[67]

At Fort Lewis, Washington, which had been sloughing off the visible signs of discrimination for many months, conscious efforts to avoid any semblance of segregation were obvious by the end of the year. In the Engineer Training Section of the Army Service Forces Training Center, where most Negro troops were then located, Negroes freely used the main exchange and theater adjacent to headquarters as well as those located in their units' areas. Championship athletic teams were organized from all Engineer unit teams to play the Medical Section for Training Center championships. A show, *The Sons of Bridges,* with a mixed cast and two orchestras, one white and one Negro, was produced. Minor altercations, of no serious consequence and of no racial significance, occurred but they were quickly controlled. "The best indication of the relationship between white and Negro troops stationed here," one observer wrote, "is evidenced by daily observation of mixed groups walking to and from the bus station." [68] Several months later the same observer, on a return trip, noted:

Racial relationship continues to be very good at Fort Lewis. No discrimination was observed either on the post or in Tacoma and Seattle. Adequate Theatres, Post Ex-

[66] Memo, Col Leonard for ASW, 3 Oct 44, ASW 291.2. See also ASF Rpt, Racial Situation in the United States, 31 Aug 44, SPINT 291.2.

[67] Memo, Col John Nash for CG ASF, 8 Nov 44, ASF DCofS File 291.2.

[68] Ltr, Maj Charles H. Flourney to CofE, 5 Dec 44, Ft. Lewis, Wash., OCE 291.2.

changes, Chapels and Service Clubs are available in the areas occupied by Negro troops; however, negro troops were observed in other Theaters and Exchanges. The general attitude is to consider them as other soldiers. . . .[69]

Though Fort Lewis received men with no better AGCT scores and civilian training than other centers and though an acute officer and instructor shortage existed there, training as well as morale were better than average: Of 1,111 Negro enlisted students enrolled in eight specialist courses, 987 or 88.8 percent satisfactorily completed their courses. Both the AWOL and the courts-martial rates for Negro troops were lower than for white troops. Of the substandard men marked for discharge processing (1,010 in November, 60 percent of them Negro) a number were returned to basic military training. One such group of 108 men was organized into a separate company with three platoons of three squads each; results were "exceptionally" good. With small squads and platoons, more individual attention could be given: thirty-six of these men went quickly into regular training units; a few were court-martialed and discharged; and the rest were retained for the completion of basic training. Officer attitudes encountered were also exceptional: "None of the officers questioned had any objections to serving with Negro troops. In fact the majority expressed their surprise that such duty was not as 'bad' as they had anticipated." [70]

---

[69] Ltr, Maj Flourney to CofE, 26 May 45, OCE 291.2.

[70] *Ibid.* Negro orientation and special services officers and Negro officers from converted medical sanitary and chemical units were assigned to the center; most Engineer officers were white.

At a number of other stations adjustment to the new directive in word and spirit was a longer process. Some camps moved the office of the exchange officer to what had been a Negro exchange, designating it the main camp exchange and transforming the main exchange into a unit or area exchange; others, after ordering all personnel to obey the directions of attendants, experimented with instructions that ushers in theaters or field houses and attendants in bowling alleys were to direct Negro patrons to specified seat locations or aisles; at still other camps word of their new privileges was assiduously kept from Negro troops. But at most posts the new directive, for all practical purposes, removed a chief bone of racial contention. Where, because of area distances or other factors, it made no marked difference in the habits of enlisted men, Negro or white, the directive nevertheless assured Negro soldiers that, in principle, the War Department had endorsed its oft-repeated assertion that all soldiers were treated alike in the eyes of the Army. This knowledge raised morale higher in many units than the construction of the most elaborate service club or exchange had achieved in many another instance.

Developments in ASF

Complementing these efforts was the development, within Army Service Forces, of a system of periodic inspections and recommendations by teams of officers. After mid-1944 Army Service Forces had control of most Negro troops within the continental United States either through their assignment to ASF units or to posts under ASF control. In

October 1944 the command devised a system making its major staff divisions directly responsible for particular activities connected with the training and use of Negro troops. Though racial relations "in general" were much better on most posts than complaints to the War Department would indicate,[71] to keep them good at posts where they had been good all along, to obtain lessons from these posts which could be applied elsewhere, and to improve conditions in areas where long-standing reputations for difficulties simply built new problems were major functions of the ASF observation teams.

ASF's Deputy Chief of Staff for Service Commands was charged with co-ordinating all policies and programs affecting Negro troops and of co-ordinating ASF policies with those of the General Staff and of the Ground and Air Forces. The Director of Plans and Operations was to expedite the movement of troops overseas and, where possible, shift a portion of the troops from Southern to Northern camps near cities with sizable Negro populations, at the same time holding conversions of existing Negro units to a minimum. The Director of Personnel was to concentrate on improving leadership in Negro units and to increase the preparation and use of orientation and recreational facilities for Negroes on posts. The Director of Military Training was to designate an officer to make frequent inspection visits on Negro training as well as distribute special instruc-

tional material. All staff agencies were to maintain at least one officer to whom racial problems could be referred. Inspection teams, composed of representatives of each of the major ASF agencies, were to make frequent trips to ASF installations.[72] Colonel Leonard, previously secretary of the Advisory Committee, became the officer in charge of co-ordination in the Office of the Deputy Chief of Staff for Service Commands. The field observation committee, known as the Leonard Committee, made intensive surveys of the larger and more critical posts and areas, making some recommendations on the spot and keeping a close check on general trends in racial matters as they affected training and morale. The work of this committee produced notable results where its recommendations were followed, but its organization so late in the war gave it a scant year of intensive activity.[73]

By this time a majority of the Army's troop strength was overseas[74] and the domestic scene, while retaining importance, was of less general concern in the employment of Negro troops. Ground Forces training stations were progressively closing. For better training and supervision, small service units were concentrated in Army Service Forces Train-

---

[71] Colonel Leonard, surveying several posts in August and September 1944 found that morale ranged from excellent at Keesler Field, Mississippi, and Fort Benning, Georgia, to poor at Camp Claiborne, Louisiana, Godman Field, Kentucky, and Walterboro Army Air Base, South Carolina. SPTR 291.2 (3 Oct 44).

[72] Memo, CofS ASF for DCofS for Sv Comds, Dir of Plans and Opns, Dir of Pers, Dir of Mil Tng, 16 Oct 44, ASF DCofS 291.2.

[73] Reports of the committee on its visits to camps and stations are in ASF DCofS 291.2 and in files of each of the member agencies. They have been cited frequently in the text of this volume.

[74] On 31 March 1945, at about the median point in this committee's activities, 5,404,000 or 66.2 percent of Army strength (8,157,386) was overseas or en route. Included in this figure was 503,998 or 72.6 percent of the Army's 694,333 Negroes. ASF Monthly Prog Rpt, sec. 6B, 31 Mar 45; *Strength of the Army*, STM-30, 1 Jan 46.

ing Centers by type.[75] Air Forces stations, generally operating under manning tables with their aviation squadrons absorbed in one or another section of the new base units, were tending, in the face of manpower shortages, to use Negro soldiers according to individual qualification and according to the stations' needs.

At the Richmond Army Air Base in 1945, for example, men of "C" Squadron, the former aviation squadron, were assigned to the motor pool as drivers, mechanics, and general duty men, and were used as cleaners, special vehicle operators, and special purpose operators in refueling, escorting, and parking planes. "And we have good success with our boys on the line," the squadron commander indicated. The field's supervisor of aircraft maintenance and supply reported that on the flight line "They are fair. They are a little bit slow, but that's only natural." [76]

The Leonard Committee's visits revealed a generally increasing awareness of the nature of its problems among higher commanders and among white and Negro junior officers. It found that the War Department's efforts were paying dividends in better discipline and training. It found many an officer whose views generally coincided with those of one commander who, remarking on the subject of improving racial relations within the Army, declared of Negro troops:

The only thing I try to do deliberately is to try very much to impress them with the idea that there is no possible discrimination here and that we are always fair. We allow them to go anywhere on the post. They are told that, and after the invariable few days in which they always go from place to place to see if we really mean it, they keep fairly well to themselves and behave quite well. I always inculcate in every new officer that he must not refer or even think about a Negro "problem" or "situation"; and to always think of and act toward them as soldiers among other soldiers. If they misbehave they are punished promptly and exactly the same as a white soldier for the same offense. We try to bestow somewhat more praise and encouragement among them than among the whites as they react well to it and need it more than the whites. One thing we never do is to "study" them as though they were something special, nor do we make any special effort to "understand" them. Normally they do not want to be "studied, understood nor uplifted." If they get the idea that you look on them as a "PROBLEM" they immediately try to qualify for it. If you treat them normally and casually they do not tend to get such an idea. . . .[77]

None of these efforts, despite their salutary effect upon the morale of Negro soldiers and upon relations between Negro and white soldiers, served of themselves to correct the major problems which the Army was facing in the employment of Negro troops. Unfortunately, by the time most of the new

[75] Accounts of training at these centers may be found in each service's installments in the serial History of Training ASF in MS OCMH.

[76] Interv, Hist Off (1st Lt Dorothy Pyle) with Capt George C. Philbrick, CO C Sq, 120th AAFBU, Richmond AAB; Interv, same, with Maj Maurice Dyer, Supervisor for Aircraft Maint and Sup, Richmond AAB; Interv, same, with Lt Col John H. Hunter, Dir of Pers and Adm, Richmond AAB, all in Fifth Installment, "Hist . . . Richmond (Va.) AAB, Apr–8 Aug 45," app. 10, 12 AF Archive 287.97-5.

[77] Brig Gen Horace L. Whittaker, ASFTC Ft. Francis E. Warren, Wyo., 20 Feb 45, Incl to Memo, ASF for members of committee formed under directive Hq ASF, dated 16 Oct 44, ASF DCofS SvC 291.2.

policies became effective the bulk of Negro units, including the large combat units, were already formed, trained, and moulded under circumstances considerably less favorable to their fullest employment. It was in the nature of America's preparation for war that this should be so, for until the problems presented themselves there was no machinery for remedying them. Nevertheless, all of the correctives of the later war years showed a greater awareness of the country's stake in the adequate use of available manpower and all of them helped create a better atmosphere for the employment of Negro troops. As guarantees of War Department support for commanders who sought to increase the morale and motivation of their men, and as guides to useful techniques in training and in the amelioration of petty frictions, as well as more serious disturbances, they were valuable to unit and higher commanders. That they did not entirely prevent future problems did not diminish their usefulness. They were additional steps toward the objective of preparing Negro units for the main business at hand—movement overseas and the further prosecution of the war.

CHAPTER XIV

Manpower and Readjustments

"A war is a confusing thing," Maj. Gen. Lewis B. Hershey, director of Selective Service, reminded the Senate Military Affairs Committee in 1943 in answer to a query about the "confusion" caused by his agency's multitudinous changes in its directions to local draft boards.[1] People who were dealing with manpower needs and allocations in 1943 agreed with him. With the major offensive of the war—the invasion of the European continent—still an uncertain number of months off, the conservation and use of manpower to provide maximum benefits for industry and agriculture as well as for the armed services were critical topics for discussion in Washington's wartime agencies throughout 1943. Negro manpower, as a generally underused part of the national total, appeared in these discussions, both in its relation to industrial and agricultural manpower and in its relation to the military services. Expedients had been proposed, tried, and discarded. New ones were on trial. But no answer to the complex problems of the equitable use of Negro manpower had been reached.

Military Manpower for 1943–45

Serious discussion of the growing manpower shortage had been under way since 1942. National service legislation to include women, the overaged, and the physically unfit had been proposed. The Army had passed through its first manpower crisis in the summer of 1942. Negro units were barely affected by it. In response to continuing pressures, a greater use of Negro manpower was planned for the 1943 increase in the strength of the Army. Though the general outlines for the absorption of a larger proportion of Negroes had been sketched and approved, the details were still to be worked out, accepted by the using services, and proved by experience.

The 1943 Troop Basis, approved in late 1942, was the first which, from the beginning, provided vacancies for a full 10.6 percent of Negroes in its augmentation of enlisted strength. The 337,750 Negroes provided in the 3,600,000-man Army planned for 1942 constituted 9.03 percent of the whole. In the 3,933,000-man augmentation needed to bring the Army up to the 7,533,000-man level authorized for 1943, 416,898, exactly 10.6 percent of the augmentation, were to be Negroes. Including Negroes already provided, a percentage of 10.02 for the entire Army would be reached by 31 December 1943. The attempt to employ Negroes in the Army in proportion to their strength in the population had succeeded, on paper at least. (*Table 9*)

[1] S. Com. on Military Affairs, 78th Cong., 1st sess., Hearings on S. 763, *Married Men Exemption (Drafting of Fathers)*, September 15, 1943, p. 80.

TABLE 9—RACIAL DISTRIBUTION, TROOP BASIS, 1943
(ENLISTED STRENGTHS)

Units and Centers	Mobilized as of 31 Dec 42		1943 Augmentation		Total by 31 Dec 43	
	White	Negro	White	Negro	White	Negro
Total..................	4,532,117	467,883	2,246,233	286,767	6,778,350	754,650
Combat units............	1,820,254	86,294	842,911	64,873	2,663,165	151,167
Service units*............	578,262	148,370	263,300	90,991	841,562	239,361
AAF and services........	1,190,363	109,637	810,000	90,000	2,000,363	199,637
Overhead*..............	363,820	65,880	64,155	9,145	427,975	75,025
RTC's..................	238,500	27,500	44,000	6,000	282,500	33,500
OCS's..................	72,200	800	0	0	72,200	800
Unassigned..............	268,718	29,402	221,867	25,758	490,585	55,160

a Includes AGF services but excludes AAF services.

b Includes men in hospitals 60 days or longer, men in replacement depots, men assigned to headquarters, station complements, and installation staffs, and men on detached lists.

Source: Tab C, Incl to AG 320.2 (11-24-42), filed in AG 320.2 (7-14-42) (1) sec. 1.

The 1943 Troop Basis was also the first based on a fairly firm knowledge of how the armed services would divide among themselves the total manpower available to them, for this troop basis was the first to operate under a system whereby nearly all men entering the armed services came through Selective Service—the result of a Presidential decision long advocated by the Army. On 5 December 1942 President Roosevelt issued Executive Order 9279, requiring all the services to recruit through the draft. The same executive order transferred Selective Service to the War Manpower Commission. The Navy began inducting its men through the Selective Service System on 1 February 1943, thereby ending the long standing Army contention that the Navy, by avoiding the use of Selective Service, was not only taking the cream of white manpower through special appeals to volunteers but also was avoiding the acceptance of its share of Negro manpower, thereby leaving in the Selective Service pool of registered manpower a larger proportion of Negroes to be absorbed by the Army alone. The War Department could henceforth use the Navy's new policy to resist Selective Service's and, later, War Manpower's efforts to force the Army to accept larger numbers of Negroes. The War Department was also aware that in specific interservice frictions the issue of Negro manpower might be used advantageously. Late in 1942 and in 1943, for example, there was considerable discussion within the Army of the Navy's siphoning off some of the best of the nation's engineering and building trades manpower for its construction battalions (Seabees). These units performed functions which, some portions of the Army felt, were not always properly those of the Navy. The War Department's Operations Division counseled:

The War Department should avoid discussion and implied criticism of Navy troop requirements. Such procedure would invite retaliatory action and would be detrimental to both services. . . . The Navy has not sought the assumption of Army responsibilities in the construction of airfields. Furthermore, the existence of construction battalions and other Navy shore units of like nature might compel absorption by the Navy Department of their quota of negro troops.[2]

Some months passed before the Navy began to take enough Negroes through Selective Service to affect the Army's accessions of Negro manpower. Beginning low, the Navy's share increased until in December 1943 the ratios of the two services stood: 1.02 Army to 1 Navy white selectee and 1.78 Army to 1 Navy Negro selectee. By the end of 1944 the Army-Navy ratio of Negroes being taken was 1 and 1, with the over-all ratio for the year being approximately 3.3 Army to 2 Navy selectees. This reapportionment of Negro inductees to both services, with the Navy eventually taking nearly as many Negroes as the Army, helped reduce, by the end of 1943, the number of Negroes who would otherwise have been earmarked for the Army by Selective Service. But joint induction alone was not responsible for the changes in the rates of induction and distribution affecting the use of Army Negro manpower in the last half of the war.[3]

Although the 1943 Troop Basis provided for a full 10.6 percent accession of Negro enlisted men, with a roughly proportionate distribution to the major

commands, the provisions of this troop basis did not, for several reasons, materialize. During the discussions of the final form of the troop basis, a number of objections to various features of it as they affected the distribution of Negro troops were voiced by the commands and by the branches. These portended the changes and developments to come during the life of this troop basis.

Army Ground Forces was critical of the continued allotment of Negroes to additional divisions and of G–3's attempts to raise the proportions of Negroes in other types of ground units. Originally, the two infantry divisions deferred from 1942 and the completed 2d Cavalry Division remained in the 1943 Troop Basis, providing a total of five Negro divisions.[4] Of the two additional infantry divisions one was scheduled for activation in March, the other in November 1943. Ground Forces succeeded in having one of the infantry divisions dropped, substituting for it nondivisional combat units.[5] Although Ground Forces continued to recommend that the remaining division be dropped, with nondivisional combat units substituted for it, G–3 would not concur in this suggestion, commenting:

The 1943 Troop Basis provides full combat support for only 78 divisions. To organize additional non-divisional combat units with Negro personnel will further reduce support already inadequate, since Negro combat units admittedly are not of the same quality as similar white units. While granting the questionable worth of Negro divisions, it appears now that we can

---

[2] Memo, OPD for DCofS, 15 Mar 43, OPD 045.7 (2–25–43), AAF 322–A Bns.

[3] Military Personnel Division, Army Service Forces, The Procurement of Military Personnel: 1 September 1939 to 1 September 1945, vol. II, exhibit 9. MS in OCMH.

[4] Ltr, CofS AGF to TAG, 30 Sep 42, AGF 320.2/276.

[5] Memo, Hq AGF for Ground G's and Rqmts, 5 Sep 42, and M/S, AGF G–1 to G–3, 1 Dec 42, AGF G–3 Plans Sec 320/1 and /32 TB 1942–43–44.

better afford to accept an additional Negro division than to further weaken our combat support for the remaining white divisions. It is planned to withhold activation of this division until late in 1943, by which time it is possible that a more profitable manner to employ Negroes will have been evolved since this matter is being given continuing study.[6]

The additional division remained in the troop basis, scheduled for activation at Fort Huachuca in December 1943.[7]

The services as well objected to the distribution of Negroes contemplated in the 1943 Troop Basis. The tentative distribution of Negroes among the services showed the same imbalance that had prevailed throughout 1942, with the Quartermaster allotment still higher than that of any other branch. The Quartermaster General requested a reduction in the number of Negroes sent to his branch, pleading a shortage of facilities, difficulty in obtaining adequate leadership, and limited sources of cadres. The Services of Supply agreed that the "efficiency of the Quartermaster service as a whole will suffer considerably and [it] will not be able to maintain its place in the team with the other services" unless the numbers of Negroes allotted it were reduced. Services of Supply recommended that Negroes allotted to the Quartermaster be reduced to 36,000, the corps' training capacity for the year. The 17,783 men remaining could be assigned elsewhere, preferably to Army Ground Forces, since the services in combat support with Ground Forces would have but a 9.3 percentage of Negroes.

G–3, however, would not sanction this realignment.[8]

The racial allocations of the new troop basis were approved by the Acting Chief of Staff, General McNarney, on 23 January 1943. Then shortages and alterations in overseas requirements began to affect the shape of both the 1943 Troop Basis as a whole and its racial allocations.

Selective Service Shortages and Quotas

At various times before 1943 Selective Service had not delivered Negroes in the numbers requisitioned, but until the middle of 1943 the Army was usually more concerned about finding places for all of the Negroes at its disposal than about shortages. It had placed larger calls on Selective Service toward the end of 1942 to bring the numbers of Negroes up to the required ratio by the end of the calendar year. These calls, ranging up to 50,000 Negroes a month, found some states unprepared to fill them. At the beginning of 1943, inductions of Negro manpower had not yet reached a proportionate level.

Early in 1943 the War Manpower Commission, facing adverse public criticism if single, apparently physically fit Negro registrants continued to remain uncalled while white husbands and fathers were being removed from many local areas and while white workers in critical industries were being reclassified by their draft boards, informed the War and Navy Departments that a final decision to take Negroes in larger num-

---

[6] Memo, G–3 for CofS, 8 Jan 43, and Memo, G–3 for CG AGF, 26 Jan 43, WDGCT 320.2 Gen (12–11–42), AGF 320.2/10.
[7] M/S 33, G–3 for AGF, 27 Jan 43, AGF 320.2/10.

[8] Memo, G–3 for CG SOS, 8 Dec 42, AG 320.2 (14 Jul 42) (36) sec. 1; Memo, G–3 for CofS, 8 Jan 43, WDGCT 320.2 Gen (1–8–43).

bers must be made.[9] The commission argued that the completion of Negro percentage quotas was desirable to reduce the rate of removal of skilled white workers from the wartime labor market. Replacements for these workers were not readily available from among civilian Negroes, Chairman Paul V. McNutt pointed out. Moreover, court action had been instituted to test the legality of quotas and separate calls in New York where a test case was in its first stages. The outcome of this case was by no means certain.[10]

Secretary Stimson assured the War Manpower Commission that the War Department's current plans called for a 10.4 percentage of Negroes by the end of 1943. Stimson reminded McNutt further that he did not consider "the present method of induction to be discriminatory in any way," so long as this percentage ratio was maintained. Making use of the limiting clause which had given Negroes some qualms in 1940, he further pointed out that the Selective Service Act provided that no man should be inducted *"unless and until"* he was acceptable to the land or naval forces for training and service and his physical and mental fitness for such training should have been determined. "While those colored registrants who are qualified physically, mentally, and morally under Army standards are acceptable," the Secretary wrote, "they are acceptable only at a rate at which they can be properly assimilated." [11]

While McNutt was certain that the acceptance of proportionate numbers of Negroes would result in higher morale among both Negro and white troops, as well as in the civilian population, he did not agree that the maintenance of racial quotas would "meet the problem of discrimination in the administration of the Selective Service and Training Act," nor did the section cited by Stimson "in any way qualify the plain mandate that registrants be inducted without discrimination on account of race or color." Therefore, McNutt informed the Secretary, as soon as current backlogs of uninducted Negroes were absorbed, Selective Service would abandon the policy of calling men by racial quotas. The War Department should be prepared, after 31 December 1943, to accept Negroes and whites in the order in which their names appeared on their local selective service rolls.[12]

So far as Stimson could see, there was no practical method of operating inductions on this basis. The matter was not simply one of separate calls and quotas, the Secretary told McNutt. When the Army reached its maximum size, continuing inductions would be based on loss replacement rates. Since most Negroes would not be in combat zones, loss replacements for Negro units would be considerably lower than for white units. A more carefully controlled induction system, aimed at maintaining but not increasing Negro proportions in the Army, would then have to be

---

[9] Ltr, Paul V. McNutt, Chairman War Manpower Commission, to SW, 17 Feb 43, AG 327.31 (9–19–40) (1) sec. 12.

[10] The case did not, in the end, affect the procedure of separate calls, nor did it, after a year and a half in the courts, settle the matter of the legality of those calls.

[11] Ltr, SW to McNutt, 20 Feb 43, AG 327.31 (9–19–40) (1) sec. 12. Italics in original.

[12] Ltr, McNutt to SW, 23 Mar 43, AG 327.31 (9–19–40) (1) sec. 12.

instituted, for otherwise the Army would be "forced to mix negro and white enlisted personnel in the same units." Stimson suggested that since he was certain that McNutt had no desire to "complicate an already difficult problem," War Manpower's proposal should be withdrawn.[13]

The War Manpower Commission did not follow Stimson's suggestion. Certain of the War Department's General Staff divisions felt that preparations should be made to counteract future War Manpower attempts to force the War Department to accept its point of view. But Selective Service, from April on, began to fall behind in its deliveries of Negro men. So long as requisitions based on population ratios remained unfilled, part of the Army's problem of what to do with Negro troops was solved and the answer to War Manpower Commission criticisms was clear. If outstanding requisitions should be filled "in a short period, [it] might prove temporarily embarrassing," G–3 observed in August, adding "however, considering the screening of Grade V personnel, such a situation appears unlikely to develop."[14] "To build a record in anticipation of continued Negro shortages and contemplated WMB [War Manpower Board] actions later on"[15] was the purpose of increasing requisitions, making certain that troop basis units existed, and reporting shortages to McNutt as they occurred.

When the 1943 Troop Basis was revised on 1 July position vacancies were

therefore retained for approximately 714,000 Negroes, or 10.4 percent of the male enlisted strength of 6,869,000 expected by 31 December. Monthly calls on Selective Service were established in numbers believed sufficient to meet the commitment made by Secretary Stimson to the War Manpower Commission. These calls provided for the placement of about 349,500 additional men, amounting to 13 percent of the total Selective Service calls for the year.[16] But, by the end of September, Selective Service was short 28,700 Negroes in its deliveries. Through the same period, separations of Negro personnel from the Army were abnormally high, totaling 44,000.[17]

Shortages in the delivery of selectees by Selective Service arose in a number of ways: through disparities between activations and authorizations for the increase of personnel in the Army; through heavier rejection rates at local boards and induction stations than expected (which, therefore, had not been offset by sufficiently large overcalls); and through changes in over-all war plans and needs. To these reasons for shortages must be added a number of special circumstances which affected the delivery and use of Negro selectees to a greater extent than whites.

The initial overrepresentation of Negroes in Selective Service Class I–A dwindled as more and more white men originally deferred were reclassified. Because of adjustments and changes in induction methods and standards, the percentages of Negroes rejected from among those examined at induction sta-

[13] Ltr, SW to McNutt, inclosing opinion of JAG, 14 Apr 43, AG 324.71 (2–17–43).

[14] M/R, G–3, 24 Aug 43, and Memo, G–3 for G–1, 27 Aug 43, both in WDGCT 291.21 (22 Aug 43).

[15] Ibid.

[16] Memo, G–3 for CofS, 13 Oct 43, WDGCT 291.21 (13 Oct 43).

[17] Ibid.

tions rose steadily during 1943 until, in September, 60.6 percent of all Negro registrants reporting to induction stations were rejected. The percentage of rejections declined slightly thereafter, but it did not again go below November's 56.1 percent. The average Negro rejection rate for the year was 53 percent, while for whites the average rate for the year was 33.2 percent.[18]

The liberalization of literacy and venereal standards in 1943 should have provided local boards with many ready men who had previously been rejected, or so the local boards thought. Negro men previously rejected for illiteracy were now returned to induction stations in large overcalls. But many of these men were now rejected again for other causes. Venereals recalled by the boards were rejected for other disorders, initially undetected or unrecorded. Many men previously rejected as illiterate were discovered to be unable to pass the new qualification tests.[19]

Selective Service, attempting to counter the effect of increasingly high rejection rates, advised its state directors in November 1942 to estimate the Negro gross call (net call plus overcall) at a higher rate than the white overcall percentage.[20] In May 1943, Selective Serv-

ice instructed its state directors that though the white gross call could be set at no more than 140 percent of the white net call, the Negro gross call could be as large as 200 percent of the Negro net call.[21] The 200 percent gross call for Negroes still did not produce the required number of inductees. In July Selective Service removed all restrictions on the size of the Negro overcall, stating that the Negro gross call might be placed "at whatever percent is necessary to deliver the Negro net call."[22] The shortages in deliveries continued just the same.

State directors, urged to fill their Negro quotas, had their own explanations for their failure to meet calls: induction stations were not examining Negroes carefully before rejecting them. "We do have evidence," the state director for Georgia reported, "that registrants are lined up and asked if they have previously been to the induction station and, if so, to hold up their hands; those who hold up their hands are asked to stand aside and they are generally not given any re-examination of any consequence and are again rejected." Moreover, the Georgia director continued:

The rejection rate is exceedingly high and it is very difficult for Georgia to fill calls for Negroes—they simply do not want them. For a long while they rejected the Negroes for urethritis and when we kicked so much about that they switched to inadequate personality, and they switched to psychoneurosis. We have been kicking about psychoneurosis for a couple of months and now they are switching to other causes for rejections but the

---

[18] Registrants Examined and Rejected at Induction Stations During 1943, app. Oa to Mil Pers Div ASF, Procurement of Mil Pers, 1 Sep 39 to 1 Sep 45, vol. V. MS in OCMH.

[19] Selective Service as the Tide of War Turns: Third Report of the Director of Selective Service, 1943–1944 (Washington, 1945), p. 208.

[20] State Director Advice No. 93, 7 November 1942, in Selective Service System, Quotas, Calls, and Inductions, Special Monograph No. 12, vol I (Washington: 1948), 204 (app. D, No. 45). The War Department, at the request of General Hershey, also advised service commanders of the necessity of higher Negro overcalls.

[21] Ltr, Selective Service to State Directors, 19 May 42, Quotas, Calls, and Inductions, p. 182.

[22] Ltr, Selective Service to State Directors, 20 Jul 43, Quotas, Calls, and Inductions, p. 183.

rejection rate, meanwhile, is steadily increasing. The men at the induction stations seem to have their orders and do not seem to have much discretion in the matter. The remedy, apparently, must come from top side.

In calling this letter to Assistant Secretary McCloy's attention, Truman Gibson noted that "This sentiment is shared by 44 state directors." [23]

Selective service directors were not alone in this sentiment. Congressmen and editors, North and South, addressed themselves to the problem during the discussions of drafting fathers and drafting women through national service legislation. Representative Charles E. McKenzie, of Louisiana, inserted in the *Congressional Record* his remarks on the subject:

Mr. Speaker, many times before have I protested the discriminatory manner in which the Selective Service Act has been interpreted and administered. It is not the fault of the local boards. Their hands are tied. The fault is here in Washington where a deliberate attempt is being made to keep Negroes, single Negroes, out of the service while white fathers are being drafted. Has it actually come to pass in America where the color of a man's skin is the basis for his being deferred, even if he is single and has no dependents. We people of the South are beginning to think so as evidenced by the following editorial from the Morehouse *Enterprise* of Bastrop, La. . . . I warn you, gentlemen of the House, that such discrimination is detrimental to the morale of the Nation. [24]

"We do not question the army's need for more men," *The Christian Century* observed during the following spring. "But it's surprising that in all the commotion about needed manpower nothing has been said about making fuller or better use of Negro citizens." Congress, this magazine felt, should investigate both the drafting and the use of Negro manpower before increasing the classes of men to be drafted. [25]

Shortages in the delivery of Negro inductees continued to the end of the year. In October, G–3 estimated that shortages in deliveries, coupled with the abnormally high attrition of 1943, would result in a total shortage of 88,000 men by the end of the year. These men were slated for use in planned units in the current troop basis which, in its October revision, contained only units which were necessary for overseas deployment by 30 June 1944, all other units having been deferred. "Due to the smallness of the reserve provided, it will be unwise to defer wholly the activation of units totaling 88,000 men if Negro fillers cannot be secured," G–3 advised. Instead, these units should be filled with any excess white personnel available. After considering G–1 and Operations Division comments on its proposal, G–3 recommended that no

are still 267 colored men in 1–A who have not been inducted—simply because there has been no 'colored call' for them." "Simply because the Government doesn't seem to want Negroes in the armed forces is no excuse," the paper said. "It is race discrimination and the colored men of Morehouse Parish feel that it is putting them in an inferior classification." See also *Married Men Exemption (Drafting of Fathers)*, Hearings . . . S. 763 . . . before the Committee on Military Affairs, United States Senate, 78th Cong., 1st sess.

[25] Editorial, "Manpower Needs and Negro Soldiers," *The Christian Century*, LXIC (April 12, 1944), 451.

---

[23] Ltr, Col James N. Keelin, State Director, Atlanta, Ga., to Col. C. G. Parker, National Headquarters, Selective Service, June 1943, and attached note, Gibson for McCloy, 21 Jun 43, ASW 291.2 NT 1943.

[24] Extension of Remarks of Hon. Charles E. McKenzie of Louisiana, November 16, 1943, *Congressional Record*, vol. 89, part 12 (78th Cong., 1st sess.), A4912. The Bastrop editorial commented on the drafting of white married men while "there

further change in calls on Selective Service be made for the rest of the year—calls had already been sent to Selective Service anyway—with "whatever shortage [which] may develop being accepted as a cushion against expected excess deliveries in 1944." New units earmarked for Negroes that could not be filled with excess whites could be deferred to absorb Negroes delivered in 1944. When the Army's strength finally reached 10.4 percent Negro, action could then be taken to restrict Negro inductions so as to maintain that percentage.[26]

The mounting shortages in the delivery of Negro inductees further weakened the impetus toward proportionate distribution and removed War Manpower's major argument for halting the use of monthly Negro quotas.[27] So long as Army requisitions for Negro inductions remained higher than Selective Service's deliveries, the War Manpower Commission could not reasonably blame the Army for its shortage of proportionate Negro strength. Actually, no defense against War Manpower action was needed. As a result of continuing discussions and dissatisfactions with national manpower policies, the Congress restored Selective Service to its independent status as of 5 December 1943,[28] thus removing the possibility that War Manpower might order the cessation of inductions by racial quotas at the end of 1943.

Though nearly 11 percent of the men sent to the Army by Selective Service during the war years were Negroes and though there was a steady increase in the number of Negroes in the Army, reaching a peak of 702,758 at the end of July 1945, their proportion never reached a 10.4 (or 10.6) percentage goal during the war. The rate of discharge and the fact that there were avenues of entry to the Army more freely available to whites than to Negroes kept the Negro percentage below its population-based proportion. Only after the end of the war, when combat veterans were discharged first and when higher percentages of Negro enlisted men volunteered to remain in the Army did the percentage of enlisted strength approach the goal. The percentage of total strength still lagged behind. (*Tables 10, 11, and 12*) As predicted by G-3, the smaller calls of 1944 were generally filled or overfilled. But in the meantime the shortages of 1943, coupled with the difficulties of shipping overseas the Negro units then in being, had worked a profound change in the organization of Negro units. Shortages had developed not only in Negro but also in white deliveries. At the same time, requirements for new units, especially in the services, soared above those originally contemplated in the 1943 Troop Basis. As the armies overseas grew larger, the requirements for service units for their support increased. With Negro units of several types, combat and noncombat, in the country and uncalled for by overseas theaters, one answer to the growing need for service units was clear. Simultaneously the reorganization of nearly all nondivisional units, combat and noncombat, offered an opportunity to reexamine the possibilities of providing Negro units of a more useful and wanted character.

[26] Memo, G-3 for CofS, 13 Oct 43, WDGCT 291.21 (13 Oct 43).

[27] Memo, G-3 for G-1, 27 Aug 43, and attached Memo for Record, WDGCT 291.21 (22 Aug 43).

[28] Public Law 197, 1943.

TABLE 10—ACCESSIONS OF ENLISTED MEN BY SOURCE
JULY 1940–AUGUST 1945

Year	Inductions		Enlistments		ERC Calls		Aggregate	
	Negro	Total	Negro	Total	Negro	Total	Negro	Total
Total.......	887,724	8,096,232	30,383	1,437,024	4,858	497,671	922,965	10,030,927
(Percent)...	(10.96)	(100.0)	(2.11)	(100.0)	(0.97)	(100.0)	(9.20)	(100.0)
1940.........	1,853	19,327	6,019	356,832	0	0	7,872	376,159
1941.........	93,399	928,998	10,367	411,832	0	120	103,766	1,340,950
1942.........	331,616	3,122,248	13,873	655,381	386	37,942	345,875	3,815,571
1943.........	291,106	2,376,312	62	4,603	3,083	278,575	294,251	2,659,490
1944.........	110,353	987,599	36	3,385	926	122,373	111,315	1,113,357
1945.........	59,397	661,748	26	4,991	463	58,661	59,886	725,400

Source: Adapted from Strength of the Army, 1 Jan 47, STM–30.

General Trends, 1943

Changes in the allocation of Negro manpower, and consequently in its ultimate employment, proceeded along two lines. The first was an attempt, supported by the Civilian Aide to the Secretary of War and the Advisory Committee on Negro Troop Policies, to devise ways and means of extending the employment of Negro troops to new types of unit and specialist fields. The second was an attempt, supported by the Chief of Staff and Army Ground Forces, to shift the emphasis from proportionate employment of Negroes in all types of units, especially combat types, to their larger proportionate use in the services, concentrating on needed labor functions.

The two lines of policy involving change were not necessarily in conflict, for, at the same time that a few Negroes went into new types of units, the bulk of Negro soldiers continued to go into the traditional types of service units. Combat, technical, and "special" units for which no immediate need could be foreseen furnished many of the men for new service units. The few new types of units activated, such as parachute, bombardment, and engineer construction units, broadened the base of Negro military experience and continued to move toward the goal that Negroes be employed in all types of units. The many new service units of established types satisfied the growing belief that the waste of Negro manpower could be avoided only by placing the bulk of Negroes in units which had a reasonable chance of success in training and of employment overseas.

The continuing shortages of manpower in 1943 affected both courses of action. The two were bolstered by an oral expression of the Chief of Staff's wishes in the spring of 1943. One morning in late April, after a general survey of mobilization and training problems with representatives of G–1 and G–3, General Marshall discussed the utilization and training of Negroes.

TABLE 11—QUARTERLY NEGRO STRENGTH AND TOTAL STRENGTH OF THE ARMY
DECEMBER 1941–DECEMBER 1945

Quarter or Month	Total Negro	Total Strength of the Army	Percent of Negro to Total	Negro Enlisted Personnel	Total Enlisted Personnel	Percent of Negro Enlisted to Total Enlisted
1941						
December....................	99,206	1,685,403	5.88	98,686	1,562,256	6.32
1942						
March......................	143,556	2,387,746	6.01	142,967	2,236,547	6.39
June.......................	178,708	3,074,184	5.81	178,032	2,867,762	6.21
September..................	255,545	3,971,016	6.44	253,952	3,673,876	6.91
December....................	399,454	5,397,674	7.40	397,407	5,000,275	7.95
1943						
March......................	504,430	6,508,854	7.75	601,423	6,010,032	8.34
June.......................	555,176	6,993,102	7.94	551,375	6,413,526	8.60
September..................	596,664	7,273,784	8.20	592,160	6,622,951	8.94
December....................	633,448	7,482,434	8.47	628,151	6,790,754	9.25
1944						
March......................	671,877	7,757,629	8.66	666,224	7,021,758	9.49
June.......................	698,911	7,992,868	8.74	692,954	7,215,888	9.60
September..................	701,678	8,108,129	8.65	695,874	7,293,480	9.54
December....................	691,521	8,052,693	8.59	685,296	7,212,210	9.50
1945						
March......................	694,333	8,157,386	8.51	687,874	7,288,292	9.44
June.......................	694,818	8,266,373	8.41	687,823	7,374,710	9.33
September..................	653,563	7,564,514	8.64	646,352	6,679,773	9.68
December....................	372,369	4,228,936	8.81	367,630	3,572,577	10.29

Source: Strength of the Army, 1 Jan 46, STM–30, p. 61.

The G–1 representative summarized the Chief of Staff's views:

a. The Chief of Staff wants the installation at Tuskegee expanded to take on the technical training of negroes for service units, particularly those kinds requiring the use of special types of heavy technical equipment.

b. Utilize more Negroes in Engineer General Service Regiments and such organizations.

c. Do not plan on the activation of more negro combat units than presently scheduled, possibility of not activating the December Division.

d. Quit catering to the negroes' desire for a proportionate share of combat units. Put them where they will best serve the war effort.[29]

General Marshall's informal proposals, while not put into effect immediately, were reflected in actions of the staff divisions from mid-1943 onward.

Screening methods were still being thought of as one answer to the problem of providing Negro units for use, but screening also involved the question of

---

[29] Memo, Col Reuben E. Jenkins for Gen White, ACofS G–1, 29 Apr 43, G–1 353–Gen.

TABLE 12—QUARTERLY NEGRO STRENGTH OF THE ARMY, BY CATEGORY
DECEMBER 1941–DECEMBER 1945

Quarter or Month	Male Officers	Enlisted Men	Nurses	Dieti- tians	Phys- ical Thera- pists	Warrant Officers	Flight Officers	WAAC and WAC		Total
								Officers	Enlisted	
1941										
December....	462	98,686	45	0	0	13	0	0	0	99,206
1942										
March.......	534	142,967	45	0	0	10	0	0	0	143,556
June........	594	178,032	76	0	0	6	0	0	0	178,708
September...	1,525	253,952	44	0	0	24	0	0	0	255,545
December....	1,921	397,246	81	0	0	26	0	19	161	399,454
1943										
March.......	2,687	498,956	165	0	0	90	0	65	2,467	504,430
June........	3,358	548,319	158	4	1	166	9	105	3,056	555,176
September...	3,859	589,253	195	8	1	336	0	105	2,907	596,664
December....	4,475	625,449	198	9	1	507	4	103	2,702	633,448
1944										
March.......	4,690	663,164	219	10	2	603	14	115	3,060	671,877
June........	4,949	689,565	213	8	2	636	32	117	3,389	698,911
September...	4,728	692,229	247	9	2	613	84	121	3,645	701,678
December....	5,027	681,376	256	9	6	656	151	120	3,920	691,521
1945										
March.......	5,073	684,097	336	7	9	685	234	115	3,787	694,333
June........	5,411	684,091	464	9	11	682	301	117	3,732	694,818
September...	5,718	642,719	466	8	10	592	312	105	3,633	653,563
December....	3,799	366,016	318	8	7	306	225	80	1,610	372,369

Source: Strength of the Army, 1 Jan 46, STM–30, p. 60.

what to do with the men remaining. To use them in purely maintenance and labor work, as sometimes suggested, would involve the Army in charges of discrimination against Negroes. On the other hand, successful screening to form units eminently suited for overseas combat use might, some feared, result in an interpretation that Negro units were generally "good" and that therefore more should be used in active theaters. One thing was certain, the Deputy Chief of Staff, General McNarney, told the members of the General Council: There

was no use having colored troops standing by and eating their heads off if they could never be used overseas. Either the men of lower qualifications who kept units from becoming efficient must be eliminated or some other use must be found for Negro troops. The War Department could not justify maintaining units which could not be shipped overseas.[30]

[30] Discussion, Min of the Gen Council, 31 May 43. The discussion arose after The Inspector General reported the overseas unreadiness of an antiaircraft battalion.

Flexible Organization and
Negro Units

The first major organizational change dictated by considerations of manpower economy was the shift from a fixed to a functional organization of nondivisional units. This change was Army-wide, but it had special effects on Negro units. As a result of deliberations culminating in the last weeks of 1942 and the beginning of 1943, the fixed brigade and regiment and, in the services, the battalion as well, virtually disappeared from the Army during 1943. The new organization provided definite advantages for Negro units so far as their training and potential deployment were concerned.

Essentially, the change to a more flexible organization involved the substitution of smaller for larger units as the fixed organization. The new organization, the "group," or the flexible battalion, was a device for grouping interchangeable units under a headquarters which, for training or operational purposes, might have none or many units under its control at a given time. Instead of an antiaircraft artillery regiment organized with a given number of battalions as prescribed in a table of organization, a group headquarters might control seven battalions for a specific function and, later, three battalions for another function. This type of organization was approved for Army Ground Forces in December 1942 and for Army Service Forces in January 1943. The process of converting existing units to the new organization continued throughout the year.

The new organization of units made possible the institution of many of the reforms in the structure and use of Ne-

gro units which had been discussed for twenty years. It gave Army Ground Forces a method within an over-all Army policy to put into practice General McNair's conviction that "colored troops can be handled more satisfactorily, and assimilated in a combat force more readily, in battalion units than in regimental units. Colored battalions can be attached to white units and given better training than they would receive if by themselves." [31] It gave the proponents of the principle that Negro troops could furnish labor while small white units provided supervision and specialists a chance to try working combinations of white and Negro troops, who, though working together, were yet not in the same unit. Negro units which formerly would have trained and operated alone could now be combined with white units under the control of a single, lower echelon headquarters.

While it required several months to reorganize all units into flexible groups, the new organization had immediate practical benefits to certain units, especially to those of service types. The companies of the 27th Quartermaster Regiment, for example, had never been physically close to their regimental headquarters. By 1943 they were spread all over the world. These companies could now be placed under headquarters physically closer to the units supervised. Elements of battalions had operated in widely separated places. The four companies of the 388th Port Battalion, for example, were assigned to widely distant stations: Company A to the Middle East, Company B to the New Orleans Port of

---

[31] 2d Ind, Hq AGF to CG Second Army, 29 Dec 42, and M/S, CG AGF to AGF G–3, 29 Dec 42, both in AGF 333/51.

Embarkation, and Companies C and D to the South Pacific. Redesignated as the 208th, 209th, 210th, and 211th Port Companies, Transportation Corps, they became in fact separate and independent.[32] They could be attached or assigned to any port or other headquarters.

The new system also promised a possible solution to some of the knottier problems in the employment of larger Negro units. An overseas area which might not wish a regiment might be willing to accept a separate battalion. One of the oldest Negro field artillery regiments was rated satisfactory for combat duty in the summer of 1942, but there was no possibility of moving it overseas in the immediate future. Ground Forces was told that unless the regiment moved from its location, where the nearest firing range was 205 miles away and where only limited facilities for combined training existed, it would be unable to maintain a satisfactory training level, aside from the effects of boredom and other morale difficulties. But there was no other suitable station available for it within the country and none overseas.[33] By November this unit, weakened by cadre losses, higher command problems, and dimming training objectives, reached the point where it fluctuated between high and low states of training and morale. Thereupon, Army Ground Forces recommended that it be redesignated a Quartermaster truck regiment for immediate use overseas. No theater desired a separate Negro field artillery regiment overseas at the

time but Quartermaster truck units were urgently needed.[34] Neither G–1 nor G–3 would sanction the conversion of this trained regiment to service use. "The constant pressure on the War Department to activate additional colored units in the combat arms and the known plans for the continued activation of such units makes it undesirable, as a matter of War Department policy, to convert a combat regiment that has had almost two years active duty training into a service regiment," G–1 said. If there was no need for a regiment of its type, G–1 suggested, conversion to another type of artillery or into two or more separate battalions might be possible.[35] Consequently, upon approval of the flexible group plan, the battalions of this regiment were among the first to be redesignated and the headquarters and headquarters battery were among the first to be disbanded.[36]

Though there was G–3 resistance to the move, the new flexible group system allowed as well the reduction of the numbers of Negro headquarters requiring high-ranking officers and exceptionally well-qualified enlisted men. Army Ground Forces, in January 1943, wished to disband the headquarters of two antiaircraft regiments, six field artillery regiments, and the one field artillery brigade. From this personnel, Army Ground Forces planned to activate an additional 155-mm. gun field artillery battalion, disbanding one similar white battalion to balance the troop basis. Later, acting on a request from the Tank

[32] Ltr, TAG to CG's NOPE, USAFISPA, USAFIME, 31 Mar 43, AG 320.2 (3–26–43) OB–I–SPOPU–M.

[33] Ltr, Hq Second Army to CG AGF, 3 Aug 42, AG 370.5–240 and 1st Ind, AGF to Second Army, 8 Aug 42, AGF 353/8 (FA Tng).

[34] Memo, Hq AGF for CofS (ACofS G–3), 2 Nov 42, AGF 320.2/16 (FA).

[35] Memo, G–1 for G–3, 21 Nov 42, WDGAP 320.

[36] Memo, Hq AGF for CofS (G–3), 12 Jan 43, AGF 321/16 (FA).

Destroyer Center, Army Ground Forces requested that Negro group headquarters be eliminated entirely. "The major purpose in organizing group headquarters is to obtain a high degree of flexibility," it stated. "In order to maintain this flexibility, it is believed that group headquarters companies should be organized with white personnel, to which could be attached all units, whether with white or Negro personnel." This could not be done, G–3 decided, for current policy required that some units of all types be organized with Negro enlisted men and that opportunities be maintained for Negro promotions up to and including the grade of colonel in each arm and service "wherein appropriate units exist." That the organization of all group headquarters with white personnel would make for a greater degree of flexibility G–3 did not doubt, but existing Negro headquarters could not be disbanded to organize white headquarters without subjecting the War Department "to a justifiable accusation of discrimination." G–3 granted permission to defer the activation of new group headquarters, since officers for them were not available. Eventually white headquarters were substituted for certain of the Negro headquarters remaining in the troop basis. The result was a material reduction in the number of Negro group headquarters.[37]

[37] Memo, AGF for G–3, 23 Jan 43, AGF 320.2/9; Memo, G–3 for CG AGF, 26 Jun 43, WDGCT 320 (1–23–43); M/S, AGF G–3 for DCofS, 4 Feb 43, AGF 320.2/9; Memo, Hq AGF for G–3, 17 Mar 43, AGF 320.2/254; Memo, G–3 for CG AGF, 23 Mar 43, WDGCT 320 (3–17–43); Memo and Memo for Record attached, Hq AGF for G–3, 26 Mar 43, AGF 321/4 (TD Units); DF, G–3 for CG AGF, 27 Mar 43, WDGCT 320 (3–26–43); M/S, Hq AGF, G–3 for CofS and AG, 30 Mar 43, AGF 321/4 (TD Units).

Shifting Manpower Allocations

For further personnel savings, with the object of getting greater use out of available manpower, surveys of manpower utilization and allocations were constant during 1943 and 1944. Revisions in tables of organization to reduce the requirements of individual types of units, changes in the troop basis, conversions of existing units to more urgently needed types, retraining programs for individuals in preparation for their use in new or related specialties, and, in certain of the technical services, the establishment of cellular units of small numbers of highly trained men who could be supplemented in the field by labor forces from units of general service types were all developments of the tight manpower situation. Though not a part of stated policy, renewed insistence that, wherever it might be done with profit, new units should be composed of Negro enlisted personnel, thus releasing white personnel for use in foreign areas or in types of units where successful Negro service was problematical, was a part of the general trend of the period.

In the late winter of 1942–43, the Transportation Corps, requiring larger numbers of port battalions, requested the addition of three port headquarters and headquarters companies and twelve battalions to the troop basis. The chief of the Transportation Corps requested that all of these units be white, but the Operations Division, which had just concluded unsuccessful attempts to have sanitary companies reorganized for greater overseas usefulness, reported to G–3 that Negro battalions could be used at the future destinations of these units. G–3 then suggested to the Services of

Supply that since this augmentation would have to be charged against the SOS reserve pool, other SOS units might be reduced to provide the personnel required for these new units. G–3 specifically suggested that Negro sanitary companies or quartermaster service battalions might be used for this purpose.[38]

The Transportation Corps still wished white units only. Services of Supply therefore requested three white headquarters and headquarters companies and ten white and two Negro port battalions. The Operations Division recommended approval of the request but not the racial proportions, whereupon G–3 reversed these proportions, with Transportation Corps' troop basis increased by ten Negro and two white port battalions.

Thereafter more and more port units were formed with Negro personnel. Similarly, most amphibian truck (Dukw) companies formed after mid-1943 were filled with Negro personnel. When twelve new Dukw companies were added to the troop basis in the late spring of 1943, Army Ground Forces and G–3 recommended that they be manned with personnel from Negro truck units. Despite the protest of the Operations Division, these and all Dukw companies activated after October 1943 used Negro enlisted personnel.[39] Most men for these units did not come from trained truck units but from disbanded medical sanitary, military police, and artillery units.

Attempts to open new types of units to Negroes were not at all successful. The revised 1943 Troop Basis provided nine Negro quartermaster depot supply companies for Army Ground Forces. This command, pointing out the difficulty of getting competent noncommissioned officers, technicians, and cadres for specialized Negro units when no parent units of the type existed, requested that they be organized with white personnel scheduled to go into Army Service Forces service and salvage collecting units. These units, requiring fewer skills, could be converted to receive Negroes. G–3 reminded Ground Forces that provisions for Negro units must be made in "compliance with law," that new methods of screening personnel at induction centers would reduce the training problem involved in the scarcity of noncommissioned officer material, and that 26 percent of Service Forces as compared with 17.5 percent of Ground Forces personnel was already Negro. Nevertheless, after advice from G–4, G–3 directed that the nine companies be activated with white personnel.[40] Similarly, when G–3 suggested informally that Army Service Forces use Negroes in the future for ordnance tire repair companies, the Ordnance Department, at a conference on the troop basis, refused to consider the possibility. These units remained white.[41]

When Army Ground Forces saved men from within its own strength by reducing table of organization require-

[38] DF, G–3 for SOS Opns Div, 11 Mar 43, WDGCT 320.2 Gen (2–13–43).

[39] Memo, G–3 for CofS, 2 Jun 43, and Memo, G–3 for CG AGF, 10 Jun 43, both in WDGCT 353 Amph (6–2–43); History of Military Training, Transportation Corps, to 30 June 1945, pp. 103–09, MS in OCMH.

[40] Memo, AGF for G–3, 19 Aug 43, AGF 321/74 (QM); Memo, G–3 for CG AGF, 24 Aug 43, WDGCT 291.21 (19 Aug 42).

[41] OO 220/28C SPOFO Mil Orgn and Equip, 2 Jul 43, and Memo, Dir Opns ASF for G–3, 3 Jul 43, both in SPMOU 322 (3 Jul 43); G–3 Memo for Record, 8 Jul 43, WDGCT 291.2 (2 Jul 43).

ments for many of its units,[42] certain of these savings provided additional vacancies for Negroes while releasing whites for duties considered more exacting. Such a reorganization was that of the motorized divisions. When fully equipped, motorized divisions included not only about 3,000 vehicles—nearly three times as many as required by the new "streamlined" standard infantry divisions—but also the additional personnel required to operate these vehicles. A major portion of this personnel was in the divisional troop transport battalion, which had a headquarters and headquarters detachment and six companies. The four partially motorized divisions— all of the existing motorized divisions except the fully motorized 4th—were reorganized as standard infantry divisions in March 1943.[43] Truck units which could be used interchangeably by several divisions, thereby saving both men and equipment, were activated. Four white battalion headquarters and headquarters detachments to control twenty-four Negro troop transport companies were authorized. With the reorganization of the 4th Motorized as a standard infantry division in June 1943 and the changing of the remaining five unactivated motorized divisions in the 1943 Troop Basis to standard infantry, five more white battalion headquarters and headquarters detachments and thirty more Negro troop transport com-

panies for attachment were provided.[44] In addition to an over-all saving of manpower, the net result was to release actual and allotted white personnel for use in other units with shortages and to absorb Negroes into units which, had they remained organic to motorized divisions, would have been white.

This method of saving manpower by the use of Negroes in positions that would release white soldiers for combat and for technical duties became more frequent as the reorganization of 1943 continued. To some extent this developing policy paralleled the philosophy of manpower use which brought women soldiers into the Army.

Women and Manpower

Aside from the aspirations of women to serve fully in the armed forces after the pattern set in the British and Canadian services, one of the major reasons urged for the formation of the Women's Army Auxiliary Corps in 1942 was the women could do many noncombatant jobs as well as and even better than men, thus releasing men for combat service.[45] During the hearings on and public discussions of the proposed corps, the question of the use of Negro women came up frequently. Some Negro groups wished

---

[42] For a detailed discussion of this process within Ground Forces, see Robert R. Palmer, "Reorganization of Ground Troops for Combat," in Kent Roberts Greenfield, Robert R. Palmer, and Bell I. Wiley, *The Organization of Ground Combat Troops,* UNITED STATES ARMY IN WORLD WAR II (Washington, 1947).

[43] Memo, G–3 for CofS, 16 Jan 43, AG 320.2 (1–16–43) (5); Memo, G–3 for CofS, 24 Feb 43, AG 320.2 (12–7–42).

[44] Memo, Hq AGF for CofS, 17 May 43, and Memo, G–3 for CG AGF, 21 May 43, both in AGF 320.2/37 (TUB 1943). The units were termed troop transport rather than truck units to assure retention of control by Ground Forces for the purposes for which they were activated.

[45] At the time of its organization, the WAAC was publicly expected to release 450 men a week for combat training (New York *Times,* July 21, 1942, p. 26). See Mattie E. Treadwell, *The Women's Army Corps,* UNITED STATES ARMY IN WORLD WAR II (Washington, 1954), especially Chapter XXX, for more detailed discussion of Negro women's service in the Women's Army Corps.

the Congress to write into the new law a protective nondiscriminatory clause similar to that contained in the Selective Service Act.[46] Such an amendment was proposed in the Senate by Senator Charles L. McNary of Oregon for Senator W. Warren Barbour of New Jersey and accepted. Similar amendments were proposed by Senators Edwin C. Johnson of Colorado and James H. Hughes of Delaware. The War Department opposed these amendments, stating in hearings that Negro units would be formed and that no amendments would be needed.[47] The amendments were not included in the bill as passed.

When Secretary Stimson announced on 15 May that Mrs. Oveta Culp Hobby, of Texas, had been made director of the new corps, Negro groups which had opposed her appointment on the ground that her southern background would not guarantee fair treatment for Negro women proposed that Stimson appoint as her assistant Mrs. Mary McLeod Bethune, Director of Negro Affairs in the National Youth Administration.[48] But Mrs. Hobby, immediately after she was sworn in, announced that among the first 400 officer trainees forty would be

Negro women and that at least two of the first companies would be Negro. Thereupon the National Negro Council, leader of the opposition to her appointment, withdrew its objections and stated that Negro women now felt confident that they would have an equal chance with white women in the new corps.[49]

Negro women were not thought of as replacements for Negro men. They were to be used wherever WAAC units were required. In the process of their use they would, like all women soldiers, release male manpower for other uses, but the manpower released did not have to be Negro. It soon developed that, whether or not protective clauses in the WAAC bill guaranteed a nondiscriminatory recruiting policy, the WAAC was not going to get a large number of Negro women. Several forces operated to restrict applications from Negro women, but one was certainly "an impression on their part that they will not be well received or treated on posts where they may be stationed."[50] Reports from Negro soldiers and from the press on conditions in training camps were of no help in recruiting women. To overcome their reluctance, the Military Personnel Division of SOS suggested an intensive recruiting campaign, conducted through the chief Negro colleges, and the establishment of a definite policy on the rights and privileges of Negro women in the service.[51]

Director Hobby had already done much to dispel the fear that Negro Waacs

[46] Statement, Edgar G. Brown, President of the United Government Employees and Director of the National Negro Council, in *Hearings . . . on H. R. 6293, January 20 and 21, 1942,* pp. 54–55; Same Statement, App to *Hearings . . . on S. 2240, February 6, 1942,* p. 33.

[47] Statements, Brig. Gen. John H. Hilldring, ACofS G–1, *Hearings . . . on H. R. 6293, May 1 and 4, 1942,* p. 15; Statements, Mrs. Helen Douglas Mankin, General Hilldring, Senators Reynolds and Chandler, *Ibid.,* pp. 44–45; Min of Gen Council, 4, 12 May 42.

[48] New York *Times,* May 16, 1942, p. 15. Age limitations and the requirement that all Waacs be commissioned from the WAAC Officer Candidate School made this appointment unlikely.

[49] Nora Baldwin, "Mrs. Hobby Sworn in as WAAC Director," New York *Times,* May 17, 1942, p. 32.

[50] Memo, Dir of Mil Pers SOS for G–1, 12 Sep 42, SPGAM/322.5 (WAAC) (8–24–42).

[51] *Ibid.*

were neither wanted nor needed. Her first public address after her installation was at Howard University before members of a college sorority on 6 July 1942. She spoke of the high qualifications of the applicants for the first officers' class, explained that the first two Negro WAAC companies, both commanded by Negro officers, would be stationed at Fort Huachuca in November,[52] and announced that she was certain that Negro women would serve faithfully and loyally in all parts of the WAAC.[53]

The assignment of Negro Waacs to posts and stations was conditioned by the same considerations that governed the location of male units: the presence of a military or civilian Negro population and the willingness of posts and stations to receive them. To clarify further the position of Negro Waacs within the corps, Military Personnel, Services of Supply, suggested that the policy of the director of the WAAC be specifically confirmed by instructing: (1) that there be no discrimination in the types of duties to which Negro women might be assigned; (2) that no lowering of standards to meet racial ratios be prescribed and that, therefore, intensive recruiting

among Negro women be inaugurated; (3) that Negro units be provided on the basis of 10.6 percent of the over-all strength of the WAAC and that this percentage be maintained in each type of unit within the WAAC, thereby paralleling the policy for men in the Army; and (4) that an eminently qualified person, preferably a Negro WAAC recruiting officer, be sent out to colleges "in order to secure the proper class of applicants for colored units of the WAAC." [54] Each of these policies was adopted.

But, by the spring of 1943, when major manpower problems had begun to assail the Army, there were still only 2,532 Negro Waacs, representing but 5.7 percent of the whole. Though the numbers of Negro Waacs increased later, they never reached 6 percent of the corps. In the manpower discussions of 1943, Negro Waacs (Women's Army Corps or WAC from July 1943) therefore played but a small part. Those in the service were occupied in post headquarters, motor pools, hospitals, and at other duties which did release men for use elsewhere, but their numbers and the prospects of their increase were not great enough to influence the solution of problems brought about by manpower shortages. Nor were their services of a nature to affect greatly the employment of Negro enlisted men. Neither in post headquarters nor in motor pools; in message centers nor in post offices; in hospitals nor in file rooms were they able to release more than a few Negro enlisted men, for relatively few Negro soldiers were so employed. Nor could Waacs themselves perform the duties

[52] Fort Huachuca had been specifically mentioned in the hearings on the WAAC bill as one of the posts which could most readily use women in uniform. In discussing the disciplinary problems of using female civilian labor at certain posts where nearby civilian facilities for their housing and protection did not exist, General Hilldring said, using Fort Huachuca as an example: "There the question is water. Water regulates the places where people live. The civilians must live in Bisbee, 40 miles away, or on the post. Fort Huachuca is one of the posts that is giving us great difficulty in this particular problem. Enlisted men there are occupying a great many positions which should be filled by civilians." Hearings . . . H. R. 6293 January 20 and 21, 1942, pp. 53–54.
[53] New York Times, July 7, 1942, p. 14.

[54] Memo, MPD SOS for G–1, 12 Sep 42, SPGAM/322.5 (WAAC) (8–24–42).

which were now proposed for the bulk of Negro enlisted men to help meet current needs of the Army.[55]

Conversions and Inactivations

Chief among the current needs for more manpower were those of Army Service Forces. In 1943 the demand for additional construction, transportation, communications, and purely labor units in overseas theaters increased beyond original expectations. In an attempt to meet these growing requirements ASF, in the first six months of the year, activated units in excess of the provisions of the troop basis. These activations created a shortage of personnel for many service and ground forces units.[56] Personnel due for induction in the last half of 1943 could be used to fill certain of these units and others yet to be activated. But for some of the units the overseas need was immediate.

Despite Army Service Forces complaints, the reserve pool of service units for emergency overseas calls remained small. On 1 July 1943 ASF units had personnel shortages totaling 70,000 men. Many units activated six months before had not yet been filled. ASF forecast that, at the scheduled induction rate, it would take two months to fill existing units if all new men inducted into the Army were used for this purpose alone. But more units were scheduled for activation in the next few months. A portion of the incoming men would have to be sent to replacement training centers to build a supply of loss replacements. Another portion, under the June 1943 regulations, would go to special training units where they would remain from one to three months. Unless a drastic revision of personnel methods and utilization was made, ASF contended, "Only further aggravation of the existing situation can result." [57]

At the same time, Army Ground Forces was complaining of shortages in its units. In June the troop basis was cut by 500,000 men in an effort to adjust activations to available manpower. Activations of the twelve divisions scheduled for the remaining months of the year, including the last Negro division, were deferred until 1944.[58] This deferment became permanent, for although it was expected that these and other divisions might be activated in 1944, actually no further divisions were activated. The War Department Manpower ("Gasser") Board estimated that 65,000 to 85,000 men could be transferred from overhead to units. But these excess men, a large number of whom were Negroes by virtue of the fifteen and over percentage of Negroes placed in overhead installations, could not be used to correct Ground Forces shortages since most of the AGF units with shortages were white and since transferring Negroes to this command would simply produce an additional excess of Negroes in existing units. Most Negro units of ground combat types were already filled and waiting while the Army tried to solve the problem of their deployment

[55] For strength statistics on Negro Wacs, see Treadwell, *Women's Army Corps*, Table 11, p. 777.
[56] Memo, G–3 for CofS, 31 Jul 43, WDGCT 220 (1 Jul 43).

[57] Incl 1 to Ltr, Hq ASF to CG's Sv Comds, Mil District of Washington, Tech Svs, TPMG, SPX 370.5 (29 Jul 43) OB–S–SPTRU.
[58] Memo, CG AGF for CofS, 2 Jun 43, and Memo, G–3 for CG AGF, 12 Jun 43, both in AGF 321/61 (Inf).

overseas. Transfer of white men from Army Service Forces to Army Ground Forces was not recommended in view of the urgent need for existing service units overseas.[59] But the transfer of white personnel from a less to a more urgently needed unit and of Negro personnel from an uncommitted Ground Forces to an immediately needed Service Forces unit was another matter.

The air base security battalions were a tempting source of personnel for the 12,000 Negro fillers needed for ASF units. In July, at ASF's request, the War Department directed Army Ground Forces to disband thirty of these battalions and their training headquarters.[60] Army Ground Forces was permitted to withdraw cadres and retain training group personnel from these units for use in amphibian truck companies, troop transport companies, and truck companies.[61] The Army Air and Ground Forces were also told to form no further Negro combat units except those already scheduled for activation. In August 1943, the Army Air Forces disbanded two white and thirteen Negro air base security battalions and distributed most of their enlisted personnel to units of the Air Service Command.[62] In the same month, Army Service Forces requested the transfer of 14,500 more Negro enlisted men for use as fillers.[63] Thirty-one battalions—13 antiaircraft, 10 field

artillery, and 8 tank destroyer—were stripped of 80 percent of their enlisted men to provide these fillers.[64] These units were left with double cadres so that they might be refilled and retrained when new inductees became available. By the end of August Army Service Forces had received, primarily from within the Army, 60,000 men for new and unfilled units. Half of these were Negroes.[65]

The End of Proportional Representation

In the meantime, formal changes within the troop basis and in the allocations of manpower to the major commands continued. Unneeded and less useful units not yet activated in the troop basis were dropped or deferred. Thus, early in 1943, 80 Negro medical sanitary companies, 1 white and 2 Negro headquarters and headquarters detachments for ordnance ammunition battalions, and 3 Negro and 10 white quartermaster laundry companies were removed from the troop basis. Their

---

[59] Memo, G–3 for CofS, 31 Jul 43, WDGCT 220 (1 Jul 43).

[60] Memo, G–3 for CG AGF, 9 Jul 43, AGF 322/6 (ABS).

[61] M/S, Hq AGF (Ground G–3 to Plans), 19–24 Jul 43, AGF 322 (ABS).

[62] Min of Gen Council, 23 Aug 43.

[63] Memo, Hq AGF for CofS, 25 Aug 43, AGF 322.999/10.

[64] These were the 234th, 235th, 319th, 321st, 393d, 394th, 458th, 492d, 493d, 538th, 790th, 819th, and 846th Antiaircraft Artillery Battalions; the 350th, 351st, 353d, 732d, 795th, 930th, 931st, 971st, 973d, and 993d Field Artillery Battalions; and the 646th, 649th, 659th, 669th, 795th, 828th, 829th, and 846th Tank Destroyer Battalions. The 364th Infantry was also used for this purpose but to not so great a degree of stripping.

[65] The 60,000 came from the following sources:

Negro EM by transfer from AGF	14,288
White EM by transfer from AAF	3,356
Negro EM from air base security units	12,966
From RTC's	8,305
From service command overhead	21,635
	60,550

Memo, ASF MPD for CG ASF, 31 Aug 43, APGAM 320.2 (30 Aug 43).

personnel was allotted elsewhere.[66] By late summer the requirements for such defensive units as antiaircraft artillery were sharply reduced, making both Negro and white units of this branch eligible for inactivation and conversion.

For the October 1943 revision of the troop basis, covering actions to be taken up to the end of the year, G–3 recommended that no further Negro combat units, other than those then active, be provided. Since overseas assignment of existing combat units was proving so difficult, G–3 said, additional Negroes should be absorbed in service units. The troop basis would continue to provide for a full proportionate accession of Negroes "as evidence of good faith" even though selective service might be unable to fill the requisitions made upon it. Under the October revision additional units were scheduled for inactivation, their personnel to be used elsewhere. For the most part these were white units of artillery, armored, cavalry, medical, ordnance, and tank destroyer types, but among them were Negro chemical, medical, and quartermaster units.[67]

Under this plan 18 antiaircraft battalions, 5 barrage balloon battalions, 32 separate antiaircraft batteries, 6 tank battalions, 1 cavalry regiment, 2 regiments and 3 battalions of seacoast artillery, 17 field artillery battalions, and 42 tank destroyer battalions, all white, were inactivated. Ten white and 6 Negro chemical smoke generator companies, 11 Negro medical sanitary companies, 18 Negro troop transport companies, 4 white and 4 Negro veterinary companies, and 8 white and 7 Negro chemical decontamination companies were also inactivated. Officers usually went with their units to the new branches. When AGF attempted to substitute Negro for white officers in units scheduled for disbandment and conversion for service uses, ASF objected and tried to get the original officers back when possible. In March 1944 G–3 estimated that by the end of the year a total of 254 combat battalions would be converted to service units. Not all of these were physical conversions, for some of these units, although provided, had not been activated. Of the 254 battalions, 43 were Negro and 211 white. The disproportionately high number of Negro battalions was traceable, G–3 said, to the relatively less advanced state of training among Negro units.[68]

The 1944 Troop Basis finally abandoned the attempt to provide Negro units by set quotas. For 1944 all units, Negro and white, were to be provided only on the basis of demonstrated and current needs. "Operational demands forecast to 30 June 1945," G–3 reasoned, "require the mobilization of a considerable additional number of service units in which Negroes can profitably be employed (port, ammunition, truck, service and dump truck companies). Generally speaking all augmentations of these types of units have been earmarked for Negro personnel." It was true that this practice had resulted in an actual decrease in the number of Negro combat units, G–3 continued, but enough had been retained to continue

[66] Ltr, TAG, 23 Feb 43, AG 320.2 (2–1–43).
[67] Memo, G–3 for CofS, 2 Oct 43, AG 320.2 (14 Jul 42) (36) sec. 1B.
[68] Incl, Employment of Negro Personnel in the Army, to Memo, G–3 for ASW, 4 Mar 44, ASW 291.2.

representation of Negroes in all arms and services. "With the smaller number of Negro combat units now provided careful selection of personnel should permit development of these units to the point where they will have battle value," G–3 concluded.[69]

After three years of attempting to maintain a balance between Negro combat and service troops and among the Negro units of the branches, G–3 thus gave up the struggle. For the rest of the war, except for replacements, most Negroes in the Army went into the services. Conversions, inactivations, and disbandments were the rule, with actions to change the missions of white and Negro units taking place both in the theaters and in the zone of interior. Through the inactivation of surplus

units; reduction in the zone of interior activities, such as interior guard and similar duties now made less essential by the progress of the war; and by closer control of theater allotments of personnel, the War Department hoped to reduce the military strain on national manpower resources.[70] The more extensive use of Negro troops in the services, it was expected, would contribute markedly to these ends. The realignment of Negro personnel for wider use in purely service units would not, in any event, lessen opportunities for shipment overseas where manpower was needed most. But, as a matter of public policy, it made the movement of the remaining combat units overseas correlatively more pressing.

---

[69] Memo, G–3 for CofS, 7 Dec 43, WDGCT 320 TB (7 Dec 43), approved 15 Jan 44 as amended, AG 320.2 (17 Aug 43) (2) sec. 1.

[70] Tab A, Detailed Plan for Implementation of 1944 Troop Basis, Memo G–3 for CofS, 20 Jan 44, AG 320.2 (17 Aug 43) (2) sec. 1, approved 21 Jan 44.

CHAPTER XV

Overseas Deployment and the Nature of Units

An additional practical consideration in the employment of Negro troops, hardly foreseen in Army mobilization plans, developed in the first year of active operations. Placing Negro units in camps within the continental limits of the United States was a constant problem to the Army, but, beginning in early 1942, assigning them overseas gradually assumed an air of high international intrigue. Combat units were more seriously affected by this development than service units, but all types of Negro units were affected by the problem of overseas deployment.

Establishing a Policy

After Pearl Harbor, General Headquarters compiled a list of units considered ready for overseas use at once or expected to be ready in the near future. These included a number of Negro units.[1] But from early 1942 on,

it became a matter of common knowledge within the General Staff that no matter what the state of readiness of Negro units happened to be, the steadily increasing number of American units departing for overseas locations would not include any large number of Negro troops until the War Department established a definite policy on their assignment and use overseas. Once established, carrying out such a policy continued to be a problem, increasingly localized as decisions on particular areas were made, but lasting up to the end of the war. The question extended beyond considerations of military utility, except in the broadest sense. It was a compound of the overseas commander's desire to avoid racial troubles in his area, of fears that the Negro units would be less adaptable and less efficient than white units of similar types, and of the objections of foreign governments and local authorities.

By March 1942, G–3 of the War Department wanted to know who was re-

---

[1] The 41st Engineer General Service Regiment was given a first priority on the basis of excellence in training, with two white general service regiments following immediately behind it. The 91st, 92d, 93d, 94th, 95th, 96th, 97th, and 98th Engineer Battalions, all of which were to become general service regiments; the 76th and 77th Engineer Light Ponton Companies, with six white ponton companies placed ahead of them; and the 18th Field Artillery Brigade, with one white and one Negro regiment, were all considered ready to go.

By 1 February, the 45th Engineer General Service Regiment and the 184th Field Artillery and, by 1 April, the 46th Field Artillery Brigade were among the units expected to be ready. Memo, ODCofS GHQ for G–3, 24 Dec 41, with Incl, GHQ 353 Tng.

sponsible for maintaining liaison with the State Department on those phases of the question which had become enmeshed in international relations. Brig. Gen. Dwight D. Eisenhower, then chief of the War Plans Division, replied that he was maintaining such a liaison. The problem was proving exceedingly difficult, he explained, for, as yet, he had found no foreign country where Negro troops would be welcomed. The War Plans Division, he said, had finally decided to send both Negro and white troops together as American troops without indicating to the authorities at their destination what their racial composition was.[2]

Though such a policy would have insured the shipment of Negro units overseas it alone was no solution, for certain areas, including American territories, were already requesting the withdrawal of Negro troops who had been sent overseas and others were requesting that none at all be sent. Reasons for the opposition of local authorities ranged from fear of miscegenation and an increase of economic unrest among local populations because of the higher rates of pay of American Negro troops to purely political considerations in countries with exclusion laws.

Governors of British West Indian and Atlantic possessions on which American bases were located were especially apprehensive lest the balance of colonial authority be disturbed by the arrival of well-paid and well-clothed American Negro troops. A delegation from Bermuda, in Washington to confer upon

the establishment of the American base there, urged that no Negro troops be sent to their islands. The 99th Antiaircraft Regiment, scheduled to be part of the garrison for Trinidad, met opposition from local British authorities, whereupon the Caribbean commander, Maj. Gen. Frank M. Andrews, recommended that a white unit be sent in its place. St. Lucia wanted neither continental Negro nor Puerto Rican troops.

Elsewhere Australia, whose "White Australia" immigration policy dated back to the establishment of the Commonwealth at the turn of the century and even farther back in some of its states, informed the War Department through the Australian Embassy in Washington that it would not agree to the dispatch of more Negro troops to Australian territory. This position was later modified to permit a limited number to enter, with the stipulation that they were to be withdrawn at the end of the Australian emergency. The Australian situation was complicated by clashes between Negro and white soldiers in which the American commander, Lt. Gen. George H. Brett, felt the civilian population might become involved. General Brett recommended the withdrawal of all Negro troops. Both Lt. Gen. John L. DeWitt, of the Western Defense Command, and Governor Ernest Gruening of Alaska informally opposed sending Negro troops to Alaska, with Governor Gruening stating that he felt the mixing of Negroes with the native Indians and Eskimos would be highly undesirable. The Air Forces requested that no Negroes of any branch be sent to Iceland, Greenland, or Labrador. Panama requested the withdrawal of a signal construction company sent

[2] Min Gen Council, 17 Mar 42, p. 4.

to the Canal Zone in the fall of 1941.[3] Chile and Venezuela advised the State Department that Negro coast artillery units would not be accepted there. The special representative to Liberia, Col. Harry McBride, advised that colored troops would not be satisfactory there, since their rate of pay would place them in a preferred status with reference to the local population. Even within the United States commanders preferred to avoid using Negro troops in defense positions.

Secretary Stimson made short shrift of the objections. Of Alaska and Trinidad he commented, "Don't yield," and, again, "No, don't yield." To the Australian proposal and to Lt. Gen. Walter Krueger's suggestion that the use of Negro troops in his Southern Defense Command be avoided because of the probability of race riots, he answered with a flat "No." On the Panama request he commented, "Tell them they must complete their work—It is ridiculous to raise such objections when the Panama Canal itself was built with black labor." On Iceland, Greenland, and Labrador he mused, "Pretty cold

for blacks" and on the proposal for Liberia he replied, "Nonsense." But for Chile and Venezuela he established a principle that was to last through most of the war when he commented, "As we are the petitioners here we probably must comply." [4]

G-1 proceeded to draw up a policy for the employment of Negro troops overseas which provided that they would not be employed in extreme northern stations and that they would not be utilized in a country against that country's will when the United States had requested the right to station troops in the country concerned. In all other cases, Negro troops would be dispatched without prior request for agreement on the part of the theater or other commander and without notation as to the color or race of personnel.[5]

No other staff agency concurred fully with the G-1 recommendations as originally written. Newer developments and existing regulations were involved in some of the nonconcurrences. Services of Supply, G-2, and G-3 recommended that the theater commanders be notified of the racial composition of shipments so that "proper arrangements" might be made for their reception. Army Air Forces objected that the retention of the proportionate repre-

[3] The Panama immigration laws, providing that Negroes whose native language was not Spanish could not be admitted to Panamanian territory, were of considerable importance in Panama's internal politics in the late thirties and during the war. By agreement between the United States and Panama, these laws were enforced in the Canal Zone, with the United States reserving the right to admit its Negro citizens to the zone for temporary work. Executive Agreement Series 452—General Relations, "Agreement between the United States of America and Panama . . . May 18, 1942" (Washington, 1945) , p. 6; Ltr, Office of Dist Engr, Panama Engr Dist to CofE, 13 Apr 42, OCE 291.2; *Annual Report of the Governor of the Panama Canal, 1942* (Washington, 1946) , p. 114.

[4] Memo, WPD for CofS, 25 Mar 42, OPD 291.2. Secretary Stimson's comments are written marginally in ink and initialed "H. L. S." See also Cable 1045, Brett to AGWAR, 25 Mar 42, in WDCSA–USAFIA Incoming Radios, Book II; Memo, DCofS GHQ for WPD, 20 Feb 42, OPD 4440–28, on attitudes of commanders and local authorities to the use of Negro troops in their areas.

[5] Memo, G-1 for TAG, 4 Apr 42, and revised proposals, 22 Apr, 30 Apr 42, both in G-1/15640-2.

sentation rule in the United States without a corresponding rule for overseas shipments would leave larger proportions of Negro troops in the United States for whom neither proper uses, stations, assignments, nor controllable percentages would be possible.[6] The War Plans Division, now redesignated the Operations Division (OPD), agreed with this objection.

The Operations Division had another reason for withholding concurrence. A message had been received from London, over General Marshall's name, stating that Negro units should not be sent to the British Isles at all.[7] This would alter entirely any policy being considered, for it was to the United Kingdom that large numbers of American units, including the very necessary aviation and general service engineers, were to be sent under the BOLERO plan. After it developed that the staff message had been sent without General Marshall's knowledge, the Operations Division determined that in planning troop shipments for the British Isles, Negro service troops would be included in "reasonable proportions."[8] G–3 now objected to the new phrasing of the revised policy directive, for the Chief of Staff had by

then (25 April) decided that there would be no positive restriction on the use of Negro troops in Great Britain, while the Operations Division was preparing to limit their use to the services. As finally issued, on 13 May 1942, the policy directive contained the original provision plus the stipulation: "There will be no positive restrictions on the use of colored troops in the British Isles, but shipment of colored units to the British Isles will be limited, initially, to those in the service categories." Theater commanders would be informed of orders moving Negro troops to their commands but they would not be asked to agree to their shipment beforehand. The policy provided as well that the commanding generals of Army Air Forces, Ground Forces, and Services of Supply would "insure" that Negro troops were ordered overseas in a proportion not less than their percentage in each command.[9]

Developing Practices

Settling upon a policy for the deployment of Negro troops overseas did not solve the problem of either their overseas locations or use. Theater commanders were still responsible for committing troops to action either in combat or in combat support. They still determined, in large measure, the types and numbers of units which they required. Their requests received the greatest attention of the War Department and of its Operations Division, whose function it was to see to it that the

---

[6] Memo, CG AAF for CofS, 14 Apr 42, G–1/15640-2.

[7] CM–IN 4619 (4-17-42), London to AGWAR, OPD 291.21 (3-4-42); Memo, OPD for G–1, 23 Apr 42, OPD 291.21/4.

[8] Memo, OPD for Exec OPD, 25 Apr 42; Memo, Exec OPD for Chief Strategy and Policy Gp and Chief Theater Gp, 25 Apr 42, OPD 291.21/4. For the BOLERO plan, and other aspects of the developing military strategy of 1942, see Maurice Matloff and Edwin M. Snell, *Strategic Planning for Coalition Warfare, 1941–1942,* UNITED STATES ARMY IN WORLD WAR II (Washington, 1953).

[9] Ltr, TAG to CG's AAF, AGF, SOS, 13 May 42, AG 291.21 (3–31–42).

theaters had the units and personnel needed to accomplish their missions. Theater commanders were known to cancel or reduce requests for certain types of units when informed that only Negro units were available. The Theater Group of Operations Division followed the practice, which (as pointed out by Brig. Gen. Patrick H. Tansey, Chief of its Logistics Group) was directly contrary to War Department policy, of asking theater commanders specifically if they "could use" or if they "desired" certain Negro units as substitutes for white units with a lesser degree of availability.[10] Commanders could still request the deletion of Negro units from movement orders. Often they could get compliance from the War Department, for few felt that the War Department could or should dictate to theater commanders in such a matter.[11] There were always some commanders who, like Lt. Gen. Delos C. Emmons in Hawaii, stated that while they were disturbed by the potential problems implied for their areas, they realized the problem facing the War Department and would therefore accept their proportion of Negro units.[12] Similarly, when General Marshall asked General Douglas MacArthur, as Supreme Commander in Australia and the Philippines, for his personal attitude and recommendations on the proposal from Australia

that no more Negro troops be sent there and that those already there either be returned to the United States or moved on to New Caledonia or India, General MacArthur replied:

I will do everything possible to prevent friction or resentment on the part of the Australian government and people at the presence of American colored troops replying your nine one seven. Their policy of exclusion against everyone except the white race known locally as the "White Australia" plan is universally supported here. The labor situation is also more acute perhaps than any place in the world. I believe however by utilizing these troops in the front zones away from great centers of population that I can minimize the difficulties involved and yet use to advantage those already dispatched. Please disabuse yourself of any idea that I might return these troops after your decision to dispatch them. You may be assured of my complete loyalty and devotion and my absolute acceptance of any decisions that you may make. I visualize completely that there are basic policies which while contrary to the immediate circumstances of a local area are absolutely necessary from the higher perspective and viewpoint. You need never have a doubt as to my fulfilling to the maximum of my ability whatever directive I may receive.[13]

But the willing acceptance of a racial problem additional to those already confronting theater commanders was not likely. Subordinate staffs often found ways to avoid accepting Negro units. Therefore, the rate of movement of Negro units overseas was slow, too slow to satisfy the military agencies in the zone

[10] Memo, Chief Logistics Gp for Chief Theater Gp OPD, 5 Feb 43, OPD File, Statistical Data Concerning Negro Troops, No. 60.
[11] Memo, G-3 for WPD, 25 Mar 42, WDGCT 291.21 (3-25-42).
[12] Memo, WPD for CofS, 25 Mar 42, OPD 291.2. To this, Secretary Stimson noted marginally, "Good."
[13] Rad 41, MacArthur to Marshall, 29 Mar 42, in OPD Exec 10, Item 7d, in answer to Rad 875, Marshall to MacArthur, 25 Mar 42, in WDCSA binder USAFIA—Outgoing Rads.

of interior who were responsible for the training and housing of Negro units, too slow to satisfy the agencies of the War Department who had to placate Negro groups and their sympathizers who kept inquiring about the use of Negroes overseas, too slow to satisfy congressmen and residents of areas which had sent large numbers of white and relatively few Negro soldiers overseas, and too slow to satisfy the Operations Division and the major commands that had to fill overseas requisitions from the troops and units available.

At the time the policy on the overseas movement of Negro troops was established, only 15,679 Negro troops were overseas, with 1,459 en route and 22,629 proposed for overseas destinations.[14] Though the actual number overseas more than tripled by the end of 1942, the percentage of Negroes overseas was still considerably less than proportionate to their over-all strength in the Army.[15]

The likelihood of solving the problem of the adequate use of Negro troops overseas seemed so slight in the spring of 1942 that The Inspector General, Maj. Gen. Virgil L. Peterson, and Brig. Gen. Benjamin O. Davis, then his assistant, questioned the wisdom of continuing to train and equip Negro units which could not be used in the various theaters. The major current effort had to be directed toward providing combat forces. Later, when new fronts opened, when requirements on existing fronts were increased, and when the United States was likely to have a freer hand in the employment of units, they counseled, Ne-

---

[14] The distribution on 12 May 42 was as follows:

Place	Present	En Route	Projected
Total...........	15,679	1,459	22,629
Alaska...........	0	0	3,825
Australia..........	6,364	186	0
British Isles........	0	811	12,887
Efate.............	3,348	0	0
Hawaii...........	0	0	1,015
India.............	35	440	2,018
Liberia...........	0	22	2,884
New Caledonia......	1,376	0	0
Panama...........	249	0	0
Tongatabu.........	1,823	0	0
Trinidad..........	2,484	0	0

Source: Memo, Col C. A. Russell, Theater Gp OPD, for Gen Eisenhower, 12 May 42, OPD 291.21/6; Memo, CofS for SW, 13 May 42, WDCSA 291.21 (5-12-42).

---

[15] Negroes were in the following places on 31 December 1942:

Place	Number	Percentage
Total.....................	53,709	5.61
Alaska......................	1,206	1.34
Northwest Service Command....	3,941	28.30
Panama......................	253	0.41
Puerto Rico..................	836	2.88
Trinidad....................	2,341	18.82
British Isles.................	7,315	6.85
Iceland.....................	213	0.59
Northwest Africa.............	8,688	4.09
Aitutaki....................	412	51.40
Canton.....................	188	8.19
Christmas...................	193	10.67
Efate......................	4,059	69.00
Espiritu Santo...............	2,360	22.75
Hawaii.....................	5,540	4.63
New Caledonia...............	1,397	5.15
Penrhyn....................	424	52.25
Tongatabu..................	1,793	47.60
Australia and New Guinea......	8,025	8.14
India, China, and Burma.......	2,523	16.32
Egypt......................	402	2.53
Kenya......................	261	100.00
Liberia.....................	1,086	92.60
Persian Gulf.................	253	4.63

Source: Monthly Strength of the Army, 31 Dec 42, AGO 320.2 (12-31-42) PM-O.

gro troops might be more readily used. In the meantime, they suggested that activation of Negro units be retarded until more places to use them were developed.[16] With the concurrent pressures of Selective Service and the need to supply more and more units to receive Negro selectees, this suggestion, though it would have helped solve the problem of overseas deployment, could not be followed.

For the remainder of 1942 the question of the deployment of Negro troops overseas continued to be a major factor contributing to the over-all problem of their general employment and placement in units. So long as few Negro units were ready for overseas shipment and so long as the heavy build-up of American forces overseas was still in the future the full solution of the problem could be deferred. But with nearly a million American troops going overseas in 1942 and with the prospect of a ten-million-man Army in the offing, the question could not lie dormant for long. The task force planned for Liberia in the late summer or early fall of 1942 was expected to take care of a number of Negro units,[17] but no comparable grouping of Negro troops was planned for any other area.

Staff Approaches and Surveys

During June 1942 the G–2 Division produced two papers on the use of Negro troops overseas, one on the Caribbean and one on other areas. The Caribbean paper suggested that local populations did not "look with favor upon the use of American negro troops on their soil," as evidenced by riots in Trinidad and Panama involving Negro troops and in Jamaica, the Bahamas, St. Lucia, and British Guiana between white and non-white elements of the local population. The paper asserted that there were no military reasons for stationing Negro troops in the tropics and that there were grave political and psychological disadvantages to doing so:

Our colored troops have a higher standard of living than the native colored troops and populations. In some instances the pay of colored troops is more than that of white foreign troops. The local authorities try to keep the native populations contented with a low standard of living. Obviously, a situation will be created which will result in an unfavorable comparison which is bound to cause local disturbances. Before the arrival of colored troops at some bases, the white and native populations were getting along well. Trouble arose as soon as our colored troops disembarked. . . .

Therefore, G–2 recommended, no Negro troops should be sent to the Caribbean or "anywhere in Latin America." [18]

To this reasoning the Operations Division, using Stimson's comments and the newly adopted policy on overseas movements to bolster its refusal to recommend changes in the policy of using Negro troops "wherever they can be used in [the] Caribbean," [19] replied that there was no record of "any considerable difficulties" in the use of Negro troops then in the Caribbean. A concession to the Panama Government on the removal of

[16] Summary Rpt of Conf with Gen Peterson and Gen Davis, OTIG, n.d., Notes on Confs re Colored Troops, OPD File Colored Question (Closed).

[17] As visualized in April 1942, Task Force 5889 (Little Joe, Structure), destined for Liberia, contained only Negro units.

[18] Memo, G–2 for CofS, 3 Jun 42, OPD 291.21/9.
[19] Routing Form, OPD, 3 Jun 42, OPD 291.21/9.

the Negro signal unit upon the completion of its job had been made, "in the interest of completing defense site agreements with Panama." This was done "purely as a compromise"; it was distinctly not desired by Secretary Stimson. On the political-economic question, the Operations Divisions observed:

While it is true that our colored troops have a higher standard of living than the native colored troops and populations and a higher wage scale than white foreign troops, it is pointed out that our white troops also are on a higher and entirely different living standard than the troops and much of the population, white or native, of countries in the Caribbean and South America. The sense of this paragraph seems to be that the War Department should defer military necessity in favor of meeting the desires of local authorities to maintain conditions which are diametrically opposite to those which the President has gone on record as stating to be the American ideals. It is believed, therefore, that any concessions which the War Department is forced to make should be held to a minimum.[20]

The Operations Division decided that there were three good military reasons for sending Negro troops to the Caribbean: (1) ". . . this theater, as well as all others, should absorb its proportionate part of the colored units now in existence or to be organized"; (2) Negroes are "peculiarly adaptable to tropic as opposed to more rigorous climates"; and (3) since the requirements for general efficiency in the Caribbean will not be so great as in the more active theaters and since Negro units are generally less efficient than white units, they can be employed in the Caribbean to release white troops for other theaters.[21] Each of these reasons would be advanced later in support of deploying Negro troops to other overseas areas.

Later in June G–2 produced a general survey which considered the attitudes of native populations, the local political, economic, and psychological disadvantages for the allied nations, and the possible action to be taken in normal as opposed to emergency situations in the employment of Negro troops in overseas areas. Greenland and Iceland disliked all foreigners, the paper said, and difficulties between their civilians and American white troops had already occurred. "Since the natives are totally unfamiliar with negroes, it is probable that they would regard them with even greater hostility," G–2 reasoned. The government and people of Canada and Newfoundland "recognize the necessity for us to send United States troops, regardless of color, to their territory," and no serious difficulties should be expected in these countries. Nor should there be "basic factors" precluding sending Negro troops to Great Britain and Northern Ireland, since "the American negro troops stationed in England during the World War created no unsolvable problems, and they were generally well treated." The British and French Pacific islands should raise no legitimate objections. On the other hand, British India, where "political difficulties . . . are of an especially complicated and grave nature," Australia, which maintained "a sharp color line," and New Zealand, which did not have a color line between whites and Maoris and did not wish to create one, should receive Negro troops only with the ac-

[20] Memo, OPD for G–2, 6 Jun 42, OPD 291.21/9.   [21] Ibid.

quiescence of their governments. Negro troops should be sent to Australia and New Zealand only in an emergency and for a limited period. "Their presence," G–2 felt, "would undoubtedly build up hostility to the United States throughout Australia." From the Middle East, British West Africa, British East Africa, the Belgian Congo, and French Equatorial Africa, no objections save the economic should be received. "Minor difficulties may arise, however, due to the French and Belgian custom of handling their colored troops with greater strictness than their white troops." Liberia, "being a colored nation," could have no objection other than the economic, but in South Africa, "the appearance of American negro troops would undoubtedly further influence the very ticklish political situation in this dominion." On the grounds that "propinquity" with white troops in garrison life would be unavoidable, that overtaxing civilian facilities would result, or that social, economic, or racial tensions already existing would be intensified, G–2 did not recommend the assignment of Negro troops to Ascension Island, Alaska, or Hawaii. Nor was their use in China looked upon favorably. "While the Chinese are not race-conscious, their Government is ready to exploit politically any action which can be distorted to appear discriminatory. They will undoubtedly complain of any Negro combat troops sent to China as second rate and will seek to make a political issue of the matter. In view of the abundant seasoned labor supply in China, the sending of negro labor troops there is superfluous," G–2 declared. G–2 recommended that it be consulted on the inclusion of Negro troops when-

ever a task force was planned for a new area.[22]

While there were points on which it might have been argued that G–2's conclusions were in error and while its predictions did not work out to the letter, country by country, the paper was a further indication that the use of Negro troops overseas was a worldwide matter, fraught with complexities as varied as any within the United States. The paper was circulated to all groups in the Operations Division and to the Secretary of War. It helped re-enforce the air of pessimistic apprehension on the whole question of the ultimate employment of Negro troops that was beginning to beshroud War Department agencies. "Very interesting and thoughtful paper," Assistant Secretary McCloy observed.[23] Should we include Negro troops in the Penhryn and Aitukaki task forces? Operations Division asked G–2 a few days later.[24] There is no objection to their use at these bases, G–2 replied.[25]

As a matter of fact, G–2 had said in the survey of foreign countries, "It is not felt that the difficulties almost certain to arise in case negro troops are used abroad should in themselves cause a decision not to so utilize our negro manpower. The military situation alone should decide whether negro troops should be accepted in any specific area. . . ."[26] But if the risks were as great as outlined, who would willingly add to the theater commanders' burdens

---

[22] Memo, G–2 for OPD, 17 Jun 42, OPD 291.21/4.
[23] Ibid., note attached.
[24] Memo, OPD for G–2, 30 Jun 42, OPD 291.21/12.
[25] 1st Ind, to Memo, OPD for G–2, 2 Jul 42, OPD 291.21/12.
[26] Memo, G–2 for OPD, 17 Jun 42, OPD 291.21/4.

the threat of civilian unrest, international displeasure and rifts, and intra-military disorders? Combined with already pressing shortages in shipping, the unsatisfactory training progress of many Negro units, and the urgency of advancing plans for offensive as well as defensive operations, it was easy to justify deferments of Negro units' movement dates. Moreover, the successive disorders between Negro and white troops in 1941 and 1942 led to a serious questioning of the psychological and emotional trust-worthiness of Negro troops in foreign countries.

Problems Overseas

In the meantime, reports from overseas areas tended to indicate that some of the problems feared by the War Department, short of full-scale disturbances, were actually materializing. Getting Negro troops into particular areas at all was sometimes a delicate operation; maintaining them in other areas was at times equally difficult. During the planning conferences for setting up the Persian Gulf Command, for example, many questions arose about the use of Negro troops at the ports. Whether Negro troops should be used at all, whether they should be used "experimentally," whether they should operate specific ports from which all native labor would be evacuated, whether they should be mixed with local labor, whether they should be permitted any contact at all with local labor, or whether the matter of their use should be left entirely with the American commander were all questions discussed in and between London and Washington before the decision was reached that Negro port units would be

used in a manner to be decided by the American commander with the understanding that "in no case should we let the impression be gained that the use of colored troops is 'experimental.' " [27] Similar questions came up whenever the employment of Negro troops in a given area was suggested.

Negro units sent early to overseas areas sometimes faced more than the problems of poor equipment and clothing that plagued many American units leaving the country in the first year of the war. The lone Negro unit sent to the Belgian Congo, Company C of the 27th Quartermaster Truck Regiment, which was employed in the construction and servicing of the southern trans-African air ferry route, became the subject of considerable diplomatic correspondence in 1942. American troops, including the quartermaster company, arrived at Matadi, Belgian Congo, on 29 August 1942. On 1 September the assistant military attaché of the Belgian Embassy in Washington referred to the War Department a message from the Belgian Government-in-Exile's Minister of Colonies protesting that, in February, at the time agreement on the proposed air line was reached, assurances were made that no Negro troops would be included in the construction party. The War Department disclaimed knowledge of such an agreement, and the assistant military attaché and the Ambassador informally

---

[27] See September 1942 exchanges in SPLS 1000, Plan for Operation of Certain Iranian Communication Facilities between Persian Gulf Ports and Teheran by U.S. Army Forces, and T. H. Vail Motter, *The Persian Corridor and Aid to Russia*, UNITED STATES ARMY IN WORLD WAR II (Washington, 1952), pp. 189ff.

advised that they had no knowledge of the "commitment" either.[28]

In the meantime, Capt. James. V. Harding, commander of the truck company, requested an immediate change of station, for upon his unit's arrival in the Congo local authorities protested so loudly that the troops were aware of the attitude of the Belgian Government. Harding reported:

Racial restrictions are extreme, and no consideration is given our Colored troops above that of the Native Negro by the local white population. . . . There are no places where our troops may go to be served food, or drink, in contrast to the freedom which is enjoyed by our white troops. . . . The Native villages are 'off limits' to all American troops due to sanitary conditions and safety precautions, and this effectively precludes any possibility of correcting the situation. . . . Our men are accorded the same pass privileges as White troops in the area, but exhibit no desire to avail themselves of such privileges as they state that a general outward and bold exhibition on the part of the populace showing Colored soldiers' presence and services are not wanted makes their status very obvious. . . . The condition of the Native population is exciting considerable comment among our men who are rapidly becoming to feel that the things they are fighting for are [a] fallacy.[29]

Belgian authorities kept asking the unit's officers why the U.S. Government had sent Negro troops over the protests of the Congo Government. When the American officers answered that they carried out their orders without question, "it is seen that information seeps back to the troops that their officers are not able to explain why they are here when they are not wanted." The heavy ve-

nereal disease rate among the only native women with whom the men could associate and a developing disrespect for the military service as a result of the conditions in which the company found itself were "playing havoc" with morale. "This unit *does not* desire [to] return to the United States," the commander continued, "but I do request your serious consideration toward sending it to a theatre where it can do its job unhampered by complete isolation and antagonism on the part of the local population." The commander added a note: he had made a personal survey of Pointe Noire, French Equatorial Africa, when moving the unit into French territory was being considered to improve the situation, but he found the colonial policy there to be no better.[30]

By the time this letter had passed through channels, with indorsements indictating that the situation was "unnecessary, disgraceful" and "getting worse," radio messages from the Commanding General, U.S. Army Forces in Central Africa, requesting authority to transfer the company to Liberia, had been received and permission to do so had been granted. The personnel of the company, less officers, were transferred.[31]

Similar problems, neither so urgent nor so simply solved as those encountered in the Congo, were developing elsewhere. Representative of these were the situations in northwestern Canada, Alaska, and in the British Isles.

The policy on the use of Negro troops overseas had stated that Negro units would not be sent to extreme northern climates, but the immediate need for

[28] Papers in OPD 322.97/3.
[29] Ltr, CO Co C, 27th QM Truck Regt, to CG SOS, 12 Sep 42, SP 320.2 (9–12–42).
[30] *Ibid.*
[31] Papers in OPD 322.97/3.

units to be used in the construction of the Alaska Highway had dictated the use of available Negro engineer units on the project. For more than a year after their arrival, the wisdom of sending the Negro engineer units so far north was debated within the receiving command, within the War Department, and in other executive agencies of the government. Travelers, observers, and residents of the areas gave conflicting reports on both their efficiency and their desirability in northern areas. The morale of many United States troops in Alaska and northwest Canada in the first year of the war was dangerously low, because of insufficient clothing, monotonous food, poor shelter, long tours of duty, and the visible contrast between troop conditions and those of contract laborers who, often employed on the same jobs, were better fed, more adequately clothed, and better paid. Few troops going to northern regions in 1942 had had specialized preparatory training, such as that later given to mountain and desert troops; nor in many cases was appropriate clothing and equipment provided for them. Often units were sent directly from the warmer camps in the continental United States without any previous cold weather experience; frequently the officers were as ignorant as their men of the proper use of the different items provided for cold weather use.[32]

For Negro troops, the problems of the Far North were greater than for the average American unit. Few Negroes in the service units sent there had had experience with living in even the colder parts of the United States; they were completely unacquainted with northern wilderness conditions. The 97th Engineer Separate Battalion, located in encampments where temperatures down to 63° below zero were encountered, was described by one observer as "pathetically ill-equipped [and] doing little else but hibernating at present. . . . As a result of worn out clothing and lack of essential equipment, their outdoor working capacity has been reduced to a small fraction of summer efficiency. . . ."[33] At the same time civilian workers, properly prepared and cared for, were continuing to work out of doors. The isolation of troops in Alaska and northwest Canada, increased in the cases of Negro units by the refusal of many towns to admit them even to their streets and shops, contributed to low morale.[34] Less sparsely populated areas registered protests similar to those of American mainland communities.

The problem was not confined to northern Canada and Alaska. Lt. Gen. Kenneth Stuart, Chief of Staff of the Canadian Army, complained informally to Lt. Gen. Joseph T. McNarney, Deputy Chief of Staff, over stationing Negro antiaircraft troops in Canada as part of the defense of the Sault Ste. Marie locks. General McNarney persuaded the Canadian general of the necessity of leaving these troops in Canada, but the objection was another indication of the general feeling toward the use of Negroes in foreign areas.[35]

---

[32] Thomas M. Pitkin, *Quartermaster Equipment for Special Forces*, QMC Historical Studies, 5. Hist Sec, OQMG, Feb 44, pp. 61, 64.

[33] Rpt of Inspection of QM Activities at Alaska and Northwestern Canada, 9 Dec 42 to 25 Jun 43, OQMG R&D Br Reading File.

[34] Memo, Secy of Interior for ASW, 14 Jun 43, inclosing Memo, Ruth Gruber for Secy of Interior, OPD 291.21/39; Memo, MPD Transportation Corps, for MPD ASF, 19 Jun 43, OPD 322.97/15.

[35] Min Gen Council, 18 Aug 42.

The decrease in efficiency of Negro troops coupled with maltreatment of equipment and supplies caused many observers, and eventually The Quartermaster General, to urge that no Negro troops, and, indeed, no troops who had not been inured to life in cold climates, be sent to the Far North.[36] But there was a powerful counterargument against removing Negro troops from the Northwest Service Command and Alaska. The difficulty of gaining overseas acceptance of Negro troops was so great that this sparsely populated area appeared to be one where, if anything, Negroes might be used in increasing numbers. "[It] eliminates to a large extent the delicate social problems involved," G–4 observed, "and in view of the numerous areas to which these troops cannot be sent, it would appear that the bulk of our forces in areas where Negro troops can be used to fulfill military requirements should be negro units." Proper training and administration would eliminate excessive maltreatment of equipment; the morale question in isolated areas affected all troops, G–4 contended, adding with a touch of irony: "It is recognized that if it were possible to assign troops born and raised in northern climates to Arctic commands, their efficiency would be greater than that of personnel from hot climates. However, it is not believed that such procedure will be practicable as existing units normally comprise personnel from various sections of the country and to break up these units would result in loss of unit training time and create other unwarranted administrative difficulties."[37] Despite later sporadic protests regarding the condition of Negro troops in the Far North, there they remained with white troops as builders of the Alaska Highway and, later, as garrison and maintenance units.

The big foreign location question of 1942 concerned the British Isles. Not long after Negro troops began to arrive, British public opinion and American travelers and journalists began to express qualms about the developing situation. All agreed that the British people readily accepted American Negro troops. The problem lay in the importation of American racial patterns to Britain by American white troops, resulting in clashes, ideological and physical, between American troops and between British civilians and American soldiers. British soldiers resented the barring of public places to American Negro troops and instructions to be "polite to colored troops, answer their queries and drift away" given to their units.[38] British townsfolk were somewhat bewildered and increasingly resentful of the intrusion of American racial mores upon their own customs. The employees of restaurants professed not to see why Negroes should be barred. Landladies who replied to white troops, "Their money is as good as yours, and we like their company" had their counterparts among the more ideologically minded who observed that "it seems silly to talk about democracy when we have white and black troops

[36] Memo, QMG for CG SOS, 4 Mar 43, SPQEQ 422.3 (Arctic Clothing).

[37] DF, G–4 for OPD, 16 Mar 43, WDGS 2905.
[38] Critic, "A London Diary," The New Statesman and Nation, XXIV (August 22, 1942), 121.

who will not talk or mix with one another."[39]

Opinions on the solution of the problem differed. As the United Kingdom became more and more crowded with American troops, plus British and Commonwealth forces and the units of other Allied nations, debate on the matter increased. Some Britons were of the opinion that the solution lay with the American Government, which should limit the numbers of Negro troops sent to Britain and use "every device of persuasion and authority" to convince white American troops that Negro troops in Britain could not be treated as they were in the States.[40] Others thought the solution lay in billeting white and Negro troops in different small towns.[41] American observers offered similar solutions; they advocated a reduction in the number of Negro troops sent to Britain and a concentration of them in port areas, where British contacts were of a more cosmopolitan nature.[42]

All of these solutions and more were tried, with varying success, but the problem of the British Isles remained with the War Department.[43] It remained a limiting factor in the ready dispatch of units overseas, for the heaviest concentration of American troops overseas was in the United Kingdom until the final invasion of Europe. Any limitation upon their use there affected the over-all employment of Negro troops overseas.

Deployment and the Future of Units

Differences in the rate of movement of Negro and white troops overseas gradually affected the projected use and training of Negro troops. As early as January 1942, the Army Air Forces contended that limitations on the overseas shipment of Negroes justified a reduction in the proportions of Negroes that it should receive. Failing to achieve a reduction in its proportion of Negro troops, the Air Forces then proposed that every task force organized in 1942 should contain one aviation squadron for each air base group, air depot group, or matériel squadron.[44] This proposal was approved, but it did not work out in practice. Shipping limitations prevented the dispatch of any but the most patently needed service troops.

For at least one type of service unit that had been activated in large numbers, the medical sanitary company, there appeared to be little or no overseas need. The Medical Department, in letters of November 1942 to all surgeons overseas, pointed out the availability of medical sanitary companies satisfactorily

---

[39] K. L. Little, "Colored Troops in Britain," *The New Statesman and Nation*, XXIV (August 29, 1942), 141. See also, "Poor Relations," *Time*, XLII (December 6, 1943), 36; George W. Goodman, "The Englishman Meets the Negro," *Common Ground*, V (Autumn, 1944), 3–11. Cf. Nevil Shute, *The Chequer Board* (New York: William Morrow, 1947) and John Cobb, *The Gesture* (New York: Harper & Brothers, 1948) for realistic, though fictional, treatments of the subject from the points of view of the British townsfolk and American white troops, respectively.

[40] Critic, "A London Diary", p. 121; Ltr, Brig Moreton F. Gage, n.d., OPD 291.21/31.

[41] Little, "Colored Troops in Britain."

[42] Memo, SOS for OPD, 24 Sep 42, OPD 322.97/4; Ltr, Coordinator of Information, London to Dir OWI, Washington, 1 Sep 42, OPD 291.21/31.

[43] On the handling of this problem by the European theater, 1942–45, see Chapter XX, below.

[44] R&RS, Hq AAF, War Orgn and Movement, to Tactical Sec, 17 Mar 42, AAF 370.22 B Expeditionary Forces—Campaigns.

MEN OF A QUARTERMASTER TRUCK COMPANY *enjoy the hospitality of a British pub and ask questions of the local constable.*

trained for employment in the theaters and suggested that surgeons urge their theater or base commanders to request these units if the need for them existed. Practically no requests for sanitary companies came from overseas commanders, for their work could usually be accomplished by other service troops or by combat units located near bases.[45] Earlier in the year, after Ground Forces transferred all sanitary companies to Service Forces as having no function in combat zones and after they were divorced from the general hospitals to which they were to have been attached, medical sanitary companies appeared to have no potential overseas usefulness at all.[46] Attempts to reorganize them as units "designed for useful work rather than merely as a method of clothing and feeding negro soldiers"[47] came to naught as proposals in early 1943 to force-ship one with each general hospital, to make them parts of antimalarial teams in which white detachments pro-

[45] Ltr, Actg TSG to All Surgeons and Defense Comds and WAF in Overseas Bases, 18 Nov 42, SPMCP 291.2; TAG Ltr, 28 Mar 42, AG 320.2 (2–26–42) MR–M–C.

[46] Memo, Surgeon Hq AGF for CG AGF, 29 May 42, and Memo, Hq AGF for G–3, 18 Jun 42, AGF 320.2/4444.
[47] DF, OPD to G–3, 23 Jan 43, OPD 320.2 (1–15–43).

vided the specialists and Negro units the labor, or to enlarge them into epidemological companies were considered and discarded.[48] While casualty evacuation units and island commands with malarial and other disease prevention problems later found them useful, sanitary companies were symbolic in 1942 and 1943 of the apparent uselessness of many Negro units, especially of those which had been formed primarily for the purpose of absorbing Negro soldiers.

Unlike medical sanitary companies, air base security battalions were in potential demand overseas. These units could perform a function which, theater commanders agreed, was a highly important one. To defend airfields without them, it was often necessary to detach infantry from divisions or use expedients that took other types of combat forces away from their primary duties. Although theater and Air Forces commanders insisted upon the need for specific units for the defense of critical airdromes, in many theaters there was strong opposition to the use of Negroes for this purpose. Yet, 175 of the 194 security battalions activated or scheduled to be activated in the 1943 Troop Basis were Negro units. G–3 feared that, instead of accepting Negro units, white units trained for other functions would be used to defend airfields while the Negro units, specifically

trained for this purpose, would remain unused in the United States.[49]

The deployment of air base security battalions faced the further handicap of doubts that, with their existing organization, these battalions, regardless of their race, were the most effective means of defending airfields. Theaters felt that the units should be more flexible. They should be readily divisible into at least two parts, for most air bases contained a number of outlying fields. The units had too many heavy weapons and yet had no protection for the unit, as such, against low-flying aircraft. Motor transport was needed in the headquarters detachment and the overall use of personnel in the units was considered excessive.[50] Little by way of increasing the effectiveness of these organizations was attempted. To increase their effectiveness greatly would have meant a severe drain on available equipment. Even so, during 1942 theater requests for air base security battalions came in such numbers and with such frequency that Army Air Forces, for a time, felt that it would be impossible to keep up with the demand unless the activation and training of these units were "expedited and augmented." [51]

In February 1943, the Operations Division reported minimum theater and defense command requests for 161 normal air base security battalions, 70 additional fixed companies, and one additional semifixed company. The United Kingdom alone wanted 50

[48] Memo, Asst to TSG to OPD SOS, 15 Jan 43, and Incl, Memo, SOS Opns for G–3, SGO 291.2–1943; Memo, SOS for TSG, 16 Jan 43, and 1st Ind, SGO to SOS Opns, 1 Feb 43, SPOPU 320.2 (1–16–43); Memo, G–3 for CG SOS, 2 Feb 43, WDGCT 320.2 Gen (1–15–43); Memo, SOS Opns for Chiefs of Svs, 6 Feb 43, SPOPU 381.2 (2–6–43); OTSG Memo for Record on Conf on Sanitary Cos, 12 Feb 43, SGO 291.2–1943.

[49] Memo, G–3 for OPD, 2 Dec 42, WDGCT 291.21 (12–2–42).
[50] Memo, OPD for G–3, 9 Feb 43, OPD 320.2 (12–2–42).
[51] Ltr, Hq AAF to CG AGF, 12 Nov 42, AAF 322–A Bns.

AIR BASE SECURITY TROOPS RACING TO THEIR HALF-TRACKS *during an alert, North Africa.*

battalions, plus 50 fixed defense companies.[52] So many requests for variants on the normal battalion indicated serious organizational problems for these units. Tests of an air base security battalion, held in the fall of 1942 at Orlando, Florida, revealed that the units, as then organized, were not equipped to defend airfields effectively. At best, their mission would have to be a delaying one in the event of a heavy ground attack.[53]

New tables of organization for the units, including a tank platoon and a transportation section, were provided by April 1943.[54] Though a few units were so reorganized, by that time the whole question of the shipment of these defensive units overseas was being restudied. The Deputy Chief of Staff directed that requests for them be justified by theater commanders,[55] with the result that most outstanding commitments were deferred or canceled. "It is unlikely that theater commanders will require negro Air Base Security Battalions, or any other negro units, to the extent of offering justifications for their use," General Arnold wrote in protesting the retention of battalions which apparently were not going to be used. Forty-nine Negro battalions with approximately 20,000 men and eleven white battalions were then awaiting shipment. Fourteen Negro battalions were overseas. Some fifty-five battalions were awaiting activation. Although

[52] Memo, OPD for G-3, 9 Feb 43, OPD 320.2 (12-2-42).
[53] Memo, AAF for G-3, 29 Dec 42, AAF 322-A Bns.
[54] T/O 7-415, 13 Apr 43.

[55] R&RS, ACofAS, Opns, Commitments, Rqmts, Theater Br to ACofAS, OC&R, Rqmts Div Air Defense Br, 11 May 43, Comment 4, AAF 381-E (Readiness).

there was continuing evidence that many of these units might have proved useful in the theaters, since other types of units continued to be diverted from their main missions for the defense of airfields, the bulk of the air base security battalions activated were not to be employed overseas.[56]

While air base security battalions and medical sanitary companies were growing both in number and in difficulty of shipment by virtue of their nature as well as their race, other units required in the theaters were left in the continental United States simply because they were Negro. If these units had Negro officers, overseas demands for them were reduced further, for certain theaters were willing to accept Negro troops if they were commanded by white officers but not if the officers included Negroes. This was a position endorsed by G–2 as a necessary "disciplinary" limitation on the shipment of Negro troops overseas.[57] In turn, the negative disposition of theaters toward units with Negro officers affected assignments and promotions in those units authorized Negro officers. The question of enlarging the number of engineer units to which Negro officers could be assigned, discussed in September 1942, was complicated by the information that units designated for early shipment to Europe were not eligible, since Negro officers were not desired in Great Britain at the time.[58] Thus, in addition to the restrictions under which

assignment agencies were operating in placing Negro officers, allowance had to be made as well for the time and place of their units' probable employment.

Unit Shortages and Shipment Policies

It was not long before requisitions began to arrive for specific types of units, service and combat, which could only be filled by the few available units of these types remaining in the country. When these units were Negro, the requests sometimes remained unfilled although Negro units were available for shipment. At times, such requests required the rapid activation or conversion of white units while available Negro units remained idle. Occasionally, such requests could be filled with little difficulty. In January 1942, the Iceland Base Command asked for three white chemical decontamination detachments, but the only decontamination units in the United States were Negro. In this case, the detachments were small, so the required number of white men could be made available from the Chemical Warfare Replacement Center at Edgewood Arsenal and especially trained for this work.[59]

At other times, filling such requests produced administrative complications which the headquarters concerned considered wasteful and unnecessary. In October 1942, among the units required for Australia, all of which were to be white, was a quartermaster sterilization battalion. But the only sterilization

---

[56] Ltr, Hq AAF to CG AGF, 23 Apr 43 and 1st Ind, AGF for AAF, 7 Jun 43, AAF 322–A Bns; Memo, ACofAS Opns, Commitments, Rqmts for DCofS, 20 May 43, AAF 322–A Bns; Memo, CG AAF for CofS (attention OPD), 29 Jun 43, AAF 370.5 I.

[57] Memo, G–2 for OPD, 17 Jun 42, OPD 291.21/12.

[58] Memo, OPD to G–1, 4 Sep 42, OPD 291.21/29.

[59] Ltr, Hq IBC to CG Fld Forces, 6 Jan 42; Ltr, CG Fld Forces to TAG, 18 Feb 42; and M/S, GHQ CWS to G–3, 3 Feb 42; all in AGF 320.2/194 (Indigo) binder 4.

battalion available was a Negro unit. "This practice of specifying white units for theaters of operation open to Negro units in this case not only eliminates the only unit available for the assignment but, in general, has undesirable results," Army Ground Forces complained to the Operations Division, through which all such requests came.[60] When the Southwest Pacific, in 1943, wanted a light tank battalion, the only one available was a Negro unit while the requisition called for a white unit only. Similar difficulties developed in furnishing an antiaircraft battalion to the Far East and a tank battalion to Europe.[61]

While some Negro combat units—the 24th Infantry in the South Pacific; the 369th Antiaircraft Artillery in Hawaii; the 76th Antiaircraft Artillery in Fiji; the 77th Antiaircraft Artillery in Tongatabu; the 99th Antiaircraft Artillery in Trinidad; and the 1st Battalion, 367th Infantry in Liberia—had been sent overseas early, others, like the 9th Cavalry, were moved to staging areas preparatory to shipment overseas only to be refused by the theaters to which they were to go. Such units had then to return to a training camp. The theaters argued that they already had enough Negro troops or that they needed another type of unit more urgently. The South Pacific, for example, wanted a cavalry regiment but it wanted no more Negro units. French control of local natives was delicate enough not to aggravate it further by the presence of additional Negro troops, the theater in-

formed the War Department. In any event white officers would be required because no local natives were commissioned officers.[62] The possibility that other combat units in the United States, especially regiments and divisions, would be required or accepted grew dimmer as the months rolled by. As the supply of white units grew, the chances of ready shipment for Negro units decreased sharply.

In spite of the fact that the three major commands had been directed to ship Negro units overseas in proportions not less than the percentages of Negro troops in the commands, under conditions such as these compliance was impossible. Army Ground Forces, when the development of this pattern was first confirmed, wanted to know if the directive had been rescinded. If it were still in force, AGF recommended, theater requirements should be filled with available troops "regardless of the fact that preferences have been expressed for white units." [63] AGF's proposal had no practical results.

In the summer of 1943, G–3 undertook to investigate the entire situation surrounding the shipment of Negro units overseas. By then the apparent inability of the War Department to ship Negro units was having effects beyond the area of the operational use of Negro troops. The whole question of the provision of Negro units, combat and service, had to be reassessed. Adherence to the formula of proportional representa-

---

[60] Memo, Hq AGF for OPD, 4 Nov 42, AGF 370.5/558.

[61] Memo for Record on G–3 M/S, G–3 Tng Br to Exec G–3, 24 Aug 43, WDGCT 291.21 (24 Aug 43); Incl to Memo, G–3 for CG AGF, 25 Aug 43, WDGCT 380.5 (2 Jan 43).

[62] New Caledonia (Patch) to AGWAR (Marshall) CM–IN 0997 (6–4–42); Memo, Hq AGF for G–3, 14 Jun 42, AGF 291.2; GNOPN/04574 (6–8–42) in G–3 291.21, vol. I; New Caledonia (Harmon) to AGWAR (Marshall), CM–IN 12580 (27 Jan 43).

[63] Memo, Hq AGF for OPD, 4 Nov 42, AGF 370.5/558.

tion of Negroes in all branches, which had already begun to weaken, was involved to the extent that G-3 was about to recommend that all Negro combat units be inactivated so that their personnel might be used for nontechnical service units, on the assumption that these, at least, could be sent to theaters and used. While all of the agencies concerned had been aware of the difficulties of shipping Negro units for some time, the question now began to spill over into the area of the possible usefulness of any Negro units, either in training in the United States or in operations in the theaters. The breaking point in G-3's tolerance of the steady worsening of the situation came in connection with the training of units for amphibious operations.

Training in combined amphibious operations was under the supervision of the Amphibious Force, Atlantic Fleet and a similar force under the Pacific Fleet. Though gas supply, service, and railhead quartermaster troops might be required for amphibious training, these supporting troops were not to be Negro, not even in the training phases. G-3 questioned the desirability of giving amphibious training to any of these supporting units, since their landings almost always came later in assault waves, thereby becoming primarily a matter of logistics. Recognizing that the responsibility for training these and such other supporting units as antiaircraft gun battalions rested with the commander of the Amphibious Force, G-3 tried to defer to his judgment in the matter. Gradually, however, the supply of white service units ran out, leaving only Negro units available. For the last three divisions to be amphibi-

ously trained in 1943, three white quartermaster service battalions in support were desired by the Amphibious Force. Moreover, a desired quartermaster truck company was to be white, for its personnel was to be used to instruct divisional personnel in Dukw operations.[64] Army Ground Forces, lacking the requested service battalions, asked permission to substitute Negro battalions.[65] The request was denied. Instead, AGF was directed to take two white service battalions from the Desert Training Center, substitute for them one Negro battalion earmarked for overseas shipment, and, to obtain the third battalion, remove one Negro battalion from the troop basis, substitute a white battalion, and activate it.[66]

Later, two tank battalions were required for amphibious training to be given on the west coast in October 1943. Army Ground Forces offered two available Negro tank battalions. The Operations Division rejected them. In discussions arising out of this incident, G-3 learned that Army Ground Forces was having difficulty employing any of its remaining Negro combat units in any form. The chief of G-3 then instructed his training branch to prepare a study citing these difficulties, and recommending, if necessary, that current policy on the provision of Negro units be reconsidered with a view to inactivating Negro combat units.

---

[64] Memo, G-3 for CG's Major Comds, 25 Mar 43, WDGCT 353 Amph (1-9-43); Incl A to Ltr, USAFAF to G-3, 8 Apr 43, AGF 353/70 (Amph Tng); Memo, G-3 for CG's Major Comds, 26 May 43, WDGCT 353 (5-18-43).

[65] Memo, Hq AGF for G-3, 18 Jun 43, AGF 353/72 (Amph).

[66] Memo, G-3 for CG AGF, 14 Jul 43, WDGCT 353 Amph (18 Jun 43).

G–3 asked Army Ground Forces and Army Service Forces to supply a list of Negro units whose estimated dates of readiness fell within the period 1 September 1943 and 1 February 1944. This list would be compared with the current six months' forecast of units scheduled for overseas movement. Both the ASF and AGF lists showed that ready units were not only on the six months' list but clearly listed there as Negro. The six months' list included, in the Pacific forecast, one Negro infantry division, the 93d, about whose shipment little discussion had been heard, since the division had been in training but a few months over a year. Moreover, the requirement of two tank battalions "which brought this matter to a head" had been canceled by the theater commander and Ground Forces had been directed to defer their training.

Except for a proposal to analyze the earmarking of units on the six months' chart to determine if last minute substitutions of white for indicated Negro units were being made a short time before shipping dates, G–3 was left with no solid facts upon which to base a recommendation. While the shipment of Negro units overseas had been slow in the past, enough other factors were involved to make it difficult to demonstrate clearly that Negro units could not be shipped in the future either because of their types or because of theater commanders' objections to their race. The six-months' charts indicated that, so far as the administrative machinery was concerned, Negro units were scheduled for shipment even though they might not leave the country as scheduled.[67]

Public Concern

The slowness of the deployment of Negro units overseas during 1942 and early 1943 produced expressions of concern in the Negro press, including doubts about the Army's intention of using any of the major units in combat. Upon the combat acquittal of Negro troops, the Negro papers felt, depended the future of the Negro in the Army and, to some extent, his position in American civil life. The commitment of the fighter squadron was of special concern to the Negro press, for it had been given to understand more and more frequently that the 99th Squadron was considered experimental by the Air Forces and that future expansion of the employment of Negro airmen depended upon the combat record of the 99th. "Today, a year and five months after the beginning of pilot training not a single one of our fliers is in combat service, although from time to time, announcement is made that numbers of them have been graduated and have received their wings," *The Crisis* commented in an editorial on Judge Hastie's resignation.[68] "There has been considerable talk that our men were not being trained to fight—not sincerely and thoroughly trained to fight," the same journal wrote after representatives of the press had observed the 93d Division on maneuvers in Louisiana in the spring of 1943. "It has been said that the Army was only going through the motions, hoping that Negro soldiers would not make good when the test came," it continued, although it reported that the

---

[67] Memo for Record on M/S, G–3 Tng to ExO G–3, 24 Aug 43, WDGCT 291.21 (24 Aug 43).

[68] "Hastie Resigns," *The Crisis*, L (February, 1943), 40. See also Pittsburgh *Courier*, February 20, 1943.

93d Division, fully equipped and well trained, was apparently being prepared for combat.[69] As the news of conversions and changes in a number of Negro units became a matter of public knowledge, the persistent questions of the Negro press became: Will any Negro combat units be left? Will any of those left be used in combat? The War Department and its major agencies were quite aware of this phase of the problem.[70]

The deployment of Negro troops overseas became, therefore, not merely a question of persuading theater commanders and foreign areas to take and use Negro troops. It became a question involving the entire organization and training policy of the Army as it affected Negro troops. It became, as well, a question of public policy. More important, from the point of view of the actual operational employment of Negro troops, it became a key question in that galaxy of queries which, by the spring of 1943, formed a cluster whose full effect was: What, now, can the Army do to salvage usable Negro troops from the host of units, holding manpower immobile, for which there is apparently no immediate use? These units included not only the proportionate absorption units created primarily to hold Negro inductees —the sanitary companies, the air base security squadrons, and the aviation squadrons for whom, even when a possible need could be foreseen, priorities for shipment were so low that space on outgoing transports could rarely be provided so long as more urgently needed units and supplies were awaiting transportation, but also the combat units which the theaters were not prepared to welcome. The Army had no clear answer to this question until after the first Negro combat unit engaged in active operations against the enemy in the summer and autumn of 1943.

[69] "Maneuvers Nail Lie," *The Crisis*, L (June, 1943), 167.

[70] Memo, ACofAS Opns, Commitments, and Rqmts for DCofS, 20 May 43, AAF 322–AB; Min Gen Council, 31 May 43.

CHAPTER XVI

Introduction to Combat: Air Phase and Aftermath

Despite the formulation of several policies on their shipment, relatively few Negro troops of any sort were overseas by the spring of 1943. None of the larger combat units, including the nondivisional units, had been actively employed in an overseas theater. The 24th Infantry Regiment went to the New Hebrides in the South Pacific in May 1942. Plans had been made to employ it in the latter phases of the campaign on Guadalcanal, but Japanese resistance there collapsed earlier than had been expected. The unit did not reach Guadalcanal until the main fighting was over.[1] There were antiaircraft and air base security units overseas but few of these had gone to active areas. Converted units were assigned their new functions with the expectation that they could then be shipped and used more speedily and effectively, but these units usually required further training in their new tasks. Brig. Gen. Benjamin O. Davis, who had spoken frequently of the desirability of sending Negro troops to active theaters, if only to counter the

growing and morale-damaging impression that they would not be sent out of the country, formally recommended in April 1943 that the Advisory Committee on Negro Troop Policies specifically propose that a Negro combat unit be sent to an active theater without delay.[2]

At the time, only 79,000 out of 504,-000 Negro troops were overseas—a little more than 15 percent of the whole. The bulk of these were service troops; two thirds of the whole were in engineer, quartermaster, and transportation units. Of ground forces Negro troops, only 7 percent of all types were overseas. Steps were being taken to return the three Negro separate infantry regiments from the defense commands to Army Ground Forces for retraining and preparation for overseas movement. The 99th Fighter Squadron was under orders to proceed to a port of embarkation. The 93d Division could be ready for shipment on 1 October 1943 if desert training were not given it and on 1 December if it received this training. But there was no assurance that it would be accepted by an active theater when ready. Proposals had been made to send the 93d to Hawaii, but this, if done, would not solve the problem, for

---

[1] Msg, CG U.S. Forces in New Caledonia for WD (AGWAR OPD), 3 Apr 44, CM–IN 1811 (3 Apr 44); Memo, Pacific Theater Sec, Theater Gp OPD for Brig Gen Carl A. Russell, 24 Apr 44, OPD Statistical Data Concerning Negro Trps (Theater Gp File).

[2] Min of Advisory Com, 2 Apr 43, ASW 291.2 NTC.

Hawaii was only a training and defense area. Moreover, the Hawaiian command was not anxious to give main defense positions to a Negro division.[3]

The Fighter Program

Of all the Negro combat units, the Air Forces' 99th Pursuit Squadron got the most attention as an immediate candidate for overseas shipment. The chief of the Army Air Forces directed in February 1942, before the unit had obtained its first pilot, that the 99th Pursuit Squadron should be prepared for foreign service as soon as possible. At the time the Air Training Command estimated that on a normal schedule the 36 pilots needed for the first squadron would not be available before 9 October 1942. If the schedule was speeded up by starting students in elementary (without preflight) training, by doubling the entry rate, and by entering pilots directly into basic training if they had completed secondary civilian pilot training under the Civil Aeronautics Administration program, 41 pilots would graduate by 3 July 1942 and 71 by October. There were 29 civilian pilot training secondary graduates available. At least 20 of these were expected to complete aviation cadet training successfully. This schedule did not provide for unit training for the squadron. To provide loss replacements for the 99th and the as yet unactivated 100th Squadron, yet another squadron would be needed.[4] To operate independently, the 99th Squadron would require its own supplementary service detachments as well. By March 1942 the Air Staff had selected the Liberia Task Force for the 99th. The 100th would see foreign service, "but it's not known at this time where it will go." [5]

As soon as it received its minimum pilot complement and hastily provided service detachments, the 99th rushed to complete its unit training and depart for overseas. Successive departure dates came and went. During the waiting period, its pilots added hours of training time, becoming so proficient as to evoke favorable comment from many observers. This additional training time, later to be weighed against it as though it was a formal part of its scheduled training, enabled distinguished visitors, military and civilian—including Secretary Stimson, Mrs. Roosevelt, and the British Ambassador, Lord Halifax—to observe the alert and anxious personnel of the squadron, with the result that before long the legend grew that the 99th, in addition to being well trained, was also made up of especially selected personnel. It was true that the original enlisted specialists sent to Chanute Field for training had been selected from a long list of applicants, but many of these men were not included in the roster of the squadron. Most of the 99th's pilots had been "selected" through the fortunate chance of

---

[3] Monthly Strength of the Army, 31 Mar 43, AG 320.2 (3–31–43) OM–R; Memo, Trp Movmt Sec OPD for Gen Handy, 15 Oct 43, OPD 320.2 (8 Oct 43).

[4] Memo, Hq Air Corps Flying Tng Comd for CofAAF, 3 Feb 42. Not sent forward "as oral

directive was received from Chief AAF," according to Memo, Lt Col Harry A. Johnson, Chief, Tng Sec, Tng and Opns Div AAF, for Lt Col Richard T. Coiner, Jr., ExO to ASWA, 9 Feb 42, enclosing above Memo for information of ASWA Robert Lovett, ASWA 291.2.

[5] Memo, Col Coiner for ASW McCloy, 9 Mar 42, ASW 291.2 (3–6–42).

meeting the requirement of previous civilian pilot training, permitting them to enter the truncated training program designed to fill the unit as quickly as possible for early overseas use. The squadron, when finally filled, included its share (as any unit filled from locally available personnel did) of men and officers who, though qualified, were not so keenly desired by Tuskegee's base units as those whom their personnel officers did not offer to the 99th. The squadron was made up of better than average Negro Army personnel, but it was hardly the handpicked, selected unit that later comments made it out to be.

The 99th Squadron, still in the United States, technically remained a part of the Liberia Task Force until January 1943 when, with the threats from Vichy West Africa and Axis forces in the Middle East removed, it was no longer necessary to provide for the air defense of Liberia. Meantime, the proposal of the Air Staff that the 99th be sent to China to join Brig. Gen. Claire L. Chennault's forces had been rejected by the Operations Division as politically dangerous, since the inexperienced squadron would there meet combat conditions that might result in heavy losses. These could reflect unfavorably upon the War Department.[6] The squadron continued its training while the Air Forces sought a place to send it. Finally the North African theater was selected, and it left Tuskegee on 2 and 3 April 1943, sailing from New York on 24 April. It left behind the 332d Fighter Group, contributing some of its personnel to the group's three partially filled squadrons. The 332d departed Tuskegee a few days

later for Selfridge Field, Michigan, where it was to train so that Tuskegee Field might be relieved of training so large a unit.

It was generally understood that when the 99th reached North Africa it would go into combat as soon as possible, for upon its performance, it was also understood, depended the future of Negroes in military aviation. As it worked out, early reports of the performance of the 99th Squadron became entwined with the future of Negroes in all other types of combat units as well.

Chill Upon the Future

In May 1943, Lt. Gen. Carl Spaatz, commanding the Twelfth Air Force in North Africa, advised General Henry H. Arnold that although the desire for an early combat test of the 99th was understood, it was believed that the squadron should be handled on exactly the same basis as other squadrons arriving in the theater.[7] Like other squadrons, therefore, the 99th was introduced to combat slowly. It was attached to the 33d Group, 64th Wing, XII Air Support Command. News reports disclosed that the 99th Squadron was used in the attack on Pantelleria in June where its first enemy plane was shot down by Capt. Charles Hall, but few details of its action there were known. In late August the squadron commander, Lt. Col. Benjamin O. Davis, Jr., was relieved for return to the United States where he was to command and complete the training of the 332d Fighter Group.

On the occasion of Colonel Davis' return, the news magazine *Time* pub-

---

[6] Memo, African–Middle East Sec, Theater Group OPD for Gen Handy, 8 Dec 42, OPD 370.5 Liberia.

[7] Memo, Secy Air Staff for ASW, 22 May 43, ASW 291.2 NT Alpha.

lished under the title "Experiment Proved?" not only an account of an interview with Colonel Davis but also hints and rumors about the current status of the squadron. So little operational data on the 99th had reached Washington, the magazine observed, that it was impossible to form a conclusive estimate of its abilities. "It has apparently seen little action, compared to many other units," the magazine reported, "and seems to have done fairly well; unofficial reports from the Mediterranean theater have suggested that the top air command was not altogether satisfied with the 99th's performance; there was said to be a plan some weeks ago to attach it to the Coastal Air Command, in which it would be assigned to routine convoy cover." [8]

Time's account appeared in its 20 September issue, on newsstands four days earlier. It was not until 19 September that General Spaatz signed a second indorsement to a report on the 99th that had originated three days before in Maj. Gen. Edwin J. House's Headquarters, XII Air Support Command. Protests and queries on *Time*'s suggestion that the Negro flyers were to be removed to less active duties therefore began to come into the War Department at about the same time that official theater reports arrived. As a matter of public policy, the War Department answered inquiries with denials that anything of the sort had been contemplated, but it was not many days before reports on the 99th Squadron had begun to affect the developing policy on the movement of Negro combat units

overseas and the formation of further Air Corps units.

General House reported to Maj. Gen. John K. Cannon, deputy commander of the Northwest African Tactical Air Force, that since 12 June when he took command of the XII Air Support Command he had visited the 99th Squadron frequently and that he was particularly impressed with its commander, Colonel Davis. "On the day of the 99th's first encounter with enemy aircraft," he wrote, "I happened to be on the airdrome and was very complimentary and encouraging to the personnel I met." Since then, he had compared the 99th with a white fighter squadron operating in the same group (33d) and with the same type of equipment. The group commander, Col. William W. Momeyer, had reported to him:

The ground discipline and ability to accomplish and execute orders promptly are excellent. Air discipline has not been completely satisfactory. The ability to work and fight as a team has not yet been acquired. Their formation flying has been very satisfactory until jumped by enemy aircraft, when the squadron seems to disintegrate. This has repeatedly been brought to the attention of the Squadron, but attempts to correct this deficiency so far have been unfruitful. On one particular occasion, a flight of twelve JU 88's, with an escort of six ME 109's, was observed to be bombing Pantelleria. The 99th Squadron, instead of pressing home the attack against the bombers, allowed themselves to become engaged with the 109's. The unit has shown a lack of aggressive spirit that is necessary for a well-organized fighter squadron. On numerous instances when assigned to dive bomb a specified target in which the anti-aircraft fire was light and inaccurate, they chose the secondary target which was undefended. On one occasion, they were assigned a mission with one squadron of this Group to bomb a target

---

[8] *Time*, XLII (September 20, 1943), 66–68.

COLONEL DAVIS HOLDING A PRESS CONFERENCE *in the War Department on his return from the MTO, 10 September 1943. Seated at right of the younger Davis is his father, General Davis: Truman Gibson, Civilian Aide, is on his left.*

in the toe of Italy; the 99th turned back before reaching the target because of the weather. The other squadron went on to the target and pressed home the attack. As later substantiated, the weather was considered operational.

The group commander went on to remark that the squadron had averaged 28 sorties per man; yet Colonel Davis had requested that his men be removed from combat for 3 days during the battle of Sicily because of fatigue, while pilots in the white squadrons of the group, with an average of 70 sorties after continuous operations for nine months, continued to fly. "Based on the performance of the 99th Fighter Squadron to date," he continued, "it is my opinion that they

are not of the fighting caliber of any squadron in this Group. They have failed to display the aggressiveness and desire for combat that are necessary to a first-class fighting organization. It may be expected that we will get less work and less operational time out of the 99th Fighter Squadron than any squadron in this group." [9]

General House observed that he had released Colonel Davis, although he did not believe that the next ranking officer would approach Col. Davis' standard; that in many discussions which he had held with officers of all professions, "in-

[9] Ltr, Hq XII Air Support Comd to Gen Cannon, Deputy Comdr, Northwest African Tactical AF, 16 Sep 43, WDCSA 291.21.

cluding medical," the consensus was that "the negro type has not the proper reflexes to make a first-class fighter pilot." On the rapid moves made within his command, "housing and messing difficulties arise because the time has not yet arrived when the white and colored soldiers will mess at the same table and sleep in the same barracks." Details were not being presented, he said, "because it is desired that administrative features not be a part of this report." He recommended that the 99th be assigned to the Northwest African Coastal Air Force and equipped with P–39's so that its P–40's could be used as replacements for active operations still to come and that "if and when" a Negro group was formed in the United States, it be kept there for defense command duties. This would release a white fighter group for movement overseas.[10]

General Cannon shared the opinion that the 99th's men lacked the stamina and lasting qualities of pilots of other squadrons. They had, he concluded, "no outstanding characteristics in which they excel in war the pilots of other squadrons of this command."[11] General Spaatz, forwarding these reports to General Arnold, added:

1. Since the arrival of the 99th Fighter Squadron in this theater, I have personally inspected the organization several times. There has been no question of their ground discipline and their general conduct. It has been excellent.

2. In processing them for combat action they were given the benefit in our training system of the supervision of instructors with much combat experience. They were processed into combat action very carefully.

3. I am forwarding this report with full confidence in the fairness of the analysis made by both General Cannon and General House. I feel that no squadron has been introduced into this theater with a better background of training than had by the 99th Fighter Squadron.[12]

With the arrival of these reports, immediately hand-carried to the chief offices concerned, the Army Air Forces recommended that the 99th be moved to a rear defense area, that the three fighter squadrons still in training be assigned to a rear defense area, thus releasing white squadrons for a forward combat area, and that the continuation of the Negro combat training program, which involved the activation and training of a medium bombardment group, be abandoned. The Air Forces recommended that this be done only with President Roosevelt's approval. It prepared a draft letter to the President for General Marshall's signature.[13]

The Air Forces attached to its recommendation an analysis indicating that the 99th had required eight months of training in comparison with three months for white units, and that its requirements in supervisory personnel had been "completely out of proportion to the results achieved."[14] Illogically, the unorthodox arrangements through which the 99th completed its training at a flying training command school while under the control of the Third Air Force, with all the attendant delays and problems of supervision, were now

[10] *Ibid.*

[11] 1st Ind, Hq Northwest African Tactical AF to Ltr cited n. 9.

[12] 2d Ind (complete), Hq Northwest African AF (Gen Spaatz) to Ltr cited n. 9.

[13] Memo, CofAS for CofS, attention ACofS G–3, 4 Oct 43, WDCSA 291.21.

[14] Memo, ACofAS Tng for ACofAS Plans, 28 Sep 43, Tab B to Memo cited n. 13.

charged against the squadron. After noting a shortage of P–40 aircraft available for training the 99th, the Air Forces declared that it had had difficulty finding "capable personnel to train for the various duties" both in this squadron and in the 332d Fighter Group. The 332d had been re-equipped with P–47's but "thru difficulties of retraining mechanics" this group was again equipped with P–40's, thus further delaying its training. When it was learned that P–40's would not be available in the theater to which the group was committed, another change was made to P–39's. With the group only half-equipped with its newest planes, training was now further delayed. The "full time duty" of the specially erected white "training" squadron, a "luxury not afforded similar white units," was also charged against the 332d Group. Time lost from the necessity for changing airplanes twice in the pilot replacement training system so that equipment in the group might be standardized was also added to the time and expense of training the group.[15]

In view of the Air Forces recommendations, General Marshall in early October 1943 directed G–3 to analyze again the entire Negro combat unit situation, ground as well as air.[16]

The 99th: Catalyst

The Air Forces' recommendations arrived at a time when, under the impact of manpower, training, and deployment problems, the whole program of providing Negro units was being pondered by both G–3 and the Advisory Committee. G–3, pursuing further the answer to the problem of the deployment of Negro troops overseas and the conversion of combat units to service types, had already sent messages to the commanding generals of the South Pacific, Southwest Pacific, North African, and China theaters asking for statements on the combat efficiency of Negro units in their theaters under hazardous conditions. Instances of unsatisfactory combat efficiency of Negro officers were specifically requested.[17]

The South Pacific theater reported no Negro combat or service units further forward than areas subject to occasional bombing; there their services were satisfactory. The theater had no instances of unsatisfactory combat service, though it asserted that individual soldiers lacked initiative and alertness and that neither Negro officers nor replacements were as effective as comparable white personnel.[18] The Southwest Pacific theater responded that though it had no Negro combat units in action, its service units had been used in forward areas under the general hazards and privations of campaigning with entirely satisfactory service. Negro officers' service, General MacArthur said, he would rate as average.[19]

From India came the report that though no other Negro units in the the-

---

[15] *Ibid.* The full-time white squadron consisted of officer and enlisted instructor personnel, activated as a separate squadron to avoid their assignment to the Negro units with which they worked. This squadron had no function except to hold white personnel training the 332d.

[16] G–3 Brief, 8 Oct 43, WDGCT 291.2 (4 Oct 43).

[17] Book Msgs to CG SPA, CINC SWPA, CG NATO, CG AMMISCA, 29 Sep 43, CM–OUT 13623, CM–OUT 13646, and CM–OUT 13647.

[18] COMGENSOPAC to AGWAR, 2 Oct 43 (SOPAC 3162).

[19] Rear Echelon GHQ SW Pacific to WAR (signed MacArthur), 2 Oct 43, CM–IN 981.

ater had been under fire, the conduct of the 823d Engineer Aviation Battalion under hazardous conditions of combat during Japanese raids on Assam in October 1942 was "magnificent." After the strafing, these engineers returned to their work promptly and began airfield repairs at once. One member of the unit received the Silver Star for action under fire during these raids; another received a Purple Heart for wounds received while removing government property from a burning warehouse. There was no known unsatisfactory combat conduct in this unit, whose only Negro officer was a chaplain reported efficient in his duties.[20]

The North African theater replied that its reports were incomplete, but that its only Negroes actively engaged in combat were in the 99th Squadron. The theater summarized the reports on the 99th sent from the Commanding General, North African Air Force, to the Commanding General, Army Air Forces, on 19 September. The conduct of Negro service units under occasional air attacks was generally satisfactory. Negro officers in the theater were generally satisfactory, but the Commanding General, Services of Supply, had stated that his Negro officers were inferior to white officers of similar grade, training, and experience.[21]

G–3 supplemented these reports with some additional information drawn from its own files. General Eisenhower had reported that during the week ending 5 August the 99th Squadron had successfully carried out difficult mis-

sions, strafing Axis communications and supply columns in Sicily. The same communication affirmed that ordnance and supply units which had landed at Gela during the earliest days of the invasion of Sicily were continuing to carry out vitally important supply assignments with the same efficiency they had previously exhibited in North Africa; that antiaircraft units were executing regular missions; and that the 41st Engineers were engaged in construction and repair work at North African invasion ports.[22] Moreover, an extract from a personal letter available to G–3 indicated that an air base security battalion in the same theater had held fast at Faid Pass when a white organization ran through it to the rear.[23] The theater reports had shown that white troops were generally preferred, G–3 noted, but combat experience had not been cited in support of this preference.

[20] Ferris to Marshall (New Delhi to AGWAR and Chungking), 6 Oct 43, CM–IN 3537.
[21] AFHQ Algiers to WAR (signed Eisenhower), 7 Oct 43, CM–IN 4335.
[22] CM–IN 3437 (5 Aug 43), Algiers to WAR (signed Eisenhower), Tab C to Memo, G–3 for CofS, 8 Oct 43, WDGCT 291.21 (4 Oct 43).
[23] Tab D to Memo, G–3 for CofS, 8 Oct 43, WDGCT 291.21 (4 Oct 43). The extract quoted by G–3 was: ". . . I don't know whether or not I told you this but Dewey's outfit held down the right flank of a certain division at Faid Pass, when a white organization ran through his lines to the rear, losing a lot of their equipment in the process. This should have panicked Dewey's men but they held together without exception. He has a total of only 4 casualties in his entire organization: 1 killed, 3 wounded—from strafing. I tell you this because I thought you might be interested in knowing how some of your men held up under fire when according to most psychological standards they should have been unnerved." This letter was written 16 May 1943; the unit referred to was the 907th Air Base Security Battalion, commanded by Lt. Col. Charles M. Dewey, a unit of the XII Air Service Command. The author of the letter later died of wounds received from a soldier of the 82d Airborne Division while he was investigating an act of discrimination against his men. Hist 909th AB Security Bn, Nov 43, AF archives.

In reporting this information to General Marshall, G-3 advised that Negro units had not yet been employed "in combat on a scale which would justify a conclusion as to their value, nor any fundamental change in the present War Department policies for such troops." Furthermore, G-3 recommended that the Army send both the 93d Division and the 332d Fighter Group to the Mediterranean area in order to provide a "just and reasonable test" of the value of large Negro units in combat.[24]

A Closer View

The report on the combat efficiency of the 99th Squadron was presented to the Advisory Committee on 13 October for discussion and comment. General White, the G-1, informed the committee that he had received similar reports from the 332d Group's commander when he was in Africa. Truman Gibson was of the opinion that contrary to general reports the 99th Squadron did not have personnel particularly selected and that white squadrons had done worse upon commitment. The squadron had had no flight leaders with combat experience and, Gibson reminded the committee, all of the facts were not currently available. He recalled that the Air Forces had initially believed that Negroes could not fly; now it believed that they lacked the ability to fight. General Davis suggested that veterans could not be made in one campaign and that therefore the program should be continued; he did not wish to criticize General Arnold, but he did not believe that the report justified scrapping the

program. General Porter informed the committee that his G-3 Division had recommended that the program be continued but that, in a study then being made, it was shown that Negroes were reluctant to follow Negro leaders. He suggested that an infantry division be developed with all white officers which, after successful combat experience, could receive substitute Negro officers. To this General Davis responded that, although available Negro leadership was limited, such a division would be discouraging. He added that training Negroes in the South put two strikes against them already; they would rather train in forty degree below zero weather anywhere else.

With the discussion rapidly moving into general philosophies on the proper training and use of Negro troops, Secretary McCloy recommended that everybody on the committee reserve his opinion until Colonel Davis, the former commander of the squadron, could be brought to Washington to discuss the matter. Before the war was over, McCloy continued, all manpower might be needed; perhaps training methods needed changing. He directed that a copy of the report be sent to Colonel Davis and that he be brought in for a conference.[25] The conference was set for 16 October, three days later.

In the meantime, G-3, the Operations Division, and General Arnold, in an agreement arrived at through Mr. McCloy, decided to submit the problem to Maj. Gen. Walter B. Smith, General Eisenhower's chief of staff in Italy. The Operations Division wished his comment on both the original Air Forces

---

[24] Memo, G-3 for CofS, 8 Oct 43, WDGCT 291.21 (4 Oct 43).

[25] Min, Advisory Com, 13 Oct 43, ASW 291.2 NT Com.

plan and the new G–3 proposal that both the 332d Fighter Group [26] and the 93d Division be sent to the Mediterranean. After discussing the matter with Maj. Gen. Thomas T. Handy, Col. Edward J. Rehmann, acting chief of OPD's Troop Movement Section, tried to brief the problem. He concluded that the reports on combat units, particularly the 99th Squadron, were "somewhat conflicting." The injection by G–3 of the question of the employment of ground forces into the problem brought up new questions, those of shipping and the acceptability of a division to the North African theater. "In view of the limited use of these units and the conflicting viewpoints it would appear desirable to have the matter fully investigated by the Theater Commander in order to obtain sufficient data to back up the proposed letter to the President," Colonel Rehmann advised. He noted that General Eisenhower's willingness to accept a division might be greater if it were not used as a substitute for the white units already planned for the Mediterranean, and that one advantage of sending a division to the Mediterranean was that from this location it could easily be sent to other theaters "in the event the unit proves its combat efficiency." [27]

A portion of the Advisory Committee

met with Colonel Davis on 16 October.[28] Colonel Davis began his answers to the committee's queries by saying that the main part of General House's letter was quoted from Colonel Momeyer's report and that what Colonel Momeyer, one of the best fighter pilots known to him, had to say, was entitled to respect. Colonel Davis then went on to state that the squadron had entered combat with certain handicaps. Because no one in the squadron had had combat experience there was a lack of confidence despite the high quality of the squadron's training. Mistakes, arising out of inexperience, occurred on the squadron's first missions. For these he would offer no excuse. On the squadron's first encounter with the enemy, over Pantelleria, it failed to maintain a flight of sixes, breaking down to twos. There was one occasion when the squadron failed to dive-bomb a target. Colonel Davis had led that mission and turned back on account of weather. No secondary target was involved. That the squadron had a reputation for disintegrating when jumped came as a surprise to him, for only the one incident, the one which he had mentioned, had been called to his attention. The squadron met fighters on 80 percent of its sorties; if there was a lack of aggressiveness, Colonel Davis felt, it was at first only. "Later we had it," he declared.

He had asked on 15 August that the squadron have 48 hours off, but he thought the circumstances should be considered. The squadron had operated continuously for two months without receiving replacements although the

---

[26] The fighter group had already been accepted by the theater in August (Eisenhower to WAR, 21 Aug 43, W7886, CM–IN 15993) ; Memo, AAF for OPD, 17 Sep 43, and DF, OPD for AAF, 27 Sep 43, both in OPD 370.5 Africa (17 Sep 43) .

[27] Memo for Gen Smith (signed E. J. R.), typed across top of OPD Memo for Gen Handy, 15 Oct 43, OPD 320.2 (8 Oct 43), photocopy on microreel 512/27 AFHQ G–3 Opns Div 59/4 on 106/F, AGO Records.

[28] Min of Mtg of Certain Members of the Advisory Com on Negro Trp Policies, 16 Oct 43, ASW 291.2 NT Com.

standard set up was 4 per month; consequently the 99th Squadron had only 26 pilots as compared with 30 to 35 in other squadrons. On heavy days, therefore, his pilots flew from three to six missions. If he had had a full quota of pilots, the strain would have been lighter.

As to the stamina of the individual pilots, Colonel Davis had noted no differences between his pilots and others; his pilots had received the same food as others, and were in good condition. Housing and messing difficulties had not arisen, although they might in winter. Each squadron had bivouacked separately and his squadron was not a member of a group except for operations. His men were more tense, but Colonel Davis attributed this to the smaller number of pilots available. He had no complaint about his pilots or their training. The impression that the squadron was not aggressive enough had not been brought to his attention in the theater. "I carried out my mission—if given a mission to bomb a target," he said, "I went ahead and bombed it." [29]

The Operations Division in the meantime went ahead with the preparation of its own recommendations for the Chief of Staff. If the conclusion on the value of Negro combat troops was not justified for ground troops on the basis of existing evidence, as G–3 had said, it certainly was for "air combat units, particularly fighters," General Handy insisted. The one fighter squadron had been made up of especially selected and very well trained personnel, Operations Division reiterated. "I do not believe we should activate any more such units and that the squadrons now in existence should be used in other than active combat areas," General Handy wrote, adding that there were several other matters to be considered in connection with G–3's recommendations. If the 93d Division was moved to the Mediterranean, it was doubtful that it would be used in combat. General Smith, Chief of Staff, Allied Force Headquarters, had stated that a maximum of sixteen divisions could be maintained in Italy. Faced with active German opposition, "one of the sixteen will certainly not be the colored division as long as tested white divisions were available." The question of over-all command of American Negro units could not be ignored. "In my opinion," General Handy stated, "our colored divisions should be employed in a theater where it can be reasonably expected that they will always serve under American high command." The chances of the 93d's entry into combat would be just as good if it went to Hawaii. He therefore recommended that the action proposed by Army Air Forces be approved, that the 93d Division be sent to Hawaii with a view to its later employment in the Central, South, or Southwest Pacific, and that the proposed letter requesting the President's approval of the alteration in the air program be dispatched over Secretary Stimson's signature.[30]

General Arnold felt that these Operations Division recommendations were all right, but noted that action should be deferred until word came from General Smith. General Handy concurred

---

[29] *Ibid.*

[30] Memo, OPD for CofS, 19 Oct 43, OPD 320.2 (8 Oct 43).

on 20 October.[31]   The whole proposal, now comprising a thick sheaf of papers, was deposited with the Deputy Chief of Staff at the end of the month, pending receipt of General Smith's comments.[32]

Expansion in the Air Program

Action on the medium bombardment group could not await decision on the continuation of the general combat program.   Consideration of this group had been under way since the spring of 1943.[33]   Complicated schedules for the training of necessary enlisted specialists, arranged so that the necessary space for the required numbers of Negro students would be available in specified classes at Air Forces training centers at the proper times, had been set up.[34]   Enlisted specialist trainees were already enrolled in some schools.   Tuskegee Field was to continue training all pilots. Bombardier-navigators, the original group coming from former Tuskegee cadets, were scheduled to enter naviga-

tion school in the Central Flying Training Command in October and to join bombardiers later at another central command school.[35]

The Air Forces' shift in policy for training flying officers had grown out of developments at Tuskegee as well as out of a recognition of the economies and improvements in training efficiency to be obtained by the use of existing school facilities.   Tuskegee had developed into a unique school. While most training fields were devoted to one specialized phase of training only, Tuskegee carried the cadet from the college training stage to graduation and initial tactical assignment, all in fields and installations within a radius of about five miles of the main post.[36]   Not only the increase in numbers of men but also the variety of activities caused administrative and training problems there. At times, portions of the field were under the Third Air Force, the Air Service Command, the Technical Training Command, and the Flying Training Command, most of which had little knowledge of the variety of activities supervised by other commands through the one small post headquarters.   By late 1943 the field was the training station for Negro pre-aviation cadets, preflight pilots, preflight bombardier-navigators, preflight bombardiers, basic pilots, advanced single-engine pilots, advanced twin-engine pilots, and pilots in transitional training in the P–40 after graduation from the advanced single-engine school.   The field also trained field artillery liaison pilots for the

---

[31] Handwritten notes on above, signed H. H. A. and C. K. G. (Col C. K. Gailey, ExO OPD).

[32] Memo for Record, O.L.N. (Col Otto L. Nelson), Asst DCofS, 27 Oct 43, WDCSA 291.21 (8 Oct 43).

[33] R&RS, CofAS for A–3, 11 Mar 43; R&RS, A–1 for A–3, 19 Mar 43; R&RS, Dir of Air Support for Dir Mil Rqmts, 17 Mar 43; R&RS, Dir of Bombardment for Dir of Mil Rqmts, 17 Mar 43, all in AAF 353–A Negro Tng; Memo, Actg Civ Aide to SW for ASWA, 1 May 43, ASWA 291.2; Memo, ACofAS Tng for Gen Giles, 10 May 43, AAF 380 Prog; Memo, R&RS, DCofAS for ACofAS Opns, Commitments, Rqmts, 10 May 43, with Staff Study for CG AAF, 10 Jun 43, and Approving Comment 10, AAF 353–A, Negro Tng; Memo, ACofAS Tng, for ACofAS Pers, 6 Oct 43, AAF 373.1Tactics and Techniques.

[34] Ltrs, ACofAS Tng to CG AAF Tng Comd, 7 Aug 43, AAF 353 Cld Tng, Binder 1; Ltrs, ACofAS Tng to CG AAF Tng Comd, 18 Sep 43, 5 Oct 43, Jun 43–Aug 44, AAF 353–A Negro Tng.

[35] Ltr, ACofAS Tng for CG AAF Tng Comd, 7 Aug 43, and Inds, AAF 353 Cld Tng, Binder 1.

[36] Hist Tuskegee Army Air Field, 1 Jan 43–29 Feb 44, AF Archives.

Ground Forces and Haitian and French colonial cadets. It also acted as a pool, holding enlisted and officer specialists awaiting assignment. The commandant of cadets had eight different types of classes to supervise. Training was so closely confined to the facilities of this field that cadets were not given standard classification tests to predetermine flying aptitudes until April 1943 when the field got its own psychological section.[37] Screening Negro applicants to determine their relative aptitude as pilots, bombardiers, or navigators, not used when all candidates were presumptive fighter pilots, began in November 1943.

Because Tuskegee was officially classified under the Advanced Training Wing of the Training Command, directives concerning the preflight schools sometimes never reached it, with the result that training there was often out of step with that at other stations. One advantage of the compact school was that all previous records of a particular cadet were always available, but "one of the disadvantages of the concentration of training at the field is trouble in the traffic pattern resulting from the various speeds of planes; neither can the over-all field be used but one runway must be operated from at a single time."[38]

Periods of crowding, followed by slack periods, were normal for the station. In late 1943 when the question of superimposing the bombardier-navigator program upon existing activities at Tuskegee came up, the station was already complaining that excess men, for whom no assignments existed, were arriving in large numbers. Tuskegee informed the Air Forces:

For the past six (6) months, enlisted men have been sent to this station, especially from technical schools of both the Air Corps and the Signal Corps, classified and trained in jobs for which, in the main, there are no positions at this station. . . . At the present time the number is approximately 120 and this station is operating under a Manning Table and has no personnel available to care for these men. No further training can be given them as they are all specialists and in most cases due to their rank are not suitable for reclassification nor for assignment to any other job on the station. Not only are these men presently at this station, but daily men are transferred into this station. . . . This is certainly a waste of manpower and malassignment of personnel and a serious imposition on this station as these men are not needed, can serve no useful purpose at this station, and constitute a serious drain upon our personnel which has to be assigned to care for them. This office has made repeated reports of this matter and to date no relief has been forthcoming.[39]

Some of these men were technical trainees scheduled for use in the now doubtful bombardment group and its supporting units. Tuskegee was falling heir to a byproduct of indecision in Air Forces headquarters. To complicate

[37] This battery of 16 tests—12 paper and pencil and 4 with apparatus—predicted success in the several aviation fields. Scores, ranging from 1 to 9, were known as stanine numbers. An over-all stanine number was assigned for the complete battery. Individual scores were given for each test, so that the cadet with a 9 in radar, a 7 in navigation, and a 6 in piloting could be assigned to the specialty in which he was most likely to succeed.
[38] Hist Tuskegee Army Air Field 1 Mar–30 Jun 44, Air Hist Gp 289.28–4, VI, 41. Quote is a paraphrase of interview with Maj Robert M. Long, Dir Advanced Single-Engine Tng, Tuskegee Army Air Field.
[39] Ltr, Hq Tuskegee Army Air Field to ACofAS Pers, Hq AAF, 4 Dec 43, AAF 220.31 Tuskegee. See also Ltr, Hq Tuskegee Army Air Field for CG AAFEFTC, Maxwell Field, 18 Nov 43, AAF 220.31 Tuskegee.

training at Tuskegee further by the addition of bombardier and bombardier-navigator training to the types already there would have been nearly intolerable.

The Air Forces, breaking quietly with the concentration of flying training at Tuskegee and avoiding thereby the previous year's experience with Jefferson Barracks, decided to schedule the new trainee classes into existing schools formerly used for white trainees only. Some of these schools were located in areas previously thought of as impossible for training Negroes.

The first class of navigation cadets, selected from men eliminated from the Tuskegee fighter pilot training program, arrived at Hondo Field, Texas, on 25 October for cadet navigation training, although a definite decision on the bombardment unit had not yet been made.[40] Since the activation of this unit was involved with the outcome of discussions on the future of Negro combat units then under way, hesitancy about continuing plans for the new bombardment group increased within Air Forces headquarters. In some conferences and communications the group was definitely mentioned as being "out"; in others, planning for the group went ahead.

"We must have a decision, a definite one soon, on the above subject," Brig. Gen. Mervin E. Gross wrote to Brig. Gen. Howard A. Craig on 20 October. The training schedule then being followed for Tuskegee would provide more pilots than could be used by the fighter group. If the bomber group was to be discontinued, no directive eliminating it had been given to the responsible chiefs of staff. If it was to be continued, the First Air Force had to be directed to prepare to receive its personnel and activate its units. If the bomber group was not to be activated, then the Air Operations, Commitments, and Requirements and the Air Training Divisions should be informed so that other uses of personnel earmarked for it could be made. Otherwise, the Air Forces would find it difficult to explain why it had trained so many men for whom it had no need.[41]

General Arnold, who, in the spring of 1943, had reacted to the suggestion of the Tuskegee commander that political pressures might force a change in the Air Forces' training program with the remark that the training program would be determined by him in the future as it had been in the past, and that it would be based only upon the foreseeable use of Negro squadrons,[42] decided on 27 October to go ahead with the bombardment group. He directed that it be organized, trained, equipped, and sent to North Africa.[43]

It would now be necessary to set up auxiliary supporting service units as well, General Gross advised.[44] Although Air Training had warned of

[40] Hist AAF Navigation School, Hondo Army Air Field, 4 Jul 42–1 Mar 44, AF Archives; Hist Hondo Army Air Field, 1 Sep–1 Nov 44, AF Archives; Memo, ACofAS Tng for Civ Aide to SW, 4 Dec 43, AAF 353 Cld Tng, Binder 2.

[41] Memo, DACofAS for Opns, Commitments, and Rqmts for Gen Craig, 20 Oct 43, AAF 353 Cld Tng, Binder 2.

[42] R&RS, DCofAS for ACofAS for Opns, Commitments, and Rqmts and ACofAS Tng, 29 Apr 43, AAF 353–A Negro Tng.

[43] Penciled note, signed "C" (General Craig), R&RS, 27 Oct 43, to Memo, Gross for Craig, 20 Oct 43, and R&RS, Gross to Col Byron E. Brugge, 27 Oct 43, both in AAF 353 Cld Tng, Binder 2.

[44] Ibid.

these needs as far back as July, it now appeared that there would be insufficient pilots to activate the Replacement Training Unit Medium Bomb Group in December as planned.[45] Delays of this type were to play a continuing part in the career of the new 477th Bombardment Group. Demands on Tuskegee for single-engine pilots continued to grow in order to meet the needs of the 332d Fighter Group and the 99th Squadron. As schedules for twin-engine training were trimmed and altered to fill these demands, one or another phase of the supply of men to the bombardment group went out of kilter.

The Air Training Division requested that Tuskegee be relieved of the responsibility of producing all types of Negro pilots because its production rate was not sufficient to meet replacement fighter requirements and, at the same time, turn out enough pilots to meet O-Day (Operational Day) requirements for the bombardment group. Restriction to the maximum production possible at Tuskegee, Air Training predicted, would mean a delay in the bomb group until July 1945. Excess Negro flying cadets could be entered in existing white schools, thus increasing the output of Negro pilots.

Instead of acquiescing or increasing facilities at Tuskegee, Headquarters, Army Air Forces, rescinded the requirements for the bombardment group on 15 November. With the exception of B–25 transition, all pilot training continued at Tuskegee, with successive O-days set for the bombardment group. O-day for the group inched forward, until it eventually reached 10 January

1945.[46] Navigators alone were trained elsewhere.

Hondo Field's first class of navigators —the first air cadets to train outside of Tuskegee—graduated on 26 February 1944, after flying a training mission to New York City which attracted national attention. By the time four classes had entered, with two of them graduating, Hondo Field had some observations to make about the Air Forces' departure in training Negro cadets at the Texas school:

The morale of negro cadets is as high as the morale of any group of cadets on the field, according to their instructors, and there is no question that they doubt the value of their opportunity here. Instructors report almost no complaining or faultfinding on their part and they state the colored cadets take additional study classes and the restrictions imposed on all cadets without losing their sense of humor.
There have been very few cases of animosity toward negro cadets from white cadets; if animosity has been felt, it has not been shown. White cadets often ask negro cadets to oppose them in games on the P. T. field. Except during P. T. hours, there is little association between the two groups, however. The strenuous class-room and flying schedule makes leisurely association a luxury which cadets seldom enjoy.
In the opinion of their instructors, it is difficult and perhaps unfair to compare the negro cadet in his ground and air work with the white cadet. Class 44–11–9–B was equal to the average white classes in flying and considerably above average in ground school. A great deal of additional effort, however, was expended by their instructors in order to master even the smallest details of ground school work.

---

[45] Comment 2, 1 Nov 43, to R&RS, note cited n. 43.

[46] Memo, ACofAS Tng for Gen Arnold, 3 Nov 43, AAF 353 NT; Ltr, ACofAS Tng to CG AAF Tng Comd, 15 Nov 43, AAF Cld Tng, Binder 2; Ltr, Hq AAF Tng Comd to CG AAF, 18 Mar 44, and 1st Ind, Hq AAF to CG AAFTC, 25 Mar 44, AAF 353 Cld Tng.

With class 44–50–N–9, on the other hand, a pronounced diminution in the quality of work has been observed and there is every reason to believe that the explanation lies in the native quality of the students, not in the quality of the instruction. Of the thirty-two cadets who entered with the class, ten had stanine scores [composite scores from special Air Corps psychological tests] of four; five had stanines of five; eleven had stanines of six; two had stanines of seven; three had stanines of eight; and one had a stanine of nine. Thus only six of the thirty-two have stanines of seven or above and no white cadet is accepted for navigation training unless his stanine score is seven or more.

Men with stanines of seven or above are doing work that compares well with accepted, standard work; the others are noticeably slower in learning and a great deal slower in retaining the material. In the opinion of their instructors these men will, inevitably, be less proficient navigators than the average white graduate.

In the most recent class to enter Hondo, however, the situation is very different; only four of the twenty-nine men have stanines below seven, these four having stanines of six. Up to the end of the period of this installment this class had done no flying, but the composite on the first examination was 78% compared to a white composite of 85%.

Though this class promises to be very much superior to 44–50–N–9, their instructors are nevertheless inclined to believe, on the basis of the first test, that the students are somewhat slower in grasping the material or at least in retaining it than are average white cadets. The evidence of the quality of work that can be expected from white and colored cadets of equal stanines is inconclusive and it does not point to any marked difference in any event. Instructors are agreed, however, that no cadets, whether white or colored, with stanine scores below seven should be accepted for navigation training.

Colored cadets live in their own barracks and have their own classroom. They eat in the same mess as white cadets and have equal privileges and enjoy access to the same recreational facilities, namely, the Cadet Club, the cadet P. X., the cadet Day Room, and (for colored officers) the Officers Club and the B. O. M.

Colored cadets fly missions prescribed by the standard details of the missions. White pilots fly the planes. Extended missions have been flown to many fields and colored cadets have received the courtesies extended to white cadets. Like white cadets, they are usually fed in the enlisted men's mess unless they land at a field that has cadets, in which event they are fed at the cadet mess.

The extension of equal access to post facilities has resulted in some grumbling by white personnel, it goes without saying. It can be said, however, that behavior by all post personnel has at all times been "correct."[47]

In the meantime, an imbalance in the production of pilots and aircrewmen, followed by a shortage of trainees, developed. By the spring of 1944, Tuskegee noted that the balance in production of pilots, bombardiers, and navigators was going askew. Originally the stanine numbers for Negroes were set at not less than 4 for pilots and bombardiers and 5 for navigators. At the same time, the white minimums were 6 and 7, respectively. In April 1944 the stanine number for all Negro aircrew trainees was raised to 5, reducing the number of men eligible for pilot training. As early as 6 March 1944, the psychological unit at Tuskegee saw Negroes with high stanines diverted from pilot to bombardier and navigator training. While Tuskegee was turning out classes of 7 to 15 twin-engine pilots, classes of 20 to 87 preflight bombardiers and bombardier-navigators were leaving the school for

---

[47] Hist Hondo Army Airfield AAF, 1 Sep–1 Nov 44, pp. 14–17, AF Archives. On stanine scoring, see footnote 37, above.

advanced training, with some of the bombardiers and navigators in these unbalanced classes having stanine pilot scores of 8 or 9 but only 6 in the specialty to which they were assigned. These assignments were often based on predetermined quotas which were filled at the expense of the pilot classes. Tuskegee, at the same time, was producing single-engine pilot replacements. Eventually, a pilot shortage resulted. The backlog of Negro applicants was soon exhausted. In the spring of 1944 applications for flying training from men in the Ground and Service Forces were discontinued, thus slowing up production further.

Not until January 1945 did the balance begin to right itself. By then applications from nonflying Negro Air Forces officers (many of them men who, originally hopeful of a cadet appointment, had chosen an Officer Candidate School appointment while on the once-long waiting lists) were readmitted; then bombardier-navigator training stopped and excess bombardier-navigators were returned for pilot training; and, in February 1945, applications from Ground and Service Forces personnel were again accepted for Air training. About the middle of March 1945, personnel again began to "pour in for Aviation Training from all headquarters." [48] On 15 March 1945, the shortage was further alleviated when the Eastern Flying Training Command again lowered pilot stanine requirements to 4. [49] The net result, as originally predicted

by Air Training, was that the 477th Group was not fully manned with pilots and aircrewmen until the early summer of 1945.

The 99th Shakes Off a Chill

By 9 December 1943, when General Arnold, returning from the Cairo Conference, briefly visited the 99th Squadron at Madna Airfield, Italy, in company with Generals Spaatz and Cannon, the career of the squadron had changed considerably since the first reports on its operations had reached the War Department in September. After several weeks of duties in which its pilots saw few enemy planes and its men wondered what its future would be, the 99th joined the 79th Fighter Group at Foggia No.3 in Italy on 17 October 1943. The 79th had been operating as an independent fighter group since the preceding March, and was already on its third compliment of pilots by the time the 99th joined it. It was flying missions "every hour on the hour." In November the group moved from Foggia to Madna, a landing strip so bogged down in mud that the units had to wait until British Basuto (East African) Engineers laid additional landing mats in order to operate. When the weather improved the 99th kept up with the older squadrons. For the men of the 79th's four squadrons, "That meant rebombing, rearming, refueling, and repairing. Damaged aircraft were repaired, props were changed and instruments adjusted practically on the spot." [50] On 30 November the 79th Group flew 26 missions, a new record. Of these the 99th flew nine.

---

[48] Hist Rpt Squadron H, Tuskegee Army Air Field, Mar 45.

[49] Hist of Tuskegee Army Air Field, 1 Mar–30 Jun 44; Hist, 2143d AAF BU . . . and TAAF, 1 Jan–28 Feb 45, 1 Mar–30 Apr 45; both in AF Archives.

[50] Hist and War Diary, 79th Fighter Gp, Sep–Dec 43, AF Archives.

Pilots of the 99th, under Maj. George S. Roberts, gained in experience and confidence in their association with the 79th Group. After two months with the 79th, the 99th, which, in the absence of a means of direct comparison, had thought of itself as a combatwise veteran of the Pantellerian and Sicilian campaigns, found that it had learned a great deal more through the adoption of the flight tactics, take-off system, and formations of the older, more experienced group. "With these changes comes more experience and with the experience comes confidence. These two attributes are precisely what pilots of the 99th Squadron are getting," the unit reported.[51] Shortly after joining the group, one 99th pilot took off with landing gear jammed by a collision before take-off, but continued and completed a dive-bombing mission. Ground crewmen of the Negro squadron were surprised and pleased when, in servicing and gassing their allotted twenty of fifty P–38's landing at Sal Sola Field, they received "splendid cooperation" from men of the 79th in their joint project.[52] Pilots of the 99th eligible for return to the United States after flying fifty missions began to request longer tours.

The unit began to feel that in its association with the 79th Group it had at last joined the air team.

By early January 1944 General Spaatz had told General Arnold that he no longer believed that this one squadron was sufficient for a thorough test of Negro flyers' capabilities. Spaatz now wanted "one or two more squadrons there to make a full group," General Arnold informed General Craig of the Air Staff. Arnold suggested that the Twelfth Air Force be queried on the dates when a second and third squadron should arrive.[53] General Craig replied on 11 January that the 332d Fighter Group had already left for the Twelfth Air Force and the 553d Fighter Squadron had been set up in the United States to furnish pilot replacements for the units overseas.[54] On the same day, the binder containing the October proposals for the further reduction of Negro air units and the reassignment of those in existence was filed without further action.[55] The fighter units were now fully deployed and their prospects for full employment were brighter than for many months past.

[51] Hist 99th Fighter Squadron, Dec 43, AF Archives.
[52] Hist 79th Fighter Gp, 1 Jan 43–1 Jan 44; War Diary, 99th Fighter Squadron, Nov 43; both in AF Archives.

[53] Memo, Gen Arnold for Gen Craig, ACofAS for Opns, Commitments and Rqmts, 6 Jan 44, AAF 353–A Negro Tng.
[54] Memo, Craig for Arnold, 11 Jan 44, AAF 353–A Negro Tng.
[55] Handwritten note to Memo for Record, Asst to the DCofS, 27 Oct 43, WDCSA 291.2 (8 Oct 43), signed O. L. Nelson, dated 11 Jan 44.

CHAPTER XVII

Conversions and Commitments

While the disposition of Negro air combat units was engaging the attention of the War Department's top echelons, the course of converting other Negro units, especially from combat to service troops, continued as part of the larger manpower policy. It soon came into conflict with the urgings of the Advisory Committee on Negro Troop Policies, the Inspector General's Office, and the Negro press and public. Each, from its own point of view, supported the desirability of putting more Negro combat and supporting units into action. Although plans for the shipment of certain units were in the making, these units had not left the United States and, under the policy of secrecy governing the movement of troops in wartime, plans for their eventual commitment could not be disclosed in more than a vague and general way. The conversion of combat units in the United States to service units for future use overseas could not be so readily concealed, and such conversions reawakened all the old fears of the Negro public and its supporters; at the same time these conversions rekindled the concern of people who felt that Negroes should share fully in battlefield losses in order to preserve population ratios. The stripping of personnel from certain units started rumors that all Negro ground combat units, and particularly the 93d Infantry Division, were

scheduled for stripping and eventual disbandment.[1]

State of the Units

The stripped combat units, like the skeletonized units of the prewar period, became symbols of the failure to use Negro manpower fully. Within Army Ground Forces there had been attempts to salvage the stripped units with their double cadres. Some wished to reduce them further to one cadre each, using the excess cadremen for Headquarters 5889 in Liberia, about to be changed from white to Negro personnel, and for quartermaster troop transport companies. Army Ground Forces G–3 wanted to use excess unassigned Negroes to refill the stripped units.[2] But in the fall of 1943 these units' priority on personnel was too low for immediate filling. Allocations of personnel then operated under rigid priorities: (1), overseas replacements; (2), alerted units; (3), unfilled units; (4), new units immediately needed; and (5), new activations. Since Negro fillers were in short supply and since existing requirements for alerted

[1] Ltr, Walter White to SW, 17 Nov 43, AGF 322/5 (93d Inf Div); Ltr, Lawrence V. Jordan, West Va. High School Principals' Conf, to SW, 17 Nov 43, AG 291.2; Ltr, Roy Wilkins, NAACP, to SW, 18 Nov 43, AG 291.2.
[2] M/S, AGF G–3 to C&RD, 29 Sep 43, AGF 320.2/6042.

service units were higher than for un-committed artillery and tank destroyer units, filling the stripped units was not at the moment feasible. Even so, certain units—one field and two antiaircraft artillery battalions—were scheduled for refilling and Army Ground Forces planned to return the others to full strength.[3]

Of ten stripped field artillery battalions, eight were eventually refilled, but six of the refilled units were later converted to engineer combat units. The other two were inactivated.[4] Six of eight tank destroyer battalions awaited fillers for several months while Army Ground Forces requested permission to inactivate them and G–3 insisted that they remain with augmented cadres until the question of refilling them was settled. All were eventually inactivated.[5]

The Inspector General in an over-all survey of the state of Negro units, found in the fall of 1943 that determining the current status of Negro units had become difficult. Simply identifying Negro units, with their changing designations, was now a problem.[6] By the time The Inspector General's survey was completed in December the status of many units had already changed. From the evidence, nevertheless, The Inspector General concluded that the Army no longer had a unified, consistent policy for the activation, training, and employment of Negro units and that the lack of a sound policy had resulted in the

ineffective use of Negro units and a corresponding waste of manpower.

Although objecting that the survey presented "no pertinent information . . . not already known to the War Department," and that the survey had not taken into consideration plans and problems in the placement of Negroes in the completed mobilization program, G–3 admitted that the study was valuable, for it "focusses attention on the seriousness of the situation and indicates that prompt, remedial action must be taken." Despite attempts to meet the manpower commitments made by Secretary Stimson, G–3 declared, failure to employ Negro combat units overseas had placed the War Department in the unenviable position of:

a. Having a backlog of combat units in the United States as indicated in the Inspector General's survey.

b. Having to deplete or inactivate these units to provide personnel for service units to avoid wasting manpower.

c. Having to answer numerous queries from negro and other allied organizations without having definite justification for failure to commit negro units to combat or for placing the preponderance of negro personnel in service units.

G–3 recommended again: (1) that all available Negro combat units be shipped without delay to active theaters and ultimately employed on missions for which they were activated and trained; (2) that when necessary they be used initially on missions other than their combat missions provided that they retain their combat identity and not be otherwise disposed of "until they have had an opportunity to prove themselves in combat, gain their share of *battle honors* and accept their share of battle losses"; (3) that pending results of the use of Negro

[3] Memo, AGF for ASW, 25 Oct 43, AGF 341/1159 GNGSE (25 Oct 43).
[4] Memo, AGF for CofS (G–3), 2 Mar 44, AGF 321/107 (FA).
[5] Memo, AGF for Cofs (G–3), 5 Nov 43, AGF 320.2/12 (TUB) (30 Oct 43)–GNGCT; Memo, G–3 for AGF, 16 Nov 43, WDGCT 322 (29 Oct 43).
[6] Memo, TIG for DCofS, 1 Jan 44, IG 312.1 Misc.

combat units in battle no change be made in combat units provided for 1944; and (4) that the Bureau of Public Relations "impress upon the nation the great importance of, and need for, service units in any war, and by suitable press releases stress not only the service functions but also the combat requirements of service troops in a war of movement and vertical envelopment and the important contributions of negro units in connection therewith." [7]

The G–3 recommendations were approved in principle by the Deputy Chief of Staff, Lt. Gen. Joseph T. McNarney, on 10 January 1944. Similar G–1 proposals calling for the early employment of Negro troops in combat and for raising morale and improving leadership were approved on 20 January. [8] The G–3 proposal on the immediate shipment of Negro units then went to the Operations Division for comment and implementation.

The Operations Division observed that all available combat units, including Negro units, were being and would continue to be shipped without delay to active theaters. Combat units, both white and Negro, had been and would continue to be used on service missions when necessary and, during such diversion from their primary missions, they would retain their identities. It was expected, the Operations Division said, that "all combat units eventually will be given the opportunity to prove themselves in combat, gain their share of battle honors and accept their share of battle losses," as G–3 proposed. The Operations Di-

vision disclaimed current contemplation of changes in the combat units provided in the 1944 troop basis, but it invited attention to "the fact that no troop basis remains firm but must be modified in accordance with a continuously changing situation." The proportions of Negroes overseas, the Operations Division demonstrated, had increased markedly; they were now, at the end of 1943, almost mathematically proportionate to their numbers in the Army. [9] Among Negro units, one division was in process of moving and another division, six tank destroyer battalions, and four field artillery battalions were on the Operations Division's list for movement by the end of July 1944. But engineer, signal, ordnance ammunition, engineer ponton, amphibious truck, chemical smoke generator, troop transport, pack, and quartermaster service units, which the Operations Division listed among "combat support units normally employed in the combat zone, theater of operations," made up the bulk of the Negro units overseas. Despite official War Department definitions, in the public mind these were no substitutes for the combat units by which battle achievement was measured. The Operations Division therefore endorsed the G–3 proposal that the Bureau of Public Relations emphasize

[7] Memo, G–3 for DCofS, 6 Jan 44, WDGCT 291.21 (1 Jan 44). Italics in original.
[8] Memo, G–1 for CofS, 13 Jan 44, WDGAP/291.2, app. DCofS, 20 Jan 44.

[9] From the best figures available the Operations Division reported that on 31 December 1943 the following distributions prevailed:

Distribution	Number of Men
Negro strength in United States............	420,445
Negro strength overseas.................	213,894
Percentage of Negroes in Army.............	8.5
Negro percentage of overseas strength.......	8.7

Memo, OPD for ASW, 21 Jan 44, OPD 322.97 (6 Jan 44), Tab D.

the importance of service units, suggesting that it do so under the supervision of G–2. In sending this comment forward through Operations Division channels, the preparing officer noted: "I have kept this short purposely. No use of entering into futile controversy. The WD gives lip service to a policy that is fraught with difficulties. OPD appears to be in the clear *now* as we must use everything." [10]

Infantry Deployment

The Operations Division had just spent several months working with the "policy that is fraught with difficulties." This staff division was thoroughly familiar with the gap between policy and practice. Time and developments in the performance of the 99th Squadron and not policy had answered the question of the deployment, if not the use, of additional fighter units and the creation of a new bombardment group. How to put into practice stated policies on the deployment of more Negro ground combat units overseas had not been fully worked out. The Operations Division, nevertheless, went ahead with tentative plans to send the 93d Division to the Pacific. With three commands in the Pacific, all of whom required additional strength, one might be willing to use the unit.

At the beginning of 1943, Lt. Gen. Millard F. Harmon, commanding Army Forces in the South Pacific Area, was asked to comment on the possibility of using a Negro division. He replied that although he needed additional divisions he would prefer white ones because every man transported over great distances in scarce ships to his area should have maximum effectiveness. If no white divisions were available, he could use a Negro division for combat and for garrisoning forward areas, including the Solomons and Bismarcks. Because of the nature of the war in the Pacific, the highest type of leadership was needed in the lower echelons of command; for this reason and because native troops in the area had no native commissioned officers, none but white officers should be sent with any Negro division.[11] In light of divisional officer policies, this last requirement could not be met.

General Emmons, in Hawaii, was then asked if a white division from among those in Hawaii might be sent to the South Pacific if a Negro division replaced it in the defense of the islands.[12] Hawaii, at the time, wanted an extra division so that units coming into the islands to replace those going out to forward areas would not, during the training and disposition period, leave a gap in island defenses. Though General Emmons had indicated that a Negro division should not be assigned the task of garrisoning either populous Oahu or the outlying Hawaiian Islands, he was requested to draw up plans for the possible use of a Negro division in the Hawaiian area, both to free a white division for combat and garrison duties in the South Pacific and to provide employment for a Negro unit. At a

---

[10] Memo, OPD for ASW, 21 Jan 44, and attached pencil note, OPD 322.97 (6 Jan 44), app. by DCofS, 28 Jan 44. Italics in original.

[11] Marshall to Harmon, 24 Jan 43, CM–OUT 8099, and Msg 274, Harmon to Marshall, 27 Jan 43, CM–IN 12580, both in OPD Log File, Jan 43.

[12] Marshall to CG Hawaiian Dept, CM–OUT 1303, 3 Feb 43.

later date, the Negro unit could be withdrawn from Hawaii and sent to the South Pacific to garrison rear areas there.[13]

The Central Pacific, despite its continuing objections, was directed in December 1943 to make plans for the use of the 93d. The theater proposed to deploy it on four less populous major islands, Kauai, Maui, Hawaii, and Molokai.[14] But it was now considered expedient that the 93d get closer to a combat area than Hawaii if possible. While movement orders directing the unit to Hawaii were being prepared, the War Department again suggested that the unit might be useful in the South Pacific where, after jungle training on Guadalcanal, it might be used as a follow-up division in the northern Solomons–New Guinea area for operations such as those in progress at Empress Augusta Bay on Bougainville.[15] At the same time the Central Pacific was informed that no proposed location for the division was final and that it would be fixed in no single location for the duration of the war.[16]

General Harmon was willing to take the 93d if he had to, but his earlier reservations still held. His area had not expected to receive an additional division during the first six months of 1944, he told the War Department. With shipping limitations in the Pacific

preventing both the building of a balanced force and the maintenance of existing units at maximum effectiveness, any available shipping could better be used to bring in replacements, service units, and rotation personnel rather than an unneeded division. However, if the 93d was sent, it could be used in the manner suggested. It could relieve first line white divisions for rest and rehabilitation, making them more speedily available for re-employment.[17] With this reluctant acceptance from General Harmon and in view of the continuing coolness of the Central Pacific, orders were issued, on 2 January 1944, changing the destination of the 93d Infantry Division from Hawaii to New Georgia in the Solomon Islands.[18]

In the same six months, means for moving two of the remaining separate infantry regiments became available. The 366th Infantry and 364th Infantry had been scheduled for the European theater, the former for February 1944 and the latter for March.[19] But all the European theater's expected requirements for separate regiments were canceled.[20] Ground Forces urged that the 364th, because of continuing difficulties in its training locations, be given some other overseas destination. The 364th was thereupon marked for rotation to

[13] Memo for Record, OPD 370.5 PTO (2–3–43) Plan for Transfer of Infantry Division from Hawaii to South Pacific, 3 Feb 43, OPD 370.5 Hawaii, sec. IV, 118.
[14] Ltr, CG USAF Central Pacific Area to TAG, 12 Dec 43, OPD 370.5 Hawaii (12 Dec 43), sec. IV, 117.
[15] Marshall to Harmon, 23 Dec 43, CM–OUT 8913, info copy to MacArthur.
[16] Marshall to Richardson, 23 Dec 43, CM–OUT 8912.

[17] COMGENSOPAC to AGWAR for OPD, info to CINCPAC, CINCWESPAC, COMSOPAC, 27 Dec 43, No. 5029, in OPD Cable File IN, 1–31 Dec 43.
[18] Memo, OPD for TAG, 1 Jan 44, issued as Ltr, TAG to CG USAFICPA, et al 2 Jan 44, OPD 370.5/AN (1 Jan 44).
[19] Incl, Tab B to Memo, AGF for G–3, 27 Sep 43, AGF 270.5/25 (2 Jan 43).
[20] Memo, AGF for OPD, 14 Oct 43, AGF 291.2/25; DF, OPD to CG AGF, 19 Oct 43, AGF 291.2/11.

Alaska for March 1944 in place of the 140th Infantry.[21]

The 366th Infantry and 372d Infantry, both of which had been in training and on security duties at their Massachusetts and New York locations since the spring of 1941, were still unallotted. There had been unsuccessful attempts to use these Negro regiments as school troops. There had been attempts to move the 372d for retraining, since Lt. Gen. Hugh Drum, commanding the Eastern Defense Command, had reported that its assignment to guard duty in the New York area was no longer necessary. With the inadequate training facilities and excessive diversions of the area, the regiment was faced with a loss of training and morale.[22] But the regiment, by the terms of its assignment to New York, could not be moved without War Department approval. The War Department, in turn, could not move the regiment without authority from the White House, for the regiment had been stationed in New York after an agreement between President Roosevelt and Mayor La Guardia.[23]

The White House, when queried on moving the unit, replied through General Watson that there was no objection to moving it provided that it was replaced by another regiment.[24] The

372d therefore remained on its New York duty. It and the 366th were frequently commented upon publicly as examples of units activated and trained over a long period of time which had not been employed overseas.[25]

The opportunity to move these regiments came as the result of conversions of other units. In November, the North African theater, which already had five air base security battalions, requested eighteen more or their equivalent for the Twelfth Air Force and for the new Fifteenth Air Force. It suggested that, if necessary, the air base security disbandment program be revised to provide the theater with units needed to cope with increasing civilian sabotage and depredations on airfields. Negro troops for these duties would be highly acceptable and a high priority for them would be arranged, the theater said.[26]

But all uncommitted air base security battalions were now disbanded. G–3 proposed that the 366th and 372d Infantry Regiments be furnished for this duty instead.[27] The Operations Division concurred and recommended again that the War Department request a White House release for the 372d Infantry. But the recommendation was returned with the notation "Leave unit there until orders from (WH) release

[21] Memo, AGF for OPD, 25 Oct 43, AGF 291.2/11; DF, OPD for G–1, G–3, and AGF, 30 Oct 43, OPD 291.21 (14 Oct 43).

[22] Memo, OPD for CofS, 20 Apr 43, OPD 322.97 (4–14–43).

[23] Ltr, TAG to CG Second Corps Area, 13 Dec 41, AG 370.5 (12-11-41) MC-C-M; Ltr, TAG to CG Second Corps Area, 26 Apr 42, AG 370.5 (4-22-42) MC-E-M; Memo, OPD for CofS, 20 Apr 43, OPD 322.97 (4-14-43).

[24] Memo, Actg SW for Secy to President, 24 Apr 43, OPD 322.97 (4-14-43); Memo, USW for CofS, 25 May 43, WDCSA 322.97 (5-25-43).

[25] Memo, Actg Civ Aide to SW for ASW, 7 Sep 43, ASW 291.2 NT–Com; Memo, Gen Davis for ASW, 10 Nov 43, ASW 291.2 NT–Com 43–44.

[26] Msg, Algiers to WAR (signed Eisenhower), 14 Nov 43, CM–IN 8975 (15 Nov 43).

[27] Memo, G–3 for DCofS, 20 Nov 43, WDGCT 291.21 (20 Nov 43), and RS, REP to Chief Orgn Mobilization Br, 15 Nov 43, attached to copy of above in G–3 files.

it." [28] The North African theater was offered the 366th Infantry and accepted it, whereupon the North African Air Force suggested on its own that an additional Negro regiment would be quite acceptable in place of the remaining air base battalions that it needed.[29] To this latter suggestion the War Department replied that the additional Negro regiment was not available, but the 65th (Puerto Rican) Regiment could be substituted.[30] The theater accepted this unit, along with the 367th Infantry Battalion, offered earlier from Liberia.[31]

The 366th, already released to Army Ground Forces for refresher training, was thus scheduled for Italy in February to serve in lieu of air base security battalions. The 364th was preparing for Alaska. The 372d remained in New York City. The 93d Division was readying for the Pacific. Plans for these units and efforts made to utilize them were not made public. The units, therefore, remained centers of public and press discussion until they were moved. When at last they were shipped, it was under circumstances peculiar to them and unique in the deployment of American military forces in World War II.

Reactions to Conversions

Not until Chicago's 930th and 931st Field Artillery Battalions, descendants of the old 8th Illinois Infantry, were converted to engineer combat battalions in January 1944 was there strong public and political reaction to the conversion of Negro units. For these units, this conversion represented the third reorganization since the beginning of mobilization. The 8th Illinois Infantry was inducted as a field artillery regiment in January 1941 and reorganized into separate battalions in January 1943. It was easy to conclude that its history of successive reorganizations indicated that it was unlikely to be used effectively at all. News that the 2d Cavalry Division was being sent overseas for disbandment had even greater impact, for two of its regiments were the old and revered 9th and 10th Cavalry. Their hold on the affections and respect of the Negro public and of many of the older Army officers was surpassed by few other regiments. Unfavorable reactions to their conversion were expected within the military establishment. By this time, concern over the fate of Negro units in general had already been expressed in many quarters. It was currently the subject of a lively debate with heavily political overtones that eventually affected the employment of the remaining Negro units.

Representative Hamilton Fish, of New York, who had spoken often in warm terms of his service in World War I as an officer of New York's 369th In-

[28] Memo, OPD for DCofS, 26 Nov 43, RF, ASGS for OPD, 2 Dec 43, and DF, OPD for G–3, 3 Dec 43, all in OPD 320.2 (20 Nov 43).
[29] Rad, AGWAR to NATO, 20 Nov 43, CM–OUT 7832; Rad, NAAF (Gen Spaatz) to CG NATOUSA, 24 Nov 43, NATOUSA–IN 15496; Rad, NATO (Eisenhower) to AGWAR (Marshall), 26 Nov 43, W6174/5807, CM–IN 16283, 26 Nov 43.
[30] Rad, WD to CG NATO, 28 Nov 43, CM–OUT 11164, 28 Nov 43; Rad WD to CG NATO, 29 Nov 43, CM–OUT 11483, 29 Nov 43; Rad, NATO to WD, 1 Dec 43, CM–IN 395, 1 Dec 43; Rad, WD to CG NATO, 4 Dec 43, CM–OUT 1992, 6 Dec 43.
[31] Book Msg, WD to Eisenhower repeated Royce for Sadler, AMSME 7712, 3 Nov 43; CG NATO (Eisenhower) to AGWAR (Marshall), W-5953, CM–OUT 23 Nov 43, Microreel 512/27 AFHQ G–3 Opns Div 52/4 on 106/F Job 10, Box 6, AGO Records.

fantry Regiment, wrote to Secretary Stimson for information on the report that Negro tank destroyer and field artillery units had been broken up. He wanted to know as well if it was true that the 24th Infantry had been in the Pacific for nearly two years performing only labor duties. "I am aware of the fact that military necessity must control the assignment of personnel in the Army," he said, "but if the planning of the General Staff were adequate such actions would not be necessary. In the circumstances, I am still wondering whether there is not a deliberate plan to keep Negro soldiers out of actual combat." He then referred to the Selective Service amendment on discrimination in training which he had sponsored in 1940, saying that "If Negro soldiers are trained as combat troops but denied service as such, such discrimination appears to be a violation of my amendment." [32]

Stimson's reply, dated 19 February 1944, was a lengthy one prepared in the Legislative and Liaison Division. It detailed the relationship of units to the course of the war, pointing out that certain defensive units, such as antiaircraft artillery, coast artillery, and tank destroyers, were no longer needed in the numbers required earlier and that service units "on a tremendous scale" were now needed to support a global war waged on many fronts. Both Negro and white units were being converted and both Negro and white units were being committed overseas in as balanced proportions as possible. Both Negro and white combat units were at times em-

ployed in labor functions. "The fact is," Fish was told, "there is no defensible reason for not so employing combat troops when necessary, and the procedure actually is to be encouraged in order to obtain maximum manpower value. As you know, rarely are all combat units in an area committed simultaneously. The decision as to when and how any unit shall be employed rests entirely with the responsible commander." [33]

It was not these, but two other statements in the letter that became the storm center for controversy. In referring to the 930th and 931st Field Artillery Battalions, the letter said:

Certain other existing Negro Field Artillery units are being converted to heavier artillery, but the 930th and 931st 155 mm. Howitzer Battalions have not been selected for conversion to heavier artillery or retention as Field Artillery owing to the unsatisfactory records of both units. To have retained these troops as Field Artillery and concurrently to have converted or stripped other Negro or white Field Artillery units with substantially higher efficiency records, would have been an uneconomical use of manpower. The present plan to convert the units to Combat Engineers is based on similar considerations.

And, on converting combat units to service units in general, it said:

. . . the War Department's selection of units to be converted has been based solely on the relative abilities, capabilities and status of training of the personnel in the units available for conversion. It so happens that a relatively large percentage of the Negroes inducted in the Army have fallen within the lower educational classifications, and many of the Negro units accordingly

---

[32] Ltr, Fish to SW, 1 Feb 44, *Congressional Record*, 90, February 9, 1944, A660.

[33] Ltr, SW to Fish, 19 Feb 44, WDLLD/250-49; *Congressional Record*, 90, February 23, 1944, 2007–2008 reprints the letter in full.

have been unable to master efficiently the techniques of modern weapons. To have committed such units to combat at the dates of conversion would have endangered operational successes as well as submitted the personnel to unnecessarily high casualty rates. Our limitations of manpower and urgent and immediate need for service units of a type whose mission could be efficiently discharged by the personnel concerned left no choice but to include Negro troops in conversions such as those mentioned in your letter.[34]

These were points of view so universally accepted within the War Department that exceptions taken to them came as a surprise. After reading the Stimson letter into the *Congressional Record*, Fish told the House that he could not agree with the Secretary's "inference that colored soldiers' efficiency ratings are so low" that they could not master modern weapons. Education among Negroes, he declared, had increased since the first World War; if the four separate regiments of that war could make good records he did not understand why their descendants could not now. It seemed strange that French Senegalese and British Indian divisions could fight superbly, that Russians with low educational standards could be war heroes, and that Japanese with less education than American Negroes had made "brave and efficient soldiers" while the War Department could not do as well with American Negroes. "Any American who is good enough to wear the uniform of his country, regardless of race, color, or creed, must be treated equally and be afforded the opportunity to serve, fight and die in defense of our free institutions, our constitutional form

of government, and for America itself," he concluded.[35]

When he saw a copy of Stimson's reply to Fish, Truman Gibson predicted to Secretary McCloy that the letter would "accentuate the greatly increasing criticisms and resulting resentments which have already reached alarming proportions." Its references to educational classifications "reduces the War Department policy with respect to Negroes to very simple terms that cannot be misunderstood." The letter, if correct, implied considerations which were "particularly unfortunate" for a public statement. "In what regard," Gibson asked, "will combat engineer units be held when it is blandly stated that men too dumb for field artillery for which they have been trained for three years can be sent into combat engineer battalions?" The letter would undoubtedly be used for political purposes. Administrative handling of the reply, Gibson felt, was poor. The letter had not been sent to him for comment and, so far as he could learn, it had gone neither through the Advisory Committee nor the McCloy office. "It suggests," he said, "that in all such cases as the Fish letter that careful consideration be given the basic policy involved and that in any event the matters be sent those of us who have some knowledge of the facts." He reiterated that temporizing solved no problems. After a conference on the disposition of the 2d Cavalry Division, Gibson had found that the "whole attitude" was "'How did Gibson find out about this?'" He reminded the Assistant Secretary that "All of these things will be found out

[34] *Ibid.*

[35] *Congressional Record*, 90, February 23, 1944, 2007–2008.

about. As a civilian, I certainly would not presume to question any decisions based on military necessity. However, the manner of procedure in the conversion of Negro units leaves the War Department open to the charge that there are other factors that are being taken into consideration." [36]

Gibson was correct about the effect of the Stimson letter. As soon as Fish's speech was over, its refrain was taken up in the Negro press, with "Stimson says Negroes too dumb to master modern weapons of war" as the main burden of their approach. Representative William L. Dawson of Chicago, at the time the only Negro Representative in the House, had already made inquiries about the converted units, saying of the stripping of the older battalions: "So far as the public was concerned, it was but a repetition of the attitude of the Army that has been all too familiar to Negroes. I am well acquainted with this attitude, having served as an officer in a regiment that fought during the last war." He, too, was exercised over the political implications of the letter. "I say to you frankly," he told the Assistant Secretary, "that the political enemies of the Commander in Chief of our armed forces are seeking to place responsibility for this unAmerican attitude squarely upon his doorstep." [37] While Republican political workers were interpreting conversions to Negroes as a general Roosevelt administration failure, Democrats blamed the Army and the War Department, with Representative Dawson telling a group of Negro Democrats

gathered in Washington for a meeting just after the Fish speech that "the failure to use Negro Americans to the fullest in this war is the diabolical work of a reactionary and prejudiced clique within the Military Establishment." [38]

Three days later, Dawson, having received no answer to his original queries, addressed a new series to Assistant Secretary McCloy, pointing out that since the Fish speech he had received

. . . hundreds of communications from every section of this country, denouncing the statements made by the Secretary of War, and demanding that I see the President to ask for the removal of the Secretary of War, or demanding that I immediately introduce a resolution for a sweeping investigation of the entire military situation with a view of finding out the sources responsible for the information upon which the Secretary of War based his letter.[39]

Dawson now wanted to know what plans had been made for the use of the Negro officers of "the units which the War Department letter states have failed so miserably" as well as information on the service schools attended by these officers and "the bases from which they were

[36] Memo, Civ Aide to SW for ASW, 23 Feb 44, ASW 291.2 NT–Alpha.

[37] Ltr, Dawson to McCloy, 19 Feb 44, WDCSA 291.2 Negroes (25 Feb 44).

[38] "Negro Democrats Urged to Laud Administration," Washington Post, February 26, 1944.

[39] Ltr, Dawson to McCloy, 28 Feb 44, ASW 291.2 NT-Combat. The Pittsburgh Courier, under the by-line of John P. Davis of its Washington Bureau, quoted Dawson as saying "Secretary Stimson should resign immediately"; a mass meeting sponsored by the Chicago Citizens Committee of 1,000 and the National Negro Council adopted a resolution calling for the removal of Secretary Stimson "for the good of the morale of all true Americans regardless of race, creed, or color" (Chicago Tribune, February 28, 1944); and the Baptist Conference of Chicago indorsed the resolution, with one minister asserting that if the President did not remove Stimson, 10,000 Negro ministers should proceed to Washington to emphasize their demand (Chicago Tribune, February 29, 1944).

formally certified for combat service and who certified them for such service." [40]

Before the War Department could begin to formulate answers to the queries arising out of the Fish-Stimson letters, news that the 2d Cavalry Division was no longer fully constituted began to filter out to the public through complaints of men of the 3d Signal Troop, left behind and converted to signal construction troops when the remainder of the division, still bearing its combat designation, left for North Africa. Inquiries about this unit began to reach the War Department. "I don't know the circumstances of the case, but evidently the men feel that they are being discriminated against because of their color." Senator Robert Taft of Ohio wrote to McCloy. "It seemed to me that perhaps you might like to look into the situation, and if you do obtain any report, I shall be glad to hear of it." [41]

Senator Taft had not mentioned the conversion of the 2d Cavalry Division, but, as a part of a long and detailed letter written the day after Taft's, Judge Hastie, now back at his old job as dean of the Howard Law School, made a logical deduction that any or all of the old Regular regiments might have shared the fate of the National Guard regiment. His letter to Stimson, the last of his attempts to influence the War Department directly, was a detailed summary of his position and an accurate delineation of the position arrived at by Negroes who

possessed pertinent facts about the course of the employment of Negro troops. He wrote:

When I read in the Congressional Record for February 24, 1944 your letter of February 19 to Congressman Hamilton Fish concerning the conversion of Negro combat units into service units, my first inclination was publicly to challenge your letter as unfair and insulting to the Negro soldier, inaccurate and lacking in candor. However, on reflection I concluded that a man of your integrity and with your sense of justice could sign such a letter only if, without personal knowledge of the facts, he had been misled by those who drafted the document. Remembering too your invitation, at the time of my resignation from your official family, that I continue to bring to your attention matters of concern to the military establishment, I determined to place before you in this letter what I believe to be important and accurate observations with reference to Army policy and practice in the disposition of Negro combat units.

Hastie began his interpretation of the problem by listing the Negro combat units existing in 1941 and indicating what was publicly known of their status in 1944. He then continued:

Despite your assurance to Congressman Fish "that any implication that the War Department is deliberately attempting to avoid sending overseas, or to keep out of combat, troops of the Negro or any other race, is entirely without foundation," the disposition of these first Negro combat regiments three years after their mobilization, deserves your further examination. Attention is directed first to the four Negro regular army regiments, the 24th and 25th Infantry and the 9th and 10th Cavalry, created in 1866 pursuant to Congressional mandate. Their maintenance in combat status is, I believe, a statutory duty. Yet, one of these regiments, the 24th Infantry, has been employed as a service unit for

---

[40] Ltr, Dawson to McCloy, 28 Feb 44, ASW 291.2 NT-Combat. Most of the officers from the two Illinois units went later to the 597th and 600th Field Artillery Battalions, 92d Division, which then became the only all-Negro staffed combat elements of the division.

[41] Ltr, Taft to McCloy, 28 Feb 44, ASW 291.2 NT-Combat (3 Mar 44).

nearly two years. I believe, Mr. Secretary, that you are entitled to know, and the public is entitled to know, whether the 9th and 10th Cavalry and the 25th Infantry have been committed to combat missions for which they have been trained or whether they too have been or are being converted to service units. These four are among the proudest regiments of our army. On the western plains, in the Philippines, with Theodore Roosevelt in Cuba, under Pershing in Mexico, they have been among our finest front line combat troops. Will you inquire, Mr. Secretary, what their missions are today? What we know about the 24th makes us apprehensive about the other three.[42]

The Taft letter, arriving at about the same time as Hastie's, went to the Legislative and Liaison Division with the request that, in answer, the matter of the legality of the conversion of the 9th and 10th Cavalry, both established by statute, be checked.[43] The prepared answer avoided mention of the legality of the conversion, but it did reveal that the entire 2d Cavalry Division was among the units converted to provide personnel for service units. No definite commitment for a cavalry division could be foreseen, Senator Taft was told. "Since the Second Cavalry Division was the only source from which such personnel could be withdrawn without delaying the war effort, the War Department was compelled to effect this change in its utilization. Needless to say, the decision would necessarily have been the same had this Division been composed of white personnel." McCloy personally added a final paragraph: "We are

taking determined steps to commit to combat, colored units just as soon as we can. We have some tactical and training problems that have to be dealt with but I think they will be solved." [44]

This first public statement that the cavalry division had been converted became the standard explanation for later inquiries.[45] When the National Association for the Advancement of Colored People made on inquiry about the division some weeks later—information on the conversion reached the public slowly—the letter to Taft was inclosed as explanation when the association was answered.[46]

Except for an acknowledgment from McCloy disavowing interpretations given the Stimson letter, Hastie had gone unanswered. His letter was not so easy to answer as many others that came into the Department on the same subject during the period, for Hastie had surveyed the whole subject of the utilization of Negro troops, placing it in the moral and ethical setting from which many Negroes viewed developing Army policies. His interpretation could not be parried, as many were, by implying that it was based on a misreading of Stimson's

---

[42] Ltr, Hastie to SW, 29 Feb 44, ASW 291.2 NT-Combat.

[43] Memo, Exec to ASW for Chief Legislative and Liaison Div, 29 Feb 44, and S/S, L&LD for ASW, 3 Mar 44, both in ASW 291.2 NT-Combat.

[44] Ltr, ASW to Taft, 6 Mar 44, ASW 291.2 NT-Combat.

[45] The 2d Cavalry Division, then arriving in Oran, had not actually been converted and inactivated in its entirety at this date. Inactivation began on 26 February 1944 and continued through 12 June 1944. AG 322 (8 Apr 44) OB-I-GNGCT-M, 11 Apr 44; 3d Ind, Hq NATOUSA, 31 Jul 44, on AG 322 (11 Jul 44) OB-I; Ltr, Hq SOS NATO, 23 Mar 44, 322-Cav (SSAG).

[46] Ltr, Roy Wilkins, Actg Secy NAACP, to SW, 23 Mar 44, ASW 291.2 NT-Combat. This was the third of a series of NAACP inquiries on conversions, but the first on the 2d Cavalry Division. See Ltrs 2 and 9 Mar 44, and Ltr, ASW to Roy Wilkins, 5 Apr 44, ASW 291.2 NT-Combat.

letter, or that, like some correspondents, his basic information was in error.[47] If changing defensive units to types more urgently needed was basic to conversions, and if Negro field artillery, infantry, and cavalry units were regarded as defensive units, "this but confirms the belief of many persons that overseas service was never intended for them, but rather they were intended from the outset for employment as glorified 'home guards,' " Hastie had pointed out. Since antiaircraft units are mainly defensive and since more of these than any other Negro combat types had found overseas assignments, there must be other reasons behind the conversion and assignment policies, he continued. The argument that inferior qualifications and unsatisfactory training records, "usually relied upon in military circles," were responsible did not hold up if it was considered that antiaircraft units had had no better men than the other units. If the Army had been primarily concerned about the "educational qualifications" of the men in combat units, during the past three years efforts would have been made to provide qualified men for these units. Instead, the combat units were denuded of their best men for cadres for other units, often of service types. "The truth of the matter is," Hastie continued, "that these original Negro combat units have been the problem children of the Army for more than two years, not because they were incompetent, but because no one wanted them." Antiaircraft units, Hastie thought, constituted a

special category, in that they could be placed in more or less permanent defensive positions where they need not be integrated with other units for use. "So the utilization of Negro Antiaircraft units in the theater of operations was adopted as the device best calculated to confound the critics of Army policy as to Negro combat troops without basically changing that policy," he concluded. There was another category of unit, Hastie said, which had not been mentioned, the air base security battalions. Their conversion was difficult to justify because of "the successful, and in at least one case distinguished, combat performance of such few of these units as fought in the North African campaign." If Negro infantry and artillery units needed strengthening, he continued, why were not qualified and trained men from air base security units sent to them rather than to the services? Then Hastie commented upon the comparisons between service and combat units suggested in the Stimson letter and upon the importance of the equitable use of Negro manpower to the future of race relations within the country:

All of this is said without intention to reflect upon the necessary and often hazardous functions of the Service Forces. Indeed, as I have read your letter to Congressman Fish, I have been struck with the apparent implication there that the Service Forces should be a dumping ground for the culls of the Ground Forces. Most remarkable of all is the suggestion that the 184th Field Artillery is being converted into "combat engineers" because of its "unsatisfactory record." I believe that I have not been alone in my thought that the functions of the combat engineers require a measure of skill and intelligence not exceeded in any other branch of the military service. Certainly, generations of the

[47] See Ltrs, ASW to Clifton E. Jones (Chicago) 21 Mar 44, ASW to Mrs. Adelaide C. Hill, Exec Secy Englewood Urban League, Englewood, N.J., 5 Apr 44, and ASW to Roy Wilkins, 5 Apr 44, all in ASW 291.2 NT-Combat.

"Engineers" at the Military Academy have so believed.

A final thought. Nothing can do more to improve the too often unsatisfactory relations between white and colored soldiers than the sharing of common experience on the field of battle. This is important now and for the future. The veterans of this war will be the greatest force for racial good will or for racial enmity in America. Prejudice and intolerance will have no place in the hearts and minds of comrades in arms who have fought and bled and conquered shoulder to shoulder.

It is respectfully submitted that it is time and past time that the matter of utilization of Negro combat units pass out of the hands of those who deal with this matter as a distasteful search for compromise born of political necessity, and into the hands of those who have the will and the understanding to exploit the great combat potential of the Negro soldier as a valuable asset in the winning of the war.[48]

Hastie's letter, tabbed "Urgent," went from the administrative assistant to Secretary McCloy, with the note: "I think it important that this be called to Mr. McCloy's attention." [49] Since McCloy had already acknowledged receipt of the copy sent him by Hastie, and since an answer involved drafts by many hands, the reply remained unprepared for the Secretary's signature for a month. In the meantime new decisions had been made, for, as soon as the winds of furor aroused by the Stimson letter reached the War Department, efforts under way for some months to solve the problem of the overseas utilization of Negro troops received renewed emphasis. Even as the Hastie letter was on its way to Stimson, the staff divisions, at McCloy's re-

quest, were drawing up new plans and studies of the problem and the Advisory Committee was preparing a formal recommendation on getting more Negroes overseas and into active combat.

The McCloy Committee Faces the Issue

By the end of February 1944 the Advisory Committee on Negro Troop Policies had before it the agreement of G–1 and G–3 and the three major commands that the shipment of more Negro units was a desirable procedure. It also had The Inspector General's survey with its evidence that the overseas Negro troop population was below its proper proportion and its conclusion that "Units containing Negro personnel have a history of activation and training, followed by a transfer of personnel and acquisition of new troops, which has necessitated units starting all over again, and for many units, this has occurred more than once." [50] And it had evidence of mounting and potential distrust of War Department intentions as shown by press comment and individual correspondence subsequent to the Fish address. Members of the committee had often suggested ways and means of shipping more units overseas, but, in the face of manpower shortages, reports of training unreadiness, and the reluctance of theaters to accept Negro units so long as white units were available, the committee as a whole had deferred action. Now, on the last day of February 1944, the committee met to consider "a formal recommendation to the Secretary of War that

[48] Ltr, Hastie to SW, 29 Feb 44, ASW 291.2 NT-Combat.
[49] RS, Office of the Admin Asst (John W. Martyn) to ASW, 3 Mar 44, ASW 291.2 NT-Combat.
[50] Memo, TIG for DCofS, 1 Jan 44, WDCSA 291.2/1 (1944 Binder).

a definite program be worked out to commit some Negro combat troops to action against the enemy." [51]

The Operations Division, unrepresented on the committee, sent Brig. Gen. Carl A. Russell, Deputy Chief, Theater Group, OPD, to the meeting by request. General Russell declared that the Operations Division sent overseas what it was offered, according to fitness and according to theater commanders' wishes. The G–1, General White, observed that all available personnel had to be used. In the midst of this discussion, Assistant Secretary McCloy arrived and announced that in a meeting just concluded with General Marshall and Secretary Stimson, the Secretary had requested that a definite proposal be presented to the staff, for he wished the use of Negro troops in combat to be placed upon the record. The War Department had not been in the habit of "dictating" to theater commanders, but, the Assistant Secretary said, with G–1 and G–3 agreeing, there were times when national policy made it necessary to dictate. "This is such a case," McCloy stated. "Ten percent of our people are colored and we have to use it. We make a farmer out of a clerk. It is a vital National Policy to make a military asset out of that part of the population." With the British using Africans in Burma [52] and with an American-Japanese unit in Italy, a Negro combat team could be sent overseas and employed, most committee members felt. After further discussion, the committee formally advised the Secretary of War:

It is the recommendation of this Committee that, as soon as possible, colored Infantry, Field Artillery, and other Combat units be introduced into combat and that if present organizations or training schedules do not permit such prompt commitment, that steps be taken to reorganize any existing units or schedules so as to permit the introduction of qualified colored combat units, as promptly as possible, into battle.

To the suggestion from General Dalton of Army Service Forces that the recommendation be made stronger, General Porter, the G–3, laconically observed, "It would take a directive of the Chief of Staff fo enforce it." [53]

In forwarding the recommendation to Secretary Stimson, McCloy amplified the committee's point of view:

There has been a tendency to allow the situation to develop where selections are made on the basis of efficiency with the result that the colored units are discarded for combat service, but little is done by way of studying new means to put them in shape for combat service.

With so large a portion of our population colored, with the example before us of the effective use of colored troops (of a much lower order of intelligence) by other nations, and with the many imponderables that are connected with the situation, we must, I think, be more affirmative about the use of our negro troops. If present

---

[51] Memo, Secy Advisory Com for the members of the Advisory Com, 28 Feb 44, ASW 291.2 NT-Combat.

[52] African troops were used in Burma, in the Mediterranean, and in the Ethiopian and Somaliland campaigns by the British. See E. E. Sabben-Clare, "African Troops in Asia," *African Affairs,* XLIV (October, 1945), 151–57; Gerald Hanley, *Monsoon Victory* (London: Collins, 1946); General Sir William Platt, "Studies in War-time Organization: (6) East African Command," *African Affairs,* XLV (January, 1946), 27–35; Brigadier F. A. S.

Clarke, "The Development of the West African Forces in the Second World War," *The Army Quarterly,* LV (October, 1947), 58–73.

[53] Min Advisory Com, 29 Feb 44, ASW 291.2 NTC.

methods do not bring them to combat efficiency, we should change those methods. That is what this resolution purports to recommend.

Secretary Stimson penned on the covering memorandum: "I concur with recommendation—H. L. S." [54]

G–3, in the meantime, prepared for Secretary McCloy a comprehensive report of the situation.[55] This material was to provide answers for any further queries from the White House and from other sources. It reviewed and refined existing policies, extending them in some instances to fit current developments. It reiterated the policy that the Army would accept and absorb 10.4 percent Negroes in its male strength, excluding "certain specialized activities such as the College Training Program and the Office of Strategic Services." [56] Negro personnel accepted would, "to the greatest practicable extent consistent with military necessity and the abilities of the individuals concerned, be distributed throughout all arms and services." [57] A corollary to this policy, G–3 said, was that since the Army "cannot afford the luxury of organizing tactical units which will remain in the United States for the duration of the war . . . the Army intends that colored units shall eventually be employed overseas to the greatest extent that their capabilities permit."

Quoting from field reports, G–3 reviewed again the difficulties in adhering to these policies. Manpower shortages and the relative preparedness of units had been responsible for conversions with the exception that in the case of the 2d Cavalry Division conversion "did not result from deficiencies on its part but rather on the unfortunate circumstance —insofar as it was concerned—that it was the only available source of urgently needed personnel. The decision of the War Department in this case would have been the same had the personnel of the 2d Cavalry Division been white." As other combat units were readied for shipment, they would be sent overseas. The War Department had made the best use of the means at its disposal; it was unfortunate, G–3 concluded, that these means divided along racial lines. But as the end of the war drew nearer, "people— *both white and colored*—of lower classification grades will gravitate toward less complicated tasks and conversions must be made. It is likewise inevitable that units with the furtherest [sic] advanced training will continue to be the first employed in battle." [58]

With the addition of data on the War Department's efforts to raise standards through special training units, this material in reduced form became the standard public explanation for War Department policies involving the conversion of Negro units to service functions. Of the special training units a typical letter remarked: "Very encouraging results have been obtained to date. In the first six months of these courses, out of 29,000 Negro trainees approximately 90% were retained in the Army and assigned to

[54] Memo, ASW for SW, 2 Mar 44, inclosing formal recommendation, WDCSA 291.2/13 Negroes (1944).
[55] Memo, G–3 for ASW, 4 Mar 44, WDGCT 291.21 (4 Mar 44), inclosing monograph, Employment of Negro Personnel in the Army, and Memo, OPD for G–3, 3 Mar 44, OPD 320.2 (3 Mar 44).
[56] Ibid.
[57] Ibid. The limitation expressed here was a new refinement of policy reflecting the problems of the half-year just past, including the abandonment of proportionate representation attempts in the 1944 Troop Basis.
[58] Ibid. Italics in original.

more advanced training. Many excellent soldiers have been developed out of men who have initially made a low score in the Army General Classification." [59] It was not long before an additional note to the effect that "recent press releases indicate that the 24th Infantry" was engaged in active combat could be added to these letters. [60]

On 6 March 1944, Stimson, McCloy, and representatives of the major agencies concerned discussed the Advisory Committee's recommendation. Two courses of action were decided upon. In accordance with the first, a radiogram went to Lt. Gen. Millard F. Harmon in the South Pacific expressing the War Department's desire that not less than one regimental combat team of the 93d Division, then arriving in the Solomons, be used in combat as soon as possible. [61] General Harmon replied that early employment met with both his and Admiral William F. Halsey's favor and that the War Department would be advised promptly on the completion of plans for use of the 93d Division. [62] The second decision was that out of the 92d Division a regimental combat team should be selected and intensively trained for shipment to an undetermined theater of operations at the earliest possible date.

The team would eventually rejoin its division. All personnel of the division would have an opportunity to volunteer for duty with the combat team. Officers for this team were to be selected on the basis of demonstrated qualifications without regard to race. The team would be trained under the most favorable provisions for terrain, instruction, equipment, ammunition, and training aids that could be made available. Ground Forces was directed to inform the War Department of the earliest date on which such a team could be ready for shipment overseas. [63]

Thus, McCloy explained to General Marshall, two methods of committing Negro ground combat troops to battle would be used: the first, the employment of existing units just as they were and the other the use of a specially selected team which, later, could impart its battle experience to the rest of the division. Under this proposal, both the proponents of introducing Negroes to ground combat through the use of a "hand-picked" unit and those who preferred a normal unit so that lessons might be drawn from the conduct of a run of the mine organization would be satisfied. [64]

The commitment of large Negro ground combat units thus proceeded under highly sponsored if not ideally planned conditions. The War Department suggested methods of use to field commanders and requested continuing reports on their progress. Once the large units were committed and definitely marked for use, it became relatively simpler to ship the smaller, supporting com-

[59] Ltr, ASW for Representative William L. Dawson, 6 Mar 44, ASW 291.2 NTC.

[60] Ltr, ASW to Roy Wilkins, NAACP, 5 Apr 44, WDCSA 291.2/23. This letter mistakenly referred to the 24th Infantry Division instead of regiment.

[61] Memo for Record, 7 Mar 44, OPD 370.5 Hawaii (7 Mar 44); CM–OUT 2853 (7 Mar 44); Memo, OPD for DCofS, 8 Mar 44, OPD 322.97 (8 Mar 44). Two-thirds of the 93d Division (9,112) had arrived in the South Pacific, 4,888 were en route, and 300 had not yet departed. Memo, Trp Mvmt Sec OPD for Gen Russell, 6 Mar 44, OPD 322.97 (8 Mar 44).

[62] CM–IN 5952 (9 Mar 44); Memo, OPD for DCofS, 9 Mar 44, OPD 322.97 (9 Mar 44).

[63] Memo, G–3 for CG AGF, 7 Mar 44, WDGCT 291.21 (7 Mar 44).

[64] Memo, ASW for Gen Marshall, 13 Mar 44, WDCSA 291.2/13.

bat units, either as separate units or as support for the larger units, especially in areas whose strength was declining. The Central Pacific was now willing to take a tank destroyer unit and General Devers, in June, queried the War Department from Algiers: "Can you send one or two colored tank battalions with the 92d? We will be delighted to have them." [65]

The commitment of Negro troops to combat, like their induction into the Army and distribution to units, was more a function of expediency in response to external circumstances—public and political pressures and considerations of morale—than a response to specific need for the units. With certain smaller units this was not the case, but with the larger units on which so much symbolic attention was focused and upon which so much administrative and training effort had been expended, this was specifically the case. The commitment of the bulk of Negro combat troops therefore followed no integrated plan for their use. It was rather an implementing of "vital National Policy" more than a response to military and strategic requirements that finally got them committed to the theaters.

Readiness for Overseas Movement

Before any shipment policy could be carried out, units had to complete their training and be processed for movement. Final preparation for overseas movement, known as POM, was a formalized procedure involving alerts, scheduled packing, tests, inspections, and departure

for staging areas where new inspections, further training, and last adjustments were made.[66] In the completion of their training and in their preparations for movement Negro units faced certain problems met less frequently or not at all by white units. These often affected the general process of employing Negro troops.

Most Negro units were small and relatively isolated "spare parts" which were trained under less than the fullest supervision. A number of the quartermaster service units, the medical sanitary units, the aviation squadrons, and the engineer separate battalions engaged in odd jobs as much as in training. Some "horrible examples" therefore turned up on The Inspector General's overseas readiness inspections. When a small Negro unit's training was poor it was likely to be very poor indeed. No balancing corollary of excellence in other units was available for contrast. That the personnel of these units had sometimes been transferred to as many as fourteen units during their training careers, that certain units had been filled and refilled many times over, and that the units themselves and their current commanders were often without blame for the conditions in which the units found themselves after months of nominal "training," did not alter the fact that these units were not ready for use.

Shipment delays added to the unreadiness of units. Some received so many

[65] Msg, Devers for Handy, 10 Jun 44, OPD In Log F–57372.

[66] A description of POM procedures, and a discussion of attendant problems as seen from the point of view of Army Ground Forces, will be found in Bell I. Wiley, "The Preparation of Units for Overseas Movement," in Palmer, Wiley, and Keast, *The Procurement and Training of Ground Combat Troops*, pp. 561–618, in this series.

warning orders that they and their administrative supervisors forgot the number. "At the end of December [1943] the job was finished off with bar and rod steel matting, and the Battalion rallied to meet its fifth (or was it sixth) warning order on January 3rd," one headquarters commented of a Negro unit.[67] Others were the victims of generally poor training histories and methods. The cited records of these units tended to influence negatively the prospects for ready use of similar units.

Some of the more highly unsatisfactory units uncovered by The Inspector General's overseas readiness inspections became examples for presentation to the General Council by General McNarney, who had a continuing concern with the adequate training of units, especially the smaller types. One of these was an aviation quartermaster company formed on 6 September 1942 by the reorganization of a truck company. All enlisted personnel had received their twelve weeks of basic training, but technical and unit training was not sufficient for the unit to perform its mission. No trucks had been assigned. In four months the unit had had only three days' training with borrowed trucks. It had never participated in combined exercises or maneuvers, had never worked with a group or any other unit as a truck company, had never been given any tests by its higher headquarters to determine its proficiency. Men of the unit had had little practice with the weapons with which they were armed; crew-served weapons had not been fired since trucks and machine gun mounts for them were not

available at the unit's station. With the record of neglect in this company General McNarney compared the record of a similar white quartermaster company, activated four days later. All personnel had had thirteen weeks of basic training. Individual technical training was adequate; unit training was complete and satisfactory. The unit had performed convoy missions for the camp quartermaster. Though it had never been on maneuvers, it had conducted several night problems under blackout conditions and had bivouacked in the field for a week. Tests conducted by its higher headquarters had found the work satisfactory; all men had fired their weapons and 60 percent had qualified.[68]

Other units, like the 387th Aviation Squadron, were declared ready before they had time to come to a point of efficient training. This unit, activated on 26 March 1943, was declared ready in July 1943. But many of its replacement fillers had only recently arrived; fifty of these were not fit for overseas duty. The unit's personnel had had a minimum of four weeks' basic training; the organization had had practically no unit training. It had had one night of field bivouac. No training or field exercises in map reading, camouflage, or chemical warfare had been given it. Discipline in general in the squadron was poor.[69]

Some cases of poor preparation were disclosed on annual inspections. The new commander of the 827th Tank Destroyer Battalion, then training at the Desert Training Center in attachment to the 93d Infantry Division, attributed his unit's difficulties in part to the inade-

[67] EAUTC, MacDill Fld, Fla., Hist Rpt, folder 1 (18 Mar 43–1 Aug 44), AF Archives.

[68] Min Gen Council, 12 Apr 43.
[69] Ibid., 9 Aug 43.

quate training young officers had received at the tank destroyer school and to the failure of former battalion and company commanders to eliminate inefficient officers and noncommissioned officers. "Many seem to feel that better replacements are not available and therefore it is best to keep the majority of the present leaders and try to train them," he explained. There were other reasons cited for the battalion's deficiencies:

a. Changes in type of unit from self propelled M-3s to towed 3 inch to self propelled M-10s.

b. Use of the Battalion as school troops from 2 January 1943 to 21 July 1943.

c. Shortages of equipment in supply branches. According to the best information available, the battalion has never been properly equipped with either organization or individual equipment.

d. Poor training in care and maintenance of equipment.

e. Lack of coordination of training by higher T.D. headquarters to produce trained battalions capable of combining the five essential elements which I consider necessary for a T. D. battalion to be successful in battle, namely:

(1) Fire power, both direct and indirect.
(2) Movement.
(3) Reconnaissance.
(4) Security.
(5) Radio Communications.

Although this battalion was activated April 20, 1942, I would rate it as unsatisfactory in all the above essential elements except direct fire. In my opinion this is due chiefly to failure to prescribe sufficient field training similar to that which a battalion will encounter against an armed enemy. Too much time is devoted to basic training and piecemeal training which does not require units to function as companies and battalions. As far as I can determine this battalion was never required to maneuver as part of a larger force and had only two battalion field exercises before I assumed command. Prior to leaving Camp Hood, no time on training schedules was allotted to indirect fire although it is the most important secondary mission of T.D. Units.[70]

The battalion, scheduled for shipment to the Central Pacific, was still not ready in February 1944. A white battalion was substituted at almost the last minute.[71]

Maneuvers revealed further unreadinesses, although the record of most small units on maneuvers was satisfactory or better. Of fifty-seven Negro service units—quartermaster, chemical, and ordnance—participating in the Sixth Maneuver period in Louisiana in the winter and spring of 1944, for example, only two were unsatisfactory. One of these, a railhead company, refused to operate on one occasion because of poor discipline among its men. It was necessary to withdraw this unit from the maneuver area and reorganize it. The other, a gasoline supply company, allowed tankers to return full and half full, through negligence.[72]

This last unit turned up five months later as one of The Inspector General's examples of an unready unit. It was no better then. Activated on 25 August 1943, it got its fillers, described as "castoffs, consisting of the sick, the lazy, the problem negroes," from the 92d Infantry Division. The whole group of 122 men

---

[70] 1st Ind, CO 827th TD Bn to CG TDC, Cp Hood. Tex., 9 Nov 43, on Ltr, Hq TDC, OTIG to CG TDC, Cp Hood, Tex., 30 Sep 43, 827 TD Files 333.1, AGO Records.

[71] Memo for Record, OPD, 4 Feb 44, OPD 370.5 Hawaii (4 Feb 44).

[72] Ltr, Hq Fourth Army to CG AGF, 25 Apr 44, AGF G-3 Sec, Misc Div, Maneuver Br, Fourth Army Maneuver Rpts, 1944.

contained only 7 with an Army General Classification Test score above Class IV. Though at authorized strength in August 1944, the unit needed replacements for both its first sergeant and for a platoon sergeant, neither of whom was sufficiently trained to hold his job. During August, thirty-four men were transferred out for physical disqualifications. Twenty-eight untrained replacements were received. The unit had had seven company commanders in a year. The current commander was not qualified to take the company overseas, but he had been left with the company because he was the only officer present for duty. This unit, General McNarney observed, was likely to be more of a handicap than assistance in a theater; it would need heroic measures, he felt, to get it into shape.[73]

In some cases, units that had completed all prescribed training and were adjudged able to perform their missions in active theaters had only one possible deficiency noted: they had a majority of their personnel in AGCT Classes IV and V.[74] In a few others, confused officer situations, in which officers had too little experience or were distributed in violation of current officer racial policies, held up shipment. In one such case, a quartermaster company had eight officers: a white captain, absent sick; a white first lieutenant, commanding but not qualified; a second lieutenant, white, with three months' service, acting as company executive; a second lieutenant, Negro, with five months' service; and four new

Negro second lieutenants, all fresh from officer candidate school, assigned to the unit for three days. No assigned officer was qualified to command. Before this unit could depart, all new officers of greater experience and qualifications had to be assigned.[75] Another small unit was held up until it could be furnished a better racial balance among officers than its one white officer commanding with all Negro lieutenants.

It would be expected that the larger Negro units, considering the circumstances of their activation, the accompanying lamentations over their desultory training records, and the difficulties in placing them overseas, would have had longer training periods in the zone of interior than comparable white units. Yet the three divisions, despite their quite different training careers, were all shipped overseas at about the same time as other divisions of their own age and somewhat in advance of some of their contemporaries.

The 93d Division, activated in May 1942, proceeded overseas in January 1944, while its sister division in point of time, the 85th, left in December 1943 and the 77th, a month older, left in March 1944. The bulk of the 92d Division, activated in October 1942, departed in September 1944, the same month that the 84th Division, activated at the same time, shipped out. There were still a number of National Guard as well as older new divisions whose commitment overseas came after a longer

---

[73] Min Gen Council, 4 Sep 44.

[74] For an example, see Status Report, 466th CA (AA) Bn (AW) (Sem), AGF 370.5/82 (CAC).

[75] Ltr, Inf Sch to CG R&SC, 9 Jan 43, 1st Ind, Hq R&SC to CG AGF, 13 Jan 43, and 2d Ind, AGF to CG R&SC, 19 Jan 43, all in AGF 210.31/1 (QMC).

period of training than that of either the 93d or 92d Division. The 2d Cavalry Division, proceeding overseas a year after activation, was a special case. After allowances for stripping and conversions from experimental to standard types of divisions are made in the cases of a number of other divisions, the Negro divisions proceeded overseas after what was about a normal training period in point of time.

Despite dire reports and predictions, the divisions had no particularly spectacular delays in their training careers. As planned in 1942, the training year of a division started fifteen days after activation, with seventeen weeks of basic and individual training, thirteen of unit training, fourteen of combined arms training, and eight weeks of review and air-mechanized training. Thus, after a year of training, a division that had not been handicapped by interruptions and stripping of personnel was about ready to proceed into maneuvers and then overseas. As both the oldest and the youngest of the Negro divisions, in its two versions the 2d Cavalry departed farthest from this pattern. The units of this division were activated at different times, with some of the units still inactive in 1942. As a result, training within the division proceeded on different levels. In May 1941, when the white units of the 3d Cavalry Brigade and the field artillery battalions showed every sign of being ready by mid-July for inspection of recruit and unit training as called for in mobilization training plans, the Negro units of the 4th Cavalry Brigade, assembled and filled more slowly, could only be expected to be prepared for recruit training inspection, since they would not complete thirteen

weeks of initial training of selectees until 5 July.[76]

Of the two Negro infantry divisions, the senior 93d had the more nearly usual training career. It was activated and trained as a unit at a single post. The younger 92d had the advantage of continuity of top command. Aside from the Regular Army 25th Infantry regiment and the 368th Infantry, activated a year before in March 1941, the 93d Division was filled with selective service men, and even the 25th and 368th, by the time the division was activated, were practically filled with new inductees as well. The 92d Division was made up wholly of newly activated units, with all but its cadre coming directly from reception centers. The cadre for the 92d Division, furnished on 31 August 1942, consisted of 128 officers and 1,200 enlisted men from the 93d Division, although the 93d had felt that, considering the training problems which it faced, three months was not enough time to prepare an adequate division cadre. In addition to the cadre for the 92d, the 93d Division provided cadres for almost every other type of unit.[77]

Except for the training problems common to most Negro units—a preponderance of slow learners, inadequate leadership in both officer and noncommissioned officer ranks, rapid turnover of enlisted and officer personnel through routine attrition and transfers to provide cadres and to rid units of unsatisfactory men, and strained morale relations—the

---

[76] Ltr, Hq 2d Cav Div, Cp Funston, Kans., to CG Second Army, 28 May 41, Div Files 353, AGO, filed with 9th Armd Div papers, AGO Records.

[77] Memo, AGF for G-1, Aug 42, AGF 333.1/1229–GNGAP–A (6–26–42); 93d Div Files, 320.2 Cadre and 320.2 Strength, AGO Records.

divisions proceeded with their training as prescribed by Army Ground Forces. Portions of the training cycle were repeated to fix training in the minds of slow learners or of new men arrived to replace men now discharged or transferred. Learning by rote was frequently used.[78] Both units received extensions of phases of their training cycles.

Despite training difficulties, observers from higher headquarters found the divisions progressing better than many had expected. General McNair of Army Ground Forces, returning from a west coast inspection trip in July 1942, reported in the War Council that the training of the 93d Division appeared to be excellent and as good as that of some of the older divisions.[79] General McNarney, after stopping at Fort Huachuca in October 1942, informed General McNair that "The 93d Division appeared to be in fine shape and General Hall doing an excellent job." [80]

The divisions went through their regularly scheduled training tests, passing some with satisfactory results and repeating others. Both infantry divisions went through the regular training cycle, with the 93d completing more of it than the 92d or, for that matter, than most other World War II divisions. The 93d's "D" (Division) exercises were held in the Huachuca Mountains in March 1943. From April to June 1943 the 93d participated in Third Army maneuvers in Louisiana, proceeding from there to the Desert Training Center (California-

Arizona Maneuver Area, "C–AMA"), where in November 1943 it went through more exercises and participated in IV Corps maneuvers. The 92d Division had the same training career except that it missed the Desert Training Center post-maneuver cycle.

Departure for maneuvers was a red-letter day for the divisions. Many smaller Negro units, especially quartermaster and engineer units, had participated regularly in maneuvers, transporting troops, maintaining roads, constructing bridges, and, at times, being thrown into combat exercises when the going became rough.

But no Negro organization as large as a division, pitted against other divisions, had participated in maneuvers prior to 1943.[81]

Before the departure of the 93d for the Louisiana Maneuver Area, its senior tactical commanders met for several conferences which emphasized that "the division would undoubtedly be under careful scrutiny primarily because it is the first Negro division to participate in maneuvers in World War II." [82] The location of the maneuver area deep in the Texas and Louisiana back country did not lessen the tension. The division suggested that it be relieved of the responsibility of furnishing umpires, usually exchanged by participating units, because the 73 required "must necessarily be comprised largely of colored lieutenants if company commanders are

---

[78] See Maj. Robert F. Cocklin, "Report on the Negro Soldier," Infantry Journal, LIX (December, 1946), 15–17.
[79] Notes on War Council, 27 Jul 42, WDCSA Files.
[80] Memo, McNarney for McNair, 11 Oct 42, AGF 354.2/7 (Desert).

[81] The two Negro regiments of the original 2d Cavalry Division had participated in the Arkansas maneuvers of 1941—the same maneuvers which had produced the original uneasiness over the use of Negro troops in Southern maneuver areas after the Gurdon incidents of that summer.
[82] Ltr, CG 93d Inf Div for IG Third Army, 25 Apr 43, 93d Div Files 250 Disc.

to retain command of their organizations and battalion and higher staffs are to function as normally composed." [83] The division staff visualized that "utilization of colored and white officers acting respectively as umpires of colored and white divisions operating against each other may result in the creation of undesirable situations. It is believed highly desirable that all umpires be white." [84] The division furnished umpires under a compromise by which units within divisions but not the divisions themselves interchanged umpires. [85]

Most worries about discipline in the division turned out to be groundless, although the greater care taken thereby may have influenced the end results favorably. Despite individual complaints of some citizens of the area, made almost immediately upon arrival of the 93d, [86] there were no racial disturbances. When the maneuvers closed the mayor of De Ridder, one of the Louisiana towns on the edge of the maneuver area, wrote to Secretary Stimson:

. . . to express my thanks and appreciation of the splendid deportment of the officers and men of the 93d Inf Div. (colored) during their stay in this area.

We anticipated no trouble before they came our way, and have given every effort to make their stay pleasant, cooperating with the officers to give the men every possible entertainment and recreation.

The troops have been very orderly and

well disciplined, causing no trouble or apprehension that could encourage criticism—for which we are thankful. [87]

Less gratifying to the 93d than its good discipline and relations with civilian communities was its movement to the maneuvers. Departure from Fort Huachuca was itself a trial which revealed weaknesses within the division. Too many units showed command and disciplinary deficiencies in managing the movement. Clothing and equipment were often in poor shape or lacking; "very frequently, the organization commander was ignorant of these facts or had no reasonable explanation." Often orders were not understood. The loading of the division was hampered by engineers' lack of knowledge of lashing techniques; much work had to be done over. Some units therefore took an inordinately long time to load. One train carried a detail as far as Douglas to complete the lashing of vehicles. In one technical company, the officers had little knowledge of what was wrong with their slow, disorganized departure. In another technical company whose loading was equally slow "the work done by its officers, when any was done at all, was of a low order." The division's chief of staff, as commander of the last train, observed the entire process. He concluded that the division had four very weak units—two of them infantry regiments—whose staffs must not have been keeping their commanders fully informed, for "if they were really on the job there could not be such consistently poor results in certain lines, particularly in the question of discipline and equip-

[83] Ltr, CG 93d Div to CG Third Army, 23 Feb 43, 93d Div Files 210.

[84] Ibid.

[85] 1st Ind to Ltr cited n. 83, above, Hq Third Army to CG 93d Div, 6 Mar 43.

[86] Ltr, Representative A. Leonard Allen (La.) to TAG, 15 Apr 43, inclosing Ltr dated 12 Apr 43 from Mrs. Lizzie Rains, Marthaville, La., and Ltr, TAG to CG Third Army, 10 May 43, both in AG 291.21 (4-15-43) OB-C.

[87] Ltr, City Council, City of De Ridder, to SW, 29 Jun 43, AG 291.2 (29 Jun 43) (19).

ment." A large number of company commanders were weak, but this was not entirely their fault, for regimental and battalion commanders were not demanding results. Unit commanders within the division, the chief of staff concluded, "have either got to get results or get relieved. They have got to be impressed with the idea that they must practice what they are supposed to preach and check the functioning of lower units by constant following up of orders and requiring an exact compliance with instructions. If they don't they are sunk and so is the Division. . . . We cannot carry anybody along—not now." [88]

In contrast to the inauspicious omens of the departure from Fort Huachuca, the maneuvers of the 93d Division against the 85th Division, conducted under the Third Army with the commander of the XV Corps, Maj. Gen. Wade H. Haislip, as director, were fairly successful. These maneuvers themselves, unlike earlier ones, began with a series of exercises and continued with problems in which the idea of winning and losing was discarded in favor of solving each problem "slowly, properly, and correctly." [89] "The maneuver was satisfactory, generally," Headquarters, Army Ground Forces, observed of one phase, adding that "men of the 93d Division obviously had received detailed, painstaking instruction, much of which was not absorbed." [90] Staff and command planning and functioning were often faulty as well. At the end of the maneuvers, Director Headquarters, as required, rated all units, with the 100th Battalion considered excellent, the 85th Division very satisfactory and the 93d, which had received the close attention of all observers, including some who came to the maneuvers extremely skeptical about the division's performance, rated unsatisfactory. But most observers concluded that the division had been well trained. Its Negro officers were generally considered satisfactory. The men of the division showed no lack of knowledge, but observers sensed a lack of will to apply that knowledge. Some of its soldiers felt, observers reported, that this was not their war. When leadership was good, especially at the noncommissioned level, the 93d performed well. Otherwise, it "fell apart." [91] But the division showed a steady improvement throughout, progressing from an unsatisfactory performance of technical duties at the beginning to satisfactory at the end.

The general feeling was that the division had performed better than expected.[92] Not all of the officers at Director Headquarters felt that it deserved so low a formal rating as it received. While they admitted that the 85th was clearly the better trained division, they did not think that its superiority was so marked as the ratings suggested.[93] Both

---

[88] Memo, Col Stanley M. Prouty, CofS 93d Inf Div, 9 Apr 43, and Memo, Prouty to Gen Miller, n.d., both in 93d Div Files 370.

[89] General Haislip in conference, 11 April, with division and principal unit commanders, quoted in Lt Francis G. Smith, Hist of Third Army, Study 17, Hist Sec AGF, 1946, p. 62; M/S, AGF Misc Div G-3 to AGF G-3, 14 Apr 43, AGF Brief of Problems, Third Army, Maneuver 2.

[90] Ltr, Hq AGF to CG Third Army, 31 May 43, AGF 354.2/75 Louisiana–1943)–GNGCT.

[91] AGF Study 17, p. 73.

[92] Ibid; Gen McNair in Gen Council, 3 May 43.

[93] AGF Study 17, pp. 73, 140, 266n. Two of the four Director Headquarters officers interviewed by the Third Army historical officer also disagreed with the 93d's unsatisfactory rating.

divisions, AGF determined, needed additional seasoning. Both left Louisiana for the Desert Training Center after the conclusion of the maneuvers in June.

The 93d was one of thirteen out of sixty-four infantry divisions trained in the United States to receive this "graduate" combined training, for the California-Arizona Maneuver Area closed in April 1944 for lack of sufficient supporting service troops in that year of manpower problems.[94] When General McNair observed the training activities of the division in August, some improvements were noted, but some of the older problems, especially slowness in executing missions and deficiencies in supervision, were still present.[95]

In the meantime, the 93d Division's personnel continued to undergo shifts and changes: enlisted men transferred out and new ones came in; the numbers of white officers decreased while the numbers of Negro officers increased. No great change occurred in the AGCT composition of the division as a result of these transfers. On 31 August 1943, the division's AGCT distribution stood: Class I, 24; Class II, 541; Class III, 2,323; Class IV, 5,616, and Class V, 6,919 (including 195 illiterates).[96] In the eighteen months between mid-1942 and the end of 1943, the number of white officers in the division decreased from 634 to 279 and the number of Negro officers increased from 250 to 575.[97]

At the close of Army maneuvers in July 1943, one infantry battalion was reorganized as a unit with all Negro officers by transferring officers from other units of the division on recommendation of unit commanders. This battalion was later reorganized again after it was observed to have made less progress than expected and after a request for a young Negro major or lieutenant colonel with a superior rating could not be filled. Company commanders, with one exception, were first lieutenants; two additional captains recommended for this battalion were not accepted. How careful the officer selection was, based on other small unit commanders' recommendations, cannot be gauged. But several of those recommended and some accepted for the battalion were later transferred out of the division as unsuitable or as surplus officers.[98]

The training of the 93d Division in Louisiana, successful particularly from the point of view that no serious disciplinary problems involving racial friction arose during the period, removed some of the reluctance about committing larger Negro units to maneuver areas for participation in exercises against white units. Third Army recommended that for fall maneuvers the 92d Division, scheduled to complete combined training on 23 October, be included in Maneuver Number 5 (6 December 1943 to 30 January 1944) and that the 2d Cavalry Division, less one

[94] Bell I. Wiley, "The Building and Training of Infantry Divisions," in Palmer, Wiley, and Keast, *The Procurement and Training of Ground Combat Troops*, p. 470.

[95] Ltr, McNair to CG DTC, 9 Sep 43, AGF 350.02/223 (AGF).

[96] AGF G-3 File folder 44 (93d Div).

[97] 93d Files 320.21, Rpts of Off Strength, AGO Records.

[98] Memo, Hq 93d Div to Distribution, 30 Jun 43, and Ltr, Hq 93d Inf Div to CO 369th Inf, 9 Jul 43, both in 93d Inf Div Files, AGO Records.

brigade, be ordered to the Desert Training Center upon completion of its combined training on 4 December 1943.[99]
Ground Forces at first suggested that the
2d Cavalry Division go instead to Louisiana, for that area was more suitable to
horse cavalry, and that the 92d, since it
was already in Arizona, go to the Desert
Training Center.[100] Plans for the 2d
Cavalry Division were altered by the
decision to send it overseas for disbandment. The 2d Cavalry was, however,
considered to have had excellent training methods. "Constant recital of duties apparently is producing results and
familiarizing individuals with their
duties," Ground Forces headquarters observed. "Planning, ingenuity, enthusiasm, military courtesy, and discipline
are outstanding. The division commander appears determined to produce
a trained combat unit." [101] The division's 4th Cavalry Brigade, located at
Camp Lockett, California, in the Southern Frontier Land Sector of the Western
Defense Command, was highly commended for its steadiness during the disturbances of the summer of 1943; squadrons of both its 10th and 28th Cavalry
helped control the giant forest fires of
September 1943 in the Cleveland National Forest. "There is no telling how
large these fires might have been had it
not been for the rapid mobilization of
your men from Lockett," the supervisor

of the national forest wrote to the commander of the brigade.[102]

The 92d Division, following the 93d
into Fort Huachuca, completed its training, including its D series, there. It
participated in the Sixth Louisiana Maneuvers from February to April 1944,
receiving a satisfactory rating at their
conclusion.[103] Most observers, both of
training at Fort Huachuca and of the
maneuvers, got the impression that the
92d was as well if not better trained
than the 93d.[104] It had the advantage of
following the 93d Division into maneuvers. Neither the qualms nor the
doubts accompanying the 93d's participation were as largely present in the
92d's exercises.

Before departing from Louisiana the
92d got the news that, in accordance
with the War Department's decision, one
combat team would begin preparations
for overseas movement upon returning
to Fort Huachuca. To the assembled
men and officers of the division its commander, Maj. Gen. Edward M. Almond,
concluding his remarks on the last phase
of the maneuvers, announced the decision and tried anew to weld his unit into
a self-respecting whole with a visible
mission:

[99] M/S, Misc Div AGF, 19 May 43, AGF Third Army Maneuvers 1943, item 94. The 2d Cavalry was to go to the Desert Training Center so as not to overburden Louisiana communities with two Negro divisions in the same period.
[100] M/S, Misc Div AGF G–3, 19 May 43, concurred in by Trp Movmts, Armd Forces, Tng, same file.
[101] Ltr, CofS AGF to CG Third Army, 18 Sep 43, AGF 253.02/028–GNGCT.
[102] Ltr, Norman J. Farrell, Forest Supervisor, Cleveland National Forest, Cal., to Brig Gen Thoburn K. Brown, 27 Sep 43, Corresp Files 4th Cav Brigade, AGO Records.
[103] Capt Jack N. Beardwood, Hist of Fourth Army, AGF Hist Sec, 1946, pp. 23ff; Ltr, Hq Fourth Army to CG AGF, 25 Apr 44, 353 GNMDC, AGF Fourth Army Manpower Rpts, 1944. Headquarters XVIII Corps, the 8th Armored, 11th Armored, 44th Infantry, and 75th Infantry Divisions also partici-pated in these maneuvers.
[104] Memo initialed J.G.C. for CG AGF, 24 Jun 43, reporting telephone conversation with Lt Gen Courtney H. Hodges, AGF 322/2 (92d Inf Div); comments in Min Gen Council, various dates.

... I told this division when it was a cadre of 1400 men and 200 Officers a year and a half ago that it had a future, and it has. I have watched it grow, I have watched the reaction of the men and the Officers. I have seen more reaction in the last two months come out on the surface than I have ever seen before. I see men salute better, perform their duties better, have a better idea of their job, and I won't say more cheerfully, because there has always been cheerfulness, except in individual cases. The 92d has a high standard of performance. It has not failed in this maneuver period. It has not failed to meet that standard. . . . It has not been but four hours ago that the Army Commander, the Corps Commander, another Corps Commander of the 21st Corps who saw the 365 at Atterbury, and three other Division Commanders told me the same thing. But I have told you before that you did not get that sort of stuff—and you don't get it—out of a book. You get it out of convincing yourself that you can do it. . . . Four days ago, I was visited by three Officers from Washington, with instructions that this Division is slated for combat duty in an active theater in the near future; that the first element to leave is a combat team, and that combat team is the 3–7–0! with the 598th following, and engineers, signal, quartermaster, medical, and other components of that combat team. Now what does that mean? There is not a man here who does not realize the importance of it. This is a Colored Division, with both white and Colored Officers. This is a cohesive military unit. You have just shown it. This is a unit that the Colored race should be proud of, and they will be before we are through; and not only the Colored race, but every American who knows enough to read about his war . . . you must take great satisfaction in the fact that you are now about to actually prove your worth.[105]

The 92d Division had transferred men to the 93d Division, the 2d Cavalry Division, and the 364th Infantry when these units left the country.[106] It now received men from the 372d Infantry and other units in preparation for its own departure. By May it had an overage both of officers and enlisted men.[107] Overstrength in enlisted men was needed to replace mentally and physically marginal men, of whom the division still had more than a thousand in August. Supervision and observation of the division during postmaneuver training and during the preparation of the 370th Regimental Combat Team for overseas movement were even closer than for the 93d Division. During the period the 92d was visited and inspected by General Marshall, Under Secretary Patterson, Maj. Gen. Ray Porter and seventeen members of his G-3 staff, General McNair and ten officers of his Ground Forces' staff, Maj. Gen. John P. Lucas and three members of his Fourth Army staff, by Maj. Gen. Louis A. Craig with five members of his XXIII Corps staff, and by visiting Mexican generals.[108]

Most impressions of the 92d and especially of its command on the eve of departure were favorable. "Almond has done a fine job," General McNair observed, "and believes that his division will fight. My own estimate of the value of these troops has risen as they emerge from the painfully slow process of drumming things into them. They are, I believe, a better outfit than the

---

[105] Comments of Gen Almond, CG 92d Div, Two-Sided Maneuvers, 7th Phase, Sixth Maneuver Period, 4 Apr 44, AGF 1944 Louisiana Maneuver Area Critiques, Sixth Maneuver Period, Seventh Phase.

[106] Interoffice Ref Sheet, 92d Div CofS to CG and GS, 14 Jan 44, Doc 354, Sheet 9, 92d Div Files.
[107] Ltr, Hq Fourth Army to CG AGF, 9 May 44, AGF 322/6 (92d Inf Div).
[108] Notes, CofS 92d Div, 15 Oct 44, Incl. 1 (Hist) Combat Efficiency Analysis, 92d Div Files.

93d when it left this country, and their future will be a most interesting contribution as to the value of negro troops." [109]   Secretary Patterson observed more guardedly that "The standard of performance was not as high as in the other divisions visited.   General Almond and his staff have worked hard, however, and deserve a good deal of credit for the way in which they are handling a difficult job.   I doubt that any one could handle the situation to better advantage." [110]

These two observations contained the kernel of representative approaches to the larger Negro units and especially to the 92d Division: that the major importance of these units was to provide documentation for the future employment of Negro troops and that their com-

manders, considering the difficulties with which they were faced, should be given all possible credit for doing as well as they did—no one was likely to do any better.   In the subsequent employment of these units both approaches were to emerge frequently.

In the meantime, Fort Huachuca from April to August 1944 was the scene of more than ordinary preparations as the 92d Division transferred men and received replacements, reorganized units and reclassified officers, dealt with the multitudinous problems of Fort Huachuca and Fry, entertained and displayed its progress for visiting dignitaries, dealt with rumors and reports in the Negro press, prepared a specially selected and constructed advance combat team, and, all the while, continued the usual training and processing for movement overseas.   The War Department and the Advisory Committee were awaiting with some curiosity the results of the larger units' assignments and their "contribution as to the value of negro troops."

[109] Memo, CofS AGF, 6 Jul 44, re USW's Inspection Trip.   This memo, according to cover note, was dictated by General McNair before he left for the ETO.   Book No. 20/23 Jun–12 Jul 44, OPD Exec Files.

[110] Ibid., Memo, USW Patterson to CofS, 4 Jul 44, re Inspection Trip to Four Divisions in the West, OPD Exec Files.

CHAPTER XVIII

Ground, Air, and the Asset Side

Decision on the means of getting more Negroes overseas and into action had barely been made when news reached the country that the first Negro infantrymen had met the enemy. With the dateline "Allied Headquarters, South Pacific, March 15," the wire services carried the story that American Negroes of the 24th Infantry were in front-line action for the first time, with Sgt. Alonzo Douglas of Chicago credited with being the first Negro infantryman to kill a Japanese in the Solomons.[1]

The 24th Infantry

The 24th Infantry, which had left the country in April 1942, had been on Efate in the New Hebrides and on Guadalcanal. From its arrival on 4 May 1942 as a part of Force 9156 (later III Island Command) to October 1942 it was charged with a large part of the perimeter defense of Efate. From October to the summer of 1943 the regiment, after consolidating its battalions, became a part of the island's mobile striking force, organized under the 24th's commander, Col. Hamilton Thorn. With the American successes on Guadal-

canal, the danger of immediate attack on the island had now passed. While the 24th continued its training and field duties, it performed base service functions, including loading and unloading ships, guarding air bases, building roads, spraying and draining as a part of mosquito control, sending daily labor details to perform quartermaster and ordnance services, and installing and maintaining wire communications for a large part of the base. These were, and continued to be, the 24th's main contribution to the Pacific war.[2]

The 24th's 2d Battalion, from about 1 March to 6 August 1943, was on detached duty on Guadalcanal, unloading ships, operating a provisional truck company, and furnishing labor details to quartermaster and ordnance dumps. The rest of the regiment moved to Guadalcanal in August, with the 1st Battalion receiving commendation from the commander of the USS *Hunter Liggett* for its speed and efficiency in unloading. The 3d Battalion was then detached in September for service at Munda for duty with the Provisional Service Command there. It operated ration dumps and a labor pool for the New Georgia Group Service Command. In the meantime, the regiment continued to return cadres

---

[1] "U.S. Negro Troops Begin Front-Line Action in Pacific," Washington *Post*, March 17, 1944. See also Frank L. Kluckholn, "U.S. Negro Troops Crack Bougainville Foe; Some from Harlem in Spirited Action," New York *Times*, March 17, 1944.

[2] AAR 24th Inf, Apr 42–Jun 43; 23 Feb–30 Jun 43; 1 Oct 43.

to the United States for new units, 11 officers and 182 enlisted men leaving in July and 5 officers and 76 enlisted men leaving in September 1943. While its units furnished men for local security in outlying areas of Guadalcanal, the regiment's chief daily duties involved supplying details for the Island Service Command, averaging 35 officers and 1,200 enlisted men.[3]

The 24th Infantry, the only Negro infantry unit continuing with all white officers, remained at these tasks until the end of January 1944, when the 1st Battalion, under Lt. Col. John L. Thomas, left Guadalcanal with naval Task Force 31 for Empress Augusta Bay, Bougainville. It landed on 30 January as a supporting unit in XIV Corps reserve.[4] While the other battalions and regimental units remained at their assigned duties at Munda and Guadalcanal, the 1st Battalion began to unload ships and work supply dumps at Bougainville, where marines and troops of the 37th Division had landed in November 1943 and where the 37th and American Divisions, plus two Fiji battalions, were still engaging the enemy.

On 29 February, two weeks after the Allied occupation of the Green Islands to the north of Bougainville had assured the cutting of Japanese communications and supply lines to Bougainville, and on the day that the Advisory Committee was meeting in Washington to frame a recommendation on the use of Negro troops in combat, the 1st Battalion, 24th Infantry, still in corps reserve, was relieved of service command duties and

attached to the 37th Division to assist in the construction of regimental reserve line positions. The battalion was assigned to the west half of the 129th Infantry reserve line. This battalion was already in position for active use against the enemy when the War Department's message urging the prompt use of Negro ground combat troops went out to General Harmon.

On 11 March, the battalion passed from XIV Corps reserve to the operational control of the 37th Division, which attached it to the 148th Infantry. It occupied the regimental reserve area. One company moved forward to reinforce the main line of resistance between the 1st and 3d Battalions of the 148th. That night this position was attacked and two men were killed.[5]

Not until the next night, 12 March—for the 1st Battalion had been organizing its sector and training its men—did the first of its combat patrols go out. Led by 2d Lt. Henry J. McAllister, the patrol moved several thousand yards out and, on its way back, about a thousand yards from the battalion's lines, encountered eight Japanese, killing one and losing one of its own men.[6] It was to this first Negro infantry patrol in a combat area that the published news release of 15 March referred.

The news release took the War Department by surprise. Would the 93d Division be as promptly used? The

---

[3] Historical Record and Hist 24th Inf, 1 Oct 43.
[4] Movement Order 12, Hq, For Area APO 709 (Guadalcanal), 18 Jan 44; Hist, 24th Inf Regt, 31 Mar 44.

[5] Company B lost Pfc. Leonard Brooks to an enemy grenade, and Pvt. Annias Jolly to enemy rifle fire. These two were probably the first Negro infantrymen to be killed by enemy grenade and rifle fire in World War II.
[6] Historical Record and Hist 24th Inf, 1 Jan–31 Mar 44; Msg, CG USAF in New Caledonia to WD, 3 Apr 44, CM–IN 1811 (3 Apr 44); 37th Div G–3 Opns Narrative.

next day an "Eyes Only" message went from General Marshall to General Harmon, advising that both the Chief of Staff and Secretary Stimson felt that initial use of the 93d Division or its elements should be permitted only after adequate preparation of the unit or units involved, for undoubtedly the first reports of the division's action would be headlined at home. News releases and theater reports would have to be kept factual; the War Department was under constant pressure for alleged failure to use Negro troops in combat. The units of the 93d should have a careful test to determine their capabilities. Anything warranting comment should be reported soon after their initial use and thereafter from time to time so that the Secretary might be kept fully informed.[7]   On 22 March another query went to the South Pacific, asking details of the extent and duration of the employment of the 24th Infantry on Bougainville, the use and location of the remainder of the regiment, future plans, personnel, casualties, and results attained so far.[8]

General Harmon assured Marshall that all reasonable measures to insure proper preparedness for the units of the 93d would be made, but the reinforced 25th Infantry Combat Team of the 93d Division was already loading for Empress Augusta Bay.   No amphibious operations were planned for these troops or for the 1st Battalion, 24th Infantry.

They were to be used initially with Fiji battalions on combat patrols and to mop up Japanese, with employment on limited operations from a base within the defense perimeter.   The War Department would be kept informed of events as they occurred.[9]

Thus, the first of the larger Negro ground combat units were committed to action, under direct suggestion from the War Department, acting under the pressure of unfavorable reactions to conversions and in the furtherance of a "national policy" which required that at least some Negro ground units be committed to combat.   Promises of reports and evaluations went along with their commitment.   In a klieg-lighted atmosphere, of which units and their officers were happily not always aware, their employment began.   Later, with the arrival of visiting observers, board members, staff representatives from higher headquarters, reporters, photographers, and interviewers, of high rank and low, troops could no longer ignore the interest focused upon them. Documentation, some objective and some not so objective, much of it out of proportion to the importance of the units or their missions, flowed into higher echelons, influencing the future use of the units concerned and the disposition of other units.   Few units, outside of the services, were employed for vital military tasks unrelated to one or another aspect of the demonstration of their abilities. The careers of Negro combat units were, therefore, as atypical as were the circumstances of their commitment to overseas duty.

---

[7] Rad, Marshall to Harmon, Eyes Only, 18 Mar 44, CM–OUT 7514 (18 Mar 44).

[8] Msg, Marshall to Harmon (OPD to CG USAFISPA) 22 Mar 44, CM–OUT 12845, OPD 322.7 (23 Mar 44). This query went out to obtain information to be used in answering questions from the public, especially those from the NAACP.

[9] Msg, Harmon to Marshall, Eyes Only, 23 Mar 44, CM–IN 16381.

The 93d Division

The 93d Division received its final movement orders in December 1943. On 11 January 1944, its advance party, under the division's commander, Maj. Gen. Raymond G. Lehman, left San Francisco for the South Pacific at the same time that its artillery units were completing firing tests at Iron Mountain. The remainder of the 93d moved to the Solomons between then and the end of February. This was the last time until the end of the war that all elements of the division were gathered in the same location. While the entire division proceeded to Guadalcanal, only its special troops and the 25th Infantry tarried there. The 368th Regimental Combat Team, without debarking, proceeded to prepare defensive positions on Banika in the Russells, arriving on 7 February. The 369th Regimental Combat Team, after a few days on Guadalcanal, proceeded in increments to islands of the New Georgia group, relieving elements of the 43d Infantry Division there. These units of the 93d Division began their careers as occupation troops, establishing guard posts, patrolling, assisting in the operation of ports, and training in jungle warfare.

The 25th Regimental Combat Team[10]

[10] In addition to the 25th Infantry, the combat team consisted of the 593d Field Artillery Battalion; Company A, 318th Engineer Combat Battalion; Company A, 318th Medical Battalion; 1st Platoon, Company D, 318th Medical Battalion; 93d Reconnaissance Troop; a detachment from the 93d Signal Company; and a detachment from the 793d Ordnance (LM) Company.

A full listing of the composition, commanders, movements, and operations of the 93d Division is recorded in Office of the Chief of Military History, Order of Battle of the United States Army Ground Forces in World War II: Pacific Theater of Operations (1959), pp. 613–27.

arrived on Guadalcanal on 17 February 1944 in the third group of 93d Infantry Division troops to reach the Solomons. It spent its first three weeks setting up camp on Guadalcanal while portions of its troops, averaging about a thousand a day, worked in the port area. When the bivouac area was in shape on 28 February, the regiment started jungle training with troops not detailed to the docks. Between then and 21 March, each battalion received about a week's training in jungle warfare, with emphasis on scouting, patrolling, perimeter defense, and rifle, grenade, and malarial training. On 22 March the combat team was ordered to move to Empress Augusta Bay, near the southern end of Bougainville,[11] where the 1st Battalion, 24th Infantry, was already being employed by XIV Corps.

The last major effort of the Japanese to dislodge Allied forces from the Torokina beachhead on Bougainville was being made at this time, though neither the troops nor their commanders could be certain of the finality of this offensive. The Japanese, with an estimated force of 25,000 on Bougainville, were expected to make strong efforts to force Allied units into the sea. Late in February, XIV Corps intelligence learned that the Japanese were concentrating a force of about 12,000 in front of Allied positions. The predicted attack came on 8 March, with a "series of vigorous but poorly coordinated attacks of a more or less piecemeal nature," all of which were repulsed with heavy Japanese and light American losses. By the end of March the main Japanese effort was over. The Japanese

[11] Ltr, Hq USAFISPA to CG Forward Area, CG 93d Div, 21 Mar 44, AG 370; Movement Order 60, Hq Forward Area APO 709, 22 Mar 44.

6th Division was, by then, practically destroyed.[12]

On 28 March, the 25th Regimental Combat Team, under the command of Col. Everett M. Yon, arrived on Bougainville, unloading by day under intermittent Japanese shelling. The next three days were spent in preparing a bivouac. On 30 March, the combat team went under the control of the American Division for training, administration, and operations.[13]

In his instructions to Maj. Gen. Oscar W. Griswold, commanding the XIV Corps, General Harmon, expanding the War Department's suggestions, emphasized the values inherent in limited offensive operations beyond the Torokina perimeter in southern Bougainville. "As a corollary," he added, "an opportunity will be afforded for the seasoning and employment of Negro combat forces." He suggested that the 25th Regimental Combat Team, supplemented if desired by the already available 1st Battalion, 24th Infantry, be used in these operations. The 24th Infantry's battalion could be replaced later by a fresh one from the same regiment. The Negro units were to work with more seasoned units under experienced leaders before going on their own.[14]

Each battalion of the 25th Infantry was therefore attached to one of the American's infantry regiments. The

593d Field Artillery Battalion and the 25th's cannon company were attached to the American's division artillery and other elements of the combat team to corresponding units of the American Division.[15] The two battalions of the Fiji Infantry Regiment, native Fijians under New Zealand and Fijian officers, whose whole combat experience had been obtained on Bougainville, were also available for use with the Negro units.

Already on Bougainville upon the arrival of the 1st Battalion, 24th Infantry, and the 25th Regimental Combat Team was the 2d Battalion of the 54th Coast Artillery, a Negro unit operating as field artillery. Later redesignated the 49th Coast Artillery Battalion,[16] this unit was among those that lost equipment and records when the *President Coolidge* sank after striking mines off Espíritu Santo on 26 October 1942. The 2d Battalion, 54th Coast Artillery, with the 172d Regimental Combat Team of the 43d Division, had been sent from Nouméa to Espíritu Santo in anticipation of the possibility of enemy attacks upon that major base supporting operations then in progress on Guadalcanal. Espíritu Santo was otherwise only lightly defended at the time.[17]

On Espíritu Santo, as part of the Island Defense, the 2d Battalion of the 54th gained experience in the use of various types of equipment, including borrowed 155-mm. and naval guns, pending arrival of replacements for its own weapons due in January 1943. Lacking

---

[12] Lt Gen M. F. Harmon, The Army in the South Pacific, OPD 314.7 PTO, Case 14; Opns Rpts, 37th Inf Div; John Miller, jr., *CARTWHEEL: Reduction of Rabaul*, UNITED STATES ARMY IN WORLD WAR II (Washington, 1959), ch. XVII.

[13] Opns Memo 57, Hq XIV Corps, 27 Mar 44; Opns Memo 9, Hq Americal Div, APO 716, 30 Mar 44; Hist, 25th Inf RCT.

[14] Ltr, CG USAFISPA to CG XIV Corps, 23 Mar 44, and Ltr, Harmon to Marshall, 30 Mar 44, copies in Orders, 93d Inf Div.

[15] Opns Memo 9, Hq Americal Div, 30 Mar 44.

[16] GO 453, Hq USAFISPA, 30 Mar 44, sub: Reorganized and Redesignated 2d Bn, 54th Coast Artillery.

[17] Harmon, The Army in the South Pacific, OPD 314.7 PTO, Case 74.

individual equipment, men learned to improvise. Occasional bombing raids, incurring no casualties and little damage, and intensive training in field artillery methods—every available man in the unit was trained as a cannoneer—contributed to the fitness of the unit. It remained on Espíritu Santo through 1943. On 4 February 1944 the unit debarked at Empress Augusta Bay where it was assigned to field artillery missions as corps artillery of the XIV Corps, thus becoming the first Negro combat support unit to engage the enemy actively in the South Pacific.[18]

The 24th Infantry on Bougainville

The 1st Battalion, 24th Infantry, while under the tactical control of the 148th Infantry from 11 to 29 March 1944, was not used for offensive operations. At the time, "the combat efficiency of the battalion was considered too low," General Griswold said. It was given a sector of the perimeter and "did an excellent job in organizing and preparing its defensive positions." [19] When the major Japanese attack against the Torokina beachhead came in March, no serious attempt was made against the 24th's sector. "In general, the troops of the battalion were inclined to be a bit 'trigger-happy,' but perhaps no more so than those of any other organization which has never had its baptism of fire," General Griswold reported.[20]

The first month's patrol work of this battalion was judged "decidedly inferior." One officer and fifteen enlisted men on a patrol reported themselves pinned down by an estimated six Japanese; though they had encountered no opposition for three hours, the officer made no attempt to extricate his patrol. One platoon of Company B, 148th Infantry, went to the rescue. Finding no opposition at all, they escorted the patrol back to the perimeter. Another patrol of the same company remained lost for several hours because, "according to the officer's statement, he was afraid to cross the barbed wire on the battalion reserve line." Another platoon did not continue an attack after being fired on, allowing an estimated half-dozen Japanese to escape.[21]

Upon the arrival of the 25th Regimental Combat Team on 29 March, the 1st Battalion, 24th Infantry, passed to the control of the Americal Division, relieving two companies on Hill 260, the scene of bitter fighting a few days before.[22] Patrols went into enemy territory but no contacts were made. Sanitary measures taken by the battalion seemed adequate, but mosquitoes were dense in the area of this hill. Japanese who had occupied it were almost universally infected with malaria. Within a month of occupying Hill 260, nearly one third of the battalion had malaria.[23] Leaving Hill 260, the battalion relieved troops of the 132d Infantry along a narrow beach running from the Torokina to the Mavavia Rivers. Patrolling, by

---

[18] Hist Rpts, 49th Coast Artillery Bn (155-mm. Gun), 15 Feb 41–Jun 44; G–3 Sec XIV Corps, Rpt of Opns on Bougainville; CG XIV Corps, Rpt of Lessons Learned in the Bougainville Operation.

[19] Rpt, CG XIV Corps to CG USAFISPA, 10 May 44.

[20] Ibid.

[21] Ibid.

[22] For an account of the Americal Division on Bougainville, see Capt. Francis D. Cronin, Under the Southern Cross (Washington: Combat Forces Press, 1951).

[23] CG XIV Corps, Rpt of Lessons Learned in the Bougainville Operation, p. 92.

24TH INFANTRYMEN PLOTTING DEFENSIVE POSITIONS, BOUGAINVILLE, *March 1944.*

now much improved, continued; clashes with the Japanese occurred north and east of Mavavia Lagoon and both sides suffered casualties.

The confidence and ability of the battalion increased. On 19 April an officer and sixteen men patrolling across the Mavavia were trapped by a company of Japanese. The patrol leader ordered his men to fight their way back across the river; twelve were able to do so, but the patrol leader and three men were pinned down by machine gun fire. A rifle platoon, supported by a platoon of medium tanks from the 754th Tank Battalion, landed from LCT's and attacked the enemy. The 24th's platoon rescued the trapped men and withdrew across the river mouth. After nearly five days of artillery and mortar fire on the area, a company of the 24th, supported by two platoons of tanks and a platoon of flame throwers, landed from LCT's and attacked along the narrow beach. Facing moderate to heavy resistance, the company cleared more than 1,000 yards of beach before nightfall while the remainder of the battalion occupied the cleared area and organized defensive positions. The advance continued the next day until midafteroon, when swampy ground near the mouth of the Moy River halted further attempts to gain ground.[24]   These constituted the first Negro infantry attacks supported by white armored troops and involving LCT's in World War II.

The 2d Battalion, 132d Infantry, took over the 24th's positions between the mouth of the Torokina and the Mavavia Lagoon while the remainder of the 24th's battalion extended their positions toward the assault company.   Through this action, more than 5,500 yards of the shore line came under the control of the American Division and its attached units.[25]   The XIV Corps commander considered the conduct of the battalion in this action to be "highly satisfactory." Subsequent patrols to the north and east as far as the Reini River he also judged "highly satisfactory."   Discipline and morale in the battalion were considered good.   "Although this battalion has in the past been employed largely on labor duties to the detriment of its training," General Griswold concluded, "its work in combat here has progressively and noticeably improved."   As of 10 May its combat efficiency was considered "good." [26]   The battalion had eleven men killed in action, two dead of wounds, and thirteen wounded during its operations in Bougainville.   It accounted for an estimated forty-seven Japanese killed in action and one prisoner of war.[27]

---

[24] Hist 24th Inf, 1 Apr–30 Jun 44.
[25] Cronin, *Under the Southern Cross.*
[26] Rpt on the 1st Bn 24th Inf and 25th RCT, 10 May 44.
[27] Hist 24th Inf, 1 Jan–30 Jun 44. The regiment as a whole already had a larger number of dead (15) from raids, accidents, and diseases.

The 25th Regimental Combat Team

When the 25th Regimental Combat Team arrived on Bougainville the main ground offensive of the Japanese—the only one since the occupation of the Torokina beachhead—had about spent itself.   After resistance on Hill 260 ended, the American Division planned to extend its outpost line of resistance along the general line of hills facing the beachhead.   Enemy artillery in these hills was still able to reach the Torokina airstrip.   The proposed hill line was divided into regimental sectors; when established by units of the American's regiments, it would be maintained by units of the 25th Infantry.

The 25th began its seasoning program under the control of the American within twenty-four hours of landing.   On 30 March, officer observers moved out with combat patrols of the American and two ammunition and pioneer platoons accompanied elements of the 132d Infantry in an attack on Hills 500 and 501.   In three days of action sixty-five Japanese were killed by this force; the 25th's platoons lost three men to sniper fire.   On 31 March Pvt. James H. O'Banner, a member of this party, became the first enlisted man of the 93d Division to kill an enemy soldier.

Before other battalions attached to the regiments of the American began their active patrolling, the 2d Battalion was temporarily detached from the 182d Infantry and assigned to a special task force from the 37th Division which included the 3d Battalion, 148th Infantry, and the two battalions of the Fiji Infantry Regiment.   The task force was directed to pursue and destroy the enemy detachments withdrawing east and north along the Laruma River. The force moved out on the morning of 2 April, heading north along the Numa Numa Trail, and halting at the Laruma River, where missions were assigned. The 2d Battalion was ordered to ford the Laruma and proceed eastward, protecting lines of communication and securing a trail junction near the mouth of Jaba Creek while the 3d Battalion, 148th Infantry, proceeded along the south bank of the river.

The 2d Battalion, 25th Infantry, crossed the river successfully, lowering men and equipment down a 60-foot river bluff by rope; Company E killed two Japanese while covering the crossing. Small skirmishes and light enemy fire occupied the battalion as it proceeded northeast. Enemy positions south of the river prohibited any advance on that side, and were bypassed by elements of the 3d Battalion, 148th Infantry. The 2d Battalion, 25th Infantry, placed considerable mortar and machine gun fire on these positions from its vantage point on the opposite shore.

On the next afternoon, 3 April, a small patrol under the regimental intelligence officer recrossed the Laruma and uncovered an enemy machine gun nest in a pocket of pillboxes. One Japanese was killed before hostile fire forced the patrol to withdraw. A platoon from Company F, after machine gun and mortar preparation, crossed the river and cleared out the machine gun position, losing five men wounded to approximately twenty Japanese dead. One man, Pvt. Wade Foggie, set up his rocket launcher under heavy fire and sent eight rounds into three enemy pillboxes, destroying them all and killing about ten

Japanese. For this action he received the division's first Bronze Star.[28] The next day Company E accompanied a party of Fiji Scouts on a patrol south of the river. On 5 April the task force completed its mission; the 2d Battalion was returned to the control of the 182d Infantry, Americal Division.

In this manner, most of the units of the 25th were introduced to combat. Patrols, consisting of members of the regiment, Fijians, and members of the Americal Division, engaged in both limited and extensive missions. In the meantime, the 593d Field Artillery Battalion was joining in the missions of the Americal's artillery. The 1st Battalion, 25th Infantry, attached to the 132d Infantry, got its first experience on 3 April. A party hand-carrying supplies to a force of the 132d in the vicinity of Hill 500 was ambushed by an enemy patrol when a part of the platoon was on the way back to the perimeter with a 132d Infantry litter case. Four men were lost —the first of the regiment to be killed in action. A member of the regimental medical detachment, Technician 3 Stephen H. Simpson, Jr., was with the 132d's patient at the time that the litter was fired on. Staying with the wounded man, he knocked out a Japanese machine gun with a hand grenade, helped the patient to the bottom of a hill, and there dressed a fresh bullet wound that the man had received during the skirmish. He and other members of the patrol improvised a litter and continued toward the rear. When darkness came, the patrol was lost in the jungle, but Simpson and the others remained with the wounded man until, guided by the sound of friendly artillery in the morn-

---

[28] GO 20, 4 Aug 44.

ing, they reached an American outpost and delivered him safely to an aid station. Company B of the 1st Battalion, in the meantime, took over a sector of the main perimeter from a company of the 132d Infantry on 4 April. Two days later, on 6 April, Company C saw its first action in conjunction with Company L, 132d Infantry, on a patrol in the vicinity of Hill 500 where, after a brief exchange of fire with an enemy force, the patrol withdrew and called for artillery fire on the area.

So far, the seasoning process had proceeded as planned and, in some cases, with better results than expected. The 593d Field Artillery Battalion was warmly welcomed by Brig. Gen. William C. Dunckel, commanding the Americal artillery, after his observers reported the accuracy of their fires and the efficiency of their construction and occupation of their positions.[29] The 2d Battalion of the 25th, returning from its mission with the 37th Division task force, was commended by the regimental commander for its count of thirty enemy dead at a cost of four minor casualties. The 3d Battalion had not as yet participated in combat patrols with elements of the 164th Infantry to which it was attached. It had been directed to organize reserve positions for the regiment. Its companies had gone on reconnaissance patrols without contacting the enemy.

On the evening of 5 April, Company K of the 25th's 3d Battalion, under the command of Capt. James J. Curran, a white officer, and Negro platoon leaders, received the mission of forming a trail block approximately 3,000 yards

from the base of Hill 250. A machine gun platoon from Company M was attached for the mission. Company K was to move out on the morning of 6 April and form the trail block during the following night. There was little time for briefing, supplying, instructing, and inspecting the company, for it was located in enemy territory and could carry on only limited activity in the dark. Capt. William A. Crutcher and three enlisted men of the 593d Field Artillery Battalion went along as artillery observers; an officer and an enlisted man of the 161st Signal Photographic Company had their cameras to make pictures for press release; Sgt. Ralph Brodin, intelligence sergeant from the Americal's 164th Infantry, was attached as combination guide and aide. All attached personnel except the 593d's enlisted men and the machine gun platoon were white.

Company K moved out about 0645. Its equipment and armament were normal, except that nine additional Browning automatic rifles had been substituted for nine M1 rifles. The light machine gun section had four guns and there was but one instead of three 60-mm. mortars. The unit carried two radios, SCR–300. The plan given to the platoon leaders was: The 1st Platoon would provide security to the front while breaking trail; a light machine gun section and company headquarters would follow. The 2d Platoon, coming next and in column, would provide security to the flanks, moving out from the trail with small finger patrols at all halts for reconnaissance and returning with reports of observations. Behind the 2d Platoon would come another machine gun section, with the 3d Platoon in the rear to provide

[29] Ltr, Hq Americal Div Arty to Offs and EM 593d FA Bn, 4 Apr 44, 93d Div Files.

security to the rear and to the immediate right and left; it also, at all halts, was to send out finger patrols and establish small outposts to the rear.

The men of the company were elated as they moved out on their first mission; the presence of newspaper men and the cameramen gave added vim to the occasion. All went well until, about 2,600 yards out and nearing its objective, the patrol entered an old Japanese hospital area containing several bamboo shelters. The 1st Platoon sent out finger patrols as planned. Shortly after halting in the shelter area, M1 fire broke out on the left front of the 1st Platoon. One patrol leader reported that his patrol had seen three Japanese, killed two. The company commander and the reporting sergeant started out to investigate. Before they reached the dead Japanese, firing broke out all around them. The patrol leader and one of his men were wounded.

With one of the 1st Platoon's patrols still out, the company commander ordered the 2d and 3d Platoons forward to join flanks with the 1st Platoon to provide security for the right and rear. The rifle platoons had moved into approximately these positions when firing resumed and machine guns were set up. Because of the dense jungle the mortar squad's men were used as riflemen, placed to the rear right of the company facing up the trail toward the 1st Platoon.

After the first rifle fire, heavy M1, automatic rifle, and machine gun fire interspersed with some Japanese fire, broke out to the front and left of the 1st Platoon. Without orders, some members of the 2d and 3d Platoons took up the fire. The 1st Section of machine guns opened fire to the right and left of the 1st Platoon; the 2d Section fired to the right and left flanks of the 3d Platoon.

His finger patrols still out, the company commander tried to order a cease fire; the order was taken up by platoon leaders and some noncommissioned officers, but after a brief silence one Japanese machine gun fired eight or nine rounds. Company K's men opened fire again. Men began to cry out that they were wounded; firing, much of it at random, continued.

The 2d and 3d Platoons, ordered to swing one squad each toward the 1st Platoon lines to bring their flanks together to meet at the trail, began moving in toward the 1st Platoon, firing sporadically in the general direction of the original position of the 1st Platoon whose men, caught in a cross fire, were now trying to take cover. Captain Curran ordered the 1st Platoon commander to reorganize his platoon and form a line about 75 yards to the rear through which the company could be withdrawn. The first sergeant, James Graham, was ordered to form the walking wounded, get a litter squad, provide security of five men, and evacuate the wounded to an aid station. These were the orders that started the movement of the entire company to the rear. The platoon sergeant of the 1st Platoon had already pulled off his pack, dropped his rifle, and disappeared. The directed movement of the 1st Platoon, whose men, highly excited as a result of being fired on from front and rear—firing which both they and the members of the other platoons insisted was Japanese fire—increased the apprehension of the men of the rear platoons, most of whom knew nothing of the orders governing the leading platoon's movements. When the company commander tried to move to the rear to help the 1st Platoon commander re-form his platoon, men crowded around him. Hoping to prevent a coalescing of the three platoons, he decided not to move with the 1st Platoon. Instead, he ordered 1st Lt. Oscar Davenport, weapons platoon leader, to withdraw his forward machine guns. Davenport, who had gone to investigate the original firing, was pinned down. He called out to the company commander, who replied, too late to cement officer solidarity and too soon to conceal rank from a sharp-eared enemy, "Don't call me captain, call me Jim." Davenport remained until all of his platoon had been withdrawn. While crawling to give aid to a wounded soldier of a nearby platoon, he was wounded. He continued toward the wounded soldier, reached him, and was administering first aid when he was hit again and killed.[30]

In the meantime, enemy firing, apparently unaimed, continued at short intervals. Sporadic bursts from Company K followed, some of it directed at any movement in the brush. The company commander reported the situation to the 3d Battalion command post and was told to withdraw about three or four hundred yards and reorganize his company. After the 2d and 3d Platoons had formed a new line as ordered, men continued to fire sporadically, pushing back each time until some lay two and three deep behind each other, firing over the heads of men in front. One backed "right over" the company commander's head and shoulder. Attempts to withdraw the men a few at a time failed, for men withdrew in groups until only the company commander and two other officers remained on the line. The new 1st Platoon line through which the company was to withdraw was a scene of confusion because men were reluctant to move off the trail and face outward as ordered. The white intelligence sergeant from the 164th Infantry, Sergeant Brodin, the sole experienced infantryman present, was of considerable help. "He walked calmly up and down carrying his carbine, telling the men there was nothing to worry about, that there were a few Japs, and that if they held everything would turn out OK," 1st Lt. Charles Schuman, the Signal Corps photographer, reported. "Sgt. Brodin suggested that my sergeant and I withdraw to the rear where we ran into Captain Curran. He was running up and down the trail trying to calm the men by shouting 'Hold your fire, hold your fire.'" At no time, Schuman continued, did he see any control exercised over the men by anyone. "I may have been in the wrong places, but I saw no leadership, no command, except Capt. Curran shouting hold your fire." Brodin commented that men fired at any moving bush. "They would listen to me because they thought I had more experience," he said. "They wanted to fight." Soon there was no patrol front; soldiers were lying about on the ground, facing and firing in all directions. Captain Curran reported again to the battalion command post, and he was ordered to bring his company back to Hill 250 to reorganize.

The first elements of Company K, with the first sergeant and the missing

---

[30] Ltr, Capt Curran, CO Co K, to CG USAFISPA, 9 May 44, sub: Posthumous Award of Bronze Star, 93d Div Files.

platoon sergeant of the 1st Platoon, reached their front lines about 1730 in the afternoon. The battalion commander met them as they crossed the Torokina River. All seemed quite upset and excited. In their opinion, the patrol had met at least a regiment of Japanese, although no survivor had seen an enemy soldier. The platoon sergeant was lying down with two or three other men; the first sergeant, in charge of litters, had "two or three men carrying him across the Torokina River," the battalion commander reported, adding, "He is rather old and fat."

Lieutenant Davenport and nine enlisted men were killed in the fight and twenty enlisted men were wounded. The dead were left behind along with equipment, including a radio, a light machine gun, a 60-mm. mortar, 30 rounds of 60-mm. ammunition, 2 Browning automatic rifles, about 18 M1 rifles, 3 carbines, and web equipment.

The entire action consumed but thirty or forty minutes but its aftermath was considerably longer. The best estimates were that not more than a squad or so of Japanese were involved and that most casualties were caused by the unit's own men. Investigation of the incident by the Americal Division, involving testimony from almost every available member of the company present, lasted from 14 April to 2 May;[31] discussion, speculation, and rumor lasted longer.

The next day a patrol from Company L went out to recover Company K's dead. This patrol ran into a fire fight about 75 yards short of its destination, losing one man in the fight and another by drowning, and returned without completing its mission. On 8 April Lt. Abner E. Jackson, 1st Platoon leader of Company K, led a carrying party of forty Company L men to the scene of the fight; six bodies were found but the men refused to touch or wrap them. Despite the threat of disciplinary action if the mission were not completed, Jackson could get only two noncoms and two privates to help him wrap the bodies. At Jackson's request, twenty men from his own Company K under the unit's new first sergeant joined his party. Three bodies and three mattress covers full of equipment were brought back. On the third day, another carrying party under the battalion commander accompanied by Jackson brought back the remaining bodies and equipment.

The 3d Battalion's units continued their patrolling for the next two weeks without further disrupting incidents or casualties. Most of the subsequent patrols of the 3d were joint patrols with the 164th, as in the initial patrols of the 25th's other battalions. On 11 April a patrol from Company K killed two of the enemy. A prisoner was taken by a Company I patrol the same day and another on 13 April.

The 2d Battalion, after its return to Americal Division control, engaged in extensive patrolling in the Torokina valley. One of the patrols from its Company F was ambushed on 8 April. A member of the patrol, Pvt. Isaac Sermon, wounded by a shot in the neck, returned

[31] Investigation of Co K, 25th Inf Patrol of 6 Apr 44, conducted by Lt Col Frank Lucas, IG Americal Div, APO 716, 14 Apr–2 May, pursuant to authority contained in 2d Ind, Interoffice Routing Slip, 14 Apr 44, attached to Memo, Hq 164th Inf for CofS Americal Div, APO 716, with allied papers, including Rpts to CO 3d Bn, 25th Inf, 93d Div; CO 1st Bn, 164th Inf, Americal Div; CO Co K, 25th Inf; SSgt Ralph E. Brodin, Hq 1st Bn, 164th Inf, Americal Div. All in 93d Div Files 333.

25TH RCT MEN KNEE-DEEP IN MUD ON A TRAIL TO HILL 165, BOUGAINVILLE, *15 April 1944.*

fire with his Browning automatic rifle and killed at least three of the enemy. After using his one magazine of ammunition, Private Sermon started crawling back to the rest of his patrol; he was shot three more times but kept going. He kept his position in the rapidly moving patrol for more than 600 yards; then he dropped from exhaustion and loss of blood and had to be carried in. He was awarded the regiment's only Silver Star for his part in this action.[32]

On the same day, 8 April, the Americal

Division ordered units of the 25th Infantry to occupy the new outpost line.[33] A provisional battalion of the 25th, including the regimental headquarters and the antitank and cannon companies, moved onto Hill 260 as the 1st Battalion, 24th Infantry, which had been going through the same seasoning process with elements of the 37th and Americal Divisions, moved off. Regiments of the Americal continued to control the battalions of the 25th as they gradually moved into position along the line of

---

[32] GO 131, 31 Oct 44.

[33] Hq Americal Div, Opn Memo 15, 8 Apr 44.

hills. Generally, the battalions of the 25th followed units of the American Division and the Fiji battalions into position as planned, remaining to organize and defend the outpost line. By 25 April, battalions of the 25th Infantry were all in outpost positions.

On 30 April control of the 25th Regimental Combat Team passed to a provisional brigade, organized under Brig. Gen. Leonard Boyd, assistant division commander, from all troops of the 93d Division then on Bougainville. The outpost line was now 12,000 yards from the Torokina bomber strip, leaving the remaining Japanese artillery out of range of the airstrips. Units of the regiment continued to patrol in co-operation with units of the American Division through May. In the meantime, troops of the 93d's 318th Engineer Battalion were constructing roads to the new positions while the 93d Reconnaissance Troop furnished security for the road builders.

Relations between men of the 25th and the veteran white troops with whom they were employed were excellent. Praise given them by officers and men of the American and by their own higher officers boosted morale. Men and officers reacted well to the knowledge that the unit was gaining experience and that some officers and men were gaining reputations as good patrol leaders. Most men and most officers considered that the unit was settling down well. Racial tensions had been pushed into the background both by enlisted men and by white officers although some Negro officers, while admitting that morale had improved, still smarted under the existing promotion policy and the lack of command positions among them. En-

listed men expressed themselves as fighting to maintain gains that Negroes had made in the past seventy years, to guarantee better jobs after the war, to "prove that we can do anything that anybody else can do," and because "If it were not for the Japs I wouldn't be here." The 25 percent or so who were not adjusting well divided roughly into two groups: those with little education, usually products of rural backgrounds, and those with urban backgrounds, who were better educated. The men of the first group viewed their missions with apathy, approaching their work halfheartedly, while the others resented being in the war at all, considering it little of their affair. Most of this minority of men lacked confidence in their leaders, white and Negro, and in their training. Some declared that their continental training in the desert had done little to fit them for jungle warfare.[34]

The Company K affair made a greater impression on the men of the regiment than most officers realized. Officers of the unit, knowing more of the problems of green troops, tended to view the episode as something that might have happened to any green troops freshly committed to action in the jungle. They realized that the men involved were

---

[34] Ltr, Div Psychiatrist (Capt George W. W. Little) to Div Surgeon, 8 May 44, sub: Psychiatrical Rpt on Front Line Conditions of the 25th CT. This report was characterized by the division commander as "a fairly accurate picture of the unique situation which exists in a colored unit whose commissioned personnel is composed of both white and colored officers"; it was, he continued, a "routine" report "used to a degree in determining the 'pulse' of this Division." Captain Little, a Negro officer, had been with the 93d Division since 21 January 1944. His previous reports had considered morale in the division low because of complex racial tensions. 1st Wrapper Ind, CG 93d Div to CG USAFISPA, 17 May 44, 93d Div Files 319.1.

somewhat shaken by the affair but there was little knowledge of its effect on the combat team as a whole. The enlisted men of the 25th, however, those who were performing and adjusting well along with those who were disgruntled, tended to view it as the result of moving the company into action without adequate preparation. They blamed the company commander for the events on this patrol. The rumor spread and was believed that the white company commander deserted his men, running to the rear under fire; that the Negro officer casualty sacrificed his life in order that his men might get back to the outpost line; and that the whole affair was being whitewashed in order to save the faces of the white officers involved. Outside the combat team, the incident became a *cause célébre* of another kind. It formed the basis of a rumor spreading through the Pacific that the 93d Division, in the invasion of Bougainville, had broken and run.[35]

Despite excellent discipline and control in many other instances, this and lesser incidents of individual and command failure combined to dampen enthusiasm for further use of the 25th Infantry on the gradually quietening Bougainville perimeter. Adverse reports sent to the War Department included a case where three men in a foxhole were approached at night by a fourth man, who jumped into the hole. In the ensuing scuffle one man was

knifed. There were no Japanese in the area at the time.[36] In another foxhole at night one of two soldiers thought he heard the enemy approaching. He fired all his own ammunition, then borrowed his companion's rifle and ammunition and fired again. When he tried to leave the foxhole, his companion attempted to stop him. In the struggle one man was shot. He was found dead in the morning in front of the foxhole. On another night a Negro officer and an enlisted man were in a foxhole closely adjoining another containing two enlisted men. The officer, thinking he heard a noise in the brush, left his foxhole, went to the neighboring position, and ordered the two soldiers to leave and investigate. Later the officer, seeing two figures in the brush, shot and killed one and wounded the other. In the morning it was revealed that these were his own two men. A company of the 25th, adjacent to a Fiji battalion, fired three mortar shells into an area close to the Fijians although half an hour earlier it had received warning that Fijian patrols were beginning to move out. On another occasion enemy infiltrators precipitated a night battle between the same company and its Fijian neighbors; though quantities of ammunition were fired, by luck alone no casualties were sustained by either unit. After ten days on the outpost line one of the 25th's battalions had not cleared sufficient fields of fire, had failed to cover the gaps between strongpoints by fire, and was erecting

---

[35] These and other rumors persisted. After the war, General Marshall described the 93d as a division whose men on Bougainville "wouldn't fight—couldn't get them out of the caves to fight." (Interv with Gen Marshall by Dr. Sidney T. Mathews, Dr. Howard M. Smyth, Maj Roy Lamson, and Maj James D. T. Hamilton, 25 Jul 49, OCMH files.)

[36] The report did not add that there was no password for the night in question; the dispersed unit had dug in too late at night to receive one. Its men had therefore been instructed to use knives against any intruder instead of firing so as not to reveal their positions to the enemy.

open-topped pillboxes to house five men each, thereby subjecting too large a group of men in one place to enemy action.[37] Easily noted incidents of this sort, failures in leadership ranging up to battalion level, as well as failures of battle discipline among individuals, Colonel Yon told his officers, "detracted from the excellent work others did and resulted in the 25th CT being rated only 'Fair' by Division and Corps in combat efficiency." The combat team nevertheless accomplished its mission, Colonel Yon felt. Battalion and company commanders of the Americal and 37th Divisions with which elements of the combat team operated stated that troops of the 25th settled down in the face of the enemy "as quickly, if not more so, than did their organizations on Guadalcanal and on New Georgia." [38]

But these and other organizations were now seasoned. They were considered dependable. The area had too little in the way of defensive troops and service troops for the widely separated positions held and developed. The 93d, with only one regiment introduced to combat, could be used to advantage, as originally suggested by General Harmon, to replace more seasoned units so that they might proceed to forge their way up the ladder of the Pacific islands toward Japan while the 93d occupied and defended forward positions already secured.

Nevertheless, the performance of the 25th Regimental Combat Team on Bou-

[37] Ltr, Gen Griswold to CG USAFISPA, 10 May 44, Combat Rpt, 1st Bn 24th Inf and 25th RCT, OPD 322.97.
[38] Ltr, Col Yon to Bn, Co, and Detachment CO's, to be read to assembled officers by Bn CO's and Separate Co CO's, 7 Jun 44, 93d Div Files.

gainville, while not without merit, produced familiar "buts" in higher commanders' estimate of the unit, all echoing the training experience and all tending to support the desirability of the original view of the most profitable employment for the Negro division. The XIV Corps commander concluded after six weeks:

(1) It is apparent that the unit had had little "jungle training"; consequently, as individuals or as a unit, they were not prepared to handle adequately problems encountered in jungle operations. Most individuals showed willingness to learn from white troops; however, their ability to learn, and to retain what has been taught, is generally inferior to that of white troops.

(2) In general, morale of all soldiers was high. However, units as a whole seemed to be unduly affected by reports of difficulties encountered by other elements of the command. Morale of the officers, especially white, seems rather low. Much of this attitude can be traced to the lack of responsibility demonstrated by their junior colored officers and non-commissioned officers.

(3) In general, discipline seems satisfactory; however, there is a tendency on the part of junior colored officers to make the minimum effort to carry out instructions. This same tendency exists among the enlisted men when they receive instructions from these junior officers. As a rule colored officers do not have control of the enlisted men. On the other hand, those units having a large proportion of white officers appear to be better controlled, trained, and disciplined.

(4) Initiative is generally lacking, especially among platoon commanders and lower grades. The presence of higher ranking officers, especially whites, is necessary to assure the tackling and accomplishment of any task.

(5) Field sanitation is generally inadequate.

(6) To date, the 25th Inf., though supposedly better trained than the 1st Bn 24th

Inf, has not progressively improved to the extent of the latter unit.

The combat efficiency of the 25th Regimental Combat Team at the time was considered fair for infantry units, good for the artillery unit.[39]

On 20 May relief of the battalions of the 25th on the outpost line by battalions of the American Division's 182d Infantry began, continuing to 12 June. Patrolling was carried on by each unit until relieved but there were few additional enemy contacts. The 93d Provisional Brigade was dissolved on 8 June 1944, just as the last elements of the 25th Infantry left Bougainville for the Green Islands north of Bougainville. The 93d Division, still under XIV Corps, passed to the control of the Southwest Pacific Area on 15 June after most of its elements moved to the Treasury Islands.[40]

The 93d Cavalry Reconnaissance Troop remained on Bougainville until 25 October 1944, continuing to operate with American forces. The reconnaissance troop, engaging in mapping patrols and protecting the engineers as they built roads, met no enemy opposition until 16 May when, on a four-day patrol mission reconnoitering and mapping the area between the Saua and Reini Rivers, one of its patrols, moving along a newly discovered trail leading west to the Reini, encountered six Japanese. Three-quarters of an hour later, it ran into an ambush near a pillbox in the same area. The rear of the patrol was subsequently attacked, and the men withdrew to high ground from which artillery fire was directed on the area. The patrol continued its mapping mis-

sion in the morning, leaving its artillery observers and heavy equipment within the perimeter. About 1020 it was ambushed again; it engaged the enemy in fire fights that lasted most of the day. The patrol leader, Lt. Charles Collins, was wounded in the leg during his fourth fire fight of the two days; he continued to command his patrol and during the fighting was wounded three more times and was then unable to continue with the rest of the patrol. Three members of the patrol stayed with him and another wounded soldier. Staff Sgt. Rothchild Webb helped his partly blinded patrol leader into a nearby swamp. After three days in Japanese-held territory, Webb successfully led Collins to safety.[41] The remaining wounded soldier and two companions, who succeeded in silencing enemy fire long enough to recover him, spent two days in the jungle before they were rescued by a friendly patrol. The troop lost three men killed in action and three wounded in these fire fights.

The 93d Reconnaissance Troop expected to join the remainder of the division in the movement from Bougainville. From 20 May to 20 June it was in reserve, standing by for movement, but on 20 June it was attached to the Americal Division for continued use on Bougainville. From 1 July to 10 July, acting as reconnaissance unit for the 182d Infantry, it participated in the battle for Horseshoe Ridge on the East-West Trail. It initiated attacks on the front and rear of the hill simultaneously; after several efforts, all elements were recalled for reorganization. Five men had been

[39] Griswold Rpt, 10 May 44, OPD 322.97.
[40] FO 1, Hq XIV Corps, 29 Jun 44.

[41] For this Webb was awarded the Silver Star. Hq USAFISPA, GO 1097, 29 Jul 44.

wounded. The attack had forced the enemy to evacuate; a handful of men, under Lt. Glen A. Allen, went up the hill in the late evening and found the Japanese leaving. They established a position on the hill and held it until reinforcements came.[42]

The 93d Reconnaissance Troop continued patrolling, setting up roadblocks and ambushes through the summer, generally acting on reconnaissance and combat patrol missions for the 164th Infantry. It employed alternating patrols in the jungles every five days during August. All missions were accomplished, some members of patrols being cited for exceptional services. After seven months on Bougainville the troop sailed to rejoin the 25th Regimental Combat Team.

Also remaining on Bougainville during this period was one other Negro ground combat unit, the 49th Coast Artillery Battalion, the 1st Battalion, 24th Infantry, having departed on 25 June for the Russell Islands. Between 4 February and 29 July, the 49th, acting as field artillery, fired 400 missions, expending 13,113 rounds. Missions were of all types: destruction, neutralization, harassment, and counterbattery. When the Japanese *6th Division* launched its March counterattack on the Torokina beachhead, the unit functioned exceptionally well during counterbattery fire, receiving credit for the destruction of several 75-mm. and 150-mm. Japanese field pieces. One officer and one enlisted man were killed and three enlisted men were wounded during this action; the unit received six Bronze Stars, two

Air Medals, and a commendation from the XIV Corps Artillery commander, Brig. Gen. Leo Kreber.

Beginning in May, part of the 49th relieved the 3d Marine Defense Battalion in seacoast defense positions, while Battery B remained as field artillery under the operational control of XIV Corps Artillery. This battery, attached to the 135th Field Artillery, moved to positions 1,000 yards outside the perimeter on the Numa Numa Trail, placing fires on enemy positions in the upper Laruma valley in support of regiments of the 37th and American Divisions.

The 49th continued with assignments on Bougainville, generally under the 68th Antiaircraft Artillery Brigade, until 26 November 1944 when, after the island was taken over by Australian forces, it was relieved of tactical duties. Not until February and March 1945 did the unit leave Bougainville for Finschhafen; even then a rear party remained with the unit's heavy ordnance equipment.[43]

After Bougainville

The 25th Regimental Combat Team left Bougainville for the Green Islands in June, unaware that the remainder of its career, along with that of the 93d Division's other regimental combat teams, was to be primarily one of security and service missions. Just before orders for the relief of the 25th arrived, the report of the investigation of Company K's patrol arrived from XIV Corps, with the conclusion and recommendation:

---

[42] The leader of this group and six enlisted men were awarded Bronze Stars for this action; three of the enlisted men were among those wounded.

[43] Hist Rpts, 49th CA Bn (155-mm. Gun), 15 Feb 41–Jun 44 and 15 Feb 41–27 Aug 45; G–3 Sec XIV Corps, Rpt of Opns on Bougainville; G–3 Opns Rpt, 37th Inf Div, Arty Sec.

The performance of Company "K," 25th Infantry as brought out in this report of investigation, is indicative of a lack of proper discipline, and small unit leadership. It is desired that training be instituted to correct these deficiencies, and be vigorously prosecuted in order to prevent like occurrences.[44]

Of the report the regimental commander commented that the 1st and 2d Battalions of the 25th had been trained, as planned, with veteran units while the 3d Battalion's units had not. Instead, Company K was sent out with but one enlisted man of the 164th Infantry. It had consistently been one of the three best companies of the regiment during the past two and a half years. It was the regimental commander's opinion that

. . . had this organization been given prior instruction and been accompanied by an experienced platoon of the 164th Infantry in its initial action, the results would have been far different. The force encountered was small but equipped with machine guns. The majority of our casualties were inflicted by other men of the company. This has resulted in many instances in jungle warfare when troops were committed without proper seasoning. Early in May a company of the 182d Infantry, a veteran of two years of jungle warfare, encountered an inferior force of the enemy east of the Saua river, became disorganized and returned to the perimeter of the 3d battalion, 25th Infantry on Hill 65 after darkness. The above facts are not offered in condonation of the failure of Company "K" to carry out its mission, but they were contributing causes. . . .[45]

───────────

[44] 1st Ind, Hq XIV Corps to CG Provisional Brigade 93d Div, on Rpt of Investigation, 15 May 44, 93d Div Files 333.

[45] 3d Ind, Hq 25th Inf (Col Yon) to CG 93d Div, 27 Jun 44, on Ltr, Hq Americal Div to CG XIV Corps, 10 May 44, 93d Div Files. See also the CG XIV Corps, Rpt of Lessons Learned in the Bougainville Operation, p. 30.

Neither this opinion nor the demurrer of the 93d Provisional Brigade's commander that the 25th Regimental Combat Team had not been adequately rated altered the course of events planned for the 93d Division. Arriving on the Green Islands, where it relieved the 3d New Zealand Division, the combat team took up its duties of security, labor, and training. Like other elements of the 93d, it was to spend the next year and a half moving from one Pacific island to another, relieving elements of other divisions going forward to engage the enemy, taking over positions which were now rear areas, loading and unloading ships, cleaning out Japanese stragglers hiding out on "secure" islands, and mounting invasions for other troops. These were the duties contemplated when the 93d Division was accepted by the theater. At first the ability of the enemy to attack the 93d's islands by air or by sea could not be discounted, but later this possibility became more and more remote. The subsequent duties performed by the 93d in the Pacific were essential, but they were not those an infantry division was normally expected to perform.

In Washington, reports on the 1st Battalion, 24th Infantry, and the 25th Regimental Combat Team were briefed and sent to General Marshall, Secretary McCloy, and Secretary Stimson. Secretary McCloy, forwarding one report to Stimson, observed:

. . . Although they show some important limitations, on the whole I feel that the report is not so bad as to discourage us.
The general tone of these reports reminds me of the first reports we got of the 99th Squadron. You remember that they were not very good, but that Squadron has now taken its place in the line and has

performed very well. It will take more time and effort to make good combat units out of them, but in the end I think they can be brought over to the asset side.[46]

To this Stimson observed: "Noted—but I do not believe they can be turned into really effective combat troops without all officers being white. This is indicated by many of the incidents herein." [47]

For the 93d, unlike the fighter squadron, there was to be no means of demonstrating improved offensive combat performance; neither the 25th Infantry nor the remaining untried units of the division would be employed for any tactical missions other than minor ones. The fighter squadrons had a different employment story now that, as Secretary McCloy expressed it, they had taken their "place in the line."

The Fighter Units

The 99th Fighter Squadron was completing its first year in combat just as the 93d's units were leaving Bougainville. On 2 June 1944, with its commanding officer, Capt. Erwin B. Lawrence, leading, it flew its 500th combat mission for a cumulative total of 3,277 sorties.[48] Public relations releases, appropriately, made much of the anniversary. Since acquiring new missions in the fall of

1943, the 99th Squadron had turned in consistently better performances, some of them with dramatic impact.

In January 1944 the 79th Fighter Group, with the 99th Squadron still operating as a fourth squadron, was assigned missions over the Anzio beachhead from Capodichino Aerodrome, near Naples. From D-day, 22 January, on, the 79th met enemy air opposition. On two successive days the 99th scored heavily over the Anzio beach where recently landed American troops were feeling the weight of massing German forces. On the morning of the 27th, fifteen of the 99th's P–40 Warhawks engaged sixteen or more Focke-Wulf 190's that were pulling out of a bomb run over the beach. They destroyed six and damaged four of the enemy planes. That afternoon, the 99th returned to the beach area, engaging twelve Focke-Wulf 190's and Messerschmitts. Three were destroyed and a fourth probable was recorded. On the next day, the 99th's share of twenty-one enemy aircraft knocked out of the air over Anzio was four destroyed.[49] "It's a grand show. You're doing a magnificent job," General Cannon declared to the 79th Group and the 99th Squadron. "You are authorized to use the following as you may see fit," General Arnold cabled General Eaker from Washington: "The results of the 99th Fighter Squadron during the past two weeks, particu-

---

[46] Brief (Col Pasco) for General Marshall, and attached Memo, ASW for Colonel Stimson, 1 Jun 44, WDCSA 370.2 (27 May 44).

[47] Memo, OSW (initialed H.L.S.) for J. J. McC., sent to Col Pasco, Gen Marshall, noted DCofS, 5 Jun 44, to Mr. McCloy, and returned to OPD for necessary action or file, WDCSA 370.2 (27 May 44). The brief, in light of Stimson's comment, contained one major error: it said that the 24th's battalions had Negro junior officers.

[48] 99th Fighter Squadron War Diary, Jun. 44.

---

[49] The squadron's full record for the period 15–28 January inclusive was: 246 aircraft airborne, 231 effective sorties, 15 noneffective (143 sorties over Anzio beachhead, 77 invasion convoy patrols); 7½ tons of bombs dropped, 12 aircraft destroyed, 2 probables, 4 damaged; one U.S. aircraft lost, two missing. In February the squadron flew another 55 missions over the Anzio-Nettuno area.

larly since the Nettuno landing, are very commendable. My best wishes for their continued success." [50] Approbation at home and abroad was noted with pleasure by men of the squadron. The Atlanta *Journal,* after carrying a news article, "Black Eagles Down 8 Planes Over Nettuno," continued editorially:

The success of the 99th U.S. Fighter Squadron in the air battles over the Nettuno beachhead Thursday will be gratifying to all Americans whatever their race or position. It should be cause for special pride among our Negroes. . . . The fine performance of the 99th in its first desperate adventure will give its members a confidence in themselves that will make the 99th a unit to be feared by the enemy.[51]

All three afternoon London papers carried the story on their front pages.

The 332d Fighter Group, under the command of Lt. Col. Benjamin O. Davis, Jr., arrived at Taranto, Italy, between 29 January and 3 February 1944, with its three full squadrons, the 100th, 301st, and 302d. On 5 February, the first of its squadrons, the 100th, became operational. The group was assigned to harbor and coastal patrol and to convoy escort missions with the Twelfth Air Force. A month later, General Eaker informed Washington that the showing of the 332d Group made him "very anxious to have them re-equipped with P-47's. I have gone over this matter thoroughly with Colonel Davis, Cannon, Twining, and Norstad and I am certain that this is the smart thing to do. You

will find also that it will take a lot of political pressure off you." [52]   The P-47 Thunderbolts would improve the range of the group, then equipped with P-39's, making them available for bomber escort duty. General Eaker restated his desire to re-equip the 332d at the same time that older groups were changed over to the newer fighters then in production. "Cannon, Twining and I believe this is a sound move," he said, adding that their reasons were countered by but one theoretical objection:

In the Anzio bridgehead battle, the colored combat pilots have demonstrated that they fight better against the German in the air than they do on ground support missions. The only point raised against this is the fact that bombardment accompanying missions are at high altitude and colored troops do not normally stand cold weather very well. The P-47 is a warm airplane, however, and we believe it will work. Colonel Davis and his colored pilots are most enthusiastic to undertake the program and I am confident that they will do a good job.[53]

Washington had planned and preferred to re-equip the 332d with P-63's, the Kingcobra, the new and improved version of the P-39,[54] but delays in proving and delivering this plane plus General Eaker's urging, provided the group with new P-47's, first used after its transfer to the Fifteenth Strategic Air Force at

[50] Msg 317, Arnold to Eaker, 4 Feb 44, OPD Log File.
[51] Editorial, "The 99th's First Battle," Atlanta *Journal,* January 31, 1944. See also, Phillips J. Peck, "The Negro in the AAF," *Flying,* XXVI (June, 1945), 24–25, 121–28.

[52] Ltr, Gen Eaker, Comdr MAAF, to Maj Gen Barney M. Giles, CofAS Hq AAF, 6 Mar 44, copy in Hist Mediterranean Allied Air Force, Dec 43–1 Sep 44, AF Archives.
[53] Hist Mediterranean Allied Air Force, copy of Query 3, Tel Conv, 14 Mar 44, Gen Eaker in Italy with Gens Craig, Giles, Hansell, *et al.* in Washington.
[54] Ltr, Actg CofAS (Gen Craig) to Gen Eaker, MAAF, 22 Mar 44; Ltr, CofAS (Gen Giles) to Gen Eaker, 25 Mar 44, copies in Hist Mediterranean Allied Air Force.

332D FIGHTER GROUP PILOTS BEING BRIEFED *before a combat mission, Italy.*

the end of May. When that happened General Eaker noted:

Yesterday we transferred the 332d, completely equipped with P–47's, to the Strategic Air Force. These colored pilots have very high morale and are eager to get started on their new Strategic task accompanying long-range heavy bombers. I talked with General Strothers, their Wing Commander, today. He has watched them closely in their indoctrination phase and he feels, as I do, that they will give a good account of themselves.[55]

---

[55] Re-equipment of Long-Range Fighter Units, Incl to Ltr, Eaker to Gen Arnold, 1 Jun 44, in Hist Mediterranean Allied Air Force.

The 332d, now assigned to the 306th Fighter Wing, flew its first mission with the Fifteenth Air Force on 7 June. On its third mission, two days later, it downed five Messerschmitt 109's over Munich.

In July the 332d was again re-equipped, this time with P–51 Mustangs, useful for long-range escort fighting like the P–47 and also for bombing, ground attacks, and reconnaissance.

Since February the 99th Squadron had been operating with the 79th Group, and then with the 324th Fighter Group, in bombing enemy positions, highways, railroads, bridges, and industrial plants. The 99th had celebrated the first anniversary of its departure for North Africa on 2 April 1944 by moving from Capodichino to Cercola Field for attachment to the 324th Group. While still with the 79th Group, beginning 8 March, it had received several P–47 Thunderbolts. This was taken by the squadron as a sign that it would remain attached to the 79th Group, which had already acquired P–47's. But on 1 April, when the last of the 99th's P–47's were transferred to the 85th Squadron, rumors broke out that the squadron was about to be detached from the 79th Group. Men and officers hoped that they would remain attached to the 79th with which they had established and maintained good relations. The news of attachment to the 324th Group, with which it had worked earlier while at Cape Bon, caused "considerable grumbling among the men . . . . Every man was proud of the attachment with the 79th Fighter Group and the policy of its commanding officer, Col. Earl Bates." During its second attachment to the 324th, the 99th operated practically independently, all reports going directly to XII Tactical Air Command (Rear). On 5 June, when the 324th left Pignatoria Airfield on which it and the 99th were stationed, attachment terminated. The squadron remained independent, operating directly under the XII Tactical Air Command while men debated the length of time that they would continue to so operate. From 11 to 29 June it was attached to the 86th Bomber Group and on the latter date was assigned to the 332d Fighter Group as originally planned.[56]

On Independence Day, 1944, the 332d flew its first operational mission with its new P–51 Mustangs. On 12 July, over southern France, the unit secured its first victories in the Mustang, one pilot, Capt. Joseph D. Elsberry, scoring three victories that day. On 15 July the group, with the 99th added, flew its first four-squadron escort mission with bombers of the Fifteenth Air Force.[57] On 18 July it shot down eleven enemy planes.

Though the youngest among them, the 332d now took its place with the 306th Wing's and, later, the Fifteenth Fighter Command's groups escorting the Strategic Air Force's bombers on their long-range missions to the Balkans and into southern France, Germany, and Czechoslovakia. Morale rose among the 332d Group's ground crews and pilots as more important missions were assigned it. Maj. Gen. Nathan Twining and Brig. Gen. Dean C. Strother visited the 332d and praised its efficiency. As more enemy aircraft were downed by the group, "everyone seemed to have had a high spirit. The Group, because of its unique set-up, attracted international attention and the pilots wanted to prove that they could make the grade."[58]

In August the 332d strafed radar installations on the coast of southern France in preparation for the invasion; on invasion day it covered Fifteenth Air Force attacks on the landing beaches. The 332d furnished fighter escort for the Fifteenth's final attack on the Plo-

---

[56] Hist, War Diary, 99th Fighter Sq, Apr–Jun 44.

[57] The junior of the four squadrons, the 302d, was inactivated and its personnel absorbed in the other three on 7 March 1945, both to eliminate the extra squadron so that the 332d might be organized as a standard three-squadron group and to solve a threatening replacement shortage.

[58] Hist 332d Fighter Group, Jul 44 Installment, AF Archives.

eşti oil refineries, accounted for thirty-six of the seventy-six aircraft destroyed on a mission to Ilandza Airdrome in Yugoslavia, strafed airdromes in the Athens area before the invasion of Greece, strafed railroad traffic from Budapest to Bratislava, and attacked targets of opportunity whenever possible. In December in missions over Germany the fighter group met its first German jet planes, the ME–262's. The 332d's commander confirmed the hopes of his men when, in his year's end message, he told them:

I cannot fail to mention the all important fact that your achievements have been recognized. Unofficially you are known by an untold number of bomber crews as the Red Tails who can be depended upon and whose appearance means certain protection from enemy fighters. The bomber crews have told others about your accomplishments, and your good reputation has preceded you in many parts where you may think you are unknown. . . . The Commanding General of our Fighter Command has stated that we are doing a good job and that he will so inform the Air Force Commander. Thus, the official report of our operations is a creditable one.[59]

The 332d's missions with the Fifteenth Air Force had their climax on 24 March 1945 when, with Colonel Davis leading, the group flew cover for B–17's in a 1,600 mile round trip attack on Berlin, the longest mission of the Fifteenth Air Force's history. One P–38 and three other Mustang groups were in this attack on the Daimler-Benz tank works, which turned out to be one of the more exciting missions of the Fifteenth Air Force's year. Before this time, only two victories over ME–262

jet planes had been confirmed by the Fifteenth Fighter Command. Over Berlin, 8 more jets were credited to Mustangs, 5 to the 31st Group and 3 to the 332d Group. The 332d probably destroyed 2 more and damaged 3 other ME–262's. It probably destroyed an ME–163 rocket plane as well. On the way back from Berlin, aircraft of the group strafed enemy ground installations and transportation, damaging 2 locomotives and 3 railroad cars. For the day's action the 332d received the Distinguished Unit Citation.[60]

Two more big days awaited the 332d. On 31 March, while on a strafing mission in the Munich area, it destroyed 13, probably destroyed 3, and damaged 1 enemy aircraft; destroyed 7 and damaged 13 locomotives, destroyed 13 and damaged 57 railroad cars, destroyed 1 and damaged 1 vehicle on flat cars; and damaged a railroad station, a roundhouse, a factory, and a warehouse. The next day, 1 April, in the Wels area, Austria, the 332d Group destroyed 12 more planes, bringing the two-day total up to 25. On 26 April the 332d concluded its combat career with 4 enemy aircraft destroyed, the last to be downed by Mediterranean-based aircraft before the end of the war.

Throughout its career, the 332d Group received its replacement pilots though morale was high enough for a number of its pilots to refuse relief when available. While the recognition that it was being used on important missions and was achieving success on those missions was a major factor in the high morale of the unit, the active

⁵⁹ Ibid., Dec 44 Installment.

⁶⁰ Hist 306th Fighter Wing, Mar 45, AF Archives; XV AF GO 3674, 9 Aug 45; WD GO 84, 5 Oct 45.

UNLOADING SUPPLIES ON THE BEACH AT HOLLANDIA

interest of higher headquarters, evidenced in the visits of Generals Eaker, Twining, and Strother and of Col. Yantis H. Taylor, the group's wing commander, was no negligible factor. The relations of the 332d with other units and its sports achievements—men of the group became basketball champions of the Fifteenth Fighter Command, placing three members on the command's all-star team—contributed to the sense of mission which gripped ground men and pilots alike. Pilots of the 332d downed over enemy territory usually managed to rejoin the group with the aid of partisans in the German occupied countries of southeastern Europe and the Maquis in France. One pilot downed in August 1944 remained in northern Italy heading a partisan band until the end of the war.

After the war, when asked about Negroes in the Air Forces, General Eaker ascribed much of the success of the units to their leadership: "They did a very good job. The reason, in my opinion, they did a good job is that they had an outstanding leader, Colonel Davis, a

West Point graduate, at the head of that group. He is a remarkable young leader." [61] However, the sense of mission, understood and furthered by Colonel Davis and by the groups's immediately higher headquarters—which assigned to the unit tasks of undeniable importance, paralleling the assignments of other units in the same command— probably had as much to do as leadership with the pride in unit and in achievement that marked the fighter group off from most other large Negro units in World War II.

The "Asset Side"

The 93d Division, in the meantime, continued its assigned missions in the Pacific. Now under control of the Southwest Pacific's Eighth Army, the 93d proceeded slowly up the island ladder of the Pacific toward the Philippines, generally relieving elements of other divisions, especially the 31st and the 41st, that were moving on to other missions. Upon its arrival in the Southwest Pacific Area, GHQ G–3, with the concurrence of GHQ G–4, gave oral instructions that the 93d Division was to have training, fatigue, and defensive missions in exactly the same proportions as those of the other divisions of the Eighth Army. [62] Despite conflicting instructions and misunderstandings on the part of both the division and the senior commanders in many of the areas occupied by the 93d's troops, this remained the policy for its

employment. [63] The 93d was to be kept in readiness to enter combat on call, although when labor requirements at Hollandia and Finschhafen mounted sharply at the end of 1944, the priority of missions was altered to place defense of areas and labor details ahead of training. [64] The 93d then had responsibility for the control and co-ordination of all labor and transportation furnished by all Eighth and Sixth Army units in the Hollandia area. For this purpose, the division assumed operational control of all Eighth Army units in the area not engaged in the operation of the army headquarters. [65] Administrative and supply responsibilities for all Eighth Army Area Command units at Hollandia, Finschhafen, and the Admiralty Islands continued with the 93d even after movement to Morotai. [66]

On their islands elements of the 93d Division generally performed security, dock, warehouse, and patrol missions. Areas occupied by the division usually had air and service units, white and Negro, on them as well, and generally included airfields, warehouses, ports, radar, radio, and antiaircraft installations. The senior 93d Division commander present was often in command of the island. Occasionally elements of the division encountered remnants of Japanese troops. In some cases while other elements of the 93d moved ahead, units as

[61] Question period following Address, Lt. Gen. Ira C. Eaker, Air Power in Modern War, 20 March 1946, Industrial Mobilization Course, The Army Industrial College, Washington.

[62] Ltr, Hq Eighth Army to CinC GHQ SWPA, 9 Dec 44, AG 370.2 (Opns).

[63] Ltr, Hq Eighth Army to CG 93d Div, 17 Nov 44, AG 353 (93d Div) (FA); Ltr, Hq Advance USAFFE to CG Eighth Army, 14 Nov, A–FEX 370.2.

[64] Ltr, Hq Eighth Army to CG 93d Div, 1 Dec 44, AG 322 (FB); 1st Ind, GHQ SWPA to CG Eighth Army, 16 Dec 44, to Ltr, Hq Eighth Army to CinC GHQ SWPA, 9 Dec 44, AG 370.2 (Opns); Ltr, Hq Eighth Army to CG 93d Div, 8 Mar 45, AG 370 (D).

[65] Ltr, Hq Eighth Army to CG 93d Div, 1 Dec 44, AG 322 (FB).

[66] FO 7, Hq Eighth Army Area Comd, 20 Mar 45.

small as a company remained behind to complete the job of rounding up remaining enemy stragglers and closing out installations. Small expeditions sometimes went out in landing craft to clear neighboring areas and islands. Occasionally enough of the enemy remained to produce fire fights of considerable size.

Though the 93d Division struck no major blows against the enemy, its role as a holding division and as administrator of large areas of the Pacific command—it had at times as high as 28,000 troops attached for administration and for operational control[67]—was on the asset side, if not wholly in the sense meant by Secretary McCloy at least in the real sense of its value to operations in the vast and undermanned Pacific. During the entire period, the 93d continued training those of its troops not engaged in other duties, preparing against the day when the division might be called upon for more critical missions.

Two of the 93d's infantry regiments had only minor encounters with the enemy in 1944. The 2d Battalion, 368th Infantry, on Vella Lavella, made several contacts while charged with the security of that island from February through June. The 369th, at Munda and elsewhere on islands of the New Georgia group, encountered no hostile forces at all. In addition to furnishing labor details, the 369th engaged in intensive training. Members of its staff flew to Bougainville, observed the jungle operations there, and returned to Munda and established a jungle patrol leader school that continued until all company officers and noncommissioned officers

completed the course. In addition, about fifty officers and petty officers of the 73d Naval Construction Battalion (Seabees) and selected officers and noncommissioned officers of the 368th Infantry attended the course. Captured Japanese rifles and machine guns, fired over troops to familiarize them with the weapons and their characteristic sounds, were used in training exercises. Battalion exercises in jungle attacks with close artillery support—the artillery barrages brought down within 200 yards of troops on the line of departure just prior to the jump-off—were staged even during packing for the move from New Georgia to Emirau, St. Matthias Group, in June 1944.

Only at the end of the year did elements of the 369th Infantry come into contact with the enemy. At Wardo on Biak, a small detachment of the 369th consisting of 15 men and one officer (later supplemented by 27 more men and another officer), sent to protect radar installations, found the enemy active. Between 6 November and 16 December, the detachment killed 38 and captured one Japanese. At the end of the year, on 31 December, a similar detachment at Wari killed eight to ten Japanese in a fire fight. By the time the 369th left Biak on 31 March 1945,[68] 74 Japanese had been killed and 34 captured, with no casualties to the 369th.

This, in general, was typical of the activities of the elements of the 93d Division, whether at Munda, Biak, Emirau, Hollandia, or Finschhafen. Some men were placed on patrol, guard, and tactical duties; some continued training; the

---

[67] Hist, Hq and Hq Co 93d Inf Div, 10 Jun 44–23 Sep 45.

[68] The 2d Battalion, 369th, remained at Biak until 1 October 1945, charged with labor, training, and security missions.

remainder were on dock, warehouse, or other service details. The 25th Infantry, for example, arrived at Finschhafen from the Green Islands on 30 October 1944. It later became responsible for the defense of the Finschhafen base, but this duty was a minor one in the regiment's work there. Finschhafen at the time was one of the busiest ports in the Southwest Pacific. Every available man in the 25th went to work in its warehouses. Later the regiment took over the greater part of dock operations. Some ninety stevedore crews were formed. Riflemen and machine gunners were re-trained as winch operators, signalmen, and checkers. For four months the regiment worked at loading and unloading ships at Finschhafen. Often the tonnage rates of the 25th's crews were better than those of the regularly organized port companies at the base.[69]

Occasionally a unit, like the 368th Infantry's landing team in late January and early February 1945, had a specific assignment calling for duties beyond these. This landing team established a perimeter guard at Toem, in the Maffin Bay area, providing security for troops evacuating supplies and disinterring bodies from the American cemetery there preparatory to closing out installations. Patrols were active continuously. The attached Battery C of the 594th Field Artillery harassed the enemy constantly, firing on area targets. On several occasions the enemy infiltrated camp areas and fire fights developed. No casualties were suffered by the landing team.

When all bodies were removed from the cemetery, and all bridges and all structures not portable destroyed, the landing team of the 368th moved on to Wakde four miles away. From Wakde patrols to the Toem mainland continued to operate for months. Company K, 368th, remained at Wakde until 2 October 1945, its patrols on occasion engaging in fire fights with enemy stragglers remaining in the Toem area.

Not until the bulk of the division—elements still remained at Biak, Wakde, Noemfoor, Middleburg, and Sansapor—arrived on Morotai, closing there on 12 April 1945, did the pattern of activity change.

An estimated five to six hundred Japanese remained on Morotai; on the nearby large island of Halmahera there were 40,000 more. The 93d Division relieved elements of the 31st Division on Morotai on 13 April, assuming responsibility for the defense and operation of all Eighth Army installations on the island. It had air support from the 80th Wing, Royal Australian Air Force, and sea support from Naval Task Unit 701.2 (PT). Combat troops of the division were instructed to kill or capture the remaining Japanese.[70]

Operations, especially on the west coast of Morotai, were intensive, with combat patrols covering ever widening areas. As a result, the remaining enemy troops, in groups of fifty or less, were unable to concentrate. The Japanese force, under the command of Col. Kisou Ouchi of the *211th Infantry Regiment*, was composed chiefly of remnants of the *2d Diversionary Unit, 36th Division Sea Transport Unit, 210th Infantry Regi-*

---

[69] Hist 25th Inf Regt, Jan 44–3 Feb 46.

[70] FO 5, Hq 93d Inf Div, 8 Apr 45; FO 7, Hq 93d Inf Div, 5 May 45; FO 8, Hq 93d Inf Div, 18 May 45.

ment, 211th Infantry Regiment, one company of the *212th Infantry Regiment, 10th Expeditionary Force,* and the *18th Shipping Engineers.* Most of these troops, with instructions to carry out raids on Eighth Army installations, were located along the west coast of the island, especially in the Tilai, Wajaboeia, Tijoe, Libano, and Sopi areas. The Japanese kept close to the better native gardens in the area. Supply barges had formerly come to Morotai from Halmahera, landing near the mouth of the Tijoe River, but PT squadrons now prevented bulk resupply of the enemy troops remaining on Morotai. Only once during the period of the 93d's occupancy were barges successful in reaching land. On 13 May, PT boats sank two of four barges but two others escaped and landed north of the Tijoe. One, on the way back to Halmahera, was intercepted and sunk; the other, beached and camouflaged, was located by 25th Infantry patrols and destroyed. There was neither organized resistance nor offensive action on the part of the enemy; the job of 93d Division patrols was to prevent consolidation of the remaining Japanese forces, who might yet engage in harassing action against the Allied base on Morotai, and to search out and capture or kill the remaining Japanese on the island.

On 15 April the first of the 93d's patrols, one from the 369th Infantry, killed four Japanese. On 21 April, the first prisoner was taken, also by the 369th. Beginning in May, landing parties went to the western and northern sectors of the island, eventually covering the entire coast line.

The disposition and number of the enemy arriving on the barge discovered in May was of the greatest interest to the 93d Division, for one of its missions was to prevent the resupply and reinforcement of the Japanese left on Morotai. On 24 May one group was located by a small patrol from Company F, 368th Infantry, led by Lt. Richard L. Crawford. The patrol trailed a pair of footprints up a stream bed from Hapo to a point two miles inland. There the trail left the stream bed and all but disappeared in the rough terrain on the north side. On a small outcropping overlooking their approach, the patrol sighted seven Japanese in clean uniforms, well equipped with pistols, but with only one rifle. One, who later proved to be a captain leading the party, stood gazing in a mirror, shaping his beard with what the patrol described as "obvious admiration." At very close range, the patrol opened fire, killing six of the seven Japanese. The seventh man, wounded, escaped. These seven, members of a Kempoi party—the dual-functioning military police and intelligence personnel—plus seven or eight well-equipped Japanese seen by the 3d Battalion, 25th Infantry, on the coast north of Libano on 13 May accounted for a total of fourteen or fifteen Japanese who had presumably arrived on the barge from Halmahera.[71]

Psychological warfare worked well for the 93d in smoking out the hungrier elements of the remaining enemy. Many of the captured prisoners carried propaganda leaflets, or said that they had heard the division's propaganda broadcasts. One prisoner, while listening to a broadcast amplified from a beach, started down to surrender. He related

[71] 93d Div G-2 Rpt 39, 28 May 45, 93d Div Files.

later that he was "very digusted" with the team for leaving the beach before he arrived. He then had to go hungry two more days before he was picked up by one of the division's patrols.[72]

A main effort of the 93d Division's patrols during the period on Morotai was to capture Colonel Ouchi alive. Ouchi, described as an egotistic commander, disliked by his men because of a tendency to allocate to himself more than a fair share of available food and supplies, successfully eluded the division's patrols for weeks, though his command post was located several times. The division was so intent on seeking him out for capture that the 93d's motto on Morotai became "Cherchez Ouchi."[73]

A 25th Infantry patrol on 11 July found traces of Ouchi in the Tijoe River area. On the last day of July, a twelve-man patrol set out to capture him. After moving about 100 yards in from the coast in the Tijoe area, the patrol came upon two Japanese, one of whom they wounded and captured. The wounded prisoner informed the patrol that a camp of ten Japanese was not far away. After administering first aid to the wounded man, the patrol located a three-hut camp, spotted six Japanese, and killed one. The other five, including some who were wounded, escaped. The patrol bivouacked near the Japanese camp. The three huts were well supplied with rice, ammunition, blankets, and grenades. The patrol decided that it was close upon Colonel Ouchi. On 2 August it scouted the surrounding area without finding the enemy until, in the late afternoon, the sound of chopping

led the patrol to a clearing with four huts in which several Japanese were sleeping. Five others, each carrying supplies, were approaching the camp. After dropping their supplies, they went to the river to bathe. The patrol surrounded them and ordered them to surrender, but they began to scatter in all directions.

Of the Japanese in the area, seven were killed, two escaped naked into the jungle, and one was taken prisoner. The prisoner turned out to be Colonel Ouchi. As the patrol started for the beach, one of the mortally wounded Japanese made a lunge for the sergeant holding Ouchi. The sergeant, "handling his carbine expertly with one hand and shooting from the hip," hit the Japanese in the temple. He fell dead at the sergeant's feet.[74] Colonel Ouchi was one of the highest ranking Japanese officers captured before the surrender of Japan.[75]

Morotai, during the period of the 93d's occupation, was the scene of considerable activity pertinent to the extension of the war in the Pacific. During the earlier weeks on the island, troops of the division, especially the 25th Infantry, then in reserve, were supplying all available men for round-the-clock port duties. The port of Morotai was then handling most of the troops and supplies used in the Australian invasion of Borneo. Working alongside Australian dock

[72] 93d Div G–2 Rpt, Weekly Summary 29, 26 May 45, covering period 19–26 May 45, 93d Div Files.
[73] Div G–2 Rpts, 93d Div Files.
[74] The 93d Cavalry Reconnaissance Troop's men in this party received the following awards: Sgt. Alfonzia Dillon, Silver Star; Technical Sgt. Albert Morrison, Pfc. Robert A. Evans, Pfc. Elmer Sloan, Bronze Stars.
[75] 93d Div G–2 Periodic Rpt 39, 4 Aug 45, 93d Div Hq Files; 93d Div Sum of Opns on Morotai, 93d Div Files; Hist 93d Cav Recon Troop, 23 Jan 44–14 Aug 45.

workers, the troops of the 93d played a large part in getting these operations under way. From 10 April to 10 July the division discharged and outloaded 311,552 tons of supplies and equipment, moved thousands of Allied troops from transports to staging areas and back to embarkation points, and improved harbor facilities, roads, and camp sites.[76]

In the last days of the war, the 93d had charge of more than 1,500 "patients" and crew from the Japanese hospital ship *Tachibana Maru*. This ship, intercepted by two destroyers, the USS *Conner* and USS *Charette*, was brought into Morotai as a prize on 6 August. The patients aboard this hospital ship had been removed from a Japanese general hospital in New Guinea. Most of them were very nearly and some completely recovered from beriberi, malaria, and other diseases. The American boarding party found mortar shells packed in boxes marked with red crosses and labeled medical supplies. Patients were sleeping in the holds—the ship carried twice its normal seven hundred—on rifles, machine guns, ammunition, and hand grenades hidden under bunks. At Morotai, the patients were removed for a thorough search of the ship, a procedure which would have been impossible, especially in the light of the later discovery of the extent of arms and ammunition available aboard the ship, had not Army troops been available to take charge of and guard the prisoners. Working parties unloading the ship found approximately thirty tons of assorted ammunition, including hand grenades, rifle, howitzer, and machine gun

ammunition, four hundred rifles and carbines, fifteen light machine guns, forty-five knee mortars, and four 8-cm. field howitzers.[77]

When hostilities ceased on 15 August 1945, the 93d Division was made responsible for the surrender of all Japanese troops in the Moluccas. Through the local Armed Forces radio station, WVTL, the Japanese on Halmahera were given instructions to meet with the division staff. After a preliminary meeting on a PT boat off the shores of Halmahera, the commander of the Japanese forces and his staff were brought over to Morotai to sign the instrument of surrender for the 40,000 Japanese troops on Halmahera. Approximately 660 stragglers were collected on Morotai itself.[78] Formal surrender of the Japanese in the Moluccas was made to the Australians after 2 September, with the 93d Division assisting.

In October the 93d Division, with the exception of the 368th Regimental Combat Team, which had already moved, proceeded to the Agusan–Del Monte Area on Mindanao where it relieved the 31st Division of its missions there. The 93d controlled supply points at Agusan and Davao, assumed command of all troops attached to the 31st Division effective 20 October, and reassumed command of the 368th and its attached troops at Zamboanga on Mindanao and on Jolo, Sanga Sanga, and Palawan. The 93d, under the discharge and transfer program effective after the close of the war, was responsible for the readjustment of

---

[76] Ltr, GHQ Co-ordinator Morotai to CG 93d Div, 9 Jul 45, 93d Div Files.

[77] CO USS *Charette* (DD581) to CinC U.S. Fleet, 17 Aug 45; Ltr, Comdr Seventh Fleet to CG 93d Div, 24 Oct 45; both in 93d Div Files.
[78] Ltr, Hq 93d Div Area Comd, to CG AFWESPAC, 9 Dec 45, 93d Div Files.

all troops in its area. It was responsible for the defense and security of Mindanao, the collecting, guarding, and evacuating of Japanese prisoners of war, and the supervision of the training and supply of all Philippine Army units within the command, including the 6th Philippine Infantry Division. On 15 November it acquired all of the Southern Islands Area Command's missions; the Mindanao-Sulu-Morotai area thereupon became the 93d Division Area Command.[79] Thereafter the 93d supplied the 6th Philippine Infantry Division, rounded up remaining stragglers, furnished leaflets to be dropped on areas suspected of harboring Japanese troops, furnished transportation for Philippine Army patrols to distant areas, and operated prisoner collecting points throughout Mindanao. As of 20 October 1945 the 93d Division had approximately 30,000 Japanese, including civilians, in its stockade. Processing and evacuating the Japanese, processing American troops for return home or transfer, classifying, storing, and evacuating surplus equipment, and operating supply points were the division's last missions.

The Asset Side?

Whether or not the 93d Division eventually moved to the asset side depended largely upon the viewer and his interpretation of the value of doing unglamorous but necessary jobs well. The diarist of the division's headquarters company prefaced one of his last installments with the apology that he realized that an account "filled with fictional adventures, hardships, and tragedies of war

would make a more powerful story" but his unit had no such heroic deeds to its credit. He would confine himself to "only actualities—nothing extraordinary, just the usual activities of a rear echelon unit" whose members were with it not by choice but by assignment. Since there was no occasion to "perform the noble, heroic and spectacular," he continued, "we have contented outselves with doing the various tasks assigned us in the shortest period of time possible and better than anyone else." His companions had seen no dead Japanese, few live ones, had had no bombings, and "only a limited few had had actual combat experience."[80] A staff officer, writing from the Moluccas, characterized the division's progress with, "And so this is just another rear area, now. Yep, 93d stuff—drag-ass along behind."[81]

At the end of the war, the 93d Division had certainly not moved to the asset side as a combat division. Walter White, while serving as a war correspondent in the Pacific,[82] had urged the White House and the War Department at home and General MacArthur in the Pacific to prepare it for a combat role. He got new denials that any other was intended for it.

White, after ten weeks in the Pacific,

[79] FO 4, AFWESPAC, 1 Nov 45.

[80] Preface, Daily Diary Hq Co 93d Inf Div, 93d Div Files.

[81] Ltr, Capt John H. S. ——— to Mrs. John H. S. ———, 10 Apr 45, 93d Div JAG Files, Off Punishment, 93d Div Files. As implied by the file location, the officer was reprimanded for writing this derogatory opinion in a self-censored letter to his wife.

[82] White, as war correspondent for the New York Post, spent considerable time in Europe, North Africa, and the Pacific during the war. See Walter White, A Rising Wind (Garden City: Doubleday, Doran, 1945), and A Man Called White (New York: Viking, 1948), Chapters XXI–XXV.

dispatched to the President, with copies to Under Secretary Patterson and Assistant Secretary McCloy, a detailed account of the career and state of morale in the 93rd. He later repeated the substance of his findings in an interview with General MacArthur. White reported that the 93d was the victim of rumor and malicious slander, all reinforced by its role as a rear echelon unit engaged primarily in labor duties. Its assignment, he observed, was viewed across the Pacific as punishment for a failure on Bougainville. To the contrary, White concluded after discussions with division and other officers, the 93d had performed its limited combat duties creditably and the rumors about it were false. Nevertheless, the division had been the victim of improper management, corrected in part by "the outstanding and most beneficial event in the history of the 93d Division," the appointment of Maj. Gen. Harry H. Johnson as commander in August 1944. General Johnson was building discipline and morale, but he occupied an unenviable position. He could not complete his job if the 93d followed his old division, the 2d Cavalry, into oblivion as "a service division." White recommended that the 93d be assembled, brought to strength, relieved of fatigue and service duties except those normal to a combat division, and trained for amphibious warfare; that it be relieved of officers who were incompetent or who disliked service with Negroes; and that it be used in combat as the only means of answering the reports about it and official policy current in the Pacific.[83]

General MacArthur, queried by the War Department in anticipation of a White House request for comment, replied to the War Department's brief of the White report. As requested by the War Department, he quoted General Griswold of XIV Corps as authority that on Bougainville the artillery did good work, the engineers fair, the infantry poor; that in training, individuals were proficient in handling and maintaining their weapons; that vehicle maintenance was of a high order, that the general level of leadership was poor despite a number of officers of "high type and adequate qualifications," and that morale was poor. The Commanding General, XIV Corps, added that under its new commander the division had taken a "new lease of life" and that under him it would improve. General MacArthur's inspectors, who, at General Johnson's request, had investigated charges of discrimination within the 93d, had reported that these charges were "without foundation in fact." Other divisions in the Southwest Pacific were all superior to the 93d "except in the matter of motor maintenance. In this item our inspection teams have shown it to be without peer among the units inspected." [84]

White, having discussed the 93d with General MacArthur at his headquarters at San Miguel on 1 March 1945, now forwarded a supplementary memorandum to the President on 8 March, stating that General MacArthur had denied that the division would be used exclusively for labor duties and that he had affirmed that it would be used in combat "providing circumstances warranted." The general had said further that the

[83] Memo, Walter White (Hollandia) for the President, 12 Feb 45, ASW's copy in WDCSA 291.2 Negroes.

[84] Rad, MacArthur to Marshall, 5 Mar 45, UAD 62716.

rumors about the division on Bougain-ville were "false and ridiculous," that he knew "from experience with the 25th Infantry and the Filipino Army he commanded that race and color have nothing whatever to do with fighting ability," that lack of ships had prevented moving the 93d and other divisions to forward areas, that the 93d would be moved from New Guinea to Morotai, and that his inspectors' reports on the division had not been too favorable. When asked for details, General Mac-Arthur told White that "it was chiefly that the men of the 93d wanted to go home. He said, laughing, that that is true and natural of all divisions overseas, regardless of race." [85]

On his return to Hollandia, White found the 93d Division planning to move from New Guinea. Steps were being taken to improve it internally. White now wrote to General MacArthur: "You certainly acted promptly after our talk of March 1 . . . ," adding, "Your action in bringing the Division together in one island for the first time since the 93rd left the States will undoubtedly have immediate effect in improvement of ef-ficiency and a sense of unity." He made new recommendations for the readying of the division, urging that its artillery be re-equipped with its own or other guns and that its officer personnel be carefully sorted to provide better leader-ship both from among white and Negro

officers. "It is my hope," he concluded, "that neither you nor the War Depart-ment will think these recommendations by a layman presumptuous. Be assured that they are made solely with the desire that the zeal of the overwhelming ma-jority of the officers and enlisted person-nel of the 93rd to contribute to the speediest winning of complete victory may be utilized to the fullest degree." [86]

Aside from the movement of the 93d Division to Morotai, which White at-tributed to his interview with General MacArthur, the only positive action taken on his report was on his statement that "One practice which has been ex-ceedingly destructive of morale, and which should be discontinued, is the in-sistent and frequent querying of officers of the 93rd Division, either by question-naires or personal interviews, as to whether or not the 93d Division can or will fight if given an opportunity." [87] As a result, after a perusal of questions sent to the 93d shortly before by Army Ground Forces,[88] all questioning of troop units "concerning or bearing upon mo-rale of, or combat relations between, racial groups" was halted, except by special permission of the Secretary of War.[89] This ruling seriously hampered Army researches into soldier attitudes for the remainder of the war.

Despite qualms about their future ca-

[85] White's dispatch to the New York *Post* describ-ing the interview, carried widely in Negro papers during the week of 26 March, reported similarly, quoting General MacArthur as saying "Any man who says that another man's fighting ability can be measured by color is wrong. I learned that in serving as a junior officer with the famous 25th Regiment. One of the greatest armies I have ever commanded was a Filipino one."

[86] Memo, Walter White (Hollandia) for the President, 8 Mar 45, and Incl, Ltr, Walter White to MacArthur, 8 Mar 45, both Incl to Memo, ExO to ASW for Brig Gen Henry I. Hodes, OPD, OPD Cld Trps-Corr.
[87] Memo, White for President, 12 Feb 45, copy in WDCSA 291.2 Negroes.
[88] Memo, Chief Current Gp OPD for Gen Hull, 2 Mar 45, OPD 322.97 (2 Mar 45).
[89] Memo, OPD for CG's AGF, ASF, AAF, 2 Mar 45, OPD 322.97 (6 Mar 45).

reers as combat units, elements of the 93d Division built a reputation for discipline, co-operation, *esprit de corps,* and excellence in their assigned duties matched by few other units in the Pacific and contrasting strongly with their training careers. To troops of the 93d one transport commander paid "his respects" after an interisland voyage with these words:

During my two years experience as a Transport Commander, I have never witnessed a unit which functioned so smoothly and efficiently nor exhibited such loyalty and esprit de corps as your troops have demonstrated.

It was indeed a pleasure to have been associated with you, your officers and men aboard and I am sure the trip will long be remembered by myself and my complement of enlisted men.[90]

Their excellent and uncomplaining work in mud and rain at POL dumps; the courteous and co-operative efficiency of their noncommissioned officers; their willingness to accept responsibility and act upon it ("an outstanding characteristic" of an entire company, one commenting officer noted); and their co-operation with men of other units, both on official duties and on joint enterprises, were frequently cited.[91] They were not only commended for leaving areas well policed but at times for leaving them "better policed than were areas of any other unit leaving this Base."[92] At Fin-

schhafen and Hollandia they were responsible for clearing up and distributing promptly an unprecedented volume of more than 210,000 bags of Christmas mail arriving in November and December 1944.[93] Not only their *esprit* and discipline in carrying out unusual and unexpected tasks were favorably commented upon. Headquarters often added comments like: "Whereas some combat units under similar instructions in the past have been content to furnish work details without interest in the job or the working conditions of their own men, the units of the 93d Division have not only furnished effective supervision for each job assigned but the higher echelons of command have maintained their control and influence by frequent inspections." [94] The results obtained, the Commanding General, Intermediate Base Section, said, "are gratifying to the Base Commanders now seriously handicapped by scarcity of labor, equipment and adequate supervision." [95]

Elements of the division given those tasks were both large and small; they were supervised by sergeants and junior and field grade officers alike. A team of five men from the 93d Signal Company, for example, under the sole direction of a sergeant, installed and operated for five weeks a communications system on Pie Beach, Hollandia, with a minimum of equipment under adverse con-

[90] SS *Lew Wallace,* Office of the Transport Comdr, to CG 93d Inf Div, 3 Nov 44. See also Memo, USS LST 589 to Lt Col M. L. Joyce, 12 Apr 45 ("The cooperation demonstrated was, by far, greater than that of any party previously transported on this vessel"); Ltr, USS LST 806 (Albert H. Burns) to CG 93d Div, 20 Oct 45. All in 93d Div Files.

[91] See numerous letters and endorsements, dated November 1944–October 1945, in 93d Division Files.

[92] Ltr, Hq Base F USASOS (Lt Col Wilfred E. Lessard, Jr., Base Area Comdr) to CO 25th Inf Regt, 14 Apr 45, 93d Div Files.

[93] Ltr, Hq USASOS to CG 93d Div, 6 Jan 45, GSCG 330.13; Ltr, Detachment 7th Base Post Office (Lt Fred W. Gish) to Hq 93d Inf Div, 13 Jan 45, 93d Div Files.

[94] 1st Ind, Hq Intermediate Sec USASOS to CG Eighth Army, 8 Jan 45, to Ltr, Hq Base F to CG Eighth Army, 1 Jan 45, IFCO 201.22.

[95] *Ibid.*

ditions.[96]   Officers and men sent to a school at Oro Bay were adjudged "outstanding in several respects. They displayed keen interest in the various subjects and worked hard in absorbing the material and information that was given them. The grades received by them on examinations were exceptionally high. Their conduct and bearing, while at this school, was excellent and their cooperation during and after classes was instrumental in making this particular class an outstanding one."[97]   The GHQ co-ordinator for Morotai, noting the many unsolicited expressions from the Australian command regarding the services given them by American forces in mounting the invasion of Borneo, declared to the Chief of Staff, Eighth Army, that "Credit for that frame of mind is due almost entirely to the very fine work done by the 93d Division. This division has not failed in one single instance to meet requirements which often placed a very heavy strain on all facilities here. This has been done in a spirit of determination and pride in accomplishment which has left a very fine impression with all agencies involved in these operations."[98]   At least one unit, in addition to the field artillery for Bougainville, got official recognition of an unspectacular but essential job in cleaning out the enemy on Mindanao and Palawan.[99]

How much of this praise was due to

the etiquette of command at the close of a successful campaign, the men of the 93d Division could not know. But they did know that no similar words speeded their way from Bougainville and they did know that they had gained a reputation for work, discipline, and maintenance in the Pacific. They had the satisfaction of knowing that in this way, if in no other, they had been an "asset" to the Pacific war.

The 24th Infantry, on the other hand, had greater satisfaction in an unusual acknowledgement of the value of garrison forces that came its way in the spring of 1945. The 24th, after its 1st Battalion's brief encounter with the enemy on Bougainville, returned to routine labor and guard duties for the South Pacific Base Command and for the Guadalcanal Island Command. In December 1944 it moved to Saipan and Tinian for garrison duty. These islands had been declared secure, but their jungles and caves were still infested with Japanese. The 24th had the task of clearing the islands of all Japanese who had not surrendered. A survey group from The Inspector General's Office, under Maj. Gen. Philip E. Brown and Brig. Gen. Elliot D. Cooke, arrived in April 1945, found the 24th still cleaning out the enemy, and reported their conduct and accomplishments to be of "such a meritorious nature" that The Inspector General brought the unit's performance to the attention of the Deputy Chief of Staff, despite the fact that "occasion rarely arises where it is appropriate for inspectors general to single out and comment upon any one unit during an over-all inspection or survey."[100]

[96] Ltr, Hq I Corps to CG 93d Inf Div, 11 Jan 45, 93d Div Files.

[97] Ltr, Hq CWSTC Base B to CG 93d Inf Div, 23 Feb 45, NBCW 220.632.

[98] Ltr, GHQ Co-ordinator Morotai to Brig Gen Clovis E. Byers, CofS Eighth Army, 9 Jul 45, 93d Div Files.

[99] Hq X Corps to CO 368th RCT, 20 Aug 45, 93d Div Files.

[100] Memo, TIG for DCofS, 14 May 45, WDSIG 330.13–24th Inf Regt.

COLONEL HEARNE RECEIVING THE SWORD OF MAJOR YOSHIHIKO NODA

The 24th Infantry, the survey group reported, had killed or captured an impressive number of the enemy, "and even today are engaged in continuous patrolling and jungle fighting against those Japanese still hiding on the island." Though the regiment as a whole had not engaged in actual combat before coming to Saipan:

It, nevertheless, conducted itself in a superior manner. Even at this late date, scarcely a day passes that members of this Regiment do not capture or kill some of the enemy and, in so doing, suffer occasional casualties themselves, yet, despite all that has been accomplished by the 24th Infantry Regiment, members of this Regiment considered that they were not eligible for the Combat Infantryman's Badge, nor that provision had been made for them to be awarded a battle clasp on the theater ribbon for the combat in which they have been engaged since assuming their task of eliminating the remaining Japanese resistance on Saipan. Nevertheless, even after three years service overseas the morale of this Regiment is high and its discipline is well worthy of emulation and praise, as is the exemplary manner of performance in all duties to which it has been assigned.[101]

---

[101] *Ibid.* The 24th killed or captured 722 of the enemy at a loss of less than a dozen of its own men killed and about twenty wounded.

Much of its record was attributed by the inspectors to the regimental commander, Col. Julian G. Hearne, Jr., who had been with the regiment for four years, advancing from battalion to regimental commander, and to "a dozen or more noncommissioned officers who have been with the Regiment since before the war and who, by example and strict adherence to traditions and customs of the Regiment and the service, have demonstrated what proper leadership can accomplish under the most trying conditions in the field." [102]

When the survey group informed the Commanding General, Pacific Ocean Areas, of the performance of the 24th, he undertook to inform the 24th that its members were eligible for both the Combat Infantryman's Badge and a battle star for their theater service ribbon. The Inspector General asked that the group's report be forwarded to the Operations Division for consideration in the future employment of Negro troops in the Pacific.[103] When informed of the matter, Under Secretary Patterson, citing the report, gave it to the press at his 31 May press conference.

The 24th left Saipan and Tinian in July 1945 and proceeded to the Kerama Islands, west of Okinawa in the Ryukyus, to continue mopping up remnants of Japanese forces there. Shortly after their arrival in early August, the Japanese capitulated. On 22 August, Colonel Hearne, with representative officers and enlisted men, accepted on Aka Island the first formal surrender of a Japanese Army garrison.

---

[102] Memo, TIG for DCofS, 14 May 45, WDSIG 330.13–24th Inf Regt.

[103] Ibid.; Memo, Deputy Chief Pacific Theater Sec OPD for Gen Hull, 16 May, OPD 330.13 (14 May 45).

CHAPTER XIX

Mountain and Plain

In readying itself for service in Italy the 370th Regimental Combat Team, commanded by Col. Raymond G. Sherman, went through a nearly complete reorganization before acting as the advance representative of the 92d Infantry Division overseas. The combat team was formed at Fort Huachuca on 4 April 1944, upon the return of the division from Louisiana.[1] During the period of intensive training for its movement overseas, substandard men failing tests in the 370th were transferred out to other units and replaced by men with higher qualifications and capabilities. Many of these were volunteers. The combat team, consisting of the 370th Infantry, the 598th Field Artillery Battalion, and detachments from each of the special units of the 92d Division, including the headquarters company, sailed from Hampton Roads on 15 July 1944. Transshipping at Oran, it arrived at Naples on 30 July.[2]

The unit, secure in the knowledge that it was well trained, in excellent physical condition, and composed of the 92d Division's best cross section of men especially selected to introduce the divi-

sion to combat, had high hopes and high morale.[3] Its arrival in Italy produced flurries of excitement and anticipation among Negro service troops in the Mediterranean area equaled only by those produced by the arrival of the 99th Fighter Squadron and the 332d Fighter Group. For Negro service troops the 92d served as a symbolic antidote to the just completed conversion of the 2d Cavalry Division in their theater. They wished it well. Some, including men from former 2d Cavalry units, began planning ways and means of requesting transfer to the 92d.[4]

When the 370th Regimental Combat Team arrived in Italy, Fifth Army had reached the south bank of the Arno River. *(Map 1)* Its troops, disposed along an approximately thirty-five mile wide front extending east from the Tyrrhenian Sea, were resting and training in preparation for the river crossing. Fifth Army was now involved in regrouping, preparatory to an attack de-

---

[1] Hq 92d Inf Div, GO 14.

[2] Maj. Paul Goodman, *A Fragment of Victory* (Army War College, Carlisle Barracks, Pa., 1952) is a detailed account of the 92d Division's operations in Italy. It offers more on divisional planning and more on the enemy aspects of the story than does this chapter.

[3] Col Sherman, Notes on 370th RCT, 92d Inf Div (remarks by Col Sherman, CO 370th RCT) to Col Harry H. Semmes, G–1 IV Corps, 10–20–44, 92d Div Files; Opns Rpt 370th Inf, Aug 44, 392–INF (370).

[4] Examples: Ltr, Pfc Percy C. Parker, 387th Engr Bn (Sep) to CO Co D, 387th Engr Bn, 24 Nov 44, with Inds; Ltr, 1st Sgt Earl Williams, 3822d QM Truck Co, to CG Repl Comd, 26 Nov 44, with Inds; Ltr, Pvt John H. Gray, 743d MP Bn, to CG Repl Comd, 31 Dec 44, with Inds. All in 92d Div 210.3 X 220.3.

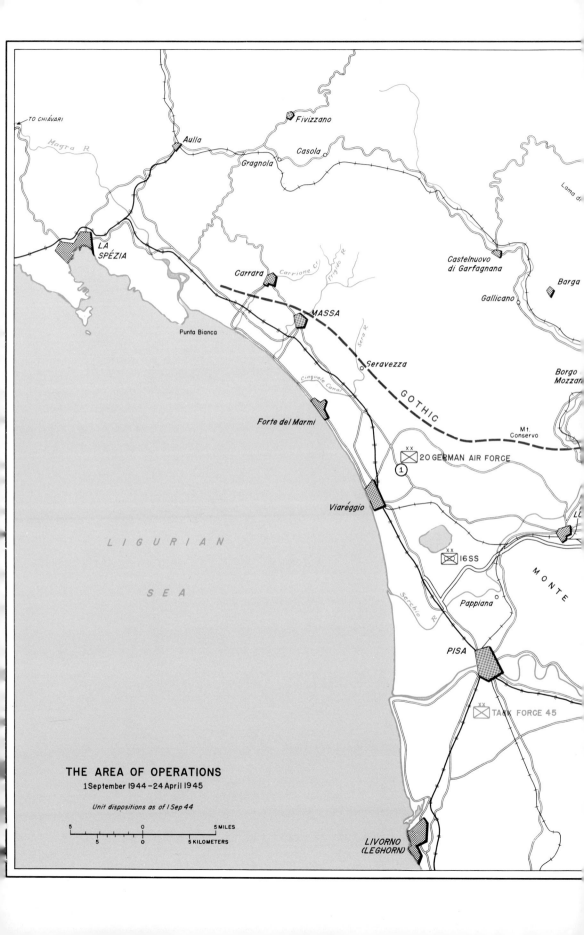

TO CHIÁVARI

Magra R.

Fivizzano

Aulla

Casola

Gragnola

LA SPÉZIA

Carrara

Carrione Cr.

Frigido R.

MASSA

Sera R.

Punta Bianca

Seravezza

GOTHIC

Castelnuovo di Garfagnana

Barga

Gallicano

Borgo Mozzar.

Lama di

Cinquale Canal

Forte del Marmi

Mt. Conservo

20 GERMAN AIR FORCE

1

L I G U R I A N

S E A

Viaréggio

16 SS

LU

M O N T E

Serchio R.

Pappiana

PISA

THE AREA OF OPERATIONS
1 September 1944 – 24 April 1945

Unit dispositions as of 1 Sep 44

5 MILES

5 KILOMETERS

TASK FORCE 45

LIVORNO (LEGHORN)

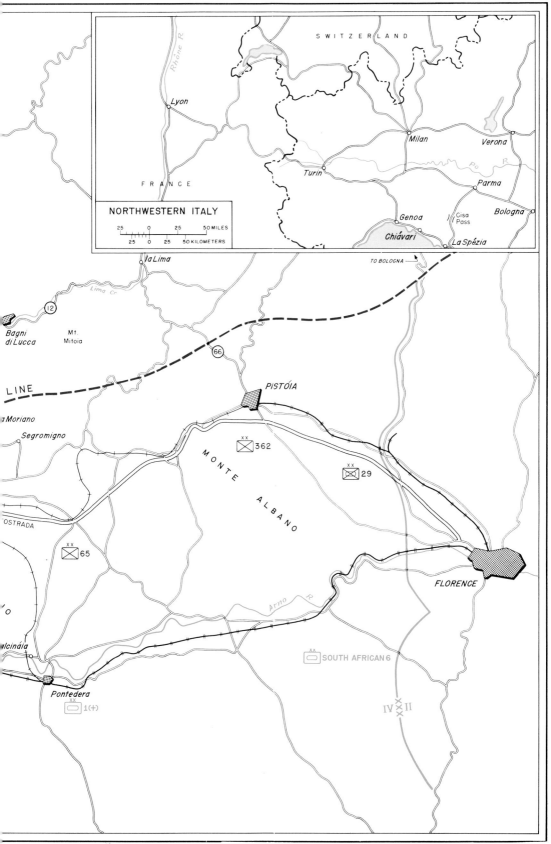

NORTHWESTERN ITALY

25   0   25   50 MILES

25   0   25   50 KILOMETERS

H. C. Brewer, Jr.

MAP 1

signed to cross the plain of the Arno and crack the Gothic Line on the southern slope of the Northern Apennines before winter caught the Allied forces in another mountain campaign. Between May and the end of July Fifth Army had lost veteran divisions amounting to about half its strength. If a major offensive were to be mounted, more troops would be needed. The arrival of the 92d Division in Italy was therefore more favorably awaited than the arrival of the 93d in the South Pacific. Upon being given its departure date in June, Lt. Gen. Jacob L. Devers expressed himself and General Sir Henry M. Wilson as "delighted" to have the 370th and as many more units as could be spared. It would be put into action as quickly as possible.[5]

At the beginning of August, IV Corps on the left, under Maj. Gen. Willis D. Crittenberger, had the task of defending the greater part of the Fifth Army front while II Corps on the right prepared for an attack on the Gothic Line to follow an Eighth Army assault to the east along the Adriatic. The IV Corps held the western thirty miles of Fifth Army's front along the south bank of the Arno River. Its Task Force 45 was on the left and the 1st Armored Division was on the right.[6] Task Force 45, formed from antiaircraft troops of the 45th Antiaircraft Artillery Brigade and attached troops, was itself symbolic of the weak-

ened infantry strength of Fifth Army. These antiaircraft units were equipped with infantry weapons on 26 July and, two days later, relieved elements of the 34th Division on the left flank of IV Corps. The antiaircraft units were still undergoing infantry retraining, rotating some elements in the front lines while others were given training in the rear. Task Force 45, as a task force and later as the 473d Infantry Regiment, had close relations with elements of the 92d Division. It described itself as "a polyglot task force of American and British antiaircraft gunners acting as infantry, with Italian Partisans, Brazilians and colored American troops fighting by their side. . . . [which] learned that different peoples can fight well together."[7]

When the 370th Regimental Combat Team arrived in the army area, the Fifth Army planned to attach it to IV Corps.[8] The 370th was to move forward on IV Corps order as soon as equipped, and Fifth Army estimated this could be done by 25 August.[9] Fifth Army headquarters did not expect the remainder of the 92d Division to arrive and be ready for use as a full division before December.

As the 370th Combat Team entered the army area, small groups of officers and enlisted men were attached to the 1st Armored Division's infantry battalions and artillery. One small group (twenty officers and twenty-three enlisted men) spent several days with the 85th Division for orientation.[10] The

---

[5] Msg, Devers to Marshall, 8 Jun 44, CM–IN 6151.

[6] *Fifth Army History*, VII, "The Gothic Line" (Capt. John Bowditch III) (Florence, Italy: L'Impronta Press, n.d.), 13–19. Unless otherwise noted, sources for this section are the *Fifth Army History*, IV Corps and 92d Infantry Division operations reports, and the operations reports, journals, and monthly histories of the elements of the 92d Division referred to.

[7] Foreword, Hist of Task Force 45, 29 Jul 44 to 28 Jan 45, Opn Rpts 105–81.1 (15093).

[8] Fifth Army OI 31, 7 Aug 44; *Fifth Army History*, VII, 15.

[9] Fifth Army OI 32, 17 Aug 44.

[10] 1st Armd Div G–3 Jnl, 17 Aug 44; Fifth Army OI 32, 17 Aug 44; Ltr, Hq Fifth Army, 17 Aug 44, AG 322.1–Y.

combat team was attached to IV Corps on 17 August and to the 1st Armored Division on 18 August. The first element of the 370th, the 3d Battalion, entered the line on the night of 23–24 August, relieving the 14th Armored Infantry Battalion near Pontedera. IV Corps was intensely interested in the efficiency of the movement of the 370th's units. "We are send [ing] a couple officers over to watch this 370th Inf on their move tonight," corps informed the 1st Armored Division. "We are not trying to watch on you, but are interested in the 370th as a unit." [11] On the next night, the 2d Battalion, 370th Infantry relieved the 6th Armored Infantry Battalion south of Pontedera. On 26 August the 1st Battalion of the 370th moved up into a reserve position. With the 598th Field Artillery Battalion moving into position on 28 August, the 370th began its battle indoctrination.[12] Key officers and noncommissioned officers of the relieved units remained in the line with men of the 370th for the first twenty-four hours. From the beginning of its operations, in marked contrast to its training history, the 370th Regimental Combat Team was in intimate contact with American white units, officers, and men.

The first of a series of distinguished visitors, including Prime Minister Winston S. Churchill, began to arrive early. Hardly had the 370th got into position when Brig. Gen. Benjamin O. Davis and the motion picture team filming *Teamwork* arrived for shots of the 92d Division "in action." Newspaper correspondents were anxious for news of the division. On 28 August, as the Eighth Army attack on the right of the Allied line was getting well under way, Lt. Gen. Mark Clark, the Army commander, visited the 370th Regimental Combat Team along with other units of the Fifth Army. General Clark was particularly anxious to welcome the 92d's troops for he understood that General Marshall desired to give them an opportunity to prove the ability of Negro troops in battle.[13] General Clark asked one colonel if he was having any major problems. He replied that the only thing he had to complain of was the slowness of promotions for some of his officers. "Give me an example," the general said. The colonel turned, called a Negro first lieutenant commanding one of his companies, and said, "Here's a good example; this man is overdue for promotion." With that, General Clark turned to his aide, "borrowed" the captain's bars off his uniform, and pinned them on the lieutenant.[14] Few actions in its career received more spontaneous approval or became more widely known among the men of the 92d and among Negro soldiers elsewhere. Few actions reinforced more strongly the belief that all problems within the division could be adjusted if higher commanders wished to and if they knew of their existence.

[11] 1st Armd Div FO 21, 23 Aug 44; 1st Armd Div G–3 Jnl, 24 Aug 44.

[12] Opns Rpt 370th Inf Regt, Aug–Dec 44; Rpt of Opns of the IV Corps in the Italian Campaign, 1–31 Aug 44.

[13] General Mark W. Clark, *Calculated Risk* (New York: Harper's, 1950), p. 392.

[14] *Ibid.* The officer was Capt. Charles F. Gandy, commanding Company F, 370th Infantry. In this account of the 92d Division all lieutenants are Negroes, all higher ranking officers white, unless otherwise identified. All enlisted men, of course, are Negroes. All supporting and attached units, unless otherwise identified, are white American units.

In the meantime, IV Corps was ready-ing for its part in the Fifth Army's re-newed offensive. IV Corps now as-sumed command of a larger sector ex-tending inland fifty-five miles, nearly to Florence, thus enabling II Corps on its right to concentrate greater strength on a reduced front to break through the Gothic Line north of Florence.[15] IV Corps would simulate a crossing in con-junction with II Corps and the British 13 Corps and be prepared, at any time after the initial attack, to follow up an enemy withdrawal across the Arno.[16]

To hold its extended line and to con-vince the enemy that the main attack was being mounted in its area, IV Corps received the 6th South African Ar-moured Division, retained the 1st Ar-mored Division, and received the al-ready famous Japanese-American 100th Infantry Battalion and the British 47th Light Antiaircraft Regiment to replace two antiaircraft battalions relieved from Task Force 45.[17]

The 370th Regimental Combat Team:
The First Six Weeks

The 370th in the Pontedera area along the Arno began to feel its way into bat-tle. During the night of 27 August its 3d Battalion command post was bombed by enemy aircraft; antipersonnel bombs caused several casualties. One platoon drove off two enemy patrols which at-tacked with machine gun support from across the river. The 598th Field Artil-lery Battalion's Battery C fired its first rounds into the enemy lines on the morn-ing of 29 August. Combat patrols of the 370th joined with those of other units along the Arno in moving into the enemy areas across the river. One twenty-two man patrol from Company F, led by Lt. Jake Chandler and accom-panied by newly promoted Capt. Charles F. Gandy, crossed the Arno on 30 August and proceeded to Calcinaia, where it destroyed a machine gun position and captured two prisoners, the first cap-tured by Negro infantrymen in Europe.

If the situation were favorable after crossing the Arno, IV Corps was to oc-cupy Mount Albano and Mount Pisano, the two major hills on the Arno Plain. Mount Pisano lay between the 370th's positions and Lucca. The 370th was ordered to join with other IV Corps units to cross the Arno at 1000 on 1 September. With its 3d Battalion on the left, its 2d Battalion in the center, and its 1st Battalion on the right, the regiment (less Company C) crossed the river as ordered. By nightfall its bat-talions had moved two to three miles north of the river. Company C crossed with Combat Command B of the 1st Armored Division, to which it was at-tached. Sniper fire and mines caused only light casualties. By 0300, 2 Sep-tember, the combat team's engineers had bridged the Arno with an armored force treadway bridge. They and the 1st Ar-mored Division engineers had already cleared mines and improved fords so that tanks might cross.

Combat Command A, 1st Armored Division, with the 370th as its infantry component and the 1st Tank Battalion in support, moved out toward Mount Pisano. The 3d Battalion, 370th Infan-try, on the left, moved around the west side of the mountain and by 2200 on 2

[15] Allied Armies in Italy Opn Order 3, 16 Aug 44; Fifth Army OI 32, 17 Aug 44.
[16] Fifth Army OI 32, 17 Aug 44.
[17] *Ibid.; Fifth Army History*, VII, 21–23.

105's of 598th Field Artillery Battalion Firing Across the Arno, *29 August 1944.*

September elements of the battalion reached the Serchio River at Pappiana, five miles north of Pisa. The 1st Battalion, on the right, its Company B riding on tanks of the 1st Tank Battalion, moved forward rapidly for six miles around the east side of Mount Pisano to reach positions on the northeast slopes. The 2d Battalion, in the center, moved over mule trails directly into the mountain mass. The enemy showed no sign of offering more than local rear guard opposition. The troops moved so rapidly that by the time the 4th Tank Battalion got its three medium tank companies into position south of the river

and registered their guns, it was unsafe to fire. Control of Mount Pisano was assured by the end of the day.

In the next three days the advance continued unchecked by an enemy who was withdrawing to his Gothic Line. The 2d Battalion, 370th Infantry, moved northwest across Mount Pisano on 3 September, reorganized, and attacked toward Lucca on the 4th. A platoon from Company F with tank support patrolled to Lucca, reconnoitered the west and south gates, and occupied them without opposition. At 0600, 5 September, two companies of the 2d Battalion continued toward the city. Company E entered

Unit of the 370th RCT Crossing the Serchio by Truck, *10 September 1944.*

the town. Company F followed at noon. The 3d Battalion, in the face of small arms, machine gun, and artillery fire, cleared the road from Pisa to Lucca; the 1st Battalion reached positions north of the *autostrada* two and a half miles east of Lucca. On the left and right flanks of the 370th and Combat Command A, Task Force 45 and Combat Combat B moved less rapidly. Task Force 45, including the 100th Battalion, was held up by extensive mine fields and Combat Command B met stronger German rear guard action on the afternoon of 4 September.

IV Corps now regrouped its forces. It planned to make it appear that it was mounting a major attack to the northwest. Though maintaining contact with the enemy and preparing to follow up further withdrawals, the corps was not to advance in strength beyond the Pistoia–Bagni di Lucca–Lucca line.[18] The 370th spent 6 September consolidating its positions around Lucca, the 7th in patrolling, and the 8th and 9th in moving forward into areas abandoned by the enemy. It moved up along the Serchio River, which bends west toward the sea at Lucca. Its mission, like that of the 1st Armored Division to which it remained attached, was to continue pressure on the enemy, preventing so far as possible his transfer of forces to the II Corps front.[19]

[18] Fifth Army OI 34, 4 Sep 44.
[19] *Fifth Army History*, VII, 79.

The general advance of Fifth Army toward the Gothic Line began the morning of 10 September. The 370th Infantry's 2d Battalion, on the left, crossed the Serchio River and moved north along its west bank. The 1st Battalion, on the right, moved north over the plain along the east side of the Serchio. The 3d Battalion remained in reserve. On 12 September positions were improved. Company A, riding on tanks, was involved in a fire fight at Ponte a Moriana. The next day all battalions moved forward again. The 1st Battalion reached Segromigno, three miles east of the Serchio; the 3d, pulled out of reserve, moved with the 2d up the river's west bank. The combat team had now reached the foothills of the Northern Apennines, and the plains of the Arno and the Serchio were left behind.

The 1st Armored Division pushed forward again on 17 September, with the attached 370th's 2d and 3d Battalions attacking northward through the hills on the west side of the Serchio. With the II Corps' breakthrough of the Gothic Line at Il Giogo Pass on 18 September, Fifth Army alerted the 1st Armored Division for movement to the II Corps front in case a rapid push into the Po Valley developed. Combat Command A was relieved from the division preparatory to movement to the Florence area on 21 September. The 370th assumed control of the former Combat Command A zone and the combat team, released from that command's supervision, was on its own.

Between then and 26 September the units regrouped as elements of the 370th took over from elements of the 1st Armored Division. The 6th Regimental Combat Team of the newly arrived Brazilian Expeditionary Force moved between the 370th's left flank and Task Force 45, which lost the 100th Battalion. The remainder of the 1st Armored Division, less Combat Command B, was released to II Corps, with responsibility for the division zone passing on 25 September to the newly created Task Force 92 (provisional) under Brig. Gen. John E. Wood, assistant division commander of the 92d, in Italy heading an advance observer's group from the 92d Division. In addition to the 370th Regimental Combat Team, Task Force 92 included Combat Command B of the 1st Armored Division and Troop D, 81st Cavalry Reconnaissance Squadron. Task Force 92's front now extended twelve miles, from Monte Conservo on the left to Monte Mitoia on the right.

When patrols of Task Force 92 made no contact with the enemy on 26 September, all elements moved forward, continuing the next day for a distance of four to five miles up the Serchio valley. The 3d Battalion, on the left, after fire fights all the way, reached positions near Bargo a Mozzano west of the Serchio River. The 1st Battalion, following Highway 12 on the east side of the Serchio valley, advanced to within a mile of the junction of Lima Creek and the Serchio River. The 2d Battalion, on the right, reached forward positions in the mountains east of the Serchio overlooking Lima Creek, near Bagni di Lucca. On 28 September, a patrol of the 2d Battalion entered Bagni di Lucca.

The next morning, 29 September, Combat Command B was relieved and Task Force 92 assumed responsibility for the full sixteen miles running from the Brazilian Expeditionary Force zone just west of the Serchio valley to a line running north from Pistóia. On the last day of the month, the 3d Battalion, 370th Infantry, crossed the Lima River and entered La Lima where Highway 66 joined Highway 12.

At the end of the month, the 370th Regimental Combat Team had advanced approximately twenty-one miles with the 1st Armored Division and IV Corps, had lost 8 men killed in action, including its executive officer, had 248 sick, wounded, or injured, and 23 missing and captured—a total loss of 279. Although it had encountered no strong resistance from the enemy, it had advanced beyond the Gothic Line in its sector and cut off Highway 12, the enemy's main east-west route of communications opposite the IV Corps front. Its men had advanced under both small arms and heavy artillery fire, had bested the enemy in small fire fights, had engaged in three river crossings and had begun to operate in the hill country of the Apennines. The 370th had worked well with the white troops of the 1st Armored Division and had shown improvement in its own increasingly independent operations. The combat team as a whole was losing the uncertainty that was at first evident. It had developed some good leaders and was on the way to developing assured team work in its smaller elements.

There were some signs from the beginning that the 370th's units, though willing, were neither the most thoroughly trained nor the most thoroughly motivated troops. More than a sea voyage was needed to bridge completely the gap between Fort Huachuca and the plain of the Arno. "They are not aggressive but will go willingly anywhere their officers take them; they will stay where

led," General Wood concluded after the first few days on the Arno Plain.[20] After the first three weeks General Wood was still of the opinion that "in combat missions they will go wherever led. They will stay as long as their leaders, anywhere." Many of the faults they then showed were those common to new troops: in the first few days they caused more damage to each other than to the enemy; jittery guards and patrols were likely to fire at "any noise or anything which moves, to challenge and fire at about the same time." Discipline slackened, with men reasoning that saluting, sanitation, maintenance, and police were not important in the combat zone.[21] But the performance of the 370th in the first few days, while not without a number of incidents which "would have been avoided by more seasoned troops," the IV Corps chief of staff observed of a report from 1st Armored Division, "was on the average as satisfactory as might be expected from a similar untried and inexperienced unit. There is no question of their will to learn, alertness and attention to duty; the nervousness exhibited is natural and may well be overcome in time." [22]

There were signs as well that the men of the 370th were learning battle lessons. "At first, when coming under artillery fire," General Wood observed, "there was a tendency to leave the danger area by withdrawing—to the rear. Quickly they learned the advantage of getting out of the fire by going forward—so as to go

---

[20] Ltr, Wood to CG 92d Div, 8 Sep 44, 92d Div Files.

[21] Ltrs, Wood to CG 92d Div, 20 and 22 Sep 44, 92d Div Files.

[22] Memo, CofS IV Corps for Brig Gen Donald W. Brann, G–3 Fifth Army, 30 Aug 44, copy in IV Corps G–3 Jnl File.

through an area registered on only once." They were also learning that a great deal of fire can do relatively little damage.[23] But there was another side to developments in the combat team: officers and staffs were relaxing their own requirements as well as their standards of expectation. Command posts were poorly organized and operated in the first few weeks; initially staffs did not operate as trained. But progress was being made "with the possible exception of some junior officers and NCOs in the proper appreciation of their responsibility for requiring what their men would cheerfully give if they know it is expected." In September there was nothing serious enough to be pessimistic about; the combat team showed every sign of building a "splendid record of accomplishment."[24]

The combat team commander, Colonel Sherman, thought, too, that the first few weeks showed promise. During this period his men were convinced that their combat team was far superior to the opposing enemy. A high *esprit de corps* developed.[25] While no determined resistance had been met, men had reacted well in fire fights and to phosphorous bombings; they had gone in to clear areas of snipers and machine guns when the opportunity offered.[26]

Shift to the Sea

On 1 October the Fifth Army line, from the sea to the IV Corps boundary, consisted of Task Force 45, the Brazilian

[23] Ltr, Wood to CG 92d Div, 20 Sep 44, IV Corps G–3 Jnl File.
[24] *Ibid.*
[25] Ltr, Hq 370th Inf to CG 92d Div, 26 Nov 44, 92d Div Files.
[26] Opns Rpt 370th RCT, Sep 44.

Expeditionary Force, Task Force 92, Combat Command B of the 1st Armored Division, and the 6th South African Armoured Division. These units were directed to continue pressure on the enemy while II Corps made the main attack. Task Force 92 was in its zone east of the Serchio River, straddling Highway 12. The 3d Battalion, 370th Infantry, moved up Highway 12 on 1 October, passing through La Lima and occupying Cutigliano and positions a mile north of the town. The 2d Battalion continued to La Lima. On the afternoon of 2 October elements of Task Force 92, on corps order, began to move to the coastal sector to exchange zones with Task Force 45, continuing until the arrival of Headquarters, 370th Regimental Combat Team, which, on 5 October, took command of the right sector of the coastal zone. Task Force 92, now consisting of the 370th Regimental Combat Team and 2d Armored Group (made up of Task Force 45's 434th and 435th Antiaircraft Artillery Battalions supported by the 751st Tank Battalion and the 894th Tank Destroyer Battalion) took over control of the entire coastal sector along Highway 1, running from Forte dei Marmi on the coast due east and southeast to the Brazilians' Serchio valley sector.

The western sector of the Fifth Army line along whose left flank Task Force 92 was now disposed faced about six constantly narrowing miles of coastal plain on the extreme left and almost impassable hill masses for the remainder of its extent on the right.

The coastal plain between the mountains and the Ligurian Sea, growing narrower as it approaches Massa and La Spézia, the next towns beyond, consists for the most part of reclaimed swamps and bogs across which run numerous canals and streams. North of the Magra River, which enters the sea beyond Massa, the mountains reach the sea. Off La Spézia, at the northern end of the plain, lay Punta Bianca, armed with heavy coastal guns trained on the plain. These guns were capable of firing beyond Massa to Forte dei Marmi. Northward through the plain ran Highway 1, the main north-south coastal road connecting Leghorn, Pisa, Viaréggio, Massa, and La Spézia.

The mountains, rising abruptly from the plains, are the Northern Apennines, sometimes called the Apuan Alps. Their rocky ridges range from 1,500 to 3,000 and sometimes 6,000 feet in height. The slopes facing southwest toward the 370th's troops were generally steep. Those to the northeast on which the enemy operated were longer and more moderate. The mountain ranges, broken into a number of individual peaks, pockets, ridges, and spurs, and cut by swift mountain streams and deep gorges, afforded the enemy excellent defensive positions as well as full observation of troops on the slopes and lower approaching hills and on the coastal plain itself. Few secondary roads usable by military vehicles existed and those that did were marked by twisting curves, steep grades, and narrow bridges. They were readily blocked either by the enemy or by landslides and mud when the fall rains set in.

With the exception of the plain itself, the only route north in this sector lay along the narrow, winding thirty-five mile long valley of the Serchio River and Lima Creek, flowing south through the heart of the Northern Apennines. Be-tween the Serchio valley and the coastal plain the main chain of the Apuan Alps barred the way with thirteen miles of massive, wild, and increasingly rugged mountains. To the east of the Serchio valley rose further mountains, cut by streams and gorges. The enemy could control the Serchio and Lima valleys, with their olive groves, vineyards, and small towns, by the use of minimum forces, for the disadvantages lay with troops attacking up the steeper cliffs from the south. By placing his positions just over the crest line of the mountains, the enemy could guard all approach routes with little trouble.

Across the coastal plain between Massa and La Spézia, turning south along the coastal mountains and across the Serchio valley, the Gothic Line curved in a generally southeastern direction across the Italian peninsula. In the Serchio valley and to the east of the river, the enemy withdrew through his well-prepared, mutually supporting, concrete pill boxes, gun emplacements, bunkers, trenches, and mine fields which made up his Gothic Line. On the west coast, German forces held their Gothic Line positions, thereby protecting their port at La Spézia and the right wing of their Ligurian army.[27]

IV Corps planned to have elements of Task Force 92 attack on 6 October in the direction of Massa, with the hill mass Mount Cauala–Mount Castiglione as the initial objective. *(Map 2)* Armored elements, with engineers attached, would push forward on the coastal plain preceding the 370th's attack. Upon arrival in the Massa area, the Brazilian Expeditionary Force would be brought

---

[27] IV Corps Opns in the Italian Campaign, Sep 44.

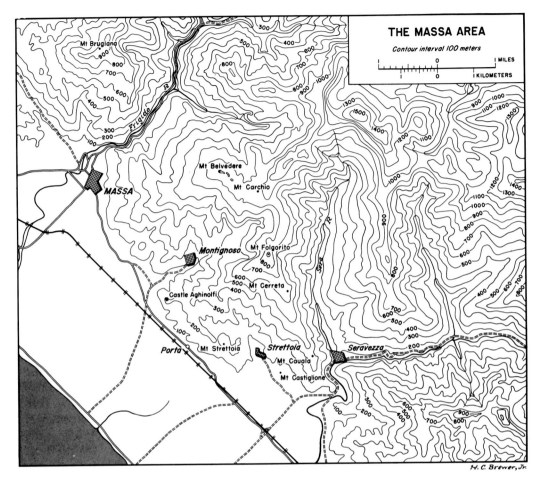

H. C. Brewer, Jr.

MAP 2

in on the right of the 92d Division's forces. The two divisions, both absorbing their new elements as they became available in the theater, would be filled and prepared for further army missions upon their arrival at La Spézia.[28]

Maj. Gen. Edward M. Almond, recently arrived in Italy preceding the 92d Division Advance Detachment, reached

Task Force 92's Viaréggio headquarters on the afternoon of 5 October, assumed command at 1800, and issued his Field Order 1 at 2000. His plan called for an attack the following morning with the two battalions of the 370th Infantry present taking Mount Cauala, the first of the series of heights guarding the southern approach to Massa. Mount Cauala stood northeast of the village of Ripa and west of Seravezza across the Sera River. The 2d Armored Group on the left would provide a diversionary attack

---

[28] Ltr, IV Corps to CG Fifth Army, 4 Oct 44, copy in IV Corps G–3 Jnl File; IV Corps OI 62, 5 Oct 44.

in the coastal plain, geared to the advance of the 370th. With Mount Cauala secured, the Task Force would take the hills beyond, move up the coast along Highway 1, capture Massa, and proceed to La Spézia.[29]

Bowed Before Massa

At 0600 on 6 October with the 1st and 2d Battalions of the 370th attacking abreast toward Mount Cauala and the 434th and 435th Antiaircraft Artillery Battalions of the 2d Armored Group providing a diversionary effort on the left flank between Highway 1 and the sea, the drive for Massa began. In a downpour of rain, slogging through "literally a sea of mud," [30] the 370th advanced about a mile while the 2d Armored Group on the left flank, initially suffering setbacks by enemy counterthrusts, made little progress in the face of harassing artillery fire. An enemy smoke screen further hampered the advance. The next day the attack resumed, with Company A pushing up the south end of Mount Cauala by 0900 while Company C tried and failed to cross the swollen Sera River. Hampered by small arms fire, Company A continued slowly up the steep rocks of the hill. By evening, when Company A was about halfway up Mount Cauala and the remaining units back in the towns were at the foot of the mountain, the attack was halted.

The next day the 370th, battalions abreast, started up the mountain again and was driven back by mortar and artillery fire on the upper slopes. On 9

October, two companies of the 2d Battalion started up the less precipitous east side under cover of darkness at 0300. By 0830, taking ten prisoners on the way up, they were at the top of the mountain. By noon heavy machine gun and mortar fire had pushed them about one third of the way back; by late evening the two companies, under fire from both flanks and from the front and believing they were in danger of being cut off from the rear, withdrew without orders to Seravezza.

The pattern for future 92d Division operations had begun. Evidences of a growing malaise within the combat team began the first day of the attack toward Massa, on 6 October. They continued to manifest themselves through the month as one after another of the combat team's units went up the slopes of Mount Cauala and neighboring heights and came down again for an infinite variety of reasons, only a few of them definitely connected with the increased tenacity of the enemy, who had decided to defend this end of the Gothic Line vigorously.

On the first day of the attack, two of the companies of the 1st Battalion failed to carry out their missions not through enemy resistance but through poor organization and control. In the case of one company the day got off to a bad start through a failure in communications. Company B was to move out upon the cessation of an artillery preparation scheduled for 0600. At that time the unit was in its assembly area a mile and a half away. It was ready to move but it received no orders to do so until 0620. It was therefore unable to take advantage of the artillery preparation. As the company advanced in column of platoons with officers forward, enemy

[29] Fifth Army OI 35, 5 Oct 44; TF 92 FO 1, 5 Oct 44.
[30] IV Corps Opns in the Italian Campaign, Oct 44.

artillery fire fell. Almost immediately contact between officers and platoons and among platoons was lost. The men became disorganized. "Things became a befuddled mess," the first sergeant said.[31] The company commander, a platoon leader, and eighteen men proceeded through enemy wire, but the rest of the unit moved back when machine gun fire fell, leaving the leading group forward. The first sergeant personally contacted each platoon in search of the platoon leaders. He was informed that they were all forward. The sergeant, in the absence of orders from his officers, rounded up one and a half squads of the 1st and 3d Platoons and part of the mortar section, organized these men into a defensive position, and sent a runner back to the battalion with information of his position. The next morning the company commander, who had spent the night forward, returned to his unit. A few hours later the remaining officers, who had spent the night back at the assembly area after being told vaguely by a chaplain that the company was dug in forward, rejoined the unit with about two dozen men. "I don't think sufficient information was disseminated and understood by all noncommissioned officers, which fact, coupled with a loss of control, particularly in the 1st Platoon, caused the affairs in question," the first sergeant observed.[32] Company B resumed the attack two mornings later. Two new officers were added, but, in the course of four days, four officers, including the company commander against his will and the two new officers, were evacuated, two for hysteria and two physically ill.

The second company had greater difficulties. On the first day, ordered to cross the Sera River and attack Mount Cauala, it moved out, crossed the river, and advanced to the enemy's wire entanglements where Lt. Alonzo M. Frazier, the leading platoon's commander, was mortally wounded. Lieutenant Frazier refused a medical corpsman's offer to take him to the rear and ordered the aidman instead to return to the rest of the platoon and have it come up and cover the wire gap. The aidman could locate only three sergeants and one private. These five started back. One was wounded on the way up the slope. The rest of the platoon was by now starting back across the river at the base of the hill. The remainder of the company, then under heavy fire on the far side of the river, did not advance at all. The company's attack the following day made no headway. On the third day, when the attack was again ordered, the men of the company refused to move, declaring that they were being made "human targets." The battalion commander assembled them and got them started, but as soon as they came under fire, the attack ceased. The company commander crossed and recrossed the Sera repeatedly trying to get his men forward, but without success.

After the failure of three daylight attempts to take Mount Cauala, a night attack was decided upon. On the night of 9–10 October the company moved out in heavy rain with all officers forward. The company got through enemy wire

[31] Statement, 1st Sgt Frank C. Clendening, Co B, 370th Inf, 16 Oct 44, 92d Div Files.

[32] Ibid. Sergeant Clendening, who had earlier received a Bronze Star, was commended for reorganizing the scattered elements of his company and setting up a defense position. Incl to Ltr, Hq 92d Inf Div TF, Actg Off in Charge to CG 92d Inf Div Task Gp, 17 Oct 44, 92d Div Files 333.1.

without a shot. When well into position, it encountered light fire, perhaps from a machine gun, a machine pistol, and a rifle, and the company streamed back through the wire and back across the Sera River despite the efforts of its officers to control it. By morning, ten men and two officers remained dejectedly alone, across the river, opposite their objective. The company was rounded up and reorganized. Again, on the night of 12 October, when other units, using scaling ladders, had again taken Mount Cauala, this company had been able to get no more than thirty men started. Mount Cauala was lost again.

The pattern for the combat career of the 92d Division emerged in these and in subsequent actions in the month of October. It repeated itself as one after another of the units of the combat team became involved in similar occurrences. General Almond placed part of the blame for these original failures on battalion command, but the problem soon showed itself to be broader and deeper than any individual's responsibility. It was a problem in faith and the lack of it —the wavering faith of commanders in the ability and determination of subordinates and enlisted men, and the continuation in the minds of enlisted men of training period convictions that they could not trust their leaders. Disorganization born of desperation soon manifested itself throughout the task force. There was no question of the lack of some individual heroism and courage among the men and officers of the task force. When four companies, using ladders to scale the cliffs, took Mount Cauala again in the early morning hours of 12 October, two of them and two reinforcing companies were forced off by

dusk. But the remaining two, Companies F and I, stuck to their positions though pinned down. Captain Gandy, commander of Company F, though mortally wounded, led the stand until 0300 the following morning when the units withdrew on regimental orders. A platoon of Company L, under Lt. Reuben L. Horner, fought off eight enemy counterattacks on Mount Strettoia while awaiting support from another unit that failed to locate it. This platoon remained until it used all its ammunition. "During my period of observation, I have heard of just as many acts of individual herosim among negro troops as among white," declared the 370th's new executive officer, Lt. Col. John J. Phelan, a veteran of six months in the Italian campaign brought in to replace the regiment's original executive officer who was killed early in September. "There is no reason to believe that there is any greater lack of individual guts among them," he told the division commander. "On the other hand, the tendency to mass hysteria or panic is much more prevalent among colored troops." [33] As he moved about the combat team's front, helping battalion and company commanders get their men started back up first one slope and then another, first across one creek and then another, he felt that he had gathered enough impressions to support this point of view. But the basis for the "tendency to panic" was not understood. Later explanations on the grounds of low test scores and poor motivation alone do not withstand close examination. A simpler basis—an all pervading lack of trust, beginning in the training

[33] Hq ExO 370th Inf to CG 92d Inf Div, 13 Oct 44, 92d Div Files.

period and now confirmed, flowing positively downward, upward, and laterally among command, commanded, and soldiers on the same firing line, accompanied by a failure in the communication of will—was apparently overlooked. This basic disbelief in the good conscience and the will to do on the part of command toward men and men toward command and both toward each other was a marked feature of the career of the 92d, especially its infantry, where belief in the importance of mission in the face of danger and belief in the reliability of both orders and fellow soldiers was of the utmost importance. It was not long before neither the men nor the officers of the division were convinced that a given job would be done and, in some instances, that it was worth the trying.

Among officers the opinion held by Company C's commander (a Negro officer) after his fourth attempt to get his men up Mount Cauala was growing: "They will not stay in their positions unless constantly watched and give as their reason for leaving the fact that the men next to them will leave anyway so there is no reason for them to stay. . . . The few good officers and noncommissioned officers in the company are not able to carry the load placed on them, no matter how hard they work. Morale is bad and I dread to make a night move, because so many of the men can slip away." [34]

Enlisted men had two approaches: what was the purpose of going up and holding a hill when there were only more hills and more Germans beyond and no one would tell them why? What was the purpose of one company's trying to scale and hold a hill when another had just been driven off? Men were willing to believe the worst, even that they were deliberately sent forward to be killed. Before leaving their battalion command post, the men of one platoon asked why they should have to occupy a hill that another company could not or would not hold. "It must be a suicide job," one said. "I hear that hill is just covered with our dead men," added another.[35] On the way out this platoon met men returning from the hill. "I asked one of the 'C' Company men why they had left the ridge," a sergeant reported, "and he told me a lot of exaggerated stories. I then spoke to my men and told them if they were going up on that ridge it would be best to do so at night, when some of the men asked me why we could not wait until morning. Then the rest of the men started going into the buildings. I went into one of the buildings and sat down." [36] When the platoon leader asked his men why they did not follow when ordered, one man replied "We would like to know more about the situation." The platoon leader repeated all that he knew but the men again refused to follow.[37] The platoon leader went to the company for information and advice. Plaster falling from the ceiling in a nearby church with a sound like small arms fire added further fears to the situation. The men decided that the noise

---

[34] Statement, Lt Robert D. Montjoy, CO Company C, 370th Inf, 15 Oct 44, 92d Div Files.

[35] Statement, 2d Lt Wesley B. Lee, 28 Oct 44, 92d Div Files.

[36] Statement, SSgt Johnny R. Walden, 3d Platoon, Co A, 370th Inf, 28 Oct 44, 92d Div Files.

[37] Statement, 2d Lt James A. Henson, 26 Oct 44, 92d Div Files.

came from approaching Germans and moved to buildings farther back.

The next morning, the platoon leader gathered his men and tried to move them out; some were eating and continued to do so, paying little attention to commands. The platoon leader, followed by a few men, moved toward the river. But the only attempt at clarifying the situation for the remaining men backfired when an officer strange to the unit arrived with assertions that no one believed. "The men seemed scared to death, so I began to talk to them with the idea of bucking up their nerve," this officer, the white commander of another company, declared. "I stated that there were no Germans up on the hill and it was just a matter of walking up there and digging in. I offered to go up there to prove this. With that a soldier turned to me with a sneer on his face and said, 'Shit.' I immediately told the soldier if he ever said that to me again, he would get a carbine slug in his head. I meant every word of the above statement. . . ."[38] While officers and men were engaged in fruitless disputation, orders came from regimental headquarters to place the platoon in arrest. The men were disarmed and arrested, the first of several groups to be so arrested. But because of the confusion surrounding these events, when orders had come from several sources and the willfully disobedient were difficult to separate from those who were awaiting clarified orders, courts-martial charges against many of these men would not hold.

Despite the evidences of disintegration, the situation did not yet seem hopeless. Some units were still performing well, but the possibilities of their continued good performance were lessened by their growing belief that men on the immediate right and left, when next one looked, might be back at the bottom of a hill or across a river where the day's action had started. "I think it is too early to definitely state whether or not negro troops could be made combat soldiers," Colonel Sherman, the 370th's commander, observed in mid-October when commenting on one of the questions continually asked higher commanders of the 92d. "Results so far—many satisfactory and many unsatisfactory—are, to my mind, inconclusive at the present time."[39]

Colonel Sherman divided the 370th's combat career up to that point into two parts: the period from arrival to 4 October, when the combat team began its move to Viaréggio, and the period from 4 October to 20 October. In the first period, he reasoned, the original high morale, the excitement of entering battle, the excellent weather, and the comparatively easy pursuit of the enemy across the Arno Plain had accounted for the team's excellent results. By the beginning of the attack toward Massa, "the romance had worn off." Operations were over much harder terrain, in much worse weather, with the daily rains turning colder and the mud getting deeper. Combat by then was an old story. Officers and men of the combat team had come to know each other's capabilities well. They could now be divided into two types: officers and men who got results and those of a poorer type who

[38] Statement, Capt Edward M. Eagan, 27 Oct 44, 92d Div Files.

[39] Sherman Notes on 370th RCT, 20 Oct 44, 92d Div Files.

spent their time "sitting around and hesitating to do anything." The majority of the outstanding officers and men became casualties quickly, often through the negligence and unreliability of the others. Units that took and held the crags of Mount Cauala were driven off, losing men and officers, when reinforcing units failed to arrive. This the men of the 370th well knew. The 370th's units could ill afford to lose as many small unit commanders as they did. As a result, Colonel Sherman felt, "Morale went down, esprit de corps departed, determined resistance on the part of the enemy began, difficult terrain was encountered, and so the natural result was that combat efficiency was lowered." [40]

"Whether all white officers would improve the action of enlisted troops is questionable," Colonel Sherman continued in answer to another of the questions frequently asked higher officers of the division. "However I believe from the standpoint of the officers only, that it would be better if all officers were either all colored or all white." [41] The executive officer, Colonel Phelan, while observing that there were leadership disadvantages in both—arising in Negro officers from the greater paucity of officer material and in white officers from a diminishing incentive "that arises from wanting to gain the respect of his men . . . he doesn't care as much as a white officer leading white troops or vice versa"—decided that "A good officer seems to achieve better results regardless of race." [42] Until now "ineffectiveness on the part of certain officers and Non-com-

missioned Officers," Colonel Sherman felt, "has been overcome by the excellent work of the outstanding officers, both colored and white, who have not only carried their own load but, in addition, the load of those ineffectives above mentioned, with the result that a high casualty rate exists among the efficient leaders and conversely a low rate among the ineffectives." [43]

To bolster crumbling units and to try out officers in new positions where they might obtain better results, officers were transferred among platoons, companies, and battalions with such frequency that at times men were barely aware of who their current commander was. Action to correct deficiencies, especially in leadership, by the reduction of noncommissioned officers and the shifting of officers from one unit to another was doomed to failure, for the supply of better material was limited. Enlisted replacements were few and those who did arrive seldom provided better material. Many of those arriving were AWOL's from the East Coast Processing Center [44] and rehabilitees from the African Disciplinary Barracks. Most of them, unhappy to find themselves in a front-line regiment, "growled a good deal." It became easy for the older members of the combat team to listen to their gripes. [45]

Though the 92d Division later esti-

---

[40] *Ibid.*

[41] *Ibid.*

[42] ExO Hq 370th Inf to CG 92d Inf Div, 13 Oct 44, 92d Div Files.

[43] 1st Ind, Hq 370th CT to CG 92d Div, 16 Oct 44, on Ltr, CG 92d Inf Div to CO 370th Inf, 13 Oct 44, 92d Div Files.

[44] Negroes from the East Coast Processing Center, where men AWOL at the time of the shipment of their units were sent, could be shipped overseas to theaters as replacements without regard to theater requirements or desires.

[45] Sherman Notes on 370th RCT, 20 Oct 44, 92d Div Files.

mated that many of its replacements, especially those from the 372d Infantry, were well trained, the replacement system in the United States, geared as it was to loss replacements for white but not Negro units, was unable to supply Negro infantry replacements in bulk. A new program expanding the training of Negro replacements in the United States was begun, but these men would not be available for several months to come. The IV Corps had already begun to worry about replacements for the division while it was still on its way to the theater. Until Negro replacements were available, the division, no matter what its efficiency, could not be used for strong offensive operations. Should it suffer heavy losses it had neither a reserve nor a replacement pool to draw upon. Not much could be expected from the overstrength of the 92d Division for, in addition to the 1,300 qualified replacements, the overstrength contained half of the division's Q-minus men from Fort Huachuca—the psychologically rather than physically unfit men of the casual camp—and 225 East Coast Processing Center AWOL's. All of the thousand-odd Q-minus men would have been included but for the War Department's desire to relieve the division of too many potential courts-martial candidates.[46]

The Full Division Arrives

In the meantime, through October, the remaining units of the 92d Division were entering Italy, bringing with them, in addition to the Q-minus and East

Coast Processing Center men, all of the other accumulated problems of Fort Huachuca and the training period. The remaining regiments of the division had suffered somewhat, inevitably, by the "selection out" of some of their best men for the 370th Regimental Combat Team. With the 92d were officers who, in August and September just before departure, had tried desperately to be relieved under the rotational policy for white officers with Negro troops, only to be met with indignant denials that the division had knowledge of any such policy—the month for departure was no time to encourage an exodus of even unwilling officers.[47] One unit, the engineer battalion, had had a typical morale-breaking ruckus illustrative of the depth and complexity of interpersonal and intergroup relations within units of the division.

The morale of this battalion came forcibly to divisional attention when, shortly after arriving in Italy and before joining the division, an unknown assailant shot an officer who lay asleep in his tent. No amount of querying could uncover the assailant's identity nor could responsibility for the weapon involved be fixed. The investigating officer, considering that there must be some truth in the many accounts so often repeated to him, summed up a "most unpleasant situation" which, he considered, "would seriously impair the effectiveness of this organization in combat:"

The EM dislike their officers; the officers dislike each other; and they all seemingly dislike their Bn Commander. Now to analyze that statement. Most of the EM have no confidence in their officers which, justi-

[46] Memo, Hq AGF for CofS, 4 Aug 44, AGF 320.2/1 (92d Div); OPD for DCofS, 9 Aug 44, OPD 370.5 Africa (4 Aug 44).

[47] Ltrs in 92d Div Files 210.3 Transfer of Offs.

fied or not, is bad. They say that there are
very few actual Engineer trained officers
amongst them; most of the officers originally being commissioned in other branches
of the service. The men don't feel these
officers are fit to lead them into combat.
One officer, a Co commander, is intensely
disliked by his men and some of the members of his Co have threatened to kill him.
One reason for the personal dislike is that
this Officer is alleged to have said he is half
white and when his men learned of this,
why their feelings mounted. The men
believe they have been unfairly treated and
cite the following examples. While at Cp
Patrick Henry they were under the impression that some of them at least were to be
allowed three day passes. Instead they
were put to work clearing fallen trees and
other debris, which resulted from a severe
storm which had swept the Area. When
many of the men under the impression
that their passes were ready for them, reported to their Orderly Room dressed to
leave, they found no passes and, when they
further discovered that the Bn Comdr and
their Co Comdr were absent on pass, why
there was a most ugly atmosphere. On the
transport coming across, the Engr Bn performed all the fatigue details aboard ship
and had no further relaxation. Even
NCO's were used on these details. The
men could not understand why, with other
units aboard the transport, they were the
only persons used for this work. It was
reported that a party was proposed by the
Bn Cmdr for the men but they refused to
attend. The statement was made that the
NCO's feel reluctant to properly perform
their duties because for almost any reason
and often w/o apparent cause, they are
reduced to the grade of Pvt. Consequently,
feeling that at any time they may be one
themselves, the NCO's don't handle Pvts as
an NCO should. The temper of the men
aboard the transport was not bettered when
they would read various items in the ship's
paper concerning the Bn Comdr or Bn
Executive Officer.[48]

Since their arrival in Italy so many additional incidents indicative of poor
leadership and command had occurred
in this unit that the investigating officer
recommended the relief of the battalion
commander. The commander not only
was not relieved; he remained to command a task force in one of the 92d Division's more disastrous ventures.

Arriving with the full division were
the remaining staff officers, many of
whom were thought by junior officers of
the 92d, white as well as Negro, to be
less than the best in judgment, knowledge, and will.[49] Staff officers, as they
arrived, were oriented in some cases by
spending a few days with veteran divisions to the east of Task Force 92, rotating headquarters staff assignments in
the meantime.

As the staff assumed its permanent
size and form, it developed standard
procedures for operating. The general
staff briefed General Almond twice daily
on the situation, at 0745 and 1700. After the morning briefing, the staff held
a planning conference in which new
plans were discussed and presented by
G–3. The plans included those for
"power patrols" as well as major operations. Most plans of a comprehensive
nature were made far in advance so that,
if corps or army called for plans for limited attacks which had to be ready in
minimum time, the 92d was ready for
every "logical objective on the whole
front of approximately 18.3 miles."
Plans, when approved and ordered executed, were transmitted to troops in operations instructions usually issued after
the 1700 conference, attended by the

[48] Asst Div TIG (Capt Charles H. Welch), Rpt
of Investigation of Shooting of 1st Lt John T.
Murphy . . . 317th Engr Combat Bn, 92d Div Files.

[49] Warman Welliver [Capt FA, 92d Div], "Report
on the Negro Soldier" Harper's, CXCII (April,
1946), 338.

executive officer of each unit as well as the staff. At the conclusion of these conferences, General Almond issued oral instructions to the units through their executive officers; these were then issued by G–3 as operations instructions as of 1800. When drafts of the instructions were approved, each unit received the appropriate paragraphs by telephone to avoid delay in transmission. For major operations, participating units were given specialized instructions, sometimes down to the tank each infantryman was to ride in an approach to an objective. But seldom did small units and individual soldiers know what was planned for units or men to their immediate right or left, nor did they know what the general plan intended to accomplish. Alternatives, when provided, were usually completely unknown. So secret were the over-all plans of the 92d Division that in the G–3 section only the chief worked on them. When the division made its February 1945 attack after long and detailed planning, not even the assistant section chiefs in G–2 and G–3 knew that the attack was going to be made until a few hours before troops crossed the line of departure.[50] In most operations detailed plans down to the platoon level were prescribed by division headquarters, giving subordinate units an opportunity to complain that the 92d's staff stifled all unit initiative.[51] The staff contended that, since the division was disposed over so large a front and since the staff had responsibility for and knowledge of both the entire front and the capabilities of division

small units and individuals, such detailed planning and supervision were necessary.[52] General Almond himself moved about his broad front with rapidity and thoroughness, endangering his own life several times as he went into division outposts. So rapid and all-inclusive were his movements that his G–3 section found that recording his whereabouts was one of the major difficulties in keeping its journal.[53]

The German command opposing soon got the impression that the 92d Division's forces were plan-bound. They would adhere strictly to plans formulated before the attack, never deviating from them. The Germans found that the scout and shock undertakings of the division were well prepared and carried out, showing good results. The front-line troops of the 92d were vigilant and in readiness for defense, but the German command considered the division, whose combat efficiency and training it judged inferior to that of other American divisions, to have made poor utilization of its terrain, to have irresolute command, and to lack tenacity. After observing the division's limited objective attacks, and learning that it was not backed by strong reserves, the German command was certain that the 92d's was a holding role only and that no strong attack would develop in its sector.[54]

As they arrived in Italy, the remaining

---

[50] 92d Div G–3 Opns Summary, 15 Oct 42–15 Nov 45, pts. II, III, V.

[51] Hq 92d Div, Ltr, Div IG to CG 92d Div, 15 Mar 45, 92d Div Files 333.3.

[52] Ibid.; Ltr, CG Fifth Army to CG MTOUSA, 14 Dec 44, OPD 322.97.

[53] 92d Div G–3 Opns Summary, 15 Oct 42–15 Nov 45, pt. II.

[54] Hq Intel Center, 7769th Hq and Hq Co, Special Investigation and Intel Rpt (report prepared after the war by a group of captured German officers representing all staff sections of OB Suedwest and some of the subordinate commands), copy in OCMH files.

units of the 92d Division prepared for entry into the line upon call. The 371st Infantry arrived at Leghorn on 18 October and began to relieve the 370th Infantry on 31 October. The 365th Infantry arrived between 29 October and 8 November, its first element entering the line on 8–9 November. The last units arrived on 22 November.

At the beginning of November, the mission of the 92d Division, now under Fifth Army control (Task Force 92 ceased to exist on 6 November), was to command its coastal sector and prepare its remaining elements for action. It was to "hold maximum enemy force in coastal area; continue to exert pressure, occupying any areas the securing of which is deemed within its capabilities" and protect the left flank of Fifth Army. That army had failed to break through to Bologna as hoped. The 92d Division's own organic elements now held the approximately twenty-mile-wide line from the sea to Barga. This, with IV Corps' line to the right, was, as General Clark described it, "the formidable half of the line that we had decided not to attack." [55] Fifth Army as a whole went into a period of active defense preparatory to resuming the offensive aimed at the Po Valley. This offensive, in conjunction with an Eighth Army attack, was tentatively planned for about 1 December.[56]

Neither this nor later Fifth Army offensives proposed for the winter materialized. The 92d Division's main mission remained the same throughout the winter. Though limited local attacks, generally in not more than company and battalion strength, were attempted and though one larger scale attack was tried in February, the division's primary mission remained defensive. The 92d planned limited objective attacks hoping to raise morale and efficiency through a successful action on its mountain front. Further unsuccessful actions, it was recognized, would damage rather than aid morale.[57] Local attacks in regimental and battalion sectors in the late fall were not promising affairs. At the end of November the 365th Infantry, just getting fully into the line, had not yet participated in more than small local patrol actions but enough had occurred in the six of his nine infantry battalions already committed to limited objective attacks for General Almond to report to General Clark that "in every case the 'melting away' tendency had been evidenced in some degree." No disaster had occurred, principally because of the defensive attitude of the enemy. In artillery, communications, supply, medical service, and troop movements, his troops had performed excellently, but his rifle units were not measuring up. Battle experience gained in attacks so far was no compensation for the loss of key leaders incurred. General Almond was not yet willing to offer final conclusions on the battle efficiency of his division. He still hoped to weld a strong force from his now fully deployed regiments. But his view at the end of November was hardly optimistic.[58]

---

[55] Clark, *Calculated Risk*, p. 3.
[56] Ltr, Hq Fifth Army to CG's II, IV, XIII Corps, CG's 6th South African Armd, 92d Inf Divs, 2 Nov 44, 92 Div Files 370.2–Y.

[57] Hq 92d Inf Div, Plan "Fourth Term," 15 Jan 45.
[58] Ltr, CG 92d Inf Div to Clark, 27 Nov 44, copy in WDSSP (MTO) (app. II) 1482.

A Fourth Hand

While the 92d Division was shuffling its troops about, reorganizing again and again its weaker units, transferring officers back and forth among units, and conducting formal investigations of its infantry units' activities, all in an earnest attempt to solve its internal problems, IV Corps and Fifth Army were concerned about maintaining the division's strength so that it could continue to hold its western end of the Fifth Army's lines. For further bolstering the numerical strength of the division, Fifth Army and the theater considered the use of Negro troops in other units, including air base security battalions.

Scattered over Italy with the Fifteenth Air Force was the 366th Infantry, with all Negro officers. It could furnish an additional regiment, in reserve or as a replacement pool, for the 92d Division. The 366th, not long after its arrival in Italy in May 1944, had been considered for infantry rather than air base guard duties at a time when the Fifth Army needed additional infantry strength for the assault on Rome. General Devers offered the 366th to Fifth Army on 30 May. Lt. Gen. Ira C. Eaker was reported to be "very favorably impressed with the colonel who is in command. He is reluctant to lose the unit, but he will concur." [59] A Fifth Army G–3 officer flew to Bari to check on the status and training of the unit and found that, because it had not been sent for combat duty, it was short of equipment. But, he reported, "the younger officers are very keen for combat," and he was very favorably impressed with them. The commanding officer of the 366th, while apparently not too overjoyed at the thought, was not seemingly antagonistic. He believed, however, that it would take him a week or ten days to get ready to move and that he should have two weeks' training before fighting. [60] The deputy G–3 recommended that the regiment be obtained by Fifth Army. Its release to the staging area at Naples was requested. [61] But General Devers decided that since it would not be ready for combat in the near future and since General Eaker required it for antisabotage duties, the offer should be withdrawn. [62]

The 366th continued to guard Air Forces installations for Fifteenth Air Force Service Command. Its elements were spread from Sardinia to the Adriatic coast. It had heard "rumors" in May that it would see action with the Fifth Army, [63] but by fall belief in these rumors had largely disappeared. The regiment maintained high morale, which it attributed to "Pride of organization, and its commander, the fact that the men know this regiment passed its combat training tests and the organization is still intact after other units have been demobilized to form Port Battalions and other types of service units." [64] Its venereal rate was low, both for the theater and for a Negro unit—30.3 per 1,000, caused by nine new cases in June.

---

[59] Memo, Fifth Army, A.M.G. for Gen Clark, 30 May 44, Mathews File, OCMH.

[60] Memo, Hq Fifth Army for Gen Gruenther, 31 May 44, Mathews File, OCMH.

[61] Msg, Fifth Army to NATOUSA, 31 May 44, MC–IN 19046, 31 May 44, AFHQ G–3 Opns, 0/00/12C (10 B 106F) ser. 40.

[62] Memo, Col Wood for Gen Brann, 2 Jun 44, Mathews File, OCMH.

[63] War Diary 366th Inf, Mar–May 44.

[64] *Ibid.,* Jun 44.

Its relations with the air units with which its detachments worked and with other Allied troops adjacent the nearly two dozen airfields that it was guarding were good. The 366th found softball exhibitions a key to good relations with foreign units. It taught New Zealanders to play ball; twenty-five New Zealand officers visited regimental headquarters for a smoker; and a group of South African officers and enlisted men demonstrated rugby for the regiment in return for its softball demonstrations. The Fifteenth Air Force complained in June that not all of the 366th's duties were being fully carried out, but by September the regiment had begun to accumulate commendations for the work of its detachments. The Fifteenth Air Force then noted perceptible improvement in the regiment's performance of its duties.[65]

With the regiment dispersed over so great an area and performing static duties, control and continued training were difficult. When General Davis, visiting the unit in September, expressed surprise that it had combat as a secondary mission, the regimental commander told him that "the regiment does not possess at present the combat efficiency attained while in the United States. Six months of guard duty have dulled the combat keenness so essential to success in battle. Continued performance of the primary mission will nullify completely the reduced combat efficiency now possessed by the regiment."[66] Its intelligence and reconnaissance platoon, for example, had

not trained since February. The regimental commander hoped that the unit could be assembled for three months of intensive training. In September, fifteen company grade officers attended a three-week leadership and battle training course from which they reported learning more than they ever had before, but otherwise the unit continued its guard duties until 28 October when Fifth Army relieved it from its Fifteenth Air Force assignments and alerted it for movement to Leghorn for attachment to the 92d Division. "Morale ran high," the unit reported, ". . . because there was anticipation that this unit would fulfill its primary mission, that of combat. . . ."[67] Thus, the 92d Division gained a fourth regiment.

The 366th arrived in Leghorn on 26 November and, upon arrival, was attached to the 92d Division. The division issued training orders and inspected and quizzed the men and officers of the regiment. It determined, for training purposes, to attach units of the regiment to its own elements, despite the concern of the 366th's commander that the regiment be given additional training and that it retain its integrity. On 30 November, the fourth day after arrival, the first of the 366th's units, Company E, entered the line attached to the 3d Battalion, 371st Infantry, then on the coast. The 366th Intelligence and Reconnaissance Platoon was attached to the division's reconnaissance troop on the following day. Its B Company was attached to the 3d Battalion, 371st; its 2d Battalion, less Company E, moved into

[65] Ltr, Hq 14th Fighter Gp (TE) to CO Co E, 23 Aug 44, and Ltr, Hq Fifteenth AF to CO 366th, 25 Sep 44. Both in Hist of 366th Inf Regt, Sep 44.
[66] Memo, Hq 366th Inf (Col H. D. Queen) for Gen Davis, 11 Sep 44.
[67] Hist of 366th Inf Regt, Nov 44; see also Hq 92d Inf, Rpt of Opns of the 366th Inf (Lt Col T. J. Arnold), n.d., 92d Div Files.

the 370th's forward positions in the Serchio valley on 2 December; its I Company went to the 371st Infantry on 5 December, its cannon company to the 370th Infantry and its antitank company to the 371st Infantry on 9 December; and its K Company to the 370th on 11 December. Its 1st Battalion, operating directly under the division and not under regimental control, relieved the 3d Battalion, 371st Infantry, in the coastal sector on 12–13 December.

In the meantime, the initial units of the 366th committed had already come under the same influences that had marked the initial efforts of the units of the 92d's regiments. The division requested an investigation of the circumstances of one company's entrance into the line and another's initial fire experience, which involved a withdrawal through the lines of an adjacent unit of the 371st, as suggested by that unit. This, the 371st's commander felt, "was more than offset by the commendable action of the company commander in organizing maneuver against an enemy machine gun. Captain Dabney was wounded during the action. The platoon which lost contact showed considerable spirit. They killed several of the enemy, including a German officer, captured 12 prisoners, and withdrew in fair order through the lines of our 3d Battalion." [68]

The 366th's commander, whose headquarters had been visited daily by the 92d's commander or members of his staff inquiring and checking on the regiment's training and efficiency, now asked for relief from his command.[69] He was evacuated for physical disability and the regiment's executive officer, Lt. Col. Alonzo Ferguson, was made commander, regimental headquarters taking control of the 1st Battalion's sector on 15 December.

With the arrival of the 366th Infantry the 92d Division was able to free some of its elements for use in other parts of the Fifth Army line where, in addition to receiving further indoctrination from more experienced units, they could ease the relief and rest problem for veteran white units in the line. The 365th Regimental Combat Team[70] on 3 December went to the eastern end of the Fifth Army line where it was attached to the 88th Infantry Division in its sector on the right of the II Corps line in the Apennines south of Bologna. The 88th Division was thus enabled to rest battalions of its 349th Infantry, to which the 365th was attached, and whose sector it later controlled.[71] The 3d Battalion of the 371st, relieved from attachment to the

---

[68] 1st Ind, CO 371st Inf (Col James Notestein) to CG 92d Div, 12 Dec 44, on Ltr, CG 92d Div to CO 371st Inf, 7 Dec 44, 92d Div Files.

[69] "1. Respectfully request that I be relieved from assignment and command of the 366th Infantry regiment for the following reasons:

a. The treatment the regiment and myself have received during the period of attachment to the 92d Infantry Division has been such as to disturb me mentally and has not been such as is usually given an officer of my grade and service.

b. To keep my record clear and up to normal expectations, before I break under the present strain as I am now physically and mentally exhausted.

2. I have been in command of this unit since 31 January, 1943 and have at all times subscribed fully to the policy of higher authority and previously have received the proper courtesy and respect in return." Ltr, CO 366th Inf Regt to CG Fifth Army, 11 Dec 44, 92d Div Files.

[70] 365th Inf Regt plus the 597th FA Bn, Co B, 317th Engr Bn, and Co A, 317th Med Bn.

[71] Hist of 349th Inf Regt, Dec 44; Hq 88th Inf Div, Dir 5, 20 Dec 44; G–3 Pers Rpt, 88th Inf Div.

370th Regimental Combat Team, replaced the 365th in the coastal sector, operating as a task force under divisional rather than regimental control. After the 2d Battalion, 366th Infantry closed into Barga for attachment to the 370th Infantry on 3 December, the 370th's 3d Battalion moved to the east to Castel di Cascio, where it was attached to the 6th South African Armoured Division's 11th Armoured Brigade on the IV Corps front. On 7 December the battalion relieved the Imperial Light Horse Kimberley Regiment in the line. The 370th Infantry now controlled but one of its own battalions, for its 2d Battalion was operating in the Gaggio Montano sector with the Brazilians, who were still planning to attack Mount Belvedere. On 18 December the 370th's 2d Battalion returned to its control.

These piebald command relationships were typical of the employment of the units of the 92d Division. Within battalions and regiments, attachment of small units back and forth for rest and adjustment of the lines was common so that, in addition to being spread over a front longer than that of other Fifth Army divisions, the development of command control, *esprit*, and discipline within elements of the division was hampered by the frequent and continuous parceling out of units first to one and then to another command.

First Reports

In Washington, the first reports of the 92d Division's career were reaching the War Department. Early in November, Truman Gibson, on behalf of the Advisory Committee for Special Troop Poli-

cies, asked Maj. Oscar J. Magee of the Intelligence Division, Army Service Forces, then about to depart on a mission to Italy, to bring back factual data on the progress of the division. Major Magee, after visits to Allied Force Headquarters, Fifth Army, and the 92d Division between 15 November and 2 December, returned with his impressions.

The 92d at this time was carrying out its assigned missions, maintaining pressure so that the enemy could not shift forces elsewhere and protecting the left flank of the Fifth Army. As a result of its recent arrival, small losses of matériel, and favorable coastal position in the line, it was "very possibly" the best fed, clothed, and equipped division in the Fifth Army. Its combat capabilities were still in process of being ascertained. "Generally speaking," Magee reported, "the work of the various components of the Division has been satisfactory since arrival overseas, with two exceptions: infantry patrol and assault . . . . In regard to assault by the infantry and observance of the rule 'Close with the enemy and destroy him with cold steel' the 92d has yet to prove its courage and tenacity. Too frequently the infantry 'melts away' under fire and an abnormal number of men hide in cellars until they are routed out by their officers." The infantry, he declared, was being "nursed along" to give it confidence, but, to date, results had been disappointing. General Almond believed the "true evaluation" of the Negro soldier's capabilities would have to await the end of the war, but Major Magee was of the opinion that it would be obtained "if and when the Division is fiercely attacked by or is thrown into an all-out offensive against German—not Fascist—troops." Efficiency and morale, he continued, were not appreciably affected by racial problems: "Racial sensitivity is strongly evident in the typical Negro officer, while distrust of a Negro's capabilities is present but less evident in the typical white officer." But, Major Magee felt, these attitudes did not affect the work at hand. No report of racial discrimination within the division should be accepted as "the true reason for any tactical or administrative action taken by the divisional leadership," he concluded. Complete trust should be placed in the "integrity, ability and impartiality of the Generals and policy-making officers whose decisions affect the 92d Infantry Division." Gibson, the report concluded, should accept "the informal invitation of Lt. Gen. Mark W. Clark, delivered through me, to 'Come and see us.' " [72]

General Clark, reflecting reports from the 92d Division to him and to his officers, reported shortly thereafter in similar vein. Allowing for the short period of actual combat, "they have performed excellently in supply and administrative matters and in such tactical operations as do not require sustained demonstration of initiative and aggressiveness on the parts of junior leaders and of the rank and file," he wrote General McNarney. The division's commander and his senior subordinates found it necessary "to lead and supervise their troops much more in detail than is normally the case." General Clark felt that the division had been well prepared for commitment; it entered combat "under no handicaps." It was true that the division's combat experience was still too brief for conclusive impressions. Its combat value still had to be demonstrated: "It is my intention to give the division increasing opportunity to assume combat responsibility and to demonstrate its ability to carry a full load in offensive operations. A further report on this subject will be submitted on the basis of future experience," he concluded. General McNarney, forwarding this report, concurred.[73]

Gibson, in sending Major Magee's report to Assistant Secretary McCloy, noted the tendency of reports on Negro soldiers to try to "prove one of two ultimate facts: either on the one hand that Negroes are no good as soldiers or on the other that they are excellent." Working toward conclusions instead of developing the full facts was a major fault of reports, making them of little value to the Army "unless the easy way out is taken of assuming that Negroes have inborn and hence incorrectible racial deficiencies that make their military use impossible." The Magee report, while revealing, omitted "most of what he [Magee] developed with me in a four hour conversation," Gibson continued. Magee reported to Gibson orally but not formally that the white officers in the 92d Division "generally disliked their assignments, had no confidence in their men and believed that the 'experiment' of using Negroes in combat would fail." One key staff officer told Major Magee that although there had been many examples of individual heroism on

[72] Memo, Hq ASF for Col Roamer (copies to ASF Brs, WDGS Secs, Civ Aide), 6 Dec 44, OPD 322.97 (6 Dec 44).

[73] Ltr, CG Fifth Army (Clark) to CG MTOUSA (McNarney), 14 Dec 44; Cover Ltr, McNarney to Gen Handy, and 1st Ind, 19 Dec 44. All in OPD 322.97.

the part of Negro officers and soldiers in the 92d, it was his belief that "the Negro generally could not overcome or escape his background of no property ownership, irresponsibility, and subservence. The Negro is panicky and his environment has not conditioned him to accept responsibilities." Said another field grade staff officer: "I don't like my assignment because I don't trust Negroes. White officers who work with them have to work harder than with white troops. I have no confidence in the fighting ability of Negro soldiers." And a third declared that "the 93rd Division was the first out, the 2nd Cavalry Division the second, and now the 92nd Division is at bat with one strike already against us."

Gibson declared that he did not believe that these attitudes were consciously developed or viciously applied, but the report on them

. . . more than justifies [the] trip because they show the nature of the problem ahead and the necessity of exercising great care in evaluating all reports from this and other Negro organizations. In the instant cases, the conclusions reached completely overlooked the effect on the men of the attitudes of the officers. Soldiers generally know how their officers feel. If they know that their officers dislike them, have no confidence in them or feel that they will not stand up under combat, the likelihood is that they will fail. . . . The problem is one of getting into the whole story and not the segments that go to prove a conclusion. Enough exists in any Negro unit to prove just about anything." [74]

Serchio Valley Counterattack

In the meantime, the 92d Division was planning further assaults on the en-

emy in conjunction with Fifth Army's proposed December offensive toward Bologna. Christmas Day was to have seen the launching of a general attack. The 370th Infantry, with the 2d Battalion, 366th, attached, was to attack east of the Serchio River to secure Lama di Sotto. Company E, 366th, and Company F, 370th, were to be the assault units. But, from mid-December, German troop movements, repairs to roads and bridges in the upper Serchio valley, and the statements of prisoners foretold a German offensive in the west, opposite the 92d Division's lightly held line. At least one German division, the *148th Grenadier*, and two Italian divisions were known to be in the area; as many as five German divisions might be based in the La Spézia region. With the port of Leghorn as an objective, such an attack, coinciding with the German counteroffensive at Bastogne then under way in the European theater, could be profitable to the enemy.

As protection against the expected counteroffensive, Fifth Army on 23 December ordered the 339th Regimental Combat Team of the 85th Division to move to IV Corps. The 337th Regimental Combat Team of the same division and the 19th and 21st Brigades of the 8th Indian Division were shifted from reserve and British 13 Corps, the 337th being attached to the 92d Division and the Indian units placed under the 92d's operational control. [75] Supporting units, including the 84th Chemical Battalion, the 755th and 760th Tank Battalions, and three American battalions and two British regiments of artillery were ordered to the Lucca area. By

---

[74] Memo, Civ Aide for ASW, 20 Dec 44, ASW 291.2 Negro Trps-Alpha.

[75] Fifth Army OI 37.

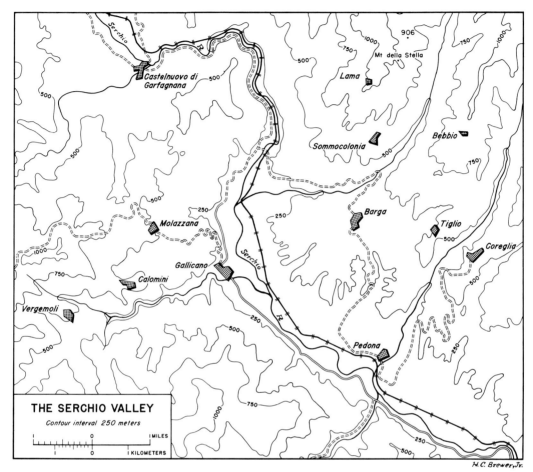

THE SERCHIO VALLEY

Contour interval 250 meters

1 MILES

1 KILOMETERS

H.C. Brewer, Jr.

MAP 3

Christmas Day both of the Indian brigades had arrived. The 92d Division returned to IV Corps control.

Movement into the 92d Division sector at the time was no lark; the 76oth Tank Battalion, which had been in Italy since the first campaign, described it as

. . . the "grimmest" move thus far made. The roads that it was necessary to cover were covered with snow and ice, the weather was extremely cold, and the total distance covered was 124 miles. . . . Several tanks "fell out" enroute due to me-chanical failures and one tank, commanded by Lieutenant John E. Visher, plunged off of the road into a flooded area and became completely submerged in water. Numerous vehicles had considerable difficulty in moving from the bivouac area because of the extremely muddy condition.[76]

In the 370th Infantry sector astride the Serchio, tanks of Company B, 76oth Tank Battalion, moved into position, with one platoon on each side of the

---

[76] Hist of 76oth Tank Bn, Dec 44.

river, to support the 92d Division's proposed Christmas Day attack. The 370th's Company G at Calomini, west of the Serchio on the left flank, was attached to the 1st Battalion in preparation for the attack; Company E of the 366th was attached to the 2d Battalion, 370th, east of the Serchio for the same purpose. The 92d Reconnaissance Troop at Bebbio and the 2d Battalion, 366th (less Company E), at Barga remained on the right flank east of the Serchio. The 370th's 2d Battalion (less Company G) moved into Sommocolonia, northernmost of the 370th's outpost towns, on the morning of the 24th. *(Map 3)*

The Christmas Day attack was called off on Christmas Eve. Antitank and machine gun fire placed on enemy positions on Christmas night brought an intense reaction from the enemy on the east bank of the Serchio. The 3d Battalion reported unusual patrol activity. Sommocolonia received some artillery and mortar fire but enemy patrols were not active and there was no close contact between elements of the 370th and the enemy. The regiment's 2d Battalion was pulled back under cover of darkness, leaving only one platoon of the 366th's Company F and a platoon of Company H in Sommocolonia. At four in the morning of the 26th the 370th's units moved to high ground west of the Serchio and south of Gallicano with the mission of digging a main defensive position across the mountain mass at that point as directed by division headquarters.

Shortly after the 2d Battalion, 370th, began its movement, the 1st Battalion at Molazzana on the west bank received machine gun fire and, at 0450, the small garrison at Sommocolonia on the east bank came under small arms and artillery fire, lasting until 0500. Half an hour later an enemy squad north of Sommocolonia engaged partisans in a fire fight. By 0700 enemy troops appeared at Molazzana and against Company G at Calomini. At 0730 Sommocolonia was surrounded by Austrian and Italian troops, some of whom were dressed as partisans. Companies A and C in Molazzana beat off repeated attacks in their area; Company G at Calomini retained possession of the town although the enemy captured a machine gun and mortar section which had been supporting the company.

The main attack, originally against Molazzana west of the Serchio, shifted late in the morning to Sommocolonia, when enemy troops moved down the draws from the vicinity of Bebbio, held by the 92d Reconnaissance Troop. The regiment ordered the reconnaissance troop to withdraw to prepared positions near Coreglia.

As the situation at Sommocolonia worsened, Lt. Graham H. Jenkins called for reinforcements at 0735. The battalion ordered a platoon of Company E to Sommocolonia. Jenkins reported fighting from door to door, and requested mortar and artillery fire, informing his battalion, "Don't worry about anything," —his men would hold.[77] Lt. John Fox, forward observer of the 366th Cannon Company, adjusted fire until it was directly on his own observation post. "That round was just where I wanted it. Bring it in 60 more yards," he called. The Germans were at his door and, he reasoned, the only way to halt

---

[77] S–2 and S–3 Jnls, 2d Bn 366th Inf.

them was to call for fire on his own position. He then called for a smoke screen to cover the withdrawal of the remaining troops. No further word came from Fox.[78] His body was discovered in the demolished observation post days later.

Efforts to reinforce Sommocolonia failed. Partisans fought the enemy in the streets, but some of the troops of the 366th, who were inside houses and unable to distinguish partisans from similarly dressed enemy, held their fire until too late. At 1145 the Sommocolonia force was ordered to withdraw but it was now surrounded. Unable to extricate itself, the force was directed to hold until dark. One officer and seventeen of the 70 men in Sommocolonia escaped as directed; the others became casualties.

German fire was now falling on the regimental and battalion command posts. The IV Corps commander, General Crittenberger, with members of his staff, arrived at the 370th's command post in the afternoon, discussed the situation with Colonel Sherman, approved steps taken by the regiment, and informed the regimental commander that the 8th Indian Division was on its way to take up defensive positions behind the 370th's lines. The 2d Battalion, 366th, was reinforced by Company F of the 370th, which was withdrawn from the west bank of the river when the main attack shifted to the 366th's sector.

The 370th, certain that its positions could be held, tried to obtain the services of a battalion of the 19th Indian Brigade, which had been motorized by the regiment on corps orders for use on the regimental right flank to prevent further encirclement. The 370th had under-

stood that the Indian troops were available for its use. Though released to the regiment by the 92d Division, the Indian battalion's commander insisted that he was still operating under his brigade; his brigade commander declined to allow his troops to be so used until directed to do so by IV Corps. The corps amended orders so that the battalion would remain under control of the 19th Indian Brigade with the mission of reinforcing the right flank of the 370th, but, with valuable time lost in jurisdictional argument, the Indian battalion could not be in position before dark.

In the meantime, Company G, 366th, on the left flank of the forces on the east bank of the Serchio, came under an intensive shelling, became disorganized, and left a gap between the river and Company F, 366th, on Barga ridge. By six in the evening, a German company was reported to be moving through this gap; by 1930 it was reported within 500 yards of the regimental command post, whereupon all command post personnel, including cooks, clerks, and staff officers, and a platoon of Company F, 370th, hastily organized under the regimental executive officer, moved out to meet the attack. Three tanks were attached and ordered to fire down the river road. The force found no trace of the enemy.

The withdrawal of Company G on the east side of the river left the right flank of the forces on the west side uncovered. The 370th ordered its 1st Battalion, on the west bank, to fall back to high ground by dawn, evacuating Gallicano in the process. The battalion of the 19th Indian Brigade and one company of the 21st Brigade arrived in the evening and were attached to the 370th,

---

[78] 598th FA Bn Jnl.

the battalion going into previously reconnoitered positions on the right flank, the company being directed to link the 92d Reconnaissance Troop in Coreglia with the 2d Battalion, 366th. By mistake the company took up positions to the rear of its intended position and therefore no link was provided. Bridges into Barga were ordered destroyed, but demolitions, later found to have been faulty, did not blow. On the west side of the river action was subsiding; Company G, 370th, in Calomini reoccupied its heavy weapons positions after pinning down the enemy with machine gun fire. The enemy retreated.

To prevent the enemy attack from developing into a further threat to Leghorn and the Fifth Army's supply lines, the 1st Armored Division moved from II Corps to the Lucca area on Fifth Army orders. The 34th Division's 135th Regimental Combat Team was attached to IV Corps and moved to the Viaréggio area. The 85th Division (less the 339th Regimental Combat Team) was already in the Lucca area. It was not yet certain that the Serchio valley attack would not develop in strength and that it would not be accompanied by a co-ordinated attack down the coast from La Spézia. Both II and IV Corps had then to readjust the positions of their divisions in line, interrupting the schedules of their units preparing for the attack on Bologna.

The next day, 27 December, the enemy resumed his attack. The 92d's forces were now assisted by a fighter-bomber group from the XII Tactical Air Force which bombed and strafed Gallicano, Vergemoli, and Sommocolonia. By 1000 German troops in white winter uniforms were in Tiglio; the 2d

Battalion, 370th, with a company of the 19th Indian Brigade attached, moved east to cover the threat. The 2d Battalion, 366th, which had taken up its new line south of Barga ridge during the night as ordered, but which lacked intrenching tools to dig in fully—none were available in the valley—now became disorganized and withdrew under enemy pressure. Between its command post at Pedona and Barga only two platoons of Company E remained. One of the battalion's 57-mm. guns, abandoned in Barga, was now turned against it by the enemy. Men from the battalion were straggling back along the roadway; all available officers of the 370th went out to gather them up and return them forward.

The battalion was practically destroyed. Men remaining were reorganized on bluffs in the rear of Pedona where the enemy advance halted. The west bank of the river remained quiet except for sporadic enemy fire.

At about 1300, Maj. Gen. Dudley Russell, commander of the 8th Indian Division, arrived at the 370th's command post, now moved to Osteria. He informed the regimental commander that he was taking command of the entire Serchio sector and directed that troops of the 370th Infantry and attachments, including the 2d Battalion, 366th, withdraw from the east bank through the lines of the Indian troops, then in position behind the combat team, and move to the west bank of the Serchio to reinforce the 1st Battalion, 370th. At 1530 orders were issued, and troops of the combat team moved through the lines of the 8th Indian Division and crossed to new positions on the west bank of the Serchio, where the 1st Battalion had been out of communication with the rest of the regiment as a result of the removal of its command post. The 8th Indian Division later decided to retain the 598th Field Artillery Battalion on its east side of the river. The field artillery, throughout, had stood firm in its positions.

The 370th Infantry formally went under operational control of the 8th Indian division on 29 December. Patrols probing forward found few Germans remaining in the area overrun by the enemy. Fighter-bombers continued to attack enemy positions in the Serchio valley. Barga was cleared by Indian troops on the 29th, Sommocolonia on the 30th, and the last day of the year patrols to Gallicano and Molazzana on the 370th's west bank and in Bebbio on the east bank met only feeble small arms resistance. But that the attack was over was not certain. On 30 December the combat elements of the 85th Division went on a two-hour alert in case either the 92d or the 8th Indian Division was again attacked.[79] By 1 January the lines were practically restored.

Winter Defense

Through January the 92d Division, like others on the Fifth Army front, continued an active defense of its lines. At the end of December, the 758th Tank Battalion, a Negro unit that had been associated with the 92d Division in its training at Fort Huachuca, arrived, and on 29 and 30 December its companies were attached to the 760th Tank Battalion. On 5 January the 135th Regimental Combat Team left the 92d Division's area to return to the 34th

Division. The 365th Regimental Combat Team returned to the 92d Division from the II Corps front the following day and went into positions in the Serchio valley sector. The valley reverted to the control of the 92d Division on 10 January following the departure of the 8th Indian Division, which went into army reserve at Pisa. General Wood took over operational control of this sector.

On 9 January Fifth Army announced the postponement of further large-scale offensives by the 15th Army Group. It directed its units to prepare for the resumption of offensive operations on or about 1 April. In the meantime, units of the army were to train and rest in preparation for a spring offensive. The IV Corps, holding its seventy-five-mile-long front with the 92d Division, the Brazilian Expeditionary Force, and the equivalent of one combat team (Task Force 45), was directed to plan a limited objective attack with its available troops to improve positions, especially in the 92d Division sector.[80] Throughout the period the Fifth Army's units were to continue to harass the enemy in order to prevent the withdrawal of German units from the IV Corps front.

The 92d Division's patrols at times reached the tops of hills in the Mount Strettoia ridge, and went into the heavily mined area north of the Cinquale Canal, sometimes taking prisoners and holding ground but as often returning without accomplishing their assigned tasks. Infantry weapons shoots, in which all infantry weapons were simultaneously fired into enemy positions at prearranged times, successfully harassed the enemy. Division engineers im-

---

[79] 85th Inf Div G–3 Opns Rpt, Dec 44.

[80] Fifth Army OI 2, 9 Jan 45.

365TH INFANTRYMEN PINNED DOWN BY ENEMY FIRE IN THE SERCHIO VALLEY *near Viareggio, 10 January 1945.*

proved roads and built a cableway from the Serchio valley up into the mountain positions of the 370th Infantry. Known as "Sherman's Skyway," the cable supplied troops located on nearly inaccessible mountain peaks and crags. The 92d Provisional Mule Pack Battalion, organized with Italian mule drivers, helped ease the mountain supply problem. This unit grew to a strength of 15 American enlisted men, 600 Italians, 372 mules, and 173 horses. The division's paper, *The Buffalo*, was published on its own presses throughout the combat period. Beginning 11 December

1944, the division G–4 Section issued *L's Bells*, a supply bulletin emphasizing conservation, improvisation, and the proper use of equipment. Units were rotated between the line and rest areas and given detailed command inspections, scheduled from February on, before their return to the line.

February Attack

In early February 1945, the 92d Division prepared for a co-ordinated limited attack, similar in objective to that originally planned for the end of December.

Designed to improve the division's positions, the attack was planned to seize the Strettoia hill mass, which dominated the coastal plain north of the Cinquale Canal, and to advance the Serchio valley positions to the Lama di Sotto ridge, overlooking the town of Castelnuova di Garfagnana two miles beyond.

The Serchio valley attack began on 4 February, with the 366th Infantry (less its 3d Battalion, then in the coastal sector between Highway 1 and the sea) on the west side of the river and the 365th Infantry on the east. Units of both regiments moved forward. The 366th occupied Gallicano and the 365th reached the foot of the Lama di Sotto ridge.

The main offensive began the next day. The 366th moved into Calomini and toward Vergemoli. Units of the 365th attacked toward Lama di Sotto, occupying the town of Lama, and taking Hill 906 and Mount Della Stella and holding them against strong enemy counterattacks. Advances continued the following day but, on the night of 7–8 February, the *2d Battalion, 286th Grenadier Regiment* of the *148th Division* counterattacked. The first counterattack, launched before dawn in company strength, was beaten off but another, in the evening, in which the entire German battalion participated, overran the town of Lama, took Mount Della Stella, and pushed the 365th's troops back 500 yards.

On the same night, the 92d Division's coastal attack got under way. The 370th Infantry moved up from reserve on the night of 7–8 February to attack the Strettoia hill mass between the 3d Battalion, 366th on the left and the 371st Infantry on the right. The 366th's 3d Battalion; Company C, 760th Tank Bat-

talion; a platoon of tank destroyers from the 701st Tank Destroyer Battalion; and the 27th Armored Field Artillery Battalion of the 1st Armored Division, operated as Task Force 1 under the command of the 92d's engineer officer. Task Force 1 was to advance along the beach from Forte dei Marmi to the Cinquale Canal, cross the canal at its mouth, and then turn inland toward Highway 1. The 370th Infantry, with its left flank on the highway and its right flank in the mountains, was to attack in column of battalions. Its leading battalion would take the first hill objective, the second would pass through to the next, and the third would pass through both to the third hill. The idea was to maintain momentum, to have troops available to counter enemy reaction, and to have the strength available to hold ground as seized, thus avoiding repetition of previous experiences of the regiment when ground, though taken, was not held by attacking troops. The left flank force on Highway 1, consisting of a company of light tanks, a company (−) of medium tanks, a platoon of tank destroyers, and attached engineers for clearing mines and filling obstacles, plus the 370th's especially trained volunteer "raider" unit made up of sixty men and three officers, was to make a diversionary attack. On the right of the 370th, the 371st was to attack in zone, keeping contact with the 370th on its left. The whole was to be a frontal assault across the entire twenty-odd miles of the 92d Division's zone.

At 0600 in the coastal mountains and a half hour later in the Sera valley zone of the 371st the main attack began. Gains were made all along the line. The 371st, finding its zone heavily mined, was slowed down and stopped after about 800 yards. The 370th's leading battalion sent companies up the first two heights by noon and began organizing these positions. Tactical planes of the 86th Fighter Squadron supported the attack by bombing and strafing enemy positions in the hills and at Punta Bianca. But by 1730, a mortar and artillery barrage, causing three officer as well as enlisted casualties, resulted in a disorganized withdrawal by the company on the farther hill just as a reinforcing company was coming up. The reinforcing company met the withdrawing troops head on. Some of its elements continued to their objective, while others joined the disorganized elements of the original company, whose remaining men were then ordered off the hill. A third company, ordered to join and extend the positions of the elements still on the hill, met the men ordered down, became disorganized themselves, and started withdrawing as well. The snowball grew and by night only one of the hills was still held. There, too, troops were confused and wavering.

On the coast, the 3d Battalion, 366th Infantry, moved out into the sea and across the mouth of the Cinquale Canal on medium tanks of the 760th Tank Battalion as planned. The battalion advanced 500 yards north of the canal and turned inland toward a coastal road paralleling Highway 1. Two tanks were disabled almost immediately by mines, blocking the movement of tanks following. Engineers could not bridge the canal and clear the mine fields because of heavy and accurate artillery fire trained on the area from coastal guns at Punta Bianca. Tanks attempting to break through the field to the road lost

four more vehicles to mines. Machine gun and mortar fire further slowed progress, but by evening the entire force had reached the north side of the canal and one company of the 1st Battalion, 370th Infantry, was crossing to reinforce the infantry. The 366th's 3d Battalion had suffered heavy casualties including Maj. Willis Polk, its commander.

On the following day, the attack resumed. The 370th and 371st made limited gains which were held against enemy counterattacks throughout the day. The 371st's high straggler losses prevented the following up of advantages gained the day before. The 370th Infantry spent the day trying to reorganize two of its battalions. It sent the remainder of its 1st Battalion on division orders to reinforce the task force in the coastal plain which, with the heights not taken, continued to suffer heavily from concentrated enemy fire from enemy positions in the hills as well as from the heavy artillery at Punta Bianca.

The beachhead now extended about 1,000 yards north and about 600 yards inland from the canal. Supporting tanks were forced to remain near the beach itself to avoid mines. Enemy counterattacks at dawn and midday were beaten off but a third, in the late evening, pushed the forces back. The remainder of the 1st Battalion, 370th Infantry, was ferried over the canal on tanks. Three light tanks of the 758th Tank Battalion fell into deep craters in the bed of the canal during the crossing and were drowned out. Supporting fighter-bombers were unable to fly because of the weather.

On the 10th, the forces in the Serchio valley, having held off counterattacks, moved to regain the ridge northeast of

Lama, attacking with two battalions of the 365th Infantry on the right and the 2d Battalion, 366th, on the left. Despite heavy enemy artillery fire, troops of the 365th's battalions re-entered Lama, captured fifty-five prisoners, and went onto parts of the ridge. But the Germans renewed their pressure and infiltrated into Lama before nightfall. Three additional enemy counterattacks the next day—one company withstood eight in all—were beaten off but a fourth caused some withdrawals.

In the heavily mined Strettoia-Sera sector, the attack also resumed on the 10th. The 3d Battalion, 371st Infantry, was now attached to the 370th Infantry. When units of the 370th again became disorganized, the 371st's troops attacked through them to seize one hill and part of another. Elements of the disorganized battalions of the 370th were rounded up during the day. By 1500 a detachment made up of men of two companies, organized and led by Lt. John M. Madison, moved up the first and then the second hill, capturing seven prisoners and two machine guns, and taking its place as left flank protection for the 3d Battalion, 371st. The 371st troops to the east contended with further counterattacks from the *285th Regiment, 148th Grenadier Division,* and elements of the supporting *Kesselring Machine Gun Battalion.*

On the coast, where Task Force 1 was still attempting to break through to Highway 1, elements on tanks moving toward strongpoints met intense automatic fire. An attack by a squad against the point from which the fire came forced the enemy to withdraw. Supplies, previously limited to small ball ammunition and some food, now came

in larger quantities, although the supply route, exposed to hostile observation and artillery fire, was still hazardous. All supplies had to be hand-carried across the canal in the absence of a bridge. The force across the Cinquale Canal had stood for forty-eight hours when an enemy attack pushed it back to a new defense line.

During the night of 10–11 February, with a heavy artillery barrage, much of it from Punta Bianca, falling on the new defense line across the canal, with a strong counterattack in progress against troops of the 371st and Lieutenant Madison's lone 370th detachment, with the 365th asking for the removal of the 2d Battalion, 366th, from its area where its own troops were holding off further counterattacks, and with the 2d and 3d Battalions of the 370th still not reorganized, General Almond decided to halt the attack.

By the morning of the 11th, troops north of the Cinquale Canal had withdrawn, according to orders received the night before, to points south of the canal. Crews burned the three stalled light tanks and destroyed the crippled medium tanks with gunfire from the remaining few operational tanks. The seventy-hour stand had cost the 760th Tank Battalion sixteen medium tanks; the 758th Tank Battalion had lost four light tanks; and the 27th Armored Field Artillery Battalion two medium tanks. The 3d Battalion, 366th Infantry, lost 2 officers and 31 enlisted men killed, 10 officers and 177 enlisted men wounded, and 48 enlisted men missing. It captured 74 prisoners.[81]

---

[81] Capt Raymond A. Diggs, Rpt of Opns of 3d Bn [366th], 8–11 Feb 45, 20 Feb 45, in Hist Rpt, 366th Inf, Feb 45.

The 371st, which was still holding approximately 800 yards in advance of its line of departure, north and west of Mount Cauala, was counterattacked frequently for the next three days by troops of the *285th Regiment*. During the attack, the 371st lost 4 officers and 17 men killed, among whom was the commander of its 3d Battalion, and 4 officers and 104 men wounded and missing. The 365th Infantry, also holding ground against counterattacks, had 1 officer and 52 enlisted men killed and 8 officers and 241 enlisted men wounded in this its first offensive action. The 370th, whose lines were generally the same as when the attack began, lost 15 officers, 3 of them killed in action, and 197 enlisted men, 13 of whom were killed in action, and took 55 prisoners, mainly from the *281st Regiment, 148th Grenadier Division.*

The result of the 92d Division's attack was that the lines of the division remained approximately the same. It had again lost a disproportionately high number of officers, including two battalion commanders and a number of its better small unit leaders. But the total impact was much greater. Neither the division nor its supervising headquarters now believed it capable of strong offensive action. Only the commander of the 365th felt that his unit had done well, but even he was not convinced of the potential value of his troops.[82]

Reorganized Again

In 15th Army Group's planning for the spring offensive, scheduled to start

in early April, it was important that the Fifth Army be able to maintain "an offensive attitude" on the west coast and be capable of capturing La Spézia "at the proper time." The early February attack by the 92d Division convinced the army group that the division, as organized, could not accomplish these tasks.

At the same time, with further reductions in 15th Army Group's strength, the 92d could not be replaced.[83] Continuing investigations of the more abortive actions in the division's career, now available in detail with recommendations for action, included recommendations that certain of its battalions, including one of the 370th's and two of the 366th's, not be used again for offensive action unless urgent military necessity required it.[84] Fifth Army planners determined, moreover, that without regard to efficiency the 92d Division, along with the Brazilian Expeditionary Force and the new Italian (Legnagno) Group, could only be considered defensive units because of the scarcity of replacements for them. For white American infantry units, enlisted and officer replacements would be available in quantities to meet estimated needs. Replacement stocks of American Negro troops would not be

---

[82] 1st Ind to CG 92d Inf Div, 21 Feb 45, on Ltr, CG 92d Inf Div to CO 365th Inf, 3 Feb 45, copy in WDSSP RG 113 (MTO) (app. II).

[83] Ltr, Hq 15th Army Gp to CG Fifth Army, 22 Feb 45, AG 370.2.

[84] The recommendation on the 370th's battalion was disapproved by General Crittenberger inasmuch as, since the events investigated, the battalion had continued in use in the absence of other troops. One of its companies had subsequently acquitted itself well at Calomini when under attack in the Serchio valley; later, after rest and retraining, it performed poorly in the February attack on the Strettoia hill mass. Ltr, Hq IV Corps, 9 Jan 45, on Investigation, IV Corps IG, 8 Jan 45; 1st Ind, Hq 92d Div to CG Fifth Army, 7 Feb 45, on Ltr, Hq Fifth Army to CG 92d Inf Div, 27 Jan 45; Ltrs, Hq 92d Inf Div, OTIG to CG 92d Div, 23 and 28 Feb 45. All in 92d Div Files.

adequate to maintain the 92d Division in any sustained offensive.[85] Neither on 1 March nor 1 April would sufficient Negro replacements be available to keep both the 92d Division and the 366th Infantry up to tables of organization levels for more than a few days in an offensive, although there should be enough replacements to maintain these units through limited operations of the type engaged in before February. If current shortages in the 366th Infantry were filled, not more than three to four hundred Negro infantry replacements all together would be on hand on 1 March.[86] As it developed, on 1 April there were 2,000 Negro replacements available for the entire 92d Division, in contrast with the 1,200 replacements available for the 442d Infantry alone.

General Marshall, in Italy with General Clark at the time of the February attack, made

. . . a dicker—a wager with Clark: that he could take those three regiments of the 92d Division and form one regiment out of them, take the one regiment made up of AAA troops who had already been converted to infantry and I would bring back the Japanese regiment, the 442d from Southern France. He was to put the Negroes in front and the Japs in reserve behind them. The Germans would think the Negro regiment was a weak spot, and then would hit the Japs. The Japanese regiment was spectacular. . . .[87]

The 15th Army Group and Fifth Army began to plan the reorganization of the 92d Division. Lt. Gen. Lucian K. Truscott, Jr., the Fifth Army commander since General Clark had assumed command of the 15th Army Group, orally directed the division to plan for a reorganization of this type.

The 92d Division proposed that the 366th be removed from the front lines and disposed of as higher headquarters might direct; that the 371st Infantry relieve the 366th and 365th in the Serchio valley; that the 473d [88] be attached to the 92d for immediate use in the coastal sector; that the 442d Infantry, upon arrival, be attached and held in a training area south of Viaréggio and that it be supplied with organizational equipment turned in by the 366th Infantry; that the 370th Infantry be relieved from front-line duty upon attachment of the 473d and that it be reorganized in a rear area by transferring into it the more outstanding officers and men from the other two organic regiments of the 92d Division; that the 365th Infantry be moved to an area south of Viaréggio to act as a

[85] Hq Fifth Army, Plans, P/114 Future Opns, 27 Feb 45, Plans 23 Jan–27 Feb 45.

[86] Memo, Fifth Army G–1 for G–3 Planning Com, 22 Feb 45, Plans 23 Jan–27 Feb 45.

[87] Interv with Gen Marshall, 25 Jul 49, by Dr. Sidney Mathews, Majs Roy Lamson and James D. T. Hamilton, and Dr. Howard Smyth, OCMH; Ltr, Gen Truscott to Gen Handy, 8 May 45, OPD Cld Trps—Corresp File. The German commander of the *148th Grenadier Division,* whose units were opposite the 92d Division during much of the

winter, comparing the two units after the war, said: "The 92d Division was a fairly good Division when units of said Division appeared in the field. The Negro soldiers, taken individually, was [sic] not courageous. As soon as the 92d Division suffered casualties, their attacks did not proceed any more. The 200th [100th Battalion, 442d] Japanese American Regiment was an excellent unit, absolutely trained for mountain warfare. They were feared by the Germans, since it was rumoured by the Germans that they were not in the habit of taking prisoners." Generalleutnant Otto Fretter-Pico, German Interrogations, III–7 Arno-Po Valley, OCMH.

[88] The 473d Infantry was activated in January 1945 from the antiaircraft units of Task Force 45. The name Task Force 45 was still used for a period thereafter to mask the conversion and to apply to the 365th Regimental Combat Team and to units of the 10th Mountain Division entering the line.

training replacement regiment for the division; and that all division elements (less the 371st, which was to continue to hold the Serchio River sector attached to Task Force 45) be moved west into a narrower sector. All of this was to be done without mentioning the transfer of units to and from the division. Attached units would wear Fifth Army insignia until a later date. When thoroughly assimilated, the two attached regiments would be assigned to the 92d Division.[89]

The reorganization of the 370th Infantry would be bound to affect the combat efficiency of the other two regiments, General Almond said in acknowledgement of concern about them expressed by Maj. Gen. Alfred M. Gruenther, Chief of Staff, 15th Army Group. But, General Almond declared, "upon studying the matter, I do not believe it will be as serious as Gruenther visualizes," for in the two remaining regiments many first sergeants, senior noncommissioned officers, and officers would remain undisturbed since all could not be utilized in the reorganized 370th. Moreover, General Almond observed:

Considering the characteristics which have manifested themselves in the infantry combat activities of this Division, I do not visualize that the combat reliability of the newly vitalized 370th Infantry will be greatly raised. I had no part in the decision in this matter, but you may rest assured that I and all those here concerned will do everything in our power to get the best available men into this regiment and to develop the material to its utmost capabilities. I do think that the divisional potentiality will be greatly increased by the

use of the 442d and 473d Infantry Regiments, and I do not visualize appreciable difficulties in their employment with our troops. I believe that the plan herewith recommended reduces the political publicity aspects of this readjustment to the minimum. In my opinion there need be no discussion of the changes in location of troop units. These are normal and have been a part of my plan for rotation of units since early November. There will necessarily be comment on changes in personnel assignments, especially key officers, but I propose to make this a gradual change over a period of three weeks.[90]

The plan, as outlined, was modified by General Truscott: The 473d would be attached to the 92d Division in its present Cutigliano sector on the division's right to avoid comment on its replacing Negro units in the coastal sector. The 365th Infantry would subsequently move to the east to the Cutigliano sector, gradually relieving the 473d and the 366th Infantry in the Serchio valley. The 365th's employment where enemy forces were scarce was considered preferable to its use as a replacement regiment for the 92d. The 371st Infantry would assemble for employment elsewhere under army control as soon as practicable. In the meantime the 92d Division's left flank could be held by the 371st and attached troops to mask the planned use of the 442d and 473d in attack. Such an attack would have to employ the reconstituted 370th, "at least in part," as well as supporting troops, General Truscott recommended, "otherwise, we are bound to occasion comment and draw unfavorable publicity, at least in the Negro press." The 366th could then be detached from the con-

---

[89] Ltr, Hq 92d Inf Div, Office CG to CG Fifth Army, 18 Feb 45, 92d Div Files.

[90] Ltr, Almond to Truscott, 18 Feb 45, cover letter to letter cited n. 89.

trol of the 92d Division. It could be converted into a general service engineer unit "without occasioning any comment whatever," for the need for engineers had been amply demonstrated by the conversion of antiaircraft units, the use of Italian engineers, and the employment of civilians. Possibly the designation "366th Infantry" might be preserved. By organizing two general service regiments all personnel of the 366th could be used, thereby avoiding returning any to replacement depots from which they might be routed back individually to the 92d Division.[91]

In approving the plan 15th Army Group directed that the reorganized 92d Division be prepared for a limited objective attack in the coastal sector at the earliest practicable date and that, for security reasons, no publicity at all be given to the reorganization of the division.[92]

By 1 March the exchange movements between the 365th Infantry and the 473d Infantry had been completed. The 366th Infantry had been withdrawn to the Viaréggio area where, in training, it was designated a reserve regiment—with the 92d Division asking that its final disposition be effected as soon as possible to avoid further speculation.[93] The 370th Infantry was in the midst of reorganization. Beginning 24 February and ending 17 March, 62 officers were transferred out and 70 transferred

in; 1,264 enlisted men and 1 warrant officer were transferred out and 1,358 enlisted men and 1 warrant officer were transferred in, giving the 370th a total strength of 139 officers, 3 warrant officers, and 2,800 enlisted men. During these changes, Truman Gibson, in response to General Clark's invitation and Assistant Secretary McCloy's recommendation, visited the division.

The Gibson Visit

Arriving on 26 February, Gibson went directly to General McNarney's Mediterranean theater headquarters where, after discussions of field commanders' recommendations that the 92d Division be taken out of the line, he was shown the latest reports on the division's career in combat. Some information on the 92d's reverses had already reached the United States through newspaper correspondents. The December counterattack was the main news of the day from Italy. The New York *Times'* Milton Bracker, after reporting the halting of the February attack, observed that the official report from 15th Army Group was "unusually detailed and candid." He concluded that the army group was trying to solve its public relations problem on the division "in view of the super-sensitivity of some Negro papers at home, which have unquestionably tended to over-emphasize the division's accomplishments. . . ." Negro correspondents in the theater as well as their white colleagues, Bracker continued, were sometimes embarrassed by their papers' handling of dispatches. "The general feeling here today was that the Fifteenth Army Group was taking no chances on

[91] Ltr, Hq Fifth Army to CG 15th Army Gp, 19 Feb 45, 92d Div Files. The designation "366th" was not available for an engineer unit, since it was already being used by the 366th Engineer Regiment.

[92] Ltr, Hq 15th Army Gp to CG Fifth Army, 22 Feb 45; Ltr, Hq Fifth Army to CG 92d Div, 23 Feb 45. Both in AG 370.2.

[93] Ltr, Hq 92d Div to CG Fifth Army, 3 Mar 45, AG 370.2.

the distortion or false play of the story of the Ninety-second's operation," he reported.[94]

Gibson, after visiting Generals Clark, Truscott, and Crittenberger, visited the 10th Mountain Division's sector, Leghorn, and Viaréggio, and the 92d Division with Maj. Gen. Otto L. Nelson, the deputy theater commander. He talked with about eight hundred officers, "hundreds" of enlisted men, and, then, with the higher commanders of the 92d Division. Reports shown to him, he observed to General McNarney, placed complete responsibility for the 92d's performance on Negro officers and enlisted men, failed to examine any underlying causes, made it seem that "everything possible had been done for the Division and yet, notwithstanding this, complete failure had resulted." He set out therefore to determine not only the facts but, where possible, the reasons behind these facts.'

Gibson felt that no extended discussion of certain facts was necessary. One of these was "melting away":

It is a fact that there have been many withdrawals by panic stricken Infantrymen. However, it is equally evident that the underlying reasons are quite generally unknown in the division. The blanket generalizations expressed by many, based on inherent racial difficulties, are contradicted by many acts of individual and group bravery. In the 365th Regiment, before large numbers of men were transferred to the 370th, certainly the generalizations do not hold.

Other facts which he regarded as similarly in no need of extended discussion

were: the "unsatisfactory promotion policy" for Negro officers, mentioned by both white and Negro officers, and the racial attitudes of the command, expressed by those white officers who commented upon it as one in which "any type of close association with Negro officers is discouraged." This policy was symbolized, Gibson felt, by the establishment of an officers' club in the attached white 894th Tank Destroyer Battalion whose rules of attendance by invitation only were intended to exclude Negro officers.[95]

Many officers of the 92d Division attributed the high rate of straggling to the deficiencies of replacements. Though the division, which pointed out that straggling had begun early in October before replacements began to arrive, disputed the accuracy of this view, Gibson suggested that the sufficiency of the retraining of replacements, most of them in low AGCT classes, could be at fault. An appeal to racial pride might be included in the battle indoctrination program of the 92d, since this had proved successful in the two artillery battalions commanded entirely by Negro officers. Promotions should be placed on a merit basis solely. Greater attention should be given to the "little things which always must be carefully considered in Negro units since they very often inflame attitudes that have been developed by conditions over which the Army has had no control."[96] Gibson found that the shifts of officers in the reorganization of the 370th Infantry, in which all of the Negro company commanders had been replaced by white

[94] Milton Bracker, "Americans Lose Ground in Italy," New York *Times*, February 14, 1945. See also "The Luckless 92nd," *Newsweek*, XXV (February 26, 1945), 34–35.

[95] Rpt, Civ Aide to Gen Nelson, 12 Mar 45, ASW files.
[96] *Ibid.*

officers, had been interpreted to mean that the division had no confidence in Negro officers; at the same time, no reclassification proceedings were pending.[97] He found little softening of the 92d Division's internal tensions as a result of its entry into combat. He observed:

It would appear that relatively isolated incidents have been permitted to develop which have resulted in having Negro officers and many of the enlisted men feel that the command is not interested in the success of the division and that decisions have been made so as to purposely reflect discredit on Negro officers and enlisted men. Nothing, of course, could be further from the truth; General Almond and all of his officers are intensely interested in turning out an efficient division from the material that was assigned them to work with. Unfortunately, the pattern of incidents overseas reflects closely the situation which General Davis and I found to exist at Fort Huachuca in 1943. . . .[98]

To this, Gibson reported, must be added the large percentage of Class IV and Class V AGCT men in the division —originally 90 percent[99]—most of whom came from civilian backgrounds where there was little opportunity for "an inculcation of pride in self or even love of country." Most of these men received their early military training under conditions which retarded the development of a combative spirit. "No similar situation has ever existed in any white unit," he said. With closer at-

tention to instilling a sense of pride and co-operation—with appeals to racial pride as pointed out in ASF Manual M–5, a project in which the 92d Division's Negro field grade officers would be happy to co-operate—the division might yet be brought to a fair efficiency. Correction of the promotion policy, the discriminatory policy symbolized by the separate officers' club, and a revision of the training schedule for replacements might help. The lesson of the 92d for the future employment of Negro troops lay in recognizing correctable deficiencies rather than in forming generalizations from the career of this particular unit, Gibson concluded.[100]

On 14 March Gibson said much the same in a press conference arranged in Rome by the public relations officer of the theater at the request of war correspondents in the area. "I agreed to participate in the conference only after being advised by officers of the theater command that there would be no objection to my engaging in a frank discussion of conditions as I observed them during my visit to the 92d Division," Gibson later told Assistant Secretary McCloy. "The fact that the reporters knew of the failure of the Division but not the underlying reasons therefor was largely responsible for my decision to talk to the reporters," he continued.[101] Gibson's views had to be taken "most seriously because he is the official representative of the War Department and is a Negro," the New York *Times'* correspondent reasoned. "He also is the first Government official to make a candid

---

[97] The division later explained that it had reclassified officers in August before proceeding overseas.

[98] *Ibid.*

[99] Division figures for March 1945 showed: Class I: 150 men, 1.1 percent; Class II: 1,361, 9.8 percent; Class III: 2,006, 14.5 percent; Class IV: 6,046, 43.7 percent; Class V, 4,085, 29.4 percent; illiterate: 202, 1.5 percent; total number of men: 13,850.

[100] Rpt, Civ Aide to Gen Nelson, 12 Mar 45.

[101] Memo, Civ Aide to SW for ASW, 23 Apr 45, OPD Cld Trps—Corresp, item 2.

publishable appraisal of the situation," this dispatch continued.[102]

But Gibson's "candid" appraisal of the situation and the heavy emphasis of the press on his figures on low literacy and on "melting away" brought down upon him the wrath of a powerful portion of the Negro press at home, already smarting under the *Times* correspondent's surmise that its emphasis on the 92d Division's accomplishments and its "supersensitivity" had brought forth the 15th Army Group's detailed account of the February attack and embarrassed their own correspondents. It did not matter that Gibson had said: "If the division proves anything, it does not prove that Negroes can't fight. There is no question in my mind about the courage of Negro officers or soldiers and any generalization on the basis of race is entirely unfounded"; nor that, after admitting that there had been "more or less panicky retreats, particularly at night when the attitude of some individual soldiers seemed to be 'I'm up here all alone; why in hell should I stay up here?'" he had added that "not all straggling and running has happened in the Ninety-second Division." Negro papers adopted a stand ranging from calls for Gibson's immediate resignation to a quiet plea that the Gibson analysis be looked at more closely for the profits which might be derived from it. "Somebody's Gotta Go!" the Chicago *Defender* editorialized: "Negroes have fought bravely and valiantly in all American wars without the generalship

of Truman K. Gibson Jr. . . . Yet no sooner does Truman Gibson Jr. come upon the scene, the Negro troops start 'melting away' in the face of the enemy. . . . It is enough our boys have to fight Nazis and Dixie race haters without having to face the venom and scorn of 'Uncle Toms.'"[103] To the Michigan *Chronicle,* the Gibson statement was "The Gibson Folly;" to Congressman Adam Powell's New York *People's Voice* it was a "smear" on the 92d.[104] To one columnist the Gibson report and the state of affairs in the 92d Division was nothing that should not have been expected in light of Army policies: "Gibson knows all these things and knew them when he stayed on and succeeded William H. Hastie when the latter could no longer stomach Army jimcrow policies. He has been an appeaser and one of the NOUVEAU Uncle Toms since taking office. He should resign at once."[105]

Two others of the larger papers, both with their own correspondents in Italy, took the interview more philosophically. "What Mr. Gibson said about the 92d is not new," the Baltimore *Afro-American* informed its readers. "Those newspapers having correspondents with the division had such reports long before Mr. Gibson went overseas. The men in the line are certainly in a better position to know the facts than are armchair warmers back home." "The term [melting away] may prick us painfully,"

[102] Milton Bracker, "Negro Courage Upheld in Inquiry," New York *Times,* March 15, 1945. See also John Chabot Smith, New York *Herald Tribune,* March 15, 1945; "A Behavior Pattern," *Newsweek,* XXV (March 26, 1945), 37.

[103] Editorial, "Somebody's Gotta Go!" Chicago *Defender,* March 24, 1945.
[104] Michigan *Chronicle,* March 24, 1945; New York *People's Voice,* March 24, 1945.
[105] George S. Schuyler in "Views and Reviews," Pittsburgh *Courier,* March 31, 1945. Schuyler's views were not necessarily those of the paper in which his column appeared.

the Norfolk *Journal and Guide* observed, "but Mr. Gibson might not have been as wrong as some would like to believe that he was. According to news reports, at times certain units of the division, or its attached units, have 'melted away' before enemy pressure just as units of white divisions have frequently 'melted away.' Situations arise on battlefields where it seems the only thing left to do, especially to inexperienced troops. Army news releases, however, carefully refrain from the use of such terms as 'melting away.' Instead, the official communique would read that 'our troops withdrew to lines they could better defend,' or something of that tactful nature." [106] The *Afro-American* had earlier given its advice to the soldiers and called for a new commander for the 92d Division: "[Gibson] didn't bite his tongue on his tour of the war front last week. . . . The *Afro* advises all soldiers overseas to fight the enemy and let us at home battle the segregation. It is plain that the 92d doesn't take our advice. It had no intention of fighting for General Almond, his lily-white staff and clubhouses. General Almond should be removed, quickly." [107]

Some of the Negro correspondents in Italy protested that the criticism of Gibson was unfair.[108] Gibson, back in Washington, observed, "It is hard for me to see how some people can, on the one hand, argue that segregation is wrong, and on the other hand, blindly defend the product of that segregation." [109]

The death of President Roosevelt on 12 April and the rapid end of the Italian and European campaigns thereafter obscured further developments in Truman Gibson's tour, which took him to the European theater before his return to Washington. But news of Gibson's interview and the reactions to it at home reached men of the 92d just in time for their spring attack.

SECOND WIND

Army group's planning called for the 92d Division to launch a diversionary attack four days before Fifth Army's main attack toward Bologna. This attack might draw in the enemy's reserves in the coastal area and, at the least, would occupy the attention of the German *148th Grenadier Division* opposite the 92d Division's lines. The 442d Regimental Combat Team would be ready by 1 April. The attack would be carried out shortly thereafter in time to permit some of the supporting troops

---

[106] Editorial, "Too Much Ado About the 92d Division Episode," Norfolk *Journal and Guide*, April 14, 1945.

[107] Baltimore *Afro-American*, Editorial, "Remove General Almond," March 24, 1945. For a similar opinion, see also Harry McAlpin, "Uncovering Washington," Philadelphia *Tribune*, March 31, 1945.

[108] "Collins George Cables From Rome: Reporters Term Criticism of Truman Gibson 'Unfair,' " Pittsburgh *Courier*, April 7, 1945.

[109] Washington *Afro-American*, April 15, 1945. See also "The Social Front: Armed Forces," *A Monthly Summary of Trends in Race Relations*, II (April, 1945), 253. This analytical journal, after pointing out that no other division had been singled out for such criticism as a division and that Gibson would have been wiser if he had released a prepared statement with no phrases which could be taken out of context, observed that "Negro newspapers have been almost unanimous in holding Jim Crow makes for less than maximum fighting efficiency, but many of them are embarrassed to find evidence of the correctness of their contention."

to be diverted, if necessary, to the main front in time for the attack there.[110]

By the time of the 92d Division's spring offensive, given the symbolic code name SECOND WIND, the 92d was no longer a Negro division. Its three infantry regiments now included one American white regiment converted from antiaircraft units (the 473d), the American-Japanese regiment (the 442d), and a practically new Negro regiment with racially mixed officers (the 370th). Its organic artillery and services remained Negro. Its attached troops, always racially mixed in the past, included one Negro (the 758th) and one white (the 760th) tank battalion, and one Negro (the 679th)[111] and one white (the 894th) tank destroyer battalion. Both of the white units had two of their companies employed elsewhere. Both of these units had had long association with the 92d Division. British and American artillery, air, and naval support would also be available. The division's 371st and 365th Infantry, scheduled to occupy the Serchio and Cutigliano sectors, would operate under IV Corps control while the 92d operated under Fifth Army control for the attack. The two detached regiments were expected to play only a holding and follow-up role in IV Corps' later attack.

The immediate objective for the 92d's diversionary attack was Massa. To avoid the heavy coastal guns at Punta Bianca, whose fires had largely

been responsible for smashing the February attempt to cross the flat, canal- and stream-crossed plain before Massa, the attack would be made to the east of the Mount Cauala–Mount Cerreta ridge along the line from Mount Folgorito through Mount Belvedere and on north to Mount Brugiana. By clearing these mountain ridges, the enemy on the Mount Strettoia hill mass might be driven out, forcing an evacuation of the heavily mined plain before Massa. The attack would then proceed to La Spézia.

The 442d Infantry, with the 599th and 329th Field Artillery Battalions, one platoon of the 894th Tank Destroyer Battalion, a company of the 84th Chemical Battalion's 4.2 mortars, and guns of the 758th Tank Battalion in support, was to drive up and around the mountains overlooking the coastal plain in order to bypass Massa and seize Mount Brugiana beyond. The 370th Infantry, with the 598th and 597th Field Artillery Battalions and guns of the 894th Tank Destroyer and 760th Tank Battalions in support, would push through the lower hills in column of battalions, branch off to the sea above the Cinquale Canal, and drive on through Massa to the Frigido River. In division reserve on the quiet right flank in the Serchio valley, the 473d Infantry was to be ready to support either the attack of the 370th or the 442d.

The offensive began at 0500 on 5 April with supporting air attacks on enemy positions and on the coastal guns at Punta Bianca and with supporting fires from British destroyers off the coast. After a ten-minute artillery barrage, the 370th on the left and 442d on the right moved out abreast. By 0645, the 370th's lead company had advanced

---

[110] *Fifth Army History,* vol. IX. The 442d was formally attached to the 92d Division on 3 April 1945 by radio message from IV Corps. Opns Rpt 442d RCT, Apr 45.

[111] The 679th Tank Destroyer Battalion arrived in Leghorn on 1–2 March 1945, moving into combat positions in support of the 92d Division on 17 March 1945. Hist 679th TD Bn.

more than two miles without significant opposition to reach the vicinity of its battalion's objective, Castle Aghinolfi, surmounting a hill that commanded the highway two miles south of Massa. This unit, Company C, assigned to spearhead the attack of the leading 1st Battalion, demonstrated what might have been done had all the regiment had equivalent leadership and determination.

Company C was completely reorganized as were all other units of the 370th. Its new commander, Capt. John F. Runyon, had one Negro and two white officers and 142 enlisted men—most of them strangers to each other—at his disposal. The company commander, personally believing that nothing was to be gained by another frontal attack on the hills before the 370th and knowing that men of the 370th and 371st "lived in mortal fear" of the hills with which they had had so many disastrous experiences, sought and got battalion permission to penetrate into the flanks of the enemy, take him by surprise, cut his communications, and, with reinforcements from the remainder of the 1st Battalion and the 2d Battalion, consolidate their position on the battalion's objective. He and his officers carefully prepared their men, telling them frankly that in the past efforts of the rifle companies of the 92d had not been satisfactory, that this time the men of Company C were going to do their job and bring credit to Negroes in combat. "The orientation had its effect," the company commander reported later. "The men knew they had a real job to do, and they seemed determined to make good. I was so gratified that I informed the Battalion Commander that I was convinced we would break through, and that he could plan his operation accordingly." [112]

The operation was so planned and, with two exceptions, went as planned. The exceptions were: (1) members of the attached platoon of the battalion headquarters company, supposed to clear mine fields, "conveniently" got lost; and (2) when the unit reached its objective reinforcements were never sent. The first of these, though disappointing, was not too serious, since the company had demolitions material and a few trained riflemen who took over. The second was disastrous for the company and, eventually, for the regiment.

Company C, with its third platoon deliberately placed in the lead position so that, since it had no officer leader, it might be better controlled, had gone out rapidly toward its objectives, so rapidly that when the company called for artillery fire, at first it had difficulty getting a response—no one on the other end could believe that the company had gone as far as it reported.

Once fire orders were acknowledged, the company got excellent artillery support enabling it to follow artillery fire as close as 100 yards without casualties. As Company C moved, cutting communications as it went, it caught the Germans by surprise, finding some at breakfast in their machine gun positions and observation posts. In one fire fight, with grenades hurled and rifles fired almost at point-blank, eight Germans, including two officers, were killed. As the now alerted enemy came out of dugouts and positions near Castle Aghinolfi, close hand-to-hand fighting ensued.

---

[112] Capt J. F. Runyon, Rpt on Co C, 370th Inf, Combined Opns 5–6 Apr 45, dated 12 Apr 45, copy in WDSSP RG 113 (MTO) (app. II) 1482.

The company's lines, with an exposed right flank, came under machine gun and mortar fire from the castle atop the hill. Reinforcements from the remainder of the units supposedly behind the lead company were called for. At first the regimental S–3 refused to accept the forward observer's word for the company's position; the 370th had not been changed enough by reorganization to believe that one of its units could move out as planned and once again Company C had to convince the regiment that it had moved as far as it had. Then the regimental executive officer informed Captain Runyon not to expect reinforcements for a long time, perhaps for days. The 370th was having trouble getting its other units to move and hold. In its 1st Battalion, the commanders of the other two rifle companies were both dead by midday and their companies were straggling away.[113] No reinforcements came to Company C. The unit was left near the castle alone.

By now, approximately 60 percent of Company C's advanced group, including one officer, were casualties. With his artillery radio, his only means of communication, fading out, Captain Runyon decided to pull back five hundred yards to prepare a defensive position. To the men remaining the order to withdraw was "a big disappointment . . . but we all knew that we were too small to hold out any longer in that exposed position." Though the withdrawal was orderly, once it began many men of the company reverted to general 370th practices. The loss of platoon commanders—two were

wounded, one in the advance group at Castle Aghinolfi and another with his platoon on one of the hills to the rear—resulted in disorganization, largely because men paid little attention to their platoon sergeants' orders. Despite pleas and orders, the men bunched up, making excellent targets. To one order to spread out, a private, paraphrasing an old spiritual, replied that he preferred to die with his friends rather than be killed alone. Enemy mortars gave the men no chance to prepare defensive positions. As soon as they started to dig in, mortars caught them again. Company C lost its radioman and its artillery observer, both of whom were wounded, and finally lost vital parts of its radio. Of the twenty-five enlisted men in the advance party when the withdrawal began, only eight who were not wounded or killed remained. Two of the four officers with the group were wounded. Captain Runyon now determined that there was but one thing to do: withdraw to his battalion lines.

The lone Negro officer in the company, 2d Lt. Vernon J. Baker, had personally destroyed an observation post, a well-camouflaged machine gun position, and a dugout during the morning, killing their eight German occupants. Baker now volunteered to cover the withdrawal of the first group, containing most of the walking wounded, and to remain to help remove the more severely wounded. Eight men and the wounded artillery observer stayed with him. Baker guarded the rear, leaving last after destroying equipment left by the killed and wounded. During the withdrawal, four different enemy machine gun crews were destroyed by the first group without loss to itself; Baker's

[113] Col R. G. Sherman, Narrative of Attack by 370th Inf, 5–8 Apr 45, WDSSP RG 113 (MTO) (app. II) 1482.

party, following, lost two men, one wounded by mortar fire and one, its only medic, killed by sniper fire. Pvt. James Thomas, the group's BAR man, located the sniper and killed him. The group encountered two machine gun nests bypassed during the morning attack. Baker, covered by Thomas' BAR, crawled up to the machine gun positions and destroyed them with hand grenades. The small party successfully evacuated its casualties to the battalion aid station.[114]

There were individual derelictions in Company C, particularly in the rear platoon that lost its leader early, causing Captain Runyon to observe that "The ideal situation with colored troops would be to have noncommissioned and commissioned officers who would never become casualties." Runyon later felt certain that if he could have had every man in Company C at the castle, he could have held. "I also feel quite certain," he added, "that if other companies of the 370th Infantry were imbued with the determination that those members of 'C' Company possessed, the high ground above Montignoso could have been taken without the assistance of the 473d Infantry." And, he continued, "Using hind sight, I am thoroughly convinced that if reinforcements had been sent up on the 5th of April and had been kept moving forward, the ground above Montignoso could have been taken with one quarter

of the casualties sustained by the 473d Infantry, and that the 370th Infantry could have done the job alone." [115]

While the remainder of the 370th was trying to get fully under way, the 442d Infantry to the right, with its 100th Battalion attacking frontally and its 3d Battalion making an enveloping move around Mount Folgorito from the east, took the ridge between Mount Folgorito and Mount Carchio on the first morning. One company of the 442d's 3d Battalion turned south to take Folgorito. Then, cutting the supply line of the enemy on Mount Cerreta where the 100th Battalion, approaching from the south, was methodically destroying bunkers one by one with bazookas and grenades, another company pushed northeast from the ridge to occupy Mount Carchio.

The 370th Infantry, after reorganizing during the night of 5–6 April, prepared to resume its attack at 0600 in column of battalions with its 2d Battalion leading. The enemy, having intercepted radio messages giving the time of the attack, laid down heavy mortar concentrations on the hills. The attack was postponed to 0800. Radio monitors then intercepted a message from a German who said that he was to be attacked at eight and that if given reinforcements he could hold. The 2d Battalion moved forward but a second mortar barrage stopped it again. Its companies began to move out of their positions. The 1st Battalion, ordered to move through the rapidly disintegrating 2d Battalion, replied that it could not move because of heavy mortar fire. The 3d Battalion was alerted for move-

---

[114] Runyon Rpt, 12 Apr 45; 1st Lt Vernon J. Baker, Narrative of Action of 5 Apr 45, dated 12 Jun 45. Copies of both in WDSSP RG 113 (MTO) (app. II). For his actions on this day and for leading a battalion advance through heavy mine fields and heavy fire the following night, Baker won the Distinguished Service Cross. GO 70, Hq Fifth Army, 10 Jun 45.

[115] Runyon Rpt, 12 Apr 45, WDSSP RG 113 (MTO) (app. II).

ment. A small enemy counterattack at noon was stopped and further attacks by the battalions of the 370th were postponed until the afternoon. At 1400 Company C was ordered to rejoin the 1st Battalion for another assault on the Strettoia hill mass. The 71 men remaining were called out and given instructions. Their company commander, Captain Runyon, sensing that they were temporarily licked and finding himself unable to muster the strength to rally their spirits, was not too sanguine about getting them out to their designated position on the same hill that they had successfully flanked the day before only to find themselves unsupported. As he, Lieutenant Baker, and a newly assigned company officer tried to work their men through a smoke screen across an open plain, Captain Runyon, relatively more successful than most commanders the unit had had since its first months in combat, was removed for temporary duty with the 473d Infantry. The men of Company C continued the move to join their battalion under another, newly assigned company commander. Each rifle company of the 1st Battalion, 370th, had now lost the commander with which it had begun the attack the day before, two by death and one by administrative action. By 1455, the first of the replacement commanders had also been killed.

The attacks were finally called off, for by late afternoon the 370th's battalion's strength was severely reduced by straggling and a battalion of the 473d Infantry was on the way. During the night, General Almond attached the 2d Battalion, 473d to the 370th. He directed this unit to make a predawn attack through the lines of the 2d Battalion,

370th, toward Castle Aghinolfi. The 1st Battalion, 370th, was ordered to move to the Serchio valley to begin the regiment's replacement of the 473d on the division's right flank. The 442d had by now gone on to secure Mount Belvedere overlooking Massa. The 371st, still on the coast, continued to support both regiments with its fire.

On the 7th, the 2d Battalion, 473d, moving through the 2d Battalion, 370th, bypassed Strettoia and seized strongpoints on the Strettoia hill mass, losing its battalion commander during the day. The 2d Battalion, 370th, cleared two more hills of the Strettoia ridge. A tank task force, consisting of elements of the 894th Tank Destroyer Battalion, the 760th Tank Battalion, and the 758th Tank Battalion, organized to support the attack and exploit the success of the 370th in the coastal zone, moved out along Highway 1. Late in the morning of the 8th—after the 3d Battalion, 370th, brought up from reserve, had failed to advance farther up Highway 1, where its Company K was dug in firmly below a hill near Porta, although the enemy had left the area during the night—control of the 370th's sector went to the 473d.

The 1st Battalion, 473d Infantry, moved to Highway 1, leaving the 370th Infantry (−) with the 3d Battalion, 473d, attached, in control of the Serchio valley sector. The 2d Battalion, 370th, moved to the Cinquale Canal, relieving the 2d Battalion, 371st Infantry, which then joined the rest of the 371st Infantry in its move to IV Corps. The 1st Battalion, 473d, with tanks of the 760th Battalion attached, attacked up Highway 1 and by noon of the 9th was on the outskirts of Massa. The 758th and 760th Tank Battalions reached the center of the city before being forced to withdraw temporarily. Despite naval and aerial attacks on the coastal guns at Punta Bianca, accurate and heavy fire continued to fall in the coastal sector through which the tank task force was operating. Approximately ten vehicles were lost during the action.

The 442d continued to move through the mountains on the right, its 2d Battalion reaching the Frigido River. When Massa was outflanked from the hills on the east, the enemy evacuated the town. The 473d Infantry occupied it on the morning of the 10th, crossing the Frigido River after dark. Tanks of the tank task force, attempting to cross the river on the 10th and 11th, were driven back; on the 12th, they succeeded in crossing.

On the 11th, the 92d Division gave responsibility for the coastal plain to the 758th Tank Battalion (−), reinforced by one company of the 370th Infantry and the antitank company of the 473d. The 758th, now the only Negro unit responsible for a sector in the 92d's zone of advance, moved forward three miles after the withdrawing enemy on the 12th, reaching Carrione Creek where strong resistance forced a temporary halt. The 442d, advancing through nearly impassable mountain terrain, had reached Carrara and occupied it on the morning of 11 April.

The units of the 92d now came up against the next of the enemy's strong defense lines, running behind Carrione Creek. The Germans had begun to commit their available reserves. A company each of the *1048th Engineer Battalion* and the *907th Fortress Battalion* were already committed and virtually destroyed. On the 14th, a battalion

758TH TANK BATTALION *75-mm. assault guns supporting the advance of the 442d Infantry up Mount Belvedere, 8 April 1945.*

of the *90th Panzer Division*, one of the two reserve divisions available to the *Fourteenth Army*, was committed. From the 14th to the 19th the advance of the 92d was slowed by the stiffening resistance of the reinforced enemy, but the attack had achieved its purpose. Its primary objectives had been secured, the enemy on its front had been badly mauled, and all reserves the enemy dared use had been committed just in time to prevent their use against the main army attack beginning on 14 April.

On the coast the guns from Punta Bianca were still covering the 92d's area with unceasingly effective fire, especially on Massa and Carrara.

These guns, which had survived aerial and naval bombardment, were now faced by the artillery of the 92d Division and attached units as soon as they came within range. All thirty-six of the 76-mm. guns of the 679th Tank Destroyer Battalion were assigned to neutralize the coastal guns. When an enemy gun fired, the tank destroyers, operating on prearranged signals to already laid guns, answered with 60 to 180 rounds, the first landing within 45 seconds after forward observers called for it. In six days the tank destroyers fired 11,066 rounds on the coastal guns; an 8-inch howitzer was brought up to aid them. By the 19th the guns on the east side of the point had stopped firing, but fire continued from those on the west side. Close-range fire destroyed several of these guns in the next twenty-four hours, but by this time the enemy was ready to withdraw rapidly, for his coastal positions were threatened by the breakthrough of IV Corps west of Bologna.

On the IV Corps front, on the right of the 92d Division, the 365th Infantry in the Cutigliano sector and the 371st Infantry, which on 9 April had taken over part of the Brazilian sector, thinly held the left half of the IV Corps' line. These units, now under corps control, were expected to continue patrolling and to harass the enemy with artillery fire while the divisions to their right made the main thrust into the Po Valley. The 371st patrolled in company strength, its units engaging in successful fire fights on 14 April and reaching the Leo River on 16 April, where their reconnaissance patrols crossed the river and hit the enemy main line of resistance. Because there was no advantage in consolidating in low ground, the

371st ordered its companies in. The regimental commander, Col. James Notestein, now fully realized something that he and the whole command of the division had sensed all along but could not demonstrate: that missions are best performed when units know what the missions are and believe that they can be accomplished. To General Almond he wrote informally:

1. In conjunction with IV Corps attack yesterday, we are given the mission of sending three combat patrols (Reinf Co, each) to: (1) kill Germans, (2) capture PW's, and (3) uncover enemy positions. As you will see from Sussell's report, attached, we finally managed to accomplish a mission. All three companies reached what appears to be the Boche MLR north of Leo River. They broke thru the outpost all along the line. "L" Co moved fast enough to overrun a Plat CP, capturing one NCO in his underwear.

2. For the first time our troops maneuvered on *level* ground, in superior numbers, with superior supporting fires. While all companies had stragglers after the Co's were hit by artillery and mortar concentrations, each outfit came back with the idea that they are good and that the Tedeschi are not invincible. You have told them these same things for six months, but this is the first time they have believed it. I don't mean to convey the idea that these Co's now can maneuver like your 1st Bn, 442, but we didn't disgrace the Division.

3. I hope this reaches you on the way into La Spezia and that your losses will not be too great.[116]

Patrols continued forward from both the 365th Infantry and the 371st Infantry. The 371st took over more of the Brazilian Expeditionary Force's sector on 18 April as the Brazilians moved out on the right. Against little resistance,

---

[116] Personal Ltr, Notestein to Almond, 15 Apr 45, item 16, T46–73.

and most of that from rear guard detachments and bypassed elements of the withdrawing enemy, both regiments moved forward. On 25 and 26 April, they began guarding prisoners of war, with the 371st's 1st Battalion (−) moving to Bologna on 27 April to relieve the Italian Legnano Group.

In the Serchio valley, the 370th Infantry (−), with the 3d Battalion, 473d Infantry, attached until 20 April, and with the support of the 597th Field Artillery Battalion, tanks, and tank destroyers made local advances in its zone, exerting pressure on the withdrawing enemy and co-ordinating with the operations of the 473d Infantry and the 442d Infantry on the coast. On 19 April, the regiment began a wide enveloping action through the mountains to meet the 442d at Aulla and to block further movement of enemy troops in an east-west direction, thus preventing the formation of another German line. On the morning of 20 April troops of the 370th entered Castelnuovo di Garfagnana and continued the pursuit northwest along the main road to Aulla. Demolished bridges and road craters made the movement of vehicles and supplies difficult. All advances were on foot. With wire communication next to impossible, radio and runners were relied on completely.

Late at night on 22 April the 3d Battalion, 370th, completed a continuous advance of over 30 hours over terrain so rough that mules could not follow much of the time. It occupied Casola after a fire fight in which eleven prisoners were taken. Supply lines were now so extended that food and ammunition began to run short.

The 1st Battalion continued to ad-vance along the main road to Fivizzano; mortar fire at Gragnola preceded a fire fight resulting in enemy casualties and fifteen prisoners. The regiment continued forward, seizing the high ground commanding Aulla and contacting the 442d Infantry then approaching the city. The advance by now was being hindered not only by abandoned and destroyed matériel, dead animals and dead enemy soldiers, blown bridges and cratered roads, but also by enemy deserters who created a problem in prisoner evacuation, most of which had to be done on foot. Patrols moving out over the road net now opening up beyond the wilder mountains reported little or no resistance.

Elements of the 92d Division on the west coast, now under temporary control of 15th Army Group, entered La Spézia on the 24th. The 473d entered Genoa on the morning of the 27th, riding through town on still operating streetcars. The last enemy pockets of resistance to surrender at Genoa were the harbor defense guns high up on Mount Maro. On the moonless, rainy night of the 27th, in a blackout, the 679th Tank Destroyer Battalion's Company A moved its twelve guns up steep streets barely wide enough for a half-track. When half-tracks failed to make the final turn, the guns were man-handled into position, where by daylight they were laid for direct fire at 400 yards on the enemy concrete emplacement openings where two 381-mm., three 152-mm., and four 90-mm. guns looked down on the city. The enemy gun tubes could not be depressed to fire on the 679th's guns. At 1430 on 28 April, with Company A's guns in position and laid and with infantry to his rear, the enemy on Mount Maro surrendered.

On 30 April, the 442d Infantry entered Turin. The 370th Infantry, after moving one battalion to the coast at Chiávari on 27 April, continued to probe to the northeast toward Cisa Pass through which the German *148th Division* and the *Italia Division* had been reported moving in an effort to escape capture. Neither the 370th nor any other unit of the 92d Division was to have the satisfaction of capturing these divisions which had opposed them for so long. They surrendered on the 29th to General Mascarenhas and the Brazilians.

New Winds Blowing

The 92d Division's war was now over. After the Italian cease-fire on 2 May the detached regiments were returned to division control. The 366th Infantry remained in training as the 224th and the 226th Engineer General Service Regiments, both marked for redeployment to the Pacific. The combat careers of both the 92d and the 366th became major ingredients in considerations for the future. Men and officers of both units had dimming views of both the future and the past. One private wrote to *Stars and Stripes* that the men of the 92d Division had been wondering and arguing among themselves about why the 473d and 442d Infantry had displaced the division's own regiments. Views and opinions differed, he said, "Yet all of us agree that it was a profound shock to us." For himself, he wanted to know "whether this was to prove that Negroes can't fight together, without the so-called inducement of a white regiment to sting us into activity;

or was it to prove (after certain unfortunate setbacks, like the setback in the Serchio Valley, where we had one regiment, yet the division was ridiculed), that we were too illiterate to fight; or that Mr. Truman Gibson's illiterate Negroes were afraid of the big bad Germans, and that we would run everytime we saw one of the master race." Whatever was proved, he continued, the men of the 92d were sure that they were not sharing in the glory of the defeat of the Germans in Italy. "Thank God the men who died did not know this. We are sorry we did not live up to the expectations of the newspapers and magazines (such as News Week) as a political division. We will try to do better next time." [117]

A senior officer, Lt. Col. Marcus H. Ray, commander of the 600th Field Artillery Battalion, one of the two artillery battalions with all-Negro officers, wrote to Truman Gibson, "now that the sound and fury raised by your press release in Rome has simmered down to an occasional bubble." He gave his view of the 92d Division's career, a reaction discernible in few of the reports of the division but one which was shared, he felt, by the "responsible officers" of his command:

Your findings on the state and training and morale of the Division were accurate but enough space was not given to the causes therefor. I realize that your release suffered "clever" editing. It is my considered opinion that the 92d, at the best, was doomed to a mediocre performance of combat duties from its very inception. The undercurrent of racial antipathies, mistrusts and preconceived prejudices made for an unhealthy beginning. The failure

---

[117] Ltr, Pvt Robert R. Thompson, Inf, in "Mail Call," *Stars and Stripes* (Italy), June 8, 1945.

to promote worthwhile Negroes and the giving of preferred assignments to white officers made for logical resentments. I do not believe that enough thought was given to the selection of white officers to serve with the 92d and further, that the common American error was made of assuming that Southern white men understand Negroes. Mixed units as we have known them have been a dismal failure. In white officered units, those men who fit into the Southern pattern are pushed and promoted regardless of capabilities and those Negroes who exhibit the manliness, self-reliance, and self-respect which are the "sine qua non" in white units, are humiliated and discouraged. In the two Artillery Battalions of the Division, officered by Negroes, it was necessary to reduce large numbers of Noncommissioned officers because they held rank only because they fitted the "pattern." Their subordinates resented and disrespected them—justly so. I was astounded by the willingness of the white officers who preceded us to place their own lives in a hazardous position in order to have tractable Negroes around them.

In the main, I don't believe the junior officers guilty of faulty judgment or responsible for tactical failures. Soldiers do as ordered but when plans sent to them for execution from higher headquarters are incomplete, inaccurate, and unintelligible, there is inevitable confusion. The method of selection and the thoroughness of the training in the Officer Candiate Schools weeded out the unfit and the unintelligent with but rare exceptions but the polishing of the officer after graduation was the duty of his senior officers. In mixed units, this, manifestly, has been impossible. I believe that the young Negro officer represents the best we have to offer and under proper, sympathetic and capable leadership would have developed and performed equally with any other racial group. Therefore, I feel that those who performed in a superior manner and those who died in the proper performance of their assigned duties are our men of the decade and all honor should be paid them. They were Americans before all else. Racially, we have

been the victims of an unfortunate chain of circumstances backgrounded by the unchanged American attitude as regards the proper "place" of the Negro. . . . Perhaps, from your vantage point, where you see the worldwide picture, it is not as dismal as my rather restricted view based mainly on the 92d Division. I do not believe the 92d a complete failure as a combat unit but when I think of what it might have been, I am heart-sick. . . .[118]

In strength the 92d Division represented less than 2 percent of Negro troops in the Army. There was a broader "world-wide picture." Generalizations from the 92d's career were therefore necessarily dangerous, especially when these generalizations were not subjected to close analysis. Men of other Negro units thought it unfair to judge the capabilities of Negro troops by this one admittedly important but also hardly representative unit. "In view of the fact that this unit's battle record is so superior to the units you have described," the commander of the 761st Tank Battalion wrote to Truman Gibson on behalf of members of his unit, "it is felt some publicity should be given the men of this battalion for their gallant fighting." [119] Troops in armored, tank destroyer, antiaircraft, engineer, quartermaster, and port battalions could

[118] Personal Ltr, Ray to Gibson, 14 May 45, WDGAP/291.2. After the war Ray succeeded Gibson as Civilian Aide in November 1945.

[119] Ltr, CO 761st Tank Bn (Lt Col Paul L. Bates) to Gibson, through channels, 13 Apr 45. This letter, which went on to outline the career of the 761st Tank Battalion, and the letter from Colonel Ray, referred to above, were personally handed to Maj. Gen. Stephen G. Henry, G–1, by Gibson, and forwarded to major agencies of the War Department by General Henry for information on a subject of "timely importance." Memo, G–1 for AGF, AAF, ASF, G–3, OPD, 5 Jun 45, inclosing copies of letters, WDGAP/291.2.

never have expected as much attention as that given to infantry divisions, but they were hardly desirous that the "proofs" offered from the 92d Division's experience should apply to them as well. They were afraid, from past experience, that they might be so applied as the division, and, later, army and theater boards, went to work on formal reports requested by the War Department.

CHAPTER XX

Service Units Around the World

Whether they were of combat, combat support, or service types, the smaller Negro units were easier for the Army to ship and to employ overseas than large units. Many of the smaller units were formally converted to other types in the theaters. Many were employed on tasks for which they had not been specifically trained. Some were at times relatively unemployed just as they had been before shipment. But for the most part they were used, generally in conjunction with larger or similar types of white units, on tasks for which their training and organization fitted them.

In greatest demand and most consistently used were Negro engineer and quartermaster units. They were also among the first to be called for and shipped overseas. There were times when special circumstances of geography, mission, readiness status, or personal preference caused delays and hesitancy in the employment of even these units. But usually they could be placed on shipment lists from the beginning, with reasonable assurance of acceptance and use at their destinations. Their shipment, especially in the deployment of American troops to the South Pacific, to Iran, and to India in early 1942, was dictated by a necessity with which other considerations, of such great importance in later months of that year, did not at first interfere. Although the first units generally had less training than those who followed they were often of greater value than similar units shipped later to fill less urgent needs.

A host of small units were employed in every theater and in almost every type of operation, forward and rear. Negro engineers were ahead of other ground and air troops in the early days at Port Moresby in New Guinea. They went in as soon as possible after the successive invasions across the broad Pacific, pushing out ahead of other ground troops at times to construct the airfields required for the planes that kept the ever-accelerating Pacific timetable on schedule. On bulldozers, in trucks, and on foot they cut their way through the frigid wilds of Canada and Alaska and through the jungles of Burma, building and improving roads for military transport. They provided a garrison for Liberia and protection for the American-built Roberts Field there. They provided antiaircraft defenses for Trinidad in the Caribbean and for the Pacific islands on the route to Australia and, later, on the route to the Philippines. Negro port and amphibious truck companies were attached to Army and Marine divisions and corps for the invasions of the Pacific islands, notably Saipan, Tinian, Iwo Jima, and Okinawa. Port companies manned great ports around the world, and sometimes places that were never ports before. Negro engineer, chemical, and quartermaster troops landed at Salerno and Anzio. A Negro barrage balloon unit, the only American unit of its type present, unleashed its captive balloons to protect the cross-Channel invasion fleet and the troops on the Normandy beaches from low-flying aircraft, while amphibious truck, quartermaster service, and ordnance ammunition companies there began jobs which were to last through V–E Day. Negro quartermaster truck and transport companies were more or less permanently attached to infantry and armored divisions fighting across Europe, many of them, through their long attachments, becoming almost integral parts of the divisions to which they were attached, some of them joining in the fighting as riflemen when needed. Medical ambulance companies attached to divisions and hospitals evacuated wounded to the rear and medical sanitary companies loaded evacuated patients aboard ship for return to hospitals in England. Companies of ordnance ammunition battalions stocked and dispensed ammunition along the routes of the armies. Smoke generator companies set their smoke pots and generators just behind front lines at Anzio and along European rivers, sometimes, as along the Garigliano, mingling their smoke positions with infantry outposts. In rear areas, at depots, bases, and ports, service units handled the supplies required to support the armies and the services, while quartermaster truckers sped them forward over the Red Ball Express route in Europe, the Motor Transport System in Iran, the Stilwell

Road in Burma, and numberless coral roads in the Pacific. Along these roads, the engineers quarried surfacing materials, built and restored bridges, moved tons of earth, constructed warehouses, depots, and living quarters, and kept the roads open for troop and supply movements. Two hospitals were manned fully and three partially by Negroes in Burma, Liberia, the South Pacific, and England. A Negro WAC unit cleared up a gigantic backlog of undelivered mail in Europe. Combat support units went into combat either as members of groups or as separate battalions assigned to corps and attached to divisions, particularly in Europe.

These were all normal functions for units of their types. But the variety in the employment of Negro troops so far outstripped anything seen in World War I or contemplated at the beginning of World War II that this fact alone is of prime significance in any account of the use of Negro troops in World War II. The sheer quantity of work performed by Negro units, often operating on round-the-clock schedules, was tremendous. None of it was accomplished without travail, for the soldiers and their officers brought with them all the problems accumulated in their training periods and acquired some new ones by virtue of their new surroundings and, in some cases, their new duties. Only in exceptional cases did their movement overseas change markedly either the will or the skill of commanders or commanded.

The use of such units was so widespread that a detailed narrative of their contributions would require a separate volume. Most small units, their designations and functions changed as the need arose, must therefore remain anonymous in this account. The ease of shipment of these units was in direct relation to the need for them; their assignment to duty was equally a function of need, though need was at times created on the spot as a headquarters found more and more duties that could be attended to if soldiers were forthcoming to perform them. The quality of their training played a less important role in their shipment, although individual unit reputations for performance in the field were directly related to the continuing use of skills acquired in training, especially in the cases of combat support and the more technical of the service units. Units shipped "in current status of training," a phrase used generally to denote a unit that had not completed its training but which was nevertheless shipped because it was needed or because it would complete its training at its destination, often performed as well as better trained units which went out to areas that had relatively less need for them. A relatively untrained unit, therefore, was often as successfully employed when faced with a visible mission and a demonstrated need for its services as a well-trained unit employed in a routine manner. Certain units, like the engineer dump truck companies, always in demand, always used, and almost always Negro, were considered of great value by the using commands and were therefore well and fully employed; others, like chemical smoke generator companies, also with a heavy Negro representation, were less generally used for their primary missions, often being put to guarding warehouses and prisoners and operating depots. When formally converted to other missions, units developed high efficiency in their new tasks when they were convinced that these tasks were of more obvious and immediate value than their former assignments. Such was the case, for example, in two quartermaster service companies whose personnel came from disbanded units. These men learned rapidly, gaining "in efficiency until approximately seventy per cent were performing technical duties and only thirty per cent were performing general service duties." [1]

Because their number and variety precludes a full-length discussion, units examined here have been chosen to illustrate the varieties of work performed by the 4,000-odd small Negro units in World War II. The soldiers in these units acquired during the war years a wider variety of technical experience than most of them would have gained in a greater number of years of civilian life. Men who had had little chance to work as interstate truckers, as heavy construction workers, and as telephone repairmen were now carrying tons of matériel in heavy trucks and trailers over strange roads, operating bulldozers and cranes in exotic ports, and stringing wire and setting up communications systems in jungles and in the war-devastated areas of western Europe. When placed against the training backgrounds of these units and their men, the achievements of both the Army and Negro soldiers in so extensive an employment cannot be lightly dismissed.

---

[1] Maj. John F. Saxon QMC, and Maj. Roy D. Geiser, QMC, "Service Units in New Caledonia," *The Quartermaster Review*, XXIV (March–April 1945)

The First Units Out

In Task Force 6814, the first large task force to be shipped to the Pacific after Pearl Harbor, were the 810th and 811th Engineer Aviation Battalions. The 811th was a new unit. Its first men arrived at Langley Field, Virginia, on 7 December 1941. It was little more than a month old when the task force departed on 23 January 1942—bound for Australia, and for later transshipment to New Caledonia should conditions met in Australia permit. The 810th, activated on 26 June 1941 at MacDill Field, Florida,[2] was a veteran unit by then current standards. The two units illustrate the differences between organizations whose relative readiness could be overlooked when need was the decisive factor in their employment. Their long careers overseas, high spots and doldrums, also illustrate the employment of Negro aviation engineers on the one hand and of Negro service units in general on the other.

The 810th, with a cadre from the 41st Engineers and four Regular officers, had a well-spent if brief six months of training before leaving the New York Port of Embarkation. Its green men learned to operate heavy equipment by building roads, bridges, and fortifications, and by doing general construction work at their home station and at other new and expanding posts.

The companies of the 810th were activated separately and therefore trained and worked at different levels. Company A, in August 1941, built a practice bomb target at Mullett Key, a small island at the entrance to Tampa

[2] GO 1, par. 1, Air Base Hq, MacDill Fld, Fla., 1942.

Bay, about twenty miles from MacDill by water. With its personnel and its four trucks, one compressor, two D-4 tractors, and one command car, it went out to the island, site of a ruined fort used during the Spanish-American War, and proceeded to clean up the flat, mosquito-ridden, swampy key. The men cleared the island of palmetto trees and brush, losing track of the number of rattlesnakes they killed though they preserved the skins to make shoes and belts for their wives and sweethearts. They repaired the island's long unused rain-catching equipment to provide a water supply. They acquired an old sixty-foot tug from the district engineer office, patched and painted it up, and operated it with their own crew, carrying supplies and men back and forth.

Other companies took over the Mullett Key project later. The men of these units acquired from their training on this subtropical island a conditioning and resourcefulness that was to stand them in good stead sooner than was then expected. At MacDill, one company participated in a local maneuver, testing theories of air base defense. Another constructed bombing targets and a drainage system at Morrison Field, Florida, and taxiways at the Charleston, South Carolina, airport. Still another, three weeks after activation, went to Lake Charles to take part in the Louisiana Maneuvers of 1941, working with a battalion of the 21st Engineer Aviation Regiment, a unit experimenting with new materials for airfield construction. This company later moved to Greenville, South Carolina, where it constructed camouflaged revetments for observation planes, and to Wilmington,

North Carolina, repeating the job for fighter planes and building asphalt connecting taxiways to the revetments. With the help of Tampa citizens, elements still at MacDill Field provided their own recreation by taking an old post theater and converting it into a service club.

The companies at Wilmington and Charleston moved to Indiantown Gap, Pennsylvania, in January 1942 to prepare for overseas movement. Headquarters Company and Company A, 810th Engineer Aviation Battalion, still at MacDill, left on New Year's Day for Savannah where, in a tented area, in cold rain and red mud, they built a complete taxiway and hardstandings for the air base. Despite the difficulties of living and working at the new base, the tense atmosphere of the month following Pearl Harbor and the obvious necessity of the work kept the unit's morale high.[3] The 810th as a whole was about as well trained in its six months as could be expected.

With one week's warning orders, the companies assembled at the New York Port of Embarkation. They discovered that they were "pretty much on our own" in making preparations, for no standard procedure had yet been worked out for moving such a unit. Seventy flatcars of automotive and heavy construction equipment were made ready and shipped to the west coast. At New York, the unit bivouacked on the SS *America,* then being converted to a troop ship in the Brooklyn Navy Yard. After two days of loading and unloading ships, it boarded the USAT *J. W. McAndrew,* which, in a convoy of six other

ships bearing the units of Task Force 6814, some of which were later to become famous as the Americal Division, departed New York for Australia on 23 January. On shipboard the 810th was joined by the relatively untrained 811th, which had spent its one month of service becoming acquainted with the experimental mats and equipment of the 21st Engineers in unusually heavy snow at Langley Field.[4]

The convoy arrived in Melbourne on 26 February, landing the next day. Only a few small forces of American troops had been through Melbourne earlier. The Australians enthusiastically greeted the appearance of the thousands of task force troops. The 810th loaded aboard a narrow-gauge railway the same day, proceeding to Camp Darley. At every street and road crossing crowds of Australian men, women, and children gathered and gave the troops aboard the train cheers of welcome. During the week in Australia, a detachment of the 810th Battalion kept busy at Melbourne docks, unloading ships and reloading them with ordnance supplies for immediate use. The remainder of the battalion went through vigorous cross-country marches to loosen ship-bound muscles. The 810th and 811th reloaded on 7 March. Aboard the USAT *Erickson,* which missed its convoy because of engine trouble, they proceeded to New Caledonia alone under the escort of a converted Allied merchantman.

In Nouméa the units, both of which were later attached to the Americal Division, went to work before unloading. Companies A, B, and C of the

---

[3] Hist 810th Engr Avn Bn From Activation to 31 Dec 43 (Lt Kenneth Z. Crumrine), AF Archives.

[4] Hist 811th Avn Bn (1st Lt Charles H. Schafer), AF Archives.

810th moved ashore to help unload ships of the task force already tied up in Nouméa harbor; the Headquarters Company remained aboard the *Erickson* in mid-channel with a French ship, the *Polynesian,* tied up alongside. The men of the 810th's company and the French crew of the *Polynesian* worked together unloading the *Erickson.* Despite the language barrier, the two crews worked well together, unloading the ship in four days instead of the estimated eight, for which the 810th company received a letter of commendation from the skipper of the *Erickson.* The 811th unloaded and proceeded thirty miles up the coast to Bouloupan to work on roads.

A part of the 810th's heavy supplies had arrived from San Francisco. When sufficient supplies had been gathered for the battalion to operate independently, it moved out to the Nepoui peninsula, 245 kilometers away. It took several weeks to move equipment up over roads and bridges never intended for heavy vehicles, but during April the battalion was ready to take over the construction of Plaine des Gaiacs airport from the civilian construction company which had started the job. This airport, to be surfaced with iron ore hauled in by truck from an ore pit seven miles away, was planned as a bomber base. It was understood by the men of the 810th that they were engaged in a race to finish their task before the American invasion of the southern Solomons, then being discussed by the Joint Chiefs of Staff. Their work was effective enough for Maj. Gen. Laurence S. Kuter to describe it with approval and in some detail to the War Department General Council. He noted as well that while

their work was continuing, a ship arrived with aviation gasoline just in time for the Battle of the Coral Sea. The port was 180 miles from the airport and after the captain of the ship anchored in an uncharted roadstead, the gasoline was unloaded and rafted ashore by the men of the 810th Battalion.[5]

While the bulk of the 810th worked at Plaine des Gaiacs, platoons of two of its companies built fighter strips and docks nearer camp. One platoon of Company C repaired an old French airfield at Koumac for emergency landings. Originally the platoon was directed merely to level and lengthen the strip, but after the first week of construction the commander of Task Force 6814, Maj. Gen. Alexander M. Patch, inspected the strip and ordered that it be made into an all-weather runway. A second platoon moved to Koumac. During the next week the company received further orders that the strip must be enlarged to handle B–17's. At least twelve parking spaces had to be built for the Flying Fortresses. The job had to be finished by the end of July. A third platoon was therefore added, plus a platoon of the 811th Battalion and twelve drivers and trucks from the 57th Engineer Combat Battalion of the Americal Division. The units worked in shifts, twenty-four hours a day, seven days a week. The field was finished on time and on 1 August a squadron of B–17's landed at Koumac. The next morning the heavy bombers took off to bomb targets in the Solomons. Units at the Plaine des Gaiacs airport, with the help of Javanese labor gangs hired to dig drainage ditches and spread the water and calcium chlo-

---

[5] Min Gen Council, 26 Aug 42.

ride used in compacting iron ore and settling dust, worked round-the-clock until the field became operational. The B–17's came in to bomb Guadalcanal before the field was completely finished; work on the field continued until the end of 1942.

Equipment for the younger 811th trickled in slowly for months. The battalion began to work on airfield projects in April, widening highways into landing strips, building dispersal areas, and constructing shelters at Tontauta, learning its job as it worked. The unit's headquarters company transported crated planes from docks to assembly points thirty-five miles from Nouméa. Two platoons, using only the available three dump trucks, a ten-ton roller, and hand tools, constructed a fighter strip at Bourake peninsula in a valley bounded on three sides by hills and by the sea on the fourth. The strip was in operation eight days after construction began. Although hastily constructed, this field was in continuous use for over a year, until artillery units on maneuvers rutted it beyond repair.

From then on the operations of the 810th and the 811th, building landing strips and maintaining airfields, were typical of the aviation engineers. Platoons and companies often operated individually on their projects. On 7 September 1942, for example, Company B of the 810th left the battalion and proceeded to Espíritu Santo in the New Hebrides. Its ship, the *Brastigi*, arrived on schedule but, during unloading, received word that a Japanese task force was headed for Espíritu Santo. The ship weighed anchor and fled, leaving two officers and forty-five men ashore without additional clothing or provi-

sions. The *Brastigi* headed for Efate, arriving the next day. The following day the ship brought the company back to Espíritu Santo, where it built a bomber field in a teakwood forest. It did not rejoin the rest of the battalion until after its arrival on Guadalcanal on 2 May 1943. In the meantime, the company acquired the battalion's first Negro officers. The remaining companies of the battalion in the intervening months constructed roads, built radar stations, and worked ration dumps, often under enemy air attack. Assembling on Guadalcanal on 15 June, the unit built installations, taxiways, and hardstandings for the Thirteenth Air Force and did small jobs, many of them not formally assigned but considered "necessary to cultivate the respect and good will of other organizations." [6]

Guadalcanal's Carney Field (Bomber One), the only field on the island from which bombers could operate efficiently, was deteriorating. It had been built months before in the rainy season. The 810th Battalion rebuilt it and in four days the taxiway was back in operation. The battalion did reconstruction jobs on other fields, built new hangers, and performed construction jobs for the Navy. With Navy and Marine Corps units it built Kili Field; after the field became operational, the battalion's Company B maintained it. Though the men of the unit, now overseas two years, were tired physically and mentally, morale remained good and efficiency high. From Christmas through 8 March 1944 there were no disciplinary problems serious enough for confinement. Malarial discipline was good. While on Espíritu

---

[6] Hist 810th Engr Avn Bn, AF Archives.

Santo, Company B, despite an epidemic on the island, had no cases, establishing a record in malaria control. After rotation began in March 1944, morale swung upward, but as quotas declined in later months—and, in some months, disappeared—the morale of the older men fell. Furloughs to Australia were limited. In light of developments in Australia, where, by mid-1944 communities were requesting that the Booker T. Washington Club at the Sydney Leave Center be closed and the Victualler's Association was proposing to close hotel bars to Negro soldiers, the theater was casting about for a substitute leave center. It finally settled upon Oro Bay, a solution heartily resented by Negro troops.[7] The 810th itself had no unit holiday until 26 June 1944, when it took the day off to celebrate its third anniversary. Despite its early arrival in the theater and despite the fact that it remained overseas until the end of the war, the 810th never went to a rest camp or had time allotted to train its replacements.[8]

Upon completion of its tour on Guadalcanal, in July 1944, the 810th Engineer Aviation Battalion was assigned to the Southwest Pacific Area's Services of Supply (USASOS) and moved to Biak, where it built a hospital for the 41st Field Hospital. Attached to Sixth Army in November, it was assigned to the Luzon invasion forces, leaving Biak on 4 January 1945 and arriving at Lingayen Gulf in the Philippines on 13 January. With its companies attached to

the 1178th and 1180th Engineer Construction Groups, a typical operational arrangement for smaller engineer units in the last years of the war, the battalion went ashore at Yellow Beach and White Beach 2 (San Fabian). After the landing, the battalion filled and laid mat on hardstandings, constructed unloading aprons, maintained roads, constructed and operated water points, built tank foundations and fire trenches, painted and erected road signs, built tent hardstands and a 1,000-bed hospital of prefabricated buildings at San Fabian, constructed a nurses area for the hospital, rebuilt and constructed bridges, replaced treadways on a Bailey bridge, strengthened and maintained ponton bridges, and made topographic surveys of proposed signal and quartermaster areas. Morale improved, since "For the first time in three years overseas, this battalion is experiencing civilization."[9] Discipline in this battalion, referred to by its men as the "rain-or-shine-we-go-all-the-time" 810th, thereafter slipped again, with one man trying to murder and succeeding in wounding an officer and another confined for assault. It was December before the battalion got all of its original men home on furlough; by then the war had been over four months.

The 811th remained on New Caledonia until the spring of 1944. At the beginning of 1943 it had enough work to keep every man busy on a twenty-hour day for seven months. New engineer units and a unit of Navy Seabees moved in and took over some of the projects. The 811th, now an experienced unit, and the Seabees started surfacing two

[7] Hist USAFFE, 1943–1945, app. 10, OCMH files.
[8] Ibid.; Notes on Conf with 810th Avn Engr Bn, 1928th Avn Engr Co, 1929th Engr Avn Co, Col George Mayo, AAF Engr, Washington, D.C., 12 Jun 45, AF Archives.

[9] Ibid.

nearly equal areas with similar equipment. The 811th finished first and helped the Seabees finish theirs. The 811th won the island record for hangar construction when a platoon of Company A put up a B–24 hangar in twenty-one days. Its Seabee neighbors held the record for constructing a radio range. When given a similar assignment, the battalion's Company C decided to wrest away the Seabees' record. It placed the same number of men on the job that the Seabees had used with the promise that for every day under the Seabees' record the soldiers would receive a day off. Despite heavy rains, the unit beat the Seabees' time by thirteen days.

After having undertaken almost every conceivable task connected with airport construction, the battalion moved to Guadalcanal in March 1944. It found mainly odd jobs waiting to be done there. The 811th, like many other Negro units, was to discover that assignment to a new headquarters often meant demonstrating all over again that it was capable of doing even the average job well.[10]

In September the 811th left for Honolulu. Despite its nearly three years on jungle islands and its return to "civilization," morale took a drop, for the unit found that Hawaii was a three-year rotation area. Morale took another drop when, assigned to Hickam Field with prospects of living in permanent barracks and running considerably ahead of schedule constructing hangars, it found

itself without warning and without reason taken off the job in midafternoon and ordered into trucks. By 1800 it had left the field, wondering what was ahead of it. Morale dropped again when, having begun to get settled at Bellows Field, it learned the reason for its sudden transfer. There had been a disturbance in civilian workers' barracks down the road from the battalion and the newly arrived Negro battalion was thought responsible. It was officially made plain later that the battalion had nothing to do with the occurrence, but by then it was settled at Bellows Field and the harm was done. While stationed at Bellows Field the 811th worked on jobs from one end of Oahu to the other until, on 10 December 1944, it entered the Jungle Training Center to prepare for further use in forward areas. After a period of amphibious training, it left Hawaii on 28 March 1945 for Iwo Jima.[11] On Iwo Jima, while building airstrips and quarters for bomber groups, its platoons kept running into holed up Japanese as their dozer blades cut into caves. The hiding Japanese were promptly captured by 811th troops or by accompanying infantry patrols.

The 810th and 811th Engineer Aviation Battalions were among the Negro units with the longest overseas careers. Almost as long, and similar in some respects, were those of the 96th and 91st Engineer General Service Regiments, which arrived in Brisbane, Australia, on 6 April 1942, organized as separate battalions. These units left the next night for Townsville aboard their same ships, arriving on 10 April. There the 96th

---

[10] Units sometimes noted that inspecting and supervisory personnel were frankly skeptical of their capabilities, especially if they had both Negro and white officers. See Ltr, Hq 376th Engr Bn, Separate, to Engr Off Peninsular Base Sec (Italy), 23 Mar 45.

[11] Hist 811th Avn Engr Bn (1st Lt Saul Cohen), 23 Sep–18 Dec 44, AF Archives.

remained for ten days, setting up its camp, furnishing labor for the Australians, and becoming acquainted with Townsville, which the troops found quite hospitable.[12] On 20 April, the 96th moved eleven miles out from Townsville where it began clearing a 7,000-foot landing strip by hand. Two companies remained in the new location until mid-June, constructing three 7,000-foot turf strips by hand. The rest of the battalion prepared to move to Port Moresby, New Guinea, where a small Australian garrison had been under Japanese air attack since 3 February.[13]

Port Moresby, on the Gulf of Papua near the southeastern tip of New Guinea, had at this time inadequate facilities for either its own defense or for the receipt of aid from Australian bases 700 miles away. Its port facilities were inadequate; its two existing airfields were small, poorly built, and so subject to continuous bombing that they were at first used only as refueling points for planes flying from Australia to attack the enemy. New fields and improvements for the existing fields and port were necessary before Port Moresby could either be defended or used as a base for operations elsewhere in New Guinea.

The 96th Engineers went to Port Moresby to improve existing prewar airfields there. On 20 April 1942, two officers and forty enlisted men departed Australia by plane to survey the area

[12] Diary 96th Engr Bn (Separate).

[13] For accounts of the status of Port Moresby and the defense of Australia in this period, see Samuel Milner, *Victory in Papua*, UNITED STATES ARMY IN WORLD WAR II (Washington, 1957), and George C. Kenney, *General Kenney Reports* (New York: Duell, Sloan and Pearce, 1949), pp. 34ff.

and prepare for the arrival of the remainder of the battalion. The rest of the battalion, less two companies, arrived at Port Moresby on 28 April, becoming the first American troop unit in New Guinea.

That night Port Moresby suffered its thirty-third enemy raid. Japanese Zero's strafed several areas, especially the airdrome at Seven-Mile where Company B of the 96th, machine-gunned by low-flying Japanese planes several times during the raid, became the first American Negro unit to come under enemy fire during the war. The arrival of twenty-six American Airacobras the next night cheered the troops of the 96th, whose companies mounted their .50-caliber machine guns and 37-mm. guns for action. Despite almost daily raids by fighters and bombers, spirits within the companies were high for the unit felt that it was "doing something" which might help to end the war.

Equipment, much of it in poor condition, arrived from Townsville on 5 May. The companies were now able to work more rapidly and effectively on their airfields. On 8 May the battalion was incorporated into the defense of Port Moresby and alerted against a possible invasion by Japanese on the way to what was to be the Battle of the Coral Sea. Raids on the landing fields increased, with both enemy and friendly planes crashing on and near the fields. To the 96th, the greatest loss possible was the occasional destruction of road graders or tractors, items which were in short supply. New steel landing mats arrived in mid-May, but unloading was delayed by the lack of proper cranes. Equipment in general was poor or lacking. The unit got its first satisfactory equipment at the end of June after the companies left in Australia rejoined.

By July, the battalion's units were all working on separate projects: Company A on Kila Drome, Company B on Seven-Mile Drome, Company C at Nine-Mile Quarry, operating rock crushers, the 1st Platoon of Company D on Bomana Field, and the 2d Platoon on Laloki Drome. Later in the summer, other engineer units arrived to take over certain of the projects; the 808th Aviation Engineer Battalion, a white unit, arrived on 26 July and took over the work on Laloki Drome; the 91st Engineers, left behind in Australia by the 96th, arrived in early September and took over the operation of Nine-Mile Quarry.

Port Moresby, mainly a way station for bombers before, was now becoming a build-up area for the fighting to come in New Guinea. Infantry and additional service units arrived in late September. To improve the port, formerly able to handle but one ship at a time, the 96th in the same month began to build a causeway from the harbor to Tatana Island, six miles away. On Tatana it built docks capable of handling six and, later, nine ships at a time.

Gradually, as messes, barracks, and roads were required by the enlarged base, the work of the 96th at Port Moresby assumed more of the nature of general engineer projects. But the 96th was still required to be prepared for supporting efforts in case of emergency. When Australian forces stopped the Japanese drive on Port Moresby on 14 September, the enemy was but thirty-two miles away. On 25 September, when the Japanese retreated toward Kokoda, north of the Owen Stanley Mountains, a 37-mm. gun and crew from the

96th went to help drive the enemy back, but by the time they arrived at Kokoda the Japanese had already left. The Japanese never got to Port Moresby but a group of the 96th, under unusual circumstances, went to Buna during the fighting there. In December 1942, Port Moresby had tanks needed by the Allied ground forces at Buna, but no one was available to unload the tanks under heavy fire and then defend the cargo until consignee troops could take them over. American and Australian officials at Port Moresby asked for volunteers from engineer units there. Nearly 150 men of the 96th, by now enlarged to a regiment, volunteered. To select the required fifteen men the regiment conducted a gunnery competition on medium field pieces. The group of fifteen men making the highest score and one officer put out to sea for Buna on 8 December. They landed the tanks on the beach there without mishap, but constant Japanese fire killed one and wounded another of the 96th's engineers.[14]

Despite frequent air attacks on Port Moresby, the 96th, primarily because of excellent precautions, lost not a single man from bombs, although it did have casualties from explosions and plane crashes. All of the airdromes in the Moresby area owed something to the work of this regiment. The construction of the Tatana causeway and docks, for which General MacArthur personally commended the unit, more than doubled the capacity of the port. In addition to the construction and maintenance of airdromes and docks, the unit was engaged in miscellaneous projects:

---

[14] Summary of Hist 96th Engr Gen Sv Regt (Lt Nils R. Holmes), 21 Apr 44.

five months of labor at the engineer dump; loading, shipping, and laying pierced steel landing mat for emergency strips; repairing and extending the runway at Kokoda during the Japanese retreat; constructing buildings for Advance Section, U. S. Army Services of Supply; and constructing a 500-bed Air Forces hospital. After an inspection and review on the anniversary of its arrival in New Guinea, Brig. Gen. Hanford McNider, then of the Combined Operational Service Command, declared to the 96th's men:

Fellow soldiers, a year ago today, when you stepped ashore as the first American troop unit in New Guinea, you were making history. You've been making it ever since. You've had a part in the building and upkeep of all our airfields; and thus you've helped make possible the destruction of the convoy in the Bismarck Sea, the flying of the infantry over the mountains, a hundred enemy actions. You've contributed your share to every crack we've taken at the Japs. You've carried out important works projects, even unloaded ships so we could eat and fight. You've built roads and the mains which give us power and light. You're one of the workingest outfits in this man's Army. All of us here are proud of you. All America will be proud of you when your record gets into the histories. Some of you have been to war with the tanks. You all know about bombs from hanging them on planes and having them hung on you. You've been good soldiers and you're going to be good soldiers. The harder we work and the better we do our jobs, the quicker you and I are going to get back where we belong—to the United States of America, which is all wrapped up in that flag which you are saluting today.[15]

This the 96th liked to hear, for the unit was convinced that it had done a good job under adverse conditions. It was a general service regiment, not an aviation engineer unit; as such its tables never called for the heavy earth-moving equipment assigned to the aviation engineers. But it knew that with inadequate and sometimes totally missing equipment it had done its job, working ahead of the planes and ground troops who would later carry the war against the Japanese forward from the fields and docks built by the 96th. It was to have this experience again, later in the war, but Port Moresby and the former outposts at Milne Bay where some of its troops were now located were becoming rear areas.

The 91st Engineers, which the 96th left behind in Australia, had a different career. The 91st, even upon departure from the United States, was neither as well nor as fully trained as the 96th. It was one of the units activated with a cadre from the 41st Engineers, the oldest Negro general service regiment, during the period when the 41st had had to abandon engineer for cadre training. The majority of the cadre were old soldiers of the arms; none had any previous training as engineers.[16] It was also one of the units whose thirteen-week basic training program was so frequently interrupted by camp labor demands that, although begun on 21 April 1941, the program, interrupted completely three times, never got beyond the ninth week. The unit left Camp Shelby for maneuvers on 28 July. From that time on the 91st remained under field conditions. It never received further formal training. It never returned to any training camp, semipermanent or otherwise, ex-

---

[15] *Ibid.*

[16] Hist Summary 91st Engineers (Capt Paul H. Miller), 4 May 44.

cept for four days spent in the staging area before leaving the New York Port of Embarkation.

The unit went to Woodstock, a railroad siding thirty miles south of Townsville, the day after disembarking in Australia. There it was to assist the 46th Engineers, a white unit, in building three landing strips. The 91st arrived in Australia without equipment. Everything that it used had to be borrowed from the 46th, a situation which, with the current shortage of all matériel in Australia, was of no help to the morale of either unit. Men worked with hand tools in clearing, in digging drains, and in culvert construction. The battalion spent twenty-four hours a day on construction without making notable progress.

On 23 April the 91st received a project of its own: the construction of an airfield and all facilities at a point outside of Giru, Queensland. But engineer separate battalions, intended primarily for labor, had no surveying equipment allotted. With only a carpenter's level, the field could not be properly laid out; drainage, slopes, grades, and alignments could not be accurately plotted. With hand tools, the unit began clearing the area for three landing strips. Only machetes were available for cutting the high grass covering the area. With all men available for handwork, hand tools soon ran out, for there were not enough to go around.

The unit rented equipment from nearby farmers, including a horse-drawn mowing machine and a farm tractor. Using an empty beer case, a section of a fourteen-inch log (felled by the farm tractor) as a wheel, a driftpin for an axle, and slender, six-foot poles for han-

STEEL BRIDGE OVER THE LALOKI *near Port Moresby, built in three weeks by an engineer company, November 1942.*

dles, the 91st devised homemade wheelbarrows. These were augmented by beer boxes rigged with wooden runners and drawn by two men holding a wooden pole on the end of a wire attached to the improvised sled. One officer, scouting Melbourne for equipment in May, found on hand only seven small, well-worn dozers and a few cargo trucks. These items finally arrived at Giru two months later, on 10 July. Other construction units, with fuller tables of equipment and higher priorities, got whatever new equipment came into the area. The 91st was occasionally able to borrow a steam shovel from the 46th Engineers, but since the 46th had first call on its use, the 91st could not depend upon it.

On the 91st projects that required heavy equipment, progress was so slow that interest lagged and morale fell. For all the work accomplished by the 91st in its first four months in Australia, it was stated to the battalion both orally and in writing that the unit might as well have stayed in the United States and continued the work it had been doing there. During the middle of August 1942 the 91st received its major equipment, including tractors, dozers, prime movers, carryalls, graders, welders, and trucks.

In the meantime the 1st Provisional Battalion of the 91st, consisting of eight officers, two warrant officers, and 528 enlisted men, was formed for shipment to the northern tip of Cape York Peninsula across from Horn Island, where a platoon of the 46th Engineers was maintaining an airfield used on the route from Townsville to Port Moresby. The provisional battalion found considerable equipment on hand to build an advance landing strip but much of the matériel was in poor condition. At one time both of the unit's two graders were deadlined for lack of fan belts. After trying to make fan belts by weaving rawhide, which slipped excessively, the unit welded sprockets from several bicycles to the crankshaft and fan pulleys. Then, by placing bicycle chains on the teeth of the sprockets, the fan belts were replaced and the machines went back on duty. The first plane landed on the new runway on 12 September; the first B–17 landed on 28 October. The 1st Provisional Battalion remained on jobs in the Cape York area until December when it joined the rest of its parent unit—by then a general service regiment and therefore entitled to more and better equipment—at Port Moresby, where it had been since 8 September.

Morale in the 91st Engineers went up during its earlier months in New Guinea. Air raids and alarms and the presence of the enemy within twenty miles of one company constructing a tactical road for the 32d Division made the outfit feel a part of the war, as it had not in Australia. The commander of the 32d Division, Maj. Gen. Edwin F. Harding, commended this company highly for the speed with which the road was completed. Again, however, the regiment was short of equipment. None of the equipment allotted to a general service regiment had yet arrived. One officer was able to "promote" a transit and a level, with but one tripod for the two instruments, before leaving Australia. This was the full surveying equipment of the unit when it arrived at Moresby.

The 91st laid out projects by guess and scrabbled in the jungle on round-the-clock schedules to complete them, only to find that projects marked for urgent completion were not used after the unit had spent all its extra time finishing them. As a result, it became increasingly difficult to call upon the men's reserve energy as the visible value of their missions diminished. The unit found that faulty planning sometimes slowed results, but the engineers got the blame. On one project, a hospital, the plans for ward tent frames were changed a total of thirteen times. On another project, completing a job begun by another unit involving poured concrete, heavily reinforced with steel, the 91st, upon removing the former unit's molds, found the concrete shot through with holes in what was to have been a water-tight structure. After exercising considerable ingenuity and laboring hard to patch and waterproof the original structure, the engineers found that it was not to be used after all. On one occasion the 91st Engineers sent an officer and ten men to Australia for schooling in diesel mechanics, since, in its previous assignment the unit had not been taught the use of diesel equipment. Along with two other general service separate engineer units, it had found in late 1942 that heavy diesel-powered equipment was suffering in the hands of men who had no knowledge of its proper use and maintenance. Unfortunately, the group sent from the 91st was not given adequate training in Australia. The men were set apart from the rest of the students and were given a course in which one ancient tractor was dismantled, and reassembled, a procedure that, the unit historian wryly commented, "did not give the men a very broad outlook or training on diesel engines." The 91st, protesting the conduct of the course, recommended that future schools be on the spot and that they employ only American instructors using American equipment.

The 91st continued to work in the Port Moresby area until mid-1944, after all other engineer and most air units had long since gone forward. Road construction and maintenance, operation of gravel pits, excavation of sites for oil storage tanks, expansion of the Tatana dock area, and construction of utilities systems, storage reservoirs, quarters, and recreational facilities were all among its projects. For some, especially dock construction—the completion of eight igloo warehouses for the quartermaster dump in four days—and for hospital projects,

it received commendations. But the 91st, which had been conditioned by its officers to expect personal hardships in furtherance of the war effort, was not helped by remaining at Port Moresby long after the war had apparently passed it by, toward the end of its stay assigned to jobs which had little visible importance, such as installing additional semipermanent structures on a base whose population was steadily dwindling.[17]

Besides engineers, units moving early to Australia and New Guinea included the 394th Quartermaster Battalion, Port, later redesignated a Transportation Corps Port Battalion. This, the oldest of the port battalions, left the United States after the engineer separate battalions just discussed, but arrived in Australia before them. It was activated with three companies on 27 June 1941 at Oakland, California. A fourth company was added on 20 January 1942, not long before the battalion sailed from San Francisco for Brisbane on 18 February 1942. After arrival on 9 March, the companies of the battalion pursued the semi-independent courses typical of port battalions. Company D (611th Port Company)[18] remained in the Brisbane area for a month, moving then to Charters Towers where it remained for a month and a half before embarking on 15 June for Port Moresby. Company C (610th Port Company) moved from Brisbane to Cloncurry, then to Mount Isa, where it stayed until it left for Port Moresby on 26 November 1942. The headquarters detachment and the two remaining companies stayed in Brisbane

---

[17] Ibid., 1 May 44, 4 May 44.
[18] Designations in parentheses indicate the numerical designation assigned after port companies became separate in 1943.

for about six weeks, moving then to Birdum in the Northern Territory. There Company A (608th Port Company) worked for two months, leaving for Milne Bay on 23 July 1942. This company was located at Milne Bay until April 1943 when it joined other units of the battalion at Port Moresby. It stayed at Moresby until November and December when, in two movements, it went to Finschhafen. The last company and the battalion headquarters were stationed at Birdum until November 1942 when they, along with Company C, moved to Port Moresby. The bulk of the battalion's work at Port Moresby was on the Tatana docks.[19]

After April 1944, when a second company left Port Moresby for Finschhafen, the battalion called on the 91st Engineers and the 55th Ordnance Ammunition Company for aid in handling cargo. Combined with the fact that at the time they were constructing tent floors and frames for units newly arrived from the United States when they themselves were still living on dirt floors after two years of foreign service, this call was a "real blow" to the fifty engineers used for port service.[20] A commendation from the 394th Port Battalion stressing the excellent spirit and fine discipline of the 91st's men, enabling the battalion to move a record amount of cargo in "a very short time," [21] did not compensate the engineers for what they thought was another sign of their slow relegation to jobs unimportant to advancing the war.

In New Guinea, meanwhile, the 96th

Engineers from the spring of 1943 worked on general engineering and airfield projects all over the island, with elements at Milne Bay, Oro Bay, and Augusta (Merauke), while the headquarters and two companies remained at Port Moresby. The full regiment, after over a year's separation, assembled at Oro Bay in June 1944 for training, rehabilitation, and preparation for a new assignment. Physical reconditioning and rest, combined with training of operators for new heavy equipment which the regiment expected to receive, occupied the unit. Courses intended to increase the skill of welders, draftsmen, machinists, mechanics, and service crews —who had been doing similar work for over two years—were recognized as being somewhat in conflict with the rest and recreational program attempted, but the regiment expected to be converted to a construction battalion (a change that did not occur) and it wanted to be prepared for anything that lay ahead. *Esprit de corps*, reflecting the regiment's record of the past two years, was high.

The regiment left Oro Bay to join a convoy for Maffin Bay on 21 July, leaving one company and a detachment behind to follow later. During a brief stop at Maffin Bay, the regiment took the occasion to remind its men that once again the role which they were playing had undeniable importance to the war effort beyond installing flooring for transient units at a dying base:

1. Every officer and man of the Ninety Sixth Engineers looks back with pride on the early days at Port Moresby. In those days, plain for all to see, on their work in maintaining and improving airdromes under fire and pushing through the Tatana

---

[19] Hist Summary 394th Port Bn (TC) 1 May 44.
[20] Hist Summary 91st Engr Regt, 1 May 44.
[21] Hq 394th Port Bn (TC) to CO Base D and 22d Port Hq (TC), APO 929, 21 Apr 44, copy attached to Hist Summary cited n. 20.

Island project depended our success in stopping the Japs. In those days the issue trembled in the balance, and every man could see his weight throwing the scales our way.

2. With a handful of worn equipment, without experience, but with no end of guts you threw yourselves into the scales. The regiment was weighed and was not found wanting.

3. Now the wheel has swung full circle and again the progress of the war depends on the work of the Ninety Sixth Engineers. The circumstances are different. We are well equipped, better than any other unit in the South West Pacific has ever been. We are taking into action twenty-two D–8's, four power shovels, eight caterpillar graders to mention only a few items. We have over two years experience behind us. The Jap is on the run. We will again be the farthest forward spearhead, building the airfield that will help make it possible for the next jump. It is literally true that the war will go as fast as the work of the Ninety Sixth Engineers.

4. We are now the people for whom one hundred million have worked together to equip and push up front. We are the people on whom a hundred million depend. Every man and officer must and will measure up to what our people expect of us.[22]

The 96th's Company C went to Wakde Island, charged with carrying out engineer construction and maintenance there. Most other troops remained aboard transports in the harbor until 3 August 1944. When the bulk of the regiment went ashore, the remnants of the Japanese garrison were still fighting a few hundred yards from the beach, and American planes from Wakde were still bombing the enemy at Sarmi, a few miles away. The regiment unloaded its supplies and equipment from Liberty ships, and reloaded them in LST's for

movement to Cape Opmarai, where the regiment debarked on 9 August. At Cape Opmarai the regiment, bivouacking in a hastily cleared site in an almost impenetrable rain forest, began work in less than twenty-four hours on an engineer road and a 500-foot over-run at the western end of the Mar airdrome. The 96th also constructed buildings, roads, gasoline bulk storage tanks, and dumps. It furnished labor in the Cape Opmarai-Sansapor area. One platoon of Company A worked on the Middleburg Island airdrome. The regiment remained in the Cape Opmarai area until April 1945.[23]

Toward the end of its stay, as this base too declined in population, and as the taxiways of Mar Drome emptied of planes, the Japanese in the hills began to harass the remaining troops on the base. In February 1945, the enemy raided a native village at Plain Creek, two miles from one outpost, and later about 150 Japanese attacked the Sansapor outpost, suffering twenty-two dead in the attack. Companies A and B of the 96th took over the defense at Table River for two days while troops of the 167th Infantry, 31st Division, to which the engineer regiment was then attached, went out in search of the attackers. All companies of the 96th sent security and reconnaissance patrols into the jungle.

The unit remained at Cape Opmarai until the base was closed out; it salvaged all the Marsden mat from Mar Drome and destroyed the runway and taxiways by cutting dozer ditches across them. It dismantled and crated storage tanks, and prepared all bridges for demolition.

---

[22] Hq 96th Engr Gen Sv Regt, GO 18, 5 Aug 44.

[23] See Robert Ross Smith, *The Approach to the Philippines*, UNITED STATES ARMY IN WORLD WAR II (Washington, 1953), ch. XVIII.

The unit was now critically short of enlisted personnel from rotation and attrition. The replacement system for Negroes was not working at all. The 96th's strength had gone down to 675 enlisted men available for duty. At the beginning of April 1945, the 96th finally received 250 replacements, but they came from the 1315th Engineer Construction Battalion, disbanded for the purpose of furnishing men to depleted older engineer units. The regiment, as its last major project, maintained roads and bridges on the supply routes of the 31st Division in the Mindanao campaign.

Though longer and more varied, the careers of these earlier engineer and port units were fairly typical of the careers of units that came after. The later units were more fully trained and equipped but they were less likely to be assigned to tasks which kept their eyes on a mission visible to the average enlisted man in the way that the work at Port Moresby and Plaine des Gaiacs appeared to the men of these first units out. Many of the later units worked almost wholly as helpers to larger white units that had the main responsibility for large construction projects. Many suffered interminably from training and leadership problems. On jobs in which units were spread over large areas the need for supervisory and administrative personnel increased proportionately to the distances separating the elements of the units. The theaters, especially the Pacific areas, thought that an overstrength in officers might help, but the War Department established no general policy for engineer units. The Corps of Engineers therefore advised theaters that since "There is no hope of reducing the number of Negro Engineer units to be sent to your Theater," [24] the theaters themselves should initiate requests giving their justifications for extra officers.[25] No general policy covering the desired overstrength was approved.

Officers were often surprised by the efficacy of the training of their units once they became operational. They stressed the importance of prior training, especially in the operation and maintenance of equipment. Said one aviation engineer battalion commander after a few months in North Africa:

My outfit has really surprised me with the construction jobs it has turned out. And our equipment and trucks have held up very well considering the circumstances. I attribute about ninety percent of our success to the excellent training that you gave the men and officers while you were with us. . . .

Like many another engineer or quartermaster unit, this one found its employment

. . . not as exciting as I thought it was going to be. You see they have held us in the rear area to do the heavy construction work after the front line outfits have built temporary fields and moved forward. The outfit has been widely separated most of the time over here. Sometimes a thousand miles or more separated the extreme elements of the battalion. The companies have learned to operate independently and I have become a flying area engineer.[26]

---

[24] Ltrs, ACofE to Engr Secs, APO's 887 (London), 885 (New Delhi), 958 (Ft. Shafter, Hawaii), 534 (Algiers), 500 (Brisbane), 11 Apr 44, CofE 320.2 (Engr, Corps of). See also, Col Arthur G. Trudeau, Rpt of Visit to NATO Engr Sec, p. 104.

[25] Trudeau, NATO Rpt, p. 104; Ltr, CofE to ASF, 22 Apr 44, CE SPEOU; Memo, Hq ASF for CofE, 24 May 44, SPMOU 322 (22 Apr 44).

[26] Personal Ltr, Lt Col Leo V. Harman, 838th Engr Avn Bn, to Capt C. E. Taylor, 3d EAUTC, MacDill Fld, Fla., 19 Nov 43, copy in EAUTC Hist Rpt, 18 Mar–1 May 43, folder 3, 1342–1C, AF Archives.

Even with the lessened control occasioned by the method of employing these and other engineer units, most observers agreed that "The amount of work done by the aviation engineers is almost unbelievable." The same factors that diminished centralized control and supervision sometimes operated to increase the actual efficiency of the isolated parts of the unit, since men, noncommissioned officers, and officers under these conditions grew relatively more interdependent and self-reliant. Tensions endemic to larger units were relieved and relations between the smaller elements and their neighbors were often tempered by the compactness of the smaller command assigned to a limited job whose meaning and value could be grasped by all involved. While nonparticipant observers continued to conclude that the efficiency of Negro service units was in direct proportion to the "efficiency, enthusiasm, ability, and number of their officers," they nevertheless felt that units performed their tasks in construction, water supply, and dump truck operations with credit.[27]

Road Builders

The first engineer and port units sent out to the Pacific were matched within a few weeks by engineer units sent to Alaska and Canada for the construction of the Alaska (Alcan) Highway from Dawson Creek to Fairbanks. Three of the seven regiments pushing this road through the northern wilderness were Negro units, all originally separate battalions later expanded to general service regiments. Their 3,695 troops ac-

counted for slightly more than a third of the 10,607 engineers on the highway.[28] The 93d General Service Regiment, arriving in April 1942, constructed the highway from Tagish north to the McClintock River and east and southeast toward Teslin; the 97th, arriving at the same time, had the section from Slana north toward the Tanana River and thence south to the Alaska-Canada border, where it would meet the 18th Engineers, a white unit building from the south. The 95th, last of the Negro regiments to arrive, began to follow the white 341st Engineers in June, improving the road cut by that regiment from Fort St. John to Fort Nelson. The Alaska Highway, evidencing something of the early American pioneer spirit as it cut through ice hills and muskeg swamps in a race against time, captured the American imagination in a way that few other projects did in the early summer of 1942 when so little else involving American forces in an aggressive role on a large scale had yet been made public. When the bulldozers of Technician 5 Refines Sims, Jr., lead cat skinner of the Negro 97th, and Pvt. Alfred Jalufka, lead driver of the white 18th Engineers, finally broke through to close the last gap in the road on 25 October 1942, the meeting between white and Negro drivers symbolized to a hopeful country the kind of unity and co-operation that foretold eventual victory. Public speakers and radio programs made much of the symbolism of the event for months to come.[29]

[27] Trudeau, NATO Rpt, p. 104.

[28] The Alaska Highway, A Report Compiled for the CG ASF (May 1945), II, OCMH.

[29] For an example, see Norman Rosten, *The Big Road* (New York: Rinehart & Co., 1946), much of which first appeared on radio networks, including those of the Armed Forces Radio Service.

OPERATING HEAVY EQUIPMENT ON THE ALASKA HIGHWAY

Having built a pioneer road, the regiments remained to improve and maintain it or to do other jobs in Alaska and the Aleutians. Units of the 97th, in addition to maintaining roads, operated terminals for trucks on the "Fairbanks Freight," the truck supply line over the highway. One company at Cathedral Rapids was charged with "glacier control," chopping glaciers off the highway by hand or building bypass roads around them when they encroached too far.[30] All three units later served in other theaters, the 93d and 97th in the Pacific, the 95th in Europe.

On the other side of the world, in Burma, 60 percent of the 15,000 American troops assigned to the construction of the Ledo Road, to run 271 miles from Ledo, Assam, to a connection with the old Burma Road to Kunming, were Negroes.[31] The first two American Army

[30] Company C 97th Engr Sv Regt Summary.

[31] Hist SOS I–BT, app. 4, Advance Sec Three, 25 Oct 44–20 May 45, OCMH. For the general background of Negro troop activity in the China-Burma-India theater, see the three volumes in UNITED STATES ARMY IN WORLD WAR II by Charles F. Romanus and Riley Sunderland: Stilwell's Mis-

units assigned to the new route were the 45th Engineer General Service Regiment and the 823d Engineer Aviation Battalion, both of them Negro units that had previously worked on airfields in Assam and elsewhere in India as the first American engineer units in the theater. Already working on the road were one bridging and several pioneer units of the British Army and 8,000 local laborers.[32]

The 45th and 823d started construction about 15 December 1942. The 45th contributed its commander, Col. John Arrowsmith, to the project as the original commanding officer of Base Section Three, headquarters for road operations at Ledo.[33]

The road, with its first section running from Ledo through the Patkai Mountains to Shingbwiyang 103 miles distant, went through previously unsurveyed territory. It followed roughly the steep narrow trail over which thousands of refugees had fled into India during the retreat from Burma.[34] Rising as high as 4,500 feet, the road ran through five ranges of the Patkais. For each mile between Ledo and Shingbwiyang, 100,000 cubic feet of earth had to be removed.[35] Steep grades, hairpin curves, and sheer drops for as much as 200 feet, all surrounded by a thick rain forest jungle, characterized this first section.

At first, equipment used on the road

was almost wholly the organizational equipment of the 45th Engineer Regiment and the 823d Engineer Aviation Battalion, supplemented by road rollers, graders, rock crushers, air compressors, and small tools available from China Defense Supply stocks.[36] By 1 January 1943 the 823d, picking up where the British forces left off, had cut five miles of point on the road. During February the work pushed ahead, the 823d coming into Japanese-held Burma at Mile 43.3.[37] Work proceeded slowly during the months thereafter as difficulties with equipment, shortages of troops, and the monsoon plagued the engineers. Landslides, washed out bridges, and swollen streams hampered progress. By the beginning of the heavy rains the roadhead had advanced so far as to be beyond practicable supply distances. Troops began to widen the road and slope the banks beyond Mile 34, with Indian tea plantation contract laborers doing most of the sloping.

Construction of the road followed the combat forces as closely as possible. On 1 April, the 45th Engineers organized to meet a possible Japanese attack. Patrols had been sighted south of the road not far from Ledo and there were reports that others were operating to the north of the road. The 45th sent patrols out in both directions, but the threat diminished within a few days.[38]

During the heavy rains, troops on the road strove to hold what they had. Thousands of Indians assisted in digging and clearing ditches. The 10th Chinese Engineers, who arrived in March

sion to China (Washington, 1953), Stilwell's Command Problems (Washington, 1956), and Time Runs Out in CBI (Washington, 1959).

[32] Planning Div, Office Dir P&O ASF (11 vols.), I, v-7, OCMH.

[33] GO 44, Hq USAF, CBI, 15 Dec 42. Base Section Three was later designated Advance Section Three and finally simply Advance Section.

[34] Hist SOS CBI, 28 Feb 42–24 Oct 44, OCMH.

[35] Hist I–B Theater, 25 Oct 44–23 Jun 45, OCMH.

[36] Hist SOS CBI, 28 Feb 42–24 Oct 44, OCMH.

[37] Hist 823d Engr Avn Bn, 1943.

[38] Hist Rpt 45th Engr Gen Sv Regt, 15 Jun 41–30 Jun 44.

Engineer Troops on the Ledo Road *building the first gravel screen to be used on the Ledo Road construction project.*

1943, worked on drainage and built re-vetments. In the following months new American units, including the 330th General Service Regiment and the 849th and 1883d Engineer Aviation Battalions, the latter two Negro units, arrived. The 330th pushed the point ahead beginning in August while the other organizations widened, improved, and bridged the road, and built adjacent airstrip and combat roads. Engineer units on the road were joined by other units necessary to road operations: three light pontoon companies, including two Negro units of this type, to bridge the swift mountain rivers and operate ferries; the 45th Quartermaster Regiment, whose trucks hauled surfacing materials and, later, supplies; and additional engineer units. Just before the end of the year, on 27 December 1943, the lead bulldozer reached Shingbwiyang, three days ahead of schedule. The most difficult part of the road was completed, but the job of widening, clearing and preventing slides, bridging, and operating the road, as well as the job of completing it through the lower lands was yet to be done. Much of the remaining route, including Myitkina and Bhamo, was still in the hands of the enemy.

The ponton companies, arriving in late 1943, went in January and February beyond Shingbwiyang to operate ferries and to build ponton bridges. The 76th, in February, moved up the Ningham Combat Trail to the Tarung River, building there a standard pneumatic float twelve-ton bridge, 470 feet long, the first in Burma and the first built in the construction of the road.[39] The bridge was not built under fire, but the company's temporary camp at the river's edge received rifle grenade fire from across the river. The 76th constructed a 540-foot ponton pier on the Tarung for the use of the 209th Combat Engineer Battalion, a white unit constructing a fixed bridge across the river. One of the 76th's platoons widened and improved the Ningham Combat Trail in order to carry ponton equipment forward to construct an eighty-foot bridge farther up-river. Since the unit had to maintain the Combat Trail to supply itself and its bridges, it sent a detachment back to Ledo to fetch dump trucks for use in this mission, but the detachment, on the way back in the now rainy season, was stopped at Mile 55 to haul gravel for washouts. The company found itself trying to maintain the Combat Trail during the monsoon without equipment. It found itself with a washed-out bridge when the Tarung River rose eleven feet in one day on 1 May. Its ferry over the Tanai could not be operated in June because of the swiftness of the rising river. The unit, stranded for six days, was moved across the river by assault boats. With the 71st Company, a white ponton unit, it then built a 775-foot bridge over the Tawang in eleven hours under the difficult conditions of the July floods. When not operating as bridge units, the ponton companies, moving at times by plane to the sites where they were needed, helped maintain roads and operate waterworks, or worked as construction troops.[40]

Certain other units came down from the road to build B-29 bases in India in early 1944. One of these, the 382d Engineer Construction Battalion, arrived at Kharagpur in late January with the mission of building a "barely operational" field there by 15 March. The unit had left its organizational equipment on the road for continued use there. It was therefore dependent upon Engineer District equipment. The unit, well disciplined and well trained for its original tasks, had few competent equipment operators for airfield construction at the start of the job. By hard work it met the target date and then went on for the next ninety days to meet the "nearly impossible 'limited operations' " date of 30 June.[41] The unit was "well rounded" by the time the job was completed. The 1888th Engineer Aviation Battalion took over the construction of Piardoba Airfield in February 1944 from another unit, inheriting a difficult schedule which it met successfully. Neither men nor officers in this unit possessed at the beginning a full knowledge of airfield construction methods, but they showed a "great will-

[39] Hist 76th Engr Light Ponton Co, 1944.

[40] Ibid; Hist 77th Engr Light Ponton Co.
[41] Hist SOS IBT, app. 12, Construction Service, 23 Apr–24 Oct 44, OCMH.

12-TON PNEUMATIC FLOAT BRIDGE BUILT OVER THE TARUNG RIVER, BURMA

ingness" which resulted in completion of their job on schedule.[42]

From the beginning the Ledo Road was a combat support road as well as a potential supply route to China. Along with construction troops, the road and the Advance Section administering it acquired troops to support combat forces as well as to maintain troops constructing the highway and the airfields and pipelines adjacent to it. The 60th Ordnance Company operated ammunition depots to stock ammunition supply points located along the road and along combat trails branching from the road.[43] Negro laundry units at Ledo and Myitkyna, and a semimobile salvage repair company were used in Advance Section Three. Truck convoys began operating as soon as enough of the road was open to enable the drivers to proceed. The 45th Quartermaster Regiment arrived in November 1943 to operate between Ledo and Shingbwiyang and stayed throughout the period of road operations.

During the monsoon, trucks became mired in mud so deep that it came up to the running boards and sometimes to the

[42] Ibid. See also "Airfield Construction in Burma" [Rpt of Lt Col Frederick A. Reickert, Chief Constr Sec AEO IB Sector CBI], Military Engineer, XXXVI (October, 1944) , 344.

[43] Hist SOS IBT, app. 4, Advance Section Three, p. 85.

hood, requiring the bulldozers of construction troops, working all the while at widening, improving, and maintaining the road, to pull and push them out.[44] One battalion maintaining the road during the monsoon season of 1944 found a hundred slides in thirty-two miles on one May day. Each slide required tractors to remove it. Tinch Slide, a 300-foot cut with its face studded with rocks of all sizes, caused constant trouble. It was often a "mess impassable to wheeled traffic." [45] Rocks weighing as much as fifteen tons were washed out by the rains and tumbled across the road, sinking into the mud and water. Many required blasting before bulldozers could edge them off the road into the river two hundred feet below.

In the early months of convoy operations truckers carried mainly supplies for the engineers and for combat troops, with little organized convoy control. The only truck outfit then based in Shingbwiyang, the 3646th Quartermaster Truck Company, whose main task was operating gravel dump trucks and jeep supply to forward areas, performed rudimentary convoy control functions. Though the engineers utilized the services of the truck companies, they wanted no part of a fleet of trucks cluttering up the trace and providing an easy target for the enemy. Their general attitude was "Get 'em in and then get 'em out quick before some damn Jap sees them and bombs hell outta the place!" [46]

Operating in the mud and muck of the

still rudimentary road, trucks and other wheeled vehicles could follow combat forces only so far as the road would carry them. In the Burma campaign, Chinese, American, and Indian combat forces were often deep in the jungles and high in the Naga Hills, far from the nearest roadhead. Neither native porters nor pack mules could reach them throughout the monsoon seasons. To supply them, the theater resorted to dropping food and supplies by air. Experimental drops in March 1943 proved the method feasible despite the absence of trained airdropping personnel, planes, or containers. For the first drops, men of laundry and ordnance units packed and dropped supplies, using basket containers and parachutes from a fighter control group and airplanes from the ferry command at Chabua. By the end of the month, a regular airdropping organization was improvised. White personnel of the 3841st Quartermaster Truck Company at Sookerating Air Base were used for warehousing, packing, and dropping, and Negro personnel of the 3304th Quartermaster Truck Company, divided into seven detachments of one officer and nine enlisted men each, were used to receive airdropped supplies at forward stations.[47]

As the airdropping mission increased in scope, the 518th Quartermaster Battalion (Mobile), a complete Negro battalion just arriving in the theater, was assigned to procuring, warehousing, packing, and loading all subsistence and other supplies for airdropping. Its headquarters and two companies worked

[44] Hist 3470th QM Truck Co for 1944.

[45] Hist Rpt 858th Engr Avn Bn, 8 Jan 44–15 Sep 45.

[46] Rpt Burma Convoy Control Station 1, Hist Motor Transport Sv, Advance Sec, I–B Theater, 3 Jan 45–30 Sep 45, app. 24, vol. II, Hist I–B Theater, vol. 27, pt. 2, OCMH.

[47] Hist SOS I–B Theater, app. 4, Advance Section Three, 25 Oct 44–20 May 45, pp. 223–24.

out of Dinjan. The other two companies went to Sookerating. The 3841st, now supplemented by additional volunteers, was attached to this unit for duty. Its personnel, split between the two bases, continued as the "kickers" who rode the planes of the 2d Troop Carrier Squadron, pushing packaged supplies from the open doors of planes in flight over the target. Two detachments of one officer and four enlisted men of the 518th went to forward areas to assist the 3304th Truck Company in its receiving and issuing duties. These Negro detachments sent back periodic reports on the effectiveness of the drops that proved valuable to the development of improved techniques. In November, 1943 when Chinese troops launched a drive into the Hukawng Valley, dropping directly to the using troops began and the 3304th was relieved of its receiving duties.[48] Nineteen Chinese and two Indian divisions as well as American units received supplies by air-dropping. The 518th Battalion continued its airdropping activities until the end of December 1944 when it was relieved to begin convoy duties. Sufficient provisional airdropping units had by now been organized and the road was about to open.[49] During the period of its airdropping activities, the 518th, with less

than ten days' instruction and orientation in its new assignment, experimented with, packed, and dropped a number of unusual items, including the first 75-mm. pack howitzer airdropped in Burma, oil and gasoline in 55-gallon drums lashed with rope around sacks of rice husks used as bumpers, ammunition carts cut into sections so that they could get through plane doors, delicate medical supplies and instruments, bulky operating tables and generators, blood plasma, and even live ducks and fresh eggs for special holidays. The 518th operated virtually a specialized subdepot, shifting its personnel about so that all learned all phases of airdropping. The unit also trained the personnel of other organizations for airdropping activities. It was proud that it used only its own personnel, other than local labor, for less technical work, and that it never allowed the planes of the air cargo squadrons to remain idle while waiting for packaged supplies.[50]

When the monsoon was over in October 1944, completion of the Ledo Road was in sight. Additional construction troops came in to reinforce the road builders. Among them were more Negro units, including the 1327th Engineer General Service Regiment, flown in from the United States,[51] and the 352d Engineer General Service Regiment, which, since January 1943, had been helping to build and maintain highways, railroads, and airfields through Iran for the Russian supply route.[52] Every avail-

[48] *Ibid.;* Unit Hist 3841st QM Truck Co, 25 Oct 42–23 Dec 44; Hist 518th QM Bn, Mobile, 1 Jan–31 Dec 44.
[49] These units, all with white personnel, later became the 1st, 2d, and 12th Air Cargo Resupply Squadrons under the Air Supply Service of the AAF. Negro aviation truck companies were attached to these units. Beginning in August 1944 and continuing through June 1945, thirteen Air Cargo Resupply Squadrons were activated in the United States and in Hollandia and the Philippines with Negro personnel. These units served in the Philippines and on Okinawa.

[50] Hist 518th Bn; Lt. Col. Abbott E. Dodge, QMC, "The Bundles for Burma Boys," *The Quartermaster Review,* XXIV (November–December 1944), 47–48.
[51] Hist I–B Theater, 25 Oct 44–23 Jun 45, OCMH.
[52] Hist 352d Engr Gen Sv Regt; Tech Intel Rpt 1943, Problems Encountered in 352d Engr Rgt, 28 May 45.

able truck and driver was being assigned to convoy service. In December 1944 thirty-six of fifty-nine quartermaster truck companies were operating in the two-way traffic between Ledo and Bhamo. Most of these were Negro units. The call now went out for volunteer truck drivers to supplement these truckers on the route to China.

By early January 1945, the first convoy was readying at Ledo to move over the road to Kunming. It began to move before the road was completed and cleared of the still fighting Japanese. At first, it was thought that a critical situation might arise over the use of Negro drivers in China but the Chinese Government, which had opposed the use of Negroes in its territory, permitted the drivers to go as far as Kunming. China requested that unless the tactical situation demanded it, Negro units not be used east of Kunming—the western Chinese had never seen Negro troops, Generalissimo Chiang explained, and he felt it better not to send them there unless required.[53] The first convoy consisted of fifty Negro and fifty Chinese drivers, the latter especially trained for the convoy and prepared to take over drivers' duties upon entering Kunming. The number of Negro drivers, after the China ruling, was reduced to ten, with two Negro war correspondents added.[54] The China restriction did not interfere with future convoys on what was now renamed the Stilwell Road.

For operations on the Stilwell Road, officially beginning 1 February 1945, fifty-eight truck companies under three group and eleven battalion headquarters were in use when the Motor Transport Service was formally organized on 25 February. Of the fifty-eight truck companies, fifty-two were Negro; the three group and nine of the battalion headquarters were also Negro. Remaining on the road for maintenance and continuing construction at this time were four engineer general service regiments, three of them Negro; seven engineer aviation battalions, four of them Negro; two dump truck companies, both Negro; two light ponton companies, one of which was Negro; and one engineer construction battalion, two engineer combat battalions, one engineer maintenance company, a heavy shop company, and a forestry company, all of which were white.[55] The first engineer unit to go to China to work on the Stilwell Road was the 858th Engineer Aviation Battalion, which moved in May 1945 to maintain the road from the Salween River to Kunming. This unit, the only Negro battalion sent to China, remained there until V–J Day as one of two battalions then working on the China end of the road. Its units, with the white 71st Light Ponton Company attached for maintenance between the Salween and the China border, eventually worked nearly five hundred miles east of Kunming.[56]

In addition to the medical dispensa-

[53] Romanus and Sunderland, *Time Runs Out in CBI*, p. 348.

[54] Ledo Road, I, VI–8, MS in OCMH; Hist SOS IBT, Adm Sec, 25 Oct 44–20 May 45, MS in OCMH. Also on the first convoy were eight white American enlisted men: one truckmaster, four section leaders, one mechanic, one medical corpsman, and one ambulance driver.

[55] GO 3, Hq Adv Sec 3, 25 Feb 45. Among the Negro truck companies were one service and one railhead company acting as truck companies. One of the remaining companies was the Indian 110th General Purpose Transport.

[56] Hist 858th Engr Avn Bn, 8 Jan 44–15 Sep 45.

ries of the engineer units located along the convoy route, the 335th Station Hospital, one of the four Negro hospitals organized for overseas duty, was located at the 80-mile mark, at Tagap, Burma. From excess personnel of this unit the 383d Station Hospital was activated as of 6 December 1944.[57] Both units operated at Tagap, the 383d attached to the 335th. With a low census, primarily of Negro troops, these two hospitals were the only ones along the road operating "strictly in the manner for which they were designed." [58]

Other units formerly working on the Stilwell Road moved to airfields, to the subbase at Myitkina, and to depots at Ledo, whose work now increased. The quartermaster section at Ledo acquired the 547th Quartermaster Depot Company, one of the two Negro units of its type "and an exceptionally good one," [59] in late 1944. After it lost this company to China in May 1945, it used the 43d Veterinary Company, converted to a composite supply platoon, and the 2d Veterinary Company on temporary duty.[60] Both of these were Negro units.

In their work on the Stilwell (Ledo) Road and on supporting and operating missions in the Advance Section of the India-Burma Theater Negro units were as fully employed as anywhere in World War II. The theater had a low priority on personnel and supplies and it was the one theater where, for most of its existence, a supply project—the construction of the Stilwell Road—took precedence over combat operations designed to pro-

vide a route for this supply project. All Negro engineer units on the road used equipment and performed tasks more complicated than anticipated for their troops; they learned to use equipment not ordinarily included in their tables of equipment. Negro troops, with their less adequate prior training and their less fully developed sense of purpose were less efficient in meeting the demands of the road than white units of similar types; the Advance Section estimated the operating efficiency of Negro troops at 70 percent that of white troops. Nevertheless the Negro units did a major share of the work on the road. Equipment operation schools, orientation lectures, and efforts to instill pride in their accomplishments were effective in most units, with at least one, the 1883d Aviation Battalion, rated "comparable to the best of the white units" in the last year of operations.[61]

Morale among Negro units on the road was judged to be higher than that of white units. There were no clashes between white and Negro troops. Racial problems were present but they involved the many races and nationalities living and working in close proximity to the road. British, Indians, Burmese, the Naga Hill people, and Chinese were on the road as well as white and Negro Americans. The differences and tensions among the many nationalities were greater than those between white and Negro American troops, but in general there were few other than individual disagreements of a sort that might take place between men of the same race or nation.[62] Recreational facilities, such

---

[57] GO 32, Hq SOS IBT, 6 Dec 44.
[58] Hist SOS IBT, app. 4, Advance Section Three, p. 116.
[59] Ibid., p. 88.
[60] Ibid., p. 89.

[61] Ibid., pp. 27, 197.
[62] Ibid., pp. 21, 197, 268.

as theaters, Red Cross clubs, and athletic contests, were open to both Negro and white troops, but separate rest camps, originally of unequal quality, caused some bitterness. There were complaints that Negro troops were more prone to use native intoxicants and drugs, and that this resulted in more clashes with the local population, especially over women. Indians complained of "barbaric" treatment by Negro troops, but these complaints were made against white troops as well.[63]

The Stilwell Road itself was sufficient incentive to cause many of the Negro troops and units to exert themselves as fully as possible. The 45th Engineers reported that in their first few months on the road morale was high because the men realized the importance of their work. The 858th Engineer Aviation Battalion found that its troops "were proud that of all the Engineer Battalions in the IBT, the 858th Engineer Aviation Battalion had been given the honor of going to China." [64] Troops in areas farther to the rear had fewer visible incentives, but, as one base general depot reported, were reasonably efficient in their duties.[65] Another base section declared that its two Negro quartermaster truck companies, operating motor pools with Indian drivers, played "an important part" in the successful operations of the area.[66] As in many other cases, headquarters reported that there was a distinct relation between leadership and

performance. General Depot 2 explained: "If the officers concerned accept and deal with the problems of the Negro soldier, there are no problems. Therefore, he becomes the same as any other soldier in time of war, willing to complete his work to the best of his ability and then return to his home." [67] The units themselves were all run-of-the mine organizations with all the endemic difficulties of Negro units and commands. Their work in the difficult projects assigned them in India and Burma, when all of their problems of training and background are considered, was a tribute to the potency of definite missions and to the adaptability and speed with which officers and men could learn both manual and leadership skills when need was greater than original skill or outlook.

Liberia Force

An early project which got under way slowly and then became moribund almost as soon as it started was the Liberia Force. In early 1942 Liberia granted the United States the unrestricted right to construct, control, operate, and defend such commercial and military airfields as might be deemed necessary by mutual agreement, and the Army was given the task of defending Liberian airfields.[68]

The task force for Liberia consisted mostly of Negro units. The officers and enlisted men of its headquarters, signal,

[63] *Ibid.*; Hist SOS IBT, app. 29, Base General Depot No. 2, p. 95, OCMH.
[64] Hist 45th Engr Gen Sv Regt for 1943; Hist 858th Engr Avn Bn, 8 Jan 44–15 Sep 45.
[65] Hist SOS IBT, app. 29, Base General Depot 2, pp. 95, 119, OCMH.
[66] Hist SOS IBT, app. 2, Opn Br of Base Section 2, p. 6, OCMH.
[67] *Ibid.*, app. 29, Base General Depot 2, p. 95, OCMH.
[68] Memo, WPD for CofS, 18 Jan 42, and Ltr, SW to Secy State, 21 Jan 42, both in WPD 4376–10; Memo, WPD for WD G–4, 24 Feb 42, OCS 20431/40; Memo, OPD for Col W. F. Dean, Rqmts Sec AGF, 7 Dec 42, OPD 320.2/DO.

OVERNIGHT STOP ALONG THE LEDO ROAD

and quartermaster detachments, five officers of the 25th Station Hospital, and personnel of the ferry command and supporting Air Corps units were white. An advance construction force, set up to prepare installations and provide defense pending the arrival of the full force, was made up of the 41st Engineer General Service Regiment (less the 2d Battalion), Co A, 812th Engineer Aviation Battalion (later redesignated the 899th Engineer Aviation Company), the 802d Coast Artillery Battery, and an advance detachment of the 25th Station Hospital.[69] These units arrived in June 1942. A detachment, with Negro enlisted men, to train the Liberian Frontier (Guard) Force, went to Monrovia. Originally the 1st Battalion, 367th Infantry, was scheduled to move at the same time, but shipping difficulties caused its deferment. The 41st Engineers received additional armament for

---

[69] Memo, WPD for CG's AGF, AAF, SOS, 16 Mar 42, WPD 381/DO (3–16–42); Ltr, Hq AGF to CG Second Army, 20 Mar 42, AGF 320.2/76 OPN; Memo, OPD for Col Wood, 25 May 42, OPD 381 Liberia (5–25–42).

BASEBALL GAME. 1ST TRANSPORT SQUADRON AND 858TH ENGINEERS, *Assam, India.*

their defense mission, making the regiment comparable to a unit of combat engineers. The 99th Squadron and its supporting service units were to join the Liberia Force later, but they were eliminated after danger of an Axis attack on Liberia diminished. The force itself had to proceed to Liberia since the United States' agreement with that country provided for it, but no commitment had been made to include air units. After being on and off alerts since April 1942, the 367th Infantry,

now a separate battalion, therefore proceeded to Liberia on 8 February 1943, arriving at Marshall, Liberia, on 10 March.[70]

Aside from building Roberts Field and access roads, troops in Liberia encountered no particular problems. All units moving out to the West African republic had been warned of the health hazards in the back country of this tropical land. The major hazard that developed was venereal disease, for the "free"

[70] Hist 367th Inf Bn, 2 Mar–18 May 44.

(unmarried) women of the villages displaced by the airfield and from coastal towns flocked to the Roberts Field area. The control measures instituted in Liberia, calling for a regulatory system complete with dispensaries and regular inspections of women housed in villages, proved satisfactory to the women and to most soldiers, who, for disciplinary and work reasons, had to be kept relatively close to the installations they were constructing. Venereal rates declined but were still higher than rates among Negro troops in the United States. Despite weekly examinations, control among the women was difficult, for Liberian men could sneak into the villages with ease, reinfecting the women.[71] Photographs of white troops and local women sent as post cards raised the question of the possible use of the "women's villages" in enemy propaganda among the peoples of Africa and Asia. The command attempted to substitute a full recreational program in an area where all recreation was limited. It was more successful with a rigid photograph censorship in Liberia.[72]

The Liberia garrison dwindled gradually as the need for defense and for specific units decreased. The nurses of the 25th Hospital were replaced by male nurses. After ten months, the 367th moved to Oran, arriving in February 1944. The 41st Engineers moved to Corsica and later to France and Germany. The 802d Coast Artillery Battery was disbanded in Liberia.[73] Instructors for the Liberia Guard Force

and hospital and air service troops remained, for Roberts Field continued to be useful to the air transport and ferry commands until the end of the war.

Rear Area Employment

It was in ports, base sections, and depots that the great majority of Negro service units were employed overseas. Aside from the bases already mentioned, the Persian Gulf, for example, had in its first priority of American troop requirements a Negro laundry platoon (the 2d Platoon, 350th Quartermaster Company) ; in its second were two Negro port battalions (480th and 481st) and one truck regiment (49th); and in its third, two Negro engineer general service regiments (357th and 352d) and two dump truck companies (435th and 436th).[74] As the worldwide deployment of the United States Army increased after mid-1944—and as the greater number of Negroes inducted in 1942 and 1943 became available in units completing their training in either their original or converted forms—the proportions of Negro troops overseas mounted rapidly. In March 1944 there were still 357,802 Negro soldiers in the United States as against the 314,075 overseas. But by December 1944, the number overseas rose to 477,421—more than twice as many as the 214,100 remaining in the United States. By April 1945 there were 511,493 Negroes overseas and 188,811 in the continental United

[71] Memo, G–1 for CofS, 14 Mar 43, with Incl, SGO (Brumfield) to G–1, 2 Mar 43, SPSP 710, WDGAP/250.1 (9–21–42).

[72] Memo, OPD for ASW, 29 Apr 43, OPD 381 Liberia.

[73] GO 23, Hq USAFIL, 22 Dec 43.

[74] Plan for Operation of Certain Iranian Communications Facilities Between Persian Gulf and Teheran by USA Forces, SPLS 1000. See T. H. Vail Motter, *The Persian Corridor and Aid to Russia,* UNITED STATES ARMY IN WORLD WAR II (Washington, 1952).

States. This was the peak overseas figure of the war.[75] Of the 477,421 overseas in December 1944, 169,678 were quartermaster troops, 111,012 were engineers, and 64,458 were transportation troops.[76]

With so large a proportion of the Negro force overseas in the services and with so many of the service troops in rear areas, a number of problems were faced by both the troops and by overseas commands. To many white troops and commanders, the sole Negro troops seen in overseas theaters were those in the ports and rear areas. This, coupled with rumors about the two Negro divisions, left a strong impression that Negro troops were not only used for little else but also that they were fitted for nothing else.[77] In the towns and villages of the war-crowded British Isles, in North Africa, and in Italy, the problem of Negro-civilian and Negro-white troop relations sometimes became acute, although Negroes and civilians often got along better than they were expected to and sometimes better than many white American troops thought they should.

With the arrival of increasingly large numbers of Negro troops in the British Isles in 1942, the European theater developed a well-defined policy intended to decrease friction between Negro and white troops and between American troops in general and the British population. This policy was extended to the Continent after the invasion. While other theaters developed varying policies, they were usually vague and undefined even though encompassed within larger War Department policies. Their specific implementation was often left to subordinate commands. In contrast, the European theater developed early a clearly stated policy which, with few exceptions, was held to for the duration of the war. The development of the policy in this theater was the result of four important factors largely absent elsewhere: the vocal interest of the British population and Government in the removal of causes for friction among the many nationalities and races of troops present in the United Kingdom; the active support of the chief American commanders for such a policy; the presence of a larger number of Negro troops in the European theater than elsewhere (154,000 in August 1944 as compared with 81,870 in the North African theater, the next largest concentration at the time) ; [78] and the institution of methods for direct observation of the effectiveness of the measures proposed.

Since the whole of the United Kingdom, including Northern Ireland, is not as large as the state of Oregon, and since much of Scotland was unsuitable for training camps and bases, the bulk of the incoming troops had to be concentrated in the already heavily populated Midlands of England. Getting along with each other as well as with the British therefore became all the more important. In July 1942 General Eisenhower's headquarters issued a statement of policy:

1. The presence of Negro troops in this Theater will present a variety of problems that can only be solved by constant and

[75] Strength of the Army, STM–30, 1 Dec 45.
[76] Ibid., 1 Jan 45.
[77] Ltr, SSgt H.A.W., Stars and Stripes (October 12, 1944) ; Benjamin C. Bowker, Out of Uniform (New York: Norton, 1946), pp. 193–212.
[78] Strength of the Army, STM–30, 1 Sep 44.

close supervision of Commanding Officers. It is the desire of this Headquarters that discrimination against the Negro troops be sedulously avoided. So far as London and other cities and leave areas where both Negro and White soldiers will come on pass and furlough, it would be a practical impossibility to arrange for segregation so far as welfare and recreation facilities are concerned. The Red Cross has been notified that Negro soldiers will be accorded the same leaves and furlough privileges as other soldiers and consequently they can expect them to come into their clubs. The Red Cross has been informed that wherever it is not possible to provide separate accommodations, the Negro soldiers will be given the same accommodations in the clubs on the same basis as White soldiers.

2. A more difficult problem will exist in the vicinity of camps where both White and Negro soldiers are stationed, particularly with reference to dances and other social activities. This Headquarters will not attempt to issue any detailed instructions. Local Commanding Officers will be expected to use their own best judgment in avoiding discrimination due to race, but at the same time, minimizing causes of friction between White and Colored Troops. Rotation of pass privileges and similar methods suggest themselves for use, always with the guiding principle that any restriction imposed by Commanding Officers applies with equal force to both races.[79]

Carrying out this directive fell primarily to Maj. Gen. John C. H. Lee, whose Services of Supply contained most of the Negro troops in the United Kingdom. To his base section commanders and commanding officers he transmitted the directive, declaring that it "sets forth clearly and unmistakably the basic principles which must guide every commanding officer in the exercise of his responsibilities of command. These

fundamental principles, enunciated by the Theater Commander, are founded on fairness, justice, and common sense. They permit of no deviation or compromise."[80]

The determination of Generals Eisenhower and Lee that internal dissensions between American Negro and white troops would not jeopardize Anglo-American relations, always under scrutiny because of the undetermined length of time that the British would have to play hosts to visiting foreign armies, gradually trickled down to lower commands. Since new units were constantly arriving, the policy had to be reiterated frequently. Some units took positive measures to prevent friction. The 28th Quartermaster Regiment with V Corps in Northern Ireland appointed three of its noncommissioned officers to a "Good Conduct Committee," inviting three white noncommissioned officers from neighboring units to join with them. These six men arranged for the selection of other noncommissioned officers from each of the companies and batteries in Northern Ireland, who discussed and carried back to their units the rules of good conduct.[81] The plan spread to II Corps, where each regiment and separate battalion, white and Negro, was asked to form a "Good Conduct Committee" to meet in joint session to discuss race relations.[82] The plan, essentially that which Judge Hastie had proposed for the Army in the United States, enabled individual soldiers to de-

[79] Ltr, Hq ETOUSA to CG's and CO's, 16 Jul 42, ETOUSA AG–Misc 291.2–A.

[80] Ltr, Hq SOS ETOUSA to Base Sec Comdrs and All CO's, 7 Aug 42, AG 291.2.
[81] Ltr, Hq V Corps to Eisenhower, 19 Aug 42, ETOUSA AG 291.2.
[82] Ltr, Hq II Army Corps to All Div and Separate Unit CO's, 6 Sep 42, ETOUSA AG 291.2.

termine for themselves how best to engender mutual respect, avoid acts which might lead to friction, and spread the word that the Red Cross was to be impartial in its treatment of soldiers.

The British Home Office at the end of August decided to inform its chief constables that it was not "the policy of His Majesty's Government that any discrimination as regards the treatment of coloured troops should be made by the British authorities" and that they should instruct local police not to approach the proprietors of "public houses, restaurants, cinemas or other places" with directions to refuse service to Negro troops. If the American authorities decided to put certain places "out of bounds" for Negro troops they could do so only by issuing an order to their own troops. British police should make themselves in no way responsible for enforcing such orders.

This circular letter, sent to General Eisenhower's headquarters for comment, elicited another affirmation of theater policy:

The Commanding General is in complete accord with the instructions the Home Office proposes to issue. This policy of non-discrimination is exactly the policy which has always been followed by the United States Army. Subordinate United States Army commanders in the European Theater of Operations are being informed of the proposed action of the Home Office.

With reference to the question of placing certain places out of bounds, we do not make any restrictions of that kind on the basis of color. The policy followed by the United States Army authorities is that places put out of bounds for United States soldiers are out of bounds to all United States Army personnel.[83]

In bringing these exchanges with the British Home Office to the attention of his commanders, General Eisenhower further informed them:

The presence of Negro troops in this theater creates a problem in inter-racial relationships much different from that in the United States. There is practically no coloured population in the British Isles. Undoubtedly a considerable association of colored troops with British white population, both men and women, will take place on a basis mutually acceptable to the individuals concerned. Any attempt to curtail such association by official orders or restrictions is unjustified and must not be attempted. Furthermore, it must be realized by all ranks that it is absolutely essential that American officers and soldiers carefully avoid making any public or private statements of a derogatory nature concerning racial groups in the United States Army. *The spreading of derogatory statements concerning the character of any group of United States troops, either white or colored, must be considered as conduct prejudicial to good order and military discipline and offenders must be promptly punished.* In the interest of military efficiency, if for no other reason, isolated incidents of friction must be eliminated.

. . . .

4. There must be continuing attention on the part of all concerned to this problem if we are to avoid distressing situations. I am taking this means of bringing the matter again to your attention because I feel that it must not be handled in a routine or perfunctory manner. *It is my desire that this be brought to the attention of every officer in this theater.* To that end, I suggest that you *personally talk this over with your next senior commander and instruct them to follow up the subject through command channels.*[84]

---

[83] Ltr, Hq ETOUSA to F. A. Newsom, Home Office, 3 Sep 42, ETOUSA AG 291.2.

[84] Ltr, Hq ETOUSA (Eisenhower) to CG's, 5 Sep 42, ETOUSA AG 291.2–B. Italics (underlining) added in SOS reproduction.

General Lee directed that every officer in the SOS read this letter and its inclosures to his immediate subordinates and then discuss it with them. Every white soldier was to be instructed and warned that "General Eisenhower means exactly what he says in par. 2 *underlined* above." [85]

Command attention to the problem of racial friction in the British Isles did not eliminate it entirely, but although the American troop population in Britain grew to more than 1,500,000 by May 1944 reports of racial incidents did not increase proportionately. As new troops came into the United Kingdom indoctrination had to continue, especially since a number of local commanders, arguing that further segregation than that permitted by issuing passes to towns and organizing dances on a unit basis was necessary to avoid trouble, took it upon themselves to add restrictions of their own. Some felt that the theater policy favored Negro soldiers, especially when officers who ignored theater policy were removed from their units and when the theater insisted that the word of a white military policeman count for no more than that of a Negro involved in a scrape. "This is a most important issue," General Lee stated, "because it cuts right down into our innermost thinking and feeling. Are we fighting this war on a clean issue or are we kidding ourselves? We've got to decide and make our decisions stick." [86]

The Red Cross, told to provide for Negroes on the same basis as for white soldiers when no separate club was available, set up a number of Negro-staffed clubs which gradually came to be known as "Colored Clubs." By February 1944 there were twenty-three of these clubs.[87] The Red Cross insisted that "We have no negro clubs. We have no white clubs. We have negro staff clubs and white staff clubs. Any negro in this Theater is welcome to any club we have. Any soldier whether he is white or black is the same." [88] But the existence of the separately staffed clubs, moved about as racial concentrations of troops altered, left a sour taste with Negro soldiers and Negro Red Cross workers, and at times led to friction when military police prevented Negroes from entering white-staffed clubs and white soldiers from entering Negro-staffed clubs.

The Red Cross clubs, like the American National Red Cross itself, were operated independently from the Army, but the close association between them and the Army overseas did not permit clear distinctions between the two institutions or their policies by the average enlisted man and officer. The Red Cross admitted that where there were no separate clubs and a Negro soldier occasionally came into white-staffed clubs, the Negro soldier himself gave little difficulty. "I must say," Edward J. Beinecke commented, "he conducts himself very well. When there has been friction, it is invariably started by the white soldier." General Lee bore out Mr. Beinecke's statement and Maj. Gen. Paul R. Hawley, theater surgeon, likewise agreed

---

[85] Ltr, Hq SOS ETO (Lee) to Maj Gen Robert M. Littlejohn, Deputy SOS Comdr, 11 Sep 42, SOS ETO 291.1.

[86] Quoted in Martin Sommers, "Lee—Batting for Eisenhower," *Saturday Evening Post*, CCXVII (September 2, 1944), 37.

[87] ARC Club Opn Cir 164, Sixth Issue, Feb 44.

[88] Edwin J. Beinecke at ETO SOS Staff Conf, Notes on Staff Conf, Hq SPS ETO, 30 Aug 43.

that Negro soldiers had caused no trouble in the nonsegregated hospitals.[89] Maj. Gen. Ira C. Eaker, commanding the Eighth Air Force, was of similar opinion, holding that where disturbances occurred white troops were responsible for 90 percent of the trouble.[90]

Although censorship excerpts cannot be taken at complete face value because of the circumstances of their origin—soldiers' letters do not necessarily reveal the full state of the individual's mind and no method of selection can guarantee an accurate cross-section of soldier opinion—they do reveal the complexity of the racial attitudes which the European theater was attempting to deal with. The majority of letters from white troops, particularly of those newly arrived, commented, month after month, and with varying degrees of amazement, on the lack of a color line in Great Britain and with indignation on the association of British women and Negro soldiers. Some explained that Negro troops had passed themselves off on the unsuspecting Irish and British as American Indians. Others declared that only the lower classes were friendly to Negroes. Some expressed fears of what their racial experience in Britain would lead to at home after the war. Others, as a result of this experience, commented unfavorably on the British people as a whole, an attitude which the theater, trying to cement Allied solidarity, considered especially disturb-

ing. Negro troops, on the other hand, expressed pleasure with the English and the Irish as they found them. Certain of their officers were happy that British custom had removed the problem of overt discrimination and public segregation from their list of troubles. They expressed themselves as satisfied with the conduct of their troops on foreign soil. A few officers not assigned to Negro troops expressed themselves as similarly pleased, though the majority voicing an opinion shared that of white enlisted men. After a time, Negro troops showed a desire to see more women of their own race. But the dominant tone of the letters was one of pleasant surprise on the part of Negro troops and an angry shock on the part of white troops. One WAC officer, after analysing censorship reports for several weeks, reported toward the end of May 1944 that "The predominant note is that if the invasion doesn't occur soon, trouble will." [91]

Official concern that no untoward racial disturbance interfere with the mounting of an invasion from the United Kingdom led to certain administrative practices in the employment of Negro troops. For the most part, port battalions and companies were separated by race in their work and in their locations. When two new units were arriving in England in September 1943, for instance, the Chief of Transportation, SOS, advised that if they were white they should be sent to the Bristol Channel "as it is inexpedient to mix white and coloured stevedore troops in the

[89] Ibid.
[90] Alfred Goldberg, "Build-up," in The Army Air Forces in World War II (Chicago: The University of Chicago Press, 1949), II, p. 656. See also Carrier Sheet, CO London Base Comd to CG ETO, 3 Oct 43, ETO AG 291.2, I (1943).

[91] Memo, Capt Susie J. Thurman, Hist Sec ETOUSA, for Col Ganoe, 29 May 44, ETOUSA Admin No. 218; Base Censor Office Special Reports, 1942–1944.

AMBULANCE MEN AT THE 14TH MAJOR PORT TRANSFERRING D-DAY CASUALTIES
en route to a field hospital in England (Southampton, 8 June 1944).

same port district." If both were Negro, they should be put in one sector,
"say Swansea and Barry." [92] Four
more arrivals, two white and two Negro,
were expected in the near future. "To
avoid mixing," the chief of operations
of the ETO Transportation Corps determined, "it is proposed placing these
as follows: Bristol Channel District, 2
battalions (white); 14th POE, 1 battal-

ion (coloured) ; and Mersey, 1 battalion
(coloured)." He had hoped to subdivide
a battalion among London, Southampton, and Plymouth "but the Authorities
are opposed to placing coloured troops in
Plymouth. Accordingly, it will apparently be necessary to restrict this battalion to London aid Southampton." [93]

Although it grew to a larger size than
most, the 14th Major Port, whose incoming battalion was originally to be divided among London, Southampton, and

[92] Comment 2, CofT SOS, APO 887 (London) to
ACofT Marine Opns SOS, 15 Sep 43, TC USFET
322.171 Arms of Service—Port Labor Bns, Railroads.

[93] *Ibid.,* Comment 4.

Plymouth, may be taken as representative of port operating headquarters employing considerable numbers of Negro units. The 14th Port, split into five groups at London, Southampton, Hull, Immingham, and Plymouth upon arrival in England in July 1943, was eventually consolidated at Southampton. It controlled all ports on the south coast of England from Southampton to Land's End, with its main port at Southampton and its main subports at Poole, Plymouth, and Portland-Weymouth. The port of Southampton alone handled a greater lift from D-day to V–E Day than any other port in the world in a comparable period of time. In the first six months after D-day, 6,444 vessels with a dead-weight tonnage of 1,781,753 and carrying 1,934,752 individuals and 170,000 vehicles cleared through Southampton alone. Total strength of the port on 31 January 1945 was 501 officers, 103 warrant officers, and 5,708 enlisted men. Assigned or attached to the port for duty from D-day to V–E Day were 23,138 officers and men. From Southampton, 2,439 LST's sailed during the period and 1,934 sailed from Weymouth. The port not only outloaded vehicles, supplies, and personnel for the far shore; it received personnel evacuated from the Continent and embarked personnel returning to the United States.[94]

Of the 27 port companies used by this port, 25 were Negro. Eight of its 15

truck companies and both of its truck battalion headquarters were Negro. Its 3 quartermaster service companies, its quartermaster fumigation company, its quartermaster gas supply company, its medical sanitary companies used for handling and unloading wounded men, and its engineer general service regiment were Negro. Its harbor-craft companies, its military police, antiaircraft, marine maintenance, combat engineer, signal, and ordnance units, were all white because most of these types, in accordance with activation policies, had few or no Negro units.

By dint of continuing efforts on the part of the British and Americans, the policy of the European theater developed in such a manner that, in proportion to the number of troops present in the United Kingdom, few incidents of open friction occurred. There were occasional street brawls, fights, and individual encounters, many of them of no more racial significance than those occurring among British and other American troops. The theater asked in 1943 that each of its larger component forces appoint a "specially selected officer" to give full-time duty to the problems of discipline and control relating to Negro troops.[95] The Services of Supply, attempting to keep its policy uniform, forbade subordinate commanders to issue instructions or directives on the subject without its prior approval.[96] The theater, in October 1943, summarized its evolved policy, calling for the

[94] Facts Worth Knowing. . . . 14th Major Port from D Day to V–E Day (Privately printed, Camelot Press, Ltd, Southampton, 1945, 8 pp.); Rpt of Visit to 14th Major Port, Southampton, 5–7 Feb 45, Rpt 27, Hq ETO GI Sec, EUCOM 333.5; Special Historical Studies, 14th Port, England, 1945, TCPT–14.0–1 (46301); A Two-Year's History of the 14th Port, 25 February 1943 to 25 February 1945, TCPT–14-0.1 (30910).

[95] Ltr, Hq ETOUSA (Maj Gen I. H. Edwards, CofS) to CG's SOS, VIII AF, V Corps, 12 Jul 43, ETO AG 250 MCS.
[96] Ltr, SOS ETO to Base Comdrs, Hq Commandant SOS, 12 Oct 43, SOS ETO AG 291.2 (7 Oct 43).

prevention of incidents and the removal of "weak and inefficient leaders." It reminded commanders that discrimination would be permitted against neither white nor Negro troops and that "Equal opportunities for service and recreation are the right of every American soldier, regardless of branch, race, color, or creed." [97] While segregation of races in areas where it was contrary to local practices and customs was declared to be not in accord with theater policy, the theater approved rotation of pass days to nearby towns and the allocation of public facilities, such as dance halls and public houses, to units through control of pass privileges or by placing these places off limits to certain units.[98]

Upon his return to Britain in 1944, General Eisenhower issued further instructions reiterating this policy and stressing that "Troops must train together, work together and live together in order to attain successful teamwork in campaign. The sharing of work opportunities and recreational facilities must be willingly accepted and utilized to unite more closely the troops of our several commands." Again commanders were reminded of their responsibilities for "exemplifying to their troops a generous attitude of respect for other troops." [99] Personnel arriving in the United Kingdom, rapidly increasing in number and bringing a renewal of old problems with them, were ordered indoctrinated on subjects affecting their stay in the British Isles. The absence of a color line in the United Kingdom

headed the list.[100] When the orientation film, *Welcome to Britain*, was made, General Lee furthered this effort by appearing in it, answering the queries of an American soldier on how American Negroes should be treated in the United Kingdom.

The European theater accomplished its purpose of preventing racial problems from interfering with the efficiency of the invasion build-up and, later, from interfering with the European campaign itself. The program did not eliminate tension, but it reduced it to the point that complaints and disturbances were often kept on a verbal level where they did no real harm. After the invasion the theater formed a General Inspectorate Section, headed by Maj. Gen. Charles H. Bonesteel. This section, so named to distinguish it from staff sections performing inspections as the term is generally understood,[101] and because its name when abbreviated would read "G.I. Section," was an outgrowth of General Marshall's concern that any neglect of combat or service troops in rear areas would endanger efforts against the enemy and present "an unfortunate reaction when these men return to civilian life." [102] Complaints "too numerous and too serious to be considered as typical of the normal soldier's discontent" were coming from soldier returnees from all theaters,[103]

---

[97] Ltr, Hq ETOUSA to CG's, 25 Oct 43, ETO AG 250.1 MDCS.

[98] *Ibid.*

[99] Ltr, Hq ETO (Eisenhower) to Lee, 1 Mar 44, copy in ETOUSA 291.2.

[100] Ltr, Hq ETO to CG's, CO's, Base Sec Comdrs, Comdts, 9 Apr 44, ETOUSA AG 461 OpGA. For example of indoctrination directive, see Ltr, Hq FUSAG to Newly Assigned Pers FUSAG, 27 Apr 44, FUSAG 291.2, copy in the 12th Army Gp 291.2.

[101] Chronological Outline of Activation and Operation of the General Inspectorate Section, Incl to Ltr, Hq ETO GI Sec to CG ETO, 3 Jun 45, p. 1.

[102] Ltr, Marshall to Eisenhower, 26 Oct 44, copy in app. A to Chronological Outline cited n. 101.

[103] *Ibid.*

but only the European theater set up a section with continuing finding functions separate from those of The Inspector General and outside the established morale and welfare agencies.[104]

The General Inspectorate Section included in its purview an examination of racial relations in the areas and installations which it surveyed.[105] Brig. Gen. Benjamin O. Davis, now Special Advisor to the Theater Commander on Colored Troops, worked closely with the General Inspectorate Section from the beginning. Later he joined it, heading one of its six field teams.[106] The other teams continued to include a check of Negro-white relations and welfare in their own agenda. These teams included limited service ex-combat men, whose conversations with other enlisted men and visits to enlisted messes and barracks gave a fuller view of soldiers' thinking than could have been obtained by officer members of the teams. The teams enabled the theater to keep a close check on developments in racial relations as well as in the area of general welfare. Field teams, in emergencies, could make corrective recommendations on the spot, including recommendations to higher commanders for the removal of weak

officers and correction of violations of general theater policies.

The organization and employment of Negro service troops in the Oise Section at the time that Supreme Headquarters, Allied Expeditionary Force, was moving to Reims was typical of the distribution and control of Negro service units on the Continent. From its Reims headquarters, the Oise Section exercised its command through depots and groups; regiments, hospitals, and battalions were commanded directly and a few engineer units were under the section engineer. The total number of units in the section at the beginning of February 1945 was 324. Their total white strength was 29,154 and total Negro strength, 14,060. The headquarters command was all white but, under the flexible group system, depots and groups were sometimes mixed, although white and Negro units under the same headquarters were usually located in different towns. For example, Chemical Depot C–939–T at Sommesous had the Negro 32d Chemical Decontamination Company at Avenay, with a detachment at Vregny, and its white depot company at Sommesous. The other three chemical depots in the section had white personnel only. Ordnance Depot O–609 at Vregny had six white ammunition and three Negro quartermaster service companies there and four Negro ammunition companies in other towns. Under the white 261st Ordnance Battalion at Depot O–612 at Maubeuge were one white bomb disposal squad and two white and three Negro ordnance ammunition companies. A separate Negro quartermaster service company was also assigned to the depot. At the Quartermaster Depot Q–180 at Reims, under the white 55th

<hr>

[104] Ltr, SHAEF to CG ETO, 13 Nov 44, AG 353.81–1 AGP; Ltr. Hq ETOUSA to CG's, Med. O. and G–1 SHAEF, 17 Nov 44, copy in app. A to Chronological Outline cited n. 101; Ltr, Hq ETOUSA to CG's, 22 Dec 44, Estimate of Hq ETOUSA, AG 322 OPCS.

[105] Memo 2, Hq ETOUSA GI Sec, 4 Jan 45, Statement of Scope of Activities, Check List. See also Memo 7, 21 March 1945, which required a general paragraph in all reports, where applicable, covering seven items, the fourth of which was discrimination against Negro troops and the fifth, white-Negro relationships.

[106] Ltr, Hq ETOUSA to CG's, 23 Jan 45, AG 322.011, resulted in General Davis' assignment to the General Inspectorate.

RED BALL EXPRESS TRUCKS MOVING THROUGH A REGULATING POINT

Quartermaster Base Depot, were a variety of quartermaster battalion headquarters, some white and some Negro, some with all white and some with all Negro units under them and some with white and Negro companies billeted either in the same or in different towns. The 123d Battalion, a Negro unit, controlled a Negro service and a Negro bakery company while the Negro 558th Quartermaster Battalion controlled a Negro and a white service company, both of them at Reims. The white 170th Battalion controlled four white and one Negro gas supply and one Negro service company. The 512th Quartermaster Group (TC), a Negro headquarters at Soissons, controlled the 476th Quartermaster Battalion (Mobile) (TC), a white headquarters at Cernay les Reims, which in turn controlled

eleven truck companies, three white and eight Negro, most of them in different towns. No clashes had occurred between military police and troops and the only difficulty between white and Negro troops occurred on the arrival of airborne troops, who had trouble with the section's white as well as with its Negro personnel. The Negro dump truck companies, attached to larger Negro and white engineer units, came in closest daily contact with the white troops. Of one of these an observer reported, "They got along well with the white soldiers with whom they were associated. They were right in the midst of the airborne troops but there had been no untoward instances whatever." [107]

During the rapid advance of the

[107] Rpt of Visit to Oise Sec, Reims, France, 17–25 Feb 45, Rpt 32, GI Sec ETO, 333.5.

armies in Europe after the breakthrough at Avranches in August 1944, the movement of large tonnages of supplies to the First and Third Armies became imperative. French railroads had been wrecked by the retreating German armies. To meet supply needs, the Transportation Corps devised the Red Ball plan on 21 August, and put it into operation four days later. The plan called for two one-way reserved highway routes marked "Red Ball Trucks Only." The original route, from St. Lô to Paris and return, was later extended to Sommesous, Reims, and Hirson. Red Ball convoys operated from 25 August to 13 November 1944. The truckers carried approximately 412,193 tons of supplies to the armies, covering a total of 121,873,929 ton-miles during this period. On the average day, 899 vehicles went forward, traveling 1,504,616 ton-miles. The average time for the trip to Paris and return was 53.4 hours; the maximum number of truck units operating on the route was 140, supplemented at the height of operations by trucks manned by personnel of combat and other service units. This number had dwindled to nineteen by the time tactical changes and the development of new ports caused the closing of the route. The majority of the units were Negro companies. Approximately 73 percent of the truck companies in the Motor Transport Service in the European theater were Negro.[108]

Supplementing the Red Ball Express and replacing it after its operations closed down were several other through highways modeled on it. The White Ball Route, carrying supplies from Le Havre and Rouen to forward areas at Beauvais and Reims for the northern French and Belgian campaigns and to rail transfer points at Paris, began operating with six companies on 25 September, clearing the ports of Le Havre and Rouen as its first mission. The B–B (Bayeaux-Brussels) Red Lion Route transported 500 tons of British petrol and other supplies daily from Bayeaux to the 21 Army Group Roadhead 1 at Brussels for approximately thirty days, beginning 16 September 1944. Four of the nine truck companies on this route were Negro units. The ABC (Antwerp-Brussels-Charleroi) Route began to operate on 30 November. The Green Diamond Route, operating from 10 October to 1 November, ran between the ports and beaches of Normandy and Dol at the northern base of the Brest peninsula, passing through Avranches and Granville on the way. Two battalions, one of which was Negro, operated nineteen truck companies on this route at the peak of operations. Two battalions, the 467th and 519th, the latter Negro, operated the POL (petroleum, oil, lubricants) routes of the Motor Transport Service. These units began to operate on D plus 8, moving forward as pipelines were laid, loading from pipe taps and storage tanks along the line, and carrying POL to forward dumps for the armies.[109] In the Advance Section, Communications Zone, gas supply companies like the 3877th, a corps unit supplying divisional troops, and the 3917th, supplying

[108] Motor Transport Service, ch. V, vol. V, pt. 2 of Hist Rpt TC in ETO, p. 7.

[109] Ibid., pp. 11–23. See also Joseph Bykofsky and Harold Larson, The Transportation Corps: Operations Overseas, UNITED STATES ARMY IN WORLD WAR II (Washington, 1957), ch. VIII.

Third Army forces from August to V–E Day, took over. These units operated forward dumps, issuing and carrying to divisional units up to 165,000 gallons of gasoline a day.[110]

In general, the work of service troops at ports and bases and on the roads was that for which they were organized, although occasionally an engineer general service regiment or a chemical unit felt that its training and usefulness were dissipated on guard, prisoner of war, or ration hauling duties.[111] The 1323d and 388th Engineer General Service Regiments, while in Britain, formed seven truck companies each within their organizations; each regiment, operating as two battalions, worked under the Normandy Base Section on the Continent. The 84th Chemical Smoke Generator Company, before moving to screen the Third Army's Moselle Crossing at Arnaville, operated as a truck unit, carrying supplies forward over the Red Ball Express route. But, for the most part, in bases and ports around the world units were used either for their primary missions or, as in the cases of engineer units on the Stilwell Road, in capacities beyond original intentions. Engineer separate battalions in the Mediterranean were originally used as general engineer labor, as planned, but gradually their work assignments changed until they were used, in the end, in practically the same manner as general service units. Lacking the training, equipment, and personnel of the general service units, their results were not always comparable to those of the more technical

units, but they became valuable reserve forces for emergency jobs.[112] General service engineers often functioned as aviation and construction units.

Most Negro units were not expected to be very successful in supervising native foreign labor. The India-Burma theater reported that it tried to have Negro port companies in Calcutta work with white port companies, supervising Indian labor, only to have the operating efficiency of all units decline. The Negro units went then to separate docks, doing all their own labor, and the white units remained at the King George docks, supervising Indian labor.[113] The Persian Gulf reported similarly that white and Negro port companies did not work together harmoniously, though white and Negro engineer units did. Initially there was resentment on the part of Iranian laborers to working under the supervision of Negro troops who had, the Iranians said, formerly been used as slave laborers in America. But, by continuing the supervisory duties of Negro troops, the problem was "gradually overcome, and towards the close of operations no difficulties were experienced." [114]

There were similar problems in North Africa and Italy where some Negro units had difficulties with both Italian civilian labor and Italian service units, the cobelligerent units formed after the Italian armistice. But the 22d Quartermaster Group which, as the 22d Quartermaster Regiment,

---

[110] "Gasoline," *The Quartermaster Review*, XXIV (May–June 1945) , 23.

[111] Cf. Rpt of Visit to Seventh Army, ETO L–1135–Fw 9.

[112] Lt Col William F. Powers, Observer's Rpt on the Engr Sv, SOS NATOUSA, in Trudeau, NATO Rpt.

[113] Hist SOS IBT, Admin Hist, 25 Oct 44–20 May 45, pp. 57f, OCMH.

[114] Ltr, Hq Persian Gulf Comd to TAG, 14 Aug 45, WDSSP 291.2.

Smoke Screen for the Third Army Crossing of the Moselle River, *November 1944.*

landed at Casablanca on 18 November 1942 in the D plus 5 convoy of the Western Task Force and which operated convoys for both American and French forces, trained 3,500 French enlisted men in the use of lend-lease vehicles in 1942. This unit piled up an efficient work record in North Africa—while assigned to the Atlantic Base Section it drove 7,311,000 truck-miles averaging 664,637 miles a month with an accident average of 1 per 30,719 miles—and operated later in the Naples and Leghorn areas under Peninsular Base Section. At Naples, beginning in October 1943,

it operated a civilian truck pool and in April 1944 it began training Italian truck companies. As a group, the 22d had both white and Negro battalions working on the same missions. It had under its control from October 1943 a total of fifteen separate Negro truck battalions, four white truck battalions, two British truck battalions, seven Italian battalions with twenty-nine companies, two Negro service companies, and miscellaneous attached Negro units. Of the 13,000 men coming under its command from October 1943 to the end of the war, only half (6,750) were Negroes, though the normal proportion at a given period was 4,500 Negroes out of 6,500 troops. Its units performed efficiently in this variegated command setup. Its two original battalions, the 37th and the 110th, and its first added battalion, the 125th, all three Negro units, were the first truck battalions in the theater to receive the Meritorious Service Plaque. As a regiment and group the unit had mixed white and Negro officers. In the interest of efficiency the unit not only permitted no segregation between officers and used a single standard in promoting whites and Negroes, but it also departed from general Army policy by promoting Negro officers to positions over white officers. Two of its companies were commanded by Negro officers with white subordinates. The 22d Quartermaster Group reported that "There is no friction or resentment against these officers having their position and command, because they are recognized as the most capable and qualified and entitled to the position, and they observe the highest degree of conduct themselves in relations to their white associates." [115]

Service Units in the Combat Zone

Most Negro service units never got close to the enemy, but some did, as elements of landing forces and through attachments to divisions and other combat units engaged at the front.

For the most part Negro units in Pacific landing forces were quartermaster, port, and engineer types, attached to divisions, engineer special brigades, construction groups, or boat and shore battalions. These units usually reverted to garrison forces once an island was declared secure. For the invasion of Angaur in the Palaus on 17 September 1944, for example, the assault echelon contained one white and one Negro engineer aviation battalion and one Negro port company among other service units needed for immediate use on the beaches. One port company and a platoon of a quartermaster service company were attached to the 81st Division for its landings; a Dukw company was attached to the assault forces. The first echelon contained a quartermaster service company, an engineer service company, and a laundry truck company. The technical, bombardment, and antiaircraft units in these echelons were white. [116]

When assault forces departed Humboldt Bay, New Guinea, on 13 October 1944 to take part in the Leyte landings on 20 October, the 394th Port Battalion's 609th Port Company had one platoon with each of the three battalions of the 34th Infantry, each aboard a different ship with the battalion to which it was attached. While the ships were under fire, the three elements of the 609th assisted in unloading troops and equipment. The three platoons finished their tasks in record time. Two then proceeded to shore where the infantry had advanced about two hundred yards in from the beach. The third platoon moved to a Navy ship and discharged cargo until nightfall. Through the night, the port troops received intense small arms and automatic

---

[115] Hist 22d QM Truck Regt (Gp); Hq Peninsular Base Sec (Col Roger W. Whitman) to Brig Gen H. S. Clarkson, Hq MTO, 19 Jul 45, WDSSP 291.2.

[116] Army Garrison Force, APO 264, 98–84.1 (15524).

weapons fire, suffering their first casualty other than men wounded in raids at Humboldt Bay.

The next morning the two platoons on shore went back into the bay to help the third platoon complete its unloading task. For the next three days, while enemy planes raided the harbor, the entire company, except the headquarters, lived and worked on the Liberty ship *D. Fields,* working five hatches from sunrise to sunset and using every available man, including cooks and kitchen police, who, since they had to be aboard to feed the men, pitched in between times. A burning Japanese bomber, hit by American antiaircraft fire, went into a dive and hit the ship while the company's gangs were working the hold, causing additional casualties. Two days later, when the company had returned to the beach, a typhoon blew in, injuring two more men. While men of the unit were salvaging cargo in another ship already damaged by enemy bombs, a hatch exploded; of the six men in the hold two were killed, one later died, and two others were severely burned.

The 609th Port Company remained on the beach through December, unloading, sorting, and delivering supplies through continuous air raids. On 10 December a nitroglycerin explosion of unknown cause demolished its entire camp area, killing and wounding several men. Despite air raids that brought more losses and despite poor lighterage, the unit averaged two to three hundred tons for each eight-hour period.[117]

In the Iwo Jima landings, beginning on 19 February 1945, the 442d and

592d Port Companies and the 471st, 473d, and 476th Amphibian Truck Companies were assigned to the Garrison Force but attached to the V Amphibious Corps (Marine) for the assault.[118] One port company remained attached to corps; the other went to the 5th Marine Division. One Dukw company was attached to the 13th Marine Regiment, one remained attached to corps, and the third was attached to the 4th Marine Division with the primary mission of hauling ammunition and cargo for the 14th Marine Regiment and evacuating casualties from the beaches. The 592d Port Company, divided into three groups, landed in the fourth wave and began unloading small boats as they arrived on the beach; three of its crane operators went to the 5th Pioneer Battalion where they operated eight-ton cranes on the beach. The Dukw companies, carrying ammunition and supplies between ship and shore and returning to ships with wounded from the beaches, were given full credit by the Marine Corps for their work in the Iwo Jima landings.[119]

For the larger landings in Europe Negro units were but a small part of the forces scheduled for the initial landings on 6 June 1944. The First Army's assault forces on D-day at OMAHA Beach had less than 500 Negroes out of 29,714

---

[117] Hist 609th Port Co (TC), Oct–Dec 44 (2d Lt Weaver A. Turner).

[118] In addition to several white quartermaster units, Negro units remaining in the Garrison Force were one aviation ordnance ammunition company, a quartermaster company, two quartermaster service companies, a salvage repair company, a truck company, an amphibian truck company, two aviation squadrons, one aviation engineer battalion, and a medical sanitary company. USAFPOA Rpt of Part in the Iwo Jima Campaign, 98–USF4–0.3 (23284).

[119] Final Rpt of CG Army Forces, Middle Pacific, 98–USF5–0.5.

troops. These were one section of the 3275th Quartermaster Service Company and the 320th Antiaircraft Balloon Battalion (VLA) (less one battery). In the force of 31,912, landing on UTAH Beach, approximately 1,200 were Negroes —troops of the remaining battery of the 320th Balloon Battalion, the 582d Engineer Dump Truck Company, the 385th Quartermaster Truck Company, and the 490th Port Battalion with its 226th, 227th, 228th, and 229th Port Companies. In the follow-up forces arriving later on D-day and on the following days there were more of the needed service troops, including quartermaster truck companies attached to divisions, the 100th Ordnance Ammunition Battalion, which was to supply ammunition to the First Army across Europe, amphibian truck companies to work across the beaches and, later, at heavily damaged ports like Cherbourg and Le Havre, and medical sanitary companies for the evacuation of the wounded to the United Kingdom.

Occasionally, special purpose units were employed in landings. At Salerno, the first Mediterranean assault landing to use smoke screens extensively, Navy and Army units laid screens on and off the beaches over an area twenty miles long to protect landing craft from enemy fire. In the D-day assault on 9 September 1943, a detachment of the 24th Chemical Decontamination Company, equipped with M1 smoke pots, and Navy personnel with generators mounted in boats screened the Paestum beaches where boats were being unloaded. During the following days the unit operated thirty-six naval mechanical generators ashore. The men laid a smoke haze daily at twilight to conceal anchorage and unloading areas from enemy bombers and screened the beaches during alerts. Smoke generally covered an area of twenty to thirty square miles. Not a single ship in the smoke cloud at Paestum was hit by enemy bombs.[120] The 24th, with other smoke companies, moved to Naples to maintain the smoke screen there. For the Anzio landings on 22 January 1944 the 24th was attached to VI Corps to provide smoke as needed. Equipped with eight Navy generators and a quantity of smoke pots it went ashore, laying its first screen on 24 January. More generators were brought in later. A British smoke unit took over the operation of smoke pots on 8 February, leaving the 24th free to operate mechanical generators, now thirty-six in number. These units ran the antiaircraft smoke screen until 24 February, when the 179th Smoke Generator Company, a white unit, arrived to extend the line to Nettuno. At Anzio, the smoke operators lived the life of front-line infantrymen, with foxholes and caves dug, the Fifth Army chemical officer reported, so that "a German shell would have to execute a corkscrew to get at them." [121] For its work at Anzio the 24th Decontamination Company received one of the first four Fifth Army plaques and the first awarded to a chemical unit. This company later operated chemical depots.

---

[120] Hist 24th Chem Decon Co; Paul W. Pritchard, "Smoke Generator Operations in the Mediterranean and European Theaters of Operation," Chemical Corps Historical Studies, 1 (Hist Sec OCofCC, n.d., 347 pp.), pp. 53–54. Fifteen of the Army smoke generator units (not counting the decontamination companies) used in these two theaters were Negro.

[121] Pritchard, op. cit., p. 59; see Col Walter A. Guild, "That Damned Smoke Again," Infantry Journal, LV (October, 1944), 25–28.

The first platoon of the 387th Engineer Battalion (separate) landed in the initial wave at Anzio, going ashore from LCT's at 0400 on 22 January 1944 with the advance shore party two miles south of Nettuno. The remainder of its Companies B and D, after sitting through two air attacks on an LST offshore, landed in the afternoon, dug foxholes, erected shelter tents, and began unloading supplies. The rest of the battalion, though arriving on D-day, had to wait, as corps troops, until the next morning to land. With hand tools, they worked on the maintenance of the overburdened roads. One sergeant blazed a shorter trail through mine fields for the medics and directed their removal of wounded soldiers. The men of the 387th unloaded ships into Dukw's and handled supplies on the beaches through many weeks of day and night air and artillery attacks. They used a large graph, posted daily, to spur unloading. For seven days the 500 men of the battalion averaged 1,940 tons a day, all handled by hand. Gradually the companies of the battalion were released from port duties. They moved to construction, operation of the engineer depot, maintenance of the runway at Nettuno airport, and operation of quarries. At times they were attached to white engineer combat and aviation units. This battalion, described by the Associated Press in a dispatch of 29 February 1944 as having been under "more fire than any other Negro unit in the Fifth Army," remained at the Anzio-Nettuno beachhead for five months. It lost four officers and eleven enlisted men killed, three officers and fifty-eight enlisted men wounded, and received three silver stars for gallantry during the period. Dur-

ing the attack on Rome it maintained the Nettuno–La Ferriere and, later, the Anzio road. It operated an asphalt mixing plant, salvaged steel, repaired submarine cable, operated trash and rubbish dumps, unloaded Bailey bridges, and furnished bulldozers, air compressors, and motorized graders to various jobs, all in heavily mined areas. For a separate battalion, intended to do only rudimentary labor, the 387th was working ahead of itself. While attached to the Negro 92d Engineer General Service Regiment for operations on 9 June 1944, one of its companies removed its first Bailey bridge. The movement of the 387th, with all the impedimenta gathered during the past few months for its varied jobs, was now difficult. "When you fill all the vehicles, you have loaded all the equipment, but have about 1005 men left over," the battalion described it.[122] It returned to Anzio at the end of June. There it took over the work of the white 540th Combat Engineers, a unit with which it had worked during the beachhead days. Then it had repaired bombed water and sewage systems; now it built and removed Bailey bridges. The battalion's companies began to work independently at new and different duties. Two of these companies, never having heard of a bridge train, were told late in June, "You are now a bridge train!"[123] They became bridge companies for the American IV Corps and the French Expeditionary Corps. The companies had to learn quickly the nomenclature and the loading method for all Bailey and treadway bridge parts, train thirty new drivers for 2½-ton trucks, and train

---

[122] Hist Rpt 387th Engr Bn (Sep), 1942–44.
[123] *Ibid.*

eight new drivers for six-ton Brockway bridge construction trucks (vehicles that mounted hydraulic cranes for lifting and placing bridge parts). Additional mechanics to maintain this equipment, which was already in poor condition, had to be found. The companies trained them. These companies delivered bridges to combat engineers, a job on which one officer and two enlisted men lost their lives. Another company took over the Fifth Army Bridge Depot on 5 July, learning all new terms, handling all types of stream crossing equipment, and learning to repair pneumatic floats, assault boats, and floating Baileys. When two other depots opened, the company operated these, acquiring first one and then two Italian engineer companies to do the bulk of the hand-loading and unloading. These depots moved by leapfrogging, following the combat units of Fifth Army. At Florence, in November 1944, one depot was flooded; the company in charge then issued Bailey bridge accessories from an assault boat.[124]

Though they were neither trained nor equipped for it, truck and troop transport units attached to divisions had frequent contacts with the enemy and sometimes joined in the fighting. Some of these units were attached so long to the same divisions that they were treated as organic units.[125] Units to which these companies were attached often had misgivings about them. They wondered if the truckers would continue their hauling when the going got tough. Some found justification for their misgivings, but the com-

mander of an infantry regiment motorized by the attachment of two Negro truck companies—companies that were "not hand-picked; they were just plain, ordinary soldiers like all the rest of us, sweating out a job that was going to be long, hard, dirty, and bloody"—described their actions as part of a special task force attacking German positions south of St. Lô when, shortly after daylight, the regiment struck the enemy:

As daylight neared, confusion mounted. Our columns clogged in endless traffic jams, bogged down in bomb craters, crawled through detours over broken fields, struggled across improvised stream crossings. All around us the night erupted with flaming towns. German artillery and bombs added to the confusion. Every once in a while a huge German tank would pound out of the darkness and cut into our column, thinking it his. Running fights ebbed and flowed about us. As daylight broke, we were literally cheek by jowl with the Germans—in the same villages, in the same fields, in the same hedgerows, in the same farm yards. A hundred sporadic fights broke out—to the front, to the flanks, to the rear, within the columns, everywhere. It was early that morning that I first became aware of the fact that our Negro truck drivers were leaving their trucks and whooping it up after German soldiers all over the landscape. This, I might add, is not hearsay. I personally saw it over and over again in the early hours of that wild morning. But in addition to my own personal observation, many reports reached me throughout the day of the voluntary participation of these troops in battle and their gallant conduct.[126]

The 3398th Quartermaster Truck Company, attached to the 6th Armored

---

[124] Ibid.

[125] See AAR 7th Armd Div Trains, 607–75.2 (8562); Hist 66th Medical Gp, 103–45.1 (11702).

[126] Address, Brig Gen Charles Lanham (formerly CO 22d Inf, 4th Div) before American Council on Race Relations, transcribed from broadcast over WMCA, New York, 12 Jul 46.

GENERAL EISENHOWER TALKS TO AN AMMUNITION HANDLER AT CHERBOURG *during a routine inspection.*

Division moving into Brittany, put out its defenses and joined an armed reconnaissance with other units in division trains when it was reported that 200 enemy troops were headed for the area where this truck company was located. Late in the afternoon eight German planes attacked the trains area. Two officers and two enlisted men of the truck company teamed up to capture a pilot parachuting from one of the three planes shot down. The company's convoys were attacked thereafter by enemy planes, and trucks were struck by shrapnel and shellfire.[127] The 57th Ordnance Ammunition Company, during the pursuit across France, found itself engaging sixty-five of the enemy at Peronne when no other American units were in the area. It killed fifty and captured the other fifteen, its members receiving two Croix de Guerre, one Silver Star, and one Bronze Star for the exploit.[128]

---

[127] The Transportation Corps in the Battle of France (Hist Rpt, TC in ETO, V), Motor Transport Brigade, pp. 9–10.
[128] Rpt 261st Ord Bn, 1944.

Another truck unit, the 666th, supplying the 101st and 82d Airborne Divisions over "Hell's Highway" to Eindhoven and Nijmegen, Holland, had trucks destroyed and drivers killed and injured by bombing. Carrying troops in support of the 82d Airborne Division in February 1945, it had several trucks shelled near Schmitt, Germany, with losses of infantrymen and drivers. Enemy shells and bombs were not this unit's main concern. It considered its greatest difficulties to be shell fragments, glass, bullets, and cartridge cases exposed in roadways when warmer weather brought thaws. In one 24-hour period the company had over a hundred punctures on its forty-odd vehicles. The 666th carried forward 2,800 tons and 17,350 soldiers for 188,587 vehicle miles over icy and snowbound roads between 1 January and 31 March 1945. For its "outstanding accomplishments" it received a formal commendation from III Corps.[129]

Medical ambulance companies were often as close to the enemy and as closely associated with forward units as the truck companies. The 588th Medical Ambulance Company, attached to the 66th Medical Group, worked in such close support of the 7th Armored Division as it spearheaded the XX ("Ghost") Corps drive across France that its ambulances were an integral part of the division so far as rations, gasoline convoys, communications, priorities in bridge crossings, and bivouac sites were concerned. Armored divisions and their medical companies moved so fast that the length of the ambulance haul to the rear was usually double that of ambulances working with infantry divisions.

Early in the Battle of the Bulge, on 20 December 1944, the enemy attacked the 7th Armored Division's Trains near Samree, Belgium. The division quartermaster, with troops of his own section, Negro troops of the attached 3967th Troop Transport Company, and white troops of a platoon of antiaircraft guns from Battery D, 203d Antiaircraft Artillery Automatic Weapons Battalion, threw up a defense and held the enemy off for about four hours while awaiting expected help from the 3d Armored Division located to the north. Medium tanks dispatched to relieve the quartermaster never arrived. The antiaircraft gunners lost their weapons to enemy fire, but not before they had knocked out two enemy tanks and run out of ammunition. The quartermaster and antiaircraft troops finally had to pull out.[130] After the Battle of the Bulge was over and the 7th Armored Division had a lull sufficient for training programs, each unit of the trains, including the 3967th, was given a 57-mm. gun and instruction in its use. Both Negro and white quartermaster units in the Bulge did what they could to hold off the enemy.[131]

These were the less usual examples among the Army's Negro service units. For the most part the quartermaster truck and service companies, the laun-

---

[129] AAR's 666th QM Truck Co, 16 Dec 43–15 Dec 44; 16 Dec 44–31 Mar 45; Feb 45.

[130] AAR Hq 7th Armd Div Trains, Dec 44; His 3967 QM Truck Co.
[131] Gen. George S. Patton, Jr., *War As I Knew I* (Boston: Houghton Mifflin, 1947), p. 194; Franl E. G. Weil, "The Negro in the Armed Forces, *Social Forces,* XXVI (1947–1948), p. 97; Visit t Advance Sec ComZ, Liège, 1–6 Mar 45, Rpt 36, G Sec, ETOUSA 333.1, FRD AGO.

dry and dump truck companies, the engineer separate and the port units performed their routine duties as assigned, within the limitations of their abilities, their leadership, and their immediate past training. There were few heroics and few chances for them. These units' employment careers, in general, were often humdrum, their efficiency run-of-the-mine, their problems only ameliorated and not solved by their assignment to overseas duties. While command problems were considerable, they were not in most cases insurmountable. Relations between white and Negro troops and between Negro troops and civilians in foreign countries were more often good than poor. The efficiency of most Negro units was not so high as it might have been but when the deficiencies of their training, both military and civilian, are considered, it was generally as high as it could have been under the circumstances. It was universally conceded to increase under conditions of good leadership, good surroundings, and definite, visible mission. Not infrequently, when these conditions obtained, the work potential increased beyond expectations.

CHAPTER XXI

Artillery and Armored Units in the ETO

Artillery

The nine separate Negro field artillery battalions remaining after the completion of the conversion program were all employed in Europe. All were heavy caliber units used as corps artillery for general support or for reinforcing the fires of one or more divisions. Because of the flexible group organization adopted by the Army in 1943 and because units were controlled by group headquarters according to the tactical needs of the day, the four Negro group headquarters controlled white and Negro battalions as the occasion demanded. The Negro battalions, similarly, were from time to time attached to one or another group, white or Negro, as required.

Of the Negro units in the Ardennes during the German counteroffensive of December 1944, one field artillery group and three field artillery battalions participated fully. The 333d Field Artillery Group, the Negro headquarters and headquarters battery present, landed in France on 29 June with the VIII Corps Artillery. The VIII Corps Artillery used the 333d Group and Negro battalions interchangeably with white units as needs arose. In the siege of Brest, for example, VIII Corps Artillery, which then had three Negro battalions and the 333d Group among the fifteen

battalions and several groups initially available to it, distributed its artillery forces into two reinforcing groups, two mixed caliber general support groups, one reinforcing battalion, and one attached group. The Negro battalions were assigned to groups and attached to divisions as required. During most of the siege the 333d Group had one Negro battalion, the 333d, and two white battalions, the 557th (155-mm. Gun, SP) and the 771st (4.5-inch Gun). The Negro 969th Field Artillery Battalion (155-mm. Howitzer), formerly attached to the 333d Group, was at first given the task of reinforcing the fires of the 2d Division and later placed under the control of the white 402d Field Artillery Group, through which it supported the 8th Division in its attack on the Crozon peninsula. The third Negro artillery unit, the 578th Battalion (8-inch Howitzer), along with three white battalions, was attached to the white 202d Field Artillery Group, one of the two general support groups responsible for counterbattery fire.[1] Neither the Negro battalions nor the groups experienced special problems as a result of their functional use. In the Negro groups, only one problem arose as a result of the attachment of white battalions to Negro group headquar-

---

[1] Rpt of Arty with the VIII Corps in the Reduction of Brest, 22 Aug–19 Sep 44.

FIELD PIECE IN THE PÉRIERS SECTOR

ters. It was solved by the group itself when one of its two Negro chaplains had to be hospitalized and was replaced by a white chaplain, thereby satisfying those who preferred spiritual assistance from one of their own race.[2]

Representative of the initial use of the Negro battalions was the earlier career of the 969th Field Artillery Battalion, which landed at UTAH Beach on 9 July 1944, under the command of Lt. Col. Hubert D. Barnes. The 969th's first mission was to reinforce the fires of the 8th Division through the 333d Field Artillery Group. On 10 July the battalion took its first positions at Lattage du Pont in the vicinity of Le Haye du Puits. At 2205 its Battery A fired the unit's first rounds in combat. The battalion commander was wounded that night, but this circumstance had little adverse effect on the unit. The battalion, under its executive officer, Maj. Einar Erickson, for the next fortnight continued to support the 8th Division through the 333d Group, and later, from 14 July, through attachment to the division. The 969th fired special missions for the 90th Division as well. On 26 July, its Battery A was attached to the 4th Armored Divi-

---

[2] 349th FA Gp AAR, Feb 45.

sion; on 1 August, the full battalion went to the 4th Armored and occupied positions near Rennes. Fighting during this period was in country filled with snipers and the battalion was at times surrounded by the enemy and strafed by enemy planes. On one occasion Battery A's first sergeant manned a .50-caliber machine gun to silence sniper fire while a march order was completed, the battalion taking credit for seventy-nine prisoners captured. In late August, the 969th began its participation in the siege of Brest, continuing until hostilities in the area ceased on 19 September. In October the battalion, still in support of the 8th Division, moved from Brest to the Bastogne area where, attached to the 174th Field Artillery Group, it remained until December.[3]

In the Bastogne-Houffalize area there were three other VIII Corps Negro field artillery units: the 333d Field Artillery Group at Atzerath supporting the 2d and later the 106th Division; the 333d Field Artillery Battalion at Schönberg attached to the 333d Group; and the 578th Field Artillery Battalion of the 402d Group at Burg Reuland. The 333d Group, after the siege of Brest, arrived at Houffalize, Belgium, on 5 October, with the Negro 333d and the white 771st Battalions attached. The group mission in December continued to be general support of VIII Corps, reinforcing the fires of the 106th Division, with the 333d Battalion reinforcing the 590th Field Artillery Battalion.

During their period in defensive positions in the Houffalize area, VIII Corps field artillery battalions had little ac-

tivity. In the 333d Group, firing was light, averaging 150 rounds a day.[4] At Burg Reuland the 578th Field Artillery, like the other units in the area, was constantly improving its billets and positions. In December, their third month in this quiet sector, all personnel were billeted in houses, log cabins, or winterized tents. Ammunition expenditure in this battalion was limited to 250 rounds per four-day period. Enemy activity consisted of occasional shelling of observation posts, harassing fire on the battalion command post, and occasional robot bombs.[5] Though the weather was damp and freezing with intermittent rain and snow, the battery positions boggy, and roads nearly impassable, the battalion found Burg Reuland "tranquil to a point almost approaching garrison conditions." Red Cross girls toured the positions with coffee and doughnuts. Troops saw USO shows and movies at least once a week, and officers and enlisted men were scheduled for trips to the Paris and Longwy rest centers. A battalion recreation center, with beer hall, bowling alley, badminton court, and game room, was operating in Burg Reuland and, for the Christmas season, men of the battalion were rehearsing a choral play.[6]

When the great German attack began on 16 December against VIII Corps' position in Belgium, Bleialf, where the 333d Field Artillery Battalion had two observation posts, was penetrated by 1100. Both observation parties withdrew by the next morning to the command post of the 590th Field Artillery

---

[3] AAR's 969th FA Bn, Jul–Dec 44.

[4] AAR 333d FA Gp, Dec 44.
[5] Ibid., Nov–Dec 44; AAR 578th FA Bn, Dec 44. See also AAR, 965th FA Bn, Dec 44.
[6] AAR 578th FA Bn, Dec 44.

Battalion, where the 333d's liaison officer was located. These two parties were the first of the 333d's men to be lost to the attacking enemy.[7] To the north from its St. Vith command post, the 402d Group was sending warning orders for a retrograde movement to its battalions. The 578th Battalion's observation post at Heckhuscheid, a town held by a battalion of the 424th Infantry, was subjected to heavy fire and attacked by the enemy. The 578th's commander, Lt. Col. Thomas C. T. Buckley, the observer, and his crew held off German infantry in a sharp fire fight in which Negro artillerymen, armed with M1 rifles picked up from the battlefield, accounted for at least half a dozen Germans.[8] The observation party then withdrew to another battalion observation post where it took twelve German prisoners. During this first day of the Ardennes campaign the 578th Battalion fired 23 missions, expending 774 rounds.[9]

The seriousness of the German attack was apparent on the following day when the slow-moving heavy artillery battalions began to suffer losses. The white and the Negro battalions of the 333d Group began to displace to prepared alternate positions on the night of the 16th, each battalion leaving one battery forward at the request of the Commanding General, 106th Division Artillery, who assured VIII Corps Artillery that his positions would be held. Forward

infantry and cavalry reconnaissance units began retreating in large and small parties, moving more rapidly than the heavy artillery units, which lost several howitzers and vehicles to enemy action. The 333d Battalion, at the end of the day, possessed only five howitzers. On 18 December the 969th Battalion, approaching Vecmont, was assigned to the 333d Group by oral order of the Commanding General, VIII Corps Artillery.

On the 19th, the Negro 578th and the white 559th Battalions, out of contact with their 402d Group headquarters and temporarily organized under the 578th's commander as Groupment Buckley, planned to return to positions at Chérain, from which a reconnaissance party had been forced the day before. The two battalions conducted reconnaissance and, with the support of three 105-mm. howitzers, occupied their positions without opposition, only to receive orders from corps artillery to move farther to the rear before they could fire a shot. The 559th suffered casualties on the highway from Houffalize, now in enemy hands; the 578th ran into tank fire but had neither casualties nor losses of matériel. "The steadiness and determination of all concerned in this trying movement when a heavy artillery battalion was fighting a rear guard action is worthy of the highest praise," the 578th commander declared.[10]

On the same day, 19 December, the 333d Group was released by VIII Corps Artillery for attachment to the newly arrived 101st Airborne Division and ordered to move to the vicinity of Bastogne. The group received its verbal

---

[7] AAR 333d FA Bn, Dec 44. For a detailed account of the German attack, see Hugh M. Cole, *The Ardennes: Battle of the Bulge*, UNITED STATES ARMY IN WORLD WAR II (Washington, 1965).

[8] AAR 578th FA Bn, Dec 44; Ltr, Hq Third Army to CG USFET, 22 Aug 45, AG 291.2.

[9] AAR 578th FA Bn, Dec 44.

[10] AAR 578th FA Bn, Dec 44.

orders at 1300, undertook reconnaissance immediately, and began to displace at 1430. By 1730 the 333d Group,
with its one white and two Negro battalions,[11] closed to its new positions. Its
command post was at Mande-St.
Etienne, with the 771st Battalion
around Flamierge, the 969th in the
Flamizoulle area, and the 333d Battalion in the vicinity of Rennamount, all
north and west of Bastogne. During the
night the enemy cut the Bastogne-
Marche highway. Reports and rumors
continued to come in indicating that the
enemy was penetrating American positions from all sides. When small arms
fire was received by the 771st and 969th
Battalions, the group commander
ordered all his units to displace toward
St. Hubert, west of Bastogne. Considerable confusion resulted from the unco-
ordinated displacement following.
Two batteries of the 771st each abandoned two mired tractors and two guns.
The 333d Battalion, receiving counterbattery and small arms fire while en
route, left three of its five howitzers behind.[12]

The 101st Division Artillery tried to
make contact with the 333d Group
headquarters throughout 20 December.
Not until early afternoon did it discover
from the group's executive officer that
the group commander had ordered his
battalions to move without consulting

101st Division Artillery. When the
units had proceeded about five miles to
the southwest along the Bastogne-Neuf-
château highway, the column was over-
taken and instructed to halt. An hour
later, the group commander ordered his
units to return to the positions just
abandoned, and they closed at 1600.
When the units arrived they found that
they had a new group commander.
The former commander announced to
his staff that he had been relieved by
Brig. Gen. Anthony C. McAuliffe of the
101st Division and that Colonel Barnes,
commander of the 969th Field Artillery
Battalion, was to take his place.[13]

Back at its old positions, the 333d
Battalion found two of its officers attempting to get the abandoned howitzers out of the mud with borrowed
tractors. The battalion reclaimed its
weapons, which were still usable. An
armored unit had already brought one
of the 771st's tractors and one gun out to
the battalion; the 771st's other three
tractors and guns were found still mired
in their positions.

A half hour later, at 1630, the 101st
Division Artillery ordered the group to
move again, first to Morhet and then to
the area around the towns of Chenogne,
Sibret, and Villeroux, about three miles
southwest of Bastogne, where elements
of the 28th Division were expected to
afford some security for the slow-moving
artillery battalions. Displacement began immediately. The 771st, still unable to remove one of its badly mired
guns, destroyed it. The battalions
closed in their new positions at about
2000, with the 771st at Sibret, south-
westernmost of the towns and the head-

[11] The 771st's attachment to the 333d Group
caused some confusion in both its racial identity
and its armament in some early published accounts,
where it was at times confused with the 969th
Battalion, called a Negro unit, and designated a
howitzer rather than a 4.5-inch gun unit. See S. L. A.
Marshall, *Bastogne: The First Eight Days* (Washington: The Infantry Journal Press, 1946), pp. 70,
206, n. 19.
[12] AAR's 333d FA Gp, 771st and 333d FA Bns,
Dec 44.

[13] *Ibid.;* Per Rpt and Jnl, 101st Div Arty, Dec 44.

quarters of the 28th Division; the 969th at Villeroux; and the 333d near Chenogne, where the group located its command post. The battalions fired light harassing missions through the night. Rear echelons reached and remained in St. Hubert and Molinfaing, though individuals, especially officers, returned to their units in the Bastogne area.

On the morning of the 21st the enemy, tightening his lines about Bastogne, approached Sibret from the south and west. Enemy tanks and mortars began to fire into the town. The commanding general of the 28th Division walked through at about 0800, ordering all personnel into the streets to defend the town. The 771st moved certain of its batteries to the northwest in search of positions with no minimum elevation so that fire could be placed on targets as close as 1,500 yards away. Heavy fire began to fall in the town and on battery positions. As vehicles of the 28th Division began to move northwest through the town toward the rear, the 771st's commander ordered his headquarters battery to follow and maintain contact. His S–3, at Chenogne for a 333d Group conference, had in the meantime received orders from group to have the 771st remain in position, firing in support of the 101st Airborne Division. The S–3, on his way back to Sibret, met one battery on its way out of Sibret and ordered it and another battery to take up new positions to the northwest of the town. Gradually the three batteries of the 771st displaced toward Chenogne. When the 28th Division evacuated Sibret at about 1000, all firing batteries of the 771st Battalion were in position near Chenogne.

Elements of the 28th Division, including one of the division's organic field artillery battalions, and the 58th Armored Field Artillery Battalion, passed through Chenogne and the positions of the 771st and 333d Battalions. German infantry and tanks now approached one of the 771st's positions and friendly infantry broke and retreated northward. Direct tank fire destroyed a gun, a tractor, and a command car of one of the 771st's batteries and another tractor moving a gun to a new position was hit. As tanks appeared over the ridge previously selected for minimum elevation fire, all units of the battalion began to move out of position without orders from their commanders. The S–2 and S–3 gathered elements of the 771st Battalion together and, on orders from VIII Corps Artillery, proceeded to Matton, France, well to the rear, where scattered elements of the battalion were gathered together over the next few days. All guns, except two, were abandoned. The battalion commander, five officers, and fourteen enlisted men joined elements of the 333d Group.[14]

In the meantime the two Negro battalions of the group remained in position, with the 333d Field Artillery Battalion in the Chenogne area and the 969th in position at Villeroux. The 333d Group headquarters moved in toward Bastogne as the enemy approached closer to Chenogne, giving movement orders to the 333d Battalion on the way. Before the 333d Battalion could move, an enemy tank fired directly into its area, hitting one prime mover and two howitzers. One howitzer and the prime

---

[14] AAR 771st FA Bn, Dec 44; AAR and Jnl 333d FA Gp, Dec 44.

mover had to be abandoned as the battalion moved toward new positions closer to Bastogne. From about 1300 to 1600 on 21 December the group headquarters maintained a temporary command post at Senonchamps with the 420th Armored Field Artillery Battalion of Combat Command B, 10th Armored Division. The group reinforced the fires of this battalion. When the enemy approached Villeroux, subjecting the 969th to heavy fire which killed its motor officer and killed and wounded several enlisted men, the 969th, on orders of the 101st Division Artillery, displaced to the northeast to a position a half mile west of Bastogne. There, as the 101st Airborne formed its perimeter defense line around the town, the three serviceable howitzers of the 333d Battalion were incorporated into the 969th Battalion. The two battalions, with men of the 969th manning the abandoned guns of the 771st, operated as one through the siege of Bastogne, reinforcing the fires of the 420th Armored Field Artillery Battalion as well as giving general support to the 101st Division Artillery. The 333d Group had only 450 rounds of high explosive shells left; missions were continually fired but with great care. All primary roads to Bastogne were now cut off and there was little possibility of resupply.

On 23 December, the third day after Bastogne had been cut off, C–47's came over with the first resupply for the besieged area, but no 155-mm. howitzer ammunition was included. Along with other units, the 333d Group's battalions were bombed on Christmas eve. They lost two battery commanders and three enlisted men. Friendly infantry lines were now within 300 to 500 yards north and west of the group command post.

On the 26th, as the 969th continued to fire its dwindling ammunition, C–47's dropped the first 155-mm. ammunition received during the siege. Late that night, the 333d Group learned that the 4th Armored Division was at Assenois, two miles from Bastogne.[15] Following the 4th Armored Division was the 590th Ambulance Company, a Negro unit then evacuating for the 10th Armored Division. Its ambulances were among the first to reach the besieged troops at Bastogne.[16]

The following day, after fifty gliders had landed with supplies, including more 155-mm. howitzer ammunition, the 333d Field Artillery Group Headquarters and Headquarters Battery, the badly depleted 333d Field Artillery Battalion, and the handful of men from the 771st Field Artillery remaining in Bastogne, were ordered by the Commanding General, VIII Corps Artillery, to displace on 28 December over the now open road to Matton, France. There, where most of the VIII Corps Artillery units which had escaped encirclement were assembled, the rear echelon of the 333d Battalion was maintaining roadblocks and a mobile reserve for security purposes. The 333d Battalion's rear echelon had tried vainly several times to send ammunition, gasoline, and ration trucks through to its batteries in Bastogne. On 26 December, one party, under Maj. Oscar Y. Lewis, group supply officer, at last succeeded in getting through with ammunition, gasoline, and rations.[17]

[15] Jnl 333d FA Gp, Dec 44.
[16] Unit Hist 590th Ambulance Co, 4 Mar 43–31 Dec 44.
[17] AAR 333d FA Bn, Dec 44.

During the siege of Bastogne, where a number of units had lost their service personnel and equipment, Technician 4 Broman Williams of 333d Group headquarters set up and maintained an improvised kitchen, feeding a thousand men daily. Other group enlisted men voluntarily carried messages under fire, salvaged abandoned trucks and carried personnel of a number of units to safety, and performed various other duties not normally assigned to them. One group soldier operated a radio for forty-eight consecutive hours without relief.[18]

The 333d Battalion, which sustained heavier losses at Bastogne than any other VIII Corps Artillery unit, lost a total of 6 officers and 222 men, 9 guns, 34 trucks, and 12 weapons carriers. Only the 58th Armored Field Artillery Battalion lost more guns (16); the other 11 battalions present lost 346 enlisted men altogether.[19] With the scarcity of trained Negro replacements, there was scant hope of rebuilding the 333d Battalion. The 333d Group, which now had the 771st, 333d, 58th Armored, and 740th Field Artillery Battalions attached to it, reorganized and re-equipped all of the battalions except the 333d, the only Negro unit then under its control. The 771st, having lost its 4.5-inch guns, was re-equipped with 155-mm. howitzers. The 333d Battalion sent the bulk of its remaining 286 men to the 578th and 969th Battalions, both of which were still engaging the enemy, and to the 333d Group's Headquarters Battery. The 333d Battalion, originally scheduled to be disbanded, remained active as a skeleton unit, performing guard and

ordnance duties while awaiting replacements. Not until the end of April 1945 did the battalion receive sufficient replacements to return to combat duties. It was then too late for it to participate further in the European campaign as an active field artillery battalion.[20]

The 969th Field Artillery Battalion's commander, Colonel Barnes, returned to his unit upon departure of the 333d Group from Bastogne. The 969th continued to support the 101st Airborne Division until 12 January when, with operations approaching normal, it was relieved and reattached to the 333d Field Artillery Group, now re-equipped and reorganized. The 333d Group returned to its old command post at Bastogne with the mission of supporting the 11th Armored Division, then advancing north toward Houffalize. As Third Army widened its hold on the area to the south of the Bulge and as the siege of Bastogne was broken, Maj. Gen. Maxwell D. Taylor, commanding the 101st Airborne, wrote to the commander of the 969th Battalion:

The Officers and Men of the 101st Airborne Division wish to express to your command their appreciation of the gallant support rendered by the 969th Field Artillery Battalion in the recent defense of Bastogne, Belgium. The success of this defense is attributable to the shoulder to shoulder cooperation of all units involved. This Division is proud to have shared the Battlefield with your command. A recommendation for a unit citation of 969th Field Artillery Battalion is being forwarded by this Headquarters.[21]

---

[18] A number received awards, generally Bronze Stars, for these actions. AAR 333d FA Gp, May 45.
[19] AAR VIII Corps Arty, Dec 44.

[20] AAR's 333d FA Bn, Jan–Jun 45; AAR 333d FA Gp, Jan 45; AAR VIII Corps Arty, Jan 45.
[21] Ltr, Hq 101st A/B Div to CO 969th FA Bn through CG VIII Corps, 3 Jan 45, copy in 969th FA Bn AAR, Jan 45.

Maj. Gen. Troy H. Middleton, forwarding this commendation to the battalion on 11 January, observed that "Your contribution to the great success of our arms at Bastogne will take its place among the epic achievements of our Army." [22] The 969th, along with other units of the 101st Division, received its Distinguished Unit Citation through Third Army on 7 February 1945, in accordance with authority granted by the War Department on 21 January. Though not the first earned, this was the first award of the Distinguished Unit Citation to a Negro combat unit in World War II.[23]

The 578th Field Artillery, moving south and west from Burg Reuland with the 559th Battalion in Groupment Buckley, reached Mierchamps, west of Bastogne, on 20 December. There the 402d Group resumed control and the groupment was disbanded. The battalion moved into several positions where it expected to be able to fire, but orders kept it moving. Along the way, the 578th gathered and attached a miscellany of troops: a battery of the 740th Field Artillery's 8-inch howitzers, a platoon of antiaircraft troops, fifty enlisted men from the 740th Field Artillery acting as infantry, and a battery of 105-mm. howitzers. All of these were white troops. On the 21st the battalion reached the Forêt du Luchy where, operating directly under VIII Corps Artillery control, it was instructed to reconnoiter and occupy a position near Flohimont so that it could fire to cover any withdrawal from Bastogne which the 101st Airborne Division might be directed to make. The 578th was convinced that now its retrograde movement would cease and the battalion could make a stand. "All concerned," the battalion commander reported, "were more than anxious to dig in and fight." Despite the battalion's expectation, a new order came from VIII Corps Artillery at 1135, directing further movement to the rear.[24] The VIII Corps Artillery, in its Matton location, was planning to move its 402d Group toward Arlon, 20 miles south of Bastogne, for attachment to III Corps Artillery now heading north with Third Army for the relief of Bastogne. The VIII Corps Artillery considered the situation too fluid on its own front to use its heavy artillery battalions profitably itself. The 578th was among the five battalions offered "on loan" to III Corps, to which the 402d Group was attached on 22 December.[25]

The III Corps Artillery directed the 578th Battalion to take positions at Nagem. By midday of 23 December all batteries were in position. From Nagem the 578th Battalion fired in general support until 26 December when the battalion moved forward, continuing to support III Corps units through the 402d Group. On 29 December the battalion was attached to the 193d Field Artillery Group, and, later in the day, ordered to operate directly under III Corps Artillery, with batteries echeloning forward over icy and slippery roads to Neunhausen, where, on 31 December, the 578th was attached to the 203d Field Artillery Group. Despite its long marches since 16 December the battalion had expended 3,455 rounds of 8-inch

[22] 1st Ind to Ltr cited n. 21.
[23] Third Army GO 31, 7 Feb 45. See below, p. (670), for the first earned.

[24] AAR 578th FA Bn, Dec 44.
[25] AAR VIII Corps Arty, Dec 44.

howitzer ammunition, firing on all but four days for an average of 288 rounds per firing day. Inspection of captured targets and target areas enabled the battalion to evaluate the effectiveness of a large portion of its fire missions. A three-volley unobserved transfer into the village of Bigonville on 24 December resulted in destruction of much of the town. Fifty-two rounds fired on enemy traffic in and around Boulaide on Christmas Day without adjustment were observed to be 100 percent effective; subsequent visits to this target area verified the effectiveness of these fires. On the afternoon of 27 December, battalion observers conducting fire in the Boulaide area immobilized two tanks, destroyed one vehicle, and scored direct hits on houses around which enemy movements had been observed. Freezing weather hampered the battalion, especially when moving to new positions; it used borrowed tanks to tow its prime movers and howitzers up steep and slippery hills.

The 578th Battalion continued in general support of III Corps, firing from Neunhausen, until 16 January. Its battalion commander, Colonel Buckley, left the unit on 8 January to assume command of the rehabilitated 333d Field Artillery Group, now returning from Matton to resume its part in the Ardennes campaign. The battalion itself was attached to the 333d Group on 26 January. While in its Neunhausen positions, the battalion received an unusual mission—on 4 January it was ordered to destroy Berle, an enemy-held village. Precision adjustment with delay fuzes was begun and four buildings were demolished before darkness made further observation impossible. The

next morning, destruction of the town continued. By late afternoon every structure in the village was demolished or severely damaged with the exception of one marked with a large red cross. Throughout the mission, the 578th's Observation Post No. 1, from which fire on Berle was directed, was continuously under mortar and occasionally under *Nebelwerfer* fire.

After the Ardennes campaign, the 578th Battalion continued across Europe in general support of VIII Corps. It was attached at times to the 333d Field Artillery Group and at times to the 402d, 174th, and 220th Field Artillery Groups. In February, after two batteries had been called on by 4th Division Artillery to assist in repulsing an enemy counterattack, the division artillery commander telephoned: "Congratulations and thanks for the effective and prompt fire." [26]

The battalion crossed the Rhine on 30 March, closing in an area near Limbach, where it was ordered to clear designated wooded areas. On the morning of 31 March, elements of each battery were formed into "infantry" platoons and squads. Armed with carbines, bazookas, and vehicular .50-caliber machine guns, the impromptu assault formations jumped off at 0930. Companies B and C cleared their assigned areas, but Company A quickly ran into machine gun and automatic pistol fire. The "reserve company," made up of headquarters battery personnel, was then committed and the advance was resumed. The unit captured sixty-one prisoners, including three officers; in its initial fire fight, Company A killed two and

---

[26] AAR 578th FA Bn, Feb 45; AAR's 333d FA Gp, Jan–Feb 45.

wounded others of the enemy. Rapid advances of infantry and armored units after the crossing of the Rhine forced the heavy battalion to move frequently but left it with few opportunities for fire. Its patrols cleared nearby wooded areas immediately after the occupation of new positions as, during April, the battalion displaced across Germany to the Czech border, firing missions at enemy-held towns and critical road junctions. On 26 April, the battalion was ordered to move to Kassell, there to take up occupation duties. Its howitzers were turned in to "ordnance and to cosmoline" on the next day, for the war in Europe was ending.[27]

After the Americans of the 11th Armored Division linked with friendly troops in Houffalize on 16 January 1945, the 969th Field Artillery Battalion, with over a hundred of the 333d Battalion's men attached as reinforcements, prepared to join the Seventh Army in the Vosges. Already in the Vosges, attached to 3d Division Artillery, was another Negro artillery unit, the 999th Field Artillery Battalion, an 8-inch howitzer unit. A sister unit of the 578th Battalion, formerly the 2d Battalion, 578th Regiment, the 999th, like the 777th Field Artillery Battalion (4.5-inch gun), had a considerably different employment career than the Negro units in the Ardennes.

The 999th arrived in Normandy on 17 July 1944 after a brief stay in England. With the commitment of Third Army and XV Corps after the capture of St. Lô, the battalion started out on 4 August with XV Corps in pursuit of the German army. In nine days it marched 180

miles in the face of enemy resistance, occupying seventeen positions near as many towns. From positions at Flacourt and at Mantes Gassicourt it fired over 2,000 rounds of ammunition and helped establish the bridgehead over the Seine that sealed off the last escape route of the German *Seventh Army*. During this rapid advance the battalion, attached to the 144th Field Artillery Group, supported the 90th and 79th Divisions and the 2d French Armored Division. After a brief attachment to First Army when that army took over the bridgehead at Mantes Gassicourt, and after a brief rest period again under XV Corps, the battalion was attached to XX Corps and the 333d Field Artillery Brigade. The XX Corps, having swept east across France, was about to assault Metz when the 999th, on 7 September, reached Chambley and began to fire in support of the 5th Division. On 10 September the battalion rejoined XV Corps and 40th Group supporting the 79th Division and the 2d French Division as they pushed the Germans across the Moselle and Muerthe Rivers. Along with XV Corps, the 999th passed to the control of Seventh Army in late October. It participated in the corps' assault on Sarrebourg, Saverne, and Strasbourg. It supported the 79th and 45th Divisions in their advance on Hagenau and, on 5 December, moved with XV Corps from Alsace back across the Vosges Mountains into Lorraine to support the 100th and 44th Divisions in their attack on Maginot Line positions near Bitche. On 21 December 1944 the battalion was relieved from XV Corps and the 194th Group and attached to the 17th Group, then supporting the 36th Division in the Colmar area. After a

---

[27] AAR's 578th FA Bn, Jan–May 45.

ARTILLERYMEN, FIRING 8-INCH HOWITZER, *help seal off the German escape route across the Seine, 20 August 1944.*

sixty-mile night march, the battalion occupied its new positions, changing them slightly when the 3d Division replaced the 36th Division. On 1 January 1945 the battalion was relieved from the 17th Field Artillery Group and attached to the 3d Division Artillery, moving on 6 January to Asubure, high in the Vosges Mountains, where it remained until 20 January. When the 3d Division issued orders for the movement it realized that the icy, steep, and winding mountain roads would make the movement difficult if not impossible. "Nevertheless you accepted the mission cheerfully," the 3d Division Artillery said in commending the battalion, "and by an extraordinary display of ingenuity and hard work

accomplished the movement in a remarkably short time. The entire matter is a splendid testimony to the efficiency and training of the 999th Field Artillery Battalion." [28]

For the elimination of the Colmar Pocket, beginning on 23 January 1945, both the 999th Field Artillery Battalion and the 969th Battalion were attached to French units. The 999th was relieved from the 3d Division on 18 January and attached to ALCA 2, a French artillery group. On 20–21 January, the 999th moved into offensive positions for the delivery of artillery preparations. The 969th, arriving at Selestat on 21 Janu-

---

[28] Ltr, Hq 3d Div Arty to CO 999th FA Bn, 7 Jan 45, copy in Hist 999th FA Bn, Jun 44–Jan 45.

ary, was attached to the 1st French Division (DMI), forming a groupment with the division's 4th Battalion. With the help of heavy artillery preparations, the attack, which started on 23 January, made good progress. The 969th Battalion alone fired 912 rounds on the first day. On 28 January, the 999th Battalion was attached to the 40th Group in the newly arrived XXI Corps; the 969th, on 25 January, was attached to the 5th French Armored Division upon commitment of that unit and, later, to the 75th Division and the 2d French Armored Division. Both battalions continued in support of the French and American divisions engaged in encircling and clearing the Colmar Pocket, a task which was completed by 8 February. Both battalions received commendations from the French and American divisions which they supported and both were among the units given the right to incorporate the arms of the city of Colmar into their insignia. Both units, when heavy artillery was no longer needed in the Colmar area, moved north to XV Corps in the Sarreguemines area where the 999th was attached to the 144th Field Artillery Group and the 969th to the 30th Field Artillery Group. Already attached to the 30th Field Artillery Group was a newly arrived Negro 155-mm. howitzer battalion, the 686th, which had landed in France on 1 February 1945 and which had begun its general support missions with the 30th Group on 10 February. The three battalions fired in general support of XXI Corps' divisions in their attacks along the Saar River and in the advance to and across the Rhine.[29]

Keeping up with the infantry and armored units so that they would be in positions within range of targets when and if needed became a problem for heavy artillery units as the spring drive of the armies across Germany picked up speed. The 999th Field Artillery was relieved of this problem when on 8 April it received a special mission that took it back to the Atlantic coast. The battalion, attached to the 13th Field Artillery Brigade under the operational control of the French Army of the Atlantic, moved by road and rail from Sarreguemines back across France to the coast. There the French were attacking German fortifications which had been blocking the entrance to the harbor of Bordeaux since the June landings. With other American artillery of the 13th Brigade, the 999th turned its guns on the German-held Ile d'Oleron at the entrance to the harbor and on Pointe de Grave across the Gironde River. The Pointe de Grave pocket was cleared out in two days. For ten days heavy artillery fired on Ile d'Oleron. When the French forces made their amphibious landing on the morning of 30 April, the artillery fires had been so heavy and accurate that German resistance was already broken. The enemy surrendered by mid-afternoon. With the rest of the units in the 13th Brigade, the 999th reloaded and, on 6 May, started back to rejoin the Seventh Army. When they arrived in Germany on 11 May, the war in Europe was over and only occupation duties awaited them.[30]

The fluid situation during the advance across central Germany and the resulting lack of targets kept the howitz-

---

[29] AAR's 999th FA Bn, Feb–May 45; 969th FA Bn, Feb–May 45; 686th FA Bn, Feb–May 45.

[30] AAR's 999th FA Bn, Feb–May 45; 144th FA Gp, Feb 45.

ers of the 969th Battalion, still in XXI Corps but then attached to the 4th Division, silent after 28 April 1945 when the battalion fired its last shots of the war. During its ten months of combat the 969th Field Artillery Battalion had fought with all four of the American armies in the European theater and with the French in the Colmar Pocket. It had fired a total of 42,489 rounds from its howitzers in support of American and French divisions.[31] On 3 May, the 969th found itself once more attached to the 101st Airborne Division under circumstances quite different from those attending its former attachment to this division at Bastogne. Though its howitzers were no longer firing, the battalion's trucks were kept busy transporting American infantry and German prisoners and the battalion assisted in processing the thousands of German prisoners pouring into the 101st Division's prisoner of war cage.

In the winter of 1944–45 additional Negro artillery groups and battalions, including the 686th already mentioned, arrived in England for transshipment to the Continent. Some of these, like the 350th Field Artillery Battalion, had been stripped, refilled, and retrained during the manpower crisis of 1943 and 1944. The 350th Battalion, retrained between April and October 1944, arrived in Scotland in December 1944, and in France on 22 February 1945. It was originally attached to the 351st Field Artillery Group, one of three Negro group headquarters and headquarters batteries arriving in Europe during the late winter months. These

units were added to the armies' artillery strength for the final attack against Germany. Theirs was generally an employment of brief intensity. When the 350th Battalion, for example, moved up into firing position on 1 March 1945, it was attached to the 413th Field Artillery Group, XXI Corps, where it supported the 63d and 70th Divisions in their attacks toward Saarbrucken. By 22 March, the battalion went into bivouac east of Bitche, France, remaining until 5 April, when it moved to Heidelberg. There it was attached to the 421st Field Artillery Group in the 44th Antiaircraft Artillery Brigade, with the mission of guarding installations—a duty which it performed until the end of the war. During April its units guarded thirty-five posts, including a prisoner of war hospital, an airfield, a repeater station, an engineer laboratory, and various dumps. In addition it operated a 245-man motorized patrol.[32]

The 686th Battalion, similarly, after firing in support of the 4th Division to which it was attached from 1 April, went to the 44th Antiaircraft Artillery Brigade on 27 April for duty with its 68th Group of the Seventh Army Security Command. During the month, the 686th Battalion displaced twenty-one times, an indication of the speed with which it had to move. As a security force, the unit was charged with maintaining order and safeguarding American troops and installations in an area about twelve miles wide and thirty miles long adjacent to the Danube.[33]

Of the remaining Negro artillery units

[31] AAR's 969th FA Bn, Feb–May 45.

[32] Hist and AAR's 350th FA Bn, Feb–May 45.
[33] Hist Summary 686th FA Bn, Apr 45.

employed in the European theater, the 777th Field Artillery Battalion and the 452d Antiaircraft Artillery Battalion had the fuller employment careers. The 777th, a 4.5-inch gun unit, was one of the Negro battalions activated in mid-1943, with cadre from the 969th and 333d Field Artillery Battalions. It was one of the units whose entire training and most of whose operational service was spent under a white group headquarters, originally the 181st and, after 30 October 1944, the 202d Field Artillery Group. After a training period just short of a year, it left Camp Beale, California, on 1 August 1944 for England, transshipping to Utah Beach on 16 September. It was one of the units that arrived just at the time when transportation for men and supplies was in great demand. Two officers and 76 men from the unit took 36 vehicles to form a portion of a truck convoy which carried men and supplies to the front, covering 3,100 miles between 25 September and 6 October. The remainder of the unit stayed in Brioquebosc, France, until 25 October 1944, when the unit set out for Tongres, Belgium, where it joined the XIX Corps as a general support unit attached to the 202d Field Artillery Group supporting the 30th Division. It participated in the Kohlschied penetration (31 October 1944 to 20 November 1944) and in the Julich sector, occupying positions at Richterich and Ubach, Germany. From 24 November it was in support of XIII Corps at Ubach and at Geilenkirchen. When the 349th Field Artillery Group, a Negro unit, became operational at Hontem, Germany, on 1 February 1945, the 777th Battalion was attached to it. The 754th, a white 155-mm. howitzer unit,

joined the 349th Group on 8 February, and the 548th, a white 155-mm. gun battalion, was attached ten days later. For the first five days of February the 777th Battalion supported the British 12 Corps through the 349th Group; on 6 February it and the 349th Group turned to general support of XVI Corps, with which it and the other attached battalions of the 349th Group operated for the remainder of the campaign in Germany. In March the 777th saw its greatest firing activity. From positions at Heidhausen, east of the Roer, the battalion fired 1,337 rounds on the night of 3–4 March. At Weiers, on 4 March, the battalion, in the presence of the corps and corps artillery commanders, fired XVI Corps' first rounds across the Rhine into Mehrum. From Altfeld, between 5 and 10 March, the battalion sank barges, destroyed vehicles, including prime movers towing guns, and fired on a troop assembly point in the pocket south of Wesel and west of the Rhine. It fired preparations and supporting fires for Operation Flash Point, XVI Corps' crossing of the Rhine. On 25 March the 777th Battalion and the 349th Group crossed the Rhine, the first of the Negro combat support units to do so.[34]

Of the Negro antiaircraft artillery units with consistent and full employment in antiaircraft duties in the European theater, the 452d Antiaircraft Artillery Automatic Weapons Battalion was one of the most active. The XII Corps, to which this unit was attached in battle, considered it to be among the

---

[34] Hist 777th FA Bn, 15 Aug 43–31 Dec 44; AAR's and Jnl 777th FA Bn, Feb–May 45; AAR's and Jnl 349th Gp, Feb–Mar 45.

best units of its type.[35] It was among the antiaircraft units whose batteries were employed in England in 1943 and early 1944 to protect military installations.[36] It spent most of its continental career protecting field artillery battalions from aerial attacks. From its arrival in Normandy on 23 June to early August 1944 it furnished antiaircraft protection for the landing beaches. In August it protected oil dumps, river crossings, and road junctions, and sent its first platoons to protect XII Corps' field artillery battalions. It made its first claims on 23 August when, out of fifteen enemy planes attacking 191st Field Artillery Battalion positions at the Sens River crossing, the 452d downed two, damaged two, and probably damaged two more. No casualties were suffered by the 191st Battalion.

Unlike many other antiaircraft battalions, the 452d was kept busy throughout its career overseas, although there were days and weeks when enemy planes were few. When protecting field artillery battalions, the 452d batteries and platoons, as was usual for antiaircraft units thus employed, were attached to a half-dozen or more field artillery units simultaneously. At one time in October 1944, the 452d platoons and batteries were protecting emplacements of the 738th, 179th, 945th, 731st, 191st, 752d, 267th, and 278th Field Artillery Battalions. All of these were white units.[37] The battalions which it protected reinforced and supported over a dozen infantry and armored divisions.

No installation defended by the 452d suffered matériel damage or personnel killed by enemy aircraft, although the battalion and the field artillery battalions which it protected suffered personnel losses from other types of enemy action. When enemy artillery fire caused casualties in the field artillery units that the 452d's platoons were protecting, men of the 452d went to the aid of men in the field artillery batteries. On one such occasion, on 27 September 1944, the platoon sergeant and an aidman of a platoon furnishing protection to a field artillery battalion went voluntarily to the aid of wounded men when they realized that the battalion's own aidmen could not give immediate attention to all casualties. When enemy shelling increased in intensity, the antiaircraft platoon and elements of the artillery withdrew, but the 452d's two soldiers remained to assist in the care and evacuation of the wounded. Another time, on 4 December 1944, three privates from a 452d platoon protecting a field artillery battalion, which had come under severe enemy artillery fire, went out to a gun position and removed five injured men to the battalion aid station, thus allowing the regular gun crew to carry on an uninterrupted fire mission.[38]

The 452d was among units informally cited for economical "shoots" after one of its batteries caused the destruction of an enemy ME–109 plane with four rounds of 40-mm. ammunition.[39] In

---

[35] Lt Col George Dyer, XII Corps: Spearhead of Patton's Third Army (Hq XII U.S. Army Corps, 1947), p. 128.
[36] Hist 452d AAA AW Bn, 1943 and 1944.
[37] AAR's 452d AAA AW Bn, Jun–Oct 44.

[38] Silver Stars: SSgt William Campbell, T/5 Zeno Ellis, Pfc Edward I. Swindell, Pfc Willie Jackson, and Pvt Samuel Johnson, Hq XII Corps, GO 3, 9 Jan 45; Hq XII Corps, GO 4, 13 Jan 45.
[39] Hq ETO, Anti Aircraft Artillery Notes, No. 6, 28 Nov 44.

March 1945, as XII Corps and Third Army drove east to the Rhine, enemy air activity increased sharply. The 452d experienced more activity during this period than at any other time since entering combat. It had 133 engagements during the month, claiming 42 enemy aircraft destroyed and 23 probably destroyed. On 17 March, two combat commands of the 4th Armored Division spearheading the advance toward the Nahe River were attacked throughout the day by Luftwaffe FW–190's and ME–109's dive bombing and strafing elements of the two commands in groups of two to five from an altitude of about 1,000 feet. Of a total of 53 planes in the area, the white 489th Antiaircraft Artillery Automatic Weapons Battalion, attached to the 4th Armored Division, destroyed 12, and the 452d, supporting corps artillery farther to the rear, engaged the remainder as they strafed artillery positions. The 452d destroyed 4 and probably destroyed 4 more.

The Nahe bridgehead, established at Bad Krueznach on 18 March, was attacked by enemy planes for the next forty-eight hours. The bridges suffered no damage and protecting antiaircraft units destroyed eleven and probably destroyed three more enemy planes. Of this total the 452d accounted for six of those destroyed and two of the probables. On 20 March, the Luftwaffe made its maximum effort against the Nahe bridgehead, sending over a total of 248 planes against positions now defended by elements of nine antiaircraft battalions. Of the aircraft attacking the area, 36 were definitely destroyed by antiaircraft fire and 14 were probably destroyed. The 452d, with 12 destroyed and 4 probables, was the high

scoring unit, followed by the 489th Battalion, which destroyed 11.

When the 5th Division reached the Rhine at Oppenheim on 22 March and a ponton bridge was begun across the river, the 452d was among the units protecting the bridge site. On the afternoon of the 23d, while the bridge was still being built, 58 enemy planes operated against the area. Of these, 19 were destroyed and 8 were probably destroyed by antiaircraft units; of these the 452d destroyed 10.[40]

The 452d did not suffer casualties from air activity until April 1945 when, in an engagement with twenty ME–109's and FW–190's, the unit had four soldiers wounded. Just before the end of the war, the German Air Force had another spurt of activity. In the first days of May, the 452d had thirteen engagements netting four planes destroyed. Its final total of claims, confirmed and approved by V–E Day when its platoons were scattered through Germany, Austria, and Czechoslovakia, was sixty-seven and eleven-twelfths destroyed, nineteen probably destroyed, and eleven damaged.[41]

Tanks and Tank Destroyers

Armored units, by virtue of their use in task forces and the attachment of their companies and platoons to infantry, had closer continuing contacts with the main stream of battle than most other small supporting Negro units. De-

---

[40] Hq ETO, Anti Aircraft Notes, No. 26, 18 Apr 45.

[41] AAR's and Opns Rpts, 452d AAA AW Bn, Aug 44–May 45, Jan–May 45. Fractions resulted when more than one unit was credited with the destruction of a plane.

spite the fact that some were attached to a number of units, seldom staying long enough with any one unit to become fully acclimatized, the employment of these units was generally normal for organizations of their types.

The 761st Tank Battalion, the first of the Negro armored units to be committed to combat, landed at OMAHA Beach on 10 October 1944 after a brief stay in England. The unit then had 6 white and 30 Negro officers and 676 enlisted men. The battalion entered France with greater confidence than most Negro units could muster upon entry into a theater of operations. It had gained assurance during the training period at Camp Hood, Texas, where it had been told by higher commanders, including the Second Army's Lt. Gen. Ben Lear, that it had a superior record and that much was expected of it. The 761st firmly believed that it owed its existence and survival and, therefore, a top performance, to Lt. Gen. Lesley J. McNair, now dead on the battlefield. Its belief in its future and its sense of responsibility were renewed when it joined the 26th Division of XII Corps, Third Army. The division commander, Maj. Gen. Willard S. Paul, in welcoming the battalion on 31 October, told the tankers and their officers: "I am damned glad to have you with us. We have been expecting you for a long time, and I am sure you are going to give a good account of yourselves. I've got a big hill up there that I want you to take, and I believe that you are going to do a great job of it." Two days later, General Patton visited the battalion and, standing on the same half-track used by General Paul, challenged the unit in characteristic Patton manner:

"Men, you're the first Negro tankers to ever fight in the American Army. I would never have asked for you if you weren't good. I have nothing but the best in my Army. I don't care what color you are, so long as you go up there and kill those Kraut sonsabitches. Everyone has their eyes on you and is expecting great things from you. Most of all, your race is looking forward to you. Don't let them down, don't let me down!" [42] The 761st, convinced that it was needed and wanted, that its first job was already laid out for it, and that the most highly regarded of armored commanders as well as the 26th Division's commander expected only the best from it, had now only to enter battle to justify its own hopes and those of men who, it felt, wished it well.

From the time that it was committed to combat on 7 November 1944 the 761st Battalion spent 183 days in action, its only pauses accounted for by the time needed to move from one task to another. In the Third Army it was attached to the 26th, 71st, and 87th Divisions, the 17th Airborne Division, and the 17th Armored Group; in the Ninth Army to the 95th and 79th Divisions and the XVI Corps; and in the Seventh Army to the 103d and 71st Divisions. With these larger units it fought in France, Belgium, Holland, Luxembourg, Germany, and Austria.

For its entry into combat on 8 Novem-

---

[42] Bn files, 761st Tank Bn; Trezzvant W. Anderson, *Come Out Fighting: The Epic Tale of the 761st Tank Battalion, 1942–1945* (Salzburger Druckerei und Verlag, 1945), pp. 15, 21. The account by Anderson, a newspaperman in civilian life who, as a noncommissioned aviation engineer, took a reduction in rank to transfer to the 761st, is one of the best of the few Negro unit histories to appear in print.

ber at Athainville east of Nancy, parts of the battalion, as was normal for separate armored units, were attached to elements of the 26th Division and placed in special task forces. The 26th Division was then preparing for XII Corps' November offensive.[43] Company A of the 761st was attached to the 104th Infantry with one platoon attached to the 101st Infantry. Company C was attached to the 328th Infantry. Provisional Task Force A contained Company K of the 101st Infantry, engineers, the 602d Tank Destroyer Battalion (−), and the remainder of the 761st Tank Battalion (excepting its mortar, assault gun, and reconnaissance platoons, in reserve), all under the command of Lt. Col. Peter J. Kopcsak, commander of the 602d Tank Destroyer Battalion.[44]

On the first day, Company A's two platoons supported the 104th Infantry's attack and capture of Vic-sur-Seille; the remaining platoon of Company A supported infantry in taking Moyenvic. Company C, attached to the 328th Infantry, used its twelve tanks in the assault on Bezange-la-Petite and a hill to the southeast.[45] On 9 November, in the season's first snowstorm, the two platoons of Company A supported the 104th Infantry, which attacked and took Chateau-Salins after four hours of fighting. Company A then turned east toward Morville-les-Vic. The remainder of the battalion in Task Force

A, with infantry mounted on its tanks, was then approaching Morville. Two platoons of Company D, with two companies of the 3d Battalion, 101st Infantry, took positions south of Salival, a small town from which enemy machine gun fire enfiladed the western slope of Hill 310 (Côte St. Jean), the 26th Division's main objective for the day. Company D shelled the town and set it afire. Infantry, at dusk, entered Salival and passed through the woods beyond.

At Morville-les-Vic, where heavy enemy mortar and artillery fire was encountered, tanks of Company B shelled the town. When they attempted to pass through, roadblocks and bazooka fire stopped the tanks. The lead tank, knocked out, blocked the narrow main road, halting the tank column. Infantry cleared the town in house-to-house fighting. In the meantime, Company C seized high ground to the northwest of Morville and held until infantry took over, while Company D, moving to the left flank from Salival to screen the attack, broke up a German counterattack. Company C, moving down from its high ground toward Morville, ran into a tank trap running from woods at the edge of the high ground to a road leading through Morville. Beyond the tank ditch were camouflaged pill boxes, by now further concealed by new-fallen snow. Company C lost nine enlisted men and one officer killed and seven tanks—four recoverable—in the action along the tank trap. Despite low visibility caused by the weather, the battalion's assault gun platoon, aided by the observations of artillery liaison planes, completed its firing missions, securing direct hits on an enemy armored vehicle and four trucks. Task Force A, finally

---

[43] For an account of the 26th Division in this, its initial campaign, see Hugh M. Cole, *The Lorraine Campaign*, in this series, Chs. VII, X, XII.

[44] Jnl 602d TD Bn, ETO L–292, 26th Inf Div (38).

[45] AAR 761st Tank Bn, Nov 44, in L–292–26th Inf Div (39); Dyer, *op. cit.*, p. 250.

getting seven tanks through Morville, went on toward Hampont, the tanks assisting the infantry in gaining a foothold in the Bois de Geline to the northeast.[46]

In its entry into battle the 761st had three experiences which, in a unit with less confidence and will to achieve, might have proved disastrous. On the evening of 7 November the 761st tank column approached a crossroads at Arracourt, France, on the way to its line of departure for the next day's attack. A French farmer, possibly a collaborationist, drove a herd of cattle into the crossroads with the result that tanks, tank destroyers, and trucks loaded with infantrymen piled up into a confused traffic jam. The 761st's commander, Lt. Col. Paul L. Bates, leading his tank column, arrested the Frenchman and got traffic moving. Just as the crossroads cleared, heavy enemy artillery fire fell, disabling one of the tanks, and an enemy patrol, infiltrating the position, opened fire with automatic weapons, seriously wounding Colonel Bates, who was evacuated for hospitalization that was to last until mid-February. The loss of its commander just before its first battle alone might have unnerved the unit, but this mishap was followed by a more unusual event, more mysterious than unnerving. Its first five tankers killed, the first American Negro tankers to die in any war,[47] were all members of the same tank crew. Their tank showed no sign of having been hit by

shell, shell fragment, or bullet, yet the men within were all dead, sitting upright in their normal crew positions, apparently untouched, and with only a look of surprise on their faces. The next day, the 761st's executive officer, acting as battalion commander, was evacuated for battle fatigue. Lt. Col. Hollis E. Hunt came forward from the 17th Armored Group to assist the battalion's acting commander. Shortly after his arrival, both Colonel Hunt and Colonel Kopcsak, commander of Task Force A, were wounded by shell fire. After Colonel Kopcsak was evacuated, Hunt, though wounded, took over command of the task force. With the evacuation of the 761st's acting commander, Colonel Hunt took over command of the tank battalion as well, a command which he retained until the end of November.

But the unit's first day's work had compensations. If the men of the 761st had brooded on what death buttoned up in a tank was like, they gave no outward sign; if they had wondered what they would do without their accustomed leaders and how well they would stand up under heavy fire, they now knew. The demonstration of leadership afforded by Colonel Hunt became an admired standard of conduct for the 761st. Around the tank companies and platoons of the 761st, the infantrymen of the units of the 26th Division were performing deeds of heroism on 8 and 9 November, one resulting in a Medal of Honor for an aidman with the 328th Infantry who, though wounded himself during the fight near Bezange-la-Petite, worked his way under fire to dress the wounds of others, giving instructions to infantrymen until his own wounds made

---

[46] AAR 761st S–2, S–3, Nov 44. Anderson, *Come Out Fighting*, pp. 20–33; Cole, *The Lorraine Campaign*, p. 323.

[47] The first member of this tank unit to lose his life was a medical aidman, Pvt. Clifford C. Adams, hit by an exploding shell while going to the aid of a wounded crewman.

it impossible for him to speak.[48]   These deeds were emulated by members of the 761st who before the unit's career was over, had won eleven Silver Stars and sixty-nine Bronze Stars, four of the latter with clusters, and nearly all for heroism under fire.[49]

On those first two days the 761st discovered as well in the crucial places—within its companies and platoons—good and trustworthy leadership to match that of its temporary commander.   The platoons of Company A attached to the 104th Regiment were commanded by the one remaining white company commander in the battalion, Capt. David Williams II, a Yale graduate about whose point of view toward service with them the men of the 761st had not always been too sure.   Just before the start of the offensive, Williams, "talking it up" with a Harlem twist, called to his men: "Now look here, ya cats, we gotta hit it down the main drag, and hip some of them unhepped cats on the other side.   So let's roll right on down ole Seventh Avenue, and knock 'em, Jack!"   This eased tension before the first tank rolled out.   The unit's own enlisted historian commented candidly:

And that guy surprised us, too, for we had our doubts about him, back in the US, but he came through, and proved that you can be wrong, and we found out that we were wrong, for Dave Williams was alright (sic).   We found that out on the battlefield, when the Jerries were sending everything our way.   In fact, we felt that Dave Williams actually *liked* killing up there,

and it became a sort of secondary 'sport' after the primary one, which of course, was 'keeping from getting killed.' [50]

On its first day, the lead tank in Company A ran into a roadblock obstructing the tank column.   A sergeant dismounted under small arms fire, attached a cable to the roadblock, and moved it off the road.   His action permitted the infantry-tank team to proceed and open the way to the successful assault and capture of Vic-sur-Seille.[51]   When the lead tank of Company B was set afire in the streets of Morville, one man within was severely wounded and the tank commander, emerging, was machine gunned and killed.   The other members of the crew, realizing that until their fire mission was completed, infantry could not proceed—a dozen or more infantry of Company K, 101st Infantry, were already dead or wounded in the street around the tank—climbed out through the turret and escape hatch, bringing their weapons with them.   They sprayed submachine gun fire on enemy foot troops and on fire positions in the upper stories of houses.   A corporal climbed back into the disabled tank through the bottom escape hatch, manned his machine gun, and silenced several enemy machine gun positions and a bazooka team firing from an upstairs window.   The tank was hit twice again, but the crew remained under it, firing individual weapons.   In the Company D action along the edge of the Bois de Geline, one tank gunner personally accounted for twenty of the enemy with his machine gun.   A tank crew,

---

[48] Cpl. Alfred L. Wilson, who died refusing aid for himself.   Cole, *The Lorraine Campaign,* p. 322n. See notes on pages 321–23 for other examples of heroism among infantrymen on these days.

[49] As of 14 Nov 45.   Ltr, CO 761st to CG 12th Army Gp, 10 Jul 45, 201.3, Bn Records; Bn Corresp Files; Anderson, *Come Out Fighting,* p. 151.

[50] Anderson, *Come Out Fighting,* pp. 25, 27.

[51] Silver Star, SSgt Ruben Rivers, Hq 26th Inf Div, GO 2 Dec 44.

after its tank had been hit and taken by the Germans, dismounted and recaptured the tank. In the heaviest action of the two days, that of Company C at the tank trap near Morville, 1st Sgt. Samuel C. Turley and 2d Lt. Kenneth W. Coleman, tank platoon leaders, organized crews from their disabled tanks into a dismounted combat group. This group successfully held off the enemy attack while crews from other trapped tanks escaped along the tank ditch. During the action, Coleman and Turley were both killed by enemy fire.[52]

During the two days there were, as well, men who re-entered tanks to pull out trapped comrades, tank commanders who strapped wounded men to their vehicles and successfully evacuated them, and men who, in exposed positions, pulled their heavy machine guns from their disabled tanks and returned German fire on foot. One tank driver, seeing seriously injured white infantrymen lying in the open, dismounted from his tank, moved across open terrain under heavy artillery and small arms fire, evacuated the men to the shelter of a disabled tank and administered first aid, and thereby saved the lives of three of the wounded. White infantrymen of Company K similarly but unsuccessfully tried to remove the body of the 761st's tank commander from his burning tank in Morville. A number lost their lives or were wounded in the attempt.[53] At the close of the second day, the 761st felt that it had won the right to its motto, "Come Out Fighting."

For the remainder of November and into December, the 761st Tank Battalion continued to support the 26th Division in its movement through the Forêt de Bride et de Koecking to Dieuze and Benestroff and toward the Sarre, where the division attacked and took Sarre Union and fought through the Maginot Line to Obergailbach on the German border. Fighting in the snow and mud against the stubborn resistance of the Germans in Lorraine was hard all the way. On 12 November two platoons of Company A repulsed an enemy counterattack at Wuisse, destroying two enemy tanks. The next day, one platoon, attached to the 2d Battalion, 104th Infantry, counterattacked on its own initiative, took Wuisse in the afternoon, and defended the town through the night.[54] On 18 November, at Guebling, when the engineers completed a bridge hastily constructed under artillery and small arms fire, 761st tanks crossed into the town to give additional support to the infantry, found heavy mine fields, and then took a "terrific beating" which prevented continuation of support on that day.[55] The crew of one tank escaped and returned for a replacement tank, and then rejoined the company at Guebling. Of the five tanks in Guebling, three were lost to antitank fire and one to mines, leaving but one tank operational in the town.[56]

Casualties in men and tanks were heavy during November—22 killed in action, 2 dead of wounds, 81 wounded, 44 nonbattle casualties, and 14 tanks

[52] Both received Silver Stars.
[53] Commendations binder, 761st Tnk Bn Files; Anderson, *Come Out Fighting*, pp. 35, 102–12.

[54] AAR 761st Tnk Bn S–2, S–3, Nov 44.
[55] War Diary, CO 101st Inf Opns Rpts, 26th Inf Div, Nov 44.
[56] AAR 761st Tnk Bn S–2, S–3, Nov 44.

lost and 20 damaged.[57] But tanks could be recovered and repaired, or replaced. On the other hand the 761st, like most other active Negro combat units, had difficulty replacing men. During its first month no replacements arrived at all and the unit ended the month with a shortage of 113 men.[58] On 4 December the first of the 761st's replacements arrived. But these were not armored force replacements—there were none—and the unit had to retrain them on the job.

The unit received numerous requests for transfer from men in the theater's service units. A number of these had to be refused because of low test scores or court-martial records. At times the unit received master and first sergeants from service units in grade, but many of these men could not be used despite their high test scores and grades. On 19 December the unit transferred 58 of its unsuitable replacements and the next day it sent 17 to other units.[59] By February it had accumulated 16 noncommissioned officers of the first four grades who had to be transferred out; at the same time it requested that 27 more replacements who had "shown no aptitude for armored training" be transferred.[60] Though it gained some excellent men both from replacements and volunteer transfer, the battalion, like other armored and artillery units, remained short of personnel much of the

time. In March it was short 10 Negro officers and 89 enlisted men. Since all of its wounded officers and a fifth of its hospitalized enlisted men returned to duty with the unit the 761st was generally able to perform its duties despite deficiencies and shortages in replacements.[61]

The 761st's work with the 26th Division in November elicited special commendation from the corps commander, in addition to commendation that went to all units of the 26th Division and XII Corps: [62]

1. I consider the 761st Tank Battalion to have entered combat with such conspicious courage and success as to warrant special commendation.

2. The speed with which they adapted themselves to the front line under most adverse weather conditions, the gallantry with which they faced some of Germany's finest troops, and the confident spirit with which they emerged from their recent engagements in the vicinity of Dieuze, Morville les Vic, and Guebling entitle them surely to consider themselves of the veteran 761st.[63]

To this General Paul added: "It is with extreme gratification that the Corps Commander's commendation is forwarded to you. Your battalion has supported this division with great bravery under the most adverse weather and terrain conditions. You have my sincere

---

[57] AAR 761st Tnk Bn Med Detachment, Nov 44 (dated 29 Nov 44) ; AAR 761st S–1, Nov 44 (dated 2 Dec 44) ; AAR Motor Office, 761st Tnk Bn, Nov 44 (dated 2 Dec 44) .

[58] Summaries of Gen Staff Secs, 26th Inf Div, G–1 Rpt, Nov 44.

[59] AAR 761st S–1, Dec 44, and Bn Files.

[60] Ltrs, 761st Tnk Bn to CG XVI Corps, 17 Feb 45.

[61] AAR's Per S–1 Rpts, 761st; Press Release, S–2 761st Tnk Bn, 6 Aug 45.

[62] Hq Third U.S. Army to CG XII Corps, 24 Nov 44, with 1st Ind, Hq XII Corps to CO's All Units Attached or Assigned to XII Corps, 28 Nov 44, XII Corps, AG 200.6; Ltr, Hq 26th Inf Div to All Members 26th Inf Div, 26 Nov 44, copies in L–292–26th Inf Div Supply Docs and attached unit rpts.

[63] Ltr, Hq XII Corps to CO 761st Tnk Bn, 9 Dec 44, AG 330.13 (G–1) , Bn Files.

wish that success may continue to follow your endeavors." [64]

When the 26th Division was relieved for a rest, beginning 9 December, the 761st Battalion was attached to the incoming 87th Division, officially committed to battle for the first time on 13 December. On 14 December the first of the 761st's tanks crossed the border into Germany. By 15 December the battalion had lost a majority of its tanks from enemy action and from mechanical failure caused by continuous commitment of all available tanks for extended periods of time. When the battalion returned to Sarre Union for four days of maintenance, only three tanks were operational. On the march from the Sarre region to Neufchâteau, Belgium, southwest of Bastogne, beginning on 24 December and ending on 30 December, again in attachment to the 87th Division, ten medium tanks dropped from the column because of maintenance failures.[65]

Beginning on 31 December, when the battalion and the 345th Infantry of the 87th Division took Rondu and Nimbermont from an enemy still fighting around Bastogne, through January the 761st engaged in successful actions at Bonnerue, Recogne, Remagne, Tillet, and Pironpie in Belgium; at Steinbach in Luxembourg, and, working with the 17th Airborne Division, at Gouvy, Hautbillan, and Watermall. Steep and icy hills and snow-covered swampy ground in the Ardennes caused wear and tear on power trains and engines and caused tanks to bog down.[66] When

at times trucks could not reach elements of the unit, the light tanks of the 761st's Company D towed ammunition trailers to supply medium tanks from dumps placed as far forward as possible.[67]

At the beginning of February the battalion moved 140 miles to Jabeek, Holland, near the German border, where it was attached briefly to the 95th Division in XVI Corps, then holding a defensive position along the Maas while waiting for Ninth Army's drive to the Rhine to begin. Supporting the 79th Division in this offensive, which began on 23 February, elements of the 761st participated in the capture of End, Holland, cut the Roermond-Julich Railway at Milich, and moved on to Erkling where they crossed the border into Germany on 3 March. The battalion then moved on to Schwannenberg, mopping up bypassed pockets of resistance and capturing prisoners left behind by the advance of the 2d Armored Division. On 7–8 March it set out to join the Seventh Army where, on 12 March, each of its medium tank companies was attached to one of the 103d Division's regiments.[68]

When the 761st arrived, the 614th Tank Destroyer Battalion (Towed), another Negro unit, was already attached to the 103d Division. The 614th, like the 761st, had five white officers; the remainder of its staff was Negro and all of its company officers were Negroes. The 614th had been with the 103d Division since 7 December. It was committed to action on 28 November when it began to relieve the 705th Tank Destroyer Battalion (SP), then supporting the 3d Cavalry Group (Mechanized). In the

[64] 1st Ind, Hq 26th Inf Div (on Ltr cited n. 63) to CO 761st Tnk Bn, AG 201.22, Bn Files.
[65] AAR 761st Motor Office, Dec 44.
[66] Ibid., Jan 45.
[67] AAR 761st Service Co, Jan 45.
[68] AAR 761st S-2, S-3, Mar 45.

3d Cavalry, one company of the 614th's towed three-inch guns was attached to each of the group's squadrons with the remainder of the battalion in reserve. At the time, the 3d Cavalry Group was protecting the north flank of XX Corps from the Moselle River to the vicinity of Ober Tunsdorf in Germany, where it maintained contact with the 90th Cavalry Reconnaissance Squadron of the 10th Armored Division, then operating in a zone between the Moselle and Saar Rivers. Before it lay the dragons' teeth, antitank ditches, and pillboxes of the Siegfried Line. On 1 December, its first day in the line, the 614th's Company A scored three direct hits on enemy-held pillboxes north of Borg. The Germans raised a white flag, but when a cavalry patrol approached they opened fire. The tank destroyers then resumed firing and the enemy retreated out of his pillboxes. The company on its first day also accounted for one German 88-mm. gun, "displaying accuracy in destroying this weapon with three rounds in the vicinity of Borg," the 3d Cavalry Group commented.[69] Late that night the 614th was relieved from the 3d Cavalry Group for movement to Luneville, France, where on Seventh Army orders, it was attached to VI Corps and, on 5 December to the 103d Division, effective upon arrival at Kuttolsheim, France.[70] There its Company A was attached to Task Force Forest, made up of the 103d Reconnais-

sance Troop, a company of the 756th Tank Battalion and a company of the 409th Infantry.[71] Company C was attached to the 411th Infantry.

The 103d Division was in process of relieving the 45th and 79th Divisions in a sector on the west bank of the flooded Zintzel du Nord River. Beginning 8 December, as elements of the 103d Division moved into line, the companies of the 614th began to fire, Company C knocking out an observation post in a church steeple, destroying a machine gun emplacement, and delivering harassing fire on enemy troops.[72]

The 103d Division's attack began before dawn on 9 December, with a crossing of the Zintzel to seize Uttenhofen and Mertzwiller on the opposite bank. The attack progressed through Griesbach and Fortsheim. In both towns observation posts in church steeples were knocked out by the 614th's guns.[73] When the attack reached the Maginot Line, German defensive positions grew stronger. In the rugged hills and woods of the Lembach-Climbach area, the 411th Infantry met particularly strong resistance. The regiment organized a task force under its executive officer to break the German hold on Climbach, a town in an open valley with high, well-defended ridges guarding its approaches. The task force contained a platoon of combat engineers, a platoon of tanks, a company of infantry, and a platoon of the 614th's towed tank destroyer guns. The force had the mission of pushing to the town of Climbach

[69] AAR 3d Cav Gp (M), Nov, Dec 44; Ltr, Hq 614th TD Bn to S-3 3d Cav Gp, 614th TD Bn AAR, Dec 44.
[70] Jnl 614th TD Bn, Dec 44; Narrative Rpt, 614th TD Bn, Dec 44; Hq Seventh Army, 3 Dec 44, AG 370.5-C.

[71] FO 3, 103d Inf Div, 7 Dec 44.
[72] Ltr, Hq Co C to S-3 614th TD Bn, 8 Dec 44, 614th TD Bn S-3 Jnl, Dec 44.
[73] Daily Rpt, ExO 614th TD Bn to S-3, 10 Dec 44.

and holding it, cutting the line of communications to Lembach.[74]

The task force left Prueschdorf at 1020 on the foggy, cold morning of 14 December. Visibility was less than 300 yards. The force, with Lt. Charles L. Thomas, commander of the 614th's Company C, in the lead armored scout car, proceeded through enemy territory, slowly ascending the steep, winding road toward Climbach. Heavy enemy small arms, automatic weapons, mortar, and artillery fire fell along the route. When within a thousand yards of Climbach, Thomas' M20 was knocked out by a shell and mine. Thomas, though wounded, dismounted from his wrecked car and helped his crew, including another wounded man, to dismount. Infantry and tanks deployed to both sides of the road. The task force commander directed the tank destroyer platoon to proceed up the road and go into firing positions. There they would place fire on the enemy in and around Climbach and act as a base of fire while the rest of the force flanked the German positions. Leaving the protection of his wrecked vehicle, Thomas ordered and directed the dispersion and displacement of two of his tank destroyers. These destroyers were soon returning the fire of the now alerted enemy, who were directing the fire of all of their ridge-top weapons upon the task force. Thomas, despite multiple wounds in his chest, legs, and left arm, continued to direct his men. Only when he was certain that his platoon commander was in full control of the situation did Thomas permit himself to be evacuated.[75]

On their exposed hillside, the ten-man tank destroyer crews went into action, loading, aiming, firing and then scooting back to their half-tracks to fire their .50-caliber machine guns at the enemy in the woods. The gun crews dwindled in size in a few minutes. One tank destroyer crew, although in the open, had better luck than the others. Its half-track bogged down in the open field but in a slight draw. The enemy poured small arms and tank fire into the position without being able to destroy it. Gun crews reduced to as few as two men went on firing, while the tank destroyers continued in action for four hours. Tanks were bogged down in the mud too far to the rear to be of any help. Three BAR men of the 411th's platoon volunteered to give flank security. The tank destroyer gunners and drivers flattened out alongside their guns and poured M1 and carbine fire into the enemy. Technician 5 Robert W. Harris, knowing that the last gun was running out of ammunition, drove his truck to the rear over fire-swept roads for a new supply. When the truck was fully loaded, he started back up the Climbach hill. About half way up, he was stopped by the task force commander, who told him that he could not go farther because enemy fire was too heavy. Disregarding the warning, Harris drove to within twenty-five yards of his gun positions, unloaded the truck, uncrated the ammunition, and began to carry it forward. The remaining men of the platoon made trip after trip under fire to carry the 54-pound ammunition boxes to the one gun still functioning. Infantrymen of the 411th infiltrated from the flanks while the tank destroyers engaged the defend-

[74] S-3 Rpt Co C 614th TD Bn, 13–14 Dec 44; S-3 Jnl 614th TD Bn, Dec 44.
[75] Hq Seventh Army, GO 58, 20 Feb 45.

ing enemy. By the time darkness came, the enemy was offering only small arms fire from Climbach itself.

This "outstanding performance of mass heroism on the part of the officers and men of Company C, 614th Tank Destroyer Battalion," the 103d Division reported, "precluded a near catastrophic reverse for the task force." Their action before Climbach, in which the platoon had more than 50 percent casualties, lost three guns, two half-tracks, and an armored car, enabled the task force to capture the town and forced the enemy to retreat from Climbach and retire to his Siegfried Line. Two infantry-tank counterattacks against the town during the night were beaten off. For its action at Climbach, the 3d Platoon, Company C, 614th Tank Destroyer Battalion, received the Distinguished Unit Citation, the first unit assigned or attached to the 103d Division and the first Negro unit to do so. In this action, in addition to a Distinguished Service Cross for Lieutenant Thomas, the platoon earned four Silver Stars, two of them awarded posthumously, and nine Bronze Stars.[76] When Maj. Gen. Charles C. Haffner, Jr., commanding the 103d Division, personally pinned their decorations on two officers and nine enlisted men at a ceremony on 28 Decem-

ber, the unit declared it "a great morale factor in our troops." [77]

Through the winter of 1944–45 the 614th Tank Destroyer Battalion remained attached to the 103d Division. It participated in the division's holding operations and limited offensives on the left flank of the Seventh Army and along the Moder River line. It fired star shells for patrols and indirect fire missions in attachment to the 928th Field Artillery Battalion, thereby relieving a critical shortage of howitzer ammunition. Its men engaged in raids and patrols with elements of the 103d Division.[78] On New Year's Day, 1945, an enemy patrol attacked a thirteen-man outpost of Company A. The outpost was isolated for about an hour while heavy small arms fire was exchanged. When the action was over, the outpost had killed nine and captured two of the enemy without suffering losses itself. On 12 January the 1st Section, 1st Platoon, Company C, directed to destroy an enemy observation post at Forbach, fired 143 rounds in forty minutes and scored 139 direct hits.

On 20 January, when the battalion joined in a planned withdrawal of the 103d Division to new defensive lines west of Hagenau, Companies A and C remained in position in order to make their withdrawal under cover of darkness. The two companies met with unusual difficulties in their withdrawal over roads covered with snow and ice. For several hours, commanders of both companies remained behind the infan-

[76] Narrative Rpt, 614th TD Bn, Dec 44; S–3 Rpt Company C 614th TD Bn, 13–14 Dec 44, Bn S–3 Jnl; Opns Rpt (Narrative, an. 1), 103d Inf Div, Dec 44, Apr 45; Personal Narrative, Sgt Dillard Booker, Third Platoon, C Company, 614th TD Bn, 614th TD 314.7. Ralph Mueller and Jerry Turk, *Report After Action: The Story of the 103d Infantry Division* (Hq, 103d Inf Div, Innsbruck, Austria, 1945), pp. 48–50; Hq 103d Inf Div, GO 88, 27 Dec 44, and GO 89, 28 Dec 44; WD GO 37, 45; Hq Seventh Army, GO 58, 20 Feb 45, and GO 141, 11 Apr 45.

[77] Narrative Rpt 614th TD Bn, Dec 44.
[78] Narrative Rpt 614th TD Bn, Jan 45, XV Corps Daily TD Rpts, Dec–Jan 44; Armd Bulls (Summaries of Armd Activity) 1st Armd Gp, Jan 45.

try force covering the withdrawal in an effort to salvage all possible matériel. One company commander and eighteen of his enlisted men arrived within friendly lines sixteen hours after the infantry covering force had withdrawn. One platoon towed one of its guns out with an ammunition vehicle. The infantry covering force, when it reached another platoon's position, insisted that the men leave and abandon their gun, but the men refused to do so. Their attempts to halt a wrecker or a tank moving to the rear failed, for withdrawing tanks had already been lost along the slippery roads and no tank driver wished to risk pulling a half-track out. Finally, the men determined to pull their gun as far as possible with their one jeep. Five hours later, fourteen cold, wet, tired soldiers, their platoon leader, and their gun, towed by a jeep, reached the new lines of the 103d Division. Despite the efforts of the men of the two companies, three guns, six half-tracks, and miscellaneous equipment had to be destroyed to prevent their falling into the hands of the enemy who, though disengaged, was expected to move rapidly into the area given up by the 103d Division. The battalion took up positions in the security and antitank defenses of the division along the south bank of the Rothbach and Moder Rivers.

During the weeks of enemy pressure and attacks against Seventh Army, coinciding with but less successful than the counterattack to the north in the Ardennes, the outposts of the 614th became as accustomed to fighting off patrols and raiding parties as did infantrymen. Typically laconic was the report of one platoon: "Last night a 6 man German patrol tried to infiltrate

our out post line. But they all were killed. Otherwise it was very quiet in this sector." [79]

In the days before the March offensive, the battalion continued patrolling and training. A carefully trained party, consisting of two officers and thirty enlisted men from the reconnaissance platoons, raided an old mill between Bischoltz and Mulhausen on 5 February, achieving perfect co-ordination and complete surprise. Each officer and enlisted man had been fully instructed not only in his own job but also in the jobs of the other men. Maps and recent air photos were carefully checked and the raid was rehearsed for three days. At 2000 the raiding party, assembling at a previously designated point, moved through the main line of resistance without drawing enemy fire. Two teams of raiders, consisting of six men each, entered the mill, while a section of machine gunners, setting up on either side of the building, covered roads outside. Eight of the enemy were killed and six prisoners captured; the raiding party itself suffered not a single casualty.[80] In describing this raid, the 103d Division's enlisted historians now termed the battalion "the crack negro 614th." [81]

With the attachment of the 761st Tank Battalion to the 103d Division on 12 March, each regiment of the 103d had one of the Negro tank and one of the

[79] 2d Recon Plat Rpt of Enemy Activities, 26 Jan 45; Jnl 614th TD Bn, Jan 45.
[80] Narrative Rpt 614th TD Bn, Feb 45; G-2 Periodic Rpt, 103d Inf Div, 6 Feb 45. The latter credits the party with only two Germans killed.
[81] Mueller and Turk, 103d Infantry Division, p. 74. This account credits the raiders with nine prisoners and one dead German. These numbers appear to be those of a subsequent force's results.

Negro tank destroyer companies attached in preparation for Seventh Army's spring offensive. When the Seventh Army's attack opened on the morning of 15 March, all elements of the 614th Tank Destroyer Battalion were used in the 103d's sector. Company A laid direct fire on Kindwiller, then formed a force under its commander, along with thirty enlisted men from the company headquarters platoon, to attack and capture the town. The dismounted task force entered the town under fire; when Capt. Beauregard King, leading his men, fell, seriously wounded, the platoon sergeant, Charles E. Parks, ran to him. King ordered him on with "Don't stop for me—finish the job!" Parks took command of the force, took the town by 1000, and captured nine prisoners in the process.[82] The 1st and 2d Reconnaissance Platoons, under the battalion commander, Lt. Col. Frank S. Pritchard, with a platoon of Company B supporting, raided Bischoltz at 1530 and took forty-one prisoners. Companies B and C supported the regiments to which they were attached with direct fire.[83] The advance continued for the next three days against little resistance until the 103d Division and its supporting troops reached Siegfried Line towns. There, on 20 March, a platoon of Company C of the 761st, supporting the 411th Infantry in its assault on Nieder Schlettenbach, neutralized 13 pillboxes and 12 machine gun positions, captured one 75-mm. antitank gun intact, and ac-

counted for 35 enemy dead. Another platoon of Company C, supporting the 409th Infantry before Riesdorf, reduced 6 pillboxes, killed 8 Germans, and took 40 prisoners. Riesdorf, well defended by pillboxes and dugouts, was a key point to the division's advance through the Siegfried Line.

On 21 March, Task Force Rhine was formed from the 761st Tank Battalion (less Company C); the 2d Battalion, 409th Infantry; the 2d Reconnaissance Platoon of the 614th Tank Destroyer Battalion; and an engineer detachment. It was to be prepared to exploit any breakthrough in the Siegfried Line and to move on to the Rhine upon order. Company C of the 761st, still supporting the 411th and 409th Regiments, neutralized 7 pillboxes and 10 machine gun positions between Nieder Schlettenbach and Erlenbach, taking 64 prisoners and counting 20 enemy dead. It then attacked pillboxes covering the approaches to Riesdorf, capturing 64 prisoners and killing 12 of the enemy at this point. The next day, Company C and infantry entered the town.

Task Force Rhine assembled at the edge of Riesdorf on the morning of 22 March. With Colonel Bates in command and the reconnaissance platoon of the 614th and the light tanks of the 761st as its point, the task force moved through Riesdorf at 1600, attacked pillboxes northeast of the town, and then split into two columns, one going north toward Birkenhordt and the other going toward Bollenborn. In the column advancing toward Birkenhordt, soldiers of Company G, 409th, rode the lead tanks, firing at everything that moved. Reaching Birkenhordt, the column advanced against small arms fire and

[82] Narrative Rpt 614th TD Bn, Mar 45; Daily Rpt, Jnl 614th TD Bn, Mar 45; Mueller and Turk, *103d Infantry Division*, p. 86.
[83] Addition to Daily Rpt Co C, 15 Mar 45, Jnl 614th TD Bn.

moved through the town until halted by two antitank guns. Corps artillery concentrations—the task force remained in constant touch by radio—were called for and the column proceeded through the town, firing at all positions that might conceal an antitank gun. The other column, attempting to enter Bollenborn, was stopped by such heavy antitank fire that it withdrew and rejoined the first column at Birkenhordt. At 1800, the 103d Division directed the task force to proceed north and east to meet the 10th Armored Division, reported to be moving toward Silz. The task force set out into the night. A crater in the road beyond Birkenhordt stopped the advance, but repairs were made in about an hour by the accompanying engineer detachment and the task force moved on, using reconnaissance by fire throughout the column to resist effectively several attempts by groups of German soldiers to halt it.

On approaching Silz, the swiftly moving column found the enemy rather than the 10th Armored Division in possession. Turning east, the column fought its way through Silz. Firing into one house, the force's guns hit an ammunition dump. The house exploded, blocking the road. Silz burned brightly, providing illumination as the task force sped through the night over strange and unmarked roads. Shortly after midnight Task Force Rhine reached Munchweiler where its machine gun fire drove enemy crews away from defending antitank guns.

Just outside Munchweiler, on the way to Klingenmunster, toward which the 36th Division was reported to be advancing—a report which, like that on the 10th Armored, proved later to be in error—Task Force Rhine overran a retreating German horse-drawn vehicle column. The task force blazed through this column, killing and wounding many of the enemy and leaving the road blocked with the wreckage of vehicles and the bodies of dead horses.

Klingenmunster itself was guarded by permanent installations. As Task Force Rhine approached the town at 0150, it was met by heavy fire, but the combined weapons of the task force were turned on the enemy, many of whom surrendered. They presented another problem. Prisoners taken earlier had been sent to the rear, but the enemy had now closed in behind the task force. Prisoners were loaded on gas and ammunition trucks and every other place where they could possibly ride as the task force moved on into Klingenmunster. One tank platoon with infantry support attempted to enter the town at about 0400 but was driven out by a combination of antitank and small arms fire and darkness. With another platoon it took up firing positions at the edge of Klingenmunster, fired all available weapons into the town, and set fire to several buildings. Task Force Rhine, seeing no sign of the expected 36th Division nor of the motorized friendly infantry which was to follow its advance, entered Klingenmunster and consolidated its positions. It now learned that the 14th Armored Division would pass through it and move on to the Rhine. By the time the contact party of the 14th Armored Division arrived, Task Force Rhine had penetrated 14 kilometers through defended enemy territory. It had destroyed 150 vehicles, 31 pillboxes, 49 machine gun nests, and 29 antitank and 4 self-propelled guns.

At least 170 of the enemy lay dead and hundreds of horses were killed or left to graze by the roadside. Twelve hundred prisoners were taken. The fire strength of the task force was such that the 761st Tank Battalion alone used slightly more than fifty tons of ammunition before it halted.[84] The 409th's infantrymen paid their tribute to the lead tank of the 761st with: "That tank commander in the first tank was wonderful! He overcame a helluva lot of obstacles even before the second tank saw them."[85]

The 103d Division reached the Rhine with the 614th Tank Destroyer Battalion still attached. It went into an interim period of occupation and mopping up in the area cleared of organized resistance. The 614th's elements aided in setting up military government for the occupied towns and in rounding up enemy stragglers and bypassed pockets. The 761st Tank Battalion, relieved from the 103d, was attached to the 71st Division, in Third Army, on 28 March, joining it at Langenselbold, Germany,

on 1 April after a 132-mile march. Companies A, B, and C were attached, respectively, to the 5th, 14th, and 66th Infantry. In the Third Army's drive across Germany to Austria, the 761st supported the division, acting at times as the sole armored spearhead for the 71st's advance toward the Danube. Tanks of the 761st entered Steyr, Austria, on 5 May, and the next day met the Russians of the 1st Ukrainian Front at the Enns River. Ten of the 761st's Tanks were part of the honor guard at the 71st Division's command post when General Lothar von Rundulic signed the surrender of his German forces in Austria.[86]

When the 103d Division resumed its pursuit of the enemy on 21 April, the 614th Tank Destroyer Battalion, with its companies attached to the division's infantry regiments, moved south toward Austria, destroying and neutralizing enemy positions and taking prisoners along the way. The battalion had its last casualties on 2 May, on the outskirts of Scharnitz, Austria, in an engagement in which one officer and six enlisted men were killed while spearheading a task force toward Innsbruck. On 3 May, one platoon from Company C joined the 411th Regimental Combat Team in a dash from Mittenwald toward the Brenner Pass where, on 4 May, they seized the pass without opposition and went beyond to meet elements of the Fifth Army's 88th Division, approaching from Italy.[87]

---

[84] Jnl and AAR 761st Tk Bn, Mar 45; Narrative Rpt 614th TD Bn; AAR 409th Inf Regt, Mar 45; Ltr, Hq 761st Tk Bn to CofS 103d Div, 3 May 45, Bn Files; Hist Data File, 103d Inf Div; Mueller and Turk, *103d Infantry Division*, pp. 96–98; Anderson, *Come Out Fighting*, pp. 67–76.

[85] Mueller and Turk, *103d Infantry Division*, p. 96. The tank commander, Sgt. Ervin Lattimore, received a Silver Star for his part in Task Force Rhine. Though wounded while leading the attack against the enemy column on the road from Munchweiler, Sergeant Lattimore refused to be evacuated, and commanded his tank on into Klingenmunster. Colonel Bates, who kept walking up and down his columns during the many halts caused by roadblocks and fire fights, talking to and jerking tired men awake during the night and early morning hours of the twelve-and-a-half-hour continuous drive, received a Silver Star as well. Bronze Stars went to a number of men and officers for their work in Task Force Rhine.

---

[86] AAR 761st Tk Bn, Apr–May 45; AAR 71st Inf Div, Apr–May 45; Clinger, Johnston, and Masel, *The History of the 71st Infantry Division* (Augsburg, 1946), pp. 57–98.

[87] Narrative Rpt 614th TD Bn, Apr–May 45; Opns Rpt 103d Inf Div, Apr–May 45.

The 784th Tank Battalion, last of the three Negro tank units to be activated, had landed on the Continent on Christmas Day, 1944, and was committed to action on 1 January 1945. It was assigned to the Ninth Army on 27 November 1944 and remained so assigned until the end of the war. The 784th, trained and led throughout its career by the same commander, Lt. Col. George C. Dalia, was attached to the 104th, the 35th, and the 84th Divisions, with individual companies attached to the 8th Infantry and 17th Airborne Divisions for brief periods.

Except for an initial incident, the 784th began its active career more quietly than other Negro armored units. On 26 December 1944, while marching to join the 104th Division, the 784th, nearing Soissons, France, heard a bomb blast followed a half hour later by a series of explosions, increasing in intensity and rapidity, coming from an ammunition train probably hit by enemy bombs. At the request of an officer from an ammunition company, the 784th furnished four tanks and three recovery vehicles, with crews, to pull the untouched cars from the train. The crews of the 784th worked all afternoon, while heavy caliber ammunition exploded,[88] and managed to save 160 carloads out of about 300.

The battalion closed into bivouac near Eschweiler, Germany, on 31 December and joined the 104th Division, which was then actively defending along the Roer River in the Duren and Merken areas.[89] Elements of the 784th, with the exception of Company C, which was

initially attached to XIX Corps as a part of corps reserve, were attached to units of the 104th; a platoon of Company D's light tanks to the 104th Cavalry Reconnaissance Troop; the 81-mm. mortar platoon to the 414th Infantry; Company A (−) and Company B (−) to the 415th Infantry; Provisional Company "X," made up of one platoon of Company A and one of Company B, to the 413th Infantry until Company C joined on 25 January. The battalion's guns were used primarily to reinforce artillery fires until 3 February, when it was released from the 104th Division for attachment to the 35th Division. During the period, the battalion "ably supported the Division in defense. . . ."[90]

When the 784th joined the 35th Division at Geilenkirchen, Germany, on 8 February 1944, the 35th had just relieved the British 52d Infantry Division in the Ninth Army's line along the Roer. The tank companies trained with the infantry regiments of the 35th Division, preparing for an offensive to begin at the end of the month. Company A, on 26 February, assisted the 134th Infantry in the capture of Hilfarth, Germany, across the Roer. The following day, a motorized attack force consisting of Company I, 137th Infantry, Company A, 784th Tank Battalion, and a platoon of tank destroyers attacked Wassenburg and took it. On the same day one platoon of Company B, attached to the 137th Infantry, participated in a successful attack on Goldrath. Task Force Byrne was organized on 28 February with the mission of liberating

---

[88] Hist 784th Tk Bn, 1944.
[89] AAR 104th Inf Div, Jan–Apr 45.

[90] Leo A. Hoegh and Howard J. Doyle, *Timberwolf Tracks* (Washington: The Infantry Journal Press, 1946), p. 222.

Venlo, Holland. It contained the 320th Infantry, motorized, the 784th Tank Battalion (less Company A), the 654th Tank Destroyer Battalion, two field artillery battalions, and attached engineer and medical units, all under the command of Col. Bernard A. Byrne, the infantry regiment's commander. On 1 March, led by the medium and light tanks of the 784th carrying a company of infantrymen, the task force attacked from Widenrath along the main road to Venlo. Bypassing resistance, except in towns and villages along the road, the task force moved so swiftly that the enemy, surprised, had no time to destroy bridges. With close co-operation between infantry and tanks, resistance met was quickly wiped out. The task force gained twenty-five miles and captured a total of twenty towns and villages. It entered Venlo by 1800. Following the task force column came the 137th and 134th Regimental Combat Teams. Company A, 784th, remained with the 134th Infantry.[91]

While the two regimental combat teams were closing into assembly areas near Venlo, mopping up scattered enemy forces bypassed by Task Force Byrne, the task force set out again at 1000 on 2 March with the mission of seizing, successively, Straelin, Nieukerk, Sevelen, Linfort, and Rhineberg. Except for scattered resistance and a few blown bridges, the task force had little trouble as it forged ahead. One tank was destroyed by *panzerfaust* fire in Straelin, but the task force was not delayed. Beyond Nieukerk, the infantry was held up by a fourteen-foot antitank

ditch blown in the road after the tanks had passed. Guns shelled the road, preventing its repair, until Sgt. Walter Hall, exposed to enemy mortar fire, managed to maneuver his bulldozer tank so as to fill the tank ditch and enable the task force to continue its mission. He then destroyed an enemy antitank gun that was harassing the column.[92] Task Force Byrne captured fifteen towns and villages during the day.

A night attack was planned for Sevelen. Here enemy paratroop resistance stiffened and slowed down the advance. Out of the task force, one light tank company, one medium tank platoon, an assault gun platoon, and a company of infantry were chosen to attack the town. This force left Nieukerk at 2200 on 2 March and entered Sevelen at about midnight, meeting little resistance until it reached the center of the town. The enemy then blew a bridge over a deep railroad cut at the south entrance to the town, trapping the force in the town and cutting it off from reinforcements and resupply. Nevertheless, at dawn, the troops resumed their attack and the town was cleared of resistance by 1100, just as reinforcements entered Sevelen by another route from the north. In addition to seizing huge stores of food and ammunition, the Sevelen force killed 53 and captured 207 of the enemy.[93]

Company A, with the 1st Battalion, 134th, and tank destroyers, drove against

---

[91] Opns Rpt 784th Tk Bn, Feb–Mar 45; AAR 35th Div, Feb–Mar 45.

[92] Bronze Star, Hq 35th Inf Div GO 26, 12 Apr 45.

[93] An Associated Press dispatch described Sevelen as a "miniature 'Bastogne,'" with the 784th's troops "mauling German parachute units in savage street fighting while cut off for eighteen hours." ("Negro Tank Outfit Repeats Bastogne," New York *Times*, March 5, 1945.)

slight resistance to a road junction west of Geldern where they made contact with the 12th Battalion, King's Royal Rifle Corps, of the British 8th Armored Division.[94] Company A was then released from attachment to the 134th Infantry. Upon its release, the regimental commander wrote to the division commander:

1. I desire to commend Company A, 784th Tank Battalion, for the splendid performance of that unit while attached to this organization for the period 25 February to 4 March 1945.
2. The Company Commander, Capt. Robert L. Groglode, 01017224, and his entire company proved indispensable to the 134th Infantry Regiment in the assaulting of Hilfarth and the Roer River and the dash to Wassenburg, Bergenlen, and Geldern.
3. Their high morale, aggressiveness, and willingness to fight deserves commendation.[95]

Within Task Force Byrne, Company B of the 784th was now attached to the 1st Battalion, 320th Infantry, and Company C to the 2d Battalion. Company A, 784th, was attached to the 137th Infantry. As troops approached the Rhine, resistance became stronger. On 4 March the 1st Battalion, 320th Infantry, and Company B, 784th, attacked Kamperbruch, Germany. The tank platoon leader believed friendly infantry to be in the eastern portion of the town when, in fact, they had been forced to withdraw by a strong German counterattack. The 784th's tanks ran into antitank guns, and lost three tanks

in the action. One tank commander, Sgt. Douglas F. Kelly, kept his crew in his vehicle when his tank was hit and immobilized, and continued to direct fire against the enemy until his ammunition began to explode. He then dismounted, made his way to an artillery command post under mortar and small arms fire and, by accurate directions, enabled the artillery to destroy four German antitank guns. Technician 5 Dave H. Adams, observing three wounded infantrymen in a burning building, left his tank, which was then pinned down by antitank fire, made his way to the burning building under heavy fire, and evacuated the wounded soldiers.[96] Kamperbruch was taken the next day.[97]

The units of the 784th continued to push toward the Rhine with the 35th Division. Company A, on 5 March, became a part of Task Force Murray, along with the 137th Regimental Combat Team, Combat Command C of the 8th Armored Division, a company of the 654th Tank Destroyer Battalion, and the 692d Field Artillery Battalion. Under the command of Col. William Murray of the 137th Infantry, this force had the mission of seizing Wesel and the Rhine bridge still intact at that point. Task Force Byrne moved ahead, with resistance stiffening toward the late afternoon of 6 March. For the next four days the two task forces fought their way ahead, meeting tenacious resistance in Ossenberg, Huck, and Milligen. On 10 March, with the 134th Regimental Combat Team relieving it, Task Force Byrne

[94] AAR 35th Div, Mar 45; Opns Rpt 784th Tk Bn, Mar 45.
[95] Ltr, Hq 134th Inf Regt to CG 35th Inf Div, 5 Mar 45, and 1st Ind, Hq 35th Inf Div to CO 784th Tk Bn, Bn Files.
[96] Bronze Stars, Hq 35th Inf Div, GO 26, 12 Apr 45.
[97] AAR 35th Div, Mar 45; Opns Rpt (Intel An.), 784th Tk Bn, Mar 45.

was dissolved. Task Force Murray cleared Ossenberg and went on to Wallach on the same day, completing its mission. Company A, 784th, was relieved from attachment to the 137th Infantry and, with the rest of the 784th, moved to Tegelen, Holland, where, from 12 to 25 March, the battalion was refitted, performed maintenance, and trained replacements.[98]

As part of the plan to exploit the XVI Corps Rhine bridgehead, the 35th Division was ordered on 25 March to move one combat team across the Rhine. Company A, 784th Tank Battalion, again attached to the 134th Infantry as part of Task Force Miltonberger, controlled by the 79th Division, crossed the river at 0800, 26 March, and assisted in the attack upon a wooded area beyond Dinslaken. In the meantime the remainder of the battalion, attached to the 137th Infantry, crossed the Rhine and began to attack toward Neukoln. Resistance, consisting mainly of rifle and *panzerfaust* fire, was slight, but the advance through the wooded area was slow. Infantry-tank co-operation was close, with tanks as well as infantry sending out patrols to uncover sources of self-propelled gun fire. In Company A's zone of advance along the autobahn north of the Rhine-Herne Canal, the enemy offered only spasmodic resistance. In Company B and C's zone south of the autobahn, resistance was heavier, but the Germans were becoming disorganized and were withdrawing steadily through the Ruhr towns instead of offering their former stiff resistance. Both infantry and tankmen took hundreds of surrendering prisoners.

Continuing the offensive from the Rhine to the Ruhr pocket, the 784th's companies attacked toward and across the Rhine-Herne Canal, supporting the infantry regiments in their attacks on Herne and Gelsenkirchen. As resistance wilted, the units continued south, with Companies B and C attached to the 17th Airborne Division on 10 April for that division's attack on Oberhausen and Mulheim. From 13 April, the battalion remained in division reserve, patrolling the wooded area around Blatz on the west bank of the Elbe, and picking up enemy soldiers and matériel left in that area during the German retreat. On occasion companies were attached to infantry for specific missions. Company D went with the 134th Infantry to clear a wooded pocket west of the Elbe on 15 April; one platoon of Company C was attached to the 654th Tank Destroyer Battalion for a security patrol mission on 16 April; one platoon of medium tanks was attached to XIII Corps to secure a truck column in the Miueste area on 18 April. The battalion moved to Immensen on 26 April, where it set up occupational governing teams for Immensen and surrounding towns. Smaller towns were governed by teams of one officer and six enlisted men each. A constant guard and patrol system was maintained during this period, which lasted until 26 May For most of June the 784th occupied and governed Kelberg and the vicinity During its combat career the battalion had 140 battle casualties from all causes, including 24 killed in action.[99]

---

[98] *Ibid.*

[99] Opns Rpts 784th Tk Bn, Apr–Jun 45; Ltr, CO 784th Tk Bn to CG 12th Army Gp, 2 Jul 45, copy in Bn Files.

The tank and tank destroyer units so far discussed, including the two battalions attached to the 92d Division in Italy, were all marked by one thing in common—the belief that they could carry out assigned missions. This will and confidence was shared by officers and men alike and, after initial demonstration, became stronger. The units differed in their training, their leadership, the caliber of their enlisted men, and, as outlined, in the nature of their employment, but so long as they were busy as supporting units they performed their duties, sometimes spectacularly but more usually as average units of their types. One other unit provided an exception to any generalization that might be made about them or about smaller units. At the same time, it provided within itself dramatic evidence that the rule of motivation combined with effective leadership was still the best guarantee of usefulness in units regardless of the efficiency of their general training or the presumed abilities of men as measured by test scores.

The 827th Tank Destroyer Battalion moved to Europe in November 1944 after its scheduled shipment to the Pacific in the spring of that year had been cancelled because of training deficiencies. Other Negro tank destroyer battalions had been converted to service troops by the spring of 1944. Some of these were considered by the 827th to have been better units than itself. The battalion executive officer, newly assigned to the unit just like the commanding officer, just before its departure for Europe, was of the opinion that the 827th had been "railroaded through the training tests." The S-3, an officer of longer service with the unit, shared this

opinion. The commander, a field artillery Reserve officer generally assigned to staff duties before coming to the 827th, was convinced upon receiving his assignment and checking into the training history and qualifications of the battalion that he had been given a mission that would lead to the conversion or inactivation of his unit.

The battalion, whose training career had been analyzed and found wanting by previous commanders, had had about two and a half years of training in the United States, but under unusual circumstances. By the time it moved overseas, it had had eight different commanders, more than one of whom had recommended that the battalion be made a service unit. It had been organized and reorganized under four different tables of organization and equipment. It was re-equipped with primary weapons four times. Starting its career with towed 75-mm. tank destroyers, it changed successively to self-propelled M10's, then to towed 3-inch destroyers, and finally to self-propelled M18's. These changes, normal as tank destroyer theories and weapons changed and improved, involved the disbandment and reconstitution of the battalion reconnaissance company, a unit which, in its final form, was looked upon by the battalion's officers as especially inefficient. With 78 to 83 percent of its personnel in AGCT Classes IV and V, the battalion had been hardly adaptable enough to weather the changes in equipment and organization to which it was subjected. Never able to create a strong group of noncommissioned officers from among its substandard men, the 827th was no luckier with its commissioned officers. It went through the experience of having its original white junior officers replaced by Negro officers who, upon the arrival of one of the unit's commanders, were blamed for most of the battalion's difficulties. The Negro officers were later removed and replaced by a new staff of white junior officers, many of whom came from other inactivated Negro tank destroyer units and who were therefore already predisposed to a jaundiced view of their new unit's future. The new white officers were no more successful, whereupon it was determined that the enlisted men, with their extremely low AGCT scores, and not their officers, were primarily at fault.[100]

By August 1944 the 827th had already failed five Army Ground Forces battalion tests. It never did complete its training. Training in indirect fire, one of the chief requirements for certain of the secondary missions of tank destroyer battalions, was waived entirely. During a round of training tests and retests in August 1944, the new battalion commander and most of his officers became firmly convinced that the unit's enlisted men could not and would not learn to maintain communications, read maps, or perform first and second echelon maintenance on their vehicles. Officers generally were convinced that their noncommissioned officers were incompetent and that no better noncommissioned officer material existed within the unit.

Preparations for overseas movement and further training in September were disrupted by two general courts-martials, one involving a meat-ax murder and the other a shooting. Both required not only considerable paper work on the part of a headquarters already swamped but also demanded the presence of the many men of the battalion concerned in the cases as witnesses. Both cases were indicative of the general state of discipline within the unit, where neither officers nor noncommissioned officers were able to control their men.

The battalion finally left Camp Hood in October 1944, and sailed from New York directly to Marseille, where it bivouacked in Delta Base Section for a month. Moving from the dock to the staging area, the battalion's vehicles became involved in several accidents, most of them attributable to carelessness. The five-day battalion march from Marseille to the Vosges to join the Seventh Army, undertaken over icy roads in December, was a nerve-destroying approach to combat for both officers and enlisted men. Accidents, speeding cases, column breaking and doubling, breakdowns from lack of lubrication, slow starts, and late arrivals marked the route. When the battalion arrived at Sarrebourg, its vehicles went to shops for immediate repairs. Seldom had a unit approached commitment to combat with less confidence or more internal disorganization.

At the time Seventh Army was adjusting its lines to cover the gap left by Third Army, which was speeding north to the Bulge. The 827th was attached to the 12th Armored Division, a SHAEF reserve unit, on 20 December 1944. The battalion sent one company into

---

[100] Rpt of Investigation, 827th TD Bn, Bibisheim, France, 15–19 Jan 45, Incl to Ltr, IG VI Corps to CG VI Corps, 21 Jan 45, SHAEF G–3 O&F, 322; 1st Ind, Hq ESFET (Main), 1 Oct 45, on Ltr, TAG to Comds, 23 May 45, AG 291.2 (23 May 45) OB–S–WDSSP, in WDSSP 291.2 (ETO).

the line on 21 December, where it supported the 714th Tank Battalion. The towed 614th Tank Destroyer Battalion was operating in the same area at the time and tried to help orient the 827th. The 827th remained in its assignment for three days, seeing no action but experiencing difficulties with discipline among its gun crews, many of whom, despite previous instructions, left their guns unguarded while they gathered firewood and built fires in violation of front-line discipline. Men leaving their vehicles was to be a continuing problem in the 827th Battalion during its short combat assignment.[101]

Seventh Army expected a German counterattack to begin at any time after 1 January.[102] The army established alternate lines for possible withdrawals and alerted its reserve units for use in case of a heavy enemy attack. On 1 January, the 12th Armored Division attached one of the 827th's companies to the 92d Reconnaissance Squadron, then maintaining a counterreconnaissance screen west of the Saar River and south of the Maginot Line. The company remained on this mission until 6 January. The 12th Armored Division requested XV Corps' permission to use other parts of the 827th in an indirect fire mission planned to increase the fire power of one of the division's artillery battalions, but XV Corps G–3 denied the request since it would involve clearance from Seventh Army and since there was a greater need to hold the battalion

for use in its primary mission.[103] Fortunate circumstances thus prevented the 827th from getting an initial assignment for which it was completely untrained.

On 6 January, Seventh Army relieved the battalion from XV Corps and attached it to VI Corps.[104] With Combat Command B, 12th Armored Division, it moved on verbal orders to join Task Force Wahl of the 79th Division, then defending the northern part of that division's lines. Before the 827th could move out, a company officer and an enlisted man shot each other when the company officer attempted to quell a disturbance among soldiers. A disgruntled soldier attacked a first sergeant in another company. The sergeant, shooting at his attacker, hit another enlisted man, an innocent bystander. The company nominated for initial commitment could not move out on time: the company commander reported that approximately 75 percent of his men were missing from their bivouac area and that many of those present were drunk.[105] Another company had to substitute and lead the battalion's march to its first combat assignment.

Task Force Wahl, under Brig. Gen. George D. Wahl, 79th Division Artillery commander, consisted of the 3d Battalion, 313th Infantry; the 315th Infantry (−); the 222d Infantry (−) of the 42d Division; Combat Command A of the 14th Armored Division; the 813th Tank Destroyer Battalion (−); and the 827th

[101] Rpt of Investigation, 827th TD Bn, AAR's 827th TD Bn.
[102] Report of Operations: The Seventh Army in France and Germany, 1944–1945 (Heidelberg, 1946), II, 560–61, 580–82.

[103] Ibid., 566; XV Corps Daily TD Rpts, Dec 44–Jan 45; Hist 827th TD Bn, Jan 45; Opns Rpt 92d Cav Recon Sq, Jan 45; Opns Rpt 12th Armd Div Arty, Jan 45.
[104] Ltr, Hq Seventh Army, 6 Jan 45, copy in Hist 827th TD Bn.
[105] Rpt of Investigation, 827th TD Bn, 15–19 Jan 45.

Tank Destroyer Battalion.[106] The 242d Infantry of the 42d Division, the 79th Division Artillery, and the 79th Reconnaissance Troop were added later. Elements of the 827th were attached to units of Task Force Wahl at 0300 on 8 January. Twelve days of combat followed in which units of the 827th, in Rittershoffen and Hatten especially, were engaged in fierce and often confused fighting—both German and American forces fought in the streets of Hatten for several days, with American forces cut off from their lines much of the time. The attachments themselves caused some confusion within the newly committed unit. On 9 January, the 827th was attached to the 813th Tank Destroyer Battalion, or at least the 813th so believed, although the attachment orders were never confirmed. The 827th thought, on the other hand, that it had been directed to "coordinate" with the 813th. In some cases, the two types of destroyers were expected to be "mixed in together." At the same time, the infantry commanders with whom elements of the 827th were operating expected to control the movements, select positions, and assign targets to tank destroyer guns and crews. Company officers within the 827th felt that the infantry commanders too often confused tank destroyers with tanks and assigned missions which destroyers could not—or were not supposed to—carry out, a tendency which the 813th, a veteran of North Africa, Italy, and Normandy with thirty months overseas, was still finding objectionable. The 827th itself expected orders to be given through its own officers, in fact, had so encour-

aged this that its crews were directed to fire only on the order of an officer, preferably an 827th officer. The procedure was enormously complicated by poor communications within the 827th. As a result, platoon officers of the 827th shuttled back and forth between their sections, trying to be everywhere at once, and 827th crews fired neither on their own initiative nor on the orders of officers strange to them. The upshot of this arrangement was that infantry commanders concluded that the 827th's crews fired only on those targets which they decided were good ones, and ignored or backed away from all others.[107]

Between 8 and 20 January the platoons and companies of the 827th had varied experiences and gave varying performances—some extraordinarily good in light of the unit's background and some extraordinarily poor by any standards. By 14 January, there existed a tangle of fact and opinion from which the unit was never to extricate itself.

One company, starting out for Oberroedorn on 9 January to fill the request of the hard pressed 3d Battalion, 313th Infantry, for more tank destroyers—this battalion had lost all but two of those attached to it—arrived with only two of the twelve guns with which it had started. The company commander sent searching parties to find the remainder of his column, and then went himself into an infantry pillbox where he remained for three and a half hours during a German attack. When he emerged, he went back to pick up his M18's, and found that seven of his destroyers were already in position though there was utter con-

---

[106] 79th Div G–3 Rpt, 7 Jan 45.

[107] Rpt of Investigation, 827th TD Bn; AAR 813th TD Bn, Jan 45.

fusion about their locations and missions. Two of the destroyers had gone into a ditch along the icy roads, one had been hit, and two others were still unaccounted for. Infantry commanders' requests for fire on particular targets often went unacknowledged while men looked for a confirming 827th officer or argued about the appropriateness of the targets. Men were found in cellars and houses instead of at their guns. On one occasion the destroyer crew refused to fire on a German tank stuck along a roadside; the infantry battalion commander ordered his company officers to shoot the entire crew if it did not fire on the tank, but by this time the Germans had recovered their tank and disappeared. A series of similar incidents, wherein men were not on their guns when needed, where gun commanders executed missions slowly or argued about positions and targets, came to a climax on 14 January when a tank destroyer parked in a barn where antitank mines were stored caught fire. The crew, when ordered by their sergeant to drive the burning destroyer out before the mines caught and exploded, refused to enter the barn. Under orders of the infantry battalion commander, an infantry lieutenant fired five times at the crew, missing each time. Another tank destroyer was brought up to tow the burning destroyer out, but by that time the fire had gone too far. In the meantime, infantrymen had carried the mines from the barn.

The infantry battalion commander, already annoyed with dilatory tactics and inefficiency within the 827th, asked for white crews to replace the Negro crews. He had been promised four white crews and, knowing that there were over 200 white replacements in his division, he had considered requesting that some of them be given him for antitank work. Crews of the 813th Tank Destroyer Battalion, which had lost during the month nineteen out of their thirty-one M10 destroyers, including four captured with the entire 2d Battalion, 314th Infantry, were already manning some of the 827th's M18's.[108] Continuing difficulties with elements of the 827th brought the VI Corps inspector general for an investigation of training and discipline within the unit.

The investigation disclosed an amazing state of affairs. Certain of the units of the 827th attached to other infantry elements of Task Force Wahl had acquitted themselves well, especially in light of their officers' estimates that their units were at best barely satisfactory, and in view of the facts that they were green and partially trained, and that the entire action took place under strafing by jet planes, against flame-throwing tanks, and in support of troops who were themselves disorganized and confused. On 9 January, for example, Company B of the 827th, then attached to the 68th Armored Infantry in Soulz-sous-Forêts, was dispatched to the area north of Hatten at 1325 to help halt an enemy attack. Sixteen enemy tanks were headed for Rittershoffen and fifteen more approached Hatten. The tanks approaching Rittershoffen (like Hatten, a village on an open plain) were fired on by the 827th's men, resulting in the destruction of eleven tanks and one full-tracked vehicle. Upon meeting this fire the remaining tanks with-

---

[108] AAR 813th TD Bn, Jan 45; Unit Jnl 3d Bn 313th Inf, Jan 45.

drew.[109]   A joint team of the 827th and 813th destroyed nine tanks at Hatten. On 10 January, 827th destroyers in Rittershoffen knocked out four more enemy tanks.[110]   Thereafter in Hatten, isolated by day and subject to resupply over the open snow-covered plain only at night, one section of a Company B, 827th, platoon continued to engage in close fighting, accounting for several enemy tanks and vehicles.   Another section, under more strenuous urging from its commander, reportedly under armed threats at times, performed well—or well enough for the 315th's infantrymen to report that they had received excellent support from the 827th.   Nevertheless, in the investigation, every officer of the 827th expressed some doubts that his men, characterized as untrainable, slow in their reactions, or stricken by fear, would ever be dependable on tank destroyers, although some officers explained that a majority of their men could be counted upon and that they had always believed that if adequate replacements could be obtained for the remainder theirs would be excellent units.[111]   Replacements had not been available in the past and, with the shortage of Negro enlisted replacements then current, hope for enough new men to make an appreciable change in the unit was practically nonexistent.

During the investigation, the elements of the 827th in Rittershoffen and Hatten continued street fighting.   The force in Rittershoffen used its guns to shell buildings and drive the enemy from them; those in Hatten knocked out two tanks at a range of 1,400 yards, and

lost one destroyer, hit by enemy fire, and its full crew.[112]

After taking testimony for four days, the inspector recommended that the 827th be withdrawn, given additional technical training, and recommitted to combat; that the men refusing to operate their guns be tried; that the unit commander be replaced with a more forceful officer; and that the noncommissioned officers be improved by making each one perform his normal duties.   The Commanding General, VI Corps, recommended instead that the unit be disbanded and that its enlisted men, excepting those who had proved themselves "to be worthy," be distributed to appropriate service units.[113]   The Commanding General, Seventh Army, approved, recommending that the battalion be inactivated and that a substitute tank destroyer battalion composed of white personnel be activated within the Seventh Army. White truck, medical ambulance, car, and smoke generator companies could be converted to Negro, both to provide white soldiers for the new battalion and service unit vacancies for the Negroes.   If higher headquarters decided that a white combat unit had to be converted to Negro to preserve a racial balance between service and combat troops, Seventh Army would convert a white engineer combat battalion instead.[114]

Now began a long administrative discussion of the disposition to be made of the 827th Battalion.   The simplest procedure would have been to adopt the

_____
[109] AAR 315th Inf 79th Div, Jan 45.
[110] AAR 813th TD Bn, Jan 45.
[111] Rpt of Investigation, 827th TD Bn.

_____
[112] Unit Hist 827th TD Bn, Jan 45.
[113] 1st Ind to Rpt of Investigation, Hq VI Corps to CG Seventh Army, 26 Jan 45.
[114] Ltr, Hq Seventh Army to CG 6th Army Gp, 31 Jan 45, AG 333.5–C, 6th Army Gp 322–3 (Jan).

VI Corps and Seventh Army recommendation, but the investigation supporting this recommendation had not reached the same conclusion. Tank destroyer battalions had now returned to high priority and were in demand.[115] The investigating officer had questioned only officers of the 827th Battalion and a few officers of units to which its elements were attached. These did not include officers of all units with elements of the 827th attached. Moreover, no enlisted men of the 827th were questioned during the investigation. On 14 February 6th Army Group therefore requested that additional testimony be taken from representative enlisted men of the unit.[116]

In the meantime, the 827th was relieved from Task Force Wahl, its last unit leaving on 23 January. The battalion returned to attachment to the 12th Armored Division, now engaged in the Colmar Pocket operation. One platoon was attached to each of the combat commands of the division on 2 February, participating with these units in the last few days of the Colmar operation.[117] The remainder of the battalion was with the division's trains. Colmar itself fell to Allied troops on 2 February, but the next day the 12th Armored Division, then in XXI Corps, was committed to continue the attack to the south and east where resistance, though scattered, was intense at some points. Combat Command B, divided into three task forces, launched an attack south

from Colmar to seize Sudhoffen, with two task forces attacking and a third in reserve. The attack progressed slowly. Task Force Boone, the reserve force consisting of a platoon of the 827th, a company of armored infantry, and a company of tanks, was committed on 4 February. It overran enemy strongpoints, destroying antitank guns and continuing the attack.[118] The other 827th platoons saw little action, for the 12th Armored Division met French forces on 6 February, sealing off the remaining Germans in the Vosges.

The uncommitted elements of the 827th, under their own commander in division trains, made up for the lack of action among the attached platoons engaged in the attack from Colmar. On the night of 5 February, the battalion commander called upon the 12th Armored Division for help. His enlisted men were becoming increasingly difficult for him to handle. They drew guns, molested civilians, and indulged in wild shootings. The division judge advocate general and inspector general went down to the 827th Battalion and conferred with the commander. As a result, 12th Armored Division asked to be relieved of the 827th Battalion.[119] Ironically, VI Corps was, during this same period, inquiring if the 79th Division still intended to award Bronze Stars to one of the 827th's crews which had performed exceptionally well in Hatten.[120]

On 12 February the 827th departed for Baccarat on verbal orders of the 12th Armored Division. There it was at-

[115] Msg, SHAEF Main to Hq ETOUSA, 13 Jan 45, OUT 1633, and Memo, Chief O&E to SHAEF G–3, 26 Jan 45. Both in SHAEF G–3 322.

[116] 1st Ind to Ltr cited n. 114, Hq 6th Army Gp to CG Seventh Army, 14 Feb 45, AG 322/3 SGS–O.

[117] Unit Jnl 827th TD Bn, Feb 45.

[118] 12th Armd Div G–3 Opns Rpt, Feb 45.

[119] 12th Armd Div G–1 Opns Rpt, Feb 45; 12th Armd Div IG Rpt, Feb 45.

[120] VI Corps G–1 Jnl, 6 Feb 45.

tached to the 68th Antiaircraft Artillery Group in XV Corps for operations.[121] It spent the remainder of the month in guard duty as prescribed by the 68th Group.[122]

The 6th Army Group's request for additional testimony concerning the performance of the 827th was complied with in March when a total of twelve enlisted men performing duties as platoon sergeants, gun commanders, gunners, drivers, and radio men were queried, primarily on their duties, training, and knowledge of map reading and first aid. The inspector concluded that the men interviewed had a satisfactory knowledge of their duties but an examination conducted after six weeks under rear area conditions could not indicate accurately the combat efficiency of an organization. Of the twelve men questioned only one gave the inspector the impression that he would prefer to return to combat rather than remain on guard duty; the others, who said that they would do as told or that they would like to return if in a tank or tank destroyer unit or if attached to a "good" division like the 79th, all hesitated "sufficiently long," in the inspector's opinion, to indicate that they did not really wish additional combat duty. The inspector recommended this time that the enlisted personnel of the 827th be transferred to a Negro infantry division.[123]

Seventh Army in the meantime nominated the 827th Tank Destroyer Battalion for use by 6th Army Group to

provide housekeeping facilities and transportation for military and civilian specialists at 6th Army Group headquarters. Since these housekeeping requirements had to be met from some source and since either conversion or retraining would take considerable time—and conversion might prove embarrassing to the theater and the War Department—the unit remained active, with its self-propelled destroyers returned to Seventh Army stocks for use by other destroyer units. To prevent its nomination for redeployment as a tank destroyer unit, the battalion was eventually named as one of those surplus to redeployment needs so that it could be returned to the United States after V–E Day for inactivation.[124]

Despite the misfortunes of the 827th —attributable largely to the state of training, discipline, and leadership within the unit as well as to the critical nature of its initial employment—the record of the smaller combat support units, including that of the armored and artillery units with the 92d Division in Italy, lent support to the older theories that Negro troops could be effectively employed in smaller units in combat support roles. Even within the 827th, smaller elements at times performed so as to lead to the belief that wiser management at one or more points in that battalion's career might have made it a useful unit.

A further type of employment for Negro troops was in the making just when the 827th was undergoing its

[121] AAR 827th TD Bn, Feb 45; Ltr, Hq Seventh Army to CG XV Corps, 12 Feb 45, AG 370.5–C.
[122] Opns Rpts 68th AAA Gp, Feb–Mar 45, CAGP–68–0.3 (42144).
[123] Ltr, Hq VI Corps, OTIG to CG VI Corps, 10 Mar 45, in Rpt of Investigation.

[124] 5th to 8th Inds, 27 Mar 45–19 Apr 45, to Ltr, Hq Seventh Army to CG 6th Army Gp, 31 Jan 45, and attached interoffice slips, 6th Army Gp 322–3 (Jan); Ltr, SHAEF G–3 Forwarded to SHAEF CofS, 19 Apr 45, GCT 322 (TK–TD) O&E.

greatest difficulties. This type of employment was to be doubly important, for the units here were to be smaller still and their roles were to require direct and close contact with the enemy— the very area in which the larger Negro units of the same type were already having their major problems.

CHAPTER XXII

Volunteer Infantry Replacements

In early December 1944, shortages of infantry rifle replacements in the European theater began to mount sharply. The theater had been experiencing rifleman shortages since July 1944, and its Ground Force Replacement Command (GFRC) had been engaged in a training program to convert basic privates from other arms and services to infantry.[1] In December the forecast of shortages increased rapidly as the supply of replacements available from the United States declined. As of 8 December, a week before the beginning of the German counterattack in the Ardennes caused further depletions, the theater estimated that there would be an overall deficiency of more than 23,000 riflemen by the end of the month.[2] Such a deficiency would effectively curtail plans for pressing the attack against Germany. By the beginning of the Ardennes counterattack, the theater had already planned to convert to infantry as many physically fit men from service units as possible. These men would be re-placed in service units by limited assignment men. Basics from new divisions were already being used to fill the infantry battalions of veteran divisions and a theater G–1 delegation was preparing to leave for Washington to present the case for more and prompter deliveries of infantry replacements. Lt. Gen. John C. H. Lee planned to release and train 20,000 additional infantry riflemen from his Communications Zone units.[3]

General Lee, after consulting with General Eisenhower and with army commanders, proposed adding to this number physically qualified men from the Communications Zone's Negro units.[4] General Eisenhower, General Bradley, and the army commanders agreed. General Lee then consulted with Brig. Gen. Henry J. Matchett, commanding the Ground Force Reinforcement Command, and Brig. Gen. Benjamin O. Davis, then Special Advisor and Coordinator to the Theater Commander on Negro Troops. General Davis responded enthusiastically and, on Christmas Day, 1944, General Davis, General Matchett, and the GFRC G–1 drew up a plan to train Negro volunteers

---

[1] Hist Ground Forces Reinf Comd, V, pt. II (6 Jun 44–8 May 45), RED VAULT, USFET. In December the term "reinforcement" was substituted for "replacement" in the ETO and the Ground Force Replacement Command became the Ground Force Reinforcement Command.

[2] Memo, SHAEF G–3 for CofS, 14 Dec 44, GCT/322–59/OE, SHAEF OCS, SGS, 370.5/2, I, 13 Oct 44–29 Dec 44.

[3] Papers in ETO AG 322 (Repl Units), Dec 44.

[4] CofS ETO ComZ, to ComZ G–1 through CofS, 15 Dec 44, item 1, ETO AG 322/49 (Repl Units).

as individual infantry replacements.[5] General Lee had already prepared a call to troops, which went out to his base and section commanders on 26 December with instructions that it be reproduced and disseminated to troops within twenty-four hours. It read:

1. The Supreme Commander desires to destroy the enemy forces and end hostilities in this theater without delay. Every available weapon at our disposal must be brought to bear upon the enemy. To this end the Commanding General, Com Z, is happy to offer to a limited number of colored troops who have had infantry training, the privilege of joining our veteran units at the front to deliver the knockout blow. The men selected are to be in the grades of Private First Class and Private. Non-commissioned officers may accept reduction in order to take advantage of this opportunity. The men selected are to be given a refresher course with emphasis on weapon training.

2. The Commanding General makes a special appeal to you. It is planned to assign you without regard to color or race to the units where assistance is most needed, and give you the opportunity of fighting shoulder to shoulder to bring about victory. Your comrades at the front are anxious to share the glory of victory with you. Your relatives and friends everywhere have been urging that you be granted this privilege. The Supreme Commander, your Commanding General, and other veteran officers who have served with you are confident that many of you will take advantage of this opportunity and carry on in keeping with the glorious record of our colored troops in our former wars.

3. This letter is to be read confidentially to the troops immediately upon its receipt and made available in Orderly Rooms.

Every assistance must be promptly given qualified men to volunteer for this service.[6]

Two days later the formal plan, based on General Davis' conference with the GFRC staff, went out to commanders. It provided that the initial quota of volunteers be kept to 2,000, the largest number the GFRC could handle at once and a number which would not reduce any service unit by more than 3.5 percent at the most. Personnel with the highest qualifications would get first priority and no man with an Army General Classification Test score lower than Grade IV would be taken. The number of volunteers would be reported by 3 January 1945 so that quotas could be allocated to units. The men selected were to report to the 16th Reinforcement Depot at Compiegne not later than 10 January 1945. They would be relieved from their present units and attached unassigned to the Ground Force Reinforcement Command. The retrained personnel would then be assigned to combat units as infantry reinforcements without regard to race.[7]

Before the plan could be carried out, a number of changes, some resulting from misunderstanding and others from apprehension, occurred. The plan itself represented a major break with traditional Army policy, for it proposed mixing Negro soldiers into otherwise white units neither on a quota nor a smaller unit basis but as individuals fitted in where needed. When the cir-

[5] Hist of Special Sec of Office of IG (29 Jun 41–16 Nov 45), Tab A to Hist OTIG, WDSS, World War II, OCMH; ETO ComZ CofS to ComZ G–1, 27 Dec 44, ETO AG 322/49 (Repl Units).

[6] Ltr, Hq ComZ ETO to Comdrs of Cld Trps ComZ, 26 Dec 44, ETO AG 322 X 353 XSGS.

[7] CofS, Hq ComZ ETO, ComZ CofS to ComZ G–1, 27 Dec 44, ETO AG 322/49 (Repl Units); Ltr, Hq ComZ ETO to CG's SOLOC, U.K. Base and Sec Comdrs ComZ, 28 Dec 44, ETO AG 322 X 353 XGA.

cular letter to troops reached Supreme Headquarters, Allied Expeditionary Force (SHAEF), Lt. Gen. Walter B. Smith, chief of staff, held that its promise to assign Negro troops *"without regard to color or race to the units where assistance is most needed, and give you the opportunity of fighting shoulder to shoulder to bring about victory"* was a clear invitation to embarrassment to the War Department. Failing to convince General Lee that he should change his letter, he put the matter to General Eisenhower:

Although I am now somewhat out of touch with the War Department's negro policy, I did, as you know, handle this during the time I was with General Marshall. Unless there has been a radical change, the sentence which I have marked in the attached circular letter will place the War Department in very grave difficulties. It is inevitable that this statement will get out, and equally inevitable that the result will be that every negro organization, pressure group and newspaper will take the attitude that, while the War Department segregates colored troops into organizations of their own against the desires and pleas of all the negro race, the Army is perfectly willing to put them in the front lines mixed in units with white soldiers, and have them do battle when an emergency arises. Two years ago I would have considered the marked statement the most dangerous thing that I had ever seen in regard to negro relations.

I have talked with Lee about it, and he can't see this at all. He believes that it is right that colored and white soldiers should be mixed in the same company. With this belief I do not argue, but the War Department policy is different. Since I am convinced that this circular letter will have the most serious repercussions in the United States, I believe that it is our duty to draw the War Department's attention to the fact that this statement has been made, to give them warning as to what may happen and

any facts which they may use to counter the pressure which will undoubtedly be placed on them.

Further, I recommend most strongly that Communications Zone not be permitted to issue any general circulars relating to negro policy until I have had a chance to see them. This is because I know more about the War Department's and General Marshall's difficulties with the negro question than any other man in this theater, including General B. O. Davis whom Lee consulted in the matter—and I say this with all due modesty. I am writing this as I may not see you tomorrow morning. Will talk to you about it when I return.[8]

General Eisenhower personally rewrote the directive, changing all but the first two sentences and making dissemination permissive instead of mandatory. "This is replacing the original & is something that can not possibly run counter to regs in a time like this," he told General Smith.[9] The new directive, officially approved by both General Eisenhower and General Lee, appeared over General Lee's signature with the same date, file number, and subject as the earlier directive, under a cover letter ordering return and destruction of all copies of the original version. The substitute letter read:

1. The Supreme Commander desires to destroy the enemy forces and end hostilities in this theater without delay. Every available weapon at our disposal must be brought to bear upon the enemy. To this end the Theater Commander has directed the Communications Zone Commander to make the greatest possible use of limited service men within service units and to

[8] Info Ltr, SHAEF OCS to Eisenhower, 3 Jan 44 [45], SHAEF OCS 291.2 I, 26 Dec 44–23 Dec 45. "Marked statement" quoted and italicized in text.
[9] Draft, "To C/S Personally DE," 4 Jan 45, SHAEF OCS 291.2 I, 26 Dec 44–23 Dec 45.

survey our entire organization in an effort to produce able bodied men for the front lines. This process of selection has been going on for some time but it is entirely possible that many men themselves, desiring to volunteer for front line service, may be able to point out methods in which they can be replaced in their present jobs. Consequently, Commanders of all grades will receive voluntary applications for transfer to the Infantry and forward them to higher authority with recommendations for appropriate type of replacement. *This opportunity to volunteer will be extended to all soldiers without regard to color or race, but preference will normally be given to individuals who have had some basic training in Infantry.* Normally, also, transfers will be limited to the grade of Private and Private First Class unless a noncommissioned officer requests a reduction.

2. In the event that the number of suitable negro volunteers exceeds the replacement needs of negro combat units, these men will be suitably incorporated in other organizations so that their service and their fighting spirit may be efficiently utilized.

3. This letter may be read confidentially to the troops and made available in Orderly Rooms. Every assistance must be promptly given qualified men who volunteer for this service.[10]

The new letter allowed for further changes in the initial plan for individual replacements but the revision appeared too late to halt the distribution of the first version completely. The Normandy Base Section, for example, had already distributed the earlier letter to the commanders of all Negro units on 28 December and had sent copies to both of its districts.[11]

_____

[10] *Ibid.;* Ltr, Hq ComZ ETO to CG's SOLOC, U.K. Base and Sec Comdrs ComZ, 26 Dec 44, ETO AG 322 x 353 XSGS, Incl to Ltr, Hq ComZ to same, 4 Jan 45. Italics in original.

[11] 1st Ind to Ltr, ComZ to Comdrs Cld Units, 26 Dec 44 (original version) Hq Normandy Base Sec to CO All Cld Units, 28 Dec 44, ETO AG 322 x 353 XSGS GA.

The revised letter could be interpreted in a number of ways. There were no Negro infantry units in the theater. The theater had long been concerned with replacements for its Negro artillery, tank, and tank destroyer units, for it had already been told that none would be available from the United States. If Negro volunteers from service units were to be retrained for combat use, the greatest immediate need was in units like the 761st Tank and 333d Field Artillery Battalions whose losses without replacements threatened their combat efficiency and, in the case of the 333d, threatened their existence. The revised letter seemed to direct that Negro volunteers would first be used for these units. But the GFRS was not equipped to convert individuals to any service other than infantry and the smaller Negro combat support units were already operating under a system, admittedly not the happiest solution, of retraining their own replacements from volunteers and replacements trained in other branches. Since the revised letter could still be interpreted to mean that any excess Negro volunteers would be placed in white units in the same manner as white reinforcements, SHAEF G–1 pressed for a further clarification. After determining that General Eisenhower did not desire to place Negro trainees in white organizations as individuals and that he preferred to form the Negro trainees into "units which could be substituted for white units in order that white units could be drawn out of line and rested," SHAEF G–1 prepared a new letter directing that the Negro volunteers be trained as reinforcements for existing Negro combat units in the theater and that any excess

VOLUNTEERS FOR COMBAT INFANTRY REPLACEMENT *learning how to assemble a BAR.*

be formed into separate infantry units for assignment to an army group. Initially, the goal would be one battalion; subsequently, if numbers warranted, this battalion would be expanded to a regiment. All other instructions were rescinded.[12]

Originally, "in fairness to all concerned," this new directive was to be

sent to all Negro units to interpret paragraph 2 of the revised letter of 26 December. After further discussions, distribution was confined to the theater G–3 and G–4, to the Commanding General, GFRC, and to General Davis. It went out under a covering letter indicating that it was an interpretation of the words "other organizations" in the revised December letter.[13] The change

[12] CRS (Staff Min Sheet), SHAEF G–1 to ETOUSA AG, 8 Jan 45; ETOUSA IRS, ETO G–1 to CG through CofS, 9 Jan 45; Ltr, Hq ETO to CG ComZ, 9 Jan 45; all in ETO AG 322/49 (Repl Units) III.

[13] IRS, ETO G–1 to ETO AG, 12 Jan 45; Ltr, Hq ComZ ETO to CG GFRC, 14 Jan 45; both in ETO AG 322/49 (Repl Units) III.

in plan did not, therefore, reach Negro troops during the period of volunteering.

By February, 4,562 Negro troops had volunteered, many of the noncommissioned officers among them taking reductions in rank to do so.[14] The first 2,800 reported to the Ground Force Reinforcement Command in January and early February, after which the flow of volunteers was stopped. The service units from which these men came parallelled closely the distribution of Negroes by branch: 38 percent came from engineer units, 29 percent from quartermaster, 26 percent from transportation, 3 percent from signal, 2 percent from ordnance, and the remaining 2 percent from units of other branches. Sixty-three percent had formerly had one of the six following military occupational specialities, in order of frequency: truck driver, duty soldier, longshoreman, basic, construction foreman, and cargo checker. Like other volunteers, they were somewhat younger than average—10 percent of the Negro riflemen were thirty years old or older as compared with 20 percent of white riflemen. They had somewhat better educational backgrounds and test scores than the average for Negro soldiers in the European theater but the differences between them and other Negro troops in these respects were not so great as the differences between them and the average white troops. Of the white riflemen in the ETO, 41 percent were high school graduates and 71 percent were in AGCT classes I, II, and III; of the Negro infantry reinforcements, 22 percent were

high school graduates and 29 percent were in classes I, II, and III; of all Negroes in ETO, 18 percent were high school graduates and 17 percent were in Classes I, II, and III.[15] The important difference between these soldiers and other Negro troops was, therefore, that they had volunteered on the basis of a call to duty under circumstances unusual to their former Army experience. Only their motivation and their method of employment set them off sharply from other Negro troops.

Retraining was conducted at the 16th Reinforcement Depot at Compiegne, which had been retraining individuals as riflemen since November. The Negro trainees were organized into the 47th Reinforcement Battalion, 5th Retraining Regiment, under the command of Col. Alexander George. According to the depot staff, the Negro volunteers approached their work with a will. There were proportionately fewer absentees and fewer disciplinary problems among the Negro trainees than among the white soldiers being retrained as infantrymen.[16]

The question of how to carry out the latest directive on the completion of the training of these infantrymen arose toward the end of January 1945. The Ground Force Reinforcement System was equipped to train individual replacements only; the newer provision that Negro trainees in excess of those needed in combat support units be trained as a battalion could not be met

---

[14] Hist of Special Sec of Office of IG (29 Jul 41–16 Nov 45), OCMH.

[15] From I&E Div Rpt B-157, 3 Jul 45. See also Shirley Star, "Negro Soldiers," in Samuel A. Stouffer, et al., *The American Soldier: Adjustment During Army Life* (Princeton: Princeton University Press, 1949), p. 588.

[16] Ltr, Gen Davis to Chief GI Sec, Hq ETOUSA, 5 Mar 45, GI Sec Rpt 33, ETO AG 333.1.

47TH REINFORCEMENT BATTALION *trainees march out for a day of intensive training, Noyon, France,*
February 1945.

by the system. In the meantime, command of the system changed and responsibility for it shifted from General Lee's Communications Zone to Lt. Gen. Ben Lear, newly arrived in the theater as deputy theater commander. General Lee now obtained a new interpretation of General Eisenhower's wishes and passed them on to General Lear. General Lee reminded General Lear that the army commanders and General Eisenhower had personally approved the original plan with the understanding that the men so trained would be used in infantry units. He informed General Lear that General Eisenhower "now desires that these colored riflemen reinforcements have their training completed as members of Infantry rifle platoons familiar with the Infantry rifle platoon weapons." These platoons would be made available to army commanders who would then provide platoon leaders, platoon sergeants, and, if necessary, squad leaders. "It is my feeling," General Lee said, "that we should afford the volunteers the full opportunity for Infantry riflemen service. Therefore we should not assign them as Tank or Artillery reinforcements unless they express such preference. To do otherwise would be breaking faith, in my opinion." [17]

The Reinforcement Command had enough volunteers to form 45 to 47 platoons, including overstrength provided to compensate for the expected lack of further reinforcements for these units.

[17] Memo, CG ComZ ETOUSA for Gen Lear, 1 Feb 45, ETO AG 322/49 (Repl Units) III.

The first 2,253 men were ready by 1 March. They were organized into 37 platoons: 25 went to 12th Army Group and 12 to 6th Army Group, joining about 10 March. A second group was distributed later, 12 platoons going to 12th Army Group and 4 to 6th Army Group. The divisions sent one platoon leader and one sergeant to meet each platoon at the 16th Depot. The possibility of receiving needed replacements, especially in early March when the spring offensive and the crossing of the Rhine were in the offing, was readily accepted by most divisions. Army group and army commanders were given discretion in the use of the platoons. They could be assigned to divisions as platoons or they could be assigned in larger groupings. They could later be grouped into units as large as a battalion if so desired.[18]

In 12th Army Group the platoons were assigned to divisions in groups of three and the divisions, retaining them as platoons, usually assigned one to each regiment. The regiments, in turn, selected a company to which the units went as a fourth rifle platoon.[19]

In most divisions, the platoons were given additional training periods of varying lengths before commitment. In others, such as the divisions headed across the Remagen Bridge, the pla-

toons arrived just in time for immediate employment. Where arrival of the Negro platoons coincided with a period of heavy fighting, their welcome as fresh replacements was warmer than in units that were then engaged in training only.[20] But divisional training periods were valuable both to the platoons and to the divisions' attitude toward accepting them. "They had had some sort of training before they joined us," one assistant division commander explained, "but we wanted to make sure they knew all the tricks of infantry fighting. We assigned our best combat leaders as instructors. I watched those lads train and if ever men were in dead earnest, they were."[21] In some cases the platoons were given the division patch and a brief indoctrination in the division's history and accomplishments, plus personal welcomes by the division or assistant division commander.[22]

In most instances, the platoons quickly identified themselves with the more than three dozen battalions and companies to which they were distributed. They were employed just as any other platoon within their companies, a point frequently noted by their regiments. Some went to veteran regiments which, like those of the 1st and 9th Divisions, had fought in Europe and Africa. Others went to newer units like the 12th and 14th Armored Divisions, and the 69th, 78th, 99th, and 104th In-

[18] Memo, ODTC ETO for Col [Paul K.] Porch, 10 Feb 45, DTC ETO 291.2 Negro Race; Ltrs, DTC ETO to Lt Gen Omar Bradley, Lt Gen Jacob L. Devers, and Maj Gen Albert Brown, 10 Feb 45, DTC 200.3 Manpower, DTC 291.2 Negro Race.
[19] G–1 Rpt, 2d Inf Div, Mar 45, 302–11.2 (10510); an. 3 (G–1 Rpt), 99th Inf Div, Mar 45, 399–33.4 (10046); an. 2 (Personnel), 104th Inf Div, Feb 45, 3104-33.4 (9455); G–1 Rpt, AAR 1st Inf Div, Mar 45, 301–11.2 (10273); AAR 8th Inf Div, Apr 45, 308–33.4 (8730); AAR 1st Army, Mar 45, 101–33.4 (10047); III Corps G–1 Jnl, Mar 45, L–595.

[20] Ltr, Hq 2d Bn 309th Inf to CO 309th Inf, 6 Jul 45, 78th Inf Div 291.2; Ltr, Hq 272d Inf to CG 69th Inf Div, 19 Mar 45, 69th Inf Div 291.2.
[21] Address, Brig. Gen. Charles Lanham (Asst Div Comdr 104th Inf Div) before American Council on Race Relations, New York City, 12 July 1946, Radio Station WMCA transcript.
[22] G–1 Rpt, AAR 1st Inf Div, Mar 45; Pers an., AAR 104th Inf Div, Mar 45.

fantry Divisions. These divisions played varying roles in the concluding months of the war. Some still met hard fighting in their marches across the Rhine and across central Germany; others found resistance collapsing all around them and spent the last weeks of the war rounding up the enemy and establishing provisional military governments.

Army and theater headquarters were considerably more interested in the careers of the platoons than were the units which, having accepted them, proceeded to employ them as they would have any other platoons. Selected divisions were required to report weekly on the strength and casualties of the platoons—their casualties were usually proportionate and in some instances relatively higher than those of comparable platoons in the same unit. Division G–1's were initially concerned about grades and promotions for the members of the platoons, many of which had arrived with all of their members rated as privates and privates first class. Strenuous efforts to determine whether the platoons had their own tables of organization with authorized ratings or whether the Negro riflemen were eligible for promotion within the tables of organization of their units and whether their members were eligible for officer candidate quotas was a question of concern both to the Reinforcement System and to the divisions. Army headquarters determined that the platoons would be assigned noncommissioned grades, a procedure considered only fair now that the Negro riflemen were not to be integrated individually, but in most instances authority for these promotions did not arrive in time to affect the organization of the platoons. Most of the

platoons, including those organized as provisional companies with the armored divisions, finished the war without ratings.

At the close of the first calendar month after the platoons joined their units, divisions had already formed their impressions of the Negro replacements. The 104th Division, whose platoons had joined while the division was defending the west banks of the Rhine at Cologne, commented: "Their combat record has been outstanding. They have without exception proven themselves to be good soldiers. Some are being recommended for the Bronze Star Medal." [23] When General Davis stopped at 12th Army Group headquarters on his way to observe the platoons a month after they had joined their units, he found that General Bradley was well satisfied with the reports of the performance and conduct of the Negro reinforcements. General Hodges stated that First Army's divisions had given excellent reports on their Negro platoons. As General Davis went down through corps and division to regiment and battalion and finally to a company—Company E of the 60th Regiment, 9th Infantry Division—he found similar reports of satisfaction. At Company E, the company and platoon commanders and several enlisted men, including the white platoon sergeant, recounted their experiences with enthusiasm. All officers and men, from the regimental commander down, reported high morale and confirmed that the platoon was functioning as planned. [24]

The 60th Infantry's Negro platoon had

[23] Pers an., AAR 104th Inf Div, Mar 45.
[24] Ltr, Davis to Chief GI Insp Sec, Hq ETOUSA, 25 Apr 45, Rpt 60, GI Insp, ETO AG 333.1.

had its first heavy going less than a fortnight before, on 5 April, when it and the other platoons of its company took Lengenbach. "This was the colored troops' first taste of combat," the regiment's combat historian recorded, "and they took a big bite." [25] Four days later one of these men, Pfc. Jack Thomas, won the Distinguished Service Cross for leading his squad on a mission to knock out an enemy tank that was providing heavy caliber support for a hostile roadblock. Thomas deployed his squad and advanced upon the enemy position. He hurled two hand grenades, wounding several of the enemy. When two of his men at a rocket launcher were wounded, Thomas took up the weapon and launched a rocket at the Germans, preventing them from manning their tank. He then picked up one seriously wounded member of the rocket launching team and, through small arms and automatic weapons fire, carried him to safety.[26]

Officers and men in other divisions gave General Davis similar reports of their satisfaction with the Negro reinforcements. One division commander, Maj. Gen. Edwin F. Parker of the 78th Division, whose Negro platoons, joining at the Remagen bridgehead, were the first Negro combat troops east of the Rhine, expressed the wish that he could obtain more of the Negro riflemen.[27] The 104th Division's G–1 noted that he gave General Davis a very satisfactory report.[28] He told the visiting general:

Morale: Excellent. Manner of performance: Superior. Men are very eager to close with the enemy and to destroy him. Strict attention to duty, aggressiveness, common sense and judgment under fire has won the admiration of all the men in the company. The colored platoon after initial success continued to do excellent work. Observation discloses that these people observe all the rules of the book. When given a mission they accept it with enthusiasm, and even when losses to their platoon were inflicted the colored boys accepted these losses as part of war, and continued on their mission. The Company Commander, officers, and men of Company "F" all agree that the colored platoon has a calibre of men equal to any veteran platoon. Several decorations for bravery are in the process of being awarded to the members of colored platoons.[29]

The three platoons attached to the three regiments of the 1st Infantry Division illustrate the range and circumstances of employment of Negro reinforcements within a single division. The 26th Infantry's platoon, continuously engaged from 12 March to 8 May, varied in strength from 36 to 31 men. They took their turn at every assignment within their company: patrolling, outposting, assault platoon, support platoon in attacks, and platoon in defense. While little time was available for training—the platoon upon arrival had had individual training only—the regiment estimated that combat efficiency went up

[25] 1st Lt Morton J. Stussman, *60th: Follow Thru* (Chr. Scheufle, Stuttgart, n.d.), p. 110.

[26] Hq Third Army GO 255, 18 Sep 45; Capt. Joseph B. Mittelman, *Eight Stars to Victory* (Washington: 9th Infantry Division Association, 1948), p. 366.

[27] Ltr, Davis to GI Insp Sec, 25 Apr 45, Rpt 60, GI Insp, ETO AG 333.1.

[28] Pers an., AAR 104th Inf Div, Apr 45.

[29] Ltr, Davis to GI Insp Sec, 25 Apr 45, cited n. 27. See also reprint of United Press dispatch on the "Dusky Devastators," one of these platoons, in Leo A. Hoegh and Howard J. Doyle, *Timberwolf Tracks: The History of the 104th Infantry Division, 1942–1945* (Washington: The Infantry Journal Press, 1946), pp. 321–22, 376–77.

from 30 percent to an estimated 80 percent by the end of the second week, a
development which the regiment
ascribed to an "increase in confidence
and training brought about by joint
integrated action in combat." [30]   Efficiency increased further in the next
weeks and the platoon took its "full
share of this almost continuous fighting
and maneuvering." [31]   Replacements
kept this platoon operating as an entity,
but the platoon assigned to Company
B, 16th Infantry, had thirty men
wounded and nine killed in action, with
the result that on V–E Day it had only
fifteen men present for duty.   When its
platoon strength fell too low to operate
as a platoon the Negro riflemen were
used as a squad or squads in a white
platoon.   Company B's Negro reinforcements participated in every battle from
12 March to 8 May.   In their first action, they were "over-eager and aggressive" and consequently suffered severe
casualties. Despite their casualties,
their success in battle was good and they
took their assigned objectives in an
aggressive manner.   White platoons
"like[d] to fight beside them because
they laid a large volume of fire on the
enemy positions."   Their discipline
was good.   They had only "three or
four" minor company punishments under the 104th Article of War and no
courts-martial offenses.[32]   The platoon
with Company B, 18th Infantry, had a
strength varying from 20 to 43 men.
It, too, was employed "in an identical
manner to any other rifle platoon in the
regiment," and, from its first contact
with the enemy on 18 March near Euden-
bach in the Remagen bridgehead, it
participated in all company combat
engagements until hostilities ceased.
The aggressiveness of this platoon was
both an asset and a drawback, for at
times it overran objectives and became
overextended.   Despite a "slightly more
pronounced" nervousness when subjected to shell fire when in defense at
night, the record of its men "as a whole
in combat was very satisfactory and the
platoon can most certainly be considered
a battle success." [33]   When this platoon's
white sergeant was wounded, he was
replaced by a Negro who performed "all
the duties of a platoon sergeant, in and
out of combat, in a superior manner." [34]
From another division came similar reports.   The Negro platoons of the 99th
Division, characterized as employed
"just as any other platoon,"

. . . performed in an excellent manner at
all times while in combat.   These men
were courageous fighters and never once did
they fail to accomplish their assigned mission.   They were particularly good in town
fighting and [were] often used as the assault platoon with good results.   The platoon assigned to the 393d Infantry is
credited with killing approximately 100
Germans and capturing 500.   During this
action only three of their own men were
killed and fifteen wounded.[35]

Units, in their own unofficial accounts,
were more laconic.   For example, the
393d's platoon, in the regiment's photographic history for its men, was described

[30] Ltr, 26th Inf to CG 1st Inf Div, 20 June 45,
Incl to Ltr, Hq XII Corps to CG Third Army, 21
Jun 45, ETO AG 353 (GNMLC).
[31] Ibid.
[32] Ltr, Hq 16th Inf to CG 1st Inf Div, 20 Jun 45,
Incl 1 to above.

[33] Ltr, 18th Inf to CG 1st Inf Div, 20 Jun 45,
Incl 2 to above.
[34] Ibid.
[35] Ltr, Hq 99th Inf Div to CG XII Corps, 21 Jun
45, ETO AG 319.1.

as "The Colored Platoon of Easy Company—one of the best platoons in the regiment." [36]

There was less satisfaction with the Negro riflemen assigned to the Seventh Army. The 6th Army Group and Seventh Army had not been included in the original discussions of the use of Negro riflemen. On the decision of General Patch, the twelve platoons assigned to Seventh Army were organized into provisional companies and sent to the 12th Armored Division, whose armored infantry battalions had relatively greater shortages than infantry division regiments. The platoons, barely trained as squads and platoons, had had no training as companies at all; the division felt that too little time was available to equip and train them before their first battle. [37] The 12th Armored Division, after its experience with the 827th Tank Destroyer Battalion a month before—it received notification to send officers to these platoons on the day that the 827th departed—"objected violently" to these platoons from the beginning. But when the reinforcements arrived they made a "good" impression. [38] The 12th Armored Division's companies were known variously as Seventh Army Provisional Infantry Companies 1, 2, and 3, or as Company D in each of the armored infantry battalions to which they were attached. [39] All of these companies were used as armored infantry in support of tanks or with tank support, but their organization varied. One was composed of four platoons, each organized into one machine gun and three rifle squads. The other two had three platoons, each with two 60-mm. mortars and several light machine guns. The companies attacked dismounted or mounted on tanks; all engaged in several actions. They were generally considered very satisfactory, improving as experience made up for their lack of training as companies and as machine gun and mortar crews. [40] When 6th Army Group's four supplementary platoons arrived on 26 March, they were similarly assigned to the 14th Armored Division, which took them with it when it moved to Third Army on 23 April. [41] In the 14th Armored Division, they were known as Seventh Army Provisional Infantry Company No. 4 or, since they were attached to the Combat Command Reserve, as CCR Rifle Company. [42]

When General Davis visited the 12th Armored Division on 19 April 1945, he found battalion and company commanders acutely conscious of the lack of company training in the Negro platoons. Even so, they felt that the units had done good work. [43] Seventh Army Provisional Infantry Company No. 1, attached to the 56th Armored Infantry Battalion, had not been committed as a unit but detachments had been used. One of these, riding on a tank near Speyer, Germany, on 23 March 1945,

---

[36] Ernest W. Fritz, compiler, *393d Infantry [99th Division] in Review: A Pictorial Account of 393d Infantry Regiment in Combat, 1944–1945* (Salt Lake City: Robert E. Freed, 1946) .

[37] G–1 Rpt 12th Armd Div, Mar 45, L–1110 (2) .

[38] 12th Armd Div G–1 Jnl, 12 Feb and 16 Mar 45.

[39] G–1 Rpt and Jnl, G–3 Opns Rpt 12th Armd Div, Mar 45.

[40] Ltr, Hq Seventh Army to CG 12th Army Gp, 23 Jan 45, ETO AG 322–C.

[41] Ibid.

[42] AAR 25th Tk Bn, Apr 45; AAR 94th Recon Sq (M) , Apr 45; Capt Joseph Carter, *The History of the 14th Armored Division* (Atlanta: Love, n.d.) , ch. XIII.

[43] Ltr, Davis to Chief, GI Insp Sec, 25 Apr 45, Rpt 61, GI Sec Files, EUCOM 333.1.

ran into heavy bazooka and small arms fire. Sgt. Edward A. Carter, Jr., voluntarily dismounted and attempted to lead a three-man group across an open field. Within a short time, two of his men were killed and the third was seriously wounded. Carter continued toward the enemy emplacement alone. He was wounded five times and was finally forced to take cover. When eight enemy riflemen attempted to capture him, Carter killed six of them and captured the remaining two. He then returned across the field, using his two prisoners as a shield, obtaining from them valuable information on the disposition of enemy troops.[44]

Similarly, the 240-man company attached to the 14th Armored Division, in combat from 5 April to 3 May 1945, failed to receive the same approving response from the division as the platoons attached to infantry regiments.[45] The 14th Armored Division, moving south through Bavaria along the Bayreuth-Nurnberg autobahn when everyone knew that the war was over, that is everyone "except the men who could hear the high-pitched, irritable whine of a sniper's bullet, the blast of a mortar shell," [46] met sporadic and spotty resistance, but resistance that was still strong enough to produce sharp, and sometimes prolonged, fire fights. The Combat Command Reserve rifle company was

mainly employed in attachment to the 25th Tank Battalion. The company's first real engagement was at Lichtenfels, where two platoons crossed the Main and, after a bitter fight, took the town.[47] But it was at Creussen, near Bayreuth, that the Negro reinforcements got the accolade of approval from the men of the 14th Armored Division. The 94th Reconnaissance Squadron had entered Creussen, site of a weapons factory, on 15 April when enemy tanks and infantry all but surrounded the town. A call for reinforcements started two platoons of tanks from the 25th Tank Battalion and one of the Negro infantry platoons toward the town. At about 1145, near Gottsfeld, the tanks were fired on by antitank guns. Four were hit and two were destroyed. The remaining tanks pulled back. The Negro infantrymen dismounted, entered the town, and, while considerable enemy artillery fire fell, cleared Gottsfeld by 1500. Tanks then moved in and before dark knocked out five enemy Mark IV's which had come out into the open just east of the town. The tank-infantry force then continued to Creussen, already relieved of much pressure as a result of the action at Gottsfeld, and moved in from the west at 1700. For the next two days, platoons of Combat Command Reserve rifle company patrolled in and around Gottsfeld and Creussen, taking prisoners. One platoon of the 94th's D Troop, observing the Negro riflemen for the first time, commented in its journal: "And were those guys good!" [48] In later fighting, when the company (less one platoon) was used as a unit, results were

---

[44] Carter received the Distinguished Service Cross. Hq Seventh Army GO 580, 4 Oct 45.

[45] Ltr, Hq 14th Armd Div to CG XX Corps, 20 Jun 45, Incl to 1st Ind, Hq XX Corps to CG Third Army, 21 Jun 45, ETO AG 353 Gen GNMTC.

[46] Carter, *14th Armored Division*, ch. XIII. This unofficial history contains a detailed account of the employment of Seventh Army Provisional Company No. 4 along with a detailed account of all units in the 14th Armored Division.

[47] Carter, *14th Armored Division*, ch. XIII.

[48] *Ibid.;* S–3 Jnl and S–3 Periodic Rpts, 25th Tk Bn, Apr 45.

less satisfactory. Poor control and discipline within the companies, especially after taking towns, was the principal fault that Seventh Army found with its Negro units.

When General Patch informed General Davis that the provisional companies were not trained to function as companies and were not performing too well as armored infantry, General Davis explained that they were never intended to be used as other than riflemen, and that, except for a week before assignment, they had had no group training. He described the use being made of them in First Army. He himself had noted that the men in the Seventh Army's companies, though they stated that they were getting along fine, lacked the enthusiasm and high morale of the Negro reinforcements in the First Army.

When General Davis' report of his visit reached General Devers, with an informal recommendation from General Lear that it should receive any action thought suitable, General Devers sent it on to General Patch with a note for his consideration to the effect that "a better solution would have been to use them as rifle platoons in an Infantry Division." Maj. Gen. Roderick Allen, commanding the 12th Armored Division, was scheduled to visit General Patch on 12 May to discuss the matter, but by then the war was over. General Patch informed his chief of staff on 11 May: "Nothing more need be done. Already Allen will be giving them Co. Tng." [49]

Thus, among men similarly trained and similarly motivated, two forms of

employment produced different results —at least in the eyes of higher headquarters if not in the eyes of the men and their immediate associates, who had no means of comparison. All the men were volunteers, and had identical training. But the men in the larger units, organized as companies with their own company administration, adding to the duties of riflemen in which they were trained those of machine gunners and mortar men in which they were not trained, operating as separate and provisional units obviously attached and not a part of the units with which they fought, lost a portion of their original enthusiasm and motivation in the process of commitment to battle. The smaller groups—operating as platoons and at times as squads—as parts of the companies to which they were attached, gained in their commitment. This was not achieved without skepticism on the part of both the Negro replacements and their associates within their companies. An officer who, as rifle platoon and company commander, led one of these platoons for nearly two months, explained that his platoon, advancing at mid-day through heavy woods, in its very first contact with the enemy

. . . discovered a German force digging in upon a hill-top. Without being discovered, it maneuvered into a position to deliver maximum fire from a distance of a scant 20 yards, and struck so powerfully and suddenly that the Germans were shot-up and dispersed before they could pick up their weapons—2 machine guns, 4 machine pistol "burp guns," several rifles and dozens of grenades.

A lucky break, we all agreed. . . .

But the soldiers of this platoon showed thereafter that this was not simply "a lucky break" since in "frequent instances

[49] Info RS, CofS Sec Seventh Army Misc Papers, envelope 9, L–1135.

after that baptismal triumph" their fellow white soldiers saw them "prove their stuff at the cost of lives and blood by advancing doggedly under fire, by aggressive noncommissioned officer leadership in house-to-house fights and in the forbidding wilderness of No-Man's Land." [50] As the men of this platoon took their places in their company, not a single incident of friction occurred between them and the white infantrymen who fought for the same towns, ate in the same chow line, sometimes gambled in the same clandestine games. The Negro troops of this platoon gradually came to be accepted not as unusual, or special, but as normal soldiers, neither better nor worse than usual. "The premise that no soldier," their commander decided, "will hold black skin against a man if he can shoot his rifle and does not run away proved to be substantially true. Most of the white men of the company soon became highly appreciative of the Negroes' help and warmly applauded their more colorful individual and combat exploits." [51]

One Negro platoon, when faced with heavy automatic weapons fire from outlying buildings in a town which another platoon was already supposed to have taken, made a hasty estimate of the situation and, realizing that its only safety was in the buildings from which its men were receiving fire, broke into a run with all weapons firing, raced three hundred yards under "a hail of enemy fire," took the buildings and, in a matter of minutes, the entire town. The battalion commander concluded:

I know I did not receive a superior representation of the colored race as the average AGCT was Class IV. I do know, however, that in courage, coolness, dependability and pride, they are on a par with any white troops I have ever had occasion to work with. In addition, they were, during combat, possessed with a fierce desire to meet with and kill the enemy, the equal of which I have never witnessed in white troops.

In a number of units whose praise of the willing efforts of the Negro volunteers during combat was high there arose an undercurrent of misgivings about retaining these troops within units once the war was over and battalions and regiments settled into occupation and garrison duties. But in this battalion two months of garrison life had brought no deterioration of relations between Negro and white soldiers:

To date, there has never appeared the slightest sign of race prejudice, or discrimination in this organization. White men and colored men are welded together with a deep friendship and respect born of combat and matured by a realization that such an association is not the impossibility that many of us have been led to believe. Segregation has never been attempted in this unit, and is, in my mind, the deciding factor as to the success or failure of the experiment. When men undergo the same privations, face the same dangers before an impartial enemy, there can be no segregation. My men eat, play, work, and sleep as a company of men, with no regard to color. An interesting sidelight is the fact that the company orientation NCO is colored, the pitcher on the softball team, composed of both races, is colored, and the bugler is colored.

The sole morale problem facing these troops two months after the conclusion of hostilities was the growing suspicion, now that a group of Negro troops had

---

[50] Lt. Robert Lewis, "Negroes Under Fire," *The Progressive and LaFollette's Magazine*, IX (September 3, 1945), 4.
[51] *Ibid.*

been transferred to this unit from another division, that they too would "soon be removing their Division patch, and the thought of this impending separation has materially affected their morale and performance thereby." [52]

This was a morale problem to many of the Negro reinforcements, for as redeployment regulations went into effect, the Negro infantrymen, having fewer points than the white troops in their units, began to be transferred to other units, including a large group that went to a combat engineer battalion constructing redeployment camps. The suspicion arose that all would eventually be returned to service units. Actually a compromise was worked out by the European theater, which declared that it could not make exceptions to redeployment regulations. A thousand or more of the reinforcements with relatively higher points were sent to the 69th Infantry Division for redeployment to the United States and the remainder, except for some who, having been transferred already, could not be readily located, went to the 350th Field Artillery Battalion, a Negro unit of low redeployment status, thus preserving their combat status and at the same time remaining with the occupation forces in Europe. The compromise was not wholly satisfactory to the troops concerned, for most of them had hoped to remain with the units with which they had fought and with whose men they had got along well. Many had hoped that their service would be "the beginning of the end of differences and discriminations on account of race and color." [53] As one of their commanders explained their and his dilemma: "These colored men cannot understand why they are not being allowed to share the honor of returning to their homeland with the Division with which they fought, proving to the world that Negro soldiers can do something besides drive a truck or work in a laundry. I am unqualified to give them a satisfactory answer." [54]

In the Negro infantry rifle platoons, the employment of Negro troops moved farthest from traditional Army patterns. Despite the multitude of problems with which the Army was faced in the use of Negro troops in World War II, at the war's end a greater variety of experience existed than had ever before been available within the American Military Establishment. For Negro troops had been used in larger numbers over a longer period of time than in any previous war. They had been used by more branches and in a greater variety of units, ranging from divisions to platoons in size and from fighter units to quartermaster service companies in the complexity of their duties. They had been used in a wider range of geographical, cultural, and climatic conditions than was believed possible in 1942. All of this was true of white troops as well, but in its manpower deliberations and in its attempts to wrest maximum efficiency and production from the manpower allotted it, the Army found that it was the

[52] Ltr, CO 2d Bn 309th Inf to CO 309th Inf, 6 Jul 45, 78th Div 291.2.

[53] Hist of Special Sec OTIG, loc. cit.; Ltr, CO 310th Inf to CG 78th Inf Div, 7 Jul 45, 78th Div 291.2.

[54] Ltr, CO 2d Bn 309th Inf to CO 309th Inf, 6 Jul 45, loc. cit. It should be noted that a large proportion of white troops did not return with their units either.

10 percent of American manpower which was Negro that spelled a large part of the difference between the full and wasteful employment of available American manpower of military age.

As World War II drew to a close the Army, as a part of its continuing inventory of its operations, turned fuller attention to the problems of Negro manpower. These had already received disproportionate administrative attention hardly justified by the results. The Army was now interested in the experience of the theaters, both to conclude the war in the Pacific and to plan for the postwar Army. Reports and more reports already existed, but the Army was now interested in the judgment of the theaters themselves. For whatever had occurred in the training and deployment phases, the crucial questions could be answered best by the experience of the theaters—the experience with Negro troops at the point of operational use. Before the war was over, stock-taking on the employment of Negro troops in World War II had already begun. Upon the basis of the direct experience of the war, the McCloy Committee began to look toward the establishment of a clearer postwar policy than there had ever been. Shortly after the war was over, on 4 October 1945, the War Department appointed a board of officers, headed by Lt. Gen. Alvan C. Gillem, Jr., to prepare a new and broad policy for the future employment of Negro troops. From the investigations and conclusions of this committee many of the changes in the employment of Negro troops after World War II would come. These deliberations and developments belong properly to a study of the postwar period, although the genesis

of the change may be found in the vastly varied experiences of the Army and the War Department in the employment of Negro troops in World War II.

Writing in the early summer of 1945, before the fighting with Japan ended, the Chief Historian of the Army, the late Dr. Walter L. Wright, Jr., provided a perceptive commentary on the Army's experience with the employment of Negro troops in segregated units during World War II: [55]

With your general conclusion regarding the performance of Negro troops, I tend to agree: They cannot be expected to do as well in any Army function as white troops unless they have absolutely first-class leadership from their officers. Such leadership may be provided, in my opinion, either by white or by Negro officers, but white officers would have to be men who have some understanding of the attitude of mind which Negroes possess and some sympathy with them as human beings. What troubles me is that anybody of real intelligence should be astonished to discover that Negro troops require especially good leadership if their performance is to match that of white troops. This same state of affairs exists, I think, with any group of men who belong to a subject nationality or national minority consisting of under-privileged individuals from depressed social strata. . . . American Negro troops are, as you know, ill-educated on the average and often illiterate; they lack self-respect, self-confidence, and initiative; they tend to be very conscious of their low standing in the eyes of the white population and consequently feel very little motive for aggressive fighting. In fact, their survival as individuals and as a people has often depended on their ability to subdue completely even the appearance of aggressiveness. After all, when a man knows that the color of his skin will automatically disqualify him for reaping the fruits of attainment it is no wonder that he sees

---

[55] Personal Ltr, Walter L. Wright, Jr., to Col John M. Kemper, 3 Jul 45, in OCMH files.

little point in trying very hard to excel anybody else. To me, the most extraordinary thing is that such people continue trying at all.

The conclusion which I reach is obvious: We cannot expect to make first-class soldiers out of second or third or fourth class citizens. The man who is lowest down in civilian life is practically certain to be lowest down as a soldier. Accordingly, we must expect depressed minorities to perform much less effectively than the average of other groups in the population. . . . So far as the war in progress is concerned, the War Department must deal with an existing state of affairs and its employment of Negroes must parallel the employment of the same group in civilian American society. Yet, it is important to remember that the civilian status of Negroes in this country is changing with a rapidity which I believe to be unique in history; the level of literacy is rising steadily and quickly and privileges other than educational are being gained every year. . . .

As to the segregation of Negroes to special units in the Army, this is simply a reflection of a state of affairs well-known in civilian America today. Yet, civilian practice in this connection differs very widely from Massachusetts to Mississippi. Since the less favorable treatment characteristic of southern states is less likely to lead to violent protest from powerful white groups, the Army has tended to follow southern rather than northern practices in dealing with the problem of segregation. Also, it is most unfortunate for the Negroes that considerations of year round climate led to the placing of most of the training camps in the southern states where conditions in the nearby towns were none too acceptable to northern white men and the unfamiliar Jim Crowism was exceedingly unacceptable to northern Negroes. My ultimate hope is that in the long run it will be possible to assign individual Negro soldiers and officers to any unit in the Army where they are qualified as individuals to serve efficiently.

Within a decade, this hope was to be realized.

Bibliographical Note

The bulk of the information used in the preparation of this volume came from the records and manuscript histories of Army agencies, units, and installations, accumulated in the two decades before December 1941 and during American participation in World War II. The records of Army (including Army Air Forces) agencies are described in *Federal Records of World War II,* Volume II, *Military Agencies,* prepared by the General Services Administration, National Archives and Records Service, The National Archives (Washington, 1951), to which the reader is referred for more detailed information about the numerous agencies concerned and their accumulation of records.

Records and manuscript histories used and cited in this work are now mostly to be found in the collections of four agencies. In the Washington, D.C. area, the Office of Military Archives of the National Archives and Records Service holds most of the pre-1940 retired Army records in the main building of the National Archives; in its World War II Reference Branch in Alexandria, Virginia, the same agency holds most of the post-1939 retired records of Army headquarters agencies and the operational records of Army ground combat units that saw action overseas. Many records of the Army Air Forces, unpublished Air Forces manuscript histories, and operational records and histories of Air units are kept by the Air University at Maxwell Field, Alabama. Records of overseas commands cited in the con-

cluding chapters are currently deposited in the regional National Archives records center at Kansas City, Missouri. Unpublished Army historical manuscripts and some other sources of information are, as indicated in the footnotes, in the custody of the General Reference Branch of the Office of the Chief of Military History.

The reader is referred to the footnotes for guidance to the wide variety of record groups used, only the most important of which are mentioned here. For both the prewar and World War II periods, the central decimal file maintained by The Adjutant General's Office (AG) is the most useful, but to get the full story of the formulation and application of policy the records of the offices of the Secretary of War and of the Chief of Staff, as well as those of the military staffs that operated under their direction, must also be consulted. The most important are the records of the Assistant Secretary of War (ASW), the Chief of Staff (OCS to 1942, WDCSA thereafter), and, among the General Staff divisions, those of the Operations Division (OPD), the Personnel Division (G-1), and the Organization and Training Division (G-3). Records of the three major commands, the Army Ground Forces (AGF), the Army Air Forces (AAF), and the Army Service Forces (bearing many separate symbol identifications, since ASF had no central file) are of major value for studying the preparation of Negro troops for service overseas. For the activities and performance of particular Negro units in the United States and overseas, the records and manuscript histories of individual units, both of the Negro units concerned and of the larger units to which these were attached, have been drawn on extensively.

Printed materials used fall into five categories. All Army historians must of necessity use official War Department publications—Army regulations, general orders, circulars, bulletins, memorandums, technical manuals, and so forth. For the actions and reactions of the Congress, the *Congressional Record* and printed records of *Hearings* of Congressional committees are obvious sources. The footnotes indicate how widely the author has made use of information and editorial comment from newspapers, including the major New York and Washington dailies and the Negro press of both North and South. He has used periodicals even more extensively than newspapers, and especially articles in service and professional journals. The last category consists of printed works in book form which, although rather frequently cited throughout the work, were of distinctly minor importance in compiling this record of the experience of the Army with Negroes, and of Negroes with the Army during World War II.

Glossary

A–1	Personnel section of an air staff; officer in charge of this section
A–2	Intelligence section of an air staff; officer in charge of this section
A–3	Operations and training section of an air staff; officer in charge of this section
A–4	Matériel and supply section of an air staff; officer in charge of this section
AAA	Antiaircraft Artillery
AAC	Army Air Corps
AAF	Army Air Forces
AAFEFTC	Army Air Forces Eastern Flying Training Command
AAFSETC	Army Air Forces Southeast Training Command
AAFTC	Army Air Forces Training Command
AAFTTC	Army Air Forces Technical Training Command
AAI	Allied Armies in Italy
AAR	After Action Report, prepared by unit concerned
ACofAS	Assistant Chief of Air Staff
Actg	Acting
AFACT	Assistant Chief of Air Staff, Training
AFCC	Air Force Combat Command
AFHQ	Allied Force Headquarters
AFWESPAC	Army Forces, Western Pacific
AG	Adjutant General
AGCT	Army General Classification Test
AGWAR	Adjutant General, War Department
A.M.E.	African Methodist Episcopal
AMMISCA	American Military Mission to China
Amph	Amphibian; amphibious
APO	Army Post Office
Armd	Armored
Arty	Artillery
ASF	Army Service Forces
ASFTC	Army Service Forces Training Center
Asst	Assistant
ASW	Assistant Secretary of War
ASWA	Assistant Secretary of War for Air
ASWAAF	Arms and Services with Army Air Forces
Avn	Aviation

AWC	Army War College
AWOL	Absent without leave
BOLERO	Build-up of U.S. forces and supplies in the United Kingdom for cross-Channel attack
CA	Coast Artillery
CofAAF	Chief of Army Air Forces
CofAC	Chief of Air Corps
CAS	Chief of Air Service
CofAS	Chief of Air Staff
Cav	Cavalry
CBI	China-Burma-India Theater
CofCAV	Chief of Cavalry
CofCH	Chief of Chaplains
CofE	Chief of Engineers
CE	Corps of Engineers
CG	Commanding General
CINCPAC	Commander in Chief, U.S. Pacific Fleet
CINCSWPA	Commander in Chief, Southwest Pacific Area
CINCWESPAC	Commander in Chief, Western Pacific
CIO	Congress of Industrial Organizations
Cir	Circular
Civ	Civilian
Cld	Colored
CMTC	Citizens' Military Training Camps
CO	Commanding officer
Com	Committee
Comdt	Commandant
COMGENSOPAC	Commanding General, South Pacific Area
COMSOPAC	Commander, South Pacific Area
COMZ	Communications Zone (between active front and rear bases)
Cp	Camp
CPT	Civilian Pilot Training
CofS	Chief of Staff
CT	Combat Team
CWS	Chemical Warfare Service
DCofAS	Deputy Chief of Air Staff
DCofS	Deputy Chief of Staff
DF	Disposition form
Dir	Director
DTC	Desert Training Center

Dukw	2½-ton 6x6 amphibian truck
EM	Enlisted men
Engr	Engineer
Enl	Enlisted
ETO	European Theater of Operations
ETOUSA	European Theater of Operations, U.S. Army
ExO	Executive officer
FA	Field Artillery
FO	Field order
G–1	Personnel section of divisional or higher staff
G–2	Intelligence section of divisional or higher staff
G–3	Operations section of divisional or higher staff
G–4	Supply section of divisional or higher staff
Gen	General
GHQ	General Headquarters
GHQAF	General Headquarters Air Force
GI Sec	General Inspectorate Section, European Theater of Operations
GO	General order
Gp	Group
H.R.	House of Representatives
IBT	India-Burma Theater
I-BT	India-Burma Theater
I&E	Information and Education
IGD	Inspector General's Department
Inf	Infantry
JAG	Judge Advocate General
JAGO	Judge Advocate General's Office
JANCWR	Joint Army and Navy Committee on Welfare and Recreation
Jnl	Journal
LCT	Landing craft, tank
L&L	Legislative and Liaison
Ln	Liaison
LST	Landing ship, tank
MAAF	Mediterranean Allied Air Force
MB	Morale Branch
Med	Medical; medium
Memo	Memorandum
Mil	Military
Mob	Mobilization
Movmt	Movement
MP	Military police

MPD	Military Personnel Division
M/R	Memorandum for record
MR	Mobilization Regulation
M/S	Memorandum slip used for informal interoffice communication
Msg	Message
MTO	Mediterranean Theater of Operations
MTOUSA	Mediterranean Theater of Operations, U.S. Army
NAACP	National Association for the Advancement of Colored People
NAAF	North African Air Force
NATO	North African Theater of Operations
NATOUSA	North African Theater of Operations, U.S. Army
NGUS	National Guard United States
NOPE	New Orleans Port of Embarkation
O	Office, as OTIG, Office of the Inspector General
OB SUEDWEST	*Oberbefehlshaber Suedwest* (Headquarters, Commander in Chief Southwest [Italy])
OinC	Officer in charge
OCofAC	Office of the Chief of Air Corps
OCAS	Office Chief of Air Service
OCofAS	Office of the Chief of Air Staff
OCD	Office of Civilian Defense
OCMH	Office of the Chief of Military History
OCS	Officer candidate school; Office, Chief of Staff
Off	Officer
OFF	Office of Facts and Figures
OI	Operations Instruction
OPD	Operations Division, War Department
OPMG	Office of the Provost Marshal General
Opns Rpt	Operations Report
ORC	Officers' Reserve Corps
Ord	Ordnance
Orgd	Organized
PofE	Port of Embarkation
Pers	Personnel
PMG	Provost Marshal General
PMP	Protective Mobilization Plan
PMS&T	Professor of Military Science and Tactics
P&O	Plans and Operations
POE	Port of Embarkation
POL	Petrol (gasoline), oil, and lubricants
POM	Preparation for Overseas Movement

Prcht	Parachute
Prog	Program
PT	Patrol vessel, motor torpedo boat
QMC	Quartermaster Corps
QMG	Quartermaster General
RA	Regular Army
Rad	Radio message; radiogram
RCT	Regimental Combat Team
R&D	Research and Development
ROTC	Reserve Officers' Training Corps
Rqmts	Requirements
R&R's	Routing and record slips
RS	Routing slip
R&SC	Replacement and School Command
RTC	Replacement Training Center
SECOND WIND	Symbolic code name for 92d Division's Spring 1945 offensive
Secy	Secretary
Sep	Separate; unit not a part of a larger unit
SGO	Surgeon General's Office
SGS	Secretary of the General Staff
SHAEF	Supreme Headquarters, Allied Expeditionary Forces
SOS	Services of Supply
Sq	Squadron
STU	Special Training Unit
Sv	Service
SW	Secretary of War
TAG	The Adjutant General
TC	Training Center; Transportation Corps
TD	Tank destroyer
Telg	Telegram
TF	Task Force
TI&E	Troop Information and Education
TIG	The Inspector General
Tk	Tank
Tng	Training
T/O	Table of organization
T&O	Training and Operations
TOE	Table of organization and equipment
Trp	Troop
TTC	Technical Training Command
TUB	Troop unit basis
USAFICPA	U.S. Army Forces in the Central Pacific Area

USAFIL	U.S. Army Forces in Liberia
USAFIME	U.S. Army Forces in the Middle East
USAFISPA	U.S. Army Forces in the South Pacific Area
USASOS	U.S. Army, Services of Supply
USFET	U.S. Forces, European Theater
USO	United Service Organizations
USW	Undersecretary of War
WAAC	Women's Army Auxiliary Corps
WAC	Women's Army Corps
WD	War Department
WDGS	War Department General Staff
WPD	War Plans (afterward, Operations) Division
ZI	Zone of interior (Continental United States)

Basic Military Map Symbols

Symbols within a rectangle indicate a military unit, within a triangle an observation post, and within a circle a supply point.

Military Units—Identification

Antiaircraft Artillery . . . .

Armored Command . . . .

Army Air Forces . . . .

Artillery, except Antiaircraft and Coast Artillery . . . .

Cavalry, Horse . . . .

Cavalry, Mechanized . . . .

Chemical Warfare Service . . . .

Coast Artillery . . . .

Engineers . . . .

Infantry . . . .

Medical Corps . . . .

Ordnance Department . . . .

Quartermaster Corps . . . .

Signal Corps . . . .

Tank Destroyer . . . .

Transportation Corps . . . .

Veterinary Corps . . . .

Airborne units are designated by combining a gull wing symbol with the arm or service symbol:

Airborne Artillery . . . .

Airborne Infantry . . . .

Size Symbols

The following symbols placed either in boundary lines or above the rectangle, triangle, or circle inclosing the identifying arm or service symbol indicate the size of military organization:

Squad . . . . •

Section . . . . • •

Platoon . . . . • • •

Company, troop, battery, Air Force flight . . . . |

Battalion, cavalry squadron, or Air Force squadron . . . . | |

Regiment or group; combat team (with abbreviation CT following identifying numeral) . . . . | | |

Brigade, Combat Command of Armored Division, or Air Force Wing X

Division or Command of an Air Force XX

Corps or Air Force XXX

Army XXXX

Group of Armies XXXXX

EXAMPLES

The letter or number to the left of the symbol indicates the unit designation; that to the right, the designation of the parent unit to which it belongs. Letters or numbers above or below boundary lines designate the units separated by the lines:

Company A, 137th Infantry . . . . A⊠137

8th Field Artillery Battalion 8

Combat Command A, 1st Armored Division . . . . A 1

Observation Post, 23d Infantry 23

Command Post, 5th Infantry Division . . . . ⊠5

Boundary between 137th and 138th Infantry . . . . ─ ||| ─
137
138

Weapons

Machine gun . . . . •→

Gun . . . . •

Gun battery . . . . ⊔⊔⊔

Howitzer or Mortar . . . . ✦

Tank . . . . ◇

Self-propelled gun . . . .

UNITED STATES ARMY IN WORLD WAR II

The following volumes have been published:

Index

INDEX

☆ U.S. GOVERNMENT PRINTING OFFICE: 1994 360—570